Marketing

THIRD EDITION

Paul Baines and Chris Fill

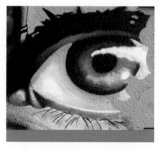

OXFORD

UNIVERSITY PRESS

OXFORD
UNIVERSITY PRESS

Great Clarendon Street, Oxford, OX2 6DP,
Unitod Kingdom

Oxford University Press is a department of the University of Oxford.
It furthers the University's objective of excellence in research, scholarship,
and education by publishing worldwide. Oxford is a registered trade mark of
Oxford University Press in the UK and in certain other countries

First edition published 2008
Second edition published 2011

Impression: 1

Published in the United States of America by Oxford University Press
198 Madison Avenue, New York, NY 10016, United States of America

British Library Cataloguing in Publication Data
Data available

Library of Congress Control Number: 2013948170

ISBN 978–0–19–965953–1

Printed in Italy by
L.E.G.O. S.p.A.—Lavis TN

Marketing

Brief Contents

Detailed Contents

Case Insights

Chapter 1: Systembolaget
Systembolaget is the world's first alcohol monopoly and remains the only retailer of alcohol in Sweden. We speak to Fredrik Thor to find out how a state alcohol monopoly with a prohibition remit can possibly market itself.

Chapter 2: BrainJuicer
How should organizations evaluate actual customer behaviour when that behaviour often differs from how customers say they will behave? We speak to BrainJuicer Labs' Managing Director, Orlando Wood, to find out more about work they undertook for their client MasterCard.

Chapter 3: MESH Planning
How should organizations measure the effectiveness of all touchpoints in interactions with customers, not just marketing communications? We speak to MESH Planning's CEO, Fiona Blades, to find out more.

Chapter 4: Glassolutions Saint-Gobain
How should organizations scan their external environments and what should they do if they identify potential threats and opportunities? We speak to Glassolutions Saint-Gobain's Marketing Director, Michael Butterick, to find out more.

Chapter 5: PJ Care
How should entrepreneurial organizations develop their marketing function in order to best serve their customers and meet shareholder financial goals? We speak to Wendy Thompson, PJ Care's general manager, sales and marketing, to find out more.

Chapter 6: Brompton Bicycles
How should organizations segment their markets given a changing customer base? We speak to Emerson Roberts, sales and marketing director for Brompton Bicycles Ltd, to find out more.

Chapter 7: Orange
We talk to Sue Wilmot, Head of Customer Strategy Delivery in the customer marketing team at Orange, to find out how they set about retaining large numbers of international customers.

Chapter 8: Domino's Pizza
How do organizations develop new propositions on a regular basis and remain competitive? We speak to Simon Wallis, Sales and Marketing Director for Domino's Pizza, to find out more.

Chapter 9: 3M
We speak to Andrew Hicks, European Market Development Manager, to find out how the company developed its pricing strategy for an innovative new product, the Visual Attention Service.

Chapter 10: *The Guardian*/BBH
How could an organization realize their objective not only to shift audience perceptions but also to change behaviours? We speak to Agathe Guerrier, Strategy Director at the advertising agency Bartle Bogle Hegarty (BBH), to find out more about the work they undertook for their client *The Guardian*.

Chapter 11: Budweiser Budvar and KASPEN/ JUNG v. MATT
How should a heritage brand in the Czech Republic design a campaign to reposition itself against competing foreign brands? We speak to Budweiser Budvar's advertising agency account director, Lubos Jahoda, to find out more.

Chapter 12: Cobalt
How should organizations develop suitable channel structures to best serve and communicate with their customers? We speak to Zena Giles, Cobalt's Legacy Officer, to find out more.

Chapter 13: BRAND sense agency
BRAND sense agency is involved with developing a holistic understanding of a brand's sensory impact. We talk to CEO Simon Harrop to find out how they go about this.

Chapter 14: RAKBANK
RAKBANK is the highly successful National Bank of Ras Al-Khaimahin, in the United Arab Emirates. We speak to Banali Malhotra, Head of Marketing, to find out how they sought to improve relationships with their customers.

Chapter 15: Oxford Instruments
How should organizations develop relationships with business partners in international markets? We speak to Lynn Shepherd, Group Director of Communications at Oxford Instruments, to find out more.

Chapter 16: Oxfam
Oxfam opened one of the world's first charity shop chains in 1948. We speak to Nick Futcher, Brand Manager, to find out how this world-renowned charity has kept pace, given major changes in the world since then.

Chapter 17: Virgin Media
What role does social media play and how should organizations incorporate it into their communication campaigns? We speak to Richard Larcombe, director of advertising and sponsorship at Virgin Media, to find out more.

Chapter 18: innocent
How do organizations develop and maintain responsible working practices and attitudes towards the environment and at the same time remain compatible with their customers' values? We speak to Tansy Drake and Dan Germain, Brand Guardian and Head of Brand and Creative at innocent, to find out more.

Chapter 19: Livity
How should organizations design their communications campaigns when targeting hard-to-reach non-traditional communities? We speak to Callum McGeogh, Creative Director, Livity, to find out more about work they undertook for their client, ChildLine, the national telephone helpline of the UK children's charity, the NSPCC.

Author Profiles

 **Paul Baines** is Professor of Political Marketing at Cranfield School of Management and Course Director, MSc Management. Paul is author/co-author of more than a hundred published articles, book chapters, and books on marketing issues. Over the last sixteen years, Paul's research has particularly focused on political marketing, public opinion, and propaganda. Paul's marketing research consultancy experience includes marketing research and strategy development projects for a variety of large, medium, and start-up organizations including a high-profile football club, a large aerospace maintenance company, a national charity, an advertising agency, an awarding body, a glass manufacturing company, and development-funded university start-ups. Paul has worked for various UK government departments on specialist communication research projects. He was a board director of the sub-regional development agency North London Limited from November 2006 to April 2008, and operates his own strategic marketing consultancy, Baines Associates Ltd. In his spare time, Paul enjoys cinema, devours current affairs, and hits the gym.

 Chris Fill is Director of Fillassociates, who develop and deliver learning materials related to marketing and corporate communications, some of which can be found online (at www.fillassociates.co.uk and www.marketing mentor.net). Formerly Principal Lecturer at the University of Portsmouth, Chris now works with a variety of private and not-for-profit organizations including several publishers. He is Visiting Professor at Poitiers Business School and Fellow of the Chartered Institute of Marketing where he was the Senior Examiner responsible for the marketing communications modules, and more recently the Professional Postgraduate Diploma module, Managing Corporate Reputation. In addition to numerous papers published in a range of academic journals, he has written over 30 books, including his internationally recognized textbook, *Marketing Communications,* now in its sixth edition. Other recent titles include *Corporate Reputation*, *Advertising*, and *Essentials of Marketing*.

Acknowledgements

As we've discovered over various editions, course textbooks are very substantial writing and research projects, resulting from the sweat and toil of lots of people, not only in their design, development, and production, but in the associated sales, marketing, and distribution tasks. The production of a textbook is only a small component of what is an integrated learning and teaching package including websites, the book itself, and the various audiovisual components. Many people contributed to the third edition of the book and its Online Resource Centre; some of those people we outline below and many others we have not, but whose contributions should be acknowledged anonymously nonetheless.

Particular thanks are due to Kelly Page, who left the author team for the third edition, but whose contributions to the first and second editions have been so important in the book's success. We would like to thank you, Kelly, particularly but not solely for your contributions to the design and delivery of what is an extensive and durable set of online resources, the excellent chapters you wrote, and the book design and marketing ideas you contributed. We wish you well.

We would like to thank our colleagues and former colleagues at Cranfield School of Management, Cardiff Business School, and the Portsmouth Business School for their support, discussions, and general input over the years. We would like to thank Dr Robert Ormrod of Aarhus University, Denmark, Ning Baines, and Mark Wilson for their contributions to the online resources for the second edition and Ning Baines, at Birkbeck, University of London and Dr Shahpar Abdollahi for their contributions to the third edition online resource centre.

As with any large textbook project, this work is the result of a co-production between the academic authors and Oxford University Press editors and staff. We would particularly like to thank Sacha Cook, former Editor-in-Chief, for persuading us to take on such a gargantuan project in the first instance. The contributions of the Development Editors over the three editions have been fundamental; thanks to Helen Cook and Sarah Lodge for their work on book development and the book's associated online resources in the second and third editions. Helen's patience, diligence, and attention to detail, shown particularly during the production of the third edition, will no doubt be invaluable as she leaves OUP to sail around the world. We would also like to thank Francesca Griffin for keeping a watchful eye over the text in the second edition and helping with the development of the DVD and the Online Resource Centre, and for her work supporting the development process for the third edition. Thanks are also due to Fiona Goodall for her sterling work as web editor: an increasingly important aspect of the whole learning package.

We would like to thank Siân Jenkins, Production Editor, for her role in shaping the final design of the book and bringing it out on schedule with the help of the design team, Charlotte Dobbs and Claire Dickinson. Thanks also to James Tomalin, Matt Greetham, and the team at Oxford Digital Media for their great video production work.

Finally, as marketers, unless our customers, students, and lecturers want to use this book, there's no use in writing and producing it, so we recognize the efforts of the marketing team, Marianne Lightowler, Marketing Director, and Katy Duff and Tristan Jones, Marketing Managers, in developing and implementing innovative sales and marketing plans for the second and third editions. In the latter case, Tristan's support of the case insight interviewing process was particularly helpful, supporting Helen Cook in ensuring the quality of the interviewees and interviews. Thanks also to Anthony Hey for his support of the video production in the latter stage of this process.

The original design for the book—going back to the first edition—was initially developed from six anonymous university lecturer participants of a focus group, who kindly agreed to meet at the OUP offices to discuss what was needed in a new marketing textbook. We would like to thank them for their support and hope that this third edition stays true to, and advances, their original concept. We've moved a step further in the third edition by including a number of original market insight contributions within the text from students, practitioners, and academics.

The authors and publishers would like to thank the following people for their comments and reviews throughout the process of developing the text and the Online Resource Centre over the last three editions.

Dr Geraldine Cohen, *Brunel University, UK*
Dr Nina Belei, *Radboud University Nijmegen, Netherlands*
Professor John Egan, *London South Bank University, UK*
Dr Fiona Ellis-Chadwick, *Open University Business School, UK*
Mike Flynn, *University of Gloucestershire, UK*
Malcolm Goodman, *Durham University, UK*
Dr Michael Harker, *University of Strathclyde, UK*
Mick Hayes, *University of Portsmouth, UK*
Nigel Jones, *Sheffield Hallam University, UK*
Dr Nnamdi Madichie, *University of Sharjah, UAE*
Alice Maltby, *University of the West of England, Bristol, UK*
Tony McGuinness, *Aberystwyth University, UK*
Richard Meek, *Lancaster University, UK*
Dr Nina Michaelidou, *Loughborough University, UK*
Dr Janice Moorhouse, *University of the West of London, UK*
William Mott, *University of Wolverhampton, UK*
Vicky Roberts, *University of Staffordshire, UK*
Chris Rock, *University of Greenwich, UK*
Professor Mike Saren, *University of Leicester, UK*
Dr Lorna Stevens, *University of Ulster, the UK*
Professor Paul Trott, *University of Portsmouth, UK*
Dr Prakash Vel, *University of Wollongong, Dubai, UAE*
Peter Waterhouse, *University of Bedfordshire, UK*
Peter Williams, *Leeds Metropolitan University, UK*
Matthew Wood, *University of Brighton, UK*
Professor Helen Woodruffe-Burton, *Northumbria University, UK*
Professor Andrea Prothero, *University College Dublin, Ireland*
George Masikunas, *Kingston University, UK*
Connie Nolan, *Canterbury Christ Church University, UK*
Neil Richardson, *Leeds Metropolitan University, UK*
Heléne Lundberg, *Mid Sweden University, Sweden*
Mike Flynn, *University of Gloucestershire, UK*
Jennie White, *University of Chichester, UK*

Dr Ann Torres, *National University of Ireland Galway, Ireland*
Dr Mikael Gidhagen, *Uppsala University, Sweden*
Dr Charles Graham, *London South Bank University, UK*
Liz Algar, *University of Essex, UK*
Dr Patrick McCole, *Queen's University Management School, UK*
Dr Elizabeth Jackson, *Newcastle University, UK*

In the third edition, we would particularly like to thank a number of lecturers, students, and practitioners who contributed market insights, including the following.

Dr Paolo Antonetti, *Warwick Business School, UK*
Paul Morrissey, *Waterford Institute of Technology, Ireland*
Will Leach, *VP, BrainJuicer Behavioural Activation Unit, UK*
Ashwien Bisnajak, *Market Intelligence Manager, Hunkemöller, Netherlands*
Dr John Habershon, *Founder, Momentum Research, UK*
Fermin Paus, *postgraduate student at the Grenoble School of Management, France*
Sofia Ekberg, *student, Södertörn University, Stockholm, Sweden*
Carolina Röhrl, *student, Södertörn University, Stockholm, Sweden*
Dr Julia Wolny, *University of Southampton, UK*
Marie O' Dwyer, *Waterford Institute of Technology, Ireland*
Dr Sarah Gilmore, *Portsmouth Business School, University of Portsmouth, UK*
Karen Knibbs, *Portsmouth Business School, University of Portsmouth, UK*

Thanks also to those reviewers who chose to remain anonymous. The publishers would be pleased to clear permission with any copyright holders that we have inadvertently failed or been unable to contact.

Preface

Welcome to the third edition of *Marketing*. You may be wondering **'Why should I buy this marketing textbook?'** The simple answer is that your marketing lecturers told us that you needed a new one! In our first edition, we were the first truly integrated print and electronic learning package for introductory marketing modules. For this, the third edition, we've gone even further. Before we started writing the third edition we went back to marketing lecturers, building on our research for the first and second editions, to identify how we could further tailor the book to meet your learning needs. Our aim with the book and its associated online resource centre is to provide an innovative learning experience to inspire the next generation of marketers to excel in this exciting and fast-moving discipline. In our research for the book, we discovered that you needed:

- updated coverage of digital and, particularly, social media marketing.
- greater integration between the wealth of material online and the textbook.
- information on what skills employers in marketing are looking for.
- a chapter dedicated to branding.
- integration of the chapters on relationship and services marketing.
- new material critiquing marketing and more content on marketing sustainability.
- more international examples to understand marketing in an international, and particularly European, context.

As with the first and second editions, the purpose of this package remains to bring contemporary marketing perspectives to life for students new to the concept of marketing, and for it to be motivational, creative, applied, and highly relevant to you. We've included brand new examples from organizations including, but not limited to, Virgin Media, innocent, Budweiser Budvar, and Domino's to help illustrate how real-life practitioners tackle marketing problems.

Marketing starts with the basic concepts from classical marketing perspectives and contrasts these with newer views from the relational and societal schools of marketing, helping you to develop your knowledge and understanding of marketing. In the third edition, there is extensive coverage of the societal implications of marketing, including chapters on marketing's contribution to society (in Chapter 1), the concept of marketing sustainability (in Chapter 18), and the critical perspective of marketing (in Chapter 19).

On the Online Resource Centre, we also provide you with web-based research activities, abstracts from seminal papers, study guidelines, multiple-choice questions, and a flashcard glossary to help you broaden and reinforce your own learning.

We aim to provide powerful learning insights into marketing theory and practice through a series of 'Insight' features—Case, Market, and Research Insights. *Marketing* is for life, purchased at level 1 or 2 or as reference reading on professional and postgraduate marketing courses, but retained and referred to throughout the course of your marketing or business degree. We sincerely hope you enjoy learning more about marketing!

Who Should Use this Book?

The main audiences for this book are:

- Undergraduate students in universities and colleges of Higher and Further Education, who are taught in English, around the world. The case material and the examples within the text are deliberately global and international in scale so that international students can benefit from the text.

- Postgraduate students on MBA and MSc/MA courses with a strong marketing component will find this text useful for pre-course and background reading, particularly because of the real-life case problems presented at the beginning of each chapter accompanied by audiovisual material presenting the solution.

- Professional students studying for marketing qualifications through the Chartered Institute of Marketing, the Direct Marketing Association, the Institute of Practitioners in Advertising, and other professional training organizations and trade bodies. The extensive use of examples of marketing practice from around the world make this text relevant for those working in a marketing or commercial environment.

New to this Edition:

- Updated with fresh insights from the latest academic and practitioner research.

- New examples of marketing practice from Europe and around the world.

- Features a new chapter on branding, condensed coverage of services and relationship marketing, and an increased coverage of critical perspectives in marketing, all in keeping with market recommendations.

- Now more concise and slightly shorter in length.

- Downloadable author podcasts summarizing each chapter.

- Additional online learning material, including weblinks, internet activities, worksheets, exercises, and further reading, all clearly signposted throughout the textbook.

- Brand new case insights and associated audiovisual material featuring well-known companies including Virgin Media, innocent, and Budweiser Budvar.

How to Use this Textbook

This text seeks to enhance your learning as part of an undergraduate or introductory course in marketing or as pre-reading for your postgraduate or professional course. However, it can also act as a 'book for life', operating as a reference book for you on matters marketing, particularly during the initial part of your career in marketing and business.

Generally, we only learn what is meaningful to us. Consequently, we have tried to make your learning fun and meaningful by including a multitude of real-life cases. If there is a seminal article associated with a particular concept, try to get hold of the article through your university's electronic library resources and read it. Reflect on your own experience if possible around the concepts you are studying.

Above all, recognize that you are not on your own in your learning. You have your tutor, your classmates, and us to help you learn more about marketing.

This textbook includes not only explanatory material and examples on the nature of marketing concepts, but also a holistic learning system designed to aid you, as part of your university or professional course, to develop your understanding through reading the text. Work through the examples in the text and the review questions, read the seminal articles that have defined a particular sub-discipline in marketing, and use the learning material on the website. This textbook aims to be reader focused, designed to help you learn marketing for yourself.

Most of you will operate either a surface or a deep approach to learning. With the surface approach, you memorize lists of information, whereas with the latter you are actively assimilating, theorizing about, and *understanding* the information. With a surface learning approach, you can run into trouble when example problems learnt are presented in different contexts. You may have simply memorized the procedure without understanding the actual problem. Deep approaches to learning are related to higher-quality educational outcomes and better grades, and the process is more enjoyable. To help you pursue a deep approach to learning, we strongly suggest that you complete the exercises, visit the weblinks, and conduct the internet activities and worksheets at the end of each chapter and other activities on the Online Resource Centre to improve your understanding and your course performance.

Honey And Mumford's Learning Styles Questionnaire

Honey and Mumford (1986) developed a learning style questionnaire that divides learners into four categories based on which aspect of Kolb's learning process they perform best at. Completion of the questionnaire, available at a reasonable price as a 40-item questionnaire (at www. peterhoney.com), provides you with scores on each of the following four categories to allow you to determine your dominant learning style. The four styles are as follows.

1 **Activists**—Where this style is dominant, you learn better through involvement in new experiences through concrete experience. You learn better by doing.

2 **Reflectors**—Where this style is dominant, you are more likely to consider experiences in hindsight and from a variety of perspectives and rationalize these experiences. You learn better by reflecting.

3 **Theorists**—Where this style is dominant, you develop understanding of situations and information by developing an abstract theoretical framework for understanding. You learn better by theorizing.

4 **Pragmatists**—Where this style is dominant, you learn best by understanding what works best in what circumstances in practice. You learn through practice.

Analysis of your learning style will allow you to determine how you learn best at the moment, and give you pointers as to what other approaches to learning you might adopt to balance how you develop. You may already have completed a learning style questionnaire at the beginning of your course and so know which learning styles you need to develop.

We believe that most textbooks are designed to particularly develop the theorist learning style. Review type questions also enhance the reflector learning style. However, in this text, we also aim to develop the pragmatist component of your learning style by providing you with Case Insights, by showing you material in which marketing practitioners discuss real-life problems with which they had to deal. Finally, we ask end-of-chapter discussion questions which require you to work in teams and on your own, as well as providing internet activities to complete and weblinks to visit, to develop your activist learning style.

We aim to enhance your learning by providing an integrated marketing learning system, incorporating the key components that you need to understand the core marketing principles. In this respect, we hope not only that this text and its associated website will facilitate and enhance your learning, making it fun along the way, but that you will find it useful to use this text, and refer back to it, throughout your student and life experiences of marketing.

Learning such an exciting discipline as marketing should be both fun and challenging. We hope that this textbook and its associated resources bring the discipline alive for you. Good luck with your learning and in your career!

How to Use this Book

This book offers a range of learning tools carefully designed to help you get the most from your study, and develop the essential knowledge and skills you'll need for your career ahead.

Learning Outcomes

Short bullet-point lists clearly identify what you can expect to learn from every chapter. This feature can also be used to effectively plan and organize your revision.

Case Insights

Learn from the real-life experiences of leading marketers working for diverse organizations, including innocent, Oxfam, and Virgin Media. Each Case Insight allows you to consider the kinds of challenges professional marketers face, and evaluate your own response to tackling the problem. In the Online Resource Centre you can also find short videos which are designed to accompany the Case Insights, and which expand on the material in the book.

Market Insights

Develop your critical thinking skills using these thought-provoking examples to help you apply the marketing theory to a leading brand or product. Questions accompany each Market Insight to test your knowledge and reinforce your learning.

Learning Outcomes

After studying this chapter, you will be able to:

▶ Define the marketing concept

▶ Explain how marketing has developed over the twentieth and into the twenty-first century

▶ Understand the exchange and marketing mix concepts in marketing

▶ Describe the three major contexts of marketing application, i.e. consumer goods, business-to-business, and services marketing

---

 Case Insight 3.1

How should organizations measure the effectiveness of all touchpoints in interactions with customers, not just marketing communications? We speak to MESH Planning's CEO, Fiona Blades, to find out more.

MESH Planning, an innovative market research agency, was set up in 2006. Fiona Blades had worked previously as an advertising planning director, seeing at first hand how organizations were seldom able to get the data they needed from traditional campaign evaluation, since these were often overly focused on TV advertising. There was also a tendency to believe that, because advertising effectiveness questions were added to **brand health monitoring**, it was advertising that caused changes in brand health when this is often not the case. In fact, MESH data shows that usage is the most influential **touchpoint** for almost all categories of offering. Results of traditional campaign analysis were always reported well after the campaign, making it too late to make interim changes. MESH Planning's response was to develop a research process to measure touchpoint effectiveness using a process called real-time experience tracking (RET). This focuses on experiences that capture the essence of what brands are made of, not interim measures.

RET fuses a number of different data sources, using traditional survey data as well as analysing experiences quantitatively, and then applying statistical measurements to them and viewing qualitative comments. Because MESH has planners (account planners and media planners) as well as researchers, the output for the client is more recommendation/action focused than findings/research focused.

Clients come to MESH because RET collects people's responses to different touchpoints, including those that they haven't been able to get before (e.g. seeing whether it is TV, online, or retail activity which drives brand consideration). The approach is faster and more cost effective than previous tools, such as **market mix modelling**. Beyond marketing campaigns, clients want to understand the impact of retail activity and the path to purchase. MESH clients have reported good results with RET: Energizer executives calculated that the new measures led to a threefold improvement in advertising cost-effectiveness, increasing Energizer's revenue in the razor category by 10% in less than four months; LG Electronics won the coveted POPAI award for retail marketing effectiveness and attributed this to working with MESH; and BSkyB re-evaluated how to spend £150m per annum using RET analytics.

Gatorade, another client, decided to re-position its offering from being in the sports drink category to sports nutrition. Its launch in Mexico included TV advertising, sponsorship, and an innovative channel strategy which used experiential channels such as gyms, fitness centres, and parks.

How could research be designed to determine, if someone experienced an experiential touchpoint, whether having this experience impacted positively on their perceptions of the brand, and specifically, those related to Gatorade's sports nutrition attributes?

 Market Insight 1.1

Blockbuster Goes Bust!

In 2010, the games and film rental company, Blockbuster, filed for bankruptcy in the USA. In 2013, the UK arm of the company, a separate legal entity, followed suit by calling in the administrators. In both cases, each company attracted a buyer and emerged from administration, albeit after closing many unprofitable stores. Dish Network bought the US Blockbuster and Gordon Brothers Europe bought the UK entity. Part of the problem was that the company was operating an out-of-date physical store retail business model in an online retail world (just like HMV who also went into administration), selling and renting DVDs, Blu-rays, and games through a network of 528 stores at a time of stiff competition from online players such as Netflix and Amazon's LOVEFILM, both of which charged a monthly subscription to a library of film and TV content. However, the film content of Netflix and LOVEFILM did not include the very latest box office hits. For this, many consumers turned to iTunes, Apple's online store selling music, film, video, and

of films through its mobile devices and steal a march on Netflix. The only problem was that US regulators wouldn't grant the company a waiver to transmit voice and data over its satellite spectrum. Meanwhile, in the UK, LOVEFILM was busily expanding its services across multiple platforms, including the iPad, Xbox360, and Xbox LIVE, and concluding content deals with Walt Disney (UK and Ireland), Warner Brothers, Studio Canal, BBC Worldwide, and ITV. Netflix, which entered the UK market in January 2012, spent £3m on advertising in the first quarter of 2012 to raise consumer awareness of its offering.

Source: BBC News (2010, 2013a,b); Mintel (2012); Newton (2012)

1 If you were a senior executive at restructuring specialists Gordon Brothers Europe, how would you seek to use the 4Ps to revive Blockbuster's marketing to appeal to more consumers?

2 Why do you think Blockbuster has found it so difficult to alter its business model?

Research Insight 1.1

To take your learning further, you might wish to read this influential paper.

Borden, N. H. (1964), 'The concept of the marketing mix', *Journal of Advertising Research*, 4, 2–7.

This easy-to-read early article explains how marketing managers act as 'mixers of ingredients' when developing marketing programmes. The marketing mix, popularized as the 4Ps, remains popular

Research Insight
Broaden your understanding and take your learning further with key journal articles and books highlighted throughout the text.

■ brings new offerings, and improvements, to market to meet latent and unserved needs;
■ seeks customer satisfaction for repeat purchases.

Visit the **Online Resource Centre** and complete Internet Activity 1.2 to learn more about how marketing innovation impacts upon society.

However, the aggregate marketing system, or marketing more generally, does not always serve the common good. Marketing is frequently criticized for doing precisely the opposite—for being unethical in nature, manipulative, and creating wants and needs where none previously existed (Packard 1960). Whilst this chapter has focused on the principles and practice of marketing, and the positive power of marketing in society, there is also a negative impact of marketing in society. This occurs both as a result of unethical marketing practice (see Chapter 18) and because of structural inequalities in the aggregate

Go Online
The Online Resource Centre contains a wealth of materials to put your knowledge to the test. Throughout the book there are QR codes providing links to each chapter's online resources.

Chapter Summary

To consolidate your learning, the key points from this chapter are summarized here.

■ Define the marketing concept.

Marketing is the process by which organizations anticipate and satisfy their customers' needs to both parties' benefit. It involves mutual exchange. Over the last 25 years, the marketing concept has changed to recognize the importance of long-term customer relationships to organizations. In addition, most definitions of marketing recognize the importance of marketing's impacts on society and the need to curtail these where they are negative.

■ Explain how marketing has developed over the twentieth and into the twenty-first century.

Whereas some writers have suggested a simple production era, sales era, marketing era development

Chapter Summary
Every chapter ends with a summary of the core themes and ideas to consolidate your learning and review the key concepts.

Review Questions

1 What is the process consumers go through when buying offerings?
2 What is cognitive dissonance and how does it relate to consumer behaviour?
3 How are the psychological concepts of perception, learning, and memory relevant to understanding consumer choice?
4 How are concepts of personality relevant to understanding consumer behaviour?
5 How are concepts of motivation relevant to understanding consumer behaviour?
6 What is the Theory of Planned Behaviour?
7 What are opinions, attitudes, and values, and how do they relate to consumer behaviour?

Review Questions
Test your understanding of the material with Review Questions at the end of every chapter.

Worksheet Summary

To apply the knowledge you have gained from this chapter and test your understanding of marketing fundamentals visit the **Online Resource Centre** and complete Worksheet 1.1.

Worksheet Summary
The online worksheets for each chapter are signposted within the text and linked by QR codes to allow you easy access to the resource. Visit the worksheet and check your knowledge and understanding of marketing fundamentals.

Discussion Questions

1 Having read the Case Insight at the beginning of this chapter, how would you advise Systembolaget to use marketing in the future (a) to maintain public support for the Swedish alcohol monopoly, and (b) to ensure that customers drink responsibly?

2 Read the section on the marketing mix within the chapter and draw up marketing mixes for the following organizations and their target customers.

A The streaming video company, Netflix, and their home audiences.
B An online travel agency specializing in luxury holidays and their wealthy clientele.

Discussion Questions
Develop your analytical and reasoning skills with these questions designed for discussion and debate.

---

re how marketing is different in the consumer (B2C), business-
keting sectors. The core principles of marketing, incorporating
marketing exchange, **market orientation**, **relationship
t logic**, are all considered. How marketing impacts positively
re this chapter seeks to provide a thorough grounding in the
se concepts are explored further in later chapters.)

Key Terms and Glossary
Key terms are highlighted in blue where they first appear in each chapter, and are also collated into a glossary at the end of the book. This offers an easy and practical way for you to revise and check your understanding of definitions when it comes to exam time.

How to Use the Online Resource Centre

www.oxfordtextbooks.co.uk/orc/baines3e/

The dedicated Online Resource Centre offers resources for both students and registered lecturers, including:

Lecturer Resources Free for all registered adopters of the textbook:

Tutorial Activities

This interactive resource is designed to reinforce practical marketing skills, and is ideal for use in seminars and tutorials. These materials provide you with a range of suggested ideas for easily integrating the textbook and its resources within your own teaching.

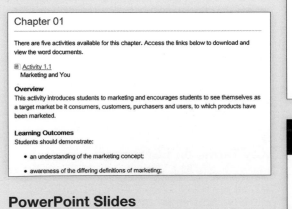

PowerPoint Slides

Accompanying each chapter is a suite of customizable slides to be used in lecture presentations.

Pointers on Answering Discussion Questions

Every chapter is accompanied by suggested answer guides to the end-of-chapter discussion questions.

Pointers for End of Chapter 10 Discussion Questions

1. Having read the Case Insight set out at the beginning of this chapter, how would you advise the marketing team at the Guardian to use marketing communications in order to change perceptions and behaviour towards the newspaper?

Pointers

- Following a suitable short introduction to set out the plan of the response, the first task should be to consider some fundamental aspects of marketing communications.

- One of these aspects is the role of marketing communications, namely, to engage audiences. Engagement can take one of two main forms; to change brand values and to change behaviours. Which type of engagement does *The Guardian* wish to achieve?

Learning Outcomes

- Define the marketing concept
- Explain how marketing has developed over the twentieth and into the twenty-first century
- Understand the exchange and marketing mix concepts in marketing
- Describe the three major contexts of marketing application, i.e. consumer goods,

---

OXFORD
UNIVERSITY PRESS

Chapter 01

1 of 5

Chapter 01 - Question 01
The key focus of the American Marketing Association's (AMA) 2007 definition of marketing is:
- organizational activities
- product components
- Shareholder returns
- Stakeholder value

Essay questions with answer guidance

Chapter 5 - Marketing Strategy

Question 1
Describe the strategic planning process.

Answer guidance
The strategic planning process commences at corporate level. Here the organization sets out its overall mission, purpose and values. These are then converted into measurable goals that apply to the whole organization. Then, depending upon the size of the organization, the range of businesses (SBUs) and/or products is determined and resources allocated to help and support each one. Each business and/or product develops detailed functional and competitive strategies and plans, such as a marketing strategy and plan.

Test Bank
This ready-made electronic testing resource is fully customizable and contains feedback for students, to help you save time when creating assessment material.

Essay Questions
Each chapter is accompanied by a set of essay questions for lecturers to use with their students, alongside clear and detailed answer guidance.

Don't forget that all of these resources can be uploaded to your institution's Virtual Learning Environment to allow students to access them directly!

Student Resources   Free and open-access material available:

Internet Activities
Arranged by chapter, the internet activities help you to undertake online research, and enhance your understanding of key marketing concepts.

Student Worksheets
Enhance your understanding of marketing frameworks and theories with a selection of task focused worksheets, designed to be completed in class or on your own.

Worksheet 1.1: Marketing Principles

Chapter Reference
Chapter 1: Marketing Principles & Society

Overview
This activity introduces you to two frameworks that help us to understand how managers can market their goods and services.

Learning Outcomes
After completing this worksheet you should be able to:
- apply McCarthy's 4P's to a good;
- apply Bitner and Boom's 7P's to a service;
- describe the exchange process;
- discuss the differences and similarities between a good and a service.

Worksheet

Choose a brand of soft drink you are familiar with and apply McCarthy's 4P's framework to this Fast Moving Consumer Good (FMCG)

4P's	Questions	Answer
Product	Product:What is the FMCG?	
Pricing	Price: How much does the FMCG cost?	
Place	Place: Where can you purchase the FMCG	

Web Links
Annotated web links allow you easy access to up-to-date and reliable marketing related sites.

Chapter Reference
Chapter 10: An Introduction to Marketing Communications

Overview
This activity introduces you to the use of internet advertising as a method for driving traffic online and the decisions that need to be considered when selecting ad placement and metrics used for ad effectiveness measurement.

Activity Description
Imagine you were the webmaster for your university or college website. You have the task of driving traffic to the website of potential new undergraduate candidates. However with a limited budget you only have the money to possible select three websites where you'd advertising the universities brand using banner advertising.

If you were to advise your college or university to advertise on the Web, what three Web pages would you recommend? Select three web pages for consideration and visit them to find out if they host banner advertising. If yes identify the following from their website corporate media rates and information:

- What is the monthly rate for a full banner advertisement at each of the websites?
- Describe the profile of the audience for each of the websites.
- Locates the sites rate card and calculate the Cost per Thousand (CPM) for each website.

Websites:
Below is a list of websites with further information about banner advertising networks:

DoubleClick: http://www.doubleclick.net/
BURST!: Media http://www.burstmedia.com/
Banner Brokers:http://www.onlinebanneradverts.co.uk/

Baines & Fill: Marketing 3e

Chapter 3: Web links

Advertising Research Foundation (ARF)
http://www.thearf.org/
Founded in 1936 by the Association of National Advertisers and the American Association of Advertising Agencies, the Advertising Research Foundation (ARF) is a non-profit corporate-membership association which is today the pre-eminent professional organization in the field of advertising, marketing and media research. Its combined membership represents more than 400 advertisers, advertising agencies, research firms, media companies, educational institutions and international organizations. The principal mission of the ARF is to improve the practice of advertising, marketing and media research in pursuit of more effective marketing and advertising communications.

Datamonitor
http://www.datamonitor.com/

Multiple-choice Questions

With a wealth of interactive multiple-choice questions for every chapter this resource gives you instant feedback, as well as page references, to help you focus on areas that need further study.

> **Question 1**
>
> Which of the following statements is correct?
>
> ✓ **Your answer:**
>
> d) Marketing is the activity, set of institutions, and processes for creating, communicating, delivering, and exchanging offerings that have value for customers, clients, partners, and society at large.
>
> **Feedback:**
>
> In their definition of marketing, the American Marketing Association (AMA) concentrates on stakeholders'; value by defining marketing as 'the activity, set of institutions, and processes for creating, communicating, delivering, and exchanging offerings that have value for customers, clients, partners, and society at large' (AMA, 2007).
>
> **Page reference:** 6

Research Insights

Throughout the textbook you'll find references to key academic papers. Connect to these articles and books using links provided.

> **Baines & Fill: Marketing 3e**
>
> Research insight 1.4
>
> **Source:** Wilkie, W. L. and Moore, E. S. (2011), 'Expanding our understanding of marketing in society', *Journal of the Academy of Marketing Science*, 40, 53–73.
>
> **Insight:** This article, building on a previous ground-breaking article (Wilkie and Moore 1999), charts 100 years of marketing thought and the extent to which marketing in society was a key consideration in scholarship during that time. It continues to expand the idea of the 'aggregate marketing system' within society, and maps the field of marketing in society by outlining extant research groups and a research agenda.
>
> **URL:** http://link.springer.com/article/10.1007/s11747-011-0277-y

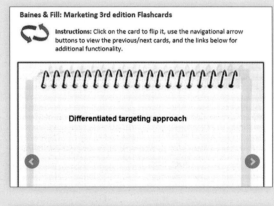

Flashcard Glossary

Learning the jargon associated with the range of topics in marketing can be a challenge, so these online flashcards have been designed to help you understand and memorize the key terms used in the book. Click through the randomized definitions and see if you can identify which key term they are describing.

Author Podcasts

Revise on the go with these audio podcasts recorded by the authors, summarizing the key points and tips for each chapter.

> **Author audio podcasts**
>
> The authors have provided audio podcasts summarizing the key learning objectives for each chapter. You can listen to these on the go, to help you revise and to give you a quick overview of each chapter.
>
> You can listen either via your computer or by downloading the files to your portable MP3 player. Note: you may need to adjust the volume settings on your PC, or you may find that wearing headphones enhances your sound. To download a file, right-click on the link. Select either 'Save Target As' or 'Save Link As' (slightly different worded options are given depending on the browser you are using).
>
> Chapter 1 (MP3, Size: 9.2MB)
> Marketing Principles and Society
>
> Chapter 2 (MP3, Size: 10.6MB)

Employability Guidance

Students, graduates, and marketing experts share their knowledge, tips, and experiences to help you get the job you really want.

Video and Digital Resources—Experience Marketing in Context

The Online Resource Centre also contains a number of video resources for both students and lecturers designed to help build knowledge and experience of marketing in a real world context.

Practitioner Insight Videos

Bespoke video case material which expands on the marketing challenges first introduced in the Case Insights section of the text. In these videos, leading practitioners from a wide variety of organizations explain how they have successfully dealt with real-life marketing dilemmas and offer students further insight into the types of issues facing professional marketers today. Lecturers can play these short videos in class to give students a sense of professional marketing in action. Students can also access these videos to assist with self study.

> **YouTube Resource Title:** What is marketing?
> **Brand and/or Topic:** Marketing
> **Resource Description:** Professor of the Department of Marketing Management. Director of ESADE's Chair of Design Management.
> **Channel:** esade
> **Link (URL):** http://www.youtube.com/watch?v=h7FIWC2NdEM
>
> **YouTube Resource Title:** Evolution of Marketing
> **Brand and/or Topic:** Marketing, Evolution
> **Resource Description:** Marketing is constantly changing - thanks to the internet. Check out the evolution of marketing from Austin Internet Marketing Agency - Three Sixty Solutions.
> **Channel:** Sherffben
> **Link (URL):** http://www.youtube.com/watch?v=mR5x9QPzCSM&NR=1

Video Library

Available to both students and lecturers, this resource offers a bank of links to marketing videos designed to demonstrate key principles and themes in practice.

Marketing Resource Bank

A suite of marketing tools and video clips are accompanied by detailed teaching notes, to provide a diverse collection of practical examples that help to illustrate key theories from each chapter.

> ### Marketing Resource Bank
>
> A suite of marketing tools and video clips accompanied by detailed teaching notes, including examples of viral marketing, online games, and TV advertisements, provides a diverse collection of practical examples to illustrate key theories in each chapter. Click here to open an Excel spreadsheet providing a breakdown of the resource bank as well as detailed descriptions of the teaching notes available.
>
> **Chapter 01: Marketing Principles and Society**
>
> - MRB 1.1: Systembolaget AB
> - MRB 1.2: RM Customer Success
> - MRB 1.3: CIM & UK Marketing Standards
> - MRB 1.4: Black Gold
> - MRB 1.5: CafeDirect
>
> **Chapter 02: The Global Marketing Environment**
>
> - MRB 2.1: Michelin Man: World Of Mobility
> - MRB 2.2: ASA: Keeping Standards High

Part One
Marketing Fundamentals

Chapter 1

Marketing Principles and Society

Learning Outcomes

After studying this chapter, you will be able to:

▶ Define the marketing concept

▶ Explain how marketing has developed over the twentieth and into the twenty-first century

▶ Understand the exchange and marketing mix concepts in marketing

▶ Describe the three major contexts of marketing application, i.e. consumer goods, business-to-business, and services marketing

▶ Understand the contribution that marketing makes to society

Case Insight 1.1
Systemboleget

Market Insight 1.1
Blockbuster goes bust!

Market Insight 1.2
Power by the Hour: Rolls-Royce's Transformation

Market Insight 1.3
KFC: A global brand with Chinese characteristics

Market Insight 1.4
Waterford Crystal: The Phoenix Rises

Market Insight 1.5
Back to the Future: Bringing Electric Cars to the Masses

Case Insight 1.1

Systembolaget AB was the world's first alcohol monopoly and remains the only retailer of alcohol in Sweden. It has a government mandate to limit the harm that might come to Swedish society from alcohol consumption. We speak to Fredrik Thor to find out how a state alcohol monopoly with a prohibition remit can possibly market itself.

It all started in 1850 with the formation in Dalarna, Sweden, of a company that was granted exclusive rights to operate outlets for the sale and serving of alcoholic drinks. This was the world's first ever alcohol monopoly and it worked so well that the model spread nationwide. In 1955, the various local monopolies were merged to form a single one—Systemaktiebolaget.

Systembolaget's mandate is to help limit the medical and social harm caused by alcohol and thereby improve public health. It aims to do this by limiting alcohol availability through the number of retail outlets (opening hours and selling rules), not endeavouring to maximize profits, not promoting additional sales, being brand-neutral, providing good customer service, and being financially efficient. But if the company is essentially designed to limit societal harm from alcohol—in effect, implementing and ensuring compliance with the government's alcohol policy— how can it market alcoholic products responsibly?

The company's marketing communication is steered by legislation, such as the Swedish Marketing Practices Act and the Swedish Alcohol Act, by Systembolaget's agreement with the State, and by the company's own internal guidelines for marketing communication in relation to alcohol products.

So, the monopoly exists to ensure that alcohol-related problems are, as far as possible, minimized. It is generally believed that if it were abolished, people would drink more and social problems would increase. But the monopoly isn't a given. It will only continue to exist as long as it has public support. Therefore the

company does everything it can to ensure that when you visit us, you like what you get.

The aim of all our communication measures has been to persuade more Swedes to support the monopoly—or at least to ensure that more people understand why it exists. The problem was that, in 2002, only 48% of Swedes actually supported the monopoly— in other words, a risky proportion of the public didn't. As Systembolaget's President said, 'If everyone knows why it exists, and people still don't want it, we shouldn't have an alcohol monopoly. But it would be awful if it were to be abolished because no one understood why it existed'.

Therefore the company defined a concrete goal in its strategic plan to boost support for the monopoly to 54% over the course of two years.

The question is how does an alcohol monopoly increase public support for its existence without promoting alcohol consumption?

Refreshing lack of promotional material at Systembolaget

Introduction

How have companies marketed their offerings to you in the past? Consider the drinks you buy, the sports teams you follow, the music you listen to, and the holidays you take. Why did you decide to buy them? Each one has been marketed to you to cater for a particular need that you have. Consider how the offering was distributed. What physical and service-based components is it made of? What societal contributions do these offerings make? Are other versions of these offerings available that meet your needs and the needs of society better? These are some of the questions that marketers should ask themselves when designing, developing, and delivering offerings to the **customer**.

In this chapter, we develop our understanding of marketing principles and marketing's impact upon society by defining marketing, comparing and contrasting American, British, and French definitions. We consider the origins and development of marketing throughout the twentieth and into the twenty-first century. We explore how marketing is different in the consumer (B2C), business-to-business (B2B), and services marketing sectors. The core principles of marketing, incorporating the marketing mix, the principle of marketing exchange, **market orientation**, **relationship marketing**, and **service-dominant logic**, are all considered. How marketing impacts positively upon society is also detailed. Therefore this chapter seeks to provide a thorough grounding in the principles of marketing. (Many of these concepts are explored further in later chapters.)

What is Marketing?

Consider your own fairly vast experience of being marketed to throughout your life. So far, you will have been subjected to millions of marketing communications messages, bought hundreds of thousands of offerings, been involved in thousands of customer service telephone or online calls, and visited tens of thousands of shops, supermarkets, and retail outlets (physical or virtual). You're already a pretty experienced customer. Our role here is to explain how professionals do the other side of marketing—how they market offerings to customers. Remember most customers are just like you and will be just as discriminating as you are when buying.

To explain how we go about marketing offerings to customers, we must first describe exactly what marketing is. There are numerous definitions, but we present three for easy reference in Table 1.1.

Visit the **Online Resource Centre** and follow the weblinks in to the CIM and AMA websites to read more about their views on 'What is Marketing?'.

The **CIM** and **AMA** definitions recognize marketing as a 'management process' and an 'activity', although many firms organize marketing as a discrete department rather than as a service across departments (Sheth and Sisodia, 2005). The CIM and AMA definitions both stress the importance of considering the customer, of determining their requirements or needs. The CIM definition refers to customer 'requirements' and the AMA to 'delivering value'. Conversely, the French definition refers to developing an offer of superior **value**. Both the AMA and French definitions refer to an 'offer' and 'offering', recognizing that marketing can be applied equally to the marketing of goods, services, ideas and in the not-for-profit sector.

The CIM definition discusses anticipating/identifying needs and the AMA discusses 'creating … offerings that have value for customers'. Both definitions recognize the need for marketers to

Table 1.1 Definitions of marketing	
Defining institution/author	Definition
The Chartered Institute of Marketing (CIM)	'The management process of anticipating, identifying and satisfying customer requirements profitably' (CIM, 2001).
The American Marketing Association (AMA)	'Marketing is the activity, set of institutions, and processes for creating communicating, delivering, and exchanging offerings that have value for customers, clients, partners, and society at large' (AMA, 2007).
A French perspective	'*Le marketing est l'effort d'adaptation des organisations à des marchés concurrentiels, pour influencer en leur faveur le comportement de leurs publics, par une offre dont la valeur perçue est durablement supérieure à celle des concurrents*', which broadly translates as 'Marketing is the endeavour of adapting organizations to their competitive markets in order to influence, in their favour, the behaviour of their publics, with an offer whose perceived value is durably superior to that of the competition' (Lendrevie *et al*., 2006).

undertake marketing research (see Chapter 3) and environmental scanning activity (see Chapter 4) to satisfy customers and, in the long term, to anticipate customers' needs.

The French definition discusses influencing the behaviour of publics, rather than customers, recognizing the wider remit of marketing in modern society. The challenge, according to the French definition, is to develop an offering that is 'durably superior' to that of the competition. Therefore this definition recognizes explicitly the importance of market segmentation and **positioning** concepts (see Chapter 6).

The CIM definition presupposes that marketing is a process with a profit motive, although it does not explicitly state whether or not this is for financial profit, or for some other form of profit, e.g. of gain in society, as in the case of a charity. The AMA definition is much clearer, arguing that marketing is a process undertaken to benefit 'clients, partners, and society at large'.

What all these definitions display is how the concept of marketing has changed over the years, from transactional concepts like pricing, promotion, and distribution, to relationship concepts such as the importance of customer trust, risk, commitment, and co-creation.

In addition, the nature of the relationships between an organization and its customers, in its offerings and its mission, are different in not-for-profit and for-profit organizations (see Chapter 16). Nevertheless, the broad principles of how marketing is used remain the same. The French and AMA definitions both recognize this widened concept of the applicability of marketing.

Visit the **Online Resource Centre** and complete Internet Activity 1.1 to learn more about the world's two leading professional marketing associations.

What's the Difference between Customers and Consumers?

What actually is a customer? And what is the difference between a customer and a **consumer**? A customer is a buyer, a purchaser, a patron, a client, or a shopper. A customer is someone who buys from a shop, a website, a business, or another customer (e.g. eBay or Amazon exchange).

Cheestrings, the calci-yummy snack for children
Source: Image courtesy of Kerry Group plc.

The difference between a customer and a consumer is that a customer purchases or obtains an offering but a consumer uses it (or eats it in the case of food).

To illustrate, consider the marketing course you are enrolled on, assuming that you are using this book as an aid to learning on the course. Did you pay your course fees yourself? Or did someone else pay them? If you did pay the fees yourself, you are the customer. If someone else paid them, they are the customer, although you make use of, and study for, the degree or course. So you are the consumer.

Another example is Kerry Food's Cheestrings, a dairy food designed to help children get their daily allowance of calcium and vitamin D to maintain healthy bones. In this case, the customer is the chief shopper, the mother/father or guardian, and the consumer is the child. Sometimes the customer and consumer can be the same person, e.g. the girl buying cinema tickets for herself and her boyfriend online.

Market Orientation

The concept of market orientation lies at the heart of marketing. Developing a market orientation is argued to make organizations more profitable, especially when there is limited competition, unchanging customer wants and needs, fast-paced technological change, and strong economies in operation (Kohli and Jaworski, 1990). In a meta-analysis of market orientation studies, Kirca *et al.* (2005) conclude that market orientation may be imperative for survival in service firms and the source of competitive advantage in manufacturing firms.

But developing a market orientation is not the same as developing a marketing orientation. So what's the difference? A company with a marketing orientation would be a company that recognizes the importance of marketing within the organization, e.g. by appointing a marketing person to CEO, or to chair of its board of directors (or trustees in the case of a charity), or to the executive team more generally in a limited company or partnership.

Developing a market orientation refers to 'the organization-wide generation of market intelligence pertaining to current and future customer needs, dissemination of the intelligence across the departments, and organization-wide responsiveness to it' (Kohli and Jaworski, 1990). So a market orientation doesn't just involve marketing, it involves all the functions of a company, gathering and responding to market intelligence (i.e. customers' verbalized needs and preferences, data from customer surveys, sales data, and information gleaned informally from discussions with customers and trade partners, from websites, and from social networking sites). Developing a market orientation means developing the following:

- Customer orientation—concerned with creating superior value by continuously developing and redeveloping offerings to meet customer needs. To do so we must measure customer satisfaction on a continuous basis and train front-line service staff accordingly.

- Competitor orientation—requires an organization to develop an understanding of its competitors' short-term strengths and weaknesses and its long-term capabilities and strategies (Slater and Narver, 1994).

- Interfunctional coordination—requiring all the functions of an organization to work together to achieve the above foci for long-term profit (as shown in Figure 1.1).

Achieving a market orientation so that an organization is internally responsive to changes in the marketplace can take an organization four years or more to develop and requires top senior management support, the development of teams to gather the necessary market intelligence data and design appropriate market-based reward systems, and management to implement the recommendations made as a result (Kohli and Jaworski, 1990).

Developing a market orientation within a company is a capability, something that not all companies can do. Organizations that manage to develop a market orientation are better at **market sensing**, i.e. understanding the strategic implications of the market for a particular organization, and acting on the information collected through **environmental scanning**. (This topic is covered fully in Chapter 4.) Colgate-Palmolive, the fast-moving consumer goods company, developed a strong market orientation by aligning their company to the task of promoting trade satisfaction, measuring the number of orders delivered on time and the number of orders completed (Day,

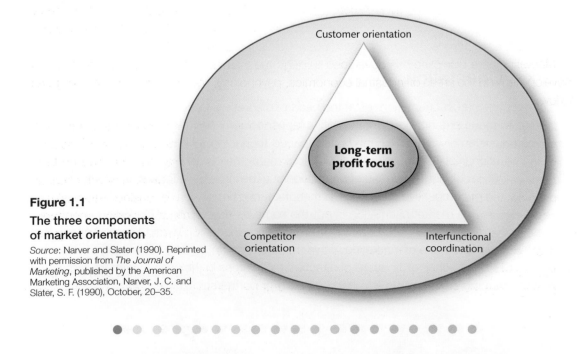

Figure 1.1

The three components of market orientation

Source: Narver and Slater (1990). Reprinted with permission from *The Journal of Marketing*, published by the American Marketing Association, Narver, J. C. and Slater, S. F. (1990), October, 20–35.

1994). Amazingly, up to the year 2000 General Electric (GE)—the American capital, expertise, and infrastructure company—had no substantial marketing organization. Instead, it had been technology driven. To orient GE towards the market, it organized its marketing function into two basic activities: go to market (e.g. segmentation) and commercial essentials (e.g. branding, communications). Then they organized their marketing teams across the company to ensure that they contained a mix of people with different skills, including instigators (who challenge the status quo), innovators who develop new offerings and processes), integrators (who build bridges across organizational functions and in the marketplace), and implementers (who execute on the new ideas). All this was backed with a process custom-designed to evaluate the success of the new approach (Comstock *et al.*, 2010).

A Brief History of Marketing

Most marketing texts present the development of marketing as a four-stage sequence as follows:

1 Production period, 1890s–1920s: characterized by a focus on physical production and supply, where demand exceeded supply, there was little competition, and the range of products was limited. This phase came after the industrial revolution.

2 Sales period, 1920s–1950s: characterized by a focus on personal selling supported by market research and advertising. This phase took place after the First World War.

3 Marketing period, 1950s–1980s: characterized by a more advanced focus on the customer's needs. This phase came after the Second World War.

4 Societal marketing period, 1980s to present: characterized by a stronger focus on social and ethical concerns in marketing. This phase took place during the 'information revolution' of the late twentieth century (Enright, 2002).

Some marketing historians regard marketing as an invention of the twentieth century (Keith, 1960), while others regard marketing as a process which evolved over a much longer period of time, without any production era ever having existed at all. Soap firms, for example, were **advertising** in the late nineteenth century in the UK, the USA, and Germany (Fullerton, 1988). The notion that marketing developed from the 1950s is probably wrong considering that self-service supermarkets operated in America from the 1930s, and products were increasingly developed based on the process of 'consumer engineering', where products were designed and redesigned, using research, to meet customer needs (see Fullerton, 1988).

Marketing as a discipline has developed through the influence of practitioners, and through developments in the areas of industrial economics, psychology, sociology, and anthropology, as follows.

- *Industrial economics influences*—our knowledge of the matching of supply and demand, within industries, owes much to the development of microeconomics. For instance, the economic concepts of perfect competition and the matching of supply and demand underlie the marketing concept, particularly in relation to the concepts of the price at which offerings are sold and the quantity distributed (see Chapter 9) and the nature of business-to-business marketing (see Chapter 15). Theories of income distribution, scale of operation, monopoly, competition, and finance all derive from economics (Bartels, 1951), although the influence of economics over marketing is declining (Howard *et al.*, 1991).

- *Psychological influences*—our knowledge of consumer behaviour derives principally from psychology, especially motivational research (see Chapter 3) in relation to consumer attitudes, perceptions, motivations, and information processing (Holden and Holden, 1998), and our understanding of persuasion, consumer personality, and customer satisfaction (Bartels, 1951). Understanding buyer psychology is fundamental to the marketing function. As marketing is about understanding customers' needs, we must empathize with our customer.

- *Sociological influences*—our knowledge of how groups of people behave derives from sociology, with insights into areas such as how people from similar gender and age groups behave (demographics), how people in different social positions within society behave (class), why we do things in the way that we do (motivation), general ways that groups behave (customs), and culture (Bartels, 1951, 1959). Our understanding of what society thinks as a whole (i.e. public opinion), and how we influence the way people think and to adopt our perspective (e.g. propaganda research), have all informed market research practice.

- *Anthropological influences*—our debt to **social anthropology** increases more and more as we use qualitative market research approaches such as **ethnography**, **netnography**, and **observation** to research consumer behaviour (see Chapters 3 and 19), particularly the behaviour of subgroups and cultures (e.g. **tweenagers**).

Differences between Sales and Marketing

When new to marketing, we might ask: what is the difference between selling and marketing? If we consider the four eras of marketing development outlined above, we would say marketing has developed from sales. But perhaps a more comprehensive answer is that sales emphasizes the process of 'product push', by creating distribution incentives for both salespeople and customers to make exchanges.

Marketing is more focused on creating 'product pull', or demand, among customers and consumers, and the offering is designed and redesigned through customer and consumer input, through research and customer insight, to meet their long term needs. Marketing activity is geared around understanding and communicating to the customer to design, develop, deliver, and determine the value in the offering, whereas sales is organized principally around enhancing the distribution of the companies' offerings once those offerings have already been designed. Sales departments are mostly concerned with the delivery part of the value creation process. However, sales as a function does and should have inputs to the design phase (through information from sales representatives), the development phase (particularly in test marketing, see Chapter 3), and the determination phase, where salespeople's informal knowledge of customers' needs is critical to the marketing process.

Whereas marketing activities stimulate demand, sales activities stimulate supply. However, the two functions should be integrated to coexist in an organization since both functions are important. Table 1.2 provides a basic summary of the differences.

What Do Marketers Do?

To answer this question, the British government worked with relevant stakeholders to map out how the marketing function operates (a role undertaken by the Skills CfA, formerly Council for Administration). Their consultation indicated that the job covered eight functional areas (see Figure 1.2), each of which is interlinked with stakeholder requirements.

Visit the **Online Resource Centre** and follow the weblink to the Skills CFA website to learn more about national occupational standards for marketing.

Table 1.2 Differences between marketing and sales

Marketing	Sales
Tends towards long-term satisfaction of customer needs	Tends towards short-term satisfaction of customer needs; part of the value delivery process as opposed to designing and development of customer value processes
Tends to greater input into customer design of offering (co-creation)	Tends to lesser input into customer design of offering
Tends to high focus on stimulation of demand	Tends to low focus on stimulation of demand, more focused on meeting existing demand

As society constantly changes, so the marketing profession also constantly changes. Marketing's place within the business profession and society more generally is often criticized. Whereas doctors, teachers, and judges are generally held in high respect (Worcester *et al.*, 2011: 136), marketing practitioners tend to be held in low esteem (Kotler, 2006). To reform marketing practice, and thereby raise its esteem, we need to:

- Make marketing a corporate staff function that operates across departments, at a strategic level, like the finance, information technology, legal, and human resource management functions.
- Ensure that the head of the marketing function reports directly to the chief executive officer (CEO).

Figure 1.2

A functional map for marketing

Source: The Marketing and Sales Standards Setting Body (2010). Reproduced with the kind permission of Dr Chahid Fourali, then head of MSSSB.

- Rename the head of corporate marketing the chief customer officer (CCO).

- Provide marketing with capital expenditure budgets in addition to operating expenditure budgets so that the marketing function can make major capital investments (e.g. in CRM projects, or sales and marketing offices in international markets).

- Ensure that the marketing function controls branding, key account management, and business development.

- Ensure that the marketing function manages external suppliers such as market research and marketing communications agencies.

- Set up, within the public limited company, a board-level standing committee, on which senior marketers sit, comparable to audit, compensation, and governance committees (Sheth and Sisodia, 2006).

On the last point, unfortunately, there are still too many major public companies with no marketing representation on their boards. A review of FTSE 350 firms in the UK by the executive search agency Norman Broadbent indicated that only 50 non-executive directors from these companies had a background in marketing (Parsons, 2013). Worse still, 57% of marketing functions within their organizations are divorced from a strategic role and 82% of marketing leaders are dissatisfied with the role and positioning of marketing within their organizations (CIM, 2009). This is unlikely to change over the next ten years unless marketers demonstrate marketing's value more in their organizations.

The Principal Principles of Marketing

Despite a hundred years or more of study, there are few true scientific principles in marketing (see also Bartels, 1944). Bartels (1951) stated in a discussion of whether or not marketing is an art or science that only two marketing generalizations exist, including:

1 As [a consumer's] income increases, the percentage of income spent for food decreases; for rent, fuel, and light remains the same; for clothing remains the same; and for sundries [miscellaneous items] increases (Engels' Law).

2 Two cities attract retail trade from an intermediary city or town in the vicinity of the breaking point (the 50% point), approximately in direct proportion to the populations of the two cities and in inverse proportion to the square of the distance from these two cities to the intermediate town (Reilly's Law of Retail Gravitation).

Clearly, things have changed since Engels produced his 'Law', especially as we now tend to buy our accommodation rather than renting it, and food is relatively less expensive than it was 60–80 years ago, so it is debatable as to whether or not the first 'Law' still applies. On the second 'Law', site location specialists for a major supermarket should locate stores near the larger of the major population centres. Again this might sound obvious as a general principle, but Reilly's Law allows retailers to determine with some degree of precision exactly where that location might be. Nowadays, multiple retail grocers, such as Carrefour in France, Sainsbury's in the UK, Coop in Denmark, and Tesco Lotus in Thailand, use complex mathematical formulae (e.g. algorithms) to determine where to locate their supermarkets, purchasing land and developing suitable properties in addition to converting existing business premises in valuable locations.

Several prominent academics have argued for the development of a 'General Theory of Marketing' (Bartels, 1968; Hunt, 1971, 1983). We continue to search for this Holy Grail of marketing theory. However, to understand the phenomenon of marketing more completely, we must first understand the following.

- The behaviour of buyers—why do which buyers purchase what they do, where they do, when they do, and how they do?

- The behaviour of sellers—why do which sellers price, promote, and distribute what they do, where they do, when they do, and how they do?

- The institutional framework (e.g. government, society, and so on) around selling/buying—why do which kinds of institutions develop to engage in what kinds of functions or activities to consummate and/or facilitate exchanges, when will these institutions develop, where will they develop, and how will they develop?

- The consequences for society of buying/selling—why do which kinds of buyers, behaviours of buyers, behaviour of sellers, and institutions have what kinds of consequences on society, when they do, where they do, and how they do (Hunt, 1983)?

The listing indicates how marketing involves a series of highly complex interactions between individuals, organizations, society, and government. We have only a limited understanding of how marketing works in theory and practice. However, we can make some more generalizations about marketing. According to Leone and Shultz (1980), these include the following.

- Generalization 1—advertising has a direct and positive influence on total industry (market) sales, i.e. all advertising done at industry level serves to increase sales within that industry.

- Generalization 2—selective advertising has a direct and positive influence on individual company (brand) sales, i.e. advertising undertaken by a company tends to increase the sales of the particular brand for which it was spent.

- Generalization 3—the **elasticity** of selective advertising on company (brand) sales is low (inelastic), i.e. for frequently purchased goods, advertising has only a very limited effect in raising sales.

- Generalization 4—increasing store shelf space (display) has a positive impact on sales of **non-staple** grocery items, such as products bought on impulse (e.g. ice cream, chocolate bars) rather than those that are planned purchases, which are less important but perhaps more luxurious types of goods (e.g. gravy mixes, cooking sauces). For instance, for impulse goods, the more shelf space you give an item, the more likely you are to sell it.

- Generalization 5—distribution, defined by the number of outlets, has a positive influence on company sales (market share), i.e. setting up more retail locations has a positive influence on sales.

As we can see, marketing techniques are still developing in a scientific sense. Most companies cannot yet describe accurately—or predict—the behaviour of their consumers, customers, and producers according to some pre-defined formulae. Therefore marketers have to make use of trial and error, and experimentation and readjustment processes.

There are some general concepts that help managers frame their actions as they develop their marketing plans and programmes. These concepts include the concept of exchange in marketing, the marketing mix for products (4Ps) and services (7Ps), market orientation, and **relationship marketing** and **service-dominant logic** for marketing.

Research Insight 1.1

To take your learning further, you might wish to read this influential paper.

Borden, N. H. (1964), 'The concept of the marketing mix', *Journal of Advertising Research*, **4, 2–7.**

This easy-to-read early article explains how marketing managers act as 'mixers of ingredients' when developing marketing programmes. The marketing mix, popularized as the 4Ps, remains popular today, although the advent of relationship marketing challenged the impersonal notion of marketers as manipulators of marketing policies, and focused more on the need to develop long-term interpersonal relationships with customers.

🔵 **Visit the Online Resource Centre to read the abstract and access the full paper.**

Marketing as Exchange

Marketing is a two-way process. It's not just about the marketing organization doing the work. The customer has to input. In fact, customers specify how we might satisfy their needs, because marketers are not mind-readers, but customers must pay for the offering. In the middle of the 1970s, there was an increasing belief that marketing centred on the exchange process between buyers and sellers and associated **supply chain** intermediaries. Exchange relationships were perceived to be economic (e.g. a consumer buying groceries) and social (e.g. the service undertaken by the social worker on behalf of society paid for by government) (Bagozzi, 1975). This recognition of the underlying exchange relationship within marketing led to the 'broadening' of marketing and the relationship marketing school of marketing (see Chapter 14). There are three main types of buyer–seller exchanges in marketing. Figure 1.3 illustrates these two-way (**dyadic**) exchanges as follows.

1 In the first exchange type, the exchange takes place between the fire service who protect the general public from fire and provide emergency planning activity and services, and the public who support them, sometimes through signing petitions to keep them in service in a particular locale, and especially through their national and local taxes, depending on the country.

2 In the second exchange type, we enter a shop, say WE—the Dutch fashion retailer—and purchase the necessary goods by paying for these with money or by credit/debit card.

3 In the third type of exchange, we have a manufacturer and a retailer. Here, the retailer (e.g. London's Hamley's toyshop) purchases goods from the manufacturer (e.g. Mattel) through a credit facility (e.g. payment in 30 days) and expects any damaged goods to be returnable, and wants the goods delivered on certain types of pallets at a certain height within a particular time limit. In return, the retailer undertakes to pay a wholesale (i.e. trade discounted) price.

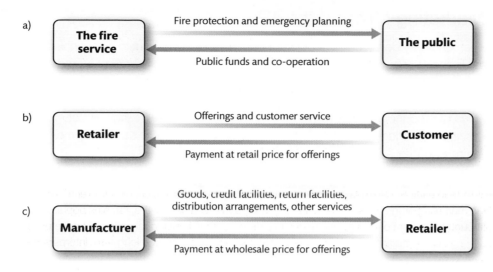

a)

The fire service → Fire protection and emergency planning → The public

The public → Public funds and co-operation → The fire service

b)

Retailer → Offerings and customer service → Customer

Customer → Payment at retail price for offerings → Retailer

c)

Manufacturer → Goods, credit facilities, return facilities, distribution arrangements, other services → Retailer

Retailer → Payment at wholesale price for offerings → Manufacturer

Figure 1.3
Simple marketing exchange processes

However, few marketing exchanges are this simple. They might involve other individual transactions and multiple combinations. For example, (2) and (3) can be combined to indicate a simple supply chain for, say, a toy manufacturer selling to shops that sell on to the general public, their customers. Through understanding how exchanges take place between members of the supply chain, we can determine where we add/do not add value to the customer experience.

Research Insight 1.2

To take your learning further, you might wish to read this influential paper.

Bagozzi, R. P. (1975), 'Marketing as exchange', *Journal of Marketing*, **39(October), 32–9.**

This important article outlined how the key consideration in marketing is the satisfaction of exchange relationships, setting the scene for widespread acceptance of social marketing methods and accelerating the search for a general theory of marketing, particularly through marketing relationships. Bagozzi wanted to answer such questions as: How do people and organizations satisfy their needs through exchange? Why do some marketing exchanges last and others fail? What is an equitable exchange? How should we go about analysing marketing exchanges? And, is the exchange concept equally applicable to all societies around the world?

@ **Visit the Online Resource Centre to read the abstract and access the full paper.**

The Marketing Mix and the 4Ps

Neil Borden originally developed the concept of the **marketing mix** in his teaching at Harvard University in the 1950s. His idea was of marketing managers as 'mixers of ingredients'—chefs who concoct a unique marketing recipe to fit the requirements of customers' needs at any particular time. The emphasis was on the creative fashioning of a mix of marketing procedures and policies to produce the profitable enterprise. He composed a 12-item list of elements (with sub-items, not reproduced here), which the manufacturer should consider when developing marketing mix policies and procedures (Borden, 1964):

1 product planning;

2 pricing;

3 branding;

4 channels of distribution;

5 personal selling;

6 advertising;

7 promotions;

8 packaging;

9 display;

10 servicing;

11 physical handling;

12 fact finding and analysis.

This list was simplified and amended by Eugene McCarthy (1960), to the more memorable but rigid 4Ps (see Figure 1.4):

1 **product**—e.g. the offering and how it meets the customer's need, its packaging, and its labelling (see Chapter 8);

2 **place** (distribution)—e.g. the way in which the offering meets customers' needs (see Chapter 12);

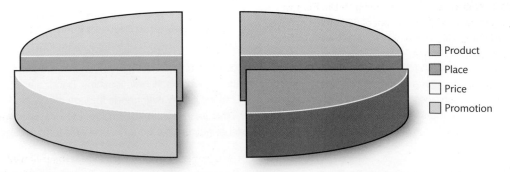

Figure 1.4
The 4 Ps of the marketing mix

3 **price**—e.g. the cost to the customer, and the cost plus profit to the seller (see Chapter 9);

4 **promotion**—e.g. how the offering's benefits and features are conveyed to the potential buyer (see Chapters 10 and 11).

The intention was to create a simpler framework around which managers could develop their planning. Although there was some recognition that all of these elements might be interlinked (e.g. promotion based on the price paid by the consumer), such interplay between these mix components was not taken into account by McCarthy's framework. (See Market Insight 1.1 for an example of why the Blockbuster video rental offering in particular and the marketing mix more generally needs redeveloping.)

Some commentators have argued that the 4Ps framework is of limited use; however, we include it here because managers continue to use it extensively when devising their marketing plans.

 # Market Insight 1.1

Blockbuster Goes Bust!

In 2010, the games and film rental company, Blockbuster, filed for bankruptcy in the USA. In 2013, the UK arm of the company, a separate legal entity, followed suit by calling in the administrators. In both cases, each company attracted a buyer and emerged from administration, albeit after closing many unprofitable stores. Dish Network bought the US Blockbuster and Gordon Brothers Europe bought the UK entity (although they later put Blockbusters back into administration). Part of the problem was that the company was operating an out-of-date physical store retail business model in an online retail world (just like HMV who also went into administration), selling and renting DVDs, Blu-rays, and games through a network of 528 stores at a time of stiff competition from online players such as Netflix and Amazon's LOVEFiLM, both of which charged a monthly subscription to a library of film and TV content. However, the film content of Netflix and LOVEFiLM did not include the very latest box office hits. For this, many consumers turned to iTunes, Apple's online store selling music, film, video, and other media content.

Dish Networks bought Blockbuster in the USA so that it could offer Blockbuster's extensive catalogue of films through its mobile devices and steal a march on Netflix. The only problem was that US regulators wouldn't grant the company a waiver to transmit voice and data over its satellite spectrum. Meanwhile, in the UK, LOVEFiLM was busily expanding its services across multiple platforms, including the iPad, Xbox360, and Xbox LIVE, and concluding content deals with Walt Disney (UK and Ireland), Warner Brothers, Studio Canal, BBC Worldwide, and ITV. Netflix, which entered the UK market in January 2012, spent £3m on advertising in the first quarter of 2012 to raise consumer awareness of its offering.

Source: BBC News (2010, 2013a,b); Mintel (2012); Newton (2012).

1 **If you were a senior executive at restructuring specialists Gordon Brothers Europe, how would you seek to use the 4Ps to revive Blockbuster's marketing to appeal to more consumers? Why might their marketing mix strategy have failed?**

2 **Why do you think Blockbuster has found it so difficult to alter its business model?**

3 **What other companies can you think of that need to revive their marketing mixes? Why do you think this?**

The Extended Marketing Mix

It might seem that what is exchanged in a service context (e.g. purchasing a holiday) is different from a goods context (e.g. buying a DVD). Therefore by the end of the 1970s it was recognized that the traditional 4Ps approach to marketing planning based on physical products (e.g. salt, CDs, alcoholic drinks) was not particularly useful for either a physical product offering with a strong service component (e.g. laptop computers with extended warranty) or services with little or no physical component (e.g. spa and massage, hairdressing, sports spectatorship) (see Chapter 14.)

Two American scholars (Booms and Bitner, 1981) incorporated a further 3Ps into the marketing mix to reflect the need to market services differently, as follows (see Figure 1.5).

1 Physical evidence—to emphasize that the tangible components of services were strategically important, e.g. potential university students often assess whether or not they want to attend a university and a particular course by requesting a copy of brochures and course outlines or by visiting the campus.

2 Process—to emphasize the importance of the service delivery. When processes are standardized, it is easier to manage customer expectations, e.g. DHL International GmbH, the German international express, transport and air freight company, is a master at producing a standardized menu of service options, such as track and trace delivery services, which are remarkably consistent around the world.

3 People—to emphasize the importance of customer service personnel, sometimes experts and often professionals interacting with the customer. How they interact with customers, and how satisfied customers are as a result of their experiences, is of strategic importance.

Consider how the extended marketing mix is used in the airline industry. For instance, the process component of the services marketing mix has been revolutionized through internet ticket booking and web check-in services. The traditional middleman, the travel agency, has had to radically alter his/her customer proposition as the major national carriers (e.g. Air France, KLM, British Airways) offer their services directly by internet to compete with a new class of lower-cost airlines also offering their services direct to the public via the internet at substantially lower prices. The travel agencies have put their own services online, customizing their holiday offerings in order to differentiate their services from the airlines and add value for the customer, offering better deals on insurance, identifying best flight connections, providing advice on best airlines, and offering affiliate hotel deals (Saren, 2006). For example, in late 2012 Thomas Cook, the tour

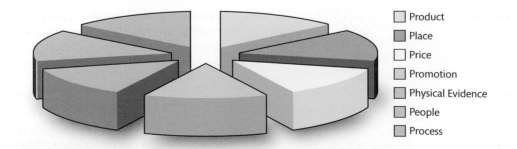

Product
Place
Price
Promotion
Physical Evidence
People
Process

Figure 1.5
The amended marketing mix for services: the 7Ps

operator, announced a flat pricing structure across all its distribution channels, online and offline, and closed down around 200 unprofitable stores (Griffiths, 2012; BBC News, 2013c).

The people, process, and physical evidence components of the airline service marketing mix are fundamental in the development of the offering. Of course, we should recognize that airlines do not offer everyone the same level of service. Most airlines offer an economy service, an economy plus service (with slightly more seating space), a business class service (with even more seating space, a better meal, personalized cabin crew service, fast-track service through passport control, and often a limousine service to and from the airport, and a first class service (with personalized menus, luxury transport to and from the airport, and luxurious in-flight seating). Table 1.3 provides a summary of the marketing mix for the airline industry.

Table 1.3 The marketing mix: the airline industry

Marketing aspect	Airline industry
Basic customer need	Safe long- and short-haul transportation, domestic and international.
Target market	Mass consumer market (economy class), businesspeople (business class), and high-net-worth individuals (first class).
Product offering	Typically, differentiated based on class of passenger, with seat size increasing, check-in and boarding times reducing, quality of food increasing, and levels of ancillary services (e.g. limousine service) increasing as we move from economy through business to first class. Some carriers focus on 'no-frills' basic services (e.g. EasyJet, Ryanair, Air Asia).
Price	Substantial difference depending on class of service, type of carrier, and purchasing approach (e.g. via internet tends to be cheaper).
Principal promotional tools	(1) Press, magazine, and radio advertising, (2) the internet, (3) billboards.
Distribution	Increasingly purchased via the internet, including third-party brokerages such as Expedia as well as through travel agents, the once-dominant but now increasingly redundant medium.
Process	Self-service via internet or aided by travel agent in retail location. Travel options increasingly customized to the customer's needs, including size of baggage allowance, class of travel, increasing availability of alternative locations. Customer and organization use of social media to air and resolve problems is increasingly important.
Physical evidence	Airline loyalty cards and souvenirs, in-flight magazines, in-flight entertainment services, food and snack meals, grooming and toiletry products provided.
People	Combination of check-in staff, customer service personnel, and cabin crew/pilot teams, all of whom interface with the customer at different points in the experience.

Relationship Marketing, Service-Dominant Logic, and Co-Creation

If marketing is about exchange, shouldn't marketing also be concerned with relationships between those parties that are exchanging value? This was the principal idea behind the development of relationship marketing in the 1990s. The relationship marketing concept spawned further evolution of marketing's conceptual foundations. There was a shift from the need to engage on transactions towards the need to develop long-term customer relationships, including relationships with other stakeholders (Christopher *et al.*, 2002; see Chapter 14) including:

- suppliers;
- potential employees;
- recruiters;
- referral markets—where they exist, e.g. retail banks partly relying on professional services organizations, including estate agents, for mortgage referrals;
- influence markets—e.g. regulatory authorities, politicians, and civil servants (see also Viney and Baines, 2012);
- internal markets, e.g. existing employees.

Hult *et al.* (2011) added shareholders and the local community to the above list. For them, the definition of marketing provided by the AMA (see Table 1.1) is inadequate because it fails to consider a wide enough set of stakeholders. The relationship marketing concept was concerned with integrating customer service, quality assurance, and marketing activity (Payne, 1993). Companies employing a relationship marketing approach stressed customer retention rather than customer acquisition. Customer retention is a particularly important strategic activity in marketing mass consumer services as research has demonstrated that when a company retains loyal customers it is more likely to be profitable compared with competitors who do not, because customers:

- will increase their purchases over time;
- are cheaper to promote to;
- who are happy with their relationship with a company are happy to refer it to others;
- are prepared to pay a (small) price premium if they are loyal (Reichheld and Sasser, 1990).

The idea of developing stronger relationships with existing customers is particularly important in mature industries where markets are saturated, such as utilities and telecommunications, the travel industry, and retail banking. Retention programmes are developed to focus marketing activity on enhancing customer service satisfaction and rewarding loyalty, building CRM (**customer relationship management**) systems, and undertaking sales promotion activities. Companies had previously been urged to develop long-term interactive relationships (Gummesson, 1987). However, relationship marketing moved the concept away from simply adopting the 4Ps to adopting an **interactive marketing** approach, paying more attention to the customer base rather than being preoccupied with market share (Grönroos, 1994).

More recently, there has been a realization that marketing needed to shift beyond a goods-based paradigm towards a new service-dominant logic (Vargo and Lusch, 2004). This new marketing

Research Insight 1.3

To take your learning further, you might wish to read this influential paper.

Vargo, S. L. and Lusch, R. F. (2008), 'Service-dominant logic: continuing the evolution', *Journal of the Academy of Marketing Science*, **36, 1–10.**

This article builds on, and updates, the authors' original ground-breaking article (Vargo and Lusch, 2004) which redefined how marketers should think about offerings, arguing that it was necessary to move beyond the idea of tangible versus intangible goods, embedded value and transactions, and other outmoded concepts derived from economics towards the notion of intangible resources and the co-creation of value and relationships. The article asserts that service is the fundamental basis of all exchanges in marketing and that value is always determined by the beneficiary.

@ **Visit the Online Resource Centre to read the abstract and access the full paper.**

paradigm sees service as *the* fundamental basis of exchange (see Research Insight 1.3). In that sense, for physical goods offerings, the good is simply the distribution mechanism. To understand this concept better, consider the difference between purchasing a music CD from a shop versus purchasing and downloading a music file from iTunes. The knowledge and technologies embedded in the offering by the company to meet the customers' needs are the source of competitive advantage. Because offerings are inherently service-based, customers become co-creators of the service experience. Therefore, in the end, the ultimate value-in-use of the offering is specified by the customer (see Market Insight 1.2 for an example).

According to Prahalad and Ramaswamy (2004a,b), organizations should use co-creation to differentiate their offerings, given that value is tied up inside the customer's experience with the organization. The co-creation experience is about *joint* creation of value, in which customers take part in an active dialogue and co-construct personalized experiences. Therefore organizations wishing to enhance customer input to co-creation should map supplier and customer processes to identify how to design their services accordingly (Payne *et al.*, 2008). For example, Boeing the airplane manufacturer incorporated feedback from both airline companies and passengers into their Dreamliner plane design before final production.

Marketing in Context

Does marketing practice change if we are marketing goods compared with services, and to consumers compared with businesses? To some degree the answer is yes. We've known since the 1960s that services were making important contributions to the US economy (Regan, 1963). Although the product has previously been the focus of marketing practice and theory,

Market Insight 1.2

Power by the Hour: Rolls-Royce's Transformation

Rolls-Royce is a global provider of integrated power systems and services to the civil and defence aerospace, marine, and energy markets. However, Rolls-Royce plc (which no longer owns the Rolls-Royce motor car brand) has completely redefined itself since the early 1970s when it was nationalized by the then Conservative government after running into financial problems. In 2012, it had underlying revenues of £12.2bn, up 33% since 2008, with an order book of £60.1bn. Product–service revenue ratios in 2012 were 46%/54% in civil aerospace, 46%/49% (5% development) in defence aerospace, 57%/43% in the marine sector, and 36%/64% in the energy sector. By comparison, after-market sales were only 20% of the civil aerospace division's revenues in 1981.

Since then, Rolls-Royce has transformed its business model from selling engines and aftercare (to ensure that the engines work properly and are maintained) to selling its customers 'power by the hour', recognizing that it is not in the engine manufacturing business, but is in the power generation integrated solutions business. In the civil aerospace sector, Rolls-Royce rents its engines to users through the TotalCare® scheme, first introduced in the 1990s, and charges airline customers based on the total number of hours flown. By collecting data from aircraft engines in flight worldwide on a continuous basis, it maintains those engines better, predicts engine failures, optimizes engine maintenance programmes, and improves future engine design. Service looks set to become

Plane flies high under Rolls-Royce power and the watchful gaze of its staff

Source: This photograph is reproduced with the permission of Rolls-Royce plc, copyright © Rolls-Royce plc 2012.

more important than ever with Rolls-Royce's product market opportunities likely to be worth around £1.79tn and the services market opportunities worth £1.38tn between 2012 and 2032.

Sources: Anon. (2009); Rolls-Royce (2012); Ryals and Rackham (2012); http://www.rolls-royce.com/about/ataglance/

1 **Why do you think Rolls-Royce has been so successful in selling the service concept?**

2 **Check out the websites of its competitors, Pratt & Whitney and GE. How do their service offerings in their civil aerospace divisions compare with Rolls-Royce's?**

3 **Can you think of other companies that have adopted a similar service-based approach? (Hint: look at the Otis Elevator Company's website on service or ADT's website on monitored burglar alarms for examples).**

it shouldn't be. Figure 1.6 shows clearly how important services are to a wide variety of economies around the world, including those in the developed world (e.g. Sweden), the developing world (e.g. Thailand), and in the lesser developed countries (e.g. Namibia). Even in China and the United Arab Emirates (UAE), services make up more than 40% of the economy—a substantial contribution.

Marketing techniques need to be adapted to the specific sector in which they are used (Blois, 1974). The context, whether it is industrial (e.g. business-to-business), consumer-based (e.g. retail),

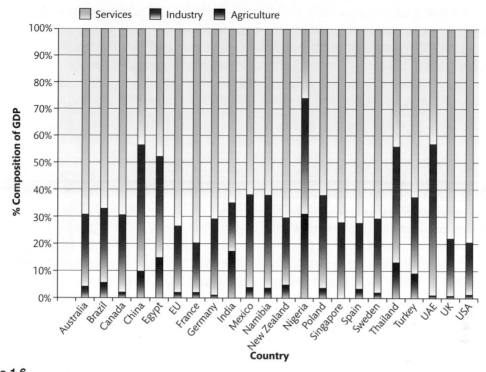

Figure 1.6

Estimated GDP % composition by sector for selected countries (year).

Note: GDP = gross domestic product. All data for 2012 excluding Singapore (2010) and India (2011).

Source: Data taken from *CIA World Factbook* (www.cia.gov). Reproduced with kind permission of CIA World Factbook.

or services-based (e.g. business-to-business services like accountancy or business-to-business products like component manufacturers), or the not-for-profit context, has an impact on the marketing tools and techniques that we use. Whether products are business-to-business or business-to-consumer, they may be either product or service, but all offerings combine some elements of the two. (We discuss the intangible nature of services further in Chapter 14 and not-for-profit marketing in Chapter 16.)

Having identified three unique contexts of marketing: consumer goods, industrial (business-to-business), and services, we briefly discuss how each of these contexts affects how we undertake marketing activities.

The Consumer Goods Perspective

Bucklin (1963) defined consumer goods as convenience goods (purchased frequently, minimum effort), shopping goods (purchased selectively), or speciality goods (purchased highly selectively). Examples of consumer goods industries include the retail car market, the luxury goods market, and multiple retail groceries. Examples of companies operating in these industries include car manufacturer Ford, French fashion house Louis Vuitton Moët Hennessey (LVMH), and Unilever, the Anglo-Dutch fast-moving consumer goods company.

The consumer goods perspective has been dominant in the history of marketing. The concept is concerned with ideas of the 'marketing mix' and the 4Ps. The consumer goods perspective, borrowing heavily from neoclassical economics, assumes that there are comparatively few suppliers within a particular industry, and that all are rivals for the **aggregated demand** (i.e. demand totalled at population rather than individual level). In fast-moving consumer goods markets (FMCG), the price at which a good is sold is clearly defined. The offering exchanged is tangible (i.e. has physical form) and exchanged between buyer and seller through retail distribution outlets. Consumption takes place at a later point in time, with demand stimulated through the **promotional mix**, i.e. advertising, personal selling, direct marketing, and public relations (see Chapter 11).

The focus of marketing in this context is on how to facilitate the rapid exchange of goods, the effectiveness of marketing in matching supplier offering to customer demand (for example, see Market Insight 1.3), and efficiency in managing the distribution of the product through the supply chain. Of particular importance in this context are the principles and practice of multichannel management and retailing (see Chapter 12).

Because of the need to stimulate demand from consumers, focus is placed on the importance of advertising (see Chapter 10) to stimulate demand and market research (see Chapter 3) to determine how to develop appropriate consumer products and how they are received by the consumers once they've launched into the marketplace. Since the advent of the world wide web in 1991, digital marketing techniques have greatly increased the amount of information that customers receive and online procurement approaches now dictate how retailers reorder goods and services from suppliers. (We cover digital marketing in Chapter 17.)

The Consumer Services Perspective

The services perspective in marketing was developed around the late 1970s and early 1980s in recognition that the goods-centric marketing approach was ill-suited to the marketing of services. Services marketing thinkers suggested that the intangible performance-dependent nature of services substantially affected the way they should be marketed (Shostack, 1977). There was a focus on the quality of service offered as a result (Grönroos, 1984), as well as a focus on the difference between customer perceptions of actual service quality and their expectations of service quality (Parasuraman *et al*., 1985).

Some commentators have questioned the use of the product analogy altogether in services marketing (Grönroos, 1998; Vargo and Lusch, 2004). On the debate about whether product and service marketing is different, it is worth noting that services:

- cannot be protected by patent;
- do not make use of packaging;
- lack a physical display;
- cannot be demonstrated in the same way.

Others have argued that there are major similarities (Judd, 1968), including the need to:

- work at full capacity;
- develop trade and service marks;
- use promotional media;
- use personal selling techniques;
- use an approach to pricing based on cost and value.

We consider services marketing in more detail in Chapter 14.

Market Insight 1.3

KFC: A Global Brand with Chinese Characteristics

How do companies tailor their offer to meet the requirements of local consumers in emerging markets? Many global brands sell their international image but do not change their positioning significantly when internationalizing. However, some markets require a significant degree of adaptation if sales success is to be achieved. This is what Yum! Brands, KFC's parent company, learned after entering China in 1987. Adapting the brand and its offering to the desires of Chinese urban consumers has been the main driver behind an astonishing success story.

KFC is by far the leading fast-food chain in China, with 5,400 restaurants (McDonald's has only 1,600) and is keen to reach 15,000 outlets. The success it has achieved to date is based on infusing a Western brand with Chinese characteristics, even if this means developing a different positioning from that which KFC has in its domestic market. Accordingly, the choice available in China is different. On average, there are 50 alternatives on the menu (the US menu has only 29 options). The type of food offered is completely different: spicy chicken, soy milk drinks, and sticky buns are what the Chinese crave. The restaurants also look and feel different—there is more space for customers to eat their meals, whilst most customers in the US take their food away and eat at home. The complex food preparation requires larger kitchens and more staff, so the overall size of the locations has to be larger. All these increased costs mean that KFC in China is more expensive than many other fast-food chains. Therefore it mainly appeals to white-collar urban consumers who are prepared to pay a higher price. The ability to adapt a global brand to Chinese expectations and desires has turned KFC's Chinese operation into a great success story, one that other Western brands entering Asian markets will be seeking to imitate.

1 **How important is it that KFC produced Chinese-specific products rather than sold its traditional range of food?**

2 **Would you define KFC China's offering as a convenience, shopping, or specialty good?**

3 **Is the KFC China retail offer purely a consumer good? Why do you say this?**

This case was kindly contributed by Dr Paolo Antonetti, Warwick Business School.

It's KFC but with a Chinese flavour
Source: © TonyV3112/Shutterstock.com

The Business-to-Business Perspective

Many marketing textbooks over-emphasize consumer goods marketing, paying inadequate attention to industrial/organizational/business-to-business (B2B) marketing. B2B marketing is essentially different from consumer marketing because the customer is a business not an individual. B2B marketing requires that marketers deal with more sophisticated customers who often buy in volume as part of a decision-making unit (with other buyers and technicians), who are trained to buy/procure professionally, and who are rewarded for buying the right propositions at the right price (see Chapter 14).

Much B2B marketing activity revolves around the need to develop strong prospects for a company's offerings, to ensure effective supply chain management operations to develop the market for a B2B offering, and to ensure that it is delivered appropriately. Because buyers typically purchase in large volumes of products or complex 'bundles' of services (e.g. customized IT software solutions sold by the German company SAP), tight specifications are usually produced with which suppliers must comply. Buyers try to ensure that they obtain the best supplier possible by offering suppliers a contract to supply for a set period of time through a bidding process.

In public sector markets, the **procurement** process is bound by strict legal guidelines for contracts valued over a set amount. This process creates substantial rivalry, with firms often submitting bids they cannot then fulfil either because they've underpriced themselves, or because they've over-promised what they can deliver; a phenomenon known as the **winner's curse** as the winning company ends up servicing an unprofitable contract (Fleisher and Bensoussan, 2004).

The emphasis in B2B markets is strongly focused on the development and building of mutually satisfying relationships based on commitment and trust (Morgan and Hunt, 1994) to win the contract in the first place and then to deliver it to the customer's specifications. Whether or not a firm meets these specifications is in part linked to the **logistics** function (i.e. warehousing, inventory management, delivery) of the firm. Consequently, B2B marketers can create a competitive advantage if they develop a strong linkage between the marketing and logistics functions, developing a strong customer service proposition through (Christopher, 1986):

- cycle time order reduction;
- accurate invoicing procedures;
- reliable delivery;
- effective claims procedures;
- inventory availability;
- good condition of goods/effective service delivery;
- few order size constraints or limited customization of services;
- effective/planned salesperson visits;
- convenient ordering systems/provision of order status information;
- flexible delivery times;
- strong after-sales support.

Marketing and Society

So far, we have considered how marketing can be characterized as operating in either the consumer, business-to-business, or services domains. What is common to all these marketing contexts is that the marketer works to satisfy the needs of customers. However, more recently, as discussed earlier, there has been a realization that marketing also impacts positively and negatively on society. Let's consider how much the marketing industry contributes positively to society (we consider the negative impacts in Chapters 18 and 19). For example, Wilkie and Moore (1999) describe the complexities of what they call the 'aggregate marketing system'. We can use the example of how marketing brings together the ingredients of an average European 'continental' breakfast. Consider the individual ingredients, for example, coffee or tea, together with Danish pastries, cold cuts of meat, salad and cheese, muesli and cereals, various fruits, the cups/plates and glasses, the oven to cook the pastries, etc. The distributive capacity of the aggregate marketing system is amazing, especially when we consider that there were over 504 million people in the EU in 2012, each of whom is brought their own unique mixture of breakfast offerings each morning (see CIA, 2013). Broadly, the aggregate marketing system in most countries works well. We're not all starving and we don't have to ration our food to preserve the amount we eat. Of course, there are certain countries in Africa, North Korea, and parts of China where people are dying of hunger, but these countries often experience imperfections in supply and demand because of political (e.g. war, dictatorship, famine) and environmental circumstances (e.g. drought). Therefore marketing plays an important role in developing and transforming society (see Market Insight 1.4). A firm which recognizes the important link between marketing and society and uses it to its advantage is the Italian firm Carpigiani, which makes *gelato* ice-cream makers. It set up Gelato University in Anzola Dell'Emilia near Bologna, taking in over 6,700 students from around the world. The course fees are low to cover the university's costs and include a voucher to purchase ice-cream-making equipment. Accordingly, over the last three years, Carpigiani's sales have increased by 23% to €113m (Anon., 2013).

 Market Insight 1.4

Waterford Crystal: The Phoenix Rises

January 22nd 2010 was a poignant day for the city of Waterford in Ireland. The world's most famous crystal brand, Waterford Crystal, shut the doors of its visitor centre for the last time, having been a national icon since 1783. The crystal manufacturing plant and adjoining visitor centre was shut when holding company, Waterford Wedgwood, went into receivership in 2009 with debts of more than $1bn, after losses of almost $100m per year.

In its heyday, 315,000 visitors per annum on average were attracted to the visitor centre in the decade prior to its closure. This was the largest tourist attraction in the region and one of the biggest in Ireland. US tourists, who have a particularly strong affinity with the Waterford Crystal brand, were the primary target market. But the catastrophic potential of losing a key element of the city's tourism infrastructure wasn't lost

Market Insight 1.4
continued

on Waterford City Council, who together with KPS Partners—the US-based equity firm who had acquired the assets of the Waterford Wedgwood Group—set in motion plans to rescue the situation. KPS recognized the intrinsic value of the Waterford Crystal brand, with its reputation for the finest craftsmanship, forged over generations in Waterford. With this commitment to the brand's home city in mind, KPS entered an agreement with Waterford City Council to open a new Waterford Crystal manufacturing facility and visitor centre in the heart of Waterford city. The new facility, branded 'The House of Waterford Crystal', opened in June 2010. The 'House of Waterford Crystal' compliments the efforts of Waterford City Council to develop the historic Viking Triangle as the core of the city's tourist offering. Both the city governors and Waterford Crystal now seek to attract a broader base of tourists. It is believed that the enhanced tourism package will help overcome the traditional dependency on the US visitor segment. The three museums in the Viking Triangle, allied to the adjacent 'House of Waterford Crystal', provide critical mass thereby, attracting a diverse tourism market. Enhanced coordination of the promotion of the city's attractions, integrated pricing and ticketing, and an improved on-line and social media presence embellish the tourism offering. The results of these initiatives are

encouraging, with Waterford Crystal at the forefront of the revival. In excess of 45,000 pieces each year are being produced using traditional hand-crafted methods. Visitor numbers are vibrant, with over 300,000 people having experienced 'The House of Waterford Crystal' by the end of 2012. Further growth is anticipated, cementing Waterford Crystal's return to its central role in the life of its home city.

Sources: Kane (2010); RTE News (2010); Taylor (2012); http://www.waterfordvisitorcentre.com/blog

1 **Evaluate the importance of iconic brands such as Waterford Crystal to local communities and societies? Can you think of other examples of brands that play such an integral role in their communities' tourism offering?**

2 **Suggest strategies to continue the growth of 'The House of Waterford Crystal' as a tourist attraction.**

3 **How can governmental agencies such as city councils align themselves with commercial brands to improve their local society?**

This case was kindly contributed by Paul Morrissey, Waterford Institute of Technology, Ireland.

Some of the world's most important inventions have come to us through the aggregate marketing system. Consider how some of the offerings outlined in Table 1.4 have affected your own life. What would we do without these inventions today? Imagine if the internet, social media networking, or mobile phones did not exist. We enjoy them because innovative individuals and companies brought these to us. Take the tin can for storing food, for example. We couldn't conceive of not having this device now and yet it is only around 200 years old. Prior to that, food was stored in earthenware pots and spoilt at a much faster rate. The cardboard carton for storing milk is ubiquitous, but was invented in 1951 in Sweden. Could you imagine ketchup not existing? It was brought to us by Heinz, based on an ancient Chinese recipe for a fish sauce called *ketsiap*! Of course, in each case, the invention outlined has been an extraordinary success. But the aggregate marketing system not only serves to bring consumers those offerings that truly meet their needs, it also serves to stop the failures getting through as well (see Chapter 8). For example, whether or not electric cars become the dominant form of car as opposed to petrol/diesel engine cars depends on the aggregate marketing system and the marketers that exist

Table 1.4 Some modern consumer products and their dates of invention

Consumer product	Product attribute	Consumer need	Inventors/pioneers[a]	Year of invention
Tin can (for storing food)	Metallic food storage device	Allowed traditionally perishable food to be stored for longer periods of time	Hall and Dorkin, UK	1810
Ketchup (from the Chinese word *ketsiap*)	A food condiment, derived from the Chinese fish-based sauce, *ketsiap*, but adapted for Western taste, using tomatoes	Designed to improve the consumer's enjoyment of their food by improving the taste and reducing the dryness of some foodstuffs	F. & J. Heinz Co., USA	1876
Diesel-fuelled internal combustion engine	An engine with an efficiency of 75% (meaning that 75% of the energy produced was used to power the engine) as opposed to 10% for the steam engines of the day	Enabled independent craftsmen to compete with large industry	Rudolph Diesel, Germany	1892
Breakfast cereals	Cereals which when added to milk provide a healthy meal	Quick and easy to prepare foodstuff which was rapidly adopted as a breakfast meal	W. K. Kellogg Foundation, USA	1906
Television	Transmission of moving images	Information, entertainment, and education	Baird Television Development Company, UK/Telefunken, Germany	1929/1932
Consumer credit card	Allowed user to purchase products and services without paying in cash at time of original purchase	Convenience of not having to pay immediately and provision of credit for a set period of time	Diner's Club, USA	1950
Carton	Cardboard liquid storage device	Allows liquid foodstuffs to be stored, packaged, and distributed in an environmentally friendly way.	TetraPak, Sweden	1951
Seat belt	The three-point seat belt as a safety system in automobiles	Saves people's lives in automobile accidents	Volvo, Sweden	1959

Table 1.4 continued

Consumer product	Product attribute	Consumer need	Inventors/pioneers[a]	Year of invention
Artificial sweeteners	Xylitol, as the sweetener is known, is used to sweeten food products such as sugar-free chewing gum and toothpastes	It sweetens food products without damaging our teeth	Cultor, Finland	1969
Personal computer	Machine allowing users to play electronic games, perform calculations, and write word-processed documents and other applications	Time-saving device simplifying complex writing/arithmetic tasks, offering recreational possibilities, i.e. game-playing	IBM, USA	1980
Mobile phone	A hand-held device for making telephone calls whilst in motion	The ability to stay in telephone contact with others regardless of one's location	NTT, Japan	1979
World wide web/web server	A system for linking hypertext documents (i.e. documents linked to other documents) via the internet; by using a web browser, users can read web pages.	Users with access to the internet can read and share information across large distances	Tim Berners-Lee, UK & Robert Cailliau, Belgium/CERN[b], EU	1990
Social networking	A website designed for personal interaction between friends and acquaintances	Provides easy and instantaneous communication between two or more people in multiple locations around the world	Facebook Inc., USA	2004
Malaria vaccine	A treatment which prevents a person from acquiring the potentially fatal mosquito-borne blood disease	Allows users to travel to malarial zones without fear of contracting the disease and ensures that those who live in malarial zones do not contract the disease.	GlaxoSmithKline, UK	2014+

[a]The named companies are not always the inventors per se; they often acquired the patents from the inventor and so were licensed to produce and distribute the invention.

[b]Conseil Européen pour la Recherche Nucléaire.

Sources: Various, including www.inventors.about.com and manufacturers' websites.

Research Insight 1.4

To take your learning further, you might wish to read this influential paper.

Wilkie, W. L. and Moore, E. S. (2011), 'Expanding our understanding of marketing in society', *Journal of the Academy of Marketing Science*, **40, 53–73.**

This article, building on a previous ground-breaking article (Wilkie and Moore 1999), charts 100 years of marketing thought and the extent to which marketing in society was a key consideration in scholarship during that time. It continues to expand the idea of the 'aggregate marketing system' within society, and maps the field of marketing in society by outlining extant research groups and a research agenda.

@ **Visit the Online Resource Centre to read the abstract and access the full paper.**

within it (see Market Insight 1.5). The aggregate marketing system impedes offerings that don't meet consumer needs (for more on the new proposition development process, see Chapter 8). Therefore it provides a number of benefits to society including the following (Wilkie and Moore, 1999):

- the promotion and delivery of desired offerings;
- the provision of a forum for market learning (we can see what does and what doesn't get through the system);
- the stimulation of market demand;
- the provision of a wide scope of choice of offerings by providing a close/customized fit with consumer needs;
- facilitates purchases (or acquisitions generally, e.g. if no payment is made directly as in the case of public services);
- saves times and promotes efficiency in customer requirement matching;
- brings new offerings, and improvements, to market to meet latent and unserved needs;
- seeks customer satisfaction for repeat purchases.

Visit the **Online Resource Centre** and complete Internet Activity 1.2 to learn more about how marketing innovation impacts upon society.

However, the aggregate marketing system, or marketing more generally, does not always serve the common good. Marketing is frequently criticized for doing precisely the opposite—for being unethical in nature, manipulative, and creating wants and needs where none previously existed (Packard, 1960). Whilst this chapter has focused on the principles and practice of marketing, and the positive power of marketing in society, there is also a negative impact of marketing in society. This occurs both as a result of unethical marketing practice (see Chapter 18) and because of structural inequalities in the aggregate marketing system (see Chapter 19).

Market Insight 1.5

Back to the Future: Bringing Electric Cars to the Masses

The race is on to produce an all-singing, all-dancing, good-looking electric car. Silent and pollution-free, with engineering underpinned by green technologies, the car must not compromise on performance, looks, or handling. Greater public concern and the need for European legislation concerning vehicle fuel emissions to combat global warming have created further stimulus for change. As car drivers are collectively a major user of oil to power their cars, a shift to electric seems obvious. Problems with oil supply and price volatility from OPEC worsen the situation.

Although many car companies now have electric car models either in development or about to launch, Renault has been a pioneer. It has brought out the Twizy (an urban compact two-seater), the Zoe (a hatchback city car), the Fluence ZE (a saloon), and the Kangoo van ZE. The business model has also changed. Instead of buying petrol at a station, the purchaser hires the battery and charges up as necessary, either from home or at a charging station. Critical questions for potential customers are: Will there be a large enough network of recharging stations or capability to power from home? Will the whole-life costs of an electric vehicle be on a par/less than the costs of owning a petrol engine car? Will the car perform as well as any hybrid/non-electric vehicle? Will the lower range before re-charging be a problem for drivers? Ralf Speth, the CEO of Indian-owned Jaguar Land Rover, has stated that even with large government subsidies, demand will not be very high. Only time will tell on whether or not he is right.

Sources: Toyota (2006); Renault (2009); Laird (2013); Neate (2013).

1 Do you think sales of electric cars will ever overtake sales of conventional petrol/diesel cars?

2 What might be a further advancement of the electric car concept in ten years' time?

3 Can you think of other well-known offerings which have taken advantage of society's increasingly strong environmental values? What are they?

Is the future of cars electric?
Source: istock © VvoeVale.

Chapter Summary

To consolidate your learning, the key points from this chapter are summarized here.

■ **Define the marketing concept.**

Marketing is the process by which organizations anticipate and satisfy their customers' needs to both parties' benefit. It involves mutual exchange. Over the last 25 years, the marketing concept has changed to recognize the importance of long-term customer relationships to organizations. In addition, most definitions of marketing recognize the importance of marketing's impacts on society and the need to curtail these where they are negative.

■ **Explain how marketing has developed over the twentieth and into the twenty-first century.**

Whereas some writers have suggested a simple production era, sales era, marketing era development for marketing over the twentieth century, others recognize that marketing has existed in different forms in different countries at different times. Nevertheless, there is increasing recognition that marketing is a more systematic organizational activity through market research, and sophisticated promotional activity, than before. There is a also move towards recognizing the need for companies and organizations to behave responsibly in relation to society.

■ **Understand the exchange and marketing mix concepts in marketing.**

The concept of exchange is important and has been considered by some to be the key to uncovering the elusive 'general theory of marketing'. Empathizing with customers to understand what they want and determining how sellers seek to provide what buyers want is a central concept in marketing. The means by which organizations deploy their marketing programmes is via the marketing mix, which comprises Product (the offering), Place (the distribution mechanism), Price (the value placed on the offering), and Promotion (how the company communicates that value). For services marketing, because of the intangible nature of the service, marketers consider an extra 3Ps, including Physical Evidence (how cues are developed for customers to recognize quality), Process (how the experience is designed to meet customers' needs), and People (the training and development of those delivering the customer experience).

■ **Describe the three major contexts of marketing application, i.e. consumer goods, business-to-business, and services marketing.**

Marketing activity divides into three types, recognizing that marketing activities are designed based on the context in which an organization operates. The consumer goods marketing approach has been dominant, stressing the 4Ps and the marketing mix. Business-to-business marketing focuses on principles of relationship marketing, particularly those required in coordinating supply chain members. Services marketing stresses the intangible nature of an offering, including the need to manage customer expectations levels of service quality and customer experience.

■ **Understand the contribution that marketing makes to society.**

The aggregate marketing system delivers to us a wide array of offerings, either directly, or indirectly through business markets, to serve our wants and needs. There is much that is positive about the aggregate marketing system and it has served to improve the standard of living for many people around the world.

 **Review Questions**

1 How do we define the marketing concept?

2 How do the American Marketing Association and the Chartered Institute of Marketing definitions of marketing differ?

3 How has marketing developed over the twentieth and into the twenty-first century?

4 What is the difference between sales and marketing?

5 What is a marketing exchange?

6 What is the marketing mix?

7 What is the services marketing mix?

8 What are the three major contexts of marketing application?

9 What is the winner's curse?

10 What contribution does marketing make to society?

Worksheet Summary

To apply the knowledge you have gained from this chapter and test your understanding of marketing fundamentals visit the **Online Resource Centre** and complete Worksheet 1.1.

Discussion Questions

1 Having read the Case Insight at the beginning of this chapter, how would you advise Systembolaget to use marketing in the future (a) to maintain public support for the Swedish alcohol monopoly, and (b) to ensure that customers drink responsibly?

2 Read the section on the marketing mix within the chapter and draw up marketing mixes for the following organizations and their target customers.

   A The streaming video company, Netflix, and their home audiences.
   B An online travel agency specializing in luxury holidays and their wealthy clientele.
   C Pharmacies (e.g. Boots, Apoteket) and their consumers.
   D A glass company supplying glass to architects.

3 Outline simple marketing exchange processes for the following buyer–seller relationships.

   A The relationship between pharmaceutical salespeople and their clients (e.g. medical practitioner, pharmacists, hospitals).
   B The relationship between a pop band of your choice and its audience.
   C The relationship between a local authority and its citizens for online services (e.g. housing, local government taxes).

4 What are the attributes of the offer, and customer needs associated with those attributes, for the following?

   A Retail bank business accounts.
   B A university (e.g. University of Gothenburg in Sweden) offering places to students on Masters programmes.
   C An Omega watch for a lady.
   D A company like Dell selling computers to businesses.
   E Watching a tennis match live at Wimbledon stadium.

Visit the **Online Resource Centre** and complete the Multiple Choice Questions to assess your knowledge of Chapter 1.

References

AMA (American Marketing Association) (2007), 'Definition of marketing', retrieve from: www.marketingpower.com/Community/ARC/Pages/Additional/Definition/default.aspx?sq=definition+of+marketing accessed 1 April 2013.

Anon. (2009), 'Britain's lonely high flier', *The Economist*, 8 January, retrieve from: http://www.economist.com/node/12887368?story_id=12887368#footnote1 accessed 10 April 2013.

Anon. (2013), 'Gelato University: Scoop!', *The Economist*, 12 January, 8.

Bagozzi, R. P. (1975), 'Marketing as exchange', *Journal of Marketing*, 3(4, October), 32–9.

Bartels, R. D. W. (1944), 'Marketing principles', *Journal of Marketing*, 9, 2 (October), 151–8.

Bartels, R. D. W. (1951), 'Can marketing be a science?', *Journal of Marketing*, 15(3), 319–28.

Bartels, R. D. W. (1959), 'Sociologists and marketologists', *Journal of Marketing*, October, 37–40.

Bartels, R. D. W. (1968), 'The general theory of marketing', *Journal of Marketing*, 32(January), 29–33.

BBC News (2010), 'Blockbuster files for bankruptcy in the US', BBC News, 23 September, retrieve from: http://www.bbc.co.uk/news/business-11397020 accessed 3 April 2013.

BBC News (2013a), 'Blockbuster goes into administration', BBC News, 16 January, retrieve from: http://www.bbc.co.uk/news/business-21047652 accessed 3 April 2013.

BBC News (2013b), 'Buyer found for Blockbuster stores, says administrator', BBC News, 23 March, retrieve from: http://www.bbc.co.uk/news/business-21912508 accessed 3 April 2013.

BBC News (2013c), Thomas Cook to cut 2,500 jobs in the UK', BBC News, 6 March, retrieve from: http://www.bbc.co.uk/news/business-21686547 accessed 3 April 2013.

Bell, D. and Shelman, M. (2011), 'KFC's radical approach to China', *Harvard Business Review*, 89(11), 137–42.

Blois, K. J. (1974), 'The marketing of services: an approach', *European Journal of Marketing*, 8, 2, 137–45.

Booms, B. H. and Bitner, M. J. (1981), 'Marketing strategies and organisation structures for service firms', in J. H. Donnelly and W. R. George (eds), *Marketing of Services*, Chicago, IL: AMA Proceedings Series, 48.

Borden, N. H. (1964), 'The concept of the marketing mix', *Journal of Advertising Research*, 4, 2–7.

Brady, D. (2012), 'Yum!'s big game of chicken', *Bloomberg Businessweek*, 4273, 64–9.

Bucklin, L. P. (1963), 'Retail strategy and the classification of consumer goods', *Journal of Marketing*, January, 51–6.

Choi, C. (2012), 'Yum! Brand's taking KFC to China's smaller cities'@, *AP Food Industry*, 6 November.

CIA (2013), *The World Factbook—European Union*, Washington, DC: CIA. Retrieve from: https://www.cia.gov/library/publications/the-world-factbook/geos/ee.html accessed 10 April 2013.

Christopher, M. (1986), 'Reaching the customer: strategies for marketing and customer service', *Journal of Marketing Management*, 2(1), 63–71.

Christopher, M., Payne, A., and Ballantyne, D. (2002), *Relationship Marketing: Creating Stakeholder Value* (2nd edn), Oxford: Butterworth Heinemann.

CIM (Chartered Institute of Marketing) (2001), 'Marketing', Glossary, available at http://www.cim.co.uk accessed 17 April 2010.

CIM (Chartered Institute of Marketing) (2009), *In Search of a Strategic Role for Marketing: Leading, Influencing or Supporting*, Cookham: Chartered Institute of Marketing.

Comstock, B., Gulati, R., and Liguori, S. (2010), 'Unleashing the power of marketing', *Harvard Business Review*, October, 90–8.

Day, G. S (1994), 'The capabilities of market-driven organisations', *Journal of Marketing*, 58(3), 37–52.

Enright, M. (2002), 'Marketing and conflicting dates for its emergence: Hotchkiss, Bartels and the fifties school of alternative accounts', *Journal of Marketing Management*, 18, 445–61.

Farzad, R. (2012), 'Jim Grant questions KFC's China strut', *Businessweek.com*, 17 October, retrieve from: http://www.businessweek.com/articles/2012-10-17/jim-grant-questions-kfcs-china-strut accessed 3 April 2013.

Fleisher, C. S. and Bensoussan, B. E. (2002), *Strategic and Competitive Analysis*, Englewood Cliffs, NJ: Prentice-Hall.

Fullerton, R. A. (1988), 'How modern is modern marketing? Marketing's evolution and the myth of the "Production Era" ', *Journal of Marketing*, 52(January), 108–25.

Griffiths, S. (2012). 'Thomas Cook ditches online discounts', TTG Digital, 19 December, retrieve from: http://www.ttgdigital.com/news/thomas-cook-ditches-online-discounts/4686194.article accessed 3 April 2013.

Grönroos, C. (1984), 'A service quality model and its marketing implications', *European Journal of Marketing*, 18(4), 36–44.

Grönroos, C. (1994), 'From marketing mix to relationship marketing: towards a paradigm shift in marketing', *Management Decision*, 32(2), 4–20.

Grönroos, C. (1998), 'Marketing services: a case of a missing product', *Journal of Business and Industrial Marketing*, 13(4/5), 322–38.

Gummesson, E. (1987), 'The new marketing: developing long term interactive relationships', *Long Range Planning*, 20(4), 10–20.

Holden, A. C. and Holden, L. (1998), 'Marketing history: illuminating marketing's clandestine subdiscipline', *Psychology and Marketing*, 15(2), 117–23.

Howard, D. G., Savins, D. M., Howell, W., and Ryans, J. K., Jr (1991), 'The evolution of marketing theory in the United States and Europe', *European Journal of Marketing*, 25(2), 7–16.

Hult, G. T. M., Mena, J. A., Ferrell, O. C., and Ferrell, L. (2011), 'Stakeholder marketing: a definition and conceptual framework', *AMS Review*, 1, 44–65.

Hunt, S. D. (1971), 'The morphology of theory and the general theory of marketing', *Journal of Marketing*, April, 65–8.

Hunt, S. D. (1983), 'General theories and fundamental explananda of marketing', *Journal of Marketing*, 47(4, Fall), 9–17.

Judd, R. C. (1968), 'Similarities and differences in product and service retailing', *Journal of Retailing*, 43(4), 1–9.

Kane, C. (2010), 'Sad end for Waterford Crystal', Independent.ie, 23 January, retrieve from: http://www.independent.ie/irish-news/sad-end-for-waterford-crystal-26625562.html accessed 4 April 2013.

Keith, R. J. (1960), 'The marketing revolution', *Journal of Marketing*, 24(January), 35–8.

Kirca, A. H., Jayachandran, S., and Bearden, W. O. (2005), 'Market orientation: a meta-analytic review and assessment of its antecedents and impact on performance', *Journal of Marketing*, 69(April), 24–41.

Kohli, A. K. and Jaworski, B. J. (1990), 'Market orientation: the construct, research propositions and managerial implications', *Journal of Marketing*, 54(April), 1–18.

Kotler, P. (2006), 'Ethical lapses of marketers', in J. N. Sheth and R. J. Sisodia (eds.), *Does Marketing Need Reform: Fresh Perspectives on the Future*, Armonk, NY: M. E. Sharpe, Chapter 17.

Laird, J. (2013), 'Is Renault's revolutionary Zoe the first truly mainstream electric car?', *TechRadar*, 29 March, retrieve from: http://www.techradar.com/news/car-tech/is-renault-s-revolutionary-zoe-the-first-truly-mainstream-electric-car-1140352 accessed 3 April 2013.

Lendrevie, J., Lévy, J., and Lindon, D. (2006), *Mercator: Théorie et Pratique du Marketing* (8th edn), Paris: Dunod.

Leone, R. P. and Shultz, R. L. (1980), 'A study of marketing generalisations', *Journal of Marketing*, 44(Winter), 10–18.

McCarthy, E. J. (1960), *Basic Marketing*, Homewood, IL: Irwin.

Marketing and Sales Standards Setting Body (2010), *Developing World-Class Standards for the Marketing Profession*, March, retrieve from http://www.msssb.org/marketing.htm accessed 17 September 2010.

Mintel (2012), *Video on Demand—UK—March 2012*, London: Mintel, retrieve from http://www.mintel.com

Morgan, R. M. and Hunt, S. D. (1994), 'The commitment–trust theory of relationship marketing', *Journal of Marketing*, 58(3, July), 20–38.

Narver, J. C. and Slater, S. F. (1990), 'The effect of a market orientation on business profitability', *Journal of Marketing*, October, 20–35.

Neate, R. (2013), 'Electric cars not mass-market solution, says Jaguar Land Rover chief', *The Guardian*, 5 March, retrieve from: http://www.guardian.co.uk/business/2013/mar/05/electric-cars-not-solution-jaguar-land-rover accessed 3 April 2013.

Newton, C. (2012), 'Dish won't turn Blockbuster Into Netflix competitor', *C/Net*, 5 October, retrieve from: http://news.cnet.com/8301-1026_3-57527262/dish-wont-turn-blockbuster-into-a-netflix-competitor/ accessed 3 April 2013.

Packard, V. O. (1960), *The Hidden Persuaders*, Harmondsworth: Penguin Books.

Parasuraman, A., Berry, L. L., and Zeithaml, V. A. (1985), 'A conceptual model of service quality and its implications for further research', *Journal of Marketing*, 49(Fall), 41–50.

Parsons, R. (2013), 'Companies acting irresponsibly by not letting marketing into c-suite', *Marketing Week*, 27 March, retrieve from: http://www.marketingweek.co.uk/news/companies-acting-irresponsibly-by-not-letting-marketing-into-c-suite/4006136.article#commentsubmitted accessed 3 April 2013.

Payne, A. (1993), *The Essence of Services Marketing*, Hemel Hempstead: Prentice-Hall.

Payne, A., Storbacka, K., and Frow, P. (2008), 'Managing the co-creation of value', *Journal of the Academy of Marketing Science*, 36, 83–96.

Prahalad, C. K. and Ramaswamy, V. (2004a), 'Co-creation experiences: the next practice in value creation', *Journal of Interactive Marketing*, 18(3), 5–14.

Prahalad, C.K. and Ramaswamy, V. (2004b), 'Co-creating unique value with customers', *Strategy and Leadership*, 32(3), 4–9.

Regan, W. J. (1963), 'The service revolution', *Journal of Marketing*, 27, 57–62.

Reichheld, F. F. and Sasser Jr, W. E. (1990), 'Zero defections: quality comes to services', *Harvard Business Review*, September–October, 105–11.

Renault (2009), *Drive the Change*, retrieve from: http://www.renault-ze.com/uk/ accessed 17 April 2010.

Rolls-Royce (2012), *Annual Report 2012*. London: Rolls-Royce plc, retrieve from: http://www.rolls-royce.com/Images/rolls_royce_annual_report_2012_tcm92-44211.pdf accessed 10 April 2013.

RTE News (2010), 'Waterford Crystal facility opens', RTE News/Ireland, 22 June, retrieve from: http://www.rte.ie/news/2010/0622/132460-waterford/ accessed 4 April 2013.

Ryals, L. and Rackham, N. (2012), 'Sales implications of servitization', February, *Presentation to the Key Account Management Best Practice Club*, Cranfield: Cranfield

School of Management. Retrieve from: http://www.som. cranfield.ac.uk/som/dinamic-content/media/Sales%20 Implications%20of%20Servitization%20White%20 Paper%20Feb%202012%20v2.pdf accessed 10 April 2013.

Saren, M. (2006), *Marketing Graffiti: The View from the Street*, Oxford: Butterworth-Heinemann.

Sheth, J. N. and Sisodia, R. J. (2005), 'A dangerous divergence: marketing and society', *Journal of Public Policy and Marketing*, 24(1), 160–2.

Sheth, J. N. and Sisodia, R. J. (2006), 'How to reform marketing', in J. N. Sheth and R. J. Sisodia (eds), *Does Marketing Need Reform: Fresh Perspectives on the Future*, Armonk, NY: M. E. Sharpe, Chapter 20.

Shostack, G. L. (1977), 'Breaking free from product marketing', *Journal of Marketing*, 41(April), 73–8.

Slater, S. F. and Narver, J. C. (1994), 'Market orientation, customer value and superior performance', *Business Horizons,* March–April, 22–7.

Taylor, J. (2012), 'Crystal clear', *Private Equity International*, 103, 24–5.

Toyota (2006), *Hybrid Synergy Drive*, retrieve from: http://www.hybridsynergydrive.com/en/top.html accessed 17 April 2010.

Vargo, S. L. and Lusch, R. F. (2004), 'Evolving to a new service dominant logic for marketing', *Journal of Marketing*, 68(January), 1–17.

Vargo, S. L. and Lusch, R. F. (2008), 'Service-dominant logic: continuing the evolution', *Journal of the Academy of Marketing Science*, 36, 1–10.

Viney, H. and Baines, P. (2012), 'Engaging government: why it's necessary and how to do it', *European Business Review*, September–October, 9–13.

Wilkie, W. L. and Moore, E. S. (1999), 'Marketing's contributions to society', *Journal of Marketing*, 63 (Special Issue), 198–218.

Wilkie, W. L., and Moore, E. S. (2011), 'Expanding our understanding of marketing in society', *Journal of the Academy of Marketing Science*, 40, 53–73.

Worcester, R. M., Mortimore, R., Baines, P., and Gill, M. (2011), *Explaining Cameron's Coalition*, London: Biteback Publishing.

Chapter 2
Consumer Buying Behaviour

Learning Outcomes

After studying this chapter, you will be able to:

▶ Explain the consumer product acquisition process

▶ Explain the processes involved in human perception, learning, and memory in relation to consumer choice

▶ Understand the importance of personality and motivation in consumer behaviour

▶ Describe opinions, attitudes, and values, and how they relate to consumer behaviour

▶ Explain how reference groups influence consumer behaviour

Case Insight 2.1
BrainJuicer Labs

Market Insight 2.1
Alfa Romeo Eases the Pain

Market Insight 2.2
Ladies' Lager Falls Flat

Market Insight 2.3
Templestay Fulfils Spiritual Potential

Market Insight 2.4
(De)shopping: To Pay or Not to Pay?

Market Insight 2.5
Celebrity Scents

Market Insight 2.6
Champagne: A Fizzling Market?

Case Insight 2.1

How should organizations evaluate actual customer behaviour when that behaviour often differs from how customers say they will behave? We speak to BrainJuicer Labs' Managing Director, Orlando Wood, to find out more about work they undertook for their client MasterCard.

The majority of consumer purchases online are made by credit or debit cards, and MasterCard has a great deal of information on these. But they are also interested in more innovative payment methods, such as e-wallets, frictionless payment paths (e.g. the iTunes model where details are stored, making payment very fast), mobile payment services, and contactless payments. These new methods have a generally low level of uptake in the UK. However, they are very likely to become a far more important part of consumer buying behaviour as mobile and social commerce develops and the online retail sector continues to grow. Therefore it's vital for MasterCard to understand them, so that it can develop its own innovative payment methods to benefit its retail partners.

However, MasterCard's level of information on new methods, and on attitudes and behaviours around online purchase in general, was low. They could track the usage of their own cards, and of new payment methods where those were linked to a MasterCard product, but they had limited visibility of usage levels of competing products (particularly new payment methods). Even more importantly, they had a limited view of consumers' behaviours around online purchase: What are the typical spend levels? What are the decision pathways? What triggers purchase? What role do attitudes and emotions play? As a result, MasterCard asked BrainJuicer Labs to investigate further.

The research project related to two sets of MasterCard customers: retail customers and consumer customers. What MasterCard ultimately wants is for retail customers to adopt its new payment methods and wants consumers to use them. The two behavioural goals are clearly linked: in order to convince retailers to adopt new payment methods, MasterCard needs to design methods which consumers will use. Therefore the project needed to be focused on understanding existing consumer behaviour around online payment, with an eye to collecting evidence which would convince MasterCard's retail partners and internal stakeholders of the benefits of new payment methods. However, the focus of the research project was not just to be around payment mechanisms, it would also need to look at the context in which those payments were taking place, if it were to be most effective and insightful.

Asking about purchase intention would let MasterCard identify a dangerous 'browser–buyer gap', where fully one-third of planned buying decisions are not executed (and spontaneous unplanned purchases only fill half this gap). Our researchers wondered what role emotions, and particularly happiness, were playing in online decision-making. Our hypothesis was that making the online user experience happy (as opposed to simply efficient) would increase spend for retailers, and that fast easy new payment methods would play a key role in this. This would allow us to build an overall case for MasterCard about the benefits of new payment methods.

Therefore the problem was to design a research programme which would allow us to evaluate the actual behaviour of financial services consumers, as opposed to their intended behaviour, and what role, if any, is played by emotions in their decision-making?

Introduction

What process did you go through when deciding which university course to study? How do you decide which restaurants to go to, or which lipstick to buy? After reading this chapter, you will understand why consumers think and behave as they do. World-class marketers have a profound understanding of customers' needs/wants and behaviours. In this chapter, we explore consumer behaviour (for business-to-business buying behaviours, see Chapter 15). We consider cognitions (thoughts), **perceptions** (how we see things), and learning (how we memorize techniques and knowledge). These are processes that are fundamental in explaining how consumers think and learn about offerings. As consumers, we are always perceiving and learning. Learning about offerings is no different from learning about concepts in general. Consider how we find out about the launch of a new offering, e.g. the BMW i3 electric car. We don't just know about it intuitively, we learn how it differs from existing petrol-powered cars, its relative benefits and disadvantages in terms of features, its price, and where it is available.

We discuss personality and motivation to illustrate how these psychological concepts affect how we buy. These are important, because offerings are often designed to appeal to particular types of people. Banks target their personal accounts at us based on our personalities and motivations. We also discuss opinions, attitudes, and values to give an understanding of how we are persuaded by **reference groups**, i.e. groups that have an influence over our decision-making. Fast-moving consumer goods companies constantly bombard us with images of celebrity endorsers, who act as our reference groups for a wide variety of offerings. Because marketing comes alive when it is interlinked into the fabric of our social lives, we consider how **social class**, lifecycles, and lifestyles influence consumer behaviour.

Consumer Behaviour: Rational or Emotional?

Consumption rose shortly after the 1950s, as citizens around the world began to prosper in relative peace after the Second World War, and industrial companies turned their attention from producing military equipment and supplies to producing consumer and industrial goods. At this time, consumers were generally thought to act rationally, according to **neoclassical economics** theory, individually maximizing their satisfaction (what economists call **utility**) based on a cost–benefit analysis of price and product scarcity (or availability). The consumer was thought to carefully measure whether or not the functional benefits of an offering outweighed its costs. Such rational purchasing decisions are considered to be based on the physical performance of the product (Udell, 1964).

However, consider an example from the Soviet Union (Russia, pre-1990). In such a strictly regulated planned economy, offerings were produced to meet basic functional needs. Nevertheless, consumers sought out televisions produced in certain factories in certain regions or countries because they thought that they were more reliable and produced better pictures. So, even when a country's government attempts to squeeze out human desires, the desire to possess the best of what is available continues anyway.

Nowadays, people are even more likely to indulge socio-psychological buying or emotional buying motives. These motives stem from a buyer's social and psychological interpretation of the offering and its performance. Consider our motivations for purchasing particular types of music, for example. Take the example of Korean pop sensation Psy's single, Gangnam Style.

Research Insight 2.1

To take your learning further, you might wish to read this influential paper.

Holbrook, M. B. and Hirschman, E. C. (1982), 'The experiential aspects of consumption: consumer fantasies, feelings and fun', *Journal of Consumer Research*, 9, 132–40.

This influential and highly cited article reconsidered how we perceive consumer behaviour, moving marketing thought away from the idea that customer behaviour is purely rational and towards a greater understanding of the irrational content of consumer decision-making, including the importance of our feelings and fantasies, and whether or not we are having fun. The authors developed a useful model contrasting the differences between the information-processing (i.e. rational) and the experiential (i.e. irrational) perspectives of consumer behaviour.

Visit the Online Resource Centre to read the abstract and access the full paper.

It had over a billion hits on YouTube within 5 months of release, making the 34-year-old Park Jae-Sang millions in YouTube, iTunes download, and celebrity endorsement revenues (Lee and Nakashima, 2012). We are likely to have bought the iTunes download because of what the music and its associated video represents to us. We buy the music because of how it makes us feel (e.g. excited, elated, happy, amused). We may even have bought it because everyone else was buying it at the time. We did not buy it because it was useful to us, or because it performed some kind of functional purpose, unless of course we are disc-jockeys (DJs).

Visit the **Online Resource Centre** and follow the weblink to the Psychology Matters website to learn more about the application and value of psychology in our everyday lives.

Proposition Acquisition

What is going on in consumers' minds when they decide whether or not to buy or, in the case of a not-for-profit consumer, acquire a particular offering? To answer this question, we need to know how offerings move from organizations to consumers. For example, consider luxury-brand Hermes' controversial crocodile skin handbags, retailing for more than US$60,000 (£37,000, €46,000). In a simplified process, the skin is sold by a crocodile farmer to the manufacturer who dries, cures, and tans it, before stitching it and sending it on to the major brand owner who stocks and retails it. At any of these stages, a different supply chain partner could be involved (see Chapter 12).

In the Hermes example, there are transactions between various buyers and sellers as raw materials are transformed into a bag, during the transactions between partners in the supply chain process (what Alderson and Martin (1965) called **transvections**). Understanding

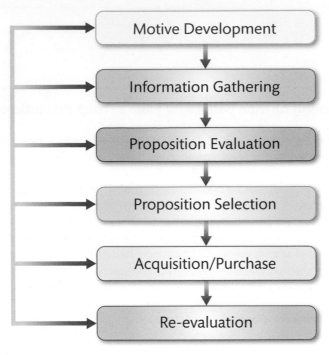

Figure 2.1

The consumer proposition acquisition process

transactions and transvections is important because this charts how propositions are developed and move from suppliers through companies to their end-users. Next, we consider the end-user component of the buyer–seller relationship—the perspective of the consumer. (We consider the buyer–seller relationship again in Chapters 14 and 15.)

The Consumer Proposition Acquisition Process

The consumer proposition acquisition process consists of six distinct stages (see Figure 2.1). The process model is useful because it highlights the importance and distinctiveness of proposition selection and re-evaluation phases in the process. In Figure 2.1, the buying process is iterative, as each stage can lead back to previous stages or move forward to the next stage.

Motive Development

The process begins when we decide that we wish to acquire an offering. This involves the initial recognition that some sort of problem needs solving. To solve the problem, we must first become aware of it. For example, a female consumer decides that she needs to buy a new dress for a party, or she's grown tired of the old one, or she thinks it's out of fashion, or to cheer herself up, or for a special occasion (e.g. engagement or hen party), or a whole host of other reasons.

Information Gathering

In the next stage, we look for alternative ways of solving our problems. Our dress buyer might ask herself where she bought her last dress, how much dresses typically cost, what

---

Research Insight 2.2

To take your learning further, you might wish to read this influential book.

Howard, J. A. and Sheth, J. N. (1969), *The Theory of Buyer Behavior*, New York: John Wiley.

Howard and Sheth's theory of the buyer behaviour process provided original and powerful insights into the psychology of buying by considering how learning theory can be applied to consumer behaviour. The buyer behaviour process consists of stimulus inputs (e.g. price, quality, service, and social settings) that feed into a perceptual process where the inputs are received and considered, and then interact with a person's attitudes and motives and existing choice criteria. This may or may not lead to purchase intention, and other outputs, including changes in attention given to the product, the extent to which the consumer understands what the brand stands for (**brand comprehension**), and their attitude towards the brand (whether they like it or not).

@ **Visit the Online Resource Centre to read more about the book.**

---

different retail outlets stock dresses, and where those retailers are located. She might ask herself where she normally buys party dresses (online or offline), what kinds of dresses are in fashion, perhaps which retailers have sales on, which store staff treat her well, and what the returns policies are of various online and offline retailers. Our search for a solution may be active, an **overt search**, or passive. In other words, we are open to ways of solving our problem but we are not actively looking for information to help us (Howard and Sheth, 1969). The search for information may be internal, i.e. we consider what we already know about the problem and the products we might buy to solve our problem. Alternatively, it might be external, where we don't know enough about our problem and so we seek advice or sup-plementary information.

Proposition Evaluation

Once we have all the information necessary to make a decision, we evaluate the proposition. But first we must determine the criteria used to rank the various offerings. These might be rational (e.g. based on cost) or irrational (e.g. based on desire). For example, the lady dress buyer might ask herself which shop is the best value for money and which is the most fashionable. A con-sumer is said to have an **evoked set** of products in mind when he/she comes to evaluate which particular product, brand, or service he/she wants to solve a particular problem. An evoked set for a party dress buyer might include Zara, H&M, Mango (MNG elsewhere in the world), or ASOS, for instance. The more affluent buyer might visit DKNY or Gucci, for example.

Proposition Selection

In most cases, the offering we select is the one we evaluate as fitting our needs best. However, we might decide on a particular offering away from where we actually buy or acquire it. For example, the party dress buyer may have checked online and made her selection but when she turned up at the retailer to try it on, the dress she wanted was not available, so she decided on an alternative on impulse at the point of purchase. Therefore proposition selection is a separate stage in the proposition acquisition process, distinct from proposition evaluation, because there are times when we must re-evaluate what we buy or acquire because what we want is not available, e.g. buying a cinema ticket for one film because the seats for the other film are sold out.

Acquisition/Purchase

Once selection has taken place, different approaches to proposition acquisition might exist. For example, our dress buyer may make a routine purchase—a dress for work. A routine purchase is a purchase made regularly. Because the purchase is regular we do not become involved in the decision-making process. We simply buy the offering again that we bought previously unless new circumstances arise. The purchase may be specialized, conducted on a one-off or infrequent basis, e.g. a ball-gown for a ball or formal event. In this case, we may become much more involved in the decision-making process to ensure that we understand what we are buying and that we are happy that it will satisfy our needs. For routine purchases, we might use cash or debit cards, whereas for infrequent purchases we might use a credit card. With infrequent purchases, the marketer might ease the pain of payment by offering credit or generous warranties. The lady buying a dress might be intending to purchase the dress, but the store's policy on returns (i.e. whether they allow this or not over what period of time) may have an impact on whether or not she actually buys a dress from a particular shop.

Acquisition also differs by channel and the prevalence of any promotional offers. For example, in the music business, global revenues from digital music grew by 8% in 2011, offsetting for the first time the decline in CD sales (Bradshaw, 2012). This shift in format has had a devastating effect on firms like Virgin Megastore France, which filed for insolvency in 2013 (Vidalon and Pennetier, 2013). Research has also indicated that selling digital music in bundles (e.g. 11 marginally appealing tracks with one hit) is likely to lose its power. In other words, it is likely to be more lucrative for music publishers to release the hit track alone, at a higher price, with the other titles bundled separately (Elberse, 2010).

Re-evaluation

The theory of **cognitive dissonance** (Festinger, 1957) suggests that we are motivated to re-evaluate our beliefs, attitudes, opinions, or values if the position we hold on them at one time is not the same as the position we held at an earlier period owing to some intervening event, circumstance, or action. This difference in evaluations, termed cognitive dissonance, is psychologically uncomfortable (i.e. it causes anxiety). For example, we may feel foolish or regretful about a purchasing decision. Therefore we are motivated to reduce our anxiety by redefining our beliefs, attitudes, opinions, or values to make them consistent with our circumstances. We will also actively avoid situations that might increase our feeling of dissonance. To reduce dissonance we might try to neutralize it by:

- selectively forgetting information;
- minimizing the importance of an issue, decision, or act;

- selectively exposing ourselves only to new information consonant with our existing view (rather than information which isn't);
- reversing a purchase decision, for instance by taking a product back or selling it for what it was worth.

The lady dress buyer might not be happy with her purchase because, although it seemed to fit her in the shop, when she tried it on at home it was too tight or ill-fitting, or it did not flatter her as much as she originally thought.

The concept of cognitive dissonance has significant application in marketing. Industrial or consumer purchasers are likely to feel cognitive dissonance if their expectations of proposition performance are not met in reality. This feeling of dissonance may be particularly acute in a high-involvement purchase (e.g. cars, holidays, or high-value investment products). We are also likely to search out information to reinforce our choice of offering. (See Market Insight 2.1 for Alfa Romeo's approach to minimizing cognitive dissonance.)

Dressed to kill—model in a stunning evening dress
Source: istock.

Research Insight 2.3

To take your learning further, you might wish to read this influential book.

Festinger, L. (1957), *A Theory of Cognitive Dissonance*, Palo Alto, CA: Stanford University Press.

A hugely influential development in psychological theory that explains how we resolve two sets of inconsistent opinions, attitudes, values, and behaviour, held at two different points, arising after we receive new information forcing us to change our initial position (e.g. on brands purchased). The theory proposed that we would change our existing opinions, attitudes, values, and behaviour to the new position to stop us from feeling the psychological discomfort associated with the inconsistent positions we hold.

@ **Visit the Online Resource Centre to read more about the book.**

Market Insight 2.1

Alfa Romeo Eases the Pain

In 2011, car manufacturer Alfa Romeo, headquartered in Turin, Italy, sold 11,563 new cars in Britain, taking a 0.6% share of the market, way behind more popular UK brands such as Peugeot, Renault, Audi/VW, GM/Vauxhall, Ford, Toyota/Lexus, BMW, and Honda. But sales were up 31% on the previous year on the back of sales of the MiTo and the Giulietta. In 2012, sales had dropped by 37% to 7,253 units. Since 2007 and the economic downturn, the car market has suffered from declining consumer confidence. Sales of new cars have dropped from a high of 2.4 million in 2007 and are projected to reach 2.34 million only in 2017. In 2012, new car registrations hit 2.04 million units, up 5.3% on the previous year.

Alfa's Giulietta: when a car looks this good, who cares about the expense?
Source: Courtesy of Alfa Romeo UK.

Given such sluggish economic growth, and the low rates of wage inflation and increases in household spending on energy and food costs, vehicle manufacturers and dealership sales personnel understand the psychological anxiety car buyers feel when purchasing new cars. The buyer's key consideration is ensuring that they obtain value

for money and that they do not feel 'ripped off'. The problem is particularly acute when customers buy new cars, because new cars are significantly more expensive than second-hand cars.

Considering that cars lose 20–30% of their value in depreciation the moment they leave the showroom, we can see why new car buyers feel vulnerable.

Market Insight 2.1
continued

Of course, there are benefits: new cars look better, incorporate the latest design features, and have reduced maintenance costs.

Car dealers work hard to reinforce the purchase decisions made by new car buyers by sending customers newsletters and offering efficient (or free three year warranty) after sales service to ensure that there are no or few maintenance problems. In many cases, new vehicles are sold with free insurance, 0% finance deals, or buy-now-pay-later schemes, all designed to reduce the post-purchase cognitive dissonance car buyers naturally feel after their purchase.

In 2012, Alfa sweetened their deal on the Giulietta, offering a time-limited offer of 0% financing and 5 years warranty with only £1,000 deposit contribution.

But with many other, more popular, car manufacturers offering so many different attractive promotions, will the promotion turn the tide of negative growth and result in an increase in market share for Alfa Romeo?

Sources: Mintel (2012c); SMMT (2012); Pollard (2012).

1 **What else could Alfa Romeo do to reduce the cognitive dissonance felt by its UK customers?**

2 **Do you think that cognitive dissonance would increase or decrease during an economic downturn?**

3 **Consider a time when you purchased an offering that left you feeling anxious. What were you purchasing?**

In Figure 2.1, the buying process is iterative, particularly at the re-evaluation phase of the acquisition process. This is because the re-evaluation of the offering leads us back to any or all of the previous phases in the product acquisition process as a result of experiencing cognitive dissonance. For example, we may have bought a games console (Wii U, etc.) but we are not completely happy with it (e.g. we think that it has poor picture/sound). If it was covered under warranty, this would lead us to the acquisition phase, where a new perfect product should be provided by the retailer. If the product was delivered in perfect working order but we simply didn't enjoy using it, we might go back to the original alternatives we selected (e.g. Xbox 360), and pick one of the other alternatives (e.g. one which might offer a larger variety of games). If we are really not sure about which games console to buy after this initial purchase, we might re-evaluate the alternatives we originally selected and then decide. If we really disliked our original purchase, and this shook our belief in what we thought was important in selecting a games console, we might go back to the information-gathering phase to get more of an idea about the offerings available. Finally, if we were extremely disappointed, we might decide that our original motive—the need to play, to relax, and to have fun—can best be solved by purchasing something other than a games console, which will still meet the same need, e.g. participation in sport.

Research by the marketing agency Razorfish identified three categories of influencer at different stages of the proposition acquisition process. These include key influencers (with their own blogs and huge numbers of Twitter followers, but who are unlikely to know them), social influencers (people in the consumer's social network, whom they might know personally, commenting in Twitter feeds and on blogs/forums), and known peer influencers (e.g. family members or part of the consumer's 'inner circle'). Of all three types, known peer influencers were the most persuasive (see section on Group Influence), but the three groups were differentially important at different points in the proposition acquisition process. For example, close family and friends exert the most influence at the motive development and information-gathering phases (the 'awareness' phase), YouTube and anonymous peer reviewers exert most influence at the proposition evaluation and selection phases (the 'consideration' phase), and close family and friends exert the most influence in the proposition selection and acquisition phases (the 'action' phase) (Sheldrake, 2011).

Perceptions, Learning, and Memory

Often consumers do not understand the messages marketers convey because they have not received, or comprehended, or remembered those messages or because the messages were unclear. Consumer understanding depends on how effectively the message is transmitted and perceived. In this section, we discuss how messages are perceived and remembered (consideration of how messages are communicated is undertaken in Chapter 10). In any one day, consumers receive thousands of messages.

Consider, for instance, a typical working woman in Paris, France, who might well be awoken by her clock radio, blaring out adverts for the *Galeries Lafayette*. While eating her breakfast, she encounters advertisements on her television. She picks up visual advertisements in the *Paris Match* magazine she is reading, say, and when she opens her post, which includes direct mail from charities (e.g. Médecins Sans Frontières) and financial service organizations (BNP Paribas etc.). On her way to the Métro station she might encounter billboards advertising, among other things, L'Oréal for instance. On the Métro, she will probably encounter more visual adverts on the train. When she arrives at work, and after being further bombarded with online ads and sponsored internet search ads, she has been subjected to hundreds of auditory, visual, and audio-visual advertising messages demanding her attention. When she retires to bed, this could have extended to thousands. If we also consider that consumers are recipients of social and interpersonal messages as well—through word of mouth and social media (e.g. Facebook and Twitter)—we begin to realize how sophisticated human perception, learning, and memory processes must be to attend to, filter, and store so many messages.

Perceptions

The American Marketing Association (AMA, 2013) defines perceptions as follows: 'based on prior attitudes, beliefs, needs, stimulus factors, and situational determinants, individuals perceive objects, events, or people in the world about them. Perception is the cognitive impression that is formed of "reality" which in turn influences the individual's actions and behaviour toward that object.' If we paid attention to all the messages we receive, rather than filtering out those we find meaningful, we would probably become overloaded, just like a computer when it crashes. The process of screening meaningful from non-meaningful information is known as **selective exposure** (Dubois, 2000).

As consumers, we are interested in certain types of offerings that are relevant to us when we receive marketing messages. So, men would not usually be interested in adverts about handbags unless they wanted to buy one as an anniversary, birthday, or travel gift. Equally, young people are not usually interested in advertising messages for pensions. If you were looking to book a flight, you would become interested in messages from airline companies and travel agents. Even vacuum cleaner adverts become interesting if your vacuum cleaner has broken down! The messages we choose to ignore and forget are removed from our perception, enabling us to process those messages that we wish to consider more effectively. So, we avoid exposure to certain messages and actively seek out others. We may also selectively expose ourselves to particular messages through the media we choose to read (e.g. certain newspapers, magazines, ezines, Facebook pages, Twitter feeds) or watch (e.g. certain terrestrial, cable, satellite, or internet TV channels). Many people do not read a daily newspaper and therefore will not see press advertisements, although they may see sponsored search ads on websites, or read, respond, and interact with Twitter posts or companies' Facebook pages. Some people do not listen to the radio often or at all. Therefore it is important to determine which **media** channels customers use.

Advertisers label this concept, representing the personal importance a person attaches to a given communication message, **involvement**. This is important because it explains a person's receptivity to communications. We are interested in their receptivity because we are interested in changing or altering their perceptions of particular offerings. We know, from earlier in the chapter, that offerings can be characterized on the basis of whether consumers use rational or emotional thinking to evaluate their relative appeal. Figure 2.2 illustrates a variety of common products and how they are generally viewed by US consumers (see Ratchford, 1987).

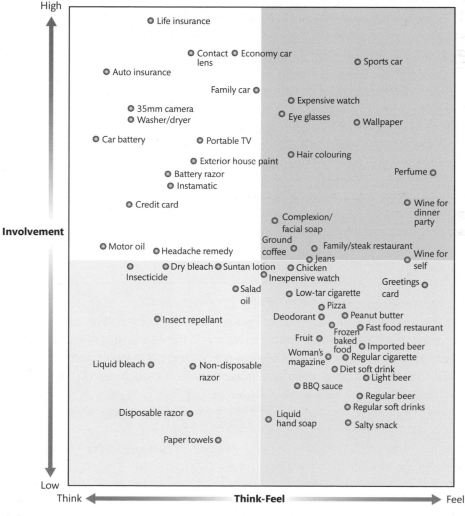

Figure 2.2

Involvement/think-feel dimension plot for common products

Source: Ratchford, B.T. (1987), 'New insights about the FCB grid', *Journal of Advertising Research*, 27(4), 24–38.

We should note that the position for a particular offering is an average of all consumers and may not represent a particular individual's decision-making well. So, for example, the purchase of life insurance was generally regarded as being in the high involvement/thinking quadrant. The positioning of this type of offering suggests the need for more informative advertising/promotion. However, an expensive watch, residing in the high involvement/feeling quadrant, suggests a need for emotional advertising. Offerings in the low involvement/thinking quadrant, such as liquid bleach, suggest the use of advertising/promotion which creates and reinforces habitual buying. Finally, offerings in the low involvement/feeling quadrant, such as women's magazines, should be promoted on the basis of personal satisfaction (Ratchford, 1987).

Another way of displaying how people think about particular offerings uses perceptual mapping, a technique used since at least the early 1960s (Mindak, 1961). Figure 2.3 indicates how customers view different male grooming brands in the UK using (brand) personality keywords. The diagram shows that L'Oréal's Men Expert range is perceived as sensuous, sophisticated, and glamorous, whilst Bull Dog is seen as tacky, quirky, and daring (we consider brand differentiation in Chapter 6). Organizations deliberately seek to position themselves in the minds of specific target audience groups. To do this properly, they must understand the nature of the group's sub-culture. However, organizations risk causing offence if they position a brand on particular dimensions which are misperceived, or perceived correctly but negatively. The Irish-based low-cost airline Ryanair drew over 7,000 complaints to the UK's advertising standards watchdog ASA after it featured an airline hostess in her underwear in one of its adverts in 2011.

Brands can thrive or die based on how their customers perceive them. Sometimes companies fail to position their offerings appropriately (see Market Insight 2.2 on the positioning of a 'ladies' lager') or need to change how their brands are perceived because they have developed negative associations. For example, premium fashion brand Burberry briefly lost its 'exclusivity' association in the UK, but not overseas, after becoming associated with white working class delinquents (so-called 'chavs', a pejorative term), causing a flood of imitations in its distinctive check pattern. By reducing the visibility of its check design, changing its styles, and cracking down on counterfeiters, the brand regained its strong positive image (Anon., 2011). Conversely, sometimes organizations position their offerings well, as Toyota did when developing the Lexus brand for the premium car market.

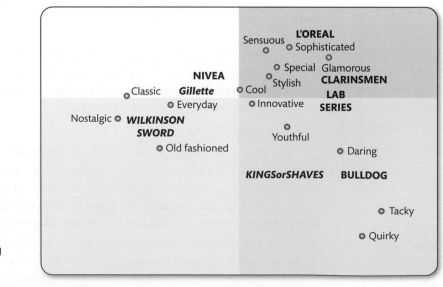

Figure 2.3

Example of a perceptual map for men's shaving brands

Source: Mintel (2009).

Market Insight 2.2

Ladies' Lager Falls Flat

In 2011, Molson Coors launched a new concept beer aimed at women, called it Animée, and backed it with a £2m advertising push. Within just 12 months, it had withdrawn the product. What happened? At the heart of this question is whether or not there is room in the market for 'beer for women'. Molson Coors thought there was, estimating the UK market to be worth around £396m. It developed Animée, a clear-filtered beer available in standard, rose, and citrus flavours, to target women drinkers. Molson Coors expected to build the UK female lager market, a market in which only 13% of all beer served is to women, compared with 33% in Ireland and 44% in Spain. The problem is that most UK women don't like beer. They regard it as too bitter and gaseous. After disappointing sales, Molson withdrew Animée, focusing instead on Corona and Coors Light, brands which already had higher proportions of women drinkers than traditional beer brands. But Molson are not the only brewer trying to woo the ladies. Carlsberg is also keen. In 2011 it launched 'Copenhagen', a 'metrosexual' beer for the 'beer-hater', though it has not explicitly targeted women, and has 130 scientists working on developing

beer that women will like. Given that a relatively high proportion of women drink Peroni, the stylish Italian lager, the trick might well be premiumization, rather than explicit feminization, of the brand. What's the conclusion? Instead of developing a women-only beer (and by definition a man-unfriendly one), brewers will focus on changing women's perceptions of drinking beer instead.

Sources: Hawkes (2012); Joseph (2012a 2012b); Willifer (2012) (see also Market Insight 4.2 in Chapter 4).

1 **What do you think men might have thought about the idea of a ladies' lager? Does it matter what they thought?**

2 **How might Molson Coors change women's perceptions of the acceptability of drinking lager in the UK?**

3 **Consider your own perceptions of lager. If you are a man, have you ever bought a 'metrosexual' type of beer in the past? (Think of: Corona, Copenhagen). What do you think of it? If you are a woman, would you have bought this type of ladies' lager? Why (not)?**

Learning and Memory

How do consumers continually learn about new offerings, their relative performance, and new trends? Learning is defined as the process by which we acquire new knowledge and skills, attitudes and values, through study, experience, or modelling others' behaviour. There are various theories of human learning, which include **classical conditioning**, **operant conditioning**, and **social learning**.

■ Classical Conditioning—Russian Nobel Laureate, Ivan Pavlov, investigated the digestive and nervous system of dogs, measuring the amount of saliva produced in response to food under certain conditions. He realized that his dog salivated before food was actually served, and set out to determine why. By carrying out a series of experiments and manipulating stimuli before the presentation of food using a bell, he realized that if he rang the bell before serving food, the dogs would associate the sound of the bell (the conditioned stimulus) with the presentation of food (the unconditioned stimulus) and begin salivating. So, classical conditioning occurs when the unconditioned stimulus becomes associated with the conditioned stimulus.

In other words, we learn by associating one thing with another—in this case, the sound of the bell with the arrival of food. This approach to learning is frequently used in marketing, for example: 1) jingles in advertising, e.g. GoCompare's annoying opera singer, Gio Compario; 2) supermarkets include bakery sections to cause consumers to buy more as they associate the smell of warm bread with eating; 3) perfume and aftershave manufacturers (e.g. L'Oréal) place free samples of products in sachets in magazines so that when readers see an advert for a particular brand of perfume/aftershave they associate the image they see with the smell, and so are more likely to purchase the product when they see its image in the future.

■ Operant Conditioning—B. F. Skinner (1954) was one of the pioneers of the behaviourist school of learning. He argued that learning was the result of operant conditioning whereby subjects would act on a stimulus from the environment. The resulting behaviour was more likely to occur if this behaviour was reinforced. In other words, operant conditioning is learning through behavioural reinforcement. Skinner termed this 'reinforcement', as the behaviour would occur more readily in connection with a particular stimulus if the required resulting behaviour had been reinforced through punishment or reward. In marketing, consider the typical in-store sales promotion. Perhaps it's a new yoghurt brand offered in a supermarket. If we don't normally eat this brand and we're curious, we might try it because there are no costs in terms of time, effort, or money in having a taste. The sales promotion provides the stimulus, the trial behaviour occurs, and if the yoghurt is liked and the consumer rewarded with a money-off coupon, the behaviour of purchasing that particular yoghurt brand is reinforced (for more on sales promotion, see Chapter 11). Supermarkets reinforce our loyalty by providing reward cards and points for purchasing particular items. The Nectar card in Britain, a reward card that links a supermarket, selected retailers, and petrol retailers to a points system, or the card and stamps system used by the retailer 7-Eleven in their convenience stores throughout the world, are examples.

■ Social Learning—this theory was proposed by the psychologist Albert Bandura, who suggested that humans are less animalistic than the Skinnerian behaviourist school of learning suggests. Bandura (1977) argued that we can delay gratification and dispense our own rewards or punishment. So, we have more choice over how we react to stimuli than Skinner proposed, who felt that we blindly followed our instinctual drives. Therefore we can reflect on our own actions and change our future behaviour. This led to the idea that we could learn not only from how we respond to situations but also from how others respond to situations. Bandura called this modelling. In social learning, we learn by observing the behaviour of others. The implications for marketers are profound. For adolescents, role models include both parents and famous athletes and entertainers, but parents are the most influential of these groups (Martin and Bush, 2000). Parents socialize their children into purchasing and consuming the same brands that they buy, actively teaching them consumer skills—materialistic values and consumption attitudes—in their teenage years. Interaction with peers also makes adolescents more aware of different products and services (Moschis and Churchill, 1978). Companies like Amazon have long recognized the power of peers, encouraging purchasers to leave reviews of products that they have previously bought. Research has demonstrated that those who read reviews are twice as likely to select a product than those who do not (Senecal and Nantal, 2004).

But what happens once consumers have learnt information? How do they retain it in their memories and what stops them from forgetting such information? Consumers do not necessarily

Some of the world's most recognizable logos
Sources: © Coca-Cola; © Google; © McDonald's; © Nike (respectively).

have the same experience and therefore knowledge of particular offerings. Knowledge develops with familiarity, repetition of marketing messages, and a consumer's acquisition of product/ service information. Marketing messages need to be repeated often as people forget them over time, particularly the specific arguments or message presented. The general substance or conclusion of the message is marginally more likely to be remembered (Bettinghaus and Cody, 1994: 67).

We enhance memorization through the use of symbols, such as corporate identity logos, badges, and signs. Shapes, creatures, and people carry significant meanings, as seen in badges, trademarks, and logos. Airlines around the world have adopted symbols, e.g. the kangaroo of Australian airline Qantas. Well-recognized symbols worldwide include the KFC 'Colonel' symbol, Intel's symbol, Apple's bitten apple logo, Coca-Cola's ubiquitous script logo, and Google's multicoloured script symbol.

Our memories, as a system for storing perceptions, experience, and knowledge, are highly complex (Bettman, 1979). A variety of memorization processes affect consumer choice, including the following:

- Factors affecting **recognition** and **recall**—less frequently used words in advertising are recognized more and recalled less. The information-processing task in transferring data from short-term to long-term memory differs for recognition (two to five seconds) and recall (five to ten seconds). Under high states of arousal, e.g. where the consumer is subject to time pressure, recognition speeds are increased whereas recall speeds are hindered. In practical terms, the more unique a campaign's message, the better it is recognized but the worse it is recalled.

- The importance of context—memorization is strongly associated with the context of the stimulus, so information available in memory will be inaccessible in the wrong context. For example, vacuum cleaner manufacturers advertising in sports magazines are unlikely to be remembered.

- Form of object coding and storage—we store information in the form it is presented to us, either by object (brand) or dimension (offering attribute) but there is no evidence that one form is organized into memory more quickly, or more accurately than the other (Johnson and Russo, 1978).

- Load processing effects—we find it more difficult to process information into our short- and long-term memories when we are presented with a great deal of information at once.

- Input mode effects—short-term recall of sound input is stronger than short-term recall of visual input where the two compete for attention, e.g. in television and YouTube advertising.

- Repetition effects—recall and recognition of marketing messages/information increase the more a consumer is exposed to them, although later exposures add less and less to memory performance.

Evidence suggests that where consumers have little experience or knowledge of an offering, provision of in-store point-of-purchase information is more successful than general advertising (Bettman, 1979). This is why brand manufacturers frequently conduct product trials in-store, offering consumers the opportunity to try the offering without expending time, money, and effort in purchasing it (see Chapter 11 for more on sales promotion). This approach places the brand in the consumer's evoked set, and helps the consumer contextualize the particular product and remember it when they shop next time. Consumer knowledge of offerings can be incomplete and/or inaccurate as consumers frequently think that they know something about an offering that is not accurate and believe this strongly (Alba and Hutchinson, 2000).

Personality

How and what we buy is also based on our personalities. **Personality** can be defined as that aspect of our psyche which determines how we respond to our environment in a relatively stable way over time. There are various theories of personality. Here, we consider three main approaches:

1 the psychoanalytic approach, which stresses self-reported unconscious desires;

2 trait theory, which stresses the classification of personality types;

3 the self-concept approach, which concerns how we perceive ourselves as consumers.

The Psychoanalytic Approach

Sigmund Freud devised a theory of motivation that considered us as irrational beings. According to Freud (1927), a person's personality is determined by their sexual development from an infant beginning with breastfeeding, to toilet training, to discovery of the genitals, through a stage of the development of hidden sexual desires from the age of about 5 years old until adolescence, and then in adolescence the individual is said to discover a sexual interest for persons of the opposite sex. Freud stated that an adult's personality is developed according to how well they cope with crises that occur during these development phases.

Freud suggested that, as individuals, we are motivated by our subconscious drives, which he saw as a system comprising three interrelated components: the id, the ego, and the superego.

- **Id**—this part of our psyche harbours our instinctual drives and urges, a kind of seething mass of needs, which require instant gratification.
- **Ego**—this part of our psyche attempts to find outlets for the urges in our id and acts as a planning centre to determine the opportunities for gratification of our urges. According to Freud, the ego is moderated by the superego.
- **Superego**—this part of our psyche controls how we motivate ourselves to behave to respond to our instincts and urges, so that we do so in a socially acceptable manner and avoid any feelings of guilt or shame. It acts as a social conscience.

(For an excellent illustration of the importance of Freud's thinking in the development of marketing and public relations, see 'Century of the Self', the four-part Adam Curtis documentary originally shown on BBC Television in the UK.)

Psychoanalytic ideas of human personality and development were applied to marketing consumer goods by the public relations specialist Edward Bernays, Freud's nephew, in America, and by many others. The application of psychoanalytic methods and concepts to the understanding of consumer behaviour became known as motivation research (Collins and Montgomery, 1969). Motivation research aimed to understand people's motivations to purchase and was undertaken extensively in the 1960s and 1970s using focus groups and qualitative research methods, particularly projective techniques of interpretation, to identify subconscious desires (see Chapter 3). According to some motivation researchers, people buy the following goods for the following reasons (Dichter, 1964; Kotler, 1965).

- Train travel—regarded as safer than airline travel by male passengers who felt less guilty about what might happen to their wives and families if there was an accident.
- Cigars—the strong smell is associated by males with virility.
- A convertible/cabriolet car—a substitute 'mistress' for the male buyer.
- Fur coats—demonstrate the financial prestige of the buyer and the sexual prowess of the wearer.

The Trait Approach

This approach to personality categorizes people into different personality types or so-called traits (pronounced 'trays'). Researchers characterize personalities according to bipolar scales, which have included the following traits:

- sociable–timid;
- action-oriented–reflection-oriented;
- stable–nervous;
- serious–frivolous;
- tolerant–suspicious;
- dominant–submissive;
- friendly–hostile;
- hard–sensitive;
- quick–slow;
- masculine–feminine.

Researchers frequently talk about the 'big five' personality dimensions: extraversion (sociable fun-loving, affectionate, friendly, talkative), openness (original, imaginative, creative, and daring), conscientiousness (careful, reliable, well-organized, hard-working), neuroticism (worrying, nervous, highly strung, self-conscious, vulnerable), and agreeableness (soft-hearted, sympathetic, forgiving, acquiescent) (McRae and Costa, 1987). An understanding of personality types helps marketers to segment customer groups (see Chapter 6) on the basis of a particular personality trait.

Car manufacturers might market offerings on the basis of personality types related to particular car attributes, e.g. safety features versus aesthetic design or handling versus social prestige of owning a particular vehicle and so on. Matzler *et al.* (2006) argue that marketers of running shoes and mobile phones should be interested in two personality traits in particular, extraversion and openness to experience, because these traits are linked to how consumers form their view of brands and their attitudinal and purchase loyalty to those brands. Interestingly, more extroverted than introverted, and people with higher levels of neuroticism, take part in social media use (de Correa *et al.,* 2010).

Visit the **Online Resource Centre** and complete Internet Activity 2.1, an online quiz, to learn more about your own personality across a number of key personality traits.

Self-Concept Approach

There is an increasing belief that people buy offerings based on the brand that they represent and its relation to the buyers' perception of their own self-concept or personality. In other words, we buy brands that resemble how we perceive ourselves. In a study of the luxury goods market, Dubois and Duquesne (1993) demonstrated how buyers of luxury goods typically divided into one of two categories.

1 Those who made their purchases based on product quality, aesthetic design, and excellence of service, motivated by the desire to impress others, their ability to pay high prices, and the ostentatious display of their wealth.

2 Those who bought luxury goods based on what they symbolize; purchasing luxury goods represented an extreme form of the expression of their own values.

Consumers buy products based on self-concept through self-giving behaviour (Mick and DeMoss, 1990). Gift-giving is a common phenomenon, particularly among family, friends, and work colleagues. It is highly symbolic, connoting love (e.g. Valentine's and Mother's/Father's Days), congratulations (e.g. wedding presents), regret (e.g. a card after offending a loved one), and dominance (e.g. clothes bought by a girl for her boyfriend to change his look). Self-giving arises from different motivations, e.g. to reward oneself, to be nice to oneself, to cheer oneself up, to fulfil a need, and to celebrate. There is a link between the purchase of clothing as a self-gift, i.e. a special purchase rather than a typical purchase, and a consumer's self-concept. An extreme example of when people purchase products to build their self-concept, although it tends to work in the short term and damages longer-term self-concept perceptions, occurs in compulsive consumer behaviour (e.g. shopping, gambling, excessive drinking).

Motivation

Abraham Maslow (1943) suggested a hierarchical order of human needs, as outlined in Figure 2.4. According to Maslow, we seek to satisfy our lower-order physiological needs first, before our safety needs, our belongingness needs, our esteem needs, and finally our need for self-actualization. There is little research evidence to confirm Maslow's hierarchy, but the concept possesses logical simplicity, making it a useful tool for understanding how we prioritize our own needs. In contemporary societies, offerings focus on solving consumer needs in the esteem and self-actualization categories, as needs in other categories are already provided for.

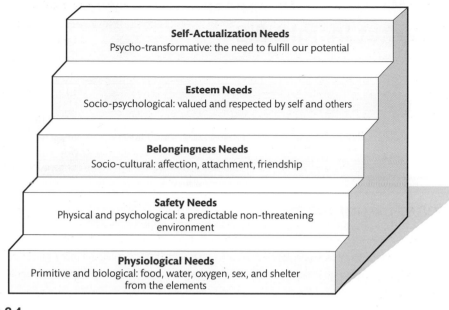

Figure 2.4

Maslow's hierarchy of needs

Source: Adapted from Maslow (1943). This content is in the public domain.

However, in the poorer parts of sub-Saharan Africa, for example, offerings operate for some citizens at the level of solving safety and belongingness needs. The implications for market-ers are that offerings aimed at the mass market in Africa in the self-actualization category (e.g. higher education, long-haul travel) are likely to fail. This does not mean that there are no market segments with this need. There are groups of people in sub-Saharan Africa whose income allows them to enjoy such offerings (see Market Insight 2.3).

There is still debate about whether consumers are motivated by rational (as outlined by Howard and Sheth, 1969) or irrational motives. Holbrook *et al.* (1986) started to consider irra-tional motives when they suggested that our wants could be latent, passive, or active, and were related to both intrinsic and extrinsic reasons, as follows:

- latent—needs are hidden, our subject is unaware of his/her need;
- passive—the costs of acquisition exceed, for the moment, the expected satisfaction derived from acquisition;
- active—the subject is both aware of his/her needs and expects perceived benefits to exceed the likely costs of acquisition.

According to Holbrook *et al.* (1986), when our needs are active they can arise either through **habit**, or through a process of choosing a brand, which the authors call **picking**. Picking is the process of deliberative selection of an offering from among a repertoire of acceptable alterna-tives, even though the consumer believes the alternatives to be essentially identical in their ability to satisfy his/her needs. It can be motivated by intrinsic or extrinsic evaluations or both. Intrinsic evaluation occurs because a consumer likes a product, perhaps because of anticipated pleas-ure from using the product. Alternatively, an extrinsic evaluation might occur because a friend mentioned that it was a great product. Extrinsic evaluations can also entail explicit cost–benefit analyses. Extrinsic reasons for purchase can be subdivided into five categories.

Market Insight 2.3

Templestay Fulfils Spiritual Potential

Tough beds and pre-dawn wake-up calls hardly sound like the stuff of a luxury holiday. And they're not. They are the brainchild of the Korea Tourist Organization's (KTO) Templestay programme, designed to help people find themselves, to self-actualize in Maslow's terminology. Activities include ceremonial chanting (*Yebul*) in praise of the Buddha three times per day (including one before dawn), sitting and walking meditation, communal vegetarian meals (*Baru Gongyang*), communal tea-drinking, lantern-making, *Sutra* (scripture) printing, and the opportunity for introspective searching conversations with Buddhist monks. KTO's Templestay marketing efforts have, in America at least, previously focused on higher-education student groups (MBAs in particular) and Taekwondo martial artists.

Such a holiday offering hardly sounds like it would be popular and yet it has been successful. The approach began after the Jogye Order, Korea's largest Buddhism sect, saw an opportunity to help the Korean government provide extra short-term accommodation during the 2002 Football World Cup, when standard hotel accommodation fell short, by providing access for tourists to its temples' spartan accommodation. Since 2002, the number of participating temples has increased to 109 from 33 with more than 2 million guests. In 2011, the programme counted 212,437 guests with 12% from overseas.

What's the moral of the (marketing) story? In an age of plenty (with all the responsibilities that possessions bring), going without and having nothing (for a time at least) is more fulfilling than one might imagine. The Korean government obviously thinks so; it has subsidized the programme to the tune of US$100m since 2004, in a bid to promote traditional Korean culture.

Sources: Kiesnoski (2009); You-Sun (2013); VisitSeoul (nd).

1 **Why do you think some people might be interested in a Templestay tourist experience?**

2 **Do you think that the Korean Tourist Organization's targeting of student and martial arts groups is appropriate? Why (not)?**

3 **Consider your own perceptions of what is important in a holiday. Which needs on Maslow's hierarchy are you looking to fulfil?**

1 Economic—concerned with expenditure of money, time, and effort spent in purchasing and consuming an offering. Economists refer to the concept of **price elasticity** of demand to explain how demand is affected when price is increased or decreased.

2 Technical—concerned with the offering's perceived quality of performance in the anticipated usage situation.

3 Social—concerned with the extent to which a purchase will enhance a person's feelings of esteem, personal worth in relation to others (cf. Maslow's hierarchy), and general adherence to group norms and effects (see section on Theory of Planned Behaviour).

4 Legalistic—concerned with what are perceived to be the legitimate demands of others (e.g. buying on behalf of a company, or for a child or spouse).

5 Adaptive—(a form of social learning) concerned with imitating others, seeking expert advice (e.g. from blogs, social networking sites, or industry and consumer magazines), or relying on the reputation of a particular company or brand in cases of uncertain or limited purchasing information.

Theory of Planned Behaviour

Theories of motivation in marketing help us understand why people behave as they do. The Theory of Planned Behaviour explains that behaviour is brought about by our **intention** to act in a certain way. This intention to act is affected by the attitude a subject has towards a particular behaviour, encompassing the degree to which a person has favourable or unfavourable evaluations or appraisals of the behaviour in question. Intention to act is also affected by the subjective norm, which is perceived social pressure to perform or not perform a particular behaviour (see section on Group Influence). Finally, intention to act is affected by perceived behavioural control, referring to the perceived ease or difficulty of performing the behaviour, based on a reflection on past experience and future obstacles. Figure 2.5 provides a graphical illustration.

For example, if we consider cigarette use, we might have different attitudes towards smoking based on our geographical location, e.g. whether we live in France or China versus Britain or New Zealand. We might think we can't give up smoking because we need a cigarette to calm our nerves (maybe we have a stressful job). Equally, we also consider the opinions significant others have towards smoking cigarettes (e.g. our spouses, children, or friends). If we place ourselves in the mind of government (de)marketers, the key elements of the theory of planned behaviour (i.e. attitudes, subjective norms, and perceived behavioural control) can help us understand how to discourage smoking. For example, we could either a) try to alter subjects' attitudes towards smoking, b) change their views on how others see them as smokers, or c) change their perceptions of how they perceive their own ability to give up (see Chapter 16 for a wider discussion of social marketing). An advertising campaign costing £2.7m launched by the UK Department of Health running over nine weeks in late 2012, actively discourages smoking by showing 'disgusting' images of cancerous tumours growing out of cigarettes whilst people smoke them. The idea is to remind people, many of whom would like to stop but can't, just how dangerous smoking is and give them the added impetus to stop (Anon. 2012a). (See also Market Insight 2.4.)

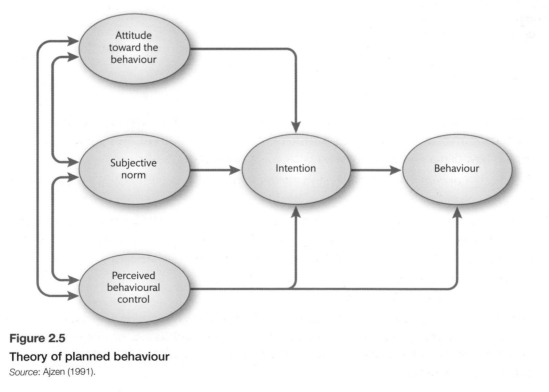

Figure 2.5
Theory of planned behaviour
Source: Ajzen (1991).

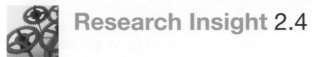

Research Insight 2.4

To take your learning further, you might wish to read this influential article.

Azjen, I. (1991), 'The theory of planned behaviour', *Organisational Behaviour and Human Decision Processes*, **50, 179–211.**

In this highly cited seminal article, the author outlines how behaviour and behavioural intention to act in a certain way are affected by the attitude the subject has towards a particular behaviour, the subjective norm, and perceived behavioural control. The author developed our understanding of the fact that how humans intend to act may not be how they end up acting in a given situation. Intention, perception of behavioural control, attitude toward the behaviour, and subjective norm all reveal different aspects of the target behaviour and serve as possible directions for attack in attempts to alter particular behaviours, making this a powerful motivational theory in marketing.

@ **Visit the Online Resource Centre to read the abstract and access the full paper.**

Market Insight 2.4

(De)shopping: To Pay or Not to Pay?

A prevalent and growing trend in retailing is when customers purchase an item, use it, and take it back for a refund without ever having had any intention of paying for it. The problem is particularly prevalent among some women when buying clothes. Of course, this approach requires retailers to operate lenient returns policies, and many do. Recent research suggests nearly 50% of British women may have bought garments and taken them back for a refund after use. This trend, known as **deshopping**, is estimated to cost US retailers up to $16bn per annum. Given the high cost to retailers (online particularly since customers cannot try on products beforehand), what should they do about it? Surprisingly, many seem reluctant to tackle the problem. A theory of planned behaviour analysis

Will this customer deshop after use?
Source: istock © kali9.

might suggest that retailers should a) try to alter buyers' attitudes towards deshopping by making it socially or morally unacceptable, b) change customers' views on how others see them as deshoppers (by trying to stigmatize this behaviour), and/or c) change deshoppers' perceptions of

Market Insight 2.4
continued

the likelihood that they can get away with this behaviour.

What have retailers done about it? One British retailer, Marks and Spencer, has reduced its returns window from 90 to 35 days, introduced dedicated returns desks (away from payment desks), and taken customers' details to check how frequently they have returned items previously. Retailers can also train staff to ask searching but polite questions of customers to establish how legitimate their return claim is, prosecute repeat offenders (assuming that they can compile the evidence needed by the police), and develop a

customer communication campaign on the demerits of deshopping.

Sources: King *et al.* (2008); Anon. (2012b); King and Balmer (2012).

1 **What attitudes do you think deshoppers use to justify their behaviour?**

2 **Have you ever deshopped? If you have: why did you do this? If you have not, do you know anybody who has?**

3 **Why do you think retailers are reluctant to tackle this problem?**

The Importance of Social Contexts

Although our own personality and other characteristics impact on how we consider and consume offerings, the opinions, attitudes, and values of others also affect how we consume, as we discovered using the Theory of Planned Behaviour. Therefore our internal perspective is determined not only by our own thoughts and personality structures but also by the input of others. Other people have an effect on our opinions, attitudes, and values. We consider these three psychological constructs next.

Opinions, Attitudes, and Values

Opinions can be described as the quick responses we might give to opinion poll questions about current issues or instant responses to questions from friends. They are held with limited conviction because we have often not yet formed or fully developed an underlying attitude on an issue. An opinion might be what we think of the latest advertising campaign for a high-profile brand. **Attitudes**, by comparison, are held with a greater degree of conviction, over a longer duration, and are much more likely to influence behaviour. **Values** are held even more strongly than attitudes and underpin our attitudinal and behavioural systems. Values are linked to our conscience, developed through the familial socialization process, through cultures and subcultures, and through our religious influences, and are frequently formed in early childhood.

The marketer needs to understand the difference between these three different mental states. Opinions are **cognitive** (i.e. based on thoughts). Attitudes are what psychologists call **affective** (i.e. linked to our emotional states). Values are **conative**, i.e. they are linked to our motivations and behaviour. Although we may have a specific attitude towards something, we do not always follow it in terms of our behaviour. In other words, we may want to be more fashionable in our dress sense but we don't bother trying new styles! VALs™ is a framework that is used to segment consumers into differing types based on their opinions, attitudes, values, and behaviours.

Visit the **Online Resource Centre** and follow the weblink to the VALs™ online survey to identify which VAL type you fall into.

Group Influence

Consumers learn through imitation (i.e. social learning). We've learnt, for instance, by observing and copying our parents and friends. As consumers we may consider our opinions, attitudes, values, and behaviour patterns compared with specific reference groups. Reference groups are groups 'that the individual tends to use as an anchor point for evaluating his/her own beliefs and attitudes. It can have great influence on one's values, opinions, attitudes and behaviour patterns. A reference group may be positive; i.e. the individual patterns his or her own beliefs and behaviour to be congruent with those of the group, or it may be negative' (AMA, 2013). However, if a consumer feels that his/her freedom to choose is being threatened, he/she may react against this intervention. So, a consumer whose decision alternative is blocked, partially or wholly, will become increasingly motivated to go against that specific decision alternative through rebellious behaviour (Clee and Wicklund, 1980). Children who are told that they cannot have particular offerings desire them more as a result (Rummell *et al.,* 2000). For example, the 'tweenage' daughter (aged between 10 and 12 years old) told by her father not to buy short skirts may very well do so, while the rebellious teenage son drinks too much alcohol against his mother's advice. This form of negative group influence occurs because of **psychological reactance**.

Consumers' assumptions about an individual's behaviour, based on identifying group membership, become automated if they are frequently and consistently made (Bargh and Chartrand 1999). This represents a form of social learning. For instance, a Swedish male consumer might purchase Abba-branded herring because this was the brand his parents ate at the breakfast table, whereas a French female beverage consumer might drink Orangina religiously because that is what her parents provided for her as a child. The link between a consumer and a particular reference group depends on how closely the consumer associates with a particular reference group. Where we do associate closely, the attachment to the brand is often assumed. For example, consumers identifying with the motorcycling genre might ride Harley-Davidson bikes because the motorcycle crowd generally buy Harley-Davidson bikes.

Message receipt is also affected by peer group pressure, through word of mouth, online and offline, whether intended or not. Members of groups tend to conform to a group norm, enhancing the self-image of the recipient and increasing the feeling of group identity and belongingness. Therefore consumers may have their own cultures and sub-cultures, which impact on how a particular marketing message may be received (see Chapter 19 on how marketing and culture interact). Some marketing messages might incorporate **celebrity endorsement** appeals, e.g. through popular culture role models who have influence over the target consumer group. H&M, the Swedish fashion retailer, has made use of renowned pop artists over the years, including Kylie Minogue and Lana Del Rey, to advertise its brands, particularly to young people. (See Market Insight 2.5 on a successful celebrity endorsement

Market Insight 2.5

Celebrity Scents

The market for celebrity-endorsed brands became apparent when Hollywood actress Elizabeth Taylor launched 'White Diamonds' in 1989, a brand that raked in global sales of nearly $1bn, making it the best-selling celebrity perfume of all time. Consequently, there has been an increasing shift towards celebrity endorsement of both men's and women's perfumes. Celebrities currently lending their faces and names to advertising campaigns include Hollywood A-listers Brad Pitt for Chanel and Charlize Theron for Christian Dior. But there has been a more recent shift towards celebrities not only endorsing the perfume by appearing in commercials but being involved in the selection of the scents and often lending their name directly to the brand. Brands like Coty, Elizabeth Arden, and Avon have all launched celebrity scents. Jennifer Lopez's 'JLo Glow' has reached $1bn in sales since its launch in 2002. Other more recent examples include 'Intimately Yours' launched by British celebrity couple David and Victoria Beckham. American singer Lady Gaga launched her 'Fame' perfume at the prestigious Harrods department store through her own company, Haus Laboratories, and Coty Inc., the US perfume company. American socialite Paris Hilton and singer Britney Spears both have more than eight lines of perfumes associated with them. Hollywood stars and American singers are not the only ones in on the act. Bollywood actresses Zeena Aman and Shilpa Shetty have also previously launched their own perfumes. With legions of followers around the world, it's no surprise that perfumiers have cottoned on to the fact that celebrity sells.

But who's buying and how are they influenced? Interestingly, a 2009 Datamonitor consumer survey found that only 9% of people cite that endorsements made by celebrities influence their buying behaviour when shopping for fragrances. So, if celebrity is not selling the perfumes, why are celebrity perfume sales booming? It could be that people are not prepared to admit to researchers that celebrities influence them. In the UK, celebrity fragrance consumers are typically

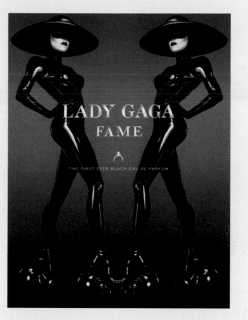

An advert for Lady Gaga's 'Fame' perfume
Source: ©Coty Inc.

between 12 and 24 years of age on the female side, the larger market, and like fruity and floral smells. But young women are also a key market for male celebrity scents, buying them for their boyfriends and husbands. Overall, Coty enjoys market leadership of both the men and women's fragrance market (15%), with second (13%) and third (12%) positions going to L'Oréal and Estée Lauder, respectively.

Sources: Datamonitor (2010); Agrawal (2012); Mintel (2012d); Rainey (2012); Uricchio (2012); Warr (2012).

1 **Why have celebrity-endorsed perfumes sold so well?**

2 **Have you ever bought a celebrity-endorsed fragrance? If you have, why? If you have not, under what circumstances would you consider buying one? (Hint: Be honest with yourself.)**

3 **Think of another celebrity-endorsement deal that you are aware of. Who is the brand, who is the endorser, and do you think that this campaign was effective?**

campaign.) Marketing campaigns frequently leverage the persuasive power of reference group membership through word-of-mouth campaigns, e.g. when consumers discuss their experiences on Twitter and Facebook. Mars Inc. got itself into hot water in 2012 when it paid various celebrities, including footballer Rio Ferdinand, to endorse its Snickers product as part of its 'You're not you when you're hungry' campaign through Twitter in the UK by sending five tweets, four of which were teasers (i.e. which did not reveal that they were sponsored advertising) and only the final one of which revealed the advertising nature of the communication. Because some of these celebrities' followers were upset because they were having products promoted to them through this medium, they made complaints to the Advertising Standards Authority (ASA) (see Chapter 4). Interestingly, the ASA adjudication, the first of its kind on the use of social media for advertising in the UK, ruled that the tweets were acceptable (Bartnett, 2012).

Word-of-mouth communication is powerful because we trust the opinions of our friends and colleagues. For example, in the beauty and personal care market (Mintel, 2011, 2012a), different influences include, in order of importance: the opinions of family and friends; the company/product website; shop assistants; passively reading articles in magazines or newspapers; proactively looking up reviews online or in magazines; actively researching using forums and chatrooms, or by reading about it on Twitter.

In the next section, we consider how consumer behaviour is affected by social class, lifestyle, and lifecycle.

Social Grade

In marketing, the term 'social grade' refers to a system of classification of consumers based on their socio-economic grouping. **Social grade** was originally developed for the IPA National Readership Survey (NRS) in the 1950s, and was subsequently adopted by JICNARS (the Joint Industry Committee for National Readership Surveys) on its formation in 1968. Social grade is a means of classifying the population by the type of work they do based on the occupation of the chief income earner, i.e. the member of the household with the largest income. NRS Ltd (the successor to JICNARS) provides social grade population estimates, not only for the National Readership Survey, but also for a number of other major industry surveys. These population estimates are obtained from the Survey's interviews with a representative sample of some 36,000 adults every year (see Table 2.1). There is a widely held belief that consumers make purchases based on their socio-economic position within society, and that different social classes have different self-images, social horizons, and consumption goals (Coleman, 1983). Such variations in attitudes, motivations, and value orientations reflect differences in occupational opportunities and demands, childhood socialization patterns, and educational influences, leading consumers to vary in their purchase behaviours across social classes (Williams, 2002). (See Market Insight 2.6 on champagne drinking and social class.)

Lifestyle

Marketers increasingly target consumers on the basis of their lifestyles (see also Chapter 6). The AMA define lifestyle as 'the manner in which the individual copes and deals with his/her psychological and physical environment on a day-to-day basis', 'as a phrase describing the values,

Table 2.1 Social grading scale

Social grade	Social status	Occupational status	Population estimate, Great Britain, age 15+ (2012) (%)	Population estimate, Great Britain, age 15+ (1982) (%)
A	Upper middle class	Professionals, chief executives, and senior managers with a large number of dependent staff	4.4	3.1
B	Middle class	Intermediate, managerial, administrative, or professional	22.1	13.4
C1	Lower middle class	Supervisory, clerical and non-manual administrative, lower managerial or early professional (e.g. junior white-collar workers based in offices)	27.4	22.3
C2	Skilled working class	Skilled manual workers	21.7	31.2
D	Working class	Semi-and unskilled manual workers	15.4	19.1
E	Those at lowest levels of subsistence	Unemployed and casual workers, pensioners or widowers with no income other than that provided by state	9.0	10.9

Source: National Readership Survey. Reproduced with the kind permission of the National Readership Survey.

attitudes, opinions, and behaviour patterns of the consumer', and 'the manner in which people conduct their lives, including their activities, interests, and opinions' (AMA, 2013). For example, a segmentation of the South Australian wine market reveals the following lifestyle types (Bruwer and Li, 2007).

- Conservative knowledgeable wine drinkers (19.2% of the population)—more likely to be male (57%), well educated, and well remunerated, this segment drinks wine frequently (particularly red), displaying connoisseur qualities when buying wine.
- Enjoyment-oriented social wine drinkers (16.2% of the population)—more likely to be female and younger, this segment likes white and sparkling wine and has an eye for value for money.
- Basic wine drinkers (23.5% of the population)—a predominantly male segment, as happy drinking beer as wine, depending on what's available.

Market Insight 2.6

Champagne: A Fizzling Market?

Champagne, the sparkling wine from the North East region of France, is often the drink of choice at weddings and on special occasions, but is most often drunk at home by Britons and occasionally in restaurants and bars/pubs. Sales of champagne dropped by 32% to £690m between 2007 and 2012, but sales of cheaper brands of sparkling wine have increased by 55% to £720m over the same period. Key brands in the UK off-trade market include Moët et Chandon, Heidsieck, Lanson, Veuve Clicquot, Etienne Dumont, and supermarket own-label.

Because of its relatively high cost, the level of champagne drinking by the different social classes is distinct. A large proportion of the professional and managerial class (AB) are champagne drinkers (37%), whereas 27% of clerical and administrative workers drink champagne (C1). By contrast, 23% of skilled manual workers (C2) tend to drink champagne. Only 13% of non-skilled manual workers, the unemployed, and those on benefits (DE) are champagne drinkers (see Table 2.2). Therefore there is a marked decrease in champagne consumption as we move down the socio-economic scale. This pattern of drinking repeats for the social classes in the drinking of sparkling wine and Cava, although a large proportion of consumers in all social grades consume sparkling wine and Cava is drunk by the fewest consumers by proportion in all social grades with the exception of those in the DE group.

Champagne, the party drink
Source: Fotolia.

It seems that there is an increasing switch to alternatives. Whilst sales have dropped in Britain, they have also dropped 4.9% in France. Only in Japan and the USA have sales increased. Given the likely continuing economic difficulties in Europe, will even better-off consumers continue to pop their champagne corks?

Sources: Evans (2012); Mintel (2012b).

1 Why do you think champagne consumption differs by social class?

2 Do you think that there is any difference by social class between those who drink champagne and those who drink sparkling wine? Why?

3 How do you think the recession in the late 2000s might have affected champagne consumption by social class?

Table 2.2 Cava, champagne, and sparkling wine consumption by social grade

Social grouping	Cava (%)	Drink any champagne (%)	Drink any sparkling wine (%)
AB	30	37	43
C1	22	27	33
C2	19	23	28
DE	15	13	23

- Mature time-rich wine drinkers (18.2% of the population)—this older male segment displays connoisseur tendencies and is interested in the provenance of his wine.

- Young professional wine drinkers (22.9% of the population)—this segment is predominantly female and employed in the professions. She tends to drink red wine, mainly at business functions.

In order to generate clusters of consumers according to different lifestyle types, marketers typically ask consumers questions around their activities, interests, and opinions (AIO). If marketers fit around a consumer's lifestyle, consumers are more likely to benefit from, and appreciate, the proposition offered. One study compared lifestyle segmentation versus demographic segmentation among the Flemish (Dutch-speaking) community in Belgium in four diverse markets (cars, tourism, political parties, and media usage). It indicated the greater predictive power of values, life visions, and aesthetic styles than gender, age, social class, and stage of life when predicting what consumers most wanted in product attributes or benefits sought (Vyncke, 2002). (We cover lifestyle segmentation in Chapter 6.)

Lifecycle

Marketers frequently hypothesize that people in the same stages of life purchase and consume similar kinds of offerings and, to some extent, this is the case. In research undertaken in America in the 1960s, Wells and Gubar (1966) determined that there were nine categories of lifecycle stage in a consumer's life, from leaving home to living as a solitary survivor, i.e. without a spouse. In contemporary society, the lifecycle concept has needed a degree of readjustment to take into account that fewer people are getting married, and at a later age, than they were in the 1960s, that there are singles with children, and increasingly there is a move by couples towards cohabiting. (See Chapter 6 for more on current lifecycle segmentation approaches.)

Visit the **Online Resource Centre** and complete Internet Activity 2.2 to learn more about how VW uses the family lifecycle to communicate its brand values to its target audience.

Most market research agencies routinely measure attitudes and purchasing patterns based on lifecycle stage to determine differences among groups. Table 2.3 indicates that there is a difference in the types of offering purchased as a result, with solitary survivors far more likely to purchase funeral plans, nursing home care, and cruise holidays, and bachelors more likely to spend their income on package and long-haul holidays and educational service products, for instance. Club 18–30, a part of the Thomas Cook Group, caused controversy in the 1990s when it used blatant sexual appeals in its advertising campaigns aimed at young people. The company's campaign, which used a series of adverts to promote the chance for holiday-makers to meet sexual partners, was banned by the ASA because although it did not offend its target market, it offended everyone else. Other tour operators, like Saga, target the older traveller, typically with more sedate appeals.

Ethnic Groups

In a globalized society, marketers are increasingly interested in how we market offerings to ethnic groups within particular populations. These groups can be large and have their own customs, so they represent an opportunity either to build a niche (ethnic) market or to consolidate

Table 2.3 The lifecycle concept

Bachelor stage: young single people not living with parents/guardians	Newly married or long-term cohabiting: young, no children	Full nest I: youngest children under 6	Full nest II: youngest children 6 or over	Full nest III: older married couples with dependent children	Empty nest I: older married couples, no children living at home, chief income earner or both in work	Empty nest II: older married couples, no children living at home, chief income earner or both retired	Solitary survivor, in work	Solitary survivor, retired
Few financial burdens. Fashion opinion leaders. Recreation oriented. Buy: basic kitchen equipment, basic furniture, cars, package and long-haul holidays, education.	Better off financially since dual wages. High purchase rate of consumer durables. Buy: cars, refrigerators, package holidays.	Home purchasing at peak. Low level of savings. Buy: washer-dryers, TV, baby food and related products, vitamins, toys.	Financial position better. Sometimes both parents in work. Buy: larger-sized family food packages, cleaning materials, pianos, child-minding services.	Financial position better still. Both parents more likely to be in work. Some children will have part-time jobs. High average purchase of consumer durables. Buy: better homeware and furniture products, magazines, and non-essential home appliances.	Home ownership at peak. Most satisfied with savings and financial position. Interested in travel, recreation, self-education. More likely to give gifts and make charitable contributions. Less interested in new products. Buy: luxurious holidays, eating out, home improvements.	Drastic cut in household income. More likely to stay at home. Buy: medical appliances and private healthcare, products which help sleep, digestion.	Medical needs will depend on age. Buy: financial, healthcare and retirement plans, meals for one.	Same medical needs as other retired group; drastic cut in income. Buy: household staples, cruise holidays, nursing home services, funeral plans.

Source: Adapted from Wells and Gubar (1966). Published by American Marketing Association.

an existing market, i.e. by appealing to a new set of consumers in addition to the old. In the USA, the Hispanic population—often immigrants from Mexico—and the Black population together represent a sizeable proportion of the total population. European countries also have sizeable ethnic populations; for example, in France there is a large Black African population and in Germany a large Turkish community. France and Britain both have large Muslim populations. In Sweden, there are large groups of Finns, former Yugoslavs, Iraqis, and Iranians. In Dubai, in the United Arab Emirates, a large community of expatriates exists, particularly from India. These groups within a country represent a potential opportunity for the marketer, if they are sizeable enough to be profitable and have similar needs. Cui (1997) proposes that in any country where there are ethnic marketing opportunities a company has four options in deciding its strategic approach.

1 Total standardization—use the existing marketing mix (see Chapter 1) without modification to the ethnic market. This is very difficult to do. Even Coca-Cola, well known for its ardent approach to standardization, adapt their Cola around the world (e.g. by adding pineapple in Indonesia to cater for local tastes).

2 Product adaptation—use the existing marketing mix but adapt the product to the ethnic market in question, e.g. Nivea's Skin Whitening Lotion sells well in Southeast Asian markets. L'Oréal has long recognized the importance of product adaptation and set up the L'Oréal Institute for Ethnic Hair and Skin Research in the USA in 2000.

3 Advertising adaptation—use the current marketing mix but adapt the advertising, particularly the use of foreign languages, to the target ethnic market by promoting the product using different associations that are more resonant with ethnic audiences (e.g. Tesco use point-of- sale promotions written in Polish to target the large number of Polish citizens who came to Britain after 2004, and stores in some parts of Finland advertise in both Swedish and Finnish to cater for the minority Swedish population).

4 Ethnic marketing—use a totally new marketing mix, e.g. Bollywood cinema is aimed at audiences in the Indian sub-continent and in diaspora around the world, using strong love and ethical themes, and a musical format.

Chapter Summary

To consolidate your learning, the key points from this chapter are summarized here.

■ **Explain the consumer product acquisition process.**

Consumer buying behaviour has rational and irrational components, although rational theories have dominated the marketing literature until now. Although there are a variety of models of consumer buying behaviour, the consumer product acquisition model is perhaps the simplest to understand, stressing how the consumer goes through six key stages in the product acquisition process including motive development, information gathering, product evaluation, product selection, acquisition, and re-evaluation.

■ **Explain the processes involved in human perception, learning, and memory in relation to consumer choice.**

The human perception, learning, and memory processes involved in consumer choice are complex. Marketers should ensure when designing advertising, when developing distribution strategies, when designing new offerings, and in other marketing tactics that they (repeatedly) explain this information to consumers in order for them to engage with the information and then subsequently retain it, if it is to influence their buying decisions.

■ **Understand the importance of personality and motivation in consumer behaviour.**

Consumers are motivated differently in their purchasing behaviour depending on their personalities and, to some extent, how they feel that their personality fits with a particular offerings. Maslow's (1943) seminal work on human needs helps us to understand how we are motivated to satisfy five key human desires. From the Theory of Planned Behaviour (Azjen, 1991), we know that how we intend to behave is not always how we actually behave, because this is affected by our attitudes towards the behaviour in question, a subjective norm (how we think others perceive that behaviour), and our own perceptions of how we can control our behaviour.

■ **Describe opinions, attitudes, and values, and how they relate to consumer behaviour.**

Opinions are relatively unstable positions that people take in relation to an issue or assessment of something. Attitudes are more strongly held and are more likely to be linked to our behaviour. Values are more strongly held still and are linked to our conscience. Marketers are interested in all three because they help us to understand consumers better and to develop marketing approaches.

■ **Explain how reference groups influence consumer behaviour.**

Reference groups, including such role models as parents, entertainers, and athletes, have an important socializing influence on our consumption behaviour, particularly in adolescence. However, where we live, what social class we come from, what lifestyle we lead, what stage of the lifecycle we are in, and which ethnic group we belong to all have an impact on our behaviour as consumers. Celebrity endorsers are powerful influencers in this regard, especially as fame is becoming an increasingly attractive quality to many consumers.

 # Review Questions

1 What is the process consumers go through when buying offerings?

2 What is cognitive dissonance and how does it relate to consumer behaviour?

3 How are the psychological concepts of perception, learning, and memory relevant to understanding consumer choice?

4 How are concepts of personality relevant to understanding consumer behaviour?

5 How are concepts of motivation relevant to understanding consumer behaviour?

6 What is the Theory of Planned Behaviour?

7 What are opinions, attitudes, and values, and how do they relate to consumer behaviour?

8 How do reference groups influence how we behave?

9 What is celebrity endorsement?

10 How does lifestyle and ethnicity influence how we buy?

11 What are the four strategies available to ethnic marketers?

Worksheet Summary

To apply the knowledge you have gained from this chapter and test your understanding of consumer buying behaviour visit the **Online Resource Centre** and complete Worksheet 2.1.

Discussion Questions

1 Having read Case Insight 2.1 at the beginning of this chapter, how does Brainjuicer Labs design a research programme which would allow Mastercard to evaluate the actual behaviour of financial services consumers as opposed to intended their behaviour, and the role, if any, played by emotions in their decision-making?

2 Describe the purchasing process you used to obtain the following using the consumer product acquisition model shown in Figure 2.1.

   A chocolate bar, e.g. Snickers or Cadbury's Dairy Milk; Plopp in Sweden;
   B long-haul flight to an exotic destination from your home country;
   C tablet computer to help you write essays and group work for your marketing course;
   D washing machine;
   E a householder receiving refuse collection services from the local council (paid for indirectly through local council taxes).

3 Use the Theory of Planned Behaviour to explain consumer motivations to pursue the following behaviours:

   A purchase of a hotel room at the Burj al Arab in Dubai, UAE;
   B a visit to the Resistance Museum in Oslo, Norway;
   C voting during an election in Afghanistan;
   D bungee jumping in New Zealand.

4 What kinds of celebrity endorsers have you noticed companies using in their advertising to persuade you to adopt the following?

   A sports apparel (e.g. Nike or Adidas);
   B luxury watches (e.g. Omega);
   C beverages (e.g. Coca-Cola or Pepsi);
   D sunglasses (e.g. Police).

5 Use PowerPoint to develop a short presentation on ethnic marketing, highlighting some examples of how different companies target ethnic groups.

@ Visit the **Online Resource Centre** and complete the Multiple Choice Questions to assess your knowledge of Chapter 2.

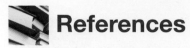 **References**

Agrawal, S. (2012), 'The rising trend of celebrity perfumes', *The Times of India*, 26 August, retrieve from: http://articles.timesofindia.indiatimes.com/2012-08-26/news-interviews/33385950_1_first-perfume-fragrance-tiger-eyes accessed 9 January 2013.

Alba, J. W. and Hutchinson, J. W. (2000), 'Knowledge calibration: what consumers know and what they think they know', *Journal of Consumer Research*, 27, 123–56.

Alderson, W. and Martin, M. W. (1965), 'Toward a formal theory of transactions and transvections', *Journal of Marketing Research*, 2(May), 117–27.

AMA (2013), *Dictionary of Marketing Terms*, retrieve from http://www.marketingpower.com/_layouts/Dictionary.aspx accessed 7 January 2013.

Anon. (2011), 'Burberry and globalization: a checkered story', *The Economist*, 20 January, retrieve from: http://www.economist.com/node/17963363 accessed 8 January 2013.

Anon. (2012a), 'Is this the most disgusting anti-smoking advert yet? Cancerous tumour seen growing out of cigarette in New Year campaign', *The Daily Mail*, 28 December, retrieve from: http://www.dailymail.co.uk/health/article-2253845/Stop-smoking-ad-Cancerous-tumour-grows-cigarette-new-anti-smoking-campaign.html accessed 8 January 2013.

Anon. (2012b), 'Retail fraud: Return to vendor—a dress on loan', *The Economist*, 3 March, retrieve from: http://www.economist.com/node/21548928 accessed 8 January 2013.

Azjen, I. (1991), 'The theory of planned behaviour', *Organisational Behaviour and Human Decision Processes*, 50, 179–211.

Bandura, A. (1977), *Social Learning Theory*, Englewood Cliffs, NJ: Prentice-Hall.

Bargh, J. A. and Chartrand, T. L. (1999), 'The unbearable automaticity of being', *American Psychologist*, 57(7, July), 462–79.

Bartnett, E. (2012), 'Rio Ferdinand Snickers tweets "acceptable" rules ad watchdog', *The Daily Telegraph*, 7 March, retrieve from: http://www.telegraph.co.uk/technology/twitter/9126724/Rio-Ferdinand-Snickers-tweets-acceptable-rules-ad-watchdog.html accessed 7 January 2013.

Bettinghaus, E. P. and Cody, M. J. (1994), *Persuasive Communication* (5th edn), London: Harcourt Brace.

Bettman, J. R. (1979), 'Memory factors in consumer choice: a review', *Journal of Marketing*, 43(Spring), 37–53.

Bradshaw, T. (2012), Digital revenues set to offset CD fall', *The Financial Times*, 24 January, 23.

Bruwer, J. and Li, E. (2007), 'Wine-related lifestyle (WRL) market segmentation: demographic and behavior factors', *Journal of Wine Research*, 18(1), 19–34.

Clee, M. A. and Wicklund, R. A. (1980), 'Consumer behaviour and psychological reactance', *Journal of Consumer Research*, 6, 389–405.

Coleman, R.P. (1983), 'The continuing significance of social class to marketing', *Journal of Consumer Research*, 10(3), 265–80.

Collins, L. and Montgomery, C. (1969), 'The origins of motivational research', *British Journal of Marketing*, 13(2, Summer), 103–13.

Cui, G. (1997), 'Marketing strategies in a multi-ethnic environment', *Journal of Marketing Theory and Practice*, 5(1), 122–35.

Datamonitor (2010), 'The Sun's celebrity-culture perfume will enjoy 15 minutes of fame', *Datamonitor Research Store*, 8 September, retrieve from: http://www.datamonitor.com/store/News/the_suns_celebrity_culture_perfume_will_enjoy_15_minutes_of_fame?productid=A525439C-8877-47D9-B115-956014B53B42 accessed 10 January 2013.

de Correa, T., Hinsley, A. W., and de Zúñiga, H. G. (2010), 'Who interacts on the Web? The intersection of users' personality and social media use', *Computers in Human Behavior*, 26, 247–53.

Dichter, E. (1964), *The Handbook of Consumer Motivation: The Psychology of the World of Objects*, London: McGraw-Hill.

Dubois, B. (2000), *Understanding the Consumer: A European Perspective*, London: FT/Prentice Hall.

Dubois, B. and Duquesne, P. (1993), 'The market for luxury goods: income versus culture', *European Journal of Marketing*, 27(1), 35–44.

Elberse, A. (2010), 'Bye-bye bundles: the unbundling of music in digital channels', *Journal of Marketing*, 74(May), 107–23.

Evans, B. (2012), 'Now even France is ditching the fizz! Recession cuts champagne sales across Europe', *The Daily Mail*, 28 December, retrieve from: http://www.dailymail.co.uk/news/article-2254290/Now-France-ditching-fizz-Recession-cuts-champagne-sales-Europe.html accessed 10 January 2013.

Festinger, L. (1957), *A Theory of Cognitive Dissonance*, Palo Alto, CA: Stanford University Press.

Freud, S. (1927), *The Ego and the Id*, Richmond: Hogarth Press.

Hawkes, S. (2012), 'A pint of Girlsberg', *The Sun*, 13 October, retrieve from: http://www.thesun.co.uk/sol/homepage/news/money/4586900/Carlsberg-plan-sweeten-beer-lager-attract-more-ladies-women-Jorgen-Buhl-Rasmussen.html accessed 8 January 2013.

Holbrook, M. B. and Hirschmann, E. C. (1982), 'The experiential aspects of consumption: consumer fantasies, feelings and fun', *Journal of Consumer Research*, 9 (September), 132–40.

Holbrook, M. B., Lehmann, D. R., and O'Shaughnessy, J. (1986), 'Using versus choosing: the relationship of the consumption experience to reasons for purchasing', *European Journal of Marketing*, 20(8), 49–62.

Howard, J. A. and Sheth, J. N. (1969), *The Theory of Buyer Behavior*, New York: John Wiley.

Joseph, S. (2012a), 'Molson Coors pulls "ladylike beer"', *Marketing Week*, 24 September, retrieve from: http://www.marketingweek.co.uk/news/molson-coors-pulls-ladylike-beer/4003968.article accessed 8 January 2013.

Joseph, S. (2012b), 'Beer should not be gender exclusive', *Marketing Week*, 28 September, retrieve from: http://www.marketingweek.co.uk/news/beer-should-not-be-gender-exclusive/4004048.article accessed 8 January 2013.

Johnson, E. J. and Russo, J. E. (1978), 'The organisation of product information in memory identified by recall times', in K. Hunt (ed.), *Advances in Consumer Research*, Vol. V, Chicago, IL: Association for Consumer Research, 79–86.

Kiesnoski, K. (2009), 'Immersing in Eastern spirituality in South Korea Templestay', *Travel Weekly*, 15 June, retrieve from: http://www.travelweekly.com/Destinations2001-2007/Immersing-in-Eastern-spirituality-in-South-Korea-Templestay/ accessed 8 January 2013.

King, T., Dennis, C., and Wright, L.T. (2008), 'Myopia, customer returns and the theory of planned behaviour', *Journal of Marketing Management*, 24(1–2), 185–203.

King, T. and Balmer, J. (2012), 'When the customer isn't right', *HBR Blog Network*, 17 February, retrieve from: http://blogs.hbr.org/cs/2012/02/when_the_customer_isnt_right.html accessed 8 January 2013.

Kotler, P. (1965), 'Behavioral models for analyzing buyers', *Journal of Marketing*, 29(October), 37–45.

Lee, Y. and Nakashima, R. (2012), 'Gangnam style' riches grow by clicks and bounds, but mostly overseas', *The New York Times*, 6 December, retrieve from: http://www.nytimes.com/2012/12/07/business/global/gangnam-style-riches-grow-by-clicks-and-bounds-but-mostly-overseas.html?_r=0 accessed 7 January 2013.

McRae, R. R. and Costa, P. T. (1987), 'Validation of the five-factor model of personality across instruments and observers', *Journal of Personality and Social Psychology*, 52, 81–90.

Martin, C. A. and Bush, A. J. (2000), 'Do role models influence teenagers' purchase intentions and behavior?', *Journal of Consumer Marketing*, 17(5), 441–54.

Maslow, A. H. (1943), 'A theory of motivation', *Psychological Review*, 50, 370–96.

Matzler, K., Bidmon, S., and Grabner-Kräuter, S. (2006), 'Individual determinants of brand affect: the role of the personality traits of extraversion and openness to experience', *Journal of Product and Brand Management*, 15(7), 427–34.

Mick, D. G. and DeMoss, M. (1990), 'To me from me: a descriptive phenomenology of self-gifts', *Advances in Consumer Research*, 17, 677–82.

Mindak, W. A. (1961), 'Fitting the semantic differential to the marketing problem', *Journal of Marketing*, 25(April), 29–33.

Mintel (2011), *Men's Grooming and Shaving Products—UK—October 2011*, London: Mintel, retrieve from: http://www.mintel.com accessed 8 January 2013.

Mintel (2012a), *Social Media: Beauty and Personal Care—UK—April 2012*, London: Mintel, retrieve from: http://www.mintel.com, accessed 7 January 2013.

Mintel (2012b), *Champagne and Sparkling Wines—UK—July 2012* London: Mintel, retrieve from: http://www.mintel.com accessed 7 January 2013.

Mintel (2012c), *Car Retailing—UK—July 2012*, London: Mintel, retrieve from: http://www.mintel.com accessed 8 January 2013.

Mintel (2012d), *Men's and Women's Fragrances—UK—September 2012*, London: Mintel, retrieve from: http://www.mintel.com accessed 8 January 2013.

Moschis, G. P. and Churchill, G. A., Jr (1978), 'Consumer socialisation: a theoretical and empirical analysis', *Journal of Marketing Research*, 15(November), 599–609.

Pollard, T. (2012), 'UK 2011 car sales analysis: winners and losers', *Car*, 8 January, retrieve from: http://www.carmagazine.co.uk/News/Search-Results/Industry-News/UK-2011-car-sales-analysis-winners-and-losers/ accessed 8 January 2013.

Rainey, S. (2012), 'The sweet smell of celebs', *The Daily Telegraph*, 27 December, retrieve from: http://www.telegraph.co.uk/news/celebritynews/9767260/The-sweet-smell-of-celebs.html accessed 10 January 2013.

Ratchford, B.T. (1987), 'New insights about the FCB grid', *Journal of Advertising Research*, 27(4), 24–38.

Rummell, A., Howard, J., Swinton, J. M., and Seymour, D. B. (2000), 'You can't have that! A study of reactance effects and children's consumer behaviour', *Journal of Marketing Theory and Practice*, 8(1), 38–45.

Senecal, S. and Nantal, J. (2004), 'The influence of online product recommendations on consumers' online choices', *Journal of Retailing*, 80, 159–69.

Sheldrake, P. (2011), *The Business of Influence: Reframing Marketing and PR for the Digital Age*, Chichester: John Wiley.

Skinner, B. F. (1954), 'The science of learning and the art of teaching', *Harvard Educational Review*, 24, 88–97.

SMMT (2012), '2012 new car market tops two million units, a four-year high', *Society of Motor Manufacturers and Traders*, News Release 5095, 7 January, retrieve from: http://www.smmt.co.uk/2013/01/2012-new-car-market-tops-two-million-units-hitting-four-year-high/ accessed 8 January 2013.

Udell, J. G. (1964), 'A new approach to consumer motivation', *Journal of Retailing*, Winter, 6–10.

Uricchio, M. (2012), 'Smell like a star: fragrance makers bet on celebrity selling power', *Pittsburgh Post-Gazette*, http://www.post-gazette.com/stories/sectionfront/life/smell-like-a-star-fragrance-makers-bet-on-celebrity-selling-power-213452/ accessed 9 January 2013.

Vidalon, D. and Pennetier, M. (2013), 'Virgin Megastore France to file for insolvency January 9', *Reuters*, 8 January, retrieve from: http://www.reuters.com/article/2013/01/08/us-virginmegastorefrance-insolvency-idUSBRE9070SV20130108 accessed 10 January 2013.

VisitSeoul (nd), 'Templestay: Finding your true self', retrieve from: http://www.visitseoul.net/en/article/article.do?_method=view&art_id=39120&lang=en&m=0004004015002&p=07 accessed 8 January 2013.

Vyncke, P. (2002), 'Lifestyle segmentation: From attitudes, interests and opinions to values, aesthetic styles, life visions and media preferences', *European Journal of Communication*, 17, 445–63.

Warr, P. (2012), 'Interview: How celebrity fragrances work', *My Daily*, 20 August, retrieve from: http://www.mydaily.co.uk/2012/08/20/celebrity-fragrance_n_1811294.html accessed 9 January 2013.

Wells, W. D. and Gubar, G. (1966), 'Life cycle concept in marketing research', *Journal of Marketing Research*, 3(November), 355–63.

Williams, T.G. (2002), 'Social class influences on purchase evaluation criteria', *Journal of Consumer Marketing*, 19(3), 249–76.

Willifer, M. (2012), 'A beer for no man', *Marketing*, 3 October, 14.

You-Sun, N. (2013), 'The spirit is willing', *Bangkok Post*, 7 January, Asia Focus Supplement, 6.

Chapter 3
Marketing Research and Customer Insight

If the adver catches the engageme can be seer in the gaze

Learning Outcomes

After studying this chapter, you will be able to:

▸ Define the terms market research, marketing research, and customer insight

▸ Describe the role of marketing information systems in the insight process

▸ Explain the role of marketing research and list the range of possible research approaches

▸ Discuss the importance of ethics and the adoption of a Code of Conduct in marketing research

▸ Note the concept of equivalence in relation to obtaining comparable data

▸ List the problems arising when coordinating international marketing research

Case Insight 3.1
MESH Planning

Market Insight 3.1
Insight Brings New Vision to Yeo Valley

Market Insight 3.2
CHP System Customer Insight: The Brief

Market Insight 3.3
CHP System Customer Insight: The Proposal

Market Insight 3.4
How Scent Sells Lingerie at Hunkemöller

Market Insight 3.5
Momentum Research: Reading People

Case Insight 3.1

How should organizations measure the effectiveness of all touchpoints in interactions with customers, not just marketing communications? We speak to MESH Planning's CEO, Fiona Blades, to find out more.

MESH Planning, an innovative market research agency, was set up in 2006. Fiona Blades had worked previously as an advertising planning director, seeing at first hand how organizations were seldom able to get the data they needed from traditional campaign evaluation, since these were often overly focused on TV advertising. There was also a tendency to believe that, because advertising effectiveness questions were added to **brand health monitoring**, it was advertising that caused changes in brand health when this is often not the case. In fact, MESH data shows that usage is the most influential **touchpoint** for almost all categories of offering. Results of traditional campaign analysis were always reported well after the campaign, making it too late to make interim changes. MESH Planning's response was to develop a research process to measure touchpoint effectiveness using a process called real-time experience tracking (RET). This focuses on experiences that capture the essence of what brands are made of, not interim measures.

RET fuses a number of different data sources, using traditional survey data as well as analysing experiences quantitatively, and then applying statistical measurements to them and viewing qualitative comments. Because MESH has planners (account planners and media planners) as well as researchers, the output for the client is more recommendation/action focused than findings/ research focused.

Clients come to MESH because RET collects people's responses to different touchpoints, including those that they haven't been able to get before (e.g. seeing whether it is TV, online, or retail activity which drives brand consideration). The approach is faster and more cost effective than previous tools, such as **market mix modelling**. Beyond marketing campaigns, clients want to understand the impact of retail activity and the path to purchase. MESH clients have reported good results with RET: Energizer executives calculated that the new measures led to a threefold improvement in advertising cost-effectiveness, increasing Energizer's revenue in the razor category by 10% in less than four months; LG Electronics won the coveted POPAI award for retail marketing effectiveness and attributed this to working with MESH; and BSkyB re-evaluated how to spend £150m per annum using RET analytics.

Gatorade, another client, decided to re-position its offering from being in the sports drink category to sports nutrition. Its launch in Mexico included TV advertising, sponsorship, and an innovative channel strategy which used experiential channels such as gyms, fitness centres, and parks.

How could research be designed to determine, if someone experienced an experiential touchpoint, whether having this experience impacted positively on their perceptions of the brand, and specifically, those related to Gatorade's sports nutrition attributes?

Introduction

What's the most persuasive ad you've seen recently? How do companies develop successful offerings? Most of us take it for granted that great companies make great offerings. But, more often than not, companies develop extraordinary propositions using research programmes designed to identify customers' changing needs. Offerings don't design themselves. They are made in the knowledge that market research and customer insight can bring. Along with marketing communications, market research is a key sub-discipline of marketing practice and a fundamental component of the marketing philosophy.

Marketing research is affected by changing technology, affecting how, where, and when we collect insight. We begin by defining the difference between 'marketing research' and 'market research'. Whereas market research is conducted to understand markets—customers, competitors, and industries—marketing research determines the impact of marketing strategies and tactics, in addition to collecting information on customers, competitors, and industries. Marketing research subsumes market research. We also cover customer insight in this chapter because it is important to understand how the knowledge generated from various insights, including research, leads to strategic marketing choices. In this chapter, we discuss **marketing information systems**. Finally, we consider the challenges of conducting international marketing research.

The first systematic data collection exercise began with the census of the Chinese people around AD 2. In Britain, the first official census of people took place in AD 1801 (Anon., 1989). However, the first marketing research department probably originated from the economic research department at P&G in the USA in 1923 to 'find out what people wanted and give it to them' (McCraw, 2000). However, research into consumer tastes, habits, and buying patterns occurred after the First World War (Arvidsson, 2004). Other pioneers included George Gallup (1901–84), who invented the Gallup public opinion survey in 1936 (Anon., 1989) and Arthur Charles Nielsen Sr, who invented TV audience rating measurement (Nielsen, 2013).

Definitions of Marketing Research and Customer Insight

Marketing research generates information to provide management with sufficient insight to make informed decisions. It follows the philosophical marketing premise that organizations must understand the motivations, desires, and behaviour of their customers and consumers to survive and thrive. We speak of market research, marketing research, and customer insight, but these terms are not interchangeable, although they are related. We outline their definitions in Table 3.1.

Visit the **Online Resource Centre** and follow the weblinks to the MRS and ESOMAR to learn more about these professional marketing research associations.

Market research is work undertaken to determine the structural characteristics of the industry of concern (e.g. demand, market share, market volumes, customer characteristics, and segmentation), whereas marketing research is work undertaken to understand how to make specific marketing strategy decisions (e.g. for pricing, sales forecasting, proposition testing,

Table 3.1 Definitions in marketing research

Term	Originator	Definition
Market Research	The International Chamber of Commerce (ICC)/ European Society for Opinion and Market Research (ESOMAR)	'Market research, which includes social and opinion research, is the systematic gathering and interpretation of information about individuals or organizations using the statistical and analytical methods and techniques of the applied social sciences to gain insight or support decision making. The identity of respondents will not be revealed to the user of the information without explicit consent and no sales approach will be made to them as a direct result of their having provided information' (ESOMAR, 2008)
	The Market Research Society (MRS)	'The collection and analysis of data from a sample or census of individuals or organizations relating to their characteristics, behaviour, attitudes, opinions or possessions. It includes all forms of market, opinion and social research such as consumer and industrial surveys, psychological investigations, qualitative interviews and group discussions, observational, ethnographic and **panel studies**' (MRS, 2010)
Marketing Research	The American Marketing Association	'Marketing research is the function that links the consumer, customer, and public to the marketer through information—information used to identify and define marketing opportunities and problems; generate, refine, and evaluate marketing actions; monitor marketing performance; and improve understanding of marketing as a process. Marketing research specifies the information required to address these issues, designs the method for collecting information, manages and implements the data collection process, analyzes the results, and communicates the findings and their implications' (AMA, 2004).
Customer Insight	Smith, Wilson, and Clark	'Customer insight is knowledge about customers which meets the criteria of an organizational strength; that is, it is valuable, rare and difficult to imitate and which the organization is aligned to make use of.' (Smith *et al.,* 2006).

and promotion research) (Chisnall, 1992). In contrast, Smith *et al.* (2006) suggest that customer insight is valuable, rare, and inimitable (i.e. not capable of being copied) knowledge about customers which an organization can make use of to formulate management decisions.

Research is a foundational element of marketing practice, but some companies value it more than others. For example, companies tend to spend between 0.5% and 1% of their revenues on research when they would be better off spending more to help fine tune their advertising and promotion (Kotler, 2005). A further problem occurs when organizations commission research, as frequently they do not provide details of an overarching strategic problem. Agencies also often fail to work with organizations to integrate into the research process all the information an organization has about its market and current situation (Cowan, 2008).

Marketing Information Systems and the Insight Process

Marketing information should be used for timely continuous information to support decision-making. The kind of information marketers need includes (Ashill and Jobber, 2001):

- aggregated marketing information in quarterly annual summaries;
- aggregated marketing information around offerings/markets (e.g. sales data);
- analytical information for decision models (e.g. SWOT, segmentation analyses);
- internally focused marketing information (e.g. sales, costs, marketing performance indicators);
- externally focused marketing information (e.g. macro and industry trends);
- historical information (e.g. sales, profitability, market trends);
- future-oriented marketing information (e.g. horizon scanning information);
- quantitative marketing information (e.g. costs, profit, market share, customer satisfaction, **net promoter score**);
- qualitative marketing information (e.g. buyer behaviour, competitor strategy information).

The above information could be provided on a continuous and/or an ad hoc basis. Continuous industry trend information is gleaned from industry reports and secondary data sources. However, the market research manager should remember to buy the reports and input the data into a marketing information system (MkIS). Other information may be obtained on an ad hoc basis by commissioning specialist market research projects (e.g. for pricing or segmentation research). This also needs to be fed into the MkIS to provide the company with an up-to-date picture. The qualitative information related to competitor strategy information is gleaned from sales reports or reports from overseas agents, for example. The main difficulty for the marketing manager is to obtain and customize the marketing information system to fit their company's specific needs, as these change according to industry, and to ensure that the data are input on a timely and continuous basis. Axelrod (1970) suggests adherence to the following 14 basic rules for building a MkIS:

1 get the top management involved;
2 set the objective for the system carefully;
3 figure out what decisions your MkIS will influence;
4 communicate the benefits of the system to users;
5 hire and motivate the right people;
6 free the MkIS from accounting domination;
7 develop the system on a gradual and systematic basis;
8 run a new MkIS in parallel with existing procedures;
9 provide results from the system to users quickly after its initiation;
10 provide information on a fast turnaround basis;
11 tie the MkIS with existing data collection procedures;
12 balance the work of the MkIS between development and operations;

13 feed valid meaningful data into the system, not useless information;

14 design a security system to ensure that different groups get different access to the information.

Fusing data from an MkIS with data from the customer relationship management (CRM) systems (see Chapter 14), including social CRM systems (i.e. software tracking customers' use of an organization's websites and presence on social media) is important. Social CRM systems provide data on purchase histories, returns, visits to e-commerce sites, dwell time on sites, sentiment analysis, and social media monitoring information, for example through proprietary software programmes such as Radian6 which allows monitoring of blogs, forums, video, and image-sharing sites (Greenberg, 2010). (See Chapter 17 on measuring social media effectiveness.)

Customer insight is derived from fusing knowledge generated from a range of sources including industry reports; sales force data, **competitive intelligence**, CRM data, employee feedback, social media analysis data, and managerial intuition. Smith *et al.* (2006) developed 12 rules for generating customer value from the insight process as follows.

1. Find data which records customers' unmet, as well as met, needs.
2. Use and synthesize multiple data sources.
3. Use information to challenge current thinking (i.e. test implicit beliefs about the market).
4. Do not rely on purely statistical analysis of quantitative data.
5. Be explicit and rigorous about managing knowledge (i.e. develop a set of clear and connected processes).
6. Begin with real needs-based segments.
7. Target value-seeking segments (i.e. rather than price-driven segments).
8. Deliver value proportional to the change achieved (i.e. greater value is achieved when the value proposition is changed substantially).
9. Change what the customer wants changing, not just change what you can change.
10. Act faster than the market changes.
11. Create a knowledge-sharing culture.
12. Create value in partnership with other functions and groups within the organization.

Cowan (2008) suggests that for organizations to genuinely make use of insight there are numerous implications for CEOs/CMOs, researchers, and insight managers.

- CEO/CMOs should recognize the importance of supporting the insight process, ask 'helicopter' (i.e. wide-scoping) questions, not try to guess the answers to strategic problems, demand evidence-based answers, and provide the necessary resources.
- Researchers: should view themselves as problem-solvers not reporters, focus on trying to gain a causal understanding, not just describing attitudes, and focus on changing the marketing situation.
- Insight managers should challenge strategy assumptions that the organization is making, challenge the 'obvious' solution since it is often wrong, analyse and combine all existing relevant data, and devote greater resources to extracting insight.

Britain's largest supermarket group Tesco uses dunnhumby, a customer analytics agency, to analyse its customer data. Each customer has a unique profile of past purchase transactions linked to lifestyle data derived from their address details. This information allows Tesco to determine the importance and use of price promotions, the degree of promotional buying, the portfolio of offerings a customer purchases, how much they spend on their groceries, and other issues (Humby, 2007). Therefore data and use of data have become a strategic asset to the firm, allowing Tesco to differentiate itself from competitors through highly effective loyalty programmes.

Commissioning Market Research

When commissioning research, the client determines whether or not he/she wants to commission an agency, a consultant, a field and tabulation (tab) agency, or a data preparation and analysis agency. Typically, a consultant might do a job that does not require extensive fieldwork, a field and tab agency when the organization can design its own research but not undertake the data collection, a data preparation and analysis agency when it can both design and collect the data but does not have the expertise to analyse it, and a **full-service agency** when it does not have the expertise to design the research and collect or analyse the data (see Market Insight 3.1 for example).

Agencies are shortlisted according to some criteria and asked to make a presentation of their services. Visits are made to their premises to check the quality of their staff and facilities, and previous reports considered to assess the quality of their work. Permission to interview or obtain references from their clients is usually requested. Each agency is evaluated on its ability to undertake work of an acceptable quality at an appropriate price. The criteria used to evaluate an agency's suitability (after proposal submission) includes the following:

- the agency's reputation;
- the agency's perceived expertise;
- whether the study offers value for money;
- the time taken to complete the study;
- the likelihood that the research design will provide insights into the **management problem**.

Shortlisted agencies are given a preliminary outline of the client's needs in a **research brief** and asked to provide proposals on research methodology, timing, and costs. After this, an agency is selected to undertake the work required. In the long term, clients are most satisfied with flexible agencies that avoid rigid research solutions and demonstrate professional knowledge of the industry, an ability to focus on the management problem and provide solutions, and consistent service quality (Cater and Zabkar, 2009).

The Marketing Research Brief

The research brief is a formal document prepared by a client organization and submitted to the marketing research agency. When marketing research is conducted in-house, the manager requiring the research prepares a brief for the market research manager. The brief outlines a

Market Insight 3.1

Insight Brings New Vision to Yeo Valley

When recession hit the UK in 2008, it also put a stop to the high revenue growth previously enjoyed by Yeo Valley, the British organic dairy manufacturer. For the previous seven years, the company had enjoyed 20–40% growth. In the midst of the recession, as consumers saved their pennies, supermarket retailers shifted their strategy to selling more own-label offerings. Although Yeo Valley supplied own-label offerings to supermarkets, it perceived the slump in demand for its branded offerings as a potential long-term threat to the company. So it hired Big Fish, a brand consultancy. They identified that the brand comprised five key factors. It was real (Yeo Valley is an English place), British, family-owned, fun, and sustainable. The agency tested these brand values by researching consumers in discussion groups of between eight and ten people. The company also researched their retail customers using telephone interviewing, using a different agency, 100% Cotton. These studies together helped Yeo Valley

design new packaging which was tested on consumers in a further round of research. 100% Cotton developed new techniques including 'triangular' research with themselves, Yeo Valley, and a retailer in the same workshop. Retailer participants included buyers, but also proposition development, technical, and customer planning teams. The result of the insight was that Yeo Valley designed new TV advertising which went viral, significantly raising brand awareness by 71% and bringing half a million new households to the brand. For the year ending May 2012, pre-tax profits doubled and turnover was up 13%.

Sources: Gosling (2012); Sims (2013); https://www.yeovalley.co.uk/

1 Do you think it was necessary to undertake all the research that they did?

2 Why do you think that Yeo Valley used different interviewing methods for retailer and consumer buyers?

3 How does the insight process used here change the relationship between the insight agency and the organization?

Research Insight 3.1

To take your learning further, you might wish to read this influential paper.

Moorman, C., Zaltmann, G., and Desphandé, R. (1992), 'Relationships between providers and users of market research: the dynamics of trust within and between organizations', *Journal of Marketing Research*, **29(3), 314–28.**

In this article, the authors investigate the role of trust between market research users and providers, developing a theory of user–provider relationships focused on personal trust. The authors indicate that trust and perceived quality of interaction between the research user and the provider contribute most to the research findings actually being implemented. The message is to use market researchers that are highly reputable and develop a good working relationship with them to ensure that the research is operationalizable.

@ **Visit the Online Resource Centre to read the abstract and access the full paper.**

Market Insight 3.2

CHP System Customer Insight: The Brief

Markus Henneberg is the director of Turbine Generators Limited (TGL), a start-up combined heat and power (CHP) system manufacturing company based in Ipswich. The company has won government funding to develop a prototype CHP system. Having just joined the company, Markus decides that the company should invest in concept testing research to determine the market potential for the CHP offering, which is likely to appeal to both domestic residential customers (who seek to replace their household boilers with a system which is 20% more efficient) and industrial customers (e.g. national house builders who run many homes off one large CHP system and require larger-scale energy efficiency). Markus expects the energy retail sector to see significant turbulence over the next five years. Whilst the CHP market is relatively new, his competitive intelligence indicates that several other similar research and development projects are being undertaken by rival start-ups and established boiler manufacturers. Accordingly, TGL would like to know whether their concept CHP system is acceptable to its potential industrial and domestic customers, what the likely market potential is for this offering, and what features are important to potential residential and industrial customers. Markus invites proposals from four market research agencies and provides them with the following information concerning TGL's research objectives. Specifically, they would like this research to do the following for both potential residential and industrial customers.

1. Indicate how both sets of potential customers perceive this offering and its expected performance.

2. Determine when/where/how existing boiler/CHP systems (and associated services) are sourced and bought and the price ranges customers are prepared to pay.

3. Compare the TGL prototype CHP product with existing alternative offerings for each market to determine which products customers perceive are best.

4. Determine what customers' decision factors are when choosing a particular supplier.

5. Evaluate the market potential of the two markets and provide an indication of the existing competition.

Markus spends two hours meeting with each of four bidding organizations, briefing them on the background to the company and outlining why he wants to conduct the research requested. Of the four companies who each submit a proposal, Markus is most impressed with the one submitted by Robinson–Bennett International. He decides to meet its Research Director to discuss their proposal.

Source: Market Research Society (MRS). Adapted and reproduced with kind permission.

1 Do you think that this brief has clear research objectives? Why do you say this?

2 Does the research brief indicate or imply that a specific methodology should be used? If so, which method does it imply?

3 What other types of research might be conducted to tackle the given research objectives?

management problem to be investigated (see Market Insight 3.2 for an example). The typical contents of a research brief include the following.

- A background summary—providing a brief introduction and details about the company and its offerings.

- The management problem—a clear statement of why the research is needed and what business decisions depend upon its outcome.

- The marketing research questions—a detailed list of the information necessary to make the decisions outlined.

- The intended scope of the research—the areas to be covered, which industries, type of customer—should be provided. The brief should give an indication of when the information is required and why that date is important (e.g. pricing research required for a sales forecast meeting).

- Tendering procedures—the client organization should outline how agencies are selected as a result of the tendering process. Specific information may be required, such as CVs from agency personnel involved in the study and referee contact addresses. The number of copies of the report required and preferences with regard to layout and format are also outlined.

The Marketing Research Process

There are numerous basic stages that guide a marketing research project (see Figure 3.1). The first, most crucial, stage involves problem definition and setting the information needs of the decision-makers. The client organization explains the basis of the problem(s) it faces to the market researcher. This might be the need to understand market volumes in a potential new market or the reason for an unexpected sudden increase in uptake of an offering. Problem definition

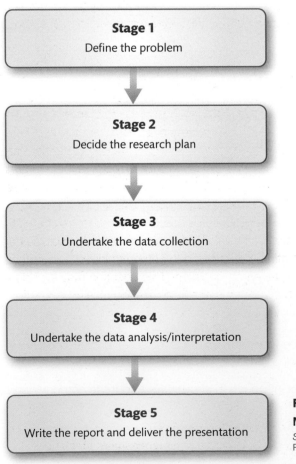

Stage 1
Define the problem

Stage 2
Decide the research plan

Stage 3
Undertake the data collection

Stage 4
Undertake the data analysis/interpretation

Stage 5
Write the report and deliver the presentation

Figure 3.1

Marketing research process

Source: Baines and Chansarkar (2002). © John Wiley & Sons. Reproduced with permission.

Carrefour, the French supermarket chain, operates globally
Source: © Carrefour.

does not always imply that threats face the organization. The initial stage allows the organization to assess its current position, define its information needs, and make informed decisions about its future.

Stage 1. Problem Definition

This process occurs when an organization provides a marketing research brief defining the management problem. Typically, the problem is described in vague terms as organizations are not always sure what information they require. An example might be Carrefour, the supermarket chain, explaining that sales are not as strong as expected in their Czech Republic stores and wondering whether or not this is due to the emergence of a competitor supermarket (see Figure 3.2). The marketing researcher then translates the management problem into a marketing research question. This subsequent problem description provides the market researcher with relatively little depth of understanding of the situation in which the supermarket finds itself, so he/she needs to discuss the problem with the staff commissioning the study to investigate further. This leads to the development of a marketing research question. This question may include a number of sub-questions for further exploration. For example, a marketing research question, and a number of more specific sub-questions, is shown in Figure 3.3.

> **Management problem**
>
> Sales at the new store have not met management expectations, possibly due to the emergence of a new competitor

Figure 3.2

Example of a management problem

MARKETING RESEARCH QUESTION

Why are sales levels not meeting management expectations?

1. Sub-question: Has customer disposable income in the area declined over the last six months?
2. Sub-question: Is a new competitor, Tesco, taking away customers?
3. Sub-question: Are customers tired/bored of the current product range in the existing supermarket?
4. Sub-question: Are customers conducting more of their shopping online?
5. Sub-question: Were management expectations set too high and/or market potential overestimated?

Figure 3.3

Example of a marketing research question

The marketing research question transforms the management problem into a question while trying to remove any assumptions made by the organization's management. Sometimes, the management problem is clear. The organization needs a customer profile, an industry profile, an understanding of buyer behaviour, or to test advertising concepts for its next campaign and so on. The more clearly the commissioning organization defines the management problem, the easier it is to design the research to solve that problem. Once the agency discusses the brief with the client, the agency provides a detailed outline of how they will investigate the problem. This document is called the research proposal. Figure 3.4 briefly outlines a typical marketing **research proposal** and Market Insight 3.3 provides an example.

The basic structure and contents of a typical research proposal should include the following:

► **Executive Summary**—a brief summary of the research project including the major outcomes and findings. Rarely more than one page in length. It allows the reader to obtain a summary of the main points of the project without having to read the full report.
► **Background to the Research**—an outline of the problem or situation and the issues surrounding this problem. This section demonstrates the researcher's understanding of the management problem.
► **Research Objectives**—an outline of the objectives of the research project including the data to be generated and how this will be used to address the management problem.
► **Research Design**—a clear non-technical description of the research type adopted and the specific techniques to be used to gather the required information. This will include details on data-collection instruments, sampling procedures and analytical techniques.
► **Personnel Specification**—the details of the people involved in the collection and analysis of the data, providing a named liaison person and outlining the company's credibility in undertaking the work.
► **Time Schedule**—an outline of the time requirements with dates for the various stages to completion and presentation of results.
► **Costs**—a detailed analysis of the costs involved in the project is usually included for large projects or simply a total cost for the project.
► **References**—typically three references are outlined so that a client can be sure that an agency has the requisite capability to do the job in hand.

Figure 3.4

A marketing research proposal outline

● ●

Market Insight 3.3

CHP System Customer Insight: The Proposal

Client's Information Needs

The client Turbine Generators Ltd, a start-up company is looking to exploit new combined heat and power system technologies in residential and industrial markets using natural gas. Its prototype system is 20% more efficient than existing boiler systems in the marketplace, producing savings in energy costs and reductions in carbon emissions. This prototype system is likely to appeal not only to householders replacing existing boiler systems but also to industries aiming to reduce their rising energy costs. Turbine Generators Ltd wishes to understand whether or not its prototype CHP system is acceptable to both residential and industrial customers, what decision factors they rely on when selecting a system of this type, what their price ranges are for comparable systems, how this system compares with existing systems available in the marketplace, and what the market potential for each of the two main markets is.

Research Objectives

The research will answer the following questions:

1. **What is the size of the marketplace for combined heat and power systems for a) residential customers and b) industrial customers?**

2. **What channels are used by existing competitors within the residential and industrial marketplaces to distribute CHP/boiler products and what are those competitors' relative market shares?**

3. **What criteria do industrial and residential customers use to evaluate the perceived value of different CHP/boiler systems before purchase?**

4. **How do industrial and residential customers rate TGL's prototype CHP system and those** of its competitors in relation to the attributes listed in research question 3? (Attributes are likely to include price, service, performance, warranty, etc.).

5. **What is the decision-making process used by a) industrial customers and b) residential customers when they seek to purchase a boiler/CHP system (and associated services)?**

Research Programme Proposed

Initially, a three-stage research programme is recommended, involving desk research, qualitative research, and quantitative research. We recommend that desk research be carried out initially to map the structure of this market offering for both industrial and residential markets. Qualitative research will be carried out before the quantitative stage to provide a stronger understanding of how potential customers perceive this new offering and the decision-making processes they go through to purchase it. This will provide a stronger understanding of how the samples should be determined in the quantitative research. Finally, quantitative research will be used to provide a stronger understanding of the market potential for the offering and a representative overview of how industrial and residential customers rate the prototype and those of its competitors on various dimensions.

Desk Research Phase

This phase will involve the systematic search of market intelligence databases, industry reports, and industry magazines, together with a trawl of the websites and publicly available company records of the main existing distributors and manufacturers in the CHP/boiler market, including members of the Energy Retail Association. The intention of this research is to pull together a market map of the distribution arrangements within both the residential and industrial markets for CHP/boiler products. Therefore the analysis aims to provide answers to the research questions 1 and 2.

Market Insight 3.3
continued

Qualitative Research Phase

Sampling

Given the potential diverse client base and the need to cover both industrial and residential markets, we recommend that we conduct a series of 20 in-depth interviews across a variety of industrial segments (identified in the desk research phase) with industrial customers (five SMEs, five medium-sized companies, five large companies, and five mixed) and a total of 12 discussion groups in different cities across the UK (by male/female in the following cities: London, Cardiff, Glasgow, Belfast, Birmingham, and Bristol). In addition to the gender mix, the groups will incorporate a mix of age groups and previous experience of buying a boiler/CHP system. The in-depth interviews with potential industrial customers will be conducted in person at the offices of the interviewee using an interview of approximately 45 minutes duration. The discussion groups will last between 60 and 90 minutes and will be held at a central location within each of the cities listed.

Data Analysis

The qualitative data will be fully transcribed before analysis. All verbatim quotes obtained in in-depth interviews and discussion groups are reviewed for the first set of interviews to ensure that our interviewers are questioning correctly before they proceed further. The analysis will use a thematic analytic approach based on research questions 3, 4, and 5.

Quantitative Research Phase

For this stage, we propose to use a computer-assisted web interviewing methodology (CAWI) for both the industrial and the residential customers. CAWI allows us to use complex question routing and skip patterns, and undertake more efficient sample management. We would aim to interview approximately 200 industrial interviewees using a judgemental sampling method, identifying appropriate companies and respondents in conjunction with TGL. For the residential customer research, we would aim to purchase six questions on a standard omnibus survey through a subcontracted research agency.

Sampling

On the industrial survey, respondents will be screened to ensure that they are the appropriate person responsible for purchasing CHP or boiler systems for their organization. We expect that this will differ and be dependent on sector, and will include a cross-section of job titles from procurement to technical managers to quantity surveyors. To determine the correct number of interviews to conduct in a given research study, we need to consider several factors including the overall objective, requirements for subset analysis, and in this case the overall size of the target universe. Given the diverse customer base and target market, we recommend using an overall sample size of 200 interviews. Using standard industrial classification (SIC) codes and company size, we will draw the sample proportionally to TGL's key intended target markets using a judgemental sampling methodology. In order to facilitate the selection of the sample, we will purchase lists of client companies from Dun & Bradstreet and/or other reputable list providers.

On the residential survey, we will use a subcontracted omnibus survey provider. Respondents will be screened to ensure that they either own or mortgage their own home. The subcontracted agency typically uses a sample size of c. 1,000 respondents and aims to ensure that the sample is representative of the UK population by questioning panels constructed using a combination of gender, working status, location, age, ethnicity, and socio-economic status. The survey uses a random sampling methodology and weighting to ensure a representative sample.

Data Analysis

On finalization of the fieldwork, collected data will be processed and tabulated. Data are then tested for statistical significance (at the 95% confidence level) where possible. Cluster analysis will be employed to determine whether or not any segments emerge from both the residential and the industrial samples. Multiple regression will be undertaken to determine the key drivers of both the residential and the industrial customers' perceptions of the prototype offering. A

Market Insight 3.3
continued

Robinson–Bennett International executive will talk through the results and answer any questions. Topline survey results are checked regularly and a response analysis is produced. This regular check allows us to identify errors as quickly as possible. The analysis aims to answer research questions 1, 3, and 4.

Reporting

We will work in partnership with TGL to ensure that the results from the research are actionable. If required, the report can be produced in PowerPoint and structured in line with the research objectives to include all aspects of the methodology and sampling. The report will be designed to include charts and tables to best depict the main findings, together with clear and concise commentary. Two copies of the report will be delivered as hard copy to TGL, with accompanying tables.

Costing and Schedule

Desk research = £5,000

Qualitative in-depth interviews = £10,000

Discussion group interviews = £24,000

CAWI set-up, sample incentives, and project management = £10,000

Omnibus survey = £5,000

Quantitative data analysis = £5,000

Qualitative analysis, data interpretation and reporting = £10,000

Total = £69,000

We suggest that the study is undertaken from the period beginning in November 2013 until the end of February 2014.

Source: The authors wish to thank the Market Research Society for permission to publish this material.

1 **How does the proposal compare with the brief in Market Insight 3.2?**

2 **Do you think that a postal survey might be a more appropriate way of reaching residential consumers? What other approaches might you select?**

3 **Do you think the research objectives are feasible given the budget requirements? Why do you say this?**

Stage 2. Decide the Research Plan

At this stage, we decide whether or not to undertake primary or secondary research or both. We would usually undertake secondary research initially to see whether someone has undertaken similar research previously. For example, if an entertainment company had recently bought a new cinema property and wanted to know who lived in the local area, it could consult secondary data sources to ascertain the characteristics of people living in the area (e.g. gender, age, population size). However, if they wanted to know what film genres customers prefer, they might survey a sample of the population.

Primary versus Secondary Research

Primary research is research conducted for the first time, involving the collection of data for the purpose of a particular project. Secondary data is second-hand data, collected for someone else's purposes. **Secondary research** (also **desk research**) involves gaining access to the results of previous research projects. This method can be a cheaper and more efficient process of data collection. We can do a large amount of secondary research free by visiting a business library or searching the internet. Other sources of secondary data include the following.

- Government sources: including export databases, government statistical offices, social trend databases, and other resources.
- The internet: including sources identified using search engines, blogs and microblogs, and discussion groups.
- Company internal records: including information housed in a marketing information/CRM system (see Chapter 14) or published reports. Where no formal marketing information system exists, we would identify sales reports, marketing plans, and research reports commissioned previously.
- Professional bodies and trade associations: these organizations frequently have databases available online for research purposes, which may include industry magazine articles, and research reports.

- Market research companies: these organizations frequently undertake research into industry sectors or specific product groups and can be highly specialized. Examples include Mintel, Euromonitor, and ICC Keynote.

Visit the **Online Resource Centre** and follow the weblinks to learn more about these market research organizations.

In practice, most research projects involve both secondary and primary research, with the desk research occurring initially to ensure that a company doesn't waste money. Primary research is undertaken to cover the gaps in a company's knowledge once all available secondary data has been evaluated. Once this initial insight is gleaned, we determine whether or not to commission a primary data study. Assuming primary research needs to be undertaken, researchers usually design their research by considering what type of research to employ. Marketing directors should understand what types of study can be conducted because this impacts on the type of information collected, and hence the data they receive to solve their management problem.

Categories of Research Design

Generally speaking, we define three categories of research design: exploratory, descriptive, and causal. These categories specify the procedure adopted for collection and analysis of the data necessary to identify a management problem.

1 **Exploratory research** is used when little is known about a particular management problem and it needs to be explored further. Exploratory designs enable the development of hypotheses. We tend to adopt qualitative methods, e.g. focus groups, in-depth interviews, **projective techniques**, and **observational studies**. Exploratory research also makes use of secondary data, **non-probability** (subjective) **samples**, case analyses, and subjective evaluation of the resultant data.

2 **Descriptive research** focuses on accurately describing the variables being considered. It uses quantitative methods, particularly questionnaire surveys (on- and offline), for example, in consumer profile studies, usage studies, price surveys, attitude surveys, sales analyses, and media research.

Figure 3.5

A continuum of research techniques

3 **Causal research** is used when we seek to determine whether one variable causes an effect in another variable. For example, when determining whether or not temperature increases cause Coca-Cola sales to increase, we might use this method. Studies into the determination of advertising effectiveness and customer attitude changes are another example. Causal designs use experiments and control groups to allow meaningful comparisons between the outcomes of the treatment group (where a variable is manipulated) and the control group (where it is not). An example might be to use slight manipulations of price increases to determine their effect, if any, on sales. The difficulty arises in determining whether or not the sales effect was caused by the price increase, or by some other unmeasured variable (e.g. an increase in compensation for the salespeople).

Qualitative Versus Quantitative Research

At the outset of a research project, we might consider whether to use qualitative research or quantitative research or a combination (see Figure 3.5). Whereas quantitative research techniques, such as surveys, emphasize theory testing, qualitative techniques explore meaning and understanding. The client (or in-house research client) may have specific budget constraints or know which particular approach they intend to adopt. However, the choice depends on the circumstances of the research project and its objectives. If much is known about the management problem based on past research/experience, it may be appropriate to use quantitative research to understand the problem further. If there is little pre-understanding of the management problem, it would be better to explore the problem using qualitative research to gather insights.

Quantitative research methods, e.g. the survey questionnaire, are designed to elicit responses to pre-determined standardized questions from many respondents. This involves collecting information, quantifying the responses as frequencies or percentages, and descriptive statistics, and analysing them statistically. Other quantitative research methods include mass observation techniques and experiments. Experiments are designed to investigate cause and effect relationships, particularly, but not exclusively, in psychological studies (see Market Insight 3.4).

Structural equation modelling is commonly used to identify how variables interact and relate with each other. **Mystery shopping** is used particularly in retailing (on- and offline), where consumers are recruited to act as anonymous buyers to evaluate customer satisfaction, customer experience quality, and the customer's own evaluation of their experiences. In contrast, **qualitative research** techniques are used to identify factors affecting the management problem. Qualitative research techniques uncover the underlying motivations behind consumers'

Market Insight 3.4

How Scent Sells Lingerie at Hunkemöller

Behavioural economics, which explores why people sometimes make irrational decisions and why their behaviour does not follow traditional economic models, has produced hundreds of fascinating academic case studies, but many businesses find it hard to apply it in a way that produces real business advantage. One exceptional example was when BrainJuicer and lingerie retailer Hunkemöller worked to create and test interventions, based around behavioural economic designs, in Hunkemöller stores in the Netherlands. Why did Hunkemöller want to use behavioural economics? There is a growing body of evidence of the immense importance of context to decision-making. This means that small interventions in the environment can have a small but significant impact on customer behaviour and sales. For instance, in a related study for a separate BrainJuicer client, introducing a brand logo at the point of sale was associated with a 4% increase in purchases for that brand. Context—for example, music, scent, and emotion—plays a huge part in shopper decisions, but shoppers hardly notice some of the most important factors, so researching it can be very difficult. The study explained how using scent in Hunkemöller stores led to a striking gain in average customer value.

BrainJuicer's Behavioural Activation Unit began by undertaking a behavioural audit of the retail environments of Hunkemöller stores, and consumers' behaviour within them, in order to design appropriate in-store interventions designed to increase sales. The experiment was designed using an alternating experimental and control store run over six weeks, alternating week on week, to measure the effect of using scent in stores as a 'prime'—making customers feel happy and romantic before buying their lingerie. Store sales data were used for effectiveness data. This work was supplemented with a short questionnaire when customers exited the store, which was designed to

BrainJuicer is an innovative UK-based market research agency

uncover the extent to which they had enjoyed their visit and noticed the intervention (the scent prime).

As a result of the experiments, Hunkemöller obtained a 20% gain in average customer basket value by rolling out a scent in all new and refurbished stores. The research also helped the company to develop protocols for undertaking behavioural economic research—running audits, creating interventions, working with a research agency to make the interventions happen and understand how to prime customer emotion and satisfaction. The results of the research offered a strong argument for continuing the experimental, hands-on research approach rooted in behavioural science, backed up with traditional data. It's a method pointing to the future of research—away from what customers say and towards what they do.

Sources: Leach and Bisnajak (2013); Goyal (2013); http://www. Hunkemöller.com/en/about-us/corporate-info.html http://www. brainjuicer.com/html/stream/labs

This case was kindly contributed by Will Leach, VP, BrainJuicer Behavioural Activation Unit, and Ashwien Bisnajak, Market Intelligence Manager, Hunkemöller.

1 Why do you think it was necessary to use a behavioural experimental approach?

2 Why is it necessary to use a control group in an experiment?

3 What other decision-making scenarios can you think of that might use the experimental approach?

opinions, attitudes, perceptions, and behaviour, adopting unstructured or semi-structured methods to elicit information from respondents.

Case studies can be qualitative or quantitative depending on the number of studies and the analytical techniques used. For example, Colgate-Palmolive might research the product lifecycle of a particular toothpaste brand in Pakistan or the UAE to identify key factors for success before launching a new brand. Other qualitative methods include social media analysis, such as the analysis of sentiment on Twitter for people mentioning a particular brand. For example, Dell employs a vice president of communities and conversations to 'listen' to customers (Crawford, 2009). A Chartered Institute of Marketing (CIM) survey identified that companies are not using social media analysis sufficiently, particularly for **sentiment analysis** and **social listening** (Halpern, 2012).

Eye-tracking research and facial coding analysis (see Market Insight 3.5) use technology, and usually small samples, to assess an audience's ability to notice marketing communications material (e.g. prices on supermarket shelves) and the emotions they display. The most common qualitative techniques are **in-depth interviews** and **focus groups**. The objective is to uncover feelings, attitudes, memories, and interpretations. These can range from an informal conversation to highly structured interviews. They might be used to seek an interviewee's perspective on a new campaign or to develop customer profiles covering a wide range of needs/preferences. Projective techniques, which uncover subconscious thoughts using picture, word, and other association techniques, can also be used in in-depth interviews and focus groups (or **group discussions** as they are also known). Focus groups normally consist of a small number of target consumers brought together to discuss various concepts, e.g. rough outlines or storyboards (see Chapters 10 and 11) for a communications campaign. A professional moderator aims to understand the thoughts, feelings, and attitudes of the group towards an offering, media, or message. **Consumer juries** consist, as do focus groups, of a collection of target consumers who are asked to rank order ideas or concepts to explain their choices. In addition to these common qualitative techniques, there is growing use of more creative qualitative techniques. For example, Goulding (2002: 10) describes Semiotic Solutions as a company that 'specializes in cultural qualitative research, drawing upon techniques borrowed from linguistic philosophy, cultural anthropology and the systematic study of signs and codes' (see Chapter 19). The company's research has formed the basis of many national and international television and brand repositioning campaigns (e.g. for British Telecommunications (BT), Tesco, and Coca-Cola). **Ethnographic studies**, which tend to use in-depth interviewing methods and/or observational methods off- and online, are frequently used, particularly to gain insights into customers' behavioural processes (e.g. Guinness has used this technique to investigate its customers' drinking habits). Netnography, a form of ethnographic study conducted online, is now an increasingly popular approach to studying consumers' online behaviour, particularly since the development of social networking sites and online communities (see Chapter 17).

Semiotic research is a research approach aimed at decoding consumer culture, which, instead of interviewing or observing people, analyses the content of advertisements and other texts to uncover the meaning of the signs and symbols contained (see Chapter 19).

Because qualitative research approaches use small samples, the results derived are not generalizable to the wider population of interest and are used to generate insights only. By contrast, quantitative research techniques are used to obtain representative samples to enable generalizability and are based on larger respondent samples, selected either randomly or to match the

Research Insight 3.2

To take your learning further, you might wish to read this influential paper.

Kozinets, R. V. (2002), 'The field behind the screen: using netnography for marketing research in online communities', *Journal of Marketing Research*, **39(1), 61–72.**

In this highly cited and pioneering article, the author coins the term 'netnography', an adapted ethnographic method, and outlines the research approach designed to make the researching of online communities faster and simpler than standard ethnographic methods and less obtrusive than traditional qualitative approaches.

Visit the **Online Resource Centre** to read the abstract and access the full paper.

population. The researcher establishes the level at which the results reflect the entire population by choosing the number and type of respondents required. One disadvantage of quantitative research is that the answers are predetermined; consequently, there is a chance that respondents do not fully express their true opinions. The major characteristics of qualitative and quantitative marketing research techniques are outlined in Table 3.2.

Table 3.2 Qualitative and quantitative research methods compared

Characteristic	Qualitative	Quantitative
Purpose	To identify and understand underlying motivations, memories, attitudes, opinions, perceptions, and behaviours	To determine the representativeness of the sample to the population, i.e. how similar is the sample to the population?
Size of sample	Involves a small number of respondents, typically less than 30	Involves a large number of respondents, more than 30
Type of information generated	Provides detailed information	Provides narrowly defined descriptive information
Degree of structuring	Uses an unstructured approach, typically with open questions	Uses a structured questioning process and frequently closed multiple fixed-response questions
Type of data analysis	Uses a non-statistical word (content-based) analysis, e.g. using NVivo qualitative analysis software	Statistical analysis, e.g. using SPSS software
Sampling approach	Uses non-probability sampling methods	Uses probability sampling techniques

Designing the Research Project

Once we know what type of research to conduct, we should consider:

- Who to question and how (the sampling plan and procedures to be used)?
- What methods to use (e.g. discussion groups or an experiment)?
- Which types of questions are required (open questions for qualitative research or closed questions for a survey)?
- How should the data be analysed and interpreted (e.g. what approach to data analysis should be undertaken)?

Research methods describe the techniques and procedures to obtain the necessary information. We could use a survey or a series of in-depth interviews. We might use observation to see how consumers purchase goods online or how employees greet consumers when they enter a particular shop, i.e. mystery shopping. We could use consumer panels where respondents record their weekly purchases or their TV viewing habits over a specified time period. Nielsen Homescan is a service where consumers use specially developed barcode readers to record their supermarket purchases in return for points, which are redeemed for household goods.

Figure 3.6 indicates the key considerations when designing qualitative and quantitative research projects. The design of marketing research projects involves determining how each of these components interrelates with the others. The components comprise the following:

- research objectives;
- the sampling method;
- the interviewing method to be used;
- the research type and methods undertaken;
- question and questionnaire design;
- data analysis.

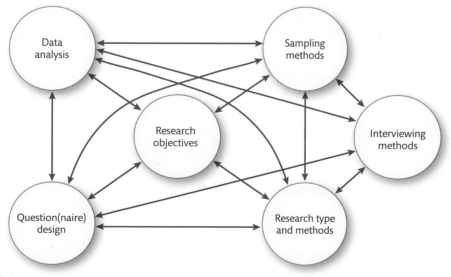

Figure 3.6

The major components of research design

Source: Baines and Chansarkar (2002). © John Wiley & Sons Limited. Reproduced with permission.

When designing research projects, we must first determine the type of approach to use for a given management problem (e.g. exploratory, descriptive, or causal). Then we determine which techniques are most capable of producing the desired data at the least cost and in the minimum time period.

To determine whether or not we've got the 'right' data, we must determine its validity (i.e. do the data correctly describe the phenomenon they measure?) and reliability (i.e. would the data be replicated in a future repeat study of the same type?). Generally, certain types of research (e.g. exploratory, descriptive, causal) use certain methods/techniques. For instance, exploratory research studies use qualitative research methods, non-probability sampling methods, and non-statistical data analysis methods. Descriptive research projects often adopt survey interviews using quota or random sampling methods and statistical analysis techniques. Causal research-ers use experimental research designs using convenience or **probability sampling** methods and statistical data analysis procedures.

Stage 3. Data Collection and Sampling

This stage involves the conduct of fieldwork and the collection of data. At this stage, we send out questionnaires, or run the online focus group sessions, or conduct a netnographic study, depending on the decisions taken in the first design stage of the fieldwork. The procedures undertaken when conducting the fieldwork might relate to how to ask the questions of the respondents—whether this be using the telephone, mail, or in person—and how to select an appropriate sample, how to **pre-code** the answers to a questionnaire (quantitative research), or how to code the answers arising out of open-ended questions (particularly with qualitative research).

The market research manager might be concerned about whether or not to conduct the research in-company or commission a field and tab agency. Other issues concern how to ensure high data quality. When market research companies undertake shopping mall intercept inter-views, they usually re-contact a proportion of the respondents to check their answers to ensure that the interviews have been conducted properly.

In qualitative research, samples are often selected on a convenience or judgemental basis. In quantitative research, we might use either probability or non-probability methods including the following.

- **Simple random sampling**, where the population elements are accorded a number and a sample is selected by generating random numbers which correspond to the individual popula-tion elements.

- **Systematic random sampling**, where population elements are known and the first sam-ple unit is selected using random number generation, but after that each of the succeeding sample units is selected systematically on the basis of an nth number, where n is determined by dividing the population size by the sample size.

- **Stratified random sampling**, where a specific characteristic(s) is used (e.g. gender, age) to design homogeneous subgroups from which a representative sample is drawn.

Non-random methods include the following.

- **Quota sampling**, where criteria like gender, ethnicity, or some other customer characteristic are used to restrict the sample, but the selection of the sample unit is left to the judgement of the researcher.

- **Convenience sampling**, where no such restrictions are placed on the selection of the respondents and anybody can be selected.
- **Snowball sampling**, a technique where respondents are selected from rare populations (e.g. high-performance car buyers). Respondents might initially be selected from responses to newspaper adverts and then further respondents are identified using referrals from the initial respondents, thereby 'snowballing' the sample.

Stage 4. Data Analysis and Interpretation

This stage comprises data input, analysis, and interpretation. How the data are input depends on the type of data collected. Qualitative data, usually alphanumeric (i.e. words and numbers), is often entered into computer software applications (e.g. NVivo) as word-processed documents or as video or sound files for content analysis. Quantitative data analysis uses statistical analysis packages (e.g. **SPSS**). In these cases, data are numeric and entered into spreadsheet packages (e.g. Microsoft Excel) or directly into the statistical computer application. Online questionnaires are useful because the data are automatically entered into a database, saving time and ensuring a higher level of data quality. If **CAPI** or **CATI** methods are used, analysis can also occur instantaneously as the interviews are undertaken. **Computer-assisted web interviewing techniques (CAWI)** allow the researcher to read the questions from a computer screen and directly enter the responses of the respondents. Using the internet, computer-aided web interviewing techniques are also commonly used, allowing playback of video and audio files.

Market research methods are used to aid managerial decision-making. Information obtained needs to be valid and reliable as company resources are deployed on the basis of the information gleaned. **Validity** and **reliability** are important concepts in quantitative market research. They aid researchers in understanding the extent to which the data obtained from the study represent reality and 'truth'. Quantitative research methods rely on the degree to which the data elicited might be reproduced in a later study (i.e. reliability) and the extent to which the data generated are bias-free (i.e. valid). Validity is defined as 'a criterion for evaluating measurement scales; it represents the extent to which a scale is a true reflection of the underlying variable or construct it is attempting to measure' (Parasuraman 1991: 441). One way of measuring validity is the use of the researcher's subjective judgement to ascertain if an instrument is measuring what it is supposed to measure (content validity). For instance, a question asked about job satisfaction does not necessarily infer loyalty to the organization.

Reliability is defined as 'a criterion for evaluating measurement scales; it represents how consistent or stable the ratings generated by a scale are' (Parasuraman, 1991: 443). Reliability is affected by concepts of time, analytical bias, and questioning error. We can also distinguish between two types of reliability, i.e. internal and external reliability (Bryman, 1989). To determine how reliable the data are, we conduct the study again over two or more time periods to evaluate the consistency of the data. This is known as the test–retest method. This measures external reliability. Another method used involves dividing the responses into two random sets and testing both sets independently using **t-tests** or **z-tests**. This would illustrate internal reliability. The two different sets of results are then correlated. This method is known as split-half reliability testing. These methods are more suited to testing the reliability of rating scales than data generated from qualitative research procedures. The results of a quantitative marketing research project are reliable if we conduct a similar research project within a short time period and the same or similar results are obtained in the second study. For example, if the marketing department of a travel agency chain interviewed 500 of its customers and discovered that 25% were in favour of a particular resort (e.g. a particular Greek island), and then repeated the study the following year and discovered that only 10% of the sample were interested in the same resort, the results of the first study can be said to be unreliable in comparison and the procurement department should not base its purchase of package holidays purely on the previous year's finding.

In qualitative research, concepts of validity and reliability are generally less important, because the data are not used to imply representativeness. Many practitioners believe that qualitative data are highly subjective anyway, so there is little need to measure reliability and validity. Qualitative data are more about the generation of ideas and the formulation of hypotheses. Validity can be assured by sending out transcripts to respondents and/or clients for checking, to ensure that what they have said in in-depth interviews or focus groups was properly reproduced for analysis. When the analyst reads the data from a critical perspective to determine whether or not this fits with their expectations, this constitutes what is termed a **face validity** test. Reliability is often achieved by checking that similar statements are made by the range of respondents, across and within the interview transcripts. Interviewees' transcripts are checked to assess whether or not the same respondent, or other respondents, have made the discussion point. Such detailed content analysis tends to be conducted using computer applications (e.g. NVivo).

Stage 5. Report Preparation and Presentation

The final stage of a research project involves reporting the results and the presentation of the findings of the study to the external or in-house client. The results should be presented free from bias. Marketing research data are of little use unless translated into a format that is meaningful to the manager or client who initially demanded the data. Presentations are often attended by senior people within the commissioning organization who may or may not have been involved in commissioning the work. Usually, agencies and consultants prepare their reports using a basic pre-written template.

Market Research Online

The internet has had a major impact on marketing research. Many companies increasingly use online methods. By 2012, online research was the most common method of research used globally (26% of all market research expenditure). The method is particularly common in Japan, New Zealand, the Netherlands, Finland, Canada, and Bulgaria, where 40%, 38%, 36%, 35%, 35%, and 35%, respectively, of market research expenditure adopted this approach (ESOMAR, 2012). Two types of panel are used in online research (Miles, 2004). Access panels, which provide samples for survey-style information, are made up of targets especially invited by email to take part, with a link to a web survey. Proprietary panels,

Research Insight 3.3

To take your learning further, you might wish to read the following influential paper:

Evans, J. R. and Mathur, A. (2005), 'The value of online surveys', _Internet Research_, 15(2), 195–219.

This highly cited paper outlines the strengths and weaknesses of undertaking online research. The article also compares online survey approaches with other survey formats, making it a particularly useful paper for those undertaking online research.

@ Visit the **Online Resource Centre** to read the abstract and access the full paper.

set up or commissioned by a client firm, are usually made up of that company's customers. To encourage survey participation, the researchers use incentives (e.g. a prize draw). However, there are pros and cons with undertaking online research (see Table 3.3).

Visit the **Online Resource Centre** and complete Internet Activity 3.1 to learn more about the Market Research Portal, a useful source of online research resources.

Table 3.3 Advantages and disadvantages of online research

The pros of online research	The cons of online research
1 Clients and analysts can see results compiled in real time	1 Demographic profile of online panels can differ from that of the general population
2 Online surveys save time and money compared with face-to-face interviews	2 If questionnaires take longer than 20 minutes to fill in, quality can suffer and they may go uncompleted
3 Consumers welcome surveys that they can fill in when they want to and often need no incentive to do so	3 Poor recruitment and badly managed panels can damage the data
4 A more relaxed environment leads to better-quality, honest, and reasoned responses	4 Technical problems, such as browser incompatibility, can mean that panellists fail to complete the survey
5 Panellist background data allows immediate access to key target audiences unrestricted by geography	5 Programming costs are higher than for offline questionnaires
6 Programming facilitates question order, allowing skipping and randomization of questions more easily	6 Sometimes survey questionnaires can be perceived as junk mail

Sources: Miles (2004: 40); Evans and Mathur (2005).

Market and Advertisement Testing

Marketing research reveals attitudes to a campaign, brand, or some other aspect of the exchange process, whereas market testing, by comparison, measures actual behaviour. There is a difference, as attitudes do not always determine action (see Chapter 2). For instance, a consumer may respond very positively to the launch of a new TV set in surveys, but family circumstances or lack of funds may mean the TV is never purchased. Market testing studies use **test markets** to carry out controlled experiments in specific country regions, where specific adverts can be shown, before exposing the 'new feature' (offering, campaign, distribution, etc.) to a full national or even international launch. Another region or the rest of the market may act as the **control group** against which results can be measured. As an example, films are often test-screened before release because of the substantial cost of producing the film in the first place.

Marketing research is used to test advertisements, whether these are in print, online, or broadcast via radio or TV. The research company Millward Brown International is renowned for this type of research. A variety of methods are used to test adverts. Typically, quantitative research is undertaken to test customer attitudes before and after exposure to see if the advert has had a positive impact or not. In addition, research occurring after exposure to the ad tests the extent to which audiences can recognize a particular advert (e.g. by showing customers a copy of a TV advert still, a print advert, or a photo online) or recall an advert without being shown a picture (we call this unaided recall). Qualitative research identifies and tests specific themes that might be used in the adverts and to test **storyboards** and **cuts** of adverts (before they are properly produced). More recently, advances in technology allow us to evaluate visual imagery more objectively, without relying on respondents' opinions. For example, technology company 3M offer a service 3M VAS (Visual Attention Service) which allows users to test communications material to see if specific sections of the communication will be noticed and in what order, using algorithms based on sophisticated eye-tracking research. Another approach to proposition and marketing communication testing uses facial coding analysis (see Market Insight 3.5).

Market Insight 3.5

Momentum Research: Reading People

One uncommon research technique to test marketing communications is the facial coding analysis undertaken by Momentum Research. The objective is to test marketing communications to see if any catch the customer's eye and determine what emotions the communication evokes at the brief moment of viewing. The method uses a two second exposure to each piece of marketing communication, with the viewer's face captured on video for facial coding analysis. One key question though is what's the point of using facial coding analysis when standard advertising tracking studies can be used? The answer is that conventional market research measures how people respond when shown communications in a research setting, with time to think and deliberate. This has a number of drawbacks. In the real world, people don't examine communications carefully and make considered judgements. A press ad, a poster site, a web ad, some packaging, or a point of sales display fails if it doesn't capture attention immediately.

Market Insight 3.5
continued

Conventional market research interrogates the conscious brain. However, when we are faced with millions of pieces of information in the real world, it is not our conscious brain which decides what will capture our attention. Within two seconds of exposing the creative material, we can see when there is unconscious engagement by a sharp focus on the object, a longer gaze duration, facial signs of thinking, and a brief nod or tilt of the head. When the communication does not engage the unconscious brain, we see an unfocused gaze and a lack of facial movement. After respondents have viewed all the communications, they are asked, as in conventional research, what they noticed, what they remembered, and what they liked or disliked and why. Non-verbal and verbal responses are recorded on an Engagement Index. As a general rule, when a communication is shown to engage through facial expressions it also brings positive verbal responses. However, it is common to have a positive verbal response without signs of unconscious engagement. Market research respondents are inclined to give approval in order to be helpful. Also, in conventional market research the communications are judged relative to one another. If there are five mediocre pack designs, at least one will stand out—simply because it is the least mediocre. With facial coding testing, the communication either captures engagement, or it doesn't. It's not a relative judgement. Because respondents are only shown each communication for two seconds, a lot of material can be tested in a short time. Including the qualitative interview, 15 minutes is usually sufficient. This means that relatively large samples can be included for a modest cost, equivalent to the cost of a small number of focus groups in a viewing studio. The following three example vignettes exemplify the approach.

> If the advert catches the eye, engagement can be seen in the gaze.

Eyetracking research measures physical stimuli rather than self-reported opinions

the Nando's logo and the cockerel). The work was combined with eye tracking and conducted by undertaking a hundred 20 minute interviews in a hall test. The results gave the client a clear and compelling answer, with one of the creative routes standing out from the rest. Combined with the qualitative interviews, the study provided Nando's with a valuable insight into all aspects of the brand personality.

Vignette 2: Diageo ready-made mixer drinks—point of sale material

How could Diageo capture the attention of Italian supermarket shoppers with their range of cocktail mixers? Three creative routes were tested with a sample of 30 to establish which one was the most engaging. Each route was also broken up into its separate creative elements: headline, tag line, main images, and colour scheme. The responses to each were then tested. After the analysis, Diageo was given clear results on the most effective in-store material, including the elements which worked most effectively. Through the qualitative interview, specific elements which were likely to be most effective in grabbing the attention of busy shoppers were also identified.

Vignette 1: Nando's Hot Sauces—new bottle designs

Four new creative routes were tested, together with the existing design, comprising 15 executions in total. The elements of the designs were tested separately (e.g.

Vignette 3: MANE France—coffee flavour testing

In a controlled trial, a number of new Nescafé cappuccino flavours were tested by capturing the facial responses of research participants at the

Market Insight 3.5
continued

moment of smelling and then tasting the coffee. The response of the eyes (e.g. widening in a fraction of a second with pleasure) and the actions of the mouth enabled us to gauge the response to each sample tested. This gave the client results directly from the unconscious brain, rather than simply relying on the considered conscious verbal responses.

Source: http://www.momentumresearch.co.uk/video.html

This case was kindly contributed by Dr John Habershon, Founder, Momentum Research.

1 How is facial coding analysis different from traditional advertising tracking methods?

2 Why is it important to collect participants' unconscious responses in research on proposition and marketing communication testing?

3 Can you think of other circumstances in which facial coding analysis would be useful?

Marketing Research and Ethics

Marketing research should be carried out in an objective, unobtrusive, and honest manner. Researchers are also concerned about the public's increasing unwillingness to participate in marketing research and the problem of recruiting suitable interviewers. The apathy among interviewees is probably associated with the growing amount of research conducted, particularly through intrusive telephone interviewing, which is increasing, and door-to-door survey interviewing, which is declining. Marketing research is increasingly conducted online, creating its own set of ethical concerns. For example, how can we verify that someone online is who they say they are? Is it acceptable to observe and analyse customer blogs and social networking site conversations? In social media research, ethical problems include the need to be open and transparent when conducting research within communities and anonymizing and paraphrasing comments (since verbatim comments can often be tracked back to a particular user in online research); however, the ethics of conducting social media research are still in development. Consequently, key organizations like ESOMAR and the MRS are still devising clear policies on the topic.

Marketing research neither attempts to induce sales nor attempts to influence customer attitudes, intentions, or behaviours. The MRS key principles outline that researchers shall (MRS, 2010: 4):

1 Ensure that participation in their activities is based on voluntary informed consent.

2 Be straightforward and honest in all their professional and business relationships.

3 Be transparent as to the subject and purpose of data collection.

4 Respect the confidentiality of information collected in their professional activities.

5 Respect the rights and well-being of all individuals.

6 Ensure that their respondents are not harmed or adversely affected by their professional activities.

7 Balance the needs of individuals, clients, and their professional activities.

8 Exercise independent professional judgement in the design, conduct, and reporting of their professional activities.

9 Ensure that their professional activities are conducted by persons with appropriate training, qualifications, and experience.

10 Protect the reputation and integrity of the profession.

The MRS Code of Conduct, based on the ESOMAR Code, is binding on all members of the MRS. Members of the general public are entitled to assurances that no information collected in a research survey will be used to identify them, or be disclosed to a third party without their consent. Data in European countries are also subject to an EU data protection directive. Respondents must be informed of the purpose of the research and the length of time that they will be involved in it. Research findings must also be reported accurately and not used to mislead. In conducting marketing research, researchers have responsibility for themselves, their clients, and their respondents/participants.

The results of research studies should remain confidential unless otherwise agreed by the client and agency, and the agency should provide detailed accounts of the methods employed to carry out the research project where this is requested by their clients.

Visit the **Online Resource Centre** and complete Internet Activity 3.2 to learn more about the Marketing Research Code of Practice adopted by ESOMAR.

International Marketing Research

Marketing researchers find it challenging to understand how culture operates in international markets and how it affects research design. Complexity in the international business environment makes international marketing research more complex because it affects the research process and design. Key decisions include whether to customize the research to each of the separate countries in a study using differing scales, sampling methods, and sizes, or to try and use a single method for all countries, adopting an international **sampling frame**. In many ways, this debate mirrors the standardization–customization dilemma common in international marketing generally (see Chapter 7).

International researchers try to ensure that comparable data are collected despite differences in sampling frames, technological developments, availability of interviewers, and the acceptability of public questioning. Western approaches to marketing research, data collection, and culture might be inappropriate in some research environments because of variations in economic development and consumption patterns. How comparable are the data related to the consumption of Burger King's offerings collected through personal interviews in the UAE, telephone interviews in France, and shopping mall intercept questionnaires in Sweden? Can an online panel be used instead across all countries? Ensuring comparability of data in research studies of multiple markets is not simple. Concepts could be regarded differently, the same offerings could have different functions, language may be used differently, even within a country, offerings might be measured differently, the sample frames might be different, and finally the data-collection methods adopted might differ because of variations in infrastructure. Table 3.4 outlines three types of equivalence: **conceptual equivalence**, **functional equivalence**, and **translation equivalence**. All three types of equivalence impact on the semantics (i.e. meaning) of words used in different countries, e.g. in developing the wording for questionnaires or in focus groups.

Table 3.4 Types of semantic equivalence in international marketing research

Type of equivalence	Explanation	Example
Conceptual equivalence	When interpretation of behaviour, or objects, is similar across countries, conceptual equivalence exists.	Conceptual equivalence should be considered when defining the research problem, in wording the questionnaire, and determining the sample unit, e.g. there would be less need to investigate 'brand loyalty' in a country where competition is restricted and product choice limited.
Functional equivalence	Functional equivalence relates to whether a concept has a similar function in different countries.	Using a bicycle in India where it might be used for transport to and from work, or France where it might be used for shopping, is a different concept from purchasing a bike in Norway where it might be used for mountain biking. Functional differences can be determined using focus groups before finalizing the research design by ensuring that the constructs used in the research measure what they are supposed to measure.
Translation equivalence	Translation equivalence is an important aspect of the international research process. Words in some languages have no real equivalent in other languages.	The meaning associated with different words is important in questionnaire design since words can connote a different meaning from that intended when directly translated into another language. To avoid translation errors of these kinds, the researcher can adopt one of the following two methods: 1. Back translation—a translator fluent in the language in which the questionnaire is to be translated is used and then another translator whose native language was the original language is used to translate back again. Differences in wording can be identified and resolved; 2. Parallel translation—a questionnaire is translated using a different translator fluent in the language which the questionnaire is to be translated into, as well as from, until a final version is agreed upon (Malhotra, 1999: 814).

Getting the language right is important because it affects how respondents perceive the questions and structure their answers.

When designing international research programmes, we need to consider how the meaning of words is different and how the data should be collected. Different cultures have different ways of measuring concepts. They also live their lives differently, meaning that it may be necessary to collect the same or similar data in a different way. Table 3.5 outlines how measurement, sampling, and data collection equivalence impacts on international research.

As we can see in Table 3.5, achieving comparability of data when conducting international surveys is difficult. Usually, the more countries included in an international study, the more likely it is that errors will be introduced, and that the results and findings will be inaccurate and liable to misinterpretation. International research requires local and international input. Therefore the extent to which one can internationalize certain operations of the research process depends on the objectives of the research.

Table 3.5 Types of measurement and data collection equivalence

Type of equivalence	Explanation	Example
Measurement equivalence	The extent to which measurement scales are comparable across countries.	Surveys are conducted in the USA using imperial systems of measurement, whilst the metric system is used in Europe. Clothing sizes adopt different measurement systems in Europe, North America, and Southeast Asia. Multi-item scales present challenges for international researchers as dissatisfaction might not be expressed in the same way in one country compared with another. Some cultures are more open in expressing opinions or describing their behaviour than others.
Sampling equivalence	Determining the appropriate sample to question may provide difficulties when conducting international marketing research projects.	The respondent profile for the same survey could vary from country to country, e.g. different classification systems are in existence for censorship of films shown at the cinema in France compared with Britain.
Data collection equivalence	When conducting research studies in different countries, it may be appropriate to adopt different data collection strategies.	Typically, data collection methods include (e)mail, personal (or CAPI), or telephone (or CATI). ■ Mail or email—used more where literacy or internet access is high and where the (e)mail system operates efficiently. Sampling frames are compiled from electoral registers, although it is now illegal in some countries to use these lists. European survey respondents can be targeted efficiently and accurately as international sampling frames do exist. ■ Telephone/CATI—in many countries, telephone penetration may be limited and computer-assisted telephone interviewing software, using random digit dialling, more limited still. Telephone penetration is around 95% in America, although European average figures are lower after the introduction of Eastern European economies. ■ Personal interviews/CAPI—used most widely in European countries favouring the door-to-door and shopping mall intercept variants. Shopping mall intercept interviews are not appropriate in Arab countries where women must not be approached in the street. Here, comparability is achieved using door-to-door interviews. In countries where it is rude to openly disagree with someone (e.g. China), it is best to use in-depth interviews.

With international projects, the key decision is to determine how much to centralize and how much to delegate work to local agencies. There is, throughout this process, ample opportunity for misunderstanding, errors, and lack of cultural sensitivity. To proceed effectively, the central agency should identify a number of trusted local market research providers on a variety of continents. Typically, an international agency will have a network of trusted affiliates who are monitored on a continual basis.

Chapter Summary

To consolidate your learning, the key points from this chapter are summarized here.

- **Define the terms market research, marketing research, and customer insight.**

  Market research is research undertaken about markets (e.g. customers, channels, and competitors), whilst marketing research is research undertaken to understand the efficacy of marketing activities (e.g. pricing, supply chain management policies). Customer insight derives from knowledge about customers which can be turned into an organizational strength.

- **Describe the role of marketing information systems in the insight process.**

  Marketing information and customer information (CRM) systems are commonly used in companies to collect, store, and analyse data, to generate and disseminate marketing intelligence, and to generate effective marketing programmes. Increasingly, companies are recognizing the importance of mining customer data and the competitive advantages that such strong customer understanding bring. Marketing information systems are important in the insight process because they aggregate data from numerous sources. The information they contain should be used to challenge current thinking and test implicit beliefs about the market, create a knowledge-sharing culture, and create value in partnership with other organizational functions and groups.

- **Explain the role of marketing research and list the range of possible research approaches.**

  Marketing research plays an important role in the decision-making process and contributes through ad hoc studies as well as continuous data collection, through industry reports, and from secondary data sources, as well as through competitive intelligence either commissioned through agencies or conducted internally with data gathered informally through sales forces, customers, and suppliers. Different methodological approaches include structural equation modelling, experiments, surveys, mystery shopping exercises, case studies, social media analysis, in-depth interviews, facial tracking and facial coding studies, ethnographic and netnographic studies, and semiotic studies.

- **Discuss the importance of ethics and the adoption of a Code of Conduct in marketing research.**

  Ethics is an important consideration in marketing research because consumers and customers either provide personal information about themselves or personal information is collected from them. Their privacy needs to be protected through observance of a professional Code of Ethics and the relevant laws in the country where the research is conducted.

- **Note the concept of equivalence in relation to obtaining comparable data.**

  International market research is complex because of the differences in language, culture, infrastructure, and other factors which intervene in the data collection process, ensuring that obtaining comparable equivalent data is more difficult.

- **List the problems arising when coordinating international marketing research.**

  International marketing research is complex because it is difficult to obtain semantic equivalence (i.e. concepts mean different things in different countries). Similarly, obtaining equivalence in measurement, sampling, and data collection can be difficult because of local variations. International research requires central coordination with local input to be effective.

 # Review Questions

1 What are the origins of market research?

2 How do we define market research?

3 How do we define marketing research?

4 How do we define customer insight?

5 What are the different types of research that can be conducted in marketing research?

6 Why is a marketing research code of conduct important?

7 What is a marketing information system and how is it used in the customer insight process?

8 What is the concept of equivalence in relation to obtaining comparable data from different countries?

9 How are the different aspects of the research process affected by differences in equivalence between countries?

 # Worksheet Summary

To apply the knowledge you have gained from this chapter and test your understanding of marketing research and customer insight visit the **Online Resource Centre** and complete Worksheet 3.1.

Discussion Questions

1 Having read Case Insight 3.1, how would you advise MESH Planning to develop a suitable research proposal for Gatorade to evaluate the effectiveness of their marketing activities? Use the outline proposal in Figure 3.4 to help you design the research.

2 Orange, the telecommunications company, wants to conduct a market research study aimed particularly at discovering what market segments exist across Europe and how customers and potential customers view the Orange brand. Advise them on the following key components.

   A Write a market research question and a number of sub-questions for the study.
   B How would you go about selecting the particular countries in which to conduct the fieldwork?
   C What process would you use when conducting the fieldwork for this multi-country study?

3 What type of research (i.e. causal, descriptive, or exploratory) should be commissioned in the following contexts? Explain why.

   A By the management of the airline Etihad in the United Arab Emirates when it wants to measure passenger satisfaction with the flight experience.
   B By Nintendo when it wants new ideas for new online games for a youth audience.
   C By the Spanish fashion retailer Zara when it wants to know what levels of customer service are offered at its flagship stores.

D   By Procter & Gamble, makers of Ariel detergent, when it wants to test a new packaging design for six months to see if it is more effective than the existing version. Fifty supermarkets are selected from one key P&G account. In 25 of them the new design is used, and in the other 25 the existing version is used.

4   You've recently won the research contract to evaluate customer satisfaction for Prêt A Manger, the food retail chain specializing in sandwiches, soups, and coffee. Your key account manager wants to increase customer satisfaction further using the knowledge gained from the study to identify potential new food offerings. Suggest a suitable research design (hint: you can advise more than one type of study) to:

A   Collect information about levels of customer satisfaction.

B   Decide what new food offerings customers might like to see.

In addition, your account manager asks you to outline what secondary data you can find in the area, detailing market shares, market structure, and other industry information, identifying specific secondary data sources and reports.

5   The following questions are concerned with international marketing research.

A   How should Boeing coordinate international marketing research to determine how to increase sales of its Dreamliner jet in the airline market?

B   Why is it difficult to achieve comparability of data across countries?

Visit the Online Resource Centre and complete the Multiple Choice Questions to assess your knowledge of Chapter 3.

References

Anon. (1989), *Hutchinson Concise Encyclopaedia* (2nd edn), London: BCA.

AMA (2004), 'Definition of Marketing Research', *American Marketing Association*, October, retrieve from: http://www.marketingpower.com/aboutama/pages/definitionofmarketing.aspx accessed 6 May 2013.

Arvidsson, A. (2004), 'On the "pre-history of the panoptic sort": mobility in market research', *Surveillance and Society*, 4, 1, 456–74.

Ashill, N. J. and Jobber, D. (2001), 'Defining the information needs of senior marketing executives: an exploratory study', *Qualitative Market Research: An International Journal*, 4(1), 52–60.

Axelrod, J. N. (1970), '14 Rules for building an MIS', *Journal of Advertising Research*, 10(3), 3–12.

Baines, P. and Chansarkar, B. (2002), *Introducing Marketing Research*, Chichester: John Wiley.

Bryman, A. (1989), *Research Methods and Organization Studies*, London: Unwin Hyman.

Cater, B. and Zabkar, V. (2009), 'Antecedents and consequences of commitment in marketing research services: the client's perspective', *Industrial Marketing Management*, 38, 785–97.

Chisnall P. M. (1992), *Marketing Research* (4th edn), Maidenhead: McGraw-Hill.

Cowan, D. (2008), 'Forum: Creating customer insight', *International Journal of Market Research*, 50(6), 719–29.

Crawford, K. (2009), 'Following you: disciplines of listening in social media', *Continuum: Journal of Media and Cultural Studies*, 23(4), 525–35.

ESOMAR (2008), *ICC/ESOMAR International Code of Marketing and Social Research Practice*, retrieve from http://www.esomar.org/uploads/public/knowledge-and-standards/codes-and-guidelines/ESOMAR_ICC-ESOMAR_Code_English.pdf accessed 6 May 2013.

ESOMAR (2012), *Global Market Research Report 2012*, retrieve from: www.esomar.org accessed 6 May 2013.

Evans, J.R. and Mathur, A. (2005), 'The value of online surveys', *Internet Research*, 15(2), 195–219.

Gosling, E. (2012), 'Big Fish puts the "heart" back into Yeo Valley identity', *Design Week*, 27 February, retrieve from: http://www.designweek.co.uk/big-fish-puts-the-%E2%80%98heart%E2%80%99-back-into-yeo-valley-identity/3034099.article accessed 6 May 2013.

Goyal, M. (2013), 'UK-based Brainjuicer finds out how chocolates can boost lingerie sales', *Economic Times of India*, 14 April, retrieve from: http://media.brainjuicer.com/media/files/The_Economic_Times_India.pdf accessed 28 May 2013.

Goulding, C. (2002), *Grounded Theory*, London: Sage.

Greenberg, P. (2010), 'The impact of CRM 2.0 on customer insight', *Journal of Business and Industrial Marketing*, 25(6), 410–19.

Halpern, K. (2012), 'In it to win it?', *Marketer*, July/August, 34–7.

Humby, C. (2007), 'R is for relevance, An antidote to CRM hype', Paper presented at the Return on Marketing Investment (ROMI) Club, May, Cranfield: Cranfield University.

Kotler, P. (2005), *FAQs on Marketing: Answered by the Guru of Marketing*, London: Cyan Books.

Leach, W. and Bisnajak, A. (2013), 'How scent sells lingerie', Paper presented at the ESOMAR Congress, 22–25 September, Istanbul

McCraw, T. K. (2000), *American Business, 1920–2000— How It Worked*, Wheeling, IL: Harlan Davidson, 49–51.

Malhotra, N. K. (1999), *Marketing Research: An Applied Approach* (3rd edn), Englewood Cliffs, NJ: Prentice Hall.

Miles, L. (2004), 'Online, on tap', *Marketing*, 16 June, 39–40.

MRS (2010), *Code of Conduct*, London: Market Research Society, retrieve from www.mrs.org.uk/standards/codeconduct.htm, accessed 6 May 2013.

Moorman, C., Zaltmann, G., and Desphandé, R. (1992), 'Relationships between providers and users of market research: the dynamics of trust within and between organizations', *Journal of Marketing Research*, 29(3), 314–28.

Nielsen (2013), 'TV Measurement', retrieve from http://www.nielsen.com/us/en/nielsen-solutions/nielsen-measurement/nielsen-tv-measurement.html accessed 6 May 2013.

Parasuraman, A. (1991), *Marketing Research* (2nd edn), Wokingham: Addison-Wesley, 280–309.

Smith, B., Wilson, H., and Clark, M. (2006), 'Creating and using customer insight: 12 rules of best practice', *Journal of Medical Marketing*, 6(2), 135–9.

Sims, J. (2013), 'Fresh perspective', *Impact*, 1, 41–44.

Part Two
Principles of Marketing Management

Part Two
Principles of Marketing
Management

Chapter 4
Marketing Environment

Learning Outcomes

After studying this chapter, you will be able to:

▶ Identify and define the three key areas of the marketing environment

▶ Describe the key characteristics associated with the marketing environment

▶ Explain PESTLE analysis and show how it is used to understand the external environment

▶ Explain the environmental scanning process

▶ Analyse the performance environment using the Porter's Five Forces industry analysis model

▶ Analyse an organization's product/service portfolio to aid resource planning

Case Insight 4.1
Glassolutions Saint-Gobain

Market Insight 4.1
Taxing Matters: Starbucks Storm in a Coffee Cup

Market Insight 4.2
The Wisdom of Crowdsourcing

Market Insight 4.3
Regulating Advertising in the UK: Cider of Sweden Ltd

Market Insight 4.4
Obesity: A Weighty Issue for Chocolate Manufacturers?

Market Insight 4.5
Britvic and AG Barr Mix Their Drinks

Case Insight 4.1

How should organizations scan their external environments and what should they do if they identify potential threats and opportunities? We speak to Glassolutions Saint-Gobain's Marketing Director, Michael Butterick, to find out more.

Glassolutions Saint-Gobain operates in all the main sectors of the glass and glazing industry in the UK. This depth of activity is a key differentiator and strength for our business, but it does make the business complex in its scope as a result. Different segments of our markets exhibit growth and contraction at different times as a consequence of a multitude of factors in the marketing environment. The task is to track and anticipate these trends to maximize their profit potential. Therefore we carry out an annual business planning and budgeting process. Key inputs to the process include sales tracking and analysis (e.g. by sector, segment, geographic region), primary market research (including surveys and key account analysis), secondary market research, sales team feedback, key competitor tracking and benchmarking, and contingency planning.

In addition, we prepare a Long-Term Strategic Plan that covers a five-year period and is presented annually to the Saint-Gobain Head Office in Paris. This Long-Term Plan is reviewed periodically throughout the year. The output of our environmental scanning is used to determine business strategy and our strategic and tactical marketing priorities. Some aspects of our operating environment don't change much from year to year, but we are acutely aware that, even in mature industries like ours, the dynamics of markets are not static. We look for changes that present both opportunities and threats to our business. A good example of this was likely changes in legal and regulatory legislation.

Changes in our industry's technical standards, such as the Building Regulations and the Window Energy Rating scheme, have a major influence on our business. Technical leadership of our industry is one of our key differentiators, and to protect this leadership

we need solutions in place to meet future technical requirements. Government legislation also affects us in ways beyond technical standards. The need to improve the energy efficiency of housing to tackle fuel poverty and reduce carbon emissions has put high-performance glass and glazing products high up the agenda. Recent Government initiatives such as the 'Green Deal' and the Energy Company Obligation (ECO) are examples of legislation that have affected our environment and presented new opportunities.

Our environmental scanning process tracked the evolution and development of the Government's policy on the 'Green Deal' and Energy Company Obligation (ECO) funding. We identified that this policy could deliver an opportunity for Glassolutions Saint-Gobain and the wider glass and glazing industry. It actually absorbed a relatively large proportion of our marketing resources to properly engage with and follow the evolution of such a large and complex initiative, but we took a conscious decision that the potential impacts, both positive and negative, were simply too great to ignore. As a business, we supported the broad aims of the policy and participated in the consultation processes that the Government organized. But we didn't always agree with the detail of how the initiatives ultimately developed. As the Government's policy on the Green Deal and ECO developed, we realized that the initiative, as it was unfolding, was unlikely to deliver any significant benefit for the glass and glazing industry.

We identified that the processes and legislative framework built for the Green Deal and ECO initiatives prevented funding from reaching the replacement window industry. This was because the cost of installing modern replacement 'A-Rated' energy-efficient windows was considered high relative to the

Case Insight 4.1
continued

carbon savings obtained. The other issue was that replacement windows deliver consumer benefits in terms of aesthetics, security, and acoustics in addition to the primary benefit of thermal insulation; ECO funding in particular is all about thermal insulation and couldn't be used to support these other benefits.

Therefore our problem was: how could we persuade government, specifically the Department for Energy and Climate Change, to reconsider how they funded green initiatives in the replacement window industry for the benefit of government, the industry, and Glassolutions Saint-Gobain?

Introduction

Have you ever wondered how organizations adapt to the changing business environment? How do companies keep up with the many changes that occur in politics, markets, and economics? What processes do they use to try to anticipate changes in technologies? We consider these and other questions in this chapter.

The operating environment for all organizations, whether they be commercial, charitable, governmental, or in the public sector more generally, is never static and seldom entirely predictable, and therefore can profoundly affect a company's course of action. We examine the nature of the marketing environment, determine environment-related issues, and provide a context for developing marketing strategies (see also Chapter 5).

Consider the degree to which an organization can influence the various environmental forces acting on it. The external environment, for example, consists of political, social, and technological influences, and organizations often have very limited influence on these. The performance environment consists of competitors, suppliers, and indirect service providers who shape the way an organization achieves its objectives. Here, organizations have a much stronger level of influence. The internal environment concerns the resources, processes, and policies an organization manages to achieve its goals. These elements can be influenced directly by an organization. Each of these three marketing environments is discussed in this chapter (see Figure 4.1).

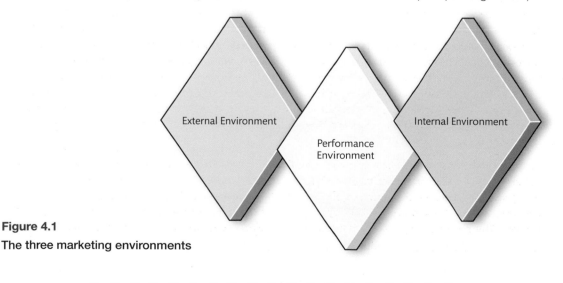

Figure 4.1
The three marketing environments

Understanding the External Environment

The external environment is characterized in two main ways. In the first, the elements do not have an immediate impact on the performance of an organization, although they might do in the longer term. In the second, although the elements can influence an organization, it is not possible to control them. This suggests that the level of risk attached to the external environment is potentially high. To make sense of the external environment, we use the well-known acronym, **PESTLE**. This is the easiest and one of the most popular frameworks for examining the external environment. PESTLE stands for the Political, Economic, Socio-cultural, Technological, Legal, and Ecological environments, as shown in Figure 4.2.

The Political Environment

When we conduct environmental scanning, we consider the political environment of the firm or organization. Although the legal environment relates to the laws and regulations associated with consumers and business practices, the political environment relates to the interaction between business, **society**, and **government** before those laws are enacted, when they are still being formed, or when they are in dispute. So, political environmental analysis is a critical phase in environmental scanning because companies can detect potential legal and regulatory changes in their industries and have a chance to impede, influence, and alter that legislation. In most marketing strategy textbooks, it is taught that the **political environment** is uncontrollable. However, there are circumstances when an organization, or an industry coalition, can affect legislation in its own favour. There is increasingly an understanding that business–government relations, properly undertaken, can be a source of **sustainable competitive advantage**

Figure 4.2
The external marketing environment

(see also Chapter 5). In other words, organizations can outperform other organizations over time if they can manage their relationships with government and regulatory bodies better than their competitors (Hillman *et al.*, 2004; Lawton and Rajwani, 2011). For example, the release of US government communications by Wikileaks shows a strong relationship between Shell Oil and the Nigerian government at every departmental level, proving useful for Shell when negotiating its oil exploration rights in that country. Mastercard and the US government also actively intervened in Russia to halt the Russian government creating its own credit company and extinguishing market opportunities for Mastercard (Viney and Baines, 2012). But companies can also fall foul of governments if they fail to play by a country's rules and regulations, written and unwritten (see Market Insight 4.1). For example, when the Oslo-based Nobel Prize Committee awarded the Peace Prize to Chinese dissident civil rights activist Liu Xiaobo, China switched its preferred trade supply of salmon from Norway to Scotland, increasing its order from 8 tonnes in the first nine months of 2010 to 4,897 tonnes in the same period of 2012 (Anon., 2012a).

Because legislation is such a technical area, few firms have the capability to understand and influence legislation without employing specialists. In such circumstances, special industry lobbyists are hired to represent clients with government decision-makers and regulators and provide strategic advice to clients on how to design their strategic communication campaigns. Generally, there are several ways in which marketers might conduct business–government relations in various countries.

- Lobbyist firms, with key industry knowledge, can be engaged either permanently or as needed.
- **Public relations** consultancies (e.g. Weber Shandwick) can be commissioned for their political services, often having members of parliament or others with a high degree of political influence serving as directors and/or advisers, in jurisdictions where this is legal.
- A politician may be paid a fee to give political advice on matters of importance to an organization, where this is legal within that particular jurisdiction, and that politician is not serving directly within the government in question on the same portfolio as that on which they are advising.
- An in-house public relations manager might handle government relations directly.
- An industry association might be contacted to lobby on behalf of members (e.g. in the European financial services industry, the Banking Federation of the EU).
- A politician may be invited to join the board of directors, board of trustees, or board of advisers of an organization to aid the company in developing its business–government relations where this is legal.

Working with parliaments, civil servants, and governments in different countries can present serious difficulties, particularly where an organization has limited market knowledge. In addition, successive governments seldom work in the same way as their predecessors, so there is a learning curve at the beginning of each electoral cycle. Generally, when conducting a public affairs campaign, it is important to:

- identify and prioritize the commercial and political issues at hand;
- develop contacts with appropriate officials in the relevant government, commission, or parliamentary departments;
- design a planning and contacts 'grid' outlining which **stakeholders** need to be contacted on what issues by which dates;

- identify key politicians and other interested parties — what Décaudin and Malaval (2008) call the deciders (key politicians who can affect regulation), the prescribers (technical experts, usually civil servants), industrial actors (e.g. other member companies in an industry body), and the general public;

- read, and try to influence, the press over the campaigning issues (Morris, 2001).

Companies or organizations often make the decision to influence governments in collaboration with other organizations, either through industry or trade bodies or together with other large companies in their industry. For example, the European Association of Tobacco Growers (UNITAB) lobbies Europe on behalf of tobacco manufacturers, declaring expenditure

JTI's controversial 'plain pack' advertising campaign
Source: Japan Tobacco International trading as Gallaher Limited in the UK.

of £875,000 via Communications et Institutions (C&I), a French PR and lobbying agency (Anon., 2012b). Sometimes companies use advertising in a bid to increase public awareness of their campaign issue and to put pressure on regulators or other government actors to acknowledge their position. For example, Japan Tobacco International (JTI) launched an issue advertising campaign in the UK criticizing potential UK legislation restricting branding and introducing plain packaging on cigarette packs, an approach that Australia has already undertaken to reduce the attractiveness and appeal of tobacco products to consumers, particularly young people, to increase the noticeability and effectiveness of mandated health warnings, to reduce the ability of the retail packaging of tobacco products to mislead consumers about the harms of smoking, and through the achievement of these aims in the long term, as part of a comprehensive suite of tobacco control measures, contribute to efforts to reduce smoking rates. JTI argued that there was no proof that plain packs would reduce smoking, that they would increase counterfeiting, and reduce government tax revenues (Gosling, 2012). The advert, which was referred to the Advertising Standards Authority after a complaint was received, related to wording used in the advertisement, which challenged whether the government 'rejected' plain packaging due to lack of evidence. The complaint was upheld and the advert has since been taken out of circulation.

The Economic Environment

Companies and organizations must develop an understanding of the economic environment because a country's economic circumstances have an impact on what economists term factor prices within a particular industry for a particular organization. These factors could include raw material, labour, building and other capital costs, or any other input to a business. The external environment of a firm is affected by the following items.

- Wage inflation—annual wage increases in a particular sector will depend on the supply of labour in that sector. Where there is scarcity of supply, wages usually increase (e.g. doctors).

- Price inflation—how much consumers pay for goods and services depends on the rate of supply of those goods and services. If supply is scarce, there is usually an increase in the price of that consumer good or service (e.g. petrol).

- **Gross domestic product (GDP)** per capita—the combined output of goods and services in a particular nation is a useful measure for determining relative wealth between countries when comparisons are calculated per member of the population (GDP per capita at **purchasing power parity**, see next paragraph).

- Income, sales, and corporation taxes—these taxes, typically operating in all countries around the world usually at different levels, substantially affect how we market different offerings (see Market Insight 4.1 for an unusual example of how public perceptions of a company's tax payments affected its reputation).

- Exchange rates—the relative value of a currency vis-à-vis another currency is an important calculation for those businesses operating in foreign markets or holding financial reserves in other currencies.

- Export quota controls and duties—restrictions are often placed on the amounts (quotas) of goods and services that any particular firm or industry can import into a country, depending on which trading bloc or country a company or firm is exporting to. In addition, countries sometimes also charge a form of tax on particular items to discourage or encourage imports and to protect their own economies.

Market Insight 4.1

Taxing Matters: Starbucks Storm in a Coffee Cup

US coffee behemoth Starbucks found itself in hot water in the UK in early October 2012 when it was revealed that the company had paid only £8.6m corporation tax on revenues of £3bn since it began operating in the UK in 1998. The company initially defended its tax payments by arguing that it was simply not making any profits and that a quarter of its 600 stores were loss-making. Critics, such as the tax pressure group UK Uncut, have argued that the company only seemingly does not make money because it pays large fees to its Dutch European headquarters for store design, trademark protection, and the use of the global brand, a commission to a Swiss affiliate when buying the coffee beans, and interest payments to the US headquarters (all so-called inter-company charges) to avoid paying tax.

One might ask why the tax issue has risen to the fore now, especially since the company's actions are legal? The answer lies in the fact that Britain has been in a deep recession since 2008 from which it is not expected to recover fully until 2018. In this public atmosphere, the idea that a company is not paying its fair share of tax has roused the public's anger. A consumer survey measuring public respect for the company recorded a net −47% respect score, beaten only by News International at −51% (a company involved in illegal phone hacking, several prosecutions, and a UK public enquiry). But the company is

not alone. Google and Amazon have also faced questioning by a UK parliamentary committee over their own legal tax avoidance schemes. As news of the tax issue became public knowledge, Starbucks' social media score plunged dramatically by late October, as people called for consumers to boycott the company. This caused Starbucks to reconsider its position, and in an open letter by UK managing director Kris Engskov, printed in the *Daily Express* on the 8th December, it announced that it would no longer claim tax deductions for inter-company charges and that it would pay 'a significant amount of tax during 2013 and 2014 regardless of whether the company is profitable during these years'.

Sources: Bainbridge (2012); Charles and Farey-Jones (2012); Lucas *et al.* (2012).

Visit the **Online Resource Centre** and follow the weblink to learn more about how Starbucks used an open letter to avert a boycott.

1 **Do you think that the company should have foreseen the potential public issue over its tax avoidance in the UK? Why do you say this?**

2 **Why do you think that it took well over a month for the company to realize the level of public anger?**

3 **Google and Amazon have come under much less public scrutiny over the same issue. Why do think this is the case?**

When operating in other countries, we should understand how exchange rates and living standards operate. We might also need to understand how prices or labour costs change if we are importing our goods and services, or components of them, from another country, i.e. our factor prices. This is known as the rate of price or wage inflation. The difficulty comes in comparing prices in one country with those in another. Should we just compare costs (what is paid for a proposition as a company) and prices of goods (at what price a good is sold, or what is paid as a consumer) through the exchange rate at any one particular time? Apparently not, as this is itself subject to political and other pressures. What economists tend to calculate is prices for a particular basket of goods—a fixed list of common items—and compare the costs in one country versus another. This is known as the purchasing power parity exchange rate. This rate allows us to compare the relative costs between two countries for a given item.

Firms usually have little impact on the macro-economic environment as they have little control over macro-economic variables (e.g. oil prices) which might affect their business, e.g. stock prices if they are multinationals listed on a major stock exchange (e.g. Hang Seng, FTSE, or Euronext). The challenge when examining the macro-economic environment is to foresee changes in the environment and how they might affect the firm's activities. If a computer company in Sweden imports silicon chips from Japan, and pays for them in Swedish kronor, but the exchange rate for the yen is rising against the krona (in other words, you get more yen per krona, perhaps because of strong Japanese export sales to Europe), then it might source its silicon chips from another country to ensure that its own prices are unaffected.

Similarly, if **inflation** drives consumer prices higher in a particularly country, it can mean that the price of goods becomes more expensive, forcing a drop in sales. Typically, during a **recession**, consumers tend to purchase fewer goods and increase their savings, and prices fall further as producers try to stimulate demand. But prices can also increase during a recession. Therefore it is important to understand general economic trends in the macro-economy and the firm's marketplace. Surveys of consumer expectations of inflation, forecasts of foreign exchange rates, wage forecasts, and lots of other financial information are frequently available from government central banks to help in this regard.

Visit the **Online Resource Centre** and complete Internet Activity 4.1 to learn more about how the contribution of service industries to the UK's national economy has changed over the last ten years.

The Socio-Cultural Environment

Lifestyles are constantly changing and consumers shift their preferences over time. Companies that fail to recognize changes in the socio-cultural environment and change their offerings typically fail. Levi Strauss, the American jeans company, has lost its way since its heyday in 1996 when sales were over $7.1bn; by 2011 sales were only $4.7bn. The company has failed to attract new generations of consumers, although it remains the world's largest jeans brand (Levi Strauss & Co., 2011; Miller, 2011). When considering the socio-cultural environment, companies need to consider the changing nature of households, demographics, lifestyles, and family structures, and changing values in society.

Demographics and Lifestyles

Changes in population proportions impact on an organization's marketing activity. In the UK (and some other European countries), immigration from Poland after EU enlargement increased the UK Polish population, with some supermarkets specifically targeting Poles by using adverts in Polish and stocking products such as borscht, meatballs, pickled vegetables, and sauerkraut soup (BBC, 2006). According to the UN Population Division (2012), by 2050 India's population is set to reach around 1.6 billion, China's is set to reach 1.3 billion, America's is due to reach 400 million, and the UK's only 73 million. Notably, some countries' populations will fall (e.g. Japan and Russia). What implications will these changes have for different consumer and industrial sectors? But it is not just total population that matters to the marketer, we are also concerned with the ages of different population groups. Figure 4.3 illustrates the relative differences in age structure in selected countries.

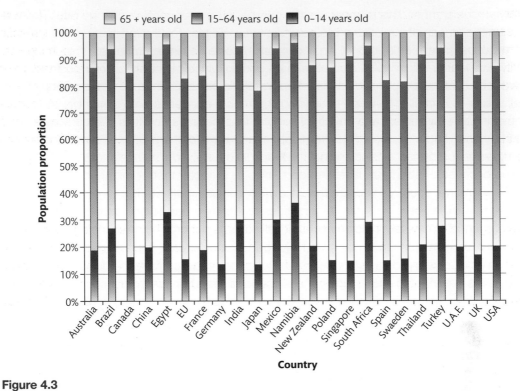

Figure 4.3

Population proportion estimates by age in selected countries

Source: CIA World Factbook (2012 estimates, row totals may not add up to 100% because of rounding).

The figure shows the relatively large proportion of people in the 65-year-old-plus age bracket (the 'silver' or 'grey' market, so-called because of the colour of their hair). Those countries with comparatively younger citizens include African and Middle Eastern countries, such as Namibia, South Africa, and Egypt. The changes and relative differences in age structure in different countries correspond to different-sized markets for brand propositions relevant to these particular communities of citizens. Clearly, the market for private pensions in Europe is likely to increase as national governments and the EU develop appropriate schemes, which bodes well for insurance and pension groups. But this is just one example; there are a whole host of offerings that might be targeted at these different groups.

People's lifestyles are also changing. In Europe, the trend is towards marrying later and a greater tendency to divorce than in previous generations. In some countries, citizens are increasingly living in single-person households. There is a rise of same-sex marriages in industrialized nations, and some countries and states within countries have legitimized these more than others (e.g. Argentina, the countries of Scandinavia, Iceland, the Netherlands, South Africa, and France). Marketers dub the homosexual segment the 'pink' market. There are obvious opportunities for the hotel leisure industry, which offers pink honeymoons, weekends, and travel facilities. The Out Now 2010 study shows a potentially large market opportunity: lesbian, gay, and transgender (LGBT) consumers living in Argentina spent a total of US$4bn on leisure and travel; in Mexico five million LGBT customers spent US$8bn, and in Brazil local LGBT consumers spend more than US$20bn annually (World Travel Market, 2010).

However, societal changes need not necessarily be demographic or lifestyle-oriented to impact on marketing. Changes are taking place within society that affect how consumers interact with an organization's marketing activity. Customers are increasingly happy to work with companies and organizations to solve problems. Howe (2006) refers to this phenomenon as **crowdsourcing**. Whitla (2009) suggests that the role and process of crowdsourcing is to identify a task or group of tasks currently conducted in-house, and then release the task(s) to a 'crowd' of outsiders who are invited to perform the task(s) on behalf of the company (for a fee or prize). This invitation might either be truly open to everyone or restricted in some way to ensure that those who respond are only those qualified to undertake the task. This approach can help marketers gain insights into both new product/service development and marketing communications. (See Market Insight 4.2 for examples of this activity and Chapter 17.)

The Technological Environment

The emergence of new technologies substantially affects not only high-technology businesses but other businesses as well. Examples include technologies that impact on productivity and business efficiency (e.g. changes in energy, transportation, information, and communication technologies). New technology also changes the way that companies go to market. For example, companies now have to make their offerings available through various channels,

Market Insight 4.2

The Wisdom of Crowdsourcing

The following three examples outline different, not always successful, uses of crowdsourcing for market ideas and solutions: the development of a name for a newly developed product, creative ideas for a print and TV advert campaign in the UK, and a new way of funding budding publishers in the Netherlands.

The development of a 'female-friendly' lager for women in Britain has been a difficult marketing challenge. Only 17% of women in Britain drink beer compared with 33% in Ireland and 44% in Spain. Previous attempts incorporated tastes of fruit and green tea but failed, so Molson Coors developed a clear low-calorie beer after undertaking a survey of 30,000 female drinkers and launched it in 2011. What do you call a clear light beer for women? That's where Molson Coors thought women could help again, and asked them to name it. They called it Animée. Unfortunately, twelve months later, after a poor sales performance, Molson Coors axed both the brand and the BitterSweet Partnership research unit that created it.

In 2009, Unilever offered $10,000 in a competition to develop ideas for its next Peperami print and TV advert campaign based on its quirky character Animal, a living representation of the pork salami snack. Using a crowdsourcing website www.ideabounty.com and its production house SmartWorks, Unilever asked for an 'unapologetic, unexpected, and incredibly memorable piece of communication'. The Unilever team was so impressed with the submissions they received that instead of picking one winning idea they selected two!

In 2010, Valentine Van Der Lande launched TenPages. com, a crowdfunding website for budding novelists in The Netherlands. The site works as a talent scout by inviting aspiring authors to submit a minimum of 10 pages of their manuscript. The public then rate the submission, effectively by buying up to 2,000 shares at £5 each and receiving a proportion of the sales revenue. If the target for funding is reached, the novelist is awarded a contract with a traditional publisher. By 2012, 65 manuscripts had been funded and 34 were available in bookshops. With such an enviable rate of author sign-up, it's small wonder that Valentine won the 2012 Cartier Women's Initiative Awards.

Market Insight 4.2
continued

Tenpages.com, the Dutch crowdfunding website for new novelists
Source: ©TenPages.com.

Sources: Sweney (2009); Taylor (2010); Anon. (2012c); Anon. (2012d); McCready (2012); www.ideabounty.com/blog/post/2485/peperami.-picks-two-winning-ideas (see also Market Insight 2.2 in Chapter 2).

1 Under what circumstances do you think crowdsourcing can be most useful to marketers?

2 Why do you think Animée was unsuccessful despite the fact that it was crowdsourced?

3 Do you know of any other companies in your own countries that have used a crowdsourcing approach? What did they use it for?

Note: In February 2014 TenPages.com ceased trading.

including mobile phone applications as well as via their traditional websites and physical stores. For example, web-only jeweller's ice.com has a mobile phone application which allows potential customers to 'try on' an item of jewelry by measuring their finger or wrist with their own mobile phone camera (Mucklow, 2012).

Changes in technology particularly affect high-technology industries, where firms must decide whether they wish to dominate that market by pushing their own particular technology standards, and especially where new technology renders existing standards obsolete (e.g. cloud computing and digital music files have taken over from the tape and vinyl record manufacturing industries).

In scanning the technological environment, we are particularly interested in research and development (R&D) trends, and our competitors' R&D efforts. Strategies to ascertain these involve regular searches of patent registrations, trademarks, and copyright assignations, as well as maintaining a general interest in technological and scientific advances. For example, in the pharmaceutical and chemical industries, companies develop new compounds based on modifications of compounds registered for patents by their competitors in a process known as **reverse engineering**.

But the reverse engineering principle does not solely operate within these industries. Companies in other industries frequently develop new propositions based on their competitors' offerings, through 'me-too' or imitation marketing strategies. In fact, this kind of imitation lies at the heart of the inability of firms to turn their technological advances into sustainable competitive advantages (Rao, 2005). The problem is that as soon as they introduce a new offering variant, it is quickly copied. The trick is to continually introduce new propositions, and to stay as close to the consumer as possible. Many companies also indulge in technology forecasting, an attempt to identify future technology trends.

For most firms, working out how to determine whether or not to invest in radical new technologies is difficult as the potential benefits are far from clear at the outset. Fear of obsolescence is usually a greater incentive to invest in new technologies than the lure of enhancement of existing propositions (Chandy et al., 2003). Therefore companies are particularly concerned about the impact of technological changes on their product and service lifecycles. However, innovation becomes a necessary condition in the strategic marketing decision-making of high-technology firms. For less technology intensive firms, innovation, whether it is process- or product/service-focused, or at least rapid adoption of new offering variants based on competitors' offerings, is still necessary to stay ahead of the competition.

The Legal Environment

The legal environment covers every aspect of an organization's business. Laws and regulations are enacted in most countries, ranging from the transparency of pricing, the prevention of restrictive trade practices, product safety, good practice in packaging and labelling, and the abuse of a dominant market position, to codes of practice in advertising, to take a small selection.

Product Safety, Packaging, and Labelling

In the European Union, product safety is covered by the General Product Safety Directive to protect consumer health and safety for both member states within the EU, and importers from third-party countries to the EU or their EU agent representatives. Where products pose serious risks to consumer health, the European Commission can take action, imposing fines and criminal sentences on those contravening the Directive. The General Product Safety Directive does not cover food safety; this is subject to another EU Directive, which has established a European Food Safety Authority and a set of regulations covering food safety. As a company operating in these sectors, it is important to keep up with changes in legislation. Failure to do so could jeopardize the business.

In the pharmaceutical industry, regulations govern testing, approval, manufacturing, labelling, and the marketing of drugs. Most countries also place restrictions on the prices that pharmaceutical companies can charge for drugs. In Japan price regulations are stipulated for individual products, whereas currently in the UK strict controls are placed on the overall profitability of products supplied by a specific company to the National Health Service under the Pharmaceutical Price Regulation Scheme. After 2014, the Scheme will use a value-based pricing mechanism (DH/ABPI, 2012). (For more on value-based pricing approaches, see Chapter 9.)

Companies that develop cosmetics and fragrances are required to comply with legislative measures designed to protect the cosmetic user and so need to ensure that products remain cosmetics and are not reclassified under different regulations, for instance those related to medicines, which makes innovation within the cosmetic industry more difficult (Gower, 2005). .

Generally, product labelling regulation in the EU tends to relate to recycling of packaging and waste to ensure that it complies with environmental regulations, whereas in the USA, for example, packaging and labelling regulations are more concerned with fair practice and ensuring that packaging does not contain misleading advertising statements. Different countries around the world have different regulations, so importers/exporters should be aware of these rules from the outset.

Codes of Practice in Advertising

Advertising standards differ around the world. In some countries, for example, the UK, advertising is self-regulated, i.e. by the advertising industry itself. In other countries, advertising is restricted by legislation. In the UK, advertising is regulated by the Advertising Standards Authority (ASA), which has a mission to apply codes of practice in advertising and uphold advertising standards for consumers, business, and the general public (see Market Insight 4.3). Such self-regulatory agencies operate in other countries, e.g. the Bureau de Vérification de la Publicité in France, and the Advertising Standards Council in India. In the EU, the European Advertising Standards Alliance oversees both statutory and self-regulatory provision in most European countries and even non-European countries covering Russia, Canada, the USA, New Zealand, and Turkey (see Chapters 10 and 11 for a more general discussion of advertising).

In the UK, for broadcast advertising communications, codes of practice exist for both radio and TV, typically with specific regulations for alcohol advertising, specifying that claims cannot be made in relation to sexual prowess, fitness or health, courage, or strength. Restrictions on the advertising of alcohol products exist in most parts of the world, e.g. alcohol products cannot be advertised before 10 p.m. in Thailand. In France, as a result of the Evin Act, which restricts advertising for alcoholic beverages, manufacturers are obliged to show a government health warning on all advertisements using the following wording: *'L'abus d'alcool est dangereux pour la santé. Consommez avec modération'*, which translates into English as 'The abuse of alcohol is dangerous for your health. Consume with moderation'. In the UK, brewers and distillers have been voluntarily placing the message 'drink responsibly' in the copy of their adverts for many years.

Government health warnings also apply to tobacco products, and tobacco advertising is now virtually banned in all forms around the world. In most Western countries, consumers are dissuaded from smoking not only through high taxes placed on tobacco to reduce consumption, and through public restrictions on where people can smoke (e.g. Sweden, India, Bahrain, Ireland, UK, etc.), but also through legislation banning and restricting advertising and requiring the placing of government health warnings on packages. In some countries, including Canada and Australia, government health warnings provide stark messages and graphic pictures. In Canada, the first country to introduce stark health messages on cigarette packs, research into tobacco products and health warning labels found that there was a relationship between the size of a health warning message and its effectiveness in stopping smoking (Hammond, 2011), part

Market Insight 4.3

Regulating Advertising in the UK: Cider of Sweden Ltd

Codes of advertising are divided into broadcast and non-broadcast practice. In the UK, the Committee of Advertising Practice (CAP) creates, revises, and enforces these Codes and comprises organizations that represent the advertising, sales promotion, direct marketing, and media industries. The Codes of Practice aim to ensure that advertising is legal, decent, honest, and truthful to ensure consumer confidence in the advertising industry. In the UK, the ASA receives complaints from members of the public and adjudicates these.

In one example a complaint was upheld against Cider of Sweden Ltd for a 2011 TV advert for Kopparberg Cider, featured in black and white, depicting people walking into an underground nightclub. Words on the nightclub's wall stated 'FIND THE VENUE YOU NEVER KNEW EXISTED', words above the club's staircase stated 'FIND THE DOOR YOU NEVER NOTICED'. The ad showed the club's dance floor with people dancing in slow motion amid flashing disco lights. The words projected on the inside wall of the club stated 'FIND THE CROWD WHO THINK EVERY NIGHT IS FRIDAY NIGHT'. Words at the bottom of the screen stated 'Enjoy Kopparberg Responsibly'. The ad then depicted three Kopparberg cider bottles in colour. The single complainant stated that the advert was likely to appeal particularly to those under 18 years of age. In their response, Cider of Sweden Ltd stated that all actors were over 25 years old, no-one was depicted with a drink, that the product was not illustrated until the end-frame and so was dissociated from the nightclub scenes, and that the band in the ad, Sleigh Bells, appealed to a target audience largely over 24 years old, and they provided MySpace and Spotify data in an attempt to prove this.

In their judgement, the ASA noted that the ads for alcohol must not appeal to people under 18 years of age regardless of the age of the actors. The ASA

suggested that a hidden underground venue and the words 'FIND THE CROWD WHO THINK EVERY NIGHT IS FRIDAY NIGHT', which convey the idea of finding excitement at every opportunity, would particularly appeal to people under the age of 18 years old. Because the song the noise-pop band, Sleigh Bells, was singing was called 'Kids' and because there was an albeit small following under 18 years of age for this band, as evidenced by the MySpace and Spotify data the company provided, the decision was upheld and the advert was banned from appearing again in its current form.

Source: ASA (2011).

1 **Do you think that the advertising industry in your home country should regulate itself or be regulated by government? Why do you say this?**

2 **In the above example, do you agree with the judgement of the ASA? Does it matter that there was only one complainant?**

3 **Can you remember an advert you've seen recently that made particularly wild claims or an advert you've seen that seriously offended you? What was it?**

Kopparberg, the Swedish cider brand, that's proud of its taste

Source: Sebastian Matthes/manox'.

Grim-looking images like these on reduce smoking cigarette packs
Source: © Commonwealth of Australia.

of the reason why Canada increased the size of the health warning in 2012 to cover 75% of the pack (CTV News, 2012), and that it is important to refresh these messages and images so that people do not ignore them (Health Canada, 2011). Australia was the first country to introduce plain packaging for all tobacco brands in late 2012. If the approach is successful in reducing smoking, particularly among young people, other countries will follow suit.

The Ecological Environment

In the 2000s, companies have become concerned with the concept of marketing sustainability (see Chapter 18 and Market Insight 4.4). Consumers are increasingly worried about the impact that companies are having on their ecological environments. For example, with food products, they are demanding more 'organic' food, incorporating principles of better welfare for the animals they consume as food products and less interference with the natural processes of growing fruit and vegetables (e.g. the use of pesticides and chemical fertilizers).

Consumers are equally concerned with ensuring that products are not sourced from countries with poor and coercive labour policies, e.g. parts of Latin America, the Far East, and Africa, a charge levelled at Nike in the 1990s. They are also keen to ensure that companies are not damaging the environment themselves or causing harm to consumers. There is a rise in 'Fairtrade' products. In Britain, for example, the Fairtrade Foundation trademarks all goods as a guarantee to indicate that that particular good has been sourced from disadvantaged producers in a developing country at a decent price to the producer. Sales of Fairtrade items include coffee, tea, banana, cocoa, flowers, wine, cotton, honey, and many others. The value of Fairtrade certified

Market Insight 4.4

Obesity: A Weighty Issue for Chocolate Manufacturers?

Food and beverage companies, like their fast food counterparts, have faced increasing pressure from governments as obesity rates increase around the world. This is particularly problematic for children (aged 5–17 years old), who eat more chocolate. Around 6–8% of children in France, England, South Korea, and the USA are obese. In Greece, the USA, and Italy around one-third of children are overweight. Only in China, Korea, and Turkey are less than 10% of children overweight. In most countries, more boys than girls are overweight and obese, with the exception of the Nordic countries, the UK, the Netherlands, and Australia, where more girls than boys are obese.

National governments have begun to scrutinize their public health policies. Several countries introduced a 'fat tax' in 2011 and 2012 (e.g. Denmark, Finland, Hungary, and France). Toms International, the Danish chocolate manufacturer, complained that the tax had lowered sales and led them to reduce their workforce as a result. The Danish government repealed the law less than 12 months later. Fat taxes are added by governments to products with a high fat content, such as confectionery (including chocolate), dairy products, and sugary foods and drinks, in a bid to reduce public consumption of high-fat foods, the obesity epidemic, and the consequent impact on public health and public healthcare budgets.

Therefore the chocolate confectionery business is an obvious potential target for government regulation. Several countries are actively discussing whether or not to introduce a 'fat tax', including Belgium, Ireland, Romania, the UK, the USA, and Italy. In the UK, the chocolate market is dominated by the trinity of chocolate makers Kraft Foods (Cadbury), Mars Inc. (Masterfoods Europe), and Nestlé. The total market grew substantially (by 11.2%) from 2009 to 2011, despite slow economic growth. Therefore, despite government health concerns, Britain seems to have a continuing love affair with chocolate. However, according to research in the UK, only 12% of those over 16 years old consider low-calorie options when buying chocolate, and 15–24-year-olds are heavier users of chocolate than older consumers. A key conundrum arises if you are CEO of one of the major chocolate manufacturers: would you seek to circumvent the obesity issue by reducing the fat content in your products (and educating consumers to buy lower-calorie options), ignore the obesity issue and therefore sell the same product (and perhaps lobby government not to introduce the tax), or pursue some mixture of these approaches?

Sources: Mintel (2012a); OECD (2012); Stones (2012).

1 What are the advantages and disadvantages to Kraft Foods (Cadbury) of producing new lower-calorie versions of their existing chocolate bars?

2 How likely do you think it is that the UK government will bring in legislation to tax high-fat food products like chocolate? Why do you think that?

3 Why do you think that Denmark repealed its fat tax law after only 12 months? What are the implications for Danish chocolate manufacturers like Toms International?

products in the UK was £1.3bn in 2011 (Fairtrade Foundation, nd). Nevertheless, despite the good intentions of these companies, consumers remain confused over whether a particular offering is organic, fairly traded, and/or ethically sourced (Murray, 2006).

One important question for marketers is: how should a company incorporate the changing trend in sustainability into its organizational processes? To answer this question, Orsato

(2006) suggests that a company can adopt one of the following four different green marketing strategies.

- Eco-efficiency—developing lower costs through organizational processes such as the promotion of resource productivity (e.g. energy efficiency) and better utilization of by-products. This approach should be adopted by firms that need to focus on reducing the cost and environmental impact of their organizational processes. Supermarket chains in Norway, and in other Scandinavian countries, have encouraged recycling for a long time.

- Beyond compliance leadership—the adoption of a differentiation strategy through organizational processes such as certified schemes to demonstrate their ecological credentials and their environmental excellence, for example, the adoption of the UN Global Compact principles or other Environmental Management System (EMS) schemes and codes. This approach should be adopted by firms that supply industrial markets, such as car manufacturers.

- Eco-branding—the differentiation of a firm's products or services to promote environmental responsibility. Examples include Duchy Originals, the British Prince of Wales' food brand, the Thai King Bhumipol's Golden Place brand, or the Toyota Prius.

- Environmental cost leadership—through offerings that provide greater environmental benefits at a lower price. This strategy particularly suits firms operating in price- and ecologically-sensitive markets, such as the packaging and chemical industries.

Whatever the company and industry, ecological trends in marketing look set to stay and develop further as the sustainability debate rages on and companies use it to develop their own competitive strategies. It is important to assess how this movement towards greener and more sustainable marketing is affecting a particular industry to ensure that a company within that industry is either not adversely affected by these changes (e.g. by non-compliance with regulatory change such as packaging) or can take advantage of the opportunities (e.g. a haulage company taking advantage of hybrid engine lorries to lower energy costs).

Information about each of these sub-environments is gathered in order for an assessment to be made about the potential impact on the organization. Organizations need to monitor all PESTLE elements, but some are more important than others. For example, pharmaceutical organizations such as GlaxoSmithKline monitor legal and regulatory developments (e.g. labelling, patents, and testing), the Environment Agency monitors political and ecological changes (e.g. flood plains for housing developments), road haulage companies should watch for changes that impact on transport development (e.g. congestion charging, diesel duty, toll roads), and music distributors should monitor changes in technology and associated social and cultural developments (e.g. downloading trends and cloud computing).

Environmental Scanning

To understand how external environments change, organizations need to put in place methods and processes to inform them of developments. The process of doing this is known as environmental scanning. **Environmental scanning** is the process of gathering information about a company's external events and relationships to assist top management in its decision-making and so develop its future course of action (Aguilar, 1967). It is the internal communication of external information about issues that may potentially influence an organization's decision-making process, focusing on the identification of emerging issues, situations, and potential threats in the external environment (Albright, 2004). Environmental scanning is an important component of the strategic marketing planning process (see Chapter 5). The development of an organization's strategic options is dependent on first determining the opportunities and threats in the environment and auditing an organization's resources.

We can gather information in environmental scanning exercises using company reports, newspapers, industry reports and magazines, government reports, and marketing intelligence reports (e.g. those published by Datamonitor, Euromonitor, and Mintel).

Visit the **Online Resource Centre** and follow the weblinks to learn more about the information and services offered provided by Datamonitor, Euromonitor, and Mintel.

Soft personal sources of information obtained through networking are also important, such as contacts at trade fairs, particularly for competitive and legal and regulatory information. Such verbal personal sources of information can be critical in fast-changing environments (May *et al.*, 2000) when reports from government, industry, or specific businesses have yet to be written and disseminated.

Small manufacturing companies, for example, tend to scan three important areas of information in environmental scanning activities (Beal, 2000).

- *Customer and competitor information*—including competitors' prices, competitors' new offerings, competitors' promotional programmes, competitors' entry into new markets and new product/service technologies, customers' buying habits, and customers' preferences, demands, and desires.

- *Company resources and capabilities*—including companies' R&D capabilities and resources, companies' websites and promotional resources, companies' sales capabilities/resources, companies' financial capabilities/resources, and companies' management capabilities/resources.

- *Suppliers of labour and funds*—including availability of external financing and availability of labour and new manufacturing technologies.

For larger companies, or small companies operating in global environments, because of the increased complexity there is a greater need to undertake effective environmental scanning. Firms successfully operating in international markets are more likely to find information on export opportunities through information from secondary sources and from market research exercises. They tend to monitor their competitors' export performance, involvement in exporting, and their export intention, and they are more likely to monitor changes in technology, in offerings, in economic conditions, and in socio-political conditions (Lim *et al.* 1996). A study of Thai small-to medium-sized food processing companies indicated that environmental scanning is a key factor for new proposition development success in sectors with high technological turbulence (Ngamkroeckjoti and Speece, 2008).

The process through which companies scan the marketing environment typically involves three stages (see Figure 4.4). In Stage 1, the focus is principally, but not exclusively, on data gathering.

Visit the **Online Resource Centre** and complete Internet Activity 4.2 to learn more about a number of sources that can be useful when conducting a scan of the marketing environment.

In Stage 2, the focus is principally, but not exclusively, on interpreting the data gathered in a process of environmental interpretation/analysis, and in the final stage, the focus is principally, but not exclusively, on strategy formulation.

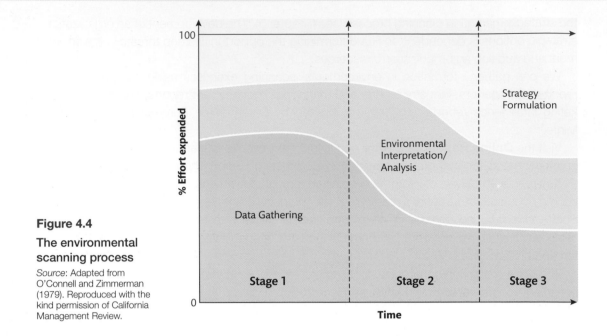

Figure 4.4

The environmental scanning process

Source: Adapted from O'Connell and Zimmerman (1979). Reproduced with the kind permission of California Management Review.

During each of the key scanning stages, there is also some activity in the other two areas so that each of the three processes dominates a particular stage but is also present at the other stages. So, in Stage 1 we might spend 60% of our time gathering data, 20% of our time undertaking environmental analysis/evaluation, and the remaining 20% of our time on strategy formulation. In Stage 2 we spend more time relatively on undertaking the environment analysis/evaluation, and in Stage 3 we spend more time relatively on strategy formulation. Environmental scanning is an activity that must be built into the strategy development and formulation process if it is to impact on company decision-making and help firms outperform their competitors by adapting to their environment.

Although the process seems relatively straightforward, and simply a matter of collecting the 'right' information, barriers to effective environmental scanning exist because it is difficult to determine what is the 'right' information. In addition, data gathering can be time-consuming. In such cases, the information gathered ceases to provide a useful input to strategic marketing decision-making. In addition, multinational corporations may see opportunities and desire organizational change, and collect the right data, to take advantage of those opportunities, but fail to actually undertake such opportunities because of **switching costs** and organizational inertia related to production, sourcing, and other business operations. In a transatlantic survey of European and American companies in the late 1970s (O'Connell and Zimmerman, 1979), American executives reported numerous frustrations in their environmental scanning exercises including the inability to move faster, managerial inhibitions related to pessimistic discussions, conflict between the desire for stability and the reality of constant change, missed opportunities due to poor timing, and problems motivating the management team to discuss the issues. European executives reported frustrations including the inability to organize for environmental scanning, difficulty matching individual executive beliefs with detectable trends, a delay between external developments and their interpretation of them, difficulty in applying a systematic approach, and problems finding relevant information.

Research Insight 4.1

To take your learning further, you might wish to read this highly influential paper.

Levitt, T. (2004), 'Marketing myopia', *Harvard Business Review*, **July–August (originally published in 1960).**

This is, perhaps the most famous and celebrated article ever written on marketing. It won the author the McKinsey Award. It has twice been reprinted in the *Harvard Business Review*. The central thesis of the article, as true today as it was in 1960, is that companies must monitor change in the external environment and keep abreast of their customers' needs or they risk decline.

@ **Visit the Online Resource Centre to read the abstract and access the full paper.**

However, some companies have developed a proactive approach by considering potential future **scenarios** facing them. For example, the multinational energy company Shell, in its analysis of the world energy market to 2050, identifies two possible future energy scenarios based on how governments and companies respond to the energy production and sustainability challenge. In its 'scramble' scenario, there is energy price volatility, no effective carbon pricing, coal and biofuels are emphasized, and renewables are forced in by legislation, with a patchwork of national standards. In the 'blueprints' scenario, effective carbon pricing is established early, energy efficiency standards are put in place, the transport sector is electrified, and new energy infrastructure develops (Royal Dutch Shell, 2012). These two scenarios help Shell to plan for alternative realities until it becomes clear which one, or neither, of the scenarios is likely to occur.

Understanding the Performance Environment

The **performance environment**, often called the microenvironment, consists of those organizations that either directly or indirectly influence an organization's operational performance. There are three main types.

1 Those companies that compete against the organization in the pursuit of its objectives.

2 Those companies that supply raw materials, goods, and services and those that add value as distributors, dealers, and retailers further down the marketing channel. These organizations have the potential to directly influence the performance of the organization by adding value through production, assembly, and distribution of products prior to reaching the end-user.

3 Those companies that have the potential to *indirectly* influence the performance of the organization in the pursuit of its objectives. These organizations often supply services such as consultancy, financial services, or marketing research or communication agencies.

Analysis of the performance environment is undertaken so that organizations can adapt to better positions, relative to those of their stakeholders and competitors. These adjustments are made as circumstances develop and/or in anticipation of environmental and performance conditions. The performance environment encompasses not only competitors but also suppliers and other organizations such as distributors, who all contribute to the industry value chain.

Knowledge about the performance arena allows organizations to choose how and where to operate and compete, given limited resources. Knowledge allows adaptation and development in complex and increasingly turbulent markets. Conditions vary from industry to industry. Some are full of potential and growth opportunities, such as cruise holidays, Fairtrade food, and the online travel and gaming industries, whereas others are in decline or at best stagnating, such as high street music stores. Rivalry may be on an international, national, regional, or local basis. The source and strength of competitive forces will vary, so that a strong organization operating in an 'unattractive' industry may have difficulty in achieving an acceptable performance. However, weaker organizations operating in 'attractive' environments may record consistently good performances.

Analysing Industries

An industry is composed of various firms that market similar offerings. According to Porter (1979), we should review the 'competitive' environment within an industry to identify the major competitive forces as this helps to assess their impact on an organization's present and future competitive positions. Numerous variables help to determine how attractive an industry is and shape the longer-term profitability for the different companies that make up the industry. Think of industries such as shipbuilding, cars, coal, and steel, where levels of profitability have been weak and unattractive to prospective new entrants. Now think of industries such as new media, oil, banking, and supermarkets, where levels of profitability have been astonishingly high. The competitive pressures in all these markets vary quite considerably, but there are enough similarities to establish an analytical framework to gauge the nature and intensity of competition. Porter suggests that competition in an industry is a composite of five main competitive forces. These are the level of threat that new competitors will enter the market, the threat posed by substitute products, and the bargaining power of both buyers and suppliers. These, in turn, affect the fifth force, the intensity of rivalry between the current competitors. Porter called these variables the Five Forces of Competitive Industry Analysis (see Figure 4.5).

As a general rule, the more intense the rivalry between the industry players, the lower their overall performance. On the other hand, the lower the rivalry, the greater will be the performance of the industry players. Porter's model is useful because it exposes the competitive forces in operation in an industry and can lead to an assessment of the strength of each of the forces. The collective impact determines what competition is like in the market. As a general rule, the stronger the competitive forces, the lower is the profitability in a market. An organization needs

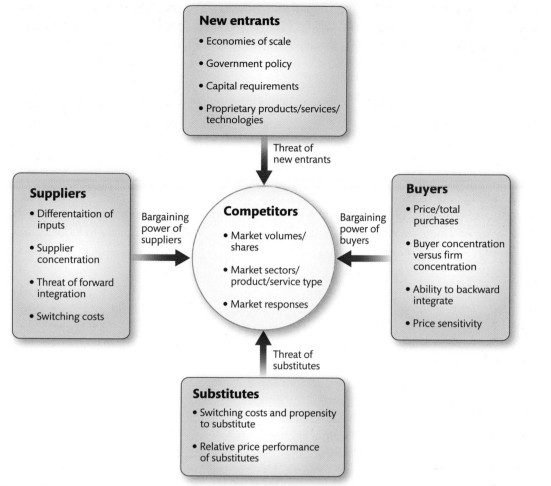

Figure 4.5

Industry analysis: Porter's five forces

Source: Adapted from Porter (1979). Reproduced with the kind permission of Harvard Business School Publishing.

to determine a competitive approach that allows it to influence the industry's competitive rules, protects it from competitive forces as much as possible, and gives it a strong position from which to compete.

New Entrants

Industries are seldom static. Companies and brands enter and exit industries all the time. Consider the UK beverage industry: it has witnessed the entrance of energy drink manufacturers such as Red Bull. This company has been competing head-on with industry stalwarts Pepsico, Coca-Cola, and GlaxoSmithKline's Lucozade, the original energy drink in the UK beverage market.

When examining an industry, we should consider whether economies of scale are required to operate successfully within it. For instance, motor manufacturing in the UK requires significant investment in plant and machinery. Unfortunately, as British labour costs are high and foreign direct investment incentives (e.g. government development grants) are not as lucrative as they once were, many British-based motor manufacturers have moved to Eastern Europe and Far Eastern countries. New entrants may be restricted through government and regulatory policy or they may be frozen out of an industry because of the capital requirements necessary to set up business. For example, in the oil and gas industry, huge sums of capital are required to fund not only exploration activities but also the extraction and refining operations.

Companies may be locked out of a market because companies already within that market are using proprietary offerings or technologies, e.g. the pharmaceutical industry where patents protect companies' investments in new medicines. The cost of a typical new patented drug in 2011 was around $1.3bn (Tufts CSDD, 2011). Few companies can compete in such a market as the set-up and ongoing R&D costs are huge. One strategic response in the industry has been a wave of consolidation (i.e. mergers and alliances) as pharmaceutical companies attempted to build critical mass in R&D, marketing, and distribution; for example, in 2009 pharmaceutical industry giants Pfizer and GlaxoSmithKline agreed to set up a joint company to develop and market their HIV/AIDS drugs in a bid to share risk and development costs (Ruddick, 2009). Ironically, whilst such mergers have resulted in less competition, they have also resulted in less R&D (LaMattina, 2011) and the launch of new chemical compounds.

Substitutes

In any industry, there are usually substitute offerings that perform the same function or meet similar customer needs. Levitt (1960) warned that many companies fail to recognize the competitive threat from newly developing offerings. He cites the American railroad industry's refusal to see the competitive threat arising from the development of the automobile and airline industries in the transport sector.

Consider the telecommunications sector in the UK. As telecommunications markets continue to converge with the development of broadband internet services, we see a variety of different companies operating in the same competitive marketspace, e.g. Everything Everywhere (Orange and T-Mobile), BT, and many others. With the long-standing development of VOIP (voice over internet protocol)—the internet telecommunication voice transmission standard—fixed-line telecommunications has become a commodity and firms operating in the area now look to develop value-added services such as video-on-demand, interactive gaming, and web-conferencing services.

Most countries' fixed-line operators have found it difficult to hold on to their original subscribers, partly because cheaper alternatives are appearing in the market (e.g. cable, internet, and fusion plans incorporating mobile and fixed lines and TV packages). It takes time for consumers to become aware of new offerings and obtain the necessary information to allow them to make a decision over whether or not to switch. Consumers consider the switching costs associated with such a decision, which, in turn, affects their propensity to substitute the offering for another. They consider the relative price performance of one offering over another. For example, if we decide we wish to travel from Amsterdam to Paris, we can fly from Schiphol airport to Charles de Gaulle airport, take the train, or drive (or hire a car and drive if we don't have one). We would consider the relative price differences (the flight is likely to be the most expensive, but not always) and we would also factor into this decision how comfortable and convenient these different journeys were hypothetically before we finally make our choice. In analysing our place within an industry, we should consider what alternative offerings exist in the marketplace, which also meet, to a greater or lesser extent, our customers' needs.

Buyers

Companies should ask themselves how much of their sales go to one individual company. This is an important question because if one buying company purchases a large volume of offerings from the supplying company, as car manufacturers do from steel suppliers, it is likely to be able to demand price concessions (price/total purchases) when there are lots of competing suppliers in the marketplace relative to the proportion of buyers (buyer concentration versus firm concentration). Buyers may also decide to increase their bargaining power through **backward integration**. For instance, a company is said to have backward integrated when it moves into manufacturing the offerings it previously bought from its suppliers. Tesco plc—the British multiple retail grocer operating in 14 markets outside the UK in 2012—also sells financial services including debt and credit services which it previously would have purchased from Visa and MasterCard **merchant** operators. As customers have tended to pay using credit/debit cards rather than cash for many years, Tesco has lowered its transaction costs by setting up its own credit/debit services. Nevertheless, for the other suppliers in a market, it means that they effectively have a new entrant into the market and hence a new competitor. Another factor impacting on a buyer's bargaining power is how price sensitive that particular company is (see Chapter 9). Depending on their trading circumstances, some companies might be more price-sensitive than other buyers. If such companies are more price-sensitive and yet there are lots of competing suppliers for their business, they are likely to display less loyalty to their suppliers. Most companies try to enhance other factors associated with an offering (e.g. after-sales service, product/service customization) to try to reduce a client company's **price sensitivity**. When analysing an industry, we should understand the bargaining power that buyers have with their suppliers as this can impact on the price charged and the volumes sold or total revenue earned.

Suppliers

When analysing a particular industry, we should determine how suppliers operate and the extent of their bargaining power. For instance, if a small number of suppliers operate within an industry (e.g. aeroplane manufacture) with a large number of competitors (e.g. national airlines and low-cost airline companies), the suppliers (e.g. Boeing and Airbus) have the stronger bargaining advantage. Conversely, in an industry (e.g. computer gaming) where there are a large number of suppliers (e.g. game production companies, game console component manufacturers) with few competitors, the buying companies (e.g. Sony, Nintendo, Microsoft) have the bargaining advantage. We should also consider whether or not the suppliers are providing unique components, products, services that may enhance their bargaining situation. In some industries, suppliers increase their market dominance by forward integrating (e.g. a toy manufacturer setting up a retail outlet to sell its own products). Forward integration not only allows a company to control its own supply chains better but also allows it to sell at lower prices, thereby increasing sales vis-à-vis competitors and profit from increased retail sales as well. Equally, if companies face high switching costs—economic, resource, and time costs associated with using another supplier—as a result a supplier has stronger bargaining power with that particular company.

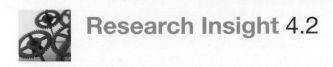

Research Insight 4.2

To take your learning further, you might wish to read this highly cited and influential book.

Porter, M. E. (1980), *Competitive Strategy: Techniques for Analysing Industries and Competitors,* **New York: Free Press.**

This book expanded Porter's first public presentation of his ideas about industry analysis in a *Harvard Business Review* article the previous year. The central tenet of the book is that industry profitability and performance is a result of the interaction of five forces: supplier power, buyer power, competitive rivalry, the availability of substitutes, and the extent of new competitive entrants into an industry. Porter's Five Forces technique for analysing industries is still widely used by marketing and strategy executives today.

@ Visit the **Online Resource Centre** to find out more about the book.

Competitors

To analyse an industry, we develop an outline of which companies are operating within that particular industry. For example, in the UK cosmetic sector, the market-leading cosmetic manufacturers are Avon European Holdings Ltd, Estée Lauder Cosmetics Ltd, L'Oréal (UK) Ltd, Procter & Gamble Ltd, the Unilever Group, and large retailers such as Boots Group plc, The Body Shop International plc, and Superdrug Stores plc. In undertaking a competitor analysis we outline each company's structure (e.g. details of the main holding company, the individual business unit, any changes in ownership), current and future developments (these can often be gleaned from reading company prospectuses, websites, and industry reports), and the company's latest financial results. We would be interested in calculating the market volumes and shares for each competitor, as market share is a key indication of company profitability and return on investment (Buzzell *et al.*, 1975).

In analysing the competitors within an industry, we are interested in different types of goods and services that competitors offer in different market sectors. Clark and Montgomery (1999) call this process of identification of competitors the supply-based approach because it considers those firms who supply the same sorts of goods and services as your own firm. However, they identify another approach to competitor identification, which they term the demand-based approach, identifying competitors based on customer attitudes and behaviour. Firms with similar offerings, as perceived by the customer, are regarded as competitors.

We are also interested in measuring market responses to any new strategy developments that our company initiates. Although this might seem obvious, research indicates that companies do not tend to consider their competitors' strategies (what the authors call 'strategic competitive reasoning'), except occasionally in relation to pricing strategy, perhaps because they do not feel that it is worth the effort (Montgomery *et al.*, 2005). Generally, managers tend to name relatively few competitors and need to focus more on competitors as determined by customer requirements (Clark and Montgomery, 1999).

Understanding the Internal Environment

An analysis of the internal environment of an organization is concerned with understanding and evaluating the capabilities and potential of the products, systems, human, marketing, and financial resources. An analysis of an organization's resources should not focus on the relative strength and weakness of a particular resource, but look at the absolute nature of the resource itself. As Thompson (1990) suggests, 'resources are not strong or weak merely because they exist … their value depends upon how they are being managed, controlled and used.' Attention here is given to two main elements, products and finance.

Portfolio Analysis

When managing a collection or portfolio of offerings, we should appreciate that understanding the performance of an individual offering can often fail to give the appropriate insight. What is really important is an understanding of the relative performance of offerings. By creating a balance of old, mature, established, growing, and very new offerings, there is a better chance of delivering profits now and at some point in the future, when the current offerings cease to be attractive and profitable. One of the popular methods for assessing the variety of businesses/ offerings that an organization has involves the creation of a two-dimensional graphical picture of the comparative strategic positions. This technique is referred to as a portfolio matrix. The Boston Consulting Group (BCG) developed the original idea and their matrix—the **Boston Box**, shown in Figure 4.6—is based on two key variables, market growth and relative market share (i.e. market

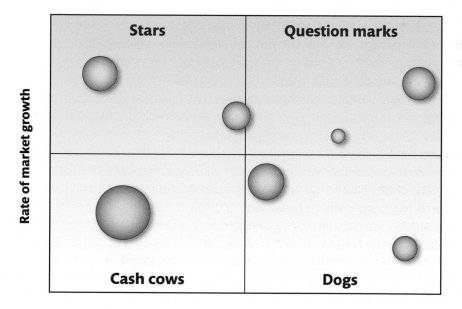

Figure 4.6

The Boston Box

Source: Reprinted from B. Hedley, 'Strategy and the business portfolio', *Long Range Planning*, 10(1), 12. © 1977, with permission from Elsevier.

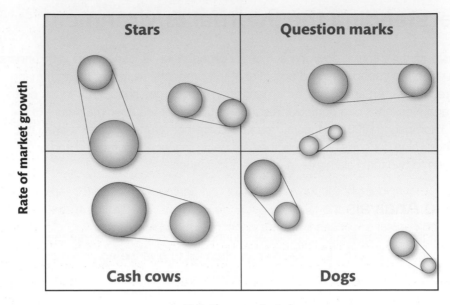

Figure 4.7

Present and future positions in the BCG matrix

Source: Reprinted from B. Hedley, 'Strategy and the business portfolio', *Long Range Planning*, 10(1), 12. © 1977, with permission from Elsevier.

share as a percentage of the share of the product's largest competitor, expressed as a fraction). Thus a relative share of 0.8 means that the product achieves 80% of the sales of the market leader's sales volume (or value, depending on which measure is used). This is not the strongest competitive position but is not a weak position either. A relative market share of 1 means that the company shares market leadership with a competitor with an equal share. A relative market share of 2 means that the company has twice the market share of the nearest competitor.

In Figure 4.7, the vertical axis refers to the rate of market growth and the horizontal axis refers to an offering's market strength, as measured by relative market share (as described in the previous paragraph). The size of the circles represents the sales revenue generated by the product. Relative market share is generally regarded as high when you are the market leader (i.e. the relative market share is 1 or greater). Determining whether or not market growth rate is high or low is more problematic and depends on the industry to some extent. In some industries, a market growth rate of 5% might be regarded as high, whereas in others this might be 10%. However, the benchmark between high and low is often taken to be 10%. This lack of clarity on what are regarded definitively as high and low rates of market growth is a key criticism of the approach.

Question marks (also known as 'problem children') are offerings that exist in growing markets but have low market share. As a result there is negative cash flow and they are unprofitable. Stars are most probably market leaders, but their growth has to be financed through fairly heavy levels of investment. Cash cows, on the other hand, exist in fairly stable low-growth markets and require little ongoing investment. Their high market share draws both positive cash flows and high levels of profitability. Dogs experience low growth and low market share, and generate negative cash flows. These indicators suggest that many of them are operating in declining markets and have no real long-term future. Divestment need not occur just because of low share. In March 2007,

Procter & Gamble decided to leave the paper business, and this involved selling off Bounty, their kitchen roll brand, and Charmin, their toilet tissue brand. They sold the business because of falling performance and because they did not see how they could achieve number 1 or 2 position in the different paper markets. Instead, they sold the business to their main rivals, SCA (Godsell, 2007). From a reverse perspective, in 2009 Coca-Cola bought a £30m stake in innocent drinks in an attempt to give it access to the smoothie market, which prior to 2008 (and the recession) had grown rapidly over the previous ten years and in which it had no presence whatsoever. By buying a minority 18% stake in innocent (which it increased by 40% to a 58% majority stake in 2010), Coca-Cola bypassed the set-up costs of developing their own 'question mark' smoothie product, thereby gaining a market presence at a relatively modest cost and giving it the option in due course to buy the company outright if it and the innocent management so desire (Reynolds, 2011).

Portfolio analysis is an important analytical tool as it draws attention to the cash flow and investment characteristics of each of a firm's offerings and indicates how financial resources can be manoeuvred to attain optimal strategic performance over the long term. Essentially, excess cash generated by cash cows should be utilized to develop question marks and stars, which are unable to support themselves. This enables stars to become cash cows and self-supporting. Dogs should only be retained as long as they contribute to positive cash flow and do not restrict the use of assets and resources elsewhere in the business. Once they do, they should be divested or ejected from the portfolio.

By plotting all a company's offerings onto the grid it becomes visually easy to appreciate just how well balanced the portfolio is. An unbalanced portfolio would be one with too many offerings clustered in one or two quadrants. Where offerings are distributed equally, or at least are not clustered in any one area, and where market shares and cash flows equate with their market position, the portfolio is financially healthy and well balanced. By analysing the portfolio in this way it becomes possible to project possible strategies and their outcomes. These are shown in Figure 4.7.

Portfolio Issues

Portfolio analysis is an important guide to strategic development, if only because it forces answers to questions such as:

- How fast will the market grow?
- What will be our market share?
- What investment will be required?
- How can a balanced portfolio be created from this point?

(See also Market Insight 4.5.)

However, the questions posed and the answers generated through use of the Boston Box do not produce marketing strategies in themselves. As with all analytical tools and methodologies, the BCG provides strategic indicators, not solutions. It is management's task to consider information from a variety of sources and then make decisions based on their judgement. The Boston Box has been criticized for providing rigid solutions to product portfolio evaluation when exceptions to the rule might exist, e.g. proposing that 'cash cow' products should not be invested in, when a company may rely solely on its 'cash cow' products to provide profits and not necessarily have new offerings in the pipeline to replace them. Equally, the Boston Box proposes that 'dog' offerings should be divested, when, in fact, they may actually be returning a profit to the company. Finding the necessary and objective data to plot the positions of products or SBUs on the two axes of relative market share and market growth rate can also be problematic. Reliable industry data may not always be available. Finally, it is not always easy to determine what market we are concerned with. For example, if we consider the smoothie market, does this include only fruit-based milkshakes, or fruit juices more generally?

Research Insight 4.3

To take your learning further, you might wish to read this influential paper.

Morrison, A. and Wensley, R. (1991), 'Boxing up or boxing in: a short history of the Boston Consulting Group Share/Growth Matrix', *Journal of Marketing Management*, 7(2), 105–29.

This highly readable and critical article outlines the history of the development of the 'Boston Box' portfolio analysis concept from academic and practitioner perspectives. The article concludes that the concept is useful in strategic planning but that those using it should be aware of its limitations, namely around the scope of the technique, the assumptions it makes, how it defines and classifies markets by share and growth, its failure to consider the political dimensions of strategy development, that there are strategic implementation difficulties of the strategies proposed in real firms, and that the matrix explains what strategy to undertake but not how to do it.

@ **Visit the Online Resource Centre to read the abstract and access the full paper.**

Market Insight 4.5

Britvic and AG Barr Mix Their Drinks

Britvic is a leading soft drinks manufacturer in Britain, Ireland, and France with many of its brands positioned as number 1 or 2 in their respective sub-categories (see Tables 4.1 and 4.2). In the UK, Britvic's product portfolio includes still and carbonated brands— Robinson's, Pepsi, 7 Up, Drench, Tango, J₂O, Britvic, Fruit Shoot, R. White's, and Pennine Spring to name a few. Britvic has tried to develop the breadth and depth of its portfolio so that it can target consumer demand in all the major soft drinks categories, through all relevant distribution channels, and across a wide range of consumption occasions. Britvic has a successful long-standing relationship with Pepsico until 2019. This relationship gives Britvic the exclusive right to distribute the Pepsi and 7 Up brands in Great Britain, and access to all new carbonated drinks developed by Pepsico for distribution in Great Britain. In 2012, Britvic agreed a merger with AG Barr, the owner of Irn-Bru, Orangina, and Tizer, among other brands, creating Barr Britvic Soft Drinks though this deal later fell through in 2013. The company would have had a combined sales revenue of more than £1.5bn.

Market Insight 4.5
continued

Table 4.1 Brand value shares in the UK take-home carbonated soft drinks market, 2009–11

	2009		2010		2011		2009–11
	£m	% share	£m	% share	£m	% share	% change
Coca-Cola (Coca-Cola GB)	1,072	48	1,156	48	1,250	48	16.6
Pepsi (Britvic)	284	13	325	13	345	13	21.5
Schweppes (Coca-Cola GB)	134	6	137	6	132	5	−1.5
Fanta (Coca-Cola GB)	114	5	116	5	127	5	11.4
Irn-Bru (AG Barr)	101	5	106	4	107	4	5.9
Dr Pepper (Coca-Cola GB)	74	3	79	3	92	4	24.3
Sprite (Coca-Cola GB)	67	3	72	3	79	3	17.9
7UP (Britvic)	36	2	41	2	46	2	27.8
Tango (Britvic)	27	1	31	1	32	1	18.5
R Whites (Britvic)	13	1	14	1	16	1	23.1
Other	135	6	156	6	165	6	22.2
Own-label	180	8	175	7	196	8	8.9
Total	**2,237**	**100**	**2,408**	**100**	**2,587**	**100**	**15.6**

Note: Totals may not add up to 100% due to rounding error.
Sources: Mintel (2012b,c); Neate (2012).

Table 4.2 Brand shares in the UK off-trade values sales of squashes and cordials, 2009–11

	2009 £m	Share %	2010 £m	Share %	2011 £m	Share %	Change 2009–11 %
Robinsons (Britvic)	216	47	218	45	218	44	0.9
Ribena (GSK)	57	12	60	12	62	12	8.8
Vimto (Nichols)	21	5	27	6	30	6	42.9
Bottlegreen (Bottlegreen Drinks)	10	2	11	2	12	2	20.0
Jucee (Princes)	8	2	5	1	7	1	−12.5

Market Insight 4.5
continued

Table 4.2 continued

	2009 £m	Share %	2010 £m	Share %	2011 £m	Share %	Change 2009–11 %
Rose's (CCE)	4	1	4	1	4	1	0.0
Kia-Ora (CCE)	3	1	3	1	4	1	33.3
Belvoir (Belvoir Fruit Farms)	3	1	3	1	3	1	0.0
Sun-Sip (Princes)	–	–	1	–	2	–	100
Ocean Spray (Princes)	3	1	2	–	2	–	33.3
Other brands	3	1	6	1	12	2	300.0
Own-label	133	29	136	28	140	28	5.3
Total	**461**	**100**	**481**	**100**	**498**	**100**	**7.6**

Note: Totals may not add up to 100% due to rounding error.

Sources: Mintel (2012b,c); Neate (2012).

Tango, the Britvic drink, that explodes with flavour

Source: Courtesy of Britvic Drinks Ltd.

1 **What are the advantages of Britvic's merger with AG Barr?**

2 **Undertake a Boston Box portfolio analysis for the combined company. What are your recommendations for brands like R White's and Tango? Why do you say this?**

3 **Can you think of three different consumption occasions when Robinson's might be the preferred drink?**

Marketing Audit

To make sense of all the information that has been collected, considered, and analysed during the strategic market analysis part of the marketing strategy process, a marketing audit is normally undertaken. Just as a financial audit considers the financial health of an organization, so a marketing audit considers its marketing health. In particular, it brings together views about the three environments. First, it considers the external opportunities and threats, where management has little or no control. Second, it considers the nature, characteristics, and any changes occurring within the performance environment, where management has partial influence. Third, the audit reviews the quality and potential of the organization's products,

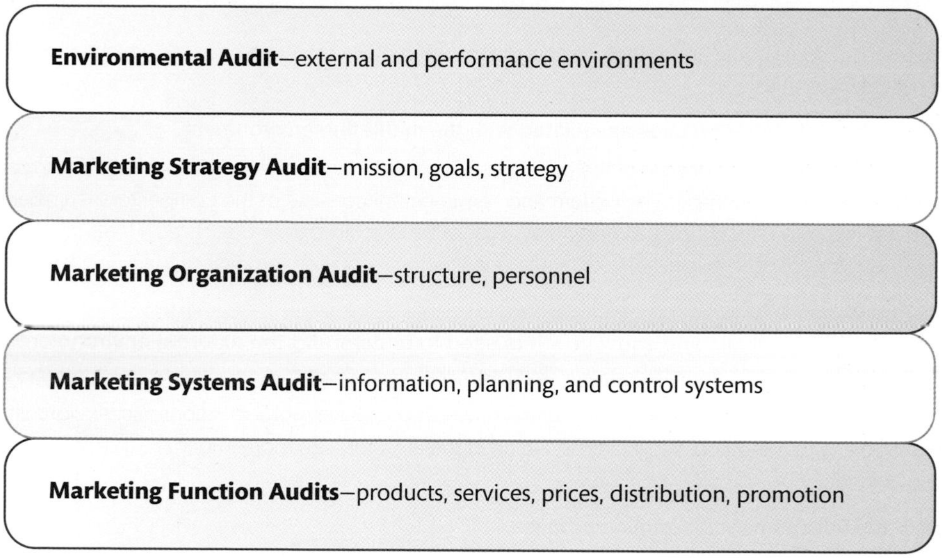

Environmental Audit—external and performance environments

Marketing Strategy Audit—mission, goals, strategy

Marketing Organization Audit—structure, personnel

Marketing Systems Audit—information, planning, and control systems

Marketing Function Audits—products, services, prices, distribution, promotion

Figure 4.8
Dimensions of a marketing audit

marketing systems, resources, and capabilities, as part of the internal environment where there is full control. The topics normally undertaken as part of the marketing audit are shown in Figure 4.8.

The audit covers the marketing environment, an organization's objectives and strategies, its marketing programmes and performance, plus the organization itself and the relevant marketing systems and procedures. We undertake marketing audits because they bring together critical information, identify weaknesses in order that they can be corrected, and provide a platform on which to build marketing strategy.

The marketing audit can be undertaken either by an internal team, led by a senior manager, or if a more objective interpretation is desired, an outside consultant can be used. Whoever conducts the audit, it should be undertaken on a regular annual basis and be regarded as a positive activity that can feed into marketing strategy. Marketing audits should not be instigated in response to a crisis.

Chapter Summary

To consolidate your learning, the key points from this chapter are summarized here.

■ **Identify and define the three key areas of the marketing environment.**

The marketing environment incorporates the external environment, the performance environment, and the internal environment. The external environment incorporates macro-environmental factors, which are largely uncontrollable and which organizations generally cannot influence. The performance environment incorporates key factors within an industry, impacting on strategic decision-making. The internal environment is controllable and is the principal means, through its resource base, by which an organization influences its strategy.

- **Describe the key characteristics associated with the marketing environment.**

  The external environment consists of the political, social, and technological influences, and organizations have limited influence on these. The performance environment consists of the competitors, suppliers, and indirect service providers shaping the way that organizations achieve their objectives. Here, organizations have more influence. The internal environment concerns the resources, processes, and policies that organizations manage to achieve their goals.

- **Explain PESTLE analysis and show how it is used to understand the external environment.**

  We considered the various components of the external marketing environment which may impact on any particular organization using the PESTLE acronym, which comprises political, economic, socio-cultural, technological, legal, and ecological factors. Some of these factors are more important than others in any particular industry.

- **Explain the environmental scanning process.**

  The environmental scanning process consists of the data-gathering phase, the environmental interpretation/analysis phase, and the strategy formulation phase. The three processes are interlinked, but, over time, more attention is focused on each one more than the others so that at the end of the process, greater effort is expended on using knowledge gleaned from the external and competitive environments to formulate strategy based on changes occurring and identified in the company's environment.

- **Analyse the performance environment using Porter's Five Forces industry analysis model.**

  The most common technique used to analyse the performance environment is Porter's Five Forces Model of Competitive Analysis. Porter concludes that the more intense the rivalry between industry players, the lower will be their overall performance. On the other hand, the lower the rivalry, the greater will be the performance of the industry players. Porter's Five Forces comprise (1) supplier bargaining power, (2) buyer bargaining power, (3) threat of new entrants, (4) rivalry of competitors, and (5) threat of substitutes.

- **Analyse an organization's product/service portfolio to aid resource planning.**

  An organization's principal resources relate to the portfolio of offerings that it carries and the financial resources at its disposal. We use portfolio analysis, specifically the Boston Box approach, to determine whether different strategic business units or product/service formulations are stars, dogs, question marks, or cash cows; each category suggests differing levels of cash flow and resource requirements to develop. It is important to undertake a marketing audit as a preliminary measure to allow proper development of marketing strategy.

 # Review Questions

1 What are the three main marketing environments?
2 What are the three stages of the environmental scanning process?
3 How might changes in the political environment affect marketing strategy?
4 How might changes in the economic environment affect marketing strategy?
5 How might changes in the socio-cultural environment affect marketing strategy?
6 How might changes in the technological environment affect marketing strategy?

7 How might changes in the legal environment affect marketing strategy?

8 How might changes in the ecological environment affect marketing strategy?

9 What are Porter's Five Forces?

10 What is product portfolio analysis and why is it useful?

Worksheet Summary

To apply the knowledge you have gained from this chapter and test your understanding of the marketing environment visit the **Online Resource Centre** and complete Worksheet 4.1.

Discussion Questions

1 Having read the Case Insight at the beginning of this chapter, how would you advise Glassolutions Saint-Gobain to persuade the Government, specifically the Department for Energy and Climate Change, to reconsider how they fund green initiatives in the replacement window industry?

2 Read Market Insight 4.4 'Obesity: A Weighty Issue for Chocolate Manufacturers'. Search the internet for further information on the obesity debate and the 'fat tax', and answer the following questions.

A What changes have taken place in the external environment to bring about the introduction of 'fat taxes' in different countries?

B How should Kraft Foods (owner of Cadbury's) ensure that they keep up to date with trends in consumer lifestyles, government legislation, and competitor new proposition development?

C What strategies in relation to proposition development and promotion could Kraft Foods adopt to ensure that they maintain their market dominance in the chocolate countline market?

3 Undertake an environmental analysis using PESTLE, by surfing the internet for appropriate information and by using available market research reports, for each of the following markets.

A The automotive market (e.g. you might be Renault, BMW, Ford, or Toyota).

B The global multiple retail grocery market (e.g. you might be Walmart, Carrefour, or Tesco).

C The beer industry (e.g. you might be InBev, Carlsberg, Heineken, Miller Brands, or Budweiser Budvar).

4 Analyse the ecological marketing environment for the cosmetics industry in a country of your choice. Look specifically at socio-cultural patterns and trends in habits, particularly in relation to male versus female grooming. You should surf the internet for appropriate documents and market intelligence material to help you develop your arguments.

5 Using the data in Table 4.3 identify the relative market shares of the various brands in the UK beer market. Use the market growth rate figure as the difference in total sales between 2009 and 2011. Then draw up a Boston Box to illustrate the product portfolio for each of the key companies and their brands.

Table 4.3 UK beer market

	2009		2010		2011		% change
	£m	%	£m	%	£m	%	2009–11
Stella Artois (AB InBev)	522	15	553	15	546	14	+4.6
Foster's (Heineken)	382	11	396	11	451	12	+18.1
Carlsberg (incl. Carlsberg Export)	389	11	454	12	446	12	+14.7
Carling (Molson Coors)	336	10	339	9	352	9	+4.8
Budweiser (AB InBev)	152	4	250	7	264	7	+73.7
Kronenbourg 1664 (Heineken)	100	3	94	3	106	3	+6.0
Beck's (AB InBev)	108	3	107	3	101	3	–6.5
John Smith's (Heineken)	96	3	94	3	96	3	–
Guinness (Diageo)	93	3	104	3	96	3	+3.2
Other brands	1,114	33	1,190	32	1,195	32	+7.3
Own-label	118	3	122	3	127	3	+7.6
Total	**3,410**	**99**	**3,703**	**101**	**3,780**	**101**	**+10.9**

Note: Totals may not add up to 100% due to rounding error.
Source: Mintel (2012d).

Visit the **Online Resource Centre** and complete the Multiple Choice
Questions to assess your knowledge of Chapter 4.

References

Aguilar, F. Y. (1967), *Scanning the Business Environment*,
New York: Macmillan.

Albright, K. S. (2004), 'Environmental scanning: radar for
success', *Information Management Journal*, May–June,
38–45.

Anon. (2012a), 'Fish farms: Salmond's salmon', *The
Economist*, 1 December, 36.

Anon. (2012b), 'Mapping the tobacco lobby in Brussels:
a smoky business', *Corporate Europe Observatory*, 6
November, retrieve from: http://corporateeurope.org/
publications/mapping-tobacco-lobby-brussels-smoky-
business accessed 5 January 2013.

Anon. (2012c), 'Is "beer for women" a viable concept?',
Marketing, 5 October, retrieve from: http://www.

marketingmagazine.co.uk/news/1152709/
beer-women-viable-concept/?DCMP=ILC-SEARCH
accessed 5 January 2013.

Anon. (2012d), 'Finalist 2012 for Europe: Valentine Van
Der Lande: TenPages.com, the Netherlands', *Cartier's
Womens' Initiative Awards*, retrieve from: http://www.
cartierwomensinitiative.com/candidate/valentine-van-der-
lande accessed 5 January 2013.

ASA (2011), 'ASA Adjudication on Cider of Sweden Ltd',
London: Advertising Standards Authority, retrieve from
http://www.asa.org.uk/Rulings/Adjudications/2011/11/
Cider-of-Sweden-Ltd/SHP_ADJ_164407.aspx accessed
5 January 2013.

Bainbridge, J. (2012), 'Taxing issues for marketing',
Marketing, 5 December, 12–13.

BBC (2006), 'Supermarkets covet Polish spend', 10 September, *BBC News*, retrieve from http://news.bbc.co.uk/1/hi/business/5332024.stm accessed 11 April 2010.

Beal, R. M. (2000), 'Competing effectively: environmental scanning, competitive strategy, and organisational performance in small manufacturing firms', *Journal of Small Business Administration*, January, 27–47.

Buzzell, R. D., Gale, B. T., and Sultan, R. G. M (1975), 'Market share—a key to profitability', *Harvard Business Review*, January–February, 97–106.

Chandy, R. K., Prabhu, J. C., and Antia, K. D. (2003), 'What will the future bring? Dominance, technology expectations and radical innovation', *Journal of Marketing*, 67(July), 1–18.

Charles, G. and Farey-Jones, D. (2012), 'Starbucks' social-media score hit by tax backlash', *Marketing*, 28 November, 4.

Clark, B. H. and Montgomery, D. B. (1999), 'Managerial identification of competitors', *Journal of Marketing*, July, 67–83.

CTV News (2012), 'Larger anti-smoking warnings now on cigarette packs', *CTV News*, 19 June, retrieve from: http://www.ctvnews.ca/health/larger-anti-smoking-warnings-now-on-cigarette-packs-1.844025 accessed 6 January 2013.

Décaudin, J-M. and Malaval, P. (2008), 'Le lobbying: techniques, intérêt et limites', *Décisions Marketing*, 50 (April–June), 59–69.

DH/ABPI (2012), 'Joint DH/ABPI statement on arrangements for pricing branded medicines from 2014', 3 August, Department of Health/Association of the British Pharmaceutical Industry, retrieve from: http://www.dh.gov.uk/health/2012/08/abpi-dh-statement/ accessed 5 January 2013.

Fairtrade Foundation (nd), 'Sales of Fairtrade certified products in the UK', retrieve from www.fairtrade.org.uk/what_is_fairtrade/facts_and_figures.aspx accessed 6 January 2013.

Godsell, M. (2007), 'Not number one, not interested', *Marketing*, 21 March, 18.

Gosling, E. (2012), 'Plain cigarette packaging: deterrent or disaster?', *Design Week*, 12 July, retrieve from: http://www.designweek.co.uk/analysis/news-analysis/plain-cigarette-packaging-deterrent-or-disaster?/3034895. article accessed 5 January 2013.

Gower, I. (ed.) (2005), *Cosmetics and Fragrances Market Report 2005*, London: Keynote.

Hammond, D. (2011), 'Health warning messages on tobacco products: a review', *Tobacco Control*, 20, 327–37.

Health Canada (2011), 'Speech by the Minister of Health The Honourable Leona Aglukkaq—Proposed Tobacco Labelling Regulations', 27 September, retrieve from: http://www.hc-sc.gc.ca/ahc-asc/minist/speeches-discours/_2011/2011_09_27-eng.php accessed 6 January 2013.

Hillman, A., Keim, G. D., and Schuler, D. (2004), 'Corporate political activity: a review and research agenda', *Journal of Management*, 30(6), 837–57.

Howe, J. (2006), 'The rise of crowdsourcing', *Wired*, Issue 14.06 (June), retrieve from www.wired.com/wired/archive/14.06/crowds.html accessed 17 April 2010.

La Mattina, J.L. (2011), 'The impact of mergers on pharmaceutical R&D', *Nature Reviews Drug Discovery*, 10, 559–60.

Lawton, T. and Rajwani, T. (2011), 'Designing lobbying capabilities: managerial choices in unpredictable environments', *European Business Review*, 23(2), 167–89.

Levi Strauss & Co. (2011), 'Fourth quarter and fiscal year 2011 financial results', *Company Press Release*, retrieve from: http://www.levistrauss.com/news/press-releases/levi-strauss-co-announces-fourth-quarter-and-fiscal-year-2011-financial-results accessed 5 January 2013.

Levitt, T. (1960), 'Marketing myopia', *Harvard Business Review*, July–August, 45–56.

Lim, J.-S., Sharkey, T. W., and Kim, K. I. (1996), 'Competitive environmental scanning and export involvement: an initial enquiry', *International Marketing Review*, 13(1), 65–80.

Lucas, L., Jopson, B., and Houlder, V. (2012), 'Starbucks ground down', *Financial Times*, 8/9 December, 8.

McCready, K. (2012), 'Q&A: Alcohol: B2C: Marketing to Women', *Marketer*, May/June, 50.

May, R. C., Stewart, W. H., Jr, and Sweo, R. (2000), 'Environmental scanning behaviour in a transitional economy: evidence from Russia', *Academy of Management Journal*, 43(3), 403–27.

Miller, Z. (2011), 'Can Levi's ever return to its 1996 peak?', *Euromonitor*, 15 June, retrieve from: http://blog.euromonitor.com/2011/06/can-levis-ever-return-to-its-1996-peak.html accessed January 2013.

Mintel (2012a), *Chocolate—UK—April 2012*, London: Mintel International Group, retrieve from www.mintel.com, accessed 5 January 2012.

Mintel (2012b), *Carbonated Soft Drinks—UK—June 2012*, London: Mintel, retrieve from www.mintel.com accessed 5 January 2012.

Mintel (2012c), *Cordials and Squashes—UK—October 2012*, London: Mintel, retrieve from www.mintel.com accessed 6 January 2012.

Mintel (2012d), *Beer—UK—December 2012*, London: Mintel, retrieve from www.mintel.com accessed 5 January 2012.

Montgomery, D. B., Moore, M. C., and Urbany, J. E. (2005), 'Reasoning about competitive reactions: evidence from executives', *Marketing Science*, 24(1), 138–49.

Morris, P. (2001), 'Dealing with Whitehall and Westminster', Hawkesmere Seminar on Lobbying, Berners Hotel, London, 4 April.

Morrison, A. and Wensley, R. (1991), 'Boxing up or boxing in: a short history of the Boston Consulting Group Share/Growth Matrix', *Journal of Marketing Management*, 7(2), 105–29.

Mucklow, G. (2012), 'The future of mobile commerce', *Econsultancy: Digital Marketing Excellence*, 17 December, retrieve from: http://econsultancy.com/th/blog/11355-the-future-of-mobile-commerce, accessed 5 January 2013.

Murray, S. (2006), 'Confusion reigns over labelling', *Financial Times*, Special Report on Responsible Business, 2.

Neate, R. (2012), 'Britvic and Irn-Bru maker AG Barr agree £1.4bn merger', *Guardian*, 14 November, http://www.guardian.co.uk/business/2012/nov/14/britvic-irn-bru-barr-merger-jobs accessed 6 January 2013.

Ngamkroeckjoti, C. and Speece, M. (2008), 'Technology turbulence and environmental scanning in Thai food new product development', *Asia Pacific Journal of Marketing and Logistics*, 20(4), 413–32.

O'Connell, J. J., and Zimmerman, J. W. (1979), 'Scanning the international environment', *California Management Review*, 22(2), 15–23.

OECD (2012), *Obesity Update 2012*, Paris: Organization for Economic Co-operation and Development, retrieve from: http://www.oecd.org/health/49716427.pdf accessed 6 January 2013.

Orsato, R. J. (2006), 'Competitive environmental strategies: when does it pay to be green?', *California Management Review*, 48(2, Winter), 127–43.

Porter, M. (1979), 'How competitive forces shape strategy', *Harvard Business Review*, March–April.

Porter, M. E. (1980), *Competitive Strategy: Techniques for Analysing Industries and Competitors*, New York: Free Press

Rao, P. M. (2005), 'Sustaining competitive advantage in a high-technology environment: a strategic marketing perspective', *Advances in Competitiveness Research*, 13(1), 33–47.

Reynolds, J. (2011), 'Innocent hints at 100% sale to Coca-Cola', *Marketing*, 24 August, retrieve from: http://www.marketingmagazine.co.uk/news/1086577/Innocent-hints-100-sale-Coca-Cola/ accessed 6 January 2013.

Royal Dutch Shell (2012), 'Shell energy scenarios to 2050', retrieve from: http://www.shell.com/global/future-energy/scenarios/2050.html accessed 5 January 2013.

Ruddick, G. (2009), 'Glaxo-Pfizer tie-up opens new era in AIDS battle', *The Telegraph*, 31 October, retrieve from www.telegraph.co.uk/finance/newsbysector/pharmaceuticalsandchemicals/6474678/Glaxo-Pfizer-tie-up-opens-new-era-in-Aids-battle.html accessed 18 April 2010.

Stones, M. (2012), 'Danish decision to ditch fat and sugar taxes welcomed', Foodmanufacture.co.uk, 14 November, retrieve from: http://www.foodmanufacture.co.uk/Regulation/Danish-decision-to-ditch-fat-and-sugar-taxes-welcomed accessed 6 January 2013.

Sweney, M. (2009), 'Unilever goes crowdsourcing to spice up Peperami's TV ads', *Guardian*, 25 August, retrieve from www.guardian.co.uk/media/blog/2009/aug/25/unilever-peperami-advertising-crowdsourcing accessed 6 January 2013.

Taylor, J. (2010), 'A new lager that's clearly for ladies', *Metro*, 15 April, 35.

Thompson, K. M. (1990), *The Employee Revolution: Corporate Internal Marketing*, London: Pitman.

UN Population Division (2012), *World Population Prospects: The 2010 Revision*, retrieve from: http://esa.un.org/unpd/ppp/Figures-Output/Population/PPP_Total-Population.htm accessed 5 January April 2013.

Tufts CSDD (2011), 'Drug developers are aggressively changing the way they do R&D', *Tufts Centre for the Study of Drug Development*, 5 January, retrieve from: http://csdd.tufts.edu/news/complete_story/pr_outlook_2011 accessed 6 January 2013.

Viney, H. and Baines, P. (2012), 'Engaging government: why it's necessary and how to do it', *European Business Review*, September–October, 9–13.

Whitla, P. (2009), 'Crowdsourcing and its application in marketing activities', *Contemporary Management Research*, 5(1), 15–28.

World Travel Market (2010), 'World's largest global LGBT study uncovers large and untapped gay markets in Latin America', *Company Press Release*, 26 October, retrieve from: http://www.wtmlondon.com/page.cfm/Action=press/libID=1/listID=1/libEntryID=43 accessed 5 January 2013.

Chapter 5
Marketing Strategy

Learning Outcomes

After studying this chapter you should be able to:

▸ Describe the strategic planning process and explain the key influences that shape marketing strategy

▸ Analyse current conditions, including competitors, and develop marketing strategies

▸ Explain the different types of strategic marketing goals and associated growth strategies

▸ Describe the concepts associated with strategic marketing action, and explain the ways in which firms engage strategically with their chosen markets

▸ Understand the main issues associated with strategy implementation, including the principles of marketing metrics

▸ Outline the key elements of a marketing plan

Case Insight 5.1
PJ Care

Market Insight 5.1
Values Matter

Market Insight 5.2
Art of War: Corporate Style

Market Insight 5.3
Console Strategies

Market Insight 5.4
Phone Strategies

Market Insight 5.5
Strategically Empowered Employees

Case Insight 5.1

How should entrepreneurial organizations develop their marketing function in order to best serve their customers and meet shareholder financial goals? We speak to Wendy Thompson, PJ Care's general manager, sales and marketing, to find out more.

PJ Care, founded in 2001, is a leading provider of specialist neurological care and neuro-rehabilitation for people with progressive or acquired neurological conditions in the UK. We specialize in the multidisciplinary care of adults and work with residents, families, charities, social services and the National Health Service to provide the highest quality care for our residents.

Our residents' care is at the heart of everything we do. We strive to nurture dignity, independence, and privacy through our purpose-built facilities, our highly trained multidisciplinary teams, the care models we offer and the therapies and activities provided. We have three specialist neurological care units, including a Day Opportunities Service in Milton Keynes, and five neurological care units and a rehabilitation service at our award-winning Eagle Wood Centre in Peterborough.

Each of our care centres is purpose built to an award-winning design to provide an environment that is:

- safe, but which allows free movement within designated areas, e.g. gardens;

- larger than average bedrooms (all en-suite) opening on to spacious communal areas with wide short corridors;

- varied, with multi-use areas for activities, therapies, family/friends visits, dining and celebrations;

- therapeutic—landscaped gardens created to suit a variety of physical and mental health needs, e.g. sensory and stimulating plants, no thorns, edible foliage, lots of pacing areas.

Over the years, we'd won a string of awards, including the Citizen Business Award 2004, Independent Healthcare Awards 2010, and Investors in People Gold Award 2011, and the company's founder Jan Flawn, a registered nurse, also won a 'First Women of Business Services Award' in 2013.

However, whilst our healthcare product and employment practices were strong, our marketing function was weak. We only have two direct competitors, and demand for beds exceeds supply, so marketing had not historically been seen as a priority. In 2011, our strategy was undertaken at the unit level. Each care centre contains between one and five units, each run by a clinician unit manager. Sales and marketing was undertaken at the unit level. Our newest centre in Peterborough, Eagle Wood Neurological Care Centre, opened in mid-2012. However, shortly before it opened, there was a low awareness of PJ Care and Eagle Wood amongst our customers in this new geographic region. We needed to increase awareness to ensure that the centre was financially viable and this required that it be operated at full capacity. At the time, the marketing department consisted of one contract marketing manager who worked 1½ days per week and there was no sales function until after the Centre opened. Our marketing budget was only 0.78% of turnover per annum.

Our problem was how do we seek to structure the marketing function, internally, from a service deliverer to strategist advisor and, externally, build our customer base and our reputation as a trusted healthcare provider?

Introduction

Have you ever thought about how organizations organize themselves so that they can make sales, achieve profits, and keep their stakeholders satisfied? This does not happen accidentally. A great deal of thought, discussion, planning, and action needs to occur, which involves getting answers to questions such as which markets the organization should be operating in, what resources are necessary to be successful in these markets, who are the key competitors and what strategies are they using, how can we develop and sustain a competitive advantage, and what is happening in the world that might affect our organization. These questions refer to issues that represent the strategic context in which organizations operate. These contextual issues can be considered in terms of four main elements: 1) the organization (and its resources, skills, and capabilities), 2) the target customers, 3) a firm's competitors, and 4) the wider environment. These are set out in Figure 5.1.

For example, Samsung's strategic context is shaped by its communications expertise and leading-edge technology skills, customers who expect a stream of added-value communication-related products, and its competitor Apple, which is number two in the smartphone market. In addition, the wider environment is becoming politically more sensitive to climate change issues, terrorism, social change, the repercussions of the economic crisis, and surges in technological development. By understanding and managing these four elements, we can develop a coherent strategic marketing plan through which offerings have a greater chance of success than if no analysis or planning is undertaken. For marketing strategy to be developed successfully, it is

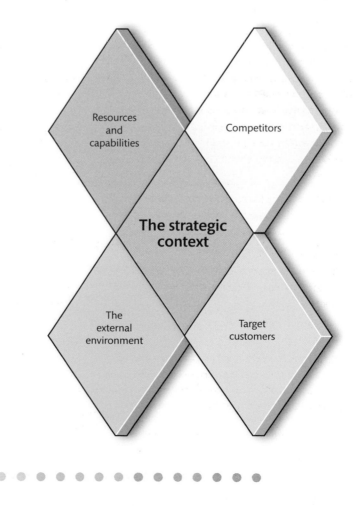

Figure 5.1

The four elements of the strategic context

necessary to understand an organization's strategic context and then to fit the marketing strategy to match the strategic context. Many organizations articulate their strategic context and their intended performance in the markets they target in terms of a framework that defines their vision, mission, values, organizational goals, and organizational strategy.

The **vision** sets out an organization's future. It is a statement about what an organization wants to become, giving shape and direction to its future. A vision should stretch an organization in terms of its current position and performance, yet also help employees feel involved and motivated to want to be part of the organization's future. According to their web site, Samsung Electronics' vision for the current decade is to 'Inspire the World, Create the Future'. As part of this vision, Samsung plans to drive $400bn in revenue and become one of the world's top five brands by 2020.

The **mission** represents what the organization wishes to achieve long term. It should be a broad statement of intention, setting out an organization's purpose and direction. It should be oriented to particular markets and customers. A mission applies to all parts of an organization, binding the many parts together. However, above all else, the mission should provide a reference point for its managers and employees to make decisions concerning which opportunities to pursue and which to ignore. It should aid investment and development decision-making. See Table 5.1 for examples of different mission statements.

Mission statements are sometimes prepared as a public relations exercise or are so generic that they fail to provide sufficient guidelines or inspiration. Some are not realistic and should be

Table 5.1 A selection of mission statements	
Organization	**Mission statement**
Tesco	To create value for customers to earn their lifetime loyalty
Coca-Cola	■ To refresh the world … ■ To inspire moments of optimism and happiness … ■ To create value and make a difference …
SAS	We provide Best Value for Time and Money to Nordic Travellers whatever the purpose of their journey
Oxfam	Oxfam works with others to overcome poverty and suffering
IBM	We strive to lead in the invention, development, and manufacture of the industry's most advanced information technologies, including computer systems, software, storage systems, and microelectronics. We translate these advanced technologies into value for our customers through our professional solutions, services, and consulting businesses worldwide
JCB	Our mission is to grow our company by providing innovative, strong, and high performance products and solutions to meet our global customers' needs. We will support our world-class products by providing superior customer care. Our care extends to the environment and the community. We want to help build a better future for our children, where hard work and dedication are given their just reward.

avoided. For example, to expect an airport such as Adelaide or Hong Kong to become the largest airport in the world is infeasible. Good mission statements are market-oriented, not product-oriented. For example, the product-oriented approach 'we make and sell lorries and trucks' is too general and runs the risk of becoming outdated and redundant. By focusing on the needs of the customers, the mission can be more realistic and have a much longer lifespan. So, 'we transport your products quickly and safely to your customers', or 'logistical solutions for your company', provides a market approach to the mission statement. Amazon.com does not per se sell books, Kindles, and DVDs (product approach): much better to say that Amazon.com 'strives to be Earth's most customer-centric company where people can find and discover virtually everything they want to buy online'. Similarly, Haier, the leading Chinese manufacturer, do not just make home appliances, 'they make lives more convenient and comfortable through innovative appliances'.

Visit the **Online Resource Centre** and complete Internet Activity 5.1 to learn more about the use of mission and vision statements by different organizations and their implications for marketing activities.

An organization's **values** must coincide with its vision and mission, because they define how people should behave with each other in the organization and help shape how the goals will be achieved. Organizational values define the acceptable interpersonal and operating standards of behaviour. They govern and guide the behaviour of individuals within the organization. Organizations that identify and develop a clear, concise, and shared meaning of values and beliefs shape the organizational culture and provide strategic direction.

Organizational values are important because they can help to guide and constrain not only behaviour but also recruitment and selection decisions. Without them, individuals tend to pursue behaviours that are in line with their own individual value systems, which may lead to inappropriate behaviours and a failure to achieve the overall goals. However, values per se do not drive a business. As Williams (2010) states, they drive the people within the business. For values to be of value and have meaning, they must be internalized within the organization. See Market Insight 5.1.

Market Insight 5.1

Values Matter

IKEA has claimed for many years that their values have affected the way they work. 'These values are as important at an IKEA store in Ireland as they are in a photo studio in Sweden or a distribution centre in China.'

Humbleness and willpower

We respect each other, our customers and our suppliers. Using our willpower means we get things done.

Leadership by example

Our managers try to set a good example, and expect the same of IKEA co-workers.

Daring to be different

We question old solutions and, if we have a better idea, we are willing to change.

Togetherness and enthusiasm

Together, we have the power to solve seemingly insoluble problems. We do it all the time.

Market Insight 5.1
continued

Cost-consciousness

Low prices are impossible without low costs, so we proudly achieve good results with small resources.

Constant desire for renewal

Change is good. We know that adapting to customer demands with innovative solutions saves money and contributes to a better everyday life at home.

Accept and delegate responsibility

We promote co-workers with potential and stimulate them to surpass their expectations. Sure, people make mistakes. But they learn from them!

However, few organizations set out how their values are derived. IBM is an exception. In an open statement Samuel J. Palmisano, Chairman, President, and Chief Executive Officer, recalls the way in which IBM's current values originated. He refers to the importance and time spent thinking, debating, and determining IBM's fundamentals. He states that in a time of great change, IBM needed to affirm reasons for being, for setting out how the company is different from others, and what should drive individual employee behaviour.

He says, 'Importantly, we needed to find a way to engage everyone in the company and get them to speak up on these important issues. Given the realities of a smart, global, independent-minded, twenty-first century workforce like ours, I don't believe something as vital and personal as values could be dictated from the top'.

So, for a three-day period, all 319,000 IBMers around the world were invited to engage in an open 'values jam' on the global intranet. Following much open debate, honesty, and involvement the employees determined the following values:

- Dedication to every client's success
- Innovation that matters, for our company and for the world
- Trust and personal responsibility in all relationships

The statement concludes with 'To me, it's also just common sense. In today's world, where everyone is so interconnected and interdependent, it is simply essential that we work for each other's success. If we're going to solve the biggest, thorniest, and most widespread problems in business and society, we have to innovate in ways that truly matter. And we have to do all this by taking personal responsibility for all of our relationships—with clients, colleagues, partners, investors, and the public at large. This is IBM's mission as an enterprise, and a goal toward which we hope to work with many others, in our industry and beyond.'

Sources: Based on www.ikea.com/ and www.ibm.com/ibm/values/us/

1 **How do these two sets of values differ?**

2 **What might be the impact on employees of seven rather than three sets of values?**

3 **Find a third set of values, this time from a not-for-profit organization, and compare these with those of IKEA or IBM.**

Teamwork matters at Ikea
Source: © IKEA

Organizational goals at the strategic level represent what should be achieved—the outcomes of the organization's various activities. These may be articulated in terms of profit, market share, share value, return on investment, or numbers of customers served. In some cases, the long-term may not be a viable period and a short-term focus is absolutely essential. For example, if an organization's financial position becomes precarious it may be necessary to focus on short-term cash strategies to remain solvent and so remove any threat arising from a takeover or administrators being called in prior to bankruptcy.

Organization or **corporate strategy** is the means by which organizational resources are matched with the needs of the organization's operations environment. Corporate strategy involves bringing together human resources, logistics, production, operations, marketing, IT, and the financial parts of an organization into a coherent strategic plan that supports, reinforces, and accomplishes the organization's goals in the most effective and efficient way. In this chapter, we are concerned with the make-up of marketing strategy and how it should support and reinforce corporate strategy.

In some very large organizations the planning process is made complicated and difficult because the organization operates in significantly different markets. In these cases the organization creates **strategic business units** (SBUs). Each SBU assumes the role of a separate company and creates its own strategies and plans to achieve its corporate goals. Therefore the Indian company Tata operates through seven SBUs, namely Information Technology and Communications, Engineering, Materials, Services, Energy, Consumer Products, and Chemicals. Each of these Tata companies operates independently. Royal Philips Electronics use four SBUs: Domestic Appliances and Personal Care, Lighting, Medical Systems, and Consumer Electronics. All of these represent significantly different markets, each with their own characteristics, customer needs, and competitors.

According to McDonald (2002: 37), a global guru of marketing planning, the strategic marketing planning process consists of a series of logical steps to be worked through to arrive at a marketing plan. These steps can be aggregated into four phases. The first phase is concerned with setting the right mission and corporate goals. The second involves reviewing the current situation or context in which the organization is operating. The third phase is used to formulate strategy, and the final phase considers the allocation of resources necessary to implement and monitor the plan.

At a broad level, the strategic marketing planning process is as follows.

- At the corporate level the organization sets out its overall vision, mission, and values.

- Measurable corporate goals are established that apply to the whole organization.

- A series of analyses and audits are undertaken to understand the external situation in which the organization intends to operate and the resources available to be used.

- Strategies are formulated and probable outcomes estimated.

- Depending on the size of the organization, the range of businesses (SBUs) and/or offerings is determined, and resources are allocated to help and support each one.

- Each business and/or offering then develops detailed functional and competitive strategies and plans, such as a marketing strategy and plan.

- The plan is implemented and the results measured and used to feed into the next planning cycle.

Marketing strategy and planning should support and contribute to the overall company strategy. However, it should also be understood that marketing strategy and planning can occur at the business, proposition, or market level (see Figure 5.2).

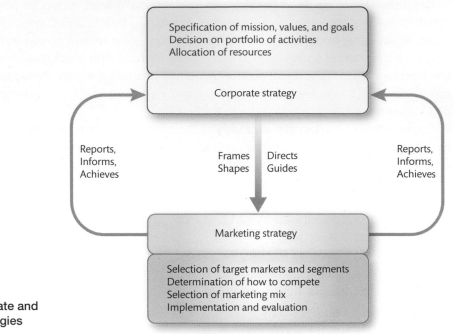

Figure 5.2

The relationship between corporate and marketing strategies

Research Insight 5.1

To take your learning further, you might wish to read this influential paper.

Mintzberg, H. (1987), 'The strategy concept: Five Ps for strategy', *California Management Review*, **30(1), 11–26.**

Mintzberg's paper made an important contribution because it argued that strategy should not be regarded as a linear sequential planning process. He shows that strategy can also be interpreted as a plan, ploy, pattern, or perspective, and as a position.

@ Visit the Online Resource Centre to read the abstract and access the full paper.

Strategic Marketing Planning—Activities

The development of a strategic marketing plan is a complex and involved process. It does not occur in linear logical steps, as implied earlier, but certain key aspects can be identified. These aspects concern three broad activities that are necessary when considering the development of marketing strategy and will form the framework through which we examine this topic (see Figure 5.3).

Figure 5.3 shows that it is necessary first to develop knowledge and understanding of the marketplace, referred to here as **strategic market analysis**. Secondly, it is necessary to

Figure 5.3
Three key activities of marketing strategy development

determine what the marketing strategy should achieve, i.e. what are the strategic marketing goals that need to be accomplished? The third decision area concerns how the goals are to be achieved. This relates directly to strategic marketing action, i.e. how the strategies should be developed as plans and how these plans should be implemented. These three activities form the basis of this chapter and are considered next.

Strategic Market Analysis

The starting point of the marketing strategy process is the development of knowledge and understanding about the target market(s) identified as part of the corporate strategy. Different people in the organization have varying levels of market knowledge and expertise, some of it accurate and up to date but some out of date and inaccurate. Therefore it is crucial that all people involved in the strategy process are well informed with accurate, pertinent, and up-to-date information.

In Chapter 4 we saw how PESTLE and environmental scanning processes can be used to understand and make sense of the external environment. We also considered Porter's (1985) Five Forces model to understand industry dynamics and how firms should compete strategically if they are to be successful in the performance environment. We also gained an insight into the importance of understanding the internal environment and how a firm's resources need to complement the external and performance environments. The task now is to assimilate this information and bring it together in a form that can be easily understood. Consideration is also given to **SWOT analysis**, explored later in this chapter. However, before these tools can be used, analysis of the performance environment, particularly our competitors and the industry's key suppliers and distributors, is required.

Analysing Competitors

The importance of understanding competitors cannot be overstated. Noble *et al.* (2002) found that organizations which pay particular attention to their competitors generally perform better than those who do not. To undertake an analysis of a firm's competitors, five key questions must be answered.

- Who are our competitors?
- What are their strengths and weaknesses?
- What are their strategic goals?
- Which strategies are they following?
- How are they likely to respond?

Who Are Our Competitors?

Competitors are those firms which provide propositions that attempt to meet the same market need as our own. There are several ways in which a need might be met, but essentially two approaches can be identified. Firms need to be aware of their direct and indirect competitors. Direct competitors provide similar propositions to the same target market, e.g. EasyJet, Flybe, and Ryanair. Direct competitors also offer a product in the same category, but target different segments; for example, Haagen-Dazs, Walls, and Green and Black's offer a range of ice creams for different target markets. Indirect competitors are those who address the same target market but provide a different proposition to satisfy the market need, e.g. Spotify, Sony, and Apple's iPod.

By understanding who the main competitors are, it becomes possible to make judgements about the nature and intensity of the competition. This also provides a view about how a firm's own marketing strategy should evolve. For example, the strategy of a market leader, which identifies little competition, will be different from that of a small firm trying to establish a small market share. The former may try to dominate the whole market, whereas the latter may attack the leader or find a small underserviced segment, called a **niche market**, and make it their own.

What Are Their Strengths and Weaknesses?

Getting information about a competitor's range of propositions and their sales volumes and values, about their profitability, prices, and discount structures, about the nature of their relationships with suppliers and distributors, and about their communications campaigns and special offers are all important. In some circumstances, getting information about new offerings that are either in development or about to be launched can be critical.

Green and Black's ice cream targets ethical consumers
Source: Courtesy of Green and Black's.

However, in addition to these marketing elements, it is important to obtain information about a whole range of other factors about competitors, not just their marketing activities. These factors include their production and manufacturing capabilities, their technical, management, and financial resources, and their processes, distribution channels, and relative success in meeting customer and market needs.

As this information accumulates and is updated over time, we use it to understand a) what a competitor's strengths and weaknesses might be and b) how to either avoid the areas where competitors are strong or exploit their weaknesses. The overall task is to determine what **competitive advantage** a competitor might have and whether this advantage can be sustained, imitated, or undermined (see section on Competitive Advantage).

What Are Their Strategic Goals?

Contrary to popular opinion, profit is not the single overriding strategic goal for most organizations. Firms develop a range of goals, encompassing ambitions such as achieving a certain market share (which is quite common), market leadership, industry recognition for technological prowess or high-quality performance, or market reputation for innovation, environmental concern, or ethical trading.

Developing a full understanding of a competitor's strategic goals is not easy and can usually only be inferred from their actions. Some firms try to recruit senior executives from competitors in to gain real insight into their strategic intentions. Although this happens quite frequently, it is not an ethical way of operating, and organizations can impose severe legal and financial constraints on employees in terms of who they can work for if they leave and the timescale in which they are not allowed to work in the industry.

Which Strategies Are They Following?

Once a competitor's goals are understood it becomes easier to predict what its marketing strategies are likely to be. These strategies can be considered through two main factors: competitive scope and positioning.

Competitive scope refers to the breadth of the market addressed. Is the competitor attempting to service the whole of a market, particular segments, or a single niche segment? If they are servicing a niche market, one of the key questions to be asked is whether they will want to stay and dominate the niche or are they simply using it as a trial before springboarding into other market segments?

Brands can be positioned in markets according to the particular attributes and benefits that they offer. Cameras might be positioned according to their technical features, whereas cosmetics are often positioned on style and fashion, frequently with campaigns led by brand ambassadors who are considered to personify the brand values. Once this is understood, the marketing mix elements are aligned to support the positioning strategy. Some brands are positioned based on price and a low-cost strategy. This approach requires a focus on reducing costs and expenses rather than investing heavily in marketing communications and/or **research and development**. We consider low-cost strategies later in this chapter.

Visit the **Online Resource Centre** and complete Internet Activity 5.2 to learn more about the importance of analysing a competitor's strategic activities

How Are They Likely to Respond?

Understanding the strategies of competitors helps inform whether they are intent on outright attack or defence, and how they might react to particular strategies initiated by others. For example, a price cut might be met with a similar reduction, a larger reduction, or none at all. Changes in the levels of investment in advertising might produce a similar range of responses.

Some market leaders believe that an aggressive response to a challenger's actions is important, otherwise their leadership position might be undermined. There are a range of responses that firms may use, reflecting organizational objectives, leadership styles, industry norms, and new strategies born of new owners. See Market Insight 5.2 on how companies can use war games to understand competitor response to changing market conditions.

Suppliers and Distributors

So far, analysis of the performance environment has concentrated on the nature and characteristics of a firm's competitive behaviour. This is important, but Porter also realized that suppliers can influence competition and he built this into his Five Forces model. However, since he published his work there have been several significant supply-side developments, notably the development of outsourcing. Outsourcing concerns the transfer of non-core activities to an external organization that specializes in the activity or operation. For example, transport and delivery services are not core activities to most companies, although they constitute an important part of the value they offer their customers. In Japan, the Hitachi Transport System, a **third-party logistics** (3PL) service, is used by companies as an outsourced provider to transport their goods. Therefore many suppliers have become an integral part of a firm's capabilities. Rather than act aggressively they are more likely to be cooperative and work in support of the firm that has outsourced the work to them.

Similar changes have occurred downstream in terms of a manufacturer's marketing channel. Now it is common to find high levels of integration between a manufacturer and their distributors, dealers, and retailers. Account needs to be taken of the strength of these relationships and consideration given to how market performance might be strengthened or weakened by the capabilities of the channel intermediary. Suppliers and distributors have become central to how firms can develop specific competitive advantages. Analysis of the performance environment should incorporate a review of key suppliers and distributors to the firm under analysis.

SWOT Analysis

Perhaps the most common analytical tool is **SWOT analysis**. SWOT stands for Strengths, Weaknesses, Opportunities, and Threats. It is a series of checklists derived from the marketing audit and the PESTLE analysis, and is presented as internal strengths and weaknesses, and external opportunities or threats. Strengths and weaknesses relate to the internal resources and capabilities of the organization, as perceived by customers (Piercy, 2002).

- A strength is something an organization is good at doing or something that gives it particular credibility and market advantage.

- A weakness is something an organization lacks or performs in an inferior way in comparison to others.

Opportunities and threats are externally oriented issues that can potentially influence the performance of an organization or offering. Information about these elements is generated through PESTLE analysis.

- An opportunity is the potential to advance the organization by the development and satisfaction of an unfulfilled market need.

Market Insight 5.2

Art of War: Corporate Style

The principles of warfare and the use of military practices have been a part of corporate and marketing strategies for a long time. However, only recently have some companies begun to use war games to help develop their offerings.

When considering the mix of components and features to include in the next version of an important offering, the development team at AVT, a consumer electronics company, knew that any upgrade would influence not just this but successive versions of the offering.

To inform the decision and to see how the competitive landscape might develop, AVT ran a war game. This consisted of cross-functional teams of product designers, marketing and sales experts, and supply-chain managers, all assuming non-familiar roles of executives in the company and in a major rival.

The three-day game revealed several new components and technologies that the competitor might include in its own update of this kind of offering. This would impact on their positioning and would require a fast and decisive response. AVT considered various strategies, so when the competitor moved as expected with its new offering, AVT was ready with its own updated version which outsold the rival over the next three years.

Xerox use corporate war games to simulate how market dynamics, competitors, or consumers might behave. One internal workshop game used proprietary software to analyse the desired outcomes that the different teams had determined. One of these was that that a particular company would begin to acquire a certain group of assets within the industry. This was proved correct within six months.

Another global high-tech electronics company, HiCom, sells a comprehensive range of specialized TV models to chains of hotels. However, as competition intensified with new entrants, HiCom wanted to know how their portfolio of offerings would be affected, and how they were positioned.

HiCom resorted to war games and created four rival teams. Each team represented a competitor, and ran a series of war games against them. Using various scenarios, the outcomes of the games indicated that rivals would use discounts on their own high-end units to get market share from lower-cost hotels.

To avoid a squeeze on profits, the company developed a strategy based on serving mid-range hotels, and leaving market segments where price competition would be fiercest. Working with the mid-range hotels offered opportunities to differentiate some of its existing offerings, and to create more customer value. HiCom went on to forge several partnerships in the industry value chain to help implement the new strategy.

The use of war games should not be one-off events, as repetition when competitors, technologies, or economic conditions change can reveal different strategies.

Sources: Anon. (2007); Horn (2011); Capozzi *et al*. (2012).

1 **To what extent do you believe that it is sufficiently realistic for executives to assume new roles and act out strategies that might be adopted by competitors?**

2 **With the development of relationship marketing concepts and partnerships, how appropriate is it to consider warfare as a viable approach for marketing strategies in the twenty-first century?**

3 **Find two companies working in an industry of your choice, visit their web sites (and other resources), and determine how similar their strategies are.**

Note: Some company names have been disguised.

■ A threat is something that at some time in the future may destabilize and/or reduce the potential performance of the organization.

SWOT analysis is used to determine an organization's strategic position. It highlights the need for a strategy to produce a strong fit between the internal capability (strengths and weaknesses) and the external situation (opportunities and threats). SWOT helps to sort through the information generated in the audit, to identify the key issues, and prompts thought about converting weaknesses into strengths and threats into opportunities, i.e. generating conversion strategies. For example, some companies have developed and run call centres for their own internal use, but saw opportunities to use their strength to run call centres for other companies. For example, a few years ago, one major computer company only used its call centre during the day. An opportunity was spotted to run the call centre at night, routing calls for a nationwide pizza company.

In inexperienced hands, SWOT often leads to long lists of items. Although the SWOT process may lead to the generation of these lists, the analyst should be attempting to identify the key strengths and weaknesses and the key opportunities and threats. These key elements should impact on strategy; if they don't, they shouldn't be in the analysis. A strength is not a strength if it does not have strategic implications and is not a strength in relation to competitors.

Once the three or four elements of each part of the SWOT matrix have been derived, a number of pertinent questions need to be asked.

1 Does the organization do something far better than its rivals? If it does, this is known as a competitive advantage (distinctive competence, differential advantage), and this can lead to a competitive edge.

2 Which of the organization's weaknesses does our strategy need to correct and is it competitively vulnerable?

3 Which opportunities can be pursued and are there the necessary resources and capabilities to exploit them?

4 Which strategies are necessary to defend against the key threats?

Figure 5.4 depicts a SWOT grid for a small digital media agency. The outcome of a successful SWOT analysis is a series of decisions that help develop and formulate strategy and goals. Note

Strengths

Quick to respond to changes in the marketing environment

Flat management encourages fast decision-making

Use of contractors enables flexibility—lowers employment costs/finance and improves customers' perception of expertise

Weaknesses

Too much work from a few clients and at non-premium rates

Few project management skills

High office and finance costs

Low customer base

Opportunities

Emerging markets such as Professional Services (e.g. dentists, lawyers, surveyors)

New distribution channels

Tax incentives to encourage eCommerce

Threats

Larger media houses buying business

Speed of technological advances

Contractors have low levels of loyalty

Figure 5.4
A SWOT analysis for a small digital media agency

Research Insight 5.2

To take your learning further, you might wish to read this influential paper.

Prahalad, C. K., and Hamel, G. (1990), 'The core competence of the organisation', *Harvard Business Review*, **68(3, May–June), 79–91.**

This paper was incredibly important because it provided a first major insight into the criticality of core competencies as a means of developing superior business performance.

@ **Visit the Online Resource Centre to read the abstract and access the full paper.**

---

that there are no more than four items in any one category, not a whole list of ten or so items. It is important to prioritize and make a judgment about what is really key. The actions that follow the identification of key issues should be based around matching opportunities with strengths and weaknesses with threats. In this example, it may be possible to diversify into professional services, a niche market (an opportunity), using particular contractors who have knowledge and relevant expertise (a strength).

Weaknesses need to be addressed, not avoided. Some can be converted into strengths, others into opportunities. In this example, entering the professional services market would probably increase the number of customers and enable premium rates to be earned. Threats need to be nullified. For example, by building relationships with key contractors (suppliers) and selected larger media houses, these threats might be dissipated, and even developed into strengths.

Visit the **Online Resource Centre** and complete Internet Activity 5.3 to learn more about the use of SWOT analysis.

Strategic Marketing Goals

The purpose of strategic market analysis is to help managers understand the nature of the industry, the way firms behave competitively within the industry, and how competition is generally undertaken. From this information it becomes easier to determine exactly what the marketing strategy should actually achieve, i.e. what the strategic marketing goals should be.

There are several types of strategic objective but four main ones are considered here. These are niche, hold, harvest, and divest goals, and are considered briefly. However, a further objective, namely growth, is considered in the next section (see Figure 5.5).

Niche objectives are often the most suitable when firms operate in a market dominated by a major competitor and where financial resources are limited. A niche can be a small segment or even a small part of a segment. Niche markets arise because it is not economic for the leading competitors to enter this segment because these customers have special needs and the leading firm does not want to devote resources in this way. To be successful in niche markets, it is important to have a strongly differentiated product offering supported by a high level of service. The Australian government identified several niche markets when exploring the development of its tourism business. It

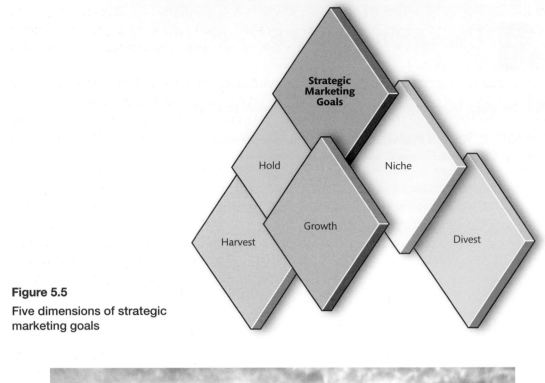

Figure 5.5

Five dimensions of strategic marketing goals

Australian Tourism has been developed around the identification of niche markets
Source: © James Fisher/Tourism Australia.

identified sports, cycling seniors, culture and the arts, backpackers, health, people with disabilities, caravanning and camping, food, wine, and agri-tourism as potential niche markets.

Hold objectives are concerned with defence. They are designed to prevent and fend off attack from aggressive competitors. Market leaders are the most likely to adopt a holding strategy as they are prone to attack from new entrants and their closest rivals as they strive for the most market share. Market leadership is important as it generally drives positive cash flows, confers privileges such as strong bargaining positions with suppliers, and enhances image and reputation. Holding strategies can take a number of forms, varying from 'doing nothing' in order to maintain market equilibrium, to implementing a counter-offensive defence, to withdrawing from a market completely.

Harvesting objectives are often employed in mature markets as firms/offerings enter a decline phase. The goal is to maximize short-term profits and stimulate a positive cash flow. By stripping out marketing communications and R&D it becomes possible to generate cash for use elsewhere. These funds generate new offerings, support 'stars', or turn 'question marks' into 'dogs' (see Chapter 4).

Divest objectives are sometimes necessary when offerings continue to incur losses and generate negative cash flows. Divestment can follow on naturally from a harvesting strategy. Typically, low-share offerings in declining markets are prime candidates to be divested. Divestment may be actioned by selling off the offering should a suitable buyer be available, or simply withdrawing from the market. For example, Procter & Gamble divested the Sunny Delight orange drink brand, General Motors sold off Saab to sports car manufacturer Spyker (Madslien, 2010), and Ford sold off Jaguar to the Indian company Tata and in 2010 completed the sale of Volvo to Geely Automobile, a Chinese motor manufacturer.

Growth

The vast majority of organizations consider growth to be a primary objective. However, there are different forms of growth and care needs to be taken to ensure that the right growth goals are selected. Growth can be intensive, integrated, or diversified.

- **Intensive** growth refers to concentrating activities on markets and/or offerings that are familiar. By increasing market share or introducing new propositions to an established market, growth is achieved by intensifying activities.

- **Integrative** growth occurs where an organization continues to work with the same propositions and same markets but starts to perform some of the activities in the value chain that were previously undertaken by others. For example, Benetton moved from designing and manufacturing their clothing products into retailing.

- Growth through **diversification** refers to developments outside the current chain of value-adding activities. This type of growth brings new value chain activities because the firm is operating with new offerings and in new markets.

The idea that growth is allied to product–market relationships is important, and Ansoff (1957) proposed that organizations should first consider whether new or established products are to be delivered in new or established markets. His product–market matrix (Figure 5.6), otherwise known as **Ansoff's matrix**, is an important first step in deciding what the marketing strategy should be. The product–market matrix is examined further in Chapter 7. See Market Insight 5.3 to learn about how growth has been achieved in the games console market.

	Present Products	**New Products**
Present Markets	Market Penetration	Product Development
New Markets	Market Development	Diversification

Figure 5.6
Ansoff's matrix
Source: Adapted from Ansoff (1957).

Market Insight 5.3

Console Strategies

The games console market is intensely competitive, but, because of the severe upfront development and launch costs, the launch of a new system is often delayed. This is because of experience curve effects, namely that as more units are sold and a market matures a console becomes cheaper to make. Games are expensive to develop but manufacturing costs are very low, which means that successful consoles are extremely profitable, even though hardware is sold at a loss to build market share.

Sony's PlayStation brand has dominated the games console market until recently. The main competition in the market has come from Microsoft, the market challenger, and the launch of Microsoft's Xbox 360 was a successful attempt to achieve market leadership. One of the reasons for Sony's previous success was that Sony established the original PlayStation as a brand. This meant that a huge consumer base was established, and one of the key attributes of the PS2 was that it was backwards-compatible with PlayStation games, thereby enabling games developed for the first machine to be used on

the PS2. In addition, it was able to play DVDs, unlike the competition, a major point of differentiation.

However, the market is dynamic, and that means it is changing and requires the competitors to update, differentiate, and launch as fast as is feasible. Market leaders sometimes like to delay the launch of new offerings in order to capitalize on the revenue streams and margins associated with established brands. In this case, it appears that Sony delayed the launch of its next-generation console based on the logistical challenges it faced in producing sufficient stock for a successful launch. Failing to satisfy market demand might have given the market challenger an opportunity to take a share. Microsoft, with their Xbox 360, sought to destabilize Sony by introducing new offerings with new attributes. Part of their strategy was to launch the Xbox 360 simultaneously in all major markets, which resulted in Microsoft gaining market leadership worldwide.

Another challenger, Nintendo, launched a radically new games console called Wii. Its main feature was that the conventional keypad was replaced with an innovative motion-sensitive controller. Sony, the market leader, responded with a built-in Blu-Ray disc player, as it was

The development of centralized platforms is a strategic goal for many entertainment-based providers.
Source: Image taken from UK Xbox 360 Dashboard Experience.

Market Insight 5.3
continued

believed that this provided the best next-generation gaming experience, and had the added advantage of being able to play high-definition movies.

For a long time competition has centred on the experience a games console generates for the participants. However, this is changing as a wider remit in the games market emerges. For example, Xbox is focusing on streaming TV shows and connecting people to their social networking sites. Lighter, faster versions have been released over the years, but now the games console industry faces severe competition from other sources, such as online games, tablets, and smartphones, as enthusiasm for mobile gaming accelerates. Sony is to offer cloud-based gaming services.

Microsoft and Sony both follow strategies which aim to dominate next-generation systems, based around games consoles as potential digital hubs replacing some current stand-alone consumer electronic devices, such as DVD players, and interconnecting with a range of electronic devices such as high-definition televisions, personal computers, MP3

players, and digital cameras. Strategies designed to establish their brands at the centre of a 'digital living room' is important for both companies mainly because of the impact this would have on their other content assets. For Sony this involves generating demand for Blu-ray gaming, video, and audio content. For Microsoft its core software businesses would be the prime beneficiary. For Nintendo, the Wii has a focus on the game-playing experience and many believe it would not be interested in the idea of living rooms as a digital hub.

Sources: Schofield (2005); Andrews (2006); Arthur (2007); Courtney et al. (2009); McCormick (2009); Anon. (2012).

1 **What markets are console manufacturers in, and, apart from using product attributes, what are the main ways in which they compete?**

2 **What do you believe are Sony's and Microsoft's strategic goals?**

3 **If an Apple product became the hub of future 'iHome' living rooms, what might be the impact on Microsoft and Sony?**

Strategic Market Action

Having analysed the industry and the main competitors, determined suitable strategic marketing goals, and performed a SWOT analysis, the final set of marketing strategy activities concerns the identification of the most appropriate way of achieving the goals and putting the plan into action—the implementation phase.

There is no proven formula or toolkit that managers can use simply because of the many internal and external environmental factors. Managers draw upon experience to know which strategies are more likely to be successful than others. Next, we consider ideas about competitive advantage, generic strategies, competitive positioning, strategic intent, and marketing planning and implementation (see Figure 5.7).

Competitive Advantage

According to Hoffman (2000: 6), **competitive advantage** is 'the prolonged benefit of implementing some unique value-creating strategy not simultaneously being implemented by any current or potential competitors along with the inability to duplicate the benefits of this strategy'. In other words sustainable competitive advantage (SCA) is achieved when an organization has a significant and sustainable edge over its competitors, when attracting buyers. Advantage can

Figure 5.7
Strategic marketing action

also be secured by coping with the competitive forces better than its rivals. Advantage can be developed in many different ways. Some organizations have an advantage simply because they are the best-known organization or brand in the market. Some achieve it by producing the best-quality offering or having attributes that other offerings do not have. For example, some pharmaceutical brands have an advantage while patent protection exists. As soon as the patent expires and competitors can produce generic versions of the drug, the advantage is lost. Some organizations have the lowest price, whereas others provide the best support and service in the industry. Whatever the advantage, the superiority has to be sustainable through time.

According to Porter (1985), the conditions necessary for the achievement of SCA are as follows.

1 The customer consistently perceives a positive difference between the offerings provided by a company and its competitors.

2 The perceived difference results from the company's relatively greater capability.

3 The perceived difference persists for a reasonable period of time. SCA is only durable as long as it is not easily imitated.

Generic Strategies

If the importance of achieving a competitive advantage is accepted as a crucial aspect of a successful marketing strategy, then it is necessary to understand how strategies can lead to the development of sustainable competitive advantages. Porter (1985) proposed that there are two essential routes to achieving above average performance. These are to become the lowest-cost producer or to differentiate the offering until it is of superior value to the customer. These strategies can be implemented in either broad (mass) or narrow (focused) markets. Porter suggested that these give rise to three generic strategies: overall cost leadership, differentiation, and focus strategies.

Cost leadership does not mean a lower price, although lower prices are often used to attract customers. By having the lowest cost structure, an organization can offer standard offerings at acceptable levels of quality, yet still generate above-average profit margins. If attacked by a competitor using lower prices, the low-cost leader has a far bigger cushion than its competitors.

Research Insight 5.3

To take your learning further, you might wish to read this influential paper.

Day, G. S. and Wensley, R. (1988), 'Assessing advantage: a framework for diagnosing competitive superiority', *Journal of Marketing*, **52(2), 1–20.**

As the title suggests, this paper considers a framework for identifying competitive advantage. It achieves this by first considering the elements of competitive advantage and then brings together both competitor- and customer-focused elements in order to identify 'points of superiority'.

@ **Visit the Online Resource Centre to read the abstract and access the full paper.**

Charging a lower price than rivals is not the critical point. The competitive advantage is derived from *how* the organization exploits its cost/price ratio. By reinvesting the profit, for example by improving product quality, investing more in product development, or building extra capacity, long-run superiority is more likely to be achieved.

A **differentiation** strategy requires that all value chain activities are geared to the creation of offerings that are valued by, and satisfy, the needs of particular broad segments. By identifying particular customer groups, where each group has a discrete set of needs, a product can be differentiated from its competitors. The fashion brand Zara differentiated itself by reformulating their value chain so that they became the fastest high street brand to design, produce, distribute, and make fashion clothing available in their shops.

Customers are sometimes prepared to pay a higher price, a price premium, for propositions that deliver superior or extra value. For example, the Starbucks coffee brand is strongly differentiated and valued, as consumers are willing to pay higher prices to enjoy the Starbucks experience. However, differentiation can be achieved by low prices, as evidenced by the success of low-cost airlines, such as the UK's Ryanair and EasyJet.

Offerings can be differentiated using a variety of criteria; indeed each element of the marketing mix is capable of providing the means for successful long-term differentiation. Differentiation can lead to greater levels of brand loyalty. For example, in contrast with low-cost ASDA, Waitrose provides a strongly differentiated supermarket service.

Focus strategies are used by organizations to seek gaps in broad market segments or in competitors' ranges. In other words, focus strategies help to seek out unfulfilled market needs. The focused operator then concentrates all value chain activities on a narrow range of offerings. Focus strategies can be oriented to being the lowest-cost producer for the particular segment or offering a differentiated offering for which the narrow target segment is willing to pay a higher price. This means that there are two options for a company wishing to follow a focus strategy. One is low cost and the other is differentiation, but both occur within a particular narrow segment. The difference between a broad differentiator and a focused differentiator is that the former bases its strategy on attributes valued across a number of markets, whereas the latter seeks to meet the needs of particular segments within a market.

Table 5.2 Types of market position	
Market leader	The market leader has the single largest share of the market. Market leadership is important as it is these offerings and brands that can shape the nature of competition in the market, set standards relating to price, quality, speed of innovation, and communications, and influence the key distribution channels. For example, Tesco was an ordinary mid-ranking supermarket in the 1980s but has since grown to become the leading UK supermarket.
Market challengers	Products that aspire to the leadership position are referred to as market challengers. These may be positioned as number two, three, or even four in the market. They actively seek market share and use aggressive strategies to take share from all of their rivals. For example, Sainsbury's and ASDA are the two main market challengers in the UK supermarket sector.
Market followers	These firms have low market shares and do not have the resources to be serious competitors. They pose no threat to the market leader or challengers and often adopt me-too strategies when the market leader takes an initiative. In the UK supermarket sector, Morrisons might be deemed a market follower.
Market nichers	Nichers are specialists. They select small segments within target markets that larger companies fail to exploit. They develop specialized marketing mixes designed to meet the needs of their customers. They are threatened by economic downturns when customers either cease buying that type of product or buy more competitively priced offerings. They are also vulnerable to changes in customer tastes and competitor innovation. Marks and Spencer's food offering is a case in point here.

Porter argues that, to achieve competitive advantage, organizations must achieve one of these three generic strategies. He argues that to fail to be strategically explicit results in organizations being 'stuck in the middle'. This means that they achieve below-average returns and have no competitive advantage. However, it has been observed that some organizations have been able to pursue low-cost and differentiated strategies simultaneously. For example, an organization that develops a large market share through differentiation and by creating very strong brands or through technological innovation may well also become the cost leader.

Competitive Positioning

Having collected industry information, analysed competitors, and considered our resources, perhaps the single most important aspect of developing marketing strategy is to decide how to compete in selected target markets. Two key decisions arise: what position do we want in the market, which is considered here, and what will be our strategic intent? Strategic intent is examined in the next section.

The position that a product adopts in a market is a general reflection of its market share. Four positions can be identified: market leader, challenger, follower, and nicher, and each has particular characteristics, as set out in Table 5.2 (see also Market Insight 5.4).

There are two main reasons for understanding the competitive positions adopted by companies. The first is to understand the way various firms are positioned in the market, and from that one can understand where the company is currently positioned and decide where it wants to be

Market Insight 5.4

Phone Strategies

The need to develop flexible business strategies in the telecommunications market is a reflection of several environmental conditions. The market is young and constantly changing as new technologies emerge on a regular basis, as new partnerships between various industry participants are forged, and as customer preferences change.

Vodafone Group plc is the world's leading mobile telecommunications company. The company has created a significant global presence in Europe, the Middle East, Africa, Asia, the Pacific, and the USA. In most countries, its mobile subsidiaries operate under the brand name 'Vodafone'. In other countries, they use dual branding in cooperation with partner networks in the marketing of global services.

Vodafone's corporate strategy has been based on a number of dimensions, most notably growth through acquisition and geographic expansion, acquiring new and retaining existing customers, and increasing customer usage by developing useful new offerings.

Vodafone's marketing strategy is based on the goal of retaining its market leadership position. This is achieved through a customer-oriented strategy based on delivering high-quality service and a stream of new offerings designed to utilize the latest technological advances. This recognizes that, as consumers become increasingly more sophisticated users of modern mobile technology, they seek added value through improvements in the offering.Vodafone's marketing objectives are:

- obtaining new customers;
- retaining customers;
- introducing new technologies and services (enabling the mobile internet, mobile TV);
- continuing to develop the Vodafone brand.

The Finnish mobile company Nokia, once the world's largest handset manufacturer, announced in 2011 that it was to collaborate with Microsoft. The goal was to develop a smartphone based on Windows Phone software as its primary smartphone platform. This was to enable it to compete more effectively with Google and Apple smartphones, to whom it had lost considerable business in the previous couple of years. By combining resources, it was hoped to drive innovation by integrating Nokia's application and content store into Microsoft Marketplace. In September 2013 it was announced that Microsoft had bought Nokia's mobile phone business for £4.6bn.

HTC, the world's fourth largest smartphone maker, based on shipments in 2012, made a major strategic move when It switched its corporate strategy. Formerly, it was a white-label manufacturer making handsets for others. Then it became a primary manufacturer for Google's Android operating system. The strategy appeared to work in 2010 and for the first two quarters of 2011. HTC marketed a series of nearly identical phones using the names: ChaCha, Salsa, Incredible, Legend, Titan, Rhyme, Sensation, Radar, Explorer, and Evo, amongst many others. However, HTC's financial results made a turn for the worse in 2011. This led to suggestions that HTC's strategy of swamping too many market sectors with too many phones failed to provide a sustainable point of differentiation and as a result had no competitive advantage relative to the other devices in the market.

Sources: Based on O'Reilly (2011, 2012), Baker (2011); Chapman (2011); BBC (2013); www.vodafone.com/section_

Market Insight 5.4
continued

article/ www.thetimes100.co.uk/case_study www.online. vodafone.co.uk/dispatch/Portal www.idc.com/

1 To what degree do you believe Vodafone's marketing strategy complements their corporate strategy?

2 If you were marketing director at HTC, how would you establish competitive advantage?

3 Which type of growth strategy has HTC been pursuing?

positioned. This shapes the nature and quantity of the resources required and the strategies to be pursued. Some of these strategies are set out in Table 5.3.

Strategic Intent

The previous section provided a general rationale about *why* organizations are positioned the way they are in markets. Consideration is now given to ideas about *how* firms engage strategically within their chosen markets. To assist, two main perspectives are explored. The first considers ideas founded on the principles of warfare. The second considers some contemporary ideas based not on outright competition but on cooperation and collaboration. Here, ideas about strategic relationships are introduced.

Table 5.3 Prime strategy characteristics

Competitive position	Prime strategies
Market leader	Attack the market—create new uses and users, or increase frequency of use
	Defend the position—regular innovation, larger ranges, price cutting and discounts, increased promotion
Market challenger	Attack the market leader—use pricing, new product attributes, sharp increase in advertising spend
	Attack rivals—special offers and limited editions, offer superior competitive advantages
	Maintain status quo
Market follower	Avoid hostile attacks on rivals
	Copy the market leader and provide good-quality products that are well differentiated
	Focus on differentiation and profits, not market share
Market nicher	Provide high level of specialization—geographic, proposition, service, customer group
	Provide tight fit between market needs and the organization's resources

Strategic Competition and Warfare

Many early ideas about competitive marketing strategies are developed from the military and based on approaches to warfare. Two main approaches can be identified: those based on attack and those on defence. For example, many organizations, especially those in the grocery sector, such as Procter & Gamble, Nestlé, Unilever, Kraft, and Heinz, will only contemplate entering or staying in a market if they have a realistic opportunity of becoming market leader or, at worst, number two. This is because the highest levels of profitability are obtained by being the market leader.

The overall size of many markets is static; therefore individual companies can only really grow by taking market share from their competitors. This can be achieved by developing superior offerings, using the right distribution channels to reach target markets, implementing effective marketing communications campaigns, and managing pricing astutely. Therefore one interpretation of marketing strategy is that it is necessary to attack to grow market share and, once this is achieved, to defend the share from predators.

Attacking Strategies

Attack strategies are mainly used to achieve growth objectives. Five main strategies (see Table 5.4) have been identified (Kotler and Singh, 1981).

Defensive strategies

Defence strategies should be in place at all times so that they can be deployed quickly and save time when faced with frontal or flanking attacks. Six main defensive strategies have been identified: position, flanking, mobile, contraction, pre-emptive and counter-offensive defences (see Table 5.5).

Visit the **Online Resource Centre** and complete Internet Activity 5.4 to learn more about attack- and defence-based strategies in the car industry.

Strategic Cooperation and Relationships

Ideas about strategy have developed from those based on competition through attack and defence strategies. An alternative perspective is to consider ways in which customer value can be increased through cooperation. By working cooperatively with other companies and their brands, relationships evolve. These in turn provide strong opportunities to add value through the differentiation of brands and considerable competitive advantage.

Cooperative relationships benefit participants through shared knowledge about offerings, markets, and competitors, can lead to improvements in product and brand performance, and help to develop stronger market positions, enabling the more efficient use of resources (Harbison and Pekar, 1998). This all adds up to a unique form of differentiation that can be of significant value to customers. For example, the rock band U2 realized that to reach a new younger audience they would have to work with new technology and develop new ways of communicating. This was achieved by working collaboratively with Apple. They made a U2 Silhouette television ad free of charge and released a single that was only available through iTunes, and Apple produced a special red and black iPod U2 (Teague, 2007).

At the corporate level, cooperative relationships, sometimes referred to as alliances, can be considered as a spectrum. At one end, cooperation is based around simple transactions. At the other end, cooperation can be formally established through a stand-alone organization where both parties share ownership.

Table 5.4 Attack strategies

Attack strategies	Explanation
Frontal attack	A head-on assault on a rival, used when there are low levels of customer loyalty, poorly differentiated offerings, and it is easy for customers to switch brands.
Flanking	Involves pressurizing a rival's vulnerable or unguarded areas. This might be a market segment that is not served very well by the existing competitors, a geographic area that is open, weak or unsatisfactory offerings, or inappropriate distribution channels. The rapid growth of low-cost airlines such as Ryanair and easyJet have been based upon flanking attacks on the established national carriers, e.g. British Airways. BA served broad markets with a differentiated service and ignored the low-cost niche segment. Ryanair spotted the flanking opportunity and have become the market leader in the new market.
Encirclement	Involves attacking a rival on all sides, literally encircling the target rival. The goal is to disrupt the competitor's strategy, causing them to reorganize resources, and to create panic as market share is taken from many sides. This can be an effective strategy when the target market is loosely segmented or when market segments are not occupied by firms who have substantial resources.
Bypass	Involves introducing new offerings or technologies that rewrite the rules of competition in the market and avoids direct conflict with a rival. For example, the introduction of compact disc technology bypassed the established magnetic-tape-based technology that previously existed.
Guerrilla	Involves irritating and slowly eroding a rival's market share through a series of unpredictable attacks on their weaker areas. This strategy is useful for small firms who have relatively few resources in situations where the target is able to defend itself relatively easily from a frontal or flanking attack. Typically, guerrilla attacks involve periods of heavily promoted price discounting, followed by differing lengths of inactivity.

Outsourcing and renewable purchasing agreements are relatively short-term cooperative arrangements. Information sharing can be seen through agreements to distribute offerings, licensing and technological collaboration represents resource and asset sharing, while cooperation based on share ownership is normally seen in mergers and acquisition activity, which has a long-term perspective. Telecommunications leaders T-Mobile and Orange developed a jointly owned company in 2012, Everything Everywhere or EE. The company combined the skills and resources of both parent organizations, particularly in network architecture and branding.

The detail concerning these various arrangements is not the focus of the strategy. What lies behind the concept of cooperation is the competitive advantage that can be developed. In particular, competitors are usually unable to determine how performance is achieved through these alliances, and even if they can, it is exceedingly difficult to replicate as they do not have the necessary or complementary resources and do have the same history of investments. All organizations in a cooperative arrangement, sometimes called a network alliance, have an advantage over their rival organizations outside an alliance. However, not all alliances and mergers are successful;

Table 5.5 Defence Strategies

Defence strategies	Explanation
Position	This involves building fortifications, 'sitting tight', and defending the current position. For example, resistance can be built around an offering, distribution channel, or geographic area. For example, Procter & Gamble developed a portfolio of hair care brands to protect their key hair care brand Pantene. Head & Shoulders and Wash & Go act as flanker brands to protect market share and to divert challengers to Pantene.
Mobile	Involves creating a moving target that is hard to attack. This requires the introduction of a regular stream of new and replacement offerings, changing market segments, and changing target markets. This can be supported by constantly repositioning offerings.
Flanking	Involves protecting the rear and the flanks, as these are potential weaknesses. By strengthening the competitive position in these segments, with new offerings, and by repositioning existing offerings, it becomes possible to deter attack. The British motorcycle industry was for many years a dominant force but produced a limited range of bikes. The industry failed to see opportunities to reach new smaller target markets that were developing as economic conditions were improving. As a result the industry was out-manoeuvred by the rapid incursion made by Japanese manufacturers Yamaha and Honda.
Counter-offensive	These strategies used as retaliation once an attacker has engaged. The aim is to hit the attacker's weakest spot, quickly and ruthlessly using various attacking options. In 2006, Microsoft used a counter-offensive defence when it entered the keyword search advertising market. This market is extremely profitable for the both Google and Yahoo, who dominate the market.
Contraction	Some markets or segments are too weak to be defended so the best action is to withdraw and concentrate resources around protecting core offerings. A strategic withdrawal strategy was used by Diageo when the company sold off Burger King to withdraw from the fast food market and concentrate on the premium drinks market (Eastham, 2002).
Pre-emptive	These strategies are built on the premise that the best form of defence is attack, and by 'getting one's retaliation in first' it becomes possible to prevent an attack. For example, by dropping product prices the overall perceived value of a market can be reduced and so deter investors and divert attackers to other markets. Alternatively, it is possible to launch a heavy-weight advertising programme or several new offerings which can deter attack.

indeed, a large number of them fail. For example, the merger between Daimler and Chrysler in 1998 proved troublesome immediately because of the clash of cultures and values between the German and US organizations. In 2007 the merger was dissolved when it was decided that both entities would be more profitable separated rather than continuing as a paired unit.

At a marketing level, alliances can be developed through key distributors and retailers to control the distribution channel. Relationships with prominent or geographically important dealers provide opportunities for exclusive distribution to reach target markets. Relationships can also be developed with strategically important customers. These customers are referred to as Key Accounts, and a large number of resources are often channelled into developing and supporting these accounts (see Chapter 15). In many markets, there is little difference between offerings, so organizations try to differentiate themselves based on the services they provide their customers, both before and after a purchase has been made. Relationships between customer and supplier can be strengthened through the provision of services, as the service is perceived to offer added value.

Relationships can also be developed with consumers. Marketing strategies designed to retain customers often use loyalty schemes and customer retention programmes. These are supported by database management and marketing facilities. Relationships can also develop through branding. Some consumers develop a strong affinity with a brand to the extent that they want to share their relationship with others and talk openly (word-of-mouth communication) about their positive brand experiences. Relationships with suppliers are important simply because competitive advantages can be developed through cost reduction, speed to market, and product differentiation.

Marketing strategy should be founded on developing customer value, and this can be achieved through a strategy based on building cooperative relationships with suppliers, customers, distributors, and other strategically relevant stakeholders. The centrality of cooperation and relationships within marketing has become an important concept for both organizations and marketing academics. Marketing has evolved from ideas that are based solely around the 4Ps (see Chapter 1). Now marketers think and act in terms of the different types of relationship that an organization has and tries to find ways of improving the right relationships with the right customers. This is referred to as relationship marketing (see Chapters 1 and 14).

Implementation

The implementation of any marketing plan is incomplete without methods to control and evaluate its performance. It is vitally important to monitor the results of the programme as it unfolds, not just when it is completed. Therefore measures need to be stated in the plan about how the results of the plan will be recorded and disseminated throughout the team. Recording the performance of the marketing plan against targets enables managers to make adjustments should it not perform as expected, possibly due to unforeseen market events.

For ease of explanation, the marketing planning process has been depicted as a linear sequential series of management activities. This certainly helps to simplify understanding about how strategy can be developed and it also serves to show how various activities link together. However, strategy development and planning, whether it be at corporate, business, or functional level, is not linear, does not evolve in preset ways, and is not always subject to a regular predetermined pattern of evolution. Indeed, politics, finance, and interpersonal conflicts all shape the nature of an organization's marketing strategy.

Marketing implementation is a fundamental process in marketing because it is the action phase of the strategic marketing process. Whereas many of the concepts in this text help us to design marketing programmes, the implementation phase is about actually doing it. In reality, then, it is the most exciting part of marketing because it is the least predictable.

The problems identified in implementing marketing strategy are not particularly well-researched. It seems likely that some companies are better at implementing marketing strategies than others. According to Piercy (1998), this may be because a company's marketing

Table 5.6 Characteristics of companies' marketing implementation capabilities

Characteristics	Explanation
Time-specific	Companies gain or lose the competencies necessary to implement a strategy based on time, e.g. senior executives or a dominant leader may retire. Company assets may be perishable, e.g. British Energy's nuclear reactors have a limited lifespan before needing to be decommissioned.
Culture-specific	Strategy may be reliant on certain cultural conditions that do not exist in other cultures, e.g. customer service standards might on average be higher in some Western countries (e.g. the USA) than in developing countries (e.g. Russia) because people tend to work harder to take account of customer needs.
Partial	Companies may be able to implement only parts of a strategy and so outsource other components, e.g. a pharmaceutical company developing a new drug with a ready customer base in Japan may not have the regulatory know-how to get the drug formally and legally listed to comply with the relevant authorities.
Latent	A company may have the actual knowledge required for the formulation of a particular strategy but not the knowledge to implement it either through poor deployment of resources or a lack of management understanding and experience.
Internally consistent	Some parts of a company might be better able to execute a strategy than others.
Strategy-specific	Companies develop capabilities to implement specific previously developed strategies but are not able to meet the needs of a new strategy, particularly where such strategies require significant organizational change.
Person-specific	Companies' implementation capabilities may depend on a single person or a particular team (e.g. a new proposition development strategy may be reliant on a particular scientist or team, causing obvious problems if they leave the company).

implementation capabilities are time-specific, culture-specific, partial, latent, internally consistent, strategy-specific, and person-specific, as outlined in Table 5.6.

Therefore the implementation of any marketing plan is far from straightforward. However, there are certain elements that impact on the implementation of most strategic marketing plans, and three of these are considered here.

- The structure and type of marketing function and the degree to which a marketing orientation prevails across the organization.

- The amount of available financial resources and how they are distributed and managed through budgets.

- The controls used to measure the effectiveness of the implementation process. These are referred to as **marketing metrics**.

Visit the **Online Resource Centre** and complete Internet Activity 5.5 to learn more about the L'Oréal business simulation game designed to help students learn about developing effective brand strategies.

Structures and Types of Marketing Organizations

How we organize ourselves to undertake the task of marketing has an impact on how effective we are. In addition, the way we organize the marketing function has an impact on how our colleagues in other professional disciplines view us and our effectiveness. According to a Chartered Institute of Marketing survey, only 10% of boardroom time is spent discussing marketing issues, and the number of CEOs with a marketing background appears to be falling (CIM, 2009a). See also Chapter 1 on the Role of Marketing.

Visit the **Online Resource Centre** and follow the weblink to the CIM to learn more about the role of marketing in organizations.

Despite the fact that brands now account for 28% of companies' total intangible value on average, according to Brand Finance, boards of directors are not required to report to investors what they are doing with their key assets—their brands. However, as Jack (2010) reports, investors appear to be more interested in how companies manage their brands. In addition, some financial analysts are beginning to accept that marketing and brand equity issues need to be taken more seriously.

Therefore marketing professionals are either less effective than their professional colleagues or they are underrated. Part of the problem and solution rests with the structure adopted by companies. McKinsey & Co. found that 81% of packaged goods companies operate a matrix structure, involving multiple reporting lines. In turn this leads to duplication and overlapping responsibilities. Because roles are not clear, there is a tendency to revisit decisions. Brand managers are prone to take on extra work in an attempt to please various groups, and to seek alignment across a large number of people. McKinsey states that these companies have so many managerial layers that their growth is curtailed. As if to illustrate this, McKinsey found that some brand managers spend as much as 80% of a working day in meetings, coordinating activities with other internal groups. All of this breeds inefficiency and reduces opportunities to create real value. A move away from matrix structures and removing two layers of management can reduce the amount of time spent in meeting to 54% (Haas *et al.*, 2010).

A further problem concerns the increasing complexity associated with contemporary brand management. Mitchell (2012) refers to globalization, the growing importance of customer experience, the significance of retailer power, the role of category management, and the recent surge in the use and influence of social media as factors that have redefined the nature of a brand manager's job. Managing increasing amounts of information, projects, and content have added layers of complexity and responsibility.

Marketing is present in all aspects of an organization, as all departments have some role to play with respect to creating, delivering, and satisfying customers. For example, employees in the R&D department designing new offerings for poorly met existing customer needs are performing a marketing role. Similarly, members of the procurement department buying components for a new offering must purchase components of specific quality and at a certain cost that will meet customer needs. In fact, we can go through all departments of a company, and find that there is a marketing role to be played in each. In other words, marketing should be distributed throughout an organization and all employees should be considered as part-time marketers (Gummesson, 1990). Marketing is not something that only people in the marketing department undertake. See Market Insight 5.5, which provides an interesting illustration of these issues.

Types of Marketing Organization

Marketers have not always been able to highlight easily the performance of their departments against the return on investment made in paying marketing salaries and budgets by senior

Market Insight 5.5

Strategically Empowered Employees

Hindustan Unilever Limited (HUL) is India's largest consumer products company. It is a household name and market leader in various categories including detergents, tea, and soaps.

At HUL's Mumbai headquarters, a strategy to become more customer orientated was launched. One of the initiatives, called 'Consumer Shoes', involved displaying all feedback concerning a cross-section of HUL's diverse product portfolio. No matter how harsh, or even savage, the comments were, they were all put up on a wall for everyone to see. Also on the wall are pictures of various types of footwear.

Staff commented on how the packaging on the toothpaste brand Fire-Freeze, a variant of Closeup, was not very good. Another observed that an ice cream competitor, Mother Dairy, had better flavours than HUL's own Kwality Walls brand.

However, unlike most feedback systems which channel customer comments, these were comments posted by HUL's employees. The strategy is for the 'Consumer Shoes wall' to empower brand teams to respond to the comments and develop an action plan.

The company admit that they used to think that interaction with customers was something that only marketing and sales should do, but now they realize that everyone in the company needs to regard consumers as their primary stakeholders.

HUL are also considering utilizing employees within the proposition development process. For example, HUL's beauty and wellness business includes 125 Lakme salons and about 20 Ayush therapy centres. In an effort to eradicate mistakes before consumers find them, HUL gave its employees big discounts to encourage them to try new versions of their Lakme Beauty Salons before they are launched.

Red Hat, the global leader in the provision of open-source software, recently changed their approach to strategy development. Teams were formed around an initial set of priorities, and through the use of wikis and other online tools, made these 'open' so that any Red Hat employee could respond with ideas and suggestions. After 5 months of idea generation the best ideas were shaped into nine strategic priorities. New teams were formed, with the task of identifying one or two of the most important strategic initiatives. They were also empowered to implement the plans without further approvals.

Today, Red Hat updates and evaluates strategy on an ongoing basis, as employees input ideas and initiatives on a continuous basis. Red Hat have placed the responsibility for planning and execution with the same people who do the work, and this has led to improved responsiveness to new opportunities or shifts in the market.

Sources: Pinto (2011); Balakrishnan (2012); Gast and Zanini (2012).

1 **Which is of greater value, consumer or employee feedback? Justify your answer.**

2 **What might be the disadvantages for HUL of using their employees to comment on the Lakme salons?**

3 **Why do so many companies continue with the annual strategy review process?**

management. As a result, organizations have developed different ways of organizing their sales and marketing functions. Some of the more frequently observed ones are presented at Figure 5.8.

In Figure 5.8a, marketing and sales are separate departments reporting to the manager in charge of a particular strategic business unit (SBU). In this situation, it is the job of the manager to coordinate the different departmental inputs into a coherent and complementary set of strategies. In Figure 5.8b, each sales and marketing department reports to a SBU manager, who will then report to a corporate headquarters. Corporate headquarters also have a corporate

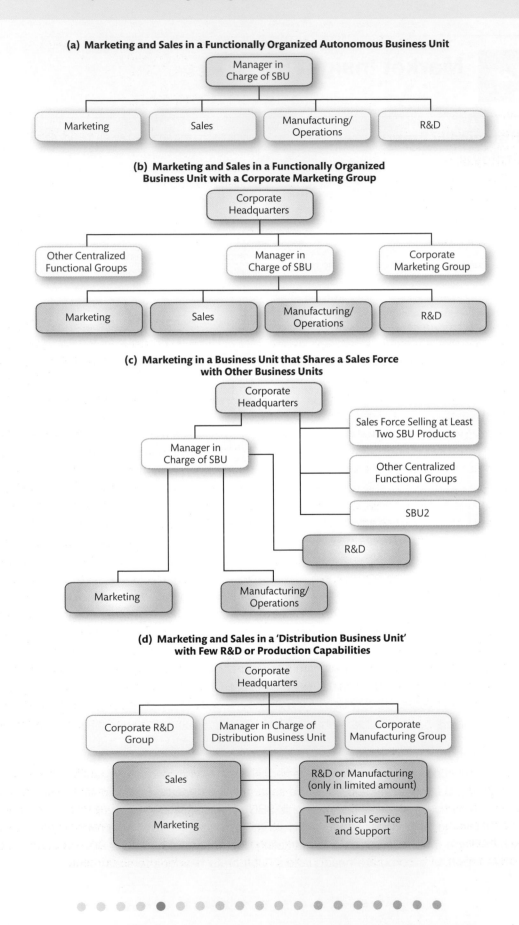

(a) **Marketing and Sales in a Functionally Organized Autonomous Business Unit**

(b) **Marketing and Sales in a Functionally Organized Business Unit with a Corporate Marketing Group**

(c) **Marketing in a Business Unit that Shares a Sales Force with Other Business Units**

(d) **Marketing and Sales in a 'Distribution Business Unit' with Few R&D or Production Capabilities**

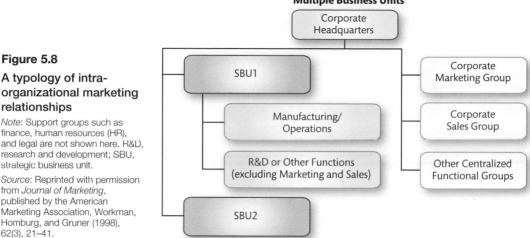

(e) Marketing and Sales in Corporate Groups Shared by Multiple Business Units

Figure 5.8

A typology of intra-organizational marketing relationships

Note: Support groups such as finance, human resources (HR), and legal are not shown here. R&D, research and development; SBU, strategic business unit.

Source: Reprinted with permission from *Journal of Marketing*, published by the American Marketing Association, Workman, Homburg, and Gruner (1998), 62(3), 21–41.

marketing group, which will tend to handle the marketing for the group as a whole (e.g. corporate identity, group market research). In Figure 5.8c, the marketing department still reports to a SBU manager, but the sales force is centralized and sells the products for other SBUs as well. In Figure 5.8d, sales and marketing operate for each individual SBU, but R&D and manufacturing are undertaken centrally across the SBUs. Finally, in Figure 5.8e, manufacturing and R&D operate for each individual SBU, but sales and marketing are corporate functions.

Marketing organizations have changed in recent years. There is now an increased emphasis on key account management, where senior marketing personnel serve important accounts or customer segments, sometimes through cross-functional teams involving sales, marketing, and supply chain management personnel, particularly in sales and operations planning (S&OP) meetings, where detailed supply and demand plans are considered and reconciled (e.g. at AstraZeneca, the pharmaceutical giant). Where firms are operating in more than one country, the role of the country manager has been reduced. As companies have globalized (e.g. Nike), and their efforts have spread across countries, senior managers now tend to operate across whole continental regions (e.g. Europe, Middle East, and Africa). In addition, product managers have lost their role as the primary marketing coordinator of sales, marketing, R&D, manufacturing, and other functions. This role has shifted to key account managers or category managers (e.g. Procter & Gamble), who oversee whole brand categories rather than individual products.

In addition, there has been an increasing shift towards outsourcing marketing activities. For example, advertising and market research have traditionally been outsourced to agencies by large multinational and many medium-sized firms. Recently, there has been an increasing shift towards outsourcing sales activities (e.g. health insurance), data warehousing (e.g. car and electrical goods manufacturers), and customer data analytics (supermarkets and financial services).

Finance and Budgeting

A marketing budget should indicate how much is to be spent on marketing activities and is an important aspect of a marketing manager's job. Yet, there are no hard and fast rules on how much should be allocated to marketing spend. A generally held view is that many companies lack a formal and proper budgeting process. When marketing budgets are properly determined, they are based on sales forecasts, often produced in association with the finance department of an organization, although usually with some input from the marketing department.

A marketing budget may be between 5% and 7% of sales revenues (excluding salaries), but exactly how much is spent on marketing activities depends on the particular industry, each firm, and the overall economic climate. For example, McKinsey & Co. report that following a recession successful companies were found to have invested over 9% more in marketing than their competitors. In addition to this, the CIM report that if a company increases its marketing spend during an economic downturn, it is likely to recover three times faster when the economy recovers (CIM, 2009b).

However, empirical work by Srinivasan *et al.* (2011) suggests that investment in both R&D and advertising during a recession should be based on the actual conditions facing the firm. Referring to this as a contingency approach, they provide a model enabling firms to determine for themselves whether and how such investments should be made.

The strongest advertisers tend to be companies in the food, beverages, and tobacco sector. Companies in the property sector spent the most on public relations. Financial services companies spent the most on sponsorship (e.g. Lloyds TSB's sponsorship of the 2012 London Olympics), retailers/wholesalers (e.g. supermarkets) spent the most on direct mail, surprisingly the public sector spent the most on email, utility companies (e.g. water, gas, and electricity companies) spent the most on promotions, business services (e.g. accountancy practices) spent the most on telephone marketing, property companies spent the most on **lead generation**, the consumer durables sector (e.g. stereos, TV manufacturers) spent the most on customer relationship management (CRM) programmes, and the food, beverages, and tobacco sector spent most on branding. Interestingly, the utility companies spent the most on internal marketing activity.

As might be expected, there are some broad differences in the pattern in which large and small firms, and those operating in consumer and business-to-business (B2B), invest in communications in periods of relative stability. Large companies in consumer markets tend to invest more heavily on most elements of the communication mix. B2B and smaller organizations, unsurprisingly, tend to invest the larger part of their budgets on less expensive activities, including direct mail, email, telephone marketing, and lead generation. Their involvement in social media is relatively limited, although a few B2B companies are actively involved in social media (see Chapter 17 for more details).

The marketing budgeting process is a political process of allocating resources within a company. Clearly, where a company can demonstrate the effectiveness of the resources it has previously used, the more likely it is to receive an increase in the budget for the next year. Over the last 15 years or so, we have seen the rise in importance of measuring marketing effectiveness. As a consequence, marketers have become increasingly excited by the idea of using marketing **metrics** to determine the effectiveness of their organization's marketing activity.

Marketing Metrics

There is increased recognition of the need to determine efficiency and effectiveness in organizational marketing efforts. In the past, marketing control has been achieved through the annual marketing plan, through analysis of company profitability, by some measure of efficiency (e.g. number of employees as a proportion of revenue or in retailing, net profit per square foot/metre of retail space), or in terms of market share or some other strategic measure. But in the past, these measures have been focused towards financial or human resource measures. More recently, there has been a considerable shift in thinking towards the need for customer-based measurements (Kaplan and Norton, 1992). There has been a move towards setting key performance indicators, which companies set and measure their progress towards in order to determine whether or not they have improved or maintained their performance over a given period of time.

Research Insight 5.4

To take your learning further, you might wish to read this influential paper.

Kaplan, R. S. and Norton, D. P. (1992), 'The balanced scorecard: measures that drive performance', *Harvard Business Review*, **January–February, 71–9.**

This seminal and much-quoted article outlines how companies should move beyond financial measures of performance, to measures incorporating financial, internal, innovation and learning, and customer perspectives. They should answer questions such as: How do we look to shareholders? What must we excel at? Can we continue to improve and create value? And how do customers see us? The paper sparked a revolution in company performance measurement practice.

@ Visit the **Online Resource Centre** to read the abstract and access the full paper.

Research indicates that British companies are now using a variety of strategic marketing metrics as key performance indicators (KPIs) in marketing. In a telephone study of 200 UK marketing and finance senior executives, nearly seven in ten respondents claimed to use the ten metrics identified in Table 5.7 (see Ambler *et al.*, 2004). The selection and use of KPIs depends on their relevance to what is being measured; however, KPIs should be selected in the context of strategic plans and associated higher-level goals (Lamont, 2012). We consider digital marketing and social media marketing metrics in Chapter 17. ScottishPower uses software that enables it to keep track of the factors that underpin its main objective, which is customer retention. These factors include the proficiency with which customer issues are resolved, and the provision of alternative interaction channels.

An organization's strategic goals should always be used to guide the way metrics are interpreted. For example, Lamont refers to ScottishPower who asked their call centre agents to offer additional services such as boiler care. As a result call time increased by 8–10%, a metric that had to be seen in terms of their retention plan, rather than a drop in their agents' productivity.

We discuss the benefits and limitations of using each of these key marketing performance metrics together with customer advocacy, as outlined in Figure 5.9, in the next section.

Profit/Profitability

Unsurprisingly, profit/profitability was the main key performance measure, where profit is broadly how much cash there is left in the business when expenses are subtracted from revenues generated. This approach indicates the 'bottom line'. It represents what is left over either for distribution to the shareholders of the business, whether that be a private or public business, or for reinvestment in the business.

However, the problem with profit/profitability is that its link with marketing activity is not always clear. The process required to determine the link requires considerable input from the finance department to measure the contributions that individual offerings make towards the overall profit levels of a business. Therefore it can be difficult to determine whether or not the marketing activity itself has led to improved levels of profitability or whether some other factor led to it (e.g. the

Table 5.7 The ten most popular key performance metrics

Rank	Metric	% Claiming to use measure	% Firms rating as very important
1	Profit/profitability	92	80
2	Sales, value, and/or volume	91	71
3	Gross margin	81	66
4	Awareness	78	28
5	Market share (volume or value)	78	37
6	Number of new products	73	18
7	Relative price	70	36
8	No. of consumer complaints or relative dissatisfaction	69	45
9	Consumer satisfaction	68	48
10	Distribution/availability	66	18

Source: Adapted from Ambler *et al*. (2004). Used with the kind permission of Westburn Publishers.

collapse of a competitor). Finally, we might have a very profitable business operating in the short term (e.g. with customers buying more of a low-value overpriced offering), but in the long term customers would defect and leave the business.

Sales

Sales value or volume is a key performance measure, where sales value is determined by measuring how many units of an offering are sold multiplied by the average unit price, and sales volume is calculated by determining how many units of an offering have been sold. The benefit of using this metric is that sales value and volume can be measured directly against individual offerings. Sales values and volumes are easier to determine and require limited input from the finance department, unlike the determination of profit/profitability. Sales values and volumes may be linked to geographical sales territories, and so when sales fall in a particular territory and efforts are made to increase them, it is relatively easy to determine whether or not those efforts have been successful.

The use of sales volumes as a marketing metric is more problematic because the profit with high-volume turnover products, particularly in brokerages where companies sell other companies' offerings, may actually be disproportionately low. In such a situation, it would be wiser to measure profit/profitability, where the data are available. However, sales values may also hide the fact that an offering is being sold at unprofitable levels. Rewarding a sales force for selling large

Figure 5.9
Key marketing performance metrics

quantities of an offering at an unprofitable level is a recipe for disaster—a recipe for the long-term decline of a company.

Gross Margin

Frequently, companies measure their performance based on the gross profit margins they can achieve in a particular industry. For example, the gross profit margin for supermarkets in the UK is around 5–8%, whereas in the USA gross profit margins are considerably lower at around 2–5%. However, supermarkets generally operate on very high volume sales. Therefore they can afford to operate on low-gross profit margins. For example, some restaurants operate a 200–300% gross margin on their wine. When gross margins for one company are compared with those of other companies in the industry, where the data are available (e.g. for publicly quoted companies), companies can determine whether or not they need to reduce their costs or increase their prices.

The problem with using gross margins as a marketing metric is that they do not always provide an indication of how much the customer is actually willing to pay. For example, smoothie manufacturers (e.g. innocent) generally operate higher gross margins (because they charge higher prices) than manufacturers in the fruit juice category (e.g. Del Monte, Minute Maid). However, if the smoothie manufacturers had set their initial prices based on typical fruit juice margins, they would never have been as successful as they have, especially when we consider that innocent Drinks, for example, achieved sales revenue of around £100m in its first ten years.

Awareness

Nearly eight in ten respondents mentioned (brand) awareness as an important marketing metric. However, although a customer may be aware of a brand, it does not mean they will buy that brand. Correspondingly, (brand) awareness is not a particularly good measure for determining the effectiveness of marketing activity, particularly in the short term, as it may take time for the increased awareness to lead to increases in sales, if it does at all.

However, (brand) awareness is a very useful metric for determining whether your marketing communications activity is entering customer consciousness. The more a target market recognizes a brand, the more likely they are to become purchasers of it. Nevertheless, building awareness may not necessarily build sales. As consumers, we can become aware of a brand, but not particularly like it and therefore not buy it. Brands can be marketed heavily but not achieve success; examples include Strand cigarettes, Ford Edsel, and Tesco 'Fresh and Easy' in the USA. Awareness does not necessarily lead to purchase.

Market Share

One of the principal measures of market performance, the measurement of market share, is enshrined in many marketing strategy models such as the Boston Consulting Group's growth–share matrix (see Chapter 4). Measuring market share is useful in determining a company's performance within the marketplace, particularly when measured relative to the market leader, because it gives an indication of how competitive a company is. Cadbury's, the confectionery company, use this metric in conjunction with other marketing metrics such as brand awareness and advertising spend (Ambler 2000).

The market share of a company (say, company A) is determined by measuring that company's sales revenues, incorporating the sales of all companies within the industry including company A, as a proportion of total industry sales revenues as follows:

$$\text{Market share}_{(\text{company A},\%)} \frac{\text{Sales revenue}_{(\text{company A, £})}}{\text{Total industry sales revenue (£)}} \times 100$$

Relative market share is determined by measuring the market share of company A against the market share of the market leader, or the nearest competitor (if company A is the market leader) as follows:

$$\text{Relative market share}_{(\text{company A, }\%)} = \frac{\text{Market share}_{(\text{company A},\%)}}{\text{Market share}_{(\text{market leader},\%)}}$$

If company A is the market leader, relative market share is a value greater than one unit. Nevertheless, a company's market share, as determined by the value of the sales, does not necessarily point to a profitable company. Many a company has started a price war (see Chapter 9) in order to try to steal market share from a competitor, only to find that prices fall generally in the industry, which inevitably leads to a decline in their own profitability.

Number of New Products

Most companies pride themselves on their capacity to innovate. However, in many industries, innovating new propositions is vital for the prosperity of the industry. For example, pharmaceutical companies manage a pipeline of new drug compounds at various stages in the process of new proposition development. When they do finally develop a drug, they quickly patent it to protect their multibillion dollar investments and to ensure that they can reap the financial rewards from its development.

In 2006, pipeline problems occurred for global pharmaceutical manufacturers AstraZeneca and GlaxoSmithKline when various high-profile compounds failed at the clinical trial stage, sending their share prices lower as a result (Griffiths, 2006). 3M (formerly the Minnesota Manufacturing and Mining Corporation), the company behind the Post-it note among other innovations, uses the proportion of sales attributable to new products as one of its marketing metrics (Ambler, 2000). (See also Case Insight 9.1.)

Nevertheless, simply developing new offerings without measuring or predicting their impact on the sales of existing offerings can be problematic, as the new offering can cannibalize the existing sales without adding any new business. In addition, this strategy may cause customer confusion as customers try to determine what they want from a variety of offers.

Mobile telephone companies quickly learned in the late 1990s and early 2000s that many consumers wanted a monthly charge service offering a limited range of telephone call packages, which included text message bundles and set levels of call time, or a pay-as-you-go plan with more limited options. What they didn't want was lots of different-priced telephone handset offers with many different call packages, offering different call charges for different times. Consumers wanted price transparency.

Relative Price

The price of a company's offerings can be indicative of how much they are valued in the marketplace. **Relative price** is determined by measuring the price of company A's offering against the price of the market's leading company, or the nearest competitor if company A is the market leader, as follows:

$$\text{Relative price}_{(\text{company A's offering, unit})} = \frac{\text{Price}_{(\text{company A's offering, £})}}{\text{Price}_{(\text{market leader's offering/nearest competitor, £})}}$$

If company A is the market leader, relative price is a value greater than one unit.

There is increasing recognition that a company that can charge a price premium *vis-à-vis* its competitors has a competitive advantage over them. One approach to measuring brand equity actually uses relative price premiums (Ailawadi *et al.*, 2003).

The problem with measuring marketing effectiveness using relative price only is that a company may only obtain a proportion of the total revenue possible in a marketplace if the price it charges is too high. In other words, a higher relative price may lead to a smaller market share if customers do not value your offering more than the competitors' offerings.

Customer Satisfaction

Many companies operate on the principle of satisfying their customers. Companies in the travel and leisure industry (e.g. First Choice, Thomson, STA, Saga) work hard to satisfy their customers and to ensure an enjoyable experience. In the past, this meant measuring service quality levels (see Chapter 14) to determine whether companies were providing the level of quality of service that customers expected. In some industries, customer satisfaction is notoriously low, but customers perceive the costs of switching their business to other providers to be too high. Retail banking services are a good example here as customers are reluctant to switch banks even when they are dissatisfied (Keaveney, 1995). Mobile phone companies (e.g. Orange, T-Mobile) measure the proportion of customers who fail to renew user contracts against the proportion of new customers acquired, termed 'churn rate' in the industry. Churn rate is a measure of disaffected customers as a proportion of new customers.

Some companies attempt to go beyond simply satisfying customers, and empower their employees to provide a high level of individual and personal help for them. For example, staff at the Ritz-Carlton hotels are authorized to spend up to $2,000 so that they can resolve a customer's problem without having to refer to a manager (Hanselman, 2012).

Nevertheless, businesses may spend too much time and effort serving customers who are neither profitable nor offer the most profit potential in the future. Generating high levels of customer satisfaction or delight may ultimately reduce shareholder value because the costs to generate such high levels of satisfaction produce lower levels of profitability. In other words, the extra costs of improving customer satisfaction from 95% to 99.5% of customers may not be worthwhile.

Customer Advocacy

According to Reichheld (2003), successful firms create exceptional growth by nurturing loyal customers. They invest huge amounts of time and effort in measuring customer satisfaction. However, most of the indices that they have previously employed are complex, produce unclear results, and do not connect to profits or growth. The net promoter score (NPS) was developed based on measuring how likely it is that a customer would recommend a firm to a friend or a colleague. The more promoters a company can gain, the bigger its growth, since the inclination to promote relates to a strong degree of loyalty and growth (Reichheld, 2003). The NPS is calculated based on the ratio of promoters to detractors. Customers are then categorized into the following groups based on their responses on a 0–10 rating scale:

(i)   promoters—those who are rated extremely likely to recommend (9–10 rating);

(ii) passively satisfied—those who are rated likely to recommend (7–8 rating);

(iii) detractors—those who are extremely unlikely to recommend (0–6 rating).

The percentage of detractors is subtracted from the percentage of promoters to produce a NPS. Companies that earn net promoter scores of greater than 75% enjoy very strong customer loyalty. By plotting a firm's NPS against the company's revenue growth rate, Reichheld (2003) found that in industries such as the airline or car rental industries, there was a strong relationship between net promoter scores and a company's revenue growth rate. The advantages claimed for NPS can be summarized as follows:

(i)   having the highest NPS in a business sector gives rise to growth rates 2.5 times higher on average than those of competitors.

(ii) Each 12-point escalation in NPS relates to a doubling of the growth rate of a firm.

(iii) Using other metrics together with NPS provides no further predictive advantage (Reichheld claims that NPS is the only metric that is needed!).

However, the NPS approach has drawn some key criticisms. Keiningham et al. (2007, 2008) have claimed that the results of the original study yielded different and contrasting results and that a single-metric approach does not outperform dual- or multimetric models.

Distribution/Availability

The extent to which an offering is distributed within the marketplace can be an important marketing metric. For example, a Hollywood blockbuster film studio will want to ensure maximum take-up of its motion pictures by many cinemas, as the more cinemas the film is shown in, the higher the box office takings will be. In other businesses, the quantity of locations within which a product is sold matter less than the quality of those locations. For example, the premium mobile phone brand Vertu is sold through specialist retail outlets only, such as Selfridges and Harrods in London, Paragon in Singapore, Brusco Gioielli in Rome, and Vertu-branded shops in countries such as Russia and Lebanon. Cosmetics companies (e.g. French cosmetics giant L'Oréal) distribute their new offerings initially through speciality cosmetics outlets and prestigious department stores, before stocking the products in supermarkets and other department stores later in the campaign.

Unilever, the world's biggest ice cream manufacturer, recognized the importance of providing confectioners, tobacconists, and newsagents (CTNs) with branded freezers to store its Heartbrand ice cream products within the many overseas markets in which it operates, such as Walls in the UK, Ola in the Netherlands, and Algida in Hungary. Providing the freezers meant that CTNs could stock more of its ice cream products as opposed to those of their competitors, until an EU ruling in a case brought by Mars forced Unilever to allow CTNs to stock a small proportion of competing brands in the Unilever freezers.

In a wide range of diverse industry sectors, distribution is critical so that customers can readily purchase a company's offerings. For this reason, companies set up sophisticated systems to link their customers' purchasing needs with their own purchasing and distribution needs. Airline yield management systems, for example, reconcile customer pricing information with live seat availability, taking into account customers' price elasticities (see Chapter 9) in order to maximize total sales revenues. Measures of distribution and offering availability are critical in this and many other industries.

The use of KPIs varies considerably, but research by Mintz and Currim (2013) indicates that a manager's use of KPIs is driven by a group of variables that describe the context in which the manager operates. They refer to 'firm strategy, metric orientation, type of marketing mix decision, firm and environmental characteristics' (Mintz and Currim, 2013: 2). They also find that use of metrics is positively associated with marketing mix performance. In particular, there is positive association between the use of marketing metrics and the performance of the marketing mix.

Managing and Controlling Marketing Programmes

There is increasing debate about how we measure the performance of marketing programmes to control them better. Most of the time, companies are not excellent at all marketing activities (e.g. the American crisp producer Frito-Lay refined the functions of selling and distribution, whereas Gillette's Personal Care Division mastered the power of advertising), and few companies master more than one or two specialist marketing functions excellently (Bonoma, 1984). Nevertheless, companies try to maximize marketing effectiveness (e.g. measured by market share growth, revenue growth, and market position) and marketing efficiency (e.g. measured by sales and marketing expenses as a proportion of gross revenue). There is some evidence that companies that succeed on one dimension, i.e. either marketing efficiency or effectiveness, succeed less on the other (Vorhies and Morgan, 2003). This makes sense because, to be effective at marketing, we have to spend more on marketing activity (which makes us marketing inefficient!).

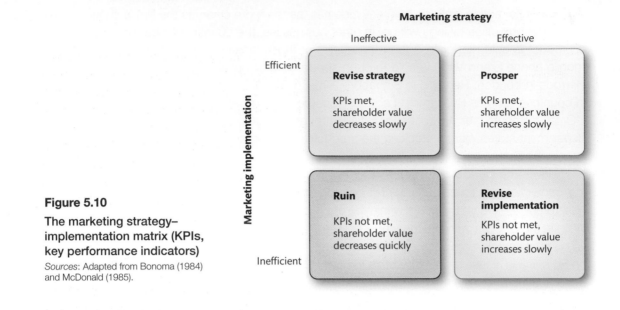

Figure 5.10

The marketing strategy–
implementation matrix (KPIs,
key performance indicators)

Sources: Adapted from Bonoma (1984)
and McDonald (1985).

Firms that can be both marketing effective and marketing efficient probably do so by changing the 'rules of the game'. They do not spend on high-cost activities like advertising to achieve effectiveness; instead they consider new and innovative approaches, which make customers pay more attention.

One problem is that marketers often consider strategy *formulation* to be problematic, but not strategy *implementation*. Managers frequently assume that implementation follows strategy as a sequential process. In fact, the two processes are often interlinked and run in parallel (Piercy, 1998). In other words, marketing strategy may be, and is, formulated on the basis of implementation considerations in the same way as implementation decisions are based on strategy formulation decisions.

In Figure 5.10, we can measure how effective and efficient our strategy has been by using the metrics for efficiency and effectiveness outlined earlier. Where we consider that marketing implementation has been efficient, but marketing strategy has not been effective, we should reformulate strategy as KPIs have not been met, otherwise we are likely to reduce shareholder value in the longer term. This situation means that we have spent marketing resources well in achieving what we set out as our strategy, but we employed the wrong strategy for what we wanted to do. The control imperative is to intervene quickly to reformulate the marketing strategy.

The dream situation is that we operate an efficient implementation plan and an effective marketing strategy. In this situation, we prosper. There is no control imperative except to maintain a watching brief to see how competition might react, as this may force us to rethink our strategy.

Where we operate inefficient marketing implementation for an ineffective marketing strategy plan, we are likely to face rapid ruin! We are spending scarce resources badly on doing the wrong things. The control imperative requires a fundamental rethink of what we are doing and how we are doing it.

Finally, where we are operating an effective marketing strategy, but implementing it inefficiently, the control imperative is to reconsider how we implement marketing programmes. Although this situation may not be disastrous in the short term, where competition is adopting a more efficient approach, it could lead to mergers, sales, or takeovers in highly competitive industry sectors.

Marketing Planning

We have considered the key activities associated with the strategic marketing planning process, essentially one of analysis, goals, and action. For organizations to be able to develop, implement, and control these activities at the offering and brand level, marketing plans are derived. This final section considers the characteristics of the marketing planning process, identifies the key activities, and considers some of the issues associated with the process.

Marketing planning is a sequential process involving a series of activities leading to the setting of marketing objectives and the formulation of plans for achieving them (McDonald, 2002: 27). A marketing plan is the key output from the overall strategic marketing planning process. It details a company's or brand's intended marketing activity. Marketing plans can be developed for periods of one year, two to five years, and anything up to 25 years. However, too many organizations regard marketing plans as a development of the annual round of setting sales targets that are then extrapolated into quasi-marketing plans. This is incorrect, as it fails to account for the marketplace, customer needs, and resources. The strategic appraisal and evaluation phase of the planning process should be undertaken first. This covers a three- to five-year period and provides a strategic insight into the markets, the competitors, and the organization's resources that shape the direction and nature of the way the firm has decided to compete. Once agreed, these should be updated on an annual basis and modified to meet changing internal and external conditions. Only once the strategic marketing plan has been developed should detailed operational or functional marketing plans, covering a one-year period, be developed (McDonald 2002). This makes marketing planning a continuous process, not something undertaken once a year or, worse, when a product is launched.

A marketing plan designed to support a particular offering consists of a series of activities that should be undertaken sequentially. These are presented in Table 5.8.

Table 5.8 Key activities within a marketing plan

Activity	Explanation
Executive summary	Brief one-page summary of key points and outcomes.
Overall objectives	Reference should be made to the organization's overall mission and corporate goals, the elements that underpin the strategy.
Product/market background	A short summary of the product and/or market to clarify understanding about target markets, sales history, market trends, main competitors, and the organization's own product portfolio.
Marketing analysis	This provides insight into the market, the customers, and the competition. It should consider segment needs, current strategies, and key financial data. The marketing audit and SWOT analysis are used to support this section.
Marketing strategies	This section should be used to state the market(s) to be targeted, the basis on which the firm will compete, the competitive advantages to be used, and the way in which the product is to be positioned in the market.

Table 5.8 continued	
Activity	**Explanation**
Marketing goals	Here, the desired outcomes of the strategy should be expressed in terms of the volume of expected sales, the value of sales and market share gains, levels of product awareness, availability, profitability, and customer satisfaction.
Marketing programmes	A marketing mix for each target market segment has to be developed along with a specification of who is responsible for the various activities and actions and the resources that are to be made available.
Implementation	This section sets out: ■ the way in which the marketing plan is to be controlled and evaluated; ■ the financial scope of the plan. ■ the operational implications in terms of human resources, R&D, and system and process needs.
Supporting documentation	Marketing plans should contain relevant supporting documentation, too bulky to be included in the plan itself but necessary for reference and detail, e.g. the full PESTLE and SWOT analyses, marketing research data, and other market reports and information plus key correspondence.

Many of the corporate level goals and strategies and internal and external environmental analyses that are established within the strategic marketing planning process can be replicated within each of the marketing plans written for individual products, product lines, markets, or even SBUs. As a general rule, only details concerning propositions, competitors, and related support resources need change prior to the formulation of individual marketing mixes and their implementation within functional level marketing plans.

The strategic marketing planning process starts with a consideration of the organization's goals and resources and an analysis of the market and environmental context in which the organization seeks to achieve its goals. It culminates in a detailed plan which, when implemented, is measured to determine how well the organization performs against the marketing plan.

Chapter Summary

To consolidate your learning, the key points from this chapter are summarized here.

■ **Describe the strategic planning process and explain the key influences that shape marketing strategy.**

The strategic planning process commences at the corporate level, where the organization sets out its overall mission, purpose, and values. These are then converted into measurable goals that apply to the whole organization. Then, depending upon the size of the organization, the range of businesses (SBUs) and/or offerings is determined and resources allocated to help and support each one. Each business and/or offering has detailed functional and competitive strategies and plans, such as a marketing strategy and plan, developed around them.

There are three key influences on marketing strategy. These are strategic market analysis, which is concerned with developing knowledge and understanding about the marketplace, strategic marketing goals, which are about what the strategy is intended to achieve, and strategic marketing action, which is about how the strategies are to be implemented.

- **Analyse current conditions, including competitors, and develop marketing strategies**

  SWOT analysis is used to determine an overall view of the strategic position and highlights the need for a strategy to produce a strong fit between the internal capability (strengths and weaknesses) and the external situation (opportunities and threats). SWOT analysis serves to identify the key issues and then prompts thought about converting weaknesses into strengths and threats into opportunities.

  An analysis of a firm's competitors involves answers to five key questions. These are: Who are our competitors? What are their strengths and weaknesses? What are their strategic goals? Which strategies are they following? How are they likely to respond?

- **Explain the different types of strategic marketing goals and associated growth strategies.**

  There are several types of strategic objective but the four main ones are niche, hold, harvest, and divest goals. However, the vast majority of organizations consider growth to be a primary objective. Although there are different ways of classifying growth, intensive, integrated, or diversified are generally accepted as the main forms.

- **Describe the concepts associated with strategic marketing action, and explain the ways in which firms engage strategically with their chosen markets.**

  Strategic marketing action is concerned with ways of implementing marketing strategies. Various concepts and frameworks have been proposed and, of these, we considered ideas about competitive advantage, generic strategies, and competitive positioning.

  There are two main perspectives of strategic intent. The first considers ideas founded on the principles of warfare. The second considers some contemporary ideas based not on outright competition but on cooperation and collaboration.

- **Understand the main issues associated with strategy implementation, including the principles of marketing metrics.**

  The implementation of most strategic marketing plans involves three main issues. These are the structure and type of marketing function and the degree to which a marketing orientation prevails across the organization, financial resources and the processes used to distribute and manage them through budgetary processes, and marketing metrics or the controls used to measure the effectiveness of the implementation process.

  Many companies now use various marketing metrics to monitor performance. These include metrics in the following areas: profit/profitability; sales, value, and volume; gross margin; awareness; market share; number of new products; relative price; number of customer complaints; consumer satisfaction; customer advocacy; distribution/availability; total number of customers; marketing spend; perceived quality/esteem; loyalty/retention; relative perceived quality.

- **Outline the key elements of a marketing plan.**

  The key elements associated with the structure of a marketing plan are overall objectives, product/market background, market analysis, marketing strategy and goals, marketing programmes, implementation, evaluation, and control. Although depicted as a linear process, many organizations either do not follow this process, do not include all these elements, or undertake many of these elements simultaneously.

Review Questions

1   What is the difference between vision and mission?

2   What are the four elements that make up the strategic context?

3   What are the key elements of the strategic planning process?

4   How might understanding a firm's competitors help develop marketing strategy?

5   Identify the key characteristics of SWOT analysis. What actions should be taken once the SWOT grid is prepared?

6   What is the difference between intensive and diversified growth?

7   How does Porter argue that firms can differentiate themselves in one of two main ways? What are they and how do they work?

8   What are the key features of attack and defence strategies?

9   What are the main marketing metrics?

10 What are the various parts of a marketing plan?

Worksheet Summary

To apply the knowledge you have gained from this chapter and test your understanding of marketing strategy visit the **Online Resource Centre** and complete Worksheet 5.1.

Discussion Questions

1   Having read Case Insight 5.1, how should PJ Care develop their strategic marketing planning function to raise their profile internally within the business and externally amongst its customers?

2   Find three examples of mission statements and associated organizational goals. Then, using these examples, discuss the value of formulating a mission statement and the benefits that are likely to arise from setting organizational-level goals.

3   If the external environment is uncontrollable and markets are changing their shape and characteristics increasingly quickly, there seems little point in developing a strategic marketing plan. Discuss the value of formulating marketing strategies and plans in the light of these comments.

4   After a successful period of 20 years' trading, a bicycle manufacturer noticed that their sales, rather than increasing at a steady rate, were starting to decline. The company, Rapid Cycles, produced a range of bicycles to suit various segments and distributed them mainly through independent cycle shops. In recent years, however, the number of low-cost cycles entering the country has increased, with many distributed through supermarkets and national retail chains. The managing director of Rapid Cycles feels that he cannot compete with these low-cost imports and asks you for your opinion about what should be done. Discuss the situation facing Rapid Cycles and make recommendations regarding their marketing strategy.

5 Explain which marketing metric(s) might be used in the following circumstances.

A A newly themed Irish pub with a marketing objective to give customers the best pub experience in the immediate area in the first year of its operation.

B A large health and fitness organization wanting to expand its chain of gymnasiums to other countries across Europe within a five-year timescale.

C The manufacturers of a designer cosmetic, such as the Gucci Pour Homme II, wishing to determine how well distributed their product is.

D A pharmaceutical company wishing to find out whether its new asthma product will be better received in the marketplace in the next 12 months compared with competing brands and if it can hold its price premium.

@ Visit the **Online Resource Centre** and complete the **Multiple Choice Questions** to assess your knowledge of Chapter 5.

References

Ailawadi, K., Lehmann, D. R., and Neslin, S. A. (2003), 'Revenue premium as an outcome measure of brand equity', *Journal of Marketing*, 67(October), 1–17

Ambler, T. (2000), 'Marketing metrics', *Business Strategy Review*, 11(2), 59–66.

Ambler, T., Kokkinaki, F., and Puntoni, S. (2004), 'Assessing marketing performance: reasons for metrics selection', *Journal of Marketing Management*, 20, 475–98.

Andrews, S. (2006), 'Game on: the battle of the superconsoles begins', *Sunday Times*, 5 November, retrieve from www.driving.timesonline.co.uk/tol/life_and_style/driving/article624345.ece accessed 25 February 2007.

Anon. (2007), 'Shall we play a game?' *The Economist*, 31 May, retrieve from: http://www.economist.com/node/9257879 accessed 9 March 2013

Anon. (2012), 'Sony announces smaller and lighter PlayStation 3', *The Telegraph*, 18 September, retrieve from: http://www.telegraph.co.uk/technology/video-games/playstation/9552598/Sony-announces-smaller-and-lighter-PlayStation-3.html accessed 1 February 2013.

Ansoff, I. H. (1957) 'Strategies for diversification', *Harvard Business Review*, 35(2), 113–24

Arthur, C. (2007), 'Retailers suspiciously coy on PlayStation 3 pre-order figures', *The Guardian*, 22 February, retrieve from: www.guardian.co.uk/technology/2007/feb/22/sonyplaystation.games

Baker, R. (2011) Nokia to partner with Microsoft under new structure, *Marketing Week*, retrieved from: www.marketingweek.co.uk/sectors/telecoms-and-it/nokia-to-partner-with-microsoft-under-new-structure/3023364.article accessed 22 January 2012.

Balakrishnan, R. (2012), 'How Hindustan Unilever is making every employee a marketer', *Economic Times*, 18 July 2012, retrieve from: http://articles.economictimes.indiatimes.com/2012-07-18/news/32730917_1_hemant-bakshi-hul-employees-feedback accessed 27 July 2012.

BBC (2013), 'Microsoft to buy Nokia's mobile phone unit', retrieved from: http://www.bbc.co.uk/news/business-23940171 accessed 17 September 2013.

Bonoma, T. V. (1984), 'Making your marketing strategy work', *Harvard Business Review*, March–April, 69–76.

Capozzi, M.M., Horn, J., and Kellen, A. (2012) 'Strategy Practice: Battle-test your innovation strategy', *McKinsey Quarterly*, December, retrieve from: https://www.mckinseyquarterly.com/Strategy/Strategy_in_Practice/Battle-test_your_innovation_strategy_3038 accessed 31 January 2013.

Chapman, M. (2011), 'Nokia fights back with Microsoft smartphones', *Marketing*, 26 October, retrieve from: www.brandrepublic.com/news/1100666/Nokia-fights-back-Microsoft-smartphones/?DCMP=ILC-SEARCH, accessed 22 January 2012.

CIM (2009a) *The Future of Marketing*, White Paper—Chartered Institute of Marketing, May, retrieve from: www.cim.co.uk/filestore/resources/agendapapers/futureofmarketing.pdf accessed 6 April 2010.

CIM (2009b) *Keep Calm and Carry on Marketing: Marketing in a Recession*, White Paper—Chartered Institute of Marketing, April, retrieve from: www.cim.co.uk/filestore/resources/agendapapers/keepcalm.pdf accessed 6 April 2010.

Courtney, H., Horn, J.T., and Kar, J. (2009), 'Getting into your competitor's head' McKinsey Quarterly, February, retrieve from: https://www.mckinseyquarterly.com/Getting_into_your_competitors_head_2281 accessed 1 February 2013.

Day, G. S. and Wensley, R. (1988), 'Assessing advantage: a framework for diagnosing competitive superiority', *Journal of Marketing*, 52(2, April), 1–20.

Eastham, J. (2002) Thin times ahead for Burger King, *Marketing Week*, 1 August, 6.

Gast, A. and Zanini, M. (2012), 'The social side of strategy', *McKinsey Quarterly*, May, retrieve from: www.mckinseyquarterly.com/Strategy/Strategy_in_Practice/The_social_side_of_strategy_2965 accessed 1 February 2013.

Griffiths, K. (2006), 'Pharmaceuticals: UK drug giants hit by pipeline problems', *The Daily Telegraph*, 27 October, 3.

Gummesson, E. (1990), 'Marketing orientation revisited: the crucial role of the part-time marketer', *European Journal of Marketing*, 25(2), 60–75.

Hanselman, A. (2012), 'Joshie the Giraffe—A Remarkable Story About Customer Delight!', *Social Media Today*, 18 May, retrieve from: http://socialmediatoday.com/andyhanselman/552313/joshie-giraffe-remarkable-story-about-customer-delight accessed 10 February 2013.

Harbison, J. R. and Pekar, P. (1998) *Smart Alliances: A Practical Guide to Repeatable Success*, San Francisco, CA: Jossey-Bass

Haas, S., McGurk, M., and Mihas, L. (2010), 'A new world for brand managers', *McKinsey Quarterly*, April, retrieve from: www.mckinseyquarterly.com/A_new_world_for_brand_managers_2564 accessed 8 March 2013.

Hoffman, N. P. (2000), 'An examination of the sustainable competitive advantage concept: past, present, and future', *Academy of Marketing Science Review*, 2000, 4, retrieve from: http://www.amsreview.org/articles/hoffman04-L 2000.pdf accessed 30 January 2013.

Horn, J. (2011), 'Playing war games to win', *McKinsey Quarterly*, March, retrieve from: https://www.mckinseyquarterly.com/Playing_war_games_to_win_2757 9 March 2013.

Jack, L. (2010), 'Building a bridge between marketing and boardroom', *Marketing Week*, 25 February, retrieve from: www.marketingweek.co.uk/in-depth-analysis/cover-stories/building-a-bridge-between-marketing-and-boardroom/3010326.article accessed 5 April 2010.

Kaplan, R. S. and Norton, D. P. (1992), 'The balanced scorecard: measures that drive performance', *Harvard Business Review*, January–February, 71–9.

Keaveney, S. M. (1995), 'Customer switching behavior in service industries: an exploratory study', *Journal of Marketing*, 59(April), 71–82.

Keiningham, T. L., Aksoy, L., Cooil, B., Andreassen, T. W., and Williams, L., (2007), 'A holistic examination of Net Promoter', *Database Marketing and Customer Strategy Management*, 15(2), 79–90.

Keiningham, T. L., Aksoy, L., Cooil, B., and Andreassen, T. W. (2008), 'Linking customer loyalty to growth', *Sloan Management Review*, 49(4), 50–7.

Kotler, P. and Singh, R. (1981), 'Marketing warfare in the 1980s', *Journal of Business Strategy*, Winter, 30–41.

Lamont, J. (2012), 'Targeting KPIs for better business performance', *KM World*, 21(8), 12–13.

McCormick, A. (2009) 'Xbox strikes back', *Revolution*, December, 20–5.

McDonald, M. H. B. (1985), 'Marketing planning and Britain's disoriented directions', *Journal of Marketing Management*, 1, 21–5.

McDonald, M. (2002), *Marketing Plans and How to Make Them* (5th edn), Oxford: Butterworth-Heinemann.

Madslien, J. (2010) Spyker boss outlines Saab plans, retrieve from: www.news.bbc.co.uk/1/hi/business/8512224.stm accessed 25 March 2010.

Mintz, O. and Currim, I. S. (2013), 'What drives managerial use of marketing and financial metrics and does metric use affect performance of marketing mix activities?' *Journal of Marketing*, 77(March), 17–40.

Mintzberg, H. (1987), 'The strategy concept: Five Ps for strategy', *California Management Review*, 30, 1, 11–26.

Mitchell, A. (2012), 'Brand managers: then and now', *Marketing*, 23(May), 28–30.

Noble, C. H., Sinha, R. K., and Kumar, A. (2002), 'Market orientation and alternative strategic orientations: a longitudinal assessment of performance implications', *Journal of Marketing*, 66(4), 25–40.

O'Reilly, L. (2011), 'Microsoft appoints UK CMO', *Marketing Week*, 11 October, retrieved from: www.marketingweek.co.uk/sectors/telecoms-and-it/microsoft-appoints-uk-cmo/3030881.article accessed 22 January 2012.

O'Reilly, L. (2012), 'HTC needs to turn up the volume on its "Quietly Brilliant" strategy', *Marketing Week*, Friday 6 January, retrieved from: www.marketingweek.co.uk/sectors/telecoms-and-it/htc-needs-to-turn-up-the-volume-on-its-"quietly-brilliant"-strategy/3033082.article accessed 22 January 2012.

Piercy, N. (1998), 'Marketing implementation: the implications of marketing paradigm weakness for the strategy execution process', *Journal of the Academy of Marketing Science*, 26(3), 222–36.

Piercy, N. (2002) *Market-Led Strategic Change: Transforming the Process of Going to Market*, Oxford: Butterworth-Heinemann.

Pinto, V.S. (2011), 'HUL to push Lakme salons, new products', *Business Standard*, 19 February, retrieve from: http://www.business-standard.com/india/news/hul-to-push-lakme-salons-new-products/425759/ accessed 30 January 2013.

Porter, M. E. (1985), *The Competitive Advantage: Creating and Sustaining Superior Performance*, New York: Free Press.

Prahalad, C. K., and Hamel, G. (1990), 'The core competence of the organisation', *Harvard Business Review*, 68(3, May–June), 79–91.

Reichheld, F.F. (2003), 'The one number you need to grow', *Harvard Business Review*, 81(12), 47–54.

Schofield, J. (2005), 'Console wars: challengers must force the pace to unseat the leader', *The Guardian*, 1 December, retrieve from: www.guardian.co.uk/ technology/2005/dec/01/microsoftbox.games1 accessed December 2007.

Srinivasan, R., Lilien, G.L. and Sridhar, S. (2011), 'Should firms spend more on research and development and advertising during recessions?', *Journal of Marketing*, 49, 75(May), 49–65.

Teague, K. (2007), 'Apple Computer, Inc: Silhouette campaign', *Encyclopedia of Major Marketing Campaigns*, 2, 131–45, retrieve from: www.warc.com

Vorhies, D. W. and Morgan, N. A. (2003) 'A configuration theory assessment of marketing organisation fit with business strategy and its relationship with marketing performance', *Journal of Marketing*, 67(January), 100–15

Williams, R. (2010), 'What Do Corporate Values Really Mean?' *Psychology Today*, 7 February, retrieve from: http://www.psychologytoday.com/blog/wired-success/201002/what-do-corporate-values-really-mean accessed 7 February 2012.

Workman, J. P., Jr, Homburg, C., and Gruner, K. (1998), 'Marketing organisation: an integrative framework of dimensions and determinants', *Journal of Marketing*, 62 (July), 21–41.

Chapter 6
Market Segmentation and Positioning

Learning Outcomes

After studying this chapter, you will be able to:

▶ Describe the principles of market segmentation and the STP process

▶ List the characteristics and differences between market segmentation and product differentiation

▶ Explain consumer and business-to-business market segmentation

▶ Describe different targeting strategies

▶ Discuss the concept of positioning

▶ Illustrate how the use of perceptual maps can assist in the positioning process

Case Insight 6.1
Brompton Bicycles

Market Insight 6.1
Tasty Additions Build Profits

Market Insight 6.2
Sport Geosegmentation: They Think It's All Over

Market Insight 6.3
Barclays Bank on Segments

Market Insight 6.4
Constructing Segments at Biacore

Market Insight 6.5
Kiasma: Positioning for Accessibility

Case Insight 6.1

How should organizations segment their markets given a changing customer base? We speak to Emerson Roberts, sales and marketing director for Brompton Bicycles Ltd, to find out more.

Brompton Bicycles is a niche British engineering company which produces folding bikes from its base in Brentford, West London. The Brompton bicycle is an engineering feat first produced by innovative owner Andrew Ritchie in 1975 from his apartment overlooking the Brompton Oratory, from which the company and the bike originally took its name. Initially, Ritchie offered the folding bike's prototype to Raleigh, the bicycle manufacturer, but they did not take up the offer. So Ritchie set up his own independent company, based around the new concept. Our product typically retails at around £900 per bike and each one is custom-made. A key selling point is the portability of the bike. Because it folds into such a small package, it can be taken on buses and trains, and even stored under office desks and in cloakrooms. For the past 5 years, we have also been working on a folding electric bike and, through sister company Brompton Dock, we have also made our bikes available throughout Britain on a commercial hire basis.

The bike's modern incarnation is custom-produced in 6 hours in a factory staffed by 115 skilled people using 1,200 parts. Each bike is quality-checked religiously before it is packed for despatch. Our bikes are particularly popular with city commuters, and sales have been growing at around 20% per year for the past eight years, bringing turnover to around £20m per year and around £2m in profit. We are making around 36,000 bikes per year. The bike has been so successful that we now export four-fifths of our production abroad to 42 markets, particularly Japan, South Korea, and Germany, countries which have a strong cycling culture. We have even opened a Brompton store in China, the world's largest market for bicycles, which serves to illustrate the company's growth potential.

Companies like Giant and Specialized have built huge markets worldwide for bicycles for leisure use. Brompton, however, saw a market opportunity for a revived market for bicycles as a mode of transport, particularly given the current trend for both keeping fit and reducing usage of cars and therefore carbon emissions. Our typical customers in the UK and Western Europe had tended to be male, middle-aged, and professional. But this was changing, not just because we had moved into new geographic markets either. It was also changing in our existing markets.

Therefore our problem was: how should we re-segment our market domestically and how should we go to market internationally?

Introduction

Ever wondered how we decide to target certain market segments with our marketing activities? Think about fashion retailers for a moment: how do they identify which people to communicate with about their new ranges? Do they base it on where you live, your age, your gender, your

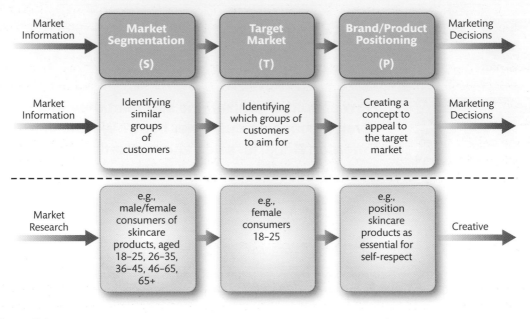

Figure 6.1
The STP Process

media usage, or something else? In this chapter, we consider how organizations decide on which segments of a market to concentrate their efforts. This process is known as **market segmentation** and it is an integral part of marketing strategy (see Chapter 5). After defining market segmentation, we explore the differences between market segmentation and **product differentiation**, to clarify the underlying principles of segmentation. We consider consumer and business-to-business market segmentation in detail. The method by which whole markets are subdivided into different segments to allocate marketing programme activity is referred to as the **STP process**, where STP refers to segmentation, targeting, and positioning (see Figure 6.1).

The STP Process

The STP process is used because of the prevalence of mature markets, greater diversity in customer needs, and its ability to help identify specialized niche segments. Marketers segment markets and identify attractive segments (i.e. who to focus on and why), identify new proposition opportunities, develop suitable positioning and **communication** strategies (i.e. what message to communicate), and allocate resources to prioritized marketing activities (i.e. how much to spend and where). Organizations commission segmentation research in order to revise their marketing strategy, investigate a declining brand, launch a new offering, or restructure their pricing policies. When operating in highly dynamic environments, segmentation research should be conducted at regular intervals to identify changes in the marketplace.

The key benefits of the STP process include the following.

■ Enhancing a company's competitive position, providing direction and focus for marketing strategies, including targeted advertising, new proposition development, and brand differentiation, e.g. Coca-Cola identified that Diet Coke was seen as 'feminine' by male consumers. Therefore the company developed Coke Zero targeted at the health-conscious male segment of the soft drinks market.

- Examining and identifying market growth opportunities through identification of new customers, growth segments, or proposition uses, e.g. Lucozade repositioned itself away from an offering that sick people used to rebrand itself as an energy drink.

- Effective and efficient matching of company resources to targeted market segments, promising greater return on marketing investment (ROMI). For example, ASDA Wal-Mart use data-informed segmentation strategies to target direct marketing messages (online and offline) and rewards to customers offering long-term value to the company.

The Concept of Market Segmentation

Market segmentation is the division of a market into different groups of customers with distinctly similar needs and proposition requirements. Alternatively, market segmentation is the division of a mass market into identifiable and distinct groups or segments, each of which have common characteristics and needs, and display similar responses to marketing actions.

Market segmentation was first defined as 'a condition of growth when core markets have already been developed on a generalised basis to the point where additional promotional expenditures are yielding diminishing returns' (Smith, 1956). It forms an important foundation for successful marketing strategies and activities (Wind, 1978; Hooley and Saunders, 1993). The purpose of market segmentation is to ensure that elements of the marketing mix, namely price, distribution, products, and promotion (and people, process and physical evidence for service offerings), meet the needs of different customer groups. As companies have finite resources, it is infeasible to produce all possible offerings for all the people all of the time. The best we can do is provide selected offerings for selected groups of people most of the time. This enables the most effective use of an organization's scarce resources.

Market segmentation is related to product differentiation. If you aim at different market segments, you might adapt different variations of your offering to satisfy those segments. Equally, if you adapt different versions of your offering, this may appeal to different market segments. For example, in fashion retailing, if you adapt your clothing range so that your skirts are more colourful, use lighter fabrics, and have a very short hemline, this styling might appeal to younger women. Alternatively, if you target older women, you might need to change the styling of your skirts by using darker heavier fabrics, with a longer hemline. The former approach is product differentiation—a focus on product offering—and the latter is market segmentation—a focus on market segments (the difference between product differentiation and market segmentation is illustrated in Figure 6.2). For example, ASOS (originally 'As Seen on Screen'), the online fashion retailer, uses a market segmentation approach, targeting 'twenty somethings'—a group of people roughly aged between 16 and 35 years, but who feel mentally in their twenties—very successfully around the world including in the UK, France, and Germany, and more recently in China and Russia (Ebrahimi, 2013).

Market segmentation was proposed as an alternative market development technique in markets with few competitors selling an identical product, i.e. imperfectly competitive markets. Where there are many competitors selling identical products, market segmentation and

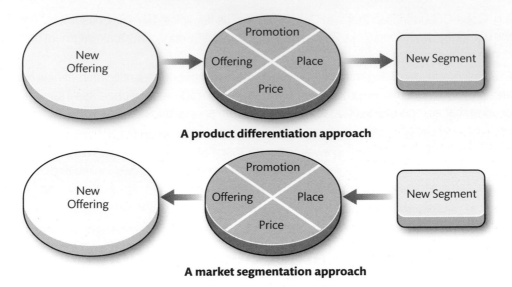

A product differentiation approach

A market segmentation approach

Figure 6.2

The difference between market segmentation and product differentiation

product differentiation produce similar results because competitors imitate each other's strategic approaches faster, and product differentiation approaches meet market segment needs more closely. Because consumers exhibit a wider range of tastes and have greater disposable income, marketers increasingly design offerings around consumer demand (market segments) rather than around their own production needs (product differentiation) (see Market Insight 6.1).

 # Market Insight 6.1

Tasty Additions Build Profits

It's a major headache for food manufacturers when food 'goes off', and the reason it does so is because the food oxidizes. The problems for food manufacturers are several. Food oxidation reduces the time the manufacturer has to sell the product, it can cause health problems for customers if it does taint and is unwittingly sold and eaten, and if customers buy it and don't eat it (and return the goods) it causes supply chain problems and unanticipated extra costs. One company that seeks to solve this problem is the Israeli food company Frutarom, which trades on the Tel Aviv and London Stock Exhanges, and sells anti-oxidants to food manufacturers (among other offerings). Established in 1933, Frutarom had become

a world-leading flavouring and fragrances company by 2006. It caters for customers in the food, beverage, functional food, flavour, fragrance, pharmaceutical, nutraceutical, and cosmetic industries. It has 31 R&D labs and 50 sales and marketing offices, and operates 28 production facilities around the world, employing around 2000 employees.

Its product Origanox™ (a mix of oregano, lemon balm, and herb spices) won an industry award (Frost & Sullivan's European Product Differentiation Excellence Award in 2012) because the product not only serves as a natural plant antioxidant but also works very effectively (enhancing the shelf-life of food products), is highly soluble, is readily available (other antioxidants are in short supply), is milder in taste than existing antioxidant formulations at lower dosage

Market Insight 6.1
continued

levels, performs well at high temperatures, masks odours, retards discoloration, and improves flavour. In addition, the product is available in oil-soluble and water-soluble formats. Because it keeps working at high temperatures, it can be used in frying but it is also efficient in cold water. Given the product's versatility, it's no wonder it won a product differentiation award. The company is also reaping the benefits: sales grew 22.3% in the first 9 months of 2012 to US$473m and net profit grew 21.5% to a rather tasty US$41m.

Sources: Bailey (2013); www.frutarom.com

1 Explain how Frutarom used a product differentiation approach to develop Origanox™.

2 What process would the company need to have adopted to have used a market segmentation approach?

3 Under what circumstances should market segmentation be used rather than product differentiation?

Research Insight 6.1

To take your learning further, you might wish to read this influential paper.

Smith, W. R. (1956), 'Product differentiation and market segmentation as alternative marketing strategies', *Journal of Marketing*, **July, 3–8.**

This seminal article explained the idea that neither supply nor demand was homogeneous (i.e. different groups wanted to produce *and* consume different things). A product differentiation approach concerns itself with bending demand to the will of supply but the reverse approach also exists, bending supply to the will of demand. This alternative marketing strategy, articulated in detail in this article for the first time, was termed market segmentation.

Visit the **Online Resource Centre** to read the abstract and access the full paper.

The Process of Market Segmentation

There are two main approaches to market segmentation. The first adopts the view that markets consist of customers that are similar. The task is to identify groups that share particular differences. This is the **breakdown method**. The second approach considers markets to consist of customers that are different. The task is to find similarities. This is known as the **build-up method** (Griffith and Pol, 1994).

The breakdown approach is the most established method for segmenting consumer markets. The build-up approach seeks to move from the individual level, where all customers are

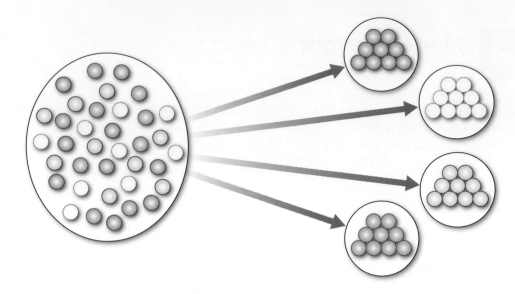

Figure 6.3
Segment heterogeneity and member homogeneity

different, to a more general level of analysis based on the identification of similarities (Freytag and Clarke, 2001). The build-up method is customer-oriented, seeking to determine common customer needs. The aim of both methods is to identify market segments where identifiable differences exist between segments—segment heterogeneity—but similarities exist between members within each segment—member homogeneity (see Figure 6.3).

Other segmentation researchers distinguish between **a priori** or **post hoc** segmentation methods, following a six- or seven-stage process of development (see Table 6.1).

In business markets, segmentation should reflect the relationship needs of the organizations involved. However, problems remain concerning the practical application and implementation of B2B segmentation. Managers frequently report that the analytical processes are reasonably clear, but it is unclear how they should choose and evaluate the various market segments (Naudé and Cheng, 2003). Segmentation theory developed in an era when a transactional goods-centric approach to marketing was predominant, rather than the service-dominant logic existing today. Under the transactional approach, resources are allocated to achieve designated marketing mix goals. However, customers within various segments have changing needs, and therefore those customers may change their segment membership (Freytag and Clarke, 2001). Consequently, market segmentation programmes should use current customer data.

Market Segmentation in Consumer Markets

To segment consumer markets, we use market information based around key customer-, product-, or situation-related criteria. These are classified as segmentation bases and include profile criteria (e.g. who are my market and where are they?), behavioural criteria (e.g. where, when, and how does my market behave?), and psychological criteria (e.g. why does my market

Table 6.1 A priori and post hoc segmentation approaches

Stage	A priori	Post hoc
1	Selection of the base (a priori) for segmentation (e.g. **demographics**, socio-economics)	Sample design—mostly using quota or random sampling approaches (see Chapter 3)
2	Selection of segment descriptors (including hypotheses on the possible link between these descriptors and the basis for segmentation)	Identification of suitable statistical methods of analysis
3	Sample design—mostly using stratified sampling approaches and occasionally quota sampling (see Chapter 3)	Data collection
4	Data collection	Data analysis—formation of distinct segments using multivariate statistical methods (e.g. cluster analysis, CHAID)
5	Formation of the segments based on a sorting of respondents into categories	Establishment of the profile of the segments using multivariate statistical methods (e.g. factor analysis) and selection of segment descriptors (based on the key aspects of the profile for each segment)
6	Establishment of the profile of the segments using multivariate statistical methods (e.g. multiple discriminant analysis, multiple regression analysis)	Translation of the findings about the estimated size and profile of the segments into specific marketing strategies, including the selection of target segments and the design or modification of specific marketing strategy
7	Translation of the findings about the estimated size and profile of the segments into specific marketing strategies, including the selection of target segments and the design or modification of specific marketing strategy	N/A

Note: N/A, stage not applicable.

Sources: Adapted from Wind (1978); and Green (1979).

behave that way?) (see Figure 6.4). A fourth segmentation criterion is contact data: a customer's name and full contact details beyond their postcode (e.g. postal address, email, mobile and home telephone number). Contact data are useful for tactical-level marketing activities, e.g. direct and digital marketing (see Chapters 11 and 17).

Table 6.2 illustrates the key characteristics associated with each of the main approaches to consumer market segmentation.

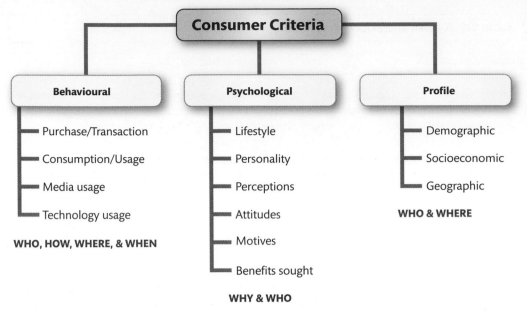

Figure 6.4
Segmentation criteria for consumer markets

When selecting different segmentation bases, the trade-off between data acquisition costs and the ability of the data to predict customer choice behaviour should be considered. Demographic and **geodemographic** data are relatively easy to measure and obtain; however, these bases suffer from low levels of accuracy in consumer behaviour predictability (see Figure 6.5). In contrast, behavioural data (e.g. **product usage**, purchase history, and media usage), although more costly to acquire, provide a more accurate means of predicting future behaviour. For example, the brand of toothpaste you purchased previously is more likely to be the brand of toothpaste you purchase in future. However, customer choices are also influenced by susceptibility to marketing communications.

Profile Criteria

One way of segmenting consumer markets is to use profile criteria to determine who consumers are and where they are located. To do this, we use demographic methods (e.g. age, gender, race), socio-economics (e.g. determined by social class, or income levels) and **geographic** location (e.g. using postcodes). For example, a utility company might segment households on geographical area to assess regional brand penetration, or an insurance company might segment the market based on age, employment, income, and asset net worth to identify attractive market segments for a new investment portfolio. These are all examples of segmentation based on profile criteria.

Demographic

Demographic variables relate to age, gender, family size and lifecycle, generation (e.g. baby boomers, Generation Y), income, occupation, education, ethnicity, nationality, religion, and social class. They indicate the profile of a consumer and are useful in media planning (see Chapter 11).

Table 6.2 Segmentation criteria

Base type	Segmentation criteria	Explanation
Profile	Demographic	Key variables concern age, sex, occupation, level of education, religion, social class, and income characteristics
	Lifestage	Based on the principle that people need different offerings at different stages in their lives (e.g. childhood, adulthood, young couples, retired)
	Geographic	The needs of potential customers in one geographic area are often different from those in another area, due to climate, custom, or tradition
	Geodemographic	There is a relationship between the type of housing and location that people live in and their purchasing behaviours
Psychological	Psychographic (lifestyles)	By analysing consumers' activities, interests, and opinions, we can understand individual lifestyles and patterns of behaviour affecting their buying behaviour and decision-making processes We can also identify similar offering and/or media usage patterns
	Benefits sought	The motivations customers derive from their purchases provide an insight into the benefits they seek from the use of an offering
Behavioural	Purchase/ transaction	Data about customer purchases and transactions provide scope for analysing who buys what, when, how often, how much they spend, and through what transactional channel they purchase
	Product usage	Segments can be derived on the basis of customer usage of the offering, brand, or product category; this may be in the form of usage frequency, time of usage, and usage situations
	Media usage	What media channels are used, by whom, when, where, and for how long provides useful insights into the reach potential for certain market segments through differing media channels, and also insight into their media lifestyle

Age is a common way of segmenting consumer markets. For example, children are targeted for confectionery and toys because their needs and tastes are different from those of older people. For example, Yoplait Dairy Crest (YDC) launched Petits Filous Plus probiotic yogurt drinks to extend the brand and increase its appeal among 4- to 9-year-olds and their parents.

Gender differences have also spawned a raft of offerings targeted at women. For example, beauty and fragrance offerings (e.g. Clinique, Chanel), magazines (e.g. *Cosmopolitan*, *Heat*), hairdressing (e.g. Pantene, Clairol), and clothes (e.g. H&M, New Look). Offerings targeted at men include magazines (e.g. *GQ*) and beverages (e.g. Carlsberg, Coke Zero). Some brands develop

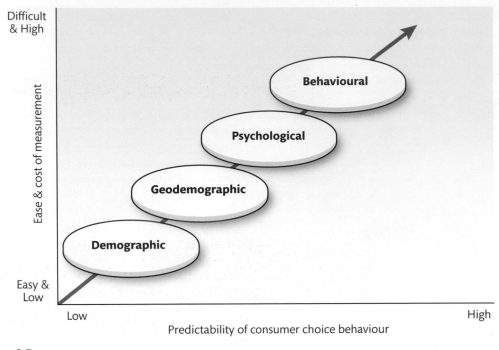

Figure 6.5

Considerations for segmentation criteria accessibility and use

Source: From Shimp. *Integrated Marketing Communications in Advertising and Promotion®, International Edition*, 7E. © 2007 South-Western, a part of Cengage Learning Inc. Reproduced by permission, www.cengage.com/permissions

offerings targeted at both men and women, e.g. fragrances (e.g. Calvin Klein) and watches (e.g. Rolex).

Income or socio-economic status is an important demographic variable because it determines whether or not a consumer can afford an offering (see Chapter 2). This comprises information about a consumer's personal income, household income, employment status, disposable income, and asset net worth. Many companies target high-net-worth individuals (e.g. Rolls-Royce, NetJets, Vertu) offering high-end exclusive offerings. However, targeting low-income earners can also be profitable. German discount supermarkets (e.g. Aldi) make a good profit from targeting low-income segments. Major supermarket groups like Carrefour and Tesco use an understanding of customer socio-economics to develop their own-label offerings. For example, Tesco Finest is developed for market segments with high disposable income, in contrast with Tesco Value marketed to the price-conscious low-income segment.

Lifecycle

Lifestage analysis posits that people have varying amounts of disposable income and different needs at different times in their lives. For example, adolescents need different offerings from single 26-year-olds, who need different offerings compared with a 26-year-old married person with young children. Major supermarkets (e.g. ASDA Wal-Mart, Tesco) have all invested in the development of offerings targeted at singles with high disposable incomes and busy lifestyles by offering 'meal for one' ranges, which compare with 'family value' and 'multipacks' targeted at families. As families grow and children leave home, the needs of parents change and their disposable income increases. Certain types of holidays (e.g. Thomas Cook's package holidays) and

Table 6.3 BMRB-TGI lifestage segmentation groups

Lifestage group	Demographic description
Fledglings	15–34, not married and have no son/daughter; living with own parents
Flown the nest	15–34, not married, do not live with relations
Nest builders	15–34, married, do not live with son/daughter
Mid-life independents	35–54, not married, do not live with relations
Unconstrained couples	35–54, married, do not live with son/daughter
Playschool parents	Live with son/daughter and youngest child 0–4
Primary school parents	Live with son/daughter and youngest child 5–9
Secondary school parents	Live with son/daughter and youngest child 10–15
Hotel parents	Live with son/daughter and have no child 0–15
Senior sole decision-makers	55, not married, and live alone
Empty nesters	55, married, and do not live with son/daughter
Non-standard families	Not married, live with relations, do not live with son/daughter, and do not live with parents if 15–34
Unclassified	Not in any group

Source: Reproduced with the kind permission of Kantar Media.

automobiles (e.g. people carriers) become more attractive to people in the lifestage when they have children. Target Group Index (TGI), a modern lifecycle classification, classifies 12–13 lifestage groups based on age, marital status, household composition, and children, e.g if they have children and the child's age (see Table 6.3). (See also Chapter 2 for a historical example of lifestage segmentation.)

Visit the **Online Resource Centre** and follow the weblink Kantar Media to learn more about the TGI.

Geographics

This approach is useful when there are clear locational differences in tastes, consumption, and preferences. For example, whereas the British celebrate Christmas with turkey dishes, Swedes often eat fish. These consumption patterns provide an indication of preferences according to differing geographical regions. Markets can be considered by country or region, size of city or town, postcode, or population density such as urban, suburban, or rural. It is often said that American beer drinkers prefer lighter beers compared with their UK counterparts, whereas German beer drinkers prefer a much stronger drink. In contrast, Australians prefer colder more carbonated beer than the British or Americans.

In addition to proposition selection and consumption, geographical segmentation is important for retail location, advertising and media selection, and recruitment. For example, recruitment to the armed forces draws people with similar demographic attributes from a variety of geographic areas. Low-cost formats might be used for retail outlets in low-income regions. Direct sales operations (e.g. catalogue sales) can use census information to develop better customer segmentation and predictive models. Interestingly, book publishers have long segmented based on geographical markets, frequently charging consumers in developing countries much less for a book than those in the developed world and trying to enforce a non-import policy so that these cheaper books do not enter Western markets. However, a recent case in the USA may hinder publishers' abilities to enforce the import ban, meaning they will no longer be able to offer developing world segments the much cheaper prices that they have previously enjoyed (Esposito, 2013).

Geodemographics

Geodemographics is a natural outcome when combining demographic and geographic variables. The marriage of geographics and **demographics** has become an indispensable market analysis tool, as it can lead to a rich mixture of who lives where (see Market Insight 6.2 for an example).

Visit the **Online Resource Centre** and complete Internet Activity 6.1 to learn more about how we use databases compiled with geodemographic data to profile market segments effectively.

Two of the best-known UK geodemographic systems are ACORN and MOSAIC. Developed by the British market research group CACI, ACORN—A Classification of Residential Neighbourhoods—demonstrates how postcode areas are broken down into six categories, 18 groups, and 62 types. The categories include groups such as:

i) affluent achievers

ii) rising prosperity

iii) comfortable communities

iv) financially stretched

v) urban adversity

vi) a not private households group

ACORN is a geodemographic tool used to identify the UK population and their demand for a variety of offerings to assist marketers so that they can determine where to locate operations, field sales forces, retail outlets, and so on. ACORN can also be used to determine where to plan marketing communications and social media marketing campaigns.

Visit the **Online Resource Centre** and follow the weblink to CACI to learn more about the ACORN system.

Another system is MOSAIC which is a geodemographic segmentation system developed by Experian and marketed globally. The system is based on the classification of 155 person types aggregated into 67 household types and 15 groups to create a three-tier classification that can be used at the individual, household, or postcode level.

Market Insight 6.2

Sport Geosegmentation: They Think It's All Over

In 2007, Sport England developed a segmentation model to enable local authorities, national governing bodies for sport (NGBs), and others working in community sport to target their scarce resources to encourage sports participation more effectively. In 2010, using fresh data, Sport England created an interactive segmentation tool allowing the creation of maps, charts, and tables to analyse segments at different geographic levels (for example, by county, local authority, county sport partnership, or postcode). The tool classifies the English population into 19 types as follows.

Source: http://segments.sportengland.org

Name	Size of Group	Description
Ben	5% of all adults, 10% of adult men	*Competitive male urbanites*: male, recent graduates with a 'work hard, play hard' attitude
Jamie	5% of all adults, 11% of adult men	*Sports team lads*: young blokes enjoying football, pints, and pool
Chloe	5% of all adults, 9% of adult women	*Fitness class friends*: young image-conscious females keeping fit and trim
Leanne	4% of all adults, 8% of adult women	*Supportive singles*: young busy mums and their supportive college mates
Helena	5% of all adults, 9% of adult women	*Career-focused females*: single professional women enjoying life in the fast lane
Tim	9% of all adults, 18% of adult men	*Settling down males*: sporty professional males, buying a house, and settling down with a partner
Alison	4% of all adults, 9% of adult women	*Stay-at-home mums*: mums with a comfortable, but busy, lifestyle
Jackie	5% of all adults, 10% of adult women	*Middle England mums*: mums juggling work, family, and finance
Kev	6% of all adults, 12% of adult men	*Pub league team mates*: blokes who enjoy pub league games and watching live sport

Market Insight 6.2
continued

Name	Size of Group	Description
Paula	4% of all adults, 7% of adult women	*Stretched single mums*: single mums with financial pressures, childcare issues, and little time for pleasure
Philip	9% of all adults, 18% of adult men	*Comfortable mid-life males*: mid-life professional sporty males with older children and more time for themselves
Elaine	6% of all adults, 12% of adult women	*Empty nest career ladies*: mid-life professionals who have more time for themselves since their children left home
Roger & Joy	7% of all adults, 6% of adult women, 8% of adult men	*Early-retirement couples*: free-time couples nearing the end of their careers.
Brenda	5% of all adults, 10% of adult women	*Older working women*: middle-aged ladies working to make ends meet
Terry	4% of all adults, 8% of adult men	*Local 'old boys'*: generally inactive older men, low income and little provision for retirement.
Norma	2% of all adults, 4% of adult women	*Later-life ladies*: older ladies, recently retired, with a basic income to enjoy their lifestyles
Ralph & Phyllis	4% of all adults, 4% of adult women, 5% of adult men	*Comfortable retired couples*: retired couples, enjoying active and comfortable lifestyles
Frank	4% of all adults, 8% of adult men	*Twilight years gents*: retired men with some pension provision and limited sporting opportunities
Elsie & Arnold	8% of all adults, 14% of adult women, 2% of adult men	*Retirement home singles*: retired singles or widowers, predominantly female living in sheltered accommodation

Source: http://segments.sportengland.org

Market Insight 6.2
continued

Sport England names its sports participation market segments

Source: © Sport England 2010

1 How useful do you think the segmentation tool will be in helping to encourage greater sports participation?

2 How might the segmentation approach be used in association with promotional media

such as advertising, direct marketing and social media?

3 What other segmentation bases could be used to encourage sports participation? How might they be used?

Visit the **Online Resource Centre** and follow the weblink to Experian to learn more about the MOSAIC system.

Psychological Criteria

Psychological criteria used for segmenting consumer markets include attitudes and perceptions (e.g. feelings about fast cars), **psychographics** or the lifestyles of customers (e.g. extrovert, fashion conscious, high achiever), and the types of **benefits sought** by customers from brands in their consumption choices.

Psychographics

Psychographic approaches rely on the analysis of consumers' activities, interests, and opinions to understand consumers' individual lifestyles and behaviour patterns. Psychographic segmentation includes understanding the values that are important to different customer types. A traditional form of lifestyle segmentation is AIO, based on customers' activities, interests, and opinions. Taylor Nelson Sofres (TNS) developed a UK Lifestyle Typology based on lifestyles, and classified the following lifestyle categories: belonger, survivor, experimentalist, conspicuous consumer, social resistor, self-explorer, and the aimless.

The Accor hotel group have used value-based segmentation to develop their brand. The Dorint-Novotel was repositioned to attract those who value personal efficiency. This involved changing the service offering by introducing efficiency-related facilities such as automated checkouts, car hire facility, 24-hour food, and wireless computing. The Dorint-Sofitel brand was repositioned by introducing fine art for the walls, real fires, fine wines, live piano in the reception, libraries, and more experienced concierge staff in order to appeal to those who valued classical styling, customization, and passion (Howaldt and Mitchell, 2007).

Benefits Sought

The benefits sought approach is based on the principle that we should provide customers with exactly what they want, based on the benefits they derive from use (Haley 1968). This might sound obvious, but consider what are the real benefits, both rational and irrational (see Chapter 2), for the different offerings that people buy, such as mobile phones and sunglasses? Major airlines often segment on the basis of the benefits passengers seek from transport by differentiating between the first class passenger (given extra luxury benefits in their travel experience), the business class passenger (who gets some of the luxury of the first class passenger), and the economy class passenger (who gets none of the luxury of the experience but enjoys the same flight). Morrissey and Baines (2011) segmented the Irish youth sports participation market based on the benefits that young people seek in sport participation (see also Market Insight 6.2), creating four segments as follows.

1. The enthusiast—cluster members exercise principally for enjoyment and fitness (strength/endurance and nimbleness) and tend to be regular exercisers.

2. The social competitor—cluster members, who tend to be regular exercises, male, and relatively young, exercise principally for interpersonal and affiliation motives. Interpersonal motives reflect individuals driven by the competitive and challenging aspects of exercise, in addition to peer recognition. Affiliation motives indicate a desire for social interaction and building of friendship through exercise.

3. The healthy looker—cluster members exercise principally for aesthetic and health motives and tend to be female and non-regular exercisers.

4. The reluctant exerciser—cluster members, who tend to be female and non-regular exercisers, exhibit below-average motivation for all motivational constructs, with interpersonal and enjoyment motives being substantially below average.

Behavioural Criteria

Product-related methods of segmenting consumer proposition markets include using behavioural methods (e.g. product usage, purchase, and ownership) as bases for segmentation. Observing consumers as they use offerings or consume services can be an important source of new ideas for new uses or proposition design and development (see Market Insight 6.4). Furthermore, new markets for existing offerings can be signalled, as well as appropriate communication themes for promotion. Purchase, ownership, and usage are three very different behavioural constructs that can be used to aid consumer market segmentation.

Usage

A company may segment a market based on how often a customer uses its offerings, categorizing these into high, medium, and low users. This allows the development of service specifications or marketing mixes for each user group. For example, heavy users of public transport might be targeted differently to heavy users of private vehicles by a coach operating company. Consumer usage of offerings can be investigated from three perspectives.

1 Social interaction perspective—symbolic aspects of usage and the social meanings attached to the consumption of socially conspicuous offerings such as a car or house are considered (Belk *et al.*, 1982; Solomon, 1983). For example, Greenpeace launched a television campaign targeting owners of four-wheel drive cars highlighting the environmental social stigma of their car purchase.

2 Experiential consumption perspective—emotional and sensory experiences are considered as a result of usage, especially emotions such as satisfaction, fantasies, feelings, and fun (Holbrook and Hirschman, 1982). For example, Oxo gravy campaigns have emphasized how usage of Oxo brings families together, and expressed family values such as love, sharing, and spending time together.

3 Functional utilization perspective—the functional usage of products and their attributes in different situations is considered (McAlister and Pessemier, 1982; Srivastava *et al.*, 1978). For example, how and when cameras are used, how often, and in what contexts.

Service providers often segment markets based on their customers' purchase behaviour. This might involve segmentation by loyalty to the service provider, or length of relationship, or some other mechanism.

Transaction and Purchase

The development of electronic technologies, such as electronic point of sale (EPOS) systems, standardized product codes, radio-frequency identification (RFID) systems, QR (quick response) codes, and integrated purchasing systems (e.g. web, in-store, telephone) has facilitated rapid growth in the collection of consumer purchase and transactional data. For example, browsing and purchase data allows Amazon to make recommendations of offerings that are more likely to appeal to consumers. EPOS systems allow retailers to track who buys what, when, for how much, in what quantities, and with what incentives (e.g. sales promotions). Companies have the ability to monitor purchase patterns in various geographical regions, at different times or seasons of the year, for various offerings, and increasingly for differing market segments. Social media can also be analysed to track what people are saying once they have purchased and used particular offerings.

Transactional and purchase information is very useful for marketers to assess who their most profitable customers are. By analysing the recency, frequency, and monetary value of purchases (RFM), marketers can identify their most profitable market segments. Customers who purchase most recently, most frequently, and spend the most would be classified as profitable customers. Transactional data are records of behaviours and provide some insight into purchasing trends. Online, we can track from where someone is accessing our website. For example, if someone is coming to us from a price comparison website, they are probably price sensitive but if they arrive from a product review website, they have probably already decided what they want and so are less price sensitive (Stiving, 2012). (Market Insight 6.3 shows an example of the combined use of usage, transactional, and attitudinal data to profile and target banking segments.)

Market Insight 6.3

Barclays Bank on Segments

Barclays, a large UK-based bank, has adopted a hybrid segmentation model, incorporating attitudinal profiles and four types of segmentation: 1) business type (personal, premier, private, small business); 2) operational segmentation by age and wealth; 3) attitudinal segmentation; 4) executional segmentation, operationalized as 'triggers, events and propensity models' (see Figure 6.6).

The executional segmentation category focuses on how individual customers are treated. One approach is through 'triggers', for example, commercially significant occurrences on a customer's account. A late payment fee might indicate that a customer's needs have changed. Or, a customer who has just taken out cash via credit card might need credit and be a target for a loan. The trigger information typically needs to be combined with an assessment of the customer's credit status to ascertain whether a loan would be an appropriate offer for a customer who has just been charged a late payment fee or an overdraft extension. Barclays also considers 'events' on customer accounts, e.g. when a customer's insurance requires renewal, or a mortgage comes to an end, or when moving house, getting married, and having children. Barclays focuses on executional segmentation by modelling customer responses to Customer Action Prompts (CAPs). This is referred to as 'propensity modelling'. The approach combines transactional data from current accounts and credit cards with external data sources to provide a picture of customers' lifestyles, lifestages, and finances. The fused data allows the development of propensity models which predict customers' likelihood of responding to particular promotional offers.

Source: Bailey *et al.* (2009) (see also Market Insight 18.3).

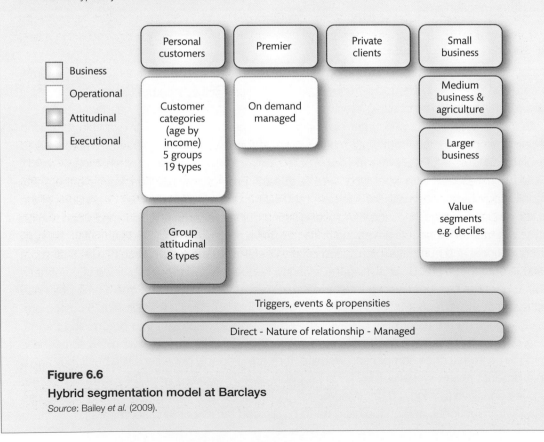

Figure 6.6

Hybrid segmentation model at Barclays

Source: Bailey *et al.* (2009).

Market Insight 6.3
continued

1 Why do you think Barclays uses a hybrid approach in their segmentation?

2 How do you think Premier customers are treated separately?

3 How do you think the segmentation approach will need to change given Barclay's repositioning towards a more ethical approach?

Media Usage

The logic of segmenting markets by frequency of readership, viewership, or patronage of **media vehicles** is well established. For example, heavy and light magazine readers might respond differently to ads with different creative appeals (Urban, 1976). Segmenting users on their media usage frequency can provide insights into whether or not a publisher attracts and retains consumers who are more or less responsive to an advertiser's communication. This information provides input when evaluating the efficiency and effectiveness of media. Furthermore, differences in frequency may lead to differences in response to repeated passive ad exposures, competing ads of other sponsors, and prior ad exposure.

Frequency of media usage has been the predominant measure of media usage experience. However, Olney *et al.* (1991) and Holbrook and Gardner (1993) have identified viewing time as an important dependent variable in a model of advertising effects. On media websites, users might be segmented by either their visit frequency or their dwell time (how long they spend on a site) among other variables.

Segmentation in Business Markets

Business-to-business market segmentation is the identification of 'a group of present or potential customers with some common characteristic which is relevant in explaining (and predicting) their response to a supplier's marketing stimuli' (Wind and Cardozo, 1974). Unfortunately, B2B market segmentation has not been as well researched as consumer market segmentation (Bonoma and Shapiro, 1983). There are two main groups of interrelated variables used to segment B2B markets (see Table 6.4). The first involves organizational characteristics, such as **organizational size** and location, sometimes referred to as **firmographics**. Those seeking to segment might start with these variables. The second group is based on the characteristics surrounding the decision-making process. Those organizations seeking to establish and develop customer relationships would normally expect to start with these variables.

Organizational Characteristics

These factors concern the buying organizations that make up a business market. There are a number of criteria that can be used to cluster organizations, including size, geography, market served, value, location, **industry type**, usage rate, and **purchase situation**. We discuss the main three categories used in Figure 6.7.

Table 6.4 Segmentation bases used in business markets

Base type	Segmentation base	Explanation
Organizational characteristics	Organizational size	Grouping organizations by relative size (MNCs, international, large, SMEs) enables the identification of design, delivery, usage rates or order size, and other purchasing characteristics
	Geographic location	Often the needs of potential customers in geographic areas are different from each other
	Industry type (SIC codes)	Standard industrial classifications (SICs) are used to identify and categorize industries and businesses
Buyer characteristics	Decision-making unit structure (DMU)	Attitudes, policies, and purchasing strategies allow organizations to be clustered
	Choice criteria	The types of offerings bought and the specifications companies use when selecting and ordering offerings form the basis for clustering customers and segmenting business markets
	Purchase situation	Segmenting buyers by how a company structures its purchasing procedures, the type of buying situation, and whether buyers are in an early or late stage in the purchase decision process

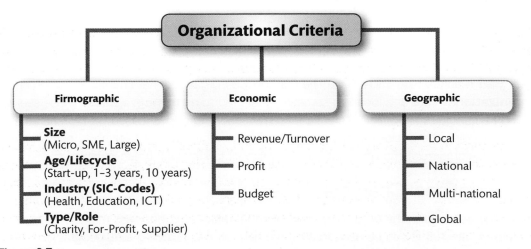

Figure 6.7

Segmentation by organizational characteristics

Organizational Size

By segmenting organizations by size, we can identify particular buying requirements. Large organizations may have particular delivery or design needs based on volume demand, e.g. supermarkets such as France's Carrefour and Britain's Tesco pride themselves on purchasing goods in sufficiently large quantities to enable them to be offered at cheaper prices. The size of the organization often impacts on the usage rates of an offering, so organizational size is linked to whether an organization is a heavy, medium, or low buyer of a company's offerings.

Geographical Location

Geotargeting is one of the more common methods used to segment B2B markets, and is often used by new or small organizations attempting to establish themselves. This approach is useful because it allows sales territories to be drawn around particular locations that salespersons can service easily (e.g. Scotland, Scandinavia, Western Europe, the Mediterranean). Alternatively, sales territories may be based on specific regions within a country, e.g. in Eastern Europe they may be based on individual nations (i.e. Poland, Czech Republic, Romania, and Hungary). However, this approach becomes less useful as the internet cuts across geographic distribution channels (see Chapters 12 and 17).

SIC Codes

Standard Industrial Classification (SIC) codes are used to understand market size. They are easily accessible and standardized across most Western countries, e.g. the UK, Europe, and the USA. However, some marketers have argued that SIC codes contain categories that are too broad to be useful. Consequently, SIC codes have received limited application, although they do provide 'some preliminary indication of the industrial segments in [a] market' (Naudé and Cheng 2003). More commonly, companies sometimes segment B2B markets using industry types (so-called 'verticals'). For example, a law firm might segment its customers into, among others, the following sectors: financial services, utilities, transport, and retailing.

Visit the **Online Resource Centre** and complete Internet Activity 6.2 to learn more about how we use SIC codes to segment business markets.

Customer Characteristics

These factors concern the characteristics of buyers within the organizations that make up a business market. Numerous criteria could be used to cluster organizations including by decision-making unit, purchasing strategies, relationship type, attitude to risk, **choice criteria**, and purchase situation.

Decision-Making Unit

An organization's decision-making unit may have specific requirements that influence purchase decisions in a particular market, e.g. policy factors, purchasing strategies, a level of importance attached to these types of purchases, or attitudes towards vendors and risk. These characteristics can be used to segregate groups of organizations for particular marketing programmes. Segmentation might be based on the closeness and level of interdependence existing between organizations. Organizational attitudes towards risk and the degree to which an organization is willing to experiment through the acquisition of new industrial offerings varies (see Market Insight 6.4). The starting point of any business-to-business segmentation is a good database

Market Insight 6.4

Constructing Segments at Biacore

Biacore International AB, a leading Swedish provider of life science tools for protein research, was bought by GE Healthcare, a unit of the General Electric Company in 2006, for SEK2.9bn ($390m) after two years of very successful growth. The company originated as a development project operating out of Pharmacia Biotech, then a leading supplier of biotechnology analytical tools. Initially, the idea of the development project was to produce a diagnosis machine to allow on-site analysis of blood samples by medical personnel (rather than having to send samples off to an external laboratory). A secondary smaller market was also identified: researchers at universities and in pharmaceutical companies interested in using the machines to characterize biomolecules. The primary market (biosensors in medical diagnostics) was estimated to be worth €400–1,000m and the secondary market (biosensors as research instruments) worth €100m. However, Pharmacia Biotech decided that the project was not viable because it had a weak position in the largest potential market (the USA) and its new product threatened to damage its relationships with its existing customers (diagnostic laboratories). It decided to scale down the project and focus only on the secondary market. In effect, its market segmentation project had failed. To understand how the diagnostic machines might be applied in research laboratories, Biacore set up launch workshops to demonstrate the biosensor machine's capabilities with potential early users, even loaning the equipment to them afterwards and discussing potential applications of the technology over protracted periods of time. This approach allowed the identification of a myriad of potential users. These interactions, through structured feedback, resulted in a series of symposia, a scientific journal, and a reference database, allowing the project to map out a whole host of potential applications, but importantly it also provided the material for new users to identify potential applications. After considerable interaction (effectively segment construction), Biacore was able to define the research market for its biosensor machines: research labs and pharmaceutical companies with high requirements concerning sensitivity, quality of data and productivity, labs and pharma companies that did not have the same high requirements, and shared laboratory environments where the technology is used in a hybrid way with other diagnostic tools (e.g. spectroscopic, fluorescent, separation). It was recognized that the company could not go on interacting with all its customers in the way that it had with early users because the cost to serve was too high and the project needed to reduce its costs in anticipation of its stock market launch. Therefore it identified a number of ideal customers for whom their offers could be standardized but, importantly, kept interacting with early users to improve its future offerings. What Biacore did very successfully was learn how to construct market segments with innovative customers rather than map an existing market that was already 'out there'. As the takeover by GE Healthcare illustrates, the real market size for their offering was far in excess of what they had originally anticipated.

Sources: Goldstein (2006); Harrison and Kjellberg (2010); www.biacore.com

1 **Why did the original approach to segmentation fail?**

2 **What segmentation method did Biacore end up using?**

3 **What other companies might use the same segmentation approach and in what circumstances?**

Sweden's Biacore International AB developed an on-site diagnostic machine for blood analysis
Source: istock © Eugene_Sim.

or customer relationship management system (see Chapter 14). It should contain customer addresses, contact details, and detailed purchase and transactional history. Ideally, it will also include the details of those buyers present in the customer company's **decision-making unit structure**.

Choice Criteria

Business markets can be segmented on the basis of the specifications of offerings that they choose. For example, an accountancy practice may segment its clients by those that seek 'compliance'-type accounting offerings such as audits and tax submission work, companies that require management accounting services, and companies that require a complex mix of both. A computer manufacturer might segment the business market for computers by those requiring computers with strong graphical capabilities (e.g. educational establishments, publishing houses) and those requiring computers with strong processing capabilities (e.g. scientific establishments). However, companies do not necessarily need to target multiple segments. They might simply target a single segment, as RM Education, an IT technological solutions provider, has done successfully in the UK education market.

Purchase Situation

Companies sometimes seek to segment the market on the basis of how organizations buy. There are three questions associated with segmentation by purchase situation that should be considered.

1 What is the structure of the buying organization's purchasing procedures? Centralized, decentralized, flexible, or inflexible?

2 What type of buying situation is present? New task (i.e. buying for the first time), modified rebuy (i.e. not buying for the first time, but buying something with different specifications from previously), or straight rebuy (i.e. buying the same thing again)?

3 What stage in the purchase decision process have target organizations reached? Are they buyers in early or late stages and are they experienced or new?

For example, a large global consulting and IT services company like Infosys from India might segment the market for IT project management services into public and private sectors. The focus might then be on fulfilling large government contracts that are put out to tender, where a group of selected buyers are offered the opportunity to bid for an exclusive franchise to deliver agreed services for a defined period of time.

Typically, in segmenting business markets, a service provider can use a mix of macro- and micro-industrial market segmentation approaches by defining the customers a company wants to target using a macro-approach, such as standard industrial classification or geographic region, and then further segmenting using the choice criteria for which they select a company. In other words, multi-stage market segmentation approaches are often adopted.

Target Markets

The second important part of the STP process is to determine which of the segments uncovered should be targeted and made the focus of a comprehensive marketing programme. Ultimately, managerial discretion and judgment determines which markets are selected and

---

Research Insight 6.2

To take your learning further, you might wish to read this influential paper.

Beane, T. P., and Ennis, D. M. (1987), 'Market segmentation: a review', *European Journal of Marketing*, **21(5), 20–42.**

This article provides a useful insight into the main bases for market segmentation and the strengths and weaknesses of the key statistical methods we use to analyse customer data to develop segmentation models. The article suggests there are many ways to segment a market, and it is important to exercise creativity when doing so.

Visit the **Online Resource Centre** to read the abstract and access the full paper.

---

exploited. Kotler (1984) suggested that, for market segmentation to be effective, all segments must be:

- **D**istinct—is each segment clearly different from other segments? If so, different marketing mixes will be necessary.
- **A**ccessible—can buyers be reached through appropriate promotional programmes and distribution channels?
- **M**easurable—is the segment easy to identify and measure?
- **P**rofitable—is the segment sufficiently large to provide a stream of constant future revenues and profits?

Kotler's approach to evaluating market segments is often referred to by the DAMP acronym, to make it easier to remember. Another approach to evaluating market segments uses a rating approach for different segment attractiveness factors, such as market growth, segment profitability, segment size, competitive intensity within the segment, and the cyclical nature of the industry (e.g. whether or not the business is seasonal, such as retailing). Each of these segment attractiveness factors is rated on a scale of 0–10 and loosely categorized in the high, medium, or low columns, based on either set criteria or subjective criteria, depending on the availability of market and customer data and the approach adopted by the managers undertaking the segmentation programme (see Table 6.5).

Other examples of segment attractiveness factors might include segment stability (i.e. stability of the segment's needs over time) and mission fit (i.e. the extent to which dealing with a particular segment fits the mission of your company). Once the attractiveness factors have been determined, the importance of each factor can be weighed and each segment rated on each factor. This generates a segment attractiveness evaluation matrix (see Table 6.6).

Decisions need to be made about whether a single offering is made available to a range of segments, a range of offerings are made to multiple segments or a single segment, or one

---

Table 6.5 Examples of segment attractiveness factors

Segment attractiveness factors	Rating		
	High (10–7)	Medium (6–4)	Low (3–0)
Growth	>2.5%	2.5%–2.0%	<2.0%
Profitability	>15%	10–15%	<10%
Size	>£5m	£1m–£5m	<£1m
Competitive intensity	Low	Medium	High
Cyclicality	Low	Medium	High

Source: McDonald and Dunbar (2004). Reproduced with permission. © Elsevier.

offering should be presented to a single segment. Whatever the decision, a marketing mix strategy should be developed to meet segment needs, which reflects the organization's capabilities and competitive strengths. Key questions around the development of the marketing mix are: How can the segment(s) be reached with appropriate communications? What is the media consumption pattern of the target audience? Where can they gain access to our offerings to purchase them? Does the offering need to be adapted for different segments and should it be priced the same or differently for all segments?

Targeting Approaches

Once segments are identified, an organization selects its preferred approach to targeting. Four differing approaches can be used (see Figure 6.8).

Table 6.6 Example of a segment attractiveness evaluation matrix

Segment attractiveness factors	Weight	Segment 1		Segment 2		Segment 3	
		Score	Total	Score	Total	Score	Total
Growth	25	6	1.5	5	1.25	10	2.5
Profitability	25	9	2.25	4	1.0	8	2.0
Size	15	6	0.9	5	0.9	7	1.05
Competitive intensity	15	5	0.75	6	0.9	6	0.9
Cyclicality	20	2.5	0.5	8	1.6	5	1
Total	100	5.9		5.65		7.45	

Source: McDonald and Dunbar (2004). Reproduced with permission. © Elsevier.

Figure 6.8
Market targeting approaches

- The **undifferentiated approach**— where there is no delineation between market segments and the market is viewed as one mass market with one marketing strategy for the entire market. Although expensive, this approach is used for markets where there is limited or no segment differentiation, e.g. housing offered by local authorities).

- The **differentiated targeting approach**—where there are several market segments to target, each being attractive to the marketing organization. To exploit them, a marketing strategy is developed for each segment. For example, HP has developed its product range and marketing strategy to target the following user segments of computing equipment: home office users, small and medium businesses, large businesses, and health, education, and government departments. A disadvantage of this approach is the loss of economies of scale because of the resources required to meet the needs of multiple market segments.

- A **concentrated marketing strategy** or **niche marketing strategy**—where there are just a few market segments. This approach is adopted by firms with limited resources to fund their marketing strategy, or who adopt a very exclusive strategy in the market. The UK's Co-operative Bank targets consumers interested in a bank with ethical lending and investment credentials. This approach is used frequently by small to medium- and micro-sized organizations with limited resources (e.g. an electrician may focus on local residences).

- A **customized targeting strategy**—where marketing strategy is developed for each customer rather than each segment. This approach predominates in B2B markets (e.g. marketing research or advertising services) or consumer markets with high-value, highly customized products (e.g. purchase of a custom-made car). For example, a manufacturer of industrial electronics for assembly lines might target and customize its offering differently for Nissan, Unilever, and SCA, given the differing requirements in assembly line processes for the manufacture of automobiles, foodstuffs, and hygiene products (e.g. hand-dryers).

Segmentation Limitations

Whilst market segmentation is a useful process for organizations to use to divide customers into distinct groups, it has been criticized for the following reasons.

- The process approximates offerings to the needs of customer groups, rather than individuals; therefore there is a chance that customers' needs are not fully met. However, **customer relationship marketing** (CRM) processes and software allow companies to develop customized approaches for individual customers. Integrating CRM processes and segmentation schemes can require considerable extra planning.

- There is insufficient consideration of how market segmentation is linked to competitive advantage (see Hunt and Arnett, 2004). The product differentiation concept is linked to the need to develop competing offerings, but market segmentation does not stress the need to segment on the basis of differentiating the offering from competitors. This angle should be integrated into the segmentation scheme if the scheme is to be more effective.

- It is unclear how valuable segmentation is to managers. Suitable processes/models to measure the market segmentation effectiveness have yet to be developed. It has been argued that much of the money spent on segmentation schemes is wasted, partly because organizations don't spend enough on these studies and partly because they don't assimilate the results of the study into the organization's strategy development processes (Incite, 2009). Therefore market segmentation is an organizational capability and some organizations are better at it than others (Poenaru and Baines, 2011).

Dibb *et al.* (2001) suggested that segmentation plans in B2B markets frequently fail because businesses fail to overcome segmentation implementation barriers including the following.

- Infrastructure barriers—culture, structure, and the availability of resources prevent the segmentation process from ever starting, e.g. there may be a lack of financial resource or political will to collect the market data necessary for a segmentation programme.

- Process issues—lack of experience, guidance, and expertise can hamper how segmentation is undertaken and managed. Typically, market research agencies and in-house market research teams use market and customer insight data and statistical software packages to undertake this task. However, because the different statistical methods provide different results, care must be taken in determining which method to use and how to interpret the results when they are produced.

- Implementation barriers—once a new segmentation model is determined, how do organizations move towards a new segmentation model? This may require a move away from a business model based on offerings (e.g. engine sizes for fleet buyers) to one based on customer needs.

Research Insight 6.3

To take your learning further, you might wish to read this influential paper.

Dibb, S. (1999), 'Criteria guiding segmentation implementation: reviewing the evidence', *Journal of Strategic Marketing*, 7(2), 107–29.

In this article, Dibb highlights an important previously unconsidered area of concern, namely, that of why segmentation schemes often fail at the implementation stage. She argues that, for segmentation to be effective, segmentation criteria should be applied before, during, and after a segmentation scheme. Extant research focused on the outcomes and inputs of segmentation rather than on what criteria can be applied before the segmentation process begins.

Visit the **Online Resource Centre** to read the abstract and access the full paper.

Positioning

Having segmented the market, determined the size and potential of market segments, and selected specific target markets, the third part of the STP process is to position a brand within the target market(s). **Positioning** is the means by which offerings are differentiated from one another to give customers a reason to buy. It encompasses two fundamental elements. The first concerns the attributes—the functionality and capability that a brand offers, e.g. a car's engine specification, its design, and carbon emissions. The second positioning element concerns the way in which a brand is communicated and how customers perceive the brand relative to competing brands. This element of communication is important as it is not what you do to an offering that is important, but 'what you do to the mind of a prospect' (Ries and Trout, 1972) that determines how a brand obtains its market positioning (see Chapter 19 on semiotics and Market Insight 6.5).

Positioning concerns an offering's attributes and design: how the offering is communicated, and the way these elements are fused together in customers' minds. It is not the offering (physical or otherwise) that is important for positioning, nor just the communication that leads to successful positioning. For example, claims (through communication) that a shampoo will remove dandruff will be rejected if the offering fails to deliver. Therefore positioning is about how customers judge an offering's value relative to competitors, its ability to deliver against the promises made, and the potential customers have to derive value from the offering. To develop a sustainable position, we must understand the market in which the offering is competing.

At a simple level, the positioning process begins during the target market selection process. Key to this process is identifying those attributes considered to be important by consumers. For a car manufacturer, these attributes may be tangible (e.g. the gearbox, transmission system, seating, and interior design) and intangible (e.g. the reputation, prestige, and allure that a brand generates). By understanding what customers consider to be the ideal standard that each attribute needs to attain and how they rate the attributes of each brand in relation to the ideal level,

Market Insight 6.5

Kiasma: Positioning for Accessibility

The meaning that a piece of art conveys, its purpose and the artist's message, fascinates many. The meaning of art has long been a source of discussion and debate. For Kiasma, the state-owned contemporary art museum in Helsinki, helping the public understand what art is trying to convey is something they wanted to address. The museum was originally opened in 1998, quickly becoming one of the most visited museums in Finland. However, the number of people enjoying the museum began to fall steadily as competition for leisure time and work commitments reduced visitor numbers. To understand people's behaviour and motivations better and to find a new way of enabling them to interact with the art, a major research programme was undertaken. The research identified five distinct segments:

1. **Passionates (15% of the population)** Those interested in high culture, middle-aged, open-minded, knowledgeable, and passionate about contemporary art.

2. **Interested (20% of the population)** Those interested in popular culture, with some interest in high culture.

3. **Moderates (34% of the population)** Those moderately interested in both popular and high culture, who would like to attend contemporary art shows.

4. **Popularists (20% of the population)** Those, often young, who are interested in popular culture but not high culture, and who have little intention of attending culture shows.

5. **Negativists (11% of the population)** Those not interested in any type of culture, not open to new ideas, and with no intention of visiting a contemporary art show.

The museum identified the Passionates, the Interested, and the Moderates as the most attractive segments to target, and developed a

The stunning Kiasma Museum of Contemporary Art in Helsinki, Finland, designed by Steven Hall Architects
Source: Finnish National Gallery/Central Art Archives/Petri Virtanen.

Market Insight 6.5
continued

new positioning strategy accordingly. The museum targeted each segment individually, based on their media habits and attitudes towards culture. The core theme for the tenth anniversary, and a central message aimed at the Interested and Moderates segments, was 'I don't quite get it …'. This focused on repositioning the art gallery as an enjoyable experience, accessible to all. This repositioning strategy was intended to help audiences overcome the intimidation felt when engaging with contemporary art. The core message was that it was not necessary to understand high culture to enjoy and be entertained by art experiences. Attendances increased as a result.

Sources: Jantti and Jarn (2009); www.kiasma.fi/

1 **Identify what types of media each of the five segments might prefer.**

2 **What problems arise when positioning cultural attractions?**

3 **Rather than positioning the Kiasma museum as accessible entertainment for everyone, how else might it have been positioned?**

and to each other, it becomes possible to see how a brand's attributes can be adapted and communicated to become more competitive.

Perceptual Mapping

Understanding the complexity associated with the different attributes and brands can be made easier by developing a visual representation of each market. These are known as perceptual maps. The 'maps' are used to determine how various brands are perceived according to the key attributes that customers value. This is important because positioning is a two-way process by which organizations seek to impose attribute perceptions onto customers and customers assimilate those perceptions, modify them, or reject them entirely. Therefore **perceptual mapping** allows the geometric comparison of how competing products are perceived (Sinclair and Stalling 1990). Typically, the closer offerings/brands are clustered together on a perceptual map, the greater the competition. The further apart the positions, the greater the opportunity for new brands to enter the market. For example, in the mobile phone market there are numerous brands competing with each other across differing attributes. Figure 6.9 shows the positioning of some key mobile phone brands in relation to general customer attributes on proposition and technology use.

Figure 6.9 illustrates several things. For example, it indicates that the Apple mobile brand (iPhone) is positioned as the mobile phone for people most comfortable with using internet technology. Blackberry is more closely associated with people who like to stand out in a crowd and enjoy eating out in trendy places. HTC is a brand more closely associated with consumers who are innovators or early adopters (see Chapter 2), whilst Sagem and Motorola brands appeal to people who prefer 'staycations' to holidaying abroad.

Perceptual mapping data reveal strengths and weaknesses that can assist strategic decisions about how to differentiate on the attributes that matter to customers the most.

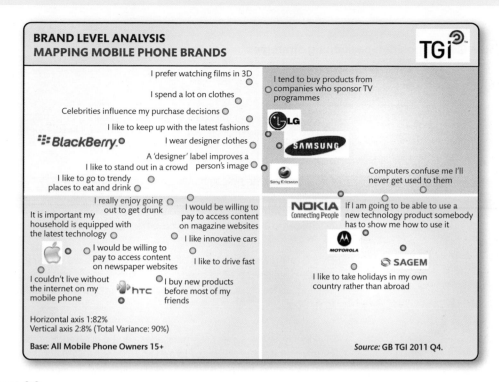

Figure 6.9

Perceptual map for UK mobile phone market

Source: © Kantar Media.

Positioning and Repositioning

Understanding brand positioning helps marketers to improve a brand's performance through modification of the marketing communications used to support a brand. Through marketing communications, especially advertising, information can be conveyed about each attribute in order to adjust customers' brand perceptions. Marketing communications can be used to position brands either functionally or expressively (symbolically) (see Table 6.7). Functionally positioned brands emphasize features and benefits, whereas expressive brands emphasize the ego, social, and hedonic satisfactions a brand brings (see Chapters 2 and 19). Both approaches make a promise: for example, for haircare, the promise is to deliver cleaner, shinier, and healthier hair (functional) or hair we are confident wearing because we want to be admired, or because it is important that we feel more self-assured (expressive). Different positioning approaches are likely to be more successful than others with particular offerings. For example, in the compact car market, Fuchs and Diamantopoulos (2010) found that direct benefit positioning (based on functional aspects) is likely to be more effective than indirect benefit positioning (based on experiential/symbolic dimensions) and that expressive positioning is more effective than functional approaches. User positioning can also provide a sound alternative to benefit positioning.

Technology, customer tastes, and competitors' new offerings are reasons why markets might change. For example, Disney acquired Lucasfilm in 2012 with a plan to launch the seventh *Star Wars* film in 2015 and others beyond. However, to be successful, Disney needs to reposition and target the new films at the generation which grew up with the *Clone Wars* cartoon and Lego Star Wars characters rather than those who watched the original trilogy in the late seventies and

Table 6.7 Proposition positioning strategies

Position	Strategy	Explanation
Functional	Product features	Brand positioned on the basis of attributes, features, or benefits relative to the competition, e.g. Volvos are safe; Red Bull provides energy.
	Price quality	Price can be a strong communicator of quality. John Lewis Partnership (the UK department store) uses the tagline 'never knowingly undersold' to indicate how it will match competitors' prices on the same items to ensure its customers always get good value.
	Use	By informing when or how an offering can be used, we create a mental position in buyers' minds, e.g. Kellogg's reposition their offerings to be consumed throughout the day, not just at breakfast (e.g. Special K).
Expressive	User	By identifying the target user, messages can be communicated clearly to the right audience. Flora margarine was initially for men and then it became 'for all the family'. Some hotels position themselves as places for weekend breaks, as leisure centres, as conference centres, or as all three.
	Benefit	Positions can be established by proclaiming the benefits that usage confers on consumers. The benefit of using Sensodyne toothpaste is that it alleviates the pain associated with sensitive teeth.
	Heritage	Heritage and tradition are sometimes used to symbolize quality, experience, and knowledge. Kronenbourg 1664, 'Established since 1803', and the use of coats of arms by many universities are designed to convey heritage to build long-term trust.

eighties (Garrahan, 2012). Thus, if the brand positioning adopted is strong, if the brand was the first to claim the position, and the position is continually reinforced with clear simple messages, there may be little need to alter the position originally adopted. Marketers should be alert and prepared to reposition their brands as the relative positions occupied by brands, in the minds of customers, will be challenged on a frequent basis, especially by competing offerings. Repositioning is often difficult to accomplish because of the entrenched perceptions and attitudes held by customers towards brands and the cost of the vast (media) resources required to make these changes.

Repositioning revolves around an offering and the way it is communicated. The following four ways outline how to approach repositioning, depending on the individual situation facing a brand. In some cases, a brand might need to be adapted before relaunch.

1 *Change the tangible attributes and then communicate the new proposition to the same market.* Nokia spent £80m in 2011 to reposition the brand globally, given a significant decline in handset sales as Apple, Samsung, and HTC took away market share. The new Nokia phone integrated the Windows 7 operating system (Brownsell, 2011). Another

Research Insight 6.4

To take your learning further, you might wish to read this influential book.

Ries, A. and Trout, J. (2006), *Positioning: The Battle for your Mind*, London: McGraw-Hill Professional.

This book by Al Ries and Jack Trout, originally published in 1981, remains the bible of advertising strategy. They define 'positioning' not as what you do to an offering to make it acceptable to potential customers, but what you do to the mind of the prospect. Positioning requires an outside-in rather than an inside-out thinking approach.

Visit the **Online Resource Centre** to read more about the book.

example of repositioning is Skoda, the Czech car manufacturer, once a household joke. Since the brand was bought by VW and new models built on the VW car platform, the brand has gone from strength to strength, giving it a UK market share of 2.6%, selling a record 53,602 vehicles in 2012 (Bell, 2013).

2 *Change the way a proposition is communicated to the original market.* The Norwegian oil and gas company Statoil Hydro was repositioned globally as Statoil by communications agency Hill & Knowlton Strategies, raising its profile in key markets across Europe, including in the UK.

3 *Change the target market and deliver the same proposition.* On some occasions, repositioning can be achieved through marketing communications alone, but targeted at a new market. For example, Lucozade was repositioned from a drink for sickly children, a niche market with limited volume sales growth, to an energy drink for busy, active, and sports-oriented people, achieved through heavyweight advertising campaigns.

4 *Change both the proposition (attributes) and the target market.* For example, Xerox have repositioned themselves from being a document company to a diversified business services company, running call centres, processing insurance claims, and even handling toll payments (Carone, 2013).

Chapter Summary

To consolidate your learning, the key points from this chapter are summarized here.

■ **Describe the principles of market segmentation and the STP process.**

Whole markets are subdivided into different segments through the STP process. STP refers to the three activities which should be undertaken sequentially if segmentation is to be successful, namely segmentation, targeting, and positioning. Market segmentation is the division of a market into different groups of customers with distinctly similar needs and offering requirements. The second part of the STP process determines which segments should be targeted with a comprehensive marketing mix programme. The third part of the STP process is to position a brand within the target market(s).

■ **List the characteristics and differences between market segmentation and product differentiation.**

Market segmentation is related to product differentiation. Given an increasing proliferation of tastes, marketers have sought to design offerings around consumer demand (market segmentation) more than around their own production needs (product differentiation).

■ **Explain consumer and business-to-business market segmentation.**

Data based on differing consumer, user, organizational, and market characteristics are used to segment a market. These characteristics differ for consumer (B2C) and business (B2B) contexts. To segment consumer goods and service markets, market information based on certain key customer-, product-, or situation-related criteria (variables) is used. These are classified as segmentation bases and include profile, behavioural, and psychological criteria. To segment business markets, two main groups of interrelated variables are used—organizational characteristics and buyer characteristics.

■ **Describe different targeting strategies.**

Once identified, the organization selects its target marketing approach. Four differing approaches exist: 1) undifferentiated, 2) differentiated, 3) concentrated or niche, and 4) customized target marketing.

■ **Discuss the concept of positioning.**

Positioning provides the means by which offerings can be differentiated from one another and gives customers reasons to buy. It encompasses physical attributes, the way in which a brand is communicated, and how customers perceive the brand relative to competing brands.

■ **Illustrate how the use of perceptual maps can assist in the positioning process.**

Perceptual maps are used in the positioning process to illustrate differing attributes of a selection of brands. They also illustrate existing levels of differentiation between brands, how our brand and competing brands are perceived in the marketplace, how a market operates, and strengths and weaknesses that can assist with making strategic decisions about how to differentiate the attributes that matter to customers in order to compete more effectively in the market.

 # Review Questions

1 Define market segmentation and explain the STP process.
2 What is the difference between market segmentation and product differentiation?
3 Identify four different ways in which markets can be segmented.
4 How do market segmentation bases differ in business-to-business and consumer markets?
5 How can market segmentation bases be evaluated when target marketing?
6 What are the different approaches to selecting target markets?
7 Describe the principle of positioning and why it should be undertaken.
8 What are perceptual maps and what can they reveal?
9 Explain three ways in which brands can be positioned.
10 Make a list of four reasons why organizations need to reposition brands.

Worksheet Summary

To apply the knowledge you have gained from this chapter and test your understanding of market segmentation visit the **Online Resource Centre** and complete Worksheet 6.1.

Discussion Questions

1 Having read Case Insight 6.1, how would you advise Brompton to segment the market for its bicycles? Consider both the domestic and international markets.

2 In a group with other colleagues from your seminar/tutor group, discuss answers to the following questions.

   A Using the information in Table 6.8 on the champagne market, and a suitable calculator, determine what are the most potentially profitable segments in the marketplace.

   B What other data do we need to determine the size of the market (market potential)?

Table 6.8 **The champagne and sparkling wine market by segment**				
Social class	Enthusiasts (%) AP = £20 F = 5/yr	Sparkling sceptics (%) AP = £10 F = 3/yr	Price driven (%) AP = £8.50 F = 3/yr	Uneducated (%) AP = £15 F = 2/yr
AB (n = 8m)	25	31	30	14
C1 (n = 14m)	23	23	32	21
C2 (n = 8m)	27	26	33	14
DE (n = 10m)	20	26	40	14

Notes: AP = average price, n = population size, F = no. of bottles purchased/year (all data hypothetical); % segment sizes per socio-economic group and segment descriptions only from Mintel (2012).

3 Discuss which market segmentation bases might be most applicable to:

   A A fashion retailer segmenting the market for womenswear.

   B A commercial radio station specializing in dance music and celebrity news/gossip.

   C A Belgian chocolate manufacturer supplying multiple retail grocers and confectionery shops across Europe (e.g. Godiva).

   D The Absolut Company, with headquarters in Sweden, supplying high-quality vodka around the world.

   E Rakbank in Dubai, United Arab Emirates, when segmenting the market for its credit card.

4 Write a one-sentence description of the attributes and benefits that are attractive to target consumers for an offering with which you are particularly familiar (e.g. Apple in the computer category or Samsung in the mobile phones category), using the statement provided. Explain how these attributes and benefits are different from those of competitors. Your positioning statement might be as follows:

[Product A] provides [target consumers] with [one or two salient product attributes]. This distinguishes it from [one or two groups of competing product offerings] that offer [attributes/benefits of the competing products].

A Briefly describe the target market segment. This should summarize the defining characteristics of the segment (e.g. demographic, psychographic, geographic, or behavioural).

B Briefly explain your reasons for believing that the attributes/benefits of your positioning statement are important for your target segment. Draw a perceptual map that summarizes your understanding of the market and shows the relative positions of the most important competing products.

Visit the **Online Resource Centre** and complete the Multiple Choice Questions to assess your knowledge of Chapter 6.

References

Bailey, E. (2013), 'Frost & Sullivan Confers Product Differentiation Excellence Award on Frutarom for Origanox™', PR Newswire, *Press Release*, 21 March, retrieve from: http://www.prnewswire.co.uk/news-releases/frost--sullivan-confers-product-differentiation-excellence-award-on-frutarom-for-origanox-199302521.html accessed 27 April 2013.

Bailey, C., Baines, P., Wilson, H., and Clarke, M. (2009), 'Segmentation and customer insight in contemporary services marketing practice: why grouping customers is no longer enough', *Journal of Marketing Management* 25(3/4), 227–52.

Beane, T. P. and Ennis, D. M. (1987), 'Market segmentation: a review', *European Journal of Marketing*, 21, 5, 20–42.

Belk, R. W., Bahn, K. D., and Mayer, R. N. (1982), 'Developmental recognition of consumption symbolism', *Journal of Consumer Research*, 9(June), 4–17.

Bell, A. (2013), 'Skoda achieves record UK sales in 2012', Contracthireandleasing.com, 8 January, retrieve from: http://www.contracthireandleasing.com/car-leasing-news/skoda-achieves-record-uk-sales-in-2012/ accessed 4 May 2013.

Bonoma, T. V. and Shapiro, B. P. (1983), *Segmenting the Industrial Market*, Lexington, MA: Lexington Books.

Brownsell, A. (2011), 'Nokia prepares £80m brand repositioning campaign', *Marketing*, 12 July, retrieve from: http://www.marketingmagazine.co.uk/article/1079542/Nokia-prepares-80m-brand-repositioning-campaign accessed 4 May 2013.

Carone, C. (2013), 'Xerox's brand repositioning challenge', *Ad Age*, 12 March, retrieve from: http://adage.com/article/cmo-strategy/xerox-s-brand-repositioning-challenge/240285/ 4 May 2013.

Dibb, S. (1999), 'Criteria guiding segmentation implementation: reviewing the evidence', *Journal of Strategic Marketing*, 7(2), 107–29.

Dibb, S., Simpkin, L., Pride, W. M., and Ferrell, D. C. (2001), *Marketing Concepts and Strategies*, Cambridge, MA: Houghton Mifflin.

Ebrahimi, H. (2013), 'ASOS bumper results always in fashion', *Telegraph*, 20 March, retrieve from: http://www.telegraph.co.uk/finance/newsbysector/retailandconsumer/9943682/Asos-bumper-results-always-in-fashion.html accessed 23 April 2013.

Esposito, J. (2013), 'The fall and rise of market segmentation', *The Scholarly Kitchen*, 22 March, retrieve from: http://scholarlykitchen.sspnet.org/2013/03/22/the-fall-and-rise-of-market-segmentation/ accessed 29 April 2013.

Freytag, P. V. and Clarke, A. H. (2001), 'Business to business segmentation', *Industrial Marketing Management*, 30(6, August), 473–86.

Fuchs, C. and Diamantopoulos, A. (2010), 'Evaluating the effectiveness of brand-positioning strategies from a consumer perspective', *European Journal of Marketing*, 44(11/12), 1763–86

Garrahan, M. (2012), 'Disney grabs a galaxy of opportunity', *Financial Times*, 1 November, 19.

Goldstein, S. (2006), 'General Electric to buy Sweden's Biacore', *MarketWatch*, 20 June, retrieve from: http://articles.marketwatch.com/2006-06-20/news/30720041_1_biacore-international-life-sciences-ge-healthcare accessed 5 May 2013.

Green, P. E. (1979), 'A new approach to market segmentation', *Business Horizons, February*, 61–73.

Griffith, R. L., and Pol, L. A. (1994), 'Segmenting industrial markets', *Industrial Marketing Management*, 23, 39–46.

Haley, R. I. (1968), 'Benefit segmentation: a decision-oriented research tool', *Journal of Marketing*, 32, 30–5.

Harrison, D. and Kjellberg, H. (2010), 'Segmenting a market in the making: industrial market segmentation as construction', *Industrial Marketing Management*, 39, 784–92.

Holbrook, M. B. and Gardner, M. P. (1993), 'An approach to investigating the emotional determinants of consumption durations: why do people consume what they consume for as long as they consume it?', *Journal of Consumer Psychology*, 2(2), 123–42.

Holbrook, M. B. and Hirschman, E. C. (1982), 'The experiential aspects of consumer behaviour: consumer fantasies, feelings and fun', *Journal of Consumer Research,* 9(September), 132–40.

Hooley, G. J., and Saunders, J. A. (1993), *Competitive Positioning: The Key to Market Success*, Englewood Cliffs, NJ: Prentice Hall.

Howaldt, K., and Mitchell, A. (2007), 'Can segmentation ever deliver the goods?', *Market Leader*, 36(Spring), retrieve from: www.warc.com, accessed 5 May 2013.

Hunt, S. D., and Arnett, D. B. (2004), 'Market segmentation strategy, competitive advantage and public policy: grounding segmentation strategy in resource-advantage theory', *Australasian Marketing Journal*, 12(1), 7–25.

Incite (2009), 'Anything but business as usual', *Incite Segmentation Newsletter*, Spring, retrieve from: http://www.incite.ws/segmentation_web/VISION%20-%20Anything%20but%20business%20as%20usual.pdf accessed 28 April 2013.

Jantti, S-M., and Jarn, C. (2009), The insightful museum—how to create a customer centred marketing strategy, *ESOMAR, Consumer Insights*, retrieve from: www.warc.com accessed 26 March 2010.

Kotler, P. (1984), *Marketing Management*, Upper Saddle River, NJ: Prentice Hall.

McAlister, L. and Pessemier, E. (1982), 'Variety seeking behaviour: an interdisciplinary review', *Journal of Consumer Research*, 9(December), 311–22.

McDonald, M. and Dunbar, I. (2004), *Market Segmentation: How to Do It, How to Profit from It*, Oxford: Elsevier.

Mintel (2012), *Champagne and Sparkling Wine—UK—July 2012*, retrieve from: www.mintel.com accessed 23 April 2013.

Morrissey, P. and Baines, P. (2011), 'Segmenting Exercise Participants by Surface Level Participation Motivation', presented at Australian and New Zealand Marketing Academy Conference, 28–30 November, Perth, Australia.

Naudé, P. and Cheng, L. (2003), 'Choosing between potential friends: market segmentation in a small company', presented at the 19th IMP Conference, Lugano, Switzerland, retrieve from: www.impgroup.org/conferences.php accessed December 2007.

Olney, T. J., Holbrook, M. B., and Batra, R. (1991), 'Consumer response to advertising: the effects of ad content, emotions, and attitude toward the ad on viewing time', *Journal of Consumer Research*, 17(March), 440–53.

Poenaru, A. and Baines, P. (2011), 'An organizational capability model of market segmentation', presented at Australian and New Zealand Marketing Academy Conference, Perth, Australia, 28–30 November.

Ries, A. and Trout, J. (1972), 'The positioning era cometh', *Advertising Age*, 24 April, 35–8.

Sinclair, S. A. and Stalling, E. C. (1990), 'Perceptual mapping: a tool for industrial marketing: a case study', *Journal of Business and Industrial Marketing*, 5(1), 55–65.

Smith, W. R. (1956), 'Product differentiation and market segmentation as alternative marketing strategies', *Journal of Marketing*, July, 3–8.

Solomon, M. R. (1983), 'The role of products as social stimuli: a symbolic interactionism perspective', *Journal of Consumer Research Conference*, 10(December), 319–29.

Srivastava, R. K., Shocker, A. D., and Day, G. S. (1978), 'An exploratory study of the influences of usage situations on perceptions of product markets', paper presented at the Advances in Consumer Research Conference, Chicago.

Stiving, M. (2012), 'Brilliant price segmentation: an example', *Pragmatic Pricing*, 4 May, retrieve from: http://pragmaticpricing.com/2012/05/04/brilliant-price-segmentation-an-example/ accessed 4 May 2013.

Urban, C. (1976), 'Correlates of magazine readership', *Journal of Advertising Research*, 19(3, June), 7–12.

Wind, Y. (1978) 'Issues and advances in segmentation research', *Journal of Marketing Research*, 15(August), 317–37.

Wind, Y. and Cardozo, R. N. (1974), 'Industrial market segmentation', *Industrial Marketing Management*, 3(March), 155–66.

Chapter 7
International Market Development

Learning Outcomes

After studying this chapter you should be able to:

▶ Define international market development as a key growth strategy

▶ Explain the different forms of international marketing strategy

▶ Identify the key drivers for international market development

▶ Describe the criteria used to identify and select international markets

▶ Examine the environmental factors that could influence the choice of international marketing strategy

▶ Explore the various methods used to enter international markets

Case Insight 7.1
Orange

Market Insight 7.1
H&M Heads East

Market Insight 7.2
On Your Trikke—New Product, New Markets

Market Insight 7.3
Coca-Cola's International Heritage

Market Insight 7.4
Google Gets Censored

Market Insight 7.5
Fueling Growth though Fast Food Franchising

Case Insight 7.1

France Telecom, owner of Orange, one of the world's leading telecommunications operators, had consolidated sales of €53.5bn in 2008 and a customer base of more than 182 million customers in 30 countries. Given such large numbers of customers what does Orange do to retain them? We talk to Sue Wilmot, Head of Customer Strategy, to find out more.

Orange offers services including mobile and fixed-line telephony, internet, and IPTV (internet TV) in 30 countries where the company operate for over 182 million customers. By the end of 2008, the Group had 122 million mobile customers worldwide and 13 million broadband internet (ADSL) customers in Europe. It is the No. 3 mobile operator and the No. 1 provider of broadband internet services in Europe and, under the brand Orange Business Services, is a world leader in provision of telecommunication services to multinational companies. The group's strategy, characterized by a strong focus on innovation, convergence, and effective cost management, aims to establish Orange as an integrated operator and benchmark for new telecommunications services in Europe. Today, the group remains focused on its core activities as a network operator, while working to develop its position in new growth activities. To meet customer expectations, the group strives to provide products and services that are simple and user-friendly.

Customers are at the heart of everything we do at Orange group. As a result, it is essential that we look after our existing customers and keep a loyal base for the future. To do this, we need to align both loyalty and retention activity to ensure that we look after our customers from the point at which they join Orange. However, there will always be instances where customers do want to leave as we work in a highly competitive industry and customers have alternatives, and therefore we need a robust retention strategy to manage this.

Customer retention as a strategy is standardized across Europe but is localized at the implementation level, given local market differences. What is highly important to some markets may not be as important to others because of the differences in customer behaviour, economic climate, maturity, and competitor situation. How we retain clients across multiple channels in different countries is based on the skills of the teams, the channel capabilities, and the systems capabilities in different countries. The market conditions are also different across Europe; for example, although involuntary churn, i.e. non-payment of bills resulting in a customer leaving an operator, is an issue for most countries, it is certainly more of an issue in Romania and Spain than in France.

These differences in retention practices and capabilities can occur for different reasons. For involuntary churn, the culture and market conditions drive how much of an issue this is in local markets. France has not been as impacted by the recent recession as much as other countries such as Romania, Spain, and the UK. This recessionary factor, coupled with a culture of high borrowing in these countries, has led to consumers finding themselves in increasingly difficult personal economic circumstances where they cannot afford to pay their bills.

When looking at customer-initiated churn, how we address churn prevention through developing contact plans from day 1 of a customer's lifecycle is key. Traditionally, the customer lifecycle has been broken into three key periods—welcome, grow, and keep. But

Case Insight 7.1
continued

if we only consider 'keeping' a customer towards the end of their lifecycle, we are often reducing our chances of being able to 'save' that customer. This is particularly the case if a customer has experienced a problem throughout their lifetime with Orange, because if we don't manage the issues and subsequent satisfaction at this point we eventually worsen the problem. By not addressing this issue and the loyalty and retention of the customer until the end of a contract, we have fundamentally missed the opportunity to retain the customer as they are already dissatisfied with us. Therefore it is not surprising that the customer wants to leave when the contract comes to an end.

Therefore the problem for us is how do we develop our customer contact plan to reduce customer churn given the different market conditions in European markets?

Introduction

Have you ever considered where the food you purchase and consume is produced or the clothes you are wearing have been manufactured? Have a look in your kitchen cupboard and your wardrobe—is it from England, Europe, China, or Southeast Asia? What about the last film you watched at the cinema. Where was it filmed—America, India, or maybe Europe? We are now consuming more products, reading more information, travelling overseas more than ever before. In 2009, we saw a collapse in global demand triggered by the biggest economic downturn in decades. What effect has this had on how, where, and to whom we export and market our offerings?

In the light of the increasing internationalization of world markets, increased foreign trade, changes in technology, and the economic impact of foreign markets, **international marketing** is essential for the survival of many organizations. Even organizations that only compete in domestic markets are affected, as they increasingly compete with foreign organizations. An understanding of international business, marketing, and globalization is essential for marketing in the twenty-first century.

This chapter explores the issues that marketers should consider when developing effective international marketing strategies and policies. This includes international market development, the criteria used to select attractive international markets, the forces in international markets that shape our activities, and the different methods for international market entry.

Types of International Organization

Before we consider the strategies and issues associated with international marketing, consideration should be given to understanding the different types of organization that operate in international markets. There are several typologies, particularly from the work of Keegan (1989), Bartlett and Ghoshal (1991), and de Mooij (1994). Their view is that organizations can be regarded as national, international, multinational, global, or transnational. These are set out in Table 7.1. Each

Table 7.1 Types of international organization

Type of Organization	Explanation
National organizations	These organizations only operate within their own domestic borders. Their marketing and sales operations are bounded by the home national boundary. The marketing policy is to serve customers with a single marketing mix.
International organizations	These organizations see their overseas operations as appendages or attachments to a central domestic organization. The marketing policy is to serve customers domestically and offer these same marketing mixes to other countries/areas.
Multinational organizations	These organizations see their overseas activities as a portfolio of independent businesses. The policy is to serve customers with individually designed country/area marketing mixes.
Global organizations	These organizations regard their overseas activities as feeders or delivery tubes for a unified global market. The policy is to serve a global market with a single marketing mix.
Transnational organizations	These organizations regard their overseas activities as a complex process of coordination and cooperation. The environment is regarded as one where decision-making is shared in a participatory manner. The policy is to serve global business environments using flexible global resources to formulate different global marketing mixes.

Sources: Adapted from Bartlett and Ghoshal (1991) and de Mooij (1994).

of these types of organization reflects their configuration and structure, and their strategic orientation towards customers and their markets.

Domestic organizations operate within their own home country boundaries using a marketing mix designed to meet the needs of the home market. Invariably this represents a standardized proposition. Some of these domestic organizations evolve into international organizations as they begin to carry out a small amount of 'overseas' work. The first step is often to use their domestically oriented marketing mix and at a later stage start to adapt it to the needs of the new 'overseas' market.

This adaption phase signals the emergence of a multinational strategy and corresponding type of organization. These organizations regard the world in which they operate as made up of discrete regions, with each requiring its own marketing mix. Each country/area reports to a world head office and performance is normally geared to meet financial targets.

As growth occurs and more and more regions are brought into an organization's scope, so it transforms into a global enterprise. Global organizations are characterized by strategies that are founded on an understanding that it is the similarities across country/area markets that are important, not the differences. Customers are seen to be part of a single global picture, and so a standardized marketing mix is preferred. All decision-making is centralized.

Transnational organizations develop out of global enterprises. These are relatively sophisticated companies which establish operations in many countries around the world, based on wholly or partially owned subsidiaries. At the hub of the operations is the headquarters. This is based in one country, but it manages the operations in all the other countries. Transnational companies seek to serve global customers by developing efficient operations. These are based on utilizing technologies to generate synergies through the 'creation, accumulation, transferring and sharing of knowledge that exists in different locations' (de Pablos 2006: 556).

Organizations need to be flexible and adapt to changing market conditions. As domestic markets stagnate, and technology and communication opportunities in particular develop, so opportunities wax and wane. In addition, organizations seek efficiency and flexibility with regard to their use of materials and resources. The use of strategic alliances and outsourcing arrangements complements this goal, and network-based organizations spanning the globe emerge.

Understanding these different types of international organization is important, not just from a structural perspective but also for the formulation and implementation of business and marketing strategies. We now explore ways in which organizations can develop their operations, the decisions they make, and the factors and issues that influence their decision-making.

Market Development

Marketing strategy is about matching market opportunities to an organization's resources (what it can do) and its objectives (what management wants to achieve). Successful strategies begin with the identification of attractive market opportunities. This can be assisted through the use of the Ansoff matrix, which is set out at Figure 7.1. Also referred to as the product–market matrix, it provides a useful basis for considering the relationship between strategic direction and market opportunities (see also Chapter 5). This matrix provides four broad strategic options available to organizations, depending on whether the product and/or the market are considered to be new to an organization.

The matrix illustrates the important point that risk increases the further strategy moves away from known positions—an existing product and/or existing market. Product development (a new proposition) and market development (a new market) typically involve greater risk than market penetration (existing offering and existing market). Diversification, a new propositions and a new market, carries the greatest risk of all. Although four types of opportunities are presented, some organizations can pursue more than one type of opportunity simultaneously. More details about the Ansoff matrix can be found in Chapter 5. Here, we pay specific attention to the strategy of 'market development'.

	Present Products	**New Products**
Present Markets	Market Penetration	Product Development
New Markets	Market Development	Diversification

Figure 7.1

Ansoff's matrix

Source: Adapted from Ansoff (1957).

A market development strategy involves increasing sales by selling existing propositions in new markets, either by gaining new customers domestically or by entering new markets internationally. Essentially the goal is to sell more of the same things, but to different people. We might target different geographical markets at home and/or abroad, or target different groups of people, perhaps a different demographic profile from our current customers. For example, Lucozade was first marketed for sick children and then rebranded to target athletes. Other examples include the use of military equipment for consumer purposes (e.g. miniature cameras in mobile phones originated from espionage), and, more controversially, the selling of cigarettes to women in the early 1930s/1940s. We currently see franchise chains such as McDonald's expanding into new geographical locations domestically by targeting new audiences through differing retail outlets such as the McCafe and airport eateries. These are good examples of developing new markets domestically for an existing offering.

Entering a new international market with an existing offering represents a much greater risk than these strategies. To build brand awareness and minimize risk, organizations often rely on the reputation of their brands in domestic markets. Honda's entry into the US market in the 1950s and the entry of the Japanese, European, and American car manufacturers into China and India over the past 10–15 years are fine examples of international market development.

Major large organizations, such as Ford, Toyota, and Samsung, use their reputation earned in well-established domestic and international markets to gain early entry in rapidly developing markets. Other examples include Cadbury Schweppes selling existing brands of chocolate bars in Africa, and McDonald's expanding their franchise and entering foreign markets such as China, Russia, and Brazil.

A key decision is whether to pursue new audiences in our domestic market or enter new international markets. Some of the main differences between domestic and international marketing include language, culture, complexity of research and decision-making, market knowledge, and marketing environment stability (see Table 7.2). For example, international markets are often seen as more unstable than domestic markets due to their sensitivity to fluctuations in currency

Table 7.2 Key differences between domestic and international marketing

Domestic marketing	International marketing
Main language	Many languages
Dominant culture	Multicultural
Research relatively straightforward	Research is complex
Relatively stable environment	Frequently unstable environment
Single currency	Exchange rate problems
Business conventions understood	Conventions diverse and unclear

Source: Fill (2009).

rates, immigration patterns, and political and trade relations. Furthermore, development in international markets requires a relatively high degree of investment by an organization and a greater understanding of the changing nature of world markets.

International Market Development

Entering international markets is a key market development strategy for organizational growth and has been a feature of civilizations for thousands of years. However, in the last century international trade saw enormous growth in both scale and complexity. With this growth, different approaches to international market development have developed.

Approaches to International Market Development

International marketing means different things to different organizations. Some organizations take an ad hoc approach, only responding to customer export enquiries when they occur. Others, such as H&M and BMW, deliberately develop an international marketing strategy in addition to their domestic strategy. However, for some, international market development is their only marketing strategy and their domestic operations are considered of minor importance. For example, the Australian beer Foster's focuses its efforts more on international markets than on the domestic Australian market. The approach selected will depend on the resources available, the industry, and the type of offering. For example, some offerings, such as information technologies, electronics, and cars, are international by nature. The high degree of investment in research and product development in these industries necessitates a move into international markets as domestic markets often do not provide sufficient sales. Irrespective of the motivation and despite the level of risk and/ or organization adaption required, there has been a growth in international marketing activities.

The EPRG classification (Perlmutter 1969), presented in Figure 7.2, was one of the first to specify the various approaches to international market development. It highlights four main approaches: **ethnocentric**, **polycentric**, **regional**, and **geocentric**.

The first two of these assume a localized approach. An ethnocentric approach views the domestic market (home market) as the most important, with foreign markets not seen to be a serious threat. With a polycentric approach, each overseas market is seen as a separate domestic market and the organization seeks to be seen as a local organization within that country. In some instances, each market has its own manufacturing and marketing operations, with only a limited overlap.

The last two adopt a more standardized approach. A regional approach groups countries together, usually on a geographical basis (e.g. Europe), and provides for the specific needs of consumers within those countries. In this instance, national boundaries are respected, but do not have the same importance as cultural differences. A geocentric approach assumes that the world is a single global market, with the organization looking for global segments (e.g. ageing market) and global opportunities to rationalize communications, production, and product development.

Another classification based on European organizations was proposed by Lynch (1994) and comprises five broad categories. These categories are based on an organization's attitudes to international markets, and the scale of the operations in markets being developed.

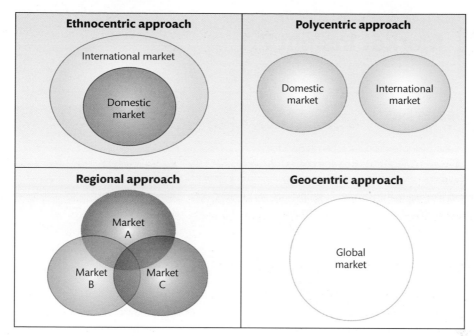

Figure 7.2
EPRG classification for international marketing

- Local-scale—these organizations operate within national and local boundaries and have little opportunity or desire to trade internationally (e.g. the local convenience store or the car repair garage).

- National-scale—these organizations focus mainly on their domestic market, but might find a number of opportunities emerging from foreign markets in the form of ad hoc customer enquiries.

- Regional-scale—these organizations focus on specific regions within Europe as opposed to operating throughout Europe (e.g. Eastern or Western Europe, Scandinavian countries) and gain experience of operating abroad on a smaller scale. For example, Norwegian and Swedish organizations have a long tradition of trade relations with other Scandinavian countries as a first experience of cross-national trade.

- European-scale—with increasing changes to the European Union and the rise in the number of member states, many organizations have turned their attention to marketing throughout Europe. Some argue that Europe is, in fact, one geographic market with a number of segments that transcend national boundaries, especially as some of the risks of international trade have been reduced or eliminated (e.g. currency). However, some will remain for ever (e.g. language, culture, infrastructure), requiring differing investment in communications, product compositions, and distribution for effective market development.

- World-scale—these organizations have a strong European base, but now operate in a range of different world markets through direct investment or joint venture, or on an **exporting** basis. For example, Unilever, BP, GlaxoSmithKline, and Nestlé derive a significant portion of sales from outside Europe. Another example is that of Hennes & Mauritz (H&M), a leading Swedish clothing retailer currently striving for world-scale operations through its market expansions into Asia (see Market Insight 7.1).

Market Insight 7.1

H&M Heads East

Hennes & Mauritz (H&M) was established in Sweden in 1947, but today H&M sells clothes and cosmetics in over 37 markets, employing more than 76,000 employees all working to the same philosophy—to bring customers fashion and quality at the best price. First-quarter 2010 net profit for the international retailer was SEK3.74bn ($514m), making H&M the number one fashion retailer across Europe, and the third largest worldwide.

With great potential for international market development, H&M has expanded substantially in recent years and today operates more than 2,000 stores across 37 countries. Germany is the biggest market, followed by France, Sweden, and the UK. However, in recent years, the retailer has undertaken aggressive expansion throughout Asia. In 2007, H&M landed in China with a splash, a particularly bright turquoise splash of images for the brand's new summery Kylie Minogue collection and the 'H&M loves Kylie' campaign promoted on thousands of billboards around Shanghai. H&M has over 21 stores throughout China with sales in 2009 of SEK1,614m.

In 2008, H&M arrived in Japan, opening two stores in Tokyo, one in Ginza followed by one in Harajuku. These stores have already proved to be the most successful store launches in H&M's history. By 2010, H&M had a total of five stores across Japan with sales in 2009 of SEK1,111m.

In 2010, H&M opened its first store in Seoul, the fashion-conscious capital of Korea, featuring international style inspiration with a full-concept store of 2,600 metres on four floors. Karl-Johan Persson, CEO of H&M, commented that 'Korea is an exciting market and H&M looks forward to bringing style-conscious shoppers in Seoul the inspiration to make their own personal fashion statement'.

Although H&M was relatively late to develop its international retail operations across Asia because of preoccupation with expansion in other foreign markets

H&M's KL store exemplifies their international development strategy
Source: © 2012 Copyright FIFOTO Photography.

(e.g. Europe, USA), its business in Asia is built on the back of 30 years of manufacturing experience from across China.

Sources: Movius (2007); Kageyama (2008); Tapper-Hoel (2010); www.hm.com.

1 Using the EPRG classification, how would you classify H&M's approach to international marketing?

2 Using Lynch's (1994) study of European organizations, how would you classify the scale of H&M's operations?

3 Why do you think H&M were 'late' to arrive in the Far East?

Research Insight 7.1

To take your learning further, you might wish to read this influential paper.

Lewis, K. S., Lim, F. A., and Rusetski, A. (2006), 'Development of archetypes of international marketing strategy', *Journal of International Business Studies,* **37(4), 499–524.**

This article provides a discussion of three separate characterizations of international marketing strategy: standardization–adaptation, concentration–dispersion, and integration–independence.

@ **Visit the Online Resource Centre to read the abstract and access the full paper.**

International Competitive Strategy

When entering international markets, the key competitive decision is to what degree should we standardize or adapt our marketing strategy? In an analysis of the rise of global competition, Hout *et al.* (1982) suggest that, from a strategic point of view, an organization can adopt a local/global, a multi-domestic, or a global competitive approach to their international marketing strategy (see Figure 7.3).

Multi-domestic Competitive Strategy

In a **multi-domestic competitive strategy**, an organization pursues a separate marketing strategy in each of its foreign markets and considers competitive activity on an independent market basis. This is also referred to as an **adaptive orientation** because an organization adapts its operations, buying, and market research to a particular country, and develops a specific market strategy for that particular market (see also Chapter 3). Through this, cultural, legal, language, communication, and geographical differences in each market are accommodated. For example, Marks and Spencer's formal businessmen's shirts suffered poor sales in the northern European market. Quality and design were identical to those sold in the UK market. However, research revealed that the M&S shirts lacked a key feature: breast pockets for items such as pens and cigarettes. Redesign resulted in an increase in sales. A central headquarters

Figure 7.3

The spectrum of competitive strategies

might coordinate financial controls, research and development activities, and marketing policies worldwide, but strategy and operations are decentralized. Each subsidiary is viewed as a profit centre and expected to contribute earnings and growth consistent with market opportunity, with competition on a market-by-market basis (Hout *et al*., 1982). See also Market Insight 7.2.

Market Insight 7.2

On Your Trikke — New Product, New Markets

In 1990, following numerous design and engineering improvements, three young middle-class Brazilians tested the first version of a small prototype vehicle. The three-wheeled vehicle, propelled by human movement using the physics principle known as 'conservation of angular momentum', became known as the 'Trikke'.

At first the Trikke was to be a fun recreational product for riding down slopes and hills. However, this changed when it was realized that the vehicle also moves on flat ground when the rider sways back and forth. There was no motor, chains, or pedals, and it did not require pedalling or pushing. Speeds of up to 30 kph(19mph) could be achieved, controlled with a handlebar brake.

The initial plan was to manufacture it in Brazil and market it in the USA. In a move similar to Honda's US market entry strategy in the 1950s, one of the inventors, Beleski, moved to Los Angeles and took a prototype with him. However, sales were less than expected.

Beleski started to attend trade shows and events, mainly in the bicycles sector. As a result of this activity a manufacturing partnership agreement was established with a Chinese firm. Two new products were introduced: one, called the Skki, was for snow use, and the other, called the Bikke, featured a small electric motor.

Potential markets included the sports equipment industry, involving cycling, golfing, fishing, skiing, windsurfing, baseball, and fitness equipment. Another was the bicycle industry, but this was going

Trikke, the bike from Brazil, propelled by human movement
Source: Image courtesy of Trikke (2013).

through enormous change as 95% of offerings were imported. Eventually a strategy to create a new category of offerings for the recreation equipment industry was formulated. Their main competitors were seen to be bicycles, skates, skis, snowboards, and gyms.

By 2006, the company was operating in over 17 countries on five continents. This was achieved through partnering agreements and the outsourcing of sales and distribution activities. Direct sales were made through the internet. The company was relatively passive, relying on the motivation of their local partners, and made little effort to develop these foreign markets.

Although the company goal was to develop a completely new sport, there remained an issue about

Market Insight 7.2
continued

how to position the brand in the future. Should Trikke be positioned as a new sport, as fitness equipment, or for family recreation? Perhaps it should be a new form of transportation, as a substitute for the bicycle, or a combination of these approaches? In addition there was concern about the channel strategy. Specialty retailers made sense because of the need to demonstrate the product. Conversely, mass retailers were important to spur market development. Depending on the positioning adopted, different marketing strategies were implied.

Company resources were limited, and this restricted the number of international markets that could be developed simultaneously. This directed them to concentrate on the US market, as once this was successful it would be much easier to enter other world markets. In 2013 the brand was available on five continents through a network of dealers

and distributors, all certified and controlled by Trikke. The brand is now promoted as 'a standing, active riding platform which can be enjoyed by nearly everyone for a variety of purposes: green transportation and mobility, fitness and weight loss, or just exhilaration'.

Sources: Fernandes *et al*. (2012); www.trikke.com/ (see also Case Insight on Brompton Bicycles in Chapter 6).

1 **What were the key international marketing problems faced by the company during its formative period?**

2 **To what extent should Trikke have adapted their brand for local international markets?**

3 **Should the firm use a niche strategy or a mass-market strategy to market the Trikke? What are the implications of each strategy?**

Visit the **Online Resource Centre** and see the weblink to the Channel 4 YouTube channel where Stephen Fry and Jonathan Ross explore the Trikke.

Global Competitive Strategy

Globalization refers to the 'process by which the experience of everyday life is becoming standardized around the world' through the free flow of four major components: goods and services, people, capital, and information (Sirgy *et al*., 2007). Globalization has been accompanied by the increasing consolidation of organizations within various industries, including pharmaceuticals, financial services, and telecommunications. Many of the newly industrialized countries (NICs), such as Poland, Slovenia, and Asian countries such as China and Taiwan, have contributed to the globalization process.

The importance and significance of increasing levels of global trade was first indicated by Levitt. He stated that 'the global cooperation operates with resolute constancy—at low relative cost—as if the entire world (or major regions of it) were a single entity; it sells the same things, in the same way everywhere' (Levitt, 1983: 92–3). However, there have also been detractors from this argument, those who argue that although it was appropriate to operate a global competitive approach to business, the key to success is to customize the offering, to adapt it to local needs (Quelch and Hoff, 1986).

A global competitive strategy represents a **standardized approach**. This requires that organizations assume that the world is one large (global) market, that they sell the same propositions in the same way throughout the world, and that they ignore local, regional, and national differences. Standardization assumes that global cultures are converging or that any cultural differences are superficial (Wind and Perlmutter, 1973; Levitt, 1983; Douglas and Douglas, 1987). The attractions of the standardization approach include improved operational efficiencies, enhanced customer preference, increased competitive leverage, and, importantly, substantial cost reductions (Herbig and Day, 1993). Those who object to this approach argue that cultural, legal, and national differences inhibit trade, especially if an organization incorrectly assumes that any differences are superficial. Communication is one of the biggest barriers to effective international marketing and is heightened when the standardization approach is used. One outcome is that advertising messages can be misunderstood (see Table 7.5).

An effective global competitive strategy comprises two elements. The first is **selective contestability**, the ability to contest successfully in any international market an organization chooses to compete in. It is based on the core marketing principles of segmentation, targeting, and positioning (STP). This requires that generic markets are divided into meaningful submarkets or segments, that the most attractive of these are then selected, and that the product is then positioned appropriately. This process lies at the very heart of devising any competitive strategy, irrespective of whether the organization is competing in a regional, national, or global market. See Chapter 6 for more about STP.

The second element is **global capability**. This concerns an organization's ability to bring its entire worldwide resources to bear on any competitive situation, regardless of location. A global brand goes far beyond an organization's physical presence in differing national markets, and

reflects the existence of a global image. It is this universal recognition that distinguishes an organization pursuing a focused strategy in numerous national markets from global players such as Ford, McDonald's, Hilton, and Google.

Visit the **Online Resource Centre** and complete Internet Activity 7.2 to learn more about how HSBC Plc positions itself as understanding local differences, with the aim of being the World's Local Bank.

Anti-Globalization Movement

The term anti-globalization most commonly refers to a political stance, a social movement, or a number of separate social movements in which participants are united in opposition to the political power of large organizations, often exercised through trade agreements. These agreements are perceived to undermine democracy, the environment, free trade, labour rights, national sovereignty, the third world, and individual privacy, among other concerns.

Protesters believe that global institutions, such as the World Trade Organization (WTO), and trade agreements not only undermine local decision-making, but also demonstrate how governments and free-trade institutions collaborate with multinational organizations such as Microsoft, McDonald's, and Google. These organizations are also perceived to have privileges that others do not, such as the right to move freely across borders, to extract natural resources, and to utilize a range of human resources. They are perceived to be able to move on after permanently damaging the natural capital and biodiversity of a nation. Activists also claim that large multinational organizations impose a global monoculture. Therefore some of the movement's common goals are to end the legal status of so-called corporate personhood and to dissolve or dramatically reform the World Bank, the International Monetary Fund, and the WTO.

Visit the **Online Resource Centre** and follow the weblinks to the documentary *The Corporation*, which presents a chilling view of how multinationals impact on local economies, society, and civil liberties.

Research Insight 7.2

To take your learning further, you might wish to read this influential paper.

Levitt, T. (1983) 'Globalisation of markets', *Harvard Business Review*, **May–June, 92–102.**

This is regarded as a seminal paper and is cited frequently. Levitt draws attention to the prevalence of global markets, considers the reasons for their development, and considers why and how organizations should offer globally standardized products that are advanced, functional, reliable, and low-priced.

@ **Visit the Online Resource Centre to read the abstract and access the full paper.**

Drivers of International Market Development

International marketing is driven by a number of key forces, as set out in Figure 7.4. The most common drivers include the following.

- Historical accident—unplanned and unforeseen events can trigger international market development. For example, in the1940s, US forces took Coca-Cola with them into the Second World War. As a result, a wider range of people experienced the drink and an opportunity arose for Coca-Cola to build the brand through a new distribution strategy. This is said to be one of the main reasons behind the growth of Coca-Cola's international marketing operations. See Market Insight 7.3.

- Excess stock—with over-production or insufficient sales, excess stock can build up. With limited opportunities for sales in domestic markets, organizations often seek out international markets to offload some of the excess stock. This is called dumping and is an international marketing version of 'clearance pricing', where excess stock is cleared into another country's market at very low prices in order to liquidate capital. There is no long-term entry strategy, just a hit and run exercise.

- Limited growth in domestic markets—one way to avoid the intensity of domestic competition when growth is limited in home markets is for organizations to enter international markets. For example, given the intense competition in the home markets of the USA and Europe, and the growth potential in the Chinese markets, the top four global brewers AB Inbev, SABMiller,

Figure 7.4
Motives for international market development

Heineken, and Carlsberg have substantially increased volumes and global presence in the last decade through overseas acquisition activity.

- Comparative advantage—certain regions and countries have developed core competencies and a reputation for producing certain products, raw resources, or workforce skills. This presents an opportunity to develop **comparative advantage**. For example, over 750 million olive trees are cultivated worldwide, with about 95% in the Mediterranean region, with the most global olive oil produced in Spain, Italy, and Greece. Certain countries offer differential labour costs and specialized skills, such as China and textile manufacturing, or India and the provision of business process outsourcing (BPOs) such as customer call centres. This presents an advantage not only in labour and operating costs, but also, for some industries, savings in transport and manufacturing costs.

- Economies of scale—for some products the cost of development and production can be high. To achieve an effective return on investment high-volume production runs are necessary, and this in turn requires large world markets. Examples include consumer electronic goods and the automotive industry. A high degree of standardization is evident in the manufacture of cars, such as the frame, engine, and transmission, with superficial changes such as air conditioning tailored for local markets. This enables car manufacturers to achieve **economies of scale** in different parts of the world (Pitcher, 1999).

- Trade liberalization—with the creation of trading blocs and the reduction of barriers to trade worldwide, we are seeing many organizations engaging in global competition with international

The iconic original VW Beetle
Source: istock.

firms in domestic markets, and domestic organizations moving abroad to compete overseas as markets open up.

- International product lifecycle—the internationalization process can occur when an offering reaches different stages of its lifecycle in different countries. For example, the original Volkswagen Beetle ceased production in Germany in 1978, but soon after commenced production and sales in South America.

- Technological changes—advances in electronic communications, such as the internet, have enabled international trade. Online channels are increasingly being used to sell into new markets because of open access and low costs. Changes in the technological infrastructure have provided SMEs with a way of increasing exports with low entry costs.

- Customer relationships—as organizations move abroad, so the effect of international marketing activities can be felt throughout the supply chain, from end-users, through intermediaries, to producers and raw material suppliers. For example, as Ford expands into foreign markets, its product components also change and suppliers will need to match the requirements of Ford's new manufacturing and assembly production process. This is also true for service-based industries. However, the difference is that there will be an increasing need to locate an organization's services much closer to the customer, either through branch offices or through subsidiaries placed strategically throughout a number of foreign markets. For example, A.C. Nielsen, one of the world's leading marketing research organizations, has research operations that span more than 100 countries.

- Transnational market segments—the growth in groups of people with similar needs but who inhabit different countries, called transnational market segments, occurs because of migration, such as Malaysians working in Australia, similarities in demographics (e.g. baby-boomers), or similarities in lifestyles (e.g. working women). From a conceptual perspective, a truly global organization should segment markets based on similar characteristics across

Market Insight 7.3

Coca-Cola's International Heritage

In the first two decades of the twentieth century, the international growth of Coca-Cola was rather haphazard. It began in 1900, when Charles Howard Candler took a jug of syrup with him on vacation to England. A modest order for five gallons of syrup was mailed back to Atlanta. The same year, Coca-Cola travelled to Cuba and Puerto Rico, and it wasn't long before the international distribution of the syrup began. Through the early 1900s, bottling operations were built in Cuba, Panama, Canada, Puerto Rico, the Philippines, and Guam (a western Pacific island). In 1920, a bottling organization began operating in France as the first bottler of Coca-Cola on the European continent. Then came the 1928 Olympics and the Second World War.

In 1926, Robert W. Woodruff, Chief Executive Officer and Chairman of the Board, committed the organization to international expansion by establishing a Foreign Department, which in 1930 became a subsidiary known as the Coca-Cola Export Corporation. By that time, the number of countries with bottling operations had almost quadrupled, and the organization had initiated a partnership with the Olympic Games that transcended cultural boundaries. Coca-Cola and the Olympic Games began their association in the summer of 1928, when an American freighter arrived in Amsterdam carrying the US Olympic team and 1,000 cases of Coca-Cola. Forty thousand spectators filled the stadium to witness two firsts: the first lighting of the Olympic flame and the first sale of Coke at an Olympiad. Dressed in caps

and coats bearing the Coca-Cola trademark, vendors satisfied the fans' thirst, while outside the stadium, refreshment stands, cafés, restaurants, and small shops called 'winkles' served Coke in bottles and from soda fountains.

During the Second World War, Coca-Cola set up bottling plants as close as possible to combat areas in Europe and the Pacific. More than 5 billion bottles of Coke were consumed by military service personnel during the war, in addition to countless servings through dispensers and mobile self-contained units in battle areas. However, the presence of Coca-Cola did more than just lift the morale of the troops. In many areas, it gave local people their first taste of Coca-Cola. When peace returned, the Coca-Cola system was poised for unprecedented worldwide growth. From the mid-1940s until 1960, the number of countries with bottling operations nearly doubled. As the world emerged from a time of conflict, Coca-Cola emerged as a worldwide symbol of friendship and refreshment. The Coca-Cola organization now operates in over 200 countries and has over 3,500 products.

Sources: Pendergrast (2000); www.thecoca-colacompany.com

1 **Identify the key market forces driving Coca-Cola's approach to internationalization.**

2 **Which marketing elements were critical for the success of Coca-Cola's international market strategy?**

3 **To what extent was Coca-Cola in the right place at the right time, or was this a planned international marketing strategy?**

national borders. Country of residence or birth is becoming increasingly less relevant as migration increases and national borders diminish.

- Organizational sustainability—the broader the range of markets served, the less likely it is that failure in one market will result in overall organizational decline. Different markets are always at different stages of development and competitive intensity. Therefore an international market portfolio will provide an organization with an increased chance of organizational sustainability.

However, whatever the motivation for international market development, a planned approach considerably increases the chances for success. Once international market entry has been decided as an organizational growth strategy, certain decisions have to be made to increase the chances of success. These include determining which foreign markets to pursue, which methods are the most suitable for entering new markets, and which strategy to adopt to appeal to the desired needs of foreign markets?

International Market Selection

The selection of international markets should be based on a consideration of a potential market's overall attractiveness. This is based on a number of factors, of which market size and growth are the two most important.

1 *Market size and growth rate* Market size refers to the number of current and potential customers. Market size can also be measured in terms of the sales value that these pool of customers represent. However, using these figures alone can be misleading, as certain regions grow in attractiveness while others decline. Ohmae (1985, 1992) points to the domination of world markets by what he calls the Triad, the three major world players comprising Europe, America, and Japan. However, times have changed and now rapid growth can be observed in Pacific Rim countries (China, Singapore, South Korea, and Taiwan), and the BRIC group (Brazil, Russia, India, and China). Although disposable income in these countries is unevenly distributed, the overall increasing prosperity of their populations has created demand for Western luxury brands to signal individual success and increasing personal wealth. Brands such as Burberry, Ralph Lauren, Land Rover, and Jaguar have experienced considerable growth in recent years. The attractiveness of these high growth rates also offsets the difficult trading conditions experienced in stable and declining markets. Whitelock and Jobber (1994) report that growth rate is a far more important consideration than market size. As if to demonstrate this point, in 2013 Honda UK announced the loss of 800 jobs at their UK plant in Swindon because of poor sales in their principal European (Mediterranean) markets. In contrast, two days later Jaguar and Land Rover announced the creation of 800 jobs at their UK Solihull factories because sales in China had increased by 72%.

2 *Market access* Accessibility refers to the extent that customers can be reached with marketing communications and through distribution and sales outlets. Media availability, industry infrastructure, channel networks, and local cultural norms can all limit or hinder market access. For example, in Japan, the monolithic structure of the industry means that the giant Sogo Sosha general trading organizations (GTCs), such as Mitsubishi Corporation and Mitsui & Co., have widespread market control. This results in few openings for foreign brands to enter the market, despite there being few legal issues or import difficulties. Other countries put high tariffs on offerings to protect local industry, or media moguls or government bodies control the use of media channels, making access to certain market segments difficult.

3 *Geographic proximity* The physical distance between the potential market and the domestic market can also have a direct impact on resources. For example, trade between Australia and the UK requires larger resources than trade between the UK and other European countries, such as France.

4 *Psychological proximity* This refers to the perceived cultural and societal similarities between countries. For example, some see greater cultural similarity between the USA and the UK than between the UK and France. Thus organizations in the UK might perceive the USA as more attractive for possible trade relations. Psychological proximity is often based on language; the UK is close to Canada, and even India, given cultural, language, and historical similarities.

5 *Established competitors* Where there is already intense market competition, it is unlikely that foreign market entrants will be received favourably.

6 *Entry costs* These can vary greatly between markets and strategies. For example, physical distribution costs can be extremely high in a country such as the USA or India where the distances between production plants and consumers can be immense. In other countries, distances might be comparably short, but marketing channels and supply chains are long and complex or lack the infrastructure to support them. For example, the telecommunications infrastructure in various African countries differs greatly from that in more established West European countries such as Germany and France.

7 *Profit potential* This refers to the number of potential customers and the profit margin that the group can generate in that market. Even though per unit profit margins might be small, a country with a large potential market might still be attractive for the overall profit generated. For example, India and China might each offer large potential profits. Powerful buying groups, low per capita income, and strong competition are all factors that can reduce profit margins.

International market selection requires sound market intelligence about the market environment and marketing opportunities. In reality, market screening can be random, driven by customer enquiries or market demand for an offering or knowledge gained through media or social networks. Visits to the potential markets will also be required for further insights and first-hand market knowledge, and to aid the development of networks and relationships. Questions useful for international market screening are detailed in Table 7.3.

Research Insight 7.3

To take your learning further, you might wish to read this influential paper.

Young, R. B., and Javalgi, R. G. (2007), 'International marketing research: a global project management perspective', *Business Horizons*, 50(2), 113–22.

This article provides a useful insight into the importance and role of marketing research as the primary mechanism through which organizations understand their current, as well as potential, customers in international markets.

Visit the Online Resource Centre to read the abstract and access the full paper.

Table 7.3 International market screening questions

Factor	Questions to consider
Market	■ At what stage is it in the growth cycle? ■ Is there sufficient future demand or potential? ■ Are there established distribution channels? ■ How sophisticated is the infrastructure?
Product fit	■ Is there an opportunity in the market for this offering? ■ Is there demand or interest for this type of offering? ■ Would the offering need to be adapted or changed in any way?
Competition	■ Who are the existing competitors in this market, national and international? ■ How intense or aggressive is the competitive environment? ■ What degree of control or influence do existing competitors have in the marketplace? ■ What are the competitive barriers to entry? ■ What is the likely competitive response to our market entry?
Market entry	■ What entry methods are feasible for this market and the organization? ■ How much would market entry cost us? ■ Do we have any contacts in the market that could assist us? ■ How similar are the culture, values, and attitudes to our domestic market?
Resources	■ What do we need to invest to enter this market? ■ Are we going to have to employ staff locally or relocate staff to enter this market? ■ What training and/or education do we require to enter this market: culture, languages, exporting skills. ■ Do we need to invest in the establishment of new or different marketing channels for market entry or can we rely on existing channels?
Trade barriers	■ What legal or regulatory factors will influence market entry or operations in the market? ■ Are the marketing communications, and/or marketing research activities similar to those used in our national market? ■ Will import tariffs or quotas apply to us? ■ Will we be able to take profits earned out of the country? ■ Are there any constraints on foreign organizations operating in this market? ■ Do we have to manufacture or produce our offering to differing quality and/or health and safety standards?

International Marketing Environment

Understanding the international marketing environment of the countries or regions of interest provides the foundation for the market assessment and selection process. An analysis of the environmental forces, as detailed in Chapter 4, for foreign markets can help to identify which countries or regions should be given priority and which market entry strategy would be most appropriate. Young (2001) argues that, in contrast with domestic marketing strategies, international marketers pay too little attention to the potential impact that global socio-cultural, economic, legal/institutional, and political developments could have on their ability to enter and trade in a foreign market successfully.

Social Factors

Social factors are very important in international marketing activities. Differences in social structures, social values, gender roles, and family composition can affect what is and what is not acceptable in international markets. The changing social structure is an important consideration. The role of women, the elderly, or the positioning of the family within society can have an impact on consumption patterns. In many Western countries family structures and the composition of households are changing as divorce rates and the number of child-free families rise. In some countries, such as the UK, America, and Australia, there are increasing numbers of new mothers returning to work, placing more reliance on grandparents for childcare responsibilities. These in turn can influence the retirement age and lifestyle patterns of older consumers in these markets. This contrasts with the composition of other markets and the greater level of cross-generation households, as found in China and Japan. Here, grandparents are considered to be a central part of the family unit and reside in the family household—the extended family unit. Migration and the associated movement of social values can also influence social factors. In Canada, for example, immigration now accounts for 67% of Canada's population growth (Martel and Chagnon, 2013). An awareness of these changes and transient social structures and values is imperative.

Cultural Factors

Culture is concerned with the beliefs, norms, and values that guide the behaviour of groups of people. It comprises language, education, religion, lifestyle, taboos, and norms. Culture affects how people define their wants and needs through consumption and how they interact. For example, DeBeers controls the majority of the world market in gem diamonds, but markets them differently to countries according to cultural norms. In the UK, a diamond ring is synonymous with getting engaged; in Spain, it is bought after the birth of a child; in Saudi Arabia, diamonds are an important wedding gift.

Culture also influences the way we interact. For example, following the movement of many call centre jobs to India, some have been transferred back to the UK. In 2005, Norwich Union (now Aviva) relocated customer calls for insurance claims back to the UK following a sequence of misunderstandings about flooding from immersion heaters. Local operators in India struggled to understand the claim as they didn't understand the heating systems. Clearly, for organizations serious about international marketing, cultural sensitivity is paramount. Table 7.4 outlines some behavioural factors that have been known to influence business conduct in international environments.

Language is a critical factor when considering entry into foreign markets. In customer relationships, it is expected that sellers will use a customer's own language. However, in many parts of the

Table 7.4 Business conduct in international markets

Factor	Description
Time	■ Attitudes towards punctuality ■ Sanctity of deadlines ■ Acquaintance time ■ Discussion time
Business cards	■ When to offer them ■ Whether to translate them ■ Who gives them first ■ How to attend to them
Gifts	■ Should they be given ■ Size/value ■ Should they be opened in front of the giver
Dress	■ Dress codes ■ Formality
Entertainment	■ Type/formality of social occasions ■ Table manners and etiquette ■ Cuisine ■ Cultural and religious taboos ■ Venues (e.g. restaurant, private home)
Space	■ Office size and location ■ Selection, quality, and arrangement of furniture
Body language	■ Greeting conventions (e.g. kiss, handshake, bow) ■ Facial and hand gestures and their meaning ■ Physical proximity ■ Touching and posture
Material possessions	■ Is it appropriate to comment and admire?

Source: Mead (1990). © John Wiley & Sons Limited. Reproduced with permission.

world, English has become the universal business language. Care needs to be given to the way marketing communications are used. There are also language issues arising for the way brand names, slogans and taglines, and product packaging are used. In French-speaking Quebec, Canada, KFC is known as PFK (Poulet Frit Kentucky); this is one of the few instances where the KFC initials are changed for the local language, even though in France it is called KFC. In several Spanish-speaking areas of the USA, KFC is known as PFK (Pollo Frito Kentucky). All forms of marketing communications have to be translated carefully to ensure correct interpretation and meaning. If communication is to be in Arabic, then is it aimed at Tunisians or Iraqis, Egyptians or Yemenis? We must also understand the style of the language and the target audience. If the audience is foreign business personnel, the vocabulary, grammar, and punctuation must reflect this. If the audience is informal or youth-oriented, then a more relaxed language should be used. Using an inappropriate language style for the wrong audience can be devastating, and incorrect translations can result in customer frustration. See Table 7.5 for some examples.

In order to adapt to cultural differences, organizations can use three internal processes (Mughan, 1993). The first of these is self-analysis, i.e. recognize a situation from the customer's

Table 7.5 Language translations

Brand name	English translation	Language	Foreign translation/interpretation
KFC	'Finger-lickin' good'	Chinese	'Bite your fingers off'
Coors	'Turn it loose'	Spanish	'Drink our beer and get diarrhoea'
Pepsi	'Come alive: you're in the Pepsi generation'	Chinese	'Pepsi brings your ancestors back from the dead'
Microsoft	Vista	Latvia	'Vista' is a disparaging term for a frumpy old woman
Motorola	'Hellomoto' ring tone	India	Sounds like 'Hello, Fatty' in India
Ford	Pinto	Brazil	'Small male genitals'
Coca-Cola	The name Coca-Cola in China was first rendered as Ke-kou-ke-la	Chinese	'Bite the wax tadpole' or 'female horse stuffed with wax'
Schweppes	Schweppes Tonic Water	Italy	Schweppes Toilet Water
Salem cigarettes	'Salem—Feeling Free'	Japan	'When smoking Salem, you feel so refreshed that your mind seems to be free and empty'
Parker Pen	'It won't leak in your pocket and embarrass you'	Mexico	'It won't leak in your pocket and make you pregnant'
Clairol	Introduced the 'Mist Stick', a curling iron	Germany	'Mist' is slang for manure. Not too many people had use for the 'manure stick'!
American Airlines	'Fly in leather'	Latin American	'Fly naked'
Electrolux	'Nothing sucks like an Electrolux'	USA	'There's nothing worse than an Electrolux'

point of view and adapt behaviour accordingly. The second is to provide cultural training, particularly for personnel working or dealing direct with distributors or customers. The third is recruitment direct from the local labour market, as this is the quickest route to widening the culture of an organization. One key characteristic found in many successful international organizations is the representation of a range of nationalities in senior management.

Consumption Attitudes

We know that perceptions can influence the way customers react to an offering or country of origin. To lower the risk of adverse perceptions and attitudes, some organizations embark on an international strategy by entering markets which have consumption attitudes similar to those in the domestic market. Examples include organizations exporting from Ireland to the UK, from Sweden to other Scandinavian markets, and from New Zealand to Australia. Through these lower-risk strategies, organizations can learn and develop knowledge before entering markets with consumption attitudes that are complex or difficult to understand.

Monitoring trends and the attitudes of customers in different countries is increasingly important in this form of market development. For a long time consumer tastes and preferences in mainland China tended to focus on mass-produced low-value and luxury fashion wear. There was no market for mid-range fashion. However, the increase in the number of young white-collar lower-middle-class women in the twenty-first century has created a demand for mid-price fashion, as evidenced by the successes of Zara, Gap, and H&M. However, this shift appears to be universal—a global trend. Movius (2007) comments, 'Fashion is not a matter of price. People tend to mix high- and low-priced items. It is a shift in customer attitude that is happening all over, including here'.

Technological Factors

The technological capability and rate of development in a market can have implications for marketing communications, new proposition development, and the overall success of a market entry strategy. In many international markets, new technology is increasingly changing the way that organizations go to market (Sclater, 2005). However, in many developing markets, radio still remains the main channel for marketing communications, with limited TV diffusion. In others (e.g. large parts of Africa), mobile phone usage far exceeds that of computers. This highlights the importance of profiling the penetration of electronic technologies and the supporting infrastructure in potential new foreign markets.

Not all demographic groups have participated in the information revolution that has occurred since the 1980s. Those who are poorer, less educated, and from rural areas have been slower to use both computers and the internet (Bikson and Panis, 1997; Tapscott, 1998). So, although certain electronic technologies have become embedded in people's lifestyles in some consumer and business markets, some groups do not share these technologies.

Many customer needs and wants are constrained by the prevailing technological infrastructure. For example, the type of fuel used for cooking will depend on a country's use of natural resources and the energy infrastructure. The type of telephone used depends on the telecommunication and economic infrastructure. Wireless telephony penetration frequently exceeds wireline (landline) penetration in developing countries. However, the needs and usage of mobile phones in developing markets differs considerably from that in mature markets. Nokia, the Finnish mobile phone manufacturer, looked for practical design features to make mobile handsets for people living in developing countries, such as India, more relevant. They learned that in hot countries, where many roads are unpaved, features such as dustproof keypads are important and of value to customers. Motorola developed a slimmed-down mobile handset with only three essential functions in order to make it easier and more practical for use by customers with poor literacy skills. Customer needs and market conditions not only shape the way customers access marketing communications messages, but can also influence proposition design.

Economic Factors

The potential of any market is also shaped by various local and international economic forces. The recent collapse in global demand led the WTO to forecast that exports worldwide would fall by approximately 9% in volume terms, the biggest contraction since the Second World War. Basic information about per capita disposable income, consumption patterns, and unemployment trends can help to draw a picture of a market's economic health. Typical ways to assess the economic potential of a market include:

- measures of per capita income;
- ownership rates of durables (e.g. cars);
- balance between urban and rural populations;
- prevailing rate of inflation;
- **gross national product (GNP)**;
- market size;
- fluctuations in currency exchanges.

When assessing a market's attractiveness, economic statistics and relevant indicators can usually be acquired from a number of sources. This may pose comparability problems, but they usually give a reasonable indication of a market's current or potential purchasing power.

Political and Legal Factors

Political and legal factors can restrict or enable international marketing opportunities. For example, some governments offer subsidies to assist particular organizations to enter foreign markets. Some governments place obstacles in the way, such as taxes and tariffs, to deter prospective importers and protect domestic industries. Measures invoked by governments to protect their domestic industries include the following:

- quotas—used to limit the amount of goods allowed into a country;
- duties—special taxes on imports, which seek to disadvantage the importer's pricing strategy;
- non-tariff barriers—these include legislation designed so that importers have to adapt their offerings, which is often expensive, before the item is legally saleable in the host country.

Governments also seek to alleviate unemployment and stimulate economic activity. As such, many countries encourage foreign investment by providing tax concessions and support of various kinds to persuade international organizations to set up their manufacturing units, or service units, in depressed areas.

Political issues can also cause difficulties for international marketers, even to the point of having to withdraw from a market or write off an entire operations plant, such as Chrysler's

Market Insight 7.4

Google Gets Censored

The economy of the People's Republic of China is the fourth largest in the world when measured by nominal GDP. With rapid industrial development and a market of more than 1.3 billion increasingly prosperous consumers, the expected rewards of doing business in China are widely recognized. China is a very desirable market for internet companies, with nearly 384 million Chinese consumers online in 2010, compared with just 10 million only a decade before. Last year, the Chinese search engine market was worth an estimated $1bn and analysts expected Google to make about $600m from China in 2010. However, doing business in China requires foreign companies to abide by the country's political and legal systems, including its strict censorship laws.

When Google launched google.cn in 2006, it agreed to the censorship of its search results to obtain market access. For four years Google censored search results, in the hope of becoming the number one search engine in China, a goal it failed to achieve as, unlike most markets, Google comes second behind Baidu, a local search operator. As a foreign organization, Google was expected to operate under the laws of the country, much as eBay is banned from listing Nazi memorabilia in Germany. Self-censorship is the cost of doing business in China, and it is a price that Google decided was worth paying. Google's decision to agree to China's requests on censorship in 2006 led to accusations it had betrayed its company motto; 'Don't be evil'. Amnesty International has consistently called on Google (Yahoo and Microsoft) to stop collaborating with the Chinese authorities and their censorship requirements,

and to respect the right to freedom of expression for web users in China. But at market entry in 2006, Google argued that it would be more damaging for civil liberties if it pulled out of China entirely.

In 2010 conditions changed. A spate of security breaches on Google email accounts, lower than forecasted ad revenues, and acknowledgment that Google's corporate policies were incompatible with the self-censorship required to operate in China led Google to question its activities. In 2010, Google stopped censoring its internet search results in China and directed all traffic from its Chinese servers to Hong Kong. This action was applauded by human rights and anti-censorship activists, now that Google challenges China to end censorship. In early 2013, Google ceased notifying Chinese users that they may be searching for censored keywords.

Various services, such as Google Drive, YouTube, Google+, Twitter, Dropbox, Facebook, and Foursquare, have all been banned by the Chinese authorities, through what is regarded as the Great Firewall of China.

Sources: Carr (2010); Davies (2010); BBC News (2010, 2013); Moskvitch (2012); www.amnesty.org www.google.com

1 Why is China seen as such an attractive market for a search engine?

2 What impact did Chinese censorship laws have on how Google entered the Chinese market in 2006?

3 Why, and how, has Google redesigned its market development strategy in China?

experience in post-revolutionary Iran (see also Market Insight 7.4 about Google in China). In some countries, a change in government may have little effect on commercial life, but in others the change can be dramatic, as in Iraq. Certain governments can restrict foreign investment and ownership by assigning market entry conditions. This might involve having to work with a local organization, which would be the majority shareholder and/or owner. Other restrictive methods within the political and legal framework include employment law, health and safety regulations, financial law, patent protection, data protection, and electronic transactions legislation.

For example, vending machines are illegal in Russia, but they are an important part of Coca-Cola's distribution strategy.

Visit the **Online Resource Centre** and complete Internet Activity 7.3 to learn more about how the international strategies of firms such as Starbucks, Apple, Google, and Primark stand up to pressures on taxation, supply and ethics.

Methods of Market Entry

There are several methods that organizations can use to enter foreign markets. This is a complex decision because of the variety of management objectives, the type of offering, and the various specific issues associated with the designated market. Six criteria should be taken into consideration when selecting the market entry method (Paliwoda 1993). These are presented in Figure 7.5. The importance of each depends on the organization's international marketing objectives. For example, how quickly they want to enter a market, how much they are prepared to invest, how much risk they are prepared to take, and how flexible they want their marketing activities in the foreign market to be.

1 *Speed and timing*: some foreign market entry methods take months, whereas others can be put into action immediately. The organization needs to review how quickly it wishes to enter the selected market.

2 *Costs:* different methods require different levels of investment. The costs and benefits of each method must be considered.

3 *Flexibility:* some methods provide organizations different levels of flexibility over its activities in the new market and future development opportunities. For example, some methods might require long-term contractual agreements or financial commitments.

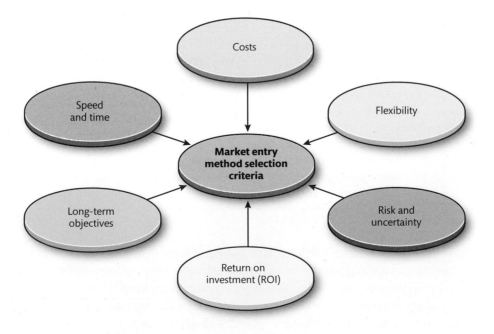

Figure 7.5
Market entry methods: selection and criteria

4 *Risk and uncertainty:* there are numerous risk factors involved with entry into new and foreign markets. Some entry methods allow for a reduction or risk and uncertainty. These include joint ventures and direct foreign investment in an international market. The latter can ease political pressure, to the pointof helping to reduce barriers to entry, such as tariffs and import quotas. However, these methods also require a larger degree of financial investment than indirect exporting or licensing.

5 *Return on investment:* the ROI needs to be considered with the first and second criteria (speed and timing, and costs). Some organizations look for a fast ROI through their market entry strategies, and thus the speed and timing of market entry is crucial to ensure a quick return on foreign investment. For example, it may take years to build a factory in a foreign market, and thus it is more suitable to develop a partnership with an existing manufacturer in the local market who can provide this resource, increasing the speed of ROI.

6 *Long-term objectives:* market entry is just the first step in a long-term strategy for international marketing. An organization needs to review what it wants to achieve in the long term from its entry into a new foreign market, as some market entry methods will provide more flexibility and leverage for long-term opportunities than others.

Entry Methods

There are several methods that an organization can use to enter international markets. Each method equates a level of risk with the potential rewards on offer through that entry method. These are presented in Figure 7.6. As with life, the higher the risk, the higher the possible rate of

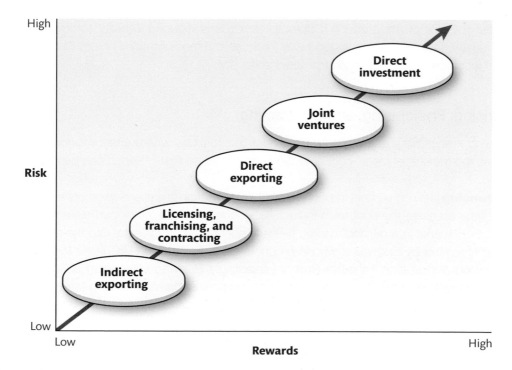

Figure 7.6
Methods of market entry

return, but as always an organization's willingness and ability to commit the appropriate managerial, financial, and operational resources is crucial to realizing the potential rewards.

Some organizations use a portfolio of methods, with the choice depending upon the importance of each international project. Nissan changed from indirect exporting to direct investment when it established a UK manufacturing base in the 1980s. Despite a relatively small share of the UK market at the time, the development of the single European market offered the potential of huge ongoing rewards.

The choice of entry method should reflect the type of offering, whether it is in the consumer or industrial sector, and the level and nature of the competition. For example, some offerings, such as fast food restaurants and coffee houses, are more suited to international franchising. Others, such as textiles and car components, are more suited to offshore manufacturing. Regional products, such as wine, cheese, chocolate, and luxury food items, are usually exported. Burgel and Murray (2000) also observe that the choice of method for international market entry, especially for start-up organizations, can often be a balance between the level of customer support that is needed and the available resources.

Indirect Exporting

Indirect exporting takes place where production and manufacture occur in the domestic market and another organization, an intermediary, is employed to sell the offering in the foreign market. For example, Australian wineries have achieved rapid growth over the last 20 years, and are now the fourth-largest exporters of wine. This has been achieved through indirect exportation to various international markets.

An exporting manufacturer seeks to benefit from an intermediary's knowledge, their contacts and business networks, and their experience in the target market. This reduces the producer's risk, but the size of the producer's potential rewards is reduced in order to compensate the intermediary. This approach is a good way for small and medium-sized enterprises (SMEs) with limited resources to test for market/product suitability.

Licensing, Franchising, and Contracting

Licensing, franchising, and/or contracting refer to situations where entry into foreign markets involves the transfer of ideas, concepts, and processes, so that offerings can be manufactured abroad.

Licensing is an agreement through which an organization (the licensor) grants another organization (the licensee) the right to manufacturer goods, use patents or particular processes, or exploit trademarks in a defined market. It is a frequent method for entry into the drinks market, as demonstrated by Budweiser whose products were made in the UK under license from the US brewing organization Anheuser-Busch. Interestingly, Budweiser is positioned in the UK as a premium drink, yet in the US domestic markets it is positioned as a working man's drink. Since its takeover by InBev, Budweiser does not need a licensing arrangement. Licensing is a low-risk and inexpensive method of generating income from foreign markets by avoiding high import tariffs and high costs of direct investment. However, this method offers little control, and possible risks of the licensee damaging the reputation and image of the licensor's name due to poor product quality and ineffective marketing. It can also create problems, as the licensee has the opportunity to develop the necessary expertise and knowledge for manufacture and to become a competitor.

Franchising involves a brand owner (the franchisor) authorizing another organization (the franchisee) the right to produce or market goods or services to certain criteria laid down by the franchisor in return for fees and/or royalties. Franchising is both a marketing channel though which market coverage can be extended and a system through which enterprises can launch and grow. Some of the most successful international marketing operations are franchise-based, including KFC, the SUBWAY® chain, and McDonald's. See Market Insight 7.5 and Table 12.2 in Chapter 12. Outside of the USA, KFC has over 15,000 restaurants in 109 countries, with more than 3,000 KFC restaurants in more than 700 cities in China alone.

The two main benefits of franchising are managerial and financial. Financially, rapid growth in market coverage and penetration can be achieved for the franchisor, with the franchisee bearing most risk through their investment in capital assets, such as equipment and premises, working capital, and other operating costs. However, the effectiveness of this form of market entry method relies on the franchisor–franchisee relationship, the commitment of the franchisee, the resources and support provided by the franchisor, and market interest in the franchise. McDonald's is established in 120 countries and serves 54 million customers every day. Consequently, it is one of the largest and most lucrative franchises in the world.

Contracting refers to situations where a manufacturer contracts an organization in a foreign market to manufacture or assemble a product in that market. This approach avoids the costs involved in the physical distribution and supply chain issues associated with producing the offering in the home market and selling it overseas. Unlike licensing, contractors have control over all marketing activities. This method is also flexible as it avoids problems of currency fluctuations, import barriers, and the high costs and knowledge required for international distribution.

Visit the **Online Resource Centre** and complete Internet Activity 7.4 to learn more about how Yum! brands uses franchising to develop its Pizza Hut, KFC, and Taco Bell brands

Direct Exporting

Direct exporting requires that the manufacturing organization distributes the offering in foreign markets, direct to customers, themselves. Here, the organization treats its international customers in the same way as its domestic market customers. It takes responsibility for finding and selecting customers, agents, and distributors, and directly supporting their efforts. The direct exporting approach is very time-consuming and expensive. However, it gives manufacturers more control and profits than is possible when using intermediaries. Further advantages include direct access to market intelligence and also the building of a clear presence in the market.

Joint Ventures

When a foreign organization and a domestic organization join forces, either by buying into each other or by establishing a separate jointly owned enterprise, a **joint venture** is created. Only by working together do the participant organizations have sufficient resources to develop or enter a foreign market. One might have cash, the other know-how and experience. Their complementary strengths facilitate success, and sometimes a joint venture is the only way an organization can enter into or gain a foothold in a foreign market. Joint ventures tend to have a limited lifespan as the needs of each party alter and develop over time. They work best in sectors where there is a high degree of local adaptation to the market. Figure 7.7 shows a list of factors that contribute to a successful joint venture partnership.

Market Insight 7.5

Fuelling Growth though Fast Food Franchising

Franchising is used by a variety of organizations to expand internationally. Some companies in the fast food sector anchor their growth around franchising. For example, Subway, founded in the USA in 1985, has 37,000 restaurants operating in more than 100 countries worldwide.

As with most franchise operations each Subway franchise owner is responsible for paying an initial franchise fee. However, they are also required to find suitable store locations, take care of the leasehold improvements and equipment, hire employees and operate restaurants, and pay an 8% royalty to the company plus a separate fee for advertising.

Subway talk of restaurants rather than stores, and identify two main types of location for them. A traditional restaurant is to be found in high streets and shopping centres. A non-traditional restaurant refers to airports, hospitals, bus and rail stations, or other sites associated with another business.

Costs vary in relation to the physical size of the restaurant. A lower-cost restaurant is one that would require fewer leasehold improvements, less seating, and fewer equipment expenditures. Moderate- and higher-cost restaurants may require extensive interior renovations, extensive seating and additional equipment. Subway suggest that the costs vary from US$106,000 to US$394,000.

All operations experience some difficulties at times. For example, Yum! Brands, who own KFC, Pizza Hut, and Taco Bell, has used franchising as its primary growth route into most countries. In China, they have adopted a direct investment strategy and own most of the restaurants, including the 889 new ones opened in 2012. When Yum! started operations in China, rather than import US managers, it employed people from other Asian economies such as Singapore, Hong Kong, and Malaysia. Yum! partnered with the state-owned enterprises and established its own distribution centres at a time when the country's transport

Much of the SUBWAY® chain's success has arisen from its franchising strategy
Source: Photo courtesy of the SUBWAY® chain.

infrastructure was poor. KFC's menu changes regularly and is explicitly Chinese, with delicacies such as rice congee with pickles, egg custard tarts, and tree fungus salad on offer. In the same way Chinese Pizza Huts reflect local tastes with squid, shrimp, and pineapple pizza on offer at the spacious low-lit, yet pricey, restaurants. In late 2012, a report on China's national broadcaster CCTV claimed that KFC's local suppliers had been using excessive antibiotics in its chickens. That resulted in an official investigation, outrage on Chinese social media, and a 41% fall in KFC China sales in early 2013. This compares with a 21% increase the previous year. McDonald's sales in China were also hit, and both companies dropped the supplier at the heart of the investigation.

Sources: Burkitt (2013); Kaiman (2013); www.franchise-international.net/page/subway-restaurants-master/osc-198.php www.economist.com/news/business/21571467-yum-brands-stumbles-china-yucky-kentucky www.yum.com/brands/china.asp (see also Market Insight 1.3).

1 In the light of Yum's! experience in China, what might be the advantages of a direct investment strategy compared with franchising?

2 To what extent is it likely that Yum's! success in China is based on an adaption strategy?

3 How might a franchisee manage the impact that local suppliers can have on their brand? Should it be their responsibility?

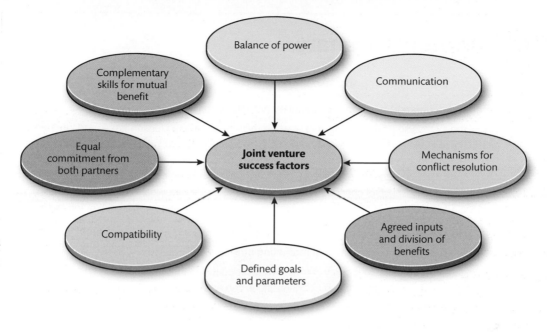

Figure 7.7
Factors contributing to the success of joint ventures

Direct Investment

Direct investment or foreign manufacture involves some form of manufacturing or production in the target country. Advantages include a commitment to the local market, fast availability of parts, and market detection of changes in the local environment. The extent of direct investment can range from the assembly of parts through to R&D-led innovation. Another means of market entry through direct investment is the acquisition or takeover of an organization in the foreign market.

 **Research Insight** 7.4

To take your learning further, you might wish to read this influential paper.

Rundh, B. (2007), 'International marketing behaviour amongst exporting firms',
European Journal of Marketing, **41(4), 181–98.**

This article provides a useful insight into factors affecting market entry through exporting to international markets for small and large organizations. Success factors relate to geographical proximity with the need for local representation and service and management commitment.

@ **Visit the Online Resource Centre to read the abstract and access the full paper.**

Chapter Summary

To consolidate your learning, the key points from this chapter are summarized here.

■ **Define international market development as a key growth strategy.**

In the light of the increasing internationalization of world markets, increased foreign trade, and international travel, international marketing has become a core activity for many organizations. A market development strategy involves increasing sales by selling existing offerings in new markets, either by targeting new audiences domestically or entering new markets internationally. International market development is growing in importance because of changes in the economic, social, and political landscape. The main considerations are the degree of risk and adjustment an organization is willing to undertake and the identification of potential opportunities within foreign markets.

■ **Explain the different forms of international marketing strategy.**

When entering international markets, a key competitive decision is whether the approach should be to standardize or adapt the marketing strategy. Organizations can adopt a local/global, multi-domestic, or global competitive international marketing strategy. The decision is based on the type of offering, the attitudes of the organization, and the resources available for market entry.

■ **Identify the key drivers for international market development.**

Many factors motivate an organization to develop markets in international markets. These include historical accident, the need to move excess stock, limited growth in domestic markets, comparative advantages, economies of scale, trade liberalization, technological changes, customer relationships, the development of transnational market segments through immigration, and organizational sustainability.

■ **Describe the criteria used to identify and select international markets.**

Assessing market attractiveness is very important as different markets have varying levels of attractiveness. Markets may be chosen according to the following criteria: market accessibility, market size, geographic proximity, psychological proximity, level and quality of competition already in the market, cost of entering the market, and the market's profit potential.

■ **Examine the environmental factors that could influence the choice of international marketing strategy.**

The analysis of environmental forces can help to identify which countries or regions should be given priority and which market entry strategy would be best suited to that country/region. Factors to consider include social, cultural, consumption attitudes, technological, economic, political, and legal factors.

■ **Explore the various methods used to enter international markets.**

The decision regarding the method of market entry is normally based on six main factors: speed and timing, costs and the required levels of investment, flexibility, risk and uncertainty, expected return on investment (ROI), and the long-term objectives. Once reviewed, organizations utilize one or more of the following methods of entry: indirect exporting; licensing, franchising, and contracting; direct exporting; joint ventures; direct investment.

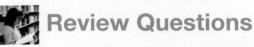 # Review Questions

1 What are the factors that influence international market development strategies?

2 Identify the key differences between multi-domestic and global competitive strategies.

3   What is the anti-globalization movement and why is it of increasing importance?

4   Which criteria should an organization use to assess the attractiveness of a foreign market?

5   Outline the main environmental factors that impact international marketing.

6   What are the different methods through which organizations can enter foreign markets?

7   What criteria should be considered when selecting an entry method to an international market?

8   What are the key differences between indirect and direct exporting?

9   Identify the benefits of using franchises in international marketing.

10 What key success factors are associated with international joint ventures?

 # Worksheet Summary

To apply the knowledge you have gained from this chapter and test your understanding of international market development visit the **Online Resource Centre** and complete Worksheet 7.1.

Discussion Questions

1   Having read Case Insight 7.1, how would you advise Orange to develop their customer Marketing strategy and communications to retain existing customers in different European countries?

2   What are the main criteria a SME should consider when deciding to enter a new international market?

3   Which of the following factors would have the greatest impact on a fashion retailer's assessment of the attractiveness of a foreign market: political, legal, social–cultural, or technological? Why?

4   Identify the key issues that a Western fast food retailing organization should consider when expanding into new international markets?

5   Marketed heavily on their country-of-origin brand image, what impact do you think joint ventures with domestic vineyards or direct investment would have on the perception of wine brands in a foreign market?

6   Take note of the country of manufacture, assembly, and origin of five of your recent purchases. Which countries and regions are represented? What impact do you think the political and legal environment has on their importation?

@ Visit the **Online Resource Centre** and complete the Multiple Choice Questions to assess your knowledge of Chapter 7.

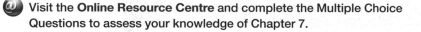

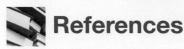

References

Ansoff, H. I. (1957), 'Strategies of diversification', *Harvard Business Review*, 25(5), 113–25

Bartlett, C. and Ghoshal, S. (1991) *Managing Across Borders: The Transnational Solution*. Cambridge, MA: Harvard Business School Press.

BBC News (2010), 'US worry at Chinese cyberattacks', *BBC News*, 14/01/2010, retrieve from: http://news.bbc.co.uk/go/pr/fr/-/1/hi/business/8458269.stm accessed 13 January 2010.

BBC (2013) Google turns off China censorship warning, retrieve from: http://www.bbc.co.uk/news/technology-20932072 accessed 2 September 2013.

Bikson, T. and Panis, C. (1997) 'Computers and connectivity: current trends', in S. Kiesler (ed.), *Culture of the Internet*, Mahwah, NJ: Lawrence Erlbaum, 407–30.

Burgel, O. and Murray, G. (2000), 'The international market entry choices of start-up organizations in high-technology industries', *Journal of International Marketing*, 8(2), 33–62

Burkitt, L. (2013), 'China spreads chicken blame', *Wall Street Journal*, 25 January, retrieve from: http://online.wsj.com/article/SB10001424127887323539804578263450081445528.html accessed 21 February 2013.

Carr, P. (2010), 'Soul searching: Google's position on China might be many things, but moral it is not', *TechCrunch*, retrieve from: www.techcrunch.com/2010/01/13/not-safe-for-wok/ accessed 13 January 2010.

Davies, C. (2010), 'Google China: Search engine's stand against censorship welcomes by campaigners', *The Guardian*, retrieve from: www.guardian.co.uk/technology accessed 13 January 2010.

de Mooij, M. (1994), *Advertising Worldwide*, Hemel Hempstead: Prentice-Hall.

de Pablos, P.O. (2006), 'Transnational corporations and strategic challenges: an analysis of knowledge flows and competitive advantage', *Learning Organization*, 13, 544–59.

Douglas, S. and Douglas, Y. W. (1987), 'The myth of globalisation', *Columbia Journal of World Business*, Winter, 19–29.

Fernandes, B.H.R., da Rocha, A., and Junior, R.S. (2012) 'Trikke Tech Inc.', *Entrepreneurship Theory and Practice*, 36, 1075–102.

Fill, C. (2009), *Marketing Communications: Interactivity, Communities, and Content* (5th edn), Harlow: Prentice Hall.

Herbig, P. A. and Day, K. (1993), 'Managerial implications of the North American Free Trade Agreement', *International Marketing Review*, 10, 15–35.

Hout, T., Porter, M. E., and Rudden, E. (1982), 'How global organizations win out!', *Harvard Business Review*, September–October.

Kageyama, Y. (2008), 'H&M opens shops in pricey Japan amid downturn', *USA Today*, 12 September, retrieve from: www.usatoday.com/money/economy/2008-09-12-213076897_x.htm accessed 10 February 2010.

Keegan, W.J. (1989), *Global Marketing Management*, Englewood Cliffs, NJ: Prentice-Hall.

Kaiman, J. (2013), 'China's fast-food pioneer struggles to keep customers saying "YUM!" ', *The Guardian*, 4 January, retrieve from: http://www.guardian.co.uk/world/2013/jan/04/china-fast-food-pioneer accessed 21 February 2013.

Levitt, T. (1983), 'The globalization of markets', *Harvard Business Review*, May-June, 2–11

Lewis, K. S., Lim, F. A., and Rusetski, A. (2006), 'Development of archetypes of international marketing strategy', *Journal of International Business Studies*, 37(4), 499–524.

Lynch, R. (1994), *European Business Strategies: The European and Global Strategies of Europe's Top Organizations*, London: Kogan Page.

Martel, L. and Chagnon, J. (2013), 'Population growth in Canada: from 1851 to 2061', *Statistics Canada*, retrieve from: http://www12.statcan.ca/census-recensement/2011/as-sa/98-310-x/98-310-x2011003_1-eng.cfm accessed 9 March 2013.

Mead, R. (1990), *Cross-Cultural Management Communication*, New York: John Wiley.

Moskvitch, K. (2012), 'Cracks in the wall: will China's Great Firewall backfire?' *BBC News*, retrieve from: http://www.bbc.co.uk/news/technology-17910953 accessed 9 March 2013.

Movius, L. (2007), 'H&M heads east with first unit in Shanghai', *WWD: Women's Wear Daily*, 17 April, 193.

Mughan, T. (1993), 'Culture as an asset in international business', in Preston, J. (ed.), *International Business: Texts and Cases*, London: Pitman, 78–86.

Ohmae, K. (1985), *Triad Power*, London: Macmillan.

Ohmae, K. (1992), *The Borderless World: Power and Strategy in the Interlinked Economy*, London: Fontana.

Paliwoda, S. (1993), *International Marketing* (2nd end), London: Butterworth-Heinemann.

Pendergrast, M. (2000), *For God, Country, and Coca-Cola: The Definitive History of the Great American Soft Drink and the Company That Makes It* (2nd end), New York: Basic Books.

Perlmutter, H. V. (1969), 'The tortuous evolution of the multinational corporation', *Columbia Journal of World Business*, January-February, 9–18.

Pitcher, G. (1999), 'Ford takes pole position in the battle for world wide domination', *Marketing Week*, 4 February, 25.

Quelch, J. A. and Hoff, E. J. (1986) 'Customising global marketing', *Harvard Business Review*, May–June, 59–68.

Rundh, B. (2007), 'International marketing behaviour amongst exporting firms', *European Journal of Marketing*, 41(4), 181–98.

Sclater, I. (2005) 'The digital dimension', *Marketer,* May, 22–3.

Sirgy, M., Lee, D.-J., Miller, C., Littlefield, J., and Atay, E. (2007), 'The impact of imports and exports on a country's quality of life', *Social Indicators Research*, 83, 245–81.

Tapper-Hoel, J. (2010), 'H&M opens its first store in South Korea', *H&M Press Release*, retrieve from: www.hm.com/pl/investorrelations/pressreleases/__prfashion.nhtml?pressreleaseid=1002 accessed 11 April 2010.

Tapscott, D. (1998), *Growing Up Digital: The Rise of the Net Generation*, New York: McGraw-Hill.

Whitelock, J., and Jobber, D. (1994), 'The impact of competitor environment on initial market entry in a new non-domestic market', paper presented at the Marketing Education Group Conference, Coleraine.

Wind Y., and Perlmutter, H. V. (1973), 'Guidelines for developing international marketing strategies', *Journal of Marketing*, 37(April), 14–23.

Young, R. B. and Javalgi, R. G. (2007), 'International marketing research: a global project management perspective', *Business Horizons*, 50(2), 113–22

Young, S. (2001), 'What do researchers know about the global business environment?', *International Marketing Review*, 18, 120–9.

Part Three
The Marketing Mix

Chapter 8

Innovation and New Proposition Development

Learning Outcomes

After studying this chapter you should be able to:

▸ Explain the nature and distinguishing characteristics of product and service propositions

▸ Identify and describe the various types of product propositions and explain particular concepts relating to the management of products, including the product lifecycle

▸ Explain the relationship between product and service offerings and describe the product/service spectrum

▸ Explore the processes and issues associated with innovating new propositions

▸ Describe how new propositions are adopted by markets

Case Insight
Domino's Pizza

Market Insight 8.1
From Socialist Product to Capitalist Brand

Market Insight 8.2
Lifecycling Online Fashion

Market Insight 8.3
Purity in Products and Services

Market Insight 8.4
Unilever Invites Innovation

Market Insight 8.5
Sensitization Takes Off in Aerospace

Case Insight 8.1

How do organizations develop new propositions on a regular basis and remain competitive? We speak to Simon Wallis, Sales & Marketing Director for Domino's Pizza, to find out more.

Our expertise and passion for delivering hot fresh pizzas has earned us numerous awards and the loyalty of millions of pizza lovers around the world. Our mission is to be the favourite pizza delivery company in the world and we have set out several priorities to enable us to achieve this goal. One of these priorities is to 'deliver consistently high-quality food on time' and another is to 'innovate in ways that matter to our team members and customers.' Speed and service are central elements that impact all parts of our business.

To satisfy these goals the development of new products that are valued by our customers is really important, yet it can be problematic and a constant challenge. For example, the environment in which we operate has changed in many ways in recent years. The economic downturn has served to flatten sales for everyone in the market. This has resulted from new consumer spending habits, a heightened interest in obesity and healthy eating issues, and new entrants who have brought fresh ideas, such as the surge of interest in Mexican products and restaurants. In addition to these external issues, new product development impacts a wide range of functions within the company and our franchisees, such as finance, operations, and logistics, as well as marketing.

Our response to these internal and external issues has been to work closely with our customers and franchisees in order to review not only the quality of our pizzas and menu choice, but also to develop and introduce new products that exceed customer expectations. Ideas for new products come from a variety of sources. These include customers, suppliers, internal sources and our Marketing Advisory Council, which consists of selective franchisees.

Appropriate ideas are then filtered across five main evaluative criteria: the franchisees, financial tests to ensure the proposition is viable, operations, and various new product development requirements including strategy, competitors, taste, and packaging. Ideas that get through these filters are developed into prospective products, which are then subject to test marketing, which include hall tests and in-store trials. Those with suitable feedback receive investment funding and are developed prior to a full market launch.

One of the problems facing Domino's Pizza is to find ways to balance the increased costs and longer operational times associated with new ingredients and products with the central tenets of service and speed on which the business is founded.

Introduction

A Samsung smartphone, a train journey from Calgary to Vancouver, a cappuccino at Costa Coffee in Stockholm, the Singapore *Straits Times* newspaper, a copy of the Brazilian magazine *Claudia*, a haircut in Hawaii, and a manicure in Manila all have one thing in common. They are all propositions or offerings. The term proposition includes the tangible and intangible attributes related not just to physical goods but also to services, ideas, people, places, experiences, and even a mix of these various elements. Anything that can be offered for use and consumption, in exchange for money or some other form of value, is referred to as a **proposition** or offering. We occasionally use the term product as well, although this has goods-centric connotations.

Tangibility refers to an item's ability to be touched and whether it can be stored. For example, a bar of soap, a Rimmel lipstick, or a Vega factory conveyor belt are all tangible products, capable of being touched and stored. A ferry trip from Wellington to Picton in New Zealand, or a visit to the hairdresser Toni & Guy, cannot be touched and are not capable of being stored. These are intangible products (i.e. services).

Soap is a purely tangible good, whereas a financial services product, such as a pension or savings account, is a pure service. They lie at opposite ends of a spectrum (see Figure 8.1). In between the pure good and the pure service lie a host of goods–services combinations. Indeed, many organizations have developed the service aspect of their offering to help differentiate themselves in the market.

This spectrum of product/service combinations incorporates strategies designed to increase the value offered to customers through improved services. However, developing the service element to provide a point of differentiation has not always been a successful strategy, as it can attract price competition. As prices fall, offerings become commoditized and customers find it difficult to separate the value offered by competing firms. To avoid this situation, some organizations have developed a third approach based around improving customer experience.

The customer experience of strategy is not based on either the tangible or intangible attributes of brands, but refers to the memories and fantasies that individuals retain or imagine as a result of their interaction with an offering (Tynan and McKechnie, 2009). Memories of experiences related to product usage, events, visits, or activities are internalized, unlike products and services which are generally external to each person. Indeed, the idea that people consume emotions is emerging as an important and influential aspect of the marketing discipline. The memories and fantasies concept is best illustrated through the activities of theme and leisure parks. For more information on customer experiences, see Chapter 14.

This chapter is used to consider the nature of products and services, before exploring issues associated with their innovation and development. We start with a consideration of the principal characteristics associated with first products and then services. The second part of the chapter examines ideas and processes related to the development of new products and services.

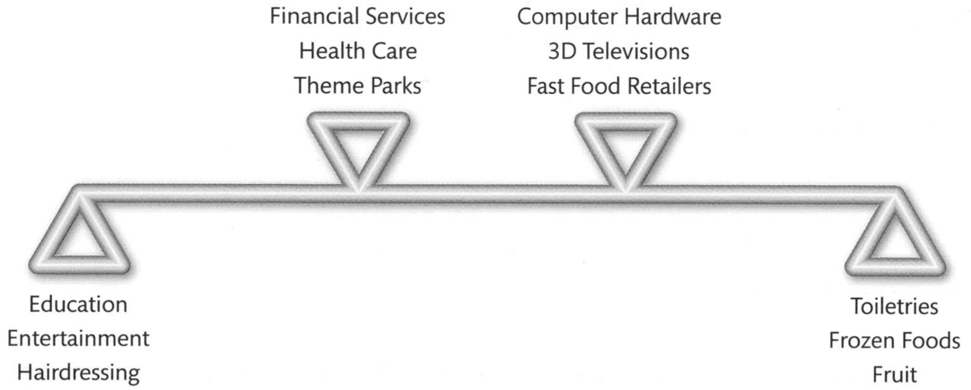

Financial Services
Health Care
Theme Parks

Computer Hardware
3D Televisions
Fast Food Retailers

Education
Entertainment
Hairdressing

Toiletries
Frozen Foods
Fruit

Figure 8.1

A spectrum of product combinations

Product Levels

When people buy products they are not just buying the simple functional aspect that a product offers; there are other complexities involved in the purchase. For example, the taste of coffee granules is an important benefit arising from the purchase of a jar of instant coffee. However, in addition to this core benefit, people are also attracted to the packaging, the price, the strength of the coffee, and also some of the psychosocial associations that we have learnt about a brand. The Cafédirect brand, for instance, seeks to help people understand its ties with the Fairtrade movement and so provide some customers a level of psychosocial satisfaction through their contribution.

To understand these different elements and benefits, we refer to three different **product forms**: the core, the embodied, and the augmented product forms (see Figure 8.2).

- The core proposition consists of the real core benefit or service. This may be a functional benefit in terms of what the offering will enable you to do, or it may be an emotional benefit in terms of how the product or service will make you feel. Cars provide transportation and a means of self-expression. Cameras make memories by recording a scene, person, or object through the use of digital processes or, originally, film.

- The embodied proposition consists of the physical good or delivered service which provides the expected benefit. It consists of many factors, for example the features and capabilities, the durability, the design, the packaging, and the brand name. Cars are supplied with different styles, engines, seats, colours, and boot space, and digital cameras are offered with a variety of picture qualities, screen sizes, pixels, zoom and telephoto features, editing, and relay facilities.

- The augmented proposition consists of the embodied offering plus all those other factors that are necessary to support the purchase and any post-purchase activities, for example credit and finance, training, delivery, installation, guarantees, and the overall perception of customer service.

When these levels are brought together it is hoped that they will provide customers with a reason to buy and to keep buying. Each individual combination or bundle of benefits constitutes added value and serves to differentiate one sports car from another sports car, one disposable camera from another. Marketing strategies need to be designed around the actual and the

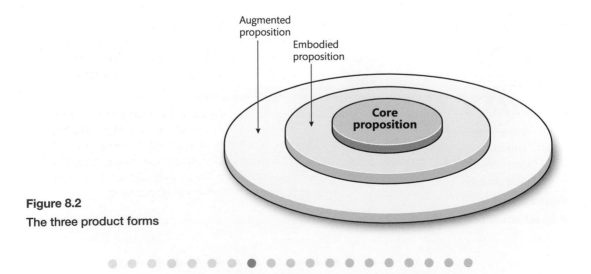

Figure 8.2
The three product forms

augmented propositions, as it is through these that competition occurs and people are able to understand how one disposable camera differs from another.

Understanding a brand and what it means to its core customers and their experience of a brand is vitally important. Pepsi's battle with Coca-Cola during the 1960s and 1970s saw it gradually reduce Coke's dominant market share. The battle culminated in 1985 when Coke abandoned its original recipe and introduced New Coke, a sweeter formulation designed to attract Pepsi's young market. Coke's customers boycotted New Coke, there was public outrage, and Pepsi temporarily became market leader. New Coke was soon dropped and the original brought back and relaunched as Classic Cola, re-establishing its credentials and retrieving the number one spot. The problem was that Coke had not appreciated the value that the proposition as a whole represented to its primary customers. The sum of the core, embodied, and augmented propositions, encapsulated as the brand Coca-Cola, drew passion from its customers and was overlooked by the market researchers when searching for a means to arrest Pepsi's progress.

The development of the internet and digital technologies has impacted on the nature of the offering and the benefits accruing from usage of the offering. This has opened opportunities for organizations to redefine their core and actual propositions, often by supplementing them with 'information' about the offering, for example providing white papers or games designed to engage website visitors with the brand. Another approach has been to transform current offerings into digital offerings, for example Napster with music downloads. A further approach is to change the bundle of offerings, sometimes achieved by presenting an online catalogue that offers a wider array than the offline catalogue.

Chaffey *et al.* (2009) refer to Ghosh (1998) and his early identification of the number of ways in which **digital value** can help augment the proposition. For example, many companies provide evidence of the awards they have won, whereas others parade testimonials, endorsements, and customer comments. These are designed to provide credibility, reduce risk, and enable people to engage with or purchase a brand. The key contribution of the internet, in this context, is that it offers digital value to customers, sometimes as a supplement and sometimes as a complete alternative to the conventional established core offering. (See Market Insight 8.1.)

 Market Insight 8.1

From Socialist Product to Capitalist Brand

The Cohiba is a relatively unknown, yet exclusive, hand-rolled Cuban cigar. It is named after the Taino Indian word for the blend of leaves that were smoked by the island's early inhabitants. The product's distinctive flavour stems from the blend of leaves from selected fields in the Vuelta Abajo region and a special fermentation process. This is reflected in the distinctive black and yellow design. The cigar was first rolled in 1966, and folklore suggests that once the Cuban President, Fidel Castro, was informed about the brand by his security guards, he became an advocate, and was frequently photographed smoking or holding the cigar.

The famous El Laguito factory produced the Cohiba cigars and distribution was closely controlled as they were exclusively for Castro and his friends. The cigar's reputation grew, mainly because of the photographic associations with Castro and because they were used as a diplomatic gift for foreign dignitaries.

Market Insight 8.1
continued

In 1982, the Cohiba was distributed internationally, on a limited basis, but was banned from sale in the USA because of the embargo on Cuban products. Despite this, the illicit nature of the brand has contributed to its popularity and a strong black market has emerged. The brand is now imbued with an association with luxury and extravagance.

At first there were three product forms: the Panetela, the Corona Especial, and the Lancero. In 1989, three new ones were added: the Robusto, the Exquisito, and the Espléndido. These six are now referred to as Cohiba's classic line. In 1992, the Siglo (meaning century) I, II, III, IV, and V, were launched. The most recent addition, in 2012, is the Cohiba Piramides Extra. These cigars are regarded as some of the finest and most popular cigars in the world.

Despite the increasing social intolerance of smoking in many parts of the world, the Cohiba cigar still stands as a product of desire, to the point of becoming

as fashionable as designer shoes and handbags. Although sales in Western countries have declined, especially in Spain, its most important market, sales in many parts of Asia, especially China, have grown considerably. The Cohiba is a simple cigar, yet it has become a luxury item, with some priced at around £40 to £50 each. A brand born of socialism and revolution is now valued by capitalists and entrepreneurs.

Source: Osborn (2011); Anon. (2012); http://www.cgarsltd.co.uk/cuban-cigars-cohiba-cigars-c-317_44_48.html

1 **How might the core, embodied, and augmented forms of a proposition be interpreted in the Cohiba cigar?**

2 **In what ways might digital value be added to the Cohiba?**

3 **Visit www.cohiba.com/ and identify any services that might be provided to support the brand.**

Classifying Products

There are two main ways of classifying products—as consumer products and business-to-business products. Consumer products are bought to satisfy personal and family needs, and industrial and business products are bought either as a part of the business's operations or to make other products for resale. Although there are some products, such as light bulbs and toilet tissue, that are bought by both consumers and businesses, we use this grouping because there are considerable differences in the way that these two types of customers buy different propositions. If you are unsure about buying behaviour issues, read Chapter 2.

Consumer Products

The first way of classifying consumer products is to consider them in terms of their durability. Durable goods, such as bicycles, music players, and refrigerators, can be used repeatedly and provide benefits each time they are used. Non-durable goods, such as yoghurt, newspapers, and plastic packaging, have a limited duration and are often only capable of being used once. Services are intangible propositions and cannot be stored.

   Durable goods often require the purchaser to have high level of involvement in the purchase decision. There is a high perceived risk in these decisions and so consumers typically spend a great deal of time, care, and energy searching, formulating, and making the final decision. As a result, marketers need to understand these patterns of behaviour, provide, and make accessible sufficient amounts of appropriate information, and ensure that there is the right type of service and support necessary to meet the needs of the target market.

Non-durable goods, typically food and grocery items, usually reflect low levels of involvement and buyers are not concerned with which particular product they buy. Risk is perceived to be low and so there is little or no need (or time usually) to shop around for the best possible price. Buyers may buy on availability, price, habit, or brand experience.

One of the key characteristics of services is that they are intangible and another is that they are perishable. This means that they cannot be touched and because they are perishable they are not capable of being stored. Therefore their use and consumption has to be based on an 'on-demand' basis. Levels of involvement may be high or low, and marketing mixes need to set up and deliver to customers' expectations. We consider services later in this chapter and in Chapter 14.

A deeper and more meaningful way of classifying consumer products is to consider how and where consumers buy them. In Chapter 2, we considered different ways in which consumers make purchases. In particular, we looked at **extensive problem solving**, **limited problem solving**, and **routinized response behaviour**. Classifying products according to the behaviour consumers demonstrate when buying them enables marketing managers to develop more suitable and appropriate marketing strategies. Four main behavioural categories have been established: **convenience products**, **shopping products**, **speciality products**, and unsought products.

Convenience products are non-durable and, as the name suggests, are bought because the consumer does not want to put very much effort, if any, into the buying decision. Routinized response behaviour corresponds most closely to convenience products as they are bought frequently and are inexpensive. Most decisions in this category are made through habit, and if a usual brand is not available an alternative brand will be selected or none at all as it would be too inconvenient to go and visit another store.

Convenience products can be subdivided into three further categories. These are staples, impulse, and emergency products and are explained in Table 8.1. All of these types of convenience products indicate that slightly different marketing strategies are required to make each of them work. However, one element common to all is distribution. If the product is not available when an emergency arises, or when a consumer is waiting to pay or walking around the supermarket, then a sale will not be made. Pricing is important, as customers know the expected price of convenience items and may well switch brands if price exceeds that of the competition.

Shopping products are not bought as frequently as convenience products, and, as a result, consumers do not always have sufficient up-to-date information to make a buying decision. The purchase of shopping products such as furniture, electrical appliances, jewellery, and mobile phones requires some search for information, if only to find out about the latest features. Consumers give time and effort to planning these purchases, if only because the level of risk is more substantial than that associated with convenience products. They will visit several stores and use the internet and word-of-mouth communications for price comparisons, product information, and the experience of other customers. Not surprisingly, levels of brand loyalty are quite low, as consumers are quite happy to switch brands to get the level of functionality and overall value they need.

Table 8.1 Categories of convenience products

Type of convenience product	Explanation
Staple products	Characteristically, staples are available almost everywhere. They include groceries, such as bread, milk, soft drinks, and breakfast cereals but they also include petrol. They are bought frequently and form the basis of our daily pattern of behaviour. In France, the daily purchase of a fresh French stick of bread or a baguette constitutes an important part of social behaviour.
Impulse products	These are products that consumers had not planned to buy but are persuaded at the very last minute to pick up and put in their trolley or basket. Typically, these items are located very near to the tills in supermarkets (the point of sale) so that whilst customers are waiting to pay for their planned or considered purchases they become attracted to these impulse items. Chewing gum, chocolate bars, and magazines are typical impulse purchases, unlike a bottle of milk or petrol which is planned.
Emergency products	Bought when a very special need arises; buyers are more intent on buying a solution than buying the right quality or image-related product. So, the purchase of a bandage when someone is cut or injured, a plumber when a pipe starts leaking in the middle of the night, or even umbrellas in the middle of summer when an unexpected downpour occurs all constitute emergency products.

The marketing strategies followed by manufacturers, and to some extent retailers, need to accommodate the characteristics of limited problem solving. Shopping products do not require the mass distribution strategies associated with convenience products. Here, a selective distribution strategy is required as, although the volume of purchases is lower and margins are higher, consumers often want the specialist advice offered by knowledgeable expert retailers.

Speciality products represent high risk, are very expensive, and are bought infrequently, often only once, and correspond to extended problem solving. People plan these purchases, search intensively for information about the object, and are often only concerned with a particular brand and in finding a way of gaining access to an outlet that can supply that brand. It is possible to find speciality products in many areas, e.g. limited edition sports equipment (Big Bertha golf clubs), rare paintings and artwork (Monet, Picasso), custom cars, watches (Rolex), haute couture (Stella McCartney), and certain restaurants and holidays. All have unique characteristics, which for buyers means that there are no substitute offerings available or worth considering.

Marketing strategies to support speciality products focus strongly on a very limited number of distribution outlets, and advertising that seeks to establish the brand name and values. The few retailers appointed to carry the item require detailed training and support so that the buyer experiences high levels of customer service and associated prestige throughout the entire purchase process.

Rolex, a speciality product
Source: Courtesy of the Rolex Watch Company Ltd.

Unsought products refer to a group of products that people do not normally anticipate buying, or indeed want to buy. Very often, consumers have little knowledge or awareness of the brands in the marketplace and are only motivated to find out about them when a specific need arises. So, a windscreen cracks or a water pipe bursts, necessitating repairs and unsought products. In a similar way, life insurance was once sold through heavy pressurized selling as people did not see the need. That has changed through legislation, but double-glazing and timeshare holiday salespeople still have a reputation for selling their offerings in this way.

Business Products

Unlike some consumer products that are bought for personal and psychological rewards, business propositions are generally bought on a rational basis to meet organizational goals. These are either used to enable the organization to function smoothly or they form an integral part of the products, processes, and services supplied by the organization for resale. In the same way as consumer products are classified according to how customers use them, so business propositions are classified according to how organizational customers use them. Six main categories can be identified: equipment goods, raw materials, semi-finished goods, maintenance repair and operating goods, component parts, and business services.

- Equipment goods cover two main areas and both concern the everyday operations of the organization: **capital equipment goods** and **accessory equipment goods**. Capital equipment goods are buildings, heavy plant, and factory equipment necessary to build or assemble products. They might also be major government schemes to build hospitals, motorways, and bridges. Whatever their nature, they all require substantial investment, are subject to long planning processes, are often one-off purchases designed to be used for a considerable amount of time, and require the involvement of a number of different people and groups in the purchase process. Accessory equipment goods should support the key operational processes and activities of the organization. Typically, they are photocopiers, computers, stationery, and office furniture. These items cost less than capital equipment goods, are not expected to last as long as capital equipment goods, and are often portable rather than fixed. Whereas a poor capital equipment purchase may put the entire organization at risk, a poor accessory purchase will at worst be frustrating and slow down activities but is unlikely to threaten the existence of the organization.

- Raw materials are the basic materials that are used to produce finished goods. Minerals, chemicals, timber, and food staples, such as grain, vegetables, fruit, meat, and fish, are extracted, grown, or farmed as necessary and transported to organizations that process the raw materials into finished or semi-finished products. They are bought in large quantities, and buyers often negotiate heavily on price. However, these buying decisions can be influenced by non-product factors such as length of relationship, service quality, and credit facilities.

- Semi-finished goods are raw materials that have been converted into a temporary state. Iron ore is converted into sheets that can be used by car and aircraft manufacturers, washing machines, and building contractors.

- **Maintenance, repair, and operating (MRO)** goods are products, other than raw materials, that are necessary to ensure that the organization can continue functioning. Maintenance and repair goods such as nuts and bolts, light bulbs, and cleaning supplies are used to maintain the capital and accessory equipment goods. Operating supplies are not directly involved in the production of the finished goods nor are they a constituent part, but oil for lubricating machinery, paper, pens, and flash drives are all necessary to keep the organization functioning.

- Component parts are finished complete parts bought from other organizations. These components are then incorporated directly into the finished product. So, for example, Ford will buy in finished headlight assemblies and mount them directly into their Ford Fusion, Focus, or Transit models as appropriate.

- Business services are intangible services used to enhance the operational aspects of organizations. Most commonly, these concern management consultancy, finance, and accounting, including auditing, legal, marketing research, IT, and marketing communications.

Product Range, Line, and Mix

To meet the needs of a number of different target markets, most organizations offer a variety of **products** and **services**. Although some offer an assortment based on an individual core product, it is rare that an organization offers just a single product. Consumer organizations, such as Gillette, offer a range of shaving products for men; industrial organizations, such as Oliver Valves, offer a range of valves for the offshore and onshore petrochemical, gas, and power generation industries. To make sense of, and understand, the relationships that one set of products have with another, a variety of terms have emerged. Table 8.2 sets out these different terms.

Visit the **Online Resource Centre** and complete Internet Activity 8.1 to learn more about the terminology relating to a product range.

Table 8.2 Product range terminology

Product term	Explanation
Product item	A distinct single product within a product line. Samsung's Galaxy S4 is a product item.
Product line	A group of closely related products—related through technical, marketing, or user considerations. For example, all the televisions offered by Samsung constitute a product line.
Product mix	The total number of product lines offered by an organization. At Samsung this would mean all the mobile devices, televisions, print solutions, domestic appliances, cameras, and accessories they offer.
Product line length	The number of products available in a product line: the 12 products available within the Samsung 'tablet' range.
Product line depth	The number of variations available within a product line. For example, if a brand of hair colourant has three pack sizes and five shades of hair colouring, that particular brand of hair care has a depth of 15.
Product mix width	The number of product lines within a product mix.

Product Lifecycles

Underpinning the product lifecycle (PLC) concept is the belief that offerings move through a sequential predetermined pattern of development similar to the biological path that lifeforms follow. This pathway, known as the **product lifecycle**, consists of five distinct stages, namely development, introduction, growth, maturity, and decline. Sales and profits rise and fall across the various lifestages of the product, as shown in Figure 8.3.

Products move through an overall cycle which consists of different stages. Speed of movement through the stages will vary, but each product has a limited lifespan. Although the life of a product can be extended in many ways, such as introducing new ways of using the product, finding new users, and developing new attributes, the majority of products have a finite period during which management needs to maximize their returns on the investment made. In Sweden, mobile phones have an overall lifespan of 9–12 months, so it is important to extend the sales period, especially through maturity. Apple and others do this through 'appstores'. The firm offers existing iPhone customers the possibility of purchasing additional applications and games (Leistén and Nilsson, 2009).

Just as the nature and expectations of customer groups differ at each stage, so do the competitive conditions. This means that different marketing strategies, relating to the offering and its distribution, pricing, and promotion, need to be deployed at particular times so as to maximize financial returns.

The product lifecycle concept does not apply to all offerings in the same way. For example, some offerings reach the end of the introduction stage and then die as it becomes clear that there is no market to sustain them. Some products follow the path into decline and then hang

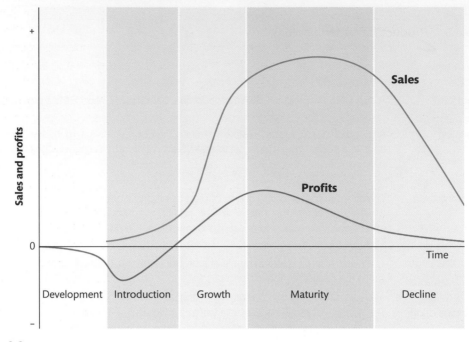

Figure 8.3
The product lifecycle

around sustained by heavy advertising and sales promotions, or they are recycled back into the growth stage by repositioning activities. Some products grow really quickly and then fade away rapidly. When the Pot Noodle products were first introduced demand grew quickly, but then died off steeply at the end of the growth stage. This was because many people did not like the taste of these early products and so there was limited repeat buying.

The brands of many fast-moving consumer goods (FMCG) are sustained through a super-market listing. Terminating a listed brand, and losing the shelf space to a competitor, is difficult to accept simply because getting the listing in the first place is so difficult and because of the substantial investment that has been put into the brand since its conception. Supermarkets will often delist an underperforming brand unless the brand owner presents a suitable variant, capable of replacing the ailing brand (Clark, 2009).

When discussing the PLC care must be taken to clarify what exactly is being described. The PLC concept can apply to a product class (computers), a product form (a laptop), or a brand (Sony). The shape of the curve varies, with product classes having the longest cycle as the mature stage is often extended. Product forms tend to comply most closely with the traditional cycle shape, whereas brand cycles tend to be the shortest. This is because they are subject to competitive forces and sudden change. So, whereas hatchback cars (product form) enjoyed a long period of success, brands such as the Ford Escort had shorter cycles and have been replaced by cars that have more contemporary designs and features, in this case the Ford Focus.

Is the PLC Concept Useful?

The PLC is a well-known and popular concept and is a useful means of explaining the broad path a product or brand has taken. It also clearly sets out that no product, service, or brand lasts for ever. In principle, the PLC concept allows marketing managers to adapt strategies and tactics to meet the needs of evolving conditions and circumstances. In this sense, it is clear, simple, and predictable. However, in practice the PLC is of limited use. For example, one problem is identifying which stage an offering has reached in the cycle. Historical sales data do not help managers identify when an offering moves from one stage to another. This means that it is difficult to forecast sales, and hence determine the future shape of the PLC curve.

The model worked reasonably well when the environment was relatively stable and not subject to dynamic swings or short-lived customer preferences. However, contemporary marketing managers are not concerned where their brand is within the product lifecycle; there are many other more meaningful ways and metrics to understand the competitive strength and development of a brand, e.g. benchmarking. Some brands do not follow the classical S-shaped curve, but rise steeply and then fall away immediately after sales reach a crest. These shapes reflect a consumer fad, a craze for a particular piece of merchandise, typified by fashion clothing, skateboards, and toys. So great care is required when using the PLC, as its role in commerce and when developing strategy is weak, but it is helpful generally as a way of explaining how brands develop. (See Market Insight 8.2.)

Market Insight 8.2

Lifecycling Online Fashion

Firms such as Oli, ColorPlus, a premium Indian casual wear brand, YesStyle.com, who offer a range of Asian fashion online, and ASOS, the UK's market leader in online fashion retailing, each have thousands of product items on their websites and can introduce hundreds of new items each week.

Understanding the principles underpinning the lifecycle can help these firms work out the length of each item's sales period, manage the stocking requirements, and plan for the introduction of new ranges. For example, in the world of online fashion the following cycle might be evident.

- Introduction—a new skirt is presented online, given lots of visibility, and is linked directly through newsletters and social media sites and also from the homepage. Some fashion leaders adopt the new skirt, while digital influencers who had been alerted previously to the launch are given access to more detailed information and, in some cases, samples.

- Growth—offline articles, online placements, and word of mouth help sales to grow. Stock management becomes critical as it is essential not to disappoint customers.

- Maturity—competition becomes intense and it is necessary to remind audiences about the offering online. More stock may be required to ensure continuity of supply. For example, a dress from the previous summer collection may still be selling well. At some point during this stage, the firm may cut the price to clear remaining stock. Sales provide an opportunity to make space in the warehouse for new offerings.

- Decline—the skirt becomes unfashionable and is replaced by a new design.

Each of these specific stages of development has different characteristics, requiring differing business and marketing approaches. This, in turn, has led to the development of software systems and applications that are geared to manage the individual characteristics of each stage. For example, Product Lifecycle Management (PLM) systems deal with online catalogues, design collaboration (enabling geographically dispersed employees to work on designs together), style information (an item's sales history), and various facilities designed to integrate order tracking, invoicing, and operations activities.

Sources: www.worldfashionexchange.com/apparel-plm.aspx www.straitstimes.com/BreakingNews/TechandScience/Story/STIStory_500942.html www.asos.com www.thetimes100.co.uk/studies/view

Market Insight 8.2
continued

In the world of online fashion, product lifecycle can be short from introduction to obsolescence
Source: © Asos.com Ltd.

1   How might the marketing activities change as an online fashion brand moves into the mature stage?

2   Use a major search engine to find the leading online fashion company in Australia, Canada, and another country of your choice. What do they all have in common?

3   Make brief notes about the needs customers have when buying fashion online. How might this change over the next five years?

Research Insight 8.1

To take your learning further, you might wish to read this influential paper.

Wood, L. (1990), 'The end of the product life cycle? Education says goodbye to an old friend', *Journal of Marketing Management*, **6(2), 145–55.**

This paper has been highlighted because it challenges the conventional wisdom about how useful the product lifecycle is. It identifies some of the problems associated with this popular concept and suggests that it is good for marketing education but not so good for marketing practitioners.

@ **Visit the Online Resource Centre to read the abstract and access the full paper.**

What is a Service?

Services are different from products. One of the distinguishing dimensions of products is that they have a physical presence. Services do not have a physical presence and they cannot be touched. This is because their distinguishing characteristic is that they are an act or a performance (Berry, 1980). A service cannot be put in a bag, taken home, stored in a cupboard, and used at a later date. A service is consumed at the point where it is produced. For example, watching a play at a theatre, learning maths at school, or taking a holiday all involve the simultaneous production and consumption of the play, new knowledge, and leisure. (See Market Insight 8.3.)

 ## Market Insight 8.3

Purity in Products and Services

Sweden's Tetra Pak revolutionized the food packaging industry, Finland's Huhtamäki Oyj is one of the world's leading manufacturers of paper cups and plates, Danish company Schur Technology is a leading North European supplier of packaging solutions, and the Norwegian company Elopak is a leading global supplier of cartons for liquid food products. Rexam is one of the world's leading consumer packaging groups supporting the beverage and healthcare markets.

What is common to all these organizations? Their skill and core competence is in packaging. They make tangible products to which, traditionally, there are few service additions.

Alternatively, Bain, McKinsey, Towers Perrin, and PwC are some of the leading management consulting organizations. Owned by IBM, PwC offers a huge range of services across many industries and sectors. Their approach to work is stated to be through 'connectedthinking'. None of these organizations make or sell any products; they provide knowledge and skills, i.e. pure services.

Sources: www.schur.com/skabeloner/ www.tetrapak.com/ www.huhtamaki.com/ www.elopak.com/ www.rexam.com/ www.pwc.com/

Packaging is a pure product
Source: © Tetra Pak image

Market Insight 8.3
continued

1 **Identify ways in which packaging might influence consumers.**

2 **Think about the role of a marketing consultant and make a list of the different types of**

knowledge that might constitute 'connected thinking'.

3 **Draw the product/service spectrum and place on it various product/service combinations.**

The service industry sector forms a substantial part of most developed economies. Not surprisingly, the range of services is enormous and we consume services in nearly all areas of our work, business, home, and leisure activities. Table 8.3 indicates the variety of sectors and some of the areas in which we consume different types of services.

The sheer number of services that are available has grown, partly because it is not always easy to differentiate products just on features, benefits, quality, or price. Competition can be very intense and most product innovations or developments are copied quickly. Services provide an opportunity to add value yet not be copied, as each service is a unique experience.

Most products contain an element of service; a product/service combination is designed to provide a means of adding value, differentiation, and earning a higher return. The extent to which a service envelops a product varies according to a number of factors. These concern the level of tangibility associated with the type of product, the way in which the service is delivered, variations in supply and demand, the level of customization, the type of relationship between service providers and customers, and the degree of involvement that people experience in the service (Lovelock *et al.*, 1999).

The product/service spectrum explored at the beginning of this chapter identifies that there are some products with little service component and some services that have little product tangibility. Many grocery products have few supporting services, just shelf-stocking and checkout operators. The purchase of new fitted bedroom furniture involves the cupboards, dressers, and

Table 8.3 Service sectors	
Sector	**Examples**
Business	Financial, airlines, hotels, solicitors, and lawyers
Manufacturing	Finance and accountants, computer operators, administrators, trainers
Retail	Sales personnel, cashiers, customer support advisers
Institutions	Hospitals, education, museums, charities, churches
Government	Legal system, prisons, military, customs and excise, police

wardrobes plus the professional installation service necessary to make the furniture usable. At the other end of the spectrum a visit to the dentist or an evening class entails little physical product-based support as the personal service is delivered by the service deliverer in the form of the dentist or tutor.

Visit the **Online Resource Centre** and complete Internet Activity 8.2 to learn more about Professional Services Marketing Group (PSMG) and the marketing of professional services.

The Nature of Services

Before moving on, it is necessary to define what a service is. As with any topic, there is no firm agreement, but for our purposes the following definition, derived from a number of authors, will be used.

A service is any act or performance offered by one party to another that is essentially intangible. Consumption of the service does not result in any transfer of ownership even though the service process may be attached to a physical product.

Much of this definition is derived from the work of Grönroos (1990), who considered a range of definitions and interpretations. What this definition provides is an indication of the various characteristics and properties that set services apart from products. The two sections that follow examine the key characteristics of services and the way in which the service mix, as opposed to the product mix, is configured.

Distinguishing Characteristics

Services are characterized by five distinct characteristics, as depicted in Figure 8.4. These are **intangibility**, **perishability**, **variability**, **inseparability**, and a lack of **ownership**. These are important aspects that shape the way in which marketers design, deliver, and evaluate the marketing of services.

 Research Insight 8.2

To take your learning further, you might wish to read this influential paper.

Shostack, G. L. (1977), 'Breaking free from product marketing', *Journal of Marketing*, 41(April), 73–80.

This passionately written paper seeks to draw a clear and distinct line between the requirements for marketing products and services. Shostack states that a marketing mix that is appropriate for products is not suitable for services. A key thrust of the paper draws on the need for an understanding of the difference between image (for products) and evidence (for services).

@ **Visit the Online Resource Centre to read the abstract and access the full paper.**

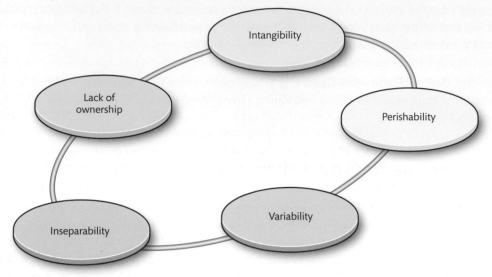

Figure 8.4
The five core characteristics of services

Intangibility

The purchase of products involves the use of most of our senses. We can touch, see, smell, hear, or even taste products before we buy them, let alone use them. Think of a trip to buy an MP3 player. It is possible to see the physical product and its various attributes, such as size and colour, to feel the weight, and to touch it. These are important purchasing decision cues, and even if the equipment fails to work properly, it is possible to take it back for a replacement. However, if a decision is made to buy additional insurance/support, this will be itemized on the receipt, but it is not possible to touch, taste, see, hear, or smell the insurance bought. Services are intangible and they are only delivered and experienced post purchase.

Intangibility does not mean that customers buy services without using their senses. What it does mean is that they use substitute cues to help make these purchasing decisions and to reduce the uncertainty because they cannot touch, see, smell, or hear the service. People make judgements based on a range of quality-related cues. These cues serve to make tangible the intangible service. Two types of cue can be identified: intrinsic and extrinsic (Olson and Jacoby, 1972). Intrinsic cues are drawn directly from the offering itself and are regarded as difficult to change. Extrinsic cues, on the other hand, are said to surround the offering and can be changed relatively easily. Brady *et al.* (2005) found that different types of service brands need different types of cue. Financial and investment-based brands prosper from the use of intrinsic cues, which stress objective information sources such as a strong reputation, industry rankings, and favourable media reviews. The reverse is true for services that have a more tangible element, such as hotels and transport services. In these circumstances, more subjective communications, such as advertising and referrals through word of mouth, are more influential.

Perishability

A bottle of shampoo on a supermarket shelf attracts a number of opportunities to be sold and consumed. When the store closes and opens again the following day, the bottle is still available to be sold and it remains available until it is purchased or the expiry date is reached. This is not the case with services. Once a train pulls out of a station or an aeroplane takes off or a film starts, those seats are lost and can never be sold. This is referred to as perishability and is an important aspect of services marketing. Services are manufactured and consumed simultaneously; they cannot be stored either prior to or after the service encounter.

The reason why these seats remain empty reflects variations in demand. This may be due to changes in the wider environment and may follow easily predictable patterns of behaviour, for example family holiday travel. One of the tasks of service marketers is to ensure that the number of empty seats and lost-forever revenue is minimized. In cases of predictable demand, service managers can vary the level of service capacity: a longer train, a bigger aircraft, or extra screenings of a film (multiplex facilities). However, demand may vary unpredictably, in which case service managers are challenged to provide varying levels of service capacity at short notice.

One of the main ways in which demand patterns can be influenced is through differential pricing. By lowering prices to attract custom during quieter times and raising prices when demand is at its highest, demand can be levelled and marginal revenues increased. Hotel and transport reservation systems have become very sophisticated, making it easier to manage demand and improve efficiency, and, of course, customer service. Some football clubs categorize matches according to the prestige or ranking of the opposition, and adjust prices to fill the stadium. In addition to differential pricing, extra services can be introduced to divert demand. Hotels offer specialist weekend breaks, such as golfing or fishing, and mini-vacations to attract retired people outside the holiday season. Leisure parks offer family discounts and bundle free rides into prices to stimulate demand.

Variability

As already stated, an important characteristic of services is that they are produced and consumed by people simultaneously, as a single event. One of the outcomes of this unique process is that it is exceedingly difficult to standardize the delivery of services. It is also difficult to deliver services so that they always meet the brand promise, especially as these promises often serve to frame customer service expectations. If demand increases unexpectedly and there is insufficient capacity to deal with the excess number of customers, service breakdown may occur. A flood of customers at a restaurant may extend the arrival of meals for customers already seated and who have ordered their meals. Too many train passengers may mean that there are not enough seats. In both these cases, it is not possible to provide a service level that can be consistently reproduced.

A different way of looking at variability is to consider a theatre. The show may be doing well and the lead actors performing to critical acclaim. However, the actual performance that each actor delivers each night will be slightly different. This change may be subtle, such as a change in the tone of voice or an inflexion, and will pass by relatively unnoticed. At the other extreme, some actors go out of their way to make their performance very different. It is alleged that the actor Jane Horrocks once remarked that during the performance of a certain theatre play she deliberately changed each evening's show to relieve the boredom.

There has been substantial criticism of some organizations which, in an effort to lower costs, have relocated some or all of their call centre operations offshore. These strategies sometimes fail as the new provider has insufficient training, or insufficient local or product knowledge, or in some cases simply cannot be understood. This type of service experience will vary among customers and for each customer. The resulting fall in customer satisfaction can lead to increased numbers of customers defecting to competitors.

The variability of services does not mean that planning is a worthless activity. By anticipating situations when service breakdown might occur, service managers can provide facilities. For example, entertainment can be provided for queues at cinemas or theme parks in order to change the perception of the length of the time it takes to experience the service (e.g. a film or a theme-park ride).

Inseparability

As established previously, products can be built, distributed, stored, and eventually consumed at a time specified by the ultimate end-user customer. Services, on the other hand, are consumed at the point they are produced. In other words, service delivery cannot be separated or split out of service provision or service consumption.

This event, where delivery coincides with consumption, means that not only do customers come into contact with the service providers, but also there must be interaction between the two parties. This interaction is of particular importance, not just to the quality of service production but also to the experience enjoyed by the customer. So, following the earlier example of a theatre play, the show itself may provide suitable entertainment but the experience may be considerably enhanced if the leading lady, Keira Knightley, Judi Dench, or Scarlett Johansson, actually performs rather than has the night off because she is unwell. Alternatively, private doctors may develop a strong reputation and should there be an increase in demand beyond manageable levels, pricing can be used to reduce or reschedule demand for their services.

The service experiences described in the preceding paragraph highlight service delivery as a mass service experience (the play) and as a solo experience (the doctor). The differences impact on the nature of the interaction process. In the mass service experience, the other members of the audience have the opportunity to influence the perceived quality of the experience. Audiences create atmosphere and this may be positively or negatively charged. A good production can involve audiences in a play and keep them focused for the entire performance. However, a poor performance can frustrate audiences, leading to some members walking out and hence influencing the perception others have of the performance and experience of the play.

Interaction within the solo experience (doctor–patient) allows for greater control by the service provider, if only because they can manage the immediate context within which the interaction occurs and not be unduly influenced by wider environmental issues. Opportunities exist for flexibility and adaptation as the service delivery unfolds. For example, a check-in operator for an airline operates within a particular context, is not influenced by other major events during the interaction, and can adapt tone of voice, body language, and overall approach to meet the needs of particular travellers.

One final aspect of variability concerns the influence arising from the mixture of customers present during the service delivery. If there is a broad mix of customers, service delivery may be affected as the needs of different groups have to be attended to by the service provider. Such a mixture may dilute the impact of the service actually delivered.

Lack of Ownership

The final characteristic associated with services marketing arises naturally from the other features. Services cannot be owned as nothing is transferred during the interaction or delivery experience. Although a legal transaction often occurs with a service, there is no physical transfer of ownership as there is when a product is purchased. The seat in a theatre, train, plane, or ferry is rented on a temporary basis in exchange for a fee. The terms associated with the rental of the seat determine the time and use or experience to which the seat can be put. However, the seat remains the property of the theatre owner, rail operator, airline, and ferry company, respectively, as it needs to be available for renting to other people for further experiences.

Research Insight 8.3

To take your learning further, you might wish to read this influential paper.

Vargo, S. L. and Lusch, R. F. (2004), 'Evolving to a new dominant logic for marketing', *Journal of Marketing*, **68, 1 (January), 1–17.**

This paper introduces the ideas concerning service-dominant logic. It sets out the conceptual underpinning for the approach by tracking back and considering previous major marketing approaches. In the paper, the authors argue that all propositions essentially embody a service and that this requires a reconsideration of how marketing should be undertaken.

@ Visit the **Online Resource Centre** to read the abstract and access the full paper.

One last point concerns loyalty schemes such as frequent flyer programmes and membership clubs, where the service provider actively promotes a sense of ownership. By creating customer involvement and participation, even though there is nothing to actually own, customers can develop an attitude based around their perceived right to be a part of the service provider.

Service-Dominant Logic

There is an emerging concept based around a group of researchers who believe that products alone are not capable of meeting all of a customer's needs (Grönroos, 2009), particularly in business markets. For customers to derive value from a product they need to consume it and that often requires a level of integration or coordination with a supplier's processes and systems. This, it is argued, resembles more of the characteristics of a service than a core product offering. Therefore marketing should be considered as a customer management process. This entails not only proposing how an offering might be of value to customers, but also requires enabling and supporting them to create the value they require through their use of the product.

This is referred to as the **service-dominant logic** (SDL) approach, and was first proposed by Vargo and Lusch (2004; see also Chapter 1). The traditional marketing management approach can be considered as product-dominant logic. So, if products alone are insufficient to meet customer needs, it is better to consider services as a more realistic means of understanding how marketing works. This idea is developed in Chapter 14, and for those interested to know more about this approach please refer to Research Insight 8.3.

Developing Propositions for Products and Services

In this section we examine the principles and approaches used to innovate and develop new propositions for both products and services.

Developing new product propositions

One of the key points that the product lifecycle concept tells us is that products do not last for ever: their usefulness starts to diminish at some point, and eventually nearly all come to an end and die. There are many reasons for this cycle: technology is changing quickly so products are developed and adopted faster; lifecycles are becoming shorter, and so new products are required faster than before. In addition to this, global competition means that if an organization is to compete successfully and survive it will need to constantly offer superior value to its customers. Therefore one of management's tasks is to be able to control the organization's range or portfolio of products and to anticipate when one product will become relatively tired and when new ones are necessary to sustain the organization and help it to grow.

The term 'new products' can be misleading. This is because there is a range of newness, relevant to both the organization and to customers. Some new products might be totally new to both the organization and the market; for example, the Dyson vacuum cleaner, with its cyclone technology, revolutionized the market previously dominated by suction-based vacuum cleaners. However, some products might only be minor product adaptations that have no real impact on a market other than offering an interesting new feature, e.g. features such as new colours, flavours, and pack sizes, and electronic facilities on CD players, digital cameras, and mobile personal players. Dyson offer their world-famous floor cleaners with a ball rather than four fixed wheels, improving manoeuvrability and providing a strong point of differentiation.

Unfortunately, these 'new' propositions do not appear at the click of a pair of fingers. They have to be considered, planned, developed, and carefully introduced to the market. In order to ensure a stream of new propositions, organizations have three main options.

- Buy in finished products from other suppliers, perhaps from other parts of the world, or license the use of other products for specific periods of time.
- Develop products through collaboration with suppliers or even competitors.
- Develop new products internally, often through R&D departments or by adapting current products through minor design and engineering changes.

Whatever the preferred route, they all necessitate a procedure or development pattern through which they are brought to the market. It would be wrong to suggest that there should be a uniform process (Ozer, 2003), as not only are there many approaches to new product development but also the procedures adopted by an organization reflect its attitude to risk, its culture, its strategy, the product and market, and, above all else, its approach to customer relationships.

The success rate of new products is consistently poor. No more than one in ten new consumer products succeed and, according to Drucker (1985), there are three main reasons for this.

1 There is no market for the product.
2 There is a market need but the product does not meet customer requirements.
3 The product's ability to meet the market need, although satisfactory, is not adequately communicated to the target market.

Successful new propositions are developed partly by understanding customer needs and competitors, and partly by developing technology to meet the identified needs. For example, when an Asian entrant to the US market for medical devices and capital equipment quickly established itself, it was thought that their lower prices were the main reason. However, when a major manufacturer reviewed their own proposition they also analysed customer needs and

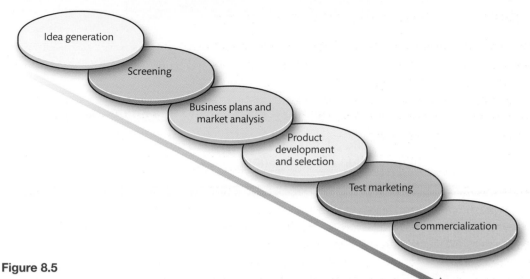

Figure 8.5
Stages within the new product development process

the nature of the competition. The results showed that the US manufacturer's products were perceived to lag slightly behind its competitor on several critical attributes that mattered more to customers than had previously been understood. It was also revealed that the competitor's product cost less to manufacture, and that the competitor had considerable room to lower its costs further. The US manufacturer's response was to close the cost gap by generating ideas that bridged 80% of the cost disadvantage. This was achieved without compromising features that users valued (Narayanan et al., 2012).

The development of new propositions is complex and high risk, so organizations usually adopt a procedural approach. The procedure consists of several phases that enable progress to be monitored, test trials to be conducted, and the results analysed before there is any commitment to the market. The most common new product development process (NPDP) is set out in Figure 8.5.

The NPDP presented here should be considered as a generalization, and it should be understood that the various phases or episodes do not always occur in the linear sequence shown. Actions can overlap or even occur out of sequence, depending on the speed, complexity, and number of people or organizations involved in the NPDP. Apart from some minor issues, the process is the same when developing new products for both consumer and business markets.

Visit the **Online Resource Centre** and follow the weblink to the Product Development and Management Association (PDMA) to learn more about the professional development, information, collaboration, and promotion of new product development and management.

Idea Generation

Ideas can be generated through customers, competitors (through websites and sales literature analysis), market research data (such as reports), R&D, customer service employees, the sales force, project development teams, and secondary data sources such as sales records. What this means is that organizations should foster a corporate culture that encourages creativity and supports people when they bring forward new ideas for product enhancements and other improvements. (See Market Insight 8.4.)

Research Insight 8.4

To take your learning further, you might wish to read this influential paper.

Kohler, T., Matzler, K., and Füller, J. (2009), 'Avatar-based innovation: using virtual worlds for real-world innovation', *Technovation*, 29(6/7), 395–407.

This interesting and topical paper considers the development of new products and services using the virtual world as the source of ideas. Through the integration of user-generated content within various virtual worlds and an interactive new product development process, the paper demonstrates through real cases how companies can tap into customers' innovative potential using the latest technology.

Visit the **Online Resource Centre** to read the abstract and access the full paper.

Market Insight 8.4

Unilever Invites Innovation

The following is a press release issued by Unilever in 2012. It demonstrates how innovation can be a strategically collaborative, open, and flexible activity for organizations.

Collaborate to Innovate: Unilever seeks help with new technical challenges to support sustainable growth

10/10/2012

London/Rotterdam—10th October 2012: Company's new Open Innovation portal receives over 1,000 ideas after six months.

Unilever, one of the world's largest consumer goods manufacturers, has released a new set of challenges to the world's innovation community to help the business deliver on its sustainable growth agenda.

In March 2012, the company's Open Innovation team launched a new online platform which offered experts the opportunity to find some of the technical solutions

it needs to achieve its ambition of doubling the size of its business while reducing its environmental impact, as set out in the Unilever Sustainable Living Plan.

Following the success of the platform, Unilever has now unveiled the details of another three research projects for which its Research & Development department is seeking external know-how.

The company hopes it will receive a similar response to when it announced its first ten open innovation 'wants' earlier this year. The platform has now received more than 1,000 submissions, ranging from ideas which tackle the challenges set by Unilever, to other technical solutions and new product ideas.

'We've been hugely impressed by the quality, ingenuity and inventiveness of the submissions that we've received since we launched our Open Innovation platform six months ago', said Jon Hague, VP Open Innovation, Unilever.

'We have a long track-record of working with external partners to develop new technologies, so we were already very aware of the strength and depth of the

Market Insight 8.4
continued

innovation talent which exists outside of Unilever. However, this was the first time we have shared our research projects in such an open forum and it's very exciting to have tapped into a new community of inventors who share our passion for sustainable innovation and creating a better future for our consumers and the environment.'

Unilever is in advanced discussions with several technology companies as a result of publishing its first set of 'wants' in March. The challenges ranged from technologies which could create lighter and more sustainable packaging, to laundry products which perform just as well with less water and lower temperatures.

The three new 'wants' which Unilever is seeking collaboration on span two of its four global categories, Homecare and Refreshments. They are:

- New technologies which break down fatty deposits left on clothes and hard surfaces in an efficient, odourless and environmentally friendly way. The solution could be incorporated as an ingredient in the detergent formulation or work as a pre-treatment application.

- New technologies which enable us to reduce the sugar in our ready-to-drink teas by 30%, without impacting on their taste or mouthfeel.

- New technologies which enable us to stabilize natural red colour cost-effectively, for use in our fruit and dairy products. The solution must maintain the stability of the colour throughout its shelf life and be water soluble.

All ideas submitted on all 13 wants will be assessed by Yet2.com, an independent open innovation consultancy, before any reach Unilever's Open Innovation team.

Visit the **Online Resource Centre** and complete Internet Activity 8.3 to learn more about how two leading FMCG companies approach the new product development process.

Unilever uses open innovation portal to source fresh product development ideas

Since Unilever's Open Innovation team was founded in 2009, the number of research projects which involve external collaboration has increased from 25% to around 60%.

Source: http://www.unilever.com/mediacentre/pressreleases/2012/collaboratetoinnovate.aspx

1 **What is the motivation for Unilever to open up its innovation processes in this way?**

2 **Make a list of the issues that might arise from this approach to innovation.**

3 **Why is innovating products difficult?**

Screening

All ideas need to be assessed so that only those that meet pre-determined criteria are taken forward. Key criteria include the fit between the proposed new product idea and the overall corporate strategy and objectives. Another involves the views of customers, undertaken using concept testing. Other approaches consider how the market will react to the idea and what effort the organization will need to make if the product is to be brought to market successfully. Whatever approaches are used, screening must be a separate activity to the idea generation stage. If it is not, creativity might be impaired.

Business Planning and Market Analysis

The development of a business plan is crucial, simply because it will indicate the potential and relative profitability of the product. In order to prepare the plan, important information about the size, shape, and dynamics of the market needs to be determined. The resultant profitability forecasts will be significant in determining how and when the product will be developed, if at all.

Product Development and Selection

In many organizations, several product ideas are considered simultaneously. It is management's task to select those that have commercial potential and are in the best interests of the organization and its longer-term strategy, goals, and use of resources. There is a trade-off between the need to test and reduce risk, and the need to go to market and drive income to get a return on the investment committed to the new product. This phase is expensive, so only a limited number of projects are allowed to proceed into development. Prototypes and test versions are developed for those projects that are selected for further development. These are then subjected to functional performance tests, design revisions, manufacturing requirements analysis, distribution analysis, and a multitude of other testing procedures.

Test Marketing

Before committing a new product to a market, most organizations decide to test market the finished product. By piloting and testing the product under controlled real-market conditions, many of the genuine issues as perceived by customers can be raised and resolved while minimizing any damage or risk to the organization and the brand. **Test marketing** can be undertaken using a particular geographical region or specific number of customer locations. The intention is to evaluate the product and the whole marketing programme under real working conditions. Test marketing, or field trials, enables the product and marketing plan to be refined or adapted in the light of market reaction, yet before release to the whole market. See Chapter 3 for more information about test marketing.

Commercialization

To commercialize a new product a launch plan is required. This considers the needs of **distributors**, end-user customers, marketing communication agencies, and other relevant stakeholders. The objective is to schedule all those activities that are required to make the launch successful. These include communications (to inform audiences of the product's capabilities and to position and persuade potential customers), training, and product support for all customer-facing employees.

Any perceived rigidity in this formal process should be disregarded. Many new products come to market via rather different routes, at different speeds and different levels of preparation. For example, LG's product development is closely aligned with its market research. They found that people wanted to get their washing done in one go at the weekend, they were concerned about the environment, and they had little or no experience or desire to do ironing. This led to the development of LG's steam washing machine. This has a large-capacity drum and uses steam rather than water (as in conventional washing machines), which is good for the environment. Steam also means fewer wrinkles, so less ironing (Barda, 2009).

Developing New Service Propositions

So far, the focus has been on the processes associated with developing new products, without reference to services. This is partly because researchers have paid much more attention to the development issues with products, and they perceive the development of new services as either problematic or very similar to that of products. This has changed in recent years as many Western economies have become increasingly service-orientated.

Möller *et al*. (2008), one of the few research groups in this area, develop ideas based on the logic that value creation is key to the development of innovative service offerings and concepts. They distinguish three service innovation strategies: established services within competitive markets, incremental service innovation targeting value-added propositions, and radical service innovation which aims to produce completely novel offerings.

Established services with a relatively stable value creation process are often generated under intense competitive behaviour to improve operational efficiency. Dell is cited as a business based on a simple concept, namely selling computer systems direct to customers. Dell's market leadership is the result of a constant focus on delivering positive product and service experiences to customers.

Incremental service innovation describes a value creation strategy in which services are developed to provide extra value. Working together, the service provider and the client can produce more effective solutions. The prime example is Google which, in addition to providing internet search services for individual consumers, provides search services for corporate clients, including advertisers, content publishers, and site managers. Google continually develops new service applications based on its back-end technology and the use of linked PCs that respond immediately to each query. Google's innovation has resulted in faster response times, greater scalability, and lower costs.

Radical service innovation is concerned with value creation generated through novel or unusual service concepts. This requires new technologies, offerings, or business concepts, and involves radical system-wide changes in existing value systems. MySQL, the world's leading open-source database software producer, uses this approach. By making the source code of the software freely available to everybody, the software is available to everyone to use and/or modify. However, all derivative works must be made available to the original developers. As a result, MySQL have been able to increase the number of users and developers, and subsequently offer their clients improved levels of service. This has led to increased financial performance.

Stages of Service Proposition Development

It is helpful to view proposition innovation in the light of the product/service spectrum introduced at the start of this chapter. Services do not always need to be seen just as an extension or add-on to a product offering; they can also be a way of creating value opportunities for clients.

Shelton (2009) considers service innovation in the context of four stages of solution management maturity. The early stages of innovation maturity are characterized by a product focus with a relatively small amount of services used only to augment and complement the products. The mature stages are characterized by much higher levels of service, some integrated with the products to provide solutions for customer problems.

- Stage 1—in this stage services are used as aftersales product support (e.g. parts and repair services). Service innovation is framed around maintaining the product and ensuring that customers are satisfied with their product purchase. As a result, customers typically view the service and product business as distinct entities.

- Stage 2—this stage is characterized by aftersales services designed to complement the core product. Here, services should improve customer satisfaction with existing products, increase loyalty, and may generate additional purchases. Sheldon refers to Hewlett-Packard's 'PC Tune-Up' which, for a fee, provides a set of diagnostics to assess and manage customers.

- Stage 3—at this stage, the portfolio includes a full line of services and products designed to provide a clearly differentiated offering aimed at solving clients' lifecycle problems. Sheldon refers to Motorola's 'Total Network Care' (TNC) which provides end-to-end support services for wireless networks. Although the service organization is often consolidated into one identifiable business, products are still core to the company. End-user customers see no major perceived boundaries between products and services.

- Stage 4—at this, the highest end of innovation maturity, firms seek to integrate the services dimension as part of their total offer. Known as 'servitization', this involves the provision of an integrated bundle of product/service solutions for the entire lifecycle of their customers, 'from cradle to grave'. These solutions are developed collaboratively with clients and therefore require a deep understanding of the customer's overall business. These firms, often market leaders, generate innovative solutions through buyer/seller collaborative processes. Solutions are developed that are of mutual value. (See Market Insight 8.5 for an example of servitization.)

Market Insight 8.5

Servitization Takes Off in Aerospace

Some organizations offer products and services as an integrated bundle, where the services are an integral part of the core product. This is referred to as 'servitization' and enables customers to create the value they require rather than be dependent on suppliers.

Examples of servitization can be seen in many sectors, but manufacturers have been prominent in developing this form of strategy. Engine manufacturers, such as Rolls-Royce operating in the aerospace industry, do not just offer engines (a product) and neither do they offer engines plus training, delivery, and maintenance services. In order to compete through differentiation rather than price, Rolls-Royce offers commercial airline customers performance-based contracts. Baines *et al*. (2009) report that these contracts link the manufacturer's compensation to product availability and the capability it delivers (e.g. hours flown). Rolls-Royce has registered trademarks for both 'Power by the Hour' and the more inclusive 'TotalCare' contracts.

Market Insight 8.5

continued

Servitization means shifting from selling engines to aerospace solutions

Source: istock.

Such contracts provide airline operators with fixed engine maintenance costs over an extended period of time (e.g. ten years). The TotalCare offering is an example of a product-centric servitization strategy.

In much the same way, GE offers a 'Complete Power Solutions' programme for its aircraft. In this, GE links its jet-engine sales with a suite of financial and operational services, hence enabling a solution across the customer lifecycle.

Sources: Baines *et al*. (2009); Shelton (2009) (See also Market Insight 1.2).

1 **To what extent is servitization a glorified service contract? What is the real value of this approach?**

2 **Make brief notes about the issues customers have when buying high-value, high-technology products.**

3 **Which other industries might make good use of a servitization approach?**

Servitization strategies have been used to create value in a number of different industries. Robinson *et al*. (2002) report their use in the chemical industry, where price-led strategies tend to dominate in a commodity context. What is noticeable is that where commodity chemical firms have implemented servitization, one of the more prominent uses has been to help build relationships and reduce both the attitudinal and physical distance between partner organizations.

Visit the **Online Resource Centre** and complete Internet Activity 8.4 to learn more about how two leading service based organizations approach the service development process.

The Process of Adoption

The process by which individuals accept and use new propositions is referred to as adoption (Rogers, 1983). The different stages in the **process of adoption** are sequential and are characterized by the different factors that are involved at each stage (e.g. the media used by each individual). The process starts with people gaining awareness of a proposition as it moves through various stages of adoption before a purchase is eventually made. Figure 8.6 sets out the various stages in the process of adoption.

In the knowledge stage, consumers become aware of the new proposition. They have little information and have yet to develop any particular attitudes towards the product. Indeed, at this stage consumers are not interested in finding out any more information.

The persuasion stage is characterized by consumers becoming aware that the innovation may be of use in solving a potential problem. Consumers become sufficiently motivated to find out more about the proposition's characteristics, including its features, price, and availability.

In the decision stage, individuals develop an attitude toward the proposition and they reach a decision about whether the innovation will meet their needs. If this is positive they will go on to try the innovation.

During the implementation stage, the innovation is tried for the first time. Sales promotions are often used as samples to allow individuals to test the product without any undue risk. Individuals accept or reject an innovation on the basis of their experience of the trial. Note the way that supermarkets use sampling to encourage people to try new food and drink products. The final confirmation stage is signalled when an individual successfully adopts the proposition on a regular purchase basis without the help of the sales promotion or other incentives.

This model assumes that the adoption stages occur in a predictable sequence, but this is not always the case. Rejection of the innovation can occur at any point, even during implementation and the very early phases of the confirmation stage. Generally, mass communications are more effective in the earlier phases of the adoption process for products that buyers are actively interested in, and more interpersonal forms are more appropriate in later stages, especially implementation and confirmation.

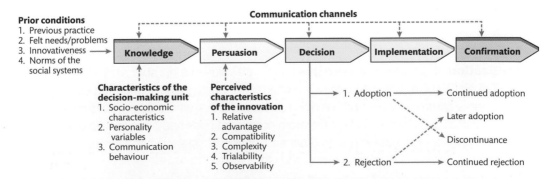

Figure 8.6

Stages in the innovation decision process of adoption

Source: Reprinted from Rogers (1983) with the permission of the Free Press. © 1962, 1971, 1983 by the Free Press.

Diffusion Theory

Consumers may have both functional and emotional motives when purchasing, but customers adopt new propositions at different speeds or timescales. Their different attitudes to risk, and their level of education, experience, and needs, mean that different groups of customers adopt new propositions at different and varying speeds. The rate at which a market adopts an innovation is referred to as the **process of diffusion** (Rogers, 1962). According to Rogers, there are five categories of adopters, as shown in Figure 8.7.

- **Innovators**—this group, which constitutes 2.5% of the buying population, is important because they have to kick-start the adoption process. These people like new ideas, and are often well-educated, young, confident, and financially strong. They are more likely to take risks associated with new propositions. Being an innovator in one category, such as photography, does not mean that a person will be an innovator in other categories. Innovative attitudes and behaviour can be specific to just one or two areas of interest.

- **Early adopters**—this group, 13.5% of the market, is characterized by a high percentage of opinion leaders. These people are very important for speeding up the adoption process. Consequently, marketing communications need to be targeted at these people who, in turn, will stimulate word-of-mouth communications to spread information. Although early adopters prefer to let innovators take all the risks, they enjoy being at the leading edge of innovation, tend to be younger than any other group, and above average in education. Other than innovators, this group reads more publications and consults more salespeople than all others.

- **Early majority**—this group, which forms 34% of the market, is more risk-averse than the previous two groups. This group requires reassurance that the offering works and has been proved in the market. They are above average in terms of age, education, social status, and income. Unlike the early adopters, they tend to wait for prices to fall and prefer more informal sources of information, and are often prompted into purchase by other people who have already purchased.

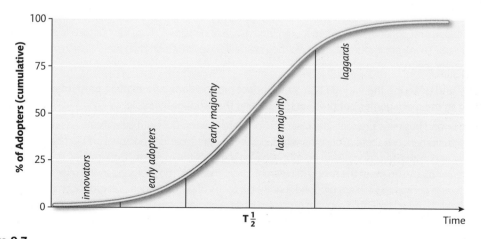

Figure 8.7

The process of diffusion

Source: Rogers (1962): fig. 5.1. © 1955, 2003 by Everett M. Rogers ©. 1962, 1971, 1983 by the Free Press.

- **Late majority**—a similar size to the previous group (34%), the late majority are sceptical of new ideas and only adopt new offerings because of social or economic factors. They read few publications and are below average in education, social status, and income.

- **Laggards**—this group of people, 16% of the buying population, are suspicious of all new ideas and their opinions are very hard to change. Laggards have the lowest income, social status, and education of all the groups, and take a long time to adopt an innovation, if at all.

According to Gatignon and Robertson (1985), the rate of diffusion is a function of the speed at which sales occur, the pattern of diffusion as expressed in the shape of the curve, and the size of the market. This means that diffusion does not occur at a constant or predictable speed; it may be fast or slow. One of the tasks of marketing communications is to speed up the process so that the return on the investment necessary to develop the innovation is achieved as quickly and as efficiently as possible.

Marketing managers need to ensure that diffusion groups are considered when attempting to understand and predict the diffusion process. It is likely that a promotional campaign targeted at innovators and the early majority, and geared to stimulating word-of-mouth communications, will be more successful as a result.

Chapter Summary

To consolidate your learning, the key points from this chapter are summarized here.

- **Explain the nature and distinguishing characteristics of product and service propositions.**

  A proposition encompasses all the tangible and intangible attributes related not just to physical goods but also to services, ideas, people, places, experiences, and even a mix of these various elements. Anything that can be offered for use and consumption, in exchange for money or some other form of value, is referred to as a proposition. Unlike products, services are considered to be processes, and products and services have different distinguishing characteristics. These are based around their intangibility (you can touch a product but not a service), perishability (products can be stored but you cannot store a service), variability (each time a service is delivered it is different but products can be identical), inseparability (services are produced and consumed simultaneously), and a lack of ownership (you cannot take legal possession of a service). These are important because they shape the way in which marketers design, develop, deliver, and evaluate the marketing of services.

- **Identify and describe the various types of product propositions and explain particular concepts relating to the management of products, including the product lifecycle.**

  Consumer and business products are classified in different ways, but both classifications are related to the way customers use them. Consumer products are bought to satisfy personal and family needs, and industrial and business products are bought either as a part of the business's operations or to make other products for resale. To meet the needs of different target markets, most organizations offer a range of products and services which are grouped together in terms of product lines and product mix. Products are thought to move through a sequential pattern of development, referred to as the product lifecycle. It consists of five distinct stages, namely development, birth, growth, maturity, and decline. Each stage of the cycle represents a different set of market circumstances and customer expectations that need to be met with different strategies.

■ **Explain the relationship between product and service offerings and describe the product/service spectrum.**

A service is any act or performance offered by one party to another that is essentially intangible. Consumption of the service does not result in any transfer of ownership even though the service process may be attached to a physical product. There is a spectrum of product/service combinations. At one extreme, there are pure products with no services, such as grocery products. At the other end of the spectrum are pure services where there is no tangible product support, such as education and dentistry. In between, there is a mixture of product/service arrangements. The product/service spectrum recognizes that many products combine physical goods with a service element.

■ **Explore the processes and issues associated with innovating new propositions**

The development of new propositions is complex and high risk, so organizations usually adopt a procedural approach. The procedure consists of several phases that enable progress to be monitored, test trials to be conducted, and the results analysed before there is any commitment to the market. The development of new services follows a similar staged process, whereby additional services are added to a core product until a point is reached where the service and the core product are integrated into a bundled offering. This is known as servitization.

■ **Describe how new propositions are adopted by markets.**

The processes of adoption and diffusion explain the way in which individuals adopt new propositions and the rate at which a market adopts an innovation. The process by which individuals accept and use new propositions is referred to as adoption (Rogers, 1983). The different stages in the adoption process are sequential and are characterized by the different factors that are involved at each stage. The rate at which a market adopts an innovation differs according to an individual's propensity for risk, and is referred to as the process of diffusion (Rogers, 1962).

Review Questions

1 Draw the spectrum of product/service combinations and briefly explain its main characteristics.
2 Identify the three levels that make up a proposition.
3 Describe the three types of convenience good and find examples to illustrate each of them.
4 What are the six types of business products?
5 What is the product lifecycle and what key characteristics make up each of its stages?
6 What are the essential characteristics of services?
7 Now that you have identified these essential characteristics, make brief notes explaining how they affect the marketing of services.
8 What are the main stages associated with the development of new product propositions?
9 What are the main proposition development stages and what is servitization?
10 Why should marketers know about the process of adoption?

Worksheet Summary

To apply the knowledge you have gained from this chapter and test your understanding of innovation and new proposition development visit the **Online Resource Centre** and complete Worksheet 8.1.

 ## Discussion Questions

1   Having read Case Insight 8.1, how should Domino's Pizza maintain their values of speed and service when faced with increased costs/operational times associated with the launch of new propositions?

2   Consider the different types of consumer offering and discuss how this knowledge can assist those responsible for marketing these offerings.

3   Working in small groups, select three service organizations and consider the extent to which they overcome the marketing problems associated with intangibility and variability.

4   As a marketing assistant assigned to a major grocery brand (of your choice), you have noticed that your main brand competitors are pursuing marketing strategies that are significantly different from those of your brand. You have mentioned this to your manager who has asked you to prepare a briefing note explaining the extent to which the product lifecycle might explain these differences. Therefore your task is to prepare a brief report in which you explain the nature of the product lifecycle, consider how it might be used to improve your brand's marketing activities, and from this highlight any difficulties that might arise when using the product lifecycle to develop strategies.

5   Discuss the view that it is not worth the huge investment necessary to develop new propositions, when it is just as easy to copy those of the market leader.

References

Anon. (2012), 'Champions of design: Cohiba', *Marketing*, 15 August, 22.

Baines, T., Lightfoot, H., Peppard, J., Johnson, M., Tiwari, A., Shehab, E., and Swink, M. (2009), 'Towards an operations strategy for product-centric servitization', *International Journal of Operations and Production Management*, 29(5), 494–519

Barda, T. (2009), 'The science of appliances', *Marketer*, May, 25–7.

Berry, L. L. (1980), 'Services marketing is different', *Business, May–June,* 24–30.

Brady, M. K., Bourdeau, B. L., and Heskel, J. (2005), 'The importance of brand cues in intangible service industries: an application to investment services', *Journal of Services Marketing*, 19(6), 401–10.

Chaffey, D., Mayer, R., Johnston, K., and Ellis-Chadwick, F. (2009), *Internet Marketing* (4th edn), Harlow: FT/Prentice Hall.

Clark, N. (2009), 'Knowing when to swing the axe', *Marketing*, February, 30–1.

Drucker, P. F. (1985), 'The discipline of innovation', *Harvard Business Review*, 63(May–June), 67–72.

Gatignon, H. and Robertson, T. S. (1985), 'A propositional inventory for new diffusion research', *Journal of Consumer Research*, 11(March), 849–67.

Ghosh, S. (1998), 'Making business sense of the internet', *Harvard Business Review*, March–April, 127–35.

Grönroos, C. (1990), *Service Management and Marketing: Managing the Moment of Truth in Service Competition*, Lexington, MA: Lexington Books.

Grönroos, C. (2009), 'Marketing as promise management: regaining customer management for marketing', *Journal of Business and Industrial Marketing*, 24(5/6), 351–9.

Kohler, T., Matzler, K., and Füller, J. (2009), 'Avatar-based innovation: using virtual worlds for real-world innovation', *Technovation*, 29(6/7, June), 395–407.

Leistén, J. and Nilsson, M. (2009), '*Crossing the Chasm: Launching and Re-Launching in the Swedish Mobile Phone Industry*, Dissertation, Jönköping International Business School retrieve from: http://hj.diva-portal.org/smash/record.jsf?pid=diva2:158025 accessed 19 March 2009.

Lovelock, C., Vandermerwe, S., and Lewis, B. D. (1999), *Services Marketing: A European Perspective*, Harlow FT/Prentice Hall.

Möller, K., Rajala, R., and Westerlund, M. (2008), 'Service innovation myopia? A new recipe for client/provider value creation', *California Management Review*, 50(3, Spring), 31–48.

Narayanan, A., Padhi, A., and Williams, J. (2012), 'Designing products for value', *McKinsey Quarterly*, October, retrieve from: https://www.mckinseyquarterly.com/Operations/Product_Development/Designing_products_for_value_3023 accessed 12 November 2012.

Osborn, A. (2011), World's biggest cigar festival opens in Havana, *The Telegraph*, 24 February, retrieve from: http://www.telegraph.co.uk/journalists/andrew-osborn/8345341/Worlds-biggest-cigar-festival-opens-in-Havana.html accessed 19 November 2012.

Olson, J. C. and Jacoby, J. (1972) 'Cue utilization in the quality perception process', in M. Venkatesan (ed.), *Proceedings of the Third Annual Conference of the Association for Consumer Research,* Association for Consumer Research, 167–79.

Ozer, M. (2003), 'Process implications of the use of the internet in new product development: a conceptual analysis', *Industrial Marketing Management*, 32(6, August), 517–30.

Robinson, T., Clarke-Hill, C. M., and Clarkson, R. (2002), 'Differentiation through service: a perspective from the commodity chemicals sector', *Service Industries Journal*, 22(3, July), 149–66.

Rogers, E. M. (1962), *Diffusion of Innovations*, New York: Free Press.

Rogers, E. M. (1983), *Diffusion of Innovations* (3rd edn), New York: Free Press.

Shelton, R. (2009), 'Integrating product and service innovation', *Research Technology Management*, 52(3, May/June), 38–44

Shostack, G. L. (1977), 'Breaking free from product marketing', *Journal of Marketing*, 41(April), 73–80.

Tynan, C. and McKechnie, S (2009), 'Experience marketing: a review and reassessment', *Journal of Marketing Management*, 25(5/6), 501–17.

Vargo, S. L. and Lusch, R. F. (2004), 'Evolving to a new dominant logic for marketing', *Journal of Marketing*, 68(1, January), 1–17

Wood, L. (1990), 'The end of the product life cycle? Education says goodbye to an old friend', *Journal of Marketing Management*, 6(2), 145–55.

Chapter 9
Price Decisions

Learning Outcomes

After studying this chapter, you will be able to:

▶ Define price, and understand its relationship with costs, quality, and value

▶ Explain the concept of price elasticity of demand

▶ Describe how customers and consumers perceive price

▶ Explain cost-, competitor-, demand-, and value-oriented approaches to pricing

▶ Understand how to price new offerings

▶ Explain how pricing operates in the business-to-business setting

Case Insight 9.1

3M is an innovative $23bn diversified technology company creating products to make the world healthier, safer, and more productive. Well-known brands include Scotch, Post-it, Scotchgard, Thinsulate, and Scotch-Brite. We speak to Andrew Hicks, European Market Development Manager, to find out how the company developed its pricing strategy for an innovative new product, the Visual Attention Service.

First set up in 1902 and now employing around 75,000 people worldwide, 3M has operations in more than 60 countries. It produces thousands of innovative products for customers and its 45 technology platforms touch nearly every aspect of modern life. The company has applied its expertise in RFID technology to deliver biometric passports and its healthcare knowledge to provide hospitals with infection prevention and detection solutions, and in 2008 it launched the MPro range of pocket projectors.

3M's enduring success is built on constant innovation. To drive this, it invests heavily in R&D, spending over $1.40bn in 2008. It is fundamentally a science-based company, producing thousands of imaginative products and leading in scores of markets—from health care and highway safety to office products and optical films for LCD displays. The company's success begins with our ability to apply our technologies, often in combination, to an endless array of real-world customer needs.

We are organized into seven business divisions: Consumer and Office, Electro and Communications, Health Care, Industrial and Transportation Business Safety, Security and Protection Services, Optical Systems, and Display and Graphics. The final division is a world leader in films that brighten the displays on electronic products, such as flat-panel computer monitors, cellular phones, personal digital assistants, and liquid crystal display (LCD) televisions.

The Digital-out-of-Home (DooH) department within the Display and Graphics division was set up in 2007. It encompasses electronic display technologies as well as software for content delivery and tools to optimize the performance of advertising messaging. DooH set up what became the 3M Visual Attention Service (3M VAS) to complement this portfolio. The service allows designers of creative messages to assess and optimize their visual impact before committing to production.

Researchers within the traffic safety business of 3M had identified that predictive attention modelling may have a commercial opportunity within the advertising industry. In the feasibility stage, the technical capability, projected costs, and potential market opportunity were assessed to determine whether to proceed with the investment required to bring the concept to market. At this stage, we undertook desk research to determine the distribution of our target market—creative agencies—by size, turnover, and specialization. Primary research with about 15 agencies helped to determine the value they would place on such a service and their likely throughput of images. These customers were given access to a beta version of the site to assess how they would use such a system. Combining the data sets allowed an estimate to be made of the potential usage levels for such a service. Through ethnographic research, 3M employees work-shadowed designers to understand the creative workflow and determine where in the process 3M VAS could offer greatest value. This research informed both the market opportunity assessment and the development of the appropriate marketing communications for this audience.

Case Insight 9.1
continued

Once we determined that there was a likely market for the product, we looked at the service, the business plan, and the marketing communications plan. We knew we had to undertake a limited release of the service to allow feedback to be gained from lead users to validate the value and market opportunity. Finally, we undertook a full commercial global launch of the service, backed by advertising and promotional campaigns, and continued customer research to refine the offer.

However, as this service was new to the world and was also not a direct substitution for an existing service, there was no reference pricing in the marketplace. When potential customers were asked what they were prepared to pay, the value they perceived varied dramatically depending on the nature of the creative work the system was being used to assess. For example, the media space costs for a national billboard campaign for a major promotion would cost hundreds of thousands of pounds.

Anything that could validate the visual effectiveness of the creative design for adverts for this type of campaign, before committing the ads to print, would be extremely valuable to the advertiser. However, the number of campaigns of this type and the quantity of creative designs considered for these campaigns is relatively small. So this would be a high-cost low-volume model.

On the other hand, thousands of designs are created every day for packaging, advertising and other marketing communications, where the level of investment and associated risk is much lower. In these cases 3M VAS would still be of value, but the price that could be charged would be considerably lower—a low-cost high-volume model.

Therefore the question for 3M was: should it launch a low-volume high-priced product or a high-volume low-priced product?

3M's Visual Attention Service tests promotional material using visual heat maps

Introduction

When did you last buy something that you thought was really expensive? Did you wonder if others would think it was expensive too? Exactly when is a price expensive and when is it not? How do companies set prices? What procedures do they use? Since price wars are self-defeating, why do companies get involved in them in the first place? These are just some of the questions we set out to consider in this chapter.

Our understanding of pricing and costing has mainly been developed through accounting practice. Economics also contributes to our understanding of pricing through models of supply and demand, operating at an aggregate level (i.e. across all customers in an industry). Psychology contributes greatly to our understanding of customers' perceptions of prices. Marketing as a field integrates all these components to provide a better understanding of how the firm manipulates price to achieve higher profits and maintain satisfied customers.

In this chapter, we provide insight into how customers respond to price changes, what economists call **price elasticity** of demand. We consider pricing decisions in relation to developing differentiated or low-cost approaches and the pricing of services. As a topic, pricing is the most difficult component of the marketing mix to understand because the price of an offering links to the cost of all the many and various elements that coalesce to make a particular proposition. The marketing manager rarely controls costs and prices of a particular offering, and usually refers to the accounting and finance department, or the marketing controller, to set prices.

Finally, we also provide an indication of how to set prices for new offerings, and how to change prices for existing offerings. As making price changes often invokes a competitive response, since competitors may also drop prices, we include a section on how to avoid price wars. In some markets, a company does not control its own price-setting, so we also consider some of the markets where prices are regulated by government.

The Concept of Pricing and Cost

Pricing

Pricing is a complex component of the marketing mix. The term **price** has come to encompass any and all of the following meanings: 'the amount of money expected, required, or given in payment for something; an unwelcome experience or action undergone or done as a condition of achieving an objective; decide the amount required as payment for something offered for sale; and discover or establish the price of something for sale' (Oxford Dictionaries 2012). In marketing terms, we consider price as the amount the customer has to pay or exchange to receive an offering. For example, when purchasing a Burger King meal for children (incorporating a burger, small apple fries, Tropicana drink, and toy), the price exchanged for the meal might be, say, $3.99, £3.59, 295 rupees, or 30 yuan depending on where you live. The £3.59 element is the price, the assigned numerical monetary worth of the kid's hamburger meal. However, the notion of pricing an offering is often confused with a number of other key marketing concepts, particularly cost and value.

Visit the **Online Resource Centre** and follow the weblink to the Professional Pricing Society (PPS) to learn more about pricing and the pricing profession.

Table 9.1 Examples of fixed and variable costs	
Fixed costs	**Variable costs**
Manufacturing plant and equipment	Equipment servicing costs
Office buildings	Energy costs
Cars and other vehicles	Mileage allowances
Salaries	Overtime and bonus payments
Professional service fees (e.g. legal, architectural)	Professional services fees (e.g. legal) in a business with a strong regulatory regime (e.g. pharmaceuticals)

Proposition Costs

To price an offering properly, we need to know what the offering costs us to make, produce, or buy. Cost represents the total money, time, and resources sacrificed to produce or acquire an offering. For example, the costs incurred to produce the Burger King kid's hamburger meal discussed above will include the cost of heat and light in the restaurant, advertising and sales promotion costs, costs of rent or of the mortgage interest accrued from owning the restaurant, management and staffing costs, and the franchise fees paid to Burger King's central headquarters to cover training, management, and marketing. Furthermore, there are costs associated with the distribution of the product components to and from farms and other catering suppliers to the restaurants. There are the costs of computer systems and purchasing systems. There are the costs of the packaging, bags, and extras like gifts and toys.

Typically, a firm will determine what their **fixed costs** are, and what their **variable costs** are, for each proposition. These items vary for individual industries, but Table 9.1 provides a general indication of what is included. Fixed costs do not vary according to the number of units of goods made or services sold, so are independent of sales volume. In a Burger King restaurant, this includes the cost of heating and lighting, rent, and staffing costs. In contrast, variable costs vary according to the number of units of goods made or services sold. For example, with the production of Burger King hamburger meals, when sales and demand decrease, fewer raw goods such as hamburger ingredients, product packaging, and novelty items such as toys are required, so less spending on raw materials is necessary. Conversely, when sales increase, more raw materials are used and spending rises.

The Relationship between Pricing and Proposition Costs

The relationship between price and costs is important because costs should be substantially less than the price assigned to a proposition, otherwise the firm will not sell sufficient units to obtain sufficient revenues to cover costs and make long-term profits (see following equations):

Total revenue $=$ volume sold $\times$ unit price

Profit $=$ total revenue-total costs

The price at which a proposition is set is strategically important because increases in price have a disproportionately positive effect on profits and decreases in price have a disproportionately negative effect on profits. For example, in one study (Baker *et al*., 2010: 5) it was identified that:

- a 1% improvement in price achieves an 8.7% improvement in operating profit;
- a 1% improvement in variable costs only achieves a 5.9% improvement in operating profit;
- a 1% improvement in volume sales achieves a 2.8% improvement in operating profit;
- a 1% improvement in fixed costs achieves only a 1.8% improvement in operating profits.

Therefore, when possible, we should increase prices every time. However, deciding how to price a proposition is not simple. Take the example presented earlier for Burger King. A firm like Burger King might well have 100 products on any one restaurant menu (including meals, individual burgers, ice creams, drinks, salads, etc.) in any one country. If we bear in mind that different countries have slightly different menus to incorporate local tastes (e.g. the Premium Kuro Burger® in Japan, where the product is served in a black bun, and the Hammour Royale® available in Jordan and much of the Middle East), we can imagine that, worldwide, Burger King must have an enormous menu of products, despite the appearance of standardization. But how do we cost and price each individual product? The first step is to determine costs but, in any one restaurant, how do we allocate fixed costs such as heat and light, rent and tax, to each of the individual products sold? Once we've allocated the fixed costs, we need to determine variable costs for each product. Once we've allocated fixed costs and determined the variable costs associated with a product, we set its initial price. But costs of components, such as heat and light, and other costs change constantly. How do we determine whether or not we need to change our prices on an item after we've set them because of changes in component costs? After all, we can't keep changing prices every time a component cost changes. So, at what point do we change a product's price?

From this short example, we can see that determining a product's cost is complex. Because of the cost of information, to increase the accuracy of the cost data, we need to spend more time collecting and analysing the data. Determining costs is an exercise where we trade-off accuracy with the benefits and costs of data collection, storage, and processing (Babad and Balachandran 1993). Determining costs and prices is more difficult when organizations are divided into separate profit centres selling on to other divisions within the same company, especially when these adopt inefficient **transfer pricing** mechanisms (Ward 1993). For example, Airbus, the airline company owned by EADS (European Aeronautic Defence and Space Company), assembles its planes using parts made in several European countries. When these parts are made by the respective divisions, they are sold on, using a process known as transfer pricing, to the main holding company which assembles the plane from its component parts.

But it's not just costs that matter; we might observe changes in demand for our products, as customers' desires change. In setting pricing levels, we must consider our customers' perceptions of prices.

Customer Perceptions of Price, Quality, and Value

Researchers are concerned with how individuals react to the way products are priced, questioning how consumers perceive prices and why they perceive them as they do. Here, we take into account individual perceptions of proposition quality and value, and their relationship to customer response to prices.

Proposition Quality

Quality is a very important concept when considering proposition pricing levels. Quality is defined as 'the standard of something as measured against other things of a similar kind; the degree of excellence of something; a distinctive attribute or characteristic possessed by someone or something' (Oxford Dictionaries, 2012). In this context, the quality of goods and services relates to standards to which that offering performs as a need-satisfier. For example, a very-high-quality car will satisfy both our aesthetic needs for aerodynamic beauty and our ego and functional needs for high-performance road-handling, speed, and power. But quality is not a single standard in an offering. It encompasses many standards as there are many levels at which our needs might or might not be satisfied.

Quality is multifaceted (i.e. different functional and non-functional needs) and multilayered (i.e. differing levels or intensities of satisfaction). Because each person has his/her own definition of quality, we prefer to talk of 'perceived quality'. We find consumers have differing views of the quality of the offering they have purchased; for example, some might be very dissatisfied, and some highly satisfied, with exactly the same offering.

The Relationship between Quality and Pricing Levels

The relationship between price and perceived quality is complex. There is an assumption that as price increases, so does quality, and that in general price reflects quality. However, research has demonstrated that there is usually only a weak relationship between price and perceived quality, although this is category dependent (Gerstner, 1985). For example, 'snob' consumers in the fashion clothing and perfume sectors (see Amaldoss and Jain, 2005; Yeoman and McMahon-Beattie, 2006) assume that higher prices reflect higher-quality garments and fragrances. The idea that price indicates quality (**perceived quality**) assumes that prices are objectively determined by market forces. In truth, people within firms set prices, often dispassionately, so as to try to obtain the maximum profit possible. Various studies to determine whether or not price bears a relation to quality found that a general price–perceived quality relationship does not exist (Gerstner, 1985; Zeithaml, 1988), except perhaps for wine and perfume (Zeithaml, 1988). Völckner and Hofmann (2007) conducted a meta-analysis of studies investigating the price–perceived quality relationship published between 1989 and 2006, and found that the price effect on perceived quality had decreased. Interestingly, they also found that the price–quality relationship is stronger in studies that investigate higher-priced products and use samples from European countries, but is weaker for services, durable goods, and respondents who are familiar with the product.

However, a study designed to understand the relationship between price and quality when price information is available online (Boyle and Lathrop 2009) found that US consumers believe that higher prices correspond to higher quality for **consumer durables** (e.g. cars, televisions), but are less likely to perceive this with non-durables (e.g. foodstuffs).

The Relationship between Perceived Value, Product Quality, and Pricing Levels

Value is defined as 'the regard that something is held to deserve; importance, worth or useful-ness of something; principles or standards of behaviour; one's judgement of what is important in life; the numerical amount denoted by an algebraic term; a magnitude, quantity, or number' (Oxford Dictionaries, 2012). In marketing terms, value refers to what we get for what we pay. It is often expressed as the equation:

$$\text{Value} = \frac{\text{quality}}{\text{price}}$$

This approach to value indicates that to increase a customer's perception of the value of an offering, we must either lower the price or increase the quality. In some ways, this is a simplistic conception of value. There are other intervening effects on the value we perceive a proposition to hold. Sometimes our initial assessment is faulty, or needs reconsideration. Sometimes as customers we are not skilled in recognizing or evaluating quality; for example, the average wine drinker would not regard him/herself as a wine connoisseur and so would find it hard to evaluate product quality properly.

Influences on Customer Price Perceptions

A Framework for Price Perception Formation

How we perceive prices as customers can be summarized in a theoretical framework (see Figure 9.1). In this framework, price perceptions are formed based on a variety of antecedents. Once we see a price, we make a judgement. This judgement is a newly formed price perception which affects our willingness to pay, which in turn affects our purchase behaviour. Price percep-tions are affected by prior beliefs, prior knowledge of reference prices, prior experiences with the product or brand under consideration, price consciousness (i.e. how aware we are of prices), our own price sensitivities (how much we are prepared to pay for things), customer characteris-tics, and cultural factors. We compare the price we see with internal reference prices (what we know of prices from experience) and external reference prices (what others tell us things should cost, perhaps through price comparison websites). **Reference prices** are price bands that

Research Insight 9.1

To take your learning further, you might wish to read this influential paper.

Völckner, F. and Hofmann, J. (2007), 'The price-perceived quality relationship: a meta-analytic review and assessment of its determinants', *Marketing Letters*, **18(3), 181–96.**

This article uses a meta-analytic approach to evaluate various studies performed between 1989 and 2006 to provide evidence that there is an increasingly weakening relationship between price and perceived quality.

@ **Visit the Online Resource Centre to read the abstract and access the full paper.**

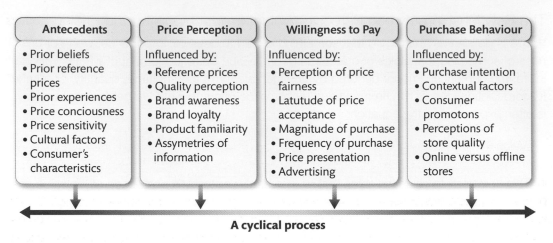

Figure 9.1

A framework for price perception formation

Source: Mendoza and Baines (2012).

customers use to judge the purchase price of offerings against. Reference prices can be viewed as predictive price expectations brought about through prior experience with those offerings or through word-of-mouth discussions with others.

Price perception formation is influenced by exposure to reference prices (internal and external), quality perceptions, brand awareness, brand loyalty, product familiarity, memory of prices (paid previously and seen previously), and asymmetries of information (the extent to which they do not know various factors about those offerings). Price perceptions affect customers' willingness to pay. Willingness to pay is influenced by perceptions of the fairness of prices set, latitude of price acceptance (customers appear willing to accept a price within a range of prices, suggesting a 'price zone of tolerance'), magnitude (absolute price) and frequency of purchase, price presentation (how prices are presented might produce different levels of willingness to pay), and advertising.

Actual purchase behaviour is then influenced by purchase intention, contextual factors (e.g. store format, location, timing, and out-of-stock situations), promotions (e.g. in-store and external promotions), perceptions of store quality, and whether or not the customer is online or in-store, partly because it is much easier to comparison shop online than it is in-store. However, price perception formation is a dynamic process. In other words, the framework indicates that once the purchase behaviour occurs, there is a recalibration of the consumer's price perception because new purchase experiences and new information may provide the stimulus for that recalibration. Therefore, the whole process is cyclical.

In the next section, we consider a number of key elements within the price perception process: willingness to pay, price consciousness, and pricing cues.

Willingness to Pay

In an online consumer survey (Sheth *et al.*, 2006) in which American consumers were asked to provide their perceptions of price (i.e. positive, negative, or neutral) across a range of product and service categories, around half of the respondents (53%) had strongly negative perceptions of the price of replacement razor cartridges and prescription drugs. Just over a quarter of respondents (27%) regarded airline pricing negatively. In contrast, only around one in ten respondents (8%) had such negative price perceptions about computers. Most consumers had neutral opinions on household appliance pricing. It appears that we are able to memorize certain prices for some items, and when companies deviate from those prices we perceive them as unfair. A key question is why some consumers see one proposition's price as fair and others don't? If we are to price an offering according to customer needs, we should understand which customers think is a fair price to pay, or what they expect to pay, or what they think others would pay.

Price Consciousness

In addition to deciding whether or not a price is fair, or what they expect to pay, or what significant others would pay, we also need to know whether or not customers are conscious of prices in a particular category. Most people do not have a good knowledge of prices. Think of your parents or a relative significantly older than you. Do they know the ticket price for a gig? Do you know the price of a good-quality dining table? As an industrial buyer, how much should you pay for the installation and servicing of a new HR system, say Peoplesoft, designed to keep records for 5,000 staff? These examples indicate that our experience of prices contributes to what we know about reference prices. Our experience is limited to what we have done previously. There are certain groups of grocery items that supermarket shoppers are more likely to know, and it is these items that supermarkets frequently discount, and advertise, to attract shoppers, rather than other lesser-known items, where prices may even be raised. Everyday items such as bread, milk, and tins of baked beans are often discounted because shoppers assume that, because these items are discounted, all other items must also be discounted. So, if people do not know the prices of particular offerings, how can they determine whether or not those prices are fair?

Pricing Cues

To be kind to grocery shoppers, estimating reference prices is subject to seasonality for some items including flowers, fruit, and vegetables (particularly exotic varieties from abroad), quality and sizes of items are not universal across companies' offerings, product designs vary over time, and customers may not purchase some goods frequently (Anderson and Simester 2003). Instead, when customers assess prices, they estimate value using **pricing cues** because they do not always know the true cost and price of the item that they are purchasing. These pricing cues include sale signs, odd-number pricing, the purchase context, and price bundling and rebates.

- *Sale signs:* Sale signs act as cues, indicating a bargain to be had. This entices the customer to purchase because it suggests to the buyer that the item is desirable to all customers and therefore may not be available if they are not quick enough to buy it. The sale sign uses the persuasive device of scarcity. The scarcer we perceive an offering to be, the more we are likely to want it (Cialdini 1993), often regardless of whether we even need it.

- *Odd-number pricing* Another pricing cue is the use of odd-number endings—prices that end in nine. Have you ever wondered why the Nintendo Wii you bought was, say, $149, or £119, or SEK1249? Why not simply round it up to $150, £120, or SEK1250? According to Anderson and Simester (2003), raising the price of a woman's dress in a national mail order catalogue from $34 to $39 increased demand by 33%, but demand remained unchanged when the price was raised to $44! The question is why did the increase in demand take place when there was an increase in price? It is unlikely that there would have been such an increase if the item had been priced at $38. The reason for this is that we perceive the first price as relative to a reference price of £30 (which is £33 rounded down to the nearest unit of ten) and more expensive, whereas the second price of $39 we perceive as cheaper than a reference price of $40 (which we rounded up to the nearest ten). (See Market Insight 9.1.)

Market Insight 9.1

The Price Is Right?

Consider a situation where you are in a coffee shop. Let's assume that it sells high-quality loose coffee beans. You are offered a choice of promotional offers on Brazilian Santos coffee beans. Their original price is £7.24 per 500g. Your choice of promotional offers is 33% extra free or 33% off the price. Which is the better offer or are they both the same? Make your choice now before reading on.

Now consider that you are in TK Maxx and you are looking to buy a particular branded jacket. Let's say it's a Ralph Lauren jacket. Its original price was £540. However, you see that it has been discounted first by 20% and then by a further 25%. Let's assume that for some reason you cannot see the final price. Would you prefer to take this double discount deal or one where the jacket was discounted once by 40%? Make your choice now before reading on.

If we revisit the coffee bean offer, the 33% extra free means we get 665g for £7.24, which is equivalent to 1.09p per gram. The 33% discount means that we get 500g for £4.85, which is equivalent to 0.97p per gram. So the better deal is the price discount, and price discounting by 33% is not the same as offering 33% extra free.

On the jacket offer, given that the original price was £540, a 20% first discount followed by a further 25% discount would mean a final price of £324. A one-off discount of 40% would mean a final price of £324. In other words, the two discounts are actually the same.

Sources: Anon. (2012a); Chen *et al*. (2012).

1 **Did you get both answers correct? If you did your mathematics is perfect and you need**

never worry again about misperceiving prices. If not, how will this knowledge affect your future promotional price shopping behaviour?

2 **When was the last time you bought a discounted product? What did you buy and why?**

3 **Ask your non-marketing friends or classmates to read the insight above and see if they get it right.**

When is a sale price a bargain?
Source: istock © jimkruger.

- *Purchase context* Our perception of risk is greater if we are continually reminded of it than if we consider it only at the point of purchase. For example, gyms use the technique of charging a monthly fee, even though they often demand a one-year membership agreement, for precisely this reason. In fact, a monthly price (instead of an annual, semi-annual, or quarterly charge) drives a higher level of gym attendance as customers are more regularly reminded of their purchase. So, the way you set your price does not just influence demand but also

Research Insight 9.2

To take your learning further, you might wish to read this influential paper.

Gourville, J. and Soman, D. (2002), 'Pricing and the psychology of consumption', *Harvard Business Review*, **September, 90–6.**

This is a useful article summarizing how marketing managers should consider not only the price at which customers are likely to purchase an offering but how the way that price is set also affects consumption. This article suggests that marketers might counter-intuitively want to draw customers' attention to the price paid so that they can achieve greater value in using the offering and generate a longer-term impact on customer retention. The article has strong implications for organizations selling subscriptions and memberships.

Visit the **Online Resource Centre** to read the abstract and access the full paper.

drives consumption (Gourville and Soman, 2002). Research shows that if we are exposed to higher-priced items first, our reference prices are anchored at the higher level, whereas if we are exposed to lower prices, they are anchored at the lower level (Smith and Nagle, 1995). Therefore it makes sense to redesign catalogues to include more expensive items in the earlier pages (Nunes and Boatwright, 2001) or in an online store to show the most expensive items on a page first by default (though the customer should be able to sort them afterwards if they wish). Location also has an impact on price perceptions. For example, we are prepared to pay more for a drink of, say, Absolut vodka from the hotel mini-bar than we are from the hotel bar or for an equivalent measure from a bottle from the supermarket. This indicates the context-specific nature of price perceptions.

Visit the **Online Resource Centre** and complete Internet Activity 9.1 to learn more about the impact that the purchase context (e.g. time of day, week, online versus telephone booking, etc.) has on the pricing of budget airline services.

Price Bundling and Rebates

Marketers highlight their prices to customers by bundling other products and services into an offering to make the price look more reasonable. For example, magazines frequently bundle gifts in with the magazine to make it appear more attractive; this is called **pure price bundling**. Sunday newspapers (in Britain, France, Thailand, Sweden) often contain numerous supplements (e.g. fashion, entertainment, property) to make the newspaper appear greater value for money. New cars are frequently sold with three years' warranty on parts to provide the customer with the knowledge that they will not have to pay for any repairs within the warranty period. Amazon had an offer where if you buy a Nintendo Wii, you also receive the Wii Sports game, one wireless Wii remote, and one Nunchuk (so-called **mixed price bundling**).

But price bundling does not always mean that the company needs to give the customer other items. We might simply be offered a rebate, i.e. given money back. Credit card companies offer cashback schemes on money spent on their credit cards as a proportion of the total amount spent.

Pricing Objectives

How a company prices its offerings depends on what its pricing objectives are. Typically, these can be financial with offerings priced to maximize profit or sales or to achieve a satisfactory level of profits or sales, or a particular return on investment. Companies may price by offering discounts for quick payment. A firm's pricing objectives could be marketing-based, e.g. pricing to achieve a particular market share (so-called market penetration pricing), or to position the brand so that it is perceived to be of a certain quality. Sometimes, companies price their propositions just to survive, e.g. pricing to discourage new competitors from entering the market by pricing propositions at a lower rate or lowering prices to maintain sales volumes when competitors lower their prices. Alternatively, a company might price to avoid price wars, maintaining prices at levels similar to its competitors—so-called competitor-oriented pricing. Finally, a company may price to achieve certain social goals. The important consideration is whether or not the pricing objective is reasonable and measurable. Often, companies pursue more than one pricing objective simultaneously, and some pricing objectives may be incompatible with each other. For example, pricing to increase cash flow by offering quick payment discounts is not compatible with maximizing profitability. However, it is compatible with obtaining a satisfactory profitability, as long as the discounts offered are not greater than the cost of the offerings sold.

Pricing Approaches

Price setting depends on various factors, including how price affects demand, how sales revenue is linked to price, how cost is linked to price, and how investment costs are linked to price (Doyle, 2000). Price setting also depends on how sales revenue relates to price. Raising prices tends to increase revenue up to a point, but then further increases in unit price produce declining increases in revenue. The relationship between price and sales revenue follows a bell curve (see Figure 9.2).

Costs also tend to vary with price in a linear fashion as higher prices reduce volume sales, producing lower total costs (see Figure 9.3). Third, investment costs, including both **working**

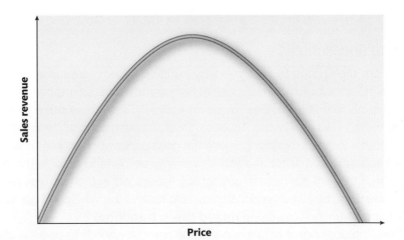

Figure 9.2

How price relates to sales revenue

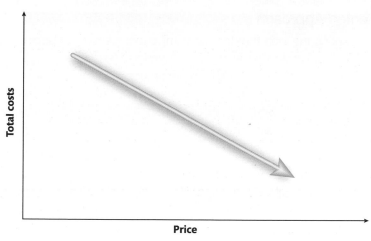

Figure 9.3
How price relates to total costs

capital and **fixed capital** (cost of plant and machinery etc.), also affect prices, with lower prices tending to require higher sales volume targets to be set with correspondingly higher levels of investment. Investments tend to be made at fixed intervals (e.g. on six-monthly cycles), with investment costs dropping compared with price increases (and sales volumes decreases), and so the relationship between investment and price looks something like a downward staircase (see Figure 9.4).

Broadly, there are four types of pricing approaches, each of which is described in the following sections:

1 the cost-oriented approach (i.e. prices set based on costs);
2 the demand-oriented approach (i.e. prices set based on price sensitivity and demand);
3 the competitor-oriented approach (i.e. prices set based on competitors' prices);
4 the value-oriented approach (i.e. prices based on what customers believe to offer value).

Figure 9.4
How price relates to investment costs

The Cost-Oriented Approach

This approach advances the idea that the most important element of pricing is the cost of the component resources that make up the product. Therefore the marketer sells output at the highest price possible, regardless of the firm's own preference or costs. If that price is high enough compared with costs, the firm earns a profit and stays in business. If not, either the firm finds a way of increasing the price or lowering costs or both, or they go out of business (Lockley, 1949). The cost-oriented approach considers the total costs of a proposition in the pricing equation but does not take into account non-cost factors, e.g. brand image, degree of prestige in ownership, or effort expended.

One approach to determining price is using mark-up pricing, often used in the retail sector. This method operates on the base of a set percentage mark-up. When used, the cost-oriented method leads to the use of list prices, with single prices set for all customers. We simply add a mark-up to the cost of X% and this constitutes the price. In British supermarket retailing the mark-up is around 6–8%, but in American supermarket retailing it is often around 4% or less. Mark-ups on wine served in restaurants are typically between 200% and 300%. The cost-oriented approach requires us first to determine the price we set that just covers our costs. This is known as break-even pricing. It represents the point at which our total costs and our total revenues are exactly equal.

To exemplify the concept of mark-up pricing further, we can use the example of a computer company selling high-quality laptop computers, which cost of £1,000 per unit to make. Suppose that the computer company uses the mark-up pricing method, adding 66.7% (or 0.67 when expressed as a decimal number between 0 and 1 and rounded up to two significant figures). The final price set is given by:

$$\text{Sales price (£)} = (\text{mark-up}^* \times \text{cost}) + \text{cost} = (0.67 \times 1{,}000) + 1{,}000 = £1{,}670$$

*Note: mark-up is expressed as a decimal between 0 and 1 (divide mark-up percentage by 100 to get a mark-up figure)

It is important to note that the gross profit margin (i.e. the proportion of the revenue which is profit) is not the same as the mark-up percentage (which is a proportion of cost). The gross profit margin in the above example is given by:

$$\text{Gross margin (\%)} = (\text{mark-up/sales price}) \times 100 = (670/1{,}670) \times 100 = 40.11\%$$

If we consider that in a supply chain there is typically more than one customer interaction, as we move along the supply chain, each partner takes their share, adding to the costs and the final selling price. A toy (e.g. a teddy bear) bought by a UK importer from a Chinese toy manufacturer based in Hong Kong, typically free on board (which means all costs after shipping are borne by the importer), brought to Britain, warehoused, stored, financed, and eventually sold at £5.90 (in cases of 12), may well have cost around £4.50 to that importer. The eventual retail price would probably be around the £10 retail price point, i.e. £9.99. The mark-up here for the retailer is expressed by:

$$\text{MU (\%)} = [(\text{sales price/cost}) - 1] \times 100 = [(£9.99/£5.90) - 1] \times 100 = 69\%$$

The mark-up for the importer is much lower at 31% = [(£5.90/£4.50) − 1] × 100. However, the importer may well buy a container of the teddy bears, comprising say 4,800 individual teddy bears (400 boxes, each containing 12 units), and sell these over the three months between August and October for the Christmas retail season. The retailer, by contrast, may sell only six boxes of 12 during the period October to December, so the retailer has to make a higher profit on a smaller volume with a wider range of items to give the customer some choice.

The cost-oriented approach does mean that we have to use a mark-up pricing approach. In some industries, prices are based on fixed formulae, set with a supplier's costs in mind. For example, in the ethical prescription pharmaceutical industry in France, Italy, and Spain government-fixed formulae dictate prices with limited scope for pharmaceutical manufacturers to negotiate, whereas in the UK and Germany the tradition has been for the country's national health authorities not to fix individual product prices but to set an overall level of profitability with which the pharmaceutical manufacturer must agree, based on a submission of their costs (Attridge, 2003).

The Demand-Oriented Approach

With the demand approach to pricing, the firm sets prices according to how much customers are prepared to pay. One of the best-known types of companies to operate this approach to pricing is the airline industry, where different groups of customers pay different amounts for airline seats with varying levels of service attached. Most airline companies operate three types of cabin service. Emirates, for instance, offers First Class, Business Class, and Economy with the following core benefits.

- First Class—offers wide aisles and individualized comfortable sleeper seats (and separate cabins with their own mini-bar and vanity desk on selected long-haul flights), seven-course meals on long-haul flights, a selection of fine wines, an award-winning in-flight entertainment service, complimentary limousine transfer service, and free entry into the Emirates Lounge executive club at selected airports.

- Business Class—offers complimentary limousine transfer service, enhanced legroom between seats (but less than First Class), double seating arrangements, luxury seating transforming into a lie flat bed, an award-winning in-flight entertainment service (but with fewer options than First Class), five-course meals on long-haul flights, and free entry into the Emirates Lounge executive club at selected airports.

- Economy Class—comfortable seating with seating arrangements in banks of three to five seats, reclining seating, and an award-winning in-flight individual entertainment service.

Other benefits, including premier access through immigration lanes, instant seat upgrades, and priority seats, are available through the Emirates membership and loyalty scheme, which has three tiers of membership, blue, silver, and gold, depending on the number of miles a passenger has flown with the carrier. In contrast, the low-cost carriers in Europe, such as Ryanair and easyJet, operate fairly sophisticated yield management approaches via online booking systems which set prices to ensure that planes operate at full capacity. Tickets are usually priced very cheaply initially to increase demand (and generally priced substantially less than the national airline carriers) and then prices increase over time as demand increases.

Companies operating a demand pricing policy should be wary of overcharging their customers, particularly where customers' requests are urgent. Examples include emergency purchases such as funeral services, or prescription pharmaceutical products for life-threatening diseases. When companies do set charges that are perceived to be unfair, they are liable to claims of **price gouging**. In 2012, several petrol stations were charged with price gouging during Hurricane Katrina in the USA under New York law which 'prohibits businesses from selling goods or services at an "unconscionably excessive price" during an "abnormal disruption of the market" ' (Bond, 2012).

The Competitor-Oriented Approach

With this approach, companies set prices based on competitors' prices, the so-called going rate. This is also called 'me-too' pricing. The advantage of this approach is that when your prices are lower than your competitors, customers are more likely to purchase from you, provided that they know that your prices are lower, which might not be the case

Price guarantee schemes like the one outlined in Market Insight 9.2 are aimed at providing customers with the peace of mind of knowing that the company they are purchasing from is competitive in price. In reality, such schemes are often expensive to operate as they require continuous monitoring of the full range of competitors' prices, and a strong focus on cost control to maintain those competitive prices. However, it is worth considering that adopting a competitor-oriented pricing strategy can lead to price wars. Sony and Amazon in the UK both ended up offering discounts of up to 97% on ebooks in 2012, particularly those by best-selling authors such as James Herbert and Jeffrey Archer. Herbert's *Ash*, with a cover price of £18.99 was

---

Market Insight 9.2

John Lewis Partnership: Still Matching Prices?

The leading British department store John Lewis Partnership owns 30 department stores, nine John Lewis at Home stores, 288 Waitrose supermarkets, a production unit, and a farm, and operates the e-commerce site Johnlewis.com. With around 81,000 staff, the John Lewis Partnership is Britain's leading department store retailer with gross sales of just over £8.7bn. What is unique about John Lewis is that it operates through a unique constitution in which the company is owned by its employees and has as its mission the 'happiness of its members'. This approach to business has been successful in a number of ways. For example, the company won Retailer of the Year and Multichannel Retailer of the Year in 2013 at the Oracle Retail Awards. Despite the economic doldrums, the company's Christmas trading statement for 2012 indicated great success at the tills with record-breaking figures up 14.8% on the same period in the previous year, partly as a result of strong performance through its website and the click and collect facility that it offers.

But John Lewis Partnership also differs in another unique way from its competitors. It offers a policy of price matching and refunds if customers can find the same product cheaper at another retailer. Its

policy, named 'Never Knowingly Undersold' has been available since 1925, perhaps the longest-running price promotion in British retailing. Things changed in 2011, when it changed the policy to match prices offered by other physical store retailers who were also online. More recently, however, John Lewis has come under flack. Some customers looking for a refund when they have identified a product sold cheaper elsewhere have not been refunded because, according to John Lewis, the product has not been exactly the same. Often this has been the result of the fact that John Lewis offers two years warranty on their electrical products, for example, while other retailers tend to offer one year. The question now for most customers though is will they continue to perceive this price promotion as fair?

Sources: Brignall (2011); www.johnlewispartnership.co.uk

1 **Do you think the cost of collecting all this competitor data on prices is justified commercially? Why?**

2 **What other data do John Lewis Partnership need to determine how customers perceive competing prices from different retailers?**

3 **Do you think it is ethical to offer a price guarantee scheme with such strict conditions? Why do you say this?**

Research Insight 9.3

To take your learning further, you might wish to read this influential paper.

van Heerde, H. J., Gijsbrechts, E., and Pauwels, K. (2008), 'Winners and losers in a major price war', *Journal of Marketing Research*, 45(5), 499–518.

This article explains that price wars initially initiate greater degrees of shopping around and increased spending, but that spending per visit drops over time. Price wars make consumers more price sensitive, helping only the store that shows an improvement in price image and the chains that already have a favourable price image. While the price war initiator can halt the decline in its market share, losers include rival mid- and high-end chains who suffer from the increased price image sensitivity.

@ **Visit the Online Resource Centre to read the abstract and access the full paper.**

selling for only 20p. Such prices are clearly not sustainable in the long term, for the retailers, the publishers, or the authors (Flood, 2012).

Price wars occur when competitors' pricing policies are almost exclusively focused on competitors rather than customers, when price is pushed downwards, and when pricing results in interactions between competitors that lead to unsustainable prices. In a review of more than 1,000 price wars, researchers found that they could usually be averted if companies responded to market-based, firm-based, product-based, and consumer-based early warning signals (van Heerde *et al.*, 2008). In other words, some firms under certain circumstances within certain industries are more susceptible to price wars than others (see Market Insight 9.3 and Table 9.2).

Market Insight 9.3

Harry Potter Price Magic!

The Harry Potter series has been a global phenomenon, making its author, J. K. Rowling, a worldwide celebrity and the inspiration behind what by 2012 has become a $15bn brand with film sales of over $7.7bn. Over 450 million copies of the seven books in the series have been sold around the world, sparking eight successful Blockbuster film tie-in movies. In 2012, *The Sunday Times* rich list placed Rowling as one of Scotland's most successful women, with a personal fortune of around £560m from books and film rights. In recognition of her fans' loyalty, in 2011 Rowling announced her own free-to-use website (www.pottermore.com). Designed to be explored alongside the Harry Potter stories and bringing the world alive for the reader, the site includes exclusive new writing about the world she created for users to discover. The Pottermore shop (www.shop.pottermore.com) is the exclusive place to buy the Harry Potter eBooks and digital audio books as Rowling, rather than her publishers (Bloomsbury in the UK and Scholastic in the US), retained ownership of the digital rights to her books. The campaign to launch the website and build brand awareness was extremely successful. A million users were accepted into the closed beta phase of the website, recruited via the 'Magical Quill'

Market Insight 9.3
continued

campaign which won *Marketing* magazine's Revolution 2012 awards for Media and Entertainment and Best Integrated Campaign.

When the seventh and final book in the Harry Potter series, *Harry Potter and the Deathly Hallows*, was released in 2007, everyone expected it to sell a lot of copies. But no one expected it to sell 11 million copies in the UK and the USA alone in the first 24 hours, breaking sales records as the fastest-selling book to date. The need to own a copy among young and old readers alike meant huge crowds of people queuing at supermarkets and bookshops around the world.

The prospect of so many customers queuing up was too much for many supermarkets. They worried that other supermarkets might steal their customers and were keen themselves to steal a march on their competitors by selling the book at a discount price. Despite the £17.99 recommended retailer price suggested by the publisher Bloomsbury, ASDA discounted the book to £5.00 in Britain after initially offering a pre-order price of £8.87. Morrison's swiftly followed suit, selling its copies at £4.99, and Tesco sold a copy for £5 if shoppers spent £50 in-store. Sainsbury's stayed above the fray, keeping its price at £8.87. Booksellers, who could not compete with the supermarkets' deep discounting, maintained prices around £10. Interestingly, the publisher made a statement that supermarkets were selling the book at cheaper prices than they had actually paid for them.

Such supermarket madness wasn't just in evidence in Britain. In Malaysia, discounting of the book to 69.90 Ringgit by supermarket groups Carrefour and Tesco, compared with the price of 109.90 Ringgit offered by booksellers, caused such an uproar that members of the Malaysian Booksellers Association threatened to return copies to the publishers. Selling the books at below cost seems like an odd way of doing business, but consider that the sales obtained from all the extra demand from customers coming in to buy their final copy of Harry would have more than compensated—now there's a spot of (marketing) wizardry!

Sources: Haycock (2007); Kaur (2007); Cobb (2007); Brown and Patterson (2009); Anon. (2012b); www.jkrowling.com http://business.timesonline.co.uk/tol/business/specials/rich_list/rich_list_search

1 Do you think it a successful pricing tactic for supermarkets to use loss-leader pricing for the new Harry Potter books?

2 The Harry Potter e-books sold at www.pottermore.com are only about £1 cheaper than the hard copies offered on the publisher's website. Do you think a lot of e-books and digital audio-books will be sold?

3 Can you think of other price wars that you have heard of or experienced? What sector were they in and what impact did they have on the competing organizations?

The magical world of Harry Potter caused price wars among supermarket chains

Source: © Pottermore Ltd.

> **Table 9.2 Circumstances under which price wars are more or less likely to occur**
>
> Circumstances under which price wars are more likely to occur
>
> 1 As market entry occurs and an entrant gains or is expected to gain a sizeable market position
> 2 When an industry possesses excess production capacity; this will also stimulate the intensity of the price war
> 3 When markets have marginal or negative growth prospects
> 4 Where market power within an industry is highly concentrated
> 5 Where barriers to exit are greater (meaning that it's more difficult to leave an industry, e.g. because of high investment costs)
> 6 Where financial conditions of at least one firm in the industry worsen or as a firm approaches bankruptcy
> 7 Where the product concerned is of strategic importance to the company
> 8 When a product is more like a commodity and so does not command a price premium
> 9 When firms introduce very similar products to one another
> 10 When there is little brand loyalty in evidence from customers
> 11 When customers are more highly price sensitive; this also increases the intensity of the price war
>
> Circumstances under which price wars are less likely to occur:
>
> 1 One or more firms have established a reputation for strong and tough responses to past price wars
> 2 Where markets have intermediate levels of market power concentration (in other words, neither suppliers nor buyers are dominant in a market)

Calculating and anticipating competitors' responses is important when setting prices and responding to competitors' price cuts. We should analyse consumer responses when a competitor starts to cut prices, but if purchase behaviour changes only modestly or temporarily, other marketing mix elements (such as promotion, distribution, or product differentiation) may be more likely to win back customers (van Heerde *et al.*, 2008).

But we do not always have to respond with a price cut in this situation. Instead, we might respond with improvements in service quality to offer the customer greater value for money as a defensive strategy to offset the competitor's price reductions (Rust *et al.*, 2000).

The Value-Oriented Approach

Even in the consumer durables category (e.g. furniture, white goods (washing machines and refrigerators), carpets), where we might expect customers to be less price sensitive, firms have long since practised pricing approaches with their customers' considerations in mind (Foxall, 1972). We term this the value-oriented approach to pricing, because prices are set based on buyers' perceptions of specific product/service attribute values rather than on costs or competitors' prices. This approach to pricing operates in direct contrast to the cost-oriented approach.

The point is that we no longer live in an era where offerings are priced at what people can afford, because resources used to make products and services are no longer scarce. Resources are now more plentiful and consumers have much of what they need. So, they are more interested in obtaining even more value from the offerings they buy. With value-based pricing, the pricing process begins with the customer, determining what value they derive from the offering and then determining price, rather than the opposite approach used in cost-oriented pricing, where costs are determined first and then the price is set.

In value-based pricing, deciding what is of value to the customer is determined using customer research first. The result may be that the company does not necessarily offer a cheaper price. In fact, it could mean a higher-priced offering. If that offering was to represent true value to the customer, they must feel that it has more benefits than equivalent offerings. A good example of a brand using this approach is L'Oréal, which has for a long time advertised its products using spokesmodels, e.g. Bollywood actress and former Miss World Aishwarya Rai, British pop sensation and television personality Cheryl Cole, and Hollywood actress Jennifer Aniston, on the basis that we should use their products 'because we're worth it'. Research indicates that brands that generate revenues over and above those obtained by an own-label or generic version of the offering gain revenue premiums, which act as a useful measure for brand equity (Ailawadi *et al.* 2003). Brand equity is important, because it contributes to company valuations when they are sold, acquired, or merged. Therefore companies are increasingly focusing on generating price premiums. Nevertheless, a price premium is useless if it's not considered fair. Consequently, when setting value-based prices, consider the following six questions.

1　What is the market strategy for the segment? What does the supplier want to accomplish?

2　What is the differential value that customers are likely to perceive? (In other words the value between this offering and the next best alternative, and this assumes that the differential value can be verified with the customer's own data.)

3　What is the price of the next best alternative?

4　What is the cost of the supplier's offering?

5　What pricing tactics will be used initially (e.g. price discounting)?

6　What is the customer's expectation of a 'fair' price? (Anderson *et al.*, 2010). (See Market Insight 9.4.)

Market Insight 9.4

The Birkin Bag—Still Worth Its Wait in Gold?

A more extreme example of the value-oriented approach to pricing is that adopted by Hermès in the development of its über-stylish, hard to get hold of, Birkin bag. The bag was named after, and first made for, British actress Jane Birkin, reportedly after she met Hermès CEO, John-Louis Dumas on a flight to Paris from London in 1984 when she complained that she could not find a leather weekend bag.

In luxury markets, people are sometimes prepared to pay more for offerings the more expensive they are, simply for 'snob' value, for the sake of their own expensiveness, or because of their uniqueness (Amaldoss and Jain, 2005; Yeoman and McMahon-Beattie, 2006; Zeithaml, 1988). The Birkin bag is a case in point, with the price ranging from a cool $10,000 to over $200,000 depending on size, skin (some are made from saltwater crocodile skin), colour, whether or not it's bejewelled, and celebrity appeal. But the custom-made bag is frequently made available only to select customers in select stores who develop relationships with particular sales assistants and only after they have spent considerable amounts of money in-store. Others spend ages on waiting lists. Kim Kardashian, the US TV star, and Victoria Beckham, the British designer

Market Insight 9.4
continued

and former singer, are fans. Beckham's collection of Hermés handbags is reportedly worth £1.5m. But as ever with fashion marketing, once an offering becomes reasonably well adopted, it starts to lose its allure. One fashion commentator asks: given that the bag is so widely available and so many people have one, is the mother of all bags now losing its appeal?

Sources: Kingston (2008); Tonello (2008); Carreon (2012); London (2012).

1 When an offering is very valuable, do you think it is harder or easier to set the price? Why do you say this?

2 What approach to pricing is Hermès using here?

3 Can Hermés marketers use price to maintain the offering's iconic status? How?

Pricing Management

Over the past few decades, marketing information systems (MkIS), database technologies, and internet-enabled technologies have been changing the rules of strategic pricing and pricing decisions. Pricing strategies such as 'real-time' or 'dynamic' pricing have increasingly developed in both B2C and B2B markets through online price comparison decision aids and online auctions.

Visit the **Online Resource Centre** and follow the weblink to Kelkoo, an example of an online price comparison decision aid.

Examples in the UK include www.comparethemarket.com and www.Gocompare.com Like their counterparts in Sweden (e.g. www.pricerunner.se) and France (e.g. www.monsieurprix. com), these companies have developed large customer databases covering all types of offerings including complex services such as gas and electricity supply, insurance, mobile phone packages, and travel, as well as standard products like cars and car breakdown cover. The implication for large companies is clear. Marketers work in a price-transparent environment, where both on- and offline customers increasingly know what prices are charged by different companies. It is important that marketers recognize that pricing is a skill and that some companies are better at pricing than others. Those companies that are excellent at pricing manage their costs and price complexity well and offer sustainability and innovation in pricing approaches (Hinterhuber and Liozu, 2012). Naked Wines founder, Rowan Gormley, managed to offer UK wine consumers lower prices by stripping out marketing costs and encouraging wine consumers to invest in new wine producers in return for preferential prices (Cave, 2012).

Visit the **Online Resource Centre** and complete Internet Activity 9.2 to learn more about the role and importance of online auctions to price-setting and consumer decision-making.

Pricing Policies

When setting prices, an organization has to trade off the factors associated with competition (how much are competitors are charging for similar offerings?), factors associated with cost (how much do the individual components that make up our offering cost?), factors associated

Price comparison websites like gocompare.com have changed the face of the purchasing of online financial service offerings
Source: Courtesy of GoCompare.com.

Research Insight 9.4

To take your learning further, you might wish to read this useful paper.

Ratchford, B. T. (2009), 'Online pricing: review and directions for research', *Journal of Interactive Marketing*, **23, 82–90.**

According to this article, the internet influences prices because it is a channel for obtaining price information and is used as a vehicle for transactions. The article reviews the literature on the impact of online information on prices, and on how the features of online markets influence online pricing. Major influences include the fact that online search can be costly and limited, the presence of switching costs, reputation, heterogeneity in search costs, heterogeneity in demand for services, and online–offline competition.

Visit the **Online Resource Centre** to read the abstract and access the full paper.

with demand (how much of this product or service will we sell at what price?), and factors associated with value (what components of the offering does the customer value and how much are they prepared to pay for them?). Most pricing decisions are trade-offs between these and other factors. So, although we outline four main pricing approaches, there are in fact many different possible pricing policies that could be used including the following.

- List pricing—an approach to pricing where a single price is set for an offering. Hotels often charge what they call 'rack rates' for hotel conferencing facilities, combining residential accommodation for a set number of delegates with daytime accommodation for a conference room, refreshments, and lunch.

- Loss-leader pricing—the price is set at a level lower than the actual cost incurred to produce it. This approach is often used in supermarkets on popular price-sensitive items (e.g. best-selling novels) to entice customers in-store. The loss incurred is made up by increasing the prices of other less price-sensitive items or absorbed as a short-term promotional cost on the basis that it brings in more customers.

- Promotional pricing—companies temporarily reduce their prices below the standard price to raise awareness of the offering to encourage trial and to raise short-term brand awareness. Such approaches incorporate the use of loss-leaders, sales discounts, cash rebates, low-interest financing (e.g. car manufacturers frequently offer 0% interest-free financing deals), and other price-based promotional incentives. (See Market Insight 9.5.)

Market Insight 9.5

Drinking Problems: Boozing at What Price?

Given perceived high levels of alcohol consumption in England and Wales, in 2012 the UK government made an initial announcement of a number of measures it suggested should be used to reduce alcohol drinking and the problems associated with it, (e.g. health and crime problems). These included a suggested 45p minimum price per unit of alcohol (about one small measure of spirits) and an end to bulk discount sales (e.g. by supermarkets) of alcohol products. Scotland—a separate jurisdiction in the UK—brought in such legislation in 2011, and proposed a 50p minimum price per unit in 2013. Australia is also considering whether or not to bring in minimum prices per unit of alcohol in a bid to stem its own drinking problems.

However, the minimum alcohol pricing approach has found many different adversaries. A leaked letter from the European Commission suggested that the approach was illegal under EU law and that duty

(a form of tax) should be raised rather than setting minimum prices per unit of alcohol. Other opposition comes, not surprisingly, from alcohol manufacturers, particularly old world (European) wine producers, who are having a tough time in the UK with rising prices anyway from existing tax increases and increasing customer price sensitivity as a result of price promotions. In the middle of 2013, the UK government decided to postpone the introduction of minimum alcohol pricing, citing the need for further research.

What is not clear as yet, since no country has introduced minimum prices per unit of alcohol, is what the effect would be. Would it penalize the poor, discriminate against low-cost suppliers from Europe and elsewhere, and produce windfall profits for major entrenched beverage companies like Diageo? Would firms push their products harder if they could not lower prices? Would it result in consumers importing their booze from overseas or would it not have any effect at all? All these questions currently remain unanswered.

Sources: Anon. (2012d); ANPHA (2012); Bainbridge (2012); Martin and Reynolds (2012).

Market Insight 9.5
continued

1 **Have a look around your local supermarket. Identify the different pricing policies used by supermarkets in your country when selling alcoholic drinks. If selling alcohol is illegal in your country, what approach do you think UK supermarkets have been using?**

2 **Why do you think the Scottish government has chosen to introduce a minimum price rather than raising the tax on alcohol in a bid to reduce alcohol consumption?**

3 **What do you think the effects of introducing a minimum price per unit alcohol would have been in England and Wales? Why do you say that?**

How would a minimum per unit alcohol price affect your consumption?
Source: istock © ansonsaw.

- Segmentation pricing—varying prices are set for different groups of customers, e.g. Unilever's ice cream is offered as various different ice cream products at differing levels of quality and price ranging from super-premium (e.g. Ben & Jerry's available in cinemas) to economy offerings (e.g. standard ice cream available in supermarkets). Economists call this approach **price discrimination**.

- Customer-centric pricing—Cross and Dixit (2005) suggest that companies can take advantage of customer segments by measuring their value perceptions, measuring the value created, and designing a unique bundle of products and services to cater to the value requirements of each segment, and continually assessing the impact this has on company profitability, taking advantage of up-selling (e.g. offering a customer a more expensive offering in the same category) and cross-selling (e.g. selling other, different offerings to the same customer).

- Pay what you want pricing— this approach to pricing allows customers to pay whatever they want. The British band Radiohead used this approach when pricing their album *In Rainbows* in 2007 (Anon., 2012c). Under certain circumstances, customers are sometimes prepared to pay more for an offering if they set the price themselves than if it is set for them (Kim *et al.*, 2009).

Pricing for New Propositions

When launching new offerings, we can adopt one of two classic pricing strategies. With the first approach, we charge an initially high price and then reduce the price, recouping the cost of the R&D investment over time from sales to the group of customers that is prepared to pay the higher price (hence 'skimming' the market). In the second approach, we charge a lower price in the hope of generating a large volume of sales and recouping our R&D investment that way (hence market penetration).

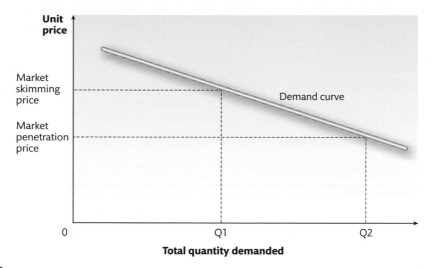

Figure 9.5

New proposition pricing strategies

Source: Adapted from Burnett (2002). Reproduced with the kind permission of the author, John Burnett.

Figure 9.5 shows both market penetration and market skimming price strategies and their hypothetical impact on quantity demanded (Q1 and Q2, respectively). For any given demand curve, the market skimming price offers a higher unit price than the market penetration price. The actual amount sold at each of these unit prices depends on the price elasticity of demand, and a more inelastic demand curve would give greater revenue from a market skimming price than a market penetration price as the quantity sold would not be so different between the two prices. On average, the market skimming price is likely to yield a lower quantity of offerings sold than the market penetration price.

The skim pricing approach is a fairly standard approach for high-technology offerings or those offerings that require substantial R&D investment initially (e.g. games consoles and prescription pharmaceuticals). For example, Nintendo dropped the price for its Nintendo 3DS machine dramatically six months after its release in 2006, an approach it does not intend to use, but may have to, for its Wii U machine launched in 2012 (Agnello, 2012).

The skim pricing approach is particularly appropriate under certain conditions (Dean, 1950; Doyle, 2000). These conditions are shown in Table 9.3.

The market penetration pricing approach is used for fast-moving consumer goods and consumer durables, where the new offering introduced is not demonstrably different from existing

Table 9.3 Conditions for effective skim pricing

1   When companies need to recover their R&D investment quickly
2   When demand is likely to be price inelastic
3   Where there is an unknown elasticity of demand since it is safer to offer a higher price and then lower it, than offer a lower price and try to increase it
4   Where there are high barriers to entry within the market
5   Where there are few economies of scale or experience
6   Where product lifecycles are expected to be short

Table 9.4 Conditions for effective market penetration pricing

1   Where there is a strong threat of competition
2   When our product/service is likely to exhibit a high price elasticity of demand in the short term
3   Where there are substantial savings to be made from volume production
4   Where there are low barriers to entry
5   Where product lifecycles are expected to be long
6   Where there are economies of scale and experience to take advantage of

---

formulations. So, if a car manufacturer introduced a new coupé, relatively similar to its previous model, which had no new features and was not significantly better than competing models, it could be priced using the market penetration pricing approach. Similarly, items aimed at capturing price-sensitive customers might use this approach. In India in 2009, the Tata Nano was launched, a small car dubbed 'the people's car' because it was priced cheaply to penetrate the market (Kurczewski, 2009). In a recessionary environment, customers are particularly sensitive to the value they receive when purchasing consumer or business-to-business offerings. The penetration approach is used under certain conditions when it is more likely to be most effective (Dean, 1950; Doyle, 2000), as outlined in Table 9.4.

Pricing in the Business-to-Business Setting

Business-to-business markets exist on the basis that firms sell offerings to one another rather than to end-users. The demand comes from the demand for the finished goods and services required by the end-user (see Chapter 15). Business markets also differ in the sense that buyers are professionally trained purchasing executives, often professionally accredited (e.g. the Chartered Institute of Purchasing and Supply in the UK), and have frequently attended training programmes to familiarize themselves with the offerings bought within their own organizations. Their function as organizational buyers is highly technical, even for an apparently simple product. For example, German buyers of stationery based in Frankfurt would typically need to know for a simple pen set in blister packaging what the market prices are for various types of stationery products and the components that make them up. For instance, the pens themselves may be bought in Italy, packaging and printing from China, refills from Germany, and the final product assembled in Bulgaria. They would typically make their purchases either at a trade fair, at their own premises after having been visited by various sales representatives, at the showrooms and offices of the various companies from which they buy, or online using an extranet website or e-procurement portal.

The buyer–seller relationship is the fundamental component of the business-to-business marketing interaction. Pricing has an important function in this relationship. If a buyer thinks he/she is being overcharged, he/she will look elsewhere. Equally, if a seller is forced to sell too cheaply and, as a result, is reprimanded by his/her superiors, he/she will not sell at that lower price in future and the relationship may be damaged. Under such circumstances, the seller may then seek to sell elsewhere.

In the business-to-business context, the discussion of price takes place between the buyer and the seller in an atmosphere where both are trying to make the best commercial decision for their organizations. The seller wants to sell at a high price to make the maximum profit, and the buyer wants to buy at a low price to lower his/her own costs and maximize profits. Their task is to resolve their mutual needs in a win–win situation.

From the business-to-business seller's perspective, there are numerous approaches to pricing including the following.

- Geographical pricing—prices are based on the customer location (e.g. pharmaceutical companies often sell their prescription drugs at different prices in different countries). This might include FOB (free on board) factory prices where the price represents the cost of the goods and the buyer must pay for all transport costs incurred. FOB destination pricing is where the manufacturer agrees to cover the cost of shipping to the destination, but not transport costs incurred on arrival at the port (air or sea).

- Negotiated pricing—prices are set according to specific agreements between a company and its clients or customers (e.g. professional services such as architectural or structural engineering practices or IT installation and servicing). This approach occurs where a sale is complex and consultative, but sales and marketing representatives should beware of conceding on price too quickly before properly understanding a client's needs (Rackham, 2001).

- Discount pricing—companies reduce the price of an offering on the basis that a customer is prepared to commit either to buying a large volume of that offering now or in the future, or paying for it within a specified time period. Large retailers work on the discount principle when buying for their stores. Their mighty procurement budgets and long experience ensure that they buy at cheaper prices from their suppliers and so lower their costs. Sometimes, discount pricing works on the basis of payment terms. For example, in the British toy and gift market, where retail buyers are used to buying their goods on credit, suppliers frequently offer their retail buyers discounts for quicker payment (e.g. 5% discount for payment within seven days, 2.5% for 14 days). However, when price is discounted, we also disproportionately reduce the operating profit (Baker et al., 2010).

- Value-in-use pricing—this approach focuses our attention on customer perceptions of the attributes of offerings and away from cost-oriented approaches. It prices offerings according to what the customer is prepared to pay for individual benefits received from that proposition, so the company must first ascertain what benefit components the customer perceives to be important, then quantify those benefit values, then determine the price equivalence of value, then rate competitive and alternative products to provide a benchmark for price determination, then quantify the value in use (i.e. the value in using our product vis-à-vis our competitors), and only then is the price actually fixed (see Christopher (1982) for a more detailed discussion). This approach is particularly used for industrial propositions, although the actual process of price determination can be complex.

- Relationship pricing—this approach to pricing seeks to understand customers' needs before pricing the offering according to those needs in order to generate a long-term relationship. This could mean offering excellent financial terms, credit or more lenient time periods for payment, or discounts based on future sales revenue or the risk involved in the purchase. The difficulty with this approach is that it relies on great trust and commitment existing between the two companies.

- Pay what you want pricing— this approach allows customers to pay whatever they want for an offering. For example, the legal services firm, CMS Cameron McKenna has offered this pricing approach to its corporate clients (Hollander, 2010).

- Transfer pricing—this occurs in very large organizations where there is considerable internal dealing between different divisions of the company and across national boundaries. Prices may be set at commercial rates, on the basis of negotiated prices between divisions, or using a cost-based approach, depending on whether the division is a cost or profit centre. The danger is that internal dealings can sometimes mean that the final offering is priced too high for a given customer. Airbus Industries, the European aircraft manufacturer owned by parent company EADS (European Aeronautic Defence and Space Company), adopts this approach when constructing its planes built from components made in different countries.

- Economic value to the customer (EVC) pricing— with this approach, a company prices an offering according to its value to the purchasing organization, typically through a comparison with a reference or market-leading offering, taking into consideration not only the actual purchase price of the offering but also the start-up and post-purchase costs to give an overall indication of how much better its pricing structure is compared with that of a competitor. A worked example of economic value to the customer (EVC) pricing is outlined in Table 9.5.

EVC pricing works by calculating total lifetime costs for an offering in comparison with a reference offering and adjustment of the purchase price to reflect the value the customer requires or the seller is prepared to offer. We use the example of a company developing CRM (customer relationship management) systems for the financial services sector. In the case of the Reference System—typically we use the market-leading offering as this acts as a well-known benchmark— the system costs £50,000 initially, but requires expenditure of a further £20,000 on start-up costs, including staff training on the system and staff time in loading and testing the software's compatibility with the firm's other software systems. Maintenance of the database developed from using the software system over a three-year period, consisting of data input, cleaning and processing time in relation to system inter-operability, and database translation issues between software packages, costs a further £30,000. Overall, the total lifetime profit from purchasing the market-leading CRM system is £100,000 because, although it costs £100,000 over three years, it also generates £200,000 in extra income.

However, our company developing CRM software systems has two alternative products, System A and System B. Let's consider System A first. Compared with the market-leading product, it offers slightly cheaper start-up costs of £15,000 because it is easier to use and requires

Table 9.5 Economic value to the customer (EVC) analysis

Cost item	Reference System	System A	System B
EVC	n/a	£70,000	£200,000
Extra revenue generated (3 years)	£200,000	£200,000	£350,000
Purchase price	£50,000	£50,000	£50,000
Start-up costs (year 1 only)	£20,000	£15,000	£20,000
Maintenance costs (3 years)	£30,000	£15,000	£30,000
Total lifetime cost (–)/profit (+)	+£100,000	+£120,000	+£250,000

less staff training. It has lower maintenance costs because data input is made easier as the software uses the majority of the company's existing database systems and so reduces software inter-operability problems. In total, the system costs £20,000 less than the reference product, but is estimated to bring in revenue of £100,000. In total, the system will cost £80,000. Therefore the economic value to the customer of purchasing System A is the total lifetime cost/profit associated with System A less the cost of the purchase of the system which equals £70,000. When we come to sell System A to our CRM system buyer, we can offer the buyer any price between £50,000 and £70,000 to remain competitive and still offer a differential price advantage over the market leader.

We can also offer our CRM buyer another system, System B. This system has the same start-up and maintenance costs as the market leader. However, it also has sophisticated predictive up-selling and cross-selling functions, allowing the client to generate higher revenue of £350,000 from the database developed compared with the £200,000 generated from the Reference System or System A. In this case, the total lifetime profit of the system is £250,000. Therefore the economic value to the customer of purchasing System B is the total lifetime cost/profit associated with System B less the cost of the purchase of the system which equals £200,000. The CRM company can offer the financial service company System B for any price between £50,000 and £200,000. In reality, however, it would probably be difficult to justify a price towards the higher figure because the extra revenue generated is uncertain.

Tendering and Bidding

In business-to-business markets, companies bid for the right to supply offerings for a fixed period of time through a competitive bidding process. In other words, a company sets up a form of competition (the tender process) where they either ask a number of selected companies (their 'preferred suppliers') or set up an open competition where they ask any number of companies to devise a proposal to supply products and services (known as a bid), to be submitted by a set deadline. Where a company does not have a pool of preferred suppliers, or wants to widen its pool of suppliers, this phase is preceded by an initial phase where the company invites 'expressions of interest' from suppliers. The submissions are screened by the company, which removes those companies that it does not want to deal with, and the rest are advanced to the next phase of the competition. The company goes on to consider the individual full bids in a ranking process, often requiring the bid submitters to make a presentation and discuss the detail of their bids individually. On the basis of those bids and the presentation, the company will make a choice of who they want to supply their company, or they take the process to a second round or subsequent rounds of bidding. Eventually, they decide which company will be awarded the temporary contract. The tendering process is a set requirement for the provision of public services and goods above certain financial values of contract in the European Union with strict rules on how the contracts must be promoted and awarded.

Private companies dealing with private companies tend to adopt the same forms of bidding and tendering, but without the same level of strict regulation. Generally, the formal tendering and bidding process takes considerable time, effort, and expense. Such bidding processes are used around the world as a means of introducing competition, particularly in the provision of public sector services, such as telecommunications, public utilities (e.g. gas, electricity, and water), transport (e.g. train, underground, monorail, maglev), oil and gas exploration, and defence contracting. The difficulty in designing, writing, and submitting a suitable contract is that the details of competitors' bids remain confidential. When trying to second-guess competitors' bid prices, we use the sales force as a source of intelligence (to pick up information from friendly companies that they supply and even colleagues in other companies at industry events). The manager should know his/her own profitability when determining the price and aim to discover the winning bidder's name and price on lost jobs, although this is not always possible (Walker, 1967). Ross (1984) argues that it is often better not to ask 'What price will it take to win this order?' but 'Do we want this order, given the price our competitors are likely to quote?'. There is the notion of the **winner's curse**, where the winning bidder obtains an unprofitable contract that he/she is duty bound to deliver because their bid price was set so low so that they won the contract.

Chapter Summary

To consolidate your learning, the key points from this chapter are summarized here.

■ **Define price, and understand its relationship with costs, quality, and value.**

Price, costs, quality, and value are all interrelated. Price is what an offering is sold for and cost is what it is bought for. When value is added to a proposition the price that can be obtained exceeds the cost. Price and cost are often confused and assumed to be the same thing. They are not. Quality is a measure of how well an offering satisfies the need it is designed to cater for. Value is a function of the quality of an offering as a proportion of the price paid.

■ **Explain the concept of price elasticity of demand.**

Price elasticity of demand allows us to determine how the quantity of an offering relates to the price at which it is offered. Inelastic propositions are defined as such because increases (decreases) in price produce relatively smaller decreases (increases) in sales volumes, whereas elastic offerings have larger similar effects. Understanding price elasticity helps us devise demand-oriented pricing mechanisms.

■ **Describe how customers and consumers perceive price.**

Understanding how customers and consumers perceive pricing helps when setting prices. Customers have an idea of reference prices based on what they ought to pay for an offering, what others would pay, or what they would like to pay. Their knowledge of actual prices is limited to well-known and frequently bought and advertised offerings. Consequently, customers tend to rely on price cues such as odd-number pricing, sale signs, the purchase context, and price bundles when deciding whether or not value exists in a particular proposition.

■ **Explain cost-, competitor-, demand-, and value-oriented approaches to pricing.**

There are a variety of different pricing policies that can be used depending on whether we are pricing a consumer or industrial offering. They tend to be cost-oriented (based on what we paid for it and what mark-up we intend to add), competitor-oriented (the so-called going rate or based on what price competitors sell an offering at), demand-oriented (based on how much of an offering can be sold at what price), or value-oriented (what attributes of the offering are of benefit to our customer and what will they pay for them).

■ **Understand how to price new offerings.**

The two classical approaches to pricing new offerings are market skimming and market penetration pricing. The former is favoured when a company needs to recover its R&D investment quickly, when customers are price-insensitive or of unknown price-sensitivity, when product lifecycles are short, andwhen barriers to entry to competitors are high. The latter is favoured when these conditions are not in existence.

■ **Explain how pricing operates in the business-to-business setting.**

A variety of pricing approaches are used in the business-to-business setting, including geographical, negotiated, discount, value-in-use, relationship, pay what you want, transfer, and economic value to the customer. Business-to-business pricing differs in that buyers are frequently expert in purchasing for their organizations. They are likely to pay particular attention to the value that they derive from the offering. Companies and organizations, particularly government organizations, frequently purchase offerings from suppliers through tenders inviting companies to submit bids containing their proposals, terms and conditions, and prices.

 # Review Questions

1   Define price, cost, quality, and value in your own words.

2   Explain the concept of price elasticity of demand, giving examples of offerings that are both price elastic and price inelastic.

3   What are pricing cues?

4   What pricing policies are most appropriate for which situations?

5   What are the main business-to-business pricing policies?

6   What are the main two approaches to pricing for new offerings?

7   When should you use price skimming as a pricing approach?

8   When should you use market penetration as a pricing approach?

9   How is business-to-business pricing different?

10 Describe in your own words the pay what you want pricing approach.

 # Worksheet Summary

To apply the knowledge you have gained from this chapter and test your understanding of price decisions visit the **Online Resource Centre** and complete Worksheet 9.1.

 # Discussion Questions

1   Having read Case Insight 9.1, should 3M launch a low-volume high-priced product or a high-volume low-priced product?

2   A range of scenarios are presented in which you are given some information on the price context. What pricing policy would you use when setting the price in the following situation (state the assumptions under which you are working when you decide on each one)?

   A   The owner of a newly refurbished themed Irish pub in a central city location (e.g. Paris or Gothenburg) wants to set the prices for his range of beers with the objective of attracting a new customer base.

B The product manager at Italian car maker Alfa Romeo wants to set the price range for the Alfa Romeo Giulietta in the UK launched in Summer 2010 (www.alfaromeogiulietta.co.uk).

C You are the manager at a large well-known consulting services organization (e.g. Boston Consulting Group) in Sweden, and your client, from a €20m turnover medium-sized import/export company, commissions a study from you on how they can improve their marketing operations. What further information would you require in order to price such a study and what pricing approach would you adopt and why?

3 How would you go about determining the price sensitivity of your customers if you were an airline marketing manager and you wanted your planes to operate at full capacity throughout the week, including very early and very late flight slots, and not just at weekends and in the mornings?

4 Identify an entrepreneur or shop owner that you know. Ask them how they set their prices for the propositions that they sell? What pricing policies do you think they use?

5 Research and examine the prices of five different items in two different jewellery shops (where possible selling similar or identical products and pack sizes in each to allow comparison). What are the average prices for each of the items and how does each shop compare with the other?

@ Visit the **Online Resource Centre** and complete the Multiple Choice Questions to assess your knowledge of Chapter 9.

References

Agnello, A. J. (2012), 'No Wii U price cut like there was for Nintendo 3DS', *Digitaltrends.com*, 30 November, retrieve from: http://www.digitaltrends.com/gaming/nintendo-no-wii-u-price-cut-like-there-was-for-nintendo-3ds/ accessed 4 January 2013.

Ailawadi, K., Lehmann, D. R., and Neslin, S. A. (2003), 'Revenue premium as a outcome measure of brand equity', *Journal of Marketing* 67(October), 1–17.

Amaldoss, W. and Jain, S. (2005), 'Pricing of conspicuous goods: a competitive analysis of social effects', *Journal of Marketing Research* 42(February), 30–42.

Anderson, E. and Simester, D. (2003), 'Mind your pricing cues', *Harvard Business Review*, September, 96–103.

Anderson, J. C.; Wouters, M., and Van Rossum, W. (2010), 'Why the highest price isn't the best price', *Sloan Management Review*, 51(2), 69–76.

Anon. (2012a), 'The psychology of discounting: Something doesn't add up', *Economist*, 30 June, 75.

Anon. (2012b), 'JK Rowling Net Worth 2012', *The Richest People,* retrieve from: http://www.therichest.org/entertainment/j-k-rowling-net-worth/ accessed 30 December 2012.

Anon. (2012c), 'Paying what you want: conscience versus commerce', *Economist*, 5 May, retrieve from: http://www.economist.com/node/21554218 accessed 4 January 2013.

Anon. (2012d), 'Alcohol pricing: time, please', *Economist*, 1 December, 35.

ANPHA (2012), 'Minimum (floor) price for alcohol draft report released', *Australian National Preventive Health Agency* retrieve from: http://anpha.gov.au/internet/anpha/publishing.nsf/Content/anphamediarelease-01112012 accessed 4 January 2013.

Attridge, J. (2003), 'A single European market for pharmaceuticals. Could less regulation and more negotiation be the answer?', *European Business Journal*, 15(3), 122–43.

Babad, Y. M. and Balachandran, B. V. (1993), 'Cost driver optimisation in activity-based costing', *Accounting Review*, 68(3), 563–75.

Bainbridge, J. (2012), 'Sector insight: wine', *Marketing*, 28 November, 25.

Baker, W. L., Marn, M. V., and Zawada, C. C. (2010), *The Price Advantage* (2nd), Hoboken, NJ: John Wiley.

Bond, S. (2012), 'Petrol stations accused of price gouging', *Financial Times*, 15 November, retrieve from: http://www.ft.com/cms/s/0/cd51b40c-2f62-11e2-8e4b-00144feabdc0.html#axzz2GY3ISGI0 accessed 30 December 2012.

Boyle, P. J. and Lathrop, E. S. (2009), 'Are consumers' perceptions of price-quality relationships well-calibrated?', *International Journal of Consumer Studies*, 33, 58–63.

Brignall, M. (2011), 'John Lewis Partnership: never knowingly undersold?', *Guardian*, 5 February, retrieve from: http://www.guardian.co.uk/money/2011/feb/05/john-lewis-never-knowingly-undersold accessed 4 January 2013.

Brown, S. and Patterson, A. (2009), 'Harry Potter and the service-dominant logic of marketing: a cautionary tale', *Journal of Marketing Management*, 25(5/6), 519–33.

Burnett, J. (2002), *Core Concepts in Marketing*, London: John Wiley.

Carreon, B. (2012), 'Has the Hermés Birkin bag lost its appeal', *Forbes*, 17 July, retrieve from: http://www.forbes.com/sites/bluecarreon/2012/07/17/has-the-hermes-birkin-bag-lost-its-appeal/ accessed 4 January 2013.

Cave, A. (2012), 'When it comes to customers, price is key', *Sunday Telegraph*, *16 September*, B10.

Christopher, M. (1982), 'Value-in-use pricing', *European Journal of Marketing*, 16(5), 35–46.

Cialdini, R. B. (1993), *Influence: The Psychology of Persuasion*, New York: Quill William Morrow.

Chen, H., Marmorstein, H., Tsiros, M., and Rao, R.R. (2012), 'When more is less: the impact of base value neglect on consumer preferences for bonus packs over price discounts', *Journal of Marketing*, 76(4), 64–77.

Cobb, C. (2007), 'Harry Potter's PR magic', *Public Relations Tactics*, August, 9–10.

Cross, R. G. and Dixit, A. (2005), 'Customer-centric pricing: the surprising secret for profitability', *Business Horizons*, 48, 483–91.

Dean, J. (1950), 'Pricing policies for new products', *Harvard Business Review*, November, 45–53.

Doyle, P. (2000), *Value-Based Marketing: Marketing Strategies for Corporate Growth and Shareholder Value*, Chichester: John Wiley.

Flood, A. (2012), 'Ebook price war sees discounts reach 97%', *Guardian*, 18 September, retrieve from: http://www.guardian.co.uk/books/2012/sep/18/ebook-price-war-discounts accessed 4 September 2013.

Foxall, G. (1972), 'A descriptive theory of pricing for marketing', *European Journal of Marketing*, 6(3), 190–4.

Gerstner, E. (1985), 'Do higher prices signal higher quality', *Journal of Marketing Research*, 22(2), 209–15.

Gourville, J. and Soman, D. (2002), 'Pricing and the psychology of consumption', *Harvard Business Review*, September, 90–6.

Haycock, G. (2007), 'UK supermarkets extend price war on Potter books', retrieve from: www.reuters.com/article/idUSL2083170420070720 accessed 4 January 2013.

Hinterhuber, A. and Liozu, S. (2012), 'Is it time to rethink your pricing strategy?', *Sloan Management Review*, 53(4), 76.

Hollander, G. (2010), 'Camerons invites legal clients to pay what they want for legal work', *The Lawyer*, 5 August 2010, retrieve from: http://www.thelawyer.com/camerons-invites-clients-to-pay-what-they-want-for-legal-work/1005236.article accessed 19 March 2012.

Kaur, M. (2007), 'Potter price war: booksellers to meet next week to decide next move', *Star*, 22 July, retrieve from: http://thestar.com.my/news/story.asp?file=/2007/7/22/nation/20070722114014&sec=nation accessed 10 April 2010.

Kim, J-Y., Natter, M., and Spann, M. (2009), 'Pay what you want: a new participatory pricing mechanism', *Journal of Marketing*, 73(1), 44–58.

Kingston, A. (2008), 'How to get the un-gettable bag', *Maclean's*, 3 March, 74.

Kurczewski, N. (2009), 'Tata Nano launched in Mumbai', *New York Times*, 23 March, retrieve from: http://wheels.blogs.nytimes.com/2009/03/23/tata-nano-launched-in-mumbai/ accessed 4 January 2013.

Lockley, L. C. (1949), 'Theories of pricing in marketing', *Journal of Marketing*, 13(3), 364–7.

London, B. (2012), 'Hermes bag for babies? Tribute to popular bag made out of Lego would make great arm candy for Suri Cruise', *Daily Mail*, 11 December, retrieve from: http://www.dailymail.co.uk/femail/article-2246336/Herm-s-Birkin-bag-kids-Tribute-popular-bag-Lego.html accessed 4 January 2013.

Martin, D. and Reynolds, E. (2012), 'Minimum price for alcohol is illegal: Europe's warning to Cameron as he pushes ahead with price hike', *Daily Mail*, 29 November, retrieve from: http://www.dailymail.co.uk/news/article-2240257/Alcohol-price-rules-illegal-European-Commission-warns-David-Cameron.html#ixzz2Gzr1lcnP accessed 4 January 2013.

Mendoza, J. and Baines, P. (2012), 'Towards a consumer price perception formation framework: a systematic review', *Proceedings of the Australia and New Zealand Marketing Academy Conference*, retrieve from: http://anzmac.info/conference/2012/papers/173ANZMACFINAL.pdf accessed 29 December 2012.

Nunes, J. C. and Boatwright, P. (2001), 'Pricey encounters', *Harvard Business Review*, July–August, 18–19.

Oxford Dictionaries (2012), 'Price', 'Value', 'Quality', retrieve from: http://oxforddictionaries.com/definition/english/price?q=price; http://oxforddictionaries.com/definition/english/quality?q=quality; http://oxforddictionaries.com/definition/english/value?q=value accessed 29 December 2012.

Rackham, N. (2001), 'Winning the price war', *Sales and Marketing Management*, 253(11, November), 26.

Ratchford, B.T. (2009), 'Online pricing: review and directions for research', *Journal of Interactive Marketing*, 23, 82–90.

Ross, E. B. (1984), 'Making money with proactive pricing', *Harvard Business Review*, November–December, 145–55.

Rust, R. T., Danaher, P. J., and Varki, S. (2000), 'Using service quality data for competitive marketing decisions',

International Journal of Service Industry Management, 11(5), 438–69.

Sheth, J. N., Sisodia, R. S., and Barbulescu, A. (2006), 'The image of marketing' in J. N. Sheth and R. S. Sisodia (eds), *Does Marketing Need Reform*, New York: M. E. Sharpe, 26–36.

Smith, G. E. and Nagle, T. T. (1995), 'Frames of reference and buyer's perceptions of value', *California Management Review*, 38(1), 98–116.

Tonello, M. (2009), *Bringing Home the Birkin: My Life in Hot Pursuit of the World's Most Coveted Handbag*, New York: HarperCollins.

van Heerde, H.J., Gijsbrechts, E., and Pauwels, K. (2008), 'Winners and losers in a major price war', *Journal of Marketing Research*, 45(5), 499–518.

Völckner, F. and Hofmann, J. (2007), 'The price-perceived quality relationship: a meta-analytic review and assessment of its determinants', *Marketing Letters*, 18(3), 181–96.

Walker, A. W. (1967), 'How to price industrial products', *Harvard Business Review*, September–October, 125–32.

Ward, K. (1993), 'Gaining a marketing advantage through the strategic use of transfer pricing', *Journal of Marketing Management*, 9, 245–53.

Yeoman, I. and McMahon-Beattie, U. (2006), 'Luxury markets and premium pricing', *Journal of Revenue and Pricing Management*, 4(4), 319–28.

Zeithaml, V. A. (1988), 'Consumer perceptions of price, quality and value: a means-end model and synthesis of evidence', *Journal of Marketing*, 52(July), 2–22.

Chapter 10
An Introduction to Marketing Communications

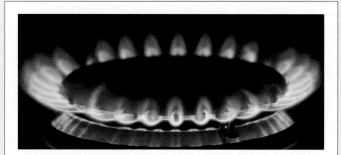

Learning Outcomes

After studying this chapter you should be able to:

▶ Describe the nature, purpose, and scope of marketing communications

▶ Explain three models of communication and describe how personal influences can enhance the effectiveness of marketing communication activities

▶ Understand the role of marketing communications

▶ Understand the models used to explain how marketing communications and advertising work

▶ Describe what culture is and explain how it can impact on the use of marketing communications

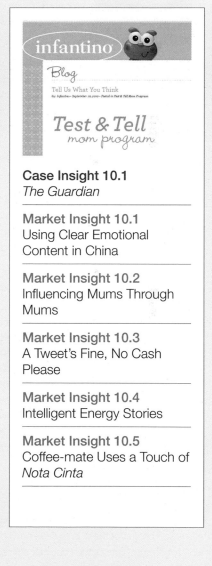

Case Insight 10.1
The Guardian

Market Insight 10.1
Using Clear Emotional Content in China

Market Insight 10.2
Influencing Mums Through Mums

Market Insight 10.3
A Tweet's Fine, No Cash Please

Market Insight 10.4
Intelligent Energy Stories

Market Insight 10.5
Coffee-mate Uses a Touch of *Nota Cinta*

Case Insight 10.1

How could an organization realise their objective to not only shift audience perceptions but to also change behaviours? We speak to Agathe Guerrier, Strategy Director at the advertising agency Bartle Bogle Hegarty (BBH), to find out more about the work they undertook for their client *The Guardian*.

The Guardian is a truly impartial media organization that is rooted in the principles of independent journalism. The Scott Trust was set up to protect this independence, and to this day *The Guardian*'s sole purpose remains the pursuit of the truth. This philosophy shapes the way they communicate: 'Facts are sacred, but comment is free'.

The Guardian is made by Progressives, for Progressives. A Progressive is a curious and connected individual who welcomes change as a positive force. Progressives are not defined by income, age, or any other demographic data.

Today's *The Guardian* is defined by its Open Operating System (OOS). By encouraging participation and debate, by welcoming contributions and challenges, they seek to provide the broadest, most comprehensive view of the world. Openness means they don't put their content behind a pay wall—a radical stance in today's media landscape. It also means that they don't believe journalists to be the only voices of authority, or to be able to complete the entire editorial process on their own—instead, what they do is initiate the creation of content, and then invite bloggers, contributors, readers, and commentators to enrich and evolve it.

The Guardian uses marketing communications in order to support the key drivers of their commercial strategy. The first of these is to drive newspaper sales which, although in structural decline, still represent nearly half of *The Guardian*'s revenues. Therefore it is strategically crucial that they defend them in a competitive marketplace.

A second driver concerns the digital reach of the brand via our desktop and mobile products. As a media brand their reach is a key driver of digital advertising revenue. Marketing and communications aim to grow their UK and international reach.

The third driver is digital engagement. Known, active, engaged users of their digital products are more valuable to us than anonymous and disengaged visitors. To this end, a strand of the marketing and communications strategy is dedicated to increasing digital engagement—registrations, participation, time spent, and frequency.

However, *The Guardian* has had to face certain problems. The first concerns their potential audience of Progressives. It was known from brand health tracking that they they weren't aware of how much *The Guardian* had changed (mainly the Open philosophy), and they scored low on image items such as 'modern', 'innovative', and 'dynamic'.

Secondly, from their trade audience (advertisers and media agencies), they knew that they were struggling with the perception of being a worthy, left-wing, pedantic, and niche newspaper brand.

In terms of direct competition, most of the traditional newspaper sector was actually suffering from a similar fate. The real threat was from the new entrants in the knowledge sector, those of the digital age-Twitter, TED, YouTube—that are really redefining people's attitudes and behaviours when it comes to seeking, consuming, and understanding news content.

Case Insight 10.1
continued

For a long time there has been little investment in the brand, with marketing spend focused on tactical campaigns, such as promoting a certain supplement or feature. The challenge now was to find a way of changing perceptions of *The Guardian* (as a dusty left-wing newspaper brand) amongst a large potential audience of digitally connected, inquisitive news readers. They wanted this audience to realize that

The Guardian had evolved and was now a radically innovative leader of the digital age.

Therefore the problem was not only how to go about shifting perceptions, but also to change behaviours by driving a larger online audience to the desktop product.

Introduction

Have you ever wondered how organizations such as *The Guardian* manage to communicate effectively with so many different people and organizations? Well, this is the first of two chapters that explain how this can be accomplished through the use of marketing communications. This chapter introduces and explains what marketing communications is. The following chapter considers the configuration of the marketing communications mix, and explains ideas about how marketing communications can be integrated and planned.

The purpose of this chapter is to introduce some of the fundamental ideas and concepts associated with marketing communications. To achieve this, the chapter commences with a consideration of communications theory. This is important because it provides a basis on which to appreciate the different ways in which marketing communications are used.

Following a definition, we explain the role and tasks of marketing communications. Again, this is important as it specifies the scope of the subject and provides a framework within which to appreciate the various communication activities undertaken by organizations. The tools and media used by marketing communications are an important aspect of this topic. Although Chapter 11 is devoted to a fuller examination of each of them, a brief overview is presented here.

Marketing communications is about developing messages that can be understood and acted on by target audiences. We present principles by which marketing messages are communicated and then consider how marketing communications might work. This chapter concludes with an overview of what culture is and how it can impact on marketing communications.

Introducing Marketing Communications

Marketing communications, or **promotion** as it was originally called, is one element of the marketing mix. It is used to communicate elements of an organization's offerings to target audiences. The offer might refer to a product, a service, or the organization itself as it tries to build its reputation. However, this is a broad view of marketing communications and we need to understand the various issues, dimensions, and elements that make up this important communication activity. For example, there are the communications experienced by audiences relating to both their use of products (how good is this food blender?) and the consumption of associated services (just how good was the service when I was in that wine bar last week?).

There are communications arising from unplanned or unintended experiences (empty stock shelves or accidents) and there are planned marketing communications (Duncan and Moriarty, 1998), which is the main focus of this and the following chapter. These are all represented in Figure 10.1 (Hughes and Fill, 2007), which is the point at which we start our exploration of marketing communications.

Figure 10.1 depicts not just the breadth but also the complexity of managing marketing communications. However, this framework fails to provide any detailed understanding, particularly of the planned marketing communications element. This component is really important because it has the potential not only to present propositions in the best possible way but also to influence people's expectations about both product and service experiences.

Organizations plan, design, implement, and evaluate their marketing communication activities. Often referred to as campaigns, these activities involve the delivery of messages either to or with target audiences through various communication tools and media.

This chapter is intended to help you understand some of the fundamental ideas associated with planned marketing communications. It sets out the broad scope of the subject and enables you to appreciate the complexity and diversity of this fascinating subject. See Market Insight 10.1 for an example of marketing communications which draws on a range of media, involves consumers, and utilizes emotional branded content.

Visit the **Online Resource Centre** and follow the weblink to the European Association of Communication Agencies (EACA) to learn more about advertising, media, and sales promotion activities across Europe.

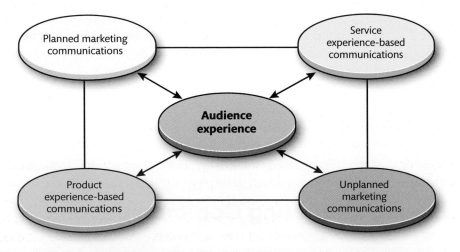

Figure 10.1

The scope of marketing communications

Source: Hughes and Fill (2007). Adapted with the kind permission of Emerald Group Publishing Limited and Westburn Publishers.

Market Insight 10.1

Using Clear Emotional Content in China

The anti-dandruff shampoo *Clear* has a supreme functional attribute; it stops and removes dandruff. However, although this was well understood and awareness levels were equally good, the Unilever brand struggled to make an impact in the Chinese market.

One of the issues concerning these types of brand is that young aspirational Chinese are reluctant to engage with a brand that blatantly demonstrates that they have a problem. This is tied up with the importance of personal image, through cultural pressure to be successful and partly because it is a driver and symbol of success.

The communications strategy for *Clear* needed to move away from one that stressed the brand's functional abilities, to one that enabled a more emotional bond to be established. This meant that *Clear* needed to be repositioned from a personal care brand to a lifestyle brand associated with success and winning.

Research had uncovered that many Chinese consumers liked local TV dramas. This was because they liked local celebrities and aspired to their images which they visualized through their own lives and success in the TV dramas.

The solution rested in the development of a tailor-made branded TV drama, called *Unbeatable*, which was developed in partnership with the Jiangsu Media Group. This enabled *Clear* to be fully integrated through the plotlines of each of the 36 episodes and reflect *Clear's* values, whilst at the same time avoid being perceived as product placement. The lead characters were young, successful, white-collared, and upwardly mobile. Launched through prime time satellite TV, the drama was linked to China's premier online video site. Digital and social platforms enabled a range of activities to be incorporated, including online character blogs, behind the scenes content, live interviews with the cast, fan forums, and a social network game plus various music videos and promotions.

The show was a huge success, attracting a third of the Chinese population, sales of *Clear* rose by 24%, and the return on marketing investment (ROMI) exceeded 700%.

Sources: Based on Hearn (2011); www.spikes.asia/winners/2011/media/entry.cfm?entryid=216&award=101&order=1&direction=1

1 **What do functional and emotional approaches mean? Find three examples of each, in any sector of your choice.**

2 **How are other anti-dandruff brands positioned in your country?**

3 **Think of two other functional and two other emotional approaches that *Clear* might use to communicate with their target audience in China or your country.**

Communication Theory

Communication theory is important as it helps explain how and why certain marketing communication activities take place. Communication is the process by which individuals share meaning. Therefore it is necessary for participants to be able to interpret the meanings embedded in the messages they receive, and then, as far as the sender is concerned, be able to respond coherently. The act of responding is important as it completes an episode in the communication process. Communication that travels only from the sender to the receiver is essentially a one-way process and the full communication process remains incomplete. This form of communication is shown in Figure 10.2.

When Marabou display their chocolate bars on a poster in the Stockholm metro, the person standing on the platform can read it, understand it, and may even be entertained by it. However, the person does not have any immediate opportunity to respond to the ad in such a way that Marabou can hear, understand, and act on his/her comments and feelings. When that same ad is presented on a website or a sales promotion representative offers that same person a chunk of Marabou milk chocolate when they are shopping in a supermarket, there are opportunities to hear, record, and even respond to the comments that the person makes. This form of communication travels from a sender (Marabou) to a receiver (the person in the supermarket) and back again to Marabou, it is referred to as a two-way communication and represents a complete communication episode. This type of communication is depicted in Figure 10.3.

Visit the **Online Resource Centre** and follow the weblink to the International Association of Business Communicators (IABC), a business network with the aim of improving marketing communications effectiveness among communication professionals.

These basic models form the basis of this introduction to communication theory. It is important that those involved in managing and delivering marketing communications understand these processes and the associated complexities. Through knowledge and understanding of the communications process, they are more likely to achieve their objective of sharing meaning with each member of their target audience. This not only helps create opportunities to interact with their audiences, but also encourages some people to develop a dialogue, the richest and most meaningful form of communication.

Understanding the way communication works provides a foundation on which we can better understand not only the way that marketing communications works, but also how it can be used effectively by organizations.

Three main models or interpretations of how communication works are considered here: the linear model, the two-way model, and the interactive model of communication.

The Linear Model of Communication

The linear model of communication, first developed by Wilbur Schramm (1955), is regarded as the basic model of mass communications. The key components of this model of are set out in Figure 10.2.

The model can be broken down into a number of phases, each of which has distinct characteristics. The linear model emphasizes that each phase occurs in a particular sequence, a linear progression, which, according to Theodorson and Theodorson (1969), enables the 'transmission of information, ideas, attitudes, or emotion from one person or group to another (or others), primarily through symbols'. The model and its components are straightforward, but it is the quality of the linkages between the various elements in the process that determines whether the communication will be successful.

The source is an individual or organization which identifies a problem requiring transmission of a message. The source of a message is an important factor in the communication process. First, the source must identify the right problem and, second, a **receiver** who perceives a source to lack conviction, authority, trust, or expertise is not likely to believe the messages sent by that source.

Encoding is the process by which the source selects a combination of appropriate words, pictures, symbols, and music to represent the message to be transmitted. The various bits are 'packed' in such a way that they can be unpacked and understood. The goal is to create a message that is capable of being easily comprehended by the receiver.

Once encoded, the message must be put into a form that is capable of transmission. It may be oral or written, verbal or non-verbal, in a symbolic form or in a sign. The channel is the means

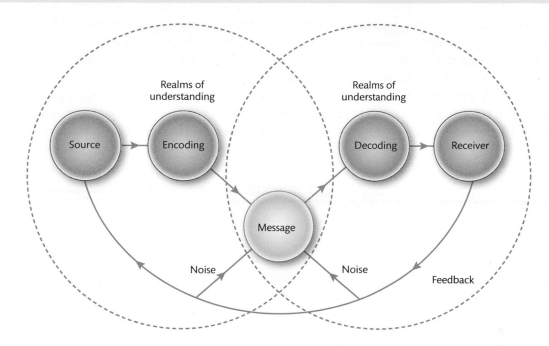

Figure 10.2

A linear model of communications

Sources: Based on Schramm (1955) and Shannon and Weaver (1962).

by which the message is transmitted from the source to the receiver. These channels may be personal or non-personal. The former involves face-to-face contact and **word-of-mouth** communications, which can be extremely influential. Non-personal channels are characterized by mass media advertising, which can reach large audiences. Ads placed in newspapers such as *The Guardian* are typical of this approach. Whatever the format chosen, the source must be sure that what is being put into the message is what they want to be decoded by the receiver.

Once the receiver, an individual or organization, has seen, heard, smelt, or read the message, they decode it. In effect, they are 'unpacking' the various components of the message, starting to make sense of it and give it meaning. The more clearly the message is encoded the easier it is to 'unpack' and comprehend what the source intended to convey when they constructed the message. Therefore **decoding** is that part of the communication process where receivers give meaning to a message.

Once the message is understood, receivers provide a set of reactions referred to as a response. These reactions may vary from an emotional response based on a set of feelings and thoughts about the message to a behavioural or action response.

Feedback is another part of the response process. It is important to know not just that the message has been received, but also that it has been correctly decoded and the right meaning attributed. However, although feedback is an essential aspect of a successful communication event, feedback through mass media channels is generally difficult to obtain, mainly because of the inherent time delay involved in the feedback process. However, feedback through **personal selling** can be instantaneous, through explicit means such as questioning, raising objections, or signing an order form. For the mass media advertiser, the process can be vague and prone to misinterpretation. If a suitable feedback system is not in place, the source will be unaware that the communication has been unsuccessful and is liable to continue wasting resources. This represents inefficient and ineffective marketing communications.

Noise is concerned with influences that distort information and, in turn, make it difficult for the receiver to correctly decode and interpret the message as intended by the source. So, if a telephone rings, or someone rustles sweet papers during a sensitive part of a film screened in a cinema, the receiver is distracted from the message.

The final component in the linear model concerns the 'realm of understanding'. This is an important element in the communication process because it recognizes that successful communications are more likely to be achieved if the source and the receiver understand each other. This understanding concerns attitudes, perceptions, behaviour, and experience—the values of both parties to the communication process. Effective communication is more likely when there is some common ground, a realm of understanding between the source and receiver.

One of the problems associated with the linear model of communication is that it ignores the impact that other people can have on the communication process. People are not passive; they actively use information, and the views and actions of other people can impact on the way information is sent, received, processed, and given meaning. One of the other difficulties with the linear model is that it is based on communication through mass media.

This model was developed at a time when first radio and then TV, with only a few channels, were the only media available. Today there are hundreds of TV channels, and audiences now use the internet, mobile phones, and an increasing array of digital equipment to manage their work, leisure, and entertainment. Increasing numbers of people engage with interactive-based communications and, in some circumstances, such as online gaming, organizations and individuals can be involved in real dialogue. Therefore the linear model is no longer entirely appropriate.

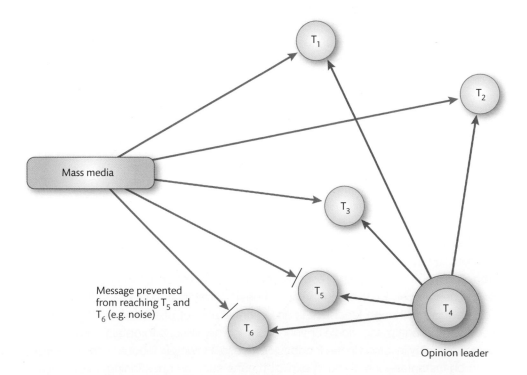

Figure 10.3

The two-step model of communications

Source: *Marketing Communications* (6th edn,) Fill, C., Pearson Education Limited (2013). Reproduced with the kind permission of Pearson Education Limited.

The Two-Step Model of Communication

One interpretation of the linear model is that it is a one-step explanation. Information is directed and shot at prospective audiences, rather like a bullet being propelled from a gun. However, we know that people can have a significant impact on the communication process and the **two-step model**, sometimes referred to as the influencer model, goes some way to reflecting their influence.

The two-step model compensates for the linear or one-step model because it recognizes the importance of personal influences when informing and persuading audiences to think or behave in particular ways. This model depicts information flowing via various media channels to particular types of people to whom other members of the audience refer for information and guidance. There are two main types of influencer. The first is referred to as an **opinion leader** and the other is an **opinion former**. The first is just an ordinary person who has a heightened interest in a particular topic. The second is involved professionally in the topic of interest. These are discussed in more detail later in this chapter, but they both have enormous potential to influence audiences. This may be because messages from personal influencers provide reinforcement and message credibility, or it may be because this is the only way of reaching the end-user audience.

The Interaction Model of Communications

This model is similar to the two-step model but it has one important difference. In this interpretation, the parties are seen to interact among themselves and communication flows among all the members in what is regarded as a communication network (see Figure 10.4). Mass media are not the only source of the communication.

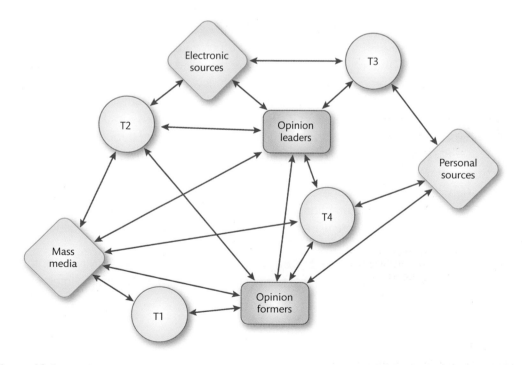

Figure 10.4
An interaction model

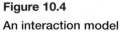

Unlike the linear model, in which messages flow from the source to the receiver, through a channel, the **interaction model** recognizes that messages can flow through various channels and that people can influence the direction and impact of a message. It is not necessarily one-way but interactive communication that typifies much of contemporary communications. In the case insight at the beginning of this chapter, the desire of *The Guardian* to be open requires the use of social media to encourage audience participation. The interaction among different people, sometimes only referring to *The Guardian* indirectly, is a good demonstration of the interaction model in practice.

Interaction is an integral part of the communication process. Think of a conversation with a friend: the face-to-face, oral-, and visual-based communication enables both of you to consider what the other is saying, and to react in whatever way is appropriate. Mass communication does not facilitate this interactional element, and therefore the linear model might be regarded as an incomplete form of the pure communication process.

Interaction is about actions that lead to a response, and much attention is now given to the interaction that occurs between people. However, care needs to be taken because the content associated with an interactional event might be based on an argument, a statement of opinion, or a mere casual social encounter. What is important here is interaction that leads to mutual understanding. This type of interaction concerns 'relationship specific knowledge' (Ballantyne, 2004). That is, the interaction is about information that is relevant to both parties. Once this is established, increased levels of trust develop between the participants so that eventually a dialogue emerges between communication partners. Therefore interactivity is a prelude to dialogue, the highest or purest form of communication.

Dialogue occurs through reasoning, which requires both listening and adaptation skills. Dialogue is concerned with the development of knowledge that is specific to the parties involved and is referred to as 'learning together' (Ballantyne, 2004: 119). The development of digital technologies has been instrumental in enabling organizations to provide increased interaction opportunities with their customers and other audiences. Think of the number of times when watching TV that you are prompted to press the red button to get more information. For example, many news programmes now encourage viewers to tweet, phone, or email comments, opinions, and pictures about particular issues. This is an attempt to get audiences to express their views about a subject and in doing so promote access to and interaction with the programme. Whereas at one time interaction only really occurred through personal selling, it is now possible to interact, and so build mutual understanding with consumers, through the internet and other digital technologies. Indeed, Hoffman and Novak (1996) claim that interactivity between people is now supplemented by interactivity between machines. This means that the interaction, or indeed dialogue, that previously occurred through machines can now occur with the equipment facilitating the communication.

Visit the **Online Resource Centre** and complete Internet Activity 10.1 to learn more about internet advertising, a form of machine interactivity with the internet.

Personal Influencers

As mentioned earlier, two main types of personal influencer can be recognized: opinion leaders and opinion formers. These are now discussed in turn.

Opinion Leaders

Studies of American voting and purchase behaviour by Katz and Lazarsfeld (1955) led them to conclude that some individuals were more predisposed to receiving information and then reprocessing it to influence others. They found that these individuals had the capacity to be more persuasive than information received directly from the mass media. They called these people opinion leaders, and one of their defining characteristics is that they belong to the same peer group as the people they influence—they are not distant or removed.

It has been reported in subsequent research that opinion leaders have a greater exposure to relevant media and as a result have more knowledge/familiarity and involvement with a certain category of offering than others. Non-leaders, or **opinion followers**, turn to opinion leaders for advice and information about offerings they are interested in. Opinion leaders are also more gregarious and self-confident than non-leaders and are more confident of their role as an influencer (Chan and Misra, 1990). Therefore it is not surprising that many marketing communication strategies are targeted at influencing opinion leaders as they will, in turn, influence others. For example, *Vogue* magazine has an 'Influencer Network', a panel of 1,000 women. These influencers provide feedback on a range of issues, including new offerings, upcoming fashion collections, and ad creatives. They are encouraged to talk about particular offerings on their social networks, raising awareness of them and of *Vogue* itself (Moses, 2011). See also Market Insight 10.2 for an example of opinion leadership.

 Market Insight 10.2

Influencing Mums through Mums

Infantino is a baby product manufacturer which developed a Test-Drive campaign to activate influencers as Infantino opinion leaders when it launched ten new products. The idea was that Mum bloggers would be encouraged to comment through multiple online platforms on the new products and so enthuse consumers about Infantino and its products.

Infantino wanted to work with bloggers who would comment authentically not only on the good but also on the not-so-good aspects of Infantino's new products, and in a way that would encourage feedback. This required careful blogger selection of people who could reach and influence others, both on- and offline.

To be an Infantino opinion leader, candidates had to be Mums who had children in the target age

range of newborn to 18 months and be located in key geographic markets. Apart from assessing their passion for baby products, potential influencers were considered in terms of their writing skills and sphere of influence. For example, the reach of their blogs, the quality of their personal web sites, and the nature of their Twitter and Facebook conversations, as well as their expertise and authority on a subject, were taken into account. Candidates were also required to complete an online survey to gauge their involvement in the category. In the end 60 mums from 24 different American states were selected to be part of the Infantino Test-Drive campaign.

The opinion leaders were sent two or three products in phases, to test for a couple of weeks. They were then required to write reviews on their blogs for each product and to share them on Twitter, Facebook, and other online platforms. The influencers also gave away products so that a wider network of mums could experience them.

Market Insight 10.2
continued

As a result, blog posts, tweets, and Facebook updates generated more than five million targeted impressions throughout the campaign. After the campaign, 96% of mums said that they would be likely to recommend Infantino products, and 86% said that they or a fellow mum had purchased Infantino products as a result of their participation in the campaign.

The next step was to create stronger influencers, or brand ambassadors. This required working with fewer bloggers, so that they could focus on authentic brand enthusiasts. The team also recognized the high quality and diversity of the bloggers' content, which means using the ambassadors to generate paid content. This means disclosing and attributing paid product reviews.

Sources: Based on DeBroff *et al.* (2012); http://blog.stay-a-stay-at-home-mom.com/2012/12/12/bloggers-wanted-infantino/ http://www.sugarinmygrits.com/2011/08/infantino-test-drive-phase-1.html

1 **Using a product or brand with which you are familiar, think about three ways in which opinion leadership might be used to develop the brand.**

2 **Think of a hobby or pastime that you might enjoy. Now, out of all your friends and social networks and contacts, who would you ask for advice about taking up the pastime? Why did you choose them?**

3 **In what way might the Infantino brand be affected if they pay their brand ambassadors for word-of-mouth communication?**

Infantino, the US baby product manufacturer, targets new mums to test and review its new offerings
Source: © Infantino.

This approach has been used to convey particular information and help educate large target audiences through TV and radio programmes. For example, TV programmes such as *Coronation Street*, *Eastenders*, and *Emmerdale*, and radio programmes such as *The Archers* (UK soaps), have been used as opinion leadership vehicles to bring to attention and open up debates about many controversial social issues, such as contraception, abortion, drug use and abuse, and serious illness and mental health concerns.

Opinion Formers

The other main form of independent personal influencer are opinion formers. They are not part of the same peer group as the people they influence. Their defining characteristic is that they exert personal influence because of their profession, authority, education, or status associated with the object of the communication process. They provide information and advice as part of the formal expertise they are perceived to hold. For example, shop assistants in music equipment shops are often experienced musicians in their own right. Aspiring musicians seeking to buy their first proper guitar will often consult these perceived 'experts' about guitar brands, styles, models, and associated equipment such as amplifiers. In the same way, doctors carry such conviction that they can influence the rate at which medicines are consumed. Drug manufacturers such as GlaxoSmithKline and Pfizer often launch new drugs by enlisting the support of eminent professors, consultants, or doctors who are recognized by others in the profession as experts. These opinion formers are invited to lead symposia and associated events, and in doing so build credibility and activity around the new proposition.

Organizations target their marketing communications at opinion leaders and formers to penetrate the market more quickly than relying on communicating directly with the target audience. However, in addition to these forms of influence, reference needs to be made to spokespersons. There are some potential problems that advertisers need to be aware of when considering the use of celebrities. First, does the celebrity fit the image of the brand and will the celebrity be acceptable to the target audience now and in the long run? If the lifestyle of the celebrity changes, what impact will the changes have on the target audience and their attitude towards

---

 Research Insight 10.1

To take your learning further, you might wish to read this influential paper.

Keller, K. L. (2001), 'Mastering the marketing communications mix: micro and macro perspectives on integrated marketing communication programs, *Journal of Marketing Management*, **17, 819–47.**

This paper provides a useful introduction to the issues, complexities, and methods of integrated marketing communications. Keller considers the micro and macro issues and describes how the two perspectives relate, as well as discussing the theoretical and managerial implications.

@ **Visit the Online Resource Centre to read the abstract and access the full paper.**

the brand? For example, the well-publicized allegations about the bad behaviour of the super-model Kate Moss led to the loss of several sponsorship and brand endorsement contracts (e.g. H&M and Burberry), although it is alleged that her overall income actually increased as a result of the negative publicity and sales through her Topshop brand soared.

The second problem concerns the impact that the celebrity makes relative to the brand. There is a danger that the receiver remembers the celebrity but not the message or the brand. The celebrity becomes the hero, rather than the proposition being advertised.

All of the models of communication discussed have a role to play in marketing communications. Mass media communication in the form of broadcast TV and radio is still used by organizations to reach large audiences. Two-way and interaction forms of communication are used to reach smaller, specific target audiences and to enable a range of people to contribute to the process. Interaction and dialogue are higher levels of communication and are increasingly used to generate personal communication with individual customers. The skill for marketing practitioners is to know when to move from one-way, to two-way, to interactive, and then dialogue-based marketing communications.

The Role of Marketing Communications

Now that we know how communication works, it is time to examine what marketing communications is and the tasks it undertakes. Marketing communications is a relatively new term for what was previously referred to as promotion. As was discussed in Chapter 1, promotion is one of the Ps of the marketing mix, and is responsible for the communication of the proposition to the target market. Although there is implicit and important communication through the other elements of the marketing mix (e.g. a high price is symbolic of high quality), it is the task of a planned and integrated set of activities to communicate effectively with each of an organization's stakeholder groups.

Fundamentally, marketing communications comprises three elements: 1) a set of tools, 2) the media, and 3) messages. The five common tools are advertising, sales promotion, personal selling, direct marketing, and public relations. In addition, a range of media, such as TV, radio, press, and the internet, are used to convey messages to target audiences.

These various tools have been developed in response to changing market and environmental conditions. For example, public relations is now seen by some to have both a proposition and a corporate dimension. Direct marketing is now recognized as an important way of developing closer relationships with buyers, both consumer and organizational, whereas new and innovative forms of communication through sponsorship, floor advertising, video screens on supermarket trolleys and checkout coupon dispensers, and the internet and associated technologies mean that effective communication requires the selection and integration of an increasing variety of communication tools and media. Communication is no longer restricted to promoting and persuading audiences as the tasks are now much broader and strategic. Today, the term marketing communications is a more appropriate and established term which reflects an organization's communication activities.

Marketing communications are used to achieve one of two principal goals. The first concerns the development of brand values. For a long time advertising, and to some extent public relations, has concentrated on establishing a set of feelings, emotions, and beliefs about a brand or organization. Brand communication seeks to make us think positively about a brand, and helps us to remember and develop positive brand attitudes in the hope that when we are ready to buy that type of offering again, we will buy brand X because we feel positively about it. *The Guardian* knew that they had to use marketing communications to change the perception that some people had of the newspaper.

The alternative and more contemporary goal is to use communications to make us behave in particular ways. Rather than spend lots of money developing worthy and positive attitudes towards brands, the view of many today is that we should use this money to encourage people to behave differently. This might be through buying the offering, or driving people to a website, requesting a brochure, or making a telephone call. This is called behaviour change and is driven by using messages that provide audiences with a reason to act, or what is referred to as a **call-to-action**. *The Guardian* had to use marketing communications to increase the number and frequency of visitors to their website, in other words a change of behaviour.

So, on the one hand, communications can be used to develop brand feelings and, on the other, to change or manage the behaviour of the target audience. These are not mutually exclusive; for example, many TV advertisements are referred to as direct-response ads because they not only attempt to create brand values but also carry a website address, telephone number, or details of a special offer (sales promotion). In other words, the two goals are mixed into a hybrid approach.

The success of marketing communication depends on the extent to which messages engage their audiences (see Market Insight 10.3). These audiences can be seen to fall into three main groups.

1 Customers—these may be consumers or they may be end-user organizations.

2 Channel members—each organization is part of a network of other organizations such as suppliers, retailers, wholesalers, value added resellers, distributors, and other retailers who join together, often freely, to make the offering available to end-users.

3 General stakeholders—organizations and people who either influence or are influenced by the organization. These may be shareholders, the financial community, trade unions, employees, local community, or others.

Therefore marketing communications involves not just customers but also a range of other stakeholders. It can be used to reach consumers as well as business audiences.

As explained in Chapter 1, the concept of exchange is central to our understanding of marketing. For an exchange to take place, there must be two or more parties, each of whom can offer something of value to the other and are prepared to enter freely into the exchange process, a transaction. There are many types of exchange but two are of particular importance: transactional exchanges and collaborative exchanges.

- **Transactional exchanges** (Bagozzi, 1978; Houston and Gassenheimer, 1987) are transactions that occur independently of any previous or subsequent exchanges. They have a short-term orientation and are primarily motivated by self-interest. So, when a consumer buys an MP3 player, a brand that they have not bought before, a transactional exchange can be identified.

- **Collaborative exchanges** (Dwyer *et al.*, 1987) have a longer-term orientation and develop between parties who wish to build long-term supportive relationships. So, when a consumer buys their third product from the same brand as the MP3 player, perhaps from the same dealer, collaborative exchanges are considered to be taking place.

These two types of exchange transactions represent the extremes of a spectrum. In mature industrial societies, transactional exchanges have tended to dominate commercial transactions, although recently there has been a substantial movement towards collaborative exchanges. Each organization has a mix of audiences, so it's not surprising that they use a range of

Market Insight 10.3

A tweet's fine, no cash please

Ideas about relationship and financial value are integral to transactional and collaborative exchanges. However, the use of tweets as social currency has started to become an alternative to the use of cash and, more pertinently, reinforces relationship value. For example, a Cape Town vending machine was programmed to dispense free 'BOS' iced tea when it received a tweet with the hashtag #tweet4t. Olympics sponsor Coca Cola enabled followers of their innocent drinks brand to 'tweet for a seat'. Everyone was invited to tweet whom they would like to take to the Olympics and why.

Perhaps the most advanced scheme was proposed by Kellogg's when they started encouraging customers to pay for their products with a tweet. Thought to be the first product–social media exchange, it demonstrates not only the value perceived to be emerging within social media, but also how offline and digital media are becoming more integrated into people's lives. The pay-with-a-tweet concept was developed for the Special K campaign using the concept that social media is a social currency, and therefore works as an exchange mechanism.

The deal was available for just four days at a pop-up store in London. In return for a product-related tweet, shoppers were entitled to a packet of Kellogg's Special K Cracker Crisps. The one-off store only sold the new under 100 calories a pack Special K Cracker Crisps snack. The promotional event was staffed by Special K girls, each wearing the heavily branded Special K red dress.

A live community board in the store displayed #tweetshop tweets and reflected the hugely positive response. Some of the tweets received included 'My first tweet and it's from #tweetshop! Brilliant! And free crisps as well!' and 'Here's to healthier crisps and turning tweets into currency'.

In many ways this event demonstrated how the use of owned media could generate earned media through word-of-mouth communication as people shared news about the new product and the idea of products for tweets.

Sources: Based on Hall (2012); Terrelonge (2012).

1 **Is the Kellogg's initiative just a short-term promotional feature, or are there longer-term opportunities for the use of social media as currency?**

2 **Identify two other brands that might benefit from this form of exchange.**

3 **Can you identify other forms of exchange not involving finance?**

Kellogg's now produce crisps under the Special K brand
Source: Kellogg's Special K Cracker Crisps © Kellogg's.

communication tools and media to suit different exchange preferences of customers, suppliers, and other stakeholder audiences.

Audiences who prefer transactional exchanges might be better engaged with advertising and mass-media-based communications, with messages that are impersonal and largely rational and product focused. Audiences that prefer more collaborative exchanges should be engaged through personal, informal, and interactive communications, with messages that are generally emotional and relationship oriented.

Shoes can be purchased from a range of different retail outlets and the store they are purchased from is often insignificant, especially as price can be an important purchasing factor. The approach adopted by the shoe company Clarks recognizes the importance of building a long-term relationship with their customers. The 'First Shoes Experience' programme run by Clarks demonstrates good marketing communications and is based on the significance of a child's first pair of shoes and what they can mean to the parents. These tiny shoes are often kept for years and years as a memento. Clarks now provide a souvenir of the occasion in the form of a free card and framed photograph of a child's very first shop visit and fitting. A simple idea that engages audiences with an important event, it also enables both the parents and Clarks to remember the event through longer-term memories. What might have been a transactional exchange is transformed into one that is more collaborative and relationship oriented.

What is Marketing Communications?

Quite naturally, definitions of marketing communications have evolved as the topic and our understanding have developed. Original views assumed that these types of communication were used to persuade people to buy offerings. The focus was on propositions, one-way communications, and persuasion, and there was a short-term perspective. In short, an organization's offerings were *promoted to* audiences.

However, this perspective has given way to the term marketing communications. This was partly a result of an increase in the tasks that the communications departments were expected to undertake and a widening of the tools and media that could be used. At the same time there has been a shift from mass to personal communications and a greater focus on integration activities. The following represents a contemporary definition of marketing communications.

Marketing communications is a management process through which an organization attempts to engage with its various audiences. By understanding an audience's communications environment, organizations seek to develop and present messages for its identified stakeholder groups before evaluating and acting upon the responses. By conveying messages that are of significant value, audiences are encouraged to offer attitudinal and behavioural responses (Fill, 2013).

There are three main aspects associated with this definition: engagement, audiences, and responses.

- Engagement—what are the audiences' communications needs and is it possible to engage with them on their terms using one-way, two-way, or dialogic communications?
- Audiences—which specific audience(s) do we need to communicate with and what are their various behaviour and information-processing needs?
- Responses—what are the desired outcomes of the communication process? Are they based on changes in perception, values, and beliefs, or are changes in behaviour required?

Therefore marketing communications can be considered from a number of perspectives. Although it is a complex activity and used by organizations with varying degrees of sophistication, it is undoubtedly concerned with the way in which audiences are encouraged to perceive an organization and/or its offerings. Therefore it should be regarded as an audience-centred activity.

The Tasks of Marketing Communications

Promotion (essentially persuasion) alone is insufficient as marketing communications undertakes other tasks in the name of engaging audiences. So, what is it that marketing communications does and why do organizations use it in varying ways? Fundamentally, marketing communications can be

used to engage audiences by undertaking one of four main tasks, referred to by Fill (2002) as the **DRIP** model. In no particular order, communications can be used to differentiate brands and organizations, to reinforce brand memories and expectations, to inform (i.e. to make aware or educate audiences), and finally to persuade them to do things or to behave in particular ways. See Table 10.1 for an explanation of each of these tasks.

Visit the **Online Resource Centre** and complete Internet Activity 10.2 to learn more about the way the fashion house Burberry uses marketing communications.

Table 10.1 The DRIP tasks for marketing communications

Marketing communication tasks	Explanation
To differentiate	In many markets, there is little to separate brands (e.g. mineral water, coffee, printers). In these cases, it is the images created by marketing communications that help differentiate one brand from another and position them so that consumers develop positive attitudes and make purchasing decisions.
To reinforce	Communications may be used to *remind* people of a need they might have or of the benefits of past transactions with a view to convincing them that they should enter into a similar exchange. In addition, it is possible to provide *reassurance* or comfort either immediately prior to an exchange or, more commonly, post purchase. This is important as it helps to retain current customers and improve profitability. This approach to business is much more cost effective than constantly striving to lure new customers.
To inform	One of the most common uses of marketing communications is to *inform* and make potential customers aware of the features and benefits of an organization's offering. In addition, marketing communications can be used to educate audiences, to show them how to use an offering or what to do in particular situations.
To persuade	Communication may attempt to *persuade* current and potential customers of the desirability of entering into an exchange relationship.

Your M&S, the bi-monthly magazine, offers fashion and style advice

Source: Image courtesy of Marks and Spencer plc 2013.

These tasks are not mutually exclusive; indeed, campaigns might be designed to target two or three of them. For example, the launch of a new brand will require that audiences be informed, made aware of its existence, and enabled to understand how it is different from competitor brands. A brand that is well established might try to reach lapsed customers by reminding them of the key features and benefits and offering them an incentive (persuasion) to buy again. For example, Your M&S is a bi-monthly magazine designed to showcase what is new in Marks and Spencer's stores and give fashion and style advice. However, it only features offerings available at M&S. The magazine is an integral part of the company's communication mix and is used, among many other activities, to engage customers with the brand and drive readers into the store to shop. To that extent, an in-house survey found that 57% of readers (i.e. nearly 2.53 million people) visited an M&S store as a result of reading the magazine. It also found that 30% of readers had bought an offering featured in its magazine (Alarcon, 2008).

The Marketing Communications Mix

The marketing communications mix consists of three main elements: 1) tools, 2) media, and 3) messages. These are considered briefly here; a fuller exposition of tools and media can be found in Chapter 11.

There are five primary tools: advertising, sales promotion, direct marketing, public relations, and personal selling. In addition to these, there are several secondary tools such as sponsorship, exhibitions and trade shows, and field marketing. The five primary tools of marketing communications are used in various combinations and with different degrees of intensity to achieve different communication goals with target audiences.

Media enable messages to be delivered to target audiences. Some media are owned by organizations (a building or delivery van can constitute media), but in most cases media to reach large audiences are owned by third-party organizations. As a result, clients have to pay media owners to send their messages through their media vehicles. Media can be classified as either paid-for or owned.

For a long time the range of available media was fairly limited, but since the early 1990s the array of media has been growing rapidly and changing the media landscape. Now there is a huge choice of paid media so that media selection has become crucial when trying to reach increasingly smaller audiences. The cost of some media can be immense, although in many cases fees are related to the number of people reached through a media vehicle. Space (or time) within traditional media is limited, and costs rise as demand for the limited space/time and audience size increases. As a generalization, space within digital media is unlimited and so contact costs fall as audience size increases.

Many of the tools, in particular advertising, use paid media to reach their audiences. However, it is important to recognize that tools and media are not the same, as they have different characteristics and are used for different purposes. The internet and Web 2.0 are media; they are not tools. For a deeper consideration of each of the elements of the mix, readers are advised to read Chapter 11.

Word of Mouth

Planned marketing communications have traditionally used paid-for media to convey messages to target audiences. However, as mentioned previously with respect to opinion formers and leaders, some messages are best relayed through personal communications. This type of communication does not involve any payment for media because communication is freely given through word-of-mouth conversation. Word-of-mouth communication is 'interpersonal communication regarding products or services where the receiver regards the communicator as impartial' (Stokes and Lomax, 2002).

Personal influence within the communication process is important. This is because customers perceive word-of-mouth recommendations as objective and unbiased. In comparison with advertising messages, word-of-mouth communications are more robust (Berkman and Gilson, 1986). Word-of-mouth messages are used either as information inputs prior to purchase or as a support and reinforcement of their own purchasing decisions.

People like to talk about their product (service) experiences. The main stimulus for behaviour is that the offering in question gave them either particular pleasure or particular displeasure. These motivations to discuss experiences vary between individuals and with the intensity of the motivation at any one particular moment. One hotel gave away teddy bears to guests on the basis that the guests would be happy to talk about their stay at the hotel, with the teddy bear acting as a prompt to provoke or induce conversation.

For every single positive comment there are ten negative comments. For this reason, word-of-mouth communication was once seen as negative, unplanned, and having a corrosive effect on a brand's overall communications. Today, organizations actively manage word-of-mouth communications to generate positive comments and as a way of differentiating themselves in the market. Viral marketing or 'word-of-mouse' communication is an electronic version of the spoken endorsement of an offering (see Chapter 17). Often using humorous messages, games, video clips, and screen savers, information can be targeted at key individuals who then voluntarily pass the message to friends and colleagues and in doing so bestow, endorse, and provide the message with much-valued credibility.

For organizations such as *The Guardian*, who target communications at 'Progressives', it is important to direct messages at those individuals who are predisposed to such discussion, as it is likely that they will propel word-of-mouth recommendations. Therefore the target is not necessarily the target market, but opinion leaders within target markets, individuals who are most likely to volunteer their positive opinions about the offering, and who, potentially, have some influence over people in their peer group. See Market Insight 10.4.

Market Insight 10.4

Intelligent Energy Stories

British Gas had a poor reputation for service and operated in a market where customers were locked into fixed-price deals and short renewal periods. As a result a switchers' market emerged and as the recession gripped and energy prices soared, it became evident that the development of a strong brand was required.

In the business market, energy was perceived as an overhead. It was not seen to be something that could be managed or used intelligently. Energy companies talked about efficiency, but there was little advice or information about how to manage energy, even among the high energy users. Not surprisingly, most businesses did not believe that they were getting the right support.

This knowledge represented an opportunity to reposition the brand and become an energy service, not just an energy supplier. From this, the positioning statement, 'intelligent energy partner', was developed.

British Gas Boilers (BGB) needed to demonstrate that they could fulfil the brand promise, and a campaign Energy Live was developed. Recognizing the value of peer support and credibility, BGB decided to use a storytelling approach, based on the experiences of five businesses. To show energy consumption and costs, the five companies were issued with a smart meter, an energy audit, and the Business Energy

Insight (BEI) service. The outcome was that the businesses saved up to 25% of their energy costs.

The Energy Live campaign was launched through the use of public relations and press. The content was based on the extent of business energy wastage and used eye-catching imagery. A variety of media, including print and documentary videos, were used to give the solution. The multimedia approach was designed to create engagement, interaction, and response, and to drive traffic to the BEI microsite. It was here that the detailed stories of the five businesses were made available through text, infographics, and video.

British Gas Boilers launched the Energy Live campaign in a bid to build its brand
Source: istock © vovan 13.

Market Insight 10.4
continued

Since the launch of the campaign, the BEI microsite has had 65,000 visitors and around 25,000 customers have signed up to BEI. Positive perceptions of BGB's service have increased by 27%, value perceptions have increased by 14%, and the perception of BGB as innovative has increased by 9%. Overall, the campaign had a positive impact on net promoter scores with an increase of 12% in just two quarters of activity. Because of the long lead times in setting up B2B energy contracts, it is too soon to comment on the impact of the campaign on overall commercial performance.

Sources: Anon. (2012); www.britishgas.co.uk/business/blog/ www.youtube.com/watch?v=70CZij16U0o www.ogilvy.co.uk/ ogilvy-one/2012/11/23/ogilvyone-uk-triumphs-at-the-b2b-marketing-awards-2012/

1 Why was it necessary for BGB to use peer comment and support in their campaign?

2 Make a list of the different elements that might compose the marketing communications mix for a B2B campaign. How does this differ from a consumer-based campaign?

3 How might BGB have made greater use of word-of-mouth communication?

How Marketing Communications Works

Ideas about how advertising, then promotion, and now marketing communications, works have been a constant source of investigation, endeavour, and conceptual speculation. To suggest that a firm conclusion has been reached would be misleading and untrue. However, particular ideas have stood out and have played a more influential role in shaping our ideas about this fascinating topic. Some of these are presented here.

The first important idea about how advertising works was based on how the personal selling process works. Developed by Strong (1925), the **AIDA** model has become extremely well known

Research Insight 10.2

To take your learning further, you might wish to read this influential paper.

Duncan, T. and Moriarty, S. (1998) 'A communication-based marketing model for managing relationships', *Journal of Marketing*, 62(April), 1–13.

This is one of the most important academic papers in the field of marketing communications. It is important because it led the transition from a functional perspective of integrated marketing communications to one that emphasized its role within relationship marketing.

@ **Visit the Online Resource Centre to read the abstract and access the full paper.**

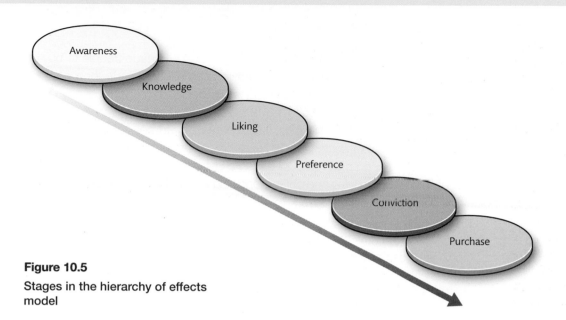

Figure 10.5
Stages in the hierarchy of effects
model

and is used by many practitioners. AIDA refers to the need to first create awareness, secondly generate interest, and then drive desire, from which action (a sale) emerges. As a broad interpretation of the sales process this is generally correct, but it fails to provide insight into the depths of how advertising works. Thirty-six years later, Lavidge and Steiner (1961) presented a model based on what is referred to as the **hierarchy of effects** approach. Similar in nature to AIDA, it assumes that a prospect must pass through a series of steps for a purchase to be made. It is assumed, correctly, that advertising cannot generate an immediate sale because there are a series of thought processes that need to be fulfilled prior to action. These steps are represented in Figure 10.5.

These models have become known as hierarchy of effects (HoE) models, simply because the effects (on audiences) are thought to occur in a top-down sequence. Some of the attractions of these HoE models and frameworks are that they are straightforward, simple, easy to understand, and, if creating advertising materials, provide a helpful broad template on which to develop and evaluate campaigns.

However, although attractive, this sequential approach has several drawbacks. People do not always process information, nor do they always purchase offerings following a series of sequential steps. This logical progression is not reflected in reality when, for example, an impulse purchase is followed by an emotional feeling towards a brand. There are also questions about what actually constitutes adequate levels of awareness, comprehension, and conviction. How can it be known which stage the majority of the target audience has reached at any one point in time, and is this purchase sequence applicable to all consumers for all purchases?

The Strong and the Weak Theories of Advertising

So, if advertising cannot be assumed to work in just one particular way, what other explanations exist? Of the various models put forward, two stand out. These are the strong (Jones 1991) and the weak (Ehrenberg, 1974) theories of advertising.

The Strong Theory of Advertising

According to Jones (1991), advertising has a strong effect as it can persuade people to buy an offering that they have not previously purchased. Advertising can also generate long-run purchase behaviour. Under the **strong theory**, advertising is believed to be capable of increasing sales for a brand and for the **product class**. These upward shifts are achieved through the use of manipulative and psychological techniques, which are deployed against largely passive consumers who, possibly because of apathy, are either generally incapable of processing information intelligently or have little or no motivation to become involved.

This interpretation is a persuasion view and corresponds very well to the HoE models referred to earlier. Persuasion occurs by moving buyers towards a purchase by easing them through a series of steps, prompted by timely and suitable promotional messages. It seems that this approach correlates closely with new offerings where new buying behaviours are required.

The strong theory has close affiliation with an advertising style that is proposition oriented, where features and benefits are outlined clearly for audiences, and where pack shots are considered important.

The Weak Theory of Advertising

Contrary to the strong perspective is the view that a consumer's brand choices are driven by purchasing habit rather than by exposure to promotional messages. One of the more prominent researchers in this area was Ehrenberg (1974), who believed that advertising represents a weak force. He believed that advertising has little impact on persuading consumers to buy offerings, mainly because consumers are active, not passive, information processors.

Ehrenberg proposed that the **ATR** framework (awareness–trial–reinforcement) is a more appropriate interpretation of how advertising works. Both Jones and Ehrenberg agree that awareness is required before any purchase can be made, although the elapsed time between awareness and action may be very short or very long. Out of the mass of people exposed to a message, a few will be sufficiently intrigued to want to try an offering (trial)-the next phase. Reinforcement follows to maintain awareness and provide reassurance to help customers repeat the pattern of thinking and behaviour. Advertising's role is to breed brand familiarity and identification (Ehrenberg, 1997).

According to the **weak theory**, advertising is employed as a defence, to retain customers, and to increase brand usage. Advertising is used to reinforce existing attitudes, not necessarily to drastically change them. This means that when people say that they 'are not influenced by advertising' they are, in the main, correct.

Both the strong and the weak theories of advertising are important because they are equally right and equally wrong. The answer to the question 'how does advertising work?' lies somewhere between the two and is dependent on the context. For advertising to work, involvement is likely to be high and so here the strong theory is the most applicable. However, the vast majority of product purchase decisions generate low involvement, and so decision-making is likely to be driven by habit. Here, advertising's role is to maintain a brand's awareness with the purchase cycle, so the weak theory is most applicable.

Visit the **Online Resource Centre** and complete Internet Activity 10.3 to learn more about the strong and the weak theories of advertising.

A Composite Approach

Most of the frameworks presented so far have their roots in advertising. If we are to establish a model that explains how marketing communications works, a different perspective is required, one that draws on the key parts of all the models. This is possible as the three key components of the attitude construct lie within these different models. Attitudes have been regarded as an important aspect of marketing communications activities, and advertising is thought to be capable of influencing the development of positive attitudes towards brands (see also Chapter 2).

The three stages of attitude formation are that we learn something (cognitive or learning component), feel something (an affective or emotional component), and then act on our attitudes (behavioural or conative component). So, in many situations we learn something, feel something towards a brand, and then proceed to buy or not to buy. These stages are set out in Figure 10.6.

The HoE models and the strong theory contain this sequential approach of learn, feel, do. However, we do not always pass through this particular sequence and the weak theory puts greater emphasis on familiarity and reminding (awareness) than the other components.

So, if we look at Figure 10.7, we can see that these components have been worked into a circular format. This means that, when using marketing communications, it is not necessary to follow each component sequentially. The focus can be on what the audience requires, and this might be on the learning, feeling, or doing components, as determined by the audience. In other words, for marketing communications to be audience centred, we should develop campaigns based on the overriding need of the audience at any one time, based on their need to learn, feel, or behave in particular ways.

▪ Learn

Where learning is the priority, the overall goal should be to inform or educate the target audience. If the offering is new, it will be important to make the target audience aware of the offering's existence and to inform them of the brand's key attributes and benefits. This is a common use for advertising as it has the capacity to reach both large and targeted audiences. Other than making them aware of the offering's existence, other tasks include showing the target

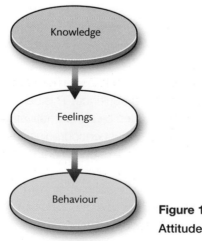

Figure 10.6
Attitude construct—linear

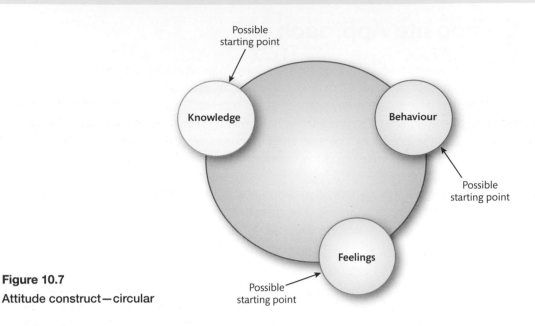

Figure 10.7
Attitude construct—circular

audience how a brand is superior to competitive offerings, perhaps demonstrating how an offering works and educating the audience about when and in what circumstances the brand should be used.

▪ Feel

Once the audience is aware of a brand and knows something about how it might be useful to them, it is important that they develop a positive attitude towards the brand. This can be achieved by presenting the brand with a set of emotional values that it is thought will appeal and be of interest to the audience. These values need to be repeated in subsequent communications to reinforce the brand attitudes.

Marketing communications should be used to involve and immerse people in a brand. So, for example, advertising or brand placement within films and music videos will help show how it fits in with a desirable set of values and lifestyles. Use of suitable music, characters that reflect the values of either the current target audience or an aspirational group, a tone of voice, colours, and images all help to create a particular emotional disposition and understanding about what the brand represents or stands for. For some people, advertising only works at an emotional level and the cognitive approach is irrelevant.

▪ Do

Most organizations find that to be successful they need to use a much broader set of tools, and that the goal is to change the behaviour of the target audience. This behavioural change may be about getting people to buy the brand, but it may often be about motivating them to visit a website, call for a brochure, fill in an application form, or just encouraging them to visit a shop and sample the brand free of payment and any other risk. This behavioural change is also referred to as a 'call to action'. See Market Insight 10.5

When the accent is on using marketing communications to drive behaviour and action, **direct-response advertising** can be effective. It is said that 40% of TV ads have a telephone number or website address. However, sales promotion, direct marketing, and personal selling are particularly effective at influencing behaviour and calling the audience to act.

Market Insight 10.5

Coffee-mate Uses a Touch of *Nota Cinta*

Coffee creamer, or whitener, is popular in Malaysia where taste and brand affinity drives brand preference. There are three main brands: F&N is the market leader followed by SBC, a private label brand, and Nestlé's Coffee-mate is the third brand. Some people continue to use the brand they grew up with, whilst others use condensed milk or fresh milk. However, the market is facing a challenge as the younger generation of Malaysians has developed a preference for black coffee.

The main brands differentiate themselves in different ways. Coffee-mate highlights taste and value, F&N stresses its versatility and Malaysian heritage, and SBC uses value pricing. Although Coffee-mate had a high level of brand awareness, it was not the first choice for the younger generation. To grow the brand it was necessary to change attitudes, and this required making an emotional connection, rather than persist with the functional approach based on taste and value.

It was decided to target young Malay couples, rather than large families, because Malays tend to marry early, are more open to experiment, and adopt new products in the initial years of their married life.

Coffee-mate adopted the 'romance and passion of a relationship' as its campaign platform, and used this to support a campaign entitled *Nota Cinta* ('love notes' in Bhasa Malaysia/Malay language). The idea was based on the simple insight that any relationship starts with a humble love note on tissue paper, a post-it note, SMS, letter, mail, or a song with a message. To connect with the digital savvy audience, Coffee-mate developed a web-based campaign—a soap, or webisodes, which featured different phases of a passionate love relationship between young

couples. Coffee-mate was presented as an integral part of the ups and downs of their relationship and the reason for stirring up the lost passion.

Viewers were driven to the micro-site where the web series was uploaded through banners, email, and blogs plus print ads, POS materials, posters, radio spots, and on-ground events. A Facebook fan page and web-based consumer contests were created to generate curiosity and interest for the webisodes. A Facebook application called *Ku Untukmu* (meaning you and me) was developed to involve couples with the brand. This enabled them to create a memorable moment for themselves, and to become familiar with the process of preparing coffee to their taste using Coffee-mate.

By the end of 2011, Coffee-mate's year-on-year sales had grown 13% in volume and 9% in value, compared with a 5% category growth. More importantly, brand involvement changed as site visits were 15% up on those expected, views of the webisode trailers were up 20%, and online contest entries were up 81%. Facebook recorded 68,000 fans during the campaign period, 540 unique videos were created by consumers using the *Ku Untukmu* application and uploaded on the brand page, and 23,105 new consumers were attracted as a result of the campaign.

Sources: Nestlé Malaysia sales records and syndicated reports; Google Analytics; Facebook records.

Courtesy: Dr Milan Agni hotri (Group Director—Brand Planning and Innovations, McCann Worldgroup Malaysia).

1 Which part of the attitude construct was the focus of the Coffee-mate campaign?

2 How did the Coffee-mate campaign try to use word-of-mouth communications?

3 What is your opinion of the Coffee-mate strategy? Justify your response.

Research Insight 10.3

To take your learning further, you might wish to read this influential paper.

Gilliland, D. I. and Johnston, W. J. (1997), 'Toward a model of business-to-business marketing communications effects', *Industrial Marketing Management*, **26, 15–29.**

An interesting paper that is based around a model that is designed to address how marketing communications works, but in a business-to-business environment. The authors introduce a number of important concepts and issues that relate to the subject in different ways.

@ Visit the **Online Resource Centre** to read the abstract and access the full paper.

Cultural Aspects of Marketing Communications

Marketing communications has the potential to influence more than just customers. Indeed, it can be used by a wide range of other stakeholders, such as suppliers, employees, religious and faith groups, trade unions, and local communities.

The tools, media, and messages used by organizations influence, and are influenced by, the culture and environment in which they operate. Culture and related belief systems are significant factors in the way organizations choose to communicate in the different areas and regions in which they operate. For example, at a broad level cases of the strong theory of advertising are observed more frequently in North America, whereas examples of the weak theory are quite prevalent in Europe.

In this final part of the chapter, consideration is given to some of the cultural issues associated with marketing communications.

Culture

Culture refers to the values, beliefs, ideas, customs, actions, and symbols that are learnt by members of particular societies. Marketing communications should be an audience-centred activity, whether those audiences are located domestically or anywhere around the globe. Therefore, as there are so many international, regional, and local communities, each with cultural variances, so the development of marketing communications for these audiences must be based on a sound understanding of their culture.

Culture is important because it provides individuals within a society with a sense of identity and an understanding of what is deemed to be acceptable behaviour. According to Hollensen (2010), it is commonly agreed that culture has three key characteristics: that culture is learned, interrelated, and shared. See Table 10.2 for a fuller account of these variables.

These boundaries between cultures are not fixed or rigid, as this would suggest that cultures are static. Instead they evolve and change as members of a society adjust to new technologies, government policies, changing values, and demographic changes, to mention but a few

Table 10.2 Characteristics of culture

Cultural characteristic	Explanation
Learned	Culture is not innate or instinctual, otherwise everyone would behave in the same way. Human beings across the world do not behave uniformly or predictably, and they learn values and behaviours that are shared with common groups. Therefore different cultures exist and there are boundaries within cultures, framing behaviours and lifestyles.
Interrelated	There are deep connections between different elements within a culture. Therefore family, religion, business/work, and social status are interlinked.
Shared	Cultural values are passed through family, religion, education, and the media. This progression of values enables culture to be passed from generation to generation. This is important as it provides consistency, stability, and direction for social behaviour and beliefs.

Source: Hollensen, S. (2007), *Global Marketing; A Decision-Oriented Approach* (4th edn), Harlow: FT/Prentice Hall.

dynamic variables. Unsurprisingly, therefore, brands and symbols used to represent brands have different meanings as they are interpreted in the light of the prevailing culture.

Culture consists of various layers. Hollensen (2010) refers to a nest of cultures, with one inside another, a structure that is similar to a 'Russian doll' (Figure 10.8).

Figure 10.8

Layers of culture

Source: *Global Marketing* (4th edn), Hollensen, S., Pearson Education Limited (2010). Used with permission.

Research Insight 10.4

To take your learning further, you might wish to read this influential paper.

Harris, G. (1996), 'International advertising: developmental and implementational issues', *Journal of Marketing Management*, 12(6), 551–60.

This paper considers the international advertising practices of several major advertisers (multinationals), and explores the extent to which they attempt to standardize their advertising across the countries in which they have a presence. The conclusion that no one organization adopts full standardization was important at the time of publication, and paved the way for the subsequent stream of research in this field.

@ Visit the **Online Resource Centre** to read the abstract and access the full paper.

Here, it can be imagined that a buyer in one country and a seller in another are faced with several layers of culture, all interrelated and all influencing an individual's behaviour.

- National culture—sets out the cultural concepts and the legislative framework governing the way business is undertaken.

- Industry/business culture—particular business sectors adopt a way of doing business within a competitive framework. The shipping business, for example, will have its own way of conducting itself based on its own heritage. As a result, all participants know what is expected and understand the rules of the game.

- Organizational culture—not only does an organization have an overall culture but the various sub-cultures also have a system of shared values, beliefs, meanings, and behaviours.

- Individual behaviour—each individual is affected by, and learns from, the various cultural levels.

Marketing communications, at both a formal and informal level, needs to assimilate these different levels to ensure that an individual's behaviour is understood and the decision-making processes and procedures within which they operate are appreciated. In many markets, there is little to separate brands (e.g. mineral water, coffee, printers). In these cases, it is the images created by marketing communications that help differentiate one brand from another and position them so that consumers develop positive attitudes and make purchasing decisions. The way in which different societies perceive these same brands is a reflection of the cultural drivers that frame people's perceptions.

Chapter Summary

To consolidate your learning, the key points from this chapter are summarized here.

- **Describe the nature, purpose, and scope of marketing communications.**

  Marketing communications, or promotion as it was originally called, is one of the Ps of the marketing mix. It is used to communicate an organization's offer relating to products, services, or the overall organization. In broad terms the management activity consists of several components. There are the communications experienced by audiences relating to both their use of products and the consumption of services. There are communications arising from unplanned or unintended experiences, and there are planned marketing communications.

- **Explain the three models of communication and describe how personal influences can enhance the effectiveness of marketing communication activities.**

  The linear or one-way model of communication is the traditional mass media interpretation of how communication works. The two-way model incorporates the influence of other people in the communication process, whereas the interactional model explains how communication flows not just between sender and receiver but throughout a network of people. Interaction is about actions that lead to a response and, most importantly in an age of interactive communication, interactivity is a prelude to dialogue, the highest or purest form of communication.

- **Understand the role of marketing communications.**

  The role of marketing communications is to engage audiences, and there are four main tasks that it can be used to complete. These tasks are summarized as DRIP, i.e. to differentiate, reinforce, inform, or persuade audiences to behave in particular ways. Several of these tasks can be undertaken simultaneously within a campaign.

- **Understand the models used to explain how marketing communications and advertising work.**

  These models have evolved from sequential approaches such as AIDA and the HoE models. A circular model of the attitude construct helps understanding of the tasks of marketing communication, namely to inform audiences, to create feelings, and a value associated with offerings, and to drive behaviour.

- **Describe what culture is and explain how it can impact on the use of marketing communications.**

  Culture refers to the values, beliefs, ideas, customs, actions, and symbols that are learned by members of particular societies. Culture is important because it provides individuals within a society with a sense of identity and an understanding of what is deemed to be acceptable behaviour. Culture is learnt, the elements are interrelated, and culture is shared among members of a society or group. Organizations that practice marketing communications in international environments have to be fully aware of the cultural dimensions associated with each of their markets. In addition, they need to consider whether it is better to adopt a standardized approach and use the same unmodified campaigns across all markets, or adapt campaigns to meet the needs of local markets.

Review Questions

1 What is the linear model of communication and each of its main elements?

2 Make brief notes outlining the meaning of interaction and how dialogue can develop.

3 What are the main differences between opinion leaders and opinion formers?

4 Explain the key role of marketing communications and find examples to illustrate the meaning of each element in the DRIP framework.

5 What constitutes the marketing communications mix?

6 What is a hierarchy of effects model?

7 What are the strong and weak theories of advertising?

8 Using examples, explain the difference between informational and emotional messages.

9 Why is the circular interpretation of the attitude construct better than the linear form?

10 Hollensen (2010) argues that culture is made up of three elements and four layers. Name them.

Worksheet Summary

To apply the knowledge you have gained from this chapter and test your understanding of marketing communications visit the **Online Resource Centre** and complete Worksheet 10.1.

Discussion Questions

1 Having read Case Insight 10.1, how would you advise the marketing team at *The Guardian* to use marketing communications to change perceptions and behaviour of Progressive newspaper-readers?

2 Consider the key market exchange characteristics that will favour the use of linear or one-way communication and then repeat the exercise with respect to interactional communication. Discuss the differences and find examples to illustrate these conditions.

3 Day Birger et Mikkelsen is a leading Danish fashion retailer, providing a range of fashion clothing for young people aged 18–35. As a marketing assistant you have just returned from a conference at which the role of personal influencers was highlighted. You now wish to convey your new knowledge to your manager. Prepare a brief report in which you explain the nature of opinion leaders and formers, and discuss how they might be used by Day Birger et Mikkelsen to improve their marketing communications. Using at least three examples, make it clear who you think would make good opinion formers for Day Birger et Mikkelsen.

4 Discuss the extent to which marketing communications should be used by organizations to persuade audiences to buy their offerings.

5 To what extent should organizations operating an advertising standardization policy consider the culture of the countries they are operating in?

@ Visit the **Online Resource Centre** and complete the Multiple Choice Questions to assess your knowledge of Chapter 10.

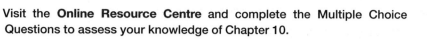

References

Alarcon, C. (2008), 'Customer titles extend reach', *Marketing Week*, 30 October, retrieve from: www. marketingweek.co.uk/in-depth-analysis/customer-titles-extend-reach/2063120.article accessed 12 July 2013.

Anon. (2012), 'Awards 2012 Case Study: Category 1: British Gas Business: 'Energy Live Challenge', *B2B Marketing Magazine*, retrieve from: http://www. b2bmarketing.net/resources/awards-2012-case-study-category-1-british-gas-business-%E2%80%98energy-live-challenge%E2%80%99 accessed 3 February 2013.

Bagozzi, R. (1978), 'Marketing as exchange: a theory of transactions in the market place', *American Behavioural Science*, 21(4), 257–61.

Ballantyne, D. (2004), 'Dialogue and its role in the development of relationship specific knowledge', *Journal of Business and Industrial Marketing*, 19(2), 114–23.

Berkman, H. and Gilson, C. (1986), *Consumer Behavior: Concepts and Strategies*, Boston, MA: Kent Publishing.

Chan, K. K. and Misra, S. (1990), 'Characteristics of the opinion leader: a new dimension', *Journal of Advertising*, 19(3), 53–60.

DeBroff, S., Schuierer, M., and Chapman, C.C., (2012), 'Case study: influencers wanted. Bevy of mommy bloggers send Infantino's test-drive campaign into high gear', *PR News*, 3 December.

Duncan, T. and Moriarty, S. (1998), 'A communication-based marketing model for managing relationships', *Journal of Marketing*, 62(April), 1–13.

Dwyer, R., Schurr, P., and Oh, S. (1987), 'Developing buyer–seller relationships', *Journal of Marketing*, 51(April), 11–27.

Ehrenberg, A. S. C. (1974), 'Repetitive advertising and the consumer', *Journal of Advertising Research*, 14(April), 25–34

Ehrenberg, A. S. C. (1997), 'How do consumers come to buy a new brand?' *Admap*, March, 20–4.

Fill, C. (2002), *Marketing Communications: Contexts, Strategies and Applications* (3rd edn), Harlow: FT/ Prentice Hall.

Fill, C. (2013), *Marketing Communications: Brands, Experiences and Participation* (6th edn), Harlow: FT/ Prentice Hall.

Gilliland, D. I. and Johnston, W. J. (1997), 'Toward a model of business-to-business marketing communications effects', *Industrial Marketing Management*, **26**, 15–29.

Hall, E. (2012), 'In London Kellogg's swaps snacks for tweets to #tweetshop', *Adage Digital*, 27 September, retrieve from: http://adage.com/article/global-news/london-kellogg-s-swaps-snacks-tweets-tweetshop/237448/?utm_source=digital_email&utm_medium=newsletter&utm_campaign=adage accessed 28 September 2012.

Harris, G. (1996), 'International advertising: developmental and implementational issues', *Journal of Marketing Management*, 12(6), 551–60.

Hearn, G. (2011), 'Asia's integration challenge', *Admap*, 46(6), 30–1.

Hoffman, D. L. and Novak, P.T. (1996), 'Marketing in hyper computer-mediated environments: conceptual foundations', *Journal of Marketing*, 60(July), 50–68.

Hollensen, S. (2010), *Global Marketing; A Decision-Oriented Approach* (5th edn), Harlow: FT/Prentice Hall.

Houston, F. and Gassenheimer, J. (1987), 'Marketing and exchange', *Journal of Marketing*, 51(October), 3–18.

Hughes, G. and Fill, C. (2007), 'Redefining the nature and format of the marketing communications mix', *Marketing Review*, 7(1), 45–57.

Jones, J. P. (1991), 'Over-promise and under-delivery', *Marketing and Research Today*, 19(40), 195–203.

Katz, E. and Lazarsfeld, P. F. (1955), *Personal Influence: The Part Played by People in the Flow of Mass Communication*, Glencoe, IL: Free Press.

Keller, K. L. (2001), 'Mastering the marketing communications mix: micro and macro perspectives on integrated marketing communication programs, *Journal of Marketing Management*, 17, 819–47.

Lavidge, R. J. and Steiner, G. A. (1961), 'A model for predictive measurements of advertising effectiveness', *Journal of Marketing*, 25, 6, 59–62.

Moses, L. (2011), 'Vogue casts 1,000 influencers for network', *Adweek*, 52, 26, 11 July, retrieved from: http:// www.adweek.com/news/advertising-branding/vogue-casts-1000-influencers-network-133299 accessed 16 December 2012.

Schramm, W. (1955), 'How communication works', in W. Schramm (ed.) *The Process and Effects of Mass Communications*, Urbana, IL: University of Illinois Press, 3–26.

Shannon, C. and Weaver, W. (1962), *The Mathematical Theory of Communication*, Urbana, IL: University of Illinois Press.

Stokes, D. and Lomax, W. (2002), 'Taking control of word of mouth marketing: the case of an entrepreneurial hotelier', *Journal of Small Business and Enterprise Development*, 9(4), 349–57.

Strong, E. K. (1925), *The Psychology of Selling*, New York: McGraw-Hill.

Terrelonge, Z. (2012), 'Kellogg's: Leave the cash at home and pay us with mobile tweets', *Mobile Entertainment,* retrieve from: http://www.mobile-ent.biz/news/read/kellogg-s-leave-the-cash-at-home-and-pay-us-with-mobile-tweets/019472 accessed 2 January 2013.

Theodorson, S. A. and Theodorson, G. R. (1969), *A Modern Dictionary of Sociology*, New York: Cromwell.

Chapter 11
Managing the Communications Mix

Learning Outcomes

After studying this chapter you should be able to:

▶ Describe the role and configuration of the marketing communications mix

▶ Explain the characteristics of each of the primary tools, media and messages

▶ Set out the criteria that should be used to select the right communication mix

▶ Describe the different activities associated with managing and planning marketing communications

▶ Consider the principles and issues associated with integrated marketing communications

Case Insight 11.1
Budweiser Budvar

Market Insight 11.1
'Mama Luchetti' Repositions Luchetti

Market Insight 11.2
To Tweet or Not to Tweet

Market Insight 11.3
Red Bull Sponsors the Fastest Human

Market Insight 11.4
British Airways Decide Not to Fly ... But to Serve at Home

Case Insight 11.1

How should a heritage brand in the Czech Republic design a campaign to reposition itself against competing foreign brands? We speak to Lubos Jahoda account director at Budweiser Budvar's advertising agency Kaspan, to find out more.

Budweiser Budvar has a 750-year tradition of brewing beer in the Czech Republic. Although there has been a long running dispute with other brewers who use the same Budweiser name, one of the current issues facing the Budvar brand concerns the decline in the size of the overall Czech beer market. Since 2009 there has been a shift towards small authentic local breweries. This is because Czechs believe that the multinationals (SAB Miller, Heineken, Molson Coors) have destroyed the essence of Czech beer by using inferior ingredients and making what is called 'EuroBeer', a universal beer that has no clear distinguishing taste or character. The big breweries have been trying to resolve the situation through innovation, as a result of which we now see loads of 'radler' beer (flavoured drinks) on the market.

Surprisingly, many customers saw Budvar as a 'big brewery team' and similar to the big breweries. We have also seen consumers move from away from Budvar towards small local breweries. But, as everyone who has ever visited the brewery knows, Budvar is more authentic than the smallest of breweries, using the same ingredients and production processes as used 118 years ago. Another problem concerns the way the brand was perceived. Budvar is seen as a very rational beer, a quality beer or 'Czech beer', but there is little emotional connection with the brand.

It was clear that we needed to reposition the Budvar brand, to differentiate it and enable Czech consumers to make an emotional connection with the brand. The question was how best to achieve this.

Research has shown that Czech people are generally more inclined to adopt a line of least resistance in order to avoid problems, and that means agreeing or saying 'yes'. However, many Czech people deeply resent such concessions and do not identify themselves with this type of compromise. This issue of dissent provided us with a pertinent platform on which to reposition the brand. This is because Budvar has repeatedly rejected various pressures. For example, we have refused to dumb down or use substitute ingredients. Budvar has also rejected the idea that we should reduce the maturing time during the brewing process. We have also refused outright to sell our brand name to our competitors, and have also said no to licensing production away from České Budějovice (Budweis).

From this insight we developed the NO campaign, which is rooted in the Czech psyche and Budvar's foundations, and can be seen in everything Budvar does, from just 'making beer' to fighting for its name and reputation across the world. The campaign had two main aims. First, at a product level, it aimed to build the image of Budvar as a quality beer, which was not associated with the multinational brewers. Second, at a brand level, it aimed to build a strong emotional link with consumers.

The question was: How should we develop this 'NO' campaign? How should we interpret and communicate the NO message without being negative? Obviously advertising was going to play a central role, but which other disciplines should we use? Which mix of media would be best at delivering the 'NO' campaign to realize the greatest impact?

Introduction

What 'touchpoints' do you have with your mobile phone provider? Perhaps these might be email, telephone, SMS, Twitter, direct mail items, and/or snail mail for personal communications? What about TV ads, webpages, articles and ads in magazines, posters, and perhaps news items that generate general brand awareness? Organizations use a variety of tools, media, and messages to engage their audiences. Collectively, these are referred to as the **marketing communications mix**—a set of five tools, a variety of **media**, and messages that can be used in various combinations, and different degrees of intensity, to communicate successfully with target audiences.

The five principal marketing communications tools are **advertising**, **sales promotion**, **public relations**, **direct marketing**, and **personal selling**. In addition, the media is used primarily, but not exclusively, to deliver advertising messages to target audiences. Although 'media' refers to any mechanism or device that can carry a message, we refer to paid-for media, processes, and systems that are owned by third parties, such as the News Corporation (who own *The Sun* and *The Sunday Times* newspapers plus the BSkyB TV platform), Condé Nast (who own *Tatler*, *Vanity Fair*, and *Vogue* magazines, among others), Singapore Press Holdings (who own the *Business Times* in Singapore), and Time Warner Inc., a 'leading media and entertainment company, whose businesses include interactive services, cable systems, filmed entertainment, TV networks, and publishing'. These organizations rent out time and space to client organizations so that they can send their messages and make content available to engage various audiences. The list of available paid-for media is expanding, but it is possible to identify six key classes. These are broadcast, print, outdoor, in-store, digital, and other (which includes both cinema and ambient media). All of these are explored in this chapter.

On completing this chapter, you should understand the main characteristics associated with the principal tools, the media, and the messages that make up the mix. It is possible to configure different mixes of tools, media, and messages to achieve different goals. This chapter also considers the marketing communications planning process and some of the issues associated with this important management activity, including **integrated marketing communications**.

The Role and Purpose of the Marketing Communications Mix

The marketing communication mix consists of five main tools, three types of media, and four forms of messages or content. These are depicted in Figure 11.1.

Up until the mid-1980s, organizations were able to use a fairly predictable and stable range of tools and media. Advertising was used to build awareness and brand values, sales promotions were used to stimulate demand, public relations conveyed goodwill messages about organizations, and personal selling was seen as a means of getting orders, particularly in the business-to-business market. However, there have been some major changes in the environment and in the way organizations communicate with their target audiences. New technology has given rise to a raft of different media and opportunities for advertisers to reach their audiences. We now have access to hundreds of commercial TV and radio channels. Cinemas show multiple films at

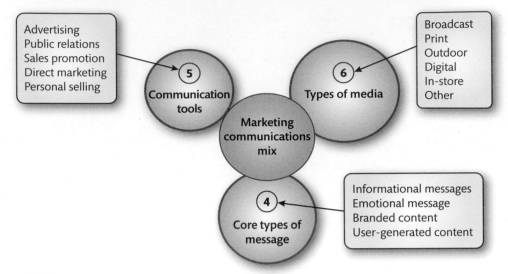

Figure 11.1

The elements of the marketing communications mix

Note: The size of the red circles denotes the relative influence of the elements.

multiplex sites, and the internet has transformed the way in which we communicate, educate, inform, and entertain ourselves.

This expansion of the media is referred to as **media fragmentation**. At the same time, people have developed a whole host of new ways of spending their leisure time; they are no longer locked-in and restricted to a few media. This expansion of media choice is referred to as **audience fragmentation**. So, although the range and type of media has expanded, the size of audiences that each medium commands has generally shrunk.

One of the key challenges for organizations is to find the right mix of tools, media, and messages that allows them to reach their target audiences effectively and efficiently. To do this they have had to revise and redevelop their marketing communication mixes. For example, in the 1990s there was a dramatic rise in the use of direct-response media as direct marketing emerged. Now, the internet and digital technologies have enabled new interactive forms of communication, where the receiver has greater responsibility for their part in the communication process and is encouraged to interact with the sender. As a result of these changes, many organizations are reducing their investment in traditional media and putting it into digital media (see Chapter 17).

Visit the **Online Resource Centre** and complete Internet Activity 11.1 to learn more about how Toyota uses an interactive website to inform its target audience about a complex proposition, the Hybrid Synergy Drive.

The role of the mix has changed from persuading customers in the short term to buy products and services, to a longer-term perspective whereby the mix facilitates communication with a wide range of stakeholders on a broader range of issues. New goals, such as developing understanding and preference, and reminding and reassuring customers, have now become accepted as important aspects of marketing communications.

The pursuit of integrated marketing communications has become a popular activity. An increasing number of organizations are trying to use the mix more efficiently, to coordinate what they say and when they say it, and to develop relationships not just with key customers, but also with key suppliers and other important stakeholders. Today, therefore, an increasing number of organizations are reformulating and integrating the mix to encourage customer retention, not acquisition.

Each of the tools of the marketing communications mix has developed in an offline environment. However, the development of the internet presents new opportunities for each of the tools to be delivered through online media. Many organizations have found that the principles through which particular tools work offline do not necessarily apply in an online environment.

The marketing communications mix is a vital part of the process that conveys added value to stakeholders. It is now expected that marketing communications, and the mix of tools, media, and messages it uses, needs to move beyond the product information model and become an integral part of an organization's overall communications and relationship management strategy. Above all else, the marketing communications mix should be utilized as an audience-centred activity. See Market Insight 11.1.

Market Insight 11.1

'Mama Lucchetti' repositions Lucchetti

Lucchetti is a pasta brand owned by Molinos, the largest food producer in Argentina. Branded as 'Mom's pasta', Lucchetti was positioned as a price-orientated value proposition. However, Molinos also owned Matarazzo, a similar pasta brand which was positioned in much the same way. In addition to this, the marketing communications across Molinos's 20 different brands lacked synergy and clear positioning. With the food market also attracting an increasing number of new entrants, all adopting similar positions, there was a need to introduce new products, such as soups, and reposition Lucchetti as a high-value emotional food brand.

Most marketing strategies tried to associate their brands with young, sexy, perfect, dynamic, and modern young women. The new strategy required a new message, away from the aspirational mother, and much more in tune with 'real' mothers. These are women who are imperfect, who make mistakes, who have fears and frustrations, who are not models, and who have an immense love for their families.

A series of new characters were developed, one of whom, 'Mama Lucchetti', was someone who can

manage a range of real-life situations. However, some of these can be unsettling, so it was necessary to soften the impact of the situations portrayed. This was achieved by using animated characters, coupled with humour and music to frame the message.

The first campaign goal was to introduce and establish the new characters. Using a storytelling approach, a series of ads were developed which showed 'Mama Lucchetti' dealing with everyday commonplace events and situations, thus enabling families to identify with the scenarios easily.

A high-intensity TV campaign, which was much more intense than that used by arch competitor Knorr, led the way. This used a new jingle and music inspired by the Muppets, which attracted children. In addition, radio ads and search engine marketing (pay per click ads) helped direct visitors to a new webpage which was different to and separate from the company's main site. By putting all the available spots online, viral marketing was stimulated. Numerous videos were shared, and a huge number of comments about the characters were tracked on Facebook and YouTube. The high volume of social media activity was unexpected, as communities formed around the different characters. Today, there are more than 50 groups created by Mama

Market Insight 11.1
continued

Lucchetti's followers, while the Facebook fan page has over two million fans.

In addition to this, the brand used public relations, sales promotions, and field marketing. The characters were used on the packaging and at points of purchase to improve identification and purchase intentions.

All this activity led to a pasta market share increase of 3.1%, which delivered a 51% increase in revenue. The soup brand market share increased by 9.5% , with revenues increasing by 37%. Consequently, the brand experienced strong growth and became the second player in all the categories.

Sources: Empresas (2009); Herrera (2009); Imizcoz (2012); Molinos (2012).

1   **Which elements of the marketing communications mix were used in the repositioning of the 'Lucchetti' brand?**

2   **How might the use of social media have helped develop the 'Lucchetti' brand?**

3   **Where and how might personal selling have been used in the campaign?**

This market insight was kindly contributed by Fermin Paus, a postgraduate student at the Grenoble School of Management.

Research Insight 11.1

To take your learning further, you might wish to read this influential paper.

Vakratsas, D. and Ambler, T. (1999), 'How advertising works: What do we really know?', *Journal of Marketing*, 63(January), 26–43.

In an attempt to understand the interaction between consumers and advertising the authors reviewed more than 250 journal articles and books. They conclude that there is no support for any particular hierarchical model that explains how advertising works. They propose that advertising should be considered in terms of affect, **cognition**, and experience (see the hierarchical model proposed in Chapter 10) and that understanding the context is absolutely imperative (e.g. goals, product category, competition, other aspects of mix, stage of product lifecycle, and target market).

@ **Visit the Online Resource Centre to read the abstract and access the full paper.**

Selecting the Right Mix of Tools

Table 11.1 sets out the principal characteristics of the five main tools of the marketing communications mix.

The principal tools presented in Table 11.1 subsume other tools such as product placement, sponsorship, and exhibitions. Although Table 11.1 suggests that the tools are independent

Table 11.1 The principal characteristics of the five main tools of the marketing communications mix

Marketing communication tools	Overview
Advertising	Advertising is a non-personal form of communication, where a clearly identifiable sponsor pays for a message to be transmitted through media. One of the distinctive qualities that advertising brings to the mix is that it reaches large, often mass, audiences in an impersonal way. The role of advertising is to engage audiences, and this engagement depends on the context in which the communication occurs.
Sales promotion	Sales promotions offer a direct inducement or an incentive to encourage customers to buy an offering. These inducements can be targeted at consumers, distributors, agents, and members of the sales force. Sales promotions are concerned with offering customers additional value, to induce an immediate sale. These sales might well have taken place without the presence of an incentive; it is simply that the inducement brings the time of the sale forward. The key forms of sales promotion are sampling, coupons, deals, premiums, contests, and sweepstakes, and, in the trade, various forms of allowance.
Public relations	Public relations is used to influence the way an organization is perceived by various groups of stakeholders. One of the key characteristics that differentiates public relations from the other tools is that it does not require the purchase of airtime or space in media vehicles, such as television magazines or online. These types of message are low-cost public, and perceived to be extremely credible. It is a management activity that attempts to shape the attitudes and opinions held by an organization's stakeholders. It attempts to co-integrate its own policies with the interests of stakeholders and formulates and executes a programme of action to develop mutual goodwill and understanding. Through this process, relationships are developed which are in the long-run interests of all parties. The key forms of public relations are sponsorship, publicity, lobbying, public affairs, issues management, crisis communications and investor relations.
Direct marketing	The primary role of direct marketing is to drive a response and shape the behaviour of the target audience with regard to a brand. This is achieved by sending personalized and customized messages, often requesting a 'call-to-action', designed to provoke a change in the audience's behaviour. Direct marketing is used to create and sustain a personal and intermediary-free communication with customers, potential customers, and other significant stakeholders. In most cases this is a media-based activity and offers great scope for the collection and utilization of pertinent and measurable data. One of the key benefits of direct marketing is that there is limited communication wastage. The precision associated with target marketing means that messages are sent to, received, processed, and responded to by members of the target audience, and no others. This is unlike advertising where messages often reach some people who are not targets and are unlikely to be involved with the brand. Some of the principal techniques are direct mail, telemarketing, email, and internet-based communications.

Table 11.1 continued	
Marketing communication tools	**Overview**
Personal selling	Personal selling involves interpersonal communication through which information is provided, positive feelings developed, and behaviour stimulated. Personal selling is an activity undertaken by an individual representing an organization, or collectively in the form of a sales force. It is a highly potent form of communication simply because messages can be adapted to meet the requirements of both parties. Objections can be overcome, information provided in the context of the buyer's environment, and the conviction and power of demonstration can be brought to the buyer when requested. The role of personal selling is largely one of representation, but it is the most expensive tool in the mix and the reach of personal selling is the most limited.

entities, each with their own skills and attributes, a truly effective mix works when the tools complement each other and work as an interacting unit. One of the challenges facing marketing communication managers is to extract the full potential from the tools selected. Only by appreciating their characteristics is it really possible to get an insight into how to select the right mix of tools for each communication task.

An overview of each of the tools should highlight a number of characteristics that are shared among them. These are the degree to which a tool and the message conveyed is controllable, the credibility of the message conveyed, the costs of using a tool, the degree to which a target audience is dispersed, and the DRIP task that marketing communications is required to accomplish. These five elements can serve as a starting point when selecting the right marketing communications mix and each is considered in turn.

Table 11.2 provides a summary of the relative strengths of each of the tools of the communications mix against these criteria. However, although depicted individually, the elements of the mix should be regarded as a set of complementary instruments, each potentially stronger when it draws on the potential of the others. The tools are, to a limited extent, partially interchangeable, and in different circumstances different tools should be used to meet different objectives. For example, in a business context, personal selling will be the predominant tool, whereas in a consumer market context, advertising has traditionally reigned supreme.

What is clear is that the nature, configuration, and use of what was once called the promotional mix has changed. No longer can the traditional groupings of tools be assumed to be the most effective forms of communication. The role of the media in the communication process is now much more significant than previously. The arrival and development of digital media expands opportunities for people and organizations to converse globally, personally, more speedily, and factually. Word-of-mouth communication also now plays a more significant part in contemporary communications, especially as communications-literate consumers are increasingly sceptical of the message conveyed by many organizations.

Visit the **Online Resource Centre** and follow the weblinks to the Federation of European Direct and Interactive Marketing Association (FEDMA) and the Institute of Promotional Marketing (IPM) to learn more about the communication tools of direct marketing and sales promotions.

Table 11.2 The relative strength of the tools of the marketing communication mix

	Advertising	Sales promotion	Public relations	Direct marketing	Personal selling
Level of control	Medium	High	Low	High	Medium
Level of cost	High	Medium	Low	Medium	High
Level of credibility	Low	Medium	High	Medium	Medium
Level of dispersion					
Consumer audiences	Low	Medium	High	High	Medium
B2B audiences	Medium	High	High	Medium	High
Primary tasks	Differentiating Informing	Persuading	Differentiating Informing	Persuading Reinforcing	Persuading

The Media

Once a client has decided on the message, decisions need to be made about how and when it is conveyed. Technically, all messages need to be delivered through media (see Tables 11.3 and 11.4). Some media are owned by the organization, for example the sales force or the signage outside a building. However, these media do not enable messages to reach a very large or targeted audience and neither do they allow for specific proposition-oriented messages to be conveyed to particular target audiences. In most circumstances, therefore, client organizations need to use the media owned by others, and pay a fee for renting the space and time to convey their messages. The next section considers the role of the media, and examines digital media before considering the principles of direct response media.

The development of digital media has had a profound impact on the way client organizations communicate with their audiences. Generally, there has been a trend to reduce the amount of traditional media used and increase the amount of digital and online media used. For example, in 2009, Gap announced that it was dropping TV advertising completely for the launch of a range of jeans and just using social media. Reports that TV and print advertising are dead are premature, but it is clear that the balance within the mix of media used by organizations is changing and new ways of delivering messages are evolving.

Visit the **Online Resource Centre** and complete Internet Activity 11.2 to learn more about the differing media that was used for the Ray-Ban 'Neverhide' campaign.

The Changing Role of the Media

For a long time commercial media have been used to convey messages designed to develop consumers' attitudes and feelings towards brands. Today, many of the messages are designed to provoke audiences into responding physically, cognitively, or emotionally. The former is

Table 11.3 Summary chart of the main forms of media by form

Class	Type	Vehicles
Broadcast	Television	Coronation Street, X Factor, Classic
	Radio	FM, Capital Radio
Print	Newspapers	*The Sunday Times, The Mirror, The Daily Telegraph,*
	Magazines: Consumer Business	*Cosmopolitan, Woman, The Grocer, Plumbing News*
Out-of-home	Billboards	96-, 48- and 6-sheet
	Street furniture	Adshel
	Transit	Underground stations, airport buildings, taxis, hot-air balloons
Digital media	Internet	Web sites, email, intranets,
	Digital television	Facebook, apps
	CD-ROM	Teletext, SkyText, various including music, educational, entertainment
In-store	Point-of-purchase	Bins, signs and displays
	Packaging	The Coca-Cola contour bottle
Other	Cinema	Pearl & Dean, Orange Wednesdays
	Exhibitions and Events	Ideal Home, The Motor Show
	Brand placement	Films, TV, books
	Ambient	Litter bins, golf tees, petrol pumps, washrooms
	Guerrilla	Flyposting

Source: Fill, C. (2009), *Marketing Communications: Interactivity, Communities and Content* (5th edn), Harlow: FT/Prentice Hall.

Table 11.4 An overview of each class of media

Class of Media	Overview
Print	Newspapers and magazines are the two main media in the print media class; others include custom magazines and directories. Print is very effective at delivering messages to target audiences as it allows for explanation in a way that most other media cannot. This may be in the form of either a picture or a photograph demonstrating how an offering should be used. Alternatively, the written word can be used to argue why an offering should be chosen and detail the advantages and benefits that consumption will provide for the user.

Table 11.4 continued	

Class of Media	Overview
Broadcast	Advertisers use broadcast media (television and radio) because they can reach mass audiences with their messages at a relatively low cost per target reached. Broadcast media allow advertisers to add visual and/or sound dimensions to their messages. This helps them to demonstrate the benefits of using a particular offering and can bring life and energy to an advertiser's message. Television uses sight, sound, and movement, whereas radio can only use its audio capacity to convey meaning. Both media have the potential to tell stories and to appeal to people's emotions when transmitting a message. These are dimensions that the printed media find difficult in achieving effectively within an advertiser's time and cost parameters.
Outdoor	Outdoor media consist of three main formats: street furniture (such as bus shelters), billboards (which consist primarily of 96-, 48-, and 6-sheet poster sites), and transit (which includes buses, taxis, and the Underground). The key characteristic associated with outdoor media is that they are observed by their target audiences at locations away from home, and they are normally used to support messages that are transmitted through primary media, namely broadcast and print. Therefore outdoor media can be seen as a secondary, but important, support media for a complementary and effective media mix.
In-store	There are two main forms of in-store media, point-of-purchase (POP) displays and packaging. Retailers control the former and manufacturers the latter. The primary objective of using in-store media is to get the attention of shoppers and to stimulate them to make purchases. The content of messages can be controlled easily by both retailers or manufacturers. In addition, the timing and the exact placement of in-store messages can be equally well controlled. There are a number of POP techniques, but the most used are window displays, floor and wall racks to display merchandise, posters and information cards, and counter and checkout displays. Packaging has to protect and preserve products, but it also has a significant communication role and is a means of influencing brand choice decisions.
Digital	Digital media embrace more than just the internet and online marketing. Although significant and extremely important, the digital media spectrum involves three key additional areas: wireless, mobile, and interactive TV. Within each of these areas there are many subsections, each of which provides a variety of media opportunities. These present clients with opportunities to communicate with their audiences in radically different ways from those previously available. Generally, most traditional media provide one-way communications, where information passes from a source to a receiver but there is little opportunity for feedback, let alone interaction. Digital media enables two-way interactive communication, with information flowing back to the source and again to the receiver, as each participant adapts their message to meet the requirements of their audience. For example, banner ads can provoke a click which takes the receiver to a new website where the source presents new information and the receiver makes choices, responds to questions (e.g. registers at the site), and the source again provides fresh information. Indeed, the identity of the source and receiver in this type of communication becomes less clear. These interactions are conducted at high speed, low cost, and usually with great clarity. People drive these interactions at a speed that is convenient to them; they are not driven by others. Space (or time) within traditional media is limited, so costs rise as demand for the limited space/time increases. To generalize, as space is unlimited on the internet, costs per contact fall as more visitors are received.

Table 11.4 continued	
Class of Media	**Overview**
Other	Two main media can be identified, cinema and ambient. Cinema advertising has all the advantages of television-based messages such as the high-quality audio and visual dimensions, which combine to provide high impact. However, the vast majority of cinema visitors are people aged 18 to 35, so if an advertiser wishes to reach different age group segments, or perhaps a national audience, not only will cinema be inappropriate but also the costs will be much higher than those for television. Ambient media are regarded as out-of-home media that fail to fit any of the established outdoor categories. Ambient media can be classified according to a variety of factors. These include posters (typically found in washrooms), distribution (e.g. ads on tickets and carrier bags), digital media (in the form of video and LCD screens), sponsorships (as in golf holes and petrol pump nozzles), and aerials (in the form of balloons, blimps, towed banners).

referred to as an attitudinal response, the latter a behavioural response. It follows that attitude- and behavioural-oriented communications require different media.

Direct-response media are characterized by the provision of a telephone number or web address. This is the mechanism through which receivers can respond to a message. Direct mail, telemarketing, and door-to-door activities are the main direct-response media, as they allow more personal, direct, and evaluative means of reaching precisely targeted customers. However, in reality, any type of media can be used, simply by attaching a telephone number, website address, mailing address, or response card. Table 11.5 sets out the main media used within direct-response marketing.

Direct-response media also allow clients the opportunity to measure the volume, frequency, and value of audience responses. This enables them to determine which direct-response media work best and so helps them become more efficient as well as more effective. Estimates vary, but approximately 25% of all TV advertisements are now direct response. Direct-response TV (DRTV) is attractive to service providers, such as those in financial services, charities, and tourism, but, increasingly, grocery brands such as Tango and Peperami have used this format. The growth in video advertising reflects the involvement of people in their online activities.

In addition, TV and online media are complementary. Consumers often research an offering online only after watching a TV ad, because TV is good at displaying ads and brand building, whereas online advertising is best at search (Berne, 2009). See also Chapter 17.

Visit the **Online Resource Centre** and follow the weblink to the Radio Advertising Bureau (RAB) to learn more about how the role and importance of radio in today's fragmented media landscape.

One aspect that is crucial to the success of a direct-response campaign is not the number of responses but the conversion of leads into sales. This means that the infrastructure to support these activities must be thought through and implemented, otherwise the work and resources put into the visible level will be wasted if customers cannot get the information they require when they respond.

Another key area of change within the media concerns content. Traditionally, content is provided by a client organization, which uses the media to interrupt and transfer their message of persuasion to their target audience, usually a mass audience. Digital media and changes in consumer behaviour now enable audiences not only to generate their own content but also to

Table 11.5 Direct-response (DR) media

Types of DR media	Explanation
Direct mail	Direct mail refers to personally addressed advertising that is delivered through the postal system. It can be personalized and targeted with great accuracy, and its results are capable of precise measurement. Direct mail can be expensive, at anything between £250 and £500 per 1,000 items dispatched. Therefore it should be used selectively and for purposes other than creating awareness.
Telemarketing	The telephone provides interaction, flexibility, immediate feedback, and the opportunity to overcome objections, all within the same communication event. Telemarketing also allows organizations to undertake separate marketing research which is both highly measurable and accountable in that the effectiveness can be verified continuously, and call rates, contacts reached, and the number and quality of positive and negative responses are easily recorded and monitored.
Carelines	Carelines and contact centres enable customers to complain about an offering and related experiences, seek advice, make suggestions regarding proposition or packaging development, and comment about an action or development concerning the brand as a whole.
Inserts	Inserts are media materials that are placed inside magazines or direct mail letters. These provide factual information about the offering and enable the recipient to respond to the request of the direct marketer. This request might be to place an order, visit a website, or post back a card for more information, such as a brochure. Inserts are popular because they are good at generating leads, even though their cost is substantially higher than a four-colour advertisement in the magazine in which the insert is carried.
Print	There are two main forms of DR advertising through the printed media: catalogues, and magazines and newspapers. Consumer direct print ads sometimes offer an incentive, and are designed explicitly to drive customers to a website where transactions can be completed without reference to retailers, dealers, or other intermediaries.
Door-to-door	Although the content and quality can be controlled in the same way, door-to-door response rates are lower than direct mail because of the lack of a personal address mechanism. Door-to-door can be much cheaper than direct mail as there are no postage charges to be accounted for.
Radio and television	Television has much greater potential than radio as a DR mechanism because it can provide a visual dimension. Originally, pricing restrictions limited the use of television in this context but, following deregulation, nearly half of all television ads now carry a response mechanism.
Digital media	The recent development of digital technologies, and the impact of digital television, internet, email, viral marketing, blogging, and social networking sites, now represents a major new form of interactive and direct marketing opportunities. Driven initially by developments in home shopping and banking facilities that were attractive to particular target groups, these facilities have now become fully interactive. As a result, these services are now accessible to a much wider audience and encompass leisure and entertainment opportunities.

discuss and consider the opinions and attitudes of others. This means that advertisers no longer have control over what is said about their brands, who says it, and when. The rise of online communities and social networking sites, blogging, wikis, and RSS feeds enable users to create content and become more involved with a brand. For example, car manufacturer Kia developed a co-creation competition to underpin a global brand campaign. The 'Power to Surprise' theme sought to elicit different meanings and interpretations from car enthusiasts across different markets. Over 250 submissions were made from people around the world, with the best entries hosted on Kia's global Facebook page. People were encouraged to share them with friends and to vote on their favourite submission. The best 13 submissions shared a prize pool of £48,000, and 10 randomly selected voters won an iPad (Chapman, 2012). See also Market Insight 11.2 about the increasing use of Twitter.

Market Insight 11.2

To Tweet or Not to Tweet

As of July 2013, Twitter had an estimated 554 million registered users, of which 200 million were active. The microblog service, which has only been in operation since 2006, is located in San Francisco, California, attracts up to 135,000 new members and hosts an average of 400 million tweets every day.

In addition to individual private users, Twitter has attracted a range of businesses seeking to promote their brands through social media. For example, a number of North American banks have created a Twitter presence, attempting to reach 'Gen Y' users. Even smaller banks have adopted Twitter in an effort to interact with these users in a less overt way than conventional advertising campaigns. In this way, smaller banks have attempted to use informal tweets from real named employees, rather than impersonal logos and pseudonyms. For example, First Arkansas Bank and Trust (FAB&T) a family-owned financial institution with only 27 banking centres, uses Twitter to emphasize its ability to 'offer the same things as big banks, that is a high level of technology and a high level of products and services, yet maintain the feel of a small operator'. Such smaller firms, which have limited resources or expertise to implement more sophisticated or time-consuming campaigns, see Twitter as a tool to facilitate expanding their reach beyond the local footprint to the online community, with the mantra of 'being in it to win it'. Instead of more obvious attempts to promote the firm or its offerings

Twitter has transformed the way in which many people and brands communicate.
Source: © Twitter.

directly, their tweets are simple, quick, and tangential, for example giving snippets of news about community events.

Some larger service organizations use Twitter as a one-to-one customer service channel, which has had the effect of generating large swathes of followers termed 'superfans', who demonstrate early adopter behaviours. For these firms, Twitter is about engaging people in conversation, leveraging both Twitter's one-to-many and one-to one capabilities. But other larger businesses remain to be convinced whether such highly visible, high-touch, 'face of the firm' provision is likely to enable them to divert customer service enquiries away from costly call centres.

Twitter has been cautious about selling its ad formats, such as 'promoted trends'. Advertisers pay about $200,000 a day to be included among Twitter's

Market Insight 11.2
continued

most popular topics, whilst trying to avoid irritating marketers' Twitter fans. In 2012, Twitter announced that it would start selling ads to small businesses for the first time (predominantly using PPC technology). Companies that have bought Twitter ads generally say that they are happy with the percentage of people who click on their ads or circulate them to other Twitter users. However, there are doubts about their ability to convert customers. Some marketers are also circumventing buying ads on Twitter by setting up bases on the service to talk directly to customers without paying anything to Twitter. For many big global corporations, Twitter still doesn't have the same mass appeal of something like a TV commercial during the Super Bowl.

Sources: Null (2009); Sausner (2009); Wheatley (2010); Halliday (2011); Ovide and Glazer (2012).

This Market Insight was written by Karen Knibbs and Dr Sarah Gilmore, Portsmouth Business School, University of Portsmouth.

1 **How can non-users (consumer and business) be encouraged to join up and start tweeting?**

2 **What are the limitations of Twitter for businesses?**

3 **Under what circumstances might Twitter add value to an organization's marketing communications mix?**

Research Insight 11.2

To take your learning further, you might wish to read this influential paper.

Kent, M. L., Taylor, M., and White, W. J. (2003), 'The relationship between web site design and organizational responsiveness to stakeholders', *Public Relations Review*, **29(1, March), 63–77.**

This paper examines the relationship between website design and organizational responsiveness to stakeholder information needs. Written at a time when there was little or no empirical evidence about the extent to which new technologies can assist organizations to develop relationships, this paper provides an interesting and readable first insight.

Visit the **Online Resource Centre** to read the abstract and access the full paper.

Marketing Communications Messages

Our consideration of communication theory in Chapter 10 confirms the importance of sending the right message, one that can be understood and responded to in context. From a receiver's perspective, the process of decoding and giving meaning to messages is affected by the volume and quality of information received and the judgement they make about the methods and how well the message was communicated. We also know that, for a message to be processed successfully, it should reflect a balance between the need for information and the need for pleasure or enjoyment in consuming the message. We can identify four main forms of message content, although they are not mutually exclusive and work together. These are informational messages, emotional messages, user-generated content, and branded content.

Messages can be categorized as either proposition-oriented and rational or customer-oriented and based on feelings and emotions. As a general, but not universal, guideline, when audiences experience high involvement (see Chapter 2) the emphasis of the message should be on the information content, with the key attributes and the associated benefits emphasized. This style is often factual and proposition-oriented. If audiences experience low involvement then messages should attempt to gain an emotional response. There are, of course, many situations where both rational and emotional messages are needed by buyers to make purchasing decisions. When the number of Facebook users reached a billion in October 2012, they celebrated with the launch of a film entitled 'Things That Connect'. The film shows people interacting with one another and with various objects. The aim was to visualize Facebook's brand strategy and show how they can facilitate the connection process, enabling people to express themselves, to feel human, and to get together (Diaz, 2012).

The presentation of messages should reflect the degree to which factual information or emotional content is required for the message to command attention and then be processed. There are numerous presentational or executional techniques, but Table 11.6 outlines some of the more commonly used appeals.

Visit the **Online Resource Centre** and complete Internet Activity 11.3 to learn more about how Bacardi uses product demonstration and a digital media format (.mp3) to inform target audiences how to make a Bacardi Mojito.

User-generated Content

The development of social media has enabled individuals to communicate with organizations, communities, friends, and family. The message content can be about brands, experiences, or events, and is developed and shared by individuals. This is referred to as **user-generated content (UGC)** and can be seen in action at YouTube, Flickr, and Twitter. Kaplan and Haenlein (2010) consider UGC to be all of the ways in which people make use of social media and it refers to the various forms of media content that are publicly available and created by end-users.

There are three main elements that can be used to identify the presence of UGC. The first is that the content needs to be freely accessible to the public. This means that it should be published either on an open website or on a social networking site accessible to a selected group of people. Second, the material needs to demonstrate creativity, and third, it should be amateur in nature, in the sense that it has not been created by an agency or professional organization.

Although there have been instances of commercial involvement in UGC, the very nature of this type of content takes the communication initiative away from organizations. As a result, marketers are listening to and observing consumers through UGC. Through this approach, many are finding out the different meanings consumers attribute to brands, which assists brand development and positioning.

Some companies invite consumers to offer content (ads), thereby crowdsourcing (see Chapter 17). For example, *Look*, a weekly fashion title, developed a campaign called 'Look

Table 11.6 Information and emotional appeals

Information-based messages

Factual	Messages provide rational logical information, and are presented in a straightforward no-frills manner.
Slice of life	Uses people who are similar to the target audience and presented in scenes to which the target audience can readily associate and understand. For example, washing powder brands are often presented by stereotypical 'housewives', who are seen discussing the brand in a kitchen.
Demonstration	Brands are presented in a problem-solving context. So, people with headaches are seen to be in pain, but then take brand X which resolves the problem.
Comparative	In this approach, brand X is compared favourably, on two or three main attributes, with a leading competitor.

Emotion-based messages

Fear	Products are shown either to relieve danger or ill-health through usage (e.g. toothpaste), or to dispel the fear of social rejection (anti-dandruff shampoos), or to discourage behaviour (anti-smoking ads).
Humour	The use of humour can draw attention, stimulate interest, and place audiences in a positive mood.
Animation	Used to reach children and as a way of communicating potentially boring and uninteresting offerings (gas/electricity, insurance) to adults.
Sex	Excellent for getting the attention of the target audience, but unless the offering is related (e.g. perfume, clothing) these ads generally do not work.
Music	Good for getting attention and differentiating between brands.
Fantasy and surrealism	Used increasingly to provide a point of differentiation and brand intrigue (e.g. Cadbury's chocolate, Coca-Cola).

What I'm Wearing'. This enabled readers to take photos of what they are wearing and upload the pictures to the *Look* website. A selection of these photos was then published in the following week's edition. The aim was to encourage consumer engagement with the brand and grow website traffic (Batten, 2012). However, UGC can work against an organization's best interests. For example, in 2012 the cider brand Frosty Jack had to remove three user-generated videos, following consumer complaints that the brand appealed to under-age drinkers. One of the videos featured a young man killing a wasp, and the others featured young men acting out various antisocial behaviours (Farey-Jones, 2012).

Branded Content

Branded content refers to the use of entertainment material delivered through paid or owned media which features a single company or brand. The recent growth in the use of branded content rests with a drive to realize the potential that 'owned' media offers. Branded content enables conversations, particularly in social media, and this serves to raise a brand's profile and its credibility.

One of the earlier forms of branded content is customer publishing. Under this model, organizations develop magazines with articles and content considered to be of interest to their customers. The magazine includes references to, and even articles and stories about, the sponsoring brand. The development and distribution of these magazines to the brand's customer base is a paid media operation.

Today consumers use a variety of platforms and so organizations, or rather their content agencies, need to develop content for use across the web, mobiles, email, video, social media, and apps (Bonn, 2012). This provides an opportunity to integrate material and allow customers to form a coherent or interconnected experience of the brand. The entertainment material is still distributed to customers, but non-customers are also included. Distribution is entirely through media owned by the brand.

Other Promotional Methods and Approaches

Media and audience fragmentation has forced organizations to adapt to changing market conditions. The switch in emphasis from mass media to digital media has also been complemented by an increase in the use of what might be regarded as support tools and media. So far, the marketing communications mix has been presented as a set of five tools and various media. However, in addition to these five primary tools, numerous other tools and communication instruments are used by organizations to reach their audiences. In many cases they can be regarded as tools or media that support the primary mix, although they can be used in their own right as stand-alone methods of communications. Some of these other tools are briefly considered here.

Sponsorship, normally associated with public relations but with strong associations with advertising, has become an important form of communication for many organizations. Sponsorship is a commercial activity, whereby one party permits another an opportunity to exploit an association with a target audience in return for funds, services, or resources (Fill, 2009). Organizations are using different forms of sponsorship activities to generate awareness and brand associations, and to cut through the clutter of commercial messages. See Market Insight 11.3 about Red Bull's innovative use of sponsorship.

Brand placement is also a form of sponsorship and represents a relationship between film/TV producers and managers of brands. Through this arrangement, brand managers are able, for a fee, to present their brands 'naturally' within a film or entertainment event. Such placement is designed to increase brand awareness, develop positive brand attitudes, and possibly lead to purchase activity.

Field marketing is about providing support for the sales force and merchandising personnel. One of the tasks is concerned with getting free samples of a product into the hands of potential customers. Another task is to create an interaction between the brand and a new customer, and yet another is to create a personal and memorable brand experience for potential customers.

Market Insight 11.3

Red Bull Sponsors the Fastest Human

In October 2012, Felix Baumgartner broke three aviation world records. These were for the height reached in a balloon, for the highest ever skydive, and perhaps the one for which he will be best remembered, the speed with which a human being has fallen, 1342.03kph (833.9mph), or Mach 1.24, or, in other words, for being the first human to break the sound barrier without mechanical propulsion.

These records were achieved when he jumped from a space capsule, Red Bull Stratos, which had been lifted by a helium balloon to a height of just over 128,100 feet, or 24 miles, above New Mexico. The successful skydive lasted for 9.09 minutes in total. It was not without difficult moments as the visor misted, and Baumgartner entered a twist, from which he was able to extricate himself before pulling the parachute after 4 minutes freefall. As the name of the capsule indicates, the whole event was sponsored by Red Bull. The mission was not just about achieving records or promoting Red Bull, but was a scientific exercise designed to improve our understanding about how the human body copes with extreme conditions. This involved aerospace medicine, engineering, pressure suit development, capsule creation, and balloon fabrication.

Red Bull's marketing communications focus on the use of sponsorship which it uses to reinforce brand associations with risk, endurance, adrenaline, and the spectacular. This event took five years to plan, and Red Bull paid not only for the capsule and the helium balloon, but also for the one-off suit designed to cope with stratospheric conditions and be sufficiently manoeuvrable in a way that most off-the-shelf spacesuits are not.

Red Bull promoted the event through its own websites, through a variety of social media channels, and by substantial public relations activities. In return for its investment, Red Bull enabled millions of people

Red Bull sponsored Felix Baumgartner's daredevil space skydive above New Mexico
Source: © Red Bull Stratos/Red Bull Content Pool.

to view the skydive live on television around the world, plus eight million concurrent views on YouTube, making this the highest ever concurrent viewing figure on the Google-owned site. Viewers saw, as one reporter put it, Baumgartner as a 'flying can of Red Bull'. Immediately after the event, Twitter reported that approximately 3.1 million tweets relating to the event had been sent.

Source: Based on Ahuja 2012; Fraser (2012); Shearman (2012); www.redbullstratos.com/cs/Satellite/en_INT/Video/What-Felix-Saw-Red-Bull-Stratos-Live-Jump-POV-021243270932859

1 How should Red Bull build on the success of this event?

2 To what extent might this event have damaged Red Bull's reputation had it been a disaster?

3 Find two other brands that sponsor extreme sports and similar events. How do they configure their marketing communication mixes?

Visit the **Online Resource Centre** and follow the weblink to see further examples of adrenaline fuelled sports events sponsored by Red Bull.

Exhibitions are held for both consumer and business markets. Organizations benefit from meeting their current and potential customers, developing relationships, demonstrating products, building industry-wide credibility, placing and taking orders, generating leads, and gathering market information. For customers, exhibitions enable them to meet new or potential suppliers, find out about new offerings and leading-edge brands, and get up to date with market developments. In business markets, exhibitions and trade shows can be an integral element of the marketing communications mix. Meeting friends, customers, suppliers, competitors, and prospective customers is an important sociological and ritualistic event in the communications calendar for many companies.

Viral marketing is a fairly recent development based on the credibility and reach associated with word-of-mouth communications. Numerous definitions have been proposed, many of which can be found in Vilpponen *et al.* (2006). According to Simmons (2006: 1), the term viral marketing refers to 'how the content—be it a joke, picture, game or video—gets around'. Developing this idea, Porter and Golan (2006: 33) refer to viral marketing in terms of how these materials are communicated and suggest that it commonly involves the 'unpaid peer-to-peer communication of provocative content originating from an identified sponsor using the internet to persuade or influence an audience to pass along the content to others'.

There are many other, largely digital, methods of communicating with target audiences: mobile communications, SMS, blogging, and podcasting to name a few. These are all considered in Chapter 17.

Marketing Communications Planning

This part of the chapter examines the issues associated with managing marketing communications activities. Management's task is to formulate and implement a communication strategy that blends the right mix of tools and media to deliver the right messages in the right place, at the right time, for the right audience. To accomplish this, there are inevitably a series of issues that need to be addressed before decisions can be made. These issues embrace a range of activities, such as developing strategy in the light of both audience and brand characteristics, agreeing communication objectives, and then formulating, implementing, and evaluating marketing communication strategies and plans, many of which need to be integrated, an important topic itself in contemporary marketing communications.

Further issues concern the creation of the right message, the configuration of the right mix of tools and media, the allocation of financial and human resources, the coordination and control of related activities, and the management of various relationships. These relationships are not just those with internal colleagues, critical as these are, but also encompass those external stakeholders who work with the organization to deliver particular elements of a marketing communications plan. For example, they might provide research information, they might be agencies that design the message (or creative as it is referred to in the trade), or they might be those who plan and buy media for the message to be conveyed to the target audience.

Marketing communications planning is a systematic process involving a series of procedures and activities that lead to the setting of marketing communications objectives and the formulation of plans for achieving them. The aim of the planning process is to formulate and convey messages to particular target audiences that encourage them to think, emote, behave, or respond in particular ways. It is the skill and responsibility of those in charge of marketing communications planning to ensure that there is the right blend of communication tools, and that they create memorable messages and convey them through a suitable media mix.

To understand what a marketing communications plan should achieve, it is helpful to appreciate the principal tasks facing marketing communications managers. These are to decide the following.

- Who should receive the messages?
- What should the messages say?
- What image of the organization/brand are receivers expected to retain?
- How much is to be spent establishing this new image?
- How are the messages to be delivered?
- What actions should the receivers take?
- How do we control the whole process once implemented?
- What was achieved?

For many reasons, planning is an essential management activity and, if planned marketing communications are to be developed in an orderly and efficient way, the use of a suitable framework is necessary. A framework for integrated marketing communications plans is presented in Figure 11.2.

The **marketing communications planning framework (MCPF)** provides a visual guide to what needs to be achieved and brings together the various elements in a logical sequence of activities. As with all hierarchical planning models, each level of decision-making is built on information generated at a previous level in the model. Another advantage of using the MCPF is that it provides a suitable checklist of activities that need to be considered. The MCPF represents a sequence of decisions that marketing managers undertake when preparing, implementing, and evaluating communication strategies and plans. This framework reflects a deliberate or planned approach to strategic marketing communications.

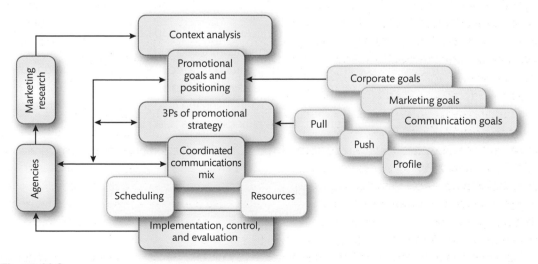

Figure 11.2

The marketing communications planning framework

Source: *Marketing Communications*, 6th edn, Fill, C., Pearson Education Limited (2013). Reproduced with the kind permission of Pearson Education Limited.

However, in practice marketing communications planning is not always developed as a linear process as depicted in this framework. Indeed, many marketing communications decisions are made outside any recognizable framework, as some organizations approach the process as an integrative and sometimes spontaneous activity. However, the MCPF approach presented here is intended to highlight the tasks to be achieved, the way in which they relate to one another, and the order in which they should be accomplished.

Elements of the MCPF

A marketing communications plan should be developed for each level of communications activity, from strategy to individual tactical aspects of a campaign. The difference between them is the level of detail that is included.

Context Analysis

The marketing plan is the bedrock of the **context analysis** (CA). This will already have been prepared and contains important information about the target segments, the business and marketing goals, the competitors, and the timescales in which the goals are to be achieved. The CA needs to elaborate and build on this information to provide the detail so that the plan can be developed and justified.

The first and vital step in the planning process is to analyse the context in which marketing communications activities are to occur. Unlike a situation analysis used in general planning models, the context analysis should be communications oriented and use the marketing plan as a foundation. There are four main components to the communications context analysis: the customer, business, internal, and external environmental contexts.

Understanding the customer context requires information and market research data about the target audiences specified in the marketing plan. Here, detailed information about their needs, perceptions, motivation, attitudes, and decision-making characteristics relative to the proposition category (or issue) is necessary. In addition, information about the media and the people they use for information about the category needs to be determined.

Understanding the business or marketing context, and the marketing communications environment in particular, is also important as these influence what has to be achieved. If the marketing strategy specifies growth through market penetration, then not only will messages need to reflect this goal but it will also be important to understand how competitors are communicating with the target audience and which media they are using to do this.

Analysis of the internal context is undertaken to determine the resource capability with respect to supporting marketing communications. Three principal areas need to be reviewed:

- people resources (are people, including agencies, with suitable marketing communications skills available?);
- financial resources (how much is available to invest in marketing communications?);
- technological resources (are the right systems and processes available to support marketing communications?).

The final area to be reviewed is the wider external context. Similar to the areas considered during the strategic analysis, emphasis is placed on the political, economic, societal, ecological, and technological conditions. However, stress needs to be given to the impact on marketing communications. For example, if economic conditions get tough, people have lower levels of disposable income. Sales promotions, promotional offers, and extended credit terms become more attractive in this context.

The context analysis provides the rationale for the rest of the plan. It is from the CA that the marketing objectives (from the marketing plan) and the marketing communications objectives are derived. The type, form, and style of the message are rooted in the characteristics of the target audience, and the media selected to convey messages should be based on the nature of the tasks, the media preferences and habits of the audience, and the resources available. See Market Insight 11.4 which explains how British Airways used the context of the Olympics to re-engage with its audiences.

Market Insight 11.4

British Airways Decide Not To Fly ... But to Serve at Home

Using the line 'To Fly. To Serve', taken from its coat of arms, British Airways launched its first major brand campaign for ten years in 2011. The aim was to give the brand a new sense of purpose, to reinforce its identity, and to provide employees a refreshed point of engagement with the brand.

At the centre of the campaign was a 90-second TV spot that paid tribute to both the early and contemporary aviators and the pilots. British Airways was a Tier One London Olympic Games sponsor and needed to use the Games as an opportunity to build on the 'To Fly. To Serve' platform. The problem was how should an airline that seeks to fly people out of the country provide realistic support for the Olympics and Team GB?

The answer rested with a 'Don't Fly. Support Team GB' campaign. This encouraged Britons to stay in the country and give support to the home team. The ad featured a British Airways aircraft taxiing by road through London to the soundtrack of 'London Calling' by The Clash. The strapline 'Don't Fly. Support Team GB and ParalympicsGB' appeared as the aircraft reached the Olympic Park.

The same message appeared in national newspapers and on outdoor posters. The campaign also ran online and in social media, using the hashtag #HomeAdvantage on Twitter. On British Airways's Facebook page, users could input their postcode and watch the aircraft taxi down their street. All this activity was supplemented

British Airways launched a surprising campaign during the Olympics urging people to 'stay at home'
Source: Produced by BBH for British Airways.

with various PR activity and experiential pop-ups. British Airways also ran a 'bag race' ad. This showed the airline's baggage handling service as a race between different pieces of luggage. Together these campaigns were specifically orientated to BA, the Olympics, and consumers. They were humorous and presented a more relaxed and contemporary view of the airline than previous campaigns.

Sources: Bacon (2012); Eleftheriou-Smith (2012); Palmer (2012); www.travelweekly.co.uk/

1 What is the context in which British Airways' 'Don't fly' was launched?

2 Explain how understanding the context shaped British Airways' campaign.

3 Find another example of how the context shaped an organization's marketing communications.

Marketing Communications Objectives

Many organizations assume that their marketing communications goals are the same as their sales targets. This is incorrect because there are so many elements that contribute to sales, such as competitor pricing, product attributes, and distributor policies, that making marketing communications solely responsible for sales is naive and unrealistic. Ideally, marketing communications objectives should consist of three main elements: corporate, marketing, and communications objectives.

- **Corporate objectives** are derived from the business or marketing plan. They refer to the mission and the business area that the organization believes it should be in.
- **Marketing objectives** are derived from the marketing plan and are sales oriented. These might be market share, sales revenues, volumes, ROI (return on investment), and other profitability indicators.
- **Communications objectives** are derived from the context analysis and refer to levels of awareness, perception, comprehension/knowledge, attitudes, and overall degree of preference for a brand. The choice of communications goal depends on the tasks that need to be accomplished.

These three elements constitute the overall set of marketing communications objectives.

They should be set out in **SMART** terminology, i.e. each should be specific, measurable, achievable, realistic, and timed. Many brands need to refine the way they are perceived by customers, commonly referred to as a brand's position. Positioning is not applicable to all communications plans, e.g. government-sponsored information campaigns do not have a positioning goal. However, most commercial and brand-oriented communication programmes need to be seen to occupy a clear position in the market. So, at this point in the planning process, the brand's positioning intentions are developed and these should be related to the market, the customers, or a product dimension (see also Chapter 6). The justification for this will have been identified in the context analysis.

Marketing Communications Strategy

The marketing communications strategy is derived from the objectives and context analysis. There are three types of strategy: pull for the end-user markets, push for the trade and channel intermediaries, and profile designed to reach all significant stakeholders. The DRIP roles of marketing communications, established in Chapter 10, can be used to elaborate the relevant strategy to be pursued. For example, if a new brand is being launched, the first task will be to inform and differentiate the brand for members of the trade before using a pull strategy to inform and differentiate the brand for the target end-user customers. For example, the UK retailer John Lewis has developed a reputation for a series of highly emotional and well-executed campaigns in the lead-up to Christmas. In the 2012 campaign, the TV ads used the Gabrielle Aplin cover of 'The Power of Love', which subsequently topped the official UK singles chart.

An organization wishing to signal a change of strategy and/or a change of name following a merger or acquisition may choose to use a profile strategy, and the primary task will be to inform about the name change. An organization experiencing declining sales may choose to remind customers of a need or it may choose to improve sales through persuasion.

A traditional pull strategy in the grocery sector used to be based on delivering mass media advertising supported by below-the-line communications, most notably sales promotions delivered in-store and through direct mail and email to registered customers (e.g. Tesco Clubcard customers). The decision to use a pull strategy should be supported by a core message that will try to differentiate (position), remind or reassure, inform, or persuade the audience to think, feel, or behave in a particular way. This approach can be interpreted as a pull/remind or pull/position communication strategy, as this describes the audience and direction of the strategy and also clarifies what the strategy seeks to achieve.

Visit the **Online Resource Centre** and complete Internet Activity 11.4 to learn more about how Honda used a pull strategy to target purchasers of its Honda Civic.

A push strategy should be treated in a similar way. The need to consider the core message is paramount as it conveys information about the essence of the strategy. Push/inform, push/position, or push/key accounts/discount might be examples of possible terminology.

Although these three strategies are represented here as individual entities, they are often used as a 'cluster'. For example, the launch of a new toothpaste brand will involve a push strategy to get the product on the shelves of the key supermarkets and independent retailers. The strategy would be to gain retailer acceptance of the new brand and to position it for them as a profitable new brand. The goal is to get the toothpaste on the retailers' shelves. To achieve this, personal selling supported by trade sales promotions will be the main marketing communications tools. A push strategy alone would be insufficient to persuade a retailer to stock a new brand. The promise of a pull strategy aimed at creating brand awareness and customer excitement needs to be created, accompanied by appropriate public relations activities and any initial sales promotions necessary to motivate consumers to change their brand of toothpaste. The next step is to create particular brand associations and thereby position the brand in the minds of the target consumer audience. Messages may be primarily informational or emotional, but will endeavour to convey a brand promise. This may be accompanied or followed by the use of incentives to encourage consumers to trial the product. To support the brand, carelines and a website, as well as a buyer reference point, will need to be put in place to provide credibility.

Communications Methods

This part of the plan is relatively complex as a number of activities need to be accomplished. For each specified target audience in the strategy, a creative or message needs to be developed. This should be based on the positioning requirements and will often be developed by an outside communications agency.

Simultaneously, it is necessary to formulate the right mix of communication tools to reach each particular audience. In addition, the right media mix needs to be determined, both on- and offline. Again, this task will most probably be undertaken by media experts. Here, integration is regarded as an important feature of the communication mix.

The Schedule

The next step is to schedule the way in which the campaign is to be delivered. Events and activities should be scheduled according to the goals and the strategic thrust. So, if it is necessary to communicate with the trade prior to a public launch, those activities tied into the push strategy should be scheduled prior to those calculated to support the pull strategy. Similarly, if awareness is a goal then, funds permitting, it may be best first to use TV and poster ads offline plus banners and search engine ads online, before using sales promotions (unless sampling is used), direct marketing, point of purchase, and personal selling.

Resources

The resources necessary to support the plan need to be determined. These refer not only to the financial issues but also to the quality of available marketing expertise. This means that internally the right sort of marketing knowledge may not be present and may have to be recruited. For example, if a customer relationship management system (CRM) initiative is being launched, it will be important to have people with knowledge and skills related to running CRM programmes. With regard to external skills, it is necessary that the current communications agencies are capable of delivering the creative and media plan. This is an important part of the plan, which is often avoided or forgotten about. Software project planning tools, simple spreadsheets, or Gantt charts can be used not only to schedule the campaign but also to chart the resources relating to the actual and budgeted costs of using the selected tools and media.

Control and Evaluation

Once launched, campaigns should be monitored. This is to ensure that should there be any major deviance from the plan, opportunities exist to get back on track as soon as possible. In addition, all marketing communications plans should be evaluated. There are numerous methods of evaluating the individual performance of the tools and the media used, but perhaps the most important measures concern the achievement of the communication objectives.

Feedback

The marketing communications planning process is completed when feedback is provided. Not only should information regarding the overall outcome of a campaign be considered but so should individual aspects of the activity. For example, the performance of the individual tools used within the campaign, whether sufficient resources were invested, the appropriateness of the strategy in the first place, whether any problems had been encountered during implementation, and the relative ease with which the objectives were accomplished are aspects that need to be fed back to all internal and external parties associated with the planning process.

This feedback is vitally important because it provides information for the context analysis that anchors the next campaign. Information fed back in a formal and systematic manner constitutes an opportunity for organizations to learn from their previous campaign activities, a point often overlooked and neglected.

Managing Communications Activities

Over the past five years there have been some sizeable changes to the way the marketing communications industry is structured, not just in the UK but across the globe. One of the most important of these has been the emergence of a number of powerful and dominant industry groups, such as WPP and News Corporation, whose business interests span cross-media ownership, content development, and delivery. The battle in 2007 between Virgin Media and BSkyB over fees to deliver Sky content through Virgin Media reflects the criticality of some of these issues. The changing industry structure is a response to several variables, particularly developments in technology, the configuration of the communications mix and media used by organizations, and the way in which client-side managers are expected to operate.

Research Insight 11.3

To take your learning further, you might wish to read this influential paper.

Jones, J. P. (1990), 'Ad spending: maintaining market share', *Harvard Business Review*, **January–February, 38–42.**

This paper provided a first and important link between advertising strategy and budgeting. The paper is built on the research findings emanating from a very large sample of brands. It draws some interesting conclusions about the level of advertising investment relative to market share.

@ **Visit the Online Resource Centre to read the abstract and access the full paper.**

There can be no doubt that technology has had a dramatic impact on the communications industry. As a result, the way organizations use the communications mix has changed considerably. Traditionally, clients working in consumer markets preferred to place the majority of their media advertising into offline mass media vehicles. Similarly, the sales force was the dominant tool of the mix used by organizations operating in business markets. Today, the use of sponsorship, direct and event marketing, and online digitally driven interactive communications is growing at the expense of offline mass media advertising and sales promotions in consumer markets. Many organizations in the business-to-business market have slashed the size of their sales forces, partly to cut costs but also to use technology more efficiently.

The reasons for these shifts in behaviour are indicative of the increasing attention and accountability that management is attaching to communication spend. Increasingly, marketing managers are being asked to justify the amounts they spend on their budgets, including advertising and sales promotion. Senior managers now want to know the return they are getting on their marketing communication investments. This is because there is pressure to use their scarce resources more effectively and efficiently so that they can meet their corporate and business-level objectives.

It might be safely assumed that the final aspect of a manager's responsibilities concerns the measurement of their marketing communications activities. This is partly correct, but measurement and evaluation should be an ongoing activity used throughout the development and implementation of a campaign. The importance of evaluating marketing communications activities should not be underestimated. The process can provide a potentially rich source of material for the next campaign and the ongoing communications that all organizations operate. Unfortunately, many organizations choose either to ignore or not to devote too many resources or too much significance to this aspect of their work. However, in an age of increasing accountability, measuring and determining just how well a campaign ran and what was accomplished is an essential part of marketing communications. Table 11.7 sets out some of the more common techniques used to measure marketing communications.

Table 11.7 Evaluation methods: marketing communications tools

Communication tool	Method of testing
Advertising	Pretesting—unfinished ads—concept testing, focus groups, consumer juries
	Pretesting—finished ads—dummy vehicles, readability test, theatre tests
	Physiological—pupil dilation, eye tracking, galvanic skin response, tachistoscopes, electroencephalographs
	Post-testing—enquiry tests, recall tests, recognition tests, sales-tracking studies, financial analysis, likeability
Sales promotion	Trial, sales, stock turn, redemption levels
Public relations	Press cuttings, content analysis, media evaluation, tracking studies, recruitment levels
Direct marketing	Response rates, sales, opening/reading ratios, trial
Personal selling	Activities, costs, knowledge and skills, sales, performance ratios, territory analysis, team outputs, customer satisfaction

Integrated Marketing Communications

So far in this chapter we have looked briefly at the five main tools, the media, and ideas about how messages should be developed. However, for these to work most effectively and most efficiently, it makes sense to integrate them so that they work as a unit. In so doing, they will have a greater overall impact. This bringing together is referred to as integrated marketing communications (IMC).

Integrated marketing communications has become a popular approach with both clients and communications agencies. Ideas about IMC originated in the early 1990s. At first, IMC was regarded as a means of orchestrating the tools of the marketing communications mix, so that audiences perceive a single consistent unified message whenever they have contact with a brand. Duncan and Everett (1993) referred to this new, largely media-oriented approach as *orchestration*, *whole egg*, and *seamless* communication. Since that time, Duncan (2002), Grönroos (2004), Kitchen *et al.* (2004), and Kliatchko (2008) have provided various definitions and valuable insights into IMC. There has been little conformity about a definition (Reinold and Tropp, 2012), so for our purposes the following definition is used:

> IMC can represent both a strategic and tactical approach to the planned management of an organization's communications. IMC requires that organizations coordinate their various strategies, resources and messages in order that they enable meaningful engagement with audiences. The main purposes are to develop a clear positioning and encourage stakeholder relationships that are of mutual value. (Fill, 2013)

Embedded within this definition are links with both business-level and marketing strategies plus confirmation of the importance of the coherent use of resources and messages. What should also be evident is that IMC can be used to support the development and maintenance of effective relationships, a point made first by Duncan and Moriarty (1998) and then by Grönroos (2004) and Ballantyne (2004). Some, such as Peltier *et al.* (2003), advocate interactive integrated marketing communications (IMC) based on the premise that all marketing communication should be based on customer databases. However, this is not a widely held view as IMC can work without having to be database fed, or interactive in that sense.

One quite common use of an integrated approach can be seen in the use of the tools. For example, rather than use advertising, public relations, sales promotions, personal selling, and direct marketing separately, better to use them in a coordinated manner. So, organizations often use advertising or sales promotion to create awareness, and then involve public relations to provoke media comment, and then reinforce these messages through direct marketing or personal selling. The internet can also be incorporated to encourage comment, interest, and involvement in a brand, yet still convey the same message in a consistent way. Mobile communications are used to reach audiences to reinforce messages and persuade them to behave in particular ways, wherever they are. However, the rise of digital media poses problems for IMC and for planning marketing communications activities. Some of these issues concern metrics and measurement, budgeting, brand control, and content development (Winer, 2009).

Another important aspect of integration concerns the question: 'What else should be integrated?' One element might be the planning and campaign development process. Using an integrated approach during the planning phase can serve to integrate clients, agencies, suppliers, and employees, as well as other resources.

IMC has emerged for many reasons, but the two main ones concern customers and costs. First, organizations began to realize that their customers are more likely to understand a single message, delivered through various sources, rather than try to understand a series of different messages transmitted through different tools and a variety of media. Therefore IMC is concerned with harmonizing the messages conveyed through each of the promotional tools, so that audiences perceive a consistent set of meanings within the messages they receive. The second reason concerns costs. As organizations seek to lower their costs, it is becoming clear that it is far more cost-effective to send a single message, using a limited number of agencies and other resources, than develop several messages through a number of agencies.

At first glance, IMC might appear to be a practical and logical development that should benefit all concerned with an organization's marketing communications. However, there are issues concerning the concept, including what should be integrated over and above the tools, media, and messages. For example, what about the impact of employees on a brand and other elements of the marketing mix, as well as the structure, systems, processes, and procedures necessary to deliver IMC consistently through time? There is some debate about the nature and contribution IMC can make to an organization, if only because there is a no main theory to underpin the topic (Cornelissen, 2003).

Although IMC has yet to become an established marketing theory, the original ideas inherent in the overall approach are intuitively appealing and appear to be of value. However, what is integration to one person may be coordination and good practice to another, and, until there is a theoretical base on which to build IMC, the phrase will continue to be misused, misunderstood, and used in a haphazard and inconsistent way.

Research Insight 11.4

To take your learning further, you might wish to read this influential paper.

Reinold, T. and Tropp, J. (2012), 'Integrated marketing communications. How can we measure its effectiveness?', *Journal of Marketing Communications*, 18(2), 113–32.

We recommend this paper for several reasons. First, it provides succinct coverage of the development of IMC. Secondly, it considers measurement issues, and thirdly, it uses the measurement perspective to consider how practitioners perceive IMC. The authors present a model for measuring IMC effectiveness that has practical applications.

Visit the **Online Resource Centre** to read the abstract and access the full paper.

Chapter Summary

To consolidate your learning, the key points from this chapter are summarized here.

■ **Describe the role and configuration of the marketing communications mix.**

Organizations use the marketing communication mix to convey messages and to engage their various audiences. The mix consists of five tools, three forms of media, and four main forms of messages or content. These elements are mixed and adapted to meet the needs of the target audience and the context in which marketing communications operate. Tools and media are not the same, as the former are methods or techniques, whereas the media are the means by which messages are conveyed to the target audience.

■ **Explain the characteristics of each of the primary tools, media, and messages.**

Each of the tools—advertising, sales promotion, public relations, direct marketing, and personal selling—communicates messages in different ways and achieves different outcomes. Each medium has a set of characteristics that enable it to convey messages in particular ways to and with target audiences. There are six main classes of media: broadcast, print, outdoor, digital, in-store, and other media. Alternatively, media can be classified according to whether it is paid, owned, or earned. Messages are a balance of informational and emotional content. Some content can be branded whilst some can be generated by users.

■ **Set out the criteria that should be used to select the right communication mix.**

Using a set of criteria can help simplify the complex and difficult process of selecting the right marketing communications mix. There are five key criteria: the degree of control over a message, the credibility of the message conveyed, the costs of using a tool, the degree to which a target audience is dispersed, and the task that marketing communications is required to accomplish.

■ **Describe the different activities associated with managing and planning marketing communications.**

There is a large range of tasks associated with managing marketing communications. At one level, there are decisions to be made about the overall strategy and direction of the marketing communications, and issues associated with the process and, of course, the content of marketing communications plans. At another level, decisions need to be made about the right mix of tools and media necessary to engage with target audiences, and about what is to be said in the message and how it is to be presented. Behind all these activities are issues associated with the management of resources, human and financial, and the agency relationships necessary to generate the communication materials. Once implemented, management is involved through control, monitoring, evaluation, and feedback processes.

■ **Consider the principles and issues associated with integrated marketing communications.**

Rather than use advertising, public relations, sales promotions, personal selling, and direct marketing separately, integrated marketing communications is concerned with working with these tools (and media) as a coordinated whole. So, organizations often use advertising to create awareness, then involve public relations to provoke media comment, sales promotion to create a trial, and then reinforce these messages through direct marketing or personal selling to persuade audiences. The internet can also be incorporated to encourage comment, interest, and involvement in a brand, yet still convey the same message. Mobile communications are used to reach audiences to reinforce messages and persuade audiences to behave in particular ways, wherever they are.

Review Questions

1 Make brief notes about the nature and role of the marketing communications mix and explain how the configuration has changed.

2 Write a definition for advertising, public relations, and one other tool from the mix. Identify the key differences.

3 Why do organizations like to use direct-response media?

4 How does media fragmentation fragment audiences?

5 What five criteria can be used to select the right mix of communication tools?

6 Write a list that categorizes the media. Find a media vehicle to represent each type of media.

7 To what extent are online and digital media likely to replace the use of traditional media?

8 Discuss the view that if marketing communications strategy is about being audience-centred then there is little need to prepare a context analysis.

9 Draw the marketing communications planning framework, without first referring to the diagram.

10 What are the principles of integrated marketing communications?

Worksheet Summary

To apply the knowledge you have gained from this chapter and test your understanding of managing the communications mix visit the **Online Resource Centre** and complete Worksheet 11.1.

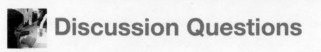

Discussion Questions

1   Having read Case Insight 11.1, how would you advise Budweiser Budvar on how to develop their 'NO' campaign? How should they communicate the NO message without being negative? What promotional tools should they use for the campaign? What mix of media would be best at delivering the 'NO' campaign to realize the greatest impact?

2   Discuss the view that the role of the marketing communications mix should change as it was developed in an age when communications were based on mass media communications.

3   Select an organization you are familiar with or would like to work for. Visit their website and try to determine their use of the marketing communications tools and media. How could their mix of tools and media be improved?

4   Select an organization in the consumer technology industry or one which you would like to work for. Visit their website and see their ad archive and read the press releases. Determine their approach to marketing communications. Now visit the website for their main competitor and determine their marketing communications. Discuss the similarities and differences.

5   Zylog is based in Sweden and manufactures and distributes a range of consumer electronic equipment. Annike Karlsson, Zylog's new marketing manager, has indicated that she wants to introduce an integrated approach to the firm's marketing communications. However, Zylog does not have any experience of IMC and their current communications agency, Red Spider, has started to become concerned that it may lose the Zylog account. Discuss the situation facing Zylog and suggest ways in which they might acquire the expertise they need. Then discuss ways in which Red Spider might acquire an IMC capability.

@ Visit the **Online Resource Centre** and complete the Multiple Choice Questions to assess your knowledge of Chapter 11.

References

Ahuja, A. (2012), 'Felix Baumgartner skydive: that was one rather helpful leap for space tourism', *The Telegraph*, 16 October, retrieve from: http://www.telegraph.co.uk/science/space/9611071/Felix-Baumgartner-skydive-that-was-one-rather-helpful-leap-for-space-tourism.html accessed 9 July 2013.

Bacon, J. (2012), 'Flying the brand flag for British Airways', *Marketing Week*, 8 November, retrieve from: http://www.marketingweek.co.uk/trends/flying-the-brand-flag-for-british-airways/4004567 accessed 14 December 2012.

Ballantyne, D. (2004), 'Dialogue and its role in the development of relationship specific knowledge', *Journal of Business and Industrial Marketing*, 19(2), 114–23.

Batten, N. (2012), 'Look launches "Look What I'm Wearing" ', *Mediaweek.co.uk*, 14 May, retrieve from: http://www.brandrepublic.com/news/1131632/Look-launches-Look-Im-Wearing/?DCMP=ILC-SEARCH accessed 20 December 2012.

Berne, S. (2009), 'Four in ten viewers driven online by TV ads', *NewMediaAge*, 19 August, retrieve from: www.nma.co.uk/four-in-ten-viewers-driven-online-by-tv-ads/ accessed 6 July 2013.

Bonn, R. (2012), 'As brands become publishers, are they getting their content right?', *The Guardian*, 22 October, www.guardian.co.uk/media-network/media-network-blog/2012/oct/22/brands-becoming-publishers-content-marketing accessed 20 December 2012.

Chapman, M. (2012), 'Kia to run global "Power to Surprise" co-creation campaign, *Campaignlive*, 4 October, retrieve from: http://www.brandrepublic.com/news/1156372/Kia-run-global-Power-Surprise-co-creation-campaign/?DCMP=ILC-SEARCH accessed 2 January 2013.

Cornelissen, J. P. (2003), 'Change, continuity and progress: the concept of integrated marketing communications and marketing communications practice', *Journal of Strategic Marketing*, 11, 217–34.

Diaz, A-C. (2012), 'Behind Facebook's emotional ad from Wieden & Kennedy', *AdAge digital*, 4 October, retrieve from: http://adage.com/article/digital/facebook-emotional-spot-wieden-kennedy/237569/?utm_source=digital_email&utm_medium=newsletter&utm_campaign=adage accessed 2 January 2013.

Duncan, T. (2002), *IMC: Using Advertising and Promotion to Build Brand*, New York: McGraw-Hill.

Duncan, T. and Everett, S. (1993), 'Client perceptions of integrated marketing communications', *Journal of Advertising Research*, 3(3), 30–9.

Duncan, T. and Moriarty, S. (1998), 'A communication-based marketing model for managing relationships', *Journal of Marketing*, 62(April), 1–13.

Eleftheriou-Smith, L-M. (2012), 'BA tells nation "Don't Fly" in support of Olympics', *Campaignlive*, 19 June, retrieve from: http://www.campaignlive.co.uk/news/1136972/ accessed 15 December 2012.

Empresas, Y. M. (2009), Mamá Lucchetti, de Madre para Molinos Rio de La Plata, www.mediosyempresas.com, 25 October, retrieve from: http://www.mediosyempresas.com/noticias/2848/repasamos+el+caso+de+exito+del+relanzamiento+de+la+linea+de+alimentos+lucchetti+.html accessed 5 April 2012.

Farey-Jones, D. (2012), 'Frosty Jack's pulls "irresponsible" user-generated videos', *Campaignlive.co.uk*, 13 June, retrieve from: http://www.brandrepublic.com/news/1136085/Frosty-Jacks-pulls-irresponsible-user-generated-videos/?DCMP=ILC-SEARCH accessed 20 December 2012.

Fill, C. (2009) *Marketing Communications: Interactivity, Communities and Content* (5th edn), Harlow: FT/Prentice Hall.

Fill, C. (2013), *Marketing Communications: Brands, Experience and Participation* (6th edn), Harlow: FT/Prentice Hall.

Fraser, G. (2012), 'Red Bull stratos Felix Baumgartner stunt worth "millions" ', *The Telegraph*, 15 October, retrieve from: http://www.telegraph.co.uk/finance/businessclub/business-club-video/consumer-and-retail-sector-vide/9610517/Red-Bull-stratos-Felix-Baumgartner-stunt-worth-millions.html accessed 16 October 2012.

Grönroos, C. (2004), 'The relationship marketing process: communication, interaction, dialogue, value', *Journal of Business and Industrial Marketing*, 19(2), 99–113.

Halliday, J. (2011), 'Boot up: Twitter hits 300m users, Motorola Atrix review, and more', *The Guardian*, 19 May, retrieve from: http://www.guardian.co.uk/technology/blog/2011/may/19/technology-links-newsbucket?INTCMP=SRCH accessed 6 July 2013.

Herrera, C. (2009), '*Lucchetti: El triunfo de la antiheroína*' Infobrand (Online), 1 December, retrieve from: http://www.infobrand.com.ar/notas/13197-Luchetti%3A-el-triunfo-de-la-antihero%EDna accessed 6 July 2013.

Imizcoz, C.L. (2012), 'Diana Arroz, la "heroína" en boca de todos que reinventó a Lucchetti', Perfil, 5 April, retrieve from: http://www.diarioperfil.com.ar/edimp/0493/articulo.php?art=23489&ed=0493 accessed 6 July 2013.

Jones, J. P. (1990), 'Ad spending: maintaining market share', *Harvard Business Review*, January—February, 38–42.

Kaplan, A.M. and Haenlein, M. (2010), 'Users of the world, unite! The challenges and opportunities of social media', *Business Horizons*, 53(1), 59–68.

Kent, M. L., Taylor, M., and White, W. J. (2003), 'The relationship between web site design and organizational responsiveness to stakeholders', *Public Relations Review*, 29(1, March), 63–77.

Kitchen, P., Brignell, J., Li, T., and Spickett Jones, G. (2004), 'The emergence of IMC: a theoretical perspective', *Journal of Advertising Research*, 44, 19–30.

Kliatchko, J. (2008), 'Revisiting the IMC construct: a revised definition and four pillars', *International Journal of Advertising*, 27(1), 133–60.

Molinos (2012), *Nuestras Marcas*, retrieve from: http://www.molinos.com.ar accessed 5 April 2012.

Null, R.A., (2009), 'Best of bank on Twitter', *Bank Technology News*, May, retrieve from: http://www.americanbanker.com/btn_issues/22_5/-378008-1.html accessed 6 July 2013.

Ovide, S. and Glazer, E. (2012), 'Twitter's slow road to IPO', *The Wall Street Journal*, 2 March, retrieve from: http://online.wsj.com/article/SB10001424052970204571404577255532594364766.html accessed 21 December 2012.

Palmer, M. (2012) Advertisers who won digital gold, ft.com, 20 August, retrieve from: http://www.ft.com/cms/s/0/b0959724-e6fc-11e1-af33-00144feab49a.html#axzz2F1Cl2HNX accessed 15 December 2012

Peltier, J.W., Schibrowsky, J.A., and Schultz, D. E. (2003), 'Interactive integrated marketing communication: combining the power of MC, the new media and database marketing', *International Journal of Advertising*, 22, 93–115.

Porter, L. and Golan, G. J. (2006), 'From subservient chickens to brawny men: a comparison of viral advertising to TV advertising', *Journal of Interactive Advertising*, 6(2), 30–8.

Reinold, T. and Tropp, J. (2012), 'Integrated marketing communications. How can we measure its effectiveness?', *Journal of Marketing Communications*, 18(2), 113–32.

Sausner, R. (2009), 'Some say Twitter's for the birds', *Bank Technology News*, 1 May, retrieve from: http://www.americanbanker.com/btn_issues/22_5/-378018-1.html accessed 21 December 2012.

Shearman, S. (2012), 'Red Bull Stratos skydive smashes YouTube records', *Marketing*, 15 October, retrieve from: http://www.brandrepublic.com/news/1154746/red-bull-stratos-skydive-smashes-youtube-records/ accessed 16 October 2012

Simmons, D. (2006), 'Marketing's viral goldmine'. *BBC News*, 14 July, retrieve from: http://news.bbc.co.uk/1/hi/programmes/click_online/5179166.stm accessed 2 January 2013.

Vakratsas, D. and Ambler, T. (1999), 'How advertising works. What do we really know?', *Journal of Marketing*, 63(January), 26–43.

Vilpponen, A., Winter, S., and Sundqvist, S. (2006), 'Electronic word-of-mouth in online environments: exploring referral network structure and adoption behavior', *Journal of Interactive Advertising*, 6(2, Spring), 71–86.

Wheatley, M. (2010), 'Avoiding the fail whale', *PM Network*, October, 31–4.

Winer, R.S. (2009), 'New communications approaches in marketing: issues and research directions', *Journal of Interactive Marketing*, 23, 108–17.

Chapter 12

Marketing Channels and Retailing

Learning Outcomes

After studying this chapter you should be able to:

▶ Describe the nature and characteristics of a marketing channel

▶ Explain the different types of intermediaries and their roles in the marketing channel

▶ Understand the different marketing channel structures and their core characteristics

▶ Explain the factors that influence the design and structure of marketing channels

▶ Describe the main elements that constitute supply chain management

▶ Consider the role and function of retailers in the marketing channel

Case Insight
Cobalt

Market Insight 12.1
Channelling Motorbikes

Market Insight 12.2
Fast Fashion and Informality

Market Insight 12.3
Getting There, On Time

Market Insight 12.4
Consistent Store Experience at Hollister

Market Insight 12.5
Tuning into iTunes

Case Insight 12.1

How should organizations develop suitable channel structures to best serve and communicate with their customers? We speak to Cobalt's Legacy Officer, Zena Giles, to find out more.

Cobalt is an independent medical charity which helps people affected by cancer and other life-limiting conditions. Each year we provide diagnostic imaging for over 18,000 patients at the Cobalt Imaging Centre in Cheltenham and with our mobile magnetic resonance imaging (MRI) scanners that travel throughout local counties and beyond. As well as cancer, our equipment is able to assist in the detection of illnesses such as dementia (including Alzheimer's disease) and multiple sclerosis (MS).

We offer training and education courses on a local, national, and international basis for doctors and healthcare professionals, ensuring that our experience and research work is widely shared. We also visit local schools, companies, and organizations, delivering cancer prevention and health education talks and workshops. In order to maintain and develop this level of service and equipment we have to raise substantial funds each year. To do this we use several formal channels including trust fundraising, corporate support, and community fundraising.

Trust fundraising involves applying to charitable trusts for lump sums of money for various projects or appeals. Each trust has a set of strict criteria that the charity must satisfy to be considered for funding. The role of Cobalt's trust fundraiser is to research the trusts that support medical charities within our area and send a 'case for support' to them to try and gain their financial support.

Corporate support includes everything from a company sponsoring an event, or choosing us as their COTY (charity of the year) to businesses taking part in payroll giving and individual employees carrying out their own fundraising activities. Cobalt's corporate support is a combination of these, and many employees will

also apply to their company for 'match funding', asking them to match what they've raised by way of a donation, so that they can give more to Cobalt.

Community fundraising encompasses what people would traditionally think of when they think of charity fundraising. It includes managing all volunteers, events, template fundraising activities, community talks and presentations, PR, and charity awareness. Cobalt's community fundraiser is responsible for Cobalt-led events, as well as coordinating outside supporter or 'third-party' events. They manage Cobalt's template fundraising, which comprises 'off-the-shelf' ready-made activities, as well as coordinating the Challenge Event and Open Garden programmes, encouraging people to take part and supporting them as they do.

Raising awareness is an important part of community fundraising and other income streams, and the role involves much of Cobalt's local PR work. The community fundraiser is also responsible for giving talks and presentations on the charity to various community groups, businesses, and schools, and they also train volunteers to deliver these.

In addition to these formal channels, we have always received legacies. These are voluntary donations made by people through their wills. However, although these are a substantial source of income, it became apparent that we needed a formalized channel within our organization to develop this funding opportunity in order to realize its full potential.

The essential problem that we faced was how should we develop an appropriate channel to reach potential legacy donors and ensure that it fits within our current multichannel structure?

Introduction

Have you ever considered the journey a bottle of water, a computer, or a bag of potatoes might take from its source (manufacturer or producer) in order to be available for you to purchase at the point you prefer? In many cases this journey can be complex, involving transactions between many organizations, countries, and people.

The organizations involved with any one journey are collectively termed a distribution, or a **marketing channel**. These are chains of organizations that are concerned with the management of the processes and activities involved in creating and moving products from producers and manufacturers to end-user customers. Each organization adds something of value before passing it to the next, and it is this interaction which provides mutual advantage (Kotler and Keller, 2009), and which underpins the concept of channel marketing.

Each of the various organizations electing to interact with others performs a specific role in the chain of activities. Some act as manufacturers and some act as agents, and others may be distributors, dealers, value-added resellers, wholesalers, or retailers. Whatever the role, it is normally specific and geared to refining, adding value, and moving a product closer to the end-user. This interaction requires coordination if participating organizations are to achieve their goals and make available final products and services that represent superior value to the channel's end-users, especially when there are multichannel activities (Yan *et al.*, 2011).

In this chapter, we consider three main elements. The first concerns the management of the intangible aspects or issues of ownership, control, and flows of communication between the parties responsible for making an offering accessible for target customers, commonly referred to as marketing channel management. The second element concerns the management of the tangible or physical aspects of moving a product from the producer to the end-user. This must be undertaken so that a customer can freely access an offering and that the final act of the buying process is as convenient and easy as possible. This is part of supply chain management, which includes the logistics associated with moving products closer to end-users. The third and final element is about retailing, a critical element of consumer markets.

Channel Management

Europe's largest clothing maker and retailer, Inditex, has seen its clothing sales rise by over 25% in recent years because it adds new stock to its fashion stores (i.e. Zara) twice a week, keeping the stock fresh and up to date with the latest fashion trends. It achieves this by manufacturing over 40% of its stock in Spain or Portugal. Although production is more costly, Inditex can get new designs into European and American stores twice as fast as if they have to wait for delivery for stock manufactured in Asia. This shows that by managing marketing channels Inditex's overall business performance has improved.

If we consider the skills Inditex need to design and assemble a range of garments, to source the materials, to manufacture, package, and then distribute the final fashion garments to its stores and other customers globally, we can see that a major set of complex operations are required. For many organizations, trying to undertake all these operations is beyond their skill set or core activity. For all organizations, there is a substantial risk associated with producing too much or too little, too soon or too late for the target market. There are risks associated with changing buyer behaviours, storage, finance, and competitors' actions, to name but a few of the critical variables.

These uncertainties can be reduced by collaborating with other organizations that have the necessary skills and expertise. Working with organizations that can create customer demand or access and manage specialist financial issues, storage, or transportation adds value and develops competitive advantage. For example, to sell its handsets in the 600,000 rural villages in India, Samsung partnered with the Indian Farmers Fertiliser Cooperative Ltd. With this new marketing channel, Samsung can now reach over 90% of these villages.

Collectively, organizations that combine to enable offerings to reach end-users quickly and efficiently constitute a marketing channel, sometimes referred to as a **distribution channel**. Organizations that combine to reduce risk and uncertainty do so by exchanging offerings which are of value to others in the channel. Therefore marketing channels enable organizations to share or reduce uncertainty. By reducing the uncertainty experienced by all members in a channel, each member is in a better position to concentrate on other tasks.

How Channels Help to Reduce Uncertainty

Marketing channels enable different types of uncertainty to be lowered in several ways (Fill and McKee, 2012). These include reducing the complexity, increasing value and competitive advantage, routinization, and providing specialization.

Reducing Complexity

The number of transactions and the frequency of contact a producer might have with each individual end-user customer would be so high that the process would be unprofitable. This volume of activity can be seen in Figure 12.1.

If an intermediary is introduced into the process the number of transactions falls drastically, as demonstrated in Figure 12.2.

The fall in the number of transactions indicates not only that costs are reduced but also that producers are better placed to redirect their attention to the needs of intermediaries. This allows

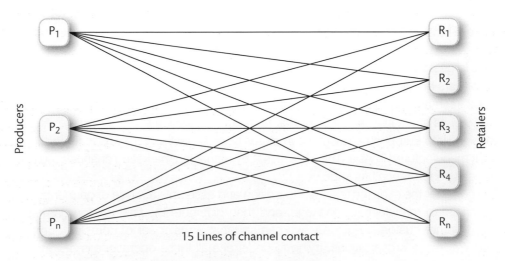
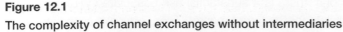

Figure 12.1
The complexity of channel exchanges without intermediaries

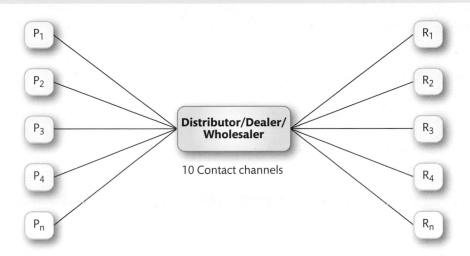

Figure 12.2
The impact of intermediaries on channel exchanges

them to focus on their core activities—production or manufacturing. In much the same way end-user customers can get much improved individual support from channel intermediaries than they would probably get from a producer.

Increasing Value and Competitive Advantage

By using intermediaries producers can reduce purchase risk, the uncertainty that customers might reject the offering. Intermediaries rather than producers have the skills and core competences necessary to meet end-user requirements (e.g. retailing). By improving the overall value that customers perceive in an offering relative to competing products and customer experience, it is possible to develop competitive advantage.

Routinization

Performance risk can be reduced by improving transaction efficiency. By standardizing or 'routinizing' the transaction process, perhaps by regulating order sizes, automating operations, managing delivery cycles and payment frequencies, distribution costs can be reduced.

Specialization

By providing specialist training services, maintenance, installation, bespoke deliveries, or credit facilities, intermediaries can develop a service that has real value to other channel members or end-user customers. Value can also be improved for customers by helping them to locate the offerings they want. Intermediaries can provide these specialist resources, whereas producers are not normally interested or able to do so. This is because they prefer to produce large quantities of a small range of goods. Unfortunately, end-user customers only want a limited quantity of a wide variety of goods.

Intermediaries provide a solution by bringing together and sorting out all the goods produced by different manufacturers in the category. They then re-present these goods in quantities and formats that enable end-user customers to buy the quantities they wish as frequently as they prefer. This is referred to as sorting and smoothing. See Table 12.1 for an explanation of these forms of specialization.

Table 12.1 Aspects of sorting and smoothing	
Aspect	Explanation
Sorting out	Grading products into different sizes, qualities or grades (e.g. potatoes, eggs, or fruit)
Accumulation	Bringing together different products from different producers to provide a wider category choice
Allocation	Often referred to as breaking bulk (by wholesalers), this involves disaggregating bulk deliveries into smaller lot sizes that customers are able (and prefer) to buy
Assorting	Assembling different collections of offerings thought to be of value to the customer (retailers and consumers)

Source: Fill and McKee (2012).

Intermediaries provide other utility-based benefits. For example, they assist end-users by bringing a product produced a long way away to a more convenient location for purchase and consumption, i.e. **place utility**. The product might be manufactured during the day but purchased and consumed at the weekend. Here manufacturing, purchase, and consumption occur at differing points in time, and intermediaries provide **time utility**.

Immediate product availability through retailers enables ownership to pass to the consumer within a short amount of time, i.e. **ownership utility**. Finally, intermediaries can also provide information about the product to aid sales and usage. The internet has led to the development of a new type of intermediary, an information intermediary (e.g. Expedia, Google). Here the key role is to manage information to improve the efficiency and effectiveness of the distribution channel, i.e. **information utility**.

There are some disadvantages to the use of intermediaries. For example, as the number of intermediaries in a channel increases, a lack of product control can develop. Some manufacturers are unable to influence intermediaries in terms of in-store merchandising, placement, and even pricing. Furthermore, intermediaries might be susceptible to competitor inducements such as trade promotions. For many manufacturers and producers, intermediaries often become a market in their own right, requiring considerable time, money, and personnel to support and develop a relationship with them.

Visit the **Online Resource Centre** and complete Internet Activity 12.1 to learn more about the role of intermediaries within the film and TV industry.

Types of Intermediary

Having seen that intermediaries play a significant role in marketing channels, we now need to consider the different types that are available. There are, of course, a number of different types of intermediary, each fulfilling different roles and providing various forms of specialization. Some of the more common ones are as follows.

- **Agents** or brokers—these act as a principal intermediary between the seller of an offering and buyers, bringing them together without taking ownership of the offering. These intermediaries have the legal authority to act on behalf of the manufacturer. For example, universities often use agents to recruit students in overseas markets (e.g. China, India).

- **Merchants**—a merchant undertakes the same actions as an agent, but takes ownership of the product.

- **Distributors** or dealers—these distribute the product. They offer value through services associated with selling inventory, credit, and aftersales service. Often used in B2B markets, they can also be found dealing directly with consumers, e.g. automobile distributors. See Market Insight 12.1 for a view of Honda's dealers and distributors.

- **Franchises**—a franchisee holds a contract to supply and market an offering to the requirements or blueprint of the franchisor, the owner of the original offering. The contract might cover many aspects of the design of the offering such as marketing, product assortment, or service delivery. The uniformity of differing branches of McDonald's and KFC is an indication of franchisee contracts. However, franchise agreements are not just used in the fast food or product sectors. Table 12.2 provides a list of the top ten franchises in 2011, spanning various categories.

Visit the **Online Resource Centre** and follow the weblink to the European Franchise Federation (EFF) to learn more about business franchise collaboration activities across Europe.

- **Wholesalers**—a wholesaler stocks goods before the next level of distribution and takes both legal title and physical possession of the goods. In B2C markets, wholesalers do not usually deal with the end-consumer but with other intermediaries (e.g. retailers). In B2B markets, sales are made direct to end-customers. Examples include Costco Wholesalers in the USA, and Makro in Europe.

 # Market Insight 12.1

Channelling Motorbikes

Honda sells over 12 million motorcycles in the Asia Oceania region alone, and the management of its distribution networks is a vital element in maintaining customer access and satisfaction. Honda produces a wide range of motorcycles, ranging from the 50cc class to the 1,800cc class, and is the largest manufacturer of motorcycles in the world in terms of annual units of production. In the region, Honda's

motorcycles are produced at sites in Japan, Indonesia, Philippines, Pakistan, and India.

In Japan, sales of Honda motorcycles (and automobiles, and power products) are made through different distribution networks. Honda's products are sold to consumers primarily through independent retail dealers, and motorcycles are distributed through approximately 11,600 outlets, including approximately 1,400 authorized dealerships. These authorized

Market Insight 12.1
continued

dealerships sell all Honda's Japanese motorcycle models, not just selected models.

Most of Honda's overseas sales are made through its main sales subsidiaries, which distribute Honda's products to local wholesalers and retail dealers. In Indonesia, Honda has recently developed its dealer network of 4,000 dealers and service shops to support sales and provide excellent aftersales service. In the USA, Honda's wholly owned subsidiary markets Honda's motorcycle products through a sales network of approximately 1,260 independent local dealers. Many of these motorcycle dealers also sell other Honda products.

In Europe, subsidiaries of the company in the UK, Germany, France, Belgium, the Netherlands, Spain, Switzerland, Austria, Italy, and other European countries distribute Honda's motorcycles through approximately 1,600 independent local dealers.

One core element of Honda's dealer strategy worldwide is its comprehensive 4S support system. This covers Sales, Service, Spare parts, and Safety. For example, in 2006 Honda provided its dealers in Thailand, Indonesia, Vietnam, and India with an easy-to-use riding simulator, called 'Riding Trainer', through which riders can get an opportunity to receive risk awareness training and riding practice and, of course, engagement with the Honda brand.

Recently a fifth S has been added, 'Second-hand (or used)' business. In Thailand, for example, the second-hand motorcycle business has been deliberately strengthened as a means of developing business. The strategy encourages potential motorcycle owners and those ready for an upgrade to purchase pre-owned Honda models, thus drawing this segment into the brand.

Sources: www.world.honda.com/ www.findarticles.com/p/articles/ http://sec.edgar-online.com

Honda is the world's largest manufacturer of motorcycles, in terms of annual units of production
Source: © Honda.

1 **Why does Honda set up subsidiary organizations in each overseas region or country?**

2 **What do you think are the benefits of the 5S support system?**

3 **What might affect Honda's dealer network (marketing channel) in the future?**

- **Retailers**—these intermediaries sell directly to end-consumers and may purchase direct from manufacturers or deal with wholesalers. This depends on their purchasing power and the volume purchased. Leading retailers include Wal-Mart, Marks and Spencer, Carrefour, and electronics retailers such as Media-Saturn.

Infomediaries are a growing type of intermediary. These are internet-based organizations designed to provide information to channel members, including end-users.

Table 12.2 Top European franchises by rank				
Rank	Franchise	Country of origin	Industry	No. of units
1	7-Eleven	USA	Food: convenience	47,298
2	Subway	USA	Food: sandwich and coffee shop	37,003
3	McDonald's	USA	Food: restaurants	33,427
4	Kumon Institute of Education Co. Ltd	Japan	Education: children	25,431
5	KFC (Yum! Brands)	USA	Food: restaurants	22,000
6	Spar	Netherlands	Food: convenience stores	13,600
7	Europcar	France	Automobile renting and leasing	13,000
8	Pizza Hut	USA	Food: restaurants	12,700
9	Burger King	USA	Food: restaurants	12,000
10	Mexx	Netherlands	Retail: clothing and footwear	11,600

Source: Franchise Europe (2013). Reproduced with the kind permission of Franchise Europe (www.franchiseeurope.com), a leading portal for the franchise industry worldwide.

Managing Marketing Channels

There are two main issues associated with the management of marketing channels. These are the design of the channel, its structure and activities, and secondly, the relationships between channel members. These are considered in turn.

Channel Design

The design of an appropriate channel, that is its structure, length, and the membership and their roles, varies according to context. For example, channels necessary to support a new product or organization start up are different from those for modifying an existing structure to adapt to changing market conditions. The channel design decision process requires consideration of three main factors.

1 The level of purchase convenience required by the different end-user customer segments to be served—the distribution intensity decision.

2 The number and type of intermediaries necessary to deliver products to the optimum number of sales outlets—the channel configuration decision.

3 The number of different types of channel to be used—the multichannel decision.

This helps us to determine the most effective and efficient way of getting the offering to the customer.

Key Considerations

When managing distribution channels, we need to consider a variety of factors to ensure that the channel suits the organization's objectives. Three broad elements need to be considered: economics, coverage, and control.

- Economics requires us to recognize where costs are being incurred and profits being made in a channel to maximize our return on investment.

- Coverage is about maximizing the offering's availability in the market for the customer, satisfying the desire to have the offering available to the largest number of customers, in as many locations as possible, at the widest range of times.

- Control refers to achieving the optimum distribution costs without losing decision-making authority over the offering—how it is priced, promoted, and delivered in the distribution channel.

Sometimes, by covering a wide range of delivery times and locations through the use of intermediaries, organizations sacrifice some control in decision-making. Intermediaries start changing the price, image, and display, as they seek to maximize sales. Think about the positions of Nokia, Samsung, and Sony. To get the maximum number of customers using their mobile phone handsets, they seek to have the maximum number of retailers and mobile phone networks promoting and selling their phones. However, the same networks and retailers also sell the handsets of their competitors, such as HTC and new entrants Huawei. As the retailers and networks compete to sign up customers, they push for lower prices, or they demand advertising subsidies to help them sell the phones. So Nokia, Samsung, and Sony may discover that their phones are being sold at very low prices, and their brand image being compromised, by retailers and networks who are desperately seeking to maximize their own sales. What happens if Motorola reduce the number of retailers or networks they deal with to increase control over their marketing mix? The danger is that their competitors will gain market share by continuing to deal with these retailers and networks. In contrast, Apple has specific policies on what distributors can and cannot discount on its products like the iPhone, whereas Google challenged the accepted mobile delivery model by launching its own online storefront for the Google Nexus One handset. All face a trade-off between economics, coverage, and control.

Visit the **Online Resource Centre** and follow the weblink to the Institute of Supply Chain Management (ISM) and the Chartered Institute of Purchasing and Supply (CIPS) to learn more about the profession and activities of managing the distribution and supply chain.

Distribution Channel Strategy

When devising a distribution channel strategy, several key decisions need to be made to serve customers and establish and maintain appropriate buyer–seller relationships. These are summarized in Figure 12.3. The first decision is selecting how the channel will be structured. If the

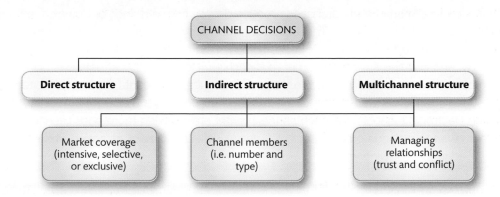

Figure 12.3
Marketing channel strategy decisions

channel requires intermediaries, we need to consider the type of market coverage we want, the number and type of intermediaries to use, and how we should manage the relationships between members in the channel. These choices are important as they can affect the benefits provided to customers.

Channel Structure

Distribution channels can be structured in a number of ways. There are three main configurations involving producers, intermediaries, and customers: 'direct', 'indirect', or 'multi' channel structures. A direct structure involves selling directly to end-user customers with little involvement from other organizations, an indirect structure uses intermediaries, and a multichannel structure combines both. These are presented in Figure 12.4. We now consider the advantages and disadvantages of each of type of channel structure.

Direct Channel Structure

In direct channels, the producer uses strategies to reach end-users directly rather than dealing through an intermediary (an agent, broker, retailer, or wholesaler) (see Figure 12.4). Have you ever

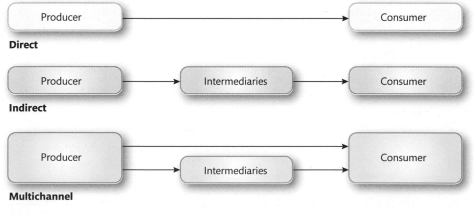

Figure 12.4
Marketing channel structures

been to a farmers' market and purchased produce directly from a farmer, or downloaded music from the website of a local band? These are examples of direct distribution. The advantages of this structure include the producer or manufacturer maintaining control over their offering and profitability, and building strong customer relationships. However, this structure is not suitable for all propositions. It is ideally suited to those who require significant customization, technical expertise, or commitment on behalf of the producer to complete a sale (Parker *et al.*, 2006). However, electronic technologies such as the internet are enabling more and differing product manufacturers to reach customers directly. Efficiency within the **direct channel structure** can be improved in the following ways.

- Processing orders and distributing the offering electronically directly to customers—Adobe Reader is free universal software manufactured by Adobe Systems Inc. that enables users to read and share electronic documents. To increase cost efficiency of delivery, the organization employs a direct structure via the internet, providing digital delivery, installation, and customer support.

- Supporting the physical distribution of the product offering directly to customers—one of the best-known examples of this is Dell Computer Corporation's system. Dell sells computer equipment through the organization's website, using telesales for product ordering, database technology for order processing, tracking, and inventory and delivery management. The organization also distributes its products through its own delivery and installation staff.

The disadvantages of a direct channel structure typically include the large amount of capital and resources required to reach customers. This means that there are virtually no economies of scale. Manufacturers might also suffer from offering a low variety of offerings, which may not meet the needs of buyers. This is especially apparent in B2C markets, such as fast-moving consumer goods (FMCGs). Imagine having to shop for bread, milk, and a soft drink at three differing retail outlets owned by each product manufacturer. Few consumers today would purchase their offerings from individual manufacturers because of the inconvenience and time costs involved. Thus, retailers fulfill the needs of end-consumers for variety, something a direct channel of distribution would not necessarily fulfill.

Indirect Channel Structure

Indirect channel structures enable producers to concentrate on the skills and processes necessary to make offerings, and use one or more intermediaries for distribution. For example, Procter & Gamble (P&G) focus their resources and expertise on developing new types of FMCGs, whereas Sainsbury's core retailing activity is to make P&G's products (and others) available to consumers.

Multichannel Structure

An increasing number of organizations are adopting a **multichannel structure** to distribute goods and services (Park and Keh, 2003). Here, the producer controls some marketing channels and intermediaries control others. For example, many airlines sell their tickets directly to consumers through the internet, but also rely on travel agents. Music labels also sell their CDs directly, using catalogues and the internet as well as independent music retailers such as Rise (on the Triangle). Consider the options for the purchase of a mobile handset. This could occur directly from the Nokia website, from a service provider such as Orange, or perhaps at Tesco while picking up some bread and milk. Samsung and Nokia use service providers, electronic retailers, and wholesale discount clubs alongside their own direct internet and telesales channels to market and deliver their mobile phone handsets.

The benefits of a multichannel structure include the following.

- Increased reach—by utilizing existing direct networks and the relationships of intermediaries a wider target audience can be reached.

- Producer control—producers have greater control over prices and communication, and can reach customers directly.

- Greater compliance—intermediaries can perceive producers to be competitors, and so comply with channel rules.

- Optimized margins—producers can improve margins from the direct channel element, and increase their bargaining power as they become less dependent on intermediaries.

- Improved market insight—by developing relationships with their direct customers, producers can derive a better understanding of their needs and markets issues.

The use of multichannel strategies has been encouraged by the growth of the internet, which has increased the efficiency with which consumers and manufacturers can interact (Park and Keh, 2003). At the same time, technologies are increasing the efficiency of information exchange between producers and intermediaries (e.g. through electronic data interchange (EDI) and extranets). See Market Insight 12.2 for an example of how a fashion house manages its distribution channels. However, the sharing of profits among channel members can be a source of conflict, especially when intermediaries perceive the producer as a competitor, as well as a supplier. This structure may also confuse and alienate customers who are unsure about which channel they should use.

Research Insight 12.1

To take your learning further, you might wish to read this influential paper.

Rosenbloom, B. (2007), 'Multi channel strategy in business-to-business markets: prospects and problems', *Industrial Marketing Management*, **36(1), 4–9.**

Rosenbloom has written extensively about marketing channels and published several books on the topic. This paper provides an interesting insight into the issues of channel strategy within a business-to-business context.

@ **Visit the Online Resource Centre to read the abstract and access the full paper.**

Market Insight 12.2

Fast Fashion and Informality

According to Amancio Ortega, the founder of Inditex, whose brands include Zara, Zara Home, Bershka, Massimo Dutti, Oysho, Stradivarius, Pull & Bear, and Uterqüe, to be successful 'you need to have five fingers touching the factory and five touching the customer'. Translation: 'control what happens to a product until the customer buys it'. In adhering to this philosophy, Inditex has developed a super-responsive supply chain. The organization can design, produce, and deliver a new garment to its 5,900 stores across 85 countries in just 24 hours in Europe and 40 hours in America and Asia. Such a pace is unheard of in the fashion business, where designers typically spend months planning for the next season.

This success stems from a holistic approach to supply chain management that optimizes the entire chain instead of focusing on individual parts. In the process, Zara defies most of the current conventional wisdom about how supply chains should be run. Unlike so many of its peers, which rush to outsource, Zara keeps almost half of its production in-house. Zara carries out all operations under the same roof at its La Coruña headquarters. Informality rules the roost, and functions such as design, production, and marketing all rub shoulders with each other. This set-up removes the need for information to travel through widely dispersed channels. It shortens delays, minimizes bureaucracy, provides the opportunity for more immediate comment and feedback, allows speedier decision-making, and lessens the potential impact of changes in circumstances such as an amendment to retail orders. This reduces the risk of loss through overproduction.

Zara's self-reinforcing system is built on three principles.

- Close the communication loop—Zara's supply chain is organized to transfer both hard data and anecdotal information quickly and easily from shoppers to designers and production

staff. It's also set up to track materials and products in real time every step of the way, including inventory on display in the stores. The goal is to close the information loop between the end-users and the upstream operations of design, procurement, production, and distribution as quickly and directly as possible.

- Stick to a rhythm across the entire chain—at Zara, rapid timing and synchronicity are paramount. To this end, the organization indulges in an approach that can best be characterized as 'penny foolish, pound wise'. It spends money on anything that helps to increase and enforce the speed and responsiveness of the chain as a whole.

- Leverage capital assets to increase supply chain flexibility—Zara has made major capital investments in production and distribution facilities, and uses them to increase the supply chain's responsiveness to new and fluctuating demands. It produces complicated products in-house and outsources the simple ones.

Sources: Vitzthum (2001); Ferdows et al. (2004); Anon. (2005); Hamilton (2007); Hansen (2012); www.zara.com

Inditex, owner of Zara, can design, produce, and deliver a new garment to its stores in 85 countries in just 24 hours in Europe and 40 hours in America and Asia.
Source: Zara/Inditex.

Market Insight 12.2
continued

1 Describe the marketing channel structure adopted by Zara.

2 Outline the advantages and disadvantages of Zara's channel strategy.

3 Choose a competitor brand, or one you are interested in, and determine their channel strategy.

Channel Intensity

Sometimes referred to as channel coverage, intensity refers to the number and dispersion of outlets an end-user customer can use to buy a particular offering. This decision concerns the level of convenience customers expect, and suppliers need to provide to be competitive. The wider the coverage the greater the number of intermediaries, which leads to higher costs associated with the management control of the intermediaries. There are three levels of channel intensity: intense, selective, and exclusive. See Figure 12.5.

Intensive distribution involves placing an offering in as many outlets or locations as possible. It is used most commonly for offerings that consumers are unlikely to search for and which they purchase on the basis of convenience or impulse, such as magazines and soft drinks or confectionery. However, retailers have increased control over the extent to which distribution is intensive. For example, a manufacturer of a new brand of yoghurt might want its new brand put on the shelves of all supermarkets; however, owing to limited shelf space, the retailers might limit their assortment to the leading brands of yoghurt.

Selective distribution occurs when a limited number of outlets are used. This is because when customers are actively involved with a purchase, and experience moderate to high levels of perceived risk, they are prepared to seek out appropriate suppliers. Those that best match their overall requirements are successful. Producers determine and control which intermediaries are to deliver the required products and level of services. Electrical equipment, furniture, clothing, and jewellery are categories where selective distribution is appropriate.

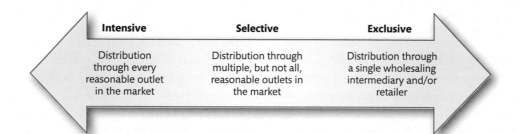

Intensive	Selective	Exclusive
Distribution through every reasonable outlet in the market	Distribution through multiple, but not all, reasonable outlets in the market	Distribution through a single wholesaling intermediary and/or retailer

Figure 12.5

Intensity of distribution continuum

Sometimes, an organization might use intensive distribution to increase awareness of its brand when entering a new market, but then move to a more selective strategy to improve control over quality and manage costs and price.

Exclusive distribution occurs when intermediaries are given exclusive rights to market an offering within a defined 'territory'. This is useful where significant support is required from the intermediary, and therefore the exclusivity is 'payback' for their investment and support. For example, high-prestige goods like Ferrari sports cars and designer fashion apparel like Chanel and Gucci adopt this type of distribution intensity.

If an offering requires complex servicing arrangements or tight control, the exclusive form of distribution may be best. The threat of price competition is also diminished, as it would be inconsistent with the positioning strategy these offerings normally adopt.

Through the internet, nearly all distribution is intensive because of the massive reach of the web. Even the smallest manufacturer can advertise and sell worldwide, using the same courier services to deliver its offerings as major firms do.

The decision about the number of intermediaries is often driven by cost considerations. The costs of intensive distribution are higher because of the number of outlets that must be served. The implications of these three strategies for distribution are summarized in Table 12.3.

Disintermediation and Reintermediation

Disintermediation concerns the reduction in the number or strength of intermediaries required in a marketing channel. There has been an active debate about whether the rate of disintermediation is increasing (Mills and Camek, 2004; Tay and Chellah, 2011). Ideas about **reintermediation** are supported by Anderson and Anderson (2002) who argue that the internet encourages intermediation, and Laffey and Gandy (2009) who believe that new roles have developed through e-commerce for new and existing intermediaries. They refer to eBay and the financial services start-up Zopa as prime examples.

The assumption is that if producers could reach their customers directly they would no longer need intermediaries, or at least they would not need so many of them. Imagine that a music publisher like Sony could reach and sell to every potential customer directly through its website (www.sony.com). Given the state of technology such as PC sound systems, CD burners, or MP3 players, customers could purchase their music directly from Sony and it could be 'distributed' electronically straight to their PCs. In such a scenario, Sony would no longer need to deal with high street music stores, leading to the disintermediation of the distribution channel. Or would this result in the growth in the number of electronic intermediaries, such as iTunes, for the distribution of music?

The technical possibility of reducing the number of intermediaries doesn't just affect 'bricks-and-mortar' intermediaries, but also electronic intermediaries. In Amazon's case, for example, more consumers could skip the intermediary and buy books online directly from publishers. Some publishers and printers have been disintermediated as some authors now sell 'ebooks' directly to the consumer. One such self-publishing author, David Gaughran, refers to the increasing number of book sales and the increasing number of authors who are avoiding traditional publishers (Gaughran, 2013). Where disintermediation does occur, it is very much dependent on the nature of the offerings distributed. Although there are significant numbers of customers who like buying directly, many customers value and prefer the role of

Table 12.3 Intensity of channel coverage

Characteristics	Exclusive	Selective	Intensive
Objectives	Strong image channel control and loyalty, price stability	Moderate market coverage, solid image, some channel control and loyalty	Widespread market coverage, channel acceptance, volume sales
Channel members	Few in number, well established, reputable stores	Moderate in number, well established, better stores	Many in number, all types of outlets
Customers	Few in number, trendsetters, willing to travel to store, brand loyal	Moderate in number, brand conscious, somewhat willing to travel to store	Many in number, convenience oriented
Marketing emphasis	Personal selling, pleasant shopping conditions, good service	Promotional mix, pleasant shopping conditions, good service	Mass advertising, nearby location, items in stock
Examples	Automobiles, designer clothes, caviar	Furniture, clothing, watches	Groceries, household products, magazines

traditional intermediaries such as bricks-and-mortar retailers for certain purchases. In fact, such is the value of some intermediaries to both customers and producers that there has been a trend towards reintermediation, the introduction of additional intermediaries into the distribution channel.

Research Insight 12.2

To take your learning further, you might wish to read this influential paper.

Mills, J. F., and Camek, V. (2004), 'The risks, threats and opportunities of disintermediation: a distributor's view', *International Journal of Physical Distribution and Logistics Management*, **34(9), 714–27.**

This paper discusses the trend in disintermediation observed in many industries. Where many recent papers see disintermediation as a phenomenon related to online transactions, this paper defines it more broadly as the removal or a weakening of an intermediary within a supply chain.

@ Visit the **Online Resource Centre** to read the abstract and access the full paper.

Managing Relationships in the Channel

An important managerial issue concerns channel relationships. Because channels are open social systems (Katz and Kahn, 1978), some level of conflict between channel members is inevitable. Conflict follows a breakdown in the levels of cooperation between channel partners (Shipley and Egan, 1992) and may well affect channel performance. Gaski (1984: 11) defined channel conflict as 'the perception on the part of a channel member that its goal attainment is being impeded by another, with stress or tension the result'.

Channel conflict may involve intermediaries on the same level (tier), for example between retailers or between agents (**horizontal conflict**). It may also occur between members on different levels (tiers), involving a producer, wholesaler, and a retailer (**vertical conflict**). These types of channel conflict are presented in Table 12.4. If strategies to prevent or avoid conflict have failed, it is necessary to resolve the conflict that erupts.

Table 12.4 Channel conflict

Types	Occurs between	Causes of conflict
Horizontal conflict	▪ Intermediaries on the same level of the same type (e.g. large grocery retailers like Tesco, Sainsbury's, and ASDA Wal-Mart) ▪ Different types of intermediaries on the same level, e.g. a high street fashion retailer (Miss Selfridge), and a large department store (Marks and Spencer)	Channel members impinge on the market territory of other intermediaries at the same level
Vertical conflict	Most frequently occurs between producer and wholesaler or producer and retailer, e.g. Unilever and Sainsbury's	▪ Intense price competition ▪ Disagreement about promotion activities ▪ Cost of services rendered ▪ Differing expectations about channel or intermediary performance ▪ Attempts to bypass intermediary and distribute directly ▪ Tough economic times ▪ Differing policies ▪ Allocation of slotting allowances for premium shelf space
Multichannel conflict	Two or more channels owned by a single manufacturer compete against each other when selling to the same market. Producers might compete with retailers by selling through their producer-owned stores, e.g. Esprit and Levi-Strauss stores compete with department stores who also carry their stock	Grey marketing—the distribution of branded goods to unauthorized dealers (Harris, 2009)

Table 12.5	Conflict resolution strategies
Strategy	**Explanation**
Accommodation	Modify expectations to incorporate requirements of others
Argument	A considered attempt to convince others of the correctness of your position
Avoidance	Removal from the point of conflict
Compromise	Meet the requirements of others half-way
Cooperation	Mutual reconciliation through cooperation
Instrumentality	Agree minimal requirements to secure short-term agreement
Self-seeking	Seek agreement on own terms or refuse further cooperation

Source: Fill and McKee (2012). Used with kind permission.

The strategies depicted in Table 12.5 vary from selfishness/stubbornness and a refusal to work with other members, through cooperation and compromise, to one that seeks to accommodate all the views of other parties, even to the extent of jeopardizing one's own position. The prevailing corporate culture, attitude towards risk, and the sense of power that exists within coalitions shapes the chosen strategy.

Visit the **Online Resource Centre** and read about the conflict that has arisen in the UK supermarket industry.

Grey Marketing

The unauthorized sale of new branded products diverted from authorized distribution channels or imported into a country for sale without the consent or knowledge of the manufacturer is referred to as grey marketing and is a source of channel conflict. Very often this is accompanied by a cut in prices. This activity is not necessarily illegal, but could fall foul of licensing agreements or trade regulations (Myers and Griffith, 1999), as Tesco discovered when it attempted to stock and sell Levi's branded jeans which it had purchased through an unauthorized supplier. The paper cited in Research Insight 12.3 provides more information about grey marketing.

Supply Chain Management

The second major issue associated with marketing channels concerns the movement of parts, supplies and finished products. Melnyk *et al*. (2009) believe that **supply chain management** (SCM) is concerned with the value creation chain of all the activities associated with physical distribution. This embraces the chain of suppliers involved in providing raw materials (upstream), through to the assembly and manufacturing stages, to distribution to end-user customers (downstream). This

Research Insight 12.3

To take your learning further, you might wish to read this influential paper.

Webb, K. L. and Hogan, J. E. (2002), 'Hybrid channel conflict: causes and effects on channel performance', *Journal of Business and Industrial Marketing*, 17(5), 338–57.

This paper discusses the role of multichannel conflict in not only reducing channel performance but also serving as a mechanism for forcing internal channel coalitions to work harder and smarter to serve their market. The findings indicate that multichannel conflict is an important determinant of both channel performance and satisfaction.

@ Visit the **Online Resource Centre** to read the abstract and access the full paper.

---

linkage is referred to as a supply chain and its coordination is commonly referred to as supply chain management. This supersedes the previous terms, logistics, and before that, physical distribution.

Integrated SCM refers to the business processes associated with the movement of parts, raw materials, work in progress, and finished goods. Unlike marketing channels, which are concerned with the management of customer behaviour, finished goods, and inter-organizational relationships, the goal of SCM is to improve efficiency and effectiveness with regard to the physical movement of products. SCM is essentially about the management of all the business activities necessary to get the right product, in the right place, for the right customer to access in a timely and convenient way (Fill and McKee, 2012).

SCM comprises of four main activities: **fulfilment**, **transportation**, **stock management**, and **warehousing**. It is argued by Brewer and Speh (2000) that SCM seeks to accomplish four main goals. These are waste reduction, time compression, flexible response, and unit cost reduction. These are explained in Table 12.6.

By achieving these four goals the efficiency of a supply chain is improved and, as a result, end-user customers can experience improved levels of channel performance. Figure 12.6 shows these activities and goals brought together in order to promote superior supply chain performance.

Management of ASDA Wal-Mart's supply chain is based on computerized scanning to inform suppliers very quickly of which products need delivery and in what quantities. More recent developments in electronic technologies, such as RFID tags, are improving the efficiency and effectiveness with which supply chain activities are managed.

Cost control is a core SCM activity given that about 15% of an average product's price is accounted for in shipping and transport costs alone. Ikea can sell its furniture 20% cheaper than competitors as it buys furniture ready for assembly, thereby saving on transport and inventory costs. The Benetton distribution centre in Italy is run largely by robots, delivering numerous goods to 120 countries within 12 days. Benetton also uses just-in-time (JIT) manufacturing, with some garments manufactured in neutral colours and then dyed to order, with very fast turnaround to suit customer requirements. However, beyond lowering costs, many organizations are increasing their focus on managing activities in order to improve customer service, meet the explosion in product variety, and harness the improvements in information and communication technologies.

Table 12.6 Supply chain management goals

Goal	Explanation
Waste reduction	By reducing the level of duplicated and excess stock in the chain, it becomes possible to harmonize operations between organizations to achieve new levels of uniformity and standardization
Time compression	Reducing the order-to-delivery cycle time improves efficiency and customer service outputs. A faster cycle indicates a smoother and more efficient operation and associated processes. Faster times mean less stock, faster cash flow, and higher levels of service output
Flexible response	By managing the order processing elements (size, time, configuration, handling) specific customer requirements can be met without causing them inconvenience and this contributes to efficiency and service delivery
Unit cost reduction	By understanding the level of service output that is required by the end-user customers it becomes possible to minimize the costs involved in delivering to that required standard

Source: Fill and McKee (2012). Adapted from Brewer and Speh (2000).

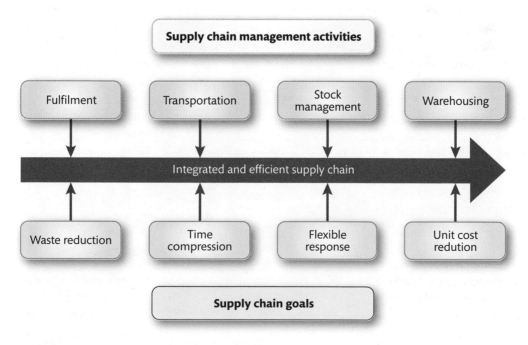

Figure 12.6

Developing high-performance supply chains

Fulfilment

Fulfilment or materials handling is about locating and picking stock, and packing and securing it before shipping the selected items or bundle to the next channel member. The increasing use of specialist software, information technology, and equipment helps manage a range of fulfilment activities. Intra-warehouse stock movement needs to be minimized, while inter-warehouse movement is optimized (Fill and McKee, 2012). Automated emails are sent out to customers following online purchase of, for example, music from iTunes, a book from Amazon, or a train ticket. Accuracy and speed of billing and invoicing customers is also vitally important, especially for customer relationships.

In the retailing sector, order-processing technologies provide quick-response programmes to help manage a retailer's replenishment of stock from suppliers. Kmart uses this kind of system, with EDI/extranets to transmit daily records of sales to suppliers, who analyse the information, create an order, and send it back to Kmart. Once in Kmart's system, the order is treated as though Kmart created it itself. Many technologies also speed up the billing cycle. For example, General Electric operates a computer-based system which, on receipt of a customer order, checks the customer's credit rating as well as whether and where the items are in stock. The computer then issues an order to ship, bills the customer, updates the inventory records, sends a production order for new stock, and sends a message back to the salesperson that the customer's order is on the way—all in less than 15 seconds. The hospitality industry also uses order-processing technology to improve service delivery efficiency. Fast food outlets such as McDonald's and KFC have for years recorded food orders through telecommunications systems, transmitting them to food preparation areas, with orders fulfilled within a matter of minutes, improving customer satisfaction in service delivery.

McDonald's and other fast food operators use electronic communications to shorten the food preparation time

Source: Used with permission from McDonald's corporation.

Transportation and Delivery

Transportation is considered to be the most important activity within SCM. Transportation involves the physical movement of products using, for example, road, rail, air, pipeline, and shipping. Sometimes transportation is just seen as a way of supplying tangible goods, but it can also be as relevant to many service organizations and the delivery of electronic (or digital) products. Consultants, IT companies, and health organizations have to move staff around, incurring transport and accommodation costs. Management of transport usually involves making decisions between usage of one or more transportation methods and ensuring vehicle capacity. Transportation methods also include electronic delivery modes such as electronic vending machines, the telephone, the internet, or EDI.

Physical Delivery

Information and communication technologies have improved physical product delivery. For example, where freight moves, the size of typical shipments and the time periods within which goods must be delivered has changed with significant economic benefits to all transportation activities. The top of the list of 'must have' systems for transportation are in-vehicle navigation and route guidance solutions to help manage transport fleets, track shipments, and optimize transportation (Dreier, 2003). Amazon's tracking system assigns a tracking number and, using proprietary software, provides information to customers in real time about where the package or shipment is located, improving customer experiences.

Electronic Delivery

As early as the introduction of the TV, radio, or even the telephone, electronic technologies have been used to deliver products. Producers of music, games, video, or software are typically unconstrained by the needs of physical distribution owing to product digitization; this has increased with the development of the internet. For example, at first Wall Street seemed to smirk at the E*Trade group's invitation to investors to make their own trades on the internet. Then the Charles Schwab Corporation jumped at the challenge, and by the late 1990s other brokerages, such as Merrill Lynch and Bank of America Investment Services Inc., were scrambling to catch up. Organizations such as travel agents, banks, and insurance companies, which have traditionally relied on customers coming to a branch or agency, have quickly moved to using ATMs, mobile telecommunications, and the internet to reach more customers. The internet has clearly added to the capacity of these electronic distribution channels, so that huge numbers of customers now bank, trade stocks, and arrange insurance and travel through electronic channels and particularly mobile phones.

Stock Management

Stock or inventory management involves trying to balance responsiveness to customer needs with the resources required to store stock. The management of both finished and unfinished goods can be critical to many organizations. For example, a balance needs to be achieved between the number of finished goods to be available when customers need it (known as speculation) against a store of unfinished goods which can be assembled at a later date or when the stock of finished goods runs low (known as postponement).

Carrying too little stock might jeopardize customer service levels, whilst carrying too much can be expensive and adds to working capital. Imagine the cost of storing all the books Amazon has listed for sale, or the storage of fashion items in the spring ready for summer demand. With JIT systems, producers and retailers carry only small inventories of merchandise, often only enough for a few days' operations. New stock arrives exactly when it is needed, rather than being stored. ASDA Wal-Mart and even Burger King use these systems to track sales to service their outlets worldwide, automatically replenishing their ingredients according to product sales.

Zero-inventory or JIT production is ideal for many organizations as it minimizes the use of resources that are often tied up in stock that doesn't sell. This must be balanced against the risk of not having the products available when customers want them.

Warehousing and Materials Handling

Supply chains involved with the exchange of goods usually require storage facilities for the periods between production, transportation, and purchase/consumption. For example books, dry goods such as sugar and canned goods, and even clothing require some level of storage between the time they leave the producer/manufacturer and when they are required to be delivered to end-user customers. See Market Insight 12.3 for examples where delivery is a critical issue.

The location, size, design, and operating systems used in warehouses are important decisions as they can impact the performance of others in the supply chain. For producers using distributors, a relatively small number of warehouses will be necessary as distributors take ownership and physical possession of stock. A higher number of warehouses are required in channels where agents' and manufacturers' representatives are preferred, as these intermediaries do not take ownership or physical possession. Organizations must decide on how many and what types of 'warehouses' it needs, and where they should be located. The type of warehouse is dependent on the type of product: tangible, digital, or perishable.

Visit the **Online Resource Centre** and use the weblink to read about how a major retailer has had to redesign and update its warehousing to cope with online sales.

Warehousing Tangible Goods

For the storage of tangible goods, such as FMCGs, an organization can use either **storage warehouses** or **distribution centres**. Storage warehouses store goods for moderate to long periods (they have a long shelf-life), whereas distribution centres are designed to move goods, rather than just store them. For products that are highly perishable with a short shelf-life, such as fruit and vegetables, distribution centres are more appropriate. Grocery chains such as Woolworths in Australia and Tesco in the UK use large cold-store distribution centres to move perishable items such as fruit and vegetables to their various retail outlets. Storage centres are more appropriate for products with a long shelf-life, or which might require stockpiling to meet seasonal demands.

Warehousing Digital 'Products'

Electronic warehousing systems, or database systems, are being used more and more for the storage of products (or product components) that can be digitized. These systems can be searched or browsed electronically, providing the user with immediate electronic delivery

Market Insight 12.3

Getting There, On Time

Ensuring that products are available for sale or use on time is critical for a large number of businesses. For example, South African brewer SABMiller revised its supply chain when its customers ran out of drinks during peak periods; on some brands the shortfall was high as 22%. Following an overhaul the group's supply chain now boasts an average stock availability of 98%.

The distribution of medicines by companies such as bioMérieux, Horiba ABX, and NovoNordisk involves a larger number of issues as human lives are at risk. As a result, logistics providers have to guarantee that products such as insulin are delivered not just securely, and on time, but in pristine condition. Warehouses and temperature-controlled trailers use probes and telesurveillance systems to ensure that temperatures are maintained within set parameters during transportation. Speed of delivery is also important, so companies such as the Norbert Dentressangle Group arrange for delivery to be made without breaking the 'cold chain'. The trucks used to transport pharmaceutical products rarely stop, and pallet unloading time is minimized. Systematic controls are carried out each time a driver stops and deviations in temperature and other problems are detected in real time.

In the IT industry, lifecycles are only 13 weeks long, so yet again on-time delivery is critical. For companies such as ASUS, production and shipments need to be timed precisely to ensure that the transition between old and new products is smooth and results in optimal sales and a minimum of old products still on the shelf. An ASUS notebook made in China takes two and a half weeks to reach North America by ocean freight. In addition, there is a further two weeks to reach customers' stores. So when Norbert Dentressangle improved the ocean schedules using faster vessels and an evening crew to turn the cargo around on the same day, transit times were slashed. This led to a competitive advantage as ASUS could get new products to market faster than their competitors.

Sources: www.norbert-dentressangle.co.uk/Client-Success/Case-studies/ www.computerweekly.com/feature/Case-study-SABMiller-revamps-supply-chain-management www.telegraph.co.uk/sponsored/business/

1 Should marketing channel managers have a greater concern for ethical issues than supply chain managers?

2 How might the Norbert Dentressangle Group (and their competitors) encourage potential clients to use their particular services?

3 Make a list of the different issues associated with the transportation of dairy products, computers, cars, and medicines.

options. For example, emerald-library.com, ABI-Inform, or ScienceDirect are electronic databases accessible through the web that store a vast array of documents electronically to facilitate customers' search for information. In addition, many organizations use data warehousing facilities where product information, or even actual products, are stored in digital form awaiting distribution. Apple iTunes is the largest music retailer in the world. By February 2013, the online store had categorized over 26 million songs, 190,000 TV episodes, 45,000 movies, and 1,500 books. This does not include the tens of thousands of games and podcasts stored electronically. Customers can find, download, play, and sync in a fraction of the time it takes to drive to a store.

We will now look more closely at one particular type of intermediary used in B2C markets, the retailer.

Retailing

Retailing encompasses all the activities directly related to the sale of products and services to consumers for personal use. These differ from wholesalers, who distribute the product to businesses, not consumers. Whether they are large retailers, such as Lotte (South Korea), Extra (Brazil), or Carrefour (France), or one of the thousands of small owner-run retailers in India, they all provide a downstream link between producers and end-consumers.

Retailers help reduce the uncertainty experienced by other intermediaries in the channel, such as wholesalers and manufacturers. This is achieved by taking small quantities of stock on a regular basis, promoting cash flows, and providing demand for their products and services.

Retailers provide consumers with access to products. As such, it is very important to find out what consumers actually want from a retailer in order to deliver value. Convenience and time utility is the primary concern for most consumers, with people increasingly being 'leisure time poor' and keen to trade-off shopping time for leisure time (Seiders *et al.,* 2000). Consequently, convenience drives most innovations in retailing, such as supermarkets, department stores, shopping malls, the web, and self-scanning kiosks in pursuit of providing customer convenience. As noted by Seiders *et al.* (2000), from a customer's perspective convenience means speed and ease in acquiring a product and consists of the following four key elements:

- access—being easy to reach;
- search—enabling customers to be easily able to identify what they want;
- possession—ease of obtaining products;
- transaction—ease of purchase and return of products.

These are outlined in more detail in Table 12.7.

Table 12.7 Retailing convenience: a customer's perspective

Element	Description
Access convenience	■ Accessibility factors include location, availability, hours of operation, parking, and proximity to other outlets, as well as telephone, mail, and internet ■ Convenience does not exist without access ■ Increasingly, customers want access to products and services to be as fast and direct as possible with very little hassle ■ Global trend, e.g. rise of convenience stores in Japan ■ Direct shopping driven by time and place utility
Search convenience	■ Identifying and selecting the products wanted is connected to product focus, intelligence outlet design and layout (servicescape), knowledgeable staff, interactive systems, product displays, package and signage, etc. ■ Solutions can be provided in the form of in-store kiosks, clearly posted prices, and mobile phones for sales staff linked to knowledge centres ■ One example of good practice is German discount chain Adler Mode Market GmbH, which uses colour-coded tags to help customers quickly spot the sizes

Table 12.7 continued	
Element	Description
Possession convenience	▪ Is about having merchandise in stock and available on a timely basis, e.g Nordstrom clothing store guarantees that advertised products will be in stock ▪ However, possession convenience has limitations for certain channels (e.g. highly customized products) ▪ The internet scores highly for search convenience, yet is generally low in terms of possession convenience
Transaction convenience	▪ The speed and ease with which consumers can effect and amend a transaction before and after the purchase ▪ A number of innovations exist here—self-scanning in Carrefour, Tesco, and Metro. Well-designed service systems can mitigate the peaks and troughs in store traffic as with the use of in-store traffic counters, as in Sainsbury's, to monitor store traffic ▪ Even with queue design, single queues in post offices and banks differ from supermarkets because of space and servicescape design ▪ Transaction convenience is a significant issue on the internet, with pure internet retailers having problems with returns and customers not prepared to pay for shipping and handling costs

Market Insight 12.4

Consistent Store Experiences at Hollister

Abercrombie & Fitch founded Hollister Co. in 2000. The Hollister concept is rooted in the Southern California surf culture, which is reflected in both their store design and clothing. The concept is standardized across its 500+ worldwide stores. Products can only be purchased in a Hollister store or through their online store.

The Ohio-based headquarters directs store operations, including how a store should be designed and presented, and how staff should behave. This requires that staff wear clothing from Hollister's product range and greet and treat customers in particular ways. In order to work in the store one must be an outgoing and courteous person with a look that fits Hollister's surf theme. The typical Hollister look is defined as natural, classic and sophisticated.

Store staff are recruited on a range of criteria including their (good) looks and outgoing disposition. They wear Hollister clothes, are styled before work each day, and are fun and friendly.

Store staff are required to greet customers with standardized phrases. According to Hollister's policy all customers should be greeted when they arrive at the store. The phrases must be said in English, regardless of where the store is located. The dress codes for female staff members allow only natural make-up and discreet earrings. Furthermore, the hair should either be left hanging or put in a braid. When it comes to the male staff, no facial hair is allowed and

Market Insight 12.4
continued

they should wear simple hairstyles. Visible tattoos and piercings are strictly prohibited in either case. Prior to any work shift, the onsite managers perform a quick inspection of their staff to verify adherence to the company's dress codes and regulations.

The main focus is on each customer's store experience. All stores are almost identical in design so that customers can easily recognize the brand no matter which country or store they are visiting. The store lighting is minimal, some would say too dark, which has led to a number of comments online. As with most major retailers, the layout and the way clothes are folded and merchandised, is prescribed. The exterior of each store should resemble a surf shack.

Sources: Chandler (2009); Palazzini (2011); Singh (2011); www.Hollister.com

This Market Insight was kindly contributed by Sofia Ekberg and Carolina Röhrl, students at Södertörn University, Stockholm, Sweden.

1 **To what extent is the Hollister brand unusual in the way that it manages the in-store experience?**

2 **Identify those types of retailers who may be more dependent than others on the value-added activities of the marketing channel.**

3 **Go to the websites of a department store (e.g. www.johnlewis.com) and a supermarket. How do they compare? Are there any retailing similarities?**

Research Insight 12.4

To take your learning further, you might wish to read this influential paper.

Glynn, M. S., Brodie, R. J., and Motion, J. (2012), 'The benefits of manufacturer brands to retailers', *European Journal of Marketing*, 46(9), 1127–49.

In this paper, the authors discuss the key values and benefits consumers derive from retailing. They consider the key benefit of convenience in retailing strategy from a customer's perspective. Convenience means speed and ease, and consists of four key elements—access, search, possession, and transaction.

Visit the Online Resource Centre to read the abstract and access the full paper.

Types of Retailer

There are numerous types of retailers. These can be classified according to the marketing strategy employed (i.e. product, price, and service) and the store presence (i.e. store or non-store retailing).

Marketing Strategy

Major types of retailers can be classified according to the marketing strategies employed, paying particular attention to three specific elements:

- product assortment;
- price level;
- customer service.

Table 12.8, although not exhaustive, provides a useful summary of these elements across the differing types of retailing channels. The types of retailing establishments can be distinguished as shown in the table.

Table 12.8 Marketing strategy and retail store classification

Type of retail store	Product assortment	Pricing	Customer service	Example
Department	Very broad and deep, with layout and presentation of products critical	Minimize price competition	Wide array and good quality	El Corte Inglés (Spain), Galeries Lafayette (France), Harrods (UK)
Discount	Broad and shallow	Low-price positioning	Few customer service options	Pound Stretcher, Dollar Dazzlers, Poundland
Convenience	Narrow and shallow	High prices	Avoids price competition	Co-op, 7-Eleven
Limited line	Narrow and deep	Traditional—avoids price competition New kinds—low prices	Vary by type	Bicycle stores, sports stores, ladies fashion
Speciality	Very narrow and deep	Avoids price competition	Standard; extensive in some	Running shops, bridal boutiques
Category killer	Narrow, very deep	Low prices	Few to moderate	Staples, Office Works, Ikea
Supermarket	Broad and deep	Some are low price; others avoid price disadvantages	Few and self-service	Tesco (UK), Woolworths (Australia), Carrefour (Europe)
Superstores	Very broad and very deep	Low prices	Few and self-service	Tesco Extra, ASDA Wal-Mart

Some department stores offer a full range of wedding dresses, accessories, and services in order to add value to their proposition
Source: © Debenhams.

- **Department stores**—these are large-scale retailing organizations that offer a very broad and deep assortment of products (both hard and soft goods), and provide a wide array of customer service facilities for store customers. Debenhams has a wide range of products including home furnishings, foods, cosmetics, clothing, books, and furniture, and provides further variety within each category (e.g. brand, feature variety). Debenhams, like many department stores, provide a wide array of customer service facilities to rationalize higher prices and minimize price competition. Value-added services include wedding registries, clothing alterations, shoe repairs, lay-by facilities, home delivery, and installation.

- **Discount retailers**—this type of retailer is positioned based on low prices combined with the reduced costs of doing business. The key characteristics here involve a broad but shallow assortment of products, low prices, and very few customer services. For example, Matalan in the UK, Kmart in Australia, and Target in the USA all carry a broad array of soft goods (e.g. apparel) combined with hard goods such as appliances and home furnishings. To keep prices down, the retailers negotiate extensively with suppliers to ensure low merchandise costs.

- **Limited line retailers**—this type of retailer has a narrow but deep product assortment and customer services vary from store to store. Clothing retailers, butchers, baked goods, and furniture stores that specialize in a small number of related product categories are all examples. The breadth of product variety differs across limited line stores, and a store may choose to concentrate on several related product lines (e.g. shoes and clothing accessories), a single product line (e.g. shoes), or a specific part of one product line (e.g. sports shoes). Examples include bookstores, jewellers, athletic footwear stores, dress shops, newsagents, etc. (see Market Insight 12.4).

- **Category killer stores**—as the name suggests, these retailers are designed to kill off the competition and are characterized by a narrow but very deep assortment of products, low prices, and few to moderate customer services. Successful examples include Ikea in home furnishings, Staples in office supplies, and B&Q in hardware.

- **Supermarkets**—founded in the 1930s, these are large self-service retailing environments offering a wide variety of differing merchandise to a large consumer base. Tesco Extra in the UK stocks products from clothing, hardware, music, groceries, and dairy products to soft furnishings. Operating largely on a self-service basis with minimum customer service and centralized register and transactional terminals, supermarkets provide the benefits of a wide product assortment in a single location, offering convenience and variety. Today, supermarkets are the dominant institution for food retailing.

- **Convenience stores, or corner shops**—these offer a range of grocery and household items that cater for convenience and last-minute purchase needs of consumers. Key characteristics include long opening times (e.g. 24/7), being family-run, and belonging to a trading group. The 7-Eleven, Spar, and Co-op are all examples. Increasingly, we are seeing smaller convenience stores threatened by large supermarket chains such as ASDA Wal-Mart and Tesco, especially as laws for longer opening times for larger stores are relaxed (e.g. Sunday trading hours in the UK).

Store Presence

We can further categorize retailers according to their presence—store or non-store retailing. Most retailing occurs through fixed stores, with existing operators having 'sunk' investment into a physical building and equipment. The physical location of a store is seen as a source of competitive advantage, providing crucial entry barriers to competitors. Several characteristics make store retailing unique from the customer viewpoint. The retail environment provides the sensation of touch, feel, and smell, which is very important for many product categories, such as clothing, books, or perfumes. Furthermore, customers can interact and seek advice with in-store staff. Once a product is selected and a purchase made, customers can walk out of the store with the merchandise in hand.

In contrast, retailing can also involve non-store retailers. These are retail transactions that occur away from a fixed store location. Examples include automatic vending machines, direct selling, and the rise of internet retailing (Bennet, 1988). Direct selling is one of the oldest retailing methods and is the personal contact between a salesperson and a consumer at a location away from a retailing environment. These activities include door-to-door canvassing and party plans, where sales presentations are made within a home to a party of guests. Examples include cosmetics companies such as Avon, Nutri-Metics skincare, and Amway household products. **Telemarketing** or telesales is another form of non-store retailing where purchase occurs over the telephone. During the 1990s, this form of non-store retailing grew extensively due to rapid developments in computer-assisted and TV shopping networks.

A more recent form of non-store retailing is the **electronic kiosk**. These are placed in shopping malls to assist the retailing experience. These computer-based retailing environments offer increased self-service opportunities, a wide array of products, and a large amount of data and information to help decision-making. Automatic vending machines provide product access 24 hours a day, seven days a week. Products distributed through vending machines are normally convenient and typically low-priced, including cigarettes, soft drinks, hot beverages, condoms, newspapers, and magazines. We also see the wide adoption of automatic teller machines (ATMs) to facilitate the delivery of financial retailing services.

Another form of non-store retailing is internet retailing. In 2011, UK sales exceeded £50bn, 12% of total national retail spend. This compares with Germany's 9%, Norway's 8%, and Italy's

1.3% (Kelkoo, 2012). UK consumers also topped the online retail spending tables in 2011, with an average annual spend of £1,500, compared with a European average of £774 on 39 items.

The key consumer categories on the internet are travel, clothes, groceries, and consumer electronics. Market Insight 12.5 provides a snapshot of the impact the leading online music retailer iTunes is having on the retailing of music.

Visit the **Online Resource Centre** and complete Internet Activity 12.2 to learn more about the variety of internet retailing sites and the importance of delivery information for the Music sector.

Market Insight 12.5

Tuning into iTunes

Online shopping is set to account for nearly 40% of all UK retail sales by 2020, with online sales reaching £50bn in 2011 and set to quadruple to £162bn by 2020. According to uSwitch, 8 million UK households spend, on average, two hours a day shopping online. The most popular online purchases are holidays, films, and music.

One organization playing a key role in the facilitation of this growth of digital music sales is Apple's iTunes Music Store (iTMS). The iTunes Store is an online business run by Apple Inc., which sells media files that are accessed through its iTunes application. Opened as the iTunes Music Store on 28 April 2003, it proved the viability of online music sales. The virtual record shop sells music videos, TV shows, movies, and video games in addition to music. iTunes now has several personalization options, and one of them is 'Just For You'. Apple dominates the market controlling more than 70% of the worldwide online digital music sales.

Apple's iTunes store allows the users to purchase songs and transfer them easily to an iPod through iTunes. The store began after Apple signed deals with the five major record labels at the time: EMI, Universal, Warner Bros., Sony Music Entertainment, and BMG (the latter two would later merge to form Sony BMG). Music by more than 600 independent label artists was added later, the first being Moby on 29 July 2003. The store now has more than 12 million songs, including exclusive tracks from numerous popular artists, and, in early 2010, Apple celebrated the downloading of the ten billionth song from Apple iTunes—the Johnny Cash song aptly titled 'Guess Things Happen That Way'.

New songs are added to the iTunes catalogue every day, and the iTunes Store is updated each Tuesday. Apple also releases a 'Single of the Week' and usually a 'Discovery Download' on Tuesdays, which are available free for one week. In the words of Apple's late CEO, Steve Jobs, 'In 1984 we introduced the Macintosh. It didn't just change Apple, it changed the whole computer industry. In 2001, we introduced the first iPod and it didn't just change the way we all listen to music, it changed the entire music industry' (Allison and Palmer, 2007).

Sources: Apple (2007); Benson (2007); Wingfield and Smith (2007); Tabini (2010).

1 **Why do you think the offline retail sale of music is declining?**

2 **Why do you think iTunes has been such a success as an online music retailer?**

3 **Consider your own recent purchases of music. Which type of retail channel did you use to purchase the music and why?**

Chapter Summary

To consolidate your learning, the key points from this chapter are summarized here.

- **Describe the nature and characteristics of a marketing channel.**

  Marketing channels are chains of organizations that are concerned with the management of the processes and activities involved in creating and moving particular offerings from producers and manufacturers to end-user customers. Marketing channels enable different types of uncertainty to be lowered by reducing the complexity, increasing value and competitive advantage, routinization, and/or providing specialization.

- **Explain the different types of intermediaries and their roles in the marketing channel.**

  An intermediary is an independent organization that operates as a link between producers and end-user consumers or industrial users. There are several different types of intermediary: agents, merchants, distributors, franchises, wholesalers, and retailers. The main role of intermediaries is to reduce uncertainty experienced by producers and manufacturers, and they promote efficiency. The key difference between the various intermediaries is that not all of them take legal title or physical possession of a product.

- **Understand the different marketing channel structures and their core characteristics**

  There are three main channel structures: 'direct', 'indirect', and 'multichannel'. A direct channel involves selling directly to end-user customers, an indirect channel involves using intermediaries, and a multichannel involves both. At the simplest level, direct channels offer maximum control, but do not always reach all of the target market. Indirect channels can maximize coverage, but often at the expense of control. This is because intermediaries start adapting the marketing mix and demand a share of the profits in return for their involvement. Multichannel strategies often result in greater channel conflict, as intermediaries perceive the manufacturer to be a competitor.

- **Explain the factors that influence the design and structure of marketing channels.**

  When establishing or adapting marketing channels, it is necessary to consider the type of market coverage that is required, the number and type of intermediaries to use, and how the relationships between channel members are to be managed. These choices are important as they can affect the value that is ultimately provided to customers.

- **Describe the main elements that constitute supply chain management.**

  Supply chain management (SCM) concerns the various suppliers involved in providing raw materials (upstream), those who assemble and manufacture products, and those who distribute finished products to end-user customers (downstream). SCM embraces four main activities—fulfilment, transportation, stock management, and warehousing—which also subsume other important activities such as order processing and purchasing. Although these are not traditionally marketing management decisions, it is important to understand that they require a marketing focus and marketing insight.

- **Consider the role and function of retailers in the marketing channel.**

  Retailing concerns all activities directly related to the sale of goods and services to consumers for personal and non-business use. Retailers provide consumers with access to products, and help reduce the uncertainty experienced by other intermediaries in the channel, such as wholesalers and manufacturers. This is achieved by taking small quantities of stock on a regular basis, promoting cash flows, and providing demand for their products and services. The different types of retailing establishments can be classified according to two key characteristics: the marketing strategy (i.e. product, price, and service) and the store presence (i.e. store or non-store retailing).

Review Questions

1 What do we mean by marketing channel management?

2 Why do organizations use intermediaries?

3 Why are economics, coverage, and control important when making marketing channel decisions?

4 What are the key elements of a channel strategy?

5 What are the advantages and disadvantages of the three different channel structures?

6 What are the advantages of using an exclusive rather than an intensive marketing channel strategy?

7 Why is supply chain management of increasing importance to marketers?

8 What are some of the reasons for channel conflict?

9 Identify six types of retailer.

10 What does the term non-store retailing mean? Identify the main types.

Worksheet Summary

To apply the knowledge you have gained from this chapter and test your understanding of marketing channels and retailing visit the **Online Resource Centre** and complete Worksheet 12.1.

Discussion Questions

1 Having read Case Insight 12.1, how should Cobalt develop a channel to engage with potential legacy donors?

2 Discuss the importance of intermediaries. In your discussion, outline the benefits and limitations of three types of intermediaries.

3 Select three direct channels and identify two types of product that are best suited to this approach. Identify the benefits of this channel strategy.

4 Convenience has become a critical issue in marketing channel decisions. Assess the arguments for and against focusing on convenience from a customer's perspective.

5 What sort of marketing channels do you believe might be most relevant in the following markets in the year 2018? Identify the three most relevant channels for each of the following product categories.
   A music and video;
   B home entertainment software (e.g. video games);
   C business application software;
   D engineering consulting advice (say on mining or construction applications);
   E financial services;

F   shampoo;

G   personal services (e.g. hairdressing, beauty therapies).

6   Consider how the roles of intermediaries in marketing channels have changed as a result of the introduction of electronic technologies.

@   Visit the **Online Resource Centre** and complete the Multiple Choice Questions to assess your knowledge of Chapter 12.

References

Allison, K. and Palmer, M. (2007), 'Into the pack: Apple takes risks in its bid to shake up the mobile market', *Financial Times*, 26 June, 11.

Anderson, E. and Anderson, R. (2002), 'The new e-commerce intermediaries', *MIT Sloan Management Review*, 43(4), 53–62.

Anon. (2005) 'The future of fast fashion', *The Economist*, 18 June.

Apple (2007), 'iTunes store tops two billion songs', *Apple Press Release*, 9 January, retrieve from: http://www.apple.com/uk/pr/library/2007/01/09iTunes-Store-Tops-Two-Billion-Songs.html accessed 6 July 2013.

Bennet, P. D. (1988), *Dictionary of Marketing Terms*, Chicago, IL: American Marketing Association.

Benson, C. (2007), 'Retail recovery', *Billboard*, 9 June, 119.

Brewer, P. C. and Speh, T. W. (2000), 'Using the balanced scorecard to measure supply chain performance', *Journal of Business Logistics*, 211(Spring), 75–95

Chandler, M. (2009), 'Shopping at Hollister Co.—Relaxing Beach or Nightclub?', 8 February, retrieve from: http://bus4411.blogspot.co.uk/2009/02/shopping-at-hollister-co-relaxing-beach.html accessed 7 July 2013.

Dreier, G. (2003), 'Technology that drives transportation', *Transport Technology Today*, 9 July.

Ferdows, K., Lewis, M. A., and Machuca, J. A. D. (2004), 'Rapid-fire fulfilment', *Harvard Business Review*, 82(11), 104–10.

Fill, C. and McKee, S. (2012), *Business Marketing*, Oxford: Goodfellow.

Franchise Europe (2012), *Top 500 Franchises in Europe*, retrieve from: www.franchiseeurope.com/top500/, accessed 2 February 2013.

Gaski, J. F. (1984), 'The theory of power and conflict in channels of distribution', *Journal of Marketing*, 48, 9–29.

Gaughran, D. (2013), 'Self-Publishing grabs huge market share from traditional publishers, 12 April, retrieve from: http://davidgaughran.wordpress.com/ accessed 22 April 2013.

Glynn, M. S., Brodie, R. J., and Motion, J. (2012), 'The benefits of manufacturer brands to retailers', *European Journal of Marketing*, 46(9), 1127–49.

Hamilton, A. (2007), 'Fast fashion, the remix', *Time*, 11 June, 54.

Hansen, S. (2012), 'How Zara grew into the world's largest fashion retailer, *New York Times*, 9 November, retrieve from: http://www.nytimes.com/2012/11/11/magazine/how-zara-grew-into-the-worlds-largest-fashion-retailer.html?pagewanted=all&_r=0 accessed 10 January 2013.

Harris, P. (2009), *Penguin Dictionary of Marketing*, London: Penguin Books.

Katz, D. and Kahn, R. L. (1978) *The Social Psychology of Organisation* (2nd), New York: John Wiley.

Kelkoo (2012), 'Online retail sales hit £50bn', *The Guardian*, 19 January, retrieve from: http://www.guardian.co.uk/money/2012/jan/19/online-retail-sales-hit-50bn accessed 7 February 2013.

Kotler, P. and Keller, K. (2009), *Marketing Management*, Englewood Cliffs, NJ: Prentice Hall

Laffey, D. and Gandy, A. (2009), 'Comparison websites in UK retail financial services', *Journal of Financial Services Marketing*, 14(2), 173–86.

Melnyk, S. A., Lummus, R. R., Vokurka, R. J., Burns, L. J., and Sandor, J. (2009), 'Mapping the future of supply chain management: a Delphi study', *International Journal of Production Research*, 47(16), 4629–53.

Mills, J. F. and Camek, V. (2004), 'The risks, threats and opportunities of disintermediation: distributor's view', *International Journal of Physical Distribution and Logistics Management*, 34(9), 714–27.

Myers, M. B. and Griffith, D. A. (1999), 'Strategies for combating grey market activity', *Business Horizons*, 42(6), 71–5.

Palazzini, M. (2011), 'Priming', 26 February, retrieve from: http://mpalazzini.blogspot.co.uk/2011/02/priming.html accessed 30 January 2013.

Park, S. Y. and Keh, H. T. (2003), 'Modelling hybrid distribution channels: a game theory analysis', *Journal of Retailing and Consumer Services*, 10, 155–67.

Parker, M., Bridson, K., and Evans, J. (2006), 'Motivations for developing direct trade relationships', *International Journal of Retail and Distribution Management*, 34(2), 121–34.

Rosenbloom, B. (2007), 'Multi channel strategy in business-to-business markets: prospects and problems', *Industrial Marketing Management*, 36(1), 4–9.

Seiders, K., Berry, L. L., and Gresham, L. G. (2000), 'Attention retailers! How convenient is your convenience strategy?' *Sloan Management Review*, Spring, 79–89.

Shipley, D. and Egan, C. (1992), 'Power, conflict and co-operation in brewer–tenant distribution channels' *International Journal of Service Industry Management*, 3(4), 44–62.

Singh, A. (2011), 'Adults puzzled by Hollister store that keeps shoppers in the dark', *The Telegraph*, 28 October, retrieve from: www.telegraph.co.uk/finance/newsbysector/retailandconsumer/8854448/Adults-puzzled-by-Hollister-store-that-keeps-shoppers-in-the-dark.html accessed 28 January, 2013.

Tabini, M. (2010), 'iTunes Store: more than 10 billion songs served', *Macworld*, 27(5), 63.

Tay, K. B., and Chelliah, J. (2011), 'Disintermediation of traditional chemical intermediary roles in the electronic business-to-business (e-B2B) exchange world', *Journal of Strategic Information Systems*, 20, 3, 217–31.

Vitzthum, C. (2001), 'Zara's success lies in low-cost lines and a rapid turnover of collections', *Wall Street Journal*, 18 May.

Webb, K. L. and Hogan, J. E. (2002), 'Hybrid channel conflict: causes and effects on channel performance', *Journal of Business and Industrial Marketing*, 17(5), 338–57.

Wingfield, N. and Smith, E. (2007), 'Jobs's new tune raises pressure on music firms: Apple chief now favors making downloads of songs freely tradable', *Wall Street Journal* (Eastern edition), A. 1.

Yan, R., Guo, P., Wang, J., and Amrouche, N. (2011), 'Product distribution and coordination strategies in a multi-channel context', *Journal of Retailing and Consumer Services*, 18, 19–26.

Part Four
Principles of Relational Marketing

Chapter 13
Branding Decisions

Learning Outcomes

After studying this chapter you should be able to:

▸ Explain the characteristics and principal types of brands and branding

▸ Examine how branding has evolved, utilizing relational and co-creation perspectives

▸ Explain how brands work through associations and personalities

▸ Understand different aspects of brand strategy and policies

▸ Describe the principal issues associated with branding in services, business, and global contexts

▸ Explore the issues and activities associated with brand equity and demonstrate why branding is important to marketing managers

Case Insight 13.1
BRAND sense agency

Market Insight 13.1
Chicken Cottage—Not Just for Muslims

Market Insight 13.2
A Finnish Association with Purity

Market Insight 13.3
SCA Rebrands and Repositions

Market Insight 13.4
Appealing Luxury Products

Case Insight 13.1

The BRAND sense agency helps clients build brands that enjoy deeper emotional connections with their consumers through both communications and the customer experience to arrive at a holistic understanding of the brand's sensory impact. We talk to CEO, Simon Harrop, to find out more.

Imagine that you are walking through a supermarket, surrounded by products in aisles and point-of-sale material all vying for your attention, when you suddenly become aware of the smell of bread, which captures your senses and sends you off in a hurry to the supermarket's boulangerie. If smell has such power in a supermarket, could it be used for advertising or enhancing the customer experience in other ways? In such a vision- and sound-cluttered promotional world, could other senses be used instead?

BRAND sense agency was set up because of a belief that brands and marketers rely too heavily on vision and words to communicate with and engage consumers. Our intuition and experience was confirmed when we carried out one of the largest ever studies into the relationship between brands and consumers across all the senses. There is a serious imbalance between how, as humans, we experience brands and how marketers seek to communicate brand propositions. Our mission is to address this imbalance, make marketing more effective, and build a business that we enjoy in the process!

Consumer behaviour is the sum of our rational and conscious relationship to the products or services that we buy and also the emotional and non-conscious influences. Consumer behaviour is the sum of experience, intention, perception, and conception of all that we buy. In the modern world, with so much choice and so much information to process, we increasingly rely on habit and non-conscious associations to make our choices.

A sensory approach involves breaking down the key elements of the emotional relationship with brands in a category and identifying differentiated emotional space that a particular brand in that category can own. We then link this emotional space to key sensory attributes. When these attributes are aligned to this emotional space, you have a strong brand. If there is dissonance between experience and brand expectation, we work with our clients to create a development programme to bring these elements into line. This has a positive influence on consumer perception and behaviour.

Our research highlighted the fact that consumers value all senses in their relationship with brands fairly much in balance. However, for certain brands in particular categories, some senses will clearly be more important than others, e.g. smell for shampoo. However, it is our contention that a multisensory approach should take a holistic view across each sense. In practice, most brands are already considering words and pictures, as

After a sensory branding treatment, this Colombian bank smells as good as it looks!

Case Insight 13.1
continued

we have seen, so most of our work involves help with smell, taste, sound, and, to a certain extent, touch.

When BRAND sense agency was approached by a major Colombian bank, a bank beset with problems in developing a differentiated proposition from other banks in the marketplace, particularly in the interior and exterior design of the branches, it wanted to make a difference, not with the common approach to branding but with a multisensory approach emphasizing sound and smell, as well as sight. Colombian banks had all tended to offer the same financial service products and even looked the same.

If you were trying to create a multisensory brand communication approach to help the Colombian bank differentiate itself in the marketplace through sight, sound, and smell, what would you do?

Introduction

Our world is full of brands—from soap powders and soft drinks to airlines and financial services, and even musicians, sports and film stars, buildings, cities and destinations, and social networks. Brands are configured in all shapes, sizes, entities. There is a huge variety in branding opportunities. As the BRAND sense agency case rightly notes, people have relationships with brands, but what exactly is a **brand**? How are they developed? Who really creates them? What exactly is the nature of these relationships? Why are they significant? These are key questions we explore in this chapter.

Branding is a process by which manufacturers and retailers help customers to differentiate between various offerings. It enables customers to make associations between certain attributes or feelings and a particular brand. If this differentiation can be achieved and sustained, then a brand is considered to have a competitive advantage. It is not necessary for people to buy brands to enjoy and understand them. Successful brands create strong, positive, and lasting impressions through their communications, and associated psychological feelings and emotions, not just their functionality through use.

Brand names provide information about content, taste, durability, quality, price, and performance without requiring the buyer to undertake time-consuming comparison tests with similar offerings or other risk reduction approaches to purchase decisions. In some categories, brands can be developed through the use of messages that are entirely emotional or image based. Many of the products in FMCG sectors, where there is low customer involvement, use communications based largely on imagery, such as Tetley in food and drink, New Look in fashion, and Revlon in cosmetics. Other sectors, such as cars or pharmaceuticals where purchase involvement tends to be higher, require rational information-based messages supported by image-based messages (Boehringer, 1996). In other words, a blend of messages may well be required to achieve the objectives and goals of the campaign.

What is a Brand?

A brand can be distinguished from its proposition or unbranded commodity counterparts by the perceptions and feelings consumers have about its attributes and performance. For example, bottled water is essentially a commodity, but brands such as Highland Spring, Aqua Falls, and Crystal Clear have all developed their offerings with imagery which serves to enhance customer feelings and emotions about the actual water in the packaging. Ultimately, a brand resides in the mind of the consumer (Achenbaum, 1993).

Brands are products and services that have added value. This value has been deliberately designed and presented by marketing managers to augment their offerings with values and associations that are recognized by, and are meaningful to, their customers. Although marketing managers have to create, sustain, protect, and develop the identity of the brands for which they are responsible, it is customer perception—the use of various senses that help fashion images of these brands, and the meaning and value that customers give to the brand—that is important. Therefore, both managers and customers are involved in the branding process.

De Chernatony and Dall'Olmo Riley (1998) identified 12 types of brand definition, but one of the more common interpretations is that a brand is represented by a name, symbol, word, or mark that identifies and distinguishes a proposition or company from its competitors. However, brands consist of much more than these various elements. Brands have character, even personalities, and in order to develop character it is important to understand that brands are constructed of two main types of attributes: intrinsic and extrinsic.

Intrinsic attributes refer to the functional characteristics of a proposition, such as its shape, performance, and physical capacity. If any of these intrinsic attributes were changed, this would directly alter the proposition. **Extrinsic attributes** refer to those elements that are not intrinsic and, if changed, do not alter the material functioning and performance of the proposition itself. These include devices such as the brand name, marketing communications, packaging, price, and mechanisms that enable consumers to form associations that give meaning to the brand. Buyers often use the extrinsic attributes to help them distinguish one brand from another, because in certain categories it is difficult for them to make decisions based on the intrinsic attributes alone. For example, many financial companies develop brands because their propositions are very complex and many consumers are reluctant or unable to give the time and effort necessary to understand them. By developing a single brand, firms such as Prudential and

Research Insight 13.1

To take your learning further, you might wish to read this influential paper.

de Chernatony, L. and Dall'Olmo Riley, F. (1998), 'Defining a brand: beyond the literature with experts' interpretations', *Journal of Marketing Management*, 14(4/5), 417–43.

This paper provides an insight to the different ways a brand can be interpreted. It was published at the end of the twentieth century, and the authors suggest some interesting perspectives that have been developed in subsequent years.

@ Visit the **Online Resource Centre** to read the abstract and access the full paper.

Zurich have tried to establish high levels of trust and reliance in their brands, as this can help to reduce customers' perceived risk and speed up the decision-making process.

Why Brand?

Brands represent opportunities for both consumers and organizations (manufacturers and retailers) to buy and sell products and services easily, more efficiently, and relatively quickly. The benefits are now considered from each perspective. Consumers like brands for the following reasons.

- They assist people to identify their preferred offerings.
- They reduce levels of perceived risk and in so doing improve the quality of the shopping experience.
- They help people to gauge the level of product/service/experience quality.
- They reduce the amount of time spent making proposition-based decisions and, in turn, decrease the time spent shopping.
- They provide psychological reassurance or reward, especially for offerings bought on an occasional basis.
- They inform consumers about the source of an offering (country or company).

Branding helps customers to identify the offerings they prefer to use to satisfy their needs and wants. Equally, branding helps them to avoid the brands that they dislike as a result of previous use or because of other image, associations, or other psychological reasoning.

Consumers experience a range of perceived risks when buying different offerings. These might be financial risks (can I afford this?), social risks (what will other people think about me wearing this dress or going to this bar?), or functional risks (will this smartphone work?). Branding helps to reduce these risks so that buyers can proceed with a purchase without fear or uncertainty. Strong brands encapsulate a range of values that communicate safety and purchase security.

In markets unknown to a buyer or where there is technical complexity (e.g. computing, financial services), consumers use branding to make judgements about the quality of an offering. This, in turn, helps consumers save shopping time and again helps reduce the amount of risk they experience.

Perhaps, above all other factors, branding helps consumers to develop relationships based on trust. Strong brands are normally well trusted, and annual surveys often announce that the BBC, Google, and Kellogg's are some of the most trusted brands. Similarly, these surveys declare those brands that are least trusted by consumers, and very often this coincides with falling sales and reducing market share. Creating trust is important as it enables consumers to buy with confidence. The branding used by Chicken Cottage, set out in Market Insight 13.1, shows how an emerging retail brand seeks to reduce different forms of uncertainty.

Many brands are deliberately imbued with human characteristics, to the point that they are identified as having particular personalities. These **brand personalities** might be based around being seen as friendly, approachable, distant, aloof, calculating, honest, fun, or even robust or caring. For example, Timberland is rugged, Victoria's Secret is glamorous, Virgin is associated with youthfulness and rebelliousness, and management consultancies such as PwC seek to be seen as successful, accomplished, and influential. Marketing communications play an important role in communicating the essence of a brand's personality. By developing positive emotional links with a brand, consumers can find reassurance through their brand purchases.

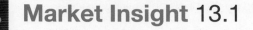

Market Insight 13.1

Chicken Cottage—Not Just for Muslims

Chicken Cottage is a halal fast-food brand with its origins in North London but which now, through franchise development, has outlets in Canada, France, Italy, Algeria, Libya, Pakistan, U.A.E, and Ireland, with restaurants due to open in Nigeria, Iran, Iraq, and Bangladesh. There are plans for 300 outlets by 2015.

Although the brand was founded on halal principles, it appeals to a wide range of customers, many of whom do not share the Islamic faith and live outside substantial Muslim populations. This was achieved partly as a result of its new product development strategy. This is based on fusing multiple tastes from multiple cultures, and by only using halal meat.

As a result Chicken Cottage has developed a product range that includes spicy and exotic products, as well as those normally expected from this type of high street outlet.

Halal principles and meat preparation are not well known among non-Muslim audiences, so the brand name and logo were created to represent an inclusive ethos and to appeal to different markets. The name Chicken Cottage represents the functional aspect of the food brand, and it also provokes images of home cooking and non-intimidating and welcoming environments. This highly emotional positioning seeks to diffuse the glare of global competitors and encourage people to approach the brand.

The logo is based on an abstract view of two chicken heads, and includes the word 'halal'. Many of their

Chicken Cottage, the UK-based halal fast-food brand, has plans for 300 outlets around the world by 2015
Source: © Chicken Cottage.

competitors promote halal conspicuously but Chicken Cottage don't use it in their signage, communications, or in-store, just in their logo. This helps attract both Muslims and non-Muslims to the restaurants.

Sources: Based on Roberts (2010); www.chickencottage.net/

1 How might Chicken Cottage develop their brand?

2 To what extent is Chicken Cottage vulnerable to the established global fast-food brands?

3 Identify two other emerging brands and their distinguishing characteristics.

Manufacturers and retailers use brands for the following reasons.

■ They can increase the financial valuation of companies.

■ They enable premium pricing.

■ They help differentiate the proposition from competitive offerings.

■ They can deter competitors from entering the market

- They encourage cross-selling to other brands owned by the manufacturer.
- They develop customer trust, loyalty/retention, and repeat-purchase buyer behaviour.
- They assist the development and use of integrated marketing communications.
- They contribute to corporate identity programmes.
- They provide some legal protection.

Branding is an important way for manufacturers to differentiate their brands in crowded marketplaces. This enables buyers to recognize the brand quickly and make fast unhindered purchase decisions. One of the brand-owner's goals is to create strong brand loyalty to the extent that customers always seek out the brand, and become better prepared to accept cross-product promotions and brand extensions.

Perhaps one of the strongest motivations for branding is that it can allow manufacturers to set premium prices. Brands such as Andrex, Stella Artois, and L'Oréal charge a premium price, often around 25–35% higher than the average price in their respective product categories. Premium prices allow brand managers to reinvest in brand development, and in some markets this is important in order to remain competitive. However, it should not be assumed that the establishment of a brand will lead to automatic success. Many brands, such as HMV and Jessops, fail, sometimes because a firm fails to invest in a brand at the level required, or because management have not recognized or accepted the need to change, adapt, or reposition their brands as market preferences have moved on.

The greater the number of product-based brands, the greater the motivation for an organization to want to develop a corporate brand. Organizations such as Aviva and Johnson & Johnson use an umbrella branding approach. This requires that they only need to invest heavily in one brand, rather than each and every product-based brand. This approach is not applicable to all sectors, although in business-to-business markets, where there is product complexity, corporate branding is an effective way of communicating and focusing on a few core brand values.

Visit the **Online Resource Centre** and complete Internet Activity 13.1 to learn more about how major organizations perceive the importance of branding and their brands.

How to Build Brands

The development of successful brands is critical to an organization's success. Keller (2009) believes that this is best accomplished by considering the brand-building process in terms of steps. The first is to enable customers to identify with the brand and help them make associations with a specific product class or customer need. The second is to establish what the brand means by linking various tangible and intangible brand associations. The third step is concerned with encouraging customer responses based around brand-related judgement and feelings. The final step is about fostering an active relationship between customers and the brand.

Figure 13.1 depicts the rational steps on the left-hand side, whereas the emotional counterpart is shown on the right-hand side. In the centre are six blocks which make up a pyramid, echoing these rational and emotional steps. Keller argues that to achieve a successful brand, or brand resonance, a foundation is necessary and that these building blocks need to be

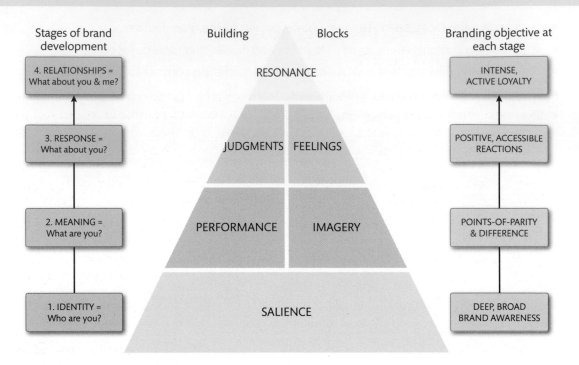

Figure 13.1

Typology of brands in real and virtual worlds

Source: 'Building strong brands in a modern marketing communications environment', Keller, K. L., *Journal of Marketing Communications*, July 2009, Taylor & Francis. Reprinted by permission of the publisher (Taylor & Francis Ltd, http://www.tandf.co.uk/journals).

developed systematically. We now apply the brand pyramid to a shampoo brand to understand the terminology further.

- Brand salience—how easily and often do customers think of the shampoo brand when thinking about hair care brands or when shopping?

- Brand performance—how well do customers believe the shampoo brand cleans and conditions their hair?

- Brand imagery—describes the extrinsic properties of the shampoo (the colour, the packaging, the product consistency, associations) and level to which these satisfy customers' psychological or social needs.

- Brand judgements—focus on customers' opinions and evaluations about the shampoo.

- Brand feelings—customers' emotional responses and reactions with respect to the shampoo brand when prompted by communications or by friends, or when washing their hair.

- Brand resonance—the nature of the relationship customers have with the shampoo brand and the extent to which they feel loyal to the brand.

Brand resonance is most likely to result when marketers create proper salience and breadth and depth of awareness. From this position 'points-of-parity and points-of-difference' need to be established, so that positive judgements and feelings can be made that appeal to the head and the heart, respectively.

Visit the **Online Resource Centre** and follow the weblink to learn more about Keller's Brand Equity model.

How Brands Work: Associations and Personalities

The development of successful brands requires customers to be able to make appropriate brand-related associations. These should be based on utilitarian functional issues, as well as emotions and feelings towards a brand. The notion of brand associations appears to be fully accepted, although what constitutes them inevitably varies among researchers.

Clayton and Heo (2011) refer to brand image, perceived quality, and brand attitude as the main dimensions of brand associations, citing work by Aaker (1991), Keller (1993), and Low and Lamb (2000) in this area. Keller (1993) believes that brand associations themselves are made up of the physical and non-physical attributes and benefits aligned with attitudes to create a brand image in the mind of the consumer. Jin and Sung (2011) claim that there is a wealth of empirical evidence to support the claim that people tend to attribute human personality characteristics to non-human entities. The symbolic meanings that brands acquire is called brand personality and is known as the set of human characteristics associated with a brand (Aaker, 1997).

These associations and images may sometimes enable consumers to construe a psycho-social meaning associated with a particular brand. The idea that consumers might search for brands with a personality that complements their self-concept is not new, as identified by McCracken (1986). Belk (1988) suggested that brands offer a means of self-expression, whether this is in terms of who they want to be (desired self), who they strive to be (ideal self), or who they think they should be (ought self). Therefore brands provide a means for individuals to indicate to others their preferred personality, as they relate to these 'self' concepts.

This emotional and symbolic approach is intended to provide consumers with additional reasons to engage with a brand, beyond the normal functional characteristics that a brand offers (Keller, 1998), which are so easily copied by competitors. Aaker (1997) developed the **Brand Personality Scale**, which consists of five main dimensions of psychosocial meaning which subsume 42 personality traits. The dimensions are sincerity (wholesome, honest, down-to-earth), excitement (exciting, imaginative, daring), competence (intelligent, confident), sophistication (charming, glamorous, smooth), and ruggedness (strong, masculine). These are depicted in Figure 13.2

Aaker's initial research was conducted in the mid-1990s and revealed that in the USA, MTV was perceived to be best on excitement, CNN on competence, Levi's on ruggedness, Revlon on sophistication, and Campbell's on sincerity. Jin and Sung (2011) believe that a brand can be associated with various demographic characteristics as gender, age, social class, and lifestyle. They also cite human personality traits and suggest that Hummer and North Face are examples of brands that are associated with ruggedness, Toyota and Dell as reliable, although recent car recalls might have damaged Toyota's strength on this dimension, iPhone and Scion with being trendy, and finally Lexus and Ralph Lauren as sophisticated.

These psychosocial dimensions have subsequently become enshrined as dimensions of brand personality. Aaker developed a five-point framework around these dimensions in order to provide a consistent means of measurement. The framework has been used frequently and cited many times by academics and marketing practitioners. For example, Arora and Stoner (2009) report that various studies have found that consumers choose brands which they feel reflect their own personality (Linville and Carlston, 1994; Phau and Lau, 2001). They prefer brands that project a personality that is consistent with their self-concepts. As Arora and Stoner (2009: 273)

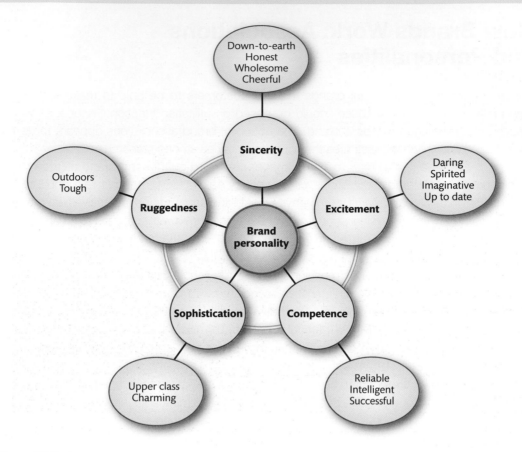

Figure 13.2

Five dimensions of psychosocial meaning

Source: Reprinted with permission from J. Aaker (1997), 'Dimensions of brand personality', *Journal of Marketing Research*, 34(August), 347–56, published by the American Marketing Association.

indicate, 'brand personality provides a form of identity for consumers that expresses symbolic meaning for themselves and for others'. Therefore brand personality can be construed as a means of creating and maintaining consumer loyalty, if only because this aspect is difficult for competitors to copy.

Customers assign a level of trust to the brands they encounter. Preferred brands signify a high level of trust and indicate that the brand promise is delivered. Therefore marketing managers need to ensure that they do not harm or reduce the perceived levels of trust in their brands. Indeed, actions should be taken to enhance trust. One way of achieving this is to use labels and logos to represent a brand's values, associations, and source (see Market Insight 13.2). For example, all Apple products are signified, and identified by, the fruit with a bite removed, and UK meat products carry a red tractor symbol. According to the National Farmers Union, the red tractor logo indicates that the meat was produced to exacting standards of food safety, kindness to animals, and environmental protection. This is intended to reassure customers about the origin and quality of the meat. A more recent symbol is that of a footprint. This refers to the carbon dioxide associated with the production and transportation of a brand. This emerged because some brands wanted a means of demonstrating the carbon savings they had made in their supply chains. Walkers Crisps and then Tesco were the first brands to use the symbol. However, as

Market Insight 13.2

A Finnish Association with Purity

Finlandia, a premium vodka brand targeted at younger upmarket drinkers, was built around functional associations with the clean, clear, natural environment of Finland. In an attempt to raise awareness of the brand, a recent campaign called 'Pure Emotion' was launched. The strategy was to be achieved by shifting brand associations to ones that engaged the target consumers emotionally. The campaign was made with the support of *The Independent* newspaper, itself a source of emotion often depicted through travel, music, and sport.

The promotion launched with advertorial content in the newspaper's *Traveller* and *Independent* magazines. Teaser ads placed on the sports pages drove readers to the promotion online at a co-branded microsite created at independent.co.uk. This was aimed at encouraging readers/users to share videos, photos, and stories of their own 'Pure Emotion' experiences.

The microsite included three 'Pure Emotion' features, with people talking about their own emotional highs and lows in music, travel, and sport. There were also three 'user-generated Pure Emotion' galleries, featuring stories, pictures, and videos from independent.co.uk users, all about emotional moments from their lives. An online competition ran, based around the users' uploaded 'Pure Emotion' content and attracted 1,213 competition entries. The microsite also featured a Finlandia advertorial and a gallery of 20 front pages of *The Independent* from the past year, underlining the emotional power of newspapers.

Text links to 'Pure Emotion' were included in *the Independent's* daily email newsletter to 80,000 subscribers and a marketing email to a 20,000-strong database. *The Independent's* campaign was tied in

The winning photo in Finlandia's 'Pure Emotion' competition
Source: Courtesy of Brown-Forman Beverages, Europe, Ltd.

with the Finlandia Vodka Pure Emotion Exhibition at Camden's Proud Gallery, showing real people's pure emotions in their own words through stories, images, and video clips. The brand also focused on its natural purity in an advertising takeover of Euston railway station.

Source: Anon. (2009a).

1 Which other brands might you suggest focus on an emotional approach? Are they successful, and why?

2 If customers buy brands with a personality that reflects their own personalities, name three brands that you purchase regularly. How do these reflect your personality?

3 Visit www.interbrand.com and find brands where the use of emotion is prominent.

Charles (2009) points out, one of the issues arising from the use of the carbon footprint symbol is that consumers do not understand what the figures mean. This will take time, just as the Fairtrade brand was not established overnight.

Visit the **Online Resource Centre** and complete Internet Activity 13.2 to learn more about the brand personality of Weightwatchers.

Types of Brand

There are three main types of brand: manufacturer, distributor, and generic.

Manufacturer Brands

In many markets, and especially the FMCG sector, retailers are able to influence the way in which a product is displayed and presented to customers. As a result, manufacturers try to create brand recognition and name recall through their marketing communications activities with end-users. The goal is to help customers identify the producer of a particular brand at the point of purchase. For example, Persil, Heinz, Cadbury, and Coca-Cola are strong manufacturers' brands, they are promoted heavily, and customers develop preferences based on performance, experience, communications, and availability. So, when customers are shopping they use the images they have of various manufacturers, combined with their own experiences, to seek out their preferred brands. Retailers who choose not to stock certain major **manufacturer brands** run the risk of losing customers.

Distributor (or Own-Label) Brands

The various organizations that make up the marketing channel often choose to create a distinct identity for themselves. The term distributor or own-label brand refers to the identities and images developed by the wholesalers, distributors, dealers, and retailers who make up the marketing channel. Wholesalers, such as Nurdin & Peacock, and retailers, such as Argos, Gap, Sainsbury's, JeronimoMartens in Portugal, and Plus Retail in the Netherlands, have all created strong brands.

This brand strategy offers many advantages to the manufacturer, who can use excess capacity, and retailers, who can earn a higher margin than they can with manufacturers' branded goods and at the same time develop strong store images. Retailers have the additional cost of promotional initiatives, necessary in the absence of a manufacturer's support. Some manufacturers, such as Kellogg's, refuse to make products for distributors to brand, although others (Cereal Partners) are happy to supply a variety of competitors.

Occasionally, conflict emerges, especially when a **distributor brand** displays characteristics that are very similar to the manufacturer's market leader brand. Coca-Cola defended their brand when it was alleged that the packaging of Sainsbury's new cola drink was too similar to their own established design.

Generic Brands

Generic brands are sold without any promotional materials or any means of identifying the company, with the packaging displaying only information required by law. The only form of identification is the relevant product category, e.g. plain flour. Without having to pay for promotional support, these brands are sold at prices that are substantially below the price of normal brands. However, although briefly successful in the 1990s, their popularity has declined and manufacturers see no reason to produce these 'white carton' products. Only firms in the pharmaceutical sector use this type of brand.

Branding Policies

Once a decision has been taken to brand an organization's offerings, an overall branding policy is required. There are three main strategies, individual, family, and corporate branding, and within these there are a number of brand combinations and variations in the way that brands can be developed.

Individual Branding

Once referred to as a multibrand policy, individual branding requires that each product offered by an organization is branded independently of all the others. Grocery brands offered by Unilever (e.g. Knorr, Cif, and Dove) and Procter & Gamble (e.g. Fairy, Crest, and Head & Shoulders) typify this approach.

One of the advantages of this approach is that it is easy to target specific segments and to enter new markets with separate names. If a brand fails or becomes subject to negative media attention, the other brands are not likely to be damaged. However, there is a heavy financial cost as each brand needs to have its own promotional programme and associated support.

Family Branding

Once referred to as a multiproduct brand policy, family branding requires that all the products use the organization's name, either entirely or in part. Microsoft, Heinz, and Kellogg's all incorporate the company name as it is hoped that customer trust will develop across all brands. Therefore promotional investment need not be as high. This is because there will always be a halo effect across all the brands when one is communicated, and brand experience will stimulate word of mouth following usage. A prime example of this is Google, which has pursued a family brand strategy with Google Adwords, Google Maps, and Google Scholar, to name a few. What is more impressive is that Google's shattering achievements have been accomplished in just ten years and without any spending on advertising or promotional materials.

Line family branding is a derivative policy whereby a family branding policy is followed for all products within a single line. Bosch is a technology company operating in the automotive industry and home markets. Many of its products are branded Bosch, but they use line branding for their Blaupunkt and Qualcast brands in their car entertainment and garden products divisions.

Corporate Brands

Many retail brands adopt a single umbrella brand, based on the name of the organization. This name is then used at all locations and is a way of identifying the brand and providing a form of consistent differentiation, and form of recognition, whether on the high street or online. Major supermarkets such as Tesco in the UK, Carrefour in France, and ASDA Wal-Mart use this branding strategy to attract and help retain customers.

Corporate branding strategies are also used extensively in business markets, such as IBM, Cisco, and Caterpillar, and in consumer markets where there is technical complexity, such as financial services. Companies such as HSBC and Prudential adopt a single-name strategy. One of the advantages of this approach is that promotional investments are limited to one brand. However, the risk is similar to family branding, where damage to one offering or operational area can cause problems across the organization. For example, the BBC experienced editorial problems with their *Newsnight* programme, which resulted in extensive and persistent negative media coverage; not only did the Director-General decide to resign, but questions about declining trust and reputation concerning the whole of the BBC surfaced.

Visit the **Online Resource Centre** and follow the weblink to learn more about IBM's corporate brand.

Branding Perspectives

So far we have assumed a largely managerial perspective with regard to the concept of brand. However, there are other perspectives to understanding brands and what they represent. These draw on sociological, psychological, and socio-cultural interpretations of brands and their consumption. We consider two important perspectives. The first considers relational issues and how people are thought to interact with brands and develop relationships through repeated consumption. The second reflects contemporary issues about co-creation and customer branding. This reverses the managerially driven view that brands are just a product of marketers.

Brand Relationships

Although branding has its roots in identification and differentiation, a 'brand-mark is a relational asset whose value to the firm is contingent on past, present and future interactions with various firm stakeholders' (Ballantyne and Aitken, 2007: 366). Fournier (1998) was one of the first researchers to introduce and utilize relationship theory to understand the roles that brands play in the lives of consumers.

Originally, relationship marketing was considered to be most relevant in inter-organizational relationships. Here, the management of relationships between buying and selling organizations is considered valid and appropriate, more so than in the relationship between an organization and a consumer. Fournier changed this when she explored ideas about consumers who think about brands as if they were human characters—the personification of brands. She also found that consumers accept attempts by marketers to personalize brands, for example, through advertising, which suggests interaction and relationship potential. She identified six facets which characterize brand relationship quality. These are love and passion, a connection between the brand and self, a high degree of interdependence, a high level of commitment, intimacy, and a positive evaluation of brand quality.

Fournier believes that it is important to understand consumer–brand relationships and that by understanding how consumers interact with brands, and the meaning that brands represent to people through consumption, marketing theory and practice can be advanced. She argues that it is necessary to consider the broad context of consumers' lives to understand the role and relationship that brands play in them. In addition, meaningful consumer–brand relationships can be observed when the brand represents the key dimension, 'perceived ego significance'. Fournier stresses the importance of understanding what consumers do with brands that adds meaning to their lives.

Perhaps the most important finding from her research concerns the meaning that consumers attribute to brands, and how this differs from those meanings intended by brand managers. This contribution has been developed in many areas, including business-to-business markets where it is now recognized that both sellers (suppliers) and buyers (their customers), and other stakeholders, co-create brand meanings. As Ballantyne and Aitken (2007) state, this indicates that brand meanings are socially constructed.

The increasing use of user-generated content in the form of blogs, tweets, wikis, and social networks now enables consumers to assume a greater role in defining what a brand means to them, something which they now share with their friends, family, and contacts, rather than with the organization itself. This means that both managers and customers are involved in the branding process. The control of brands used to reside with brand owners. Today, this influence has shifted to consumers as they redefine what brands mean to them, and how they differentiate among similar offerings and associate certain attributes or feelings and emotions with particular brands.

However, as Bengtsson (2003) argues, there is doubt about whether consumers really want a relationship with brands or even if they do have a relationship with them. His doubt concerns whether relationship theory is appropriate when examining the way consumers interact with brands.

de Lencastre and Côrte-Real (2010) believe a brand to be a sign and use **semiotics**, the science of signs, as a basis for a model that considers the different components of the relationships among them. They attempt to integrate the multiple facets of the brand concept and define three main brand dimensions. These are the identity sign itself, the marketing object to which the sign

 Research Insight 13.2

To take your learning further, you might wish to read this influential paper.

Fournier, S. (1998), 'Consumers and their brands: developing relationship theory in consumer research', *Journal of Consumer Research*, 24(4), 343–73.

This article has already been characterized as a modern classic by Bengtsson (2003), such is its significance and contribution to our understanding about marketing and consumer research. This paper discusses the need to incorporate relationship marketing theory with branding and explores the types of relationships people form with brands.

@ **Visit the Online Resource Centre to read the abstract and access the full paper.**

refers, and the market response to the sign (see also Chapter 19). One of the points they make is that brands today are largely regarded as socio-cultural concepts in which relational and community issues replace the former power-based managerial perspective whereby brand managers assumed control over a brand.

Visit the **Online Resource Centre** and follow the weblinks to learn more about brand semiotics.

Brand Co-creation

The managerial perspective assumes that manufacturers or service providers develop and manage brands, while individual consumers can only influence brand meaning or perception of the brand. This requires marketers to perform three essential branding activities. Pennington and Ball (2009) suggest that these are to enable identification and differentiation, to maintain consistency, and to communicate the existence and attributes to customer and marketing channel audiences.

In recent years this perspective and process has been challenged as there is increasing evidence that brands can be created by customers. In customer branding, the customer attaches a name, term, or other feature that enables them to identify one seller's good or service as distinct from those of other sellers (AMA, 2012). This is commonly referred to as co-creation, and there are many examples indicating that it is not a recent phenomenon.

Pennington and Ball (2009: 455) define customer branding as 'a process in which a customer, or customers, define, label and seek to purchase a subset of an otherwise undifferentiated or unbranded product. The customer can be anywhere along the value chain, including intermediate and end-user customers'.

In conventional branding processes, a business is able to influence external stakeholders and customers through promises of value creation, and internally as means of employee branding and organizational identity. Where there is customer branding, the organization surrenders control of the brand's ability to convey these and other clear messages to customers and employees (Pennington and Ball, 2009).

In conventional branding activities, communication about a brand flows from the marketer to the consumer. In co-creation contexts, it is the customer who knows what they want, badges it, and requests it by the badge they have provided or by some other characteristic that others will recognize. In other words, in customer branding, the flow is reversed.

Pennington and Ball (2009: 459) identify three key conditions that need to be met for customer branding to occur. First, there must be a variety of offerings in the market, secondly the delivery and quality of offerings must be unacceptable, and thirdly customers must be able to obtain a reliable and satisfactory alternative from within the marketing channel. As the authors phrase it, 'for the customer to expend the effort to take over branding activities that the marketer is not performing, the customer must show certain needs, perceptions and abilities'.

Ideas about brand co-creation are not confined to product or service offerings. For example, Juntunen (2012) found that a range of stakeholders, not just customers, are involved in corporate brand co-creation. These include employees, relatives, friends, university researchers, students, employees and managers of other companies, advertising agencies, financiers, lawyers, graphic designers, and customers. She revealed that stakeholders engage in various sub-processes of corporate brand co-creation, even before a company is formed (Kollmann and Suckow, 2007). These include inventing the corporate name before a company is established, developing a new

Research Insight 13.3

To take your learning further, you might wish to read this influential paper.

Muzellec, L., Lynn, T., and Lambkin, M. (2012), 'Branding in fictional and virtual environments: introducing a new conceptual domain and research agenda', *European Journal of Marketing*, 46(6), 811–26.

Muzellec and colleagues wrote this paper with the aim of introducing and exploring ideas about virtual brands. They argue that the brand concept may now be detached from physical embodiment and extended to the fictional and computer-synthesized worlds. The paper helps to explain the concepts of protobrands and reverse product placement.

@ **Visit the Online Resource Centre to read the abstract and access the full paper.**

corporate name, updating the logo and communications material, and developing the proposition and the business after establishment of the company.

Brand Strategies

Brands constitute a critical part of an organization's competitive strategy, so the development of strategies to manage and sustain them is important. However, the original idea that brands provide a point of differentiation has been supplemented, not replaced, by an understanding of the relational dimension. As we saw in Figure 13.1 through Keller's brand pyramid, brands provide a way in which organizations can create and maintain relationships with customers. Therefore brand strategies need to encompass relationship issues and to ensure that the way a customer relates to a brand, including the meanings they assign, offers opportunities for cross-selling customers into other offerings in an organization's portfolio.

Brand Positioning

We saw in Chapter 6 that a comprehensive segmentation strategy involves targeting and positioning brands. Positioning is concerned with the processes associated with creating and altering the perceptions consumers have about a firm's products or brands (Crawford, 1985). In other words, brand positioning is not about a brand's physicality, it is about the place the brand occupies in a consumer's mind (Ries and Trout, 1972).

Brand positioning is a strategic activity that is used to differentiate and distinguish a brand, so that a consumer understands the brand, not just remembers it. As Tudor and Negricea (2012) rightly state, branding and positioning are interrelated. A credible position cannot be sustained without a strong brand, and a brand cannot be developed or preserved without the audience perceiving a justifiable position.

In addition to the largely transactional positioning strategies set out in Chapter 6, some brands attempt to position themselves as relational brands. The aim is to attract relationship-orientated buyers—people who, as Crosby (2012: 10) indicates, appreciate and seek 'recognition, appreciation, personalization, customization, exceptional customer service, fairness, reciprocity, information sharing, honesty/trustworthiness, cooperative problem solving and harmonious interactions' with their chosen brands.

To help achieve this, brands need to make relational promises. As examples, Crosby (2012: 10) refers to Nordstrom, BMW, Whole Foods, and American Express, whose promise is '… personalized concierge services and travel consultants to help unlock a world of VIP treatment and benefits'. Of course, successful brand positioning is not a one-off activity. Customer interactions and perceptions can alter as contexts evolve. This can mean that brands need to be repositioned and so different, increasingly relational, promises are developed as personal unique positions are sought out.

Brand Name

Choosing a name for a brand is a critical foundation stone because, ideally, it should enable all of the following to be accomplished:

- be easily recalled, spelled, and spoken;
- be strategically consistent with the organization's branding policies;
- be indicative of the offering's major benefits and characteristics;
- be distinctive;
- be meaningful to the customer;
- be capable of registration and protection.

Sometimes a crisis can stimulate a change of name. For example, Research in Motion, or RIM, changed its official name to Blackberry in January 2013 when its share value fell by 90%. Although changing the name alone does not stop the cause of the crisis, it can trigger a change in culture, values, and approach. Brand names need to transfer easily across markets, and to do so successfully it helps if customers can not only pronounce the name but can also recall the name unaided. Problems can arise through interpretation. For example, Traficante is an Italian brand of mineral water, but in Spanish it means drug dealer. Clairol's curling iron 'Mist Stick' had problems when launched in Germany because 'mist' is slang for manure (see Chapter 7).

One of the reasons that high-profile grocery brands are advertised so frequently is to create brand name awareness, so that when a UK customer thinks of pet food they think of Felix or Winalot, or a Swedish customer thinks of Mjau and Doggy. Names that are difficult to spell or pronounce are unlikely to be accepted by customers. Short names such as Lego, Mars, Sony, Flash, or Shell have this strength.

Brand names should have some internal strategic consistency and be compatible with the organization's overall positioning. Ford Transit, Virgin Atlantic, and Cadbury Dairy Milk are names that reflect their parent company's policies that the company name prefixes their product brand names. Some brand names incorporate a combination of words, numbers, or initials. The portable 'sat nav' TomTom Via 130 and Canon's EOS 600D digital camera use names that do not inform about the functionality, but use a combination of words and numbers to reflect the parent company, the product line to which they belong, and a hint of their technological content. A brand's functional benefit can also be incorporated within a name as this helps to convey

Lego is a short name which is easy to pronounce
Source: © Lego.

its distinctive qualities. Deodorant brands such as Sure and Right Guard use this approach, although Lynx relies on imagery plus fragrance and dryness.

Most brands do not have sufficient financial resources to be advertised on TV or in any main-stream media. Therefore it is not possible to convey brand values through imagery and brand advertising. For these brands it is important that the name reflects the functionality of the offering itself. So, the super adhesive brand No More Nails, Cling Film, and Snap-on-Tools all convey precisely what they do through their names. For these brands, packaging and merchandising is important in order to communicate with customers in-store.

Increasingly, brands are being developed through the use of social media. This is essentially about people talking, either spontaneously to one another, through blogs, or through formal or informal communities, about brands that they have experienced in some way. The role of brand

TomTom products do not inform about functionality but reflect the name of the parent company
Source: © TomTom.

managers is to listen to these conversations, and then adapt their brands accordingly (see Chapter 3). What this suggests is that the control and identity of a brand has moved from the brand-owner to the consumer.

Finally, brands can represent considerable value to their owners and so names need to be registered and protected for two main reasons. First, brand name protection helps organizations prevent others from copying and counterfeiting the brand. Although copying products is now commonplace, preventing the use of the brand name helps protect the brand-owners and enables them to maintain aspects of their brand positioning. The second reason for name registration is that the searches required when registering a name mean that the organization will not infringe the rights of others who already own the name. This can avoid costly legal arguments and delays in establishing a brand.

Visit the **Online Resource Centre** and complete Internet Activity 13.3 to learn more about generating brand names.

Rebranding

Brands need to flex according to time and contextual dynamics. Traditionally, this flexing was seen as a managerial reaction or anticipation of changing customer needs, and environmental and competitor conditions. The process is referred to as **rebranding**, and encompasses ideas associated with repositioning a brand. So when Burton Foods rebranded as the Burton Biscuit Company, it was a strategic signal of their innovation focus on biscuits, their past internal achievements, and their international growth ambitions. See also Marketing Insight 13.3.

According to Lambkin and Muzellec (2008), rebranding can be observed at three levels in an organization: corporate, strategic business unit (SBU), and product. These terms are explained in Table 13.1

Table 13.1 Level of rebranding

Level of rebranding	Explanation
Corporate	Refers to the renaming of a whole corporate entity, often signifying a major strategic change or repositioning. Some well-known examples are the merger of United and Continental airlines, to form United, tobacco giant Philip Morris to Altria, and listings company Yell to Hibu.
SBU	Occurs within large corporations where a subsidiary or division within a larger corporation is given a unique name to create a distinct identity separate from the parent. For example, Aviva launched Quotemehappy.com, an internet insurance brand. Alternatively, large organizations seek to realign a division closer to another brand in its portfolio, e.g. hotel group Accor rebranded its Etap brand to Ibis Budget.
Product	Occurs for many reasons, including tactical adjustments in the light of competitor activity, a desire to become a global brand, or to reap economies of scale in marketing communications. For example, the Marathon chocolate bar became Snickers.

Source: Adapted from Lambkin and Muzellec (2008).

Market Insight 13.3

SCA Rebrands and Repositions

Based in Stockholm, SCA is a leading global hygiene and forest products company which develops and produces sustainable personal care, tissue, and forest products. It markets a range of brands across personal care, tissue, packaging, paper for print publications, and solid wood products. It even owns 2.6 million hectares of forest.

In 2007, SCA acquired Procter & Gamble's European tissue business, including the kitchen towel brand Bounty and the toilet tissue brand Charmin. Under the terms of the acquisition contract, SCA were required to rebrand these products.

Bounty was rebranded as Plenty in 2009. The name was designed to convey the product's versatility around the home and so drive greater sales. The Plenty name was also expected to provide synergies across SCA's European markets.

A major £8m campaign was necessary to support the rebrand. A large proportion of this was spent on TV featuring the strapline 'Bounty is now called Plenty—same great towel, brand new name'. In addition, outdoor and press ads were used to communicate the name change and reinforce the message about product versatility. In-store activities including promotional and experiential programmes, were used to drive product trial.

The packaging featured the same easily recognizable logo for continued on-shelf stand-out. It also maintained the new Good Housekeeping Institute seal of approval, as evidence of the product's quality.

A targeted consumer PR campaign was used throughout the year to provide continued awareness and brand credibility. Online, a new brand website (www.plenty.co.uk) was also developed. The overall purpose of the campaign was to reassure consumers that the product maintained the same high performance characteristics and value for money.

In 2010, the toilet tissue brand Charmin was rebranded as Cushelle. This was also supported by a similar £10m campaign. The new brand featured a Cushelle Koala, which was used on the advertising, packaging, and embossed tissue. This character replaced the Charmin Bear. The name and the koala icon were chosen to reflect the product's softness, and to appeal to families and those loyal to Charmin. Each new pack featured a purple swoosh which was labelled 'formerly Charmin'. The message 'same irresistible product, brand new name' was used to reassure consumers. Market share rose by 6.9% and its value by 13.2% within 12 months.

In 2011, in an attempt to attack market leader Andrex, SCA repositioned its toilet tissue brand Velvet from 'soft and sustainable' to an ethical luxury brand. A £10.5m campaign focused on SCA's three trees sustainability initiative, which promises to plant three new trees for every one tree it uses in the production of its products. SCA repositioned both Velvet and Cushelle so that each had a clear point of differentiation to challenge Andrex, which had a broad emotional position for the mass market.

Sources: Anon. (2009b); Baker (2010, 2011); Bolger (2013); www.sca.com

1 To what extent was the repositioning of Velvet necessary in the light of the rebranding of Charmin into Cushelle?

2 Why did SCA stagger the rebranding of the two key brands purchased from Procter & Gamble?

3 Identify two other brands, in a market of your choice, that have been rebranded. Were they successful?

O2's marketing strategy involved them moving away from the functionality of handsets and tariffs to other aspects of their business, such as money, ticketing, and charity initiatives. To support this initiative a new slogan 'Fresh thinking, new possibilities' was developed. This enables the various O2 divisions to put into practice the 'Fresh thinking, new possibilities' principle. A campaign was developed for consumers to share this idea and perceive O2 to be radically different from its competitors (O'Reilly, 2012).

Muzellec and Lambkin (2006) define rebranding as 'the creation of a new name, term, symbol, design or a combination of them for an established brand with the intention of developing a new, differentiated position in the mind of stakeholders and competitors'. This is based on the traditional managerial interpretation of a brand. In the light of ideas about co-creation, rebranding might be better considered, especially at the product level, as something that evolves as stakeholders attribute fresh meanings to a brand.

Brand extensions

Brand extensions are a way of capitalizing on the recognition, goodwill, and any positive associations of an established brand (Hem *et al.*, 2003), and using the name to lever the brand into a new market. Mars successfully leveraged their confectionery bar into the ice-cream market and, in doing so, deseaonalized their sales by providing income in the summer when chocolate sales are normally at their lowest.

The attractiveness of brand extension is that time and money does not need to be spent building awareness or brand values. The key role for marketing communications is to position the new extended brand in the new market and give potential customers a reason to try it.

Successful brands are usually associated with a set of enduring brand values, often co-created by the brand and its loyal customers. These values provide the means through which brand extensions become possible, but understanding these values can be critical. For example, Harley-Davidson's (HD's) values are essentially rugged and masculine, born out of the power and rumble associated with the motorbike. This had contributed to the development of the HD brand but was not understood or recognized when the chain of HD shops began selling wine coolers, baby clothes, and fragrances. This alienated its very loyal customers and the inappropriate products were withdrawn. Harley-Davidson had developed a strong brand by sticking consistently to making big classic US motorbikes and being proud about it. By moving away from this core activity and associating itself, through brand extensions, with categories that did not reflect the strong masculine values, the brand alienated its customers and threatened the strength of the brand itself (Anon., 2006).

Licensing

Brand licensing the trademark of an established brand and using it to develop another brand is proving to be another popular way of using brands. In return for a fee, one company permits another to use its trademark to promote other offerings over a defined period of time in a defined area. Companies such as Disney use licensing because it provides revenue at virtually no cost and constitutes a form of marketing communications that takes the brand to new customers and markets. On the downside, brand licensing can lead to brand proliferation to the extent that the market is swamped with brand messages that fail to position the brand properly. In addition, problems with manufacturing or contractual compliance can lead to costly legal redress.

For a long time licensing was a marketing activity that was the preserve of child-related toys, characters, and clothing. Now licensing is used increasingly with adult brands, such as Gucci, Armani, Coca-Cola, and sports teams such as Manchester United, Formula One, and the Australian national cricket team.

Visit the **Online Resource Centre** and complete Internet Activity 13.4 to learn more about how Disney uses licensing.

Co-branding

Co-branding occurs when two established brands work together on an offering. The principle behind co-branding is that the combined power of the two brands generates increased consumer appeal and attraction. It also enables brands to move into markets and segments where they would normally have great difficulty in establishing themselves. Another reason for co-branding is that it enables organizations to share resources based on their different strengths. The co-branding arrangement between Microsoft and the UK charity NSPCC (National Society for the Prevention of Cruelty to Children) gives the charity access to the financial resources of Microsoft for marketing communications to reach new donors and raise awareness of their cause. Microsoft benefits from its association with a softer brand, one that helps reposition Microsoft as a brand that cares.

Brand Preference or Relevance

Conventional brand strategies are based on competition for **brand preference**. According to Aaker (2012: 44) this is about 'my brand being better than yours' and requires making sure that customers prefer your brand of fruit juice rather than those of your competitors. This is achieved by innovations that lead to claims based on 'faster, cheaper, better", resulting in a more attractive, reliable, or less costly brand promise. Inevitably competitors respond very quickly, nullifying any short-term gains.

Unfortunately, preference strategies have little impact, as the evidence shows that there is little or no shift in sales or market share. This is mainly due to brand and market inertia. Brand preference competition works if the goal is customer retention, but as Aaker (2012: 44) states, 'it can lead to price and margin erosion and a decline into irrelevance".

An alternative, and little used, strategy is to compete on the basis of being the most relevant brand. The key is to create propositions that have particular characteristics that are so attractive to a segment that any competitive offering that does not have the desirable characteristic will be rejected. Aaker refers to these defining characteristics as 'must haves', and they include 'personality, organizational values, social programs, self-expressive benefits, or community benefits'. Aaker refers to innovations such as SalesForce.com advocating cloud computing, Cirque du Soleil reinventing the circus, and Kevlar, the branded ingredient which created a new subcategory in the body armour market.

Competing through **brand relevance** can generate real growth and is far more effective than the 'faster, cheaper, or better' strategies. It requires innovations which lead to the creation of new categories or subcategories, all of which reflect changes in the market and involve substantial risk and new business models, Aaker claims.

Sector Branding

Brands work in different ways according to the prevailing environment. Here we consider branding within services, inter-organizational or business marketing, and global contexts.

Service Brands

The development of brand strategies for services is important simply because the intangibility of services requires that customers be helped to understand the value associated with a service offering. Essentially, a brand provides a snapshot of the value and position offered by a service. Brands convey information about the standard of service and, in doing so, seek to achieve two main goals. First, brands can reduce the uncertainty associated with the purchase of services, especially when there are no tangible elements on which to base purchase decisions. Consider the complexity and risk associated with buying financial services, such as insurance, pensions, and savings products. Developing strong brands enables these risks to be rolled up into a single identity, one that is familiar and trusted. Just think of Virgin Money, a relative newcomer to the financial services market but already well established and growing quickly. The use of sampling and free trials is a popular approach to reducing risk in service-based purchases.

The second goal is to reduce the amount of time people spend searching for a particular service, especially when they are unfamiliar with a particular market or category. When travelling, many visitors to a city will stay at hotels such as Marriott, Travelodge, Holiday Inn, or Hilton because the brands say something about the standard of service that can be expected. Branding shapes customer expectations and can provide a quick answer to a purchase decision. Advertising can also be used to help tangibilize the benefits of a service rather than the features that can be limited or boring, or both. Credit cards often promote the feature of a 0% balance transfer, but they also demonstrate the benefits by showing holidays, electrical goods, or fashion items bought as a result of using the credit card.

Good services branding involves the use of logos and symbols plus straplines and slogans. These can also help to make the intangible more tangible by relating to some of the core benefits a brand offers. Many service providers use their physical facilities to shape the environment so that customers feel at ease and are attracted into the service process. Booms and Bitner (1981) termed this the **servicescape** and refer to the need to consider customer expectations and their emotional states. Branding the environment using signs, colours, clothing, and other physical items can provide recall of previous use of the service provider and also influence customer expectations. Consider the environment and overall design of fast food restaurants such as McDonald's and Burger King. These servicescapes are designed and replicated in high streets across the globe, are easily recognized, and convey information about the type of food offered and the standard of service. Empirical research by Harris and Ezeh (2008) reinforces the view that restaurant managers should actively manage their servicescapes.

The role of marketing communications in the development of these brands is important. Customers use information provided by the organization either to learn about the service provider prior to a service encounter or to reinforce actual brand experience. Marketing communication is used to convey messages not just about product functionality but also the emotional aspects of brands, often referred to as brand personality. Communications help frame customer expectations and so impact on customer experience.

The emotional dimension of service brands has grown in significance as it becomes increasingly difficult to establish and maintain functional differentiation. Through the use of marketing communications, brands seek to develop trust and a positive attachment and identification with a brand's values. This can lead to an emotional preference for a brand and so establish a form of competitive advantage that is difficult to copy. Just as the ownership of prestige brands such as designer fashion brands, trainers, cars, and watches can be used to convey status, so ownership (and display) of many prestige service brands can convey similar status and position—for example, travelling first class, use of platinum credit cards, and being a member of certain clubs or societies.

Finally, not all services are able to develop strong brands; they simply do not have the resources or inclination. However, communications should still be an important part of their marketing. Those delivering services where the credence properties are dominant and customers are unable to distinguish the quality of service can emphasize their professionalism. This can be achieved by displaying certificates and diplomas, having a long list of professional qualifications on their business cards, and referring in their sales literature and websites to the number and types of client they have worked with.

To conclude this section we present a comment made by respondents to a research survey undertaken by Marquardt *et al.* (2011: 54). These services marketing practitioners said that 'the most effective means of building brand meaning for business-to-business services is to promote superior, deeper, and richer customer experiences'. The significance of brand meaning and its link to customer experience is important. We consider customer experience marketing in Chapter 14.

Branding in Business-to-Business Markets

The benefits that can accrue from branding in industrial markets or business-to-business (B2B) marketing (Shipley and Howard, 1993) are no different from those in consumer markets. Some argue that branding in business markets is not appropriate or necessary, but this view is not widely held any more (Kuhn *et al.*, 2008). However, there are some specific B2B context branding issues that can be distilled into four main dimensions: functional and product use benefits, emotional, self-expressive, and relational benefits. These are set out in Table 13.2.

Many people assert that business markets have been slow to develop brands and that B2B product-based branding is a relatively underdeveloped area (Mudambi, 2002). In support of this view, Roper and Davies (2010) remark on the scarcity of true business brands. However, many believe that branding in a B2B context is very often corporate branding rather than product branding, and, more importantly, that branding can influence business purchasing decisions.

There could be many reasons for this underdeveloped use of branding, one of which may be the nature of organizational decision-making processes and associated group activities. Mudambi (2002) concludes that branding is not of equal significance to all organizational buyers, nor is it important in all B2B buying situations. Bendixen *et al.* (2004) and Zablah *et al.* (2010) find that delivery, price, and the services offered are consistently more important to buyers than a brand name.

As a counter argument both Shipley and Howard (1993) and Michell *et al.* (2001) suggest that brand strategies are used widely by B2B organizations. This is primarily because product and corporate branding can be important contributors to successful performance. This is, in part, a reflection of the increasing awareness of the importance of relationships within business

Table 13.2 Benefits derived from branding

Brand benefit	B2B example
Functional advantages	Product performance and high quality associations
	Superior service and support associations
	Specific application and/or location advantages
Emotional advantages	Improved confidence and trust through a reduction in uncertainty.
Self-expressive advantages	Buyer-related personal and professional satisfaction
Relational advantages	Larger and stronger networks and collaboration opportunities

markets. For example, a partnership might develop whereby the brand, among other things, provides reassurance for a buyer, who in turn supports the brand on a regular or even frequent basis and pays the brand's price premium. As a result, business brands not only provide solutions on a continuous basis for certain customers, but they may also become integral to a long-term relationship. Lindgreen *et al.* (2010) observe that organizational buyers make decisions using emotional benefits and self-expressive benefits (such as personal and professional satisfaction) in addition to the functional elements. Indeed, work by Roper and Davies (2010: 584) provides timely empirical evidence that B2B brands can have a demonstrable personality and that 'industrial brands can benefit from the concept of brand image and personality'.

To develop business brands, three core elements need to be managed. These are symbolic devices, communication, and behaviour. Together these might be considered to be the branding mix. In corporate reputation management, these elements are referred to as the Identity Mix (Birkigt and Stadler, 1986). All organizations use symbolism to signal who they are and what they stand for. Logos, company names, straplines, colours, architecture, design, workwear, and delivery vehicles are all symbols. Communication can be considered in terms of management communication (internal and external), organization communication (public relations), and marketing communication. These need to be integrated around a central theme or strategic platform. The behaviour of employees and managers, not only with one another but with external stakeholders, is often overlooked in the branding and reputation management process. One of the key tasks is to align the values employees have with the organization's values, and this requires training, communication, and attention by management. Some of the issues associated with internal branding are discussed later in this chapter.

To build corporate brands, organizations must develop modern integrated communication programmes with all their key stakeholder groups. Stakeholders demand transparency, accountability, and instant, often online, access to news, developments, research, and networks. This means that inconsistent or misleading information must be avoided. In addition, the leading contributors to the strength of a corporate brand are seen to be their products and services, followed by a strong management team, internal communications, public relations, social accountability, change management, and the personal reputation of the CEO.

Table 13.3 B2B Customer clusters	
Name of cluster	Characteristics
Highly tangible	Require messages that stress quantifiable and objective benefits of the product and company
Brand receptive	Require messages that emphasize the support of a well-established and highly reputable manufacturer; the emotional and self-expressive benefits should be stressed
Low-interest	More likely to respond to brand-based communications that highlight the importance of the purchase decision and which are supported with processes and procedures that assist the ordering systems

Source: Adapted from Mudambi (2002).

Mudambi (2002) suggests that there are three types, or clusters, of B2B customers based upon the way they each perceive the importance of branding in the organizational purchase decision process. These are set out in Table 13.3

Communications for the low-interest cluster need to stimulate interest in the offering and associated purchase decision, perhaps by using testimonials and mini-cases highlighting customers who have experienced similar purchase situations.

Internal Branding

Employees are an integral part of a brand, if only because they interact with customers and other stakeholders. They deliver the functional aspects of an organization's offering and they also deliver the emotional dimensions, particularly in service environments. Through interaction with these two elements, long-term relationships between sellers and buyers can develop. Both scholars and practitioners rightly emphasize the need to integrate internal audiences in brand development.

This process, whereby employees are encouraged to communicate with stakeholders so that organizations ensure that what is promised is realized by customers, is referred to as 'living the brand'. Welch and Jackson (2007) consider some of the issues associated with internal communication. They suggest that internal corporate communication refers to communication between an organization's strategic managers and its internal stakeholders, with the purpose of promoting *commitment* to the organization, a sense of *belonging* (to the organization), *awareness* of its changing environment, and *understanding* its evolving goals, such as that operated by Convergys and at White Stuff.

The success of many corporate and service brands is founded on the strength of the internal dimension. The greater the degree to which staff believe and uphold the values, mission, and vision of an organization, the more likely reputation and performance goals will be achieved. Slowly, more energy is being put into the internal aspect of B2B marketing activities.

Global Branding

Brands can be considered in terms of the markets they operate in, sometimes referred to as scope. **Brand scope** can vary from operating in local and domestic markets, to selected foreign markets, and across a range of international markets. Townsend *et al.* (2010) provide a useful typology of brands (see Table 13.4).

The scope or reach of a brand is a result of decisions to enter different geographical regions to achieve particular goals. As organizations extend their scope, so their branding and marketing strategies must adapt to influence local cultures and customer needs. However, global branding is characterized by a consistency of marketing strategies—a transfer of the same strategy across all markets as practised by IBM, AT&T, and China Mobile. See Market Insight 13.4 for the attraction of Western luxury brands to consumers in China and India.

Table 13.4 A hierarchy of brand scope

Brand scope	Criteria and characteristics	Examples
Domestic Brand	A brand with a presence only in the home market and managed locally	White Stuff Timothy Taylor Thornton's William Hill
International brand	Sold across a few country markets and managed largely by the home market, often using local agents in international markets Positioning, identity, image, distinguishing characteristics including attributes, associations, and identifiers of the brand virtually identical to the home market	Eddie Stobart Ideal Standard
Multidomestic brand	Sold across multiple country markets and managed through decentralized management with local control Positioning, identity, image, distinguishing characteristics including attributes, associations, and identifiers of the brand varying across markets	Ferrero Samsung Philips Diageo GM Caterpillar
Global brand	Sold across multiple country markets with distribution located in three major developed continents; centralized brand management coordinates local execution The core essence of the brand remains unchanged; positioning, identity, image, distinguishing characteristics including attributes, associations, and identifiers maintain a high degree of consistency across worldwide markets	Coca Cola McDonald's IBM Apple Google

Source: Adapted from Townsend *et al.* (2010).

Research Insight 13.4

To take your learning further, you might wish to read this influential paper.

Holt, D. B., Quelch, J. A., and Taylor, E. L. (2004), 'How global brands compete',
Harvard Business Review, **82(9), 68–81.**

This is an important paper which all those interested in global marketing and global brands should read. The authors review the ways global brands compete and reflect on the need for companies to manage their national identities as well as their 'globalness'.

Visit the **Online Resource Centre** to read the abstract and access the full paper.

One of the most influential advocates of global branding was Theodore Levitt, whose work on globalization is considered in Chapter 7. Levitt (1983) argued that a global market for uniform products and services requires transnational organizations to standardize their products, packaging, and communications to achieve a common positioning that would be effective across cultures. Growth was to be achieved by selling standardized products all over the world (Holt *et al.*, 2004). However, there are few pure examples of this practice, as even 'global' brands such as McDonald's and Coca-Cola adjust their propositions to suit some local market needs.

The way in which an organization manages its brands and associated products with respect to one another is known as a brand portfolio. According to Townsend *et al.* (2009), citing Douglas *et al.* (2001), it seems as if global branding has become more significant, as they observe organizations focusing on core brands and implementing brand portfolio structures to encourage brand consistency across international markets. However, as different brands within a portfolio are targeted at different market segments, including different geographical markets, it is not unusual for global companies such as Samsung and Toyota to carry international brands within the portfolio.

In addition to the economics of globalization, prestige and status advantages are associated with global brands, which also manifest themselves in terms of improving brand equity (Johansson and Ronkainen, 2005), higher quality, prestige, and intention to purchase (Steenkamp *et al.*, 2003).

Whatever the merits, the purity of the global brand concept has not been entirely realized as issues of adaptation to local market needs has led to a need to achieve a balance between these two extremes. For example, Coca Cola adapt the taste to meet the needs of local markets, even across Europe. So, as the consumption of different offerings naturally varies across countries (e.g. chocolate, milk, coffee, cars), it is unsurprising that we find manufacturers and producers vary their marketing strategies. What this means is that marketers need to determine which elements can be standardized (e.g. products, name, packaging, service), and which need to be adapted to meet local needs, typically language, communications, and voice-overs.

Visit the **Online Resource Centre** and follow the weblinks to see how Interbrand and Millward Brown rank the world's top 100 brands.

Market Insight 13.4

Appealing Luxury Products

Many luxury products have their roots in Western economies. Of the many factors that constitute luxury products, history, geography, and quality are regarded as critical attributes. This suggests that location or country of origin is important and might be a barrier for some countries wishing to produce luxury products.

As countries such as China and Brazil experience rapid economic growth, many of the wealthy in these regions like to purchase luxury brands. This is a way of signalling their success and preference for high-quality products. For example, during the years when the Chinese economy grew rapidly, sales of Western luxury brands, such as Louis Vuitton, Gucci, Omega, Versace, Hugo Boss, and Burberry, boomed and became popular with the newly rich.

In China today, different types of luxury brands can be identified. For the really affluent there are low-profile exclusive luxury niche brands, and there are also emerging brands, created by independent designers, many of whom have yet to have a world presence.

Increasingly, rich Chinese seek out luxury brands that have a long history, very high prices, and a low profile, even to the point of no logo or identifying marks. For example, once the very wealthy Chinese used to drink Château Lafite Rothschild; now they prefer the wine brand La Tache, an as yet little known super-premium brand produced in Bourgogne, France.

Mass luxury brands such as Louis Vuitton and Gucci are now perceived to be unsuitable, partly because they are available throughout the world. Brands such as Marco Polo, Joop, and the German handbag-maker Bree are regarded as emerging brands, and are often discovered through overseas visits and word of mouth. Chinese consumers, particularly those in key urban areas, now seek uniqueness and individualism in the brands they choose to buy.

In 2012, the Indian government allowed foreign companies to establish majority-owned (more than

Handbag maker Bree, made in Germany, loved in China
Source: © Bree.

51% shareholding) single-brand stores in India on the condition that they would source 30% of their products from Indian vendors. This poses a problem for some luxury brands such as Louis Vuitton, who, although they source products from India, hesitate to set up a manufacturing base there.

Sources: Liu (2012); Rathmore (2012).

1 What might be the future for mass luxury products if they are available everywhere to everyone?

2 Why might some luxury brands not wish to set up a manufacturing base in India?

3 Identify three similar products from three luxury brands and identify their country of manufacture.

Brand Equity

Brand equity is a measure of the value and strength of a brand. It is an assessment of a brand's wealth, sometimes referred to as goodwill. Financially, brands consist of their physical assets plus a sum that represents their reputation or goodwill, with the latter far exceeding the former. So, when Premier Foods, who own Branston sauces and Ambrosia Creamed Rice, paid £1.2bn to buy Rank Hovis McDougall (RHM), who own Oxo, Hovis, and Mr Kipling cakes, in 2006, they bought the physical assets and the reputation of RHM brands, the sales of which amount to £1.6bn annually (OFT, 2007).

Brand equity is considered important because of the increasing interest by various stakeholders in measuring the return on promotional investments and pressure to value brands for balance sheet purposes. A brand with a strong equity is more likely to be able to preserve its customer loyalty and fend off competitor attacks.

There are two main views about how brand equity should be valued—from a financial and from a marketing perspective (Lasser *et al.*, 1995). The financial view is founded on a consideration of a brand's asset value that is based on the net value of all the cash the brand is expected to generate over its lifetime. The marketing perspective is grounded in the images, beliefs, and core associations consumers have about particular brands, and the degree of loyalty or retention a brand is able to sustain. Measures of market awareness, penetration, involvement, attitudes, and purchase intervals (frequency) are typical. However, Feldwick (1996) suggests that there are three factors associated with brand equity:

- brand value, based on a financial and accounting base;
- brand strength, measuring the strength of a consumer's attachment to a brand;
- brand description, represented by the specific attitudes customers have towards a brand.

Brand equity is strongly related to marketing and brand strategy because this type of measurement can help focus management on brand development. However, there is little agreement about what is to be measured and how and when it is measured. Ambler and Vakratsas (1998) argue that organizations should not seek a single set of measures simply because of the varying circumstances and contextual factors that impinge on brand performance. In reality, the measures used by most firms share many common elements.

Stahl *et al.* (2012) researched the relationship between brand equity and customer lifetime value (CLV), composed of customer acquisition, retention, and profitability. They found that brand equity has a 'predictable and meaningful impact on CLV'. They conclude that brand equity is a multidimensional concept, because the components of brand equity exert different effects on acquisition, retention, and profit. Most interestingly, they suggest that brand management and customer management should be integrated, so that they work together in organizations and are not separated.

Chapter Summary

To consolidate your learning, the key points from this chapter are summarized here.

- **Explain the characteristics and principal types of brands and branding.**

  Brands are products and services that have added value. Brands help customers to differentiate between the various offerings and to make associations with certain attributes or feelings with a particular brand. There are three main types of brands: manufacturer, distributor, and generic.

- **Examine how branding has evolved, utilizing relational and co-creation perspectives.**

  Definitions and types of brands (e.g. virtual brands) have evolved and emerged as potentially powerful socio-cultural concepts in which relational and community issues replace the former managerial perspective involving senders and receivers, and the control of one party over another. A co-created brand, or customer branding, can be seen when a customer attaches a name, term, or other feature that enables them to identify one seller's good or service as distinct from those of other sellers.

- **Explain how brands work through associations and personalities.**

  Brands are capable of triggering associations in the minds of consumers. These associations may sometimes enable consumers to construe a psychosocial meaning associated with a particular brand. This psychosocial element can be measured in terms of the associations consumers make in terms of five key dimensions: sincerity, excitement, competence, sophistication, and ruggedness. Brand personality provides a form of identity for consumers that expresses symbolic meaning for themselves and for others.

- **Understand different aspects of brand strategy and policies.**

  Brand strategies need to encompass relationship issues and to ensure that the way a customer relates to a brand, including the meanings they assign, offers opportunities for cross-selling customers into other products and services in an organization's portfolio. Brand names, policies, and relevance strategies are important.

- **Describe the principal issues associated with branding in services, business, and global contexts.**

  Branding is important in various sectors. These include services, because the intangibility of services requires that customers are helped to understand the value associated with a service offering. In business markets, branding is increasingly regarded as important because research shows that buyers make decisions based on emotional benefits and self-expressive benefits, not just on utilitarian elements. The management of global brands requires that there is brand consistency across all markets.

- **Explore the issues and activities associated with brand equity and demonstrate why branding is important to marketing managers.**

  Brand equity is a measure of the value of a brand. It is an assessment of a brand's wealth, sometimes referred to as goodwill. Financially, brands consist of their physical assets plus a sum that represents their reputation or goodwill, with the latter far exceeding the former. There are two main views about how brand equity should be valued, namely financial and marketing perspectives.

Review Questions

1. How have definitions of brands changed over the past 50 years?
2. What is the difference between intrinsic and extrinsic attributes?
3. Why is branding important to consumers and organizations?

4 What are the main types of brand?

5 Why is it necessary to consider the broad context of consumers' lives in order to understand the role and relationship that brands play in them?

6 Explain the phrase coined by Ballantyne and Aitken (2007) that 'brand meanings are socially constructed'.

7 What is a protobrand and why are they significant?

8 What are Aaker's five dimensions of psychosocial meaning?

9 What is the difference between preference and relevance brand strategies?

10 Write brief notes explaining the two main views about brand equity.

Worksheet Summary

To apply the knowledge you have gained from this chapter and test your understanding of branding decisions visit the **Online Resource Centre** and complete Worksheet 13.1.

Discussion Questions

1 Having read Case Insight 13.1 at the beginning of this chapter, how would you advise BRAND sense agency to develop a sensory marketing campaign for its retail bank client? Consider sight, sound, and smell not only for the brand itself but also for the retail environment of the bank.

2 If brands are capable of having a personality, are they therefore susceptible to personality disorders? Justify your answer.

3 When Ingrid Stevenson was appointed brand manager for a range of well-established fruit juices, one of her first tasks was to understand the market and how consumers related to the brand. How might an understanding of Aaker's brand personality scale help her in this task?

4 To what extent are ideas about co-creation and socially constructed meaning relevant to business-to-business brands?

5 The British celebrity chef Gordon Ramsay owns and runs a series of high-profile restaurants. He is opening restaurants worldwide, stars in his own ground-breaking chef/food-based TV programmes, and has a number of books and other business interests. Discuss the view that celebrities cannot be brands as they do not meet the common brand criteria.

References

Aaker, D. A. (1991), *Managing Brand Equity*, New York: Free Press.

Aaker, D. A. (2012), 'Win the brand relevance battle and then build competitor barriers', *California Management Review*, 54(2), 43–57.

Aaker, J. (1997), 'Dimensions of brand personality', *Journal of Marketing Research*, 34, 347–56.

AMA (2012) Dictionary Definition, retrieve from: http://www.marketingpower.com/_layouts/Dictionary.aspx?dLetter=B accessed 2 November 2012.

Ambler, T., and Vakratsas, D. (1998), 'Why not let the agency decide the advertising', *Market Leader*, 1, 32–7.

Anon. (2006), Extension brand failures: Harley Davidson perfume', 5 November, retrieve from: http://brandfailures.blogspot.com/2006/11/extension-brand-failures-harley.html accessed 13 July 2013.

Anon. (2009a), 'Creative solution: Finlandia', *Campaign*, 4 September, 24.

Anon. (2009b), 'Bounty returns as Plenty under SCA stewardship', SCA Press Release, 9 February, retrieved from: www.talkingretail.com/products/product-news/bounty-returns-as-plenty-under-sca-stewardship accessed 10 March 2013.

Achenbaum, A. A. (1993), ' The mismanagement of brand equity', in ARF Fifth Annual Advertising and Promotion Workshop, 1 February.

Arora, R. and Stoner, C. (2009), 'A mixed method approach to understanding brand personality', *Journal of Product and Brand Management*, 18(4), 272–83.

Baker, R. (2010), 'Charmin rebrands to Cushelle, *Marketing Week*, 25 January, retrieved from: www.marketingweek.co.uk/charmin-rebrands-to-cushelle/3009084.article accessed 10 March 2013.

Baker, R. (2011), 'Velvet to take on Andrex with new positioning', *Marketing Week*, 27 September, retrieved from: www.marketingweek.co.uk/velvet-to-take-on-andrex-with-new-positioning/3030466.article accessed 10 March 2013.

Ballantyne, D. and Aitken, R. (2007), 'Branding in B2B markets: the service-dominant logic', *Journal of Business and Industrial Marketing*, 22(6), 363–71.

Belk, R. (1988), 'Possessions and the extended self', *Journal of Consumer Research*, 15(2), 139–68.

Bendixen, M., Bukasa, K. A., and Abratt, R. (2004), 'Brand equity in the business-to-business market', *Industrial Marketing Management*, 33, 371–80.

Bengtsson, A. (2003), 'Towards a critique of brand relationships', *Advances in Consumer Research*, 30, 154–8.

Birkigt, K. and Stadler, M. M. (1986) *Corporate Identity, Grundlagen, Funktionen, Fallspielen*, Landsberg am Lech: Verlag Moderne Industrie.

Boehringer, C. (1996), 'How can you build a better brand?', *Pharmaceutical Marketing*, July, 35–6.

Bolger, M. (2013), 'Getting fresh', *Marketer*, March–April, 24–7.

Booms, B. H. and Bitner, M. J. (1981), 'Marketing strategies and organization structure for service firms', in J. H. Donnelly and W. R. George (eds), *The Marketing of Services*, Chicago, IL: American Marketing Association.

Charles, G. (2009), 'Get to grips with the carbon agenda', *Marketing*, 30 September, 26–7.

Clayton, M. and Heo, J. (2011), 'Effects of promotional-based advertising on brand associations', *Journal of Product and Brand Management*, 20(4), 309–15.

Crawford, M. C. (1985), 'A new positioning typology', *Journal of Product Innovation Management*, 2, December, 243–53.

Crosby, L. A. (2012), 'Relational brands', *Marketing Management*, Summer, 10–11.

de Chernatony, L. and Dall'Olmo Riley, F. (1998), 'Defining a brand: beyond the literature with experts' interpretations', *Journal of Marketing Management*, 14(4/5), 417–43.

de Lencastre, P. and Côrte-Real, A. (2010), 'One, two, three: a practical brand anatomy', *Brand Management*, 17(6), 399–412.

Douglas, S. P., Craig, C. S., and Nijssen, E. J. (2001), 'Integrating branding strategy across markets: building international brand architecture, *Journal of International Marketing*, 9(2), 97–114.

Feldwick, P. (1996), 'What is brand equity anyway, and how do you measure it?', *Journal of Marketing Research*, 382, 85–104.

Fournier, S. (1998), 'Consumers and their brands: developing relationship theory in consumer research', *Journal of Consumer Research*, 24(4), 343–73.

Harris, L. C. and Ezeh, C. (2008), 'Servicescape and loyalty intentions: an empirical investigation', *European Journal of Marketing*, 42(3/4), 390–422.

Hem, L., de Chernatony, L., and Iversen, M. (2003) Factors influencing successful brand extensions, *Journal of Marketing Management*, 19(7/8), 781–806.

Holt, D. B., Quelch, J. A. and Taylor, E. L. (2004) 'How global brands compete', *Harvard Business Review*, 82(9), 68–81.

Jin, S-A. A. and Sung, Y. (2010), 'The roles of spokes-avatars' personalities in brand communication in 3D virtual environments', *Brand Management*, 17(5), 317–27.

Johansson, J. K. and Ronkainen, I. A. (2005), 'The esteem of global brands', *Brand Management*, 12(5), 339–54.

Juntunen, M. (2012), 'Co-creating corporate brands in start-ups', *Marketing Intelligence and Planning*, 30(2), 230–49.

Keller, K. L. (1993), 'Conceptualizing, measuring, and managing customer-based brand equity', *Journal of Marketing*, 57(January), 1–22.

Keller, K. L. (1998), *Strategic Brand Management: Building, Measuring, and Managing Brand Equity*, Upper Saddle River, NJ: Prentice-Hall.

Keller, K. L. (2009), 'Building strong brands in a modern marketing communications environment', *Journal of Marketing Communications*, 15(2/3), 139–55.

Kollmann, T. and Suckow, C. (2007), 'The corporate brand naming process in the net economy', *Qualitative Market Research*, 10(4), 349–61.

Kuhn, K-A. L., Alpert, F., and Pope, N. K. L. (2008), 'An application of Keller's brand equity model in a B2B context', *Qualitative Market Research*, 11(1), 40–58.

Lambkin, M. and Muzellec, L. (2008), 'Rebranding in the banking industry following mergers and acquisitions', *International Journal of Bank Marketing*, 26(5), 328–52.

Lasser, W., Mittal, B., and Sharma, A. (1995), 'Measuring customer based brand equity', *Journal of Consumer Marketing*, 12(4), 11–19.

Levitt, T. (1983), 'The globalization of markets', *Harvard Business Review*, May–June, 2–11.

Lindgreen, A., Beverland, M. B., and Farrelly, F. (2010), 'From strategy to tactics: building, implementing, and managing brand equity in business markets', *Industrial Marketing Management*, 39, 1223–5.

Linville, P. and Carlston, D. E. (1994) 'Social cognition of the self', in P. G. Devine, D. L. Hamilton, and T. M. Ostrom (eds), *Social Cognition: Impact on Social Psychology*, San Diego, CA: Academic Press, 143–93.

Liu, J. (2012), 'New generation of luxury brands gets attention', *China Daily*, 8 October, retrieve from: http://www.chinadaily.com.cn/bizchina/2012-10/08/content_15800258.htm accessed 16 November 2012.

Low, G. S. and Lamb C. W. (2000), 'The measurement and dimensionality of brand associations', *Journal of Product and Brand Management*, 9(6), 350–68.

McCracken, G. (1986), 'Culture and consumption: a theoretical account of the structure and movement of the cultural meaning of consumer goods', *Journal of Consumer Research*, 13, 71–84.

Marquardt, A.J., Golicic, S. L., and Davis, D.F. (2011), 'B2B services branding in the logistics services industry', *Journal of Services Marketing*, 25(1), 47–57.

Michell, P., King, J., and Reast, J. (2001), 'Brand values related to industrial products', *Industrial Marketing Management*, 30(5), 415–25.

Mudambi, S. (2002), 'Branding importance in business-to-business markets: three buyer clusters', *Industrial Marketing Management*, 31(6), 525–33.

Muzellec, L. and Lambkin, M. (2006), 'Corporate rebranding: destroying, transferring or creating brand equity?', *European Journal of Marketing*, 40(7/8), 803–24.

Muzellec, L., Lynn, T., and Lambkin, M. (2012), 'Branding in fictional and virtual environments: introducing a new conceptual domain and research agenda', *European Journal of Marketing*, 46(6), 811–26.

OFT (2007), www.oft.gov.uk/shared_oft/mergers_eaoz/361227/premier.pdf, accessed 2 December 2007

O'Reilly, L. (2012), 'O2 brand campaign to trumpet new strategy', *Marketing Week*, 7 March, retrieve from: http://www.marketingweek.co.uk/news/o2-brand-campaign-to-trumpet-new-strategy/4000482.article accessed 13 March 2013.

Pennington, J. R. and Ball, D. A. (2009), 'Customer branding of commodity products: the customer-developed brand', *Brand Management*, 16(7), 455–67.

Phau, I. and Lau, K. C. (2001), 'Brand personality and consumer self-expression: single or dual carriageway?', *Journal of Brand Management*, 8(6), 428–44.

Rathmore, V. (2012), 'Luxury brands set to flaunt "Made-in-India" tag; Indian suppliers see opportunities', *Economic Times*, 3 October 2012, retrieve from: http://articles.economictimes.indiatimes.com/2012-10-03/news/34239005_1_luxury-goods-makers-luxury-brands-single-brand-stores accessed 16 November 2012.

Ries, A. and Trout, J. (1972), 'The positioning era cometh', *Advertising Age*, 24 April, 35–8.

Roberts, J. (2010), 'Young, connected and Muslim', *Marketing Week*, 24 June, retrieve from: http://www.marketingweek.co.uk/young-connected-and-muslim/3014934.article accessed 9 November 2012.

Roper, S. and Davies, G. (2010), 'Business to business branding: external and internal satisfiers and the role of training quality', *European Journal of Marketing*, 44(5), 567–90.

Shipley, D. and Howard, P. (1993), 'Brand-naming industrial products', *Industrial Marketing Management*, 22(1), 59–66.

Stahl, F., Heitmann, M., Lehmann, D. R., and Neslin, S. A. (2012), 'The impact of brand equity on customer acquisition, retention and profit margin', *Journal of Marketing*, 76 (July), 44–63.

Steenkamp, J. E., Batra, R., and Alden, D. L. (2003), 'How perceived brand globalness creates brand value', *Journal of International Business Studies*, 34(1), 53–65.

Townsend, J. D., Cavusgil, S. T., and Baba, M. L. (2010), 'Global integration of brands and new product development at General Motors, *Journal of Product Innovation Management*, 27, 49–65.

Tudor, E. and Negricea, I. C. (2012), 'Brand positioning—a marketing resource and an effective tool for small and medium enterprises, *Journal of Knowledge Management, Economics and Information Technology*, 11(1), 182–90.

Welch, M. and Jackson, P. R. (2007), 'Rethinking internal communication: a stakeholder approach', *Corporate Communications*, 12(2), 177–98.

Zablah, A. R., Brown, B. P., and Donthu, N. (2010), 'The relative importance of brands in modified rebuy purchase situations', *International Journal of Research in Marketing*, 27(3), 248–60.

Chapter 14
Managing Relationships and Customer Experiences

Learning Outcomes

After studying this chapter you should be able to:

▶ Appreciate the nature of perceived value, and describe the differences between the transactional and the relationship approach to marketing

▶ Describe what is meant by the term service processes, 'service encounters', and the principles associated with measuring service quality

▶ Outline the principles and economics of customer retention and consider the merits of loyalty programmes

▶ Understand the principles of trust, commitment, and customer satisfaction, and explain how they are interlinked

▶ Explain the term 'customer experiences', how it has evolved, and how it might be measured

Case Insight 14.1

RAKBANK is the highly successful National Bank of Ras Al-Khaimah in the United Arab Emirates. We speak to Banali Malhotra, Head of Marketing, to find out how they sought to improve their customer relationships.

It is very difficult these days to get by without a credit card. Hotel bookings, car rentals, holidays, entertainment, and internet purchases are nearly impossible to make without these pieces of plastic. At RAKBANK, the highly successful National Bank of Ras Al-Khaimah in the United Arab Emirates, our strategy involved us entering the fiercely competitive credit card market. This market was dominated by our competitors' use of Gold and Platinum credit cards. These were positioned on a prestige platform and, supported by a range of associated privileges, but they all required an annual fee and various extra charges.

The problem we faced was that customers resented paying these fees and were disenchanted with the financial services community. This dissatisfaction was rooted in the hidden charges and the service fees that were nearly always glossed over in the marketing communications used by our competitors. Their messages centred on financial freedom and desirable lifestyles, but there is no mention of their gratuitous annual fees, extortionate interest rates, complicated cancellation procedures, and poor customer service.

RAKBANK was a late entrant into this overcrowded and disgruntled market and we needed to find a strong point of differentiation, something that would resonate with our customers and encourage them to value and maintain their relationship with RAKBANK.

Our research indicated that there was a need for a premium product, one that offered the prestige perception and privileges, but at a cost advantage to customers. This suggested that something between the Gold and Platinum cards, which currently dominated the market, might be successful. We also needed customers to evaluate the RAKBANK offering by comparing products on the basis of their features and benefits, and service, but not price.

RAKBANK identified four main segments. These are credit card customers, business entrepreneurs, high-net-worth individuals, and local people who need personal loans. We developed our strategy on the well-established principle that the delivery of high product quality and above-average service levels leads to improved customer satisfaction levels. This in turn promotes higher levels of customer perceived value. We believed that once customers experienced our superior customer service, they would be more likely to take up other product offerings from RAKBANK. However, we needed to find a range of incentives to first attract and then retain customers, and so realize higher revenues from the lifetime value generated by these customers.

Suggest a name for a credit card that RAKBANK could use to enter the market. What key product incentives are necessary to attract and retain customers?

Introduction

Have you ever said to a friend when leaving a gig or a theme park or when watching a DVD, 'Wow that was great, what a fantastic experience'? If you have, then it is likely that the event has given you a memorable and positive emotional feeling. These are referred to as **customer experiences**.

Although ideas about the importance of providing a superior customer experience have only emerged in recent years, companies such as RAKBANK in the UAE now recognize its importance. The goals are to drive up customer service and enable customers to associate great experiences with their brand. However, this contemporary approach is currently practised by only a small, but increasing, number of organizations.

To understand this development, we must explore ideas about customer value, build on our knowledge of services, and then explore issues related to relationship marketing. All of these concepts have made significant contributions to the rise of customer experience marketing. As we saw in Chapter 8, services are important because they impact immediately on people and their perception of an organization. Therefore it is important to understand how marketing activities enhance the performance of service providers.

In this chapter, we consider service processes, and how these impact on the **service encounter**, the point at which a service is provided and simultaneously consumed. We also look at service marketing and how services can be measured. Before reading further, it may help to read the section on service characteristics in Chapter 8.

Relationship marketing focuses on the nature of the relationship and interaction between buyers and sellers (largely in inter-organizational contexts), not products and prices. The more frequent and intense these exchanges become, the more the strength of the relationships between buyers and sellers increases. It is this fundamental relational perspective that has provided the infrastructure for understanding and developing this different approach to marketing, which has evolved into customer experience marketing.

Understanding Perceived Value

Customers buy offerings for the benefits that arise from using them. Customers do not buy products and services purely for their features. They buy offerings that enable them to do what they want to achieve. Consumers do not buy toothpaste just because it has a red stripe or a minty taste. What they buy is a clean mouth, fresh breath, or white gleaming teeth, depending on their segment characteristics. In the same way, business customers buy solutions to business problems, not stand-alone products. These benefits and solutions constitute value-for-customers, and represent the main reasons why one offering is selected in preference to another. For both consumers and business customers, value is determined by maximizing the benefits they can achieve and by reducing or minimizing the sacrifices associated with an offering. **Perceived value** equates to benefits minus the sacrifices, or the 'net satisfaction' derived from consuming and using an offering, not just the costs involved in obtaining it.

Another way of viewing these solutions and benefits is to consider them as (customer) needs. Customers seek to satisfy their needs through their purchase of offerings. Therefore by satisfying these needs it becomes possible to deliver value for customers.

Kothandaraman and Wilson (2001) argue that the creation of value is dependent on an organization's ability to deliver high performance on the benefits that are important to the customer, and this, in turn, is rooted in their competency in technology and business processes, or core competences. Doyle (2000) suggests that customer value should be based on three principles.

1 Customers will choose between alternative offerings and select the one that (they perceive) will offer them the best value.

2 Customers do not want product or service features; they want their needs met.

3 It is more profitable to have a long-term relationship between a customer and a company than a one-off transaction.

Value is the customer's estimate of the extent to which an offering can satisfy their needs. For example, RAKBANK's customers determine the value of the bank's service, as they consider alternative solutions and weigh up the benefits and costs associated with RAKBANK's proposition and service delivery, relative to their needs. Therefore, value is relative to a customer's needs, expectations, and experience of competitive offerings. Value can be derived from sources other than propositions and prices. For example, value can be generated through the provision of additional services, such as:

- training or support facilities, for example those normally provided by Carphone Warehouse for their customers;

- through association with a highly regarded brand, for example the co-branding arrangements between Adidas and Porsche and between Disney and Mattel;

- legal or insurance provision, for example the financial support provided by government and some regional councils for start-up entrepreneurs and small businesses;

- joint working relationships between government and building/finance schemes such as those associated with the Private Finance Initiative.

Menon *et al.* (2005) refer to these as add-on benefits and suggest that they may be more important than the core benefit arising from proposition and price attributes. However, above all else it is the relationships between buyers and sellers that are considered to represent real value (Simpson *et al.*, 2001), if only because they are longer lasting and difficult for competitors to copy or destroy. Indeed, the creation and the sharing of value are regarded as critical aspects of buyer–seller relationships (Anderson, 1995).

Lefaix-Durand *et al.* (2009) point out that that the customer value concept should be considered from two complementary perspectives. These are *value-to-customers* and *value-of-customers*. *Value-to-customers* focuses on the net value customers realize from using the offerings provided by suppliers. *Value-of-customers* assumes a supplier's perspective of the net value they derive from their customers (Ulaga and Eggert, 2005). Emerging ideas about value are driven largely by the service-dominant logic (SDL) group, introduced in Chapters 1 and 8. This perspective considers relationships as a function of value, or what is known as value-in-use.

Grönroos (2009) argues that value cannot be created by suppliers but can only be realized by customers when utilized through the use of their own processes, resources, and capabilities. Grönroos considers that value should be considered to consist of two fundamental elements; value propositions and value creation. Suppliers develop *value propositions* which are essentially suggestions or promises of value embedded in their offerings. Customers fulfill *value creation* when incorporating offferings into their processes. For example, the benefits (value) arising from the use of a manufacturing software system only occur once the system is installed and operationalized by a manufacturer. So, a software developer might offer (the value proposition) to tailor their software to meet the needs of a particular buyer and install it for them. This means that the system can be installed faster and more accurately, and be of greater benefit to the buyer, than a system that is not tailored to their needs. The manufacturer only derives value when the software system is running and supporting their manufacturing processes.

Suppliers can assist customers by creating opportunities to engage with their value-generating processes. The level of interaction between the parties might vary from zero to the full participation that is co-creation. So, a spectrum of different value propositions can be considered, leading to various forms of value creation.

Movement along the continuum can be interpreted as a change in the way value is created. Ribeiro *et al*. (2009) identify four core value strategies. These are exchange (or commodity) value, added-value, performance-value, and value co-creation strategies.

- **Commodity-value**—transactional exchange relationships are characterized by an exchange of basic resources. Sellers provide a core offering, but it is buyers who assume full responsibility and the resources to create the value they require out of the resources transacted.

- **Added-value**—suppliers can choose to provide buyers with resources necessary to help them create the required value. This approach is referred to as an 'added value' strategy and examples include providing training, financial assistance, or installation support. As a result of these interactions, parties become closer and stronger, so that the original value perceived in the exchange of propositions and prices gradually gives way to a focus on the relationship, which itself becomes of value.

- **Performance-value**—further along the continuum organizations provide 'performance value' strategies. Here, value is created by the activities of buyers and sellers working together for mutual benefit, but value is still passed from one to another. Also known as value-in-use, examples include joint product development and projects to enhance the buyer's software systems, and processes and initiatives designed to improve manufacturing efficiencies (see Market Insight 14.1).

Market Insight 14.1

Cisco Brings Performance Value

Cisco, said to be the world's largest manufacturer and supplier of networking equipment, has created a virtual organization designed to provide added value and efficiencies in the value chain, for all business partners, suppliers, and customers. Part of this strategy has been accomplished through its use of web-based applications that focus on internet, intranet, and extranet applications, designed to link all aspects of its value network.

For example, the company openly encourages its customers' engineers to solve their technical problems through use of Cisco's self-help web-based technical support pages and network configurator. By making these facilities easy to use, not only is Cisco better placed to manage staffing (time and costs) required for technical support, but it also encourages customers to become more involved in Cisco applications, allowing them to reduce their own organization's systems difficulties. As a result, customer organizations are able to share technical knowledge, and through their satisfaction provide positive word-of-mouth referrals.

Sources: http://www.cisco.com/cisco/web/support/index.html
https://learningnetwork.cisco.com/community/certifications
http://www.cisco.com/web/learning/le27/learning_learning_
partner_connection_home.html

Market Insight 14.1
continued

1 Identify the key elements that support the relationship between Cisco and its customers' engineers.

2 What might be the disadvantages associated with the Cisco approach of involving customers in the process?

3 Think of ways in which Cisco might co-create value with a major cable manufacturer.

Cisco, the world's largest manufacturer and supplier of networking equipment, created a virtual organization to provide added value and efficiencies in the value chain

Source: © Cisco (2013).

- **co-creation value**—collaborative relationships are characterized by value that is created by both parties as a form of co-production or through 'value co-creation' (Sheth and Uslay, 2007). This occurs where both organizations work together for mutual benefit, and value is generated together, not traded by a supplier to a buyer as in performance value. More information about these different value strategies can be seen in Table 14.1.

  Visit the **Online Resource Centre** and complete Internet Activity 14.1 to learn more about how the Automobile Association (AA) uses its interactive website to provide added-value services and information to AA members.

Table 14.1 Characteristics of value strategies

Defining characteristics	Value Strategies			
	Commodity	Value added	Performance	Value co-creation
Value-generating drivers	Product quality Delivery performance Market price	Service support Personal interactions Product and service quality	The konw-how of others Time to market Performance from both (costs, revenues, productivity)	Joint and radical innovation Leveraging new competencies
Management intention	Attract and satisfy	Customer retention (implicit: profit, satisfaction, loyalty, risk, reduction, etc.)	Interactions to establish, develop and facilitate cooperative relationship and mutual benefit	Coordinating relationships among companies in a network to seek new resources and value networks
Duration Adaptation	Discrete Little or no adaptation	Continous, but discrete hiring Process adaptations	Continous and long-term contracts Process adaptations	Continous, mutual cooperation contracts Adaptations and business creation
Description of value offering	'We offer good products and competitive prices'	'We offer excellence'	'We customize, we build on order for the customer'	'Our customers, suppliers and other partners got us here and will take us wherever it need be to generate value'
Management structure	Functional hierarchial: marketing, sales, R&D, etc.	Process and functions like: customer service manager. CRM manager	Customer and market managers/ cross-functions and levels	Business managers
Capabilites	Production Delivery Promoting-communicating Process leverage Relationship Mastery and integration into the customer's business model Radical innovation Setting up networks			

Source: Ribeiro et al. (2009).

Service Processes

Having considered ideas about value and value creation, we now turn our attention first to services, and then to relationships. Services are considered to be processes, and a substantial part of the academic literature on services is based on a process perspective. A process is a series of sequential actions that leads to pre-determined outcomes. So, a simple process might be the steps necessary to visit a dentist, whereas a complex process might be the actions necessary to manage passengers on a two-week luxury cruise.

If processes are an integral part of the operations performed by service organizations, in the general sense, what are they processing? Lovelock *et al.* (1999) argue that these processes are directly related to two variables. First, the intensity of the equipment used to deliver a service and, second, the intensity of people involved in the provision of the service. On the one hand, a haircut is people intensive but the failure of a network server is equipment oriented. Lovelock *et al.* present a four-cell categorization of services based on tangible and intangible actions on people's bodies, minds, and physical assets. The categories involve four different processes: people processing, possession processing, mental stimulus processing, and information processing.

People Processing

In this type of processing people have to present themselves physically so that they become immersed within the service process. This involves them spending varying amounts of time actively cooperating with the service operation. So, people taking a train have to physically go to the station and get on a train and spend time getting to their destination. People undergoing dentistry work will have made an appointment prior to attending the dentist's surgery, will sit in the chair and open their mouths, and cooperate with the dentist's various requests. They have physically become involved in the **service process** offered by their dentist.

From a marketing perspective, consideration of the process and the outcomes arising from participation in the service process can lead to ideas about what benefits are being created and what non-financial costs are incurred as a result of the service operation. For the dentistry example, a comfortable chair, background music, non-threatening or neutral to warm decor, and a pleasant manner can be of help.

Possession Processing

Just as people have to go to the service operation for people processing, so objects have to become involved in possession processing. Possessions such as kitchen gadgets, gardens, cars, and computers are liable to break down or need maintenance. Cleaning, storing, and repairing, plus couriering, installation, and removal services are typical possession-processing activities.

In these situations, people will either take an item to the service provider, or invite someone in to undertake the necessary work. In possession processing the level of customer involvement is limited compared with people processing. In most cases the sequence of activities is as follows. For an object to be attended to, a telephone call is often required to fix an appointment. Then the item either needs to be taken to the service provider or the customer must wait for an attendant to visit. A brief to explain the problem/task/solution is given before returning at an agreed time/location to pay and take away the repaired item. This detachment from the service process enables people to focus on other tasks. The key difference here is that the quality of the service is not dependent on the presence of the owner or representative of the possession while the service operation takes place.

Mental Stimulus Processing

These types of service try to shape attitudes or behaviour. To achieve this, these services have to be oriented to people's minds, hence the expression mental stimulus processing. So, examples of these types of services are education, entertainment, professional advice, and news. In all of these, people have to become involved mentally in the service interaction and give time to experience the benefits of this type of service.

Service delivery can be through one of two locations. First, services can be created in a location that is distant to the receiver. In this case, media channels are used to deliver the service. Alternatively, services can be delivered and consumed at the point at which they originate, i.e. in a studio, theatre, or hall. One of the key differences here is the form and nature of the audience experience. The theatre experience is likely to be much richer than the distant format. Digital technology has enabled opportunities for increased amounts of interactive communication, even though the experience will be different from the original. In the same way, online or e-learning in its purest form has not yet become an established format, perhaps because learners need to spend some of their learning time in interaction with their co-learners and in the presence of a tutor, for example the use of summer schools operated by the Open University and the increasing success of blended learning programmes.

Information Processing

The final type of service concerns information processing, the most intangible of all the services. Transformed by advances in technology, and computers in particular, information processing has become quicker, more accurate, and more frequent. The use of technology is important, but we should not exclude people, as individuals have a huge capacity to process information. For example, one key issue that RAKBANK and other organizations need to consider concerns the degree to which people should become involved in information processing. They could deliberately route customers away from people processing by reducing the number of clerks and counters, and into information processing by pushing online and ATM operations: easyJet reduces costs by making it difficult for customers to telephone the company and seek advice from expensive staff. Their approach is to drive people to their website and use the FAQs to answer customer queries.

Service Encounters

The development of service marketing strategies involves understanding the frequency and the ways in which customers contact service providers. Once this is understood, strategies that maintain required levels of service can be developed, but the processes and linkages that bring the elements of the services marketing mix and associated systems together can be reformulated. Therefore service marketing strategy should be based on insight into the ways in which customers interact with or contact a service. The form and nature of the customer encounter is of fundamental importance.

A **service encounter** is best understood as a period of time during which a customer interacts directly with a service (Shostack, 1985). These interactions may be short and encompass all the actions necessary to complete the service experience. Alternatively, they may be protracted, involve several encounters, several representatives of the service provider, and indeed several locations in order for the service experience to be completed. Whatever their length, the quality of a service encounter impacts on perceived service value which, in turn, influences customer satisfaction (Gil *et al.* 2008).

Originally the term 'encounter' was used to describe the personal interaction between a service provider and customers. A more contemporary interpretation needs to include all those interactions that occur through people and their equipment and machines with the people and equipment belonging to the service provider (Glyn and Lehtinen, 1995) as set out in Market Insight 14.2. As a result, three levels of customer contact can be observed: high-contact services, medium-contact services, and low-contact services (see Table 14.2). This demarcation of customer contact levels is necessary because it provides a sound base on which to develop services marketing activities.

One of the interesting developments in recent years is the decision by some organizations to move their customers from high-contact to low-contact services. Clear examples of this are to be found in the banking sector, with first ATMs, then telephone banking, and now internet banking, all of which either lower or remove personal contact with bank employees. Further examples include vending machines, self or rapid checkout facilities in hotels, and online ticket purchases.

Visit the **Online Resource Centre** and follow the weblink to the British Bankers Association (BBA) to learn more about the marketing of financial services.

 # Market Insight 14.2

Waving Aside Service Encounters

Whether it is Hong Kong, Auckland, Amsterdam, or London, the huge numbers of people traveling by trains, buses, trams, ferries, and metro systems brings service problems not only in terms of seating capacity and general comfort but also in terms of the time and queues associated with purchasing travel tickets and enabling people to keep moving. At peak times, queuing for tickets can be frustrating and cause enormous delays.

Ticket offices provide people with an opportunity to discuss their requirements on an interpersonal basis with a member of staff. However, this is an expensive and, at times, a time-poor use of resources. There are many people who know what (ticket) they need, and self-service ticket machines are a way of providing a service for people who do not want or need a personal service encounter. There are an enormous number of people who make the same journey each day. In much the same way, airlines use e-ticketing and on-airport self-check-in solutions, such as kiosks, and off-airport self-check-in through kiosk, web, and mobile check-in applications.

Wave and pay services, like Oyster on the London Underground, are becoming increasingly popular

Source: Courtesy of Transport for London. The Oyster brand and logo are registered trademarks of Transport for London.

Market Insight 14.2
continued

In London, the Oyster card, a pay-as-you-go card, enables travellers to wave the card a few centimetres from a point-of-sale terminal on entry and exit from the underground transport system and the amount for the journey is debited from the card. Plans to introduce wave and pay ticketing across the tube, buses, the Docklands Light Railway, tram services, and National Rail services is expected to be implemented in 2013. This system will give passengers with contactless-enabled Eurocard, Mastercard, or Visa cards the ability to pay using existing Oyster card readers.

In Hong Kong, the Octopus card is based on a smartcard which incorporates near-field communication (NFC). This enables two devices to exchange data when they are adjacent. Here the 'wave and pay' card is used not only for transport and ticketing services but also for a whole range of purchases, including supermarkets, restaurants, gift shops, and even hospitals and cinemas.

The chip technology can be embedded in a variety of products, such as watches, key chains, ornaments, and smartphones. It is expected that next-generation Samsung and Apple smartphones will enable users to 'wave and pay'.

Sources: Brignall (2006); Harris (2008); Oates (2009); Laja (2012); Wheatley (2012).

1 How would you classify 'wave and pay' as a form of service encounter with transport systems?

2 How might B2B marketers make use of 'wave and pay'?

3 How might a symbol or logo which indicates that a card uses contactless technology assist in the marketing of this service?

Table 14.2 Levels of customer contact

Contact level	Explanation
High-contact services	Customers visit the service facility so that they are personally involved throughout the service delivery process, e.g. retail branch banking and higher education
Medium-contact services	Customers visit the service facility but do not remain for the duration of the service delivery, e.g.consulting services and delivering and collecting items to be repaired
Low-contact services	Little or no personal contact between customer and service provider. Service is delivered from a remote location, often through electronic means, e.g. software repairs and television and radio entertainment.

Key Dimensions of Services Marketing

Many of the strategies appropriate to the marketing of services relate to the particular characteristics that are relevant to each service context and specific target customers. However, the marketing of services can be improved if we understand how customers evaluate service performance. How might a RAKBANK customer judge the quality of the bank's services? This is potentially very difficult as complex services, such as surgery or stockbroking, have few tangible clues upon which to make a judgement about whether the service was extremely good, good, satisfactory, poor, or a disgrace. Customers purchasing physical goods can make judgements about the features, style, and colour prior to purchase and during purchase, and even return faulty goods after consumption. This is not possible with some types of services, especially people-processing services.

Zeithaml (1981) determined a framework that categorizes different services which, in turn, influence the degree to which market offerings can be evaluated. Three main properties were identified.

- Search properties are those elements that help customers to evaluate an offering prior to purchase. Physical products tend to have high search attributes that serve to reduce customer risk and increase purchase confidence.

- Experience properties do not enable evaluation prior to purchase. Sporting events, holidays, and live entertainment can be imagined, they can be explained, and they can be illustrated, but only through the experience of the performance or the feel of sitting in an audience of 100,000 people can proper evaluation of the service experience be made.

- Credence properties relate to those service characteristics that customers find difficult to evaluate even after purchase and consumption. Zeithaml (1981) refers to complex surgery and legal services to demonstrate the point.

As demonstrated earlier, most physical goods are high in search properties. However, services reflect the strength of experience and credence characteristics that, in turn, highlight their intangibility and their variability.

This classification has been challenged on the basis that it does not entirely reflect contemporary service markets (Garry and Broderick, 2007). Whereas the original classification vested expertise in the service provider, emerging research recognizes customer expertise and sophistication. With more information, customers have increasing skills and abilities to make judgements about the quality of service offerings prior to purchase. According to Garry and Broderick, this increased focus on customer attributes should also be matched with a consideration of the attributes we associate with service encounters. Here, they consider issues relating to information accessibility, time and interactivity, and, finally, the level of customer centricity present within a customer experience.

Many organizations recognize the importance and complexities associated with the marketing of services. As a result they often develop and plan their marketing activities in such a way that they help and reassure their customers prior to, during, and after purchase. This is achieved through the provision of varying levels of information to reduce perceived risk and to enhance the service experience. Two techniques, branding and internal marketing, are instrumental in delivering these goals in services marketing.

However, understanding service encounters, customer satisfaction, and associated service measurement techniques fails to lead to an understanding beyond the moment of truth, or the point at which the service is actioned. Understanding and measuring the experience that customers take away as a result of an interaction is much more pertinent and insightful.

Measuring Service Quality and Performance

Measuring the quality of a service encounter has become a major factor in the management of service-based organizations. **Service quality** is based on the idea that customer expectations of the service they will receive shape their perception of the actual service encounter. In essence, therefore, customers compare perceived service with expected service.

So, if the perceived service meets or even exceeds expectations, customers are deemed to be satisfied and are much more likely to return in future. However, if the perceived service falls below what was expected, they are more likely to feel disappointed and not return.

Various models have been proposed to help organizations manage and provide a consistent level of service. Primarily, these have been based on performance measures, disconfirmation (the gap between expected and perceived service encounter), and importance-performance ideas (Palmer, 2005) (see Table 14.3).

Each of these approaches has strengths and weaknesses but the one approach that has received most attention is **SERVQUAL** developed by Parasuraman *et al.* (1988). For some, it represents the benchmark approach to managing service quality.

SERVQUAL is a disconfirmation model and is based on the difference between the expected services and the actual perceived service. Inherently, this approach assumes that there is a gap between these variables, and five particular types of GAP have been established across service industries.

- **GAP 1—the gap between the customer's expectations and management perception**. By not understanding customer needs correctly, management directs resources into inappropriate areas. For example, train service operators may think that customers want places to store bags, whereas they actually want a seat in a comfortable safe environment.

- **GAP 2—the gap between management perception and service-quality specification**. In this case, management perceives customer wants correctly but fails to set a performance standard, fails to clarify it, or sets one that is not realistic and hence unachievable. For example, the train operator understands customer desire for a comfortable seat but

---

Table 14.3 Three approaches to service quality measurement

Contact level	Explanation
Performance measures	Derived from the manufacturing sector, this approach simply asks customers to rate the performance of a service encounter. SERVPERF is the standard measurement technique.
Disconfirmation	This approach is based on the difference between what is expected from a service and what is delivered, as perceived by the customer. SERVQUAL is the standard measurement technique.
Importance-performance	Seeks to compare the performance of the different elements that make up a service with the customer's perception of the relative importance of these elements. IPA (importance-performance analysis) is the standard measurement technique.

fails to specify how many should be provided relative to the anticipated number of travellers on each route.

- **GAP 3—the gap between service quality specifications and service delivery**. In this situation the service delivery does not match the specification for the service. This may be due to human error, poor training, or a failure in the technology necessary to deliver parts of a service. For example, the trolley buffet service on a train may be perceived as poor because the trolley operator was impolite because he/she had not received suitable training or because the supplier had not delivered the sandwiches on time.

- **GAP 4—the gap between service delivery and external communications**. The service promise presented in advertisements, on the website, and in sales literature helps set customer expectations. If these promises are not realized in service delivery practice, customers become dissatisfied. For example, if an advertisement shows the interior of a train with comfortable seats and plenty of space, yet a customer boards a train only to find a lack of space and hard seating, the external communications have misled customers and distorted their view of what might be realistically expected.

- **GAP 5—the gap between perceived service and expected service**. This gap arises because customers misunderstand the service quality relative to what they expect. This may be due to one or more of the previous gaps. For example, a customer might assume that the lack of information when a train comes to a standstill for an unexpectedly long period of time is due to ignorance or a 'they never tell us anything' attitude. In reality, this silence may be due to a failure of the internal communication system.

Using this GAPS approach five different dimensions of service quality have been established.

1 Reliability—the accuracy and dependability of repeated performances of service delivery.
2 Responsiveness—the helpfulness and willingness of staff to provide prompt service.
3 Assurance—the courtesy, confidence, and competence of employees.
4 Empathy—the ease and individualized care shown towards customers.
5 Tangibles—the appearance of employees, the physical location and any facilities and equipment, and the communication materials.

The SERVQUAL model consists of a questionnaire containing 22 items based on these five dimensions. When completed by customers it provides management with opportunities to correct areas where service performance is perceived to be less than satisfactory and learn from and congratulate people about the successful components.

Although SERVQUAL has been used extensively, there are some problems associated with its use. These difficulties concern the different dimensions customers use to assess quality, which varies according to each situation. In addition, there are statistical inconsistencies associated with measuring differences and the scoring techniques plus reliability issues associated with asking customers about their expectations after they have consumed a service (Gabbott and Hogg, 1998). Finally, ideas about measuring satisfaction are being overtaken as understanding about customer experience becomes more widely known. This is explored at the end of this chapter.

Visit the **Online Resource Centre** and complete Internet Activity 14.1. This will help you learn about the five gaps between actual and expected service quality: reliability, responsiveness, assurance, empathy, and tangibles.

Research Insight 14.1

To take your learning further, you might wish to read this influential paper.

Parasuraman, A., Zeithaml, V., and Berry, L. L. (1988), 'SERVQUAL: a multiple-item scale for measuring consumer perceptions of service quality', *Journal of Retailing*, 64(1), 5–37.

This is a classic article, structured in five sections, that describes the development of SERVQUAL, the multiple-item scale for measuring service quality. It also provides an interesting discussion regarding the scale's properties and its potential applications.

@ Visit the **Online Resource Centre** to read the abstract and access the full paper.

Principles of Relationship Marketing

As part of our exploration of customer experiences we now turn our attention to ideas about relationship marketing. To appreciate how experiences and relationships are interconnected we must first look at fundamental ideas about the exchanges that occur between a pair of buyers and sellers. Two main types can be identified: market and collaborative exchanges.

Market (or discrete) exchanges occur where there is no prior history of exchange and no future exchanges are expected between a buyer and seller. In these transactions, the primary focus is on the proposition and price. This is often referred to as 'transactional marketing', and the 4Ps approach to the marketing mix variables (the Marketing Management school of thought) is used to guide and construct transaction behaviour. Buyers were considered to be passive and sellers active in these short-term exchanges.

However, the assumption that buyers were passive was soon challenged by the notion that, in reality, buyers are active problem-solvers and seek solutions that are efficient and effective. Research into business markets identified that purchasing is not about a single discrete event; rather it is about a stream of activities between two organizations. These activities are sometimes referred to as episodes. Typically, these may be price negotiations, meetings at exhibitions, or a buying decision, but they all take place within the overall context of a relationship. This framed the Relationship Marketing school of thought, in which the buyer–seller relationship was the central element of analysis. This meant that the focus was no longer the offering, or even the individual buying or selling firm, but the relationship and its particular characteristics over time.

Therefore **relationship marketing** is based on the principle that there is a history of exchanges and an expectation that there will be exchanges in the future. Furthermore, the perspective is long term, envisaging a form of loyalty or continued attachment by the buyer to the seller. Price, as the key controlling mechanism, is replaced by customer service and quality of interaction between the buyer and seller. The exchange is termed collaborative because the focus is on both parties seeking to achieve their goals in a mutually rewarding way and not at the expense of one another. See Table 14.4 for a more comprehensive list of fundamental differences between transactional and collaborative-based marketing.

Table 14.4 Characteristics of market and collaborative exchanges

Attribute	Market exchange	Collaborative exchange
Length of relationship	Short term Abrupt end	Long term A continuous process
Relational expectations	Conflicts of goals Immediate payment No future problems (there is no future)	Conflicts of interest Deferred payment Future problems expected to be overcome by joint commitment
Communication	Low frequency of communication Formal communication predominates	High frequency of communication Informal communication predominates
Cooperation	No joint cooperation	Joint cooperative projects
Responsibilities	Distinct responsibilities Defined obligations	Shared responsibilities Shared obligations

Although market exchanges focus on propositions and prices, there is still a relational component, if only because interaction requires a basic relationship between parties for the transaction to be completed (Macneil, 1980).

Dwyer *et al*. (1987) refer to relationship marketing as an approach that encompasses a wide range of relationships, not just with customers but also those that organizations develop with suppliers, regulators, government, competitors, employees, and others. From this, relationship marketing might be regarded as all marketing activities associated with the management of successful relational exchanges.

RAKBANK and others recognize that the role of collaboration in relationship marketing is important. However, many organizations maintain a variety of relationships with their different customers and suppliers, some highly collaborative and some market oriented or, as Spekman and Carroway (2005: 1) suggest, 'where they make sense'.

Visit the **Online Resource Centre** and follow the web link to Association for the Advancement of Relationship Marketing (AARM) to learn more about continuing professional development in relationship marketing.

The Economics of Relationship Marketing

Early ideas about marketing considered the subject to be a social anathema because of the perception that it persuaded and manipulated people into purchasing offerings that they did not really want (Packard, 1958). These particular fears and misgivings have generally been overcome, only for a further myth to emerge—namely, that all customers are good customers. This is patently not true as it is now clear that some customers are far more attractive and of greater value than other customers.

Research Insight 14.2

To take your learning further, you might wish to read this influential paper.

Reichheld, F. F. and Sasser, E. W. (1990), 'Zero defections: quality comes to services', *Harvard Business Review*, **September, 105–11.**

Often quoted by authors and researchers, this paper by Reichheld and Sasser finds that a small increase in the number of retained customers can lead to a disproportionately large increase in profitability, and has helped propel a wealth of research and interest in relationship marketing. By definition, loyal customers are less likely to switch and therefore incur lower sales and service costs. They also help, through word-of-mouth, to recruit new customers, so the net result is that they all contribute to higher profits.

Visit the **Online Resource Centre** to read the abstract and access the full paper.

This view has been substantiated through our understanding of the economic and financial issues associated with customer management. From an understanding of transaction economics, ideas emerged about how customer relationships might be advantageous. Relationship cost theory identified benefits associated with stable and mutually rewarding relationships. Such customers avoided costly switching costs associated with finding new suppliers, whereas suppliers experienced reduced quality costs incurred when adapting to the needs of new customers.

Reichheld and Sasser (1990) identified an important association between a small (e.g. 5%) increase in customer retention and a large (e.g. 60%) improvement in profitability. So, a long-term relationship leads to lower relationship costs and higher profits. It is on this simple, yet crucial, principle that many organizations develop and run loyalty programmes. Many of the major airlines find it difficult to keep their high-mileage business customers, so they develop loyalty schemes, referred to as frequent flyer programmes (FFP), in which they reward travellers with free air miles for paid mileage undertaken with them. A typical FFP scheme, such as the one offered by British Airways, includes not only a mileage scheme, but also offers a range of added-value services such as graded membership status (and privileges), worldwide lounge access, seating preference records, meal preferences, and priority on busy flights.

Since this early work there has been general acceptance that customers who are loyal not only improve an organization's profits but also strengthen its competitive position (Day, 2000) because competitors have to work harder to dislodge or destabilize their loyalty. It should be noted that some authors suggest that the link between loyalty and profitability is not that simple (Dowling and Uncles, 1997), and others argue that much more information and understanding is required about the association between profitability and loyalty, especially when there may be high costs associated with customer acquisition (Reinartz and Kumar, 2002). However, the relationship marketing concept is considered to consist of two main elements, namely customer attraction and customer retention.

By undertaking a customer profitability analysis, it is possible to identify those segments that are worth developing. This, in turn, enables the construction of a portfolio of relationships, from which

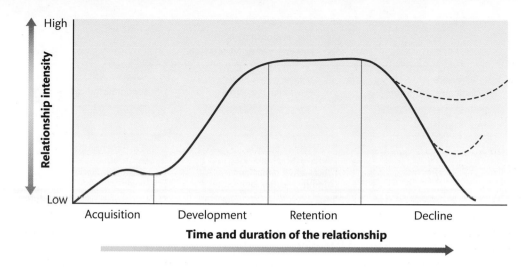

Figure 14.1
The customer relationship lifecycle

it is possible to identify relationships that have the potential to provide mutually rewarding benefits. This provides a third dimension of the customer dynamic, namely customer development.

The Customer Relationship Lifecycle

Understanding the economics associated with relationship stability and profitability uncovers three main stages within customer relationships. These are customer acquisition, development, and retention. This suggests similarities to the phases or stages of development associated with the product lifecycle concept. Taking this idea one step further allows us to develop a **customer relationship lifecycle**. This consists of four main stages, namely **customer acquisition**, development, retention, and finally decline or termination.

Just as different strategies can be applied to different phases of the product lifecycle, so it is possible to observe that customers have different requirements as a relationship evolves. These requirements are reflected in the intensity of the relationship held and the level of intensity will vary through time. See Figure 14.1 for a visual depiction of the customer relationship lifecycle.

Key to this concept is the differing level of relationship intensity that determines each stage. Bruhn (2003) suggests that there are three primary elements, or indicators (as he refers to them), that make up this intensity dimension. These are the psychological, behavioural, and economic indicators, and are depicted in Figure 14.2.

The psychological intensity indicators are based on a customer's judgement about the quality of the relationship and the amount of trust in, and commitment to, the seller or supplying organization. These are important foundations for establishing and maintaining ongoing mutually rewarding two-way relationships. Behavioural intensity indicators refer to the manner and scope of a customer's search for information, including word-of-mouth communication as well as their purchasing behaviour. Economic intensity indicators refer to both the profit contribution and the lifetime value a customer represents.

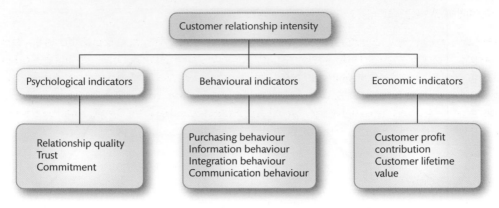

Figure 14.2
Elements of customer relationship intensity

These three indicators signal the intensity of a relationship. They vary through time and help explain the characteristics associated with each of the relationship stages.

Customer Acquisition

The customer acquisition stage is marked by three main events. First, both buyers and sellers search for a suitable match. Second, once a suitable partner has been found, there is a period of initiation or 'settling in' during which both parties seek out information about the other before any transaction occurs. The duration of this initiation period will depend partly on the strategic importance and complexity of the propositions and partly on the nature of the introduction. If they are introduced to each other by an established and trusted organization, certain initiation rights will be shortened.

The third phase is characterized by socialization, whereby once a transaction occurs the buyer and seller start to become more familiar with each other and gradually begin to reveal more information about themselves. The seller is able to collect payment, delivery, and handling information about the buyer and as a result is able to prepare customized outputs. The buyer is able to review the seller's offerings and experience the service quality of the seller.

Customer Development

During the development phase, sellers encourage buyers to purchase increased quantities, to try other products, to engage with other added-value services, and to vary delivery times and quantities. The degree to which buyers respond to the supplier's overtures depends on a variety of factors. Some of these concern their economic and production needs; others will reflect their competitive environment, their purchasing strategies, and their overall drive to become more involved with the supplier.

The **customer development** stage is critical, as not only do the number and value of transactions increase but also the socialization processes started during acquisition continue as buyer and seller begin to understand each other's requirements and goals. It is also during this stage that sellers develop a better understanding of the wider array of their buyer's stakeholder relationships. This can have a significant influence on the nature of the supplier's relationship with the buyer, often indicating the depth to which the relationship aspires.

Customer Retention

The retention phase is characterized by greater relationship stability and certainty. As a result the relationship becomes stabilized, displaying greater levels of trust and commitment between the partners. This, in turn, allows for increased cross-buying and product experimentation, joint projects, and product development. More commonly, suppliers provide customer loyalty schemes in order to increase the volume and value of products and services bought, and to lock in their customers by creating relationship exit barriers.

Customer Decline

In many cases, relationships become destabilized and higher levels of uncertainty emerge. This might occur after a long period of relationship stability or after a short period immediately after acquisition. The reasons for this are many and varied, and range from purchasing agreements and loyalty programmes that are not sufficiently attractive to lock in the customer to changes in the wider environment such as legislative, climatic, or economic developments. As a result, the **customer decline** period is concerned with the demise of the relationship and termination becomes a serious problem or episode for the parties to manage.

The likely process is that the buying organization decides to reduce its reliance on the seller and either notifies them formally or begins to reduce the frequency and duration of contact and moves business to other competitive organizations. Customer recovery strategies are required at the first sign that the relationship is waning.

Loyalty, Retention, and Customer Satisfaction

The customer relationship cycle implies that customers who keep coming back to buy from a particular supplier are loyal. One problem with this suggestion is that what is understood to be 'loyalty' may actually be nothing more than pure convenience or habit. A person who regularly attends the same supermarket is not necessarily consciously loyal to the supermarket brand, but happy with the convenience of the location and the overall quality and value of the products and services offered. Loyalty might be better appreciated in the context of a football supporter who travels to all away and home fixtures (regardless of domestic commitments), is a member of the club, buys into the merchandise and credit card offerings, and defends their club, even when they are relegated at the end of the season.

This cycle of customer attraction (acquisition), development, retention, and eventual decline represents a major difference from the 4Ps approach. The relationship approach is customer centred, and therefore complements marketing values more effectively than the 4Ps model. However, although the focus has moved from proposition and prices to relationships, questions remain about whose relationship it is that is being managed. Early interpretations of relationship marketing focused on suppliers' attempts to develop relationships with customers. In other words, they were 'customer relationships' and this meant there was an imbalance or one-sidedness within the relationship. Today, relationship marketing recognizes the need for balanced customer–supplier relationships in which participants share the same level of interest, goodwill, and commitment towards each other.

Table 14.5 Types of loyalty	
Type of loyalty	Explanation
Emotional loyalty	This is a true form of loyalty and is driven by personal identification with real or perceived values and benefits
Price loyalty	This type of loyalty is driven by rational economic behaviour and the main motivations are cautious management of money or financial necessity
Incentivized loyalty	This refers to promiscuous buyers, those with no one favourite brand, who demonstrate through repeat experience the value of becoming loyal
Monopoly loyalty	This class of loyalty arises where a consumer has no purchase choice owing to a national monopoly. Therefore this is not a true form of loyalty

Types and Levels of Loyalty

The concept of loyalty has attracted much research attention, if only because of the popularity of this approach. Table 14.5 represents some of the more general types of loyalty that can be observed. These hierarchical schemes suggest that consumers are capable of varying degrees of loyalty. This type of categorization has been questioned by a number of researchers. Fournier and Yao (1997) doubt the validity of such approaches, and Baldinger and Rubinson (1996) support the idea that consumers work within an evoked set and switch between brands. This view is supported on the grounds that many consumers display elements of curiosity in their purchase habits, enjoy variety, and are happy to switch brands as a result of marketing communication activities and product experiences.

Loyalty at one level can be seen to be about increasing sales volume, i.e. fostering loyal purchase behaviour. However, high levels of repeat purchase are not necessarily an adequate measure of loyalty, as there may be a number of situational factors determining purchase behaviour, such as brand availability (Dick and Basu, 1994). At whichever level of loyalty, customer retention is paramount and neither behavioural nor attitudinal measures alone are adequate indicators of true loyalty. O'Malley (1998) suggests that a combination of the two is of greater use, and that the twin parameters of relative attitudes (to alternatives) and patronage behaviour (the recency, frequency, and monetary model), as suggested by Dick and Basu, offer more accurate indicators of loyalty when used together.

Visit the **Online Resource Centre** and complete Internet activity 14.2. This will help you learn about the four general types of loyalty and how these four types of loyalty can exist for one offering across different customers and situations.

Loyalty and Retention Programmes

The number of customer loyalty programmes offered by organizations has grown significantly in recent years. These range from supermarket-based points schemes and frequent flyer reward programmes offered by airlines to attract and retain high-margin business customers to discounts and loyalty bonus formats designed to retain contract-based customers such as those

The Clubcard launched in the 1990s helped Tesco achieve market domination via the customer insight it provided

Source: © Tesco plc.

associated with mobile phones and financial services (e.g. car insurance). One of the more visible schemes has been the Clubcard offered by Tesco, which has been partly responsible for Tesco's market dominance.

Firms such as RAKBANK understand that these schemes are important not only because they help retain customers, but also because they allow for the collection of up-to-date customer information. These data can be used to target marketing communication campaigns and to make product purchase decisions, volumes, and scheduling in order to make savings in the supply chain.

There has been a proliferation of loyalty cards, reflecting the increased emphasis on keeping customers rather than constantly finding new ones, and there is some evidence that sales lift by about 2–3% when a loyalty scheme is launched. Yet there is little evidence to support the notion that sales promotions are capable of encouraging loyalty. Schemes do enable organizations to monitor and manage stock, use direct marketing to cross and up-sell customers, and manage their portfolio in order to increase a customer's spending. However, questions still exist about whether 'loyalty' is developed by encouraging buyers to make repeat purchases or whether these schemes are merely sales promotion techniques that encourage short-term retention purchasing patterns.

This expansion in the number of loyalty programmes leads Capizzi *et al.* (2004) to suggest that five clear trends within the loyalty market can be identified. These are set out in Table 14.6. These trends suggest that successful sales promotions schemes will be those that enable members to perceive significant value linked to their continued association with a scheme. That value will be driven by schemes run by groups of complementary brands which use technology to understand customer dynamics and communications that complement their preferred values.

The medium-term goal might be that these schemes should reflect customers' different relationship needs and recognize the different loyalty levels desired by different people. Market Insight 14.3 describes some of the loyalty schemes used by airlines.

Visit the **Online Resource Centre** and complete Internet Activity 14.3 to learn more about how to increase customer loyalty.

Table 14.6 Five loyalty trends

Trend	Explanation
Ubiquity	The proliferation of loyalty programmes in most mature markets. Many members have little interest in them other than the functionality of points collection
Coalition	Schemes are run by a number of different organizations in order to share costs, information, and branding (e.g. Nectar) and appear to be the dominant structure industry model
Imagination	Opportunities to exploit technologies and niche markets will depend on creativity and imagination in order to get customer data to feed into the loyalty system
Wow	To overcome consumer lethargy and boredom with loyalty schemes, many rewards in future will be experiential, emotional, and unique in an attempt to appeal to lifestage and aspirational lifestyle goals—wow them
Analysis	To be competitive, the use of customer data analytics and business intelligence is becoming critical, if only to feed CRM programmes. Collect and analyse customer information effectively

Source: Adapted from Capizzi *et al*. (2004).

Market Insight 14.3

Airborne Alliances Build Loyalty

As costs have increased and competition intensified, airlines around the world have formed strategic alliances. These collaborative schemes require members to share routes, facilities such as executive lounges, and, of course, customers. Three main alliances have emerged.

- The Oneworld Alliance consists of 13 airlines, including Qantas, American Airlines, and British Airways, and together they fly to 149 countries.

- The Star Alliance has 25 member airlines, including Air China, Singapore Airlines, and United, and fly to more than 1,293 airports in 185 countries.

- The SkyTeam has 19 members, including Air France, Delta Airways, and China Airlines, and collectively they serve over 900 destinations.

SkyTeam, the airline alliance enabling customer loyalty
Source: © SkyTeam.

The use of loyalty schemes in the airline industry is well established. These enable airlines to add value and help to brand their propositions by de-commoditizing their services and offerings. Frequent Flyer

Market Insight 14.3
continued

Programmes (FFPs) are now regarded as a key part of an alliance's success. Within an alliance each airline has their own loyalty programme, with its own procedures and complexities. In addition to these, alliances offer a single alternative loyalty programme which is integrated with the home airline's primary loyalty programme.

Alliance schemes have several membership tiers based on usage. The membership tiers in the Oneworld alliance are branded Emerald, Sapphire, and Ruby. In the Star Alliance there are two premium levels, Silver and Gold. These schemes offer seamless travel, better usage of amenities at airports, and, through compatible loyalty schemes and code-sharing, the transference of frequent flyer miles from various alliance-based carriers which helps to build customer loyalty to their alliance, not an airline.

Sources: http://www.cheapflights.co.uk/travel-tips/airline-alliances/ accessed 15 November 2012; http://www.itcinfotech.com/Uploads/GUI/knowledgecentre/Airline_alliances_and_Frequent_Flyer_Programs.pdf accessed 15 November 2012.

1 Do you think that operating both an airline and an alliance loyalty scheme is a good use of resources? Justify your view.

2 How might Star Alliance Members retain customers in a recession?

3 Some organizations choose not to offer a loyalty scheme, preferring to offer low prices. Does this offer customers better value?

Relationship Trust, Commitment, and Satisfaction

It is difficult to find agreement about a definition of trust, as many authors fail to specify clearly what they mean when using it (Cousins and Stanwix, 2001). However, there is a general consensus that trust is an element associated with personal, intra-organizational, and inter-organizational relationships, and is necessary for their continuation. Gambetta (1988) argues that trust is a means of reducing uncertainty in order for effective relationships to develop.

Cousins and Stanwix also suggest that, although trust is a term used to explain how relationships work, often it actually refers to ideas concerning risk, power, and dependency, and these propositions are used interchangeably. From their research on vehicle manufacturers, it emerges that B2B relationships are about the creation of mutual business advantage and the degree of confidence that one organization has in another.

Trust involves judgements about reliability and integrity and is concerned with the degree of confidence that one party to a relationship has that another will fulfil their obligations and responsibilities. The presence of trust in a relationship is important because it reduces both the threat of opportunism and the possibility of conflict which, in turn, increases the probability of buyer satisfaction. It has been claimed that the three major outcomes from the development of relationship trust are satisfaction, reduced perceived risk, and continuity (Pavlou, 2002).

- Perceived risk is concerned with the expectation of loss and therefore is tied closely to organizational performance.

- Trust that a seller will not take advantage of the imbalance of information between buyer and seller effectively reduces risk.

- Continuity is related to business volumes, necessary in online B2B marketplaces, and the development of both on- and offline enduring relationships. Trust is associated with continuity and therefore, when present, is indicative of long-term relationships.

Trust within a consumer context is important as it can reduce uncertainty. RAKBANK, for example, understood that many potential customers distrusted banks because of the hidden annual fees and cynical charges relating to credit cards. Strong brands provide sufficient information for consumers to make calculated purchase decisions in the absence of full knowledge. In a sense, consumers transfer their responsibility for brand decision-making, and hence brand performance, to the brand itself. Through regular brand purchases, habits or 'routinized response behaviour' develop. This is important not just because complex decision-making is simplified, but because the amount of communication necessary to assist and provoke purchase is considerably reduced.

The presence of trust within a relationship is influenced by four main factors (Young and Wilkinson 1989): the duration of the relationship, the relative power of the participants, the presence of cooperation, and various environmental factors that may be present at any one moment. Although pertinent, these are quite general factors, and Morgan and Hunt (1994) established what are regarded today as the key underlying dimensions of relationship marketing. In their seminal paper, they argued that it is the presence of both commitment and trust that leads to cooperative behaviour, customer satisfaction, and ultimately successful relationship marketing. **Commitment** is important because it implies a desire that a relationship continues and is strengthened because it is of value. Morgan and Hunt proposed that commitment and trust are the **key mediating variables** (KMV) between five antecedents and five outcomes. See Figure 14.3.

According to the KMV model, the greater the losses anticipated through the termination of a relationship, the greater the commitment expressed by the exchange partners. When relationship partners share similar values, commitment increases. Morgan and Hunt proposed that building a relationship based on trust and commitment can give rise to a number of benefits. Some of these include developing a set of shared values, reducing costs when the relationship finishes, and increasing profitability as a greater number of end-user customers are retained because of the inherent value and satisfaction they experience. Cooperation arises from a relationship driven by high levels of both trust and commitment (Morgan and Hunt, 1994).

Ryssel *et al*. (2004: 203) recognize that trust (and commitment) has a 'significant impact on the creation of value and conclude that value creation is a function of the atmosphere of a relationship rather than the technology employed'. Trust and commitment are concepts that are central to relationship marketing.

Customer Satisfaction

A natural outcome from building trust and developing commitment is the establishment of customer satisfaction. This is seen as important because satisfaction is thought to be positively related to customer retention which, in turn, leads to an improved return on investment and hence profitability. Unsurprisingly, many organizations seek to improve levels of customer satisfaction, with the intention of strengthening customer relationships and driving higher levels of retention and loyalty (Ravald and Grönroos 1996). So, the simple equation is build trust, drive satisfaction, improve retention, and increase profits.

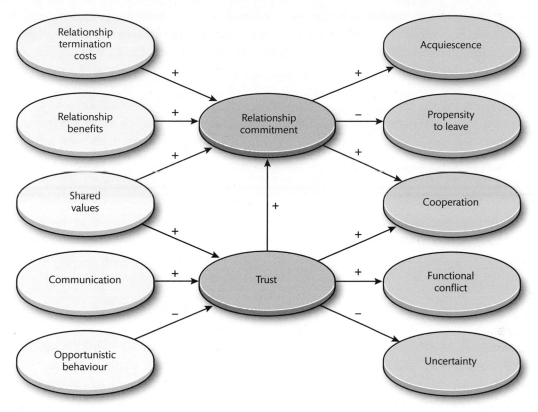

Figure 14.3

The KMV model of relationship marketing

Reprinted with permission from R. M. Morgan and S. D. Hunt (1994), 'The commitment–trust theory of relationship marketing', *Journal of Marketing*, 58(July), 20–38, published by the American Marketing Association.

Research Insight 14.3

To take your learning further, you might wish to read this influential paper.

Morgan, R. M. and Hunt, S. D. (1994), 'The commitment–trust theory of relationship marketing', *Journal of Marketing*, 58(July), 20–38.

This well-known paper examines the role of trust and commitment in buyer–supplier relationships. The authors present the KMV model to explain various behavioural and cognitive aspects associated with exchange partnerships. Using social exchange theory, it is argued that, through mutually beneficial exchanges, trust and commitment develop which, in turn, lead to longer-lasting relationships.

Visit the Online Resource Centre to read the abstract and access the full paper.

However, customer satisfaction is not driven by trust alone. Customer expectations play an important role and help shape a customer's perception of product/service performance. Customers compare performance against their expectations and through this process feel a sense of customer satisfaction or dissatisfaction. More recent ideas suggest that the perceived value of a relationship can be more important than trust when building customer satisfaction (Ulaga and Eggert, 2006).

So, if expectations are met, customer satisfaction is achieved. If expectations are not met, customers will be said to be dissatisfied. This simplistic interpretation can be misleading because satisfaction does not always imply loyalty (Mittal and Lassar, 1998). What may be seen as loyalty may be nothing more than convenience or even inertia, and dissatisfaction need not result in brand desertion (O'Malley, 1998). Cumby and Barnes (1998) provide a useful insight into what contributes to customer satisfaction:

- core product/service—the bundle of attributes, features, and benefits that must reach competitive levels if a relationship is to develop;
- support services and systems—the quality of services and systems used to support the core product/service;
- technical performance—the synchronization of the core product/services with the support infrastructure to deliver on the promise;
- elements of customer interaction—the quality of customer care demonstrated through face-to-face and technology-mediated communications;
- affective dimensions of services—the subtle and non-core interactions that say something about the way the organization feels about the customer.

This is a more useful insight into what it is that drives customer satisfaction because it incorporates a wide range of factors and recognizes the importance of personal contact. Customer satisfaction and the quality of customer relationships are related, in differing ways, among differing people and contexts. However, one factor that is common to both is the perceived value of the interaction between parties.

Customer Service and Relationship Management

The delivery of a superior level of customer service and the management of relationships have for a long time been regarded as the responsibility of the sales force. However, this perspective has also changed, and it is now expected that a range of employees have a responsibility for satisfying customer needs. Managing trust and reputation, reducing risk, and providing high levels of customer satisfaction and experience are now regarded as an expectation that all suppliers need to meet. Two elements of customer management are considered here. The first is customer contact centres, and the second is customer relationship management systems (CRM).

Customer Contact Centres

Many organizations try to help their customers contact them. This can be achieved via a customer contact centre. Instead of customers contacting a variety of people in different offices, all of whom require training and support, and receiving assorted messages, it makes sense to have a single point of contact. Very often, this task is outsourced to a specialist company trained in product support and company policy. Specialist organizations can reduce costs, improve efficiency, and enhance a client's reputation through the quality of interaction with customers. Using digital technology to manage voice, web, interactive TV, email, mobile, and fax-originated messages, contact centres enable customers to complain about a product performance and related experience, seek product-related advice, make suggestions regarding product or packaging development, and comment about an action or development concerning the brand as a whole. Very often, this access is referred to as a 'careline'—a dedicated telephone and email connection. In addition, organizations can use contact centres to provide outbound calls, often to generate sales leads or to provide market information.

Carelines and contact centres have enormous potential to support brands. The majority of calls to carelines are not complaints, but are from people seeking advice or help about products. Food manufacturers provide cooking and recipe advice, cosmetic and toiletries companies provide healthcare advice and application guidelines, and white goods and service-based organizations can provide technical and operational support. When complaints are dealt with in a prompt, courteous, and efficient manner, people are more likely to repurchase a brand than if the service was not available. Carelines are essentially a post-purchase support mechanism which facilitates feedback and intelligence gathering. They can warn of imminent problems (product defects), provide ideas for new products or variants, and, of course, provide a valuable method to reassure customers and improve customer retention levels.

CRM Systems

The development of **customer relationship management** (CRM) systems has been a significant development in the way organizations have attempted to manage their customers (see Market Insight 14.4 for an example). CRM applications were originally developed as sales force

---

 Market Insight 14.4

Banking on CRM

When First Direct launched as a 24/7 telephone bank in 1989, the brand was positioned for people who didn't have time to visit a bank branch or didn't enjoy the experience. Using information to feed the bank's value proposition, First Direct very quickly established itself as the number one provider in terms of customer satisfaction and the number of recommendations offered by customers.

Today, the target market is referred to as the 'Mass Affluent' and interaction with their 1.2 million customers is facilitated through a variety of channels, although over 80% of transactions are now conducted online. First Direct's CRM system is regarded as central and paramount to the coordination of the variety of communication, consumer insight, and service support activities that the bank undertakes.

Customer communications through phone, SMS, written correspondence, and the internet require service representatives to have a single view of all relevant interactions. In addition, First Direct encourages the use of podcasts, vodcasts, and text message banking. They also need a view of customer preferences, products, and enquiries.

The CRM system is required to integrate all the channel activities and provide real-time

Market Insight 14.4
continued

information at any time. It is possible for a First Direct agent to engage online customers through text chat and then switch to co-browsing, whereby both are looking at the same screen and so they are enabled to resolve any misunderstanding or difficulties.

As part of the development of their multi-channel strategy, First Direct has embraced mobile technology. Through the addition of a smartphone app, customers can access their accounts, and make payments and transfers, from wherever they are. This move recognizes First Direct's orientation towards understanding and then meeting customer needs for banking on the move. CRM technology enables this strategy to be implemented.

A Social CRM strategy is also now in place inviting customers to become part of the bank's community, and to contribute to their thoughts and ideas about how the bank and its customers can grow.

Sources: Garrett *et al.* (2007); Hauck (2012).

First Direct, a telephone banking pioneer, now embraces a multichannel strategy including mobile, internet, and social CRM
Source: Courtesy of First Direct.

1 **Do you think CRM systems provide customers with added value or are they just a means by which organizations can achieve their business goals?**

2 **Search the web, identify two online banks, and compare their offers.**

3 **Is the outsourcing of customer contact centres to a different country in the customers' best interests?**

support systems (mainly sales force automation) and later applications were designed for supplier organizations to enable them to manage their end-user customers. They have subsequently evolved as a more sophisticated means of managing direct customers and are now an integral part of customer contact centres.

The principal aim of CRM systems is to provide superior value by enabling suppliers to have access to real-time customer information. This helps suppliers to anticipate and satisfy customers' needs effectively, efficiently, and in a timely manner. To make this happen, a complete history of each customer needs to be available to all staff who interact with customers. This is necessary to answer two types of questions. First, there are questions prompted by customers about orders, quotations, or products, and, second, questions prompted by internal managers concerning, for example, strategy, segmentation, relationship potential, sales forecasts, and sales force management.

CRM applications typically consist of call management, lead management, customer record, and sales support and payment systems. However, CRM systems are invariably treated as add-on applications that are expected to resolve customer interface difficulties without any change to current business operations and regardless of changing customer needs (Maklan *et al.*, 2011). Unsurprisingly, many clients have voiced their dissatisfaction with CRM, as many of the promises and expectations have not been fulfilled. According to Joe Ferrara, regarded as an industry expert, these systems have failed for being no more than 'flat, static contact management systems that haven't evolved to encompass the growing volumes of external data that salespeople need to leverage, and in particular, data from social media' (Davey, 2012).

Sood (2002) suggests that problems have arisen with CRM implementation because technology vendors have not properly understood the need to manage all relationships with all major stakeholders. Disappointment with CRM systems can also be regarded as a failure to understand the central tenets of a customer-focused philosophy and the need to adopt a strategic business approach to managing customer relationships. If the centrality of concepts such as trust and commitment are not understood, and no willingness to share information and achieve a balanced relationship is displayed, the installation of databases and data warehouses will not change the quality of an organization's relationships with its customers.

O'Malley and Mitussis (2002) also refer to the failure of CRM systems in terms of internal political power struggles and associated issues about who owns particular systems and data. Where an organization has not established a customer-oriented culture or begun to implement enterprise-wide systems and procedures, it is probable that access to certain data might be impeded or at least made problematic. Nguyen (2011) points to several issues associated with CRM, including the one-to-one dilemma, relationship symmetry, and data tracking and usage.

It is important to understand that even the most sophisticated CRM systems are based on data about an organization's contacts and its transactions with them. Although these can be processed to supply one-touch real-time multidimensional views of any relationship, they do not manage it. That, as ever, is the challenge for the people involved.

Visit the **Online Resource Centre** and follow the weblink to CRM Today to learn more about CRM systems, applications, news, and research.

Customer Experiences

The thrust of this chapter has been an exploration of ideas about perceived value and the evolution of marketing practices related to services marketing, which then transformed into customer relationships. The focus is now extended into customer experiences (Maklan and Klaus, 2011).

The idea that providing a superior customer service might help in the (repeat) purchase decision process is something that many organizations now appreciate. For a long time it was assumed that product quality and pricing were sufficient differentiators. However, product quality is no longer a viable means of establishing competitive advantage, simply because of shortening lifecycles and improved technologies. Service, although difficult to deliver in a consistent way, is very hard to replicate and has become an important aspect of customer management.

Although generating customer satisfaction is important, it provides an incomplete picture. Of greater interest is **customer experience**. As Prahalad and Ramaswamy (2004: 137) suggest, cited by Iyanna *et al.* (2012), the literature on value is no longer embedded in goods and services, or indeed relationships, but 'is now centered in the experiences of consumers'. Customer value is regarded by an increasing number of academics and practitioners as the central marketing activity (Iyanna *et al.*, 2012), and that value is now central to customers' experiences. The

Research Insight 14.4

To take your learning further, you might wish to read this influential paper.

Meyer, C. and Schwager, A. (2007), 'Understanding customer experience', *Harvard Business Review*, **February, 117–26.**

This paper looks at how firms can benefit from adopting a customer experience perspective. It provides a clear understanding of what customer experience is practically and discusses the managerial issues that can be avoided by utilizing an experience view rather than a relationship only view. It also contains a useful table showing how customer relationship management differs from customer experience management.

Visit the **Online Resource Centre** to read the abstract and access the full paper.

implications for marketing are clearly stated by Meyer and Schwager (2007: 118) when they say that 'customer experience encompasses every aspect of a company's offering—the quality of customer care, of course, but also advertising, packaging, product and service features, ease of use, and reliability'. For a deeper understanding of the issues arising from the adoption of a customer experience perspective see Research Insight 14.4.

The importance and significance of customer experience to both individuals and society was first established by Pine and Gilmore (1998) when they referred to the 'experience economy'. Chang and Horng (2010) suggest that themed restaurants, such as Starbucks and the Hard Rock Café, are prime examples of customer experience. These brands are not just about the consumption of coffee, but a situation or environment in which the consumption of services occurs and relationships are developed, but in total provide a meaningful or valuable customer experience. Ismail *et al*. (2011) refer to the trend towards creating unique experiences

Starbucks offers coffee and a service experience
Source: Courtesy of Starbucks Coffee Company.

for customers with a view to developing a competitive advantage, something that is particularly sustainable for those in the service sector, as replication is very difficult.

Before exploring the characteristics and issues associated with customer experience, it is helpful to consider how the concept is defined. Unfortunately, there have been several attempts to define this concept but little consensus. Some of the more notable ones are set out in Table 14.7.

There are some similarities across many of these definitions. For example, customer experience is seen to be an individual event, and concerns emotional reactions following direct and indirect interaction with an organization. It is also related to events prior to, during, or after

Table 14.7 Definitions of experience

Reference	Definition
Csikszentmihalyi (1977: 36)	The individual is experiencing flow when he has 'a unified flowing from one moment to the next, in which he is in control of his actions and in which there is little distinction between self and environment, between stimulus and response, between past, present and future'.
Holbrook and Hirschman (1982; cited by Carù and Cova 2003)	Experience is defined as a personal occurrence, often with important emotional significance, founded on the interaction with stimuli which are the products or services consumed.
Carbone and Haeckel (1994: 8)	'The take-away impression formed by people's encounters with products, services, and businesses, a perception produced when humans consolidate sensory information.'
Schmitt (1999: 60)	From a customer perspective: 'Experiences involve the entire living being. They often result from direct observation and/or participating in the event—whether they are real, dreamlike or virtual'.
Shaw and Ivens (2002: 6)	'An interaction between an organization and a customer. It is a blend of an organization's physical performance, the senses stimulated and emotions evoked, each intuitively measured against customer experience across all moments of contact.'
Gentile et al. (2007: 397)	'The customer experience originates from a set of interactions between a customer and a product, a company, or part of its organization, which provoke a reaction. This experience is strictly individual and implies the customer's involvement at different levels (rational, emotional, sensorial, physical and spiritual). Its evaluation depends on the comparison between a customer's expectations and the stimuli coming from the interaction with the company and its offering in correspondence of the different moments of contacts or touch-points.'
Ismail et al. (2011)	Emotions provoked, sensations felt, knowledge gained and skills acquired through active involvement with the firm pre-, during, and post-consumption.

Source: Adapted from Ismail et al. (2011).

consumption. Perhaps one crucial point is that it is not possible for two people to have or to share the same experience (Pine and Gilmore, 1998). As a result, the task of managing and measuring customer experiences is inherently complex (see Market Insight 14.5).

To help disentangle some of this complexity, Pine and Gilmore derive four distinct realms of experience based on two dimensions. These dimensions concern a customer's participation in an experience (weak/passive or active/strong), and an individual's connection with the

---

Market Insight 14.5

Leopard Experiences

Leopard is a business-to-business global financial services provider. When a major customer moved a substantial part of its business to a rival, senior management at Leopard were galvanized into reviewing their processes and procedures for managing customer relationships. One of the reasons for the urgency could be traced to a recent internal account review that resulted in this particular account being categorized as 'superior'. Something was clearly wrong.

To understand the situation a mini-audit was initiated to look into the existing customer experience programmes, those responsible, and the performance. This revealed that that the company's analysis focused on lead-tracking and buying patterns, and that most of the knowledge about customers was based on opinion, and nothing else. For example, Leopard's only customer experience management (CEM) metric was based on an annual direct mail customer satisfaction survey, where the wording had not changed in three years. In addition, it appeared that the majority of employees assumed that customer experience was the job of marketing or sales.

It was critical to prevent further customer defections, and so a relationship survey of the company's top customers was initiated. During the design of the pilot survey, one important observation was that customer responses to feedback about customer experience information was different from that encountered during a typical sales call. So, instead of a conversation structured around individual transactions, the focus shifted towards relationship development.

The survey was designed so that responses could be compared by location, service platform, and vertical market. It became clear that 'experiences' were critical to overall satisfaction and that these differed in each vertical market. It was also realized that customer experience goals would be needed for each stage of the value chain. Summary scores from the survey were compared with customer sales revenue, and four types of customer were identified.

- Model customers: good summary scores; good revenue. Requirement = Maintain.
- Growth customers: good summary scores; higher potential revenue. Requirement = Cross-selling and up-sell.
- At-Risk customers: low scores; good revenue. Requirement = Decisive intervention.
- Dangling customers: low scores; low revenue. Requirement = Rescue or abandon.

Subsequent analysis showed that there were several discrepancies. For example, the Growth segment had three times as many customers as any of the others, yet some of these customers didn't buy as much as those in other quadrants. One of the largest remaining customers was clearly in the At-Risk quadrant.

The results of the survey led to various actions. First, customer experience became an integral part of the strategic planning process. Second, discussions were held with customers about the initial survey results, and agreement reached about what the team planned to do. Each team was also required to send out transaction surveys of customers' experiences about service installation and repair on a regular basis. Each team set experience goals for itself and scheduled relationship surveys. In addition,

Market Insight 14.5
continued

support staff became involved with customers on a regular basis, many helping to resolve customer issues.

A year later, current experience data had replaced ill-informed opinion at Leopard. At monthly operations meetings, vertical-market general managers reviewed key customer experience issues, and actions taken, before they reviewed the financial information. Discussions about relationship issues became a central element of quarterly executive strategy discussions and, of the many positive outcomes,

customer defections within each vertical-market group fell by an average of 16%.

Source: Adapted from Meyer and Schwager (2007).

1 To what extent is customer experience capable of being measured?

2 Explain the key differences between customer satisfaction and customer experience.

3 List different ways in which customer experience with Leopard might be improved.

environment of the experience or environmental relationship (from absorption/weak to immersion/strong). The four realms that emerge from these dimensions are educational, entertainment, aesthetic, and escapist.

- **Educational realm**—occurs when a individual learns and enhances their skills and knowledge as a result of the events unfolding before them (Pine and Gilmore, 1999; Oh *et al.*, 2007).

- **Entertainment realm**—occurs when a individual views a performance, listens to music, or reads for pleasure. The experience is absorbed passively (Pine and Gilmore, 1999).

- **Aesthetic realm**—occurs when an individual passively appreciates an event or environment but leaves without affecting or altering the nature of the environment (Pine and Gilmore, 1999; Oh *et al.*, 2007).

- **Escapist realm**—occurs when individuals become completely immersed in their environment and actively participate so that they affect actual performances or occurrences in the environment (Pine and Gilmore, 1999; Oh *et al.*, 2007).

This approach has subsequently led to research that focuses on the ways in which experiences are produced, narrated, and mediated (Lofgren, 2008).

Visit the **Online Resource Centre** and follow the weblinks to see how the Customer Experience Professionals Association (CCPA) supports the industry.

Experience quality

We have previously considered SERVQUAL, the leading approach to measuring service quality. Although SERVQUAL has many benefits and is used extensively, it is not suitable for measuring experience quality. SERVQUAL does provide a measure of customer satisfaction but, as Maklan and Klaus (2011) argue, it focuses largely upon customers' assessment of the service process and human interactions and is not a suitable vehicle to measure customer experiences.

Chang and Horng (2010) refer to the study of the quality of life experience by Csikszentmihalyi and LeFevre (1989: 2404). They investigated how people evaluate and feel about their own experiences. This led them to define experience quality as 'how customers emotionally evaluate their experiences as they participate in consumption activities'. These authors are keen to point out that the evaluation of experience quality is not just about emotions, but putting more emphasis on the emotional nature of experience quality can 'reveal more of the characteristics of experience that underlie contemporary experience marketing'.

Therefore, they conceptualize **experience quality** as a customer's emotional judgement about their total experience, and they identify five dimensions for the construct. These are the physical surroundings, service providers, other customers, customers' companions, and the customers themselves. Chang and Horng (2010: 2415) refer to four sub-dimensions of the physical surroundings (atmosphere, concentration, imagination, and surprise), and that the dimension of 'customer themselves' has two sub-dimensions (cognitive learning and having

fun). Their study concludes that the development of 'elaborate physical surroundings to elicit positive customers' emotional perceptions of experience quality is significant for experience design. Customers are commonly more impressed with service settings with atmosphere.'

Visit the **Online Resource Centre** and follow the weblinks to explore more about customer experience.

In this chapter we have seen how the evolution of marketing thought and practice has moved from understanding different types of value creation, to the importance of service encounters and customer satisfaction, through to the significance of relationship marketing and collaboration and trust. There is now increasing agreement that the creation of value through customer experience is, or should be, central to the marketing activities of all organizations, regardless of sector or context.

Chapter Summary

To consolidate your learning, the key points from this chapter are summarized here.

- **Appreciate the nature of perceived value, and describe the differences between the transactional and the relationship approach to marketing.**

  Value is a customer's estimate of the extent to which an offering can satisfy their needs. Value can be generated in many ways, not just through propositions and prices. One important source of value is the relationship generated through buyer–seller interaction. Organizations interact with other organizations to provide superior value for their customers. Transactional exchanges are characterized by short-term, proposition-oriented, or price-oriented exchanges, whilst collaborative exchanges are characterized by a long-term orientation where there is complete integration of systems and processes and the relationship is motivated by partnership and mutual support.

- **Describe what is meant by the term service processes, 'service encounters', and the principles associated with measuring service quality.**

  A process is a series of sequential actions that leads to pre-determined outcomes. Four main service process categories can be identified: people, possession, mental stimulus, and information processing.

A service encounter is best understood as a period of time during which a customer interacts directly with a service (Shostack, 1985). There are three levels of customer contact: high-contact services, medium-contact services, and low-contact services. As more services are introduced, so opportunities for service variability and service failure also develop. Service quality is based on the idea that a customer's expectations of the service they will receive shapes their perception of the actual service encounter. In essence, customers compare perceived service with expected service. SERVQUAL is a major model used to measure service quality. It is a disconfirmation model and is based on the difference between the expected service and the actual perceived service.

■ **Outline the principles and economics of customer retention and consider the merits of loyalty programmes.**

Relationship marketing is based on the premise that retained customers are more profitable than transactional-marketing-based customers. Loyalty is an important concept within relationship marketing. The critical point is that different customers represent different value to organizations. This suggests that there are many different forms of loyalty and that different marketing strategies are required to reach each of them.

■ **Understand the principles of trust, commitment, and customer satisfaction and explain how they are interlinked.**

There are several key concepts associated with the management of customer relationships. The main ones are trust, commitment, and satisfaction. These are interrelated, and the management of customer relationships should be based on the principles of reducing the influence of power and the incidence of conflict to build customer trust, gain customer commitment, and, through loyalty and retention, generate customer satisfaction. This approach should increase the perceived value of the relationship for all parties.

■ **Explain the term 'customer experiences', how it has evolved, and how it might be measured.**

Customers' experience an emotional transition and response through interactions with an organization and its offerings. This individuality of experience implies there are different types or levels of experience, such as rational, emotional, sensorial, physical, and spiritual. The development of customer experience marketing has been built on evolving ideas concerning service encounters, perceived value, relationship marketing, and customer satisfaction.

 # Review Questions

1 What are the main types of service processes and identify their main characteristics?
2 Explain the term 'service encounter'.
3 How does an understanding of the relevant search, experience, and credence properties of a service influence the way they are marketed?
4 Name the five dimensions of service quality and explain their key characteristics.
5 Distinguish clearly between the three main methods used to measure service quality.
6 What are the key differences between transaction marketing and relationship marketing?
7 Why is trust an important aspect of relationship marketing?
8 Why do so many CRM systems fail to live up to expectations?

9 Make notes for a short presentation in which you explain the term customer experience and track its evolution.

10 What dimensions are used by Csikszentmihalyi and LeFevre (1989) to measure experience quality?

 # Worksheet Summary

To apply the knowledge you have gained from this chapter and test your understanding of managing relationships and customer experiences visit the **Online Resource Centre** and complete Worksheet 14.1.

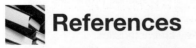 # Discussion Questions

1 Having the read the Case Insight at the beginning of this chapter, how would you advise RAKBANK to develop a loyalty programme to attract and retain customers and improve customer experiences?

2 To what extent is the traditional marketing mix a useful basis to develop marketing strategies for service organizations?

3 Westcliffe and Sons make a range of fruit juice drinks. Their business falls into two main segments, consumers and business users, such as local councils and catering companies. Recent sales figures suggest that orders from some catering companies are down on previous years, and some have stopped buying from them altogether. The marketing director of Westcliffe has reported that he cannot understand the reason for the decline in business as product quality and prices are very competitive. Advise the marketing director about the key issues he should consider and discuss how the company should re-establish itself with the catering companies.

4 Consider the view that loose or arms-length B2B customer relationships can be just as productive as those that are intense and close.

5 Using PowerPoint, prepare a short presentation in which you explain the meaning of customer experience.

@ Visit the **Online Resource Centre** and complete the Multiple Choice Questions to assess your knowledge of Chapter 14.

References

Anderson, J. (1995), 'Relationships in business markets: exchange episodes, value creation and their empirical assessment', *Journal of the Academy of Marketing Science*, 23(4), 346–50.

Baldinger, A. and Rubinson, J. (1996), 'Brand loyalty: the link between attitude and behaviour', *Journal of Advertising Research*, 36(6), 22–34.

Brignall, M. (2006), 'Wave and pay cards set to put an end to queues', *The Guardian*, 16 December, retrieve from: www.guardian.co.uk/money/2006/dec/16/creditcards.debt accessed 13 July 2013.

Bruhn, M. (2003), *Relationship Marketing: Management of Customer Relationships*, Harlow: FT/Prentice Hall.

Carbone, L. P. and Haeckel, S. H. (1994), 'Engineering customer experiences', *Marketing Management*, 3(3), 8–19.

Carù, A. and Cova, B. (2008), 'Small versus big stories in framing consumption experiences', *Qualitative Market Research*, 11(2), 166–76.

Capizzi, M., Ferguson, R., and Cuthbertson, R. (2004), 'Loyalty trends for the 21st century', *Journal of Targeting Measurement and Analysis for Marketing*, 12(3), 199–212.

Chang, T-C. and Horng, S-C. (2010), 'Conceptualizing and measuring experience quality: the customer's perspective', *Service Industries Journal*, 30(14), 2401–19.

Cslkszentmlhalyl, M. (1977), *Beyond Boredom and Anxiety*, San Francisco, CA: Jossey-Bass.

Csikszentmihalyi, M. and LeFevre, J. (1989), 'Optimal experience in work and leisure', *Journal of Personality and Social Psychology*, 56(5), 815–22.

Cousins, P. D. and Stanwix, E. (2001), 'It's only a matter of confidence! A comparison of relationship management between Japanese and UK non-owned vehicle manufacturers', *International Journal of Operations and Production Management*, 21(9), 1160–80.

Cumby, J. A. and Barnes, J. (1998), 'How customers are made to feel: the role of affective reactions in driving customer satisfaction', *Customer Relationship Management*, 1(1), 54–63.

Davey, N. (2012), 'CRM sucks and collaboration's a crock: relationship management's big rethink, retrieve from: http://www.mycustomer.com/topic/social-crm/crm-sucks-and-collaboration-crock-relationship-management-s-big-rethink/159432 accessed 15 November 2012.

Day, G. (2000), 'Managing market relationships', *Journal of the Academy of Marketing Science*, 28(1), 24–30.

Dick, A. S. and Basu, K. (1994), 'Customer loyalty: toward an integrated framework', *Journal of the Academy of Marketing Science*, 22(2), 99–113.

Dowling, G. R. and Uncles, M. (1997), 'Do customer loyalty programs work?' *Sloan Management Review*, 38(4), 71–82.

Doyle, P. (2000), *Value Based Marketing*, Chichester: John Wiley.

Dwyer, R. F., Schurr, P. H., and Oh, S. (1987), 'Developing buyer–seller relationships', *Journal of Marketing*, 51 (April), 11–27.

Fournier, S., and Yao, J. L. (1997), 'Reviving brand loyalty: a reconceptualisation within the framework of consumer-brand relationships', *International Journal of Research in Marketing*, 14(5), 451–72.

Gabbott, M. and Hogg, G. (1998), *Consumers and Services*, Chichester: John Wiley.

Gambetta, D. (1988), *Trust: Making and Breaking Co-operative Relations*, New York: Blackwell.

Garrett, A., Roopalee, D., Wilson, H., and Clark, M. (2007), *First Direct Comes of Age*, Cranfield Customer Management Forum.

Garry, T. and Broderick, A. (2007), 'Customer attributes or service attributes? Rethinking the search, experience and credence classification basis of services'. In *Proceedings of the 21st Service Workshopof the Academy of Marketing*, 15–17 November, University of Westminster: Academy of Marketing, 24–39.

Gentile, C., Spiller, N., and Noci, G. (2007), 'How to sustain the customer experience: an overview of experience components that co-create value with the customer', *European Management Journal*, 25(5), 395–410.

Gil, I., Berenguer, G., and Cervera, A. (2008), 'The roles of service encounters, service value, and job satisfaction in business relationships', *Industrial Marketing Management*, 37(8), 921–39.

Glyn, W. J. and Lehtinen, U. (1995), 'The concept of exchange: interactive approaches in services marketing', in W. J. Glyn and J. G. Barnes(eds), *Understanding Services Management*, Chichester: John Wiley, 89–118.

Grönroos, C. (2009), 'Marketing as promise management: regaining customer management for marketing', *Journal of Business and Industrial Marketing*, 24(5/6), 351–9.

Harris, M. (2008), 'Leaving the wine cheats high and dry', *The Sunday Times*, 4 April, retrieve from: http://www.thesundaytimes.co.uk/sto/ingear/tech_and_net/article83926.ece accessed 13 July 2013.

Hauck, E. (2012), 'First Direct's CRM strategy review', retrieve from: http://eduardohauck.wordpress.com/2011/07/06/firstdirects-crm-strategy-review/ accessed 15 November 2012.

Holbrook, M. and Hirschman, E. (1982), 'The experiential aspects of consumption: fantasies, feelings, and fun', *Journal of Consumer Research*, 9, 132–40.

Ismail, A. R., Melewar, T. C., Lim, L., and Woodside, A. (2011), 'Customer experiences with brands: Literature review and research directions', *Marketing Review*, 11(3), 205–25.

Iyanna, S., Bosangit, C., and Mohd-Any, A. A. (2012), 'Value evaluation of customer experience using consumer generated content', *International Journal of Management and Marketing Research*, 5(2), 89–102.

Kothandaraman, P. and Wilson, D. (2001), 'The future of competition: value creating networks', *Industrial Marketing Management*, 30(4), 379–89.

Lovelock, C., Vandermerwe, S., and Lewis, B. (1999), *Services Marketing: A European Perspective*, Harlow: FT/Prentice Hall.

Lefaix-Durand, A., Kozak, R., Beauregard, R., and Poulin, D. (2009), 'Extending relationship value: observations from a case study of the Canadian structural wood products industry', *Journal of Business and Industrial Marketing*, 24(5/6), 389–407.

Lofgren, O. (2008), 'The secret lives of tourists. Delays, disappointments and daydreams', *Scandinavian Journal of Hospitality and Tourism*, 8(1), 85–101.

Laja, S. (2012), 'Transport for London's contactless tickets roll out behind schedule', *Government Computing*, retrieve from: http://www.governmentcomputing.com/news/2012/may/22/contactless-tickets-tfl-delay-wave-pay accessed 16 November 2012.

Macneil, I. R. (1980), *The New Social Contract*. New Haven, CT: Yale University Press.

Maklan, S. and Klaus, P. (2011), 'Customer experience: are we measuring the right things?' *International Journal of Market Research*, 53(6), 771–92.

Maklan, S., Knox, S., and Peppard, J. (2011), 'Why CRM fails—and how to fix it', *Sloan Management Review*, 52(4), 77–85.

Menon, A., Homburg, C., and Beutin, N. (2005), 'Understanding customer value in business-to-business relationships', *Journal of Business to Business Marketing*, 12(2), 1–38.

Meyer, C. and Schwager, A. (2007), 'Understanding customer experience', *Harvard Business Review*, February, 117–26.

Morgan, R. M. and Hunt, S. D. (1994), 'The commitment–trust theory of relationship marketing', *Journal of Marketing*, 58(July), 20–38.

Mittal, B. and Lassar, W. M. (1998), 'Why do consumers switch? The dynamics of satisfaction versus loyalty', *Journal of Services Marketing*, 12(3), 177–94.

Nguyen, B. (2011), 'The dark side of CRM', *Marketing Review*, 11(2), 137–49.

Oates, J. (2009), 'Westminster readies "wave and pay" parking meters', *The Register*, 29 October, retrieve from: www.theregister.co.uk/2009/10/29/westminster_parking_scheme/ accessed 13 July 2013.

Oh, H., Fiorie, A. M., and Jeoung, M. (2007), 'Measuring experience economy concepts: tourism applications, *Journal of Travel Research*, 46, 119–32.

O'Malley, L. (1998), 'Can loyalty schemes really build loyalty?' *Marketing Intelligence and Planning*, 16(1), 47–55.

O'Malley, L. and Mitussis, D. (2002), 'Relationships and technology: strategic implications', *Journal of Strategic Marketing*, 10, 225–38.

Palmer, A. (2005), *Services Marketing*, Maidenhead: McGraw Hill.

Packard, V. (1958), *The Hidden Persuaders*, London: Penguin.

Parasuraman, A., Zeithaml, V., and Berry, L. L. (1988), 'SERVQUAL: a multiple-item scale for measuring consumer perceptions of service quality', *Journal of Retailing*, 64(1), 5–37.

Pavlou, P. A. (2002), 'Institution-based trust in interorganisational exchange relationships: the role of online B2B marketplaces on trust formation', *Journal of Strategic Information Systems*, 11(3–4), 215–43.

Pine, B. J. and Gilmore, J. H. (1998), 'Welcome to the experience economy', *Harvard Business Review*, July-August, 97–105.

Pine, B. and Gilmore, H. (1999), *The Experience Economy: Work is Theatre and Every Business a Stage*, Boston, MA: Harvard Business School Press.

Prahalad, C. K. and Ramaswamy, V. (2004), *The Future of Competition: Co-creating Unique Value with Customers*, Boston, MA: Harvard Business School Press.

Ravald, A. and Grönroos, C. (1996), 'The value concept and relationship marketing', *European Journal of Marketing*, 30(2), 19–33.

Reichheld, F. F. and Sasser, E. W. (1990), 'Zero defections: quality comes to services', *Harvard Business Review*, September, 105–11.

Reinartz, W. J. and Kumar, V. (2002), 'The mismanagement of customer loyalty', *Harvard Business Review*, July, 86–94.

Ribeiro, A. H. P., Brashear, T.G., Monteiro, P. R. R., and Damzaio, L.F. (2009), 'Marketing relationships in Brazil trends in value strategies and capabilities', *Journal of Business and Industrial Marketing*, 24(5/6), 449–59.

Ryssel, R., Ritter, T., and Gemunden, H. G. (2004), 'The impact of information technology deployment on trust, commitment and value creation in business relationships', *Journal of Business and Industrial Marketing*, 19(3), 197–207.

Schmitt, B. H. (1999) *Experiential Marketing*, New York: Library of Congress Cataloguing-in-Publication Data.

Shaw, C. and Ivens, J. (2002) *Building Great Customer Experiences,* New York: Palgrave Macmillan

Sheth, J. N. and Uslay, C. (2007), 'Implications of the revised definition of marketing: from exchange to value creation', *Journal of Public Policy and Marketing*, 26(2), 302–7.

Shostack, G. L. (1985), 'Planning the service encounter', in J. A. Czepiel, M. R. Solomon, and C. F. Surprenant(eds), *The Service Encounter*, Lexington, MA: Lexington Books, 243–54.

Simpson, P. M., Sigauw, J. A., and Baker, T. L. (2001), 'A model of value creation: supplier behaviors and their impact on reseller-perceived value', *Industrial Marketing Management*, 30(2), 119–34.

Sood, B. (2002), *CRM in B2B: Developing Customer-centric Practices for Partner and Supplier Relationships*, retrieve from: www.intelligentcrm.com/020509/508feat2_2.shtml accessed 13 July 2013.

Spekman, R. E. and Carroway, R. (2005), 'Making the transition to collaborative buyer–seller relationships: an emerging framework', *Industrial Marketing Management*, 35(1), 10–19.

Ulaga, W. and Eggert, A. (2005), 'Relationship value in business markets: the construct and its dimensions', *Journal of Business-to-Business Marketing*, 12, 1, 73–99.

Wheatley, T. (2012), 'Excited about wave and pay? It's old news in Hong Kong', CNN.com, retrieve from: http://business.blogs.cnn.com/2011/02/01/excited-about-wave-and-pay-its-old-news-in-hong-kong/ accessed 16 November 2012.

Young, L. C. and Wilkinson, I. F. (1989), 'The role of trust and co-operation in marketing channels: a preliminary study', *European Journal of Marketing*, 23(2), 109–22.

Zeithaml, V. A. (1981), 'How consumer evaluation processes differ between goods and services', reprinted in C. Lovelock,(ed.), *Services Marketing* (2nd), Upper Saddle River, NJ: Prentice Hall, 1991.

Chapter 15
Business-to-Business Marketing

Learning Outcomes

After studying this chapter you should be able to:

▶ Explain the main characteristics of business markets and understand the different types of organizational customers

▶ Describe the different types of offerings that are sold and bought in business markets

▶ Set out the main processes and stages associated with organizational buying and purchasing

▶ Understand the principles of key account management

▶ Explain what business-to-business marketing is and the marketing issues associated with professional service firms

▶ Compare business and consumer marketing

Case Insight 15.1

How should organizations develop relationships with business partners in international markets? We speak to Lynn Shepherd, the Group Director of Communications at Oxford Instruments, to find out more.

Oxford Instruments sells a wide range of high-technology tools and systems to customers in research and industrial markets all over the world. Its core technologies allow the analysis, manipulation, and fabrication of matter at the atomic and molecular level, so nanotechnology is the prime sector that drives our growth strategy.

We operate in two main markets, the research/academia and industrial markets. In the former we work with highly educated well-informed customers. These include university professors, heads of research labs, and physics-based experts working within niche markets with very specific requirements. Our high-end cutting edge products sell in low volumes and are highly priced. As a result the buying decisions are usually very complex, and are based around a tender process. These transactions are very relationship dependent, are not cyclic, and on the whole are all in niche markets, where sometimes the buying cycle lasts for five years!

In the industrial market there is little interest in the technology behind the instrument. In addition to a sole trader running a scrap yard, our customers include buyers in multinational companies, government agencies (e.g. NASA), and quality control managers in a range of industrial sectors from food to cement, through automotive and petrochemicals. What is common to them all is that they want to press a switch and get a result quickly. This makes for a less complicated purchase decision process, which involves fewer people and

stages, and is often concluded in a matter of weeks. Although these industrial products sell in higher volumes than those in the research market, they are not mass produced.

In both of these markets it is vital that our sales team establishes a relationship with the customer. For us, relationship marketing is a key ingredient of our marketing activity. Customer relationships must be maintained and nurtured as the reputation of our brand is a key influence on potential purchasers and must be protected.

The growth of our company involves finding and analysing emerging or rapidly growing markets such as Russia, Turkey, and Korea. We identify countries where governments are investing in nanotechnology and industrial growth. Our challenge then involves learning and understanding these new markets, and although the differences in some instances may be small, they are critical. We need to know the potential growth of a target market and determine what might be the optimal method of entering a market. We use a variety of methods including distributor marketing, installing a territory manager, and establishing a wholly owned office.

The essential problem that we faced when we identified India as a potential market was to determine which entry method would be most effective to help establish the credibility of Oxford Instruments and build mutually profitable business relationships.

Introduction

For many of us marketing is concerned with consumer products—those that we buy and consume on a fairly regular basis. However, there is also a colossal market that is often hidden from our daily view of the world. This is referred to as the **business market** and **business-to-business marketing** is concerned with the marketing of offerings that are bought and sold between organizations.

Some of the characteristics of business-to-business (B2B) marketing are very different from those associated with **consumer marketing**. There are numerous reasons for these differences and their impact varies among organizations. In this chapter, we explore the nature and impact of these characteristics. We highlight the main types of business-to-business organizations, learn about the different types of goods and services, and develop an understanding about the way organizations make buying decisions, who makes them, and what purchasing strategies can be used.

A traditional perception of business marketing activity is that it concerns salespeople selling products with services attached (Leigh and Marshall, 2001). In many ways this was true, but now that the answers to most prior-to-purchase questions and much customer order-taking is an online activity, the sales department has shifted its role. Now salespeople are intent on increasing customer productivity, with a focus on managing relationships. Previously, its thrust was tactical, but now it is more strategic (Piercy, 2006).

Citing Vargo and Lusch (2004), Storbacka et al. (2009: 892) state that there 'has been a significant shift from product to service (or solution) selling ("servitisation") in many business-to-business interactions'. Research by Storbacka et al. (2009) shows that sales is increasingly about process, rather than a series of separate transactions carried out by a specific function. They claim that the sales process is much more relational than it used to be. Second, the sales function now involves close working links between sales and operations, especially as sales increasingly becomes linked with information gathering, processing, and interpretation, resource mobilization, and delivery. This makes sales much more cross-functional than it used to be. Finally, they observe the increasing emphasis on customer issues, and also on sales metrics, suggesting that the sales function has shifted from an operational to a strategic activity.

A key part of B2B marketing is associated with managing the relationships that can develop between organizations and the people who represent them. Therefore managing customers is vitally important, and one task is to identify and manage those customers that are important to the success of the organization. This is referred to as **key account** management, and we examine this topic because it is becoming an important aspect of B2B marketing. Although the chapter focuses on the differences and characteristics of business marketing, we conclude with a reflection of the similarities that exist between business and consumer marketing.

What is Business-to-Business Marketing?

Just imagine the complexity associated with the design and construction of Boeing's 787 Dreamliner, the King Abdullah Economic City project between Jeddah and Rabigh in Saudi Arabia, the Russky Island bridge in Vladivostok, or the Skipark 360° in Stockholm. A vast network of organizations, large and small, is involved in specifying, negotiating, buying and

The design and construction of an airliner involves a vast number of parts, materials, sub-assemblies, and services which necessitates a huge network of organizations.
Source: istock © Martin_Petit.

selling, building, delivering and storing, and then replacing parts and materials as they become used. The operational difficulty alone is enormous, and the value of the materials, components, labour, and energy involved far exceeds consumer spending in the soap, beauty, or confectionery markets. The market for goods and services bought and sold between businesses is simply huge.

To make a car, a manufacturer must try to create value: they do this by buying a range of finished and part-finished items, assembling them, and distributing the completed cars to dealers who sell them to consumers or businesses (fleet-buyers). The array of parts and finished items that the manufacturer buys involves a huge number of suppliers. This is the business market. The actions undertaken by a supplier of a brake system in order to influence the car manufacturer to select their system rather than a competitor's constitute business-to-business marketing.

In a number of ways, B2B marketing is fundamentally different from consumer goods or services marketing because organizational buyers do not consume the products or services themselves. Unlike consumer markets, where goods and services are consumed individually, invariably by the people who buy them, the essence of business markets is that organizations, not individual people, undertake the act of purchase.

Far larger than the consumer market, the business market comprises many types and sizes of organization. Each organization interacts with a selection of others and forms relationships of varying significance and duration. This web of interaction is referred to as a network. Although organizations are often structurally and legally independent entities, a key characteristic is that they are also interdependent. That is, they have to work with other organizations, to varying degrees, to achieve their goals.

Characteristics of Business Markets

Business markets are characterized by a number of factors, but the main ones are the nature of demand, the buying processes, international dimensions, and, perhaps most importantly, the relationships that develop between organizations in the process of buying and selling. These are shown in Figure 15.1 and are examined in turn.

The Nature of Demand

There are three key aspects of demand in business markets: derivation, variance, and elasticity. Demand in business markets is ultimately derived from consumers (Gummesson and Polese, 2009). This may seem a little odd, but consider the demand for building trains. When Banverket, the Swedish Railway Administration, and Bombardier Transportation, considered developing a 'Green Train', the goal was to develop a new generation of high-speed super-efficient trains that meet the special technical and traffic requirements in the Nordic Countries. Part of the project team's calculation was to estimate the number of people prepared to make train journeys and what they are prepared to pay. Even though each train is the result of hundreds of organizations interacting with one another, it is train passengers (consumers) who actually stimulate demand for the construction of trains.

Demand is variable because consumer preferences and behaviour fluctuate. The demand for rail journeys, for example, usually declines following a major train accident or a significant increase in fares. It also increases in response to petrol price rises and calls for consumers to be more environmentally aware. The subsequent impact could be felt on rail operators, support services, train manufacturers, and the whole array of suppliers and subcontractors in the market. All of this suggests that organizations should monitor and anticipate demand. See Market Insight 15.1 for an example.

Figure 15.1
Key characteristics of business markets

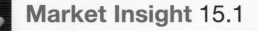

Market Insight 15.1

Baltic Baker Predicts and Responds

In many industries demand fluctuates for a number of reasons. These might involve falling prices, rapid technological change, or even volatility where frequent variation in product demand can cause companies to swing between having no stock to periods of over-production and surplus capacity. This, in turn, can impact on the rate and size of investment made by organizations as they flex themselves in anticipation of 'foreseeable' demand.

For example, the food group VAASAN produces a variety of fresh bakery products and breads for sale in retail chains, restaurants, and hotels. The Northern European group has subsidiaries in Finland, Norway, and Sweden, and in addition is also one of the largest thin crisp and crisp-bread producers in the world.

One of the critical success factors in the food industry concerns the production of the right products, for the right customers at the right time, and in VAASAN's case, across the Nordic region. The company aims for a minimum on-time delivery rate of 98.5% Unfortunately, each of the group's subsidiaries had developed different methods of predicting customer demand. This represented a business risk, so a standardized process was necessary in order to predict fluctuations in customer demand and adjust production and delivery schedules to meet them.

The solution lay in a demand planning system that gathered and analysed data from multiple sources. These included the company's enterprise resource planning (ERP) system and data warehouse, plus expert opinions from its sales analysts and customers.

This combination of historical sales data and expert prediction allows VAASAN to identify trends in customer demand and generate rolling forecasts. This in turn enables the group to predict its raw materials requirements and to adjust workforce planning and production scheduling to prepare for any anticipated rise in customer orders.

When the Swedish subsidiary won new customers and increased the range of products available to

Vaasan, the Northern European baker, is one of the largest thin crisp and crisp-bread producers in the world
Source: © Vaasan.

consumers, demand increased by 30%. The demand forecasting solution was used to predict the total sales volumes at each of the new customer's outlets. This in turn gave VAASAN sufficient time to plan and adjust the manufacturing schedule at its bakeries in order to increase the daily production volumes. Not only are customers happy and relationships strengthened, but capacity utilization and plant efficiency is improved significantly, thus minimizing the business risk of over- or under-production.

Source: Adapted from www.cafod.org.uk/policy_and_analysis/public_policy_papers www-01.ibm.com/software/success/cssdb.nsf/cs/STRD-8YKKDA?OpenDocument&Site=cognos&cty=en_us

1 **From where is the demand for bakery products derived?**

2 **Do you believe that demand for bakery products is elastic or inelastic?**

3 **How else might a marketing manager overcome this type of volatility?**

Demand is essentially inelastic. If suppliers raise their prices, most manufacturers will try to absorb the increases into their own cost structures to avoid letting their customers down in the short term, or because they are tied into fixed price contracts. Incorporating these price increases, at least over the short to medium term, means that there is price inelasticity. In the medium term, manufacturers can eliminate the original parts, redesign the proposition, or search for new suppliers.

The Buying Processes

The buying processes undertaken by organizations differ in a number of ways from those used by consumers. These differences are a reflection of the potential high financial value associated with these transactions, product complexity, the relatively large value of individual orders, and the nature of the risk and uncertainty. As a result, organizations have developed particular processes and procedures, which often involve a large number of people. What is central, however, is that the group of people involved in organizational purchasing processes are referred to as a decision-making unit, and that the types of purchases they make are classified as **buyclasses**, all of which are made in various **buyphases**. Details about these processes are outlined in the section The Decision-Making Unit: Processes.

International Dimensions

In comparison with consumer markets, B2B marketing is much easier to conduct internationally. This is because the needs of businesses around the world are far more similar to one another than the needs of consumers, whose preferences, tastes, and resources vary. As a result, an increasing number of B2B organizations are moving into international markets. This is often enabled by advances in technology, most notably the internet, which permit organizations enormous geographical coverage.

In comparison with B2C markets, B2B organizations benefit from a smaller variety of product functionality and performance. This is partly because the various trading associations across the world have agreed standards relating to content and performance. This means that buying and selling of products and services, wherever located, are relatively simple and the trading environment is reasonably well-regulated and controlled. Many industries (e.g. the steel, plastic, chemicals, and paper industries) all have commonly agreed standards, which facilitate inter-organizational exchange processes. In B2C markets there are numerous issues concerning consumer culture and values and the adaptation of products and promotional activities to meet various colour, ingredient, stylistic, buying process, packaging, and language requirements.

Visit the **Online Resource Centre** and follow the weblink to ABBA, the Association for B2B Agencies to learn more about B2B organizations.

Relationships

If there is one characteristic that separates business marketing from consumer marketing, it is the importance of relationships. In B2C markets, the low **perceived value** of the products and the competitive nature of the market, which makes product substitution relatively easy, makes relationships between manufacturers and consumers relatively more difficult to establish. In business marketing, the interaction between buyers, sellers, and other stakeholders is of major

Research Insight 15.1

To take your learning further, you might wish to read this influential paper.

Dwyer, R. F., Schurr, P. H., and Oh, S. (1987), 'Developing buyer–seller relationships', *Journal of Marketing*, 51(April), 11–27.

This paper is one of the most cited by other researchers in the subject area. Its popularity is based on the critical observation that buyer–seller exchanges are not discrete activities or events, but a part of ongoing relationships. The authors present a framework for developing buyer–seller relationships that links into marketing strategy.

Visit the **Online Resource Centre** to read the abstract and access the full paper.

significance. The development and maintenance of relationships between buying and selling organizations is pivotal to success. Interdependence, collaboration, and in some cases partnership over the development, supply, and support of products and services are considered core elements of B2B marketing. Strong inter-organizational relationships are referred to as 'embedded ties'. Noordhoff *et al.* (2011) refer to these as a close and reciprocal relationship between a customer firm and a supplier firm. It is accepted that embedded ties improve relational and business performance outcomes because they are understood to facilitate the transfer of complex, sensitive, and even tacit knowledge between partners (Reagans and McEvily, 2003) and improve innovation.

The importance of relationships in B2B marketing should not be underestimated. More information about relationship issues and concepts can be found in Chapter 14.

Types of Organizational Customers

Once referred to as industrial marketing, the term B2B marketing has now been adopted because it recognizes the involvement of a range of other non-industrial suppliers, agents, and participants. The government, the non-profit sector, and charities and institutions in most countries are responsible for a huge level of B2B activity. Consider the transactions necessary to support various government functions. For example, the huge range of offerings necessary to support the pharmaceutical and medical supplies in the health service, and the products and infrastructure necessary to maintain the prison and military services, all represent a major slice of B2B activity.

It is possible to categorize organizations by their size (revenue or number of employees), namely large, medium, and small organizations. Macfarlane (2002) refers to global and national organizations, the public sector, small and medium-sized enterprises (SMEs), and small office/

home office (SOHOs). However, this approach is too general and fails to accommodate different buyer needs and purchasing procedures. Here, three broad types of B2B organizations are identified: commercial, government, and institutional organizations. See Table 15.1 for a brief outline of their principal characteristics.

All of these types of B2B organizations—commercial, government, and institutions—buy goods and services on an inter-organizational basis. Consumers are only involved through their interaction with retailers or as end-users of health treatments, education, or policing for which no direct financial exchange occurs. The type of marketing activities used to encourage repeat exchanges between these various types of organization can be considerable. However, one common strategy has been the more overt approach to developing relationships through cooperation and collaboration.

Table 15.1 Key types of business organizations

Type of organization		Key characteristics
Commercial	Distributors	Wholesalers, value added resellers, retailers and distributors/dealers. Not only do they smooth the progress of products through the marketing channel but they should also add value to them by providing storage (through distribution centres), services (such as training), or financial support (such as credit facilities). See Market Insight 15.2.
	OEMs	Original equipment manufacturers (OEMs) refers to one company relabelling a product, incorporating it within a different product, in order to sell it under their own brand name and offering its own warranty, support, and licensing. For example, Toyota may have a contract with a headlight manufacturer to supply them with a certain quantity of headlight assemblies. Toyota is the OEM because they build these headlight assemblies into their different cars and sell the car as a Toyota, without identifying the manufacturer of the headlight assembly.
	Users	Users are organizations that purchase goods and services that are then consumed as part of their production and manufacturing processes. Therefore users consume these parts and materials and they do not appear in the final product offering but do contribute to its production. Toyota will purchase many support materials, for example, machine tools, electrical manufacturing equipment, vending machines, office furniture, and stationery. None of these can be identified within the cars they produce.
	Retailers	Retailers need to purchase goods in order to resell them just as other organizations do. However, the buying processes are not always as complex or as intricate as those normally associated with organizational buying and the group of people who make purchase decisions—the decision-making unit (DMU). Suppliers need to understand their retailers and their markets.

Table 15.1 continued

Type of organization	Key characteristics
Government	The value of the business undertaken by governments is very high. Health, policing, education, transport, environmental protection, and national defence and security are a few of the areas that require public investment. Many of the larger projects that concern governments and associated ministries are large and complex, and involve a huge number of stakeholders. Although similar in many ways to commercial purchasing procedures and guidelines, those in the government sector are subject to political objectives, budget policies, accountability, and EC Directives (van Weele, 2002).
Institutions	Institutions include not-for-profit organizations such as churches and charities, community-based organizations such as housing associations, and government-related organizations such as hospitals, schools, museums, libraries, and universities. Characteristically, institutions tend to form large buying groups. Through collaboration the group is able to negotiate greatly reduced prices and much larger discounts, usually related to bulk purchases.

Research Insight 15.2

To take your learning further, you might wish to read this influential paper.

Achrol, R. S. (1997), 'Changes in the theory of interorganizational relations in marketing: toward a network paradigm', *Journal of the Academy of Marketing Science*, 25(1), 56–71.

Achrol sets out how the then-established vertically integrated, multidivisional type of organization started to be replaced by new forms of network organization consisting of large numbers of functionally specialized firms tied together in cooperative exchange relationships. He considers four main types, the variables involved, the economic rationale, and the types of coordination and control mechanisms necessary for organizations to adapt to the new environment.

@ **Visit the Online Resource Centre to read the abstract and access the full paper.**

Table 15.2 Types of business goods and services

Type of goods	Explanation
Input goods Raw materials, semi-manufactured parts, and finished goods	Input goods have been subjected to different levels of processing (*raw materials*, *semi-manufactured parts*, and *finished* goods), and they lose their individual identities and become part of the finished item.
Equipment goods Otherwise known as capital or investment goods	These are necessary for manufacturing and operations to take place. Land and buildings, computer systems, and machine tools are all necessary to support the production process, but they cannot be identified in the finished product.
Supply goods Otherwise known as maintenance, repair, and operating materials (MRO) items	These goods and services are 'consumables' as they are necessary to keep production processes and the organization running. For example, lubricants, paints, screws, and cleaning materials may all be necessary to maintain a firm's operations. Computer or IT servicing is necessary to maintain operations and to avoid down-time, whilst accounting audits are a legal requirement.

Types of Business Goods and Services

Just as there are a variety of types of organizations in the business sector, so the offerings available are equally varied and complex. Table 15.2 sets out the three principal business types of goods and services.

Most organizations, at various points in their development, have to decide whether to make/supply their own products and services or buy them in from outsourced providers. This 'make or buy' decision can have far-reaching effects not only on the strategic and operational aspects of an organization, but also on the purchasing function and its role within an organization.

Outsourcing is an increasingly popular activity practised by a wide range of organizations. As a result, purchasing behaviours have had to adapt accordingly which, in turn, has impacted on business marketing. The development of 'lean management' techniques has enabled organizations to concentrate on their core processes and to outsource all other activities. As organizations have become 'leaner', they dramatically reduce their use of resources and the importance of purchasing increases (Durham and Ritchey, 2009).

Visit the **Online Resource Centre** and complete Internet Activity 15.1 to learn more about how the internet is used to market computing software to business customers.

Organizational Buyer Behaviour

Only by appreciating the particular behaviour, purchasing systems, people, and policies used by an organization can suitable marketing and selling strategies be implemented. This section builds on the introduction to buyer processes made earlier in this chapter and the **organizational buyer behaviour** and segmentation information introduced in Chapter 6. It considers some of the key issues associated with the way organizations purchase the goods and services necessary to achieve their corporate goals.

Two definitions of organizational buyer behaviour reveal important aspects of this subject. First, Webster and Wind (1972) defined organizational buying as 'the decision making process by which formal organizations establish the need for purchased products and services and identify, evaluate and choose among alternative brands and suppliers'. This adopts a buying organization's perspective and highlights the important point that organizational buying behaviour involves processes rather than a single static one-off event. There are a number of stages, or phases, associated with product procurement, each one often requiring a key decision to be made.

A second definition, by Parkinson and Baker (1994: 6), cited by Ulkuniemi (2003), states that organizational buying behaviour concerns 'the purchase of a product or service to satisfy organizational rather than individual goals'. This takes a neutral perspective but makes the point that organizational buyer behaviour is about satisfying organization-wide needs and hence requires marketers to adopt processes that take into account the needs of different people, not a single individual.

Organizational buying behaviour is about three key issues.

- The functions and processes buyers move through when purchasing products for use in business markets.

- Strategy, where purchasing is designed to assist value creation and competitive advantage, and to influence supply chain activities.

- The network of relationships that organizations are part of when purchasing. The placement of orders and contracts between organizations can confirm a current trading relationship, initiate a new set of relationships, or may even signal the demise of a relationship.

What should be clear is that organizational buying behaviour is not just about the purchase of goods and services. In addition to this fundamental task, it is concerned with the strategic development of the organization, creating value, and the management of inter-organizational relationships, all key issues in B2B marketing. These issues overlap each other and are not discrete items.

Hollyoake (2009) argues that business marketing is increasingly about managing buyers' experiences and interactions. This involves creating expectations, often referred to as the brand promise, and then delivering products and services against these promises. It is important that a customer's evaluation of their experience is ahead of what was expected. Hollyoake develops these ideas to consider 'ease of doing business' as a measure of the supplier–customer relationship and to discover the key dimensions of the customer experience. He suggests that experiences are founded on four pillars: trust, interdependence, integrity, and communication. These ideas are also explored in Chapter 14.

Grönroos (2009) develops the principles about expectations into a new perspective of (business) marketing, referred to as **promise management**. These ideas are rooted in what

Grönroos sees as the purpose of contemporary marketing, namely as a value creation process. Firms are involved in developing and delivering value propositions (promises). These propositions of value can only be realized once an offering is consumed, and that can only be done by customers. Therefore value creation is experienced only by customers as value fulfilment.

Decision-Making Units: Characteristics

Although organizations usually designate a 'buyer' who is responsible for the purchase of a range of offerings, in reality a range of people are involved in the purchasing process. The purchasing process is a means by which an organization creates value. Therefore it is an integral part of an organization's value at some point in the future. This group of people is referred to as either the **decision-making unit (DMU)** or the **buying centre**. In many circumstances these are informal groupings of people who come together in varying ways to contribute to the decision-making process. Certain projects, usually of major significance or value, require a group of people to be formally constituted who have responsibility to oversee and complete the purchase of a stipulated item or products and services relating to a specific project.

DMUs vary in composition and size according to the nature of each individual purchasing task. Webster and Wind (1972) identified a number of people who undertake different roles within buying centres and these are set out in Figure 15.2.

- **Initiators** start the whole process by requesting the purchase of an item. They may also assume other roles within the DMU or wider organization.

- **Users** literally use the product once it has been acquired and they will also evaluate its performance. Users may not only initiate the purchase process but are sometimes involved in the specification process. Their role is continuous, although it may vary from the highly involved to the peripheral.

- **Influencers** very often help set the technical specifications for the proposed purchase and assist the evaluation of alternative offerings by potential suppliers. These may be consultants hired to complete a particular project. For example, an office furniture manufacturer will regard

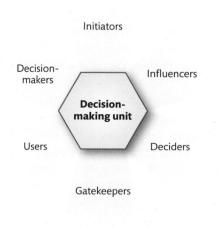

Figure 15.2

Membership of the decision-making unit

Source: Fill and McKee (2012). Reproduced with the kind permission of Goodfellow Publishers.

office managers as key decision-makers but understand that specifiers such as office design-ers and architects influence the office manager's decision about furniture decision (see Market Insight 15.2).

- **Deciders** are those who make purchasing decisions, and they are the most difficult to identify. This is because they may not have formal authority to make a purchase decision, yet are suf-ficiently influential internally that their decision carries the most weight. In repeat buying activi-ties, the buyer may also be the decider. However, it is normal practice for a senior manager to authorize expenditure decisions involving sums over a certain financial limit.

- **Buyers** or purchasing managers select suppliers and manage the process whereby the required products are procured. Buyers may not decide which product is to be purchased, but they influence the framework within which the decision is made. They will formally under-take the process whereby products and services are purchased once a decision has been made to procure them. For example, they may be formal buyers and kick-start the purchase of a type of lubricant because the stock figures have fallen to a threshold level that indicates that current supplies will be exhausted within three weeks. Therefore they will assume the roles of both an initiator and a buyer.

- **Gatekeepers** have the potential to control the type and flow of information to the organiza-tion and the members of the DMU. These gatekeepers may be assistants, technical personnel, secretaries, or telephone switchboard operators.

Market Insight 15.2

Alibaba Connects Global Buyers and Suppliers

The roles of influencers and decision-makers are important in the B2B buying process. When faced with risk, decision-makers buy from familiar companies. By providing appropriate information, opportunities can arise for building credibility and providing a sound platform for a long-term customer relationship.

Alibaba.com is an online marketplace with more than 36.7 million members, made up of small business buyers and suppliers, who can contact and trade with each other. Alibaba launched a UK campaign encompassing TV, outdoor, and online, targeting small and medium businesses in 2009. Using the proposition 'working for you', it featured potential entrepreneurs, with the strapline 'Whatever your business, get Alibaba.com working for you'.

One ad featured Minster Giftware, a small family business in Nottingham. The company is a direct importer and supplier of furnishing accessories to companies of all sizes throughout Europe. The ad showed how the owner, through using Alibaba.com, was able to research products, find samples and suppliers in just a single day, and then arrange three factory visits prior to launching a whole new product range at extremely competitive prices. Therefore Alibaba.com enables suppliers to reach potential decision-makers, as well as buyers and influencers.

'Gandys', established in 2011 by brothers Rob, Paul, and Matt Forkan, is a footwear brand based on stylish and fun flipflops. To find the right manufacturer to help them build their ideal flipflop they used Alibaba.com. After entering their requirements in the simple-to-use online system, they were provided with a list of suitable product

Market Insight 15.2

continued

manufacturers. Following discussions with several nominated suppliers, a few prototypes were developed. This helped secure significant investment in their business, and in 2012 their flipflops were in 60 boutiques across the UK, with plans to more than double these in 2013.

Sources: http://www.alibaba.com/others/ibdm/emea_worksforyou/success-stories.html http://www.alibaba.com/activities/ibdm/goodideas/stories.html?tracelog=uksite_mggs_1208#.UXFV1LXrzi4

1 **What do you think is the main difference between an influencer and an opinion former? (Hint: see Chapter 10).**

2 **Think of an industry or sector with which you are familiar and try to determine possible influencers.**

3 **Visit the Alibaba website (www.alibaba.com) and list the advantages and disadvantages of using the site from a marketing perspective**

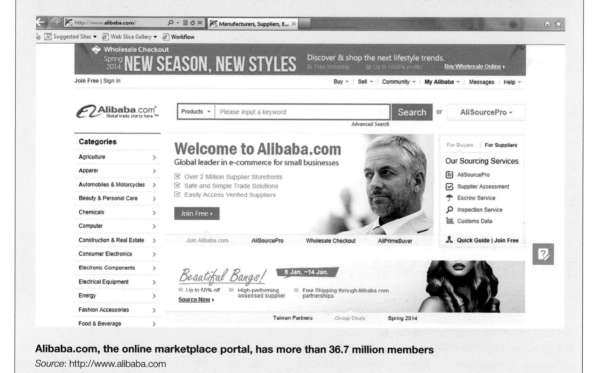

Alibaba.com, the online marketplace portal, has more than 36.7 million members

Source: http://www.alibaba.com

The size and form of the buying centre is not static. It can vary according to the complexity of the product being considered and the degree of risk that each decision is perceived to carry for the organization. Different roles are required and adopted as the nature of the buying task changes with each new purchase situation (Bonoma, 1982). All of these roles might be subsumed within one individual for certain decisions. It is vital for seller organizations to identify members of the buying centre, and to target and refine their messages to meet the needs of each member of the centre.

Membership of the DMU is far from fixed, and this fluidity poses problems for selling organizations simply because it is not always possible to identify key members or shifts in policy or requirements. As Spekman and Gronhaug (1986) point out, the DMU is a 'vague construct that can reach across a number of different functional roles with any number of individuals participating or exerting influence at any one time'. Therefore it is worth noting that, within this context, the behaviour of DMU members is also largely determined by the interpersonal relationships of the members of the centre.

The Decision-Making Unit: Processes

Organizational buying decisions vary in terms of the nature of the offering, the frequency and the relative value of purchases, their strategic impact (if any), and the type of relationship with suppliers. These, and many other factors, are potentially significant to individual buying organizations. However, there are three main types of buying situations. Referred to by Robinson *et al.* (1967) as buyclasses these are **new task**, **modified rebuy**, and **straight rebuy**. These are summarized in Table 15.3.

Buyclasses

New Task

As the name implies, the organization is faced with a first-time buying situation. Risk is inevitably large at this point as there is little collective experience of the product/service or the relevant suppliers. As a result of these factors there are normally a large number of decision participants. Each participant requires a lot of information and a relatively long period of time is needed for the information to be assimilated and a decision to be made.

Table 15.3 Main characteristics of the buyclasses

Buyclass	Degree of familiarity with the problem	Information requirements	Alternative solutions
New buy	The problem is fresh to the decision-makers	A great deal of information is required	Alternative solutions are unknown; all are considered new
Modified rebuy	The requirement is not new but is different from previous situations	More information is required but past experience is of use	Buying decision needs new solutions
Rebuy	The problem is identical to previous experiences	Little or no information is required	Alternative solutions not sought or required

Source: Fill, C. (2009), *Marketing Communications: Interactivity, Communities and Content* (5th edn), Harlow: FT/Prentice Hall.

Modified Rebuy

Having purchased a product, uncertainty is reduced but not eliminated, so the organization may request through their buyer(s) that certain modifications be made to future purchases—for example, adjustments to the specification of the product, further negotiation on price levels, or perhaps an arrangement for alternative delivery patterns. Fewer people are involved in the decision-making process than in the new task situation.

Straight Rebuy

In this situation, the purchasing department reorders on a routine basis, very often working from an approved list of suppliers. These may be products that an organization consumes in order to keep operating (e.g. office stationery), or may be low-value materials used within the operational value-added part of the organization (e.g. the manufacturing processes). No other people are involved with the exercise until different suppliers attempt to change the environment in which the decision is made. For example, a new supplier may interrupt the procedure with a potentially better offer. This may stimulate the emergence of a modified rebuy situation.

Straight rebuy presents classic conditions for the use of automatic reordering systems. Costs can be reduced, managerial time redirected to other projects, and the relationship between buyer and seller embedded within a stronger framework. One possible difficulty is that both parties perceive the system to be a significant exit barrier should conditions change, and this may deter flexibility or restrict opportunities to develop the same or other relationships.

The use of electronic purchasing systems at the straight rebuy stage has enabled organizations to empower employees to make purchases, although control still resides with purchasing managers. Employees can buy direct online from a catalogue list of authorized suppliers. The benefits are that employees are more involved, the purchasing process is speeded up, costs are reduced, and purchasing managers can spend more time with other higher-priority activities.

Visit the **Online Resource Centre** and follow the weblink to Electronic Commerce Europe, the biggest online trade network in the world, for more information on the use of electronic B2B purchasing.

Buyphases

Organizational buyer behaviour (OBB) consists of a series of sequential activities through which organizations proceed when making purchasing decisions. Robinson *et al*. (1967) referred to these as buying stages or buyphases. The following sequence of buyphases is particular to the new task situation just described. Many of these buyphases are ignored or compressed according to the complexity of the offering and when either a modified rebuy or straight rebuy situation is encountered.

Need/Problem Recognition

The need/recognition phase is about the identification of a gap. This is the gap between the benefits an organization is experiencing now and the benefits it would like to have. For example, when a new product is to be produced there is an obvious gap between having the necessary materials and components and being out of stock and unable to build. Therefore the first decision is about how to close this gap. There are two broad options: outsourcing the whole or parts of the production process, or building or making the objects oneself. The need has been recognized and the gap identified. The rest of this section is based on a build decision being taken.

Product Specification

As a result of identifying a problem and the size of the gap, influencers and users can determine the desired characteristics of the product needed to resolve the problem. This may take the form of either a general functional description or a much more detailed analysis and the creation of a detailed technical specification for a particular product. What sort of photocopier is required? What is it expected to achieve? How many documents should it copy per minute? Is a collator or tray required? This is an important part of the process, because if it is executed properly it will narrow the supplier search and save on the costs associated with evaluation prior to a final decision. The results of the functional and detailed specifications are often combined within a purchase order specification.

Supplier and Product Search

At this stage, the buyer actively seeks suppliers for the necessary product(s). There are two main issues at this point. First, will the product match the specification and the required performance standards? Second, will the potential supplier meet the other organizational requirements such as experience, reputation, accreditation, and credit rating? In most circumstances, organizations review the market and their internal sources of information and arrive at a decision that is based on rational criteria.

Wherever possible, organizations work to reduce uncertainty and risk. By working with others who are known, of whom the organization has direct experience, and who can be trusted, risk and uncertainty can be substantially reduced. This highlights another reason why many organizations prefer to operate within established networks that can provide support and advice when needed.

Evaluation of Proposals

Depending on the complexity and value of the potential order(s), the proposal is a vital part of the process and should be prepared professionally. The proposals from the shortlisted organizations are reviewed in the context of two main criteria: the purchase order specification and the evaluation of the supplying organization. If the potential supplier is already a part of the network, little search and review time is needed. If the proposed supplier is not part of the network, a review may be necessary to establish whether it will be appropriate (in terms of price, delivery, and service) and whether there is the potential for a long-term relationship or whether this is a single purchase that is unlikely to be repeated.

Supplier Selection

The DMU will normally undertake a supplier analysis and use a variety of decision criteria, according to the particular type of item sought. A further useful perspective is to view supplier organizations as a continuum, from reliance on a single source to the use of a wide variety of suppliers for the same product. Jackson (1985) proposed that organizations might buy an offering from a range of different suppliers to maintain a range of multiple sources (a practice of many government departments). She labelled this approach 'always a share', as several suppliers are given the opportunity to share the business available to the buying centre. The major disadvantage is that this approach fails to drive cost as low as possible, as the discounts derived from volume sales are not achieved. The advantage to the buying centre is that a relatively small investment is required and little risk is entailed in following such a strategy.

At the other end of the continuum are organizations that only use a single source supplier. All purchases are made from the single source until circumstances change to such a degree that the buyer's needs are no longer being satisfied. Jackson referred to these organizations as 'lost for good'; because once a relationship with a new organization has been developed they are lost for good to the original supplier. An increasing number of organizations are choosing to enter alliances with a limited number of, or even single source, suppliers. The objective is to build a long-term relationship, and to work together to build quality and help each other achieve their goals. Outsourcing manufacturing activities for non-core activities has increased considerably.

Evaluation

The order is written against the selected supplier, which is then monitored and evaluated against such diverse criteria as responsiveness to enquiries, modifications to the specification, and timing of delivery. When the product is delivered it may reach the stated specification but fail to satisfy the original need. In this case, the specification needs to be rewritten before any future orders are placed.

Developments in the environment can impact on organizational buyers and change both the nature of decisions and the way they are made. For example, the decision to purchase new plant and machinery requires consideration of the future cash flows generated by the capital item. Many people will be involved in the decision, and the time necessary for consultation may mean that other parts of the decision-making process are completed simultaneously.

Visit the **Online Resource Centre** and complete Internet Activity 15.1. This will aid learning about the seven buying phases that organizations go through when purchasing industrial goods and services.

Buyphases	Buyclasses		
	New task	**Modified rebuy**	**Straight rebuy**
Problem recognition	Yes	Possibly	No
General need description	Yes	Possibly	No
Product specification	Yes	Yes	Yes
Supplier search	Yes	Possibly	No
Supplier selection	Yes	Possibly	No
Order process specification	Yes	Possibly	No
Performance review	Yes	Yes	Yes

Table 15.4 **The buygrid framework**

Buygrids

When the buyphases are linked to the buyclasses, a buygrid is determined. This grid is shown in Table 15.4.

The buygrid serves to illustrate the relationships between buyphases and buyclasses. It is important because it highlights the need to focus on buying situations or contexts, rather than on offerings. Even though this approach was developed over 40 years ago, it is still an important foundation for this topic.

According to the buyphase model, buyers make decisions rationally and sequentially, but this does not entirely match with practical experience. For example, such a long and complex process is not evident in every buying situation and differs according to the kind of products and services bought, the experience and resources available to organizations, and the prevailing culture. In other words, there are many variables that can influence organizational buying behaviour.

The Role of Purchasing in Organizations

All organizations have to buy a variety of offerings to operate normally and achieve their performance targets. What we have set out so far are the general principles, types, and categories associated with organizational buying. However, the way in which organizations buy products and services varies considerably and does not always fit neatly with the categories presented here. Professional purchasing is not only an important (if not critical) feature, but for many organizations it is also an integral part of their overall operations and strategic orientation (Ryals and Rogers, 2006; Pressey *et al.*, 2007).

In the past, an organization's purchasing activities could have been characterized as an 'order-delivery response function'. Purchasing departments signed orders and the right deliveries were made at the right place and the right time, and then invoiced correctly. The goal was to play off one supplier against another, and as a result reduce costs and improve short-term profits. Purchasing departments used to be regarded as an isolated function within organizations, a necessary but uninteresting aspect of organizational performance. That perspective changed towards the end of the last century. Now organizations reduce the number of their suppliers, sometimes to just one, and **strategic procurement** (as it is often termed) is used to negotiate with suppliers on a cooperative basis in order to help build long-term relationships. Purchasing has become an integral part of an organization's operations.

One of the main reasons for this changed approach was research that showed that business performance improves when organizations adopt a collaborative, rather than adversarial, approach to purchasing and account management (Swinder and Seshadri, 2001). However, there are several other related issues that have changed the role of purchasing, namely customer sophistication, increasing competition, and various strategic issues.

Customer Sophistication

Owing to increasing customer sophistication, organizations are trying to differentiate their offerings and become more specialized. Organizational purchasing has to follow this movement and also become more specialized, otherwise the organization will become increasingly ineffective in meeting customer needs.

Increasing Competition

With increasing competition, margins have been eroded. As a result, more attention has been paid to internal costs and operations. By influencing purchasing costs and managerial costs associated with dealing with multiple suppliers, the profitability of the organization can be directly impacted. Consequently, the importance of purchasing polices, processes, and procedures within organizations have increased.

Strategic Issues

There are several strategic issues related to the purchasing activities undertaken by organizations. First, there is the 'make or buy' decision. Should organizations make and/or assemble products for resale, or outsource or buy in particular products, parts, services, or sub-assemblies and concentrate on what is referred to as core activities or competences? Second, the benefits that arise through closer cooperation with suppliers and the increasing influence of buyer-seller relationships and 'joint value creation' have inevitably led to a tighter, more professional, and integrated purchasing function. The third strategy-related issue concerns the degree to which the purchasing function is integrated into the organization. New IT systems have raised the level of possible integration of purchasing and operations to the extent that the competitive strength of the organization is enhanced (Hemsworth *et al.,* 2008). As if to highlight the variation

Nokia and Skype joined R&D efforts for VOIP mobile service
Source: Courtesy of Skype.

in approaches to purchasing behaviour, Svahn and Westerlund (2009) identify six principal purchasing strategies used by organizations.

■ The 'price minimizer' purchasing strategy refers to a buyer's efficiency orientation where the main purchasing goal is to seek the lowest price for the offering. To help achieve this, the buyer actively promotes competition among several potential suppliers.

■ The 'bargainer' purchasing strategy focuses on a dyadic buyer–seller relationship. Here, the buyer's strategy is to achieve operational efficiency through long-term collaboration with a selected supplier (Håkansson and Snehota 1995; Anderson and Narus, 1999).

■ The 'clockwiser' purchasing strategy refers to network relationships that function predictably and precisely, just as a clock works. Again, the goal is strict efficiency, achieved through the vigilant integration of production-based integrated control systems and IT, and the careful coordination of the value activities performed by each supply network partner (Glenn and Wheeler, 2004).

■ The 'adaptator' purchasing strategy focuses on adapting the manufacturing processes between the exchange parties. This can arise during the purchase of one major product or service when the seller is required to accommodate its offering to the particular needs of the buyer.

■ The 'projector' purchasing strategy occurs between buyers and sellers who are development partners. This can occur during projects when partners develop their offerings in close collaboration, after which the joint development project is completed and the parties continue the development work independently. As an example of this strategy, we could explore the collaboration between Nokia and Skype. These major players in the information and communication technology industry joined their development efforts in order to develop a radically novel type of mobile phone that utilizes the voice-over-internet service (the free-call system created by Skype).

- The 'updater' purchasing strategy is based on collaboration in research and development. Here, collaboration between partners is continuous and the nature of the relationship is not a dyad but a supply network. This collaboration is intentional as demonstrated by Intel and various PC manufacturers, who produce updated versions of personal computers as a result of constant co-development.

Customer Portfolio Matrix

These six core strategies reflect the complexity and the variety of purchasing activities undertaken by buying organizations. Most supplying organizations have a mixture of different types of customers or accounts. Each account varies in terms of frequency of purchase, types of products and services bought, prices paid, delivery cycles, time taken to pay, the level of support required, purchasing strategies, and many other factors. These variables are partly a reflection of the strength of the relationship between buyer and seller, and they impact on the profitability each account represents to the seller.

Therefore it makes sense to categorize customers to determine their relative profitability. This, in turn, enables sellers to allocate resources to customers according to their potential to deliver profits in the future. One useful approach, called a **customer (or account) portfolio matrix**, brings together the potential attractiveness and the current strength of the relationship between seller and buyer (see Figure 15.3).

The relationship dimension incorporates the strengths from a customer's perspective relative to competitors. For example, a strong relationship is indicative of two organizations working closely together, whereas a weak relationship suggests that they have little interest in each other. Customer attractiveness refers to total revenue spend, average rate of growth, and the opportunities a buyer represents to the seller in terms of profit potential. These calculations can be complicated and involve a measure of management judgment. For clarity, these scales are presented as high or low, strong or weak. However, they should be considered as a continuum, and accounts can be positioned on the matrix not just in a sector but at a particular position within a sector. As a result, strategies can be formulated to move accounts to different positions which, in turn, necessitate the use of different resources.

'Must-Have Customers' in Sector A in Figure 15.3 enjoy a close business relationship and are also attractive in terms of their profit potential. Many of these customers are assigned key account status (see the section on Key Account Management), but all represent investment opportunities and resources should be allocated to develop them all.

'Good-to-Have Customers' in Sector B are essentially prospects because, although they are highly attractive, their relationship with the seller is currently weak. In this situation, marketing resources should be allocated on a selective basis that is proportional to the value that each prospect represents: high investment for good prospects and low for the others.

Relationships with customers in Sector C are strong, but they do not offer strong potential. Therefore these 'Need-to-Have Customers' are important because they provide steady background business that is marginally profitable, so resources need to be maintained. Where it is identified that some of these customers are supported by a relatively large sales team, significant cost-savings can be achieved relatively quickly. There is little reason to invest in the 'Do-Not-Need Customers' in Sector D. Relationships with these customers are weak and, as they are

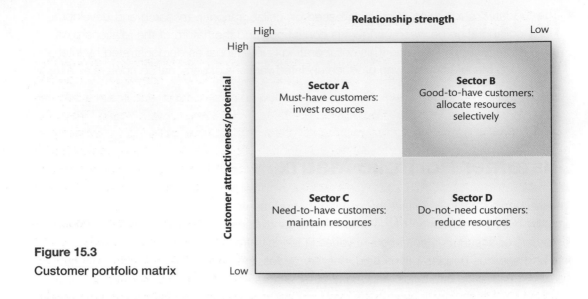

Figure 15.3
Customer portfolio matrix

relatively unattractive in terms of profit potential, many of these customers should be 'let go' and released to competitors. They represent a net drain on the selling organization. Therefore customers in this sector should receive little support and freed-up resources should be directed to customers in sectors A and B.

One of the benefits of developing a customer portfolio matrix is that it becomes easier to allocate sales channels to customers. Multichannel marketing decisions are important and should be rooted within the customer portfolio matrix. A range of channel strategies that relate to the channel needs of business customers and to any end-user target consumer segments can be identified (Payne and Frow, 2004). These can be considered to be part of a spectrum. At one end channels can consist of a dedicated personal key account manager (highly personalized sales channel), and at the other end the channel can be purely electronic with no personal contact at all. In the middle, there will be a range of different combinations of personal and electronic channels (see Figure 15.4).

In reality, most business customers will use a mixture of online and offline resources wherever possible and according to their specific needs. Therefore it is important for selling organizations to identify and allocate the most appropriate set of channels for their customers, based on the business potential each customer represents. These channels can be changed as the intensity of a customer relationship and their attractiveness develops over time.

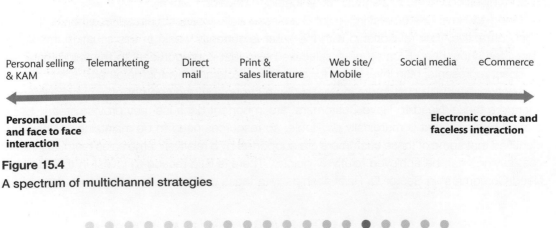

Figure 15.4
A spectrum of multichannel strategies

Professional Services Marketing

Professional service firms (PSFs) can be distinguished as an independent type of organization. They provide services to all other organizations and can be found in many sectors, including engineering, architecture, IT and software, and management consultancy and financial services companies such as PricewaterhouseCoopers, Deloitte, KPMG, and Ernst & Young. They offer highly complex and customized services that are created and delivered by highly qualified personnel (Reid, 2008). PSFs possess authority which is granted by the community in which they operate. For example, accounting firms delineate international accounting standards which in turn impact financial markets. They are governed by an ethical code and exhibit a professional culture (Thakor and Kumar, 2000).

According to Gummesson (1978), a professional service is provided by qualified people, is advisory, focuses on problem solving, and is an assignment from the buyer to the seller. Typical services include management, accounting, law, engineering, surveying, and medicine, and are often referred to as 'knowledge engines for business' (Lorsch and Tierney, 2002: 14).

Greenwood *et al.* (2005: 661) define PSFs as 'those whose primary assets are a highly educated (professional) workforce and whose outputs are intangible services encoded with complex knowledge'. They use this understanding to identify two characteristic dependencies that serve to segregate PSFs from goods-producing organizations. The first dependency concerns a client's dependency on the PSF due to the imbalance of information held by the two parties. The second concerns the dependency on its professional workforce and the high levels of mobility necessary to generate the PSF's outputs (see Market Insight 15.3 for an example of how a PSF rescued a parts supplier).

 ## Market Insight 15.3

PSF Rescues Parts Supplier

Aero Inventory, an aftermarket supplier of aircraft parts supporting airlines, MROs, and supply chain specialists, went into administration in 2011. Its reputation was at an all-time low following a period of late deliveries, poor customer service, stagnant sales, and some financial reporting issues. Professional services firm KPMG were appointed as administrators, who in turn appointed an agency, BPW, to repair relationships with key industry buyers. One important goal was to steer the brand away from negative associations and to reposition it as a trustworthy, reliable, and efficient partner.

The first task was to find out what had gone wrong. The blame was put on poor internal communication which not only delayed deliveries, but also confused sales representatives and clients. The business model was based on clients phoning for quotes from various suppliers. They then waited up to two weeks to get a paper quote. These would then be compared, and there was little or no opportunity to get or give a re-quote. It was slow, costly, and very inefficient.

A simpler and more efficient customer purchase process was required. The answer involved introducing an e-commerce platform. This enabled a name change from Aero Inventory to Aeroinv.com. This helped customers not only to access the brand but also to build their quote online and receive immediate feedback.

Raising the brand profile so that it could be seen to be strong and viable was also important. This was

Market Insight 15.3
continued

achieved by attending, and using a branded stand, at all the prominent aviation trade shows around the world during the year. Updated and refreshed marketing materials, such as brochures, PDFs of case studies, and brand videos, were soon noticed. Ads were taken in the trade press, including *Aviation Week*, *Aircraft Technology*, and *Engineering & Maintenance*, to build brand values rather than drive immediate sales. Word of mouth among journalists that Aeroinv.com was investing again spread quickly. As a result of these activities over a thousand new customers registered, one of whom, Turkish Airlines, credited the new ads for making it aware of the aircraft parts supplier.

A loyalty scheme was introduced to encourage repeat business. They also launched a free delivery service for parts that weigh less than 20kg. A programme of discounts and special services for high-value clients was devised. One of these, the 'Aircraft On Ground' (AOG) service, was targeted at airlines that had to take an aircraft out of service. Delivery was free for AOG clients.

By segmenting data about clients it became easier to shape and tailor the content and target emails more accurately. As a result, opening rates improved from 16–19% to 22–25%.

Aeroinv.com gained 3,000 new customers within the first six months. Sales of over £1.5m a month were recorded each month from May to September. Annual turnover is expected to top £16m in the first year, with e-commerce business worth around £10m.

Sources: Singh (2011); Bolger (2012); www.aeroinv.com/ www.oxxygen.co.uk/aeroinv-com-business-turnaround/ http://www.kpmg.com/uk/en/issuesandinsights/articlespublications/newsreleases/pages/kpmg-launches-aeroinv-com.aspx

1 **What value might client organizations perceive when using a PSF?**

2 **To what extent do PSFs influence industry standards and regulations? When might there be an ethical issue with PSFs in this role?**

3 **Find two PSFs in the same industry, and consider their brand identities and reputation. What are the differences and similarities?**

An important question concerns what it is that characterizes a PSF. Greenwood *et al*. (2005) identify two core characteristics. The first is that the outputs of PSFs are intangible and are normally applications of complex knowledge. This makes it difficult for customers to compare and evaluate the relative competence of suppliers, and thus makes clients dependent on the professionals delivering these services.

The second defining characteristic concerns the engine of this knowledge. This is generated from a highly educated workforce, professionals who are qualified and skilled at customizing complex knowledge to different client situations. PSFs have to attract and retain qualified people who can develop close ties with each client.

These two core characteristics shape the marketing strategies of PSFs. To simplify the outputs into understandable units of information and so convince clients of its superior competence, PSFs strive to develop superior reputations. In order that the workforce continues to deliver complex knowledge and foster the relationships, it is necessary to attract and retain suitable professionals who possess high levels of mobility.

As Greenwood *et al*. (2005) acknowledge, here lies an interesting and self-fulfilling cycle of activities. The quest for suitable professionals is assisted by the development of corporate reputation, as the latter helps attract the best recruits. A strong reputation can lower marketing costs

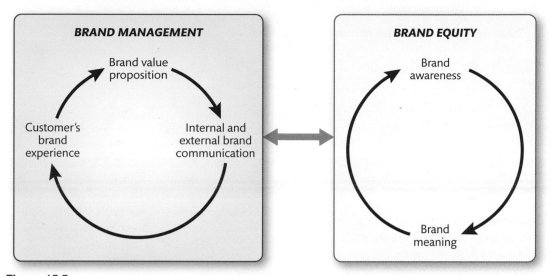

Figure 15.5

B2B service brand process

Source: Marquardt *et al.* (2011).

as clients seek out higher-status firms (Podolny, 1994). A brand name that carries a high reputation facilitates the charging of premium fees (Krishnan and Schauer, 2000).

PSFs, especially the larger multinational consultancies, invariably adopt relational marketing strategies designed to retain rather than acquire clients. According to Reid (2008), their marketing activities are then geared to generating a financial return and building a business network. However, it is the quality of the client relationship that is critical. This can be both formal (e.g. project briefings) and informal (e.g. social). This in turn requires a range of technical and interpersonal skills, and for the organization to have a clear brand vision and identity which is internalized by the professional workforce.

For PSFs, the key to successful marketing is the development of a strong reputation, and this involves the creation and maintenance of a corporate brand. Marquardt *et al.* (2011) have developed a service brand process model (see Figure 15.5). This is useful because it identifies three brand management components. The first is the need to develop a compelling brand value proposition, or promise. The second is the use of internal and external communications to inform and influence stakeholders, particularly clients, about the brand. The third and final component concerns customers' experiences with the brand and the realization of the brand promise. These are directly affected by interactions with the professional workforce (Berry, 2000). Indeed, there is general agreement that the development of a strong corporate reputation has to be founded on a workforce that embodies and identifies with the mission and values of the organization (Roper and Davies, 2010). The issue of customer experience is examined in Chapter 14. Collectively, these managerial components impact on the development of brand equity, which Marquardt *et al.* (2011) see as a composite of brand awareness and brand meaning.

To conclude this section on PSFs, it is helpful to consider the range of elements that constitute the **corporate communication mix**. The mix provides a series of cues through which stakeholders develop impressions about an organization. The mix can be considered to be composed of five main elements. These are symbolic, management, marketing, organizational, and behavioural communications, and are presented in Table 15.5.

Table 15.5 The corporate communication mix

Form of corporate communication	Explanation
Symbolic	Communications concerning the visual aspects of an organization. These encompass names, letterheads, logos, signage, emblems, colour schemes, architecture, and the overall appearance of all the design aspects associated with the company.
Management	Communications by managers who have a responsibility for the deployment of resources. These communications can be directed to internal or external audiences.
Marketing	Communications designed to engage customer-orientated audiences with regard to the promotion of an organization's offerings.
Organizational	Communications aimed at a range of stakeholders, not just customers, that are designed to build identification, commitment, and relationships with an organization, and are not sales-orientated.
Behavioural	Communications that emanate from the interactions, decisions, tone of voice and overall empathy between employees and with others outside the organization.

Source: Fill (2013). Based on Birkigt and Stadler (1986); van Riel and Fombrun (2007). Reprinted with the kind permission of Pearson Education.

Through the use of the different elements of corporate communication, organizations seek to build strategies that differentiate the firm. Berry (2000: 131) argues that there is 'a conscious effort to be different, a conscious effort to carve out a distinct brand personality'. He also argues that organizations need to represent something that is important to their customers. In the PSF sector, this is represented by superior knowledge, the one critical element that clients want to be associated and use to compare propositions.

Key Account Management (KAM)

It should be clear from the previous section that not all customers represent the same potential and profitability. However, it is quite common for a small number of customers to contribute to a disproportionately large part of an organization's income and profitability. As a result, these organizations often become essential to the firm's survival. The term **key accounts** has become the established term for referring to those customers who are considered to be strategically important. A key account might offer the supply side company opportunities to learn about new markets or types of customers. It might provide access to new and valuable resources, offer involvement with other key organizations, or just be symbolically valuable in terms of influence, power, and stature. Size alone is not sufficient for key account status. Establishing key accounts and the supporting infrastructure represents a significant investment for organizations and an opportunity cost.

Visit the **Online Resource Centre** and complete Internet activity 15.2 to learn more about the use of **sales force automation (SFA)** applications to aid the management of key client accounts.

So, why have so many organizations established and formalized their key account strategies? There are many reasons, some particular to each organization; however, the main ones relate to changes in the competitive environment and changes in industry structure.

Changes in the Competitive Environment

In an increasingly complex and competitive environment, where product lifecycles appear to be getting shorter and differentiation difficult to sustain, the need to find new ways of enhancing business performance has intensified. One of the ways in which this can be achieved is to provide a range of services that are tailored to the needs of each customer.

Many types of service can be customized; for example, customized training, advantageous financial arrangements, extranets, customer-driven delivery routes and timings, product support, and advice facilities. However, it is through the provision of added-value services that relationships are often developed and maintained. Establishing key accounts is a natural extension of providing particular services for key customers. Not only does this enhance the profile of these customers, both internally and externally, but it also helps to focus resources on particular customers and their individual needs.

Changes in Industry Structure

Many organizations have centralized their purchasing activities, a move driven by two main factors. The first is industry consolidation, a process by which a few organizations grow larger by merging or acquiring their competitors, so that the industry is concentrated around a small number of large organizations. Industry consolidation has increased substantially in recent years. Second, in industries where consolidation has not been significant, many organizations have moved towards centralizing their purchasing departments, processes, and functions as a means of achieving cost savings, improving effectiveness and efficiencies, and, in doing so, improving profits. ABB Sweden is a global corporation operating in a variety of industry segments, including power generation, pulp and paper, water, and chemicals. Brehmer and Rehme (2009) evaluate the way in which ABB Sweden used three different approaches to key account programmes, recognizing sales opportunities, customer demands, and a need to be more customer focused.

The result of both of these actions is that there are a smaller number of purchasing units responsible for a larger proportion of business. For business marketers and suppliers generally, these trends towards industrial concentration and purchasing centralization mean that competition is increased and marketing strategies need to be much more customer specific. Key account programmes are used with the deliberate intention of building relationships, often achieved by influencing levels of trust and commitment in order to generate more business.

However, in relationships between manufacturers and retailers (e.g. the grocery business), the presence of a key account relationship does not appear to have any significant benefit on the amount of resources allocated to the supplier's products (Verbeke et al., 2006).

Development stages within a cycle	Explanation
	Table 15.6 Key account management development stages
Exploratory	Suppliers identify and isolate those customer accounts that have key account potential.
Basic	In this transactional period, exchanges are used by both parties to test each other as potential long-term partners.
Cooperative	An increasing number of people from both parties become involved in the relationship.
Interdependent	Mutual recognition of each other's importance. Very often single supplier status is conferred.
Integrated	Both parties share sensitive information and undertake joint problem-solving. The relationship is regarded as a single entity.
Disintegrated	The termination or readjustment of the relationship can occur at any time.

Key Account Relationship Cycles

Key accounts do not just appear and flourish; they are the result of careful management, nurturing, and time. Key accounts represent a particular strength of relationship and, as with good wine, need time to develop to reach full potential. Consequently, each key account will, at any one moment in time, be at a particular stage of relationship development (Millman and Wilson, 1995). Key accounts can be plotted through various stages of a **KAM development cycle**. One such cycle is shown in Table 15.6.

The time between stages is not fixed and varies according to the nature and circumstances of the parties involved. The stages can be negotiated quickly in some cases, or may become protracted. The titles of each of the stages reflect the relationship status of both parties rather than of the selling company (e.g. prospective) or buying company (e.g. preferred supplier).

Managing Key Accounts

Key account managers provide the main link between their employer and their key account customers. They provide a route through which information flows, preferably in both directions. They must be capable of dealing with organizations where buying decisions can be either protracted and delayed (Sharma, 1997) or quick and demanding. However, key account managers do not operate alone and are not the sole point of contact between organizations. Normally, there are a number of levels of interaction between the two organizations, to the extent that there could be 'an entire team dedicated to providing services and support to the key account' (Ojasalo, 2001: 109).

Research Insight 15.4

To take your learning further, you might wish to read this influential paper.

Speakman, J. I. F. and Ryals, L. (2012), 'Key account management: the inside selling job', *Journal of Business and Industrial Marketing*, 27(5), 360–9.

Written by two highly reputable authors, this paper investigates the various roles undertaken by key account managers. In particular, the research shows that key account managers are able to adapt and use a combination of management behaviours and that these are modified during periods of conflict.

@ **Visit the Online Resource Centre to read the abstract and access the full paper.**

Therefore key account managers assume responsibility for all points of contact within the customer organization.

The value that a customer derives from a particular offering will have a significant influence on the level of attention given by the buyer to the supplier's programme. Furthermore, the level to which an organization uses centralized buying procedures will also impact on the effectiveness of a KAM programme. Unsurprisingly, key account sales behaviours cannot be the same as those used in field sales roles. So, as the majority of key account managers are drawn internally from the sales force (Hannah, 1998; cited by Abratt and Kelly, 2002), it is necessary to ensure that they have the correct skills mix, or are trained appropriately. Abratt and Kelly found six factors that were of particular importance when establishing a KAM programme. These were: the suitability of the key account manager, knowledge and understanding of the key account customer's business, commitment to the KAM partnership, delivering value, the importance of trust and the proper implementation and understanding of the KAM concept.

In addition to the interpersonal relationships that exist between the customer's contact person and the supplier's key account manager, there are also inter-organizational relationships that may concern system and policy issues. These will vary in strength and some may not be compatible with the tasks facing the key account manager (Benedapudi and Leone, 2002).

A Comparison of B2B and B2C Buying Characteristics

So far in this chapter, we have considered various characteristics of the business market. These include the different types of offerings, the variety of customers, the processes used to buy business products and services, professional service firms, and the key account management systems used by suppliers to reach and develop relationships with business customers. What do these factors contribute to our understanding of B2B marketing?

Overall, the marketing of offerings between organizations is not the same as consumer goods marketing and, because there are a number of fundamentally different characteristics, diverse marketing strategies and operations need to be implemented to meet the needs of business customers.

Differences

Business marketing can be distinguished from consumer marketing by two main factors: first the intended customer, which is an organization not an individual; second, the intended use of the offering, which is to support organizational objectives. As a result, different marketing programmes are required to reach and influence organizational buyers as opposed to consumers.

In the business sector, organizations buy a range of offerings either to make new products or to enable production processes to operate successfully. Defined processes and procedures are used to buy offerings, and the decisions attached to securing the necessary materials, unlike consumer-based decisions, very often involve a large number of people.

Many of the key differences between consumer and business marketing are rooted in the principal characteristics associated with the respective buying behaviours. These are set out in Table 15.7.

Table 15.7 A comparison of buying characteristics in organizational and consumer markets

	Consumer buying characteristics	Organizational buying characteristics
No. of buyers	Many	Few
Purchase initiation	Self	Others
Evaluative criteria	Social, ego, and level of utility	Price, value, and level of utility
Information search	Normally short	Normally long
Range of suppliers used	Small number of suppliers considered	Can be extensive
Importance of supplier choice	Normally limited	Can be critical
Size of orders	Small	Large
Frequency of orders	Light	High
Value of orders placed	Light	Heavy
Complexity of decision-making	Light to moderate	Moderate to high
Range of information inputs	Moderate	Moderate to high

Source: Fill and McKee (2012). Used with permission of Goodfellow Publishers.

One of the main characteristics is that there are far fewer buyers in organizational markets than in consumer markets. Even though there may be several people associated with a buying decision in an organization, the overall number of people involved in buying packaging products or road construction equipment, for example, is very small compared with the millions of people who might potentially buy a chocolate bar. The financial value of organizational purchase orders is invariably larger and the frequency with which they are placed is much lower. It is quite common for agreements to be made between organizations for the supply of materials over a number of years. Similarly, depending on the complexity of the product (e.g. photocopying paper or a one-off satellite), the negotiation process may also take a long time.

Although there are differences, many of the characteristics associated with consumer decision-making processes can still be observed in the organizational context. However, organizational buyers make decisions that ultimately contribute to the achievement of corporate objectives. To make the necessary decisions, a high volume of pertinent information is often required. This information needs to be relatively ███████████████████████████████ and logical style. The needs of the buyers are ███████████████████████████████ Goals, such as promotion and career advance ███████████████████████████████ employee satisfaction combine to make org ███████████████████████████████ raining and the development of expertise are ███████████████████████████████

Similarities

Although there are many differences between the B2C and B2B sectors, there are an increasing number of areas where the two converge. Two of the most important similarities emerge through market orientation, regardless of the sector in which an organization operates. Both have a customer orientation and work backwards from an understanding of customer needs. Both need the ability to gather, process, and use information about customers and competitors to achieve their objectives.

In addition, both types of supplier desire positive relationships with their customers. It does not matter whether they are consumers or organizations; what is wanted is that the relationship is continued for mutual benefit. The fundamental notion that organizational decision-making is basically rational in nature and that consumer decision-making is more unstructured and emotionally driven is questionable. For example, many personal purchases are of such technical complexity (e.g. financial services) that consumers need to adopt a more rational factual-based approach to their buying. Some business-oriented decisions are made on the basis of social contacts, consisting mainly of family and friendship networks.

Wilson (2000) explores some of these issues of similarity and observes that consumers use a wide range of inputs from other people, and not just those in the immediate family environment, when making product-related purchase decisions. This is similar to the group-buying dynamics associated with the DMU. He also suggests that the rationality normally associated with organizational decision-making is misplaced, because in some circumstances the protracted nature of the process is more a reflection of organizational culture and the need to follow bureaucratic procedures and to show due diligence. In addition, issues concerning established behaviour patterns, difficulties, and reluctance to break with traditional purchasing practices, intra- and inter-organizational politics and relationships, and the costs associated with supplier switching all contribute to a more interpretative understanding of organizational decision-making. Further support for this view is given by Mason and Gray (1999), who refer to the characteristics of

Research Insight 15.5

To take your learning further, you might wish to read this influential paper.

Gummesson, E. and Polese, F. (2009), 'B2B is not an island!', *Journal of Business and Industrial Marketing*, **24(5/6), 337–50.**

This conceptual paper is based on network theory and case study research. It considers customers as part of value networks and treats B2B and B2C as elements within a larger marketing context, not as independent categories. This represents a new approach to understanding B2B and B2C marketing and makes this article a timely contribution.

@ Visit the **Online Resource Centre** to read the abstract and access the full paper.

decision-making in the air travel market and note some strong similarities between consumers and business passengers. See Market Insight 15.4 for a similar consideration of Alenia, an aeronautical company.

It is also interesting to observe the similarities between the extended problem-solving, limited problem-solving, and routinized response behaviour phases of consumer buying and the new task, modified rebuy, and rebuy states associated with organizational buying. There is a close match between the two in terms of purpose, approach, and content. Risk and involvement are relevant to both categories and, although the background to both may vary, the principles used to manage the various phases and conditions are essentially the same, just deployed in different ways.

One further area of similarity concerns branding. In consumer markets, branding is common practice and for a long time was not thought to be of direct concern to business marketers. Now, however, B2B organizations use a variety of branding approaches. Ingredient branding (Intel Inside and Lycra), cause-related branding, cooperative advertising, and dual branding, in addition to joint advertising and sales promotion activities, are all used to raise perceived value (Bengtsson and Servais, 2005). Traditionally, trucking companies have not paid much attention to the way they present themselves. When Eddie Stobart recognized this in the UK trucking market, he used it as a branding opportunity. In addition to the distinctive livery, he ensured that his trucks were always clean, that his drivers wore the company's green shirt and tie, and that his operation ran efficiently and always on time. As a result, the Eddie Stobart brand stands out and helps justify a substantial price premium (Hague, 2006).

It is important to recognize that, although there are some substantial differences between consumer and business marketing, there are also several areas where there are distinct similarities. This suggests that the principles of marketing apply equally to the consumer and business markets, and, when planning and implementing marketing programmes, particular care should be given to understanding the nature and characteristics of the buying processes and procedures of the target market.

Eddie Stobart, the supply chain company, takes branding very seriously
Source: Eddie Stobart Ltd.

 # Market Insight 15.4

Alenia's Networking Flags Some Similarities

As if to demonstrate the similarities rather than the differences, Gummesson and Polese (2009) consider the various B2B, C2B, B2C, and C2C combinations that can be identified in different industries. Alenia Aeronautica, a Finmeccanica Company, supplies Boeing, Airbus, and the US Department of Defense, among others, with various specialized units. The industry is experiencing rapid change, with the number of prime suppliers reduced from seven or eight to two or three, whereas the number of smaller prime suppliers has fallen from over 50 to just five to eight.

Once there were over 1,000 component suppliers, now there are just 50.

However, all of these organizations are involved in a complex interacting network, and all contribute value to the whole chain of suppliers. The Alenia–Boeing relationship is direct B2B, as is Boeing's relationships with the airlines that buy their aircraft. The airlines have close B2C relationships with their customers, essentially passengers. When passengers interact with passengers it is C2C (chat rooms, blogs, communities), but when they interact with the airline with a view to influencing them about food, comfort, entertainment, or air quality issues, this is often through the cabin crew

Market Insight 15.4
continued

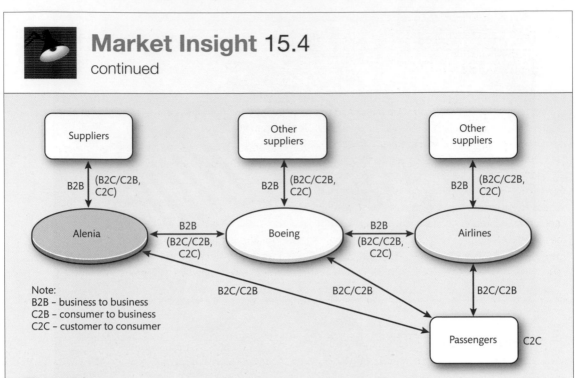

Figure 15.6

Aeronautica Alenia's network of relationships

Source: Gummesson, E. and Polese, F. (2009) 'B2B is not an island!', *Journal of Business and Industrial Marketing*, 24(5/6), 337–50 © Emerald Group Publishing Limited. All rights reserved.

This Boeing 787 fuselage panel is produced in Grottaglie, Italy

Source: Alenia Aeronautica media gallery.

Market Insight 15.4
continued

and represents C2B interaction. This information is then manifested in future orders to Airbus and passed back to Alenia, albeit as indirect interaction, in the form of specifications, updates, and revision. This, in turn, gets passed on by Alenia to its supply network as orders. Alenia is increasingly asking for access to information arising either through the C2C interaction or through Airbus's relationships with the different airlines. Early information means that the development process can be speeded up and so add value to the network. See Figure 15.6 for a representation of these various relationships and interactions.

1 **What are the implications of Alenia's various indirect relationships for its marketing activities?**

2 **How might Alenia's marketing programmes meet B2B and B2C needs?**

3 **Think of an industry with which you are familiar and make a list of the different B2B, B2C, C2B, and C2C relationships.**

Chapter Summary

To consolidate your learning, the key points from this chapter are summarized here.

■ **Explain the main characteristics of business markets and understand the different types of organizational customers.**

Business markets are characterized by four main factors: the nature of demand, the buying processes, international dimensions, and the relationships that develop between organizations. There are a range of organizations that make up business markets and these are classified as commercial, government, and institutional. These organizations buy products and services to make goods for resale to their customers, but they also consume items that are required to keep their offices and manufacturing units functioning.

■ **Describe the different types of offerings that are sold and bought in business markets.**

Products and services bought and sold through business markets are categorized as input goods, equipment goods, and supply goods.

■ **Set out the main processes and stages associated with organizational buying and purchasing.**

Organizational buying behaviour can be understood to be a group buying activity in which a number of people with differing roles make purchasing decisions that affect the organization and the achievement of its objectives. Buying decisions can be understood in terms of different types of decisions (buyclasses) and different stages (buyphases).

■ **Understand the principles of key account management.**

Some suppliers refer to some of their strategically important customers as key accounts. Relationships with these customers move through various stages, called key account management development cycles. Each stage is marked by particular characteristics and part of the role of the key account manager is to ensure that all contact between the supplier and the customer builds on strengthening the inter-organizational relationship.

■ **Explain what business-to-business marketing is and the marketing issues associated with professional service firms**

B2B marketing is concerned with the identification and satisfaction of business customers' needs. This requires that all stakeholders benefit from the business relationship and associated transactions. Customers derive satisfaction by purchasing offerings that are perceived to provide them and/or their organizations with particular value. Professional service firms focus on developing their reputation as the main means of differentiation.

■ **Compare business and consumer marketing**

Both have a customer orientation and work backwards from an understanding of customer needs. In addition, both require information about customers and competitors to achieve their objectives. There is a close match in terms of the purpose, approach, and content between the extended problem-solving, limited problem-solving, and routinized response behaviour phases of consumer buying and the new task, modified rebuy, and rebuy states associated with organizational buying.

Review Questions

1 In note format and in your own words set out the essential purpose of B2B marketing.

2 What are the key characteristics associated with B2B markets?

3 What are the different types of organizations that make up the business market?

4 Name four of the different types of people that make up a DMU.

5 Distinguish clearly between buyphases and buyclasses.

6 What is the customer portfolio matrix?

7 How are key accounts different from house or major accounts?

8 What different phases are associated with key account development cycles?

9 What are the key differences and similarities between B2B and B2C marketing?

10 What are the main characteristics of the B2B marketing mix?

Worksheet Summary

To apply the knowledge you have gained from this chapter and test your understanding of business-to-business marketing visit the **Online Resource Centre** and complete Worksheet 15.1.

Discussion Questions

1 Having read Case Insight 15.1, what market entry approach and methods do you believe Oxford Instruments should use to enter India in order to build mutually profitable business relationships?

2 Discuss the main characteristics of business marketing and consider whether there is really any major difference when compared with consumer marketing.

3 AstraVera Ltd has been developing a conveyor belt designed to meet new government-driven hygiene standards. The problem in many manufacturing, packaging, and assembly plants is that floors underneath conveyor belts can become wet and hence present a danger to people working around the equipment. The new belt has a trough incorporated in it, which runs along its entire length. Spillages feed into the trough where collection sumps and filters remove the excess liquids before they overflow to the floor (developed from Spear 2006). Make brief notes advising AstraVera's marketing manager about marketing the new conveyor.

4 Working in small groups, select three B2B organizations and identify the main influences on their marketing activities. To what extent is it possible to prioritize these influences and does this matter?

5 Using PowerPoint, prepare a short presentation in which you explain the meaning of buyclasses, buyphases, and buygrids.

@ Visit the **Online Resource Centre** and complete the Multiple Choice Questions to assess your knowledge of Chapter 15.

References

Abratt, R. and Kelly, P. M. (2002), 'Perceptions of a successful key account management program', *Industrial Marketing Management*, 31(5), 467–76.

Achrol, R. S. (1997) 'Changes in the theory of interorganisational relations in marketing: toward a network paradigm', *Journal of the Academy of Marketing Science*, 25(1), 56–71.

Anderson, J. and Narus, J. A. (1999), *Business Market Management: Understanding, Creating, and Delivering Value*, Upper Saddle River, NJ: Prentice Hall.

Benedapudi, N. and Leone, R. P. (2002), 'Managing business-to-business customer relationships following key contact employee turnover in a vendor firm', *Journal of Marketing*, 66(April), 83–101.

Bengtsson, A. and Servais, P. (2005), 'Co-branding in industrial markets', *Industrial Marketing Management*, 34(7), 706–13.

Berry, L.L. (2000), 'Cultivating service brand equity', *Journal of the Academy of Marketing Science*, 28, 128–37.

Birkigt, K. and Stadler, M.M. (1986), *Corporate Identity, Grundlagen, Funktionen, Fallspielen*, Landsberg am Lech: Verlag Moderne Industrie.

Bolger, M. (2012), 'Case Study: Aeroinv.com. Brand take-off', *Marketer*, 26 October.

Bonoma, T. V. (1982), 'Major sales: who really does the buying?', *Harvard Business Review*, 60(3), 111–18.

Brehmer, P-O. and Rehme, J. (2009), 'Proactive and reactive: drivers for key account management programmes', *European Journal of Marketing*, 43(7), 8961–84.

Durham, J. and Ritchey, T. (2009), 'Leaning forward; removing design inefficiencies and improving quality', retrieve from: http://www.hhnmag.com/hhnmag/jsp/articledisplay.jsp?dcrpath=HFMMAGAZINE/Article/data/07JUL2009/0907HFM_FEA_planning&domain=HFMMAGAZINE 1 July 2009, accessed 24 July 2013.

Dwyer, R. F., Schurr, P. H., and Oh, S. (1987), 'Developing buyer–seller relationships', *Journal of Marketing*, 51(April), 11–27.

Fill, C. (2013), *Marketing Communications: Brands, Experiences and Participation* (6th edn), Harlow: FT/Prentice Hall.

Fill, C. and McKee, S. (2012), *Business Marketing*, Oxford: Goodfellow.

Glenn, R. R. and Wheeler, A. R. (2004), 'A new framework for supply chain manager selection: three hurdles to competitive advantage', *Journal of Marketing Channels*, 11(4), 89–103.

Greenwood, R., Li, S. X., Prakash, R., and Deephouse, D. L. (2005), 'Reputation, diversification, and organizational explanations of performance in professional service firms', *Organization Science*, 16(6), 661–73.

Grönroos, C. (2009), 'Marketing as promise management: regaining customer management for marketing', *Journal of Business and Industrial Marketing*, 24(5/6), 351–9.

Gummesson, E. (1978), 'Towards a theory of professional services marketing', *Industrial Marketing Management*, 7(2), 89–95.

Gummesson, E. and Polese, F. (2009), 'B2B is not an island!', *Journal of Business and Industrial Marketing*, 24(5/6), 337–50.

Hague, P. (2006), 'Branding in business to business markets', White Paper, retrieve from: www.b2binternational.com/library/whitepapers, accessed 13 July 2013.

Håkansson, H., and Snehota, I. (1995), *Developing Relationships in Business Networks*, London: Routledge.

Hannah, G. (1998), 'From transactions to relationships: challenges for the national account manager', *Journal of Marketing and Sales*, 4(1), 30–3.

Hemsworth, D., Sánchez-Rodríguez, C., and Bidgood, B. (2008), *Total Quality Management and Business Excellence*, 19(1/2), 151–64.

Hollyoake, M. (2009), 'The four pillars: developing a bonded business-to-business customer experience', *Database Marketing and Customer Strategy Management*, 16(2), 132–58.

Jackson, B. (1985), 'Build customer relationships that last', *Harvard Business Review*, 63(6), 120–8.

Johnson, W. J. and Lewin, J. E. (1996), 'Organizational buying behavior: toward an integrative framework', *Journal of Business Research*, 35, 1–15.

Krishnan, J. and Schauer, P. C. (2000), 'The differentiation of quality among auditors: evidence from the not-for-profit sector', *Auditing*, 19(2), 9–25.

Leigh, T. W. and Marshall, G. W. (2001), 'Research priorities in sales strategy and performance', *Journal of Personal Selling and Sales Management*, 21(2), 83–93.

Lorsch, J. W. and Tierney, T. J. (2002), *Aligning the Stars*, Boston, MA: Harvard Business School Press.

Macfarlane, P. (2002), 'Structuring and measuring the size of business markets', *International Journal of Market Research*, 44(1), 7–31.

Marquardt, A. J., Golicic, S. L., and Davis, D. F. (2011), 'B2B services branding in the logistics services industry', *Journal of Services Marketing*, 25(1), 47–57.

Mason, K. J. and Gray, R. (1999), 'Stakeholders in a hybrid market: the example of air business passenger travel', *European Journal of Marketing*, 33(9–10), 844–58.

Millman, T., and Wilson, K. (1995), 'From key account selling to key account management', *Journal of Marketing Practice: Applied Marketing Science*, 1(1), 9–21.

Noordhoff, C. S., Kyriakopoulos, K., Moorman, C., Pauwels, P., and Dellaert, B. G. C. (2011), 'The bright side and dark side of embedded ties in business-to-business innovation', *Journal of Marketing*, 75(September), 34–52.

Ojasalo, J. (2001), 'Key account management at company and individual levels in business-to-business relationships', *Journal of Business and Industrial Marketing*, 16(3), 199–220.

Parkinson, S. T. and Baker, M. J. (1994), *Organizational Buying Behavior: Purchasing and Marketing Management Implications*, London: Macmillan.

Payne, A. and Frow, P. (2004), 'The role of multi-channel integration in customer relationship management', *Industrial Marketing Management*, 33, 527–38.

Piercy, N. F. (2006), 'The strategic sales organization', *Marketing Review*, 6, 3–28.

Podolny, J. M. (1994), 'Market uncertainty and the social character of economic exchange', *Administrative Science Quarterly*, 39(3), 458–83.

Pressey, A., Tzokas, N., and Winklhofer, H. (2007), 'Strategic purchasing and the evaluation of "problem" key supply relationships. What do key suppliers need to know?', *Journal of Business and Industrial Marketing*, 22(5), 282–94.

Reagans, R. and McEvily, B. (2003), 'Network structure and knowledge transfer: the effects of cohesion and range, *Administrative Science Quarterly*, 48(2), 240–67.

Reid, M. (2008), 'Contemporary marketing in professional services', *Journal of Services Marketing*, 22(5), 374–84.

Robinson, P. J., Faris, C. W., and Wind, Y. (1967), *Industrial Buying and Creative Marketing*, Boston, MA: Allyn & Bacon.

Roper, S. and Davies, G. (2010), 'Business to business branding: external and internal satisfiers and the role of training quality', *European Journal of Marketing*, 44(5), 567–90.

Ryals, L. J. and Rogers, B. (2006), 'Holding up the mirror: the impact of strategic procurement practices on account management', *Business Horizons*, 49, 41–50.

Sharma, A. (1997), 'Who prefers key account management program? An investigation of business buying behaviour and buying firm characteristics', *Journal of Personal Selling and Sales Management*, 17(4), 27–39.

Sheth, J. N. (1973), 'A model of industrial buyer behavior', *Journal of Marketing*, 37(October), 50–6.

Singh, R. (2011), 'KPMG administrators launch Aero Inventory business', *Accountancy Age*, 14 September, retrieve from: http://www.accountancyage.com/aa/news/2109079/kpmg-administrators-launch-aero-inventory-business accessed 28 November 2012.

Speakman, J. I. F. and Ryals, L. (2012), 'Key account management: the inside selling job', *Journal of Business and Industrial Marketing*, 27(5), 360–9.

Spear, M. (2006), 'Smooth movers', retrieve from: www.foodmanufacture.co.uk/news/fullstory.php/aid/3445/Smooth_movers.html accessed 29 November 2012.

Spekman, R. E., and Gronhaug, K. (1986), 'Conceptual and methodological issues in buying centre research', *European Journal of Marketing*, 20(7), 50–63.

Storbacka, K., Ryals, L., Davies, I. A., and Nenonen, S. (2009), 'The changing role of sales: viewing sales as a strategic, cross-functional process', *European Journal of Marketing*, 43(7/8), 890–906.

Svahn, S. and Westerlund, M. (2009), 'Purchasing strategies in supply relationships', *Journal of Business and Industrial Marketing*, 24(3/4), 173–81.

Swinder, J. and Seshadri, S. (2001), 'The influence of purchasing strategies on performance', *Journal of Business and Industrial Marketing*, 164, 294–306.

Thakor, M.V. and Kumar, A. (2000), 'What is a professional service? A conceptual review and bi-national investigation', *Journal of Services Marketing*, 14(1), 63–82.

Ulkuniemi, P. (2003), *Purchasing Software Components at the Dawn of Market*, retrieve from: http://herkules.oulu.fi/isbn9514272188/ accessed 13 July 2013.

van Riel, C. B. M. and Fombrun, C. J. (2007), *Essentials of Corporate Communication*, London: Routledge.

van Weele, A. J. (2002), *Purchasing and Supply Chain Management* (3rd edn), London: Thomson.

Vargo, S.L. and Lusch, R.F. (2004), 'Evolving to a new dominant logic for marketing', *Journal of Marketing*, 68(1), 1–17.

Verbeke, W., Bagozzi, R. P., and Farris, P. (2006), 'The role of key account programs, trust, and brand strength on resource allocation in the channel of distribution', *European Journal of Marketing*, 40(5/6), 520–32.

Webster, F. E. and Wind, Y. (1972), *Organizational Buying Behaviour*, Englewood Cliffs, NJ: Prentice Hall.

Wilson, D. F. (2000), 'Why divide consumer and organisational buyer behaviour?', *European Journal of Marketing*, 34(7), 780–96.

Chapter 16
Not-For-Profit Marketing

stop. FULL STOP.

Learning Outcomes

After studying this chapter, you will be able to:

▸ List some key characteristics of not-for-profit organizations

▸ Explain why not-for-profit organizations do not always value their customers

▸ Analyse stakeholders and develop appropriate engagement strategies

▸ Describe and assess cause-related marketing campaigns

▸ Understand how marketing can be, and is, used to achieve social and political change in society

▸ Explain how marketing is used for charitable fund-raising

Case Insight 16.1
Oxfam

Market Insight 16.1
How The 'Gu' Saved Bilbao

Market Insight 16.2
Kellogg's: The Serial Giver

Market Insight 16.3
Duchy Originals: Food Fit for a Prince

Market Insight 16.4
THINK! Scaring Drivers and Riders

Market Insight 16.5
Obama's Big Data Wins Election

Case Insight 16.1

Founded in 1942, as the Oxfam Committee for Famine Relief, Oxfam opened one of the world's first charity shop chains in Oxford in 1948. But given major changes in the world since then, particularly in relation to climate change and the advance of information and communication technologies, how has this world-renowned charity kept pace? We speak to Nick Futcher to find out more.

Oxfam GB is an independent development, relief, and campaigning organization that works with others to overcome poverty and suffering, employing around 1,070 people in the UK. When it launched its first shop, it attracted donations ranging from false teeth and stuffed animals to a houseboat! Today our shop network, stretching from the High Street to cyberspace, forms an integral part of Oxfam's Trading Division. Oxfam GB is part of Oxfam International set up in 1995—a worldwide family of organizations sharing common values and working together for change and development. Oxfam GB's global programme works through eight regions worldwide, offering strategic funding, supporting long-term development programmes, delivering emergency relief in times of crisis, and campaigning for a fairer world. Currently, Oxfam's primary organizational focus is combating climate change and mitigating its effects on the poorest people in the world.

Basic marketing techniques employed by Oxfam include TV and outdoor advertising, online advertising, mailings, and face-to-face recruitment. Such techniques have been developed and refined over time. Fundamentally, it pays to be innovative. Oxfam were the first to introduce regular giving with our £2 a month initiative, and started the first online charity 'shop' through a combination of auctions of donated goods in 1996.

Oxfam's supporters range from individuals, institutional donors, trusts and corporations, all the way through to community fundraising groups. There are a variety of individual supporter types that are all pivotal to Oxfam's work. Such supporters include regular donors, one-off donors, legacy leavers, fundraisers, campaigners, volunteers, those who donate goods, those who buy from Oxfam shops, and those who attend Oxfam events.

In developing our marketing activities, all our advertising must adhere to the rules and regulations set out by the Advertising Standards Agency (ASA) and the Fundraising Standards Board (FRSB), who oversee an independent and transparent scheme for fundraising. This is important because we aim to ensure that public confidence in charitable giving is increased.

Oxfam's fundraising helps overcome poverty and suffering throughout the world. Oxfam, as a charity, uses marketing for a variety of overarching objectives. The first is to facilitate fundraising—the cornerstone of charitable organizations. This transmits into a variety of marketing strategies within different teams to promote how easy, fun, and ultimately rewarding supporting Oxfam is. These can range from our events team producing targeted communications to advertise Oxjam, Oxfam's month-long music festival spread across venues all over the UK, to direct mailing for emergency cash appeals and development projects. Oxfam shops represent a more traditional and recognizable touchpoint for engaging supporters, and remain a key mechanism for our Trading Division to raise funds. Oxfam is also a campaigning organization, and marketing is a tool that allows us to inform people

Case Insight 16.1
continued

of upcoming activities and ways to get involved, such as petitioning and demonstrating, to raise awareness, and to help effect lasting change.

Our organizational priority for the short to medium term will remain mitigating the effects of climate change on the world's poorest people. However, the troubled economic climate of recent times has made planning for the future in marketing terms more difficult. Because giving to a charitable cause is largely dependent on engagement with the issues a charity works on, maintaining and consolidating existing

support is vital, particularly in a difficult economic climate. However, research was indicating that Oxfam was becoming more distant in the minds of the UK public. Although people respected and trusted us (over 99% of the UK public knew who we are), they had a limited understanding of what we do and didn't feel close to us as a brand. There was considerable potential to improve knowledge of, and involvement, in Oxfam's aims and values.

The key question was: how should we go about repositioning ourselves?

Introduction

Over the last 40 years, the role of marketing in not-for-profit organizations has grown substantially as these organizations have realized the value of marketing in developing a strong understanding of customers and other stakeholders. But have you ever wondered what would happen if a charity fully met its strategic objectives? Should it cease to exist? Are the techniques we use in commercial marketing relevant in a not-for-profit environment, where the remit is not to enrich shareholders? Is there any difference in how we use marketing techniques in a social environment—for example, when governments use marketing to reduce binge drinking, or increase fruit and vegetable consumption to five or six portions a day, or increase voter registration? In this chapter, we answer some of these questions.

So far our attention has been centred on commercial organizations, those intent on making profits. However, there are other types of organizations—for example, those that operate in the not-for-profit sector. Kotler and Levy (1969) pioneered the ground-breaking application of marketing to not-for-profit enterprises. So, for example, marketing is now readily used by local government, churches, museums, charities, universities, political parties, zoos, public hospitals, and many others, all of which operate without profit as their central goal.

Despite the similarities between not-for-profit and commercial marketing highlighted by Kotler and Levy, there are some key differences in how marketing is used, particularly in relation to marketing communications. Rothschild (1979) indicates that these key differences include the following.

- Proposition—with not-for profit offerings, there is a weaker unique selling proposition, i.e. weaker direct benefits, making it more difficult to direct customer or target audience behaviour in the way desired. For example, giving to charity provides us with a sense of 'doing good' but this feeling may not be sufficient to induce many people to give.

- Price—this important component of the marketing mix has different connotations in not-for-profit situations. For example, in a political marketing context, what is the price when marketing a political party? Is it the effort needed to vote, or the economic costs of voting for one party versus another? In relation to charities, the amount donated is often left to the discretion of the donor and is largely determined by the donor, rather than being specified by the seller as in a commercial transaction.

- Involvement—whereas we speak of high and low involvement in commercial situations regarding how consumers become involved with an offering to learn more about it during the purchasing process, the involvement in non-business situations displays more extreme tendencies. People often either really engage with a charity or political party or cause, for example, or show strong reactions against it.

- Segmentation—in the not-for-profit environment, it may be necessary to develop a campaign to drive behaviour in all targets rather than a specific audience, as in commercial markets. For example, a road safety campaign might wish to encourage all adults to drive at, or below, the speed limit, although there may well be sub-groups who need specific targeted messages (e.g. young male drivers who may persistently break the speed limit).

Another key difference in the strategic marketing of not-for-profit organizations is the need to continually check the marketing strategy against the environment, the available resources, and the organization's values (Hatten, 1982). In the latter case, the values of the organization have an impact not only on why the organization exists but also on how it goes about its marketing activities, including fundraising, promotional programmes, and operational programme developments. Table 16.1 outlines the mission statements for a variety of national and international not-for-profit organizations. For commercial organizations, the mission statement usually revolves around being the best in a particular marketplace and consequently achieving high levels of profit. In the not-for-profit sector, mission statements revolve around causes. The *raison d'être* of a charity is to solve a particular societal problem—in effect, to extinguish the need for its own existence. Of course, if a charity did indeed help to remove the problem it was designed to create (e.g. a tuberculosis charity ceasing to operate because there were no more cases of tuberculosis in the world), it would simply amend its mission. Like any other organization, a charity interacts with its environment and must stay relevant within the context that it operates to attract funding.

 Research Insight 16.1

To take your learning further, you might wish to read this influential paper.

Kotler, P. and Levy, S. J. (1969), 'Broadening the concept of marketing', *Journal of Marketing*, **33(1, January), 10–15.**

In this seminal article, the authors proposed that marketing techniques and concepts, as typified by the 4Ps, could be applied to non-business organizations and therefore could be applied to the marketing of organizations, persons, and ideas. It provoked a considerable debate at the time, with some writers suggesting that the concept of marketing had been broadened too far.

@ **Visit the Online Resource Centre to read the abstract and access the full paper.**

Table 16.1 A selection of mission statements from not-for-profit organizations

Organization	Mission statement
WWF—World Wildlife Fund (International)	WWF's mission is to conserve nature and reduce the most pressing threats to the diversity of life on Earth. Our vision is to build a future where people live in harmony with nature.
The Alannah and Madeline Foundation (Australia)	**Our Mission** The Alannah and Madeline Foundation's mission is keeping children safe from violence. **Our Vision** The Alannah and Madeline Foundation's vision is that every child will live in a safe and supportive environment. **Our Values** Caring; friendliness; valuing difference; including others; respect; responsibility
City of London Police (UK)	**Mission Statement** We will provide a high-quality police service in the City of London and work with the community, other organizations, and agencies to promote a safe, peaceful, and crime-free environment. **Our Values** <ul><li>To be sensitive, open and fair to the public and our own staff.</li><li>To encourage equal opportunities.</li><li>To encourage participation and consult the public and our staff.</li><li>To treat people as individuals.</li><li>To act with honesty, compassion, courtesy, and patience.</li></ul>**Force Priorities** <ul><li>Deter criminal terrorist activity.</li><li>Deter economic crime activity.</li><li>Prevent, deter, and positively respond to public disorder.</li><li>Provide high quality community policing.</li></ul>
China Charity Federation (China)	Our programmes include the following areas. <ul><li>Delivering much needed assistance at the scene of natural disasters.</li><li>Equipping the handicapped to better cope with their limitations.</li><li>Caring for orphans and the aged who would otherwise be neglected.</li><li>Providing medical equipment and supplies to relieve and prevent illness.</li><li>Aiding education so that everyone can be well educated.</li><li>Generally alleviating suffering and helping people to help themselves.</li></ul>
Médecines Sans Frontières (France, International)	Médecins Sans Frontières (MSF) is an international independent medical humanitarian organization that delivers emergency aid to people affected by armed conflict, epidemics, natural disasters, and exclusion from healthcare. MSF offers assistance to people based on need, irrespective of race, religion, gender, or political affiliation.

Table 16.1 continued	
Organization	**Mission statement**
Great Ormond Street Hospital (GOSH) Charity (UK)	Our mission is to provide world-class clinical care and training, pioneering new research and treatments in partnership with others for the benefit of children in the UK and worldwide. In everything we do, we work hard to live up to our three core values: pioneering, world class, and collaborative.

Source: Organizations' websites.

Key Characteristics of Not-for-Profit Organizations

The key characteristics that impact on marketing include the presence of multiple stakeholders, transparency in the organization's mission and finances, the presence of multiple objectives in business and social terms, a different orientation compared with commercial organizations, and, finally, different customer perceptions (see Figure 16.1). We consider each of these characteristics below.

Multiple Stakeholders

Although for-profit or private sector organizations interact with a range of stakeholders to achieve their business goals, their focus is firmly on customers and shareholders. What is different about not-for-profit organizations is their concern for a wider group of stakeholders. **Stakeholders**

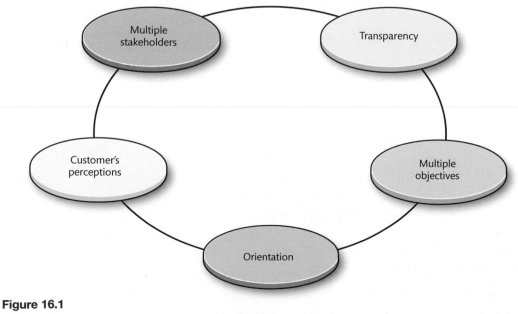

Figure 16.1

Key characteristics of not-for-profit organizations

are groups with whom the organization has a relationship, and which impact on the operations of the organization, and include shareholders (or trustees), regulatory bodies, other charity or not-for-profit partners, supply chain partners, employees, and customers. In private companies, revenue is distributed from customers to shareholders; it is initially converted into profits by the organization, and shareholders are rewarded with a dividend as a share of the profits earned. Companies also have stakeholders, but those stakeholders have less influence on how the organization's profits are distributed.

Not-for-profit organizations provide offerings, but their customers or users seldom pay the full costs incurred by the organization to provide them. Many not-for-profit organizations rely on stakeholders to finance the organization's operations. Instead of revenue from customers being used to reward shareholders, there are usually no profits to be redistributed as those who fund the organization do not require a return on their resource provision. For example, central government, local council taxpayers, lottery funding for special projects, and business rate taxes, to name but four sources of income, fund city councils in the UK. Charities are supported by individual and corporate donations. Museums may rely on a mixture of grants, lottery allocations, entrance fees, and individual donations and bequests. Zoos may also rely on a mixture of grants, entrance fees, and individual donations.

Because they serve a range of stakeholders, not-for-profit organizations do not always value their beneficiary customers (i.e. those who receive their charitable services) as much as they should, and they sometimes fail to explain sufficiently to donors (i.e. supporter customers) how those donations are used. The difficulties arising when trying to satisfy multiple stakeholder groups are outlined in Table 16.2, which considers beneficiary and supporter customers and

Table 16.2 Why not-for-profit organizations do not always seem to value their customers

Reasons for not valuing beneficiaries	Reasons for not valuing supporters	Interactive reasons for undervaluing customers
Many not-for-profits exist in a monopolistic situation, which potentially creates an arrogant culture towards beneficiaries.	Donors claim to be approached too often for donations and do not feel sufficiently appreciated.	Dealing with multiple stakeholders can cause inter-group tension as one group's call on resources takes precedence over others. For example, a high-value donor for a university might want their donation to be used in a way that is different from the management of the university.
Demand far outstrips supply creating problems in delivering a consistent quality of service.	Volunteer service workers can often feel undervalued and under-supported.	
Lack of market segmentation for beneficiaries undertaken. Research into beneficiary customers' needs is not common because funds available are seen as better used for funding operations.		

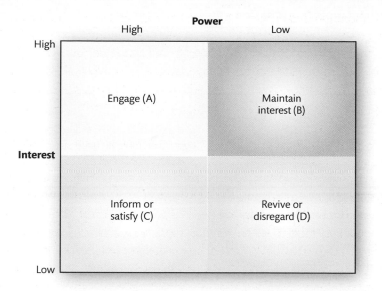

Power

Figure 16.2
The stakeholder mapping matrix
Source: Scholes (2001).

explains why charities sometimes fail to satisfy, and undervalue, these groups of customers (see Bruce, 1995).

It is important for not-for-profit organizations to determine which of the different stakeholders have the most interest in their activities and the most power to affect their organization's performance. A common method used to distinguish between the interests and power of stakeholders is the stakeholder mapping matrix, outlined in Figure 16.2.

The matrix can be used to identify four types of stakeholder, based on the high/low levels of interest that they have in an organization and the level of power they exert over it. Those with high levels of interest and power (group A) are key stakeholders that need to be continuously engaged. They might be funding bodies or powerful regulators, for example. Those with high interest but low levels of power (group B), for example individual donors to charities, should be informed about that charity's activities to maintain their interest. Group C represents those organizations with high power but low interest. It is important for the not-for-profit to increase information flow to these organizations to increase their interest so that they can exert their power in the not-for-profit's favour (as a funding body might), or alternatively to keep them satisfied if they intend to exert their power against the not-for-profit (as a regulator might). Finally, an organization's relationships with those stakeholders who have little power or interest should either be disregarded or revived (see Market Insight 16.1 for an example).

Transparency

The use of public money and donations in not-for-profit organizations requires that their source and allocation is easily understood, audited, and tracked. Such public scrutiny or transparency of funding is a feature that distinguishes these organizations from their private sector counterparts. For donations to continue to flow, not-for-profit organizations must demonstrate trust, integrity, and honesty. For example, charities in the UK are governed by a different set

Market Insight 16.1

How The 'Gu' Saved Bilbao

Until 1997, Bilbao had been a decaying former steel and shipbuilding city, the capital of the Basque country in Spain, with little prospect of improvement, and an unemployment rate of 25%. When city planners decided that they needed to revive the city, they came up with a brave plan. Why not build an art gallery? But what kind of art gallery and how would it succeed in regenerating the area? If it really was to revitalize the area, it had to have a strong architectural presence, be a spectacular tourist attraction in its own right, and house attractive art collections which would bring leisure and tourist customers. Tourism can provide a powerful motor for economic investment.

If an art gallery was to be the key draw in Bilbao, what kind of art gallery would it be and who might partner with the Basque government to develop the concept? Then city officials had a brainwave. Why not ask the Solomon R Guggenheim Foundation if they were interested in developing a museum in Bilbao? After all, the Guggenheim Foundation had developed the Peggy Guggenheim Collection in Venice. The Foundation's Board of Trustees received the proposal warmly, not least because they had developed a long-term plan to develop Guggenheim museums in a number of international locations. In 1991, after long negotiations, the Basque Government Minister for Culture, the Deputy General of the Provincial Council of Bizkaia, and a member of the board of trustees of the Solomon R Guggenheim Foundation signed the Development and Programming Services Agreement for the Guggenheim Museum Bilbao. Nearly six years later the museum finally opened its doors to visitors, becoming an instant overnight sensation. Within a year, it had received 1.3 million visitors.

The mission of the Guggenheim Museum Bilbao is 'to collect, conserve, and study modern and contemporary art, to exhibit the art of our times from a variety of perspectives in the context of art history, and to reach a broad and diverse audience. As one of the cornerstones of the Guggenheim Museum Network, and a symbol of the Basque Country's vitality, we hope to promote an understanding, appreciation, and enjoyment of art and its values in an iconic architectural setting'. From the mission statement, it is easy to see the importance of the museum in maintaining the Basque country's cultural heritage.

In 1997, the Deutsche Guggenheim opened in Berlin, to complete the Guggenheims in New York, Venice, and Bilbao. To celebrate contemporary Middle Eastern art, the Foundation intends to open a new Guggenheim Museum in the Middle East, located in the cultural district of Saadiyat Island, Abu Dhabi, United Arab Emirates, in 2017; five years later than originally planned. As China and India develop their own tourist markets, it's probably only a matter of time before they negotiate a Guggenheim Museum in their countries too.

Sources: Marling (2003); BBC (2012); Hall (2012); www. guggenheim-bilbao.es www.guggenheim.org/abu-dhabi (see also Market Insight 1.4).

Visit the **Online Resource Centre** and follow the weblink to the BBC World Service programme *Witness* to learn more about the Guggenheim Bilbao.

1 Who do you think were the key stakeholders in the process of developing the Guggenheim Museum Bilbao?

2 Who do you think the key stakeholders are now in developing the audiences for the collections that are shown to attract the visitors?

3 What are the risks in marketing terms in opening the new Guggenheim Museum, Abu Dhabi? How might these risks be minimized?

of regulatory requirements which require them to provide considerably greater information on how they are governed compared with their commercial counterparts. Charities' executive teams are overseen by boards of trustees, often unpaid volunteers who are senior and experienced people who have some interest in running the organization. In parallel, the executive teams of private or public limited companies are overseen by paid executive and non-executive directors.

Private sector organizations declare the minimum financial information required—just enough to comply with customs and excise requirements. Sometimes not-for-profit organizations overcompensate, providing considerable details of their internal procedures and processes. This is because they do not want to be judged as financially incompetent, and they want to avoid adverse media coverage and the negative perceptions that follow. However, a serious outcome might be that future funding streams are curtailed or even terminated because a charity is seen to have insufficient funds to cover its activities. Equally, providing detailed outlines of organizational structures and plans can also provide competitors with valuable competitive intelligence, which could be detrimental to the organization.

Multiple Objectives

In the manufacturing and other sectors, profit is a central overriding goal. Investment decisions are often based on the likely rate of return and resources are allocated according to the contribution (to profit) they will make. Profit provides a relatively easy measure of success. As the name suggests, in the not-for-profit sector, profit is not the central overriding goal. Not-for-profit organizations have a range of goals—a multiple set of tasks that they seek to achieve. These include generating awareness, motivating people to be volunteers, distributing information, contacting customers, raising funds, allocating grants, and **lobbying** members of parliament for changes in regulations or legislation. Other goals include increasing their geographical spread to reach new people who might benefit from the organization's activities and campaigning to get media attention about a particular issue. In the non-profit sector, performance measurement is challenging, because there a wider set of objectives are used.

Orientation

As a general rule, rather than manufacturing, distributing, and selling a physical product, organizations in the not-for-profit sector are oriented to delivering a service. Developing a market orientation (see Chapter 1) is important, because the stronger the market orientation, the stronger the organization's market performance, particularly for smaller charities (Seymour *et al.*, 2006). How the not-for-profit raises its funding has an impact on the organization's market orientation. In a study of Portuguese not-for-profits, those organizations relying on private funding, as opposed to state funding were found to be more market-oriented (Macedo and Pinho, 2006) and more likely to be successful in fundraising.

Not-for-profit organizations need to create positive awareness about their cause or activities. The principal focus of the organization is to motivate and encourage people to become involved and identify with the aims of the organization, which may then lead to financial contributions and/or volunteering support (e.g. by working in a charity's shop, or by contributing financial, marketing, or other professional services expertise).

Raising funds is an ongoing critical activity in the not-for-profit sector. The payment handed over by a customer to a charity does not operate in the same way as the payment by a customer for a banking service at the point of receiving the service. Raising funds for a charity requires people or donors to contribute money, so the expectations of not-for-profit customers are different from those of commercial firms. This leads to a greater focus on engaging supporters to become part of, and identify with, the ethos of the not-for-profit organization rather than simply being a customer.

Customers' Perceptions

Customers of private sector organizations realize that in exchange for an offering they are contributing to the profits of the organization they are dealing with. Customers have a choice, and organizations compete to get their attention and money. In the not-for-profit sector, customers do not always have a choice. Donors are free to give to one charity rather than another, or not to give anything at all. In the public sector, choice is limited, although governments do try to provide some choice (e.g. in school provision). In reality, however, there is little practical opportunity for the public to choose among different public services in the same way as in the private sector. For example, services provided by local councils, such as dinner services (called meals-on-wheels) for the elderly and infirm, magistrate's courts, or building regulations and planning, are effectively

single source; there is no choice or alternative supplier. In these cases, pressure to deliver a superior level of service interaction can often be based on an individual's own sense of duty and integrity rather than on any formal organizational service policy and training.

Visit the **Online Resource Centre** and follow the weblink to the National Council of Non-profit Associations (NCNA) to learn more about the challenges and developments facing non-profit organizations.

Types of Not-for-Profit Organization

We can classify four main types of not-for-profit organizations: 1) charities, 2) the **social enterprise** sector, 3) the public sector, and 4) political parties and campaigning organizations. How marketing is used in each of these organizations is considered further in this section.

Charities

The increasing success experienced by many charities has resulted partly from improved commercial professionalism and the adoption of many ideas from the private sector, together with greater collaboration with the private sector through **cause-related marketing** activities. However, there has also been a simultaneous increase in the number of charities in the marketplace. This means that there is greater competition as more charities chase a finite number of donor contributions.

The act of making a donation to a charitable organization is the culmination of a decision-making process involving a wide range of variables. Attitude to the cause, personal involvement or related experience, and trust in the charity to use the funds appropriately are critical to encouraging donations to be made. Consequently, charities seek to develop empathy with potential donors and build trust from which an initial transaction or donation can be made. The acquisition of a new donor is relatively expensive compared with the low costs associated with the collection of monthly standing orders and direct debits. Costs are minimized when repeat donations occur, so charities, just like private sector organizations, practice relationship marketing principles (see Chapter 14).

NSPCC ●
™

Cruelty to children must stop. FULL STOP.

The NSPCC's highly successful Full Stop! Campaign brought in £250m of donations above the usual fund-raising initiatives over an eight-year period
Source: © NSPCC.

The process of giving is based on a strong emotional involvement with the objectives of the charity. This means that charities try to communicate through messages that invoke an emotional response in their target donors. A powerful example of a British charity that has used an emotional appeal in its fundraising to good effect is the National Society for the Prevention of Cruelty to Children (NSPCC). Its Full Stop! campaign, launched between 1999 and 2007 to stop cruelty to children, brought in £250m of donations above the usual fund-raising initiatives (NSPCC, 2013). Charities need to provide people with a rationale, a reason to give money.

Charities also try to raise funds by working in partnerships with commercial organizations in cause-related marketing campaigns. According to Kotler (2000), companies increasingly differentiate themselves by sponsoring popular social causes to win the public's favour. Such an approach, known as cause-related marketing, is recognized as a useful way of developing a positive brand image for the private companies as it builds not only customer loyalty, but also employee respect. The charity gains vital income from this partnership. The American Marketing Association defines cause-related marketing, which Americans term cause-marketing, as follows.

> Promotional strategy that links a company's sales campaign directly to a non-profit organization. Generally includes an offer by the sponsor to make a donation to the cause with [the] purchase of its product or service. Unlike philanthropy, money spent on cause marketing is a business expense, not a donation, and is expected to show a return on investment. (AMA, 2013)

This type of campaign associates a company's sales with the mission or campaign of a not-for-profit organization and includes a promise to make a donation for each offering bought. However, cooperation between the two organizations can take many forms. Traditionally, these schemes are based on sales promotions, whereby a donation to the charity is made as a percentage of sales. H&M, the Swedish fashion retailer, has partnered with WaterAid to launch the H&M for Water collection for the Summer 2013 range, modelled by global superstar Beyoncé, with 25% of sales from the H&M for Water collection donated to H&M for WaterAid (WaterAid, 2013).

This approach is an increasingly attractive proposition for organizations as several reports have found that a very large proportion of consumers (85%+) agree that when price and quality are equal, they are more likely to buy an offering associated with a 'cause' or good deed. Therefore companies are increasingly likely to differentiate themselves by co-opting social causes (Kotler, 2000). Other relationships, for example those between pharmaceutical companies and medicine distribution charities, are based on the company providing free product and technical knowledge ('gifts in kind'). (See Chapter 18 for more on corporate social responsibility (CSR).)

In numerous markets, including the UK, Ireland, and Poland, supermarket retailer Tesco has run an initiative called Tesco for Schools and Clubs where customers save vouchers that can be redeemed for computers for their local schools. The scheme worked on the basis that during the 10-week promotional period each year, customers received one voucher to donate to a school or club of their choice for every £10 spent in a Tesco store. Schools or clubs then collect these vouchers to redeem them for computers and other equipment from a catalogue. Since the original programme was launched in 1992, the scheme has donated £185m to schools and clubs in the UK (Tesco, 2012). The scheme rewarded Tesco in many ways, including increased customer loyalty, stronger community relationships, and attraction of new shoppers into their stores, and it also helped to ensure the computer literacy of school leavers and potential employees. A good example of a global cause-related marketing campaign is Kellogg's *Breakfast for Better Days™* initiative (see Market Insight 16.2).

Cause-related marketing can affect consumers' overall attitude towards the sponsoring company or brand, as well as a consumer's cognitive knowledge of the brand (i.e. what they know).

Market Insight 16.2

Kellogg's: The Serial Giver

Kellogg's has a long history of manufacturing and marketing breakfast cereals. The company was originally set up in 1906 as the 'Battle Creek Toasted Corn Flake Company' in Michigan, USA. The company went from strength to strength. By 1930, despite the depression, the company's founder W. K. Kellogg set up the W. K. Kellogg Foundation, investing in particular in children's education. Today, the company operates in 180 countries across the world, and holds well-loved brands such as Corn Flakes, All-Bran, Frosties, Special K, Pop-Tarts, and, after a 2012 acquisition from Procter & Gamble, Pringles. In 2012, the company had net sales of $14.2bn, with an operating profit of $2.0bn, and an employee base of around 31,000 people worldwide. To support the company's global brand positioning, it spent $1.1bn on advertising.

As well as high turnover targets, the Kellogg Company also has grand corporate responsibility ambitions. It seeks to provide one billion cereal and snack servings to people in need around the world by 2016 to help alleviate hunger through the global *Breakfast for Better Days™* initiative. Between 2008 and 2012, the Kellogg Company donated $68m to $129m in products to charitable organizations worldwide. In

one initiative, Kellogg's support breakfast clubs, which provide children who come to school hungry with free breakfasts. In the UK, Kellogg's have invested £2m since 1998 to set up and support breakfast clubs, with more than 500 running by 2012, partly through cause-related marketing promotions. Similarly, Kellogg Canada has donated more than C$1m and 2.5 million pounds (1.1 million kg) of food between 2007 and 2012 and works extensively with Breakfast Clubs of Canada.

Sources: Coughlan (2012); Kellogg's (2012a,b); Anon. (2013c); http://www.kelloggs.com/en_US/our-history.html http://www.giveachildabreakfast.co.uk/about_breakfast_clubs.aspx

1 How well do you think Kellogg's corporate social responsibility initiatives fit its corporate strategy?

2 Do you think that Kellogg's spends sufficient resources on its corporate social responsibility initiatives? Why do you say this?

3 How important is it that a company promotes not just the cause-related marketing initiative but the fact that the company is undertaking the initiative in the first place?

Cause-related marketing campaigns are more effective when they are used over time and when there is a strong fit between the brand and the cause (Till and Nowak, 2000). The perceived fit between the company and the cause is important to the effectiveness of the campaign. Nevertheless, there are risks to the not-for-profit organization. The charitable organization's most important asset is its name, and as cause-related marketing is a business transaction, it is subject to contract and so there is a risk that the charity will suffer reputational damage (Gifford, 1999). Cause-related marketing should be used as part of a wider CSR strategy (Steckstor, 2012). To reduce the risk, charities should not sell their association at less than it is really worth. They should also obtain the fee up front and control all uses of their name (Gifford, 1999).

Visit the **Online Resource Centre** and complete Internet Activity 16.1 to learn more about cause-related marketing.

Social Enterprises

A new form of organization has emerged in recent years, one with a format and purpose that has captured the imagination of many different people, including people in commercial business, people working in the social sector, volunteers, academics, and leading political parties. In the UK, the government considers a social enterprise to be an enterprise that 'is a business with primarily social objectives whose surpluses are principally reinvested for that purpose in the business or in the community, rather than being driven by the need to maximize profit for shareholders and owners' (BIS, 2011: 2). Social enterprises blend social objectives with commercial reality. There is a drive to make a profit, but any surplus is reinvested into the enterprise and not redistributed as a reward to owners. In the UK, Fairtrade schemes, Welsh Water (Glas Cymru), Jamie Oliver's Fifteen, the Co-operative Group, charities, and even farmers' markets are all examples of social enterprise organizations (see Market Insight 16.3). Elsewhere around the world, examples include Groupe SOS in France, which offers products/services to the disadvantaged and socially

Research Insight 16.2

To take your learning further, you might wish to read this influential paper.

Varadarajan, P. R., and Menon, A. (1988), 'Cause-related marketing: a coalignment of marketing strategy and corporate philanthropy', *Journal of Marketing*, 52(July), 58–74.

The authors of this article detailed programmes undertaken by organizations that mixed corporate philanthropic objectives with marketing strategy, sparking decades of discussion around whether or not business should work with charities or leave charity to charities, and how to measure the effectiveness of cause-related marketing programmes. The article outlines how cause-related marketing can be conducted at the strategic, quasi-strategic, and tactical levels within a company, and warns of the differences between cause-related and cause-exploitative marketing.

Visit the Online Resource Centre to read the abstract and access the full paper.

Market Insight 16.3

Duchy Originals: Food Fit for a Prince

Much has changed in the UK food industry in the last 20 years. Organic farming is now commonplace and consumers are increasingly concerned not just about what they eat, but about how what they eat has been produced. One visionary food brand which has long heralded sustainable farming values is Duchy Originals, launched by HRH The Prince of Wales in 1992, using produce from the Duchy's Home Farm at the Highgrove Estate in Gloucestershire. At the company's ten-year anniversary, he explained the rationale behind the venture: 'I wanted to demonstrate that it was possible to produce food of the highest quality, working in harmony with the environment and nature, using the best ingredients and adding value through expert production'. Importantly, the organization's profits are seeded to the Prince's Charities Foundation. But it hasn't all been plain sailing. The Duchy Originals brand saw a decline during the economic recession of the late 2000s, with losses of around £3.3m in one year. Since then, the brand has been taken over by exclusive distributor Waitrose, the quality multiple retail grocer.

This proves to have been a smart move as The Prince of Wales Charitable Foundation received £2.8m from Waitrose in 2012, with sales up a third on the previous year. Duchy Originals from Waitrose now sells around 260 products and exports to 25 countries including Belgium, Japan, Australia, and Taiwan. But Prince Charles is not the only one selling royal food. HM King Bhumipol Adulyadej of Thailand's Golden Place brand has been going from strength to strength since 2001. It seems that everyone now wants food fit for royalty, and the fact that profits go to charity makes it even tastier.

Sources: Anon. (2013d); http://www.duchyoriginals.com/ http://www.goldenplace.co.th/

1 Do you think that this social enterprise would be able to survive if it did not have the patronage of HRH The Prince of Wales?

2 Do you think it was a good idea to make Waitrose the exclusive distributor for the brand? Why do you say this?

3 Take a look at the website of another social enterprise with which you are familiar. How does the business model compare?

---

excluded, and Specialisterne in Denmark, which specializes in software testing and employs mainly people with Asperger's syndrome, a form of autism.

However, social enterprises are not restricted in format. The sector is very diverse and includes public limited companies (PLCs), community enterprises, cooperatives, housing associations, charities, and leisure and development trusts, among others. All of these can adopt social enterprise values.

Public Sector

The term public sector covers a very wide range of activities based around the provision of local and central government services, and services provided by government agencies. These services are essentially concerned with satisfying social needs and benefiting society as a whole. The public sector in many countries has grown on the back of the ideas embedded within the welfare state, although many of these countries have privatized their telecommunication, water, gas, and electricity provision. Now the different types of services provided are founded on the principle of improving the social context in which people live their lives.

Public sector organizations operate in industrial, governmental, consumer, and societal markets, and their marketing activities are driven by a complex web of stakeholder relationships. Marketing in the public sector is governed by three main forces: 1) social, 2) economic, and 3) political. The interaction of these forces within an increasingly uncertain and unstable environment makes the provision of customer choice of service problematic, although not impossible.

Internal marketing is crucial in these organizations, although at times rather unsophisticated in comparison with private sector counterparts. Rather than refer to buyers and sellers, the public sector approach is based more on official terms such as providers and users, where resources and not investment comprise the primary criterion, although this approach is changing. One distinguishing characteristic of the public sector concerns the political tensions that arise between the various stakeholder groups. For example, the conflict between central and local government is crucial, and perceptions of who is responsible for taxation, and why tax rates rise faster than inflation, reflect the power imbalance between the participants.

But governments also use marketing to bring about societal change. The idea that marketing techniques could be used in this way was first discussed by Kotler and Zaltman (1971). There is debate over the extent to which advertising, for example, can really change people's views and behaviour on social issues. For example, during the 1995 Divorce Referendum in Ireland, the Irish people narrowly voted for divorce (50.3%) to be made legal. Given that there was no precedent to overturn a referendum in Irish history, the 'No' lobby challenged the result in court, arguing that the Irish government had behaved unconstitutionally by spending around 500,000 Irish Punts ($750,000) on advertising the referendum and, in particular, supporting the 'Yes' campaign. The judge in the High Court case cast doubt on the idea that advertising could affect the way people voted on such an important issue, but analysis by Harris *et al.* (1999) indicates that the advertising may indeed have had an effect on the result. In other words, advertising can change peoples' attitudes, even on important value-based issues such as divorce and religion. Nevertheless, most social marketing campaigns are clear cut, and are designed to advance social causes to the benefit of a particular audience by changing social attitudes and behaviours (see Research Insight 16.3). Social marketing campaigns are typically, but not exclusively, run by public sector organizations. Some examples are as follows.

- Government health departments encouraging healthy eating (i.e. the Danish six-a-day campaign to encourage people to eat more fruit and vegetables), exercising, cessation of smoking and other behaviours, or government departments of transport encouraging road safety (see Market Insight 16.4).

- The British Heart Foundation campaign to educate the general public about how to administer first aid to a person suffering a heart attack to increase their chances of survival through a television advertising campaign featuring football star turned actor Vinny Jones.

Visit the **Online Resource Centre** and follow the weblink to the Healthcare Communication and Marketing Association Inc. (HCMA) to learn more about marketing communications and the healthcare service profession.

- The police or other emergency services use social marketing campaigns to reduce undesirable behaviour, either as an alternative or a complement to law enforcement. For example, the City of London Police have used handbills and posters to inform the general public about their crime-reduction security operations, and social marketing communications including cinema advertising have been used as part of the Wales Arson Reduction Strategy (JAG, 2011).

WARNING!
Thieves Operate in this area

Over the last few weeks there has been an increase in thefts from unattended cars in the City. This has taken place in both car parks and on the street.

- Some of the items stolen had been left on view within the vehicle.

- If you can, take your belongings with you rather than leaving them in the car.

- Even that old coat on the back seat, it may be worthless but thieves won't know that. They may break in to see if you've left any money or cards in one of the pockets.

For emergencies or where a crime is being committed please dial 999. Alternatively please contact the City of London Police switchboard to report any other concerns on **020 7601 2222**.

For more advice on the security of your vehicle, please visit www.cityoflondon.police.uk

CITY OF LONDON POLICE

The City of London Police use handbills and posters to inform the general public about their crime-reduction security operations

Source: Photo courtesy of the Commissioner of Police for the City of London.

Marketing does have the potential to improve mass communication in terms of ensuring the receipt of the message and the positive processing of that message. However, some have argued that wholesale application of social marketing has considerable ethical implications, and therefore that public oversight bodies should be developed to regulate social marketing techniques (Laczniak *et al*., 1979). One example of a campaign that caused public concern was when the US State Department, in the wake of the September 11 bombing, spent $5m purchasing

Market Insight 16.4

THINK! Scaring Drivers and Riders

Watch the petrol station screen advert at: https://www.gov.uk/government/news/think-urges-motorcyclists-to-stay-in-control.

Imagine that you are a marketing executive in a government transport department. How would you design a campaign to encourage drivers to take more care when driving near motorcyclists? How would you encourage riders to drive more safely? The difficulty in designing a suitable message for the target audiences arises from several concerns. Most people either think that they are good car drivers or bike riders, or that an accident won't happen to them. THINK! is the road safety campaign created by the UK Department of Transport. Launched in 2000, the campaign aims to reduce behaviour that contributes to road casualties and fatalities, including the use of mobile phones to speak or text while driving, driving when tired, not wearing a seatbelt, driving after taking legal or illegal drugs, anti-social driving such as tailgating, and paying insufficient attention to motorcyclists. The campaigns use different tactics to engage the audience, ranging from softer, more positive messages to hard-hitting campaigns which remind people of the consequences of risky or careless driving behaviour.

One promotional campaign is based around an important road safety issue—accidents involving motorcyclists. Incredibly, motorcyclists make up only 1% of the traffic on roads but account for 19% of deaths from traffic accidents. As a result, the UK Department for Transport is running a two-pronged campaign: one prong is aimed at encouraging motorcyclists to drive 'defensively', frightening them into watching out for potential dangers whilst riding, and the second is aimed at car drivers to frighten them into being more vigilant when driving by watching out for bikers. The campaign works with industry partners, including the Motorcycle Industry Association, *Motor Cycle Monthly* magazine, Devitt Insurance and Yamaha, to develop and

get out the message. Posters, leaflets, and other promotional material were distributed to motorcycle dealerships and retailers across the UK through other partner organizations such as the Motorcycle Retailers Association, Motorcycle Industry Training Association, British Motorcyclists Federation, Motorcycle Action Group, retail brands including Shark and Furygan, and major motorcycle dealers including Kawasaki. As part of the campaign, a short 10 second advert, showing on advertising screens in petrol stations, uses the fear appeal, initially showing an eye which then zooms back to reveal the helmeted face of a stricken female biker, lying dead on the road, with flashing police lights reflecting in her helmet. At the same time, the words appear 'When pulling out at junctions, take longer to look for bikes.

LOOK REACT STAY IN CONTROL

Expect the unexpected.
Give yourself time to react.   THINK!

The UK Department for Transport's Think! Campaign sought to improve the safety of motorcycle riding through posters, broadcast adverts and social media
Source: DfT © 2013.

Market Insight 16.4

continued

Think!' The campaign is also disseminated through the Think! Biker Facebook page and Think! Twitter channel.

Source: DfT (2013).

1 Watch the advert. Do you think this advert will be effective? Why do you say this?

2 Why do you think the campaign uses the fear appeal? Could another less hard-hitting approach have been used effectively?

3 Do you think that it is ethical for a government department to use the fear appeal in a road safety campaign? Why do you say this?

airtime on Middle Eastern and Asian TV stations to broadcast a series of adverts in a campaign called the 'Shared Values Initiative' designed to convince the Muslim world that America was not waging war on Islam. In the end, the US State Department pulled the ads after serious criticism in the media and Al Jazeera and other channels in certain countries refused to air them (Fullerton and Kendrick, 2006). The problem was that many people viewed the broadcasts as **propaganda** rather than advertising.

But when is social marketing propagandist? O'Shaughnessy (1996) has argued that social marketing and social propaganda are distinctly different, but admits that they are related fields. Social marketing is usually based on audience wants, identified through audience research, whereas propaganda is one-way communication and evangelical (i.e. the propagandist is convinced of the message's own rightness and uses research only as a means of increasing the

Research Insight 16.3

To take your learning further, you might wish to read this influential paper.

Michie, S., van Stralen, M. M., and West, R. (2011), 'The behaviour change wheel: a new method for characterizing and designing behaviour change interventions', *Implementation Science*, **6(1), 42–53.**

In this highly readable article, the authors undertake a systematic literature review to identify frameworks for behaviour change interventions. They synthesize a new framework, based on 19 identified extant behaviour change intervention frameworks, which they call the 'COM-B system'. The COM-B system explains how behavioural change should be analysed from the perspective of the capabilities, opportunities, and motivations that target audiences have to change their behaviour, leading to the design of nine intervention functions including education, persuasion, incentivization, coercion, training, enablement, modelling, environmental restructuring, and restrictions.

@ Visit the **Online Resource Centre** to read the abstract and access the full paper.

propaganda's effectiveness). Propaganda also typically uses language aimed at uniting or instilling minority grievances.

The idea that marketing can also be used to counter negative social ideas, or grievances, has a long pedigree. Edward Bernays, the grandfather of the public relations industry and nephew of psychoanalyst Sigmund Freud, wrote a far-sighted article on how America should use marketing and public relations techniques to help people 'see' the true alternative between democracy and fascism, and democracy and Nazism, during the Second World War (Bernays, 1942).

Political Parties and Campaigning Organizations

The of use of marketing by political parties and third-party interest groups has increased in the last 50 years since the development of TV and mass media broadcasting worldwide. Scientific methods of assessing market and public opinion have transformed how political campaigns are now run. In addition, charities and other campaigning organizations use marketing techniques to influence legislation and public opinion. With the development of globalized industries, the interplay between marketing and politics has increased further, and so marketing methods associated with political campaigning are increasingly used by companies to influence legislators and regulators (e.g. in the European Parliament, on Capitol Hill in Washington, DC, and at World Trade talks). Regulators go on to influence the legislation associated with those commercial markets.

Marketing is used by political parties to bring about an exchange of political support (e.g. votes, petitions, donations, volunteering) for political influence (e.g. legislative change/amendments). Political and electoral campaigns have existed for thousands of years, but the uptake of marketing techniques in these campaigns has increased with the advent of broadcasting, particularly since TV became commonplace in people's households in the 1950s. Political marketing has been likened to a marketing–propaganda hybrid, mixing marketing and propaganda. This is particularly the case in America, where negative campaigning is rife (O'Shaughnessy, 1990), using 30-second and 15-second advertising spots to pour out malicious attacks on political opponents. A well-known example of such an advertising campaign is former US President Lyndon B. Johnson's 'daisy spot' TV campaign against Barry Goldwater in the 1964 American presidential election, where a young girl picks leaves off a flower to a narrative of Goldwater's nuclear countdown. Broadcast TV adverts (known in America as 'spots') can be particularly emotive, and the image of the young girl creates mental associations around the future of our children and the potential threat of nuclear Armageddon. This powerful image created fear in its audience, and the audience automatically associated that fear with voting for the opposition candidate Barry Goldwater. The British Conservative Party used a similar approach against the Labour Party in the late 1990s, painting Tony Blair with 'demon eyes' to insinuate that he was the devil. Although the spot was controversial and widely condemned in the media, it won an effectiveness award from *Campaign* magazine (Culf, 1997). More recently, the National Rifle Association (NRA) has used controversial campaign ads to criticize President Obama's pledge to tighten gun laws after the Sandy Hook elementary school attack which killed 26 people.

Visit the **Online Resource Centre** and follow the weblink to the National Rifle Association (NRA) website to learn more about their campaign.

Marketing is used by political parties in representative democracies to provide citizens and voters with information on current and potential political programmes for running the country. In the process, parties aim to improve social cohesion, democratic participation, and citizen belongingness. Unfortunately, the recent use of political marketing in post-war democracies worldwide also seems to have occurred in parallel with a decline in political participation. Whether or not there is a correlation is difficult to determine. What is clear is that citizens seem to be increasingly disengaged from political parties. Some argue that marketing has been over-used, thereby damaging public trust; however, the truth is more likely to be that marketing techniques can be used to market a poor party or candidate just as much as they can be used to market an excellent party or candidate. In politics, it is difficult to determine which is which until the party comes into power. The disaffection and disappointment that citizens and voters then feel can fuel later disengagement. In that sense, politics is a credence service (see Chapter 14). In many countries around the world, there are different legal requirements for political advertising compared with commercial advertising. In Britain, political advertising regulations allow comparison of political parties and adverts as long as they are 'decent' and in 'good taste'. In 2001, the BBC refused to air a party election broadcast by the Pro-Life Alliance Party as it contained graphic footage of an abortion (House of Lords, 2003). It is more difficult to determine that a political advert must be truthful, as politics is often a matter of opinion and judgement. In contrast, advertising claims for commercial products must always adhere to the guidelines on taste, decency, and truthfulness (for more on the ethics of political advertising, see Chapter 18).

The political marketing offering includes political representation. Considering political representation to be a political service provided to companies or voters gives us a better understanding of the political party's reason for existence in relation to its target markets. As marketing techniques, such as advertising and market research, are increasingly used in political campaigns (and have been since the 1930s in the UK), there is increasing use of strategic marketing techniques such as market positioning and market segmentation (see Chapter 6).

Most marketing campaigns for political campaigns (corporate or party political) have historically been undertaken by specialized marketing and PR agencies on an ad hoc basis, although political parties and multinational corporations are increasingly conducting their political marketing activity in-house. In America, political consultants are more specialized, undertaking work in such areas as polling, petition management, fundraising, strategy, media buying, advertising, public affairs, grassroots lobbying, law, donor list maintenance, online campaigning, and campaign software consulting. The internet and social media have become important areas for generating campaign finance and grassroots support, particularly in the US. The internet looks set to become the future battleground of political campaigning in elections around the world (see Market Insight 16.5).

As with the use of marketing for social campaigning, its input into politics strikes concern into many who think that politics should not adopt such techniques. Marketing has played a strong role in bringing about revolution against Soviet-allied governments in Serbia, Georgia, and the Ukraine, where American political consultants were advising opposition parties which deployed 'revolutionary symbols and slogans' to encourage activists to take to the streets (Sussman and Krader, 2008). Given marketing's ability to influence the general public, the question arises: what is and what is not a legitimate use of marketing in the political sphere?

Under certain circumstances, it is possible to influence the political environment, and therefore the political agenda (see Chapter 4), in favour of an organization's strategy. Charities and not-for-profit organizations frequently focus on campaigning to change legislation or government policy agendas (a process known as lobbying or public affairs). The organization Purpose.com in the US has had considerable success working with companies like Google and Audi and organizations like the Bill & Melinda Gates Foundation to build mass movements online to support particular causes. For example, Audi hopes to enter the Indian car market, and part of its entry strategy involves designing and promoting clean water machines (Anon., 2013a).

Often, lobbying or public affairs campaigns use stunts to obtain media publicity to influence public opinion and, in turn, influence parliamentary opinion in the countries concerned. For example,

Market Insight 16.5

Obama's Big Data Wins Election

The 2012 US presidential election was the most expensive political contest ever, a feat enjoyed seemingly every election season, costing each presidential candidate over US$1bn each. In the end, despite a fierce contest, Barack Obama was returned with 332 votes to Mitt Romney's 206 of the total of 538 electoral college votes available. In the popular vote, Obama obtained 65,917,258 votes (51%) to Romney's 60,932,235 votes (47%).

The two candidates ran on very different campaign platforms, with Obama using the slogan 'Forward' and Romney using the slogan 'Believe in America'. Interestingly, according to Ipsos USA data taken towards the end of the campaign during the National Party Conventions, whilst Obama was seen by 'swing voters' as more 'likeable', 'eloquent', 'is a good person', and 'would be fun to meet in person', Romney had the lead on being seen as 'effective in Washington', 'will protect American jobs', and 'a man of faith', important perceptions which had stronger links to voting intention. However, Romney still didn't win. The question is: why?

One perspective is that Obama had a much more finely honed election campaign machine. The 2012 election was the 'big data' election. The campaign was particularly focused on digital marketing. The mybarackobama.com website from 2008 was resurrected. The digital campaign encouraged the dissemination of user-generated content, and so Obama courted 33 million Facebook 'likes', and 246 million views and 240,000 subscribers on YouTube. In comparison, Romney only managed 23,700 subscribers and 26 million views on YouTube. In this election, it wasn't the super-expensive TV ads that won it. It was the micro-targeted messages aimed at persuadable voters both to get out their vote and raise money using predictive analytic software programmes and voter data (e.g. geodemographics,

party registration data, and consumer data fused together). Obama's campaign sent 20 times more emails than Romney's between 11 August and 10 September, though only 85% made it into people's inboxes compared with Romney's 93%. Obama's open rate was also much higher (10.7% vs. 6.4%). In 2008, digital marketing was a game changer for US political marketing campaigns, now social marketing is a prerequisite. With predictive analytics software and the semantic web, expect even more targeted communication in 2016.

Sources: Anon. (2012); Braun and Gillum (2012); Gilson (2012); Harnden *et al*. (2012); Lynch (2012); MacMillan (2012); Mortimore *et al*. (2013).

1 **Why do you think that social media has become so important in US political campaigning?**

2 **How important is social media in election campaigns in other countries; for example, in countries in Europe, Asia, or Africa?**

3 **Do you think that social media is best used for raising support or for procuring donations? Why do you say this?**

The 2012 US presidential was a 'big data' election, where data are used to send finely-tune targeted communications to voters

Source: istock © Hocus Focus Studio.

the global environmental organization Greenpeace has long campaigned against nuclear policy in many countries around the world. It is probably best known in this regard for staging a protest against France's nuclear testing in the Pacific in 1985, when its ship *Rainbow Warrior* was bombed in Auckland Harbour, New Zealand, by French secret service agents (BBC, 2006).

Therefore we can see that publicity is important in pressure group campaigning. Typically, pressure groups try to advance policy change despite government opposition. Thus the publicity serves to highlight the cause and to bring supporters from the general public, who can then volunteer their time or provide donations in the same way that they would do with a charity.

Fundraising

An important role for marketing in charitable organizations is the generation of funds from donors and donor organizations. Whereas commercial organizations are typically funded by their customers (and invested in by shareholders), charitable organizations may generate funds from a variety of sources including government departments, non-governmental organizations (NGOs), and foundations (e.g. The Bill & Melinda Gates Foundation), and international agencies (e.g. the UN, the WHO, the World Bank), in addition to individual donors and customers. In some countries (e.g. China) there may be restrictions on whether or not international charitable organizations can solicit funds from the general public. The marketing role in such countries is used more to generate supporters and volunteers than for fundraising. In most countries, marketing has a key role to play in generating awareness of the need for funding, to stimulate giving, and in profiling supporters (Mindak and Bybee, 1971). Common techniques used to solicit funds include the following promotional approaches.

- Door drops—unaddressed mail is posted to an address often within specific targeted locations.
- Press/magazine inserts—details of the charity and its appeal are printed as a loose-leaf insert in a particular publication.
- Direct mail—targeted addressed mail is delivered to an address either online or offline.
- Direct response TV (DRTV)— advertisements for specific charities encourage viewers to make donations online or by ringing specific telephone numbers.
- Directly via a charity's website or through social media campaigns. However, charities are not making as much use of these channels as they either could or should (Waters *et al.,* 2009; Mintel, 2012). In New Zealand, the Australia and New Zealand Banking Group (ANZ) launched a donation service through Twitter for the Poppy Day Appeal to support veterans and ex-service people and their families in times of need (Mintel, 2012).
- Face-to-face donor recruitment—volunteers attend shopping malls or other areas of high potential donor footfall and solicit donations directly, usually for frequent giving through direct debit schemes (i.e. automatic monthly cash transfers from one's bank account).
- Face-to-face donation solicitation—volunteers attend shopping malls, as above, but with the aim of obtaining cash donations, often by rattling their donation tins.
- Corporate donations—a company makes a donation to a particular cause, although some companies donate a fixed proportion of their income. For example, in the UK companies that gave a high percentage of community contributions in relation to their pre-tax profits include

HESCO Bastion Ltd (44.8%), Avon Cosmetics (25.7%), Richer Sounds (19%), and Spar UK (13.9%) (Lillya, 2013).

- Major gifts—these are typically solicited from wealthy philanthropists, sometimes given as a legacy. For instance, when a philanthropist dies they make a sizeable gift in their wills to a particular charitable organization or social enterprise (e.g. Berkshire Hathaway financier Charles Munger gave $110m in his will to the University of Michigan (Anon., 2013b)).

Visit the **Online Resource Centre** and complete Internet Activity 16.2 to learn more about how the internet is improving the effectiveness and efficiency of fundraising activities for charitable organizations.

Many charities work on the principle that donors increase in loyalty over a period of time and shift from being non-supporters to infrequent donors. Infrequent donors are more likely to become more regular donors, a proportion then move onto giving major gifts, and, finally, even fewer donors leave legacies in their wills enabling charities to inherit their financial resources. Figure 16.3 shows how as donors increase in loyalty, and therefore giving, the size of each group drops.

Most charitable organizations and social enterprises recognize that some marketing techniques are more effective than others in raising income. Of the methods outlined above, direct marketing methods tend to be a relatively ineffective and expensive approach to fundraising compared with major gift, trust, and corporate donation solicitation, although charities have been successfully using face-to-face donor recruitment tactics widely in the last ten years or so (Sargeant *et al.,* 2006). Giving cheques/cash and via direct debit are now the most popular ways of giving to charity in the UK (Mintel, 2012). Over seven in ten adults in the UK population donate to charity (Mintel, 2012; Charities Aid Foundation, 2012). The estimated total amount donated in the UK in 2011–2012 was £9.3bn, down £2.3bn on the previous year after adjusting for inflation (CAF/NCVO, 2012). This compares favourably with the donation rate in other countries (see Table 16.3). The world's most generous countries, in terms of the extent to which people are prepared to donate their money and time to both organizations and strangers, are (in order) Australia, New Zealand, Ireland, Canada, and Switzerland (Charities Aid Foundation, 2012).

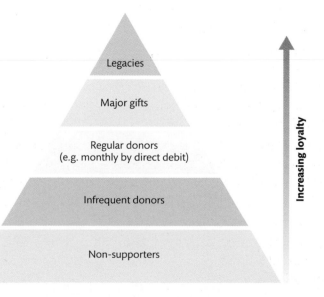

Figure 16.3
The fundraising loyalty ladder

Table 16.3 World Giving Index 2012

Rank	Country	Percentage of population giving money to charities	Percentage of population who have volunteered time for an organization in the last month	Percentage of population who have helped a stranger in the last month	World Giving Index score (average of previous columns)
1	Australia	70	38	64	57
2	New Zealand	68	41	63	57
3	Ireland	72	35	60	56
4	Canada	64	35	68	56
5	Switzerland	71	34	60	55
6	USA	60	39	65	55
7	Netherlands	77	39	46	54
8	UK	73	29	58	53
9	Sri Lanka	58	52	50	53
10	Austria	69	30	58	52
11	Lao People's Democratic Republic	64	32	53	50
12	Sierra Leone	29	45	75	50
13	Malta	83	21	40	48
14	Iceland	67	26	47	47
15	Turkmenistan	17	61	62	47
16	Guyana	36	33	67	45
17	Qatar	64	18	53	45
18	Hong Kong	70	13	50	44
19	Germany	49	28	56	44
20	Denmark	67	20	45	44
21	Guinea	28	42	61	44
22	Guatemala	46	33	51	43
23	Trinidad & Tobago	45	25	60	43
24	Myanmar	36	40	52	43
25	Thailand	73	18	36	42
26	Luxembourg	58	28	41	42
27	Kuwait	41	19	67	42
28	Norway	43	38	45	42
29	Angola	24	39	61	41
30	Italy	62	16	45	41

Source: Charities Aid Foundation (2012).

Unfortunately, UK charities tend not to present performance metrics such as market share (i.e. in relation to competition for donations), donor loyalty, retention, and satisfaction to top management, which indicates that marketing is still not used fully in not-for-profit organizations (Bennett, 2007). Equally, other strategic management concepts including SWOT analysis (see Chapter 5), the Balanced Scorecard (a technique for measuring organizational performance), and resource and capability analyses are also not being applied systematically in the not-for-profit context (Kong, 2008).

Corporation donations are also important, though in the UK in 2011–2012, they contributed only around 5% of the total income of charities and even the most generous companies tended to give less than 0.4% of their pre-tax profits (DSC, 2011). By comparison, the most charitable companies in the US were more generous (see Table 16.4).

Table 16.4 America's top ten most charitable companies 2012

Rank	Company	Sector	Donation (US$m)	2011 donation as percentage of 2010 pre-tax profits
1	Alcoa Inc.	Materials	$36.6	6.7
2	Merck & Co.	Pharmaceuticals	$72.6	4.4
3	General Mills Inc.	Food manufacturing	$88.7	4.0
4	Kroger Co.	Grocery retailing	$69.7	4.0
5	Xerox Corporation	Document management	$27.0	3.3
6	Target Corporation	Retailing	$146.0	3.3
7	Goldman Sachs Group Inc.	Investment banking	$337.0	2.6
8	Safeway Inc.	Grocery retailing	$21.6	2.5
9	Northwestern Mutual Life Insurance	Financial services	$17.0	2.4
10	Starbucks Corporation	Food retailing	$30.5	2.1

 Research Insight 16.4

To take your learning further, you might wish to read this influential paper.

Porter, M. E. and Kramer, M. R. (2002), 'The competitive advantage of corporate philanthropy', *Harvard Business Review*, 80(12), 56–68.

In this highly cited article, the authors argue that firms must look beyond the public relations value of their social contributions. The key to successful philanthropy is to focus giving on the context in which the firm

Research Insight 16.4
continued

operates. They explain how Cisco Systems set up the Cisco Networking Academy to train computer network administrators to alleviate a potential constraint on the company's growth, i.e. lack of available trained employees. Interestingly, the authors argue that philanthropy can be the most cost-effective way for a company to improve its competitive context, given that under these circumstances companies can leverage the efforts and resources of not-for-profit organizations and other institutions to make systemic changes.

Visit the **Online Resource Centre** to read the abstract and access the full paper.

Chapter Summary

To consolidate your learning, the key points from this chapter are summarized here.

■ **List some of the key characteristics of not-for-profit organizations.**

Not-for-profit organizations are differentiated from their commercial counterparts in numerous ways. Not-for-profit organizations tend to have multiple stakeholders and, because there are no shareholders, any profit earned is often reinvested in the organization. Because not-for-profit organizations do not distribute funds to shareholders, and are social enterprises, public sector organizations, or charities, there is a need for transparency in determining how these organizations operate as they are claiming to act for the common good. Accordingly, they have multiple objectives, rather than a simple profit motivation. Historically, they have not been strongly market oriented, but this is changing as not-for-profit organizations become more experienced in marketing. Customers' perceptions of not-for-profit organizations differ from those of their commercial counterparts because the not-for-profit typically has a unique mission and set of values and a non-financial organizational purpose.

■ **Explain why not-for-profit organizations do not always value their customers.**

Not-for-profit organizations frequently do not value their beneficiary customers because they exist in a monopolistic situation, demand far outstrips supply, a lack of market segmentation activity exists, and research into customer needs is not seen as a priority for expenditure and investment. Not-for-profit organizations frequently also undervalue supporter customers because typically they approach them to solicit funds too often and do not sufficiently appreciate them when they do give. Volunteer service workers who generously give their time can often feel undervalued. Because not-for-profit organizations have multiple stakeholders, problems can arise between these groups, which need resolution but which can often lead to customers feeling undervalued as those tensions are resolved.

■ **Analyse stakeholders and develop appropriate engagement strategies.**

A common way of analysing stakeholders is by mapping them on a power–interest matrix to identify four types based on the level of interest they display in an organization and the level of power they exert. Those with high levels of interest and power (group A) are key stakeholders in need of continuous engagement. Those with high interest but low levels of power (group B) should be informed about the organization's activities to maintain their interest. Group C represents those organizations with high power but low interest.

Here, it is important either to increase information flow to these organizations to increase their interest so that they can exert their power in the not-for-profit's favour, or alternatively to keep them satisfied if they intend to exert their power against the not-for-profit. Finally, an organization's relationships with those stakeholders who have little power or interest (Group D) should either be disregarded or revived.

■ **Describe and assess cause-related marketing campaigns.**

A cause-related marketing campaign occurs when companies and non-profit organizations form marketing alliances. Often, these marketing campaigns are focused on sales promotions developed for mutual benefit where the purchase of a commercial offering is linked to donations to a charitable third-party organization. Such campaigns tend to work best where there is a strong strategic fit between the commercial organization and the not-for-profit organization, particularly in relation to the audiences targeted and when the campaign runs over the longer term.

■ **Understand how marketing can be, and is, used to achieve social and political change in society.**

Only in the last 50 years have we embraced the use of marketing for social and political causes. Marketing is now commonly used in government information campaigns to drive positive behavioural change and improve citizens' well-being; however, we can question whether or not government should have this role and the ethics of using marketing in social and political campaigning. The use of marketing techniques in election campaigns has a longer pedigree and is now very common in most democracies worldwide. In this scenario, marketing is used to understand the electorate's wants/needs and to provide them with a set of party policies and leaders which suit those needs. In addition to the use of marketing by government to influence society, and by political parties to gain support and votes, marketing is used by third-party organizations (e.g. pressure groups) to drive legislative change in lobbying campaigns, particularly by courting publicity and the media's support more generally.

■ **Explain how marketing is used for charitable fundraising.**

Funds can be raised from donors using a variety of techniques including the following: door drops, where unaddressed mail is posted to addresses in targeted locations; press/magazine inserts; direct mail, online or offline; direct response TV (DRTV) advertisements encouraging viewers to make donations online or by ringing specific telephone numbers; charity websites and through social media; face-to-face donor recruitment; face-to-face donation solicitation; corporate donations; major gifts.

 # Review Questions

1 What key differences exist in marketing communications for not-for-profit versus for-profit organizations?

2 Can you name the main types of not-for-profit organization reviewed?

3 What are the key characteristics of not-for-profit organizations?

4 Why do not-for-profit organizations sometimes not value their beneficiaries?

5 Why do not-for-profit organizations sometimes not value their donors?

6 What axes are used on a stakeholder analysis matrix?

7 How is marketing used to raise funds for charitable organizations?

8 What is cause-related marketing?

9 How do we assess cause-related marketing programmes?

10 How is marketing used in political campaigning?

Worksheet Summary

To apply the knowledge you have gained from this chapter and test your understanding of not-for-profit marketing visit the **Online Resource Centre** and complete Worksheet 16.1.

Discussion Questions

1   Having read Case Insight 16.1 on Oxfam, how would you use marketing and PR techniques in future campaigns to:

   A   further improve the positive brand associations people have of Oxfam and its mission?
   B   recruit more supporters to the charity, particularly those who give on a monthly basis by direct debit?
   C   raise awareness of how Oxfam is distributing funding to its supporters?

2   Working in small groups, select three different not-for-profit organizations and consider the following.

   A   How do their 'propositions' differ from each other?
   B   What is the nature of price in each case?
   C   What is the nature of customer involvement for each proposition?
   D   How can the audiences for these 'products' be segmented, if at all?

3   Read the section on stakeholder mapping and draw up maps for the following organizations.

   A   An international medical charity undertaking work to alleviate the suffering of people living with HIV/AIDS in sub-Saharan Africa.
   B   The US Republican Party as it develops its campaign plan for the 2016 presidential election.
   C   A government department developing a campaign to increase citizens' consumption of fruit and vegetables in Denmark.
   D   The UK social enterprise *Fifteen*, the restaurant chain set up by celebrity chef Jamie Oliver.

4   Discuss reasons why charitable organizations should, or should not, communicate with donors on details of what the charity has achieved with their donations.

5   Visit the marketing sections of the websites of the following organizations for ideas on how they engage with their audiences.

   A   The police service in the country in which you were born.
   B   The largest charity in Europe (hint: Google this first).
   C   The European Parliament.
   D   A social enterprise with which you are familiar (if you are not, visit the website of HRH Prince Charles's company Duchy Originals, or France's Groupe SOS).

   Visit the **Online Resource Centre** and complete the multiple choice questions to assess your knowledge of Chapter 16.

References

AMA (2013), 'Dictionary: Cause marketing', retrieve from: http://www.marketingpower.com/_layouts/Dictionary. aspx?dLetter=C accessed 21 April 2013.

Anon. (2012), 'Brand Obama vs. brand Romney. Who's winning', *Marketing Week*, 30 October, retrieve from: http://www.marketingweek.co.uk/trends/brand-obama-vs-brand-romney-whos-winning/4004528. article accessed 21 April 2013.

Anon. (2013a), 'The business of campaigning: profit with purpose', *Economist*, 26 January, 60.

Anon. (2013b), 'Financier Munger gives largest gift in UM history, for grad hall', *CBS Local*, 18 April, retrieve from: http://detroit.cbslocal.com/2013/04/18/financier-munger-makes-largest-gift-in-um-history-for-grad-hall/ accessed 21 April 2013.

Anon. (2013c), 'Kellogg Company launches *Breakfasts for Better Days*™ hunger relief initiative', *PR Newswire*, 25 February, retrieve from: http://www.prnewswire. com/news-releases-test/kellogg-company-launches-breakfasts-for-better-days-hunger-relief-initiative-193058821.html accessed 21 April 2013.

Anon. (2013d), 'Prince Charles's Duchy Originals sees profits jump after bumper sales', *Telegraph*, 3 January, retrieve from: http://www.telegraph.co.uk/finance/ newsbysector/retailandconsumer/9777533/Prince-Charless-Duchy-Originals-sees-profits-jump-after-bumper-sales.html accessed 21 April 2013.

BBC (2006), 'NZ rules out new Greenpeace probe', 2 October 2006, retrieve from: http://news.bbc. co.uk/1/hi/world/asia-pacific/5398170.stm accessed 21 April 2013.

BBC (2012), 'Witness: The Guggenheim Bilbao', *BBC World Service*, 21 October, disseminated 13:50 GMT, retrieve from: http://www.bbc.co.uk/programmes/ p00z560n accessed 21 April 2013.

Bennett, R. (2007), 'The use of marketing metrics by British fundraising charities: a survey of current practice', *Journal of Marketing Management*, 23(9/10), 959–89.

Bernays. E. (1942), 'The marketing of national policies: a study of war propaganda', *Journal of Marketing*, 6(3), 236–45.

BIS (2011), *A Guide to Legal Forms for Social Enterprise*, Department of Business Innovation and Skills, November, retrieve from: http://www.bis.gov.uk/assets/ BISCore/business-law/docs/G/11-1400-guide-legal-forms-for-social-enterprise.pdf accessed 21 April 2013.

Braun, S. and Gillum, J. (2012), '$2bn price tag for presidential election', *Yahoo! News*, 7 December, retrieve from: http://news.yahoo.com/2-billion-price-tag-presidential-election-013546258--election.html accessed 21 April 2013.

Bruce, I. (1995), 'Do not-for-profits value their customers and their needs?', *International Marketing Review*, 12(4), 77–84.

CAF/NCVO (2012), UK Giving 2012: *An Overview of Charitable Giving in the UK 2011/2012*, London: Charities Aid Foundation/National Council for Voluntary Organizations, retrieve from: https://www.cafonline.org/ PDF/UKGiving2012Full.pdf accessed 21 April 2013.

Charities Aid Foundation (2012), *World Giving Index 2012: A Global View of Giving Trends*, December, retrieve from: https://www.cafonline.org/PDF/ WorldGivingIndex2012WEB.pdf accessed 20 April 2013.

Coughlan, S. (2012), 'Parents failing to give children breakfast', *BBC News*, 16 October, retrieve from: http://www.bbc.co.uk/news/education-19951590 accessed 21 April 2013.

Culf, A. (1997), Demon eyes ad wins top award', *Guardian*, 10 January, retrieve from: http://www. guardian.co.uk/politics/1997/jan/10/past.andrewculf accessed 20 April 2013.

DfT (2013), 'Think! urges motorcyclists to "stay in control"', Department for Transport, Press Release, 18 April, retrieve from: https://www.gov.uk/ government/news/think-urges-motorcyclists-to-stay-in-control accessed 21 April 2013.

DSC (2011) 'May 2011: Little sign of government action to boost charitable giving from companies', Directory for Social Change, Press Release, retrieve from: http:// www.dsc.org.uk/PolicyandResearch/Pressreleases/ LittlesignofGovernmentactiontoboostcharitable givingfromcompanies accessed 21 April 2013.

Fullerton, J., and Kendrick, A. (2006), *Advertising's War on Terrorism: The Story of the US State Department's Shared Values Initiative*, Spokane, WA: Marquette Books.

Gifford, G. (1999), 'Cause-related marketing: ten rules to protect your non-profit assets', *Nonprofit World*, 17(4), 11–13.

Gilson, D. (2012), 'The crazy cost of becoming president, from Lincoln to Obama', *Mother Jones*, 20 February, retrieve from: http://www.motherjones.com/ mojo/2012/02/historic-price-cost-presidential-elections accessed 21 April 2013.

Hall, C. (2012), 'Louvre and Guggenheim Abu Dhabi delayed', *Financial Times*, 25 January, retrieve from: http://www.ft.com/cms/s/0/35377308-470c-11e1-bc5f-00144feabdc0.html#axzz2R8LgdoYG accessed 21 April 2013.

Harnden, T., Gye, H., and Warren, L. (2012), 'After Obama routs Romney in electoral college AND popular votes to win four more years as president here comes the real challenge', *Daily Mail*, 7 November, retrieve from: http://www.dailymail.co.uk/news/article-2229053/US-Presidential-Election-results-2012-Comeback-kid-Obama-headed-White-House-2nd-term.html#ixzz2RCEDbNjV accessed 21 April 2013.

Harris, P., Lock, A., and O'Shaughnessy, N. (1999), 'Measuring the effect of political advertising and the case of the 1995 Irish Divorce Referendum', *Marketing Intelligence and Planning*, 17(6), 272–80.

Hatten, M. L. (1982), 'Strategic management in not-for-profit organisations', *Strategic Management Journal*, 3, 89–104.

House of Lords (2003), 'Judgments—Regina v. British Broadcasting Corporation (Appellants) ex parte Pro-Life Alliance (Respondents)', retrieve from: http://www.publications.parliament.uk/pa/ld200203/ldjudgmt/jd030515/bbc-3.htm accessed 20 April 2013.

JAG (2011), *Wales Arson Reduction Strategy: A Review by the Joint Arson Group*, St. Asaph, Denbighshire, North Wales Fire and Rescue Service, November, retrieve from: http://www.nwales-fireservice.org.uk/media/64363/wars_review_final_nov_2011.pdf accessed 21 April 2013.

Kellogg's (2012a), *Kellogg Company 2012 Annual Report*, retrieve from: http://investor.kelloggs.com/files/doc_financials/annual_reports/KELLOGG_12AR.pdf accessed 21 April 2013.

Kellogg's (2012b), *Corporate Responsibility Report*, retrieve from: http://www.kelloggcompany.com/content/dam/kelloggcompanyus/corporate_responsibility/pdf/2012CR/2012_ExecutiveSummary.pdf accessed 21 April 2013>

Kong, E. (2008), 'The development of strategic management in the non-profit context: intellectual capital in social service non-profit organizations', *International Journal of Management Reviews*, 10(3), 281–99.

Kotler, P. (2000), 'Future markets', *Executive Excellence*, 17(2), 6.

Kotler, P. and Levy, S. J. (1969), 'Broadening the concept of marketing', *Journal of Marketing*, 33(1, January), 10–15.

Kotler, P. and Zaltman, G. (1971), 'Social marketing: an approach to planned social change', *Journal of Marketing*, 35(3, July), 3–12.

Laczniak, G. R., Lusch, R. F., and Murphy, P. E. (1979), 'Social marketing: its ethical dimensions', *Journal of Marketing*, 43(Spring), 29–36.

Lillya, D. (2013), *The Guide to UK Company Giving 2013/2014* (9th edn), London: Directory of Social Change.

Lynch, M. (2012), 'Barack Obama's big data won the 2012 US election', *Computerworld*, 13 November, retrieve from: http://www.computerworld.com/s/article/9233587/Barack_Obama_39_s_Big_Data_won_the_US_election accessed 21 April 2013.

MacMillan, G. (2012), 'Beyond politics: what can you learn from the US election?', *Marketing*, 31 October, 10–12.

Macedo, I. M. and Pinho, J. C. (2006), 'The relationship between resource dependence and market orientation: the case of non-profit organisations', *European Journal of Marketing*, 40(5/6), 533–63.

Marling, S. (2003), 'Back from the brink: how one building gave a community a new lease of life—reviving an industrial city with an art gallery sounds unlikely, but Bilbao did so in spectacular style', *Daily Telegraph*, 11 January, 12.

Michie, S., van Stralen, M.M., and West, R. (2011), 'The behaviour change wheel: a new method for characterizing and designing behaviour change interventions', *Implementation Science*, 6(1), 42–53

Mindak, W. A. and Bybee, H. M. (1971), 'Marketing's application to fundraising', *Journal of Marketing*, 35(July), 13–18.

Mintel (2012), 'Charitable Giving—UK—May 2012', London: Mintel. Retrieve from: www.mintel.com.

Mortimore, R., Baines, P., Worcester, R., Young, C., and Clark, J. (2013), 'Asymmetric political image effects and the logic of negative campaigning', *Academy of Marketing Science Conference*, 15–18 May, Monterey, CA.

NSPCC (2013), *A Pocket History of the NSPCC*, London: National Society for the Prevention of Cruelty to Children, retrieve from: http://www.nspcc.org.uk/what-we-do/about-the-nspcc/history-of-NSPCC/history-of-nspcc-booklet_wdf75414.pdf accessed 21 April 2013.

O'Shaughnessy, N. (1990), *The Phenomenon of Political Marketing*, London: Macmillan Press.

O'Shaughnessy, N. (1996), 'Social propaganda and social marketing: a critical difference? ', *European Journal of Marketing*, 30(10/11), 62–75.

Porter, M. E. and Kramer, M. R. (2002), 'The competitive advantage of corporate philanthropy', *Harvard Business Review*, 80(12), 56–68

Rothschild, M. L. (1979), 'Marketing communications in non-business situations or why it's so hard to sell brotherhood like soap', *Journal of Marketing*, 43(Spring), 11–20.

Sargeant, A., Jay, E., and Lee, S. (2006), 'Benchmarking charity performance: returns from direct marketing in fundraising', *Journal of Nonprofit and Public Sector Marketing*, 16(1/2), 77–94.

Scholes, K. (2001), 'Stakeholder mapping: a practical tool for public sector managers', in G. Johnson and K. Scholes (eds), *Exploring Public Sector Strategy*, London: FT/Prentice Hall, 165–84.

Seymour, T., Gilbert, D., and Kolsaker, A. (2006), 'Aspects of market orientation of English and Welsh charities', *Journal of Nonprofit and Public Sector Marketing*, 16(1/2), 151–69.

Steckstor, D. (2012), *The Effects of Cause-Related Marketing on Customers' Attitudes and Buying Behavior*, New York: Gabler Verlag.

Sussman, G. and Krader, S. (2008), 'Template revolutions: marketing US regime change in Eastern Europe', *Westminster Papers in Communication and Culture*, 5(3), 91–112.

Tesco (2012), *Corporate Responsibility Review 2012*, Cheshunt: Tesco plc. Retrieve from: http://www.tescoplc.com/files/pdf/reports/tesco_cr_review_2012.pdf accessed 21 April 2013.

Till, B.D. and Nowak, L.I. (2000), 'Toward effective use of cause-related marketing alliances', *Journal of Product and Brand Management*, 9(7), 472–84.

Varadarajan, P.R. and Menon, A. (1988), 'Cause-related marketing: a coalignment of marketing strategy and corporate philanthropy', *Journal of Marketing*, 52(July), 58–74.

WaterAid (2013), 'Beyoncé launches new H&M campaign', WaterAid UK, 21 March, retrieve from: http://www.wateraid.org/uk/news/news/beyonce-launches-new-h-and-m-campaign accessed 21 April 2013.

Waters, R.D., Burnett, E., Lamm, A., and Lucas, J. (2009), 'Engaging stakeholders through social networking: how nonprofit organizations are using Facebook', *Public Relations Review*, 35, 102–6.

Part Five
Critique and Change in Marketing Practice

Chapter 17
Digital and Social Media Marketing

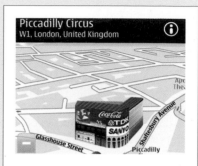

Learning Outcomes

After studying this chapter you should be able to:

▶ Define digital marketing and social media marketing

▶ Explain how digital marketing is evolving from Web 1.0 to Web 3.0

▶ Discuss key techniques in digital marketing and social media marketing

▶ Review how practitioners measure the effectiveness of social media marketing

▶ Discuss crowdsourcing and explain how online communities can be harnessed for marketing purposes

Case Insight
Virgin Media

Market Insight 17.1
Readable Stores and Shoppable Magazines

Market Insight 17.2
hairybaby.com: Using Irish Wit and Humour to Sell T-Shirts Online

Market Insight 17.3
easyJet Pays to Take Off!

Market Insight 17.4
Kony 2012: Viral Phenomenon

Market Insight 17.5
McDonald's: On Location!

Case Insight 17.1

What role does social media play and how should organizations incorporate it into their communication campaigns? We speak to Richard Larcombe, director of advertising and sponsorship at Virgin Media, to find out more.

Virgin Media pioneered the concept of 'quad play' by becoming the first UK provider of all four broadband, TV, mobile, and home phone services. We have a fantastic fibre-optic network at our disposal and focus on delivering brilliant entertainment and communication services to high-value customers. Our interactive television service is equally compelling, bringing together broadcast TV, thousands of hours of on-demand programming, and the best of the web in a single set-top box powered by TiVo. As a result, Virgin Media has become the fastest growing pay-TV company in the UK since its introduction. We also operate the most popular virtual mobile network in the UK and are one of the largest providers of fixed-line home phone services in the country. This combination of next-generation services, built for the mainstream, is a powerful proposition which sets us apart and will continue to drive our growth.

However, a number of our competitors, including BT, Sky, and TalkTalk, are following our lead and have started offering similar bundles of services. One of the things that sets us apart, however, is the power of our fibre-optic network, which enabled us to double the speeds of millions of broadband customers this past year and deliver superfast broadband as standard. The launch of Virgin TV Anywhere takes Virgin Media TiVo's functionality and content onto computers, tablets, and smartphones for use both inside and outside the home. By leveraging the capabilities of Virgin Media TiVo, we're bringing our multiple platforms together and enabling our customers to take their favourite content with them across their choice of screens.

Therefore our communications campaigns need to be designed to hit our objective of building better connections with consumers by bringing people closer to the brand and making Virgin Media more valuable to their entertainment and communications lifestyle. We aim to take the relationship beyond our offerings to build a personal connection with our customers and non-customers and, by providing easy access to help, allowing consumers to discover, navigate, and curate their own entertainment. We also wanted to continuously grow our communities and increase engagement with the brand. One of the ways we did this was by building a community of Virgin Media evangelists to bring people closer to our content and providing them with valuable content to build social interest and encourage sharing and conversation. We also work hard to create and facilitate a fun and active environment that customers and non-customers want to be part of.

Therefore social media is a fundamental component of our marketing. It enables us to maintain an always-on approach through earned media, harnessing the power and considerable influence of prospects and customers. Our Go-to-Market approach (see Figure 17.1 splits across four key areas: Consideration (which falls into three segments—passive search, trigger points and active search), Convert (the sale), Care (maintaining the relationship), and Cultivate (growing the relationship). Social cuts through every element.

We operate in a very fast-moving and competitive market, and some of our competitors have significantly greater marketing budgets. Nevertheless, we need to maintain our broadband leadership and

Case Insight 17.1
continued

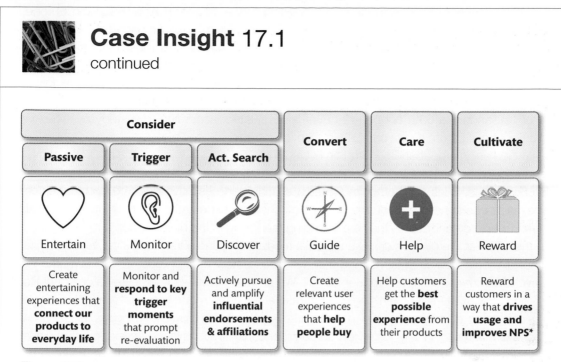

Figure 17.1

Virgin Media uses a set of customer management principles to guide its social media strategy

Note: *NPS, net promoter score (see Chapter 5 for more details).

we knew that superfast broadband could become a real point of differentiation for us. Because we can't rely on advertising spend alone to cut through and create impact, our campaigns need to disrupt, differentiate through the humour of the brand, and be demonstrative in execution. Part of this advertising campaign would involve Usain Bolt, our brand ambassador, and officially the world's fastest man.

Therefore our problem was how could we use social media to support our advertising campaign featuring Usain Bolt, and execute the above strategic objectives to promote superfast broadband?

Case compiled in conjunction with Richard Larcombe, director of advertising and sponsorship at Virgin Media.

Introduction

Consider for a moment your own personal use of digital technologies and social media. How many times did you login to your Facebook, Twitter, or LinkedIn account? When logged in did you update your status, write a tweet, 'like' a post, or pin a photo? Did you download an **app** or complete a survey? Did you watch or share any YouTube videos, or post comments, rate others' videos, or share them with anyone? Have you used a smartphone to transfer money from your bank account or to receive a mobile token (e.g. the Orange Wednesday's textcode that allows you to obtain two for the price of one tickets on Wednesdays)? Increasingly, many of the social interactions and information exchanges in which we engage are facilitated by digital and social media technologies. As people change how they communicate, the marketing profession has turned to digital and social media marketing to complement and, sometimes replace, traditional marketing channels and activities.

By 2012, internet penetration stood at 15.6% in Africa, 27.5% in Asia, 63.2% in Europe, 40.2% in the Middle East, 78.6% in North America, 42.9% in Latin America/Caribbean, and 67.6% in Oceania/Australia (Internet World Stats, 2012). The world's most networked-ready economy—a measure of the degree to which economies leverage information and communication technologies for enhanced competitiveness—in 2012 was Sweden, with Singapore ranking second and Finland third. The United Kingdom ranked tenth, the Netherlands sixth, UAE 30th, China 51st, and India 69th out of 142 countries evaluated, according to a study by INSEAD/World Economic Forum (Dutta and Bilbao-Osorio, 2012).

With increasing broadband penetration (increasingly via mobile devices), the adoption of digital and social media marketing techniques have become common. **Blogs**, **microblogs**, social networking sites, wikis, and other multimedia sharing services have become commonplace. These digital phenomena are not simply altering consumer expectations of their interaction with the web or with organizations, they are changing marketing in the digital space.

In this chapter, we discuss digital and social media marketing. First, we define various digital and social media marketing terms, and then we discuss how the approach to digital marketing has evolved from channel push to market pull. We provide a review of some key areas of digital marketing spend: internet advertising, search marketing, email marketing, viral marketing, social media marketing, advergaming, and mobile marketing. We define crowdsourcing and explain how it is used in marketing. Finally, we review some wider considerations in the development of digital marketing strategy and how practitioners measure the effectiveness of social media marketing.

Digital Marketing

Digital marketing is an established, and increasingly important, subfield of marketing brought about by advancements in digital media technologies and digital media environments. Digital marketing extends beyond internet marketing, making use of mobile telephony, digital display advertising, and other forms of digital media. Marketing in the digital age does not exist in a silo, independent of other marketing principles (e.g. pricing, distribution, or customer service). It is interdependent with other more traditional communication channels (e.g. press, radio, television) and distribution channels (e.g. retail outlets). Integrating digital marketing campaigns into marketing communications plans (see Chapter 11) and channel distribution plans (see Chapter 12) requires detailed consideration if they are to be effective, not least because the digital environment is not simply another channel but a channel in which consumers often behave differently. Therefore digital marketing should be considered more widely because digital media allows consumers to interact with other consumers, quite often outside the control of the organization around which they might be interacting.

A variety of terms are used in the digital marketing and social media marketing fields including as e-marketing, digital marketing, direct marketing, interactive marketing, and social media marketing among many others. Whilst these terms are sometimes incorrectly used interchangeably, in fact they each have their own specific meaning (see Tables 17.1 and 17.2).

Internet marketing is just one form of digital marketing specific to the use of internet-only technologies (e.g. web, email, intranet, extranets). This excludes the use of some digital broadcast media. However, it includes a wide array of resources, such as internet advertising, direct email, advergaming, and social media marketing (see Table 17.2 and section on Digital Marketing Activities). Throughout the rest of this chapter, we focus on digital marketing and social media marketing.

Table 17.1 Defining digital marketing terms

e-marketing	Process of marketing accomplished or facilitated through the use of electronic devices, applications, tools, technologies, platforms, and/or systems. It is not limited to one specific type or category of electronic technology (e.g. internet, TV), but includes both older analogue and developing digital electronic technologies.
Digital marketing	Management and execution of marketing using specifically digital electronic technologies and channels (e.g. web, email, digital TV, wireless media, and digital data about user/customer characteristics and behaviour) to reach markets in a timely, relevant, personal, interactive, and cost-effective manner.
Direct marketing	'A specific form of marketing that attempts to send its communications direct to consumers using addressable media such as post, internet, email, and telephone and text messaging' (Harris, 2009).
Interactive marketing	Refers to marketing that moves away from a transaction-based effort to a conversation (i.e. two-way dialogue) and can be described as a situation or mechanism through which marketers and a customer (e.g. stakeholders) interact usually in real time. Not all interactive marketing is electronic (e.g. face-to-face sales).

Table 17.2 Types of digital marketing activities

Type	Detail
Internet marketing	A form of digital marketing also referred to as i-marketing, web marketing, and online marketing, specific to the use of internet-only-based technologies (e.g. web, email, intranet, extranets) for the marketing of an offering (includes internet advertising, email marketing, social media marketing).
Internet advertising	A form of marketing communication that uses the internet for the purpose of advertising—delivering marketing messages to increase website traffic (i.e. click-through) and encourage product trial, purchase, and repeat purchase activity (i.e. conversion). Examples include display advertising, classified listings, rich media ads, search marketing, and advertising on social media sites.
Search marketing	A form of internet marketing that seeks to increase the visibility of websites in search engine results pages (SERPs) through the use of website **search engine optimization (SEO)** tactics and **search engine marketing (SEM)** activities (e.g. paid placement, contextual advertising, and paid inclusion).
Email marketing	A digital form of direct marketing using electronic means to communicate messages directly, increase loyalty, and build relationships with audiences of individuals who have given their permission (e.g. opt-in) to be sent messages through email (e.g. newsletters). Spam, in contrast, consists of unsolicited or undesired email messages.

Table 17.2 continued

Type	Detail
Mobile marketing	A form of digital marketing which enables organizations to communicate and engage with their audience in an interactive and relevant manner through any mobile device or wireless network (e.g. smartphone).
Viral marketing	A 'form of marketing whose prime aim is to encourage consumers to pass on a promotional message or idea, whether it be a statement, video clip, or email. Viral marketing is dependent on fast and high pass-along rates from consumer to potential consumer and is reliant on friends and acquaintances sharing information, ideas and of course video clips which are most frequently placed on YouTube' (Harris, 2009).
Online retailing (e-tailing)	A type of e-commerce used for business-to-consumer (B2C) transactions, click-and-collect (where the goods are delivered to a local store for easy collection rather than posted to someone's residence where delivery may occur when the addressee is not present), and mail order services (see Market Insight 17.1 and Chapter 12).
Advergaming	The use of video and online games to advertise a product, organization, or idea. Advergames encourage repeat website traffic and reinforce brand loyalty.
Social media marketing (SMM)	'Social media marketing (SMM) is a form of internet marketing that utilises social networking websites as a marketing tool. The goal of SMM is to produce content that users will share with their social network to help a company increase brand exposure and broaden customer reach' (WhatIs.com, 2013).

Market Insight 17.1

Readable Stores and Shoppable Magazines

Traditionally, reading fashion magazines was accompanied by passive salivation over the haute couture looks carefully crafted by editors and their creative teams. Brands would send their best and latest garments to magazine editors, and these provided material for editorial pages. Magazines like *Vogue* and *Elle* would shoot photo stories and write editorial reviews on their pages featuring clothes for customers to covet. This was meant to encourage readers to purchase in-store, phoning the

relevant retailer (a long list of store phone numbers was traditionally printed on the last pages of each magazine) or buying on the internet. Either way, the link between seeing and acting was far from seamless.

More recently, online brands such as Net-a-Porter and ASOS have started creating their own magazine style pages, where clothes are presented in a more glamorous way than the 'off the hanger' look required for their online store. The setting of those editorial shots is the stuff of artistry and fantasy, incorporating elements of glamour and far-away locations. The difference now is that users can click directly from this virtual world into the real-life experience of buying and

Market Insight 17.1
continued

owning the particular garment displayed. Bloggers have also taken on the mantle of providing readers with exquisite images, creating desire for the products and trends featured. Seeing an opportunity in the social aspect of fashion, there has been an increase in start-ups and apps (e.g. TheSartorialist.com and Lookbook.nu) encouraging users to share the looks and products they like with others. From here it was just a matter of time before those looks became monetized and linked to purchase opportunities.

Apps such as Pose already allow users to contribute looks they like to an app, which then links directly to purchase opportunities of the identified garments from relevant retailers. Another app, Kalei.do, provides users with a changing kaleidoscope of images from third-party sites—blogs as well as branded sites—allowing users to purchase the same or similar items from other brands with different price-points directly from within the app. If those examples and the popularity of Pinterest is anything to go by, the boundaries between editorial and purchase have become increasingly blurred.

1 **In the multichannel world, do you think fashion editors are still important? How might their role as trendsetters have changed?**

2 **How do apps like Pose and Kalei.do change the conventional fashion channel management model?**

3 **How does the merging of content and distribution, as presented above, impact on the consumer's buying behaviour?**

Sources: Anon. (2012a); Kansara (2012).

This market insight was kindly contributed by Dr Julia Wolny, University of Southampton.

ASOS sells dazzling cloths from magazine-style webpages
Source: This picture is the property of ASOS.com.

Marketing's Digital Evolution

Few people remain unaffected by the incredible growth of digital technologies. Developments include the world wide web (i.e. Web 1.0), the proliferation of mobile handsets and interactive digital TV in the 1990s, and the increasing popularity of text messaging (SMS), through to the introduction of 3G mobile phone technology and the rapid development and adoption of digital social media resources (e.g. Web 2.0). Each technological change has impacted on marketing practice. Recently, with the proliferation and acceptance of social media (e.g. Twitter and Facebook) and the shift to 4G mobile phone technology, other marketing opportunities have rapidly opened up.

In the first ten years of the web (i.e. Web 1.0), it was used as a static publishing and retailing channel. Nevertheless, it was revolutionary in form, content, and its ability to disseminate content compared with other electronic channels such as TV and radio. However, it was still used as a one-way asymmetrical channel, with a focus on the technology and the website as opposed to consumers' needs. de Chernatony and Christodoulides (2004) argued that brands were positioned through website factors such as the speed of site content download, the site's visual appearance and brand synergy, ease of site navigation, offline personal support and the offering of different rewards through online rather than offline channels.

In these early days, marketers replicated offline marketing and publishing efforts, often using brochure-ware sites lacking in dynamic content and interactivity, thereby following a traditional 'marketing push' approach (see Chapter 10).

The development of digital media and the rise of Web 2.0 (i.e. the social web) technology saw a further evolution in marketing away from a hierarchical one-sided mass communication model. Web 2.0 used more participatory technologies (e.g. social channels and online communities), rather than just information or transactional channels. These newer digital technologies facilitated the practice of user-generated, co-created, and user-shared content with a focus on the active (not passive) user/participant rather than the website or marketer (as per Web 1.0). The change was from a focus by marketers on website content to facilitating user participation, and therefore from a one-way model of passive communication of information 'pushed' through to target audiences, to a multichannel and multi-user approach in which web users were empowered to 'pull' down information and/or interact with the organization and content, as well as with each other (consumer-to-consumer). The best example of this was eBay, which empowered web users to sell just about anything to each other.

The next iteration, Web 3.0, is called the **semantic web**. Web 3.0 'is about the web itself understanding the meaning of all the content and participation … semantic web analysis is a term encompassing techniques to infer meaning in (including the sentiment of) contributions made to the social web (Web 2.0). The semantic web (Web 3.0) allows for that meaning to be built in to all published data' (Sheldrake, 2011: 154). For example, on the semantic web, it would be possible to compare the relationship between your online bank statement and your personal calendar to identify periods of high expenditure (Beaumont, 2008). The semantic web will make content more findable, e.g. by search engines, and linkable, e.g. by social media (Feigenbaum, 2012). Online search, social media, online advergaming, and mobile marketing all differ considerably from earlier forms of internet marketing, and semantic technologies will effect even greater change in each of these areas. Table 17.3 illustrates how the web has shifted from the provision of static information resources through to providing greater social interaction to a self-organizing, intelligent social web. The web becomes increasingly about consumer pull

Table 17.3 The digital evolution of marketing

Feature	Web 1.0 (the web)	Web 2.0 (the social web)	Web 3.0 (the semantic web)
Marketing focus	Website or branded content	User-generated content, community participation	User-generated content, community participation, greater measurement and prediction of target audience response (i.e. an artificially intelligent web)
Approach	Push	Push and pull	Push and pull
Market role	Audience	Participants	Participants
Audience behaviour	Passive	Passive and active	Passive, active, and facilitated by the web
Interactivity	Engagement with websites	Engagement with websites and other people online	Interactivity between websites and other people
Product offering	Production	Co-production	Co-creation
Communication model	Monologue (one-to-many)	Dialogue (one-to-one, many-to-many)	Predictive dialogue (one-to-many, many-to-many)
Control	Control over information transfer by marketer	Control of information transfer by marketer and consumer	Greater control of information transfer by marketer through intelligent software, but consumer retains ultimate control
Timeline (common use)	1991–2003	2004–2014	Beyond 2014
Market research focus	Navigability and usability studies	Social media analysis	Predictive sentiment and tonality analysis

(rather than organization push), enabling ever greater customer participation, co-creation of offerings (not just mass production), dialogue, and shared control over the form and content of a brand's messages, marketing activities, and offering. For example, the Dutch bank ING Direct was forced to take one of its TV adverts, which customers deemed was making light of mental health issues, off air in Canada after it faced a backlash on social media (Fisher, 2013).

The changing nature of the socio-technical environment means that many marketing executives must reconsider how brand management and marketing activities more generally need to change to suit the digital environment, recognizing that it operates differently from other channels (see Market Insight 17.2). There is also a corresponding increase in marketing spend on digital channels. Not all companies have been quick to take advantage, however. Procter &

Market Insight 17.2

hairybaby.com: Using Irish Wit and Humour to Sell T-Shirts Online

Social media has evolved over the last few years to become an important part of most companies' online marketing strategy. An increasing number of SMEs are embracing social media in order to raise awareness of their company and/or brands and to connect with the public. One such SME is hairybaby.com, an Irish company established in 2004 that has grown to become Ireland biggest online custom-designed T-shirt and hoodie provider. On the company's website www.hairybaby.com, they sell a variety of T-shirts and hoodies which celebrate Irishness, using a fun approach and Irish wit and humour. Most of the images, slogans, and characters on their T-shirts and hoodies are designed to remind people of their youth and tap into nostalgia.

hairybaby.com is a good example of a company that uses social media as a large part of its online marketing strategy. The company makes minimal use of traditional media. Instead, through the use of Facebook and Twitter, it engages with existing and new customers to create a buzz about the hairybaby.com brand. The company focuses a lot of its resources and creativity on Facebook, where it posts inventive and creative posts that encourage interaction and often asks its customers to collaborate on new T-shirt ideas. In addition, it also runs Facebook competitions for its fans and features images of Irish celebrities endorsing and wearing its merchandise. The company's use of Facebook has created positive word of mouth, and has led to increased traffic to their website and Twitter page.

hairybaby.com has found that the market for its products keeps growing as Irish consumers have developed a real affinity for the brand, purchasing the products for themselves or as a gift for someone else. It has also found that the recent exodus of Irish job seekers to foreign shores has been positive for its brand as hairybaby.com T-shirts have become

hairybaby.com uses Irishness and wit to sell its clothes online

Source: hairybaby.com.

Market Insight 17.2
continued

one of the big seasonal sellers for expats in places like New Zealand, Australia, the USA, and Canada. hairybaby.com provides a specific Irish identity overseas for a generation that has departed Irish shores.

1 Visit the company's website www.hairybaby.com. Comment on what you see as the personality of the brand. How does hairybaby.com merchandise appeal to consumers' hedonic/emotional needs?

2 Why is the use of social media such a good fit for the hairybaby.com brand? Why do you think the company has made little use of traditional media?

3 Visit hairybaby.com's Facebook page. Comment on the techniques being used by the company to engage with their consumers on Facebook.

Sources: Daly (2011); Leech (2011); Naughton (2012); www.hairybaby.com

This market insight was kindly contributed by Marie O'Dwyer, Waterford Institute of Technology, Ireland.

Research Insight 17.1

To take your learning further, you might wish to read this influential paper.

Kane, G. C., Fichman, R. G., Gallaugher, J., and Glaser, J. (2009) 'Community relations 2.0', *Harvard Business Review*, **87(11 November), 45–50.**

This paper draws on the study of more than two dozen firms, describing the changes brought about by social media and how managers should take advantage of these changes.

@ Visit the **Online Resource Centre** to read the abstract and access the full paper.

Gamble (P&G) has admitted that it needs to make 'fundamental shifts' from TV advertising to digital marketing. By 2010, P&G was still spending £136m out of £203m on TV advertising in the UK (Eleftheriou-Smith, 2012).

Visit the **Online Resource Centre** and follow the weblink eMarketer.com to learn more about the adoption, use, and evolution of electronic technology for marketing practice.

Digital Marketing Activities

Digital marketing encompasses a number of activities (see Figure 17.2). Today, there is considerable growth in search marketing, social media marketing, advergaming, and mobile marketing. In the twenty or so years that search engine technology has existed, it has become commonplace

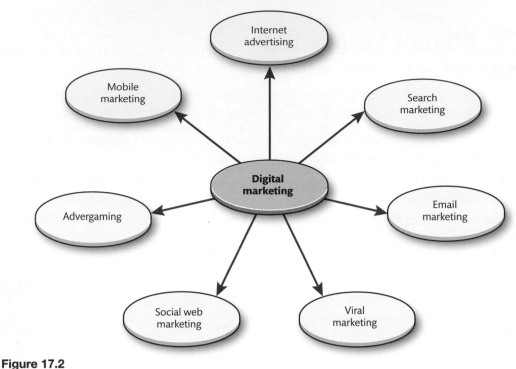

Figure 17.2
Digital marketing activities

in how we work online. McKinsey, the global consultancy company, estimates that search technology added 1.2% to US gross domestic product (GDP), and 0.9% to the German economy, 0.9% to the French economy, 0.5% to the Brazilian economy, and 0.5% to the Indian economy (Bughin *et al.,* 2011). There has also been considerable growth in mobile subscriber connections to 6.0 billion globally in 2012 and to an estimated 3.2 billion unique users (Anon., 2012b), making mobile technologies and associated wireless digital services a very attractive platform for marketing activities. Therefore the internet is becoming increasingly important in how we live our lives. In Canada, Japan, India, and China, the internet holds greater influence than family and friends over how consumers make decisions (Vogt and Alldredge, 2012).

Internet Advertising

Internet advertising is an important source of online consumer information, especially as the number of internet users continues to increase. It is a form of marketing communication that uses internet-based resources for the purpose of advertising, delivering messages to drive traffic to a website (**click-through rate**), and also to encourage trial, purchase, or repeat-purchase activity (**conversion rate**) (Cheng *et al.,* 2009). Specific online advertising formats include display advertising (e.g. banner ads), rich media ads (e.g. embedded multimedia ads, pop-up ads, **interstitials**), online video-streamed ads, search engine marketing, email advertising, classified listings, and sponsored advertising on social media networks (e.g. Twitter).

In 2011, online advertising spend was around £4.78bn in the UK (IAB, 2013), exceeding TV advertising spend at £4.36bn (Thinkbox, 2012). Growth was evident in search engine marketing (up 18% to £2.77bn), and particularly strong for dedicated tablet advertising (up 2,288% on 2010, generating £2.45m) and affiliate search listings (up 3012% to £38.73m). Display advertising on emails declined (down 71% on 2010 to £7.86m), as did interruptive formats (e.g.

pop-ups, which declined by 14.4% in 2010 to £20.89m) (IAB, 2013). Given these changes in spending, marketers need to plan their media spend carefully to ensure its effectiveness.

Major considerations when using internet advertising to increase brand awareness and encourage click-through to a target site include the following.

- Cost—internet adverts are still relatively cheap compared with traditional advertising.
- Timeliness—internet adverts can be updated at any time with minimal cost.
- Format—internet adverts are richer, using text, audio, graphics, and animation. In addition, games, entertainment, and promotions can be incorporated.
- Personalization—internet adverts can be interactive and targeted to specific interest groups and/or individuals.
- Location-based—using wireless technology and geo-location technology (GPS), internet advertising can be targeted to consumers wherever they are (e.g. near a restaurant or theatre).
- Intrusive—some internet advertising formats (e.g. pop-ups) are seen as intrusive and suffer more consumer complaints than other formats.

Visit the **Online Resource Centre** and follow the weblink to the Interactive Advertising Bureau (IAB) to learn more about developments and standards for internet advertising activities.

Search Marketing

The growth in digital content available through the web has given rise to a number of interactive decision aids used to help web users locate data, information, and/or an organization's digital objects (e.g. pictures, videos). The main two types of decision aids are a search directory (web directory) and/or a search engine.

A **search directory** is a human-edited database of information. It lists websites by category and subcategory, with categorization usually based on the whole website rather than one page or a set of keywords. Search directories often allow site-owners to submit their site directly for inclusion, and editors review submissions for fitness. The first directory of websites (webservers) was categorized by Tim Berners-Lee in 1992, during the early development of the web. Today, popular examples include the Yahoo! Directory and the Netscape-owned Open Directory Project (ODP). ODP has categorized over 5.3 million sites, in 590,000 categories, and has been constructed and maintained by a community of 70,000 editors (Anon., 2012c).

In contrast, a **search engine** operates algorithmically or uses a mixture of algorithmic and human input to collect, index, store, and retrieve information on the web (e.g. webpages, images, information, and other types of files), making this information available to users in a manageable and meaningful way in response to a search query. Information is retrieved by a webcrawler (also known as a spider), which is an automated web-browser that follows every link on the site, analysing how it should be indexed, using words extracted from page and file titles, headings, or special fields called meta-tags. These indexed data are then stored in an index database for use in later queries. When a user enters a query into a search engine (typically using keywords), the engine examines its index and provides a listing of best-matching webpages according to its criteria on search engine result pages (SERPs). There are only a few dominant search engines in the market, with Google leading the global market share rankings with 84%, followed by Yahoo! Search at 8%.

Search Marketing Methods

Search engine marketing (SEM) is one of the main forms of internet advertising, with a UK spend of £2.77bn in 2011 accounting for about 58% of total UK online ad spend (IAB, 2013). Its aim is to promote websites by increasing their visibility in SERPs. SEM methods include search engine optimization (SEO), paid placement, contextual advertising, digital asset optimization, and paid inclusion (SEMPO, 2010).

- Search engine optimization occurs when a website's structure and content is improved to maximize its listing in organic search engine results pages using relevant keywords or search phrases. Marketing agencies spend about 20% of their client's budgets on SEO (Econsultancy, 2012). According to Forrester Research, total expenditure in Western Europe will reach €2bn by 2016 (O'Reilly, 2012). Increasingly, there is recognition that SEO and social media are interlinked. Dunphy (2012) argues that 'every share, like, re-tweet, +1, subscription, and pin means one more endorsement for your website, simultaneously increasing your social capital and your search creditability. By gaining a massive amount of social shares, you're not just boosting your SEO signals and your site visibility—you're also creating content with value for your customer base'.

- **Paid placement** or **pay per click (PPC)** is an advertising model used when advertisers pay their host only when their sponsored ad or link is clicked. Advertisers bid on keywords or phrases relevant to their target market, with sponsored/paid search engine listings to drive traffic to a website. The search engine ranks ads based on a competitive auction and other related criteria (e.g. popularity, quality). Google AdWords, Yahoo! Search Marketing, and Microsoft adCenter are the three largest ad-network operators with all three operating under a bid-based model.

- **Contextual advertising** is a form of targeted advertising, with advertisements (e.g. banners, pop-ups) appearing on websites, with the advertisements themselves selected and served by automated systems based on the content displayed to the user. A contextual advertising system scans the text of a website for keywords and returns advertisements to the webpage based on what the user is viewing. Google AdSense was the first major contextual advertising programme.

- **Digital asset optimization (DAO)** or SEO 2.0 is the optimization of all an organization's digital assets (e.g. .doc, .pdf, video, podcasts, music files, images, and other digital media) for search, retrieval, and indexing.

- **Paid inclusion** occurs when a search engine company charges fees related to inclusion of websites in their search index. Some organizations mix paid inclusion with organic listings (e.g. Yahoo!), whereas others do not allow paid inclusion to be listed with organic lists (e.g. Google and Ask.com).

All these search marketing methods allow marketers to match users with content according to their interests. Search engines and directories take a different approach, but one thing unites them—search marketing is one of the most cost-effective methods of digital marketing. However, SEM is declining slightly in importance as digital marketers look increasingly to shift budget into mobile and social channels (O'Reilly, 2012). See Market Insight 17.3 for a review of the UK flight sector's search marketing activities and easyJet's search performance in 2009.

Market Insight 17.3

easyJet Pays to Take Off!

An analysis of key search terms used by UK consumers when searching online for flights was conducted for the third quarter of the year in 2009. This independent research, conducted by Greenlight, identified 3,200 of the most commonly used search terms by UK webusers, which cumulatively deliver 28.1 million searches for flight-related terms. The term 'Flight' accounted for 59% of all flight-related searches. Short-haul destinations, largely within Europe, accounted for almost 5.3 million searches in December 2009, with queries for flights to Palma and Rome cumulatively accounting for 16% of these. The analysis also reported the most visible websites using these keywords, which topped the lists for organic and paid search listings.

■ Organic listings—in natural search, with 89% visibility, SkyScanner.net ranked at position one on page one of Google for 445 of the 3,200 keywords analysed. TravelSupermarket.com followed with 72% visibility, followed closely by expedia.co.uk (57%), easyJet.com (52%), and lastminute.com (48%).

■ Paid placement—in paid search it was a very different picture, with easyJet attaining a 65% share of voice. This was achieved through bidding on 29 of the 30 keywords analysed. BMI Baby followed with 51%, then British Airways (43%), Aer Lingus (43%), and TravelSupermarket (36%).

Sources: Greenlight (2009); Cowen (2009); www.easyjet.com

1 **What is the difference between natural and paid placement in search engine marketing?**

2 **What factors do you think influence how a website is ranked in a search engine's natural (organic) search listings?**

3 **Why do you think easyJet.com was ranked higher in paid placement than in organic listings?**

easyJet, clearly visible in the skies and on the internet
Source: © easyJet plc.

Email Marketing

Permission-based email marketing is a highly cost-effective form of digital marketing (Waring and Martinez, 2002; Cheng *et al.,* 2009). It is a method of marketing by email, which the recipient of the message consents to receive. As a marketing tool, it is easy to use and costs little to send, but does incur greater costs when personalizing messages (e.g. labour) and where a database must be developed or purchased. Nevertheless, it can reach millions of willing prospects in minutes. According to a US Direct Marketing Association (DMA) report (Magill, 2011), email marketing is expected to generate a return on investment of US$39.40 for every US$1 spent in 2012, dropping to $35.02 by 2016, although this is still considerably higher than the return forecast to be earned by other marketing channels, for example, social media and mobile marketing. Email marketing includes 'opt-in' and 'opt-out' mailing lists, email newsletters, and discussion list subscriptions. Email, when used properly, goes beyond simply sending a sales message. It helps build a brand's relationship with consumers. For example, 69% of UK consumers reported that they preferred to receive brand communications this way (Experian, 2012). It helps create trust, retain customers, build customer referrals, and generate revenues.

Importantly with email marketing, the communicator only sends the message to those who have agreed to receive messages. This is the opposite to **spam**, unsolicited email, which clogs email servers and uses up much-needed internet bandwidth. McAfee (2012) reported that worldwide monthly spam, whilst in decline, reached nearly 1.2 trillion messages in the second quarter of 2012 compared with just over 0.4 trillion legitimate email messages, at an estimated total end-user cost of around $14bn per year worldwide (Rao and Reiley 2012). For the marketer, the difficulty is in sending messages which stand out from this clutter (Table 17.4 provides a list of important considerations when designing successful permission-based email marketing campaigns).

Viral Marketing

Viral marketing occurs when people communicate, often provocative, content to their peers. Typically, the content originates from an identified sponsor. One of the best examples of viral marketing occurred when the team behind the Hollywood movie *The Blair Witch Project* promoted the film using viral marketing techniques, turning a low-budget horror film into a worldwide box office hit in 1999 (Chang and Heath, 2001). To encourage 'buzz', as viral marketing is often referred to (or more properly electronic word of mouth (eWOM)), the filmmakers pretended that the *Blair Witch* story was real and that the film was actually not a film at all but a documentary which charted the demise of the film-makers. Only after the film hit the cinemas was the truth revealed.

Contemporary viral marketing campaigns, like Scottish soft drink maker AG Barr's 'baby' advert in 2012, are often controversial. In the 'baby' advert, a mother in her hospital bed explains to her husband that she wants to call their child the name Fanny (an old-fashioned female name, but one which now has another sexual meaning in Britain). Initially, the new father is against the idea but after taking a slurp of Irn-Bru he changes his mind. The tagline is 'Irn-Bru gets you through'. What was particularly interesting about this TV ad, though, was that it had notched up a million hits on YouTube after a single tweet from a well-connected fan. Social media analysis indicated that after one person's initial tweet, the ad was viewed 100,000 times within 24 hours. After the television broadcast of the ad, the YouTube ad recorded a further 300,000 views in 48 hours (Kiss, 2012). The problem for marketers though is this: who do we target with viral messages in the first place?

Table 17.4 Fundamentals of email marketing

Make the campaign targeted—80/20 rule	Think carefully about the target audience; exclude those not relevant and design the campaign to communicate key benefits
	Pay attention to the 20% who are most engaged with your brand and responsive to email offers
Gain and confirm permissions	Provide a mechanism for list members to opt in or opt out of the relationship
	Confirm this opt-in when a consumer joins
	Allow members to choose different email offerings such as newsletter, discount offers, and offering-specific updates
	Include options in the unsubscribe process to retain members
Personalize	First-name personalization has become standard. Studies show that personalization can increase response rates by 64%
Message and copy	Email is often read in the preview screen on laptops/desktops so ensure that the key message is contained within this frame. Increasingly, email is now opened on a Smartphone, so consider offering mobile-friendly formats.
	Keep your message simple—short copy works better
	Design to draw the reader to the call-to-action increases response rates
	Thank the purchaser and use consumer preferences to guide copy and offers
Subject line	Message more likely to be opened if the subject conveys the email's value/benefits
	Limit subject line to 35 characters
	Test subject lines to determine effectiveness
	Subject lines deserve special attention where the aim is to get consumers to pass along emails, as they tend to be kept throughout an email chain
Source address: 'From'	Ensure: the from address is consistent with who the recipient opted in to; you comply with privacy regulations and the recipient can recognize this; the brand name (B2C) or salesperson's (B2B) name appears in the 'from' field
Test, test, and retest	Where possible, test subject line, call-to-action, time-of-day, frequency, incentive, etc. on a statistically valid sample
Track, report, and mine results	Use an email system that allows tracking and reporting on all elements of the campaign, including opens, clicks, pass-along, unsubscribe, and bounce-backs
	Mine customer data for insights and analyse message frequency coupled with response rates
Collect and follow-up responses	Ensure responses come through to you and dictate how often they are received
	Follow-up responses are more likely to warrant higher value or interested prospect
Spam blocking	Check if the system allows a domain delegation to lower risk of being blocked by spam filters

Sources: IMT (1999); Phelps *et al.* (2004); Glass (2006); Westlund (2009).

Phelps *et al.* (2004) categorize people receiving viral messages into four types: 1) those who receive a lot of viral messages and pass them on (viral mavens), 2) those who receive few messages but pass them on (high-opportunity infrequent senders); 3) those who receive many but send few on; 4) those who receive few and send few on (both of which they call infrequent senders). When setting up a viral campaign, it is important to target the people most likely to relay your messages (i.e. the viral mavens). The problem is that there is no clear demographic data identifying these people.

Another key question arises for the marketer: how do you design viral campaigns so that they are more likely to be transmitted and advocated to other people? A series of studies provides some help in understanding this question. Phelps *et al.* (2004) suggest that the content of the marketing material most likely to be passed on evoked strong emotions (humour, fear, sadness, or inspiration). Other studies have confirmed that strong emotion ensures messages are passed along (Dobele *et al.,* 2005, 2007; Eckler and Bolls, 2011) but that positive message content is more likely to be transmitted than negative messaging (Eckler and Bolls, 2011). Rules of thumb to improve the transmissibility of viral messages include ensuring that (Dobele *et al.,* 2005):

- the imagination of the audience is captured by making the message fun or intriguing;
- the message is attached to an offering that is easy to use (e.g. collapsible scooters) or highly visible (e.g. Gucci baguette bags);
- messages are well-targeted;
- messages have a credible source;
- a variety of company communication technologies are used (e.g. SMS, websites, social media).

Whilst the use of emotion in viral campaigns is important, we need to understand what type of emotion should be used in what context (see Market Insight 17.4 for an example of a viral campaign playing on emotion). Joy, for example, should be used for irreverent or fun brands, or those targeting young consumers. Sadness and fear appeals (when accompanied with a suggested solution) are best used by social marketers. Anger is best used by single-issue campaign groups. Disgust appeals are most effective when aimed at young men for rebel-style brands (Dobele *et al.,* 2007). Interestingly, whilst some studies indicate that women are more likely to pass on viral messages (Phelps *et al.,* 2004), others have suggested that men are more likely to pass them on (Dobele *et al.,* 2007). There is no definitive research suggesting how effective viral videos are when targeted at men and women, people of different age groups, and from different cultures (Eckler and Bolls, 2011). However, recent research suggests that contagious messages are more effective than those targeting 'influentials', i.e. people likely to pass on messages widely (Berger and Milkman, 2012).

We also know that people have different motivations for forwarding viral messages, depending on the context. Ho and Dempsey (2010) suggest that these motivations are fourfold as follows: 1) the need to be part of a group, 2) the need to be individualistic, 3) the need to be altriuistic, and 4) the need for personal growth. In truth, though, we do not fully understand what makes one viral video work when another flops (see Market Insight 17.4).

Social Media Marketing

According to a report by Nielsen/NM Incite (2012), individuals worldwide are spending increasing amounts of time visiting social media sites, particularly via their mobile phones and through applications. People were particularly likely to report purchasing via social media websites/online

Market Insight 17.4

Kony 2012: Viral Phenomenon

Kony 2012 was a campaign launched by Invisible Children, a US pressure group campaigning to bring about the arrest of indicted war criminal Joseph Kony, the leader of the Lord's Resistance Army (LRA) in Africa in 2004. The group's stated aims are 1) to make Kony famous in order to create global awareness of LRA atrocities, 2) to increase protection of civilians from LRA attacks, 3) to pressure international governments to support regional efforts to stop the LRA, and 4) to see Joseph Kony and his commanders captured by regional forces and tried by the International Criminal Court. In 2012, Invisible Children released a documentary film on YouTube. The film depicted the dreadful plight of Africa's children forcefully recruited into Kony's LRA, which operated in Uganda until 2006 and thereafter in the border regions of the Central African Republic, South Sudan, and the Democratic Republic of Congo. Importantly for viral design, the documentary dealt exclusively in the currency of emotion, incorporating an interview with an ex-child soldier sobbing when describing his brother's killing. The clip secured nearly 92,000,000 views in the first four months after its release. Therefore this viral campaign illustrates how social media can be used for grassroots lobbying and political campaigning. The campaign was controversial. The Prime Minister of Uganda, Amama Mbabazi, protested that the viral documentary suggested that Uganda is at war and unconcerned with capturing Kony, a charge Mbabazi denies vehemently. What is strange, though, is that the clip went viral at all, because it was too long, about someone few people previously knew, from a charity few had ever heard of, and contained a very negative tone. It was an experiment, but one which worked surprisingly well.

Sources: Mbabazi (2012); Warman (2012); Baines and O'Shaughnessy (2013); http://invisiblechildren.com/kony/

The Kony 2012 YouTube clip racked up nearly 92,000,000 views in the first four months after its release, making it a viral superstar
Source: Courtesy of Invisible Children.

1 Why do you think the Kony 2012 campaign was so successful?

2 How and why were people motivated to access the video on YouTube?

3 What other viral campaigns have you seen? Were they successful and, if so, why (not)?

product reviews in the entertainment, home electronics, travel and leisure, food/beverages, and fashion sectors, especially if they came from the Asia-Pacific, Latin American, or Middle Eastern regions. According to the 2012 Chief Marketing Officer (CMO) survey, 7.4% of marketing budgets are spent on social media marketing, with that figure predicted to grow to 10.8% within 12 months and 19.5% within five years (Moorman, 2012). Further research has identified the movement of marketing spend away from traditional areas. FMCG giants Coca-Cola and Unilever announced a move away from campaign-led microsites to investments in community channels like Facebook and YouTube (Cooper, 2010), joining Dell, Starbucks, P&G, Ford, and American Express in using the social web to converse, connect, and learn from the communities within which their organizations coexist.

Therefore **social media marketing** (SMM) is a form of digital marketing that describes the use of the social web and social media (e.g. social networks, online communities, blogs, wikis) or any online collaborative technology for marketing activities (e.g. sales, public relations, research, distribution, customer service). Marketers are increasingly investing in social networks (e.g. Facebook, LinkedIn, QQ in China), video-sharing sites (e.g. YouTube), image-sharing sites (Flickr, Pinterest), blogging platforms (WordPress), and microblogs (Twitter) to increase the **social capital** of their brands.

Growing a Brand's Social Capital

Whereas human capital is embodied in the skills and knowledge acquired by an individual, social capital is embodied in the relations among individuals (Coleman, 1988), i.e. within the social structures and networks within which we live and work. Exploratory research attests to strong connections between social network usage on Facebook and an individual's social capital (Ellison *et al.,* 2007). An analysis of the global top ten socially engaged media brands in 2012, based on one week in September, highlighted the following brands: Samsung, Amazon, Red Bull, Nokia, Nike, Coca-Cola, McDonald's, MTV, Disney, and Walmart (Li, 2012). Ellison *et al.* (2007) found a positive correlation between use of the social web and a firm's financial performance.

The development of social media marketing is impacting on where managers spend their budgets. It is also challenging the way we communicate, share information, interact, and create (or produce) an offering. When anybody on the internet can create, comment on, or share information about what companies, brands, organizations, or people do, what they represent, and how they work (see Market Insight 4.1 on Starbucks in Chapter 4), we no longer have the power or control we thought we had over how we are perceived in the marketplace. Changing media habits and growth in digital and social media mean that CMOs can see that one day many traditional marketing and communication models/principles will no longer work (Court *et al.,* 2005). The advent of social media has turned marketing practice upside down. Many previously held beliefs no longer hold. Examples include the following ideas: brand managers own and orchestrate brands, the web is for finding information, companies use marketing communications to control their messages, consumers purchase offerings promoted by marketers, and, finally, providing a forum for customers to talk is dangerous and risky (Hanna *et al.,* 2011). Social media marketing leaders have dedicated in-house teams (e.g. Virgin Media). Next, we discuss four key areas where social media marketing differs from other digital marketing activities.

Sharing Control

Sharing **control** refers to the ability of users in a computer-mediated environment to access content at will, create and modify content to pertain to their needs, and share this content with consumers, companies, or third parties. Habitat UK, the British furniture retailer, offended people when it used trending, but inappropriate, **hashtags** to get noticed by a wider audience to announce a 20% discount on its Spring 2009 collection (Chamberlin, 2011). It included #iranianelection and #mousavi hashtags in its tweets in the middle of the Iranian election riots!

Surprisingly, despite being denounced on Twitter for spamming and taking advantage of Iran's political situation, the company took months to apologize (BBC, 2009).

This exemplifies how social digital technologies have changed who controls (or thinks they control) organization-branded communications and the changing mindset regarding the role and purpose of marketing (Christodoulides, 2009). The brand manager, who used to be the 'custodian' of the brand, is now the 'host', whose main role is not to control, but to facilitate sharing, participation, connectivity, and the co-creation of an offering, regardless of whether that is good or bad (Mitchell, 2001). There has been a shift from being in control of conversations to shaping conversations by providing the following (see Mangold and Faulds, 2009).

- Networking platforms (e.g. Facebook, Flickr, Foursquare).

- Blogs and social media tools to engage customer—because customers like to give feedback on a broad range of issues.

- Both internet and traditional promotional tools to engage customers.

- Information on, for example, correct product usage.

- Exclusivity—because people like to feel special.

- Offerings that are designed from the perspective of consumers' desired self-images and with talking points to make advocacy easier; for example, JetBlue the US budget airline makes leather seats and televisions available to its customers.

- Support for causes that people value; for example, the Italian fashion retailer Benetton used a disabled German model, Mario Galla, and a transsexual from Brazil, Lea T, in its Spring/Summer 2013 advertising (Chapman, 2013).

- Memorable stories—the UK food and beverage company innocent outlines the story of the foundation of the firm on its website. The story has it that three friends set up a stall to sell smoothies at a London music festival. A sign above the stall reads 'Should we give up our jobs to make these smoothies?' and people are asked to throw their empties into one of two bins marked either 'Yes' or 'No', where 'Yes' wins. Needless to say, 'Yes' won.

User-generated and Co-created Content

The social web enables users to generate, share, and comment on content (van den Bulte and Wuyts, 2007). The OECD definition of **user-generated content (UGC)** is a) content made available over the internet, b) which reflects creative effort, and c) is created outside professional routine and practices (Wunsch-Vincent and Vickery, 2007). Therefore content is created by general users, not producers (e.g. videos contributed to YouTube). When UGC is created with a marketing benefit, it is also called vigilante marketing, defined as 'unpaid advertising and marketing efforts, including one-to-one, one-to-many, and many-to-many commercially orientated communications, undertaken by brand loyalists on behalf of the brand' (Muniz and Jensen Schau, 2007: 35). Using desktop software, consumers can create promotional content to rival professionally-produced content. Examples of UGC have been created by fans for Apple iPod, Coca-Cola, Nike, and Volkswagen, among other brands. In contrast, **co-created content** is content or applications created through social interaction. Contributions to Wikipedia are typical examples of co-creation.

UGC and co-creation are important concepts because marketers can derive an understanding of consumer perceptions of the brand and brand attributes from the content resulting from these processes. They provide vivid examples of compelling messages from the perspective of brand loyalists. As social web channels increase in frequency and prominence, so will UGC and co-creation (Muniz and Jensen Schau, 2007).

Community and Social Networks

Social media enables individuals and organizations to connect to each other within the social milieu in which we live, work, and study (Simmons, 2008). For marketers, the challenge lies in deciding how to engage in these social communities, and how to inspire communities to form around particular brand values? How can organizations participate in the dialogue and add value? What marketers should not be doing is trying to control brand communities, because 'brand communities' are actually 'best viewed not as brand communities, but as passionate communities supported by brands that share and reinforce that community's values' (Bubula, 2012).

Social networking sites have seen massive growth since their inception. There were an estimated 190 million unique Twitter users and 837 million Facebook users worldwide by the end of 2012 (Dembosky and Bradshaw, 2013). In Britain in 2011, 60% of British internet users were using online social networking sites, up from 17% in 2007, and this figure rose to 90% among those under 25 years old (WIP, 2012). China presents a different social networking graph. Unlike the USA, Europe, and Australasia, Facebook does not rank in the top social networks in the country, and most access to services is undertaken via mobile phones rather than laptop/desktop computers. QQ/QZone (owned by Tencent) has more than 700 million active users monthly for social gaming, Sina Weibo (a microblogging service) has around 400 million users, Tencent Weibo (also for microblogging) has 200–250 million users, WeiXin (a voicemail-based social networking service) has around 100 million users, as has Douban (used for networking around special interest groups and topics) and RenRen (a Chinese version of Facebook which facilitates online networking) (Fong, 2012).

Social networking requires a cultural shift for marketers and has differing levels of engagement. New communities coalesce and disperse quickly, and are often led by different people at different times for differing reasons. Table 17.5 provides a list of the major reasons why individuals and small and medium-sized business use social networks.

Conversations and Dialogue

Social media marketing is not about mass marketing, but about facilitating real conversations around the organization, the brand, or an individual. Commerce is reliant on human conversation and the interaction between people; however, traditionally, business has been divorced from real conversations. Instead, marketing has focused heavily on a traditional one-way monologue or sales pitch. To engage in these digital conversations requires trust and transparency, and involves authentic engagement in a real two-way dialogue. However, the social web does not make these conversations happen; it just supports them. By understanding how the social web supports the conversation, businesses can open up interactions with individuals and communities. For example, Twitter and Facebook are regularly used by companies to respond to customer care queries and concerns. But the important point is real conversation, i.e. authenticity. When Ernst & Young hired an agency to manage its university/college-recruiting presence on Facebook, the results were poor. Only when the organization enlisted a group of interns who were active Facebookers to contribute did the conversation become more authentic and draw more traffic, contributing to the company's rapid rise in *Business Week* magazine's ranking of top firms that college students want to work for (Kane *et al.*, 2009).

Visit the **Online Resource Centre** and complete Internet Activity 17.1 to learn more about how Ernst & Young use Twitter to maintain an ongoing real dialogue with their followers.

Table 17.5 Reasons for social networking site use

Consumer		SME use	
Reason	%	Reason	%
Send private or direct messages to individuals	80	Attract new customers	91
Respond to a post or update	77	Cultivate relationships	86
Share personal thoughts/updates	74	Increase awareness	18
Share personal photos	72	Communicate the brand online	73
Read updates posted by my networks	68	Receive feedback	46
Meet/connect with new people	52	Interact with suppliers	14
Share general news or articles I have read	51		
Join groups of personal or professional interest	48		
Play games	41		
Find deals or discounts	31		
Find a new job/browse for work opportunities	24		
Share purchases I have made	23		

Sources: Michaelidou *et al.* (2011) Base: 100 UK SMEs; Mintel (2012) Base: 1,525 social network users aged 16+.

Measuring Social Media Effectiveness

As social media, e.g. blogs, wikis, games, and social networking sites, are increasingly used as part of the marketing manager's planning (for communications and for research), there is an increasing need to understand whether what marketers are doing in social media is working or not. Web activity is amazingly measurable, because web users leave traces of their presence and activity on the various sites they visit. However, the process of measuring social media effectiveness requires a detailed seven-fold process (CIM, 2013).

1. Start by looking at measurement metrics (Table 17.7 provides a detailed list of the social media activities that can be measured).

2. Review your social media campaign objectives. for example, was your motivation to i) build traffic on your website, ii) improve brand perceptions, iii) deepen relationships with

customers, iv) learn from the community, v) drive purchase intent, vi) foster dialogue, vii) promote advocacy, viii) facilitate support, or ix) spur innovation (see Murdough, 2009; Owyang and Lovett, 2010).

3. Map your campaign—in this phase the brand owner identifies how the brand is consumed on the web by showing a) brand generated content, b) consumer-generated content, c) consumer-fortified content (e.g. by showing online locations where consumers can go to distribute content relating to the brand), and d) exposure to content consumers (e.g. favourable product reviews on websites).

4. Choose the criteria and tools of measurement by a) determining the criteria for assessing effectiveness and b) selecting the most appropriate software measurement tools (e.g. Radian6).

5. Establish a benchmark (e.g. by measuring where your company is in relation to some of the metrics in Table 17.6).

6. Undertake the campaign, and then analyse the outcomes and propose changes by comparing the outcomes against your proposal benchmarks to assess the variance between the two. This makes it possible to ascertain what changes are necessary to meet the benchmark targets.

7. Continue to measure on a daily, weekly, monthly, and quarterly basis.

Table 17.6 List of social media marketing metrics

1. Number of Twitter followers	2. Number of click-throughs (inbound via Facebook)	3. Net positive mentions across channels	4. Net product reviews (total volume, positive, negative)
5. Volume of outbound updates per day	6. Other activity on Facebook (discussions, events, downloads, event RSVPs, etc.)	7. Net negative mentions across channels	8. Net recommendations across all channels (and per channel)
9. Volume of inbound tweets per day	10. Number of daily visitors to the blog	11. Customer support or service requests on Twitter per day/hour	12. Response to promotional offers (track codes, hash tags, etc.)
13. Number of outbound re: (replies) generated per day	14. Number of unique visitors to the blog per post/article	15. Average number of re: (reply) updates to complete a customer service request	16. Event attendance (physical and virtual)
17. Number of retweets generated per day	18. Number of comments per day	19. Average amount of time to close out a customer service request	20. Net number of transactions
21. Number of click-throughs (inbound via Twitter)	22. Number of comments per post	23. Net number of positive outcomes to customer service requests (resolution)	24. Net sales volume (total, by product, by category, etc.)

Table 17.6 continued

25. Number of Facebook fans	26. Number of daily inbound visits to website from blog	27. Net number of negative outcomes to customer service requests (no resolution)	28. Net number of transacting customers
29. Volume of updates per day	30. Number of inbound links visits to website from blog per unique post	31. Net potential reach	32. Average buyrate/ frequency of transaction in a selected group/ subset
33. Number of 'likes' per day	34. Number of views and downloads (video)	35. Net frequency of interactions/touches per customer in a selected group/ subset	36. Average yield/ amount per transaction in a selected group/ subset
37. Number of 'likes' per update	38. Number of downloads (audio/ podcast)	39. Net unique visitors to website	40. Conversions
41. Number of comments per day	42. Number of downloads (pdf, other written content)	43. Net number of unique visitors inbound from seeded links across SM channels (and per channel)	44. Share of voice (e.g. via Radian6)
45. Number of comments per update	46. Volume of mentions (brand or associated keyword) across channels	47. Net online transactions (e-sites)	48. Influence (e.g. via Klout, Peerindex, Kred)

Sources: Adapted from Blanchard (2011) and Vocell (2012).

 Research Insight 17.2

To take your learning further, you might wish to read this influential paper.

Hoffman, D. L. and Fodor, M. (2010), 'Can you measure the ROI of your social media?', *MIT Sloan Management Review*, 52(1), 41–49.

This article suggests that, rather than considering the organization's investment in social media, what should be considered are the customers' investments, i.e. their motivations to use and continue using an organization's social media resources. Return on investment (ROI) from this perspective, the authors argue, stresses long-term more fruitful customer relationships.

@ **Visit the Online Resource Centre to read the abstract and access the full paper.**

Advergaming

Advergaming or in-game advertising (IGA) is another form of digital marketing, often coupled with sales promotions that provide rewards in terms of incentives and novel and fun entertainment. Advergaming uses computer and video games to deliver advertising. Advergames consist of membership models of multiplayers (e.g. *World of Warcraft*), applications downloaded to a mobile device or added to an online social network, or online viral games where the game is passed from user to user. Most advergames require users to register, allowing the collection of data for marketing research and other marketing initiatives, and mix interactivity, gaming, and advertising.

The UK has more online and console gamers than anywhere else in Europe, with 68% of men and 59% of women playing games, compared with 63% and 54%, respectively, in Germany, and 61% and 52% in France (Anon., 2011).

With the rise in apps on social networking sites and smartphones, the development of hyper-reality virtual worlds (e.g. *Second Life*) and advergaming, obtaining perceived playfulness and enjoyment from digital resources has increased in importance. Perceived playfulness is the degree to which a current or potential user believes that the technology brings a sense of enjoyment and/or pleasure (Sledgianowski and Kulviwat, 2009). Individuals with a more positive playfulness belief in the specific technology view their interactions with technology more positively, and they are inclined to use the technology more often and transfer this feeling to associated brands (e.g. advertisers).

Two rising trends in digital gaming platforms are the increasing use of social networks and the penetration of smartphones. In 2007, Facebook opened up its platform allowing outside web developers to create free software programs that members of the social networking site could use to entertain and inform each other. Games such as *FarmVille* or *Angry Birds* were rapidly taken up. Facebook has more than 9 million applications (Darwell, 2012), allowing Facebook users to send each other virtual hugs, share movie picks, and play games. For example, Zynga's *Farmville*, King.com's *Bubble Witch Saga*, and Zyna's *City Ville* all have 10 million or more monthly active users (Socialbakers, 2013). Every month, 235 million Facebook users engage with platform applications (Lunden, 2012). By the end of 2012, the Google Play app store was offering almost as wide a range as Apple's store at 675,000 and 700,000 apps, respectively, and achieved 25 billion apps downloaded, a figure Apple had achieved in the first half of 2012 (Reisinger, 2012). On an average day in November 2012, Apple's app store was selling $15m per day of apps compared with $3.5m for Google Play. The largest markets for sales were the US, Japan, the UK, and Australia (Whitney, 2012).

What is interesting from a marketing perspective is that how people behave in online virtual worlds is not necessarily how they behave in real-life, opening up the intriguing idea of segmenting consumers based on the characteristics of their avatars rather than their own real-life characteristics (Hemp, 2006; Kaplan and Haenlein, 2009). Given the impressive statistics around game adoption, and the effectiveness of in-game advertising on brand recognition, recall, and revenue, in-game advertising is an important digital marketing activity.

Mobile Marketing

Increasingly, we can access digital technologies, share information, socialize online, and play games on the move. The number of mobile internet users has grown exponentially as the wireless infrastructure and mobile devices required to support the mobile internet have evolved. The global mobile market reached 6.0 billion by year-end 2011; and Asia and the Pacific remained the world's largest region, accounting for 48% (2.9 billion) of global mobile connections, mainly due to strong growth in India and China (Anon., 2012b). However, the developing world has far fewer mobile internet subscriptions, though this is likely to increase substantially between 2013 and 2018. Smartphone shipments are expected to increase substantially from 660 million in 2012 to 1.16 billion units by 2016 (Blagdon, 2012). Netbook and tablet computers, e-readers (e.g. Amazon's Kindle), media players (e.g. iTouch), and gaming devices (e.g. Wii) all provide internet access and a myriad of possibilities for the mobile marketer.

Mobile marketing is the set of practices that enables organizations to communicate and engage interactively with their audiences through any mobile device or network (MMA, 2009). With the added benefits of store-and-send technology giving the option of message storage, mobile marketing is quick, inexpensive, and reaches markets wherever they are, despite limitations in message content. Mobile marketing differs from traditional mass marketing across four elements (Shankar and Balasubramanian, 2009).

1. Scope of audience—mobile marketing audiences are restricted to owners of mobile devices who opt in to receive communications.

2. Type and format of messages—bandwidth capacity and tight screen size constraints restrict the format and type of message possible.

3. Location-based targeting—location- and time-based targeting of messages is facilitated through mobile devices;

4. Response tracking—marketers can better track and measure audience responses to mobile messages.

See Table 17.7 for the many differing types of mobile marketing.

Table 17.7 Types of mobile advertising methods	
Type	**Description**
Text message	Mobile version of direct marketing used for sweepstakes, voting in contests, instant wins, offering consumer statistics, and other data.
Games	Branded offerings can range from simple puzzles to custom multiplayer to multilevel advergames.
Mobile ads	Mobile versions of adverts, some of which offer discounts or coupons and hence new ways to connect with customers (e.g. Orange Wednesday discount two-for-one offer at cinemas).
Interactive voice response (IVR)	Opt-in consumers receive mobile phone calls from star endorsers, celebrity endorsers, or customer service personnel.
WAP sites and banner ads	Websites translated for wireless devices to access and download content and to display adverts.

Table 17.7 continued

Type	Description
Ringtones	Giveaways of brand-related tones and screensavers or wallpaper.
Viral	Promotions and UGC designed to spread from peer to peer about brands and branded messages on mobiles.
Geotargeting	Use of GPS and location-based tracking software to target consumers with offerings or store-based offers at the point of purchase (e.g. Foursquare, the location-based social networking website for mobile devices).
Sponsorships/ subsidizing call costs	Consumers offset the cost of a mobile service, programme, and content with advertising.
Applications (apps)	Branded software applications for mobile devices, consumers to pull added-value information, customer service, and/or entertainment when and where they want it.
QR codes	QR codes, which look a little like barcodes, contain details which, when read by a compatible app on mobile phones, allow users to read the code and trigger specific actions such as downloading a file or launching a website (Nicholls, 2011).
Near-field communications (NFC)	A set of standards for smartphones which allow phones to communicate with other digital devices when in close proximity to allow, for example, payment transactions (e.g. credit card contactless payments), data exchange, for identity documents, and a whole host of other uses including box office ticketing. Assa Abloy, the Swedish-based world leader in door-opening solutions, uses NFC to open doors (e.g. in hotels instead of magnetic cards or physical keys).

 ## Research Insight 17.3

To take your learning further, you might wish to read this influential paper.

Shankar, V. and Balasubramanian, S. (2009), 'Mobile marketing: a synthesis and prognosis', *Journal of Interactive Marketing*, **23, 118–29.**

This article presents the conceptual underpinnings of mobile marketing and a synopsis of relevant literature. The authors discuss four key issues: drivers of mobile device adoption, the influence of mobile marketing on customer decision-making, formulation of mobile marketing strategy, and mobile marketing in a global context.

Visit the **Online Resource Centre** to read the abstract and access the full paper.

Given that customers have the opportunity to access marketers' offerings on multiple devices, providing a range of support and content provision is of increasing importance (Shankar and Balasubramanian, 2009). Kodak, which went bankrupt in 2012 but is likely to re-emerge as a more streamlined business in late 2013 (Anon., 2013), began developing iPhone apps in 2008 to support its imaging services. The first was a connection to the Kodak online photosharing gallery which allows customers to upload pictures and share their online album direct from their iPhone. This was followed by the Kodak Pic Flick, an app that allows people with certain WiFi-enabled Kodak products (e.g. digital frame or printer) to simply 'flick' a photo from their iPhone direct to their frame or printer.

Social media marketing is also frequently undertaken via smartphones. This is creating both a challenge and an opportunity for marketers, in matching services and content to the market through the most suitable mobile devices. Market Insight 17.5 shows how McDonald's targeted consumers in Finland and China with location-based promotional offers direct to their mobile phones.

 # Market Insight 17.5

McDonald's: On Location!

In 2009, leading global advertiser McDonald's conducted a location-targeted campaign in Finland. Powered by NAVTEQ LocationPoint Advertising, a subsidiary of Nokia, McDonald's trialled the delivery of location-relevant mobile ads to users of Nokia Ovi Maps when they were within a certain distance of one of McDonald's 82 restaurants in Finland. NAVTEQ is the leading global provider of maps, traffic, and location data (digital location content), enabling navigation, location-based services, and mobile advertising around the world.

The ad campaign promoted a McDonald's cheeseburger for €1. Consumers who clicked on the ads saw the details of the promotion, and could receive driving or walking directions to the nearest store location. The campaign delivered a 7% click-through rate (CTR), and 39% of those who clicked through selected the click-to-navigate option, which offered 'drive to' or 'walk to' navigation to the nearest McDonald's location, using Nokia's Ovi Maps navigation.

In 2012, Finnish developer Rovio partnered with McDonalds China to launch a location-based promotional campaign using the *Angry Birds* game, which also features in-game McDonalds advertising. Gamers have the opportunity to unlock various game content, such as game modes, stages, and power-ups, depending on which restaurant they are visiting, and they can also vote for their favourite restaurant.

Mobile marketing and location-based services bring personalization to promotional campaigns, providing greater relevance and immediacy to the consumer as well as driving impulse sales that might not previously have occurred otherwise.

Sources: Murphy (2010); Buczkowski (2012); www.navteqmedia.com

1 What does mobile as a marketing channel give to advertisers?

2 What was the key content and service strategy of the McDonald's mobile campaign?

3 Why do you think this campaign is seen as a good example of effective location targeting?

Market Insight 17.5
continued

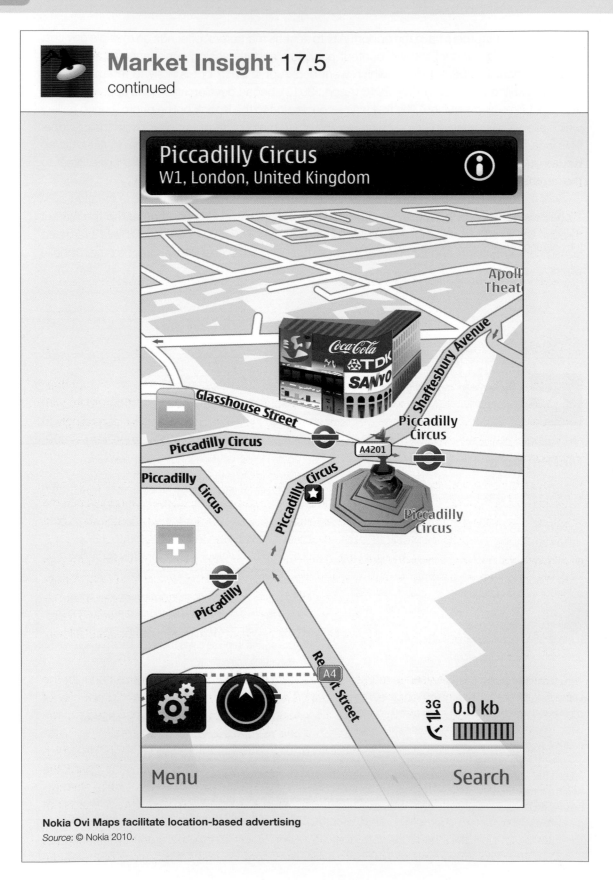

Nokia Ovi Maps facilitate location-based advertising
Source: © Nokia 2010.

Research Insight 17.4

To take your learning further, you might wish to read this influential paper.

Winer, R. (2009), 'New communications approaches in marketing: issues and research directions', *Journal of Interactive Marketing*, 23(2), May, 108–17.

This article addresses the wider current context within which developing digital channels are influencing how organizations engage and participate in a dialogue with customers and their marketing activities. It reviews the challenges that these present from the perspective of the marketing manager.

@ Visit the **Online Resource Centre** to read the abstract and access the full paper.

Crowdsourcing

Whilst the previous discussion was concerned with social media, technologies, and marketing, we now consider how marketers make use of social media to interact and co-create with communities through the technique of crowdsourcing. Crowdsourcing is used increasingly in marketing. The term **crowdsourcing** was first coined by Jeff Howe in *Wired* magazine in 2006. Various definitions exist for the term.

- 'Crowdsourcing, a term that combines "crowd" and "outsourcing", loosely means engaging a large group of people to come up with an idea or solve a problem. Some companies use the process to draw on the knowledge and opinions of a wide body of internet users to create better products and marketing plans, or solve other problems' (Vallone, 2011).

- 'Crowdsourcing represents the act of a company or institution taking a function once performed by employees and outsourcing it to an undefined (and generally large) network of people in the form of an open call. This can take the form of peer-production (when the job is performed collaboratively), but is also often undertaken by sole individuals. The crucial prerequisite is the use of the open call format and the large network of potential labourers' (Howe, 2006: 5).

Crowdsourcing can be used in marketing in different ways, with different requirements for the role of the crowd, the end-goal, how the crowd is remunerated, and the size and diversity of the crowd necessary for the task. However, it's probably most helpful to think of it used in three main categories: the crowdsourcing of 1) routine activities, 2) content, and 3) creative activities (see Table 17.8). One example of the crowdsourcing of routine activities was reCAPTCHA (which stands for Completely Automated Public Turing test to tell Computers and Humans Apart), the initiative to digitize books by supplying websites with CAPTCHA protection from **bots** attempting to access restricted sites. The CAPTCHA test requires users to retype images of words not recognized by optical character recognition (OCR) machines, and in so doing helps to digitize the internet archive and the archives of the *New York Times*. iStockphoto and openstreetmap are good examples of companies which crowdsourced content, respectively stock photography

Table 17.8 Forms of crowdsourcing (CS)

Consideration	CS of routine activities	CS of content	CS of creative activities
Role of the crowd	Provision of time, the ability to process information	Provision of content (especially information)	Provision of solutions, ideas, knowledge
Goal	Division of labour (integrative)	Division of labour (integrative)	Winner takes all (selective)
Remuneration	Micro-payments	Micro-payments or volunteer	Micro- to high payments
Size of the crowd	Very important	Very important	Of little importance
Diversity of the crowd	Not important	Very important	Very important
Commercial examples	reCAPTCHA	iStockPhoto, openstreetmap	InnoCentive, Wilogo

Source: Adapted and translated from Burger-Helmchen and Pénin (2011).

and location-based data for street mapping (see also Table 17.9 on iStockPhoto). Companies which have used crowdsourcing for creative activities include InnoCentive (see also Table 17.9) and Wilogo, which use crowdsourcing mechanisms for research and development projects and to produce logo designs, respectively.

Crowdsourcing is becoming increasingly ubiquitous in marketing as organizations seek to use it to reduce their marketing costs, reduce the time taken to undertake a particular task, find and use skills and labour that do not exist in-house, obtain information and market intelligence, design new products and services, and design promotional material. One of the key considerations when setting up a crowdsourcing task is how to motivate the crowd to take part. One common rule of thumb suggests that 90% of visitors to the site will consume the content (see the task), 9% will partially engage (read the task, consider taking part or request further information), and 1% will fully engage (e.g. provide a submission). See Table 17.9 for examples of early pioneers and recent users of crowdsourcing in marketing.

Legal and Ethical Considerations

With the rise in digital resources and their increasing use for marketing activities, come complications and changes to legislation and regulated business practices. The types of legal, ethical, and regulatory issues that marketers need to consider include the following.

- Jurisdiction—where does digital marketing activity take place? Commercial law is based on transactions within national boundaries, but digital marketing exposes both individual

Table 17.9 Pioneer and recent users of crowdsourcing

Organization	Date (first use)	Details
Pioneer users		
Threadless	2000	Began selling T-shirts with designs developed and rated by its user community, instead of expensive designers, in an ongoing competition process. Winning designers received $2,000 prize money and $500 voucher to spend at Threadless. Submitters of winning slogans received $500 prize money.
iStockPhoto	2000	Sells royalty-free stock images, media, and design elements using material sourced online from a crowd of largely amateur artists, designers, and photographers. Contributors receive a percentage of the purchase price when their images are downloaded. A smaller group of contributors screen new applicants and maintain the image database, earning a higher percentage from work downloaded.
InnoCentive	2001	Began life as a spin-off company from US pharmaceutical giant Eli Lilly. InnoCentive works by posting online R&D and scientific challenges for its crowd of users to solve. Winning contributors are paid a large financial incentive and InnoCentive takes a fee for hosting the challenge.
More recent users		
innocent	2011	Crowdsourced a TV advert by inviting fans to submit an ad and then asked other fans to evaluate the various submissions. The submitter of the winning ad received £5,000 (Lake 2011).
Ford	2012	Developed the first-ever spectator-filmed commercial using US racing drivers Tanner Foust and Greg Tracy by incorporating film from spectators during the race. Ford flew six active Ford Facebook fans to experience the shoot in Key West, Florida (Roat 2012).
LEGO®	2012	Developed its product innovation platform LEGO® CUUSOO, released initially as a beta version, to invite users to submit LEGO product ideas and get them rated by other users. Any idea which receives 10,000 votes is considered by the LEGO product review board for production. If a user's LEGO idea is chosen, the submitting user receives a 1% royalty on total net sales of that product. Initial ideas receiving more than 10,000 votes included the Exo Suit and the Back to the Future™ Time Machine (see Kronsberg 2012).

organizations and the community to information, transactions, and social activity outside these boundaries (e.g. EU legislation and Microsoft).

- Ownership—who owns the content we create and share? Copyright law is a national issue, and the copyright laws (what can and cannot be used without the originator's permission) differ from one country to another. Some countries do not have copyright or intellectual property protection, and so ideas, designs, etc. sent to those countries can be taken and used without the agreement of the copyright holder. The value of copyright is also being questioned with the increase in user-generated and co-created content, and the rise of the Creative Commons (CC) free licence system.

■ Permissions—do we have the right permissions to upload and share content? Privacy legislation is also national or regional, and the right of an individual or organization to use information is subject to this legislation. A new EU-wide **cookies** law, which came into place in 2012 requires companies to make it clear to users when they are saving a cookie onto someone's computer. Although some countries have no privacy legislation, the European Union Data

Protection Directive has resulted in Europe becoming one of the most highly regulated jurisdictions in the world when it comes to data protection requirements. However, that doesn't directly govern the activities of organizations founded in the USA (e.g. Microsoft, Facebook).

Visit the **Online Resource Centre** and complete Internet Activity 17.2 to learn more about privacy and the use of cookies for online observational research.

■ Security—how secure are the data and information we share? Information and transaction security and protection from fraud and identity theft is another area of increasing change. Legislation varies from country and region, with further differences evident in the laws that govern and protect consumer and business interests (e.g. distance selling regulations, consumer protection (e-commerce) regulations).

■ Accessibility—does everyone who wants access have access? Disability and discrimination legislation also require consideration. As more services and marketing information is being shared digitally, the right to access and usability for all becomes an important agenda item for the dissemination of information and services.

Chapter Summary

To consolidate your learning, the key points made throughout this chapter are summarized here.

■ **Define digital marketing and social media marketing.**

Digital marketing is the management and execution of marketing using digital technologies and channels (e.g. web, email, digital television, internet) to reach markets in a timely, relevant personal, interactive, and cost-efficient manner. It is related to, but distinct from, e-marketing, direct marketing and interactive marketing. Social media marketing is a form of digital marketing which uses social networking sites to produce content that users will share and which will in turn create exposure of the brand to customers and thereby increase or reinforce its customer base.

■ **Describe how digital marketing has evolved from Web 1.0 to Web 3.0.**

In the beginning of the internet, the marketing focus for Web 1.0 was the creation of static websites for branded content and information sharing. Later, Web 2.0 was characterized by greater audience engagement and an interactivity between the website and the user. This facilitated the development of user-generated content, the co-creation of content and brand communities, where like-minded users meet to network and socialize online. The next iteration of the web, Web 3.0, will be characterized by the web becoming artificially intelligent, thereby recognizing links and relationships between data sources, allowing the prediction of audience response and greater audience targeting.

- **Discuss key techniques in digital marketing and social media marketing.**

  Key techniques in digital marketing include internet advertising, search marketing, email marketing, viral marketing, social media marketing, advergaming, and mobile marketing. Within the area of social media marketing important considerations include the following: it is rapidly increasing in importance and marketers are expected to increase their expenditure on it significantly by 2016; marketers must share control over their brands with their online users; users will co-create content and generate their own content; customers will develop their own brand communities which marketers should seek to contribute to rather than usurp; it is about dialogue, conversation, and listening rather than monologue and transmitting; and the measurement of effectiveness

- **Review how practitioners measure the effectiveness of social media marketing.**

  In order to measure the effectiveness of a social media campaign, marketers should follow a seven-step process which includes identifying a set of appropriate social media metrics, reviewing the social media campaign objectives, and mapping the campaign by highlighting links to brand-generated content, consumer-generated content, consumer-fortified content, and exposure to content(ed) consumers choosing the criteria and tools of measurement, establishing a benchmark, undertaking the campaign, and measuring it frequently.

- **Discuss crowdsourcing and explain how online communities can be harnessed for marketing purposes.**

  Crowdsourcing is the process of outsourcing a task or group of tasks to a generally large 'crowd' of people. It is used in marketing to outsource routine activities, obtain content (e.g. Ford/copy for adverts), or obtain creative input (e.g. Lego/new product development).

Review Questions

1 Define how digital marketing differs from interactive and internet marketing.
2 What is Web 3.0 and how might it change marketing?
3 Compare and contrast the difference between 'pull' and 'push' approaches to digital marketing.
4 What are the benefits of internet advertising and advergaming?
5 What is by social media marketing?
6 How do we measure the effectiveness of social media marketing?
7 What is the difference between user-generated and co-created content?
8 Why do some online adverts go viral and others do not?
9 How is the growth of mobile devices (e.g. smartphones) impacting on marketing?
10 What marketing activities can crowdsourcing support?

Worksheet Summary

To apply the knowledge you have gained from this chapter and test your understanding of digital and social media marketing visit the **Online Resource Centre** and complete Worksheet 17.1.

Discussion Questions

1 Having read Case Insight 17.1 at the beginning of this chapter, how could Virgin Media use social media to support its marketing communications campaign to promote superfast broadband?

2 Do you think that digital resources are redefining marketing?

3 Why is the principle of sharing control of a brand and organizational information so difficult for the marketing profession to adopt?

4 Children and men have been playing games for years, making them obvious targets for advertising. What changes in gaming channels do you think have increased the wider appeal and reach of advergaming to other target audiences?

5 Privacy and ownership of digital information is increasingly challenged. When participating on Facebook I think I control my own data and information, but do I? Discuss.

@ Visit the **Online Resource Centre** and complete the Multiple Choice Questions to assess your knowledge of Chapter 17.

 # References

Anon. (2011), 'Survey: More than half UK, French and German adults are gamers', *VG 24/7*, 8 August, retrieve from: http://www.vg247.com/2011/08/08/survey-more-than-half-uk-french-and-german-adults-are-gamers/ accessed 17 February 2013.

Anon. (2012a), 'Net-a-Porter to become "media brand" ', *Drapers*, 10 February, retrieve from: http://www.drapersonline.com/news/ecommerce/net-a-porter-to-become-media-brand/5033516.article accessed 5 January 2013.

Anon. (2012b), 'Global mobile statistics 2012. Part A: Mobile subscribers; handset market share; mobile operators', *MobiThinking Report*, retrieve from: http://mobithinking.com/mobile-marketing-tools/latest-mobile-stats/a#uniquesubscribers accessed 11 February 2013.

Anon. (2012c), 'The best search directories', *Pandia*, retrieve from: http://www.pandia.com/resources/search-directories.html accessed 3 February 2013.

Anon. (2013), 'Court approves $844m Kodak Bankruptcy financing', *Bloomberg Businessweek*, 23 January, retrieve from: http://www.businessweek.com/ap/2013-01-23/court-approves-844m-kodak-bankruptcy-financing accessed 11 February 2013.

Baines, P. and O'Shaughnessy, N. J. (Eds.) (2013), *Propaganda,* Vols I–IV, London: Sage Publications.

BBC (2009), 'Habitat sorry for Iran tweeting', BBC News, 24 June, retrieve from: http://news.bbc.co.uk/1/hi/8116869.stm accessed 3 February 2013.

Beaumont, C. (2008), 'Tim Berners-Lee: The web that thinks', *The Telegraph*, 20 March, retrieve from: http://www.telegraph.co.uk/technology/3356768/Tim-Berners-Lee-The-web-that-thinks.html accessed 11 February 2013.

Berger, J. and Milkman, K.L. (2012), 'What makes online content viral?', *Journal of Marketing Research*, 49(April), 192–205.

Blagdon, J. (2012), 'IDC forecasts 1.16 billion smartphones shipped annually by 2016', *The Verge*, 29 March, retrieve from: http://www.theverge.com/2012/3/29/2910399/idc-smartphone-computer-tablet-sales-2011 accessed 11 February 2013.

Blanchard O. (2011), *Social Media ROI*, Indianapolis, IA: Que.

Bubula, M. (2012), 'The myth about brand communities', *Admap*, November, 20–1.

Buczkowsk, A. (2012), 'Angry Birds and McDonald's: location-based marketing campaign in China', *Geoawesomeness.com*, 25 October, retrieve from: http://geoawesomeness.com/?p=1949 accessed 26 January 2013.

Bughin, J., Corb, L., Manyika, J., *et al.* (2011), 'The impact of internet technologies: search', McKinsey and Company, July, retrieve from: www.mckinsey.com accessed 11 February 2013.

Burger-Helmchen, T. and Pénin, J. (2011), 'Crowdsourcing: définition, enjeux, typologie' (trans. Crowdsourcing: definition, stakes, typology), *Revue Management et Avenir*, January, 41, 254–69.

Chamberlin, B. (2011), 'Social media 101: Social media disasters', *IBM Market Insights*, retrieve from: http://www.slideshare.net/HorizonWatching/social-media-101-social-media-disasters accessed 3 February 2013.

Chang, V. and Heath, C. (2001), The Blair Witch Project (A), Case No. M295A, Stanford Graduate School of Business Case, retrieve from: https://gsbapps.stanford.edu/cases/detail1.asp?Document_ID=1527 accessed 3 February 2013.

Chapman, M. (2013), 'Benetton to feature trans-sexual Brazilian model in Spring/Summer campaign', *Marketing*, 23 January, retrieve from: http://www.marketingmagazine.co.uk/sectors/retail/article/1168021/Benetton-feature-trans-sexual-Brazilian-model-Spring-Summer-campaign/ accessed 3 February 2013.

Cheng, J.M.-S., Blankson, C., Wang, E.S.-T., and Chen, L.S.-L. (2009), 'Consumer attitudes and interactive digital advertising', *International Journal of Advertising* 28(3), 501–25.

Christodoulides, G. (2009), 'Branding in the post-internet era', *Marketing Theory*, 9, 1, 141–4.

CIM (2013), 'How to measure the impact of your social media campaign', *Chartered Institute of Marketing, Marketing Expert [Forum]*, retrieve from: www.cim.co.uk accessed 17 February 2013.

Coleman, J. S., (1988), 'Social capital in the creation of human capital', *American Journal of Sociology*, 94, 95–120.

Cooper, W. (2010), 'Coke drops campaign in favour of social media', *New Media Age*, 14 January, retrieve from: www.nma.co.uk accessed 15 January 2010.

Court, D. C., Gordon, J. W., and Perrey, J. (2005), 'Boosting returns on marketing investment', *McKinsey Quarterly*, 2, 37–47.

Cowen, M (2009), 'EasyJet tops table for paid-search terms', *Travel Weekly (UK)*, 4 September.

Daly, J. (2011), 'Spirit of the fighting Irish', *Irish Examiner*, 17 December, retrieve from: http://www.irishexaminer.com/weekend/spirit-of-the-fighting-irish-177353.html accessed 26 January 2013.

Darwell, B. (2012), 'Facebook platform supports more than 42 million pages and 9 million apps', *Inside Facebook*, 27 April, retrieve from: http://www.insidefacebook.com/2012/04/27/facebook-platform-supports-more-than-42-million-pages-and-9-million-apps/ accessed 11 February 2013.

de Chernatony, L. and Christodoulides, G. (2004), 'Taking the brand promise online: challenges and opportunities', *Interactive Marketing*, 593, 238–51.

Dembosky, A. and Bradshaw, T. (2013), 'Twitter puts modesty before inflated values', *Financial Times*, 26/27January, 15.

Dobele, A., Toleman, D., and Beverland, M. (2005), 'Controlled infection! Spreading the brand message through viral marketing', *Business Horizons*, 48, 143–9.

Dobele, A., Lindgreen, A., Beverland, M., Vanhamme, J., and van Wijk, R. (2007), 'Why pass on viral messages? Because they connect emotionally', *Business Horizons*, 50, 291–304.

Dunphy, J. (2012), 'SEO and social media get married', Econsultancy, 24 December, retrieve from: http://econsultancy.com/uk/blog/11406-seo-and-social-media-get-married accessed 11 February 2012.

Dutta, S. and Bilbao-Osorio, B. (eds) (2012), *The Global Information Technology Report: Living in a Hyperconnected World*, Geneva: World Economic Forum/INSEAD, retrieve from: http://www3.weforum.org/docs/Global_IT_Report_2012.pdf accessed 26 January 2013.

Eckler, P. and Bolls, P. (2011), 'Spreading the virus: emotional tone of viral advertising and its effect on forwarding intentions and attitudes', *Journal of Business Research*, 11(2), 1–11.

Econsultancy (2012), 'UK search engine marketing benchmark report 2012', Econsultancy / Net Booster, March, retrieve from: http://econsultancy.com/uk/reports/uk-search-engine-marketing-benchmark-report accessed 11 February 2013.

Eleftheriou-Smith, L-M. (2012), 'P&G Marketing Chief admits it needs to fundamentally shift how it operates', Marketingmagazine.co.uk, 14 March, retrieve from: http://www.brandrepublic.com/news/1122108/ accessed 10 February 2013.

Ellison, N., Steinfield, C., and Lampe, C. (2007), 'The benefits of Facebook friends: exploring the relationship between college students use of online social networks and social capital', *Journal of Computer-Mediated Communications*, 12(4), 1143–68.

Experian (2012), 'Prepare to share: younger consumers turn up the data heat as they share information across channels', *Company Press Release*, August, retrieve from: http://www.experian.co.uk/marketing-information-services/big-data-press-release-august12.html accessed 16 February 2013.

Feigenbaum, L. (2012), 'BBC's adoption of semantic web technologies: an interview', *CMS Wire*, 29 October, retrieve from: http://www.cmswire.com/cms/information-management/bbcs-adoption-of-semantic-web-technologies-an-interview-017981.php accessed 11 February 2013.

Fisher, E. (2013), 'ING Direct pulls ad after social media backlash: mental health is no joke', *Yummymummy.ca*, 22 January, retrieve from: http://www.yummymummyclub.ca/blogs/eileen-fisher-gigamom/20130122/ing-direct-pulls-ad-after-social-media-backlash accessed 16 February 2013.

Fong, H. (2012), '5 things you need to know about Chinese social media', *Forbes*, 25 November, retrieve from: http://www.forbes.com/sites/ciocentral/2012/10/25/5-things-you-need-to-know-about-chinese-social-media/ accessed 17 February 2013.

Glass, K. (2006), 'Top 10 tips for targeted email marketing', *B&T Weekly*, 3 November, 21.

Greenlight (2009), 'Market share benchmarks in Google search', *Flight Sector Report* [Report], Q2 2009, retrieve from: www.greenlightsearch.com/sectorreports/flights.html accessed 4 April 2010.

Hanna, R., Rohm, A., and Crittenden, V.L. (2011), 'We're all connected: the power of the social media ecosystem', *Business Horizons*, 54(3), 265–73.

Harris, P. (2009), *Penguin Dictionary of Marketing*, London: Penguin Books.

Hemp, P. (2006), 'Avatar-based marketing', *Harvard Business Review*, June, 48–57.

Ho, J. Y. C. and Dempsey, M. (2010), 'Viral marketing: motivations to forward online content', *Journal of Business Research*, 63, 1000–6.

Hoffman, D. L. and Fodor, M. (2010), 'Can you measure the ROI of your social media?', *MIT Sloan Management Review*, 52(1), 41–9.

Howe, J. (2006), 'The rise of crowdsourcing', *Wired*, Issue 14.06(June), retrieve from: http://www.wired.com/wired/archive/14.06/crowds.html accessed 26 January 2013.

IAB (2013), 'Digital adspend tables: 2003-2012', *Internet Advertising Bureau*, 18 January, retrieve from: http://www.iabuk.net/research/library/digital-adspend-tables-2003-2012 accessed 11 February 2013.

IMT (1999). *Permission Email: The Future of Direct Marketing*, retrieve from: www.imtstrategies.com accessed 9 September 2001.

Internet World Stats (2012), 'Internet usage statistics: The internet big picture', June, *Internet World Stats*, retrieve from: www.internetworldstats.com/stats.htm accessed 26 January 2013.

Kane, G. C., Fichman, R. G., Gallaugher, J., and Glaser, J. (2009), 'Community relations 2.0', *Harvard Business Review*, 87(11, 1 November), 132–42.

Kansara, V. A. (2012), 'The next chapter of content and commerce integration', *Business of Fashion*, 20 November, retrieve from: http://www.businessoffashion.com/2012/11/fashion-2-0-the-next-chapter-of-content-and-commerce-integration.html accessed 5 January 2013.

Kaplan, A. M. and Haenlein, M. (2009), 'Consumer use and business potential of virtual worlds: The case of "Second Life" ', *International Journal on Media Management*, 11, 93–101.

Kiss, J. (2012), 'Secrets of a viral ad campaign on Twitter: visualisation', *Guardian*, 31 December, retrieve from: http://www.guardian.co.uk/media/interactive/2012/dec/31/twitter-viral-marketing?INTCMP=SRCH, accessed 3 February 2013.

Kronsberg, M. (2012), 'How Lego's great adventure in geek-sourcing snapped into place and boosted the brand', *Fast Company*, 2 February, retrieve from: http://www.fastcompany.com/1812959/how-legos-great-adventure-geek-sourcing-snapped-place-and-boosted-brand accessed 2 February 2013.

Lake, C. (2011), '10 things that have been crowdsourced in 2011', *Econsultancy*, 23 March, retrieve from: http://econsultancy.com/uk/blog/7323-10-things-that-have-been-crowdsourced-in-2011 accessed 2 February 2013.

Leech, M. (2011), 'Social media: no pressure to do it all', *Bank of Ireland-All about Business*, 27 May, retrieve from: http://allaboutbusiness.ie/hub/article/social_media_no_pressure_to_do_it_all accessed 26 January 2013.

Li, A. (2012), 'Top 10 brands with highest social media engagement this week', *Mashable*, 23 September, retrieve from: http://mashable.com/2012/09/22/top-10-brands-social-media/ accessed 11 February 2013.

Lunden, I. (2012), 'Facebook says it now has 235m monthly gamers, app center hits 150 monthly visitors', *TechCrunch*, 14 August, retrieve from: http://techcrunch.com/2012/08/14/facebook-says-it-now-has-235m-monthly-gamers-app-center-hits-150m-monthly-users/ accessed 11 February 2013.

McAfee (2012), 'McAfee threats report: second quarter 2012', Report, retrieve from http://www.mcafee.com/uk/resources/reports/rp-quarterly-threat-q2-2012.pdf accessed 11 February 2013.

Magill, K. (2011), 'Email remains ROI king. Net marketing set to overtake DM, says DMA', *Magill Report*, 4 October, retrieve from: http://www.magillreport.com/Email-Remains-ROI-King-Net-Marketing-Set-to-Overtake-DM/ accessed 16 February 2013.

Mangold, W.G. and Faulds, D.J. (2009), 'Social media: the new hybrid element of the promotion mix', *Business Horizons*, 52, 357–65.

Mbabazi, A. (2012), 'Kony 2012 "gives impression Uganda is still at war" says Ugandan PM-video', *Guardian*, 18 March, retrieve from: http://www.guardian.co.uk/world/video/2012/mar/18/kony-2012-ugandan-pm-video accessed 3 February 2013.

Michaelidou, N., Siamagka, N. T., and Christodoulides, G. (2011), 'Usage, barriers and measurement of social media marketing: an exploratory investigation of small and medium B2B brands', *Industrial Marketing Management*, 40, 1153–9.

Mintel (2012), 'Social media and networking—UK—May 2012', *Mintel Report*, retrieve from: www.mintel.com accessed 12 February 2013.

Mitchell, A. (2001), *Right Side Up: Building Brands in the Age of the Organised Consumer*, London: HarperCollinsBusiness.

Moorman, C. (2012), 'Social media spend continues to soar', *CMO survey.org*, 6 March, retrieve from: http://www.cmosurvey.org/blog/social-media-spend-continues-to-soar/ accessed 11 February 2013.

MMA (2009), 'Buy mobile marketing', *Mobile Marketing Association*, retrieve from: http://mmaglobal.com/about/content_category/research/10/341

Muniz, A. M., and Jensen Schau, H. (2007), 'Vigilante marketing and consumer-created communications', *Journal of Advertising*, 36(3, Fall), 35–50.

Murdough, C. (2009), 'Social media measurement: it's not impossible', *Journal of Interactive Advertising*, 10(1), 94–9.

Murphy, D. (2010), 'McDonald's scores with cheesy location-based campaign', *Mobile Marketing Magazine*, retrieve from: http://www.mobilemarketingmagazine.co.uk/content/mcdonalds-scores-cheesy-location-based-campaign accessed 3 February 2013.

Nielsen/NM Incite (2012), 'State of the media: the social media report 2012', *Company Report*, retrieve from http://blog.nielsen.com/nielsenwire/social/2012/ accessed 16 February 2013.

Naughton, P. (2012), 'Social media for SMEs in Ireland', *BeFound.ie*, 7 August, retrieve from: http://www.blog.organicseospecialists.com/social-media-networking/187-social-media-for-smes-in-ireland-.html accessed 26 January 2013.

Nicholls, S. (2011), *Social Media in Business: Succeeding in the Internet Revolution*, London: Bookinars.

O'Reilly, L. (2012), 'Search marketing spend to slowdown', *Marketing Week*, 7 June, retrieve from: http://www.marketingweek.co.uk/news/search-marketing-spend-to-slowdown/4002084.article accessed 11 February 2013.

Owyang, J. and Lovett, J. (2010), 'Social marketing analytics: A new framework for measuring results in social media', Altimeter Group, 22 April, retrieve from: http://www.slideshare.net/jeremiah_owyang/altimeter-report-social-marketing-analytics accessed 17 February 2013.

Phelps, J.E., Lewis, R., Mobilio, L., Perry, D., and Raman, N. (2004), 'Viral marketing or electronic word-of-mouth advertising: examining consumer responses and motivations to pass along email', *Journal of Advertising Research*, December, 333–47.

Rao, J.M. and Reiley, D.H. (2012), 'The economics of spam', *Journal of Economic Perspectives*, 26(3), 87–110.

Reisinger, D. (2012), 'Can Apple's app store maintain its lead over Google Play', *c|net*, 27 September, retrieve from: http://news.cnet.com/8301-1035_3-57521252-94/can-apples-app-store-maintain-its-lead-over-google-play/ accessed 21 February 2013.

Roat, O. (2012), 'Four recent examples of clever crowdsourcing campaigns', *Mainstreethost*, 22 August, retrieve from: http://blog.mainstreethost.com/four-recent-examples-of-clever-crowdsourcing-campaigns, accessed 2 February 2013.

SEMPO (2010), *State of Search Engine Marketing Report* (The Search Engine Marketing Professional Organization), 25 March, retrieve from: www.sempo.org/news/03-25-10 accessed May 2010.

Sheldrake, P. (2011), *The Business of Influence: Reframing Marketing and PR for the Digital Age*, Chichester: John Wiley.

Shankar, V. and Balasubramanian, S. (2009), 'Mobile marketing: synthesis and prognosis', *Journal of Interactive Marketing, Tenth Anniversary Special Issue*, 23(2), 118–29.

Simmons, G. (2008), 'Marketing to postmodern consumers: introducing the internet chameleon', *European Journal of Marketing*, 42(3/4), 299–310.

Sledgianowski, D., and Kulviwat, S. (2009), 'Using social network sites: the effects of playfulness, critical mass and trust in a hedonic context', *Journal of Computer Information Systems*, 49(4), 74–83.

Socialbakers (2013), 'Games applications: Facebook statistics', retrieve from: http://www.socialbakers.com/facebook-applications/category/8-games/ accessed 17 February 2013.

Thinkbox (2012), 'TV advertising reached record high in 2011', Press Release, 7 March, retrieve from: http://www.thinkbox.tv accessed 11 February 2013.

van den Bulte, C., and Wuyts, S. (2007), *Social Networks and Marketing*, Boston, MA: Marketing Science Institute.

Vallone, J. (2011), 'Crowdsourcing could predict terror strikes, gasoline prices'", *Investors' Business Daily*, 29 August, 5.

Vocell, J. (2012), '5 Social media metrics you should be monitoring', *Social Media Today*, 17 October, retrieve from: http://socialmediatoday.com/jvocell/914271/5-social-media-metrics-you-should-be-monitoring accessed 2 February 2013.

Vogt, C. and Alldredge, K. (2012), '2012 Digital Influence Index', *Fleishman Hillard/Harris Interactive Report*, retrieve from: http://push.fleishmanhillard.netdna-cdn.com/dii/2012-DII-White-Paper.pdf accessed 16 February 2013.

Waring, T. and Martinez, A. (2002), 'Ethical customer relationships: a comparative analysis of US and French organisations using permission-based email marketing', *Journal of Database Marketing*, 10(1), 53–70.

Warman, M. (2012), 'Joseph Kony 2012: a model of modern campaigning", *Daily Telegraph*, 8 March, retrieve from: http://www.telegraph.co.uk/news/worldnews/africaandindianocean/uganda/9131355/Joseph-Kony-2012-a-model-of-modern-campaigning.html accessed 3 February 2013.

Westlund, R. (2009), 'Best practices for email marketing', *AdWeek* 50(31 August), E2–6.

WhatIs.com (2013), 'Social media marketing', retrieve from: http://whatis.techtarget.com/definition/social-media-marketing-SMM accessed 2 February 2013.

Whitney, L. (2012), 'Google Play surges, but Apple's app store is still No.1', c|net, 20 December, retrieve from: http://news.cnet.com/8301-1035_3-57560218-94/google-play-surges-but-apples-app-store-is-still-no-1/ accessed 17 February 2013.

Winer, R. (2009), 'New communications approaches in marketing: issues and research directions', *Journal of Interactive Marketing*, 23(2, May), 108–17.

WIP (2012), *World Internet Project International Report, World Internet Project* (4th edn), retrieve from: www.worldinternetproject.net accessed 17 February 2013.

Wunsch-Vincent, S. and Vickery, G. (2007), *Participative Web: User-created Content*, Geneva: OECD, retrieve from http://www.oecd.org/internet/interneteconomy/38393115.pdf accessed 3 February 2013.

Chapter 18

Marketing, Sustainability, and Ethics

Learning Outcomes

After studying this chapter, you will be able to:

▸ Define sustainable marketing and its implications for marketing practice

▸ Define marketing ethics

▸ Explain the common ethical norms applied in marketing

▸ Describe the role of ethics in marketing decision-making

▸ Understand how ethical breaches occur in marketing programmes and activities.

Case Insight 18.1
innocent

Market Insight 18.1
Unilever's Sustainability Challenge

Market Insight 18.2
Living with AIDS at Anglo American

Market Insight 18.3
Barclays Caught Rate-Fixing

Market Insight 18.4
Ethical Content, In Context

Market Insight 18.5
Alleged Bribery at Rolls-Royce

Case Insight 18.1

How do organizations develop and maintain responsible working practices and attitudes towards the environment and at the same time remain compatible with their customers' values? We speak to Tansy Drake, Brand Guardian at innocent to find out more.

Our purpose at innocent is *to make healthy, natural food and drinks that help people live well and die old*. It's accompanied by five company values which are to be responsible, generous, commercial, entrepreneurial, and natural. They steer our behaviour and how we're going to get there.

Some flinch at a reference to death in a business context, but we believe it gives us some backbone and something really important to aim for. Both our purpose and values crystallized as the company grew, but doing business responsibly has always been intuitive to innocent's business approach.

It was a central value shared by all three founding members, and subsequently by all employees. So there's never been a decision as such to do business in a particular way. It was just the responsible way. We are a business, so we need to be commercial, and we do that in an entrepreneurial way. But that doesn't exclude being responsible and generous. And we will

always make natural things and be ourselves at work. This explanation hangs in every loo at our offices.

To give substance to our values we have a permanent sustainability team, as well as champions in every part of the business. With that in mind we've tried to make our packaging as low-impact as possible.

Our little bottles were our first products, and so in 2002 we started on the journey to have the world's first 100% recycled plastic bottle. We finally achieved it in 2008 but soon found that the quality of the plastic isn't high enough at that level. We dropped back down to 35% and have now edged it up to 50%—but beyond that it isn't good enough for our premium products.

The essential problem we face is that as customers perceive highly recycled bottles to be low quality, how do we stick to our principles and ensure a high level of recyclable content without losing sales?

Introduction

What is sustainable marketing and why is everyone talking about it? Why are banks reconsidering their ethical policies? When are advertising and marketing communications coercive? When should companies give back to their communities? What is 'good' marketing behaviour and what is 'bad' marketing behaviour? Are corporate social responsibility initiatives a good idea, or are they cynically used to further organizational interests? These are the sorts of question considered in this chapter.

We begin by discussing marketing's shift towards sustainable economic development and the sub-discipline of sustainable marketing, defining it and explaining its implications for marketing practice. We then discuss what ethics are, before applying ethical principles to the marketing context. We outline how ethical situations impact on the marketing decision-making process. Four main ethical approaches to marketing decision-making are outlined. Ethical situations arising in product, promotion, price, and distribution programmes are explained. We consider ethical issues in international marketing, i.e. whether or not different cultures should have different moral rules, and finally we discuss the important topic of bribery.

Understanding **marketing ethics** is important because we need to understand the ethical, legal, and social dimensions of marketing decision-making and develop the analytical skills to consider ethical problems. There has been an increased interest in business ethics and the responsible company as a result of the following.

- An increasing belief that business performance should not negatively impact on the environment and society in which it operates.

- Government legislation, e.g. the American Sarbanes–Oxley Act 2002 set up an oversight board for the US accounting profession to ensure high standards of financial reporting.

- An increase in global trade and the rise of the multinational corporation with multi-country interests, particularly in developing countries.

- The rise of global media companies operating on a continual 24 hour/seven days a week basis, such as the BBC World Service, CNN, Al Jazeera, and Asia News, with the potential to damage corporate reputations worldwide.

- Increasing belief that climate change (i.e. global warming) is affected by industrial activity and modern consumer lifestyle choices, and that this will have profound implications for future generations.

Sustainable Marketing

Supporters of the concept of **sustainable marketing** accept the limitations of marketing philosophy, acknowledging the need to impose regulatory constraints on the market mechanism in economic development (van Dam and Apeldoorn, 1996), particularly the impact of marketing activity on the environment. Sustainable economic development was first outlined at the United Nations Conference on the Human Environment in Stockholm in 1972, where it was regarded as development that met the needs of current generations without imposing constraints on the needs of future generations (WCED, 1987). Recent examples of negative corporate environmental impact include the following.

- 2010: BP—More than 200 million gallons of oil were released into the Gulf of Mexico after an oil rig explosion in the Macondo Well killed 11 people. The oil spill affected around 1,000 miles of shoreline, killing thousands of birds, around 153 dolphins and other local wildlife. The disaster caused BP to lose half its share value, and estimated costs for the disaster total $40bn (Bryant, 2011). BP's contractor, Transocean, shared some blame for the incident, receiving a fine of $1.4bn from the US authorities (BBC News, 2013a), and BP is suing another contractor, Halliburton, separately over what it believes to be its contribution to the incident (Rushe, 2012).

- 2005–2012: News International—the row over the hacking of phones by investigative reporters, including those of Prince William, Queen Elizabeth II's grandson, and murdered schoolgirl

Milly Dowler, whilst working on stories for British weekly *News of the World* (NOTW) between 2006 and 2011 led to the closure of the NOTW, the failure of News Corporation's bid for satellite broadcaster BSkyB, the establishment of the Leveson Inquiry into press standards, several arrests of key company figures, and the probable break-up of News Corporation, its parent company, into two separate groups, one focused on publishing and the other on TV and satellite broadcasting (BBC News, 2013b).

- 2012: Standard Chartered, the UK bank, was fined around $670m by the US Federal Reserve, New York's Department of Financial Services, the US Treasury Department's Office for Foreign Assets Control (OFAC), and the US Department of Justice to settle charges that it had violated US sanctions on Iran, Burma, Libya, and Sudan by undertaking thousands of illegal financial transactions between 2001 and 2007 (BBC News, 2012a).

Sustainable marketing is an attempt to broaden the concept of marketing beyond simple economic development. It introduces maxims, known as the three Es of sustainability.

1 Ecological—marketing should not negatively impact upon the environment.

2 Equitable—marketing should not allow or promote inequitable social practices.

3 Economic—marketing should encourage long-term economic development as opposed to short-term economic development.

Sustainable marketing can be characterized as the 'third age' of green marketing (Peattie, 2001). In the first age, ecological green marketing (c.1960s/1970s) was concerned with automobile, oil, and agrichemical companies which encountered environmental problems in the production process. The second age, environmental green marketing (c.1980s), saw the development of the green consumer, i.e. people who purchased an offering to avoid negative environmental impacts (e.g. cosmetic products that had not been tested on animals), and companies did try to develop a reputation for being green by offering green products. Sometimes this failed, as when cosmetic suppliers to The Body Shop were found to have tested their products on animals, although The Body Shop later ensured that its suppliers complied with a strict code of practice.

Peattie and Crane (2005) argued that green marketing was too heavily focused on the purchasing component of consumption. Sharma *et al*. (2010) suggest that this is because the sustainability debate has not considered the business-to-business dimension sufficiently. They suggest that sustainable marketers should focus on positioning and demand stimulation for recycled and remanufactured products and build-to-order offerings, as well as considering supply chain management issues such as enabling materials recovery from end-consumers, designing offerings to enable their dismantlement, enabling **reverse logistics** for recycling and remanufactured offerings, and reducing supply by offering build-to-order offerings (Sharma *et al*., 2010).

The third age of green marketing is sustainable green marketing. In the third age, to pursue sustainable marketing policies successfully, companies need to lengthen the time horizons under which they achieve returns on their investments. This requires emphasis on the full costs of purchase rather than simply the price paid. Proposition development activities should fully consider, equitably, inputs and cooperation from members of the supply chain. Companies need to adopt environmental auditing methods (e.g. to include costs for disposal as well as development, delivery, and consumption), and organizations may discourage consumption in certain cases (Bridges and Wilhelm, 2008), or at least encourage more mindful consumption where consumers consume in a way which reflects a caring for self, society, and nature, and encourage temperance rather than acquisitive, repetitive or aspirational over-consumption behaviour

Sainsbury's 'Switch the fish' campaign in the UK encouraged consumers to eat more sustainable fish
Source: © J Sainsbury plc.

(Sheth *et al.*, 2011). For example, Sainsbury's 'Switch the fish' campaign in the UK encourages consumers to eat more sustainable fish than the five endangered species cod, haddock, tuna, salmon, and prawns (Benady, 2013; see also Market Insight 18.1), and The Norwegian Seafood Council promoted the fact that its cod, fished from Norwegian waters, is from sustainable stocks (Bolger, 2013). In 2013, Coca-Cola launched a worldwide campaign on obesity, partnering in

 # Market Insight 18.1

Unilever's Sustainability Challenge

In 2010, Unilever's CEO Paul Polman proudly launched an ambitious sustainability plan called the Sustainable Living Plan. He claimed that Unilever wants to make a positive contribution to society and help solve environmental and social challenges. Among other targets, the company committed itself to halving its environmental footprint by 2020, whilst doubling revenues. Some question the feasibility of such a bold plan, warning that if the financial objectives are not met, investors might be less willing to believe in Polman's visionary leadership.

Market Insight 18.1
continued

Unilever is a multinational corporation, manufacturing and marketing many popular brands including Flora, Dove, and Lynx. To get an idea of the company's sphere of influence, around two billion consumers use Unilever brands every day worldwide. The Sustainable Living Plan seeks to assess in depth the impact that the company's offerings have on society and the environment, setting ambitious targets that go beyond internal operations. To achieve its ambitious environmental goals, the company needs to persuade its customers to behave more responsibly and buy ethical alternatives—a challenge because although a majority of consumers express concern about the environment, only a small segment consistently behave according to their attitudes. A year after the launch of the plan, Unilever reported on its progress. Although internal operations are more sustainable, chief marketing officer Keith Weed admitted that changing consumer behaviour is proving more difficult than expected. This is surprising because one of the reasons for launching the Sustainable Living Plan was

to respond to consumer pressure and social concern for environmental issues. Therefore Unilever will need to redouble its efforts to engage consumers to reach its sustainability targets.

Sources: Skapinker (2010); Baker (2012); Polman (2012); Bainbridge (2013).

1 **Why do you think that Unilever has decided to launch the Sustainable Living Plan?**

2 **What do you think are the major impacts that Unilever's offerings have on the environment and society?**

3 **How could the company try to engage its customers more effectively? Why do you think some customers are not supporting sustainability initiatives despite stating interest in environmental and social issues?**

This Market Insight was kindly contributed by Dr Paolo Antonetti, Warwick Business School.

the UK (until 2015) with StreetGames, a sport participation charity, by introducing smaller bottles (375ml) and by displaying detailed calorie content on-pack (Mintel, 2013).

Although companies are increasingly recognizing the negative impacts they have on society (**externalities**), many are also increasingly trying to contribute positively to societal development through corporate social responsibility programmes. We consider this topic next.

Corporate Social Responsibility

Corporate social responsibility (CSR) initiatives have become increasingly common. Many companies publish annual CSR or sustainability reports (e.g. BAT, GSK). Increasingly, governments and supranational organizations actively encourage CSR initiatives (e.g. the UN Global Compact project). CSR practitioners and academics continue to try to demonstrate the commercial effectiveness of CSR programmes to determine whether or not being 'good' translates into being profitable.

Despite any obvious return, businesspeople and companies have given to charity for centuries. Famous cases include the John Paul Getty foundation in the USA based on profits from the oil industry, which funds art and social projects, and Anglo American, the mining conglomerate which provides welfare support for its employees living with HIV/AIDS in Africa (see Market Insight 18.2).

Market Insight 18.2

Living with AIDS at Anglo American

Anglo American is one of the world's largest mining companies. Headquartered in London, its operations span Africa, Europe, South and North America, Australia, and Asia. In 2011, the company enjoyed underlying profits of $6.1bn, with a total of around 100,000 permanent employees. The company enjoys strong profits and is a pioneering employer. In 2002, it made the decision to offer free antiretroviral treatment to those employees who contract HIV/AIDS and it offers free voluntary HIV/AIDS testing. In South Africa, around 17% of Anglo's South African staff is living with AIDS. Ensuring that they live a normal life and that there are no new infections is key to Anglo's policy. In 2011, for instance, Anglo American tested 110,000 employees and gave free antiretroviral drugs to 4,700 employees. Of course, the company is also concerned with other areas of sustainability, not only employee health. In 2011, the company achieved many of its sustainable policy goals including, among others, zero fatal injuries, a more diverse workforce, the creation/sustenance of 47,070 jobs through enterprise development initiatives, and compliance of 94% of all sites with ISO14001 environmental management certification, and its waste targets exceed those required by law. The company designed and is rolling out a group-wide carbon management programme ECO_2MAN. In 2011, the company spent around $130m on projects to support community development. To assess a project's performance, Anglo American encourages a peer review process including the views of communities affected and NGOs. As a result, it admits that not all its initiatives have been as effective as it would like. Despite these valiant efforts, the company did not reach the Global Top 100 world's most sustainable companies in 2013. However, other companies from the extractive industries (e.g. mining and energy) did, including Belgium's Umicore at No.1, Norway's Statoil at No.2, and Finland's Neste Oil at No.3.

Sources: Anon. (2012a,b, 2013); www.angloamerican.com
www.global100.org/annual-lists/2013-global-100-list.html

Anglo American's concern for its employees' healthcare includes free AIDS tests and treatment
Source: © Anglo America Plc.

Market Insight 18.2
continued

1 Do you think Anglo American has more responsibility to pursue a CSR agenda because it operates in developing countries than a company operating in a wealthier country with less deprivation in the population? Why do you say this?

2 What impact, if any, do you think the company's HIV/AIDS policy has had on Anglo American's revenues?

3 What other companies can you think of that have similar types of policies in relation to their employees? (Hint: check out the 2013 Global 100 list of the world's most sustainable companies.)

The rationale for developing CSR initiatives, irrespective of their financial contribution, is based around the following ideas (Buchholz, 1991: 19).

- Corporations have responsibilities that go beyond the production of their offerings at a profit.

- These responsibilities involve helping to solve important social problems, especially those they helped to create.

- Corporations have a broader constituency of stakeholders than shareholders alone.

- The impacts of corporations go beyond simple marketplace transactions.

- Corporations serve a wider range of human values that cannot be captured solely by a focus on economic values.

A central theme of CSR is that corporations have a responsibility to society that goes beyond the pursuit of profit (Martin, 2002). However, determining responsibility is not a simple exercise. A counter-argument is that in order to make life-saving drugs available at little or no cost to patients who cannot afford them, there is a need to share the costs widely in society rather than expect drugs companies to foot the bill. We don't expect airlines to offer free flights to the unemployed, for example. One key problem associated with CSR programmes is whether or not stakeholders view the company's CSR programme as sincere, particularly as customers punish companies they regard as insincere (van de Wen, 2008) by boycotting them (e.g. UK consumers' boycotting Starbucks over its tax affairs; see Chapter 2).

CSR can sometimes be seen as a 'gentle soap for washing dirty hands' (Debeljak *et al.*, 2011: 12). In other words, it is used by companies in industries regarded as unsustainable (e.g. oil and gas, tobacco and alcohol) because managers believe that it is important (Cai *et al.*, 2011), presumably because it helps them to improve their companies' reputations.

Visit the **Online Resource Centre** and complete Internet Activity 18.1 to learn more about some of the ethical debates that have occurred over the years surrounding sportswear manufacturing.

The pharmaceutical example illustrates the ethical difficulties inherent in marketing decision-making. Therefore we turn to the topic of ethics next.

Ethics and Marketing

Ethics, as a sub-discipline of philosophy, has been around for over 2,000 years. It is defined as 'moral principles that govern a person's behaviour or the conducting of an activity' and 'the branch of knowledge that deals with moral principles' (Oxford Dictionaries, 2013). Ethics can be divided into the following types.

- **Normative ethics**—concerned with the rational enquiry into standards of right and wrong (i.e. norms), good or bad, in respect of character and conduct and which *ought to be* accepted by a class of individuals.

- **Social or religious ethics**—concerned with what is right and wrong, good and bad, in respect of character and conduct. It does not claim to be established merely on the basis of rational enquiry and makes an implicit claim to general allegiance to something (e.g. God, Allah).

- **Positive morality**—a body of knowledge generally adhered to by a social group of individuals, concerning what is right and wrong, good and bad, in respect of character and conduct.

- **Descriptive ethics**—concerned with the study of the system of beliefs and practices of a social group from the perspective of being outside that group.

- **Meta-ethics**—a form of philosophical enquiry that treats ethical concepts and belief systems as objects of philosophical enquiry in themselves.

Considering morality in business gives rise to the question of how should a 'good' businessperson behave? To determine how to apply ethics to marketing, we must redefine what marketing is. The Chartered Institute of Marketing's definition is 'the management process responsible for identifying, anticipating and satisfying customer requirements profitably'. So, how does ethics relate to marketing? We could suggest that marketing ethics is concerned with how we go about the process of identifying, anticipating, and satisfying customer requirements. The application of ethical principles might consider what meaning is given to the term 'profitable'. Islamic readers would not be entirely happy with the ultimate objective of a firm being to achieve profit. They might feel that it is more worthy for a firm to aspire to value maximization (Saeed *et al.*, 2001). Because there are both prescriptive and descriptive components of ethics, we define marketing ethics as: 'The analysis and application of moral principles to marketing decision-making and the outcomes of these decisions'.

Ethical Norms in Marketing Decision-Making

Norms are suggestions about how we ought to behave. Professional marketing organizations typically have a code of professional practice that requires members to behave and act in a professional manner, as do many companies and organizations. The Chartered Institute of Marketing (CIM), the world's largest member-based marketing organization, requires its members to (CIM, 2012):

- demonstrate integrity, bringing credit to the profession of marketing;
- be fair and equitable towards other marketing professionals;
- be honest in dealing with customers, clients, employers, and employees;
- avoid the dissemination of false or misleading information;

Research Insight 18.1

To take your learning further, you might wish to read this influential paper.

Hunt, S. D. and Vitell, S. (2006), 'The general theory of marketing ethics: a revision and three questions', *Journal of Macromarketing*, 26(2), 143–53.

This article builds upon one of the most highly cited paper in marketing ethics (Hunt and Vitell, 1986), which defined the study of marketing ethics. This updating paper suggests that the original 1986 theory required revision because the model was applicable in any ethical decision-making situation, not just in business and management contexts, and required empirical testing. The authors argue that ethical judgments lead to intentions and on to behaviour. Our intentions are made on the basis of whether an action is right in itself (i.e. deontological ethics) and whether our intentions are right (i.e. teleological ethics).

@ **Visit the Online Resource Centre to read the abstract and access the full paper.**

- demonstrate current knowledge of the latest developments and show competence in their application;
- avoid conflicts of interest and commit to maintaining impartiality;
- treat sensitive information with complete confidence (except where it is illegal to do so);
- negotiate business in a professional and ethical manner;
- demonstrate knowledge and observation of the requirements of other (professions') codes of practice;
- demonstrate due diligence in using third-party endorsement, which must have prior approval;
- comply with the governing laws of the relevant country concerned.

In ethics, these norms typically include five general approaches: 1) deontological ethics, 2) teleological ethics, 3) managerial egoism, 4) utilitarianism, and 5) virtue ethics (see Table 18.1).

We now outline each approach. We do not need to determine the differences between each of these approaches at this stage. Read through each section, and the associated examples, to understand the differences. You might wish to read through this section several times before moving onto the next section.

Deontological Ethics

Deontological ethics proposes that the rightness of an action is not determined by the consequences of that action (Mautner, 1999). Rather, deontological ethics emphasizes the importance of codes of ethics, such as those outlined by the Market Research Society (MRS) governing market research in Britain or by ESOMAR, the world association for market research. Deontological approaches propose that we have not only a moral duty to ensure customer satisfaction via the finished offering, but also a duty to ensure integrity in how the offering is produced and marketed (see Market Insight 18.3)

Table 18.1 The main normative approaches to ethical decision-making	
Ethical approach	**Explanation**
Deontological ethics	An ethical approach where the rightness or wrongness of an action or decision is not judged to be based exclusively on the consequences of that action or decision
Teleological ethics	An ethical approach where the rightness or wrongness of an action is determined by its consequences
Managerial egoism	An ethical approach recognizing that a manager ought to act in his/her own best interests and that an action is right if it benefits the manager undertaking that action
Utilitarianism	An ethical approach developed by English philosopher Jeremy Bentham which suggests that an action is right if, and only if, it conforms to the principle of utility, whereby utility is maximized (i.e. pleasure, happiness, or welfare), and pain or unhappiness minimized, more than any alternative
Virtue ethics	A form of ethical approach associated with Aristotle stressing the importance of developing virtuous principles, 'right' character, and the pursuit of a virtuous life

Teleological Ethics

Teleological ethics proposes that the rightness of an action depends only on the value of the consequences (Mautner, 1999). Therefore an organization is acting morally if it does not intend harm to come from its actions but harm is caused by accident anyway, or if its behavior is 'bad' but 'good' consequences result (e.g. bribing a warlord to allow food aid distribution in

Research Insight 18.2

To take your learning further, you might wish to read this influential paper.

Laczniak, G. R. and Murphy, P. E. (2006), 'Normative perspectives for ethical and socially responsible marketing', *Journal of Macromarketing*, **26(2), 154–77.**

This article presents a set of normative ethical perspectives for improving the practice of marketing, including putting people first, achieving a standard in excess of law, being responsible for whatever is intended as a means or ends of a marketing action, cultivating better moral imagination in employees, articulating and embracing a core set of ethical principles, adopting a stakeholder orientation to ethical marketing decisions, and delineating an ethical marketing decision-making protocol.

@ Visit the **Online Resource Centre** to read the abstract and access the full paper.

Market Insight 18.3

Barclays Caught Rate-Fixing

In 2012, the British bank Barclays had a very bad year. It admitted fixing the London inter-bank offer rate (LIBOR), and was fined £290m by the UK's Financial Services Authority (FSA) and the US Department of Justice and the Commodity Futures Trading Commission (CFTC). The rate is one of the most important interest rates in the world of financial services, underscoring trillions of pounds of loans and finance contracts. The resultant outcry, including a summons to a UK House of Commons Treasury Select Committee meeting, caused the resignation of the Chairman Marcus Agius, the Chief Executive Bob Diamond, and the Chief Operating Officer Jerry del Missier, all within a week of the details of the fines being made public. Barclays was not the only bank trying to fix the rates. The Swiss bank UBS was also fined a total of £940m for LIBOR rate-fixing.

In early 2013, Antony Jenkins, Barclays's new Chief Executive, demanded that staff sign up to a strict new code of ethical conduct. Staff performance will now be judged against measures such as 'respect, integrity, service, excellence and stewardship' with a view to shifting employees' performance perspectives from the short term to the longer term. Incentives for sales staff will be based on customer service rather than product sales. Barclays seems to have really taken its new ethical values to heart. In 2013, it announced the closure of the tax planning unit of Structured Capital Markets, a unit which had provided tax avoidance services for its clients and is rumoured to have secured £1bn in profits. Whilst the tax avoidance planning services were legal, they were no longer acceptable ethically given the tough financial environment in which the UK government resides.

Sources: BBC News (2013c); Benady (2013); Brownsell (2013a,b); Treanor (2013) (see also Market Insight 4.1).

1 Do you think the ethical policy that Barclays has developed will help to ensure that a scandal like LIBOR fixing will never happen again? Why do you say this?

2 Do you agree with the Barclays' chief executive's decision to shut down its tax planning unit in the Structured Capital Markets division? Why do you say this?

3 Look up the ethical policies of two other global banks on their websites. How are they similar and how do they differ?

a developing country in a CSR programme). Utilitarianism and virtue ethics are subsets of teleological ethics.

Managerial Egoism

The rationale for egoism is the pursuit of our own interests, or self-interest. We assume that the interests of marketing managers are in agreement with the interests of the organization's owners or directors (but they may not be). Under these circumstances, the ethical principle of **managerial egoism** is the maximization of shareholder value or stakeholder value (for a non-profit organization). If managers aim to maximize their own self-interest within the free market, economic welfare is maximized across the population, according to Adam Smith (1776). If we adopt the managerial egoist principle, we conclude that companies should set their marketing programmes to maximize shareholder or stakeholder value. The celebrated economist Milton Friedman suggested that managers should only have responsibility to maximize shareholder returns as they 'lack the wisdom and ability to resolve complex social problems' (Friedman

1979: 90). Economists have long suggested that markets are amoral. The free market mechanism does not work to promote ethical decisions, but it does work to supply the optimal amount of goods and services in a society. Managerial egoism is a subset of teleological ethics.

There is a view that marketers should not concern themselves with ethics as long as they uphold the law and manage their own self-interest, as unethical behaviour is subject to sanction in the marketplace. Firms will pursue their own self-interest and act ethically anyway (Gaski, 1999). There is some evidence to suggest that companies offering services rather than goods might require employees to be more ethical, as there is a greater opportunity for unethical behaviour because of the greater interaction between company and customer and the trust generated from this interaction (Rao and Singhapakdi, 1997).

If marketers act according to the law or a company's self-interest only, this can be regarded as a moral minimum. Most societies require companies to go beyond this. The problem with this ethical approach is that it is not always possible to determine whether a company is pursuing a managerial egoist approach (i.e. acting in their own self-interest because ultimately this will benefit others) or a shareholder value maximization approach. The two sometimes appearto be the same. The cynic will wonder whether a company that goes beyond its legal duties and apparently acts according to higher morals (e.g. Ben & Jerry's, Guaranty Trust Bank) is simply trying to win over public opinion and maximize long-term shareholder value, rather than be ethical.

Utilitarianism

An ethical approach originally developed by the English philosopher Jeremy Bentham, **utilitarianism** suggests that an action is right if, and only if, its performance will be more productive of pleasure or happiness or welfare, or more preventive of pain or unhappiness, than any alternative (Mautner, 1999). Utilitarian arguments are concerned with the consequences of an action. Most ethical arguments proposed by marketers are utilitarian. Marketing itself could be argued to be utilitarian as it is concerned with satisfying consumer needs and wants at the market level (Nantel and Weeks, 1996).

Utilitarianism is concerned with 'producing the greater good for the greatest number of people'. The problem is that the maximization of one group's utility can lead to the minimization of another group's utility. To determine the utility associated with a particular decision, we determine the 'costs' and 'benefits' which, quite often, are more or less impossible to quantify. Where an offering may save lives, such as with life-saving drugs or health treatments, the losers may pay with their lives and the gainers survive, particularly where that offering is in scarce supply.

To explain this further, consider a train operating company trying to improve its health and safety record by, for instance, improving safety instrumentation (i.e. signalling and track equipment). In such a situation, the company has to decide exactly how much to spend on protecting passengers' health and safety needs. The costs of purchasing and fitting equipment to reduce what industrial safety engineers call the **fatal accident rate (FAR)** are passed on to the customer. A decision on whether or not to fit the equipment, and how much to spend, requires a calculation of the likely reduction in risk of accidents against how likely the passengers are to pay the increased prices. Otherwise, the company will need to absorb the extra costs. However, the following question arises: is this an acceptable approach? Many would argue that it is not, stating that if even one life lost or damaged can be avoided, the company must improve the health and safety of all passengers regardless. Rationing supplies is an extreme example of utilitarianism, as occurs in wartime, and occurred with electricity supply in Chile in 1999, with petrol in Iran and diesel in China in 2007, and an extension of rationing to diesel in Iran in 2012.

In Rawls' *Theory of Justice* (Rawls, 1972), he argues that in a just society the following two conditions must be met.

1 'Each person is to have an equal right to the most extensive total system of equal basic liberties compatible with a similar system of liberty for all' (Liberty Principle).

2 'Social and economic inequalities are to be arranged so that they are both:

   a) to the greatest benefit of the least advantaged; and

   b) attached to offices and positions open to all under the conditions of fair equality of opportunity' (Difference Principle).

The application of the Difference Principle to marketing situations suggests that vulnerable groups in society should not be disadvantaged further by marketing decisions. It is to this principle that the international media implicitly appeal when criticizing international pharmaceutical companies, oil and gas companies, and banks for what they term to be excessive profiteering. This approach to ethical decision-making would suggest that we have a duty to help the disadvantaged, particularly where they are likely to be adversely affected by our actions.

Virtue Ethics

Previous normative ethical theories, i.e. managerial egoist, utilitarian, and deontological, provide marketers with decision-making approaches that can be used to choose between alternative courses of 'right' action. In direct contrast, **virtue ethics** stresses the importance of developing virtuous principles, with 'right' character, and the pursuit of a virtuous life. This branch of ethics is associated principally with Aristotle (Mautner, 1999). Virtue ethics proposes the development of good character, suggesting that we should aim to develop the virtuous organization. But what virtues should organizations strive to develop? The idea is that if we live a virtuous life, virtuous decision-making develops naturally.

Many organizations claim to be virtuous. The values statements of some pharmaceutical and oil and gas companies emphasize the importance of 'integrity'. Enron, the US energy company, which inflated its own earnings and ended in collapse, extolled its own virtues in its mission statement. But exactly what are virtuous principles and how are they operationalized? Aristotle, in *Nicomachean Ethics*, defines virtue as 'a settled disposition of the mind which determines choice' (Mautner, 1999). He defines 11 virtues comprising bravery, self-control, generosity, magnificence, self-respect, balanced ambition, gentleness, friendliness, truthfulness, wittiness, and justice. Although a company, as a company, does not have a character in the same way that a person does, its employees do. Therefore it is possible to consider how these virtues *might* relate to a company. For example, generosity might relate to the development of CSR programmes, or incentives given to employees or channel partners. Table 18.2 outlines each virtue and how it might be applied to organizations.

Visit the **Online Resource Centre** and complete Internet Activity 18.2 to learn more about Switzerland's ABB (Asea Brown Boveri), which topped Forbes' list of the world's most ethical companies in 2013.

The Ethical Decision-Making Process

Having defined four main ways in which we analyse how an organization ought to behave, we consider how organizations go about making ethical decisions. A manager initially has to perceive that an ethical dilemma exists before undergoing the ethical decision-making process

Table 18.2 Moral virtues applied to companies

Moral virtue	Application in business and marketing
Bravery, valour	In relation to innovation/new product/service development and long term as opposed to short-term goal-setting
Self-control in respect of bodily pleasure	Not given to excessive pricing or profit-taking
Generosity	Development of CSR/philanthropy, or in terms of discounted offerings or other incentives given to employees/others
Magnificence	Aiming to build a large enterprise with a well-defined mission which serves its stakeholders well
Self-respect or pride	Openly communicating to stakeholders the good and bad news associated with a company's operations
Having some ambition but not in excess	Competitive but not at all costs and not combative within an industry
Gentleness or good temper	The use of a balanced approach to dealings with stakeholder relations, e.g. industrial relations, consumer boycotts
Friendliness	The will to join forces with competitors in the same industry where necessary, e.g. for purposes of self-regulation, to develop industry standards, and an exemplary approach to customer service and satisfaction
Truthfulness	In relation to financial integrity and other stakeholder communications
Wittiness	Taken to mean intelligence and a company's ability to redefine the 'rules of the game' without taking itself too seriously
Justice	The audits of one's own ethical approaches and the initiation of reward/ punishment when these are disregarded

(Hunt and Vitell, 2006). Critically, if no ethical dilemma is perceived, no consideration of alternative action can take place. Further, determining if a situation has ethical content is specific to individual cultures. People from some cultures are more likely to perceive ethical breaches than others. However, there are also some universal standards. For example, bribery is universally condemned worldwide and most countries have laws making bribery of public officials illegal, although it still happens in practice (see later section on Bribery). Early attempts to devise frameworks of how to act ethically involved asking ourselves the following reflective questions (Laczniak and Murphy, 1993).

- Does the contemplated action violate the law (legal test)?

- Is this action contrary to widely accepted moral obligations (duties test)?

- Does the proposed action violate any other special obligations that stem from the type of marketing organization in focus (special obligations test)?

- Is the intent of the contemplated action harmful (motives test)?

- Is it likely that any major damage to people or organizations will result from the contemplated action (consequences test)?

- Is there a satisfactory alternative action that produces equal or greater benefits to the parties affected than the proposed action (utilitarian test)?

- Does the contemplated action infringe on property rights, privacy rights, or the inalienable rights of the consumer (rights test)?

- Does the proposed action leave another person or group less well off? Is this person or group already a member of a relatively underprivileged class (justice test)?

An elaborate model of ethical decision-making is shown in Figure 18.1. The authors cite five key issues for ethical consideration including **bid rigging**, **price collusion**, bribery, falsifying research data, and advertising deception. In bid rigging, subcontractors submit false bids, perhaps producing offerings that are too expensive knowing that they will form part of the final contract. Sometimes, companies might agree not to submit a bid so that another company can successfully win a contract. **Collusion** occurs when companies collaborate on submitting bids for some competitions but not others. With price collusion, companies either conspire to set prices or limit production, which has similar effects.

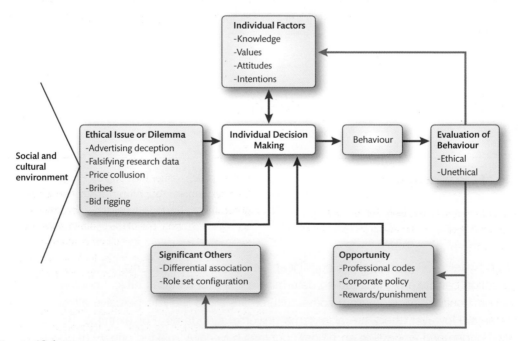

Figure 18.1

A contingency model of ethical decision-making in a marketing organization

Source: Reprinted with permission from *Journal of Marketing*, published by the American Marketing Association, Ferrell and Gresham 1985, 49(3), 84–96.

Research Insight 18.3

To take your learning further, you might wish to read this influential paper.

Ferrell, O. C. and Gresham, L. G. (1985), 'A contingency framework for understanding ethical decision making in marketing', *Journal of Marketing*, **49 (Summer), 87–96.**

A highly cited, very readable paper outlining how ethical marketing decisions are contingent on the ethical issue itself, the social and cultural environment, individual factors (such as attitudes and values), significant others, and the opportunity (i.e. professional codes with which one operates, corporate policy), focusing academic attention on the fact that ethical marketing decisions are dependent on the circumstances in which the decision-making occurs for the first time.

@ **Visit the Online Resource Centre to read the abstract and access the full paper.**

How a person in an organization responds to situations with ethical content depends on their social and cultural environment (see Market Insight 18.4). Although bribery is illegal in most countries worldwide, it remains more prevalent in some countries than in others (see section on Bribery). How an employee makes a decision on an ethical issue is affected by their own knowledge, cultural background, values, and attitudes, and whether or not the company has a code of ethics, a corporate ethical policy, and guidelines on rewards/punishment for ethical and unethical behaviour.

Market Insight 18.4

Ethical Content, In Context

How would you react if you were in the following situations at work? Consider the ethical content of each of the following situations.

■ You work for a Western defence company (i.e. USA, UK, France, Sweden) and have just visited an African nation where you are likely to be awarded a multimillion dollar contract to supply the government with missile technology, which they state that they intend to use only for the defence

of their nation, rather than aggression against their neighbours. Your African contact within the government asks for a large 'facilitation payment', equivalent to about 5% of the contract value, for arranging the contract. If you do not arrange the payment, you are unlikely to get the contract and could lose your job. Do you arrange the 'facilitation payment'?

■ An advertising agency devises an awareness-raising campaign for a new scent aimed at affluent women in Denmark. The campaign uses a well-known model in a highly sexually provocative pose,

Market Insight 18.4
continued

which your research indicates does not offend the affluent female target audience and captures their attention. However, it is possible that the campaign might offend others. Should you commission the campaign anyway?

■ You work for an oil and gas company in an African country during an election year. You think that the leading political party in power is in a position once it forms a government to increase your production capacity by extending your oil rights, but to obtain this you need to donate a 'large gift' to the party. Should you make the donation?

1 Go through each of the above situations and identify what you would do in the circumstances. Why would you act in this way?

2 What other marketing situations can you think of with ethical content?

3 How important is it for an organization to have clear ethical policies? Do you think that they can provide guidelines for all the ethical situations that employees might find themselves in?

A person's ethical decision-making is shaped by how they interact with people who are part of their reference group. Association with others behaving unethically, combined with the opportunity to be involved in such behaviour oneself, is a major predictor of unethical behaviour (Ferrell and Gresham, 1985). Therefore the behaviour of superiors determines how employees behave and is the most important factor influencing ethical/unethical decisions. Next, we consider how ethics impacts on distribution, promotion, products, and pricing decisions.

Distribution Management and Ethics

Distribution and production policy can have major ethical dimensions. Ethical breaches in distribution management occur when, for example, companies collude over production quotas, when companies abuse their monopoly status, and when companies overcharge or exploit supply chain partners. The following sections provide examples of companies and situations where ethical breaches have occurred.

■ Collusion—the European Commission fined Spain's Telefonica €66.9m and Portugal Telecom €12.3m after they allegedly agreed not to compete with each other in the Iberian telecom market between September 2010 and December 2011 (Mock, 2013).The best known and most tolerated global example of production collusion is that which takes place in the oil industry, through OPEC (the Organization of Oil-Exporting Countries) which co-manages oil production quotas in countries such as Nigeria, Saudi Arabia, Iran, Venezuela, and elsewhere.

■ Abuse of monopoly status— China Telecom and China Unicom have both been accused of abusing their monopoly status of the telecommunications market in China (Gu, 2012). The European Commission fined Microsoft €561m for failing to adhere to previous EU anti-monopoly judgments regarding Microsoft's dominance of the browser market with Internet Explorer (Halfacree, 2013).

- Exploitation of supply chain partners—a well-known example in Western markets takes place between supermarkets and their suppliers, particularly those supplying multinational supermarket groups. European countries have brought in legislation to stop supermarkets from wielding excessive power. For instance, in France the Châtel Act replaced the Loi Galland, which forbade supermarkets from charging so-called **listing fees**. The new act strengthens legislation to stop supermarkets selling at below-cost prices and is aimed at increasing competition in the sector. All discounts and services provided by the distributor to the supplier now require stipulation upfront in an annual agreement (see Boutin and Guerrero, 2008).

Promotion and Ethics

There are many advertising issues prompting ethical consideration, e.g. shock and sexual appeals in advertising, the labelling of consumer products, the use of propaganda and advertising in political campaigns, and marketing to children.

The Use of Sexual and Shock Appeals

Advertisers use emotional appeals because they capture attention. We are persuaded by them because we are less likely to consider objections about why we might not agree with the message. For French philosopher, Jean Baudrillard (2005), advertising has an erotic element to it, seducing us to buy. But the ethical question arises because a substantial proportion of adverts use sexual themes explicitly (e.g. naked or semi-naked models, sometimes male, but mostly female) to advertise their products. For example, sexual appeal was used to advertise Axe, the Unilever deodorant brand, in India as part of the 'Any excuse to get dirty' campaign.

Many critics argue that sexual appeals exploit women, and men, as sex objects. The fashion industry has consequently decided not to use models under the age of 16 years. Others argue that sexual appeals in advertising might be appropriate for the offering in question, i.e. a perfume. The difficulty arises in determining how far to go when using sexual appeals. For what offerings is it appropriate, in what countries, and targeted at people of what ages? Interestingly, a cross-cultural study found that young consumers in China hold similar attitudes towards the use of sex appeal in advertising as US consumers and even more favourable attitudes than Australian consumers (Liu *et al.*, 2009). Consumers also generally tend to prefer mildly erotic ads to non-erotic ads. When erotica is used in cause-related advertising, it appears to be received more favourably if it is congruent with the cause and more by women than men (Pope *et al.*, 2004).

Shock advertising appeals have also created controversy. Perhaps the best examples of shock advertising appeals are those used by governments to reduce tobacco smoking. Australia uses approximately 82.5% of the space on a cigarette packet to depict pictures and text encouraging people not to smoke, including graphic images of people with nasty ailments such as mouth and throat cancer (Anon., 2012c). Special interest groups also use shock advertising. The NSPCC, the UK children's charity, used a hard-hitting message about child-beating in its Full Stop advertising campaign to raise funds. PETA, the US vegan campaigning organization, is also well known for its shocking ads and stunts, some depicting meat eaters as murderers and others combining sexual and shock appeals, using celebrities such as Hollywood stars Pamela Anderson and Alicia Silverstone.

However, it has been argued that shock appeals are limited in their effectiveness because, when encountering a dismaying image, viewers neutralize the messages in a process psychologists

Pamela Anderson models for PETA in an anti-meat-eating campaign
Source: Courtesy of PETA, www.peta.org

call 'emotional forgetting', or they avoid looking at the image in the first place (see Chapter 2 on 'selective exposure'). It is important for an advertiser to determine what level of shock is appropriate to get the audience's attention without offending or harming them.

Product Labelling

The key ethical issue with product labelling is whether or not labels mislead the buying public. Proper labelling is particularly important in the food, pharmaceutical, and cosmetic industries, as we literally consume these products or absorb them into our bodies. Increasingly, food products, and particularly meat products in Europe and elsewhere, are required to demonstrate their country of origin. For Europe's Muslims, whether or not food products are correctly labelled **halal** is important, as Muslims believe that animals should be slaughtered according to the custom of cutting the animal's throat while it is alive and then draining its blood. Some animal rights groups condemn the practice, and Sweden, Norway, Iceland, Switzerland, and Poland have banned 'ritual slaughter' despite the fact that it is allowed under EU law (Hasan, 2012; BBC News, 2012b).

Unscrupulous companies can, and do, circumvent product labelling rules by importing food products from one country, processing them in another, and claiming that they come from the country where they are processed. In most countries of the European Union, regulations were created after the EU passed the EC Packaging and Packaging Waste Directive 94/62/EC to govern the composition of packaging and its recycling. However, guidelines on advertising claims are not contained in this act and are covered in Britain by the Trading Standards Service, which investigates misleading packaging and labelling on behalf of the consumer.

Propaganda and Political Advertising

In many countries, political advertising is exempt from the rules and regulations associated with traditional advertising. In America, for instance, freedom of speech (enshrined in the Fifth Amendment) allows a highly negative approach to political advertising based on 15- and 30-second advertising spots used to assassinate the character of political opponents. An excellent example was the Swift Boat Veterans for Truth special interest group campaign against John Kerry in the 2004 US presidential election, which aimed to attack John Kerry's patriotism in a dishonest and unjust way and thereby damage his chances of winning the presidency. In Britain, political advertising on billboards, in cinemas, and in magazines is exempt from the advertising rules set by the Advertising Standards Authority (ASA). Political parties are not expected to be truthful, i.e. to validate their claims, unlike their commercial counterparts. Broadcast political advertising is illegal; instead, a system of party political broadcasts operates. The ethical question is: should politicians be exempt from the rules and regulations associated with traditional marketing activity?

However, political advertising is not solely undertaken by political parties. Other organizations also undertake political advertising (see Chapter 16). Some political adverts are propagandist. One pertinent example is a campaign by the Israeli Defence Forces (IDF) who, in 2012, disseminated a poster on Twitter boasting of their killing of Hamas leader Ahmed Jabari (Crann, 2012). However, both the American and British military have used propaganda methods in their bid to justify the Iraq War, partly through the practice of **embedding** journalists in allied combat units, but also through press censorship and event staging (see Baines and Worcester, 2005).

Visit the **Online Resource Centre** and follow the weblink to the Advertising Standards Authority (ASA) to learn more about advertising rules and regulations.

Marketing tools and techniques are not solely used by governments either. They are also used by terrorist groups. Terrorist groups use propaganda videos to market the cause of suicide bombing through the use of visual rhetoric distributed through the Qatari TV station Al Jazeera and on the internet (O'Shaughnessy and Baines, 2009).

It is critical to realize that an understanding of marketing and public relations provides users with the means to persuade mass groups of people. The question arises as to whether or not it is legitimate for governments and special interest groups (including terrorists) to use these means to persuade citizens and electorates about the legitimacy of war or terrorist action before, during, and after the event.

Marketing to Children

Scholars have frequently commented on whether or not children should be targeted for advertising, given their immature views of time, money, and identity. In a research study on marketing to children in Britain, undertaken on behalf of Business in the Community (BITC) by Research International and Lightspeed Research, researchers found evidence that children are targeted in promotional campaigns and that parents are concerned by this. For example:

- Children are more exposed to marketing than before and parents increasingly feel that they are losing control of the marketing directed at their children.

- Parents are particularly concerned about the marketing channels used (e.g. internet, mobile phone, social media, and advergames) which target children directly.

- Inappropriate marketing to children damages the brand, making it less likely that marketers will get past the parent as gatekeeper.
- More appropriate marketing methods are informative and help parents to feel more in control.
- Consumers are willing to support companies that communicate with children in a responsible way.
- Marketers, especially advertisers, should use the means of communication appropriately and educate parents and children alike on newer and less traditional communication media (see Daniels and Holmes, 2005).

One company under pressure in relation to its promotion to children is McDonald's, as its offerings appeal particularly to children through the use of licensed characters and celebrity endorsement. Child obesity is regarded as a problem in many countries (e.g. Australasia, Britain, EU generally, and the USA). One perspective suggests that the problem is caused by food advertising to children, although the evidence is unclear as it could also be inactive lifestyles and lack of exercise. Nevertheless, fast food retailers such as McDonald's, KFC, and Burger King are coming under increasing pressure to make their menus healthier.

Products and Ethics

In marketing, we should consider whether or not an offering complies with industry health and safety. Companies must follow strict guidelines on product quality. Where consumers have concerns about a particular company's product quality, they can inform a government body which will then be charged with looking into the case on the consumer/customer's behalf. For instance, the US Consumer Product Safety Commission, the UK's Office of Fair Trading, Sweden's National Consumer Agency, Dubai Municipality's Central Laboratory Department (DCLD), and the EU's Health and Consumer Protection Directorate-General all perform this role. Most countries have organizations charged with ensuring product quality; however, the same degree of protection for ensuring service quality does not exist, probably because it is more difficult to monitor service quality, decide on minimum service standards, and determine whether or not breaches have been made. Agencies also provide consumer information. For instance, the UK's Office of Fair Trading provides information on such services as buying warranties for electrical goods, funerals, buying and selling your home, holidays, pawnbroking, ticket agents, and private dentistry—industries where sharp practice frequently occurs.

Visit the **Online Resource Centre** and follow the weblinks to the various consumer agencies and government fair trading bodies to learn more about regulations and guidelines organizations must follow to ensure the health and safety of consumers and the conduct of fair business practice.

Breaches in product quality can be extremely serious, leading to loss of life and grave injury, particularly in the food industry. For this reason, many countries have separate official bodies charged with ensuring food safety guidelines, e.g. the American Food and Drug Administration, Britain's Food Standards Agency, France's Agence Française de Sécurité Sanitaire des Aliments (AFSSA), and the bi-national Food Safety Australia and New Zealand (FSANZ) organization covering both territories. Pertinent examples of recent defective products causing death, injury, and inconvenience include the following.

1   In 2008, Sanlu (and other Chinese milk producers) were involved in a major scandal in China when they were found to have added melamine, a banned substance in food worldwide, to milk to falsely improve protein test readings. Around 300,000 infants became sick as a result and approximately six died (Spencer, 2008). Sanlu declared bankruptcy the same year, and the Chinese authorities passed sentences on the perpetrators ranging from long prison terms to two death sentences (BBC News, 2010).

2   Between 2009 and 2011, Toyota were forced to recall more than 9 million cars worldwide after faults were found with poorly fitted floor mats and sticking accelerator pedals, costing the company an estimated $3bn in total (Sager, 2013).

3   In 2013, Ikea was forced to recall almond cakes, obtained from a single Swedish supplier, from 23 countries after Chinese customs officials found that they contained traces of sewage bacteria (Collins, 2013).

However, determining when to recall products is a difficult ethical problem. Where a risk of injury is likely, a product should be recalled. This might occur when:

- a serious consumer illness or injury is caused by product contamination;
- there are similar complaints of illness or injury that apply to a specific product;
- a design or manufacturing failure could result in potential harm to consumers;
- there is defective product labelling that could result in potential harm to consumers, or where a product has been tampered with.

Pricing and Ethics

An important consideration in marketing ethics is whether or not the price of an offering is 'fair'. Key considerations concern **price gouging**, where the price of the offering is far higher than what is considered reasonable, **price discrimination**, where the price of an offering is set differently for certain groups of people, and price collusion, where competitors work together to set prices or distribution targets to the detriment of consumers and excluded competitors.

Price gouging occurs when a company charges more than governments perceive is fair for their offerings. It occurs when companies operate a demand pricing formula (see Chapter 9) where demand is very high, leading to very high prices being charged to customers. One example was the pricing of antiretroviral drugs in South Africa prior to 2002, when major global pharmaceutical companies charged very high prices for AIDS/HIV treatments despite generic versions being available at far lower prices. Of course, the issue was complicated by these companies holding global patents, but the issue raised by the world's media was not the legality of the situation but its morality.

Price discrimination involves setting different prices for different groups of people. Thus, price discrimination is linked to market segmentation (see Chapter 6). It is not unethical in itself when the product is differentiated for different groups. The practice is more questionable where there is no difference in the offer, and the price remains the only difference. Nevertheless, price discrimination occurs frequently. For instance, signs at tourist sites in different countries often show the price for foreigners versus the cost for domestic nationals (e.g. at the Taj Mahal in India, the price to visit the monument for international visitors is 25 times that of the cost for Indian nationals).

Price discrimination also occurs on airlines, e.g. easyJet and Ryanair use so-called **yield management** systems to sell airline tickets based on different prices being charged depending on the time of booking. Women's haircuts are frequently more expensive than men's, although there is some scope for the argument that the service provided is more attentive and takes longer. Until new European Union rules came into effect in 2012, women could obtain cheaper car insurance, sometimes by up to 40%, than men in Britain (King, 2012) from specialists such as Sheila's Wheels.

In some markets, the concept of price discrimination goes further, with each customer potentially paying a different price through **haggling** (see Kimes and Wirtz, 2003). Haggling is more common in some markets than in others (e.g. house and car buying in Europe), and in some countries compared with others (e.g. Middle Eastern and Southeast Asian countries such as Egypt, Morocco, Thailand, and Indonesia as opposed to West European countries like France, Sweden, and the UK). Do you remember the last time you haggled when buying something? Where were you? What were you buying?

Price Collusion

Some of the world's best-known companies have been fined for price collusion. In 2007, the US Department of Justice and the UK Office of Fair Trading fined British Airways (now part of International Airlines Group) £148m and £121.5m, respectively, after the company fixed fuel price surcharges with rival Virgin Atlantic between 2004 and 2006 (BBC News, 2007). BA eventually only paid half the fine in 2012 after protracted negotiations with the Office of Fair Trading (Russell 2012).

In 2012, the European Union fined Royal Philips Electronics (of the Netherlands) €313.4m, South Korea's LG Electronics €295.6m, a Philips–LG joint venture €391.9m, Panasonic €157.5m, Samsung €150.8m, Toshiba €28m, and Technicolor €38.6m for conspiring to set up two cartels which fixed the price of picture and display tubes for television and computer screens, in addition to market sharing, customer allocation, and commercial information exchange (Kanter, 2012).

Price collusion is regarded as unethical because it results in unfair, and higher, charges to customers, and it can stifle innovation—as competitors do not need to develop better competing offerings. In addition, as a result consumers do not benefit from improvements in quality and/or performance.

Universalism/Relativism in Marketing Ethics

Some cultures are less likely than others to perceive ethical dilemmas. Ethicists say that different groups of people see ethical situations from two perspectives. Under one perspective, ethicists suggest that universal ethical codes of practice should exist because there are some things that are simply 'wrong', no matter what the colour or creed of the people concerned (e.g. murder, bribery, extortion). This is termed universalism. The opposite argument, termed cultural relativism, suggests that different groups consider ethical situations from different viewpoints and that there is nothing wrong with this (e.g. gifts, corporate entertainment). The debate in international marketing ethics concerns itself with this dichotomy, i.e. cultural relativism versus ethical universalism.

For example, how should a director of a Western company ensure that local managers do not use bribery to ensure access to certain markets for the company's offerings? This problem is alleged to have occurred with the pharmaceutical manufacturer GSK in China (BBC News, 2013d). The excuse often made for bribery is that if managers didn't act this way, managers in other companies would, and they would win the business. From a cultural relativist perspective, such practice is ethically unacceptable, except where bribery might lead to a greater good, say widespread distribution of health-giving pharmaceuticals, whereas the universalist perspective suggests that bribery is a fundamental ethical breach regardless of the circumstances. In a study outlining American–Thai differences in ethical behaviour, American marketers were more likely than their Thai counterparts to perceive unethical marketing behaviours to be serious (Marta and Singhapakdi, 2005). In a separate study of how Thai managers made ethical decisions, Singhapakdi *et al*. (2000a) stated that one approach to improve ethical decision-making by Thai marketing managers would be to encourage idealism—the degree to which individuals 'assume that desirable consequences can, with the "right" action, always be obtained'—rather than relativism, where 'an individual rejects universal moral rules' (Forsyth, 1980).

Idealism could be encouraged through training programmes and communication of clear company policies on ethical matters. In another study, Singhapakdi *et al*. (2000b) found that there is a very strong positive relationship between a marketer's religiousness and their degree of idealism. In other words, the more religious you are, the more likely you are to hold universal ethical principles. Less religious marketers reject universal moral principles when evaluating situations with ethical content and the consequences of situations when examining them retrospectively.

A study of marketing ethics in Korea by Kim and Chun (2003) found that Koreans perceived the seriousness of ethical problems in order of importance as follows:

1 bribery;

2 unfair price increases;

3 exaggerated advertising;

4 sexual discrimination.

They found in their research that younger Koreans were less likely to perceive situations as having ethical content generally, whereas the older generation perceived less ethical content in bribery situations. Overall, they felt that a lack of ethical concern would have a negative impact on Korean business, affecting company performance, if there was no education on marketing ethics.

Microcultural differences have a big impact on perceived ethical problems, according to a study of the Javenese, Batak, and Indonesian-Chinese managers in Indonesia (Sarwono and Armstrong, 2001). Each subculture responded differently to situations with ethical content. As a result, the authors suggested that Indonesian managers and expatriates operating in Indonesia should undergo cultural training, including evaluating ethical perceptions held by local managers, together with the establishment of formalized codes of conduct.

Bribery

Transparency International, the international organization with a mission to stamp out bribery and corrupt practices around the world, published a Bribe Payers Index based on survey data to determine the propensity of companies to bribe public officials from 21 leading exporting nations shortly after the OECD Convention on Combating Bribery of Foreign Public Officials in International Business Transactions was introduced. In 2011, the worst perceived offender was Russia, followed closely by China. Companies in the top four countries least likely to pay bribes were in the Netherlands, Switzerland, Belgium, and Germany. The worst offending industries from which bribe payers were most likely to originate included public works contracts and construction, and utilities. Therefore companies in these industries have a greater need to provide ethical training, confidential helplines, and robust whistle-blowing procedures to allow employees

Research Insight 18.4

To take your learning further, you might wish to read this influential paper.

Saeed, M., Ahmed, Z. U, and Mukhtar, S-M. (2001), 'International marketing ethics from an Islamic perspective: a value-maximization approach', *Journal of Business Ethics*, **32, 127–42.**

This article explains why, in the search for a global ethical marketing framework, it is important to redefine the purpose of marketing from profit maximization to value maximization to ensure its adherence with the Qur'an and the teachings of the Holy Prophet. The authors argue that current Western approaches to international marketing based on profit maximization can lead to *Dhulum* (injustice/exploitation/oppression). The article outlines the implications of an Islamic ethical code of practice for the implementation of the marketing mix.

@ **Visit the Online Resource Centre to read the abstract and access the full paper.**

to highlight ethical breaches to senior managers without fear of penalty. Where bribery occurs, it is used to attempt either to influence potentially adverse legislative programmes, or to obtain favourable contracts at another company's expense. In order to comply with the UK Bribery Act 2010 companies must put in place procedures to deter employees from paying bribes (see Market Insight 18.5).

Market Insight 18.5

Alleged Bribery at Rolls-Royce

A former employee turned whistle-blower, Dick Taylor, alleged that Rolls-Royce had bribed the son of a former Indonesian president to win the Garuda airline engine contract by offering $20m and a Rolls-Royce car in 1990. Taylor's allegations, made as reply comments to Rolls-Royce news stories, caused Britain's Serious Fraud Office (SFO) to investigate further. In China, Rolls-Royce is also alleged to have made payments to an executive handling an order worth $2bn for engines Rolls-Royce supplied to Air China in 2005 and China Eastern Airlines in 2010. Rolls-Royce opened an internal enquiry, passing

its findings to the British SFO's investigators. It also appointed Lord Gold, a Conservative peers, to review its compliance procedures. The company outlined the following statement on bribery to its stakeholders.

Principles

- We are committed to conducting our activities in a wholly ethical manner, free from any form of bribery or corruption. We are committed to maintaining a high level of awareness among our employees, our suppliers and others with whom we do business of the latest rules and regulations relating to anti-bribery and corruption.

Market Insight 18.5
continued

- We comply with the applicable legislation on bribery and corruption wherever we operate and we cooperate appropriately with officials of the relevant government agencies.

- We only appoint intermediaries to represent our interests in the sales process who can demonstrate they fully comply with the principles of this Code and avoid bribery and corruption. We actively manage these intermediaries to ensure they continue to comply with these principles.

- We will exercise due caution when making charitable donations to ensure that they are appropriate and proportionate.

Bribery can be defined as "the receiving or offering of an undue reward to a public official or private individual in order to influence them in the exercise of their duty". Indirect bribery is when a payment is made via an intermediary.

We will:

- require any intermediaries in the sales process to comply with a code of ethics that is at least comparable to ours and to applicable laws;

- conduct thorough due diligence and only select intermediaries that meet our ethical requirements;

- only make payments to intermediaries that are proportionate, proper and legitimately due in relation to the services provided;

- ensure that internal controls are in place to prevent bribery and corruption; and

- ensure staff receive training to prevent bribery and corruption.

We will not:

- offer, promise or accept, directly or indirectly, anything of value that could be construed as a bribe; and

- pursue business that requires us or Rolls-Royce to engage in unethical or illegal activity.

Additionally, managers are expected to:

- set a personal example in promoting honesty and integrity in their business conduct.

Facilitation payments

Making a payment or a gift to an official to encourage or induce them to act more swiftly may appear to be an acceptable practice, or customary in some parts of the world. However, such payments or gifts, often known as 'facilitation payments', are illegal in many countries. Common circumstances in which facilitation payments are requested are:

- when obtaining permits, licences or other official documents to qualify a person to do business in a foreign country;

- when processing government papers such as visas or work orders;

- to provide security services for company people or assets; and

- to provide access to utilities such as water or power.

The company does not condone the making of facilitation payments.

If, however, you are faced with a situation in which a payment is demanded by an official and the demand is accompanied by a threat to your personal safety, you may pay. However, you must report this to your local senior manager as soon as possible, who must in turn notify the Director of Security and the Head of Business Ethics and Compliance or local ethics manager. Any such facilitation payments must be appropriately and accurately recorded.'

Sources: Rolls-Royce (2009); Milmo (2012); Miller (2013); Monaghan (2013).

1 **How should Rolls-Royce ensure that the bribery and corruption component of their ethics code of conduct is fully understood by its employees and contractors?**

2 **Is it *always* unethical to pay bribes when doing business? Might there be a circumstance in which it is ethical to pay a bribe?**

3 **Can you think of other companies that have been mired in bribery allegations? Look into the case of TeliaSonera in Uzbekistan, for example.**

Chapter Summary

To consolidate your learning, the key points from this chapter are summarized below:

■ **Define sustainable marketing and its implications for marketing practice.**

Sustainable marketing has been termed the third age of green marketing and is concerned with ecological, equitable, and economic impacts of marketing practice. It is concerned with ensuring that marketing activities meet the needs of existing generations and, in doing so, do not compromise meeting the needs of future generations. As a result, companies are re-imagining marketing practices, for example, by recovering the costs of investment financing over longer payback periods, by emphasizing the full costs of purchase to customers, by considering all members of the supply chain and ensuring that they are paid equitably, and by demarketing consumption to vulnerable groups of consumers or those who are overconsuming.

■ **Define marketing ethics.**

Marketing ethics is concerned with how marketers go about the marketing process. In particular, it is the application of moral principles to decision-making in marketing and the consideration of the outcomes of those decisions.

■ **Explain the common ethical norms applied in marketing.**

Marketing ethics can be divided into normative and descriptive branches, which distinguish between how we *ought* to act in a given marketing decision-making situation and how people *actually behave* when making marketing decisions. There are five main normative approaches to marketing decision-making: deontological ethics (doing the *right* thing because it's the *right* thing to do), teleological ethics (the *right* thing to do is the thing with the right consequences), managerial egoism (doing the *right* thing because it's the best thing to do), utilitarianism (doing the *right* thing for the largest number of people), and virtue ethics (doing the *right* thing for everyone), each of which can be applied to any given ethical situation.

■ **Describe the role of ethics in marketing decision-making.**

Models of marketing decision-making outline the importance of the ethical content of a situation, the importance of 'significant others', employees' values, and the ethical training given by a company in line with its own ethical policy. Hunt and Vitell's (2006) model of marketing decision-making is the best known, stressing the importance of considering what is the *right* thing to do (deontological norms) and what are the *right* intended outcomes for us to follow (teleological norms).

■ **Understand how ethical breaches occur in marketing programmes and activities.**

Ethical breaches can occur in all areas of an organization's marketing activity including distribution, pricing, promotion, and product policies. From a services marketing perspective, the people and process components of the extended marketing mix are particularly appropriate, as ethical breaches are often undertaken by employees who may or may not be following company ethical guidelines and codes of conduct appropriately.

 # Review Questions

1 What is sustainable marketing?

2 How will sustainable marketing impact on marketing practice?

3 How do we define marketing ethics?

4 What are the common ethical norms applied in marketing?

5 What role does ethics in marketing play in the marketing decision-making process?

6 What are key ethical considerations when pricing offerings?

7 What are key ethical considerations when promoting offerings?

8 What are key ethical considerations when distributing offerings?

9 What are key ethical concerns when developing the product offering?

10 What is bribery?

 # Worksheet Summary

To apply the knowledge you have gained from this chapter and test your understanding of marketing, sustainability, and ethics visit the **Online Resource Centre** and complete Worksheet 18.1.

Discussion Questions

1 Having read Case Insight 18.1, how should innocent achieve a high level of recyclable content in their bottles without making the offering look less attractive and hence lose sales?

2 Go online to find examples of companies that have a strong stance on sustainable marketing. Are there any common characteristics across these companies? (Hint: take a look at any of the following companies' websites and search for their sustainability credentials: Britain's Marks and Spencer, Sweden's SCA, France's Danone, Nigeria's Guaranty Trust Bank).

3 Re-read the section of the chapter on normative ethics. Consider SSL International plc's condom product Durex, designed to reduce the proportion of people sustaining sexually transmitted diseases (STDs) and women having unwanted pregnancies. To what extent might it be appropriate for SSL International to promote condom usage to young children, particularly in 1) Catholic countries and 2) African countries? Discuss this ethical problem using the following normative ethical approaches (check the definitions in the Glossary if necessary):

   A managerial egoism—the principle of managerial self-interest;
   B utilitarianism—the principle of the greater good for the greater number of people;
   C deontological ethics—the principle of duty-based ethics.

4 Consider whether or not it is unethical to act in the following ways in the following circumstances:

   A You are a salesperson working for a South African construction company trying to secure a road-building contract in Nigeria. You know that if you do not pay a 'commission' to the public official in charge of tendering for the project, you will not win the contract. Should you pay the 'commission' or do you have other choices of action?
   B You are a London-based banker. A potential new client in Dubai insists on taking you to a very exclusive restaurant at the Burj al Arab at her expense to discuss a loan she requires to purchase a new building for her rapidly expanding business. Should you accept?

C   You are a farmer supplying a large chain supermarket in Copenhagen with selected prime cuts of meat products. The supermarket requests an upfront 'listing' fee of 170,000 Danish krone before they can accept you as a supplier. You can then expect high-value orders of millions of krone. Should you pay the 'listing fee' to the supermarket? Would the situation be different in France? Why?

Visit the **Online Resource Centre** and complete the **Multiple Choice** Questions to assess your knowledge of Chapter 18.

References

Anon. (2012a), 'Making AIDS history', *Guardian*, 3 December, retrieve from: http://www.guardian.co.uk/sustainable-business/anglo-american-world-aids-day accessed 15 April 2013.

Anon. (2012b), 'Getting a second opinion on community development performance', *Guardian*, 16 October, retrieve from: http://www.guardian.co.uk/sustainable-business/anglo-amercian-community-development accessed 15 April 2013.

Anon. (2012c), 'Canada's graphic cigarette pack warnings rank high', *CP24*, 14 November, retrieve from: http://www.cp24.com/news/canada-s-graphic-cigarette-pack-warnings-rank-high-1.1037491 accessed 15 April 2013.

Anon. (2013), 'Schumpeter. Sex, drugs and hope: how big business fought AIDS in South Africa', *Economist*, 13 April, 69.

Bainbridge, J. (2013), 'The *Marketing* interview. Jon Goldstone: Unilever', *Marketing*, 16 January, 22–3.

Baines, P, and Worcester, R. (2005), 'When the British Tommy went to war, public opinion followed', *Journal of Public Affairs*, 5(1), 4–19.

Baker, R. (2012), 'Unilever: Sustainability marketing is biggest challenge', *Marketing Week*, 12 December, retrieve from: http://www.marketingweek.co.uk/news/unilever-sustainability-marketing-is-biggest-challenge/4001322 article on 12th December 2012, accessed 13 April 2013.

Baudrillard, J. (2005), *The System of Objects* (trans. James Benedict), London: Verso Books.

BBC News (2007), 'BA's price fix fine reaches £270m', Wednesday 1 August, retrieve from: http://news.bbc.co.uk/1/hi/business/6925397.stm accessed 16 April 2013.

BBC News (2010), 'Timeline: China milk scandal', *BBC News*, 25 January, retrieve from: http://news.bbc.co.uk/1/hi/7720404.stm accessed 13 April 2013.

BBC News (2012a), 'Standard Chartered hit by $300m in Iran fines', *BBC News*, 10 December, retrieve from: http://www.bbc.co.uk/news/business-20669650 accessed 14 April 2013.

BBC News (2012b), 'Polish ritual slaughter illegal, court rules', *BBC News*, 28 November, retrieve from: http://www.bbc.co.uk/news/world-europe-20523809 accessed 13 April 2013.

BBC News (2013a), 'Transocean agrees to pay $1.4bn oil spill fine', BBC News, 3 January, retrieve from: http://www.bbc.co.uk/news/business-20905472 accessed 14 April 2013.

BBC News (2013b), 'News Corp will start its new life with $2.6bn after split', *BBC News*, 8 March, retrieve from: http://www.bbc.co.uk/news/business-21720220 accessed 13 April 2013.

BBC News (2013c), 'Timeline: LIBOR fixing scandal', *BBC News*, 6 February, retrieve from: http://www.bbc.co.uk/news/business-18671255 accessed 16 April 2013.

BBC News (2013d), 'GlaxoSmithKline finance head banned from leaving China', *BBC News*, 18 July, retrieve from: http://bbc.co.uk/news/business-23352844, accessed 20 July 2013.

Benady, D. (2013), 'Reinventing sustainability', *Marketing*, 27 February, 26–7.

Bolger, M. (2013), 'Case study: Norwegian Seafood Council: Marketing splash', *Marketer*, March/April, 20–3.

Boutin, X. and Guerrero, G. (2008), 'The "Loi Galland" and French consumer prices', June, retrieve from: www.insee.fr/en/indicateurs/analys_conj/archives/june2008_d1.pdf accessed 16 April 2013.

Bridges, C.M. and Wilhelm, W.B. (2008), 'Going beyond green: the "why" and "how" of integrating sustainability into the marketing curriculum', *Journal of Marketing Education*, 30(1), 33–46.

Brownsell, A. (2013a), 'Barclays orders staff to "buy in" to ethical values', *Marketing*, 20 February, 5.

Brownsell, A. (2013b), 'Barclays plots regeneration', *Marketing*, 20 February, 12–13.

Bryant, B. (2011), 'Deepwater Horizon and the Gulf oil spill–the key questions answered', *Guardian*, 20 April, retrieve from: http://www.guardian.co.uk/environment/2011/

apr/20/deepwater-horizon-key-questions-answered accessed 13 April 2013.

Buchholz, R. A. (1991), 'Corporate responsibility and the good society. From economics to ecology: factors which influence corporate policy decisions', *Business Horizons*, 34, 4, 19–31.

Cai, Y., Jo, H., and Pan, C. (2011), 'Doing well while doing bad? CSR in controversial industry sectors', *Journal of Business Ethics*, 108(4), 467–80.

CIM (2012), 'The Chartered Institute of Marketing. The code of professional standards 2012', retrieve from: http://www.cim.co.uk/Files/codeofprofessionalstandards10.pdf accessed 16 April 2013.

Collins, N. (2013), 'Ikea recalls cakes from 23 countries after sewage bacteria found', *Telegraph*, 5 March, retrieve from: http://www.telegraph.co.uk/foodanddrink/foodanddrinknews/9910417/Ikea-recalls-cakes-in-23-countries-after-sewage-bacteria-found.html accessed 13 April 2013.

Crann, J. (2012), 'The soapbox: Twitter no place for propaganda wars', *Times Herald*, 16 November, retrieve from: http://www.mjtimes.sk.ca/Opinion/Columns/2012-11-16/article-3122333/The-Soapbox%3A-Twitter-no-place-for-propaganda-wars/1 accessed 16 April 2013.

Daniels, J. and Holmes, C. (2005), *Responsible Marketing to Children: Exploring the Impact on Adults' Attitudes and Behaviour*, London: Business in the Community.

Debeljak, J., Krkač, K., and Bušljeta Banks, I. (2011), 'Acquiring CSR practices: from deception to authenticity', *Social Responsibility Journal*, 7(1), 5–22.

Ferrell, O. C. and Gresham, L. G. (1985), 'A contingency framework for understanding ethical decision making in marketing', *Journal of Marketing*, 49(Summer), 87–96.

Forsyth, D. R. (1980), 'A taxonomy of ethical ideologies', *Journal of Personality and Social Psychology*, 39(1), 175–84.

Friedman, M. (1979), 'The social responsibility of business is to increase profit', in T. Beanchamp and N. Bowie (eds), *Ethical Theory and Business*, Englewood Cliffs, NJ: Prentice Hall.

Gaski, J. E. (1999), 'Does marketing ethics really have anything to say? A critical inventory of the literature', *Journal of Business Ethics*, 18, 315–34.

Gu, M. (2012), 'An introduction of the anti-monopoly law in China', *China Law Vision*, 23 October, retrieve from: http://www.chinalawvision.com/2012/10/articles/competitionantitrust-law-of-th/an-introduction-of-the-antimonopoly-law-in-china/ accessed 16 April 2013.

Halfacree, G. (2013), 'Microsoft hit with €561m fine', *Bit-Tech*, 7 March, retrieve from: http://www.bit-tech.net/news/bits/2013/03/07/microsoft-eu-fine/1 accessed 16 April 2013.

Hasan, M. (2012), 'Halal hysteria', *New Statesman*, 9 May, retrieve from: http://www.newstatesman.com/politics/politics/2012/05/halal-hysteria accessed 13 April 2013.

Hunt, S.D. and Vitell, S. (1986), 'A general theory of marketing ethics', *Journal of Macromarketing*, 6(1), 5–16.

Hunt, S.D. and Vitell, S. J. (2006), 'The general theory of marketing ethics: a revision and three questions', *Journal of Macromarketing*, 26(2), 143–53.

Kanter, J. (2012), 'Europe fines electronics makers $1.92m', *New York Times*, 5 December, retrieve from: http://www.nytimes.com/2012/12/06/business/global/europe-fines-7-companies-for-picture-tube-price-fixing.html?_r=0&adxnnl=1&adxnnlx=1366130644-/WEXfmLEpfKw/Kuo3CwqAA accessed 16 April 2013.

Kim, S. Y. and Chun, S. Y. (2003), 'A study of marketing ethics in Korea. What do Koreans care about?', *International Journal of Management*, 20(3), 377–83.

Kimes, S. E. and Wirtz, J. (2003), 'Has revenue management become acceptable? Findings from an international study on the perceived fairness of rate fences', *Journal of Service Research*, 6(2), 125–35.

King, M. (2012), 'Women count cost of car insurance as EU gender rules come into force', *Guardian*, 21 December, retrieve from: http://www.guardian.co.uk/money/2012/dec/21/women-car-insurance-eu accessed 13 April 2013.

Laczniak, G. R. and Murphy, P. E. (1993), *Ethical Marketing Decisions: The Higher Road*, Englewood Cliffs, NJ: Prentice Hall.

Liu, F., Cheng, H., and Li, J. (2009), 'Consumer responses to sex appeal advertising: a cross-cultural study', *International Marketing Review*, 26(4/5), 501–20.

Maitland, I. (2002), 'Priceless drugs: how should life-saving drugs be priced?', *Business Ethics Quarterly*, 12(4), 451–80.

Marta, J. K. M. and Singhapakdi, A. (2005), 'Comparing Thai and US businesspeople: perceived intensity of unethical marketing practices, corporate ethical values and perceived importance of ethics', *International Marketing Review*, 22(5), 562–77.

Martin, R. L. (2002), 'The virtue matrix: calculating the return on corporate responsibility', *Harvard Business Review*, 80, 5–11.

Mautner, T. (ed.) (1999), *Penguin Dictionary of Philosophy*, London: Penguin.

Miller, R. (2013), 'SFO "considering end to Rolls-Royce bribe enquiry', *Times*, 23 March, retrieve from: http://www.thetimes.co.uk/tto/business/industries/engineering/article3721522.ece accessed 13 April 2013.

Milmo, D. (2012), 'Rolls-Royce faces bribery claim inquiry', *Guardian*, 9 December, retrieve from: http://www.guardian.co.uk/business/2012/dec/09/rolls-royce-faces-bribery-inquiry accessed 15 April 2013.

Mintel (2013), 'Coca-Cola brings anti-obesity push to the UK—11th April 2013', London: Mintel International Group, retrieve from: www.mintel.com accessed 15 April 2013.

Mock, V. (2013), 'EU fines Telefonica and Portugal Telecom', MarketWatch, 23 January, retrieve from: http://www.marketwatch.com/story/eu-fines-telefonica-and-portugal-telecom-2013-01-23 accessed 16 April 2013.

Monaghan, A. (2013), 'Rolls-Royce commissions Lord Gold review amid bribery allegations', *Telegraph*, 10 January, retrieve from: http://www.telegraph.co.uk/finance/newsbysector/industry/9794281/Rolls-Royce-commissions-Lord-Gold-review-amid-bribery-allegations.html accessed 15 April 2013.

Nantel, J. and Weeks, W. A. (1996), 'Marketing ethics: is there more to it than the utilitarian approach?', *European Journal of Marketing*, 30(5), 9–19.

O'Shaughnessy, N. J. and Baines, P. (2009), 'The selling of terror: the symbolisations and positioning of jihad', *Marketing Theory*, 9(2), 227–41.

Oxford Dictionaries (2013), *'Ethics'*, retrieve from: http://oxforddictionaries.com/definition/english/ethics?q=ethics accessed 16 April 2013.

Peattie, K. (2001), 'Towards sustainability: the third age of green marketing', *Marketing Review*, 2, 129–46.

Peattie, K. and Crane, A. (2005), 'Green marketing: legend, myth, farce or prophesy?', *Qualitative Market Research*, 8(4), 357–70.

Polman, P. (2012), 'Captain Planet—Interview with Paul Polman', *Harvard Business Review*, June, 112–18.

Pope, N. K. L., Voges, K. E., and Brown, M. R. (2004), 'The effect of provocation in the form of mild erotica on attitude to the ad and corporate image: differences between cause-related and product-based advertising', *Journal of Advertising*, 33(1), 69–82.

Rao, C. P. and Singhapakdi, A. (1997), 'Marketing ethics: a comparison between services and other marketing professionals', *Journal of Services Marketing*, 11(6), 409–26.

Rawls, J. (1972), *A Theory of Justice*, Cambridge, MA: Harvard University Press.

Rolls-Royce (2009), 'Global Code of Ethics', London: Rolls-Royce plc, retrieve from: http://www.rolls-royce.com/Images/ethicscode_eng_tcm92-13314.pdf accessed 13 April 2013.

Rushe, D. (2012), 'BP sues Halliburton for Deepwater Horizon oil spill clean-up costs', *Guardian*, 3 January, retrieve from: http://www.guardian.co.uk/business/2012/jan/03/bp-sues-halliburton-over-deepwater accessed 14 April 2013.

Russell, J. (2012), 'OFT halves British Airways fine to settle price fixing probe', *Telegraph*, 19 April, retrieve from: http://www.telegraph.co.uk/finance/newsbysector/transport/9214396/OFT-halves-British-Airways-fine-to-settle-price-fixing-probe.html accessed 15 April 2013.

Saeed, M., Ahmed, Z. U., and Mukhtar, S-M. (2001), 'International marketing ethics from an Islamic perspective: a value-maximization approach', *Journal of Business Ethics*, 32, 127–42.

Sager, I. (2013), 'The most expensive product recalls', *Bloomberg Businessweek*, 17 January, retrieve from: http://images.businessweek.com/slideshows/2013-01-17/the-most-expensive-product-recalls#slide11 accessed 13 April 2013.

Sarwono, S. S. and Armstrong, R. W. (2001), 'Microcultural differences and perceived ethical problems: an international business perspective', *Journal of Business Ethics*, 30, 41–56.

Sharma, A., Gopalkrishnan, I. R., Mehotra, A., and Krishnan, R. (2010), 'Sustainability and business-to-business marketing: a framework and implications', *Industrial Marketing Management*, 39, 330–41

Sheth, J. N., Sethia, N. K., and Srinivas, S. (2011), 'Mindful consumption: a customer-centric approach to sustainability', *Journal of the Academy of Marketing Science*, 39, 21–39.

Singhapakdi, A., Salyachivin, S., Virakul, B., and Veerayangkur, V. (2000a), 'Some important factors underlying ethical decision-making of managers in Thailand', *Journal of Business Ethics*, 27, 271–84.

Singhapakdi, A., Marta, J. K., Rallapalli, K. C., and Rao, C. P. (2000b), 'Towards an understanding of religiousness and marketing ethics: an empirical study', *Journal of Business Ethics*, 27, 305–19.

Skapinker, M. (2010), 'Long-term corporate plans may be lost in translation' *Financial Times*, 23 November.

Smith, A. (1776), *The Wealth of Nations*, London: Penguin, 1982.

Spencer, R. (2008), 'China reveals 300,000 were made ill by tainted milk', *Telegraph*, 2 December, retrieve from: www.telegraph.co.uk/news/worldnews/asia/china/3540917/China-reveals-300000-children-were-made-ill-by-tainted-milk.html accessed 13 April 2013.

Treanor, J. (2013), 'Barclays closes controversial tax avoidance unit', *Observer*, 9 February, retrieve from: http://www.guardian.co.uk/business/2013/feb/09/barclays-closes-tax-avoidance-unit, accessed 16 April 2013.

van Dam, Y.K. and Apeldoorn, P.A.C. (1996), 'Sustainable marketing', *Journal of Macromarketing*, 16, 45–56.

van de Wen, B. (2008), 'An ethical framework for the marketing of corporate social responsibility', *Journal of Business Ethics*, 82(2), 339–352.

WCED (World Commission on Environment and Development) (1987), *Our Common Future—The Brundtland Report*, Oxford: University University Press.

Chapter 19
Critical and Postmodern Perspectives in Marketing

Learning Outcomes

After studying this chapter, you will be able to:

▶ Assess the negative impact that marketing has on society

▶ Define the possible meanings and key features of postmodern marketing

▶ Discuss the reversal of production and consumption in the postmodern context

▶ Explain the important role of semiotics in consumption

▶ Understand how to deconstruct marketing 'texts', including advertisements

Case Insight 19.1
Livity

Market Insight 19.1
Flogging a Dead Horse

Market Insight 19.2
Reality TV: Engaging Brands

Market Insight 19.3
Back to the Past: Return of the Trabant

Market Insight 19.4
Cadbury's Not-So-Secret Secret

Market Insight 19.5
Deconstructing Gaga's 'Fame'

Case Insight 19.1

How should organizations design their communications campaigns when targeting hard-to-reach non-traditional communities? We speak to Callum McGeogh, Creative Director of Livity, to find out more about work they undertook for their client ChildLine, the national telephone helpline of the UK children's charity NSPCC.

Twelve years ago, the founders were two youth marketers disillusioned with selling stuff to kids. They believed instead that they could infiltrate marketing budgets to 'sell' the social messages that get drowned out by the very same brands that they were going to hijack. So, we created Livity, the Youth Engagement Agency. Our purpose was to make a measurable positive impact on the lives of young people in order to make Britain a better place to live (and still make time to play hide and seek). Described by one client as 'a marketing agency with a youth club in the middle of it', our agency's unique set-up gives us the benefit of real-time ethnographic insight into the audience we create and co-create our campaigns, platforms, content, and training for.

We open the doors of our Brixton HQ to over 5,000 annual visits from young people, every day of the working week, to give them the chance to make more of their lives, partly by contributing to our in-house magazine *Live*. This direct engagement with our community is one of the primary reasons behind our success. Fusing community and enterprise creates opportunity, understanding, and innovation. Our open-door policy brings contributors from all social backgrounds, ranging from graduates, school and college students, to young people recently released from prison, or excluded from school or in care. Because life for young people changes quickly, they reserve the right to change their minds, and to defy categorization and expectations, which they frequently do. Consequently, the Livity office is a bustling place, inspiring new thinking, providing fresh perspectives,

and delivering ongoing ethnographic understanding of youth audiences. Our engagement with young people takes place through provision of work experience, mentoring, consultation, and apprenticeships. It gives us an opportunity for the mutually beneficial exchange of ideas and information, informing every campaign we deliver. For example, we often know about new trends in technology, communication, lifestyle, and social issues months, and sometimes years, ahead of the curve.

When the NSPCC wanted to increase young people's awareness of the brand and the helpline number, and to increase their propensity to contact ChildLine (via phone or website), especially if they were in distress, Livity was an obvious first choice. One of ChildLine's key audiences is a black and minority ethnic (BME) audience, particularly older teens and boys, who are often harder to reach and engage. Because urban music, social media, MC-ing and performance is at the heart of the BME target audience's culture, we thought it could be used as a way to help them express themselves. We felt that strategic use of video and YouTube could be the entry point for a social media platform which our audience would be eager to view but also create, comment, and share content online. But this strategy would need to be supported by digital marketing, PR, and partnerships.

Therefore our problem was: how would we design the campaign to raise awareness of ChildLine using young people's affiliation for music?

Introduction

Do organizations seduce us into buying offerings or experiences we think we want but don't need? Have you ever felt that a company's advertising represses your individuality? Do you think that marketing theory and/or marketing practice need to be reformed? Is all marketing activity benevolent and beyond reproach? Have you read aspects of this textbook and wished that marketing practice was somehow different? We discuss some of these questions and more in this chapter.

Critical marketing and **postmodern marketing**, the key areas considered in this chapter, are very different topics from those considered in mainstream marketing. Both marketing sub-disciplines are anti-foundational. In other words, both critique the foundations of marketing. Postmodern marketing emerged in the late 1980s, but was kick-started in the UK with the writings of Brown (1995, 1997). Critical marketing emerged formally around the same time (Murray and Ozanne, 1991; Alvesson, 1994), although Tadajewski (2010) has argued that there has been a critical tradition in marketing since the 1930s. From Hetrick and Lozada's (1999) perspective, critical marketing is anti-marketing theory (e.g. by critiquing its inherent weaknesses in failing to promote the greater societal good), whilst postmodern marketing is marketing anti-theory (e.g. by critiquing how supposed marketing maxims do not operate in the way that they are said to do). However, not everyone would agree that critical marketing is anti-marketing (Burton, 2001). Saren (2009) has also suggested that critical marketers can adopt three different perspectives, only one of which might be labelled anti-marketing.

1) Oppositional—to critique mainstream marketing from both inside and outside the discipline.

2) Revivalist—by working inside the discipline to encourage it to return to its original methods in order to be more sceptical and critical.

3) Therapeutic—by working inside the discipline to encourage the uptake of a wider set of methodological techniques in order to become more critical.

We will seek to define each of these two marketing sub-disciplines throughout this chapter. We discuss critical and postmodern marketing because marketing textbook authors have been criticized for not including a critique of marketing in the past (Burton, 2001), as the following comment demonstrates: 'Marketing management texts work up a managerial world devoid of discordance … awash with manufactured consensus' (Hackley, 2003: 1327). We genuinely hope that readers of this text will recognize that although much of this textbook deals with marketing from a managerialist and pro-marketing perspective, because that is the dominant perspective in the marketing discipline, we also seek to balance this orientation by encouraging you as marketing scholars and practitioners to become more critical of how marketing operates, and to assess and re-assess its performance and the performance of the academics who teach you. As Tadajewski (2010) explains, it is important that you, as marketing scholars, do not rote learn marketing theories and assess them uncritically.

In this chapter, we provide an insight into what is critical marketing, what is postmodern marketing, how production and consumption are reversed in postmodern marketing, what is semiotics and its role in consumption, and, finally how marketing texts (i.e. anything which conveys a message) can be deconstructed. First, we consider the critical marketing perspective.

The Critical Marketing Perspective

Some consider the ideology of marketing to be suspect, believing it to be rooted in big business, mass consumer sovereignty, and excess supply over demand and ever-increasing consumption (Brownlie and Saren, 1992). Our argument is that not all marketing's contributions to society are good. As a consequence, we should develop a critical approach to understanding marketing. To truly understand the discipline, we should study both mainstream and critical marketing, as they are interdependent (Shankar, 2009). For Saren (2011: 95), 'critical marketing analysis and concepts have an important role at the theoretical level in problematizing hitherto uncontentious marketing areas to reveal underlying institutional and theoretical dysfunctionalities'. For Brownlie (2006), mainstream marketing thought does not sufficiently consider how social relations in marketing are culturally and historically conditioned and that more pluralistic research methods need to be used to right this wrong. A critical approach to marketing ensures that we consider the following.

- The need to evaluate and re-evaluate marketing activities, categories, and frameworks, and to improve them so that marketing operates in a desirable manner within society.

- How marketing knowledge is developed and the extent to which this is based on our contemporary social world. For example, much of current marketing knowledge is based on American (and certainly Western) practice and research. What implications does this have for the rest of the world? Otherwise marketing can, 'be learned from the many varieties of market that exist rather than concentrating on branded, mass consumption products in developed economies' (Easton, 2002).

- How do the historical and cultural conditions in which we operate, as consumers and as students of marketing, impact on how we see marketing as a discipline?

- How marketing can benefit from other intellectual perspectives, e.g. social anthropology, social psychology, linguistics, philosophy, and sociology (see Burton, 2001).

Some key topics in critical marketing are marketing as manipulation, commodity fetishism, and the nature of need and choice (see also Tadajewski, 2010). We consider each of these in turn.

Marketing as Manipulation

Over the whole of its life, marketing has been open to the charge that it serves its own masters rather than consumers, and that it supports the **capitalist** rather than the labouring classes. Packard (1960) was the first to offer a really detailed critique of how marketing persuaded its target audiences, which he argued was often covert and manipulative, and, importantly, frequently without people understanding how they were being persuaded. Marketers and public relations officers frame their communications in a certain way to make them more persuasive. **Framing** is both the action of presenting persuasive communication and the action of audiences in interpreting that communication so as to assimilate it into their existing understanding (see Scheufele and Tewksbury, 2007). This framing can take place via the framing of situations (e.g. by highlighting sales promotions available for a fixed time only), attributes (e.g. by highlighting the usage features of, say, a mobile phone), choices (e.g. by showing a potential car buyer options across the range), actions (e.g. buy now, pay later schemes), issues (e.g. BP explaining its version of why the Deep Water Horizon incident occurred), responsibilities (e.g. the NSPCC explaining the need to stamp out child cruelty by donating funds), and news (e.g. companies explaining their versions of why a chief executive has been replaced) (see Hallahan, 1999).

The problem arises when framing is taken too far. At this point is some marketing promotion really corporate propaganda? For example, Levi Roots, the man behind the Reggae Reggae sauce company, explained to investors on the British reality TV investment show *Dragon's Den* that his sauce was developed from his grandmother's recipe and that he had been selling it for 15 years at the Notting Hill Carnival. After winning the funding and setting up the company, it emerged that his 'heritage' story was 'his marketing ploy' or, to put it less euphemistically, a complete lie (Barnes, 2011).

Visit the **Online Resource Centre** and complete Internet Activity 19.1 to learn more about manipulative practices in marketing.

Commodity Fetishism

This perspective, derived from Marxist economic theory (Marx, 1867), proposes that society is increasingly overly dominated by consumption, thereby fetishising it (i.e. placing supreme importance on it). Marx suggested that, prior to industrialization, goods were produced for their use-value. In other words, a producer manufactured a product for a user and exchanged it directly with the customer. After industrialization, the social relationship between producer and user changed in a way which, Marx argued, exploited the workers for their labour, as they became removed from the product they produced and paid on a piece rate rather than on a share of the financial return generated as a result of the labour. In the process, the commodity produced acquired exchange-value as it became tradable with other commodities within the capitalist market system, benefiting the capitalist (i.e. the investor). Marx felt that the rigid pursuit of capitalism was so doctrinal that it represented a religious ideology. In that sense, the commodities produced as a result of capitalist endeavour took on a religious aura, worshipped by those who were 'mystified' (i.e. seduced) by their perceived value (Sherover, 1979). The idea that we are worshipping consumption is linked to the notion of whether or not marketers are meeting our wants and needs. An unwelcome example of how consumer and worker needs were subverted in favour of those of the capitalist is that of the Horsemeat Scandal which took place in Europe in 2012 (see Market Insight 19.1).

Market Insight 19.1

Flogging a Dead Horse

On 16 January 2013, the Food Safety Authority of Ireland reported traces of equine DNA in products labelled 'beef' burgers supplied to Silvercrest Foods in Ireland and Dalepak Hambleton in Britain. As a result, ten million burgers were removed from shelves by supermarket retailers including Aldi, Lidl, Tesco,

Iceland, and Dunnes Stores. Frozen meat at Freeza Meats Company in Northern Ireland was found to contain 80% horsemeat, forcing Asda to withdraw its supplies from the shelves. Later, Findus UK 'beef' lasagne, supplied by French company Comigel, was found to contain 100% horsemeat. Worse, the French company had supplied 28 different companies in 13 European states. It quickly became apparent that Britain and Ireland were not the only countries

Market Insight 19.1
continued

affected. Swiss food giant Nestlé was forced to remove two pasta meals from supermarkets in Italy and Spain. German discount chain Lidl was forced to remove ready meals from its Finnish, Danish, and Swedish stores after finding that certain meat products were contaminated with horsemeat. Other contaminated products were found in other European countries including France, Austria, Norway, the Netherlands, and Germany. Unsurprisingly, consumers and politicians alike were shocked and appalled at the idea that the food they were eating was something other than it purported to be. If they were eating horse labelled as beef, what else might they be eating? For a short while, consumer trust was shattered. Kantar Worldpanel, the market research company, reported that burger sales in Britain recorded a 43% drop in the four weeks after the scandal broke and sales of frozen ready meals went down 13% over the same period.

The key question is: who was at fault? Was it the local authorities (who enforce food safety), the retailers (who stock and test the products), the criminals who mislabelled and switched the product, the suppliers (who process and produce the product), the food standards agencies in the countries concerned, or even the consumer (for buying ever cheaper products from their supermarkets)?

Sources: Anon. (2013a); Lucas (2013); Press Association (2013).

1 What marketing factors, if any, do you think led to the scandal arising?

2 Who do you think was at fault? Why do you say this?

3 From a marketing perspective, what do you think can be done to rebuild consumer trust?

Findus UK 'beef' lasagne, supplied by French company Comigel, was found to contain 100% horsemeat
Source: istock © OlgaMiltsova.

Need and Choice

The dominant view perpetuated by mainstream marketing theorists and practitioners is that marketing works towards meeting the needs of customers and consumers. However, Alvesson (1994), who comes from outside the marketing discipline, has completely rejected this notion. He argues that people in affluent societies seek more and more offerings without gaining any further long-term satisfaction from such consumption, because much of the consumption is superficial anyway and because appealing to people's fantasies and highlighting their imperfections (so as to encourage them to reduce these feelings of inadequacy by buying a particular offering) leads to narcissistic tendencies. Inherent in marketing is the notion that more choice is good, when in fact more choice leads to customer confusion and a decline in trust (Newman, 2001). The problem is that, as Saren (2007) contends, for many people 'to have is to be'. In other words, the meaning of life for many is consumption (see Research Insight 19.1). A further problem is that some customers are persuaded and manipulated into purchasing offerings that they do not necessarily want or which are unfit for their requirements. For example, financial services companies in the UK have been charged with mis-selling payment protection insurance (PPI). By 2013, British banks had had to put aside £14bn to settle customers' compensation claims (Osborne, 2013). Another example, and part of the reason behind the economic recession after 2008, is that banks were irresponsible in their lending policies by lending to people who could ill afford the repayments. Worthington and Durkin (2012) discuss how banks, together with irresponsible customers (who, they argue, borrowed more than they should have), actually destroyed value in the banking sector.

Although the aggregate marketing system (Wilkie and Moore, 1999; see also Chapter 1) distributes life-saving medicines, food, and important utilities (e.g. heat and light), it also distributes arms, alcohol, tobacco, and gambling products. These are products most would regard as dangerous to our health and well-being. Of course, in many cultures around the world, people enjoy drinking, smoking, and gambling. However, we are fooling ourselves, especially if we use these to excess, if we think that we are really satisfying our own needs and not causing ourselves harm, as

Research Insight 19.1

To take your learning further, you might wish to read this influential paper.

Saren, M. (2007), 'To have is to be? A critique of self-creation through consumption', *Marketing Review*, **7(4), 343–54.**

This highly readable article critiques the notion that consumers link their identity to their consumption activity and thereby derive satisfaction. Saren argues that the consumption process, seen from the critical theoretical perspective, actually leads to a never-ending cycle of desire which is never satisfied, and so a consumer's identity can never be complete.

Visit the Online Resource Centre to read the abstract and access the full paper.

all three can have addictive properties to varying degrees. Equally, the products of the arms indus-try are used to defend countries, but if access to these goods is not sufficiently restricted, they can also be used for great evil. A case in point is the lack of restrictions in the USA on access to the purchase of guns, which have been used in countless massacres over the years including the murder of 20 schoolchildren and six staff at the Sandy Hook Elementary School in Connecticut in 2012. What might seem obvious to an observer, namely that guns should either be severely restricted to certain types of firearm and/or certain kinds of people, is less obvious in many parts of America, where the National Rifle Association (NRA) presents itself as a powerful lobbying pres-ence in Congress, and where the right to bear arms is enshrined in the US constitution.

Therefore, unless told otherwise by government regulators, the aggregate marketing system (Wilkie and Moore, 1999) will distribute anything. If prostitution and soft drugs, such as cannabis, were made legal in Britain, the aggregate marketing system would distribute them. It already does this in the Netherlands, for instance, where these practices are no longer illegal. In that sense the aggregate marketing system in itself is inherently amoral. Not immoral, i.e. designed to harm, but amoral, i.e. designed without any care as to whether it harms or not. The system is only made moral by the decisions made by government and other institutional actors who regu-late the aggregate marketing system. Illegal offerings can be marketed in almost the same way as legal offerings. For example, this has occurred via the 'dark web'—hidden websites where illegal goods and services are sold, including drugs, forged passports, guns, and stolen credit card details, among other ill-gotten booty (see Franklin, 2013). Examples of these websites are Farmer's Market and DarkMarket, both of which have since been shut down by law enforcement officials operating in cooperation across various parts of the world.

Other Controversies

There are many other controversies in critical marketing. Of particular concern to critical market-ers are those situations in which one group is unfairly disadvantaged over another, in which one group exerts its power over another (e.g. the Fairtrade Movement was set up to ensure that in the coffee market, for example, shippers, roasters, and retailers pay fair prices to the supplying farmers, who are mostly located in developing countries such as Kenya and Colombia). Some controversies include the following.

- Is the price paid by companies and organizations in wealthier countries for supplies obtained in poorer countries fair? In her seminal text *No Logo*, Klein (1999) outlined how major mul-tinational corporations such as Nike and The Gap were exploiting migrant labour in foreign countries to produce expensive branded goods (see also Ellis *et al*., 2010: 219). The apparent moral dilemma incurred here, and the consumer backlash against these brands at the time, has at least in part led to the rise of the Fairtrade Movement (see Chapter 18).

- To what extent should the propositions and ideas of one country be marketed over the proposi-tions and ideas of another country? This is known as cultural imperialism. What are the cultural implications? For example, China has blocked Twitter, Facebook, and Google from operating, preferring instead to set up its own search engine (Baidu), microblogging site (Weibo) and social networking site (QQ).

- How much should we consume of any one particular offering or idea? When should govern-ments step in to limit consumption? In Sweden, alcohol retailing is run by the state alcohol monopoly Systembolaget (see Chapter 1) in order to ensure that public health is not adversely impacted by over-consumption of alcohol.

- Are some producers or buyer groups more powerful than others, and what impact, if any, does this have on society? For example, France's Free, the country's second-largest internet service provider, upgraded its modem software to block ads from Google in a bid to force Google to pay it fees to access its network of subscribers. However, after lobbying from advertisers and newspaper websites (and presumably Google), the French government forced Free to remove the ad block (Anon., 2013b). Is this fair?

- Does the shift from customer research to customer surveillance benefit customers? For example, retailers are using mannequins integrated with facial recognition software of the type used by law enforcement agencies to track the age, sex, and race of their customers as they pass through or by a store. Depending on whether or not data on individual customers is stored, and on how this data is used and stored, such an approach has serious ethical implications (Clark, 2012).

These examples illustrate imbalances in power structures between consumers, producers, retailers, and other actors. The question which arises for marketers is how should these relationships be structured to ensure that they are fair to all concerned?

Postmodern Marketing

In this next section, we consider another anti-foundational sub-discipline of marketing, namely, postmodern marketing. Many writers do not bother defining postmodernism per se, or define it in relation to its exact opposite, modernism. For some, postmodernism is 'impervious' to definition (Heartney, 2001). Some describe it in such detail, and with such a diverse range of terms, that it is rendered indecipherable. The term 'postmodern' is said to have first gained currency in architecture, where it denotes 'a rejection of the functionalism and brutalism of modern architecture (high-rise slums, impersonal box-like office blocks)' (Mautner, 1999). Postmodernism is therefore reactionary. As a movement, it disputes the way things are, and should be, and strives to be different in its approach.

Postmodern marketing pokes fun at the received ideas of major foundational thinkers. In the sense that it is **anti-foundational** to marketing, it is similar to critical marketing. It is different in the sense that it does not necessarily seek to reform marketing, and it is certainly irreverent. In other words, postmodern marketing thinkers aim to show up, and poke fun at, our established beliefs. Postmodernism has been defined as 'an **incredulity** towards **meta-narratives**' (Lyotard, 1984), meaning that postmodern marketers are critical and disbelieving of overarching belief systems (i.e. meta-narratives), which are often taken for granted and inherent in the discipline. Meta-narratives underpin the legitimacy of a concept in activity (Mautner, 1999). Such meta-narratives in Western society include beliefs in capitalist economic progress, the importance of scientific advancement, the idea of an objective reality and the independent subject (or man as an unbiased rational observer), and, more generally, that society exists for the good of its members and that knowledge is worth seeking for its own sake (Mautner, 1999). Some potential meta-narratives in the marketing sphere, the techniques associated with them, what their opposing meta-narratives might be, and in which chapters the existing meta-narratives are considered further are outlined in Table 19.1. (Use Table 19.1 to reflect on the received wisdom of particular concepts in marketing and their opposing concepts. This will help you to gain a more balanced perspective of marketing theory and practice.)

Table 19.1 Potential existing and opposing meta-narratives in marketing

Existing meta-narrative	Marketing knowledge and techniques interrogated	Opposing meta-narrative	Existing meta-narrative considered in ...
The consumer decision-making process is rational.	The proposition acquisition process	The consumer decision-making process is predominantly irrational.	Chapter 2
The marketing environment is capable of being understood.	SWOT and PEST analysis	The marketing environment is inherently chaotic and incapable of being pre-ordained.	Chapter 4
That marketing strategy development can be logically and easily predetermined.	The marketing planning process	Marketing strategy is an iterative, interactive, and experimental process with uncertain outcomes.	Chapter 5
That market segments can be identified, targeted, and clearly positioned.	The STP process of segmentation, targeting, and positioning	Markets are fragmenting and people are increasingly incapable of being grouped and targeted using the same positioning strategies.	Chapter 6
The marketing mix principle is still relevant in a consumption- rather than a production-oriented society	The marketing mix	The marketing mix principle is irrelevant in a multichannel world and other service-based dimensions are more important, especially in a co-creative consumption environment.	Chapters 1, 8–12 & 14
Consumers must become involved in advertising before they can act upon it.	AIDA process of awareness–interest–desire–action	Consumers do not become involved in advertising consciously (assuming they do at all). Instead the suggestive nature of advertising forces people to act and they are then forced to rationalize their interest and desire post hoc.	Chapter 10
To improve customer satisfaction for services we must focus on improving service quality by meeting customers' expectations.	The SERVQUAL measurement paradigm	Customer satisfaction is not always important. Under certain circumstances, where customers are wrong or do not know what they want/need, employee satisfaction might actually be more important in the long term.	Chapter 14
Marketing practitioners understand how and when to make ethical decisions.	The ethical decision-making process	Marketing practitioners do not understand how and when to make ethical decisions because they are frequently unskilled in applied moral philosophy for business.	Chapter 19

Postmodernism indicates a break with the old ways of thinking and the re-enchantment, or resurrection, of new ways of thinking. We say resurrection because postmodernism typically conjures up old associations and re-places them in a new light, providing us with new insights into old ideas. In art, French artist Michel Duchamp's urinal, a piece of work he entitled Fountain, complete with his signature, rocked the art world in 1917. He suggested that a signed urinal was a work of art! By doing this, Duchamp was making a statement about the quality of existing art, questioning why urination was taboo in French society.

How does the concept of postmodernism manifest itself in the way consumers consume? Postmodern marketing emphasizes the value of linking with an offering rather than simply using it, focusing on co-creation of meaning in its use, rather than simply a transference of meaning from the producer to the consumer. For the postmodern marketer, the consumer actively participates in the brand experience, and does not simply act as a recipient of advertising messages (see Cova, 1996).

There is increasingly a belief among consumer researchers that postmodern consumers are incapable of being grouped and segmented according to their needs (see Chapter 6). The postmodern consumption era is defined by the celebrated late French cultural critic and philosopher Jean Baudrillard (1995) as characterized by the fragmentation and trivialization of our values, images, and symbols. Fragmentation occurs in everyday life experiences and results in a loss of commitment to a single lifestyle (Firat and Shultz, 1997). In these circumstances, the consumer consumes (rather than just purchases), becoming both a customizer and producer of (self-)images in each consumptive experience (Dittmar, 1992; Firat *et al.*, 1995; Gabriel and Lang, 1995).

Modern, as opposed to postmodern, marketing suggests that value for the consumer is materialized in the prescribed benefits of the bundle of product attributes offered to the consumer, and customer satisfaction is obtained from value inherent in this bundle. But in postmodern markets, production and consumption are reversed. By this, we mean that there is emphasis on the consumption experience, as opposed to what is actually being consumed or purchased (see Market Insight 19.2). In service-based markets, this linkage between production and consumption is further pronounced, as production and consumption are considered to be inseparable (see Chapter 14). In postmodern service markets, the emphasis leads to an exaggeration of the importance of process in some cases—of the importance of form over content. For example, in American and British political campaigns, the increasing use of marketing has led to a perceived slickness of the electoral machinery—a development of the form of citizen politics but not a corresponding development in the substance, the policy, of politics. However, politics is just one example.

As a distinct area of thought in marketing, postmodernism has a set of central conditions and key features, which focus on the following concepts (Firat and Shultz, 1997).

- Hyper-reality—postmodern markets are hyper-real, where illusory and fantastical experiential components of brands are represented to us instead of the functional concrete attributes of brands. Reality is constituted through hype and simulation.

- Fragmentation of markets—in postmodernity, there is recognition that we are individuals with multiple or **multiphrenic** (from 'multi' meaning many and 'phrenia' meaning mind) personalities without commitment to a single lifestyle, acting in different ways in different circumstances, at different times, with different people, in different cultures. Experiences with products and services are disjointed and disconnected as a result.

Market Insight 19.2

Reality TV: Engaging Brands

An obvious example of the phenomenon of the reversal of production and consumption is the commonplace nature of reality TV ('living soap') shows, where audiences take part in voting for the outcomes of the show, and frequently appear on the show as contestants or stars. Examples of such shows include *Big Brother*, first developed by Dutch production company Endemol in the late nineties, quickly copied in the UK, and exported to many countries around the world including Australia, Russia, countries of the Middle and Far East, and many more. Other examples have included *Pop Idol*, developed in the UK but exported to the USA (as *American Idol*) and elsewhere, albeit with slightly different formats. *X-Factor* has been particularly successful in the UK, and *Britain's Got Talent* was exported to the USA and Australia. What's particularly clever about *X-Factor*, to take one example, is that Simon Cowell, the show's supremo, found a new way to simultaneously find new musical talent and sell music to masses of music buyers, whereas in the past artists were found by touring clubs where they were playing and music was sold through retail outlets. Critical to the show's success is the generation of customer engagement through social media. In the USA, in late 2012, *X-Factor* generated a huge response: 522,000 social media mentions per episode, compared with 132,000 per episode in 2011.

But reality TV isn't just a phenomenon in the West; it's taken Africa by storm as well. The *Big Brother Stargame* involves participants from 14 African countries competing for a top prize of $300,000. The show is screened across Africa in 47 different countries. No surprise then that Coca-Cola Nigeria has decided to become the headline sponsor. It seems that the desire to be famous is universal.

Sources: Halperin (2012); Ugorji (2012); www.bigbrother.com

1 In what ways are production and consumption reversed in these examples, from the perspective of the TV audience?

2 Why do you think audiences want to engage so much with the shows on social media?

3 Do you think that it is ethical to take advantage of consumers' desires to become famous for marketing purposes?

The *Britain's Got Talent* reality show format has been sold successfully around the world
Source: © Rex Features.

- Reversal of production and consumption—in postmodern times, when produce is plentiful, we no longer satisfy our needs but our desires. This change in emphasis requires a complete change in focus on production and consumption. Instead of producing what we need, manufacturers have shifted marketing emphasis to producing what we desire, a level of product and particularly service development more focused on experiential phenomena. Instead of simply passively accepting an offering, consumers have shifted to actively interpreting brands and how they are used.

- Decentred subject—consumers are becoming dominated by the things they consume and the experiences they have. Instead of simply having one self operating in different purchase situations, consumers have many selves operating in different consumption experiences.

- **Juxtaposition** of opposites is a style frequently used in postmodern advertising to appeal to consumers using ironic advertising treatments (Proctor, 2000). Whereas the modern world can be described in extremes using unipolar and black-and-white differentials, such as good *or* evil, nice *or* nasty, in the postmodern world we use bipolar dimensions, known as **dialectics**, such as good *and* evil, nice *and* nasty, to explain events, things, places, or other phenomena. For example, Unilever has run the 'dirt is good' campaign for many years for its Persil/Omo brands.

Elliot (1997) argues that consumption in the postmodern era has changed over the latter part of the twentieth century across five such dialectics, which he states include the following:

1 the material versus the symbolic;

2 the social versus the self;

3 desire versus the satisfaction;

4 rationality versus irrationality;

5 creativity versus constraint.

A reconsideration of marketing using these dialectics is useful because it allows us to reflect on how marketing and consumption really operate rather than how we are told they ought to operate. We consider each of these dialectics in the following sections.

 **Research Insight** 19.2

To take your learning further, you might wish to read this influential paper.

Elliot, R. (1997), 'Existential consumption and irrational desire', *European Journal of Marketing*, 31(3/4), 285–96.

This article considers marketing in the contemporary world from the perspective of five dialectics—material/symbolic, social/self, desire/satisfaction, rationality/irrationality, and creativity/constraint—to provide insights into consumption from cultural, social, and psychological perspectives. Elliot argues that the consumption process is an end in itself, and that consumers derive personal meaning and identity from the consumption process, not just from obtaining the offering.

@ **Visit the Online Resource Centre to read the abstract and access the full paper.**

The Material versus the Symbolic

Consumption experiences have moved from satisfying mere needs to satisfying symbolic needs (Levy, 1959). Consumers are consuming not only the material components of offerings but also the actual meaning that they represent to them. We re-perceive ourselves as consumers, not merely as purchasers of petrol from, say, a BP petrol station, but as purchasers of petrol from a company that we may, or may not, associate with environmental catastrophe. As postmodern consumers, we are (not) buying corporate image and activism, just as much as we are consuming their offerings.

Luxury goods (e.g. Birkin handbags, Omega watches, and Maserati cars) are products that sell at very high retail price points. They are sold not purely on their functionality but on their **aesthetic**—visual and sensory—value. The Birkin handbag is the epitome of arrival, the Omega watch the epitome of style and sophistication, and the Maserati the epitome of understated distinctiveness. But although we might expect luxury goods to be sold on the basis of their symbolism, there is an increasing shift towards marketing any offering on its symbolism. Witness the movement by some companies towards ethical branding, e.g. Pampers with its tie-up with UNICEF for baby vaccination, and the Nigerian Guaranty Trust Bank. These companies are not simply selling their offerings, but also their stance on particular issues. Marks and Spencer aims to become the world's most sustainable major retailer by 2015, implementing a programme they call Plan A, by cutting their own, their customers', and their suppliers' carbon emissions, by reducing waste, by reducing their use of natural resources, through fair partnerships and employment practices, and by working to improve their customers' health and wellbeing (M&S, 2012).

A key feature of postmodern marketing is the development of offerings that feature a new theme on an old product. Brown (2001) calls this retromarketing or 'the revival or

Marks and Spencer aims to become the world's most sustainable major retailer by 2015 through its Plan A programme
Source: Image courtesy of Marks and Spencer plc 2013.

relaunch of a product or service brand from a prior historical period, which is usually but not always updated to contemporary standards of performance, functioning, or taste'. In 2012, Chanel—the iconic French perfume house—developed an advertising campaign around the long deceased, but continuingly alluring, 1950s American film star Marilyn Monroe, featuring the interview in which she revealed that all she wore to bed was Chanel No.5 (see also Market Insight 19.3). Confectionery brand Galaxy also unveiled a retro-style advertising campaign in 2013 with a deceased Hollywood film star, Audrey Hepburn, eating the chocolate bar in an open-top car on Italy's Amalfi coast. Abbott Mead Vickers BBDO, the agency behind the ad, resurrected the strapline, 'Why have cotton when you can have silk?'—the same strapline that it used between 1987 and 2000 (Anon., 2013c). However, retromarketing need not be focused only on promotion. Hasbro, the US toymaker, resurrected Furby, the best-selling toy in the late 1990s, re-engineered for the 2010s with a digital campaign targeting 8–12-year-old girls (Charles, 2012).

Visit the **Online Resource Centre** and follow the weblink to the website of Stephen Brown to learn more about his writings on postmodern marketing and retromarketing. See also the weblink for the Chanel retro perfume ad featuring Marilyn Monroe.

Retromarketing seeks to induce feelings of pseudo-nostalgia. We say pseudo-nostalgia because many consumers are unlikely to have experienced the original brand. So, postmodern marketers try to reproduce an 'authentic' version of the previous model but enhance it in some way to bring it into the present. Retro brands are reminiscent of histori-cal periods, temporal connections, and their attendant national, regional, and political associations (Brown et al., 2003).

Visit the **Online Resource Centre** and complete Internet Activity 19.2 to learn more about retromarketing and the revival of a brand from a historical period.

Research Insight 19.3

To take your learning further, you might wish to read this influential paper.

Brown, S., Kozinets, R. V., and Sherry, J. F., Jr (2003), 'Teaching old brands new tricks: retro branding and the revival of brand meaning', *Journal of Marketing*, 67(3), 19–33.

This interesting and engaging article uses a netnographic research approach to understand why two retro brands, specifically the Volkswagen New Beetle and *Stars Wars 1: The Phantom Menace* were successful. It concludes that for brands to be successful they must understand the importance of the 4As of retro branding: allegory (brand story), aura (brand essence), arcadia (idealized community), and antinomy (brand paradox). Crucially, the article also explains that retro brand image-making is a co-created process which occurs at a social community, as well as an individual, level.

@ **Visit the Online Resource Centre to read the abstract and access the full paper.**

Market Insight 19.3

Back to the Past: Return of the Trabant

The Trabant car was the laughing stock of Europe. The national car of the Communist German Democratic Republic in the days before the fall of the Berlin Wall in 1989 and the reunification of Germany, it could barely muster 88kph (55mph), was powered by a 37cc two-stroke engine, cost less than £1,000, and measured about 3.4 metres long by 1.5 metres wide. Because of the old communist system of central planning, it could take years after ordering to finally take delivery of the car. So it was a bit of a surprise that the new electric model, the nT, unveiled as a concept car at the Frankfurt Motor Show in 2009 will reach up to 120kph (75mph), uses an electric powertrain, will cost somewhere between £7,000 and £9,000, and will be about 15 centimetres longer and wider. It will even have a range of 156 miles—not bad for an electric car—and will be powered through a rooftop solar panel. The new model will be also rather better

equipped than the old: in true capitalist style it comes with all **mod cons** including a satellite navigation system and an iPod player. Herpa, the German company behind the new car, will soon put the car into production. The question is: will German drivers buy it? At the 2012 Frankfurt Motor show Herpa were still looking for investors to raise the funds to bring the car to market. Some key questions need to be answered before they will part with their cash: will drivers love it as a retro fun brand or hate it as a symbol of the darker side of East Germany's past under Soviet occupation?

Sources: Hall (2009); Korzeniewski (2009); Autocar (2012).

1 **What do you think would prevent the Electric Trabant nT being made?**

2 **To what extent might the Trabant's old communist associations impact on consumer uptake?**

3 **Have you come across any other retro offerings recently? Did you feel nostalgia for these brands?**

The Trabant, a retrotastic iconic brand from the Cold War era, threatens to return to production

Source: © Herpa.

However, the fact that the retro brand is really a copy makes it inauthentic. The fact that some consumers will not have encountered the original version makes the new version, to that group of consumers at least, a copy without an original. This is what Baudrillard (1995) refers to as a **simulacrum**. A simulacrum is a copy without an original. A simulacrum develops through successive evolutionary image phase changes comprising different stages of (mis)representation:

1 an image that reflects a profound reality (a *good* likeness);

2 an image that masks and denatures a profound reality (a *bad* likeness);

3 an image that masks the absence of a profound reality (something that plays at being an appearance);

4 an image that has no relation to any reality whatsoever (a simulacrum, a copy without an original, or a simulation).

The concept of the simulacrum helps us to understand how images are produced, and reproduced, in postmodern times, particularly through electronic media. When numerous simulacra come together, we encounter a play of illusion and phantasm (i.e. ghost-like fleeting appearance), effectively a theme park. One example of such inauthenticity and simulation is the inauthentic 'authentic' Irish theme pubs, supposedly made to resemble original Irish drinking dens, and deliberately made to look as if they have heritage by appearing older in décor than they really are. Commercialization can undermine the idea of authenticity to consumers (Grayson and Martinec, 2004). For Baudrillard, Disneyland and Las Vegas are the perfect examples of places incorporating simulacra. Using fake fantastic worlds, with no reference to any myth or children's folklore (unlike in Europe, for example, where some theme parks conveyed the fantastical worlds of celebrated Danish author Hans-Christian Andersen), Disney quite literally created a Mickey Mouse world, complete with its own fantastical themes. This use of fantasy and illusion, with no real basis in reality, produces a hyper-reality.

Therefore marketers must decide carefully when to bring back elements of a brand's heritage or co-opt the heritage of other retro brands.

The Social versus the Self

Consumer offerings have always meant more to us than just what they can do functionally. In the postmodern environment, offerings not only affirm who we are to ourselves but who we are to others. There is social status in owning particular offerings (e.g. a Birkin bag) or using certain services (e.g. a stay at Raffles in Singapore). Our possession and use of these offerings projects meaning about us to others within a cultural context. What is particularly different in the postmodern environment, is how easy it is to change ourselves, to be someone different. For example, in cyberspace, our anonymity—consuming unknown from behind a computer screen—means that we can behave differently if we want to because we can operate as multiple selves, consuming in different patterns on different sites than we might do otherwise if we were to buy the same things in person. But this pattern of buying is increasingly transgressing the real as well as the virtual world, as consumers' individual identities become fragmented, as they become isolated from existing communities, knowing fewer people in the area where they live, but more people across the world and across cyberspace.

Whereas marketers have tended to focus on rational consumer buying motives, there is increasing recognition that consumers buy using irrational motives and favour experiences over possessions (see Market Insight 2.3 on the Templestay programme in Korea). Cova (1997) talks of deconsumption, where consumers reject the acquisition of material possessions in favour of experiences. Whereas families in the 1800s may have had 150–200 possessions in their home, a typical family at the beginning of the twenty-first century may have many thousands of possessions (Wilkie and Moore, 1999). As the postmodern consumer loses contact with community in the traditional sense, time-starved as he/she is, he/she increasingly craves satisfaction through **emotion** shared with others, particularly through experiences.

   A reaction against rampant individualism and over-consumption in the postmodern world is the rise of anti-consumption protest movements, e.g. the Occupy Movement. Occupy is an international protest organization whose principal aim is to target the social and political inequality caused by large corporations and the global financial system. In Britain, Occupy London occupied St. Paul's Cathedral after their efforts to occupy the entrance to the London Stock Exchange was thwarted by police and local authorities (BBC News, 2012). Another example is the international Buy Nothing Day, begun in Mexico in 1992 as a reaction against over-consumption, where people are exhorted to buy nothing on the last Saturday in November each year under the strapline 'Shop £€$$ Live More' (Sims, 2012). In various parts of the world, there has been a reaction against what some see as over-advertising. For example, Sao Paolo banned billboard advertising in 2007 (Burgoyne, 2007). Rome also considered this in 2011 after 10,000 people signed a petition to bring in a new law

(Kington, 2011). In Beijing, the city's administration has banned luxury advertising terms in billboard ads over concerns that aspirational adverts might create an 'unhealthy political climate' in highlighting the wealth gap between rich and poor (Moore, 2011).

   Visit the **Online Resource Centre** and complete Internet Activity 19.3 to learn more about the international Buy Nothing Day and other international anti-consumption protest groups.

A brilliant Italian anti-consumerist graffito explains 'consumption consumes you!'
Source: Image by Edgar Fabiano.

According to data from the World Values Survey (2008), different country populations have different degrees of interest in consumer activism, based on their desire to take part in consumer boycotts. Consumer activism, a key component of the anti-globalization movement, is particularly high in Sweden and Canada. However, very high proportions of people in other countries (e.g. Egypt and Russia) indicate that they would never take part in a consumer boycott.

However, consumer boycotts are becoming more prevalent (see Market Insight 4.1 on the boycott of Starbucks in the UK). People tend to boycott, or not boycott, for the following four reasons (Klein *et al.,* 2004):

1 the desire to make a difference;

2 the scope for self-enhancement, e.g. by a reduction, or a feeling of solidarity with others;

3 counter-arguments that inhibit boycotting, e.g. don't use the product enough, boycotting it will cause other problems;

4 the cost to the boycotter of constrained consumption, e.g. the cost of purchasing competing brands.

Consumers in Britain are increasingly consuming from an ethical/political standpoint. They are quite prepared to boycott brands they think do not deserve their custom, a trend that is not simply a passing middle-class fad (Shaw *et al.*, 2006). One pertinent example of a consumer boycott on political grounds was the animosity that American consumers showed towards French wine as a result of a lack of French support of American military action in the Second Iraq War (Ettenson and Klein, 2005). The difficulty for the managers of French wine companies in this example is that there was not much they could do about their government's defence policy. However, one approach might be to undertake corporate responsibility programmes highlighting environmental causes to offset some of the negative associations consumers might have about their government's stance, or even to advertise more during a boycott to try to rebut some of the negative associations that various groups are trying to attach to the brand.

In the cyberspace-connected world, the global village, brands live and die in the glare of the public. Brands which offend communities can quickly find themselves boycotted.

Desire versus Satisfaction

Whereas in the modern era, the focus was on satisfying the consumer, particularly through functional appeals, in the postmodern era, the focus shifts to consumer desire. Not so much satisfying desire, because desire can never be satisfied, but simply allowing the consumer to recognize that desire exists and to experience its effects.

For Baudrillard (1968), such rational appeals to consumer choice (see Chapter 2) fail to explain why particular brands and commodities are so in demand. For him, economic concepts of consumer decision-making needed to be replaced with a theory of the value of signs, which recognizes the importance of symbolism, and desire, as opposed to need (Cherrier and Murray, 2004). Postmodern marketers recognize the consumer shift away from simple satisfaction of functional needs. Although advertising has long fed our desires as consumers, in postmodernity, as consumers, we also want others to see our desires met.

In postmodernity, such desire, even for its own sake, is accepted and acceptable. The consumer is left with the message that it is good to desire something just for the sake of experiencing it, and not because one actually needs it. Consequently, appeals to consumer desire as opposed to consumer rationality are persuasive because they appeal to the subconscious, often through sexual appeal and the satisfaction of previously taboo desires (Elliot, 1999). For some marketing commentators, this shift towards satisfying consumer desire is a step too far. For them, marketing is increasingly being used to increase consumption to the benefit of capitalist exploitation 'by creating a logic of signs and codes that has no other virtue but to serve a system of competitive power where consumer needs are purely dominated' (Cherrier and Murray, 2004). The implication for marketers is that it is important to understand the limits consumers place on the extent to which they allow brand owners to seduce them. When seduction is inauthentic (i.e. over the top or when it is clearly manipulative), consumers are likely to react negatively.

Rationality versus Irrationality

Consumers buy and consume products and services because they have fun with them, enjoy their use, and gain pleasure from them. These are outcomes of our consumption experience. Although this might seem like common sense, for many years consumer behaviourists stressed that consumers consider functionality, the results of the use of the offering, as primary customer considerations. But our evaluative criteria for brand selection are also psychosocial (e.g. aestheticism, play) rather than simply economic. Inputs to the purchasing decision are based on considerations of time, as well as money, hedonism as opposed to problem-solving, right-brain thinking as opposed to left-brain thinking, exploratory behaviour as opposed to information-acquisitive behaviour, and personality type rather than customer characteristics such as lifestyle or social class. Environmental inputs into this experiential consideration of consumer decision-making stress the following:

- syntactic forms of communication—how something is said—as opposed to semantic forms—what is actually said;
- non-verbal as opposed to verbal stimuli;
- subjective features, as opposed to objective functions, of an offering.

The experiential consumer decision-making process is particularly appropriate to buying situations involving consumer experiences of entertainment, arts, and leisure products, such as visits to museums (Goulding, 1999). Other such experiences might include visits to dry ski slopes, and travel and leisure generally.

In making decisions about what we consume, we may use different frames of reference at different points in time to evaluate our experiences. Postmodernists suggest that we are 'multi-phrenic', a kind of consumer multiple personality (dis)order where we may simultaneously want something and not want it at the same time, or want very different things at the same time, or want very different things at different times for the same purpose. This knowledge is important, because many marketing models and theories wrongly assume that consumers are rational, when frequently they do not behave this way. Much market research practice is predicated and designed on the assumption of customer rationality, meaning that a fundamental rethink may be necessary in that discipline.

Creativity versus Constraint

In the postmodern world, opposing social forces exist. By this we can question whether advertising reflects reality or reality reflects advertising. In other words, are our needs reflected in the advertising or is the advertising reflected in our needs? There is, to some extent, a backlash by

Research Insight 19.4

To take your learning further, you might wish to read this influential paper.

Holbrook, M. B. and Hirschmann, E. C. (1982), 'The experiential aspects of consumption: consumer fantasies, feelings and fun', *Journal of Consumer Research*, 9(2), 132

This definitive article was the first to really challenge the received impression that consumers buy goods purely on a rational basis. Holbrook and Hirschmann have suggested that existing consumer behaviour models do not take account of irrational and experiential considerations. They stress the experiential process of consumer purchasing. Our cognitions of—thoughts about—the brand may not only encompass our current memories but also information from our subconscious, imagery rather than simply knowledge and structure, and fantasies and daydreams.

@ Visit the **Online Resource Centre** to read the abstract and access the full paper.

many citizen-consumers against the kind of materialism that advertising supports. Constant advertising of an offering leads to the idea that materialism in society is good, that feeding our materialistic desires is worthy of our attention and action. In many, this creates a kind of **psychological reactance** (see Chapter 2), and a desire to adopt a different and opposing frame of reference. Consumption from this new frame of reference, in a creative way, is a way of restoring the freedom that those postmodern consumers feel they are in danger of losing. This leads to the development of new forms of tribal behaviour (Cova, 1997), where consumers develop entire communities around the symbolic consumption of offerings. An example of such a community includes Nike+, the community for Nike product owners which allows them to track their sports activities, set personal goals, and improve their performance in a social media environment. Another example is the Harley Owners Group, which brings Harley Davidson motorcycle owners together—an activity group which predated the internet communities more common today. The implication for marketers is that they cannot always control how customers interact with their brands, nor should they try (see also Chapter 17).

Semiotics and Deconstruction

Semiotics can be defined as 'a discipline that provides a structure for studying and analysing how signs function within a particular environment' (Zakia and Nadin, 1987). Its defining feature 'is that it takes the culture and not the consumer as the object of study' (Lawes, 2002). In undertaking semiotic analysis, we are particularly concerned with the analysis of signs. A sign can be anything that represents meaning, and includes sensory information, such as visuals/pictures, sound/music, taste, smell, touch/pain, and cultural forms, such as film, dance, gesture, mime, architecture, and more. We might use the term 'symbols' interchangeably here with 'sign', as the sign symbolizes something to the viewer. Semiotics has the power to allow us, as marketers or social analysts, to embed the macroanalysis of consumer decision-making into a theory of cultural interaction. As a result, we can link the consumer to his/her purchasing environment to determine how the two mutually reinforce each other.

To understand semiotics further, we need to understand the concept of sign. For the celebrated Swiss linguist Ferdinand de Saussure, the linguistic sign is a dyadic relationship between the **signified** (e.g. caviar from the Caspian and Black Sea regions) and sound images known as the **signifier** (e.g. the spoken word 'caviar'). For de Saussure, the meaning conveyed by language was formed not only from the words used but also from the way that the words interacted with each other. The idea is that, for example, two words when put together mean more than the sum of their parts. This concept had not been explicitly recognized in linguistics until de Saussure's work. To get some idea of the power of combining concepts with apparently different meanings consider, Cadbury's 'Joyville' campaign (see Market Insight 19.4).

de Saussure's concept of signs was built on further by C. S. Peirce (1931–58), who felt that rather than being dyadic, sign processes (or symbolism) are in fact a function of a triadic process. Peirce argued that a sign was anything that gives us an impression of something (its object

Market Insight 19.4

Cadbury's Not-So-Secret Secret

In 2012 and 2013, Cadbury Dairy Milk launched €1.5m and £7m TV integrated marketing communication campaigns in Ireland and Britan, with TV ads supported by nationwide sampling tours and digital marketing campaigns around the fictional place of 'Joyville'—a positioning strategy it has committed to until 2022. The story of the ad focuses upon a young factory worker who follows a boss through umpteen secret passages and rooms into a room with a safe containing the Cadbury Dairy Milk secret ingredient, which is the fact that it contains a glass and a half of dairy milk in each bar. The ad, reminiscent of the Roald Dahl story *Charlie and the Chocolate Factory*, seeks to celebrate the dairy milk taste of Cadbury's Dairy Milk chocolate. The boss who explains that this information about the secret recipe is being given on a 'need to know basis' is asked by the surprised apprentice, 'You do realize this is on the front of every pack?' The advert ironically plays on the idea that no-one knows that Cadbury Dairy Milk contains milk when in fact

everyone does. It seeks to remind consumers of that fact and draw attention to its creamy taste—hence the importance of the sampling activity supporting the campaign.

Sources: Anon. (nd); Joseph (2013); Reynolds (2013); http://www.cadburydairymilk.co.uk/

To view the official advert shown in the UK and Ireland, search for 'Cadbury dairy milk—the not-so-secret secret (official TV ad)'

1 **What is the danger of using concepts with irony when advertising or branding products?**

2 **Watch the video using the address given. Do you think that the ad and the concept works? What does the ad convey to you?**

3 **Can you think of any other ads that use the concept of the juxtaposition of opposites? (Hint: check out Viktor and Rolf's perfume ad for 'Flowerbomb'). What attributes do they convey to you?**

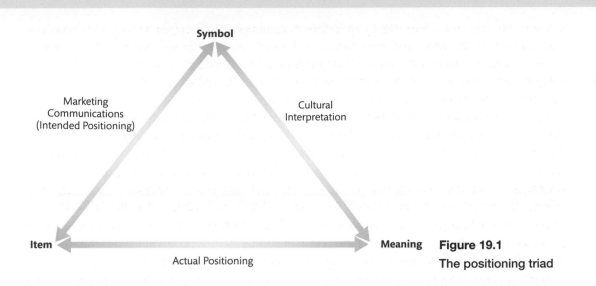

Figure 19.1
The positioning triad

(or 'item' as it may not be physical)) projected at somebody (its interpreter) in some respect (its context) (Mick, 1986). What results from this triadic interrelationship is some sort of understanding projected from the object, which holds some sort of interpretation in our minds. Peirce calls this understanding that we have as a result the 'interpretant', which is neither the interpreter nor the interpretation, but which is in fact a concept shared within the culture in which it is disseminated. To make these concepts easier to understand, we have relabelled the 'interpretant' as 'meaning' and the 'object' as 'item'.

Figure 19.1 illustrates what we've called the positioning triad, demonstrating the three-way relationship between the Item (that which we are communicating something about), the Symbol (what we intend to communicate about the item), and the Meaning (the interpretation of the symbol within a cultural context). What is useful about this concept is that it provides us with a clearer understanding of how the **positioning process**—the way that an offering is perceived in the minds of the customer—in marketing communications works (see Chapters 6 and 10). In Figure 19.1, the intended meaning of the item is conveyed as a symbol through the marketing communication process. This meaning, once received by the audience, develops in a concept through shared understanding of its meaning. On the basis of how a culture perceives the item, its symbolism is either reinforced or altered, and it is correspondingly positioned or repositioned as part of the ongoing marketing communications process.

Visit the **Online Resource Centre** and complete Internet Activity 19.4 to learn more about symbolism and the marketing and consumption experience.

In analysing semiotics, we take an outside-in approach, looking at how an audience interprets communications, in the sense of the meanings that these communications convey (Lawes, 2002). But how do we analyse those meanings? Semioticians often talk of 'texts' (i.e. from a linguistic perspective, not to be confused with the modern-day text message, SMS) and therefore anything that conveys meaning is regarded as a 'text'. Semiotic analysis of competitor advertising can be useful in understanding what messages an advertiser seeks to convey, and how they convey these messages within the cultural context of the consumer. It can be used as an alternative to undertaking positioning studies (see Chapter 6), as it provides us with an insight into how the advertiser requires the audience to see their offering (Harvey and Evans, 2001) and as a complement to a traditional positioning study (Baines *et al.*, 2013). If we can decode the signs that the advertiser intends to present, we can understand their positioning strategies. With positioning studies, we do not necessarily see how the company is trying to position itself (intended positioning); what we see instead is how the company actually ends up positioned in the minds of customers ('the Meaning'). There is a clear difference between the two.

In the postmodern world, pictures interact with words to show some sort of meaningful interaction. There is free playing between image and word (Scott, 1992). Such works might be interpreted in different ways. Approaches to analysis include the use of the deconstruction linguistic technique, commonly associated with French philosopher Jacques Derrida. In **deconstruction**, the aim is to revisit what the 'text' is trying to convey. The reader looks at gaps, inconsistencies, and underlying 'absences' in the text (Derrida, 1967). The textual analysis breaks the text down into privileged themes, and then determines the 'binary opposites' (e.g. man/woman, white/black, right/wrong) of those privileged themes as the hidden or absent meaning of the work, and essentially proposes that this is what that work was really trying to say.

Postmodern advertisements tend to possess distinctive features in that they use an irrational appeal (to emotion rather than reason), adopt 'feminist' stances (appealing to anti-masculine sentiment), and destroy widely held ideas in society (meta-narratives) about how things should be perceived (see Proctor *et al.*, 2001). An example of a postmodern marketing campaign is the one supporting the launch of Lady Gaga's own perfume, 'Fame' (see Market Insight 19.5).

 Market Insight 19.5

Deconstructing Gaga's 'Fame'

Lady Gaga, the pop icon, who boasts a legion of Twitter followers (her 'little monsters'), launched her own perfume in 2012 with global perfume manufacturer Coty to much fanfare. The Fragrance Shop labelled the perfume the best-selling UK celebrity scent of 2012. The scent, made of black fluid which turns transparent when sprayed, contains the smell of belladonna (a poisonous flower), tiger orchidea, apricot, saffron, and honey drops. The perfume launch commercial plays on the dark side of fame. However, judging by the number of people who watch reality TV shows which offer the opportunity to achieve off-the-shelf fame, the desire to obtain fame remains strong. Fame is seen as desirable, bringing riches, glory, adulation, and admiration.

The ad, a high-fashion production in the style of her pop videos, contains blood-curdling screams, dark, moody, aggressive, and overtly sexual imagery, and a naked Gaga scaled by tiny barely clad men in a scene reminiscent of Gulliver's Travels (the image used for the perfume's print ads). The imagery/aura around the brand is distinctly occultist, on several levels. Apparently, Gaga had wanted her perfume to have fragrance notes of ingredients frequently used in ritual magic. Other occultish symbolism includes the perfume's main ingredient, belladonna. In an interview for the launch of the perfume, Gaga calls it a 'slutty, seductive' perfume, explaining that people become famous through the process of seducing others, but that fame has a dual nature. It can be both good/evil, frightful/delightful, paranoid/trusting, following/leading, supernatural/ordinary, and happy/sad (note: our deconstruction, not Gaga's!). In deconstructing, we can see that Gaga's perfume commercial is a short horror film which allows us to rehearse the arguments against fame, take part in a conspiracy against it, but secretly desire it. As Gaga's 'Fame' consumers, we are the exact opposite of famous; we are in fact ordinary trusting followers seeking the extraordinary. Her perfume gives us the opportunity to transpose ourselves into a fame fantasy (despite its evils), albeit temporarily.

Market Insight 19.5
continued

Given the sales volumes achieved in the first week—six million bottles according to one of her own tweets—Lady Gaga knows a thing or two about the art of seduction and how to perpetuate her own fame.

Sources: Anon. (2012); Bergin (2012); London (2012); Luoma (2012) (see also Market Insight 2.5: Celebrity Scents).

To view the advert, search for 'Lady Gaga—Fame—Full Official Commercial' on YouTube. To see the singer explain her perfume concept, search for 'Lady Gaga Fame_Gaga Interview' on YouTube.

1 What, in your view, are the advantages of using the deconstruction technique?

2 Watch the video using the addresses given. Regardless of your gender, do you think the ad and the concept work? What other dialectics does the ad convey to you?

3 Identify another postmodern ad (Hint: if you're stuck, try haircare brand GHD's 'Rapunzel' ad, part of the 'Twisted Fairytales' series). What do you think the advertisers are trying to convey, to whom, and for what purpose?

Chapter Summary

To consolidate your learning, the key points from this chapter are summarized here.

■ **Assess the negative impact that marketing has on society.**

The critical marketing perspective suggests that marketing impacts negatively on society. The perspective calls for us to (re)evaluate marketing activities, categories, and frameworks to improve them, so that marketing operates in a desirable manner within society. It seeks to critique the nature of marketing knowledge and question in whose interests existing frameworks, approaches, and techniques operate. It questions the historical and cultural conditions in which marketing operates, and questions the legitimacy of marketing in order to provide new insights into how it ought to operate. Finally, the critical marketing perspective suggests that we have much to learn from other disciplines (e.g. social anthropology, social psychology, linguistics, philosophy, sociology) and that too rigid a philosophical stance, e.g. solely scientific (i.e. positivist) approaches, is bad for the development of the discipline and of society at large.

■ **Define the possible meanings and key features of postmodern marketing.**

From a postmodernist perspective, marketers need to rethink how we go about segmenting our markets, as markets are fragmenting, about how our consumers choose offerings, because they are irrational as well as rational beings, and being careful not to characterize them as being of one type, as we display different selves in purchasing and consumption. Therefore postmodernism in marketing is an orientation, a way of thinking and rethinking, about how we experience the marketing world around us. It denotes a break with the past, with the old concepts of marketing, towards a new theory of how marketing should interact with customers in the future. Increasingly, customers are more involved with the process of production and consumption, and co-produce those consumer offerings and experiences in a situation where proposition development begins from the perspective of consumption first and production second. The customer becomes dominated or owned by his/her experiences rather than the reverse. Marketing in the postmodern world has dialectical features with seemingly opposite characteristics existing simultaneously, focusing on the material/symbolic, social/self, desire/satisfaction, rational/irrational, and creativity/constraint dimensions.

■ **Discuss the reversal of production and consumption in the postmodern context.**

In postmodernity, when produce is plentiful, we no longer simply satisfy our needs but also our desires. The change in emphasis requires a complete shift in focus from production to consumption. Instead of producing what consumers need, manufacturers must shift emphasis to producing what they desire—a level of product and service development more focused on experiential phenomena. Instead of passively accepting an offering, consumers have shifted to actively interpreting brands and how they are used, and are increasingly involved in the co-creation of them in a metaphorical, symbolic, and literal sense.

■ **Explain the important role of semiotics in consumption**

Semiotics is the science of signs. A sign can be anything that represents meaning and includes sensory information such as visuals/pictures, sound/music, taste, smell, and touch/pain, and cultural forms such as film, dance, gesture, mime, and architecture. In analysing signs, we use linguistic concepts developed by de Saussure to determine what is signified by a signifier. Peirce took the concept further by identifying a concept that he called the 'interpretant', which indicates the shared cultural meaning that derives as a result of the image projected from the object. Semiotics is used by marketers to understand such image-meanings, to embed the macroanalysis of consumer decision-making into a theory of cultural interaction. As a result, we can link the consumer to his/her purchasing context to determine how the two interact with each other. Semiotic analysis is particularly useful as a technique to analyse competitors' intended positioning strategies.

■ **Understand how to deconstruct marketing 'texts', including advertisements**

Semioticians often talk of 'texts', and anything that conveys meaning as a 'text'. Approaches to analysis of 'texts' include the deconstruction linguistic technique associated with the French philosopher Jacques Derrida. In deconstruction, the aim is to determine what the 'text' seeks to convey by revisiting its meanings. The reader searches for gaps, inconsistencies, and underlying 'absences' in the text (Derrida 1967). The textual analysis breaks the text down into privileged themes, and then determines a series of 'binary opposites' (e.g. dark/light, right/wrong) of those privileged themes as the hidden or absent meaning of the work. Once these binary opposites have been determined, the deconstruction technique proposes that the lesser non-privileged binary opposite is often what the focus of the work was *really* about.

Review Questions

1 What is critical marketing and what is postmodern marketing?
2 Name the key concepts in critical marketing.
3 What are the key features of postmodernism in marketing according to Elliot?
4 What is a simulacrum?
5 How are postmodern markets becoming increasingly fragmented?
6 When postmodernists say that production and consumption are reversed, what do they mean?
7 What is the juxtaposition of opposites and why might it be useful in marketing?
8 What is semiotic analysis?
9 What are the three components of the positioning triad?
10 What is deconstruction and how might it be useful in marketing?

 **Worksheet Summary**

To apply the knowledge you have gained from this chapter and test your understanding of critical and postmodern perspectives in marketing visit the **Online Resource Centre** and complete Worksheet 19.1.

Discussion Questions

1 Having read Case Insight 19.1, how would you advise Livity to design their campaign to raise awareness of ChildLine using young people's affiliation for music? (Hint: consider why traditional promotional approaches might not work.)

2 Do you think some commodities are fetishised more than others? Identify four offerings where you think this is the case and discuss the nature of the relationships between manufacturer, retailer, and consumer. To what extent are these relationships exploitative?

3 Explain how each of the following dialectic postmodern concepts is relevant in marketing the following two offerings: 1) material versus symbolic, 2) social versus self, 3) desire versus satisfaction, 4) rationality versus irrationality, and 5) creativity versus constraint.

 A The Mini car (owned by BMW Group).
 A The Star Trek conventions (see www.startrek.com).

4 Identify another retro brand not outlined in the chapter (e.g. from your own country or somewhere else). What social, political, and historic connections is the brand trying to conjure up? Do you think it will be successful? Why do you say this?

5 Re-read the section on semiotics and deconstruction. Then have a look at 'The Guardian—The Three Little Pigs' advert on YouTube (see also the Case Insight in Chapter 10). What 'binary opposites' can you identify in this ad?

@ **Visit the Online Resource Centre and complete the Multiple Choice Questions to assess your knowledge of Chapter 19.**

 **References**

Alvesson, M. (1994), 'Critical theory and consumer marketing', *Scandinavian Journal of Marketing*, 10(3), 291–313.

Anon. (nd), 'Cadbury launches Joyville campaign', *Adworld*, not dated, retrieve from: http://www.adworld.ie/news/read/?id=8404ee99-70f7-440e-8c1b-8cc6ae0bc645 accessed 1 April 2013.

Anon. (2012), 'Lady Gaga sells six million bottles of her 'Fame' perfume in a week', *NME*, 23 September, retrieve from: http://www.nme.com/news/lady-gaga/66269 accessed 31 March 2013.

Anon. (2013a), 'Nestlé finds horsemeat in pasta dishes', *Fijilive*, 19 February, retrieve from: http://fijilive.com/news/2013/02/nestle-finds-horsemeat-in-pasta-dishes/52114.Fijilive accessed 26 March 2013.

Anon. (2013b), 'France v Google', *Economist*, 12 January, 8.

Anon. (2013c), 'Galaxy ads to "star" Hepburn', *Marketing*, 27 February, 10–11.

Autocar (2012), 'New electric Trabant', *Autocar*, not dated, retrieve from: http://www.autocar.co.uk/car-news/new-cars/new-electric-trabant accessed 26 March 2013.

Baines, P., Crawford, I., O'Shaughnessy, N. J., Worcester, R., and Mortimore, R. (2013), 'Positioning in political marketing: how semiotic analysis can support traditional survey approaches', *Journal of Marketing Management*, DOI:10.1080/0267257X.2013.810166

Barnes, R. (2011), 'Brand health check: Levi Roots', *Marketing*, 30 November, 22.

Baudrillard, J. (1968), *The System of Objects* (trans. J. Benedict), London: Verso Books, 2005: 195.

Baudrillard, J. (1995), *Simulacra and Simulation* (trans. S. F. Glaser), Ann Arbor, MI: University of Michigan Press.

BBC News (2012), 'Arrests over Occupy London Stock Exchange camp', *BBC News*, 2 May, retrieve from: http://www.bbc.co.uk/news/uk-england-london-17919750 accessed 31 March 2013.

Bergin, O. (2012), 'Lady Gaga inspired by Gulliver's Travels for "Fame" fragrance advert', *Telegraph*, 17 July, retrieve from: http://fashion.telegraph.co.uk/beauty/news-features/TMG9404906/Lady-Gaga-inspired-by-Gullivers-Travels-for-Fame-fragrance-advert.html accessed 31 March 2013.

Brown, S. (1995), *Postmodern Marketing*, London: Routledge.

Brown, S. (1997), *Postmodern Marketing 2: Telling Tales*, London: International Thomson Press.

Brown, S. (2001), *Marketing: The Retro Revolution*, London: Sage.

Brown, S., Kozinets, R. V., and Sherry, J. F. (2003), 'Teaching old brands new tricks: retro branding and the revival of brand meaning', *Journal of Marketing*, 67 (July), 19–33.

Brownlie, D. (2006). 'Emancipation, epiphany and resistance: on the underimagined and overdetermined in critical marketing', *Journal of Marketing Management*, 22(5/6), 505–28.

Brownlie, D. and Saren, M. (1992), 'The four Ps of the marketing concept: prescriptive, polemical, permanent, and problematic', *European Journal of Marketing*, 26(4), 34–47.

Burgoyne, P. (2007), 'Sao Paolo: the city that said no to advertising', *Business Week*, 18 June, retrieve from: http://www.businessweek.com/stories/2007-06-18/s-o-paulo-the-city-that-said-no-to-advertisingbusinessweek-business-news-stock-market-and-financial-advice accessed 31 March 2013.

Burton, D. (2001), 'Critical marketing theory: the blueprint?', *European Journal of Marketing*, 35(5/6), 722–43.

Charles, G. (2012), Furby toy set for relaunch', *Marketing*, 26 September, 10.

Cherrier, H. and Murray, J. B. (2004), 'The sociology of consumption: the hidden facet of marketing', *Journal of Marketing Management*, 20, 509–25.

Clark, L. (2012), 'Mannequins are spying on shoppers for market analysis', *Wired.co.uk*, 23 November, retrieve from: http://www.wired.co.uk/news/archive/2012-11/23/mannequin-spies-on-customers?page=all accessed 30 March 2013.

Cova, B. (1996), 'The postmodern explained to managers: implications for marketing', *Business Horizons*, November–December, 15–23.

Cova, B. (1997), 'Community and consumption: toward a definition of the "linking value" of products or services', *European Journal of Marketing*, 31(3–4), 297–316.

Derrida, J. (1967), *Of Grammatology* (trans. G. C. Spivak), Baltimore, MD: Johns Hopkins University Press.

Dittmar, H. (1992), *The Social Psychology of Material Possessions*, Hemel Hempstead: Harvester Wheatsheaf.

Easton, G. (2002). 'Marketing: a critical realist approach', *Journal of Business Research*, 55(2), 103–9.

Elliot, R. (1997), 'Existential consumption and irrational desire', *European Journal of Marketing*, 31(3–4), 285–96.

Elliot, R. (1999), 'Symbolic meaning and postmodern consumer culture', in D. Brownlie, M. Saren, R. Wensley, and R. Whittington (eds), *Rethinking Marketing: Towards Critical Marketing Accountings*, London: Sage, 112–25.

Ellis, N., Fitchett, J., Higgins, M., J *et al*. (2010), *Marketing: A Critical Textbook*, London: Sage.

Ettenson, R. and Klein, J. G. (2005). 'The fallout from French nuclear testing in the South Pacific: a longitudinal study of consumer boycotts'. *International Marketing Review*, 22(2), 199–224.

Firat, A. F. and Shultz, C. J., II (1997), 'From segmentation to fragmentation: markets and modern marketing strategy in the postmodern era', *European Journal of Marketing*, 31(3–4), 183–207.

Firat, A. F., Dholakia, N., and Ventakesh, A. (1995), 'Marketing in a postmodern world', *European Journal of Marketing*, 29(1), 239–67.

Franklin, O. (2013), 'Unravelling the dark web', *GQ* (British), February, 184–9.

Gabriel, I. and Lang, T. (1995), *The Unmanageable Consumer: Contemporary Consumption and its Fragmentations*, London: Sage.

Goulding, C. (1999), 'Contemporary museum culture and consumer behaviour', *Journal of Marketing Management*, 15, 647–71.

Grayson, K. and Martinec, R. (2004), 'Consumer perceptions of iconicity and indexicality and their influence on assessments of authentic market offerings', *Journal of Consumer Research*, 31, 296–311.

Hackley, C. (2003), ' "We are all customers now…." Rhetorical strategy and ideological control in marketing management texts', *Journal of Management Studies*, 40(5), 1325–52.

Hall, A. (2009), 'Trabant is back but this time without the smoke', *Daily Telegraph*, 14 August, 12.

Hallahan, K. (1999), 'Seven models of framing: implications for public relations', *Journal of Public Relations Research*, 11(3), 205–42.

Halperin, S. (2012), ' "X-Factor" sees significant social media strides', *Hollywood Reporter*, 19 December, retrieve from: http://www.hollywoodreporter.com/live-feed/x-factors-social-media-strategy-405485 accessed 26 March 2013.

Harvey, M. and Evans, E. (2001), 'Decoding competitive propositions: a semiotic alternative to traditional advertising research', *International Journal of Market Research*, 43(2), 171–87.

Heartney, E. (2001), *Movements in Modern Art: Postmodernism*, London: Tate Publishing.

Hetrick, W. and Lozada, H. (1999), 'Theory, ethical critique and theexperience of marketing', in D. Brownlie, M. Saren, R. Wensley, and R. Whittington (eds), *Rethinking Marketing: Towards Critical Marketing Accountings*, London: Sage, 162–76.

Holbrook, M. B. and Hirschmann, E. C. (1982), 'The experiential aspects of consumption: consumer fantasies, feelings and fun', *Journal of Consumer Research*, 9 (September), 132–40.

Joseph, S. (2013), 'Cadbury returns to Joyville in £7m TV push', *Marketing Week*, 8 February, retrieve from: http://www.marketingweek.co.uk/news/cadbury-returns-to-joyville-in-7m-tv-push/4005635.article, accessed 1 April 2013.

Kington, T. (2011), 'Romans revolt over billboard jungle', *Guardian*, 26 December, retrieve from: http://www.guardian.co.uk/world/2011/dec/26/rome-revolt-billboard-jungle accessed 31 March 2013.

Klein, J. G., Smith, N. C., and John, A. (2004), 'Why we boycott: consumer motivations for boycott participation', *Journal of Marketing*, 68(July), 92–109.

Klein, N. (1999), *No Logo*, London: Flamingo.

Korzeniewski, J. (2009), 'Electric Trabant revival slated to debut at Frankfurt', 14 August, *Autobloggreen*, retrieve from: http://green.autoblog.com/2009/08/14/electric-trabant-revival-slated-to-debut-at-frankfurt/ accessed 26 March 2013.

Lawes, R. (2002), 'Demystifying semiotics: some key questions answered', *International Journal of Market Research*, 44(3), 251–64.

Levy, S. (1959), 'Symbols for sale', *Harvard Business Review*, 37(July/August), 117–24.

Lucas, L. (2013), 'Horsemeat scandal sheds light on tastes', *Financial Times*, 14 March, retrieve from: http://www.ft.com/cms/s/0/7b6700d0-8bfa-11e2-8fcf-00144feabdc0.html#axzz2OsS38aHH accessed 26 March 2013.

Luoma, S. (2012), 'Lady Gaga's "Fame" perfume named most popular UK scent', *DigitalSpy*, 24 December, retrieve from: http://www.digitalspy.co.uk/showbiz/news/a447062/lady-gagas-fame-perfume-named-most-popular-uk-scent.html accessed 31 March 2013.

Lyotard, J-F. (1984), *The Postmodern Condition*, Paris: Les Éditions de Minuit.

M&S (2012), 'Our Plan A Commitments 2010–2015', retrieve from: http://plana.marksandspencer.com/media/pdf/ms_hdwb_2012.pdf accessed 26 March 2013.

Marx, K. (1867), *Capital: Critique of Political Economy*, Vol.1, London: Penguin, 1990.

Mautner, T. (1999), *Dictionary of Philosophy*, London: Penguin.

Mick, D. G. (1986), 'Consumer research and semiotics: exploring the morphology of signs, symbols and significance', *Journal of Consumer Research*, 13, 196–213.

Moore, M. (2011), 'China bans luxury advertising in Beijing', *Telegraph*, 22 March, retrieve from: http://www.telegraph.co.uk/news/worldnews/asia/china/8398097/China-bans-luxury-advertising-in-Beijing.html accessed 31 March 2013.

Murray, J. B. and Ozanne, J. L. (1991), 'The critical imagination: emancipatory interests in consumer research', *Journal of Consumer Research*, 18(2), 129–44.

Newman, K. (2001), 'The sorcerer's apprentice? Alchemy, seduction and confusion in modern marketing', *International Journal of Advertising*, 20, 409–29.

Osborne, H. (2013), 'PPI—Facts and figures from the "biggest mis-selling scandal of all time" ', *Guardian*, 4 March, retrieve from: http://www.guardian.co.uk/money/2013/mar/04/ppi-facts-figures-biggest-mis-selling-scandal accessed 27 March 2013.

Packard, V. O. (1960), *The Hidden Persuaders*, Harmondsworth: Penguin Books.

Peirce, C. S. (1931–58), *Collected Papers*, ed. C. Hartshorne, P. Weiss, and A. W. Burks, Cambridge, MA: Harvard University Press.

Press Association (2013), 'How the horsemeat scandal unfolded—timeline', *Guardian*, 15 February, retrieve from: http://www.guardian.co.uk/world/2013/feb/08/how-horsemeat-scandal-unfolded-timeline accessed 28 March 2013.

Proctor (2000), *Strategic Marketing: An Introduction*, London: Routledge.

Proctor, S., Papasolomou-Doukakis, I., and Proctor, T. (2001), 'What are television advertisements really trying to tell us? A postmodern perspective', *Journal of Consumer Behaviour*, 1(3), 246–55.

Reynolds, J. (2013), 'Cadbury plots Joyville roll-out to wider brand range', *Marketing*, 13 February, 5.

Saren, M. (2007), 'To have is to be? A critique of self-creation through consumption', *Marketing Review*, 7(4), 343–54.

Saren, M. (2009), 'Commentary. Modes of engagement for critical marketing: oppositional, revivalist and therapeutic', *Journal of Marketing Management*, 25(7–8), 843–8.

Saren, M. (2011), 'Critical marketing: theoretical underpinnings', in G. Hastings, K. Angus, and C. Bryant (eds), *The Sage Handbook of Social Marketing*, London: Sage, 95–107.

Scheufele, D. A. and Tewksbury, D. (2007), 'Framing, agenda setting and priming: the evolution of three media effects models', *Journal of Communication*, 57, 9–20.

Scott, L. M. (1992), 'Playing with pictures: postmodernism, poststructuralism, and advertising visuals', *Advances in Consumer Research*, 19, 596–611.

Shankar, A. (2009), 'Reframing critical marketing', *Journal of Marketing Management*, 25(7–8), 681–96.

Shaw, D., Newholm, T., and Dickinson, R. (2006), 'Consumption as voting: an exploration of consumer empowerment', *European Journal of Marketing*, 40(9/10), 1049–67.

Sherover, E. (1979), 'The virtue of poverty: Marx's transformation of Hegel's concept of the poor', *Canadian Journal of Political and Social Theory (Revue Canadienne de Théorie Politique et Sociale)*, 3(1), 53–66.

Sims, A. (2012), 'Buy nothing day? There must be a better way to protest', *Guardian*, 21 November, retrieve from: http://www.guardian.co.uk/world/shortcuts/2012/nov/21/buy-nothing-day-better-way accessed 31 March 2013.

Tadajewski, M. (2010), 'Towards a history of critical marketing studies', *Journal of Marketing Management*, 26(9–10), 773–824.

Ugorji, C. (2012), 'TV reality show: Coca-Cola continues to refresh Big Brother Africa as BBA-7 launches', Coca-Cola Nigeria News Release, 3 May, retrieve from: http://afriktainmentmedia.blogspot.co.uk/2012/05/tv-reality-show-coca-cola-continues-to.html accessed 26 March 2013.

Wilkie, W.L. and Moore, E.S. (1999), 'Marketing's contributions to society', *Journal of Marketing*, 63, 198–218.

Worthington, S. and Durkin, M. (2012), 'Co-destruction of value in context: cases from retail banking', *Marketing Review*, 12(3), 291–307.

World Values Survey (2008), Online Data Analysis (Step-1): Study Selection, retrieve from: http://www.wvsevsdb.com/wvs/WVSAnalizeStudy.jsp accessed 31 March 2013.

Zakia, R. D. and Nadin, M. (1987), 'Semiotics, advertising and marketing', *Journal of Consumer Marketing*, 4(2, Spring), 5–12.

Glossary

accessory equipment goods these support the key operational processes and activities of the organization.

account portfolio matrix *see* customer portfolio matrix.

adaptative orientation a firm believes that each country should be approached separately as a different market, buying or conducting market research into the particular country and developing specific market strategy for that particular market.

advergaming (or in-game advertising (IGA)) the use of video and online games to advertise a product, organization, or idea. Advergames encourage repeat website traffic and reinforce brand loyalty.

advertising a form of non-personal communication, by an identified sponsor, that is transmitted through the use of paid-for media.

aesthetic consideration of what is beautiful or in good taste, particularly in art.

affective a psychological term referring to our emotional state of mind. Values are affective because they are linked to our feelings about things.

aggregated demand demand calculated at the population level rather than at the individual level.

AIDA a hierarchy of effects or sequential model used to explain how advertising works. AIDA stands for awareness, interest, desire, and action (a sale).

AMA the American Marketing Association is a professional body for marketing professionals and marketing educators based in the USA, operating principally in the USA and Canada.

Ansoff's matrix the product–market matrix provides a useful framework for considering the relationship between strategic direction and market opportunities.

anti-foundational a reaction against the development of something or an idea. An attempt to destroy the foundations of something, someone, or an idea.

anti-globalization a term most commonly ascribed to the political stance of people and groups who oppose certain aspects of globalization. Participants are united in opposition to the political power of large corporations, as exercised in trade agreements and elsewhere, which they say undermines democracy, the environment, labour rights, national sovereignty, the third world, and other concerns.

app third-party application software designed for mobile and other smart devices. They enable a brand to be connected with a user as they move around.

a priori method segments are pre-determined using the judgement of the researchers beforehand.

art use of imitation, imagination, and creative flair, typically to make, draw, write, build, or develop something.

artefact a term derived from archaeology to denote man-made objects retrieved from dig sites, but used in a metaphorical sense in marketing to indicate cultural meanings and brands.

asynchronous delays in interaction or information exchange ranging from a few seconds to even longer such as a few days or weeks.

ATR a framework developed by Ehrenberg to explain how advertising works. ATR stands for awareness–trial–reinforcement.

attack strategies derived from military origins, these strategies seek to achieve growth objectives.

attitudes refers to mental states of individuals that underlie the structuring of perceptions and guide behavioural response.

audience fragmentation the disintegration of large media audiences into many smaller audiences caused by the development of alternative forms of entertainment that people can experience. This means that to reach large numbers of people in a target market, companies need to use a variety of media, not just rely on a few mass media channels.

backward integration when a company takes over one or more of its suppliers, it is said to be backward integrating. Taking over a buyer is forward integrating.

behavioural economics the study of the psychology of consumer decision-making, particularly seeking to explain irrational decision-making and behaviour.

benefits sought by understanding the motivations customers derive from their purchases it is possible to have an insight into the benefits they seek from product use.

bid rigging when organizations conspire to determine which company or companies should win a particular contract.

blogs frequent web-based publication of personal thoughts and weblinks made accessible to a wider online audience that supports audience feedback.

Boston Box a popular portfolio matrix, commonly also referred to as the BCG, developed by the Boston Consulting Group.

bot an automated program that performs specific commands when instructed (as in robot). Examples include chat room hosts who greet visitors, and 'spiders' that access websites to retrieve their content for search engine indexes.

brand multidimensional and emotional constructs which people use to embrace an abstract object or a set of associations in the mind.

brand association a concept relating to the psychosocial meanings people are encouraged to make with some brands.

brand comprehension refers to what we understand the brand to mean to us in both in functional terms, i.e. how it solves a particular problem, and emotional terms, i.e. whether or not we like it and how we relate to it.

branded content use of entertainment material delivered through paid or owned media which features a single company or product/service brand.

brand equity a measure of the value of a brand. It is an assessment of a brand's physical assets plus a sum that represents their reputation or goodwill.

brand extensions a term used to refer to the process when a successful brand is used to launch a new product into a new market.

brand health the overall condition of a brand relative to the context in which it operates.

brand licensing in return for a fee, one company permits another to use its trademark to promote other products over a defined period of time in a defined area.

brand personality the set of human characteristics that some individuals associate with a brand.

Brand Personality Scale dimensions used to measure brand personality.

brand placement the planned and deliberate use of brands within films, television, and other entertainment vehicles with a view to developing awareness and brand values.

brand positioning a strategic activity that is used to differentiate and distinguish a brand.

brand preference ensuring that customers choose your brand rather than those of your competitors.

brand relevance the creation of brand characteristics that are so attractive that any competitive brand that does not have the desirable characteristic is rejected.

brand scope the range of international markets in which a brand operates.

breakdown method the view that the market is considered to consist of customers who are essentially the same, so the task is to identify groups that share particular differences.

briefs written documents used to exchange information between parties involved with the development and implementation of a campaign.

build-up method considers a market to consist of customers that are all different, so here the task is to find similarities.

business markets characterized by organizations that consume products and services for use within the manufacture/production of other products or for use in their daily operations.

business-to-business activities undertaken by one company, which are directed at another.

business-to-business marketing the marketing of products and services that are bought and sold between organizations.

buyclasses the different types of buying situations faced by organizations.

buyers people who select suppliers and manage the buying process whereby the required products and services are procured. They formally undertake the process whereby products and services are purchased once a decision has been made to procure them.

buying centre *see* decision-making unit.

buyphases a series of sequential activities or stages through which organizations proceed when making purchasing decisions.

call-to-action a part of a marketing communication message that explicitly requests that the receiver act in a particular way.

capital equipment goods buildings, heavy plant, and factory equipment necessary to build or assemble products.

capitalism the political system in which private (as opposed to governmental) capital and wealth is the predominant means of producing and distributing goods.

category killer a large retail outlet typically positioned in out-of-town locations, specializing in selling one area of products with the aim of killing off the competition, e.g. DIY stores such as Homebase in the UK and Toys Я Us in the USA, France, and UK, and other countries. These stores are characterized by a narrow but very deep product assortment, low prices, and few to moderate customer services.

causal research a technique used to investigate the relational link between two or more variables by manipulating the independent variable(s) to see the effect on the dependent variable(s) and comparing effects with a control group where no such manipulation takes place.

cause-related marketing a campaign where a company is linked to a charity or social cause with the express intention of building its own customer goodwill, providing the charity with an increase in resource, and the company with either a concomitant increase in sales of its product/service or a reputational dividend.

celebrity endorsement usually famous or respected members of the public, used by advertisers to market specific goods and services because they are perceived to be expert or knowledgeable or because of their ability to display particular attractive qualities.

channel conflict is where one channel member perceives another channel member to be acting in a way that prevents the first member from achieving its distribution activities.

choice criteria denotes the principal dimensions on which we select a particular product or service. For a hairdresser, this might be price, location, range of services, level of expertise, friendliness, and so on.

CIM the Chartered Institute of Marketing is a professional body for marketing professionals based in the UK, with study centres and members around the world.

classical conditioning a theory of learning propounded by Russian physiologist Ivan Pavlov, who carried out a series of experiments with his dogs. He realized that if he rang a bell before serving food, the dogs would automatically associate the sound of the bell (conditioned stimulus) with the presentation of the food (unconditioned stimulus), and begin salivating. Classical conditioning occurs when the unconditioned stimulus becomes associated with the conditioned stimulus.

click-through rate (CTR) the amount of traffic on a website.

client brief a written document developed by clients to provide their appointed agencies with key information about their markets, goals, strategies, resources, and contacts. Client briefs should provide the agency with an insight into the client's task or communication problem that needs to be resolved.

co-branding the process by which two established brands work together on one product or service. The principle behind co-branding is that the combined power of the two brands generates increased consumer appeal and attraction.

co-created content (CCC) is the act of interacting, creating content or applications, by at least two people.

coding in a survey when answers are assigned numbers in order to allow them to be more easily analysed; they can be either pre-coded (i.e. analysed before the questionnaire is completed, when answers are set) or coded after the questionnaire is completed (when closed questions are used).

cognition knowing or perceiving something, typically as a result of rational thought.

cognitive a psychological term relating to the action of thinking about something. Our opinions are cognitive. Cognitions are mental structures formed about something in our minds.

cognitive dissonance a psychological theory proposed by Leon Festinger in 1957 which states that we are motivated to re-evaluate our beliefs, attitudes, opinions, or values if the position we hold on them at one point in time does not concur with the position held at an earlier period owing to some intervening event, circumstance, or action.

collaborative exchanges a series of economic transactions between parties who have a long-term orientation towards, and are primarily motivated by, concern for each other.

collusion when a group of competitor companies conspire to control the market, often at the expense of the consumer/customer, and typically in relation to price fixing.

commitment a desire that a relationship should continue.

communication the sharing of meaning created through the transmission of information.

communications objectives goals related to the outcome of a marketing communications campaign. Normally set in terms of desired levels of awareness, perception, comprehension/knowledge, attitudes, and overall degree of preference for a brand.

comparative advantage the ability to produce goods and/or services at a lower opportunity cost than other firms or individuals.

competitive advantage achieved when an organization has an edge over its competitors on factors that are important to customers.

competitive intelligence the organized, professional, systematic collection of information, typically through informal mechanisms, used for the achievement of strategic and tactical organizational goals.

computer-assisted personal interviewing (CAPI) an approach to personal interviewing using a hand-held computer or laptop to display questions and record the respondents' answers.

computer-assisted telephone interviewing (CATI) an approach to telephone interviewing using a laptop or desktop computer to display the questions to the interviewer who reads them out and records the respondent's answers.

computer-assisted web interviewing (CAWI) an approach to online interviewing where the respondent uses a laptop or desktop computer to access questions in a set location to which the respondent must go. Questions are automatically set based on the respondent's answers.

conative a psychological term relating to our motivations to do something. Attitudes are conative because they are linked to our motivations to do things.

concentrated marketing strategy (niche marketing strategy) recognizes that there are segments in the market. However, a concentrated strategy is implemented by focusing on just one or two or a few market segments.

conceptual equivalence the degree to which interpretation of behaviour, or objects, is similar across countries.

consumer the user of a product, service, or other form of offering.

consumer durables manufactured consumer products that are relatively long-lasting (e.g. cars or computers) as opposed to non-durables (e.g. foodstuffs).

consumerism a movement concerned with the protection of consumers', as opposed to producers', interests.

consumer juries consist of a collection of target consumers who are asked to rank in order ideas or concepts put to them and to explain their choices.

consumer marketing refers to marketing activities undertaken directly to influence consumers, as opposed to other businesses.

context analysis the first stage of the marketing communications planning process. It involves the analysis of four main contexts (or situations)—the customer, business, internal, and external environmental contexts—in order to shape the detail of the plan.

contextual advertising a form of targeted advertising, on websites, with advertisements selected and served by automated systems based on the content displayed to the user.

contracting is where a manufacturer contracts an organization in a foreign market to manufacture or assemble the product in the foreign market.

control (digital media) the ability of users in a computer-mediated environment to access content at will, and create, modify, and share the content.

control (distribution) means achieving the optimum distribution costs without losing decision-making authority over the product offering and the way it is marketed and supported. Therefore this is about maximizing your capacity to manage all the marketing mix decisions.

control group a sample group used in causal research, which is not subjected to manipulation of some sort. *See* causal research.

convenience products non-durable goods or services, often bought with little pre-purchase thought or consideration.

convenience sampling a method used to select respondents where the criteria for selection are not restricted and the selection of the respondents is left entirely to the judgement of the researcher and the chance of selection beforehand is unknown.

convenience stores or corner shops offer a range of grocery and household items that cater for convenience and last-minute purchase needs of consumers. Key characteristics include long opening times (e.g. 24/7), usually family run, and often belong to a trading group.

conversion rate a form of marketing communication to encourage, trial, purchase, or repeat purchase activity from a website.

cookie an electronic 'token'—a piece of data or record transmitted by a webserver to a client computer. More simply put, a cookie is a small text file found on your hard drive that allows information about your web activity patterns to be stored in the memory of your browser.

corporate communication mix the particular configuration of the symbolic, management, marketing, organizational, and behavioural elements of communication.

corporate objectives the mission and overall business goals that an organization has agreed.

corporate social responsibility (CSR) typically a programme of social and/or environmental activities undertaken by a company on behalf of one or more of its stakeholders to develop sustainable business operations, foster goodwill, and develop the company's corporate reputation.

cost leadership a strategy involving the production of goods and services for a broad market segment, at a cost lower than all other competitors.

counter-implementation the behaviour employees exhibit when they resist tasks associated with the implementation of strategic programmes, whether intentionally or unintentionally, which is often motivated by anxiety.

coverage is about maximizing the amount of contact and value (or benefits) for the customer (in terms of product offering availability). This is the marketer's desire to have the product available to the maximum number of customers, in the maximum number of locations, across the widest range of times.

credit crunch a period of economic turbulence during which economies around the world entered recession. The turbulence was caused by lax regulation in banking markets and the improper securitization of sub-prime mortgage debt, which led to very low rates of inter-bank lending and difficulties in obtaining consumer and wholesale credit (hence the term credit crunch).

critical marketing the process of scrutinizing marketing theory and practice from an anti-foundational perspective to identify unintended adverse societal consequences and discord.

CRM *see* customer relationship management.

crowdsourcing when an organization outsources a function originally undertaken by its employees to a group ('crowd') of people either as an open call or in a more restricted way.

cultural anthropology a branch of study concerned with observing and explaining cultural differences in human behaviour.

culture the values, beliefs, ideas, customs, actions, and symbols that are learned and shared by people within particular societies.

customer the person who purchases and pays for (or initially requests and specifies, in the case of a non-financial transaction) a product, service, or other form of offering from a company or organization.

customer acquisition all marketing activities and strategies used by organizations to attract new customers.

customer development a period during which buyers and sellers become more familiar with each other's propositions and needs.

customer decline the concluding and terminal stage of a buyer–seller relationship

customer experience the individual feelings and emotions felt through interactions with an organization and its offerings.

customer portfolio matrix a 2 × 2 grid that is used to reflect the strength of the relationships between a buyer and seller and the profitability that each account represents to the seller.

customer relationship lifecycle the stages a customer moves through during their relationship with an organization. These stages are customer acquisition, development, retention, and decline or termination.

customer relationship management (CRM) software systems that provide all staff with a complete view of the history and status of each customer.

customer relationship marketing all marketing activities and strategies used to retain customers. This is achieved by providing customers with relationship-enhancing products and/or services that are perceived to be of value and superior to those offered by a competitor.

customer retention all marketing activities and strategies used by organizations to keep current customers.

customer satisfaction a state of mind reached when the provision of goods or services meets or exceeds a customer's pre-purchase expectations of quality and service.

customized targeting strategy in which a marketing strategy is developed for each customer as opposed to each market segment.

cuts adverts are initially produced in cartoon format, complete with dialogue, before they are produced, filmed, and edited.

deciders people who make organizational purchasing decisions, often very difficult to identify.

decision-making unit (DMU) a group of people who make purchasing decisions on behalf of an organization.

decision-making unit structure the attitudes, policies, and purchasing strategies used by organizations provide the means by which organizations can be clustered.

decoding that part of the communication process in which receivers unpack the various components of the message, and begin to make sense and give the message meaning.

deconstruction a form of textual analysis, associated with French philosopher, Jacques Derrida, used to uncover hidden or 'absent' meanings by breaking the text down into privileged themes, then determining the binary opposites of those privileged themes as the hidden or absent meaning of the work, and essentially proposing that this is what the work was really trying to say.

defence strategies derived from military origins, these strategies need to be deployed quickly and save time when faced with frontal or flanking attacks.

demographic key variables concerning age, sex, occupation, level of education, religion, and social class, many of which determine a potential buyer's ability to purchase a product or service.

deontological ethics a form of ethical approach by which the rightness or wrongness of an action or decision is not judged to be exclusively based on the consequences of that action or decision.

department store a large-scale retailing institution that has a very broad and deep product assortment (both hard and soft goods), with the provision of a wide array of customer service facilities for store customers.

descriptive ethics (ethno-ethics) concerned with the study of system of beliefs and practices of a social group from the perspective of being outside that group.

descriptive research a research technique used to test, and confirm, hypotheses developed from a management problem.

deshopping the deliberate purchase of an item where there is an intention to return it for a refund after a single use.

desk research see secondary research.

dialectics the art of investigating the truth of opinions by considering that which is said from opposing perspectives to determine which of the two opposite forces is dominant.

dialogue the development of knowledge that occurs when all parties to a communication event listen, adapt, and reason with one another about a specific topic.

diaspora peoples dispersed from, or who have emigrated from, their homeland. Often used in relation to the Jewish peoples.

differentiated targeting approach recognizes that there are several market segments to target, each being attractive to the marketing organization. To exploit market segments, a marketing strategy is developed for each segment.

differentiation a strategy through which an organization offers products and services to broad particular customer groups, who perceive the offering to be significantly different from, and superior to, its competitors.

digital asset optimization (DAO) the optimization of all an organization's digital assets for search, retrieval, and indexing.

digital marketing the process of marketing accomplished or facilitated through the application of electronic devices, appliances, tools, techniques, technologies, and/or systems.

digital value the means by which digital processes and systems can be used to provide customers with enhanced product and service value.

direct channel structure where the product goes directly from the producer to the final customer.

direct exporting involves the manufacturing firm itself distributing its product offering to foreign markets, direct to customers.

direct investment or foreign manufacture, some form of manufacture or production in the foreign or host country is sometimes necessary.

direct marketing a marketing communications tool that uses non-personal media to create and sustain a personal and intermediary-free communication with customers, potential customers, and other significant stakeholders. In most cases this is a media-based activity.

direct-response advertising advertisements that contain mechanisms such as telephone numbers, website addresses, email, and snail mail addresses. These are designed to encourage viewers to respond immediately to the ads. Most commonly used on television and known as DRTV.

direct selling is one of the oldest forms of retailing methods. Defined as the personal contact between a salesperson and a consumer away from the retailing environment, this type of retailing may also be called in-home personal selling.

discount retailers this type of retailer involves comparatively low prices as a major selling point combined with the reduced costs of doing business.

disintermediation the reduction in the number or strength of intermediaries that are required in a marketing channel.

distribution see place.

distribution centres are designed to move goods, rather than just store them.

distribution channel see marketing channel.

distributor brands brands developed by the wholesalers, distributors, dealers, and retailers who make up the distribution channel. Sometimes referred to as own-label brands.

distributors organizations that buy goods and services, often from a limited range of manufacturers, and normally sell them to retailers or resellers.

diversification a strategy that requires organizations to grow outside their current range of activities. This type of growth brings new value chain activities because the firm is operating with new products and in new markets.

divest a strategic objective that involves selling or killing off a product when products continue to incur losses and generate negative cash flows.

DRIP the four primary tasks marketing communications can be expected to accomplish: differentiate, reinforce, inform, and persuade.

dumping some organizations need to get rid of excess stock and, with limited opportunity for sales in domestic markets, seek overseas markets in which to offload some of this stock.

durable goods goods bought infrequently, which are used repeatedly, and which involve a reasonably high level of consumer risk.

dyadic essentially means two-way. A commercial relationship that is dyadic is an exchange between two people, typically a buyer and a seller.

early adopters a group of people in the process of diffusion who enjoy being at the leading edge of innovation and buy into new products at an early stage.

early majority a group of people in the process of diffusion who require reassurance that a product works and has been proven in the market before they are prepared to buy it.

economies of scale the reduction in cost of each additional unit as production increases and operational efficiencies are realized.

ego a Freudian psychoanalytical concept which denotes that part of our psyche that attempts to find outlets for the urges in our id, moderated by the superego.

elasticity an economic concept associated with the extent to which changes in one variable are related to changes in another. If a price increase in a good causes a decline in volume of sales of that good, we say the good is price elastic and specify how much. If it causes no change or very little change, we say it is inelastic.

electronic kiosks are being placed in shopping malls to assist the retailing experience. Mediated by hypermedia web-based interfaces, these computer-based retailing environments offer consumers increased self-service opportunity, wide product assortments, and large amounts of data and information aiding decision-making.

elicitation techniques a technique of disguising questioning so that information is obtained without the imparter recognizing what they are divulging.

email marketing direct marketing using electronic mail as a means to communicate messages directly, increase loyalty, and build relationships with an audience who have given their permission.

embedding (journalists) refers to the practice of the government inviting selected journalists to report on military activity while based inside units involved in major combat operations. This provides the journalist with some degree of protection, but exposes them to the same risks from enemy combatants as the soldiers. Thus, it could be argued that their journalistic impartiality is compromised as a result.

emotion mental feeling or disturbance arising instinctually.

encoding a part of the communication process when the sender selects a combination of appropriate words, pictures, symbols, and music to represent a message to be transmitted.

engagement refers to the moment of audience captivation, achieved through the delivery of messages that are relevant, meaningful, of interest, and/or which arouse curiosity.

environmental scanning the management process internal to an organization designed to identify external issues, situations, and threats that may impinge on an organization's future and its strategic decision-making.

ethnocentric approach views the domestic market (home market) as the most important, and overseas markets as inferior with foreign imports not seen as representing a serious threat.

ethnographic studies involve an approach to research that emphasizes the collection of data through participant observation of members of a specific subcultural grouping and observation of participation of members of a specific subcultural grouping.

ethnography a subdiscipline derived from cultural anthropology as an approach to research, which emphasizes the collection of data through participant observation of members of a specific subcultural grouping and observation of participation of members of a specific subcultural grouping.

evoked set a group of goods, brands, or services for a specific item brought up in a person's mind in a particular purchasing situation and from which he/she makes a decision as to which product, brand, or service to buy.

exclusive distribution is where intermediaries are given exclusive rights to market the good or service within a defined 'territory', and thus a limited number of intermediaries are used.

exhibitions events when groups of sellers meet collectively with the key purpose of attracting buyers.

experience quality the emotional evaluation by customers of their experiences as they participate in consumption activities.

exploratory research a research technique used to generate ideas to develop hypotheses based around a management problem.

exporting manufacturing goods in one country, but selling them to customers overseas in foreign markets.

extensive problem-solving occurs when consumers give a great deal of attention and care to a purchase decision where there is no previous or similar product purchase experience.

externalities negative impacts that arise as a result of economic development, e.g. on the environment, to society, and so on.

external pacing occurs where the speed, sequence, and content are controlled by the sender of the message/information.

extrinsic attributes those elements that, if changed, do not alter the material functioning and performance of the product itself.

face validity the use of the researcher's or an expert's subjective judgement to determine whether an instrument is measuring what it is designed to measure.

fatal accident rate (FAR) a term used in industrial safety engineering to denote how many people would be killed under certain hypothetical conditions. Typically, the FAR is calculated with a view to minimizing the number of fatalities in any given industrial scenario.

feedback a part of the communication process referring to the responses offered by receivers.

field marketing a marketing communications activity concerned with providing support for the sales force and merchandising personnel.

firmographics an approach to segmentation of business-to-business markets using criteria such as company size, geography, standard industrial classification (SIC) codes, and other company-oriented classification data.

fixed capital the cost of plant, equipment, and machinery owned by a business.

fixed costs costs that do not vary according to the number of units of product made or service sold. For instance, fixed costs in the pharmaceutical market would include manufacturing plant costs. In a service business like the airline industry, fixed costs would include the cost of purchasing the plane.

flippancy to be disrespectful by treating something serious with less importance than others expect.

focus a strategy based on finding gaps in broad market segments or in competitors' product ranges.

focus group *see* group discussion.

fragmentation refers to the process of the trivialization of our value systems and the corresponding break-up of associated market segments, the break-up of consumer identities, and a weak commitment to a single consumer lifestyle.

framing the dual action by which communicators present ideas and concepts, and members of an audience interpret those concepts by assimilating them into their pre-existing cognitive schema.

franchise where a company offers a complete brand concept, supplies, and logistics to a franchisee who invests an initial lump sum and thereafter pays regular fees to continue the relationship.

franchising a contractual vertical marketing system in which a franchisor licenses a franchisee to produce or market goods or services to certain criteria laid down by the franchisor in return for fees and/or royalties.

fulfilment activities associated with locating and picking stock, packing, and shipping the selected items to the next channel member.

full-service agency an advertising agency that provides its clients with a full range of services, including strategy and planning, designing the advertisements, and buying the media.

functional equivalence relates to whether or not a concept has the same function in different countries.

gatekeepers people who control the type and flow of information into an organization and in particular to members of the DMU.

generic brands brands sold without any promotional materials or any means of identifying the company.

geocentric approach sees the world as a single market—global, with the organization looking for global segments (e.g. ageing market) and global opportunities to rationalize communications, production, and product development.

geodemographic this approach to segmentation presumes that there is a relationship between the type of housing and location that people live in and their purchasing behaviours.

geographic in many situations the needs of potential customers in one geographic area are different from those in another area. This may be due to climate, custom, or tradition.

geographic proximity closeness of the market in physical terms to the domestic market.

global capability the willingness and capability to operate anywhere in the world with a direct result in global brand recognition.

globalization refers to increasing global connectivity, integration, and interdependence in the economic, social, technological, cultural, political, and ecological spheres.

government the system of organization of a nation state.

grey marketing the unauthorized sale of new branded products diverted from authorized distribution channels or imported into a country for sale without the consent or knowledge of the manufacturer.

gross domestic product (GDP) a measure of the output of a nation—the size of its economy. It is calculated as the market value of all finished goods and services produced in a country during a specified period, typically available annually or quarterly.

gross national product (GNP) total domestic and foreign added value claimed by residents of a state.

group discussions (or focus group) a group discussion on a pre-selected series of topics among 8–12 people introduced by a moderator, where group members are encouraged to express their own views and interact with one another.

habit a repetitive form of behaviour, often undergone without conscious rational thought in a routine way. However, the processes underlying the routinization process are voluntary (i.e. controllable) rather than reflexive (uncontrollable).

haggling when a customer argues with a supplier, usually a retailer, over the price to be paid for a good or service and is successful in obtaining a discount.

halal a term referring to what is permissible under sharia law and most typically used in Western societies when referring to permissible foodstuffs. For a food to be halal it must not contain alcohol, blood or its by-products, or the meat of an omnivore or carnivore. In addition, where the food is from an animal, a Muslim must have pronounced the name of Allah before slaughtering the animal.

harvesting a strategic objective based on maximizing short-term profits and stimulating positive cash flow. Often used in mature markets as firms/products enter a decline phase.

hashtag a word or a phrase prefixed with the symbol #, often used in microblogging to group messages about similar topics.

hierarchy of effects (HoE) general sequential models used to explain how advertising works. Popular in the 1960s–1980s, these models provided a template that encouraged the development and use of communication objectives.

hold a strategic objective based on defending against attacks from aggressive competitors.

horizontal conflicts may arise between members of a channel on the same level of distribution.

host country a country in which international marketing operations take place.

hybrid channel conflict conflict is bound to occur when producers compete with retailers by selling through their producer-owned stores.

hybrid channel structure where some products go directly from producer to customers and others go through intermediaries.

hyper-reality a play of illusions and phantasms, an imaginary world, made up of simulacra.

id a Freudian psychoanalytical concept referring to the part of our psyche that harbours our instinctual drives and urges.

incredulity disbelief of someone, or towards something (e.g. an idea).

in-depth interview a qualitative research method used to identify hidden feelings, memories, attitudes, and motivations of the respondents using a face-to-face interview approach.

indirect channel structure where the product goes from the producer through an intermediary, or series of intermediaries such as a wholesaler, retailer, franchisee, agent, or broker, to the final customer.

indirect exporting takes place where production and manufacture of the product offering occurs in the domestic market and involves the services of other companies (intermediaries) to sell the product in the foreign market.

industrial marketing and purchasing group (IMP) IMP represents a school of thought about relationship marketing.

industry type (SIC codes) standard industrial classifications (SIC) are codes used to identify and categorize all types of industry and businesses.

inflation when prices rise.

influencers people who help set the technical specifications for a proposed purchase and assist the evaluation of alternative offerings by potential suppliers.

information utility the provision of information about the product offering before and after sales. It can further provide information about those purchasing it.

initiators people who start the organizational buying decision process.

innovators a group of people in the process of diffusion who like new ideas, and are most likely to take risks associated with new products.

inseparability a characteristic of a service, one that refers to its instantaneous production and consumption.

intangibility a characteristic of a service, namely that it does not have physical attributes and so cannot be perceived by the senses—cannot be tasted, seen, touched, smelt, or possessed.

integrated marketing communications (IMC) a process associated with the coordinated development and delivery of a consistent marketing communication message(s) with a target audience.

integrative a growth strategy based on working with the same products and the same markets but starting to perform some of the activities in the value chain that were previously undertaken by others.

intensity of channel coverage number of intermediaries to use when they want or need it.

intensive a growth strategy that requires an organization to concentrate its activities on markets or products that are familiar.

intensive distribution means placing your product or service in as many outlets or locations as possible in order to maximize the opportunity for customers to find the good or service.

intention in the consumer context, this is linked to whether or not we intend, are motivated to, purchase a good or service.

interaction model the flow of communication messages that leads to mutual understanding about a specific topic.

interactive marketing is more accurately described as creating a situation or mechanism through which a marketer and a customer (or stakeholders) interact, usually in real time.

interactivity as such, interactivity is about the interchange between two or more parties (i.e. people or machines) and the effect one party has on the other's response.

intermediary an independent business concern that operates as a link between producers and ultimate consumers or industrial end-users. It renders services in connection with the purchase and/or sale of the product offering moving from producers to consumers.

internal marketing the application of marketing concepts and principles within an organization. Normally targeted at employees with a view to encouraging them to support and endorse the organization's strategy, goals, and brands.

international marketing marketing activity that crosses national boundaries.

internet advertising a form of marketing communication that uses the internet for the purpose of 'advertising'; delivering marketing messages to increase website traffic.

internet marketing (or online marketing) a form of electronic marketing limited in technical context and thus a tool-based definition denoting the use of internet-based technologies only (e.g. web, email, intranet, extranets, etc.) for marketing.

interstitials webpages that are displayed before an expected content page, often to display advertisements.

intrinsic attributes the functional characteristics of a product, such as its shape, performance, and physical capacity.

inventory management *see* stock management.

inverted production/consumption a concept indicating that the traditional pattern of consumption following production is changing in postmodern times to a pattern of production following consumption, e.g. in reality television where the viewer votes on which contestants should enter/leave a particular show.

involvement the greater the personal importance a person attaches to a given communication message, the more involvement they are said to have with that communication.

irony to say one thing and mean the opposite is to be ironic, often as a form of humour. To have something happen to you when the opposite was expected indicates an ironic event.

joint venture when two organizations come together to create a jointly owned third company.

This is an example of cooperative as opposed to competitive operations in international marketing.

juxtaposition to place items beside each other, with connotations of contrast.

KAM development cycle the development stages experienced by organizations as relationships with key account customers develop.

key accounts business customers who are strategically significant and with whom a supplier wishes to build long-lasting relationships.

key mediating variables (KMV) commitment and trust, used within the Morgan–Hunt model of relationship marketing.

laggards a group of people in the process of diffusion who are suspicious of all new ideas and whose opinions are very hard to change.

late majority a group of people in the process of diffusion who are sceptical of new ideas and only adopt new products because of social or economic factors.

lead generation activities undertaken by a company or organization to develop lists of prospective customers.

licensing a commercial process whereby the trademark of an established brand is used by another organization over a defined period of time in a defined area, in return for a fee, to develop another brand.

lifestage analysis is based on the principle that people need different products and services at different stages in their lives (e.g. childhood, adulthood, young couples, retired, etc.).

limited line retailers this type of retailer has a narrow but deep product assortment and customer services that vary from store to store.

limited problem-solving occurs when consumers have some product and purchase familiarity.

listing fee when a retailer charges a supplier a fee to allow the supplier to supply the supermarket. This fee is not typically related to any discounts already provided to the retailer. Such fees are illegal in France.

lobbying the process employed by companies, charities, and third-party interest groups to develop and build relationships with regulatory and political bodies in order to influence legislation in their favour or in order to advance a particular cause.

logistics the process of transporting the initial components of goods, services, and other forms of offering, and their finished products, from the producer to the customer and then on to the consumer.

logistics management broadly, the coordination of activities of the entire distribution channel to deliver maximum value to customers—from suppliers of raw materials to the manufacturer of the product, to the wholesalers who deliver the product, to the final customers who purchase it.

maintenance, repair, and operating (MRO) products, other than raw materials, that are necessary to ensure that the organization is able to continue functioning. Often referred to as consumables.

management problem a statement that outlines a situation faced by an organization requiring further investigation and subsequent organizational action.

managerial egoism a form of ethical approach to the effect that a manager ought to act in his/her own best interests and that an action is right if it benefits the manager undertaking that action.

manufacturer brands created and sustained by producers who seek widespread awareness and distribution because there is high demand for these brands.

market development strategy involves increasing sales by selling existing or 'old' products in new markets, either by targeting new audiences domestically or entering new markets internationally.

market (discrete) exchange a type of transaction between a buyer and a seller where the main focus is on the product and price.

marketing channel an organized network of agencies and organizations which together perform all the activities required to link producers and manufacturers with consumers, purchasers, and users to distribute product offerings.

marketing communications mix the five key communication tools used by organizations to reach consumers and other organizations with product- and organization-based messages. These tools are advertising, sales promotions, public relations, direct marketing, and personal selling.

marketing communications planning framework (MCPF) a model of the various decisions and actions that are undertaken when preparing, implementing, and evaluating communication strategies and plans. It reflects a deliberate or planned approach to strategic marketing communications.

marketing ethics the analysis and application of moral principles to marketing decision-making and the outcomes of these decisions.

marketing information systems a system incorporating ad hoc and continuous market and marketing research surveys, together with secondary data and internal data sources, for the purpose of decision-making by marketers.

marketing metrics a measure or set of measures that senior marketers use to assess the performance of their marketing strategies and programmes.

marketing mix the list of items a marketing manager should consider when devising plans for marketing products, including product decisions, place (distribution) decisions, pricing decisions, and promotion decisions. Later, the mix was extended to include physical evidence, process, and people decisions to account for the lack of physical nature in service products.

marketing myopia a term coined by Harvard Business School professor Theodore Levitt to denote the mindset that some companies get into when they completely fail to identify new competitors within their industry, which result from the development of substitute products and services.

marketing objectives marketing goals to be accomplished within a particular period of time. Usually referred to in terms of market share, sales revenues, volumes, ROI (return on investment), and other profitability indicators.

marketing research the design, collection, analysis, and interpretation of data collected for the purpose of aiding marketing decision-making.

market mix modelling a research process which uses multiple regression analysis based on customer survey data to ascertain the relative contributions of different promotional techniques on a customer-based dependent variable (e.g. awareness, intention to buy).

market orientation refers to the development of a whole-organization approach to the generation, collection, and dissemination of market intelligence across different departments and the organization's responsiveness to that intelligence.

market segmentation the division of customer markets into groups of customers with distinctly similar needs.

market sensing an organization's ability to gather, interpret, and act on strategic information from customers and competitors.

materialism a tendency to place superior value on physical objects rather than on spiritual or intellectual pursuits.

measurement equivalence concerns the extent to which the methods by which the researcher collects and categorizes essential data and information from two or more different sources are comparable.

media facilities used by companies to convey or deliver messages to target audiences. Media is the plural of medium.

media fragmentation the splintering of a few mainstream media channels into a multitude of media and channel formats.

media usage data on what media channels are used, by whom, when, where, and for how long provides useful insight into the reach potential for certain market segments through differing media channels, and also insight into their media lifestyle.

media vehicle an individual medium used to carry advertising messages.

merchant a merchant performs the same functions as an agent, but takes ownership.

meta-ethics a form of philosophical enquiry that treats ethical concepts and belief systems as objects of philosophical enquiry in themselves.

meta-narrative an overarching belief system, held by the majority. Might also be called the received wisdom. Examples in contemporary Western society are the belief in the need to maintain capitalist economic growth and the need for continual scientific advancement.

metric in a marketing sense, a measure or set of measures used to assess the performance of marketing strategies and programmes.

microblogs see blogs.

mission a statement that sets out an organization's long-term intentions, describing its purpose and direction.

mixed price bundling when a product or service is offered together with another typically complementary product or service, which is also available separately, in order to make the original product or service seem more attractive (e.g. a mobile phone package with text messages and international call packages included in the price).

mobile marketing is the set of practices that enable organizations to communicate and engage with their audience in an interactive and relevant manner through any mobile device or network.

mod cons a colloquialism, an abbreviated form of modern conveniences.

mode of transfer a transmissive process is the method by which something travels from source or sender to a receiver.

modernist a style of thought based on logic and associated with the ideals and assumptions of the Enlightenment period advocating capitalist economic growth and the importance of scientific advancement, among other ideals.

modified rebuy the organizational processes associated with the infrequent purchase of products and services.

monitoring activities related to ensuring that brand development remains on-schedule and in line with the stated objectives and performance targets.

multichannel structure the use of multiple sales channels to provide a variety of customer touchpoints.

multi-domestic competitive strategy an organization pursues a separate marketing strategy in each of its foreign markets while viewing the competitive challenge independently from market to market.

multiphrenic the many-minded consumer, who can want different kinds of consumer experiences all at the same time or at different times in the same sort of circumstances. A kind of consumer multiple personality disorder.

mystery shopping this form of research is designed to evaluate standards of customer service performance received by customers and is commissioned either within one's own organization or within a competitor's organization.

neoclassical economics refers to a meta-theory of economics predicated on delineating supply and demand based on rational individuals or agents each seeking to maximize their individual utility by making choices with a given amount of information.

netnography the branch of ethnography which seeks to analyse internet users' behaviour.

net promoter score a system for measuring the loyalty of customer relationships by determining the extent to which customers are prepared to advocate an organization.

new task the organizational processes associated with buying a product or service for the first time.

niche market a small part of a market segment that has specific and specialized characteristics that make it uneconomic for the leading competitors to enter this segment.

niche marketing strategy *see* concentrated.

noise influences that distort information in the communication process and, in turn, make it difficult for the receiver to decode and interpret a message correctly.

non-durable goods low-priced products that are bought frequently, used just once, and incur low levels of purchase risk.

non-probability sampling a sampling method used where the probability of selection of the sample elements from the population is unknown. Typical examples include quota, snowball, and convenience sampling approaches.

non-staple in the grocery context, grocery products that are not a main or important food.

non-store retailers retailing activities resulting in transactions that occur away from the retail store.

non-tariff barrier obstacle to international markets from a non-fiscal source (e.g. product safety legislation).

normative ethics concerned with the rational enquiry into standards of right and wrong, good or bad, in respect of character and conduct and which ought to beaccepted by a class of individuals.

observation a research method that requires a researcher to watch, and record, how consumers or employees behave, typically in relation to either purchasing or selling activities.

observational study a study where behaviours of interest are recorded, e.g. mystery shopping and mass transit studies.

omnibus survey a regular survey made up of questions from several different clients at any one time, each buying one or more questions and spreading the cost of the survey between them.

online marketing *see* internet marketing.

online retailing a type of electronic commerce used for business-to-consumer transactions and mail order forms of non-shop retailing.

operant conditioning a learning theory developed by B. F. Skinner, which suggests that when a subject acts on a stimulus from the environment (antecedents), this is more likely to result in a particular behaviour (behaviour) if that behaviour is reinforced (consequence) through reward or punishment.

opinion followers people who turn to opinion leaders and formers for advice and information about products and services they are interested in purchasing or using.

opinion formers people who exert personal influence because of their profession, authority, education, or status associated with the object of the communication process. They are not part of the same peer group as the people they influence.

opinion leaders people who are predisposed to receiving information and then reprocessing it in order to influence others. They belong to the same peer group as the people they influence; they are not distant or removed.

opinions refer to observable verbal responses given by individuals to an issue or question and are easily affected by current affairs and discussions with significant others.

opportunity cost the difference between the revenues generated from undertaking one particular activity compared with another feasible revenue-generating activity.

organization or corporate strategy the means by which the resources of the organization are matched with the needs of the environment in which the organization decides to operate.

organizational buyer behaviour the characteristics, issues, and processes associated with the behaviour of producers, resellers, government units, and institutions when purchasing goods and services.

organizational goals the outcomes of the organization's various activities, often expressed as market share, share value, return on investment, or numbers of customers served.

organizational size grouping organizations by their relative size (MNCs, international, large, SMEs) enables the identification of design, delivery, usage rates, or order size and other purchasing characteristics.

organizational values the standards of behaviour expected of an organization's employees.

original equipment manufacturers (OEMs) the process whereby one company purchases and relabels a product and then incorporates it within a different product in order to sell it under a different (their own) brand name.

overt search the point in the buying process when a consumer seeks further information in relation to a product or buying situation, according to the Howard–Sheth model of buyer behaviour.

ownership utility goods are available immediately from the intermediaries' stocks; thus ownership passes to the purchaser.

pacing the control of the speed and sequence of information transfer.

paid inclusion can provide a guarantee that the website is included in the search engine's natural listings.

paid placement *see* pay per click.

panel studies studies that use information collected from a fixed group of respondents over a defined period of time.

pastiche something made up of different parts, especially in relation to music or picture, or a work of art composed in the style of another, often well-known, artist.

pay per click (PPC) advertising that uses sponsored search engine listings to drive traffic to a website. The advertiser bids for search terms, and the search engine ranks ads based on a competitive auction as well as other factors.

perceived quality a relative subjective measure; we talk of perceived quality because there is no truly objective absolute measure of product or service quality.

perceived risk the real and imagined risks that customers consider when purchasing products and services.

perceived value a customer's estimate of the extent to which a product or service can satisfy his/her needs.

perception a mental picture in our heads based on existing attitudes, beliefs, needs, stimulus factors, and factors specific to our situation, which governs the way we see objects, events, or people in the world about us. Our perceptions govern our attitudes and behaviour towards whatever we perceive.

perceptual mapping a diagram, typically two-dimensional, of 'image-space' derived from attitudinal market research data, which display the differences in perceptions that customers, consumers, or the general public have of different products/services or brands in general.

performance environment organizations that directly or indirectly influence an organization's ability to achieve its strategic and operational goals.

perishability a characteristic of a service, which recognizes that spare or unused capacity cannot be stored for use at some point in the future.

permission-based email marketing (opt-in) opt-in email or permission marketing is a method of advertising by electronic mail wherein the recipient of the advertisement has consented to receive it.

personal selling the use of interpersonal communications with the aim of encouraging people to purchase particular products and services, for personal gain and reward.

personality that aspect of our psyche that determines the way in which we respond to our environment in a relatively stable way over time.

PESTLE an acronym used to identify a framework that examines the external environment. PESTLE stands for the political, economic, socio-cultural, technological, legal, and ecological environments.

picking in the context of consumer behaviour, this word has a different meaning from the same term used in common parlance. It is the process of deliberative selection of a product or service from among a repertoire of acceptable alternatives, even though the consumer believes the alternatives to be essentially identical in their ability to satisfy his/her need.

pitch a presentation, made by competing agencies, in order to win a client's account (or business).

place or distribution is essentially about how you can place the optimum amount of goods and/or services before the maximum number of members of your target market, at times and locations that optimize the marketing outcome, i.e. sales.

place utility the relocation of an offering to enable more convenient purchase and consumption.

political environment that part of the macroenvironment concerned with impending and potential legislation and how it may affect a particular firm.

polycentric approach each overseas market is seen as a separate domestic market, and each country is seen as a separate entity, and the firm seeks to be seen as a local firm within that country.

positioning the way that an audience of consumers or buyers perceives a product or service, particularly as a result of the marketing communications process aimed at a target audience.

positive morality a body of doctrine that is generally adhered to by a social group of individuals, concerning what is right and wrong, good and bad, in respect of character and conduct.

post hoc method where segments are deduced from research.

postmaterialist emphasizes self-expression and quality of life, as opposed to economic and physical security.

postmodernism a rejection of modernist thought and approach, which at its heart contravenes and pokes fun in an irreverent way at the existing received wisdom as a way of drawing attention to itself and challenging the existing order.

postmodern marketing is a rejection of modernist and traditional thought in marketing, demonstrated by the contravention and poking of fun in an irreverent way at the existing received wisdom so as to draw attention to itself and challenge the existing order in marketing thought.

pre-code in surveys, in order to speed up data processing, answers to questions are assigned a unique code e.g. male 1, female 2, so that they can easily be analysed.

pressure group an organization that campaigns to change legislation in a particular area, and frequently seeks publicity to support its cause.

price the amount the customer has to pay to receive a good or service.

price collusion occurs when companies conspire to fix, raise, and maintain prices, and allocate sales volumes in their industries.

price discrimination occurs where the price of a good or service is set differently for certain groups of people.

price elasticity the percentage change in volume demanded as a proportion of the percentage change in price, usually expressed as a negative number. A score close to zero indicates that a product or service price change has little impact on quantity demanded, whereas a score of –1 indicates that a product or service price change effects an equal percentage quantity change. A value above –1 indicates a disproportionately higher change in quantity demanded as a result of a percentage price change.

price gouging occurs when a seller sets the price of a good or service at a level far higher than what is considered reasonable.

price sensitivity the extent to which a company or consumer increases or lowers their purchase volumes in relation to changes in price. Thus, a customer is price insensitive when unit volumes drop proportionately less than increases in prices.

pricing cues proxy measures used by customers to estimate a product or service's reference price. Examples include quality, styling, packaging, sale signs, and odd-number endings.

primary activities the five direct activities within the value chain necessary to bring materials into an organization, to convert them into final products or services, to ship them out to customers, and to provide marketing and servicing facilities.

primary research a technique used to collect data for the first time that has been specifically collected and assembled for the current research problem.

probability sampling a sampling method used where the probability of selection of the sample elements from the population is known. Typical examples include simple random, stratified random, and cluster sampling methods.

process of adoption the process through which individuals accept and use new products. The different stages in the adoption process are sequential and are characterized by the different factors that are involved at each stage.

process of diffusion the rate at which a market adopts an innovation. According to Rogers, there are five categories of adopters: innovators, early adopters, early majority, late majority, and laggards.

procurement the purchasing (buying) process in a firm or organization.

product anything that is capable of satisfying customer needs.

product class a broad category referring to various types of related products, e.g. cat food, shampoo, or cars.

product differentiation when companies produce offerings that are different from competing firms.

product forms the three different levels of elements and benefits that each product offers users: the core, the embodied, and the augmented forms.

product lifecycle the pathway a product assumes over its lifetime. There are said to be five main stages: development, introduction, growth, maturity, and decline.

product lines groups of brands that are closely related in terms of their functions and the benefits they provide.

product mix the set of all product lines and items that an organization offers for sale to buyers.

product placement the planned and deliberate use of brands within films, TV, and other entertainment vehicles with a view to developing awareness and brand values.

product usage segments are derived from analysing markets on the basis of their usage of the product offering, brand, or product category. This may be in the form of usage frequency, time of usage, and usage situations.

professional service firms organizations that deliver highly complex and customized services, created and delivered by highly qualified personnel

projective techniques an indirect questioning approach that encourages the subject to reveal their hidden feelings, values, and needs using word association, role playing, pictorial construction, and completion tests, for example.

promise management the process of enabling promises to be made to/with customers, making promises to them, and keeping promises by meeting the expectations that have been created by promises.

promotion the use of communications to persuade individuals, groups, or organizations to purchase products and services.

promotional mix the combination of five key communication tools: advertising, sales promotions, public relations, direct marketing, and personal selling.

propaganda a technique used by a communicating party expressing opinions or activities to influence the opinions or activities of a receiving party, to direct them towards a pre-determined agenda drawn up by the communicating party, often using psychological and symbolic manipulations.

proposition a product or service that represents a promise made to customers and stakeholders.

psychographic (lifestyles) analysing consumers' activities, interests, and opinions, we can understand individual lifestyles and patterns of behaviour, which in turn affect their buying behaviour and decision-making processes. On this basis, we can also identify similar product and/or media usage patterns.

psychological proximity perceived cultural and societal similarities between countries.

psychological reactance when a consumer perceives their freedom to pursue a particular decision alternative is blocked, wholly or partially, they become more motivated to pursue that decision alternative.

public relations a non-personal form of communication used by companies to build trust, goodwill, interest, and ultimately relationships with a range of stakeholders.

pull strategies marketing communication strategies used to communicate directly with end-user customers. These may be consumers but they might also be other organizations within a business-to-business context.

purchase situation this approach segments organizational buyers on the way in which a buying company structures its purchasing procedures, the type of buying situation, and whether buyers are in an early or late stage in the purchase decision process.

purchase/transaction data about customer purchases and transactions provides scope for analysing who buys what, when, how often, how much they spend, and through what transactional channel they purchase. This provides very rich data for identifiable 'profitable' customer segments.

purchasing power parity an economic theory that seeks to determine the relative value of currencies between countries, so that there is an equivalence of purchasing power.

purchasing power parity exchange rate a measure used to determine relative wealth of the population based on the cost of an identified basket of goods, which allows us to compare the wealth of one population with another.

pure price bundling when a product or service is offered together with another typically complementary product or service, which is not available separately, in order to make the original product or service seem more attractive (e.g. a CD with a music magazine).

push strategies marketing communication strategies used to communicate with channel intermediaries. These may be dealers, wholesalers, distributors, and retailers, otherwise referred to as the 'trade' or channel buyers.

qualitative research a type of exploratory research using small samples and unstructured data collection procedures, designed to identify hypotheses, possibly for later testing in quantitative research. The most popular examples include in-depth interviews, focus groups, and projective techniques.

quantitative research research designed to provide responses to pre-determined standardized questions from a large number of respondents involving the statistical analysis of the responses.

quota a non-tariff barrier that limits imports to an agreed percentage of the market.

quota sampling a method used to select respondents where the criteria for selection are restricted but the final selection of the respondents is left to the judgement of the researcher and the chance of selection beforehand is unknown.

random digit dialling a procedure used in telephone interviewing to provide a randomized sample of telephone numbers using specialized software programs.

rebranding the creation of a new name, term, symbol, or design, or a combination of these, for an established brand.

recall a measure of advertising effectiveness based on what an individual is able to remember about an ad.

receivers individuals or organizations who have seen, heard, smelt, or read a message.

recession a fall in a country's gross domestic product for two or more successive quarters in any one year.

recognition when new images and words presented are compared with existing images and words in memory and a match is found.

re-intermediation the increase in the number or strength of intermediaries that are required in a marketing channel.

reference group group that an individual uses to form his/her own beliefs and attitudes. A reference group can be positive, in which we align our opinions, attitudes, values, or behaviour with theirs, or negative, in which we are repelled by their behaviour and seek to dissociate our opinions, attitudes, values, and behaviour from theirs.

reference price the price band against which customers judge the purchase price of goods and services in their own minds.

regional approach grouping countries together, usually on a geographical basis (e.g. Europe), and providing for the specific needs of consumers within those countries.

relationship intensity the depth of trust and commitment and overall feelings a customer perceives in a relationship.

relationship marketing the development and management of long-term relationships with customers, influencers, referrers, suppliers, recruiters, and employees.

relative price denotes the price of company A's product/service as a proportion of the price of a comparable product/service of, typically, the market-leading company (B) or its nearest competitor (if A is the market leader).

reliability the degree to which the data elicited in a study are replicated in a repeat study.

research and development (R&D) the department within an organization in charge of using basic and applied science to develop new technologies, which are, in turn, used to develop new product, process, and service specifications, which can be leveraged into the development of new or reformulated customer propositions.

research brief a formal document prepared by the client organization and submitted to either an external market research provider (e.g. a market research agency or consultant) or an internal research provider (e.g. in-house research department) outlining a statement of the management problem and the perceived research needs of the organization.

research proposal a formal document prepared by an agency, consultant, or in-house research manager and submitted to the client to outline what procedures will be used to collect the necessary information, including timescales and costs.

resellers organizations that purchase goods and services from wholesalers, distributors, or even direct from producers and manufacturers, and make these available to organizations for consumption.

retail audit panel studies undertaken for retailers providing competitor (pricing) and market information.

retailers organizations that purchase goods and services from wholesalers, distributors, or even direct from producers and manufacturers, and make these available to consumers.

retailing all the activities directly related to the sale of goods and services to the ultimate end consumer for personal and non-business use. This is also called the retail trade.

retromarketing the practice of resurrecting a brand or iconic product from the past and re-marketing it.

reverse engineering the process of developing a product from the finished version (e.g. from a competitor's prototype) to its constituent parts rather than the usual approach from component parts to a finished product.

reverse logistics the process of returning goods in a physical distribution channel. This might be a flow from customer to manufacturer via a retailer (e.g. for repair or replacement).

routinized response behaviour a form of purchase behaviour which occurs when consumers have suitable product and purchase experience and where they perceive low risk.

sales force automation (SFA) occurs when firms computerize routine tasks or adopt technological tools to improve the efficiency or precision of sales force activities.

sales promotion a communication tool that adds value to a product or service with the intention of encouraging people to buy now rather than at some point in the future.

sampling equivalence concerns the extent to which samples representative of their populations are comparable across countries.

sampling frame a list of population members from which a sample is generated, e.g. telephone directories, membership lists.

scenarios pictures of the future that show how different outcomes may result from different strategic decisions.

science the pursuit of knowledge through a systematic method based particularly on the use of mathematical principles and the collection of empirical data, and in particular relation to studies of the natural world.

search directory a database of information maintained by human editors. It lists websites by category and subcategory, usually based on the whole website rather than one page or a set of keywords.

search engine operates algorithmically or using a mixture of algorithmic and human input to collect, index, store, and retrieve information on the web and making it available to users in a manageable and meaningful way in response to a search query.

search engine marketing (SEM) a set of marketing methods to increase the visibility of a website in search engine results pages (SERPs).

search engine optimization (SEO) attempts to improve rankings for relevant keywords in search results by improving a website's structure and content.

search marketing a form of internet marketing that seeks to increase the visibility of websites in search engine results pages.

secondary research a technique used to collect data that has previously been collected for a purpose other than the current research situation. The process is often referred to as desk research.

selective contestability the ability to disaggregate generic markets into meaningful submarkets or segments, select those most attractive, and position the product offering appropriately.

selective distribution where some, but not all, available outlets for the good or service are used.

selective exposure the process associated with how consumers screen out the information that is not consider meaningful or interesting.

semantic web the semantic web (also known as Web 3.0) is an enhancement of the social web (Web 2.0) but made more intelligent and responsive to users' needs by incorporating context-understanding programs to automatically find and act upon web-based information.

semiotics the science of signs and how they convey meaning in their representation.

sentiment analysis analysis of social media (e.g. on Twitter, Facebook) to determine whether or not people's comments are positive, negative, or neutral (or some other categorical variation).

service any act or performance offered by one party to another that is essentially intangible and where consumption does not result in any transfer of ownership.

service delivery the means through which services are experienced by customers.

service-dominant a core orientation that considers marketing to be a customer logic management process, in which services (not products) are the principal consideration for value creation.

service-dominant logic (SDL) asserts that organizations, markets, and society are concerned fundamentally with exchange of service, based on the application of knowledge and skills. Therefore it rejects the notion of dualism between goods and services marketing by arguing that all offerings provide a service.

service encounter an event that occurs when a customer interacts directly with a service.

service failure an event that occurs when a customer's expectations of a service encounter are not met.

service processes a series of sequential actions that lead to pre-determined outcomes when a service is performed correctly.

service quality a measure of the extent to which a service experience exceeds customers' expectations.

service recovery an organization's systematic attempt to correct a service failure and to retain a customer's goodwill.

servicescape the stimuli impacting on the customer in the service environment. The concept is similar to the atmospherics present in a retail environment.

services mix a combination of different service elements, including products.

servitization an integrated bundle of products and services where the services are an integral part of the core product.

SERVQUAL a disconfirmation model designed to measure service quality. It is based on the difference between the expected service and the actual perceived service.

shopping product a type of consumer product that is bought relatively infrequently and requires consumers to update their knowledge prior to purchase.

signified a term used in linguistics, developed by Ferdinand de Saussure to refer to something being discussed, e.g. French sparkling wine from the Champagne region of France (*see* signifier).

signifier a term used in linguistics, developed by Ferdinand de Saussure to refer to sound images used to represent something, e.g. the spoken word 'champagne' is used to refer to the signified French sparkling wine (*see* signified).

simple random sampling a method used to select respondents from a known population frame using randomly generated numbers assigned to population elements.

simulacrum the concept of a copy without an original, advanced by French philosopher Jean Baudrillard. A simulacrum comes into being through successive image-change phases, and after successive reproduction the end-copy is so different from the original that it is no longer a copy but a simulated version only.

SMART an approach used to write effective objectives. SMART stands for specific, measurable, achievable, realistic, and timed.

snowball sampling a method used to select respondents from rare populations where the criteria for selection are based on referral from an initial set of respondents typically generated through newspaper advertisements or some other method, and this set of respondents refers another set of respondents, and the process repeats.

social anthropology the scientific discipline of observing and recording the way humans behave in their different social groupings.

social capital is the relations among individuals, the social structures, and networks within which we live and work.

social class system of classification of consumers or citizens, based on the socio-economic status of the chief income earner in a household, typically into various subgroupings of middle- and working-class categories.

social enterprise a business whose primary objectives are essentially social and whose surpluses are reinvested for that purpose in the business or in the community, rather than dispersed to the owners.

social grade a system of classification of people based on their socio-economic group, usually based on the household's chief income earner.

social learning social learning theory, advocated by Albert Bandura, suggests that we can learn from observing the experiences of others, and in contrast with operant conditioning we can delay gratification and even administer our own rewards or punishment.

social listening the process of obtaining and analysing user commentary in social media.

social media marketing a form of marketing that utilizes social networking websites. The aim is to generate content that users share within their social networks to help a company develop a brand.

social or religious ethics is concerned with what is right and wrong, good and bad, in respect of character and conduct. It does not claim to be established merely on the basis of rational enquiry and makes an implicit claim to general allegiance to something (e.g. God).

society the customs, habits, and nature of a nation's social system.

spam unsolicited email, the junk mail of the twenty-first century, which clogs email servers and uses up much-needed bandwidth on the internet.

speciality products these are bought very infrequently, are very expensive, and represent very high risk.

sponsorship a marketing communications activity, whereby one party permits another an opportunity to exploit an association with a target audience in return for funds, services, or resources.

SPSS Statistical Package for the Social Sciences, a software package used for statistical analysis marketed by SPSS, a company owned by IBM.

stakeholders people with an interest, a 'stake', in the levels of profit an organization achieves, its environmental impact, and its ethical conduct in society.

standardized approach a firm operates as if the world were one large market (global market), ignoring regional and national differences, selling the same products and services the same way throughout the world.

stock management managing the balance between the anticipated number of finished goods required by customers, and a sufficient store of unfinished goods which can be assembled at a later date or when the stock of finished goods runs low.

storage warehouses store goods for moderate to long periods.

storyboards before advertisements are made, an outline of the story that the advertisement will follow is produced showing key themes, characters, and messages.

STP process the method by which whole markets are subdivided into different segments for targeting and positioning.

straight rebuy the organizational processes associated with the routine reordering of good and services, often undertaken from an approved list of suppliers.

strategic business unit an organizational unit which, for planning purposes, is sufficiently large to exercise control over the principal strategic factors affecting its performance. Typically abbreviated to SBU, these might incorporate an entire brand and/or its sub-components, or a country region, or some other discrete unit of an organization.

strategic market analysis the starting point of the marketing strategy process, involving analysis of three main types of environment: the external environment, the performance environment, and the internal environment.

strategic procurement the long term assignment of a single supplier, or a few suppliers, in order to develop mutually beneficial purchasing relationships.

stratified random sampling a method used to select respondents from known homogeneous subgroups of the population where subgroups are determined on the basis of specific criteria.

strong theory a persuasion-based theory designed to explain how advertising works.

superego a Freudian psychoanalytical concept, which denotes the part of our psyche that controls how we motivate ourselves to respond to our instincts and urges in a socially acceptable manner.

supermarket a large self-service retailing environment, which can be defined as a large-scale departmental retailing organization that offers a wide variety of differing merchandise to a large consumer base.

supply chain management formed when organizations link their individual value chains.

support activities the indirect activities necessary to facilitate the primary activities within the value chain.

sustainable competitive advantage when an organization is able to offer a superior product to competitors, which is not easily imitated and enjoys significant market share as a result.

sustainable marketing marketing activities undertaken to meet the wants/needs of present customers without comprising the wants/needs of future customers, particularly in relation to negative environmental impacts on society.

switching costs the psychological, economic, time-related, and effort-related costs associated with substituting one product or service for another or changing a supplier from one to another.

SWOT analysis a methodology used by organizations to understand their strategic position. It involves analysis of an organization's strengths, weaknesses, opportunities, and threats.

synchronicity refers to the degree to which a user's input into a system/channel and the response they receive from the system/channel are simultaneous.

synchronous immediate, or near-immediate, 'real-time' information exchange.

systematic random sampling a method used to select respondents from a known population using an initial random number generated to determine the first sample respondent but where each subsequent sample respondent is selected on the basis of the *n*th respondent proceeding, where *n* is determined by dividing the population size by the sample size and rounding up.

tangibility possessing the characteristics of something that is physical, i.e. it can be touched. As a result, it has form. When products are tangible they have physical presence.

tariff barrier a financial tax on imported goods.

telemarketing or telesales is a form of non-store retailing where purchase occurs over the telephone.

teleological ethics a form of ethical approach by which the rightness or wrongness of an action or decision is judged primarily on the intentions of the decision-maker.

test marketing a stage in the new product development process, undertaken when a new product is tested with a sample of customers or is launched in a specified geographical area, to judge customers' reactions prior to a national launch.

test markets regions within a country used to test the effects of the launch of a new product or service, typically using regional advertising to promote the service and pre- and post-advertising market research to measure promotional effectiveness.

time utility manufacture, purchase, and consumption might occur at differing points in time; time utility bridges this gap.

touchpoint an occasion when a consumer engages with a brand including those not directly associated with advertising activities.

transactional exchanges short-term economic transactions between parties who are primarily interested in products and prices. Participants are primarily motivated by self-interest.

transfer pricing typically occurs in large organizations and represents the pricing approach used when one unit of a company sells to another unit within the same company.

transportation the physical movement of products using, for example, road, rail, air, pipeline, and shipping.

translation equivalence the degree to which the meaning of one language is represented in another after translation.

transvections a term proposed by Alderson and Miles to denote the relationships (transactions) that occur in the development of a product or service that crosses between company (i.e. product/service) ownership boundaries to produce a finished product or service. We would now consider such cooperation in manufacturing from the perspective of supply chain management as vertical integration or cooperation.

trust the degree of confidence that one person (or organization) has in another to fulfil an obligation or responsibility. Trust is achieved by reducing uncertainty, the threat of opportunism, and the possibility of conflict, while at the same time building confidence, the probability of buyer satisfaction, and longer-term commitment, necessary for effective relationships to be sustained.

***t*-test** a statistical test of difference used for small randomly selected samples with a size of less than 30.

tweenagers pre-adolescent children, typically taken to be between the ages of 9 and 12, who are hence about to enter their teenage years.

two-step model a communication model that reflects a receiver's response to a message.

undifferentiated approach there is no delineation between market segments, and instead the market is viewed as one mass market with one marketing strategy for the entire market.

user-generated content (UGC) content made publicly available over the internet which reflects a certain amount of creative effort and is created by users not professionals.

users people or groups who use business products and services once they have been acquired and who then evaluate their performance.

utilitarianism an ethical approach originally developed by English philosopher and social reformer Jeremy Bentham which postulates that an action is right if, and only if, it conforms to the principle of utility, whereby utility—pleasure, happiness, or welfare—is maximized, or pain or unhappiness minimized, more than any alternative..

utility a measure of satisfaction or happiness obtained from the consumption of a specific good or a service in economic thought, typically measured as an aggregate.

validity the ability of a measurement instrument to measure exactly the construct it is attempting to measure.

value the regard that something is held to be worth, typically, although not always, in financial terms.

value chain a term determined by Michael Porter that refers to the various activities an organization undertakes and links together in order to provide products and services that are perceived by customers to be different and of superior value.

value creation the benefits derived by a customer resulting from the incorporation of particular products and services.

value proposition the benefits promised by a supplier if their products or services are used.

values beliefs of a social group or individual, that are held with some conviction, often learned from parents and formed early in life, and tend to change less and less with age, which define how we ought to behave.

variability a characteristic of a service, one that refers to the amount of diversity allowed in each step of service provision.

variable costs costs that vary according to the number of units of product made or service sold. For instance, variable costs in the pharmaceutical market would include plastic bottles in which to place the pills. In a service business like the airline industry, variable costs would include airline meals.

vertical conflict conflict between sequential members in a distribution network, such as producers, distributor, and retailers, over such matters as carrying a particular range or price increases.

vividness the ability of the technology to produce a sensually rich experience. Based on sensory breadth and depth.

viral marketing the unpaid peer-to-peer communication of often provocative content originating from an identified sponsor using the internet to persuade or influence an audience to pass along the content to others.

virtue ethics principally associated with Aristotle, this branch of ethics stresses the importance of developing virtuous principles, with 'right' character, and the pursuit of a virtuous life.

vision how an organization sees its future and what it wants to become.

warehousing facilities used to store tangible goods for the periods between production, transportation, and purchase/consumption.

weak theory a view that suggests advertising is a weak force and works by reminding people of preferred brands.

wholesalers stock products not services before the next level of distribution.

winner's curse terminology associated with the bidding process in commercial markets where a company ends up submitting a bid at a price that is unprofitable or not very profitable just to win the contract.

word of mouth a form of communication founded on interpersonal messages regarding products or services sought or consumed. The receiver regards the communicator as impartial and credible as they are not attempting to sell products or services.

working capital in accounting terms, this represents a company's short-term financial efficiency and is the difference between its current assets (what it owns) and its current liabilities (what it owes).

Wünderkind a German term referring in this context to an exceptionally bright (i.e. intelligent) person.

yield management a system for maximizing the profit generated from activities, which carefully manages price to ensure full utilization of capacity while balancing supply and demand factors.

z-test a statistical test of difference used for large randomly selected samples with a size of 30 or more.

Index